D1093979

CHILDREN OF LUCIFER

OXFORD STUDIES IN WESTERN ESOTERICISM

Series Editor
Henrik Bogdan, University of Gothenburg

CHILDREN OF LUCIFER
The Origins of Modern Religious Satanism
Ruben van Luijk

OXFORD STUDIES IN WESTERN ESOTERICISM

Children of Lucifer

THE ORIGINS OF MODERN RELIGIOUS SATANISM

Ruben van Luijk

OXFORD
UNIVERSITY PRESS

OXFORD
UNIVERSITY PRESS

Oxford University Press is a department of the University of Oxford. It furthers
the University's objective of excellence in research, scholarship, and education
by publishing worldwide. Oxford is a registered trade mark of Oxford University
Press in the UK and certain other countries.

Published in the United States of America by Oxford University Press
198 Madison Avenue, New York, NY 10016, United States of America.

Library of Congress Cataloging-in-Publication Data
Names: Luijk, Ruben van, author.
Title: Children of lucifer : the origins of modern religious satanism / Ruben van Luijk.
Description: New York : Oxford University Press, 2016. | Includes bibliographical references and index.
Identifiers: LCCN 2015044388| ISBN 978–0–19–027510–5 (cloth : alk. paper) |
ISBN 978–0–19–027512–9 (epub)
Subjects: LCSH: Satanism—History.
Classification: LCC BF1548 .L85 2016 | DDC 133.4/2209—dc23 LC record
available at http://lccn.loc.gov/2015044388

9 8 7 6 5 4 3 2 1
Printed by Sheridan, USA

Contents

Acknowledgments xi
Practical Indications for the Reader xiii

Introduction: Mostly for Academic Readers 1
    Defining Satanism 2
    Available Literature 7
    Hypothesis, Framework, and Methodology of This Study 12

1. The Christian Invention of Satanism 16
    A Short Biography of the Devil 16
    Constructing Worshippers of Satan 22
    Exorcising the Devil's Fifth Column 31
    The Satanist Conspiracy of Witchcraft 35
    Black Magic and the Black Mass 40
    The Affair of the Poisons 45
    Satanists before the Modern Age? 56

Intermezzo 1 The Eighteenth Century: Death of Satan?

2. The Romantic Rehabilitation of Satan 69
    The Satanic School of Poetry 69
    God, Satan, and Revolution 76
    Poetry, Myth, and Man's Ultimate Grounds of Being 87
    Satan's New Myths: Blake and Shelley 91
    Satan's New Myths: Byron and Hugo 99
    How Satanist Were the Romantic Satanists? 108

3. Satan in Nineteenth-Century Counterculture 113
    Sex, Science, and Liberty 114
    Satan the Anarchist 116
    (Re)constructing Historical Satanism 121

Satan in Nineteenth-Century Occultism 126
Children of Lucifer 147

Intermezzo 2 Charles Baudelaire: Litanies to Satan

4. *Huysmans and Consorts* 164
"Down There" 164
Huysmans Discovers Satanism 168
Péladan, Guaita, and Papus 171
Joseph Boullan 175
The Remarkable Case of Chaplain Van Haecke and Canon Docre 185
Intermediary Conclusions 188
Competing Concepts of Satanism 194
Aftermath 200

5. *Unmasking the Synagogue of Satan* 207
The Unveiling of Freemasonry 208
Taxil before Palladism 216
Excursus: Taxil's Sources 220
The Rise and Fall of Palladism 223
The Great Masonic Conspiracy 231
How Freemasons Became Satanists 239

6. *Unmasking the Synagogue of Satan: Continued and Concluded* 242
Fighting Democracy by Democratic Means 244
Hidden Temples, Secret Grottos, and International Men of Mystery 249
A Few Words on Satan in Freemasonry, and on Neo-Palladism 263
The Jewish Question 270
By Way of Conclusion 278

Intermezzo 3 Nineteenth-Century Religious Satanism:
Fact or Fiction?

7. *Paths into the Twentieth Century* 294
The Church of Satan 295
Precursors and Inspirations 299
Aleister Crowley, or the Great Beast 666 306
The Other Tradition: Attribution 314
The Heritage of Romantic Satanism 321
The Paradox of Antireligious Religion 328
Reviving "Black" Magic 336

8. *Tribulations of the Early Church* 344
Satan and Set; LaVey and Aquino 344
The Satanism Scare, or, The Virulence of Old Legends 356
Nazism, the Western Revolution, and Genuine Satanist Conspiracies 364
LaVey's Last Years 377

Intermezzo 4 Adolescent Satanism, Metal Satanism, Cyber-Satanism

Conclusion 386
     Attribution 388
     Rehabilitation 391
     Appropriation 395
     Application 402

NOTES 409
BIBLIOGRAPHY 567
INDEX 607

Acknowledgments

MY FIRST DEBT of gratitude is to Daniela Müller, who adopted and promoted the project of this study at an early date, when I was still a rather ragged and only recently graduated student, finding me an institutional home on more than one occasion. She is the real *Doktorvater* of this study, and I hope this publication justifies her unflinching trust. Next I would like to mention Theo Salemink, my copromoter, whose untiring enthusiasm and inexhaustible suggestions for new literature and new venues of investigation stimulated me immensely; in addition, his wizardry in circumnavigating certain practical hindrances proved essential in launching my research. Wouter Hanegraaff supported and supervised this project at an early stage: his acute criticism of my earliest chapters was of great value to me. When academic bureaucracy prevented him from continuing this role, he was replaced by Gerard Rouwhorst, who spared me many a headache by his unfailing references to literature on more theoretical issues.

Although an unlikely place for this research, the Faculty of Catholic Theology of Tilburg University at Utrecht provided me with a hospitable institutional bedding for pursuing my dark studies during the first five years of this project. When the harsh spirit of modern efficiency also engulfed this last oasis of academic respite, the Faculty of Philosophy, Theology, and Religious Studies of the Radbouduniversity at Nijmegen kindly opened its doors for me, thanks to generous financial support by the now-defunct interfaculty focus group for Culture, Religion, and Memory.

Finally I thank my inspiring colleagues in the Noster Werkgroep Nieuwe Spiritualiteit, especially Johanneke Berghuijs; the helpful personnel of all libraries, archives, and other institutions I consulted, in particular Rens Steenhard of the Vredespaleis at The Hague and Brigitte Hegelauer of Mission Eine Welt; Ab de Jong, Marcel Poorthuis, Hans de Waardt, Iris Gareis, Peter Paul Schnierer, Per Faxneld, Syds Wiersma, Michael Siefener, Annemarie

Bos, Burton H. Wolfe, and Olivier van Praag, for the help and information they gave me; Dr. Christina Pumplun, for reading Faust with me; Cyril Kuttiyanikkal and Lut Callaert, for being roommates; the two anonymous reviewers, for their comments that allowed me to add some final retouches; Céline Giron et Mortimer Malaisé, pour leur hospitalité et amitié; and my parents, for their understanding, even when they couldn't always understand.

Practical Indications for the Reader

∿ ───────────────────────────────────────

ALL TRANSLATIONS FROM other languages in this publication are mine, unless otherwise noted in the notes. Unless otherwise noted, any emphasis within quoted texts is from the original.

Initial capitals within cited texts have been changed as the flow of my text demanded. For brevity's sake, gods and other (im)personal entities of mixed, neutral, or unknown sex are referred to as "he" or "him." No theological or ideological statement is implied.

As is by now common usage in scholarly literature, I capitalize Satanism, in accordance with the English-language convention for denoting religions (compare Christianity, Judaism, Buddhism, etc.). Except in specific cases, however, I have avoided the epithet "Satanic" for matters regarding Satanism (e.g., "Satanist philosophy") because it literally signifies something belonging to or sharing traits with Satan and is commonly understood as "diabolically evil."

The bibliography contains all the relevant publications I have consulted. Periodicals are listed separately, but primary and secondary sources have been compiled within one alphabetical list for quick consultation by inquiring readers. Archival sources and websites are listed in the notes only.

To ensure the readability of the text and because of the lack of a real *status qæstionis* regarding many aspects of the history of Satanism, I chose, in most cases, to allocate discussions of specialized scholarly literature to the notes. Specialist readers should consult these, as they contain much additional information. Endnotes toward the beginning of a chapter or section list or discuss the most relevant literature regarding that particular topic.

CHILDREN OF LUCIFER

What yesterday was still religion is no longer such today;
and what to-day is atheism, tomorrow will be religion.

LUDWIG FEUERBACH, *The Essence of Christianity*, trans. George Eliot

Introduction

(Mostly for academic readers)

⌐＿ _____

WALKING THROUGH THE university library one day, my eye fell on a pulp paperback entitled *The World's Weirdest Cults*. I immediately surmised that Satanism would be among the religions featured in the book. Indeed, seven of the sixteen chapters in the little book turned out to be centered on Satanist "cults" of one kind or another.[1] My hunch in this respect was not based on some eerie premonition. Authors of pulp paperbacks are by no means exceptional in considering Satanism among "the world's weirdest cults." To this day, the word "Satanism" conjures images of the bizarre, the sinister, the lurid, the monstrous, the perverse, and the downright evil. This attitude is reflected in much of the literature, both academic and nonacademic, that deals with the subject or happens to refer to it in passing and also in the reactions of many people, both academic and nonacademic, to whom I mentioned the subject I was working on.

Such associations naturally make Satanism an excellent tool for blackening other people's reputations. Throughout history, persons and groups alleged to practice Satanism of some kind or another make up a long list, which includes the Essenes,[2] the Gnostics,[3] the Hindus,[4] the Jews and the Cathars,[5] the Templars,[6] the Goliards,[7] several medieval and early modern Roman Catholic popes,[8] adherents of tribal religions,[9] the Protestants and the Anabaptists,[10] John Milton,[11] François Henri de Montmorency-Bouteville, Maréchal de Luxembourg,[12] Madame de Montespan,[13] the Illuminati,[14] the Presbyterians,[15] Robespierre, Marat, and Danton,[16] the Mormons,[17] the Rosicrucians,[18] magnetists and spiritists,[19] Giuseppe Mazzini and Giuseppe Garibaldi,[20] Otto von Bismarck,[21] Giacomo Leopardi,[22] Charles Baudelaire,[23] Grigori Rasputin,[24] the Chinese Tongs,[25] Karl Marx,[26] Friedrich Nietzsche,[27] the San Francisco Vigilantes,[28] Pope Pius IX and Pope Leo XIII,[29] Cardinal Mariano Rampolla,[30] Aleister Crowley,[31] J. R. R. Tolkien,[32] Robert Johnson,[33] Adolf Hitler,[34] the SS,[35] Julius Evola,[36] supporters of the New Age Movement,[37] the Wiener Aktionstheater,[38] the Beatles,[39] the Manson Family,[40] Communists,[41] McDonalds,[42] Procter & Gamble,[43] Walt Disney,[44] Cardinal Ratzinger,[45] and all American presidents since George Bush Sr.[46]

DEFINING SATANISM

This enumeration is by no means exhaustive, as even a cursory reading of this book will show. If anything, it highlights the need for a proper demarcation of the subject. This means establishing at least a working definition of Satanism. Despite the spontaneous images that the term conjures in the minds of most people, this is not so straightforward an endeavor as it may seem. From the outset, an almost Babylonian confusion of tongues has surrounded the terminology around Satanism. The word and its derivation "Satanist" appeared for the first time in French and English in the sixteenth century during the European Wars of Religion.[47] In publications from this period, Roman Catholic authors directed it against Protestant Christians, and vice versa, while both applied the epithet to Anabaptists. Their polemical use of the term did not necessarily mean that they thought their religious counterparts were self-consciously and secretly worshipping the devil—although mutual abuse might occasionally spill over into such allegations, particularly with regard to the Anabaptists—but rather that Roman Catholic veneration for "graven images" or Protestant adherence to "heresy" *implied* being a fellow traveler on Satan's bandwagon. In the early nineteenth century, the terms "Satanist" and "Satanism" acquired even broader meanings and came to designate a person or thing with a "Satanic character," a person or thing inherently evil or wicked. When Prosper Merimée (of *Carmen* fame) wrote in an 1842 letter to an anonymous female friend that she was making "quite rapid progress in Satanism," he did not mean to say that she held regular rituals for the fallen angel but that she was growing increasingly "ironic, sarcastic, and even diabolic."[48] Only toward the end of the nineteenth century did the word "Satanism" come to hold the significance that it still has, for historians of religion, B-film directors, and the general public alike, namely, as the intentional and explicit worship of Satan.[49] This is not to say that the concepts and practices embodied in this word did not exist prior to that time.

In this book, I use the term "Satanism" only in its third, most recent significance. As a provisional hypothesis to guide us through the mire of historical material, I define Satanism as the *intentional, religiously motivated veneration of Satan*. At first glance, this may seem a fairly straightforward definition that even those who are not experts may instinctively agree with. Looking more closely into the matter, however, it will soon become apparent that things are not so simple. Therefore, some prefatory clarifications.

In using the phrase "intentional veneration," I hope to make clear that I speak of Satanism only in the case of a (allegedly) purposely religious choice. Thus, I do *not* enter into interpretations of historical phenomena as "Satanism" from a theological or philosophical viewpoint— such as "National Socialism was Satanism because it was an instrument of the devil in spreading evil."[50] This kind of analysis presumes an ability to discern the "real" place of things in the cosmic order (or disorder) and their hidden or invisible identity behind the "mask" of historic facts. A strong tendency toward such "theological" definitions or identifications of Satanism is especially apparent in the large body of nonacademic or pseudo academic literature on the subject originating from Christian subculture(s), but it is also discernible in the rare historical accounts that Satanists themselves have given of their religion. In contrast with this, this study is about the origins and history of (assumed) intentional Satanisms; in other words, it is about Satanism as a deliberate religious option clearly demarcated by (assumed) acts or utterances.

I do not concern myself, as may be deduced from the foregoing, with suppositions about the interference of supernatural actors in this history. Whether Satan and his company have an ontologically tangible presence, and, if so, in what way and through what intermediaries he chooses to operate, is beyond my range of expertise. The answers to these and comparable questions ultimately depend on personal religious (or nonreligious) inclination and cannot be decided through simple historical inquiry—although I do not presume that my own attitudes on this matter will be impossible to detect in the pages that follow.

When I talk about "religiously motivated" veneration, I mean that this veneration must have a religious character. Otherwise this would be a book about not the history of a religious movement but the history of a mythological symbol with religious origins (although both subjects are inevitably and intricately intertwined, as we will see). Elucidating, however, what it is exactly that we mean by the word "religious" is no easy task. As of yet scholars have not agreed upon a proper definition of religion.[51] One of the first attempts was by the nineteenth-century historian of religion E. B. Tylor, who defined religion as "belief in supernatural beings."[52] This restriction of the religious domain to "the supernatural" has now been discarded by many scholars. First, "the supernatural" is a term that itself is not easy to define, and the implication would be to reduce religion to a kind of reversed communicating vessel with modern Western science (which, incidentally, is exactly what Tylor proposed).[53] Moreover, a number of religions do not fit easily within this definition (e.g., some tribal religions, pantheism, Taoism). Many modern religious movements in particular embrace forms of religiosity that do not entail "belief in supernatural beings," properly speaking—the various manifestations of "self-religion" especially come to mind.[54]

Other schools of religious studies have sought to define religion by stressing social or ritual parameters. The consequences of this choice become clear when we study the definition of Satanism used by Massimo Introvigne, a leading expert on the history of esoteric movements. In Wouter Hanegraaff's *Dictionary of Gnosis and Western Esotericism*, Introvigne defines Satanism as "the adoration, in an organized and ritual form, of the figure known in the Bible as the devil or Satan."[55] In his monograph *Enquête sur le satanisme*, the same definition can be found in a greater profusion of words: "From a historical or sociological point of view, Satanism can be defined as the adoration or veneration, by groups organized as a movement, through repeated practices of a cultic or liturgical character, of the personage that is called Satan or devil in the Bible."[56] Both variants make clear his evident adherence to notions that declare the social and the ritual to be essential components of religion. I, on the contrary, do not consider either of these components as formal preconditions essential for the demarcation of religion or Satanism. Rites and rituals, whether real or imagined, certainly play an important role in the history of Satanism. But what makes a Satanist a Satanist, whether real or imagined, is not his performance of certain ritual actions, but his relation to Satan. In the same way, more generally speaking, it is not the social or ritual act in itself that makes religion religious, but the implied *significance* of this act. Bowing before a king is not religion (except, of course, when this king is considered divine); bowing before a god or the image of the clan's totem is. Nor can I agree with those scholars who deem the social dimension an essential part of religion. An individual alone in his room who is praying, conducting a ritual, or giving expression to his convictions about the universe in words or art is, in my opinion, essentially still *practicing religion.* Especially at present, with the ever-growing fragmenting and individualization of the Western religious landscape, it seems of crucial importance to maintain the fact that it is still religion that we encounter here.[57]

For the purposes of this book, therefore, I opt for a broader definition of religion. To this end, I adopt the concise formula of Robert Bellah, who defined religion as "a set of symbolic forms and acts which relate man to the ultimate conditions of his existence."[58] I tacitly assume, by the way, that Bellah really meant to write "a set of symbolic forms and acts which relate man to *what he perceives to be* the ultimate conditions of his existence." Furthermore, as will become evident later in this study, I adopt a broad interpretation of Bellah's "symbolic forms and acts" (broader, possibly, than Bellah may have intended).

Shrewd readers may observe that this interpretation places the essence of the religious—that which makes a religion religion—in the suppositions it explicitly or implicitly presents regarding "man's ultimate grounds of existence"; in other words, regarding a "general order of existence," to borrow Clifford Geertz's celebrated phrase.[59] This is indeed my conviction. It must be made clear that this does not imply that religion is identical to individual belief. Although it might be hard to imagine how a religion could come into being with none of its original participants believing its suppositions, a religion that presents suppositions with none of its adherents individually believing them is perfectly feasible. Individual belief, that is to say, is just one possible locus of the religious—a locus, moreover, that can only be studied through its expression in external forms and acts. Neither, it should be added, does this centrality of significance imply that the study of religion must be confined to explicit doctrinal statements or the evolution of theological discourses, as more traditional "histories of the church" were wont to do. Ritual, traditional custom, law, liturgy, and art (may) all belong to the symbolic forms and acts by which man relates himself to what he thinks to be the ultimate grounds of his existence and gives expression to suppositions about a general order of existence.

In applying this definition, I may label some groups as religious who would not consider themselves thus, or who would even categorically deny this classification. If I do so, this is partly because I believe that their rejection of the religious label is ideologically conditioned by the specific history of modern Western civilization, and it is the task of the historian of religion to attempt to supersede such time-limited conceptions regarding his domain of investigation. This is not to diminish the significance of the religious-critical attitude that explicit or implicit self-categorizations like these express. As a matter of fact, the historical genesis of this attitude, which began roughly three centuries ago in the West, will prove to be an essential part of the story of this book. Even our current use of the word "religion" may be intimately linked with this historical process, as it presupposes a notion that the religious can be separated from other domains of human society or human existence, an idea that seems to be relatively modern.[60]

Concerning the last point: the fact that our concept of religion as a separate category may have been gestated by the particular historical evolution of the West does not invalidate the use of the term, in my opinion. The particular experience of Western civilization may well have led to genuinely valuable insights—indeed, our trust in the validity of the academic and scientific endeavor implicitly depends on this conviction. It is important to realize, however, that people in different places and in different times did not necessarily and do not necessarily share this relatively sharp categorization. Nor does it mean that we should accept without scrutiny current popular conceptions regarding religion, and what it is and is not, as the last word in matters of definition and demarcation.[61]

I am aware that Bellah's definition leaves us with certain methodological and ontological problems of its own.[62] Our purpose for the moment, however, is not to find an indisputable, watertight definition for religion, but to find a useful tool to separate genuine Satanism from the host of other phenomena that have been associated with it in prior literature or popular and theological lore. And even with a broad definition of religion such as this, I can disclose beforehand, the history of (what-may-or-may-not-be) Satanism presents us with cases that create a formidable challenge to any attempt at categorization. It might not be coincidental that such cases often also give rise to the most tantalizing questions and insights regarding the nature of religion, Western civilization, and human nature in general.

Let's return to our provisional definition. In *Enquête sur le satanisme*, it might be noted, Introvigne speaks of Satanism as "adoration or veneration" of Satan. For my own definition, I prefer the latter designation (intentional, religiously motivated *veneration* of Satan). Many practitioners of modern or even older forms of Satanism certainly would not describe their relation to Satan in terms of "adoration" or "worship." And especially with regard to nontheistic religious practices, these words do indeed seem inapt. I therefore opt for the "milder" alternative of "veneration."

This is a minor issue; I note it only in passing. Of greater importance is the ambiguous interpretation that the word "Satan" may represent. In its simplest form, I take it to refer to any mythological being designated by the biblical name of "Satan" or meant to make intentional reference to him. For the purposes of this study, I also include under this heading those biblical entities that were identified or closely associated with Satan in the early Christian tradition, such as Lucifer, Beelzebuth, Leviathan, and the Serpent. Thus, any intentional, religious veneration of these mythological personages *after* they were integrated into the Christian hierarchy of evil is considered Satanism by me. This does not mean, of course, that the choice of (for example) Lucifer as an object of veneration, rather than Satan, is arbitrary. Often it is highly significant, and wherever appropriate, I aim to indicate these significances in the chapters that follow.

What I categorically do *not* propose, however, is to extend the mythological complex encapsulated under the heading of Satan to deities or mythological entities from other religious systems because of their presumed typological associations with the Judeo-Christian Satan (e.g., as alleged representatives of evil, of the chthonic, of sexuality or vitality, or merely because of their non-Christianity or their fierce looks), as often occurs in both Christian and Satanist traditions. Thus, a worshipper of Shiva is not a Satanist, even though he may be considered as such by some Christians, and even though some Satanists might include Shiva within their particular pantheon or pandemonium. Neither, and this is an even more fundamental point, does Satan equate with evil. Satan as a mythological figure has been given different shapes and different meanings in the various traditions in which he appears; he is, and was, not always a representative of evil. He only assumes this role in a localized, predominantly Christian tradition that started shortly before the beginning of the Common Era and has subsequently not remained unchallenged.[63]

A final, related difficulty in defining Satanism is the question of how much "Satan" we need before we can speak of Satanism. Some religious groups or individuals that manifest a veneration for Satan also venerate other, nonconnected mythological entities—most often, surprisingly enough, stemming from the Judeo-Christian heritage, such as Jehovah, Christ, or the Virgin Mary, but sometimes originating from a wide variety of other religious sources, such as Set, Loki, Kali, Marduk, or other non-Christian deities.[64] There is, clearly, no objective criterion for establishing when "Satanism" is most appropriate in these circumstances, or when some other term might do better. In general, one should be extremely careful in applying religious labels—*any* religious labels, but that of Satanism in particular. As a rule of thumb, therefore, I only use the term "Satanism" when the veneration of Satan (or the biblical entities associated with him) has a clear dominance. In other cases, when veneration for the fallen angel is merely one aspect among others or a subordinate facet in a wider religious system, it seems better to speak of religions that display *elements of Satanism*. In all these cases, it must be emphasized, I use the term "Satanism" merely as a historical or sociological nomer, without any ethical or theological value judgment implied.

Recently, two scholars of twentieth-century Satanism have suggested a different approach to the question of its definition. In a series of articles, Kennet Granholm has argued that, because of its pejorative connotations, the term "Satanism" should be reserved as "a valid denominator for groups and philosophies which appropriate the figure of Satan and attribute significance to it, and that identify as Satanists."[65] I wholeheartedly agree (although not necessarily with his definition, on which more later). When I discuss groups or individuals in this volume that Granholm would identify (and rightly so) as non-Satanist or post-Satanist, I do so because I think they are of historic relevance to the development of Satanism, not because I want to imply they belong to this category.

I will not follow in this study Granholm's further suggestion to adopt the denominator "Left-Hand Path" as a more promising analytical term. First, that is because the subject of this study *is* Satanism, not Left-Hand Path spirituality. As a historical occurrence, Satanism is both a current religious variety that can be placed within a wider gamut of Left-Hand Path religion and a broader phenomenon that has also manifested itself outside the Left-Hand Path milieu. In other words, not all Satanisms have been left-handed. In addition, I do not concur with his assertion that Satanism "is not a particular useful analytical category."[66] To the contrary, as a historian, I found it very useful to detect hidden trails in the history of religion and of ideas, and to connect these with broader developments outside the domain of esotericism. I hope this assertion will be borne out by the present volume.

A very different approach has been proposed by Jesper Aagaard Petersen, which he most crisply formulated in his introduction to the 2009 Ashgate volume *Contemporary Satanism*. First, in analogy with Colin Campbell's category of "cultic milieu," Petersen propounds to isolate a "Satanic milieu" as a broad subcultural field engaging in "satanic discourse." Satanism sensu stricto, that is, in an organized, religious form, forms part of this "fuzzy" movement that produces reinterpretations of and identifications with Satan and Satanism.[67] After reading the present history of (proto)Satanisms, one can easily see the potential usefulness of such an approach. Time and again, we see more or less articulated expressions of (proto)Satanism emerge from a broader bedding of dissident subculture: that of practitioners of demonic magic in the seventeenth century; that of radical, Romantic, and/or Decadent intellectuals in the "long" nineteenth century; and that of members of (occult) counterculture in the twentieth century.

We should take care, however, to reify this concept of milieu, as Petersen immediately hastens to point out himself. Satan and the Satanic often consist of no more than an aside for the actors in these mostly incoherent and inconsistent subcultures; it is only when their expressions on this subject are isolated by historical research and reassembled into narrative that a significant pattern emerges. For this study, I felt more at ease with the concept of "tradition," in the loose sense that Per Faxneld also adopts: as a chain of utterances, mostly textual in our case, that is picked up, elaborated, and extended over time.[68]

Apart from his idea of a "Satanic milieu," Petersen also formulates "a minimum definition of the satanic discourse of organized Satanism within the satanic milieu," mentioning four common traits: "self-religion, antinomianism, the use of certain 'S'-words and a formulated ideological genealogy, often in some relation to Anton Szandor LaVey."[69] As the last point immediately leads one to suspect, this definition is mainly useful for present-day, (post)LaVeyan Satanism. And even there, exceptions are bound to occur. If we descend into earlier history, most of these traits lose their validity. What remains is "the use of certain 'S'-words," as Petersen puts it. In the same article, he elaborates that these must be employed "as positive terms," and he furthermore emphasizes "a certain emic self-designation . . . to differentiate between prejudice and modern Satanism proper." Although I can understand his motives here, I have grave objections against the emic element that both he and Granholm incorporate in their definitions. Precisely because of the negative connotations surrounding the term "Satanism" (not to mention the sometimes very real consequences for life and limb that this label can entail), it is not to be taken for granted that those venerating Satan will stand up and declare themselves as such. (The Middle East *yezidi* may be a case in point.) Furthermore, as with the term "religion" we discussed earlier, I would like to maintain the prerogative of the academic scholar to categorize the world according to his own insights.

AVAILABLE LITERATURE

The difficulties of definition and the bridal gown of associations that goes with the term "Satanism" give the task of writing its history much of its special charm, yet they make it a particularly challenging undertaking as well. Another challenging factor is the exceedingly ragged state of serious research on the subject. The historian is confronted with the double-edged problem that certain aspects pertaining to the history of Satanism (early modern witchcraft, the Satanism Scare, some of the Romantic Satanists) have engendered bookshelves or even libraries of scholarly literature, while other aspects (early modern pacts with the devil, 1960s "Swinger Satanism") have been virtually or totally neglected. Thus, the historian is either wading through an enormous sea of literature or desperately looking for information in obscure or popular publications. Moreover, where there is an abundance of literature, mostly only a small part of this is concerned with the questions that interest a historian of Satanism, and this mostly in a cursory manner. There is a profusion of critical research into the life and work of figures such as Byron, Blake, and Huysmans, for instance, but matters concerning their attitudes toward Satan and Satanism are often treated in passing or receive a mere mention. For many aspects of the history of Satanism, there exists no real *status quæstionis* in the academic sense of the word, or only the most rudimentary scholarly discussion.

In a way, this applies to the history of Satanism in its totality as well. There is a small bookshelf of works that deal exclusively with this subject. Most of these, however, either are sensational pulp books of the type I described in the opening paragraph or are written from within a religious perspective and/or living tradition of polemic use of the Satanism trope. The latter include alarmist treatises from fundamentalist Christian (and increasingly also Islamic) provenance, as well as the occasional historiographical efforts from within the Satanist community itself, which often display considerably more wit and less paranoia but a similar lack of academic rigor.[70] In general, I used these publications not as references but as sources (that is to say, as sources for the existence of certain beliefs and ideas about Satanism).

If we put these clearly unscholarly publications aside, it becomes conspicuous how few academic or academically inclined authors have in fact attempted to give a historical overview of Satanism. The attempt has been made, however, and delving into the academic libraries of the Western world, we can find about half a dozen titles that fit the bill, particularly if our conception of "serious historical literature" is not too narrow. As an academic treatment is traditionally opened by an "overview of the available literature," I discuss these works one by one below.

Gerhard Zacharias's book *Satanskult und Schwarze Messe: Die Nachtseite des Christentums. Eine Beitrag zur Phänomenologie der Religion* might be an appropriate starting point.[71] Originally published in 1964, and reprinted four times since, this monograph breathes much of the attitudes of its time of conception. Zacharias (a former Roman Catholic priest turned Greek Orthodox pastor and Jungian therapist) describes Satanism as the nondualistic "night-side of Christianity," an outlet for the "Dionysian energies" repressed by the Christian religion. This allows him to connect a great deal of phenomena with Satanism that unaware readers might think unconnected with it, such as the above-mentioned Aktionstheater of the Vienna avant-garde of the 1960s, with which Zacharias was personally acquainted.[72] The result is rather chaotic. And to add to this chaos, his book does not in fact purport to be a history of Satanism at all, but rather a "phenomenological" treatment of the subject. This means that clearly fabricated allegations of devil worship are indiscriminately mixed with reports of actual instances of the practice of Satanism, because both, according to the author, have equal "religion-phenomenological and psychological" reality. This probably is an incorrect understanding of the nature of phenomenology: of course, mere accusations of Satanism and actually practiced forms both have a certain presence in reality, but they are not real in the same way. At any rate, it proves an unworkable starting point, even for Zacharias himself, it seems, given the many historical statements he nevertheless strews across the pages of his book. As a coherent history of Satanism, thus, *Satanskult und Schwarze Messe* disappoints. The most important reason one might have for consulting the book is the wealth of original source materials it presents, in both their original languages and German translations.

Much the same applies to Karl H. Frick's three-volume *Satan und Die Satanisten: Ideengeschichtliche Untersuchungen zur Herkunft der komplexen Gestalt "Luzifer/Satan/ Teufel," ihrer weiblichen Entsprechungen und ihrer Anhängerschaft.*[73] Like Zacharias's book, this work displays erudition of an impressive but sadly incoherent kind. Most conspicuously, Frick seems to have fallen for the popular misconception that equates orgies and sex rites with Satanism. In the first volume, which deals with all kinds of devil and devil-like figures in antique and premodern religion, we are confronted with deliciously irrelevant diversions about subjects like sacred orgies, anthropophagy, ritual defloration, and "sacred sodomy."[74] The second volume is about Satanists before 1900, while the last volume covers twentieth-century Satanism. Here again, however, Frick's lack of a clear delimitation of his subject matter plays tricks on him, inducing him to include groups in his history that have no place for Satan in their theology or philosophy at all, like the Christian Agapemonites in the nineteenth century, or the Left-radical Rote Armee Fraktion and the existentialist philosophers in the twentieth century.[75]

The German-language region seems to be particularly rich in historical treatments of Satanism. A third work that has its provenance here is Josef Dvorak's *Satanismus: Schwarze Rituale, Teufelswahn und Exorzismus, Geschichte und Gegenwart.* First published in 1989, this books stands out because it's the only one in this list written by a self-proclaimed Satanist. Dvorak was an Austrian seminary student who became a Left-wing therapist in the Vienna of the 1960s, where he cofounded the ("Satanist") Aktionstheater. After he encountered Satan during an LSD trip, he became a "Satanologist" (as he likes to call himself), gaining notoriety when the Crowleyanite rituals he conducted were broadcast on Austrian television.[76] His book, unfortunately, betrays the fact that it has been written by an occultist rather than by a professional historian. A lot of psychoanalysis, number magic, references to Hitler, and personal reminiscences meet the eager reader proceeding through its pages. In the end, *Satanismus* is best regarded as an interesting roller-coaster ride through Dvorak's own bookshelves: highly readable, certainly, but overly *improvistu* and insufficiently annotated.

At the moment, the best German-language introduction to the subject of Satanism is without doubt *Satanismus: Mythos und Wirklichkeit* by Joachim Schmidt. It provides a clear-headed, balanced, and to-the-point account of the history of Satanism. The most important objection that can be raised against Schmidt's book is that it is indeed an introduction, and with a mere 231 pages and a total of 115 endnotes it is not sufficient for the specialist or for the reader with more than a general interest. Another objection might be that while the varieties of Satanism that Schmidt distinguishes certainly are lucidly described, his descriptions are not connected in a historical account that provides deeper or original insights. More unfortunate is the fact that he succeeds in doing something for which academic writers are often, and often justly, derided: turning a gloriously wild and fascinating subject into something that is basically a bit dreary.

Given that they were the cradle both of today's living tradition of religious Satanism and of the most recent wave of Satanism anxieties to date, the almost total lack of full-blown academic treatment of the history of Satanism from Anglophonic regions is striking. Apart from a few articles of note, I personally am aware of just two exceptions.[77] The first, from 1970, Arthur Lyons's *The Second Coming: Satanism in America,* I hesitate to include in this survey.[78] It was reissued in an updated version under the title *Satan Wants You* in 1988, with a revised text to account for the Satanism Scare that had recently swept the United States.[79] This revision did not notably affect the part of the book concerned with Satanism's pre-1966 history, which features scholarship that was already outdated in 1970 (with an uncritical implementation of Margaret Murray's thesis regarding European witchcraft as the most flagrant example). The almost nonexistent annotation suggests that this book was never meant for a specialist readership at all. Nevertheless, it is still frequently quoted in scholarly literature, predominantly with regard to the emergence of 1960s California Satanism. Even here, however, the book should be used with caution. Much of its information was derived directly from Anton LaVey, with whom Lyons was personally acquainted, and the author's all-too-evident sympathy for the self-styled Black Pope has invited just criticism.[80]

A much better English-language history is provided by *Lure of the Sinister: The Unnatural History of Satanism*, by the English freelance writer Gareth J. Medway, published in 2001 by New York University Press.[81] This is, it must be said, a bit of an oddball work. Despite its pulpy title, it is well researched and decently annotated. Despite being well researched and decently annotated, it is a rollicking read: Medway's is one of the few serious titles on the subject that actually manages to be very funny at times. What, again, is lacking, is a coherent historical vision on the emergence of Satanism. Medway's amusing style makes one almost forget that his book is in fact largely a collection of anecdotes. In addition, the main thrust of the book seems to be in debunking myths of Satanism. Actually practiced Satanism is treated in a series of often unconnected asides, sometimes of a brevity verging on rashness (for instance, when Medway classes Baudelaire the first modern Satanist without really elaborating on his statement).[82] This emphasis is understandable: Medway clearly wrote the book in reaction to the Satanism Scare of the 1980s and 1990s, which takes up most of the book. Medway's own (freely admitted) background as "a Pagan and a priest of Themis in the Fellowship of Isis" might have been another factor in determining this emphasis. It seems best, therefore, to read *Lure of the Sinister* for what it is: primarily a book aimed at dispelling some of the tenacious myths that surrounded Satanism in the 1990s, less a work about what it actually was and how it came to be.

Without a doubt the best overview of the history of Satanism currently available is Introvigne's *Enquête sur le satanisme: Satanistes et antisatanistes du XVIIe siècle à nos jours*, which originally appeared in 1994 in Italian under the title *Indagine sul satanismo*.[83] Introvigne, who has an academic background in philosophy and law, is a noted specialist in the field of new religious movements and a cofounder of CESNUR, a research institute in Turin dedicated to the study of new varieties of religion. His *Enquête sur le satanisme* may be considered the pioneering study of the field, densely packed with information about practically every individual and every group historically connected with the subject. He neatly avoids wandering into endless irrelevancies by adopting a sharp definition of Satanism (which I amply discussed above). In addition to this, he manages to give a coherent narrative of the seemingly chaotic history of the subject. To this purpose, he proposes to approach the history of Satanism as the constant ebb and flood of Satanism, on the one hand, and anti-Satanism, on the other hand. Briefly summarized: every time Satanism surfaces in the West, this engenders a reaction in larger society. This anti-Satanism, however, tends to succumb to exaggerations; and in the wake of its ensuing discredit, new Satanist movements arise.[84] Using this model, Introvigne is able to draw a creative connection between the many appearances of Satanism as a mythical and polemic construct, and the historical instances of actually practiced veneration for the fallen angel.

I would like, first, to eulogize Introvigne's tremendously rich book, without which I could not have written this study, or at least would have faced an immensely more daunting task. The fact that I will disagree with Introvigne's findings and conclusions on more than one occasion does not mean that I do not appreciate his work. Rather, it is because Introvigne can be considered the sole conversation partner in this venture, the only earlier author to propose an elaborate and coherent reconstruction of the historical genesis of contemporary religious Satanism. On this level, the scholarly discussion in this book virtually amounts to a dialogue with *Enquête sur le satanisme*. When I differ in opinion with Introvigne about specific facts or episodes in the history of Satanism, I have indicated so in the text or the accompanying notes. Here, I would like to single out some more general differences in approach between his study and mine which are best made explicit beforehand.

First, Introvigne uses a very specific definition of Satanism, and he begins his history with the first actual instance he knows to fit this definition: the Affaire de Poisons at the end of the seventeenth century. Thus, the long history of Christian mythmaking about Satanism that preceded the seventeenth century does not receive any substantial treatment in his account. (In the same way, the Romantic Satanists are completely ignored, probably because Introvigne does not consider them religious Satanists—a conclusion I share, but for different reasons.) These choices automatically give his story a certain direction and inclination. Reading Introvigne, one gets the impression that it was the emergence of actual Satanism that initiated the flux of Satanism/anti-Satanism, while, in reality, the stereotype of the Satanist—even if he or she was not called by that name—had been present long before. In my view, this way of presenting Satanism creates a certain imbalance vis-à-vis the historical facts.

Second, Introvigne's pendulum discussion of Satanism/anti-Satanism itself is in itself a weak point. It remains vague how a waning credibility of anti-Satanism would induce people to become Satanists. If I understand Introvigne correctly, he says that Satanism has actually always been present throughout modern history—somewhere hidden in the underground of occultism, where it was born and is continually reborn as "an extreme version of the tendencies and contradictions" present in society at large.[85] The periodical waning of anti-Satanist sentiments merely allows this underground Satanism to take center stage again and recruit new disciples, thereby provoking a new wave of anti-Satanism.[86] This idea seems overly schematic to me, and Introvigne's eagerness to distinguish historical periods of Satanism and anti-Satanism sometimes induces him to see Satanists where there are no clear historical indications of their presence. In this study, I would like to propose a more subtle interplay between anti-Satanism and Satanism, which are both involved in the creation and transmission of a certain tradition *about* Satanism. And I would like to introduce a third partner in this exchange, namely, fiction, or the imaginative arts—in our case, predominantly literature.[87] In this respect, among others, the Romantic Satanists clearly have their appropriate place.

Of course, these matters partly reflect the inevitable consequences of a choice of approach: one cannot write about every possible aspect of a subject. A different approach might thus provide additional insights. This also applies to a third remark I wish to make. Introvigne labels religious Satanism as a typically modern phenomenon, even calling it the Jungian shadow of modernity.[88] Nowhere, however, does he go into detail regarding what exactly the relation between Satanism and the emergence of modern society might be. Even more fundamentally, the historical reasons for Satanists having become Satanists remain rather obscure in *Enquête sur le satanisme*. Certainly, the particular historical context of each new Satanist movement is described, but one does not really come to *understand* their motives through the pages of Introvigne's book. They mostly remain historical occurrences, not fellow human beings who make choices that we can understand people can make in their given historical circumstances. Again, this could partly be a mere matter of methodological or stylistic choice. But I suspect that Introvigne's personal inclinations may have played a role as well.[89] Although he never steps outside the pale of academic integrity in *Enquête sur le satanisme*, reading this book leaves one with the impression that his sympathies lie elsewhere.

As mentioned above, there exists a relatively extensive literature on the Satanism Scare of the closing decades of the previous millennium, and sometimes these publications contain a few pages or a chapter on the wider historical background and/or on currently practiced forms of actual Satanism. I have not included these in my overview here. The same applies to books and articles that concentrate on the current practice of religious Satanism. Recent works of preponderantly young scholars have given this field of research an important impetus toward maturity: their publications will be noted in the last chapter. It would mean gross injustice, however, to conclude this introduction without mentioning the work of the Swedish historian of religion Per Faxneld. In 2006, he published a history of Satanism before Anton LaVey, which I was unfortunately unable to consult because it is published in Swedish only.[90] In addition, he conducted doctoral research into the history of Satanism during roughly the same period as I did, concentrating especially on gender aspects. During our contacts, it turned out we had been following each other as shadows, often probing into the same areas and mostly reaching more or less similar conclusions. It must be underlined here that we both formulated these conclusions in complete independence, although we subsequently benefited from our mutual insights. Apart from this, I have profited especially from his pioneering research on more marginal figures in the history of Satanism, such as Ben Kadosh and Stanislaw Przybyszewski, which I refer to in intermezzo 3. Faxneld's monumental dissertation, *Satanic Feminism: Lucifer as the Liberator of Woman in Nineteenth-Century Culture*, was published in 2014, just in the nick of time for me to incorporate some of its findings into my study. Because it does not purport to be a general history of Satanism, I will not discuss it here. But I heartily recommend it as a companion volume to the present publication, for anyone who is interested in the sometimes surprisingly prominent role played by Satan in nineteenth-century cultural discourse or who has a craving for yet more deliciously obscure byways from the Satanic history of the West.

HYPOTHESIS, FRAMEWORK, AND METHODOLOGY OF THIS STUDY

While it is essential to remember, as we have seen, that veneration for Satan does not necessarily equal veneration of evil, it is, of course, precisely the traditional Christian role of Satan as the chief mythical representative of malevolence that makes the existence of a religious Satanism fascinating. *How did it come about that individuals and groups in modern Western society came to venerate a former symbol of evil?* That is the prime question that the existence of modern Satanism brings up, and it is the central question that runs through this book.

To help answer this question, I adopted two tools for categorization. These are *attribution* and *identification* or *appropriation*; attribution being the mechanism of attributing the practice of Satanism to others, and identification being identifying oneself with this attributed concept of Satanism, or with the figure of Satan, or both.[91] These tools allow us to sift through historical reports of Satanism and separate them according to whether they ascribe practices or ideas to others (mostly as part of a polemical discourse) or describe actual practiced forms of Satanism. Clearly, however, there is more involved in selecting this angle of approach. It implies that I believe that attribution preceded identification, and that grasping and showing this fact is an essential prerequisite for placing Satanism in its proper historical context. As mentioned above, I chose a different approach here from the one implicitly or explicitly selected by Introvigne in his *Enquête sur le satanisme*. It also implies that I consider Satanism to be an *invented tradition*, to use the well-known phrase of H. B. Hobsbawm.[92] Although this approach to the subject, like any other, inevitably entails certain preconceptions, I hope its usefulness will be borne out in the pages that follow.

To ensure clarity, it might be advisable to specify the two possible meanings of "attribution" in the context of Satanism. First, attribution may refer to the application of what I have termed the "theological" definition of Satanism to certain groups or individuals: that is, designating these as Satanists out of general theological or philosophical considerations without necessarily postulating the existence of a sociologically real and intentionally practiced veneration for Satan. For example, nihilists may be called Satanists because they "satanically" disrupt society, not because they are believed to stage rituals to worship the devil. Second, attribution may entail the ascription to others of an intentional, religiously motivated veneration for Satan: in other words, of actually and deliberately *practiced* Satanism, according to the definition used in the present work. The last variant is the most important for our investigation, but the two are intimately linked to each other in the evolution of Satanism and continue to exist side by side.

In practice, this means that the chapters that follow have a threefold thrust. First, I search for real Satanists, using the provisional definition and the concept of attribution to determine the veracity of historical descriptions of Satanism and describe their place in the wider framework of history. Second, I indicate how these cases of ascribed or actual Satanism contributed to the conceptual construct of Satanism. Third, I aim to locate and describe the transition from attribution to identification that gave rise to (modern) religious Satanism, as well as its historical context.[93] This last aspect means that this study includes extensive discussions of groups or individuals that fall outside the scope of our definition of Satanism properly speaking, such as the Romantic Satanists and their heirs in nineteenth-century (counter)culture. I have chosen to do this where I believe they embody or represent crucial steps in the shift from attribution to identification, or make clear in what way the emergence of modern religious Satanism is linked to the emergence of modern Western society. For the same reasons, I discuss certain cases of evident attribution more extensively than they might be thought to merit at first glance.

There have also been methodological considerations of a more practical kind. As we have noted already, the history of Satanism extends over a period of hundreds of years, while the historical genesis of Satan may date back almost three millennia. It is clearly impossible for a single person with limited time at his disposal to give an account covering such a period of time based on a comprehensive examination of primary sources. Especially with regard to the subjects covered in chapter 1, I relied heavily on secondary literature—secondary literature, that is, by specialists on the specific historical periods or episodes under consideration; only in exceptional cases have I relied on general histories of Satanism as my only reference. Even here, nevertheless, I have attempted to remain in touch with the buried realities of history by consulting key primary texts; in order to enable the reader to do likewise, I have freely strewn samples of this material throughout my narrative. For the subsequent chapters, I profited extensively from the work of earlier scholarship as well. In addition, however, I chose to anchor my interpretations in a wide reading of published original texts of every description. For chapter 4, moreover, I dug deeply into primary sources (mostly letters and personal documents by Huysmans and Boullan or their consorts). Yet the added value of this book, I hasten to add, does not lie in the unearthing of new historical information from archival sources. Rather, it is to be found in its fresh take on a tangled historical subject that has received scarce academic attention and that has seldom been presented with ample breadth and precision in the past.

The breadth of this book's subject has also enforced other limitations on the scope of my investigation. For practical academic reasons, it was necessary to focus my research on a particular period of history. I chose to concentrate especially on the nineteenth century—a lucky choice, it turned out, as this period of history proved to be a vital stage in the transition from attribution to identification that was essential in the emergence of modern Satanism. In addition to this chronological emphasis, I was also forced to adopt geographical limitations in my choice of material. To some extent, these were dictated by the subject matter itself. If we define Satanism as the intentional, religious veneration of Satan, it is a phenomenon that can occur only in societies that are part of or have been in contact with the Judeo-Christian heritage. Within this spectrum, my focus is essentially directed toward Western civilization. Thus the Islamic world was excluded from this survey, although it adopted the Judeo-Christian Satan and developed its own variety of views on him.[94] In chapters 2 and 3, which deal with the Romantic Satan and his influences, English and French literatures are the principal works discussed, with some extensions into other European literatures. Time and means prohibited a proper exploration of, for instance, German literature, although I think this would most certainly have added interesting additional insights.[95] Chapter 4, about Huysmans, is naturally focused on France, while chapters 5 and 6 predominantly deal with France as well, with important ramifications, however, for the wider Roman Catholic world. The final chapters tell about the rise of modern religious Satanism in the twentieth century, and they are in large measure concerned with America, the trend-setting region with regard to Satanism during this period.

Given the many aspects of our subject and the manifold approaches it allows, the present work cannot be anything more than a sketch and a proposal for a comprehensive history of Satanism. In connection with this fact, a last fundamental aspect of the methodology of this book should be clarified as well. This is not, in any way, a functionalist assay. I will not delve deeply into possible sociological, economic, psychological, or anthropological causalities that may have instigated people to become Satanists, or to think of other people as Satanists. While all these approaches may yield greater understanding of our subject at different levels of the complex texture of reality, I have adopted a (for want of a better word) *narrativist* methodological framework. A historical narrative, I think, should seek to give plausible interpretations and interconnections among verifiable traces of the past and order them into a meaningful description of what likely occurred. Although I certainly believe significant patterns can be discerned in history, and in the history of Satanism as well, the complexity of humans and human interaction is such that the ensuing historical events tend to be unique and can only be adequately described and explained by an account of the sequel of events themselves. This, I think, is the terrain par excellence of the historian.[96] The "origins of modern religious Satanism," mentioned in the subtitle of this book, thus refer to the *historical* origins of Satanism, not to the economic, sociological, or psychological mechanisms that might have been involved in its gestation.

If considered like this, academic historiography has indeed much similarity to the religious venture itself, in the fact that it assumes that a "story" can and should be found in reality, and in the fact that it formulates propositions about reality that cannot be falsified or verified in a strictly empirical way. Of course, there remain important differences between the two—the most important being the fact that a proper historical narrative always refers to verifiable sources and adheres to rational plausibility as its primary principle of argument. I think we certainly should take care to retain this difference, which really is no more than a courteous bow to our readers that signals our fundamental readiness to be questioned and refuted. Otherwise, I believe historians may cherish the extension of their profession into the domain of meaning, as it is precisely this that gives the historical discipline much of its value.[97] History is about myths of origins— mostly about *our own* myths of origin. History also allows us to connect with other human beings—most ostentatiously with the unrecoverable estranged other from the past, but just as well with the present-day other around us, with whom we can discover a shared humanity and construct a shared history.

Both these elements are important, if not essential, constituents of our humanity. Mircea Eliade once wrote in this respect that reading (or writing) a good history of religion should be something of a religious experience itself. By permitting us to relive the existential dilemmas of others, in other cultures or other times, we will be confronted with questions that relate us to the ultimate grounds of our own existence.[98] In narrating the history of Satanism that follows, I hope to enable the reader, and myself, to relive some of the existential dilemmas that Western society has confronted in the past, thus allowing us to gain greater understanding of not only the human choices involved in the emergence of this unusual religion, but also who we are or want to be ourselves.

To him I'll build an altar and a church,

And offer lukewarm blood of new-born babes.

CHRISTOPHER MARLOWE, *Doctor Faustus*, Act I, scene v, lines 13–14

1

The Christian Invention of Satanism

THE CONCEPT OF Satanism is an invention of Christianity. As we will see presently, it was within the context of Christian religion and of a society shaped by Christian religion that the idea of Satanism first arose.[1] In the big picture, moreover, the emergence of Satanism is fundamentally linked to Christianity by the pivotal role that the latter religion played in the proliferation of the concept of the devil. If we define Satanism as the intentional religious veneration of Satan, it follows that there can be no Satanism without (a) Satan. This chapter will accordingly open with a short account of the genesis of this mythological entity. We then follow the trail of the concept of Satanism as it arose and developed within the Judeo-Christian world. At the same time, we will keep a watchful eye on the reality behind the concept and consider the presence of real forms of Satanism in premodern and early modern history. In particular, we discuss the so-called Affair of the Poisons from late seventeenth-century France, as well as some other specific instances of possible Satanism from the early modern era. As already mentioned, however, our tour of exploration will start with a concise account of the birth of Satan himself.

A SHORT BIOGRAPHY OF THE DEVIL

From early on in history, humans have attested a tendency to blame or fear spiritual entities for causing misfortune.[2] In local communities, misfortune was associated with certain places, animals, or people, with archaic deities, or with certain times of the year when spirits roamed. In more centralized societies, religious specialists compiled inventories of spiritual beings responsible for misfortune in ritual texts and long lists of names. Knowing the correct appellations of these potentially dangerous beings offered some measure of control and the opportunity to protect oneself through ritual.[3] As the spirit world was characterized by great ambivalence, the boundary lines between spiritual beings that brought misfortune and those that did not were not clearly drawn. They fluctuated according to place, time, ethnic identity, and profession. In formulas of exorcism and protection, the spiritual beings that are warded off include entities personifying the chaotic, classes of beings preying on men, gods of neighboring peoples, and local gods that could be beseeched by enemies to do one harm. Sometimes, these spells end with a plea to protect the supplicant against "every god and every goddess who assumes manifestations when they are not appeased"— evidently out of concern that a spiritual being whose name was forgotten in the list might otherwise pierce the protective shield established by ritual.[4]

The same divine or superhuman entities might thus fulfill both "malign" and "benign" roles, depending on the circumstances. Ancient Greek religion provides a well-known illustration of this phenomenon. The gods of Olympus displayed behavior that may be described as amoral. They were generally well-disposed toward humans but were also capable of doing harm when thwarted. Their opponents, the titans, stood for the unruly forces of primeval chaos that had to be combated and subdued to allow the ordered, habitable world to exist. Yet no strict ethical or ontological juxtaposition between titans and Olympic gods existed, as is demonstrated by the fact that Zeus himself originally sprang from the race of the former. Similarly, the term "demon" (daimon) was devoid of exclusively malevolent implications and was liberally applied to both greater and lesser divine beings.[5] According to Plato, demonic possession was responsible for passionate feelings of love, prophetic trance, and insanity; the latter was not even considered to be simple misfortune, but a sign of the presence of the gods conferring divinatory powers. Socrates (Plato tells us) claimed to be inspired by such a personal δαιμον.

Historical struggles among nations might be reflected in the topography of the spiritual realm as well. Where one culture conquered or submerged another, the conquered set of gods was often assimilated into the pantheon of the conqueror or denigrated into lesser but more malign entities. In addition, divergent cultural or linguistic evolutions could lead to strikingly different ascriptions in the world of the gods. A famous and often-quoted example of the latter phenomenon is the case of the *asuras* and *devas* in Indo-Iranian religion. In the Indian Rig Veda, *ásura* meant something like "lord," especially in the significance of "leader of a fighting force". It could be applied to both friend and foe. Later on, the *asuras* became a specific class of beings that was considered inimical to the *devas*, the Vedic gods. In Iranian religion, meanwhile, "ahura" retained its old significance of "lord," even becoming part of the appellation of the supreme god, Ahura Mazda. At the same time, the warriorlike "daevas" were relegated to the status of hostile spirits.[6]

In brief, a certain moral ambiguity is characteristic of conceptions about the spiritual sphere in the ancient world.[7] As far as we know, the crisp division in the divine domain between a "good" and a "bad" (set of) god(s) is a relatively late innovation in the history of religion. The Egyptian god Seth in its later aspects may provide a rare, tentative instance of the evolution of such a spiritual representative of evil. Egyptian religion, one of the most ancient we know about, tells about a god of origin called Atum, "The Complete One." From him all other gods sprang. One of these was Seth, god of the desert and of the wastelands, "great in strength." The Dutch Egyptologist Te Velde, in his authoritative dissertation on the subject, characterized Seth as a "god of confusion." He was a disturber of order, a bringer of storm and tumult, a "hot tempered, lecherous god" who killed his brother Osiris and sexually harassed Osiris's son Horus.[8] But despite these seemingly unpleasant traits, it would be dangerously anachronistic to describe him as an incorporation of absolute evil. Rather, Seth represented a necessary aspect by which the divine manifested itself. As one of the fiercer aspects of the divine, he is sometimes depicted as a protector of the sun barque during its nightly voyage, defending it against the Apopis snake, an entity of chaos that threatens to devour the sun.[9] His cult flourished in certain parts of Egypt, with faithful followers giving their children names like "Seth is great," "Seth is gracious," and "Seth rules."[10]

As god of the desert, Seth was also associated with foreign lands and foreign people. Names of foreign gods in international treaties, for instance, were usually translated as "Seth" in the Egyptian versions of the texts. When Egypt experienced a period of territorial expansion under the Rammesides, the cult of Seth was greatly stimulated; several Rammaside pharaohs took on a second name incorporating that of Seth. As the "divine foreigner," the god in a way represented the new, non-Egyptian subjects of the pharaoh. This association may have opened the door for the eventual demonization of Seth. When Egypt embarked on a long period of foreign domination after the invasion of the Assyrians, Seth became the symbolic representative of alien rule. His name and image were erased from monuments and inscriptions; a ritual "to overthrow Seth and his gang" was enacted in Egyptian temples, during which the disfavored god was addressed as "lord of lies," "king of deceit," and "gangleader of criminals."[11] Yet this demonization was never universal, it seems, and as late as the Roman period, we can find indications that Seth was still worshipped in outlying oases.[12]

If we leave aside the equivocal case of Egypt's "god of confusion," Zoroastrianism must be considered the first religion that presents us with a supreme mythological representative of evil. Founded by Zoroaster or Zarathustra between 600 and 1000 BCE, this innovative Iranian religion reinterpreted the world in radical dualist terms. From the beginning, it claimed, two spiritual entities opposed each other in the universe: Ahura Mazdā, or Ormuzd, the principle of goodness and light, and Angra Mainyu, or Ahreman, the principle of darkness and evil. Initially, Angra Mainyu was a general designation that simply meant "evil spirit." As Zoroastrianism evolved, it gradually developed into a proper name for the deity of evil.[13]

In an unprecedented way, this sharp divide between a god of good and a god of evil was applied to the rest of reality as well. Thus the spiritual world was conceived of as consisting of two opposing camps: Ahreman was supported by the daevas, the old warrior gods now considered evil spiritual beings, while Ormuzd was assisted by a host of good divinities. In the animal world, certain animals (predominantly insects and reptiles) were said to be created by the evil spirit: killing these *khrafstra* was a sacred duty to the Zoroastrian faithful.[14] Last but not least, humanity was divided into two camps as well. The Zoroastrian believers who followed the precepts of Ahura Mazdā would share in his final victory over the evil spirit. The evildoers and unbelievers, however, were to be destroyed in the final fire, along with their spiritual master. Interestingly, Zoroastrian texts also express great anxiety about groups of people who were said to worship the daevas in a more specific way. These "Ahremanists" were described as secretly gathering at night in order to celebrate their own reverted liturgy and recite their own daevanic revelation; the Zoroastrian scribes also claimed that they liked to feast on putrefying human flesh and cover themselves in human excrement.[15]

It is against this historical canvas that we must place the slow evolution of Satan. The oldest traces of the designation "satan" can be found in the collection of Hebrew writings that would later form the Jewish Tenach and the Christian Old Testament. The Hebrew word שָׂטָן is commonly translated as "adversary," "opponent," or "accuser"; related meanings of "obstructer" and "tester" have been proposed as well.[16] In five places in the Tenach—the majority of cases—the word indicates human opponents; in four places, it is used for non-human actors. Thus in Numbers 22:22–35, the *mal'ak Yahweh* (the Messenger or Angel of Yahweh) is called a "satan" when he blocks the passage of Balaam on his way to curse the people of Israel. The word "satan" here simply means that the angel is a "physical" obstructer standing in Balaak's way.

This satan is clearly a different personality from the satan that appears in a vision of the prophet Zechariah dealing with the disputed status of a Hebrew high priest (Zechariah 3:1–2). In the vision, the high priest is pictured standing before the Angel of Yahweh, while *hássátan*, "the accuser," is on his right side to accuse him. The Angel of Yahweh rebukes this accuser, however, and vindicates the priest's position. A similar role of accuser is fulfilled by the most well-known "satan" in the Jewish Tenach, the one figuring in the prologue to the book of Job, which is commonly dated to the sixth century BCE. The first two chapters of this book describe how the "sons of god" are gathered before Yahweh. Among them appears an angel who is, once again, simply indicated as "the accuser." When he reports that he has "roamed throughout the earth, going back and forth on it," Yahweh asks him if he has noted the exceptional piety of his servant Job. The angel responds that Job's exceptional piety is not surprising, as Yahweh has made him prosper in all ways. What will remain of Job's dedication if his wealth and health are taken away? Yahweh takes up the challenge and allows the angel to strike Job with disaster and disease.

Obviously, thus, there is a connection between a "satanic" angel and misfortune in the book of Job. Yet the "satan" that we find here, most modern scholarship agrees, is not a distinct mythological personality incorporating evil, but rather the job description of a heavenly functionary whose office it is to report on humankind and test its virtue.[17] The idea of a universal opposing spiritual force that is responsible for misfortune is absent in the Hebrew Bible, which has as one of its central themes the status of Yahweh as the only true and genuinely powerful deity. Misfortune is attributed either to human infringements of Yahweh's prescriptions or to the inscrutable divine will itself. This is the theme of many of the Psalms and also, eventually, of the book of Job, which after the prologue is completely devoted to poetical disputations about the righteousness of Yahweh's distribution of fortune and misfortune, while the accuser angel is never mentioned again.

Some biblical scholars have argued that the "inner dynamics" of developing monotheisms like the Hebrew cult of Yahweh more or less inevitably lead to a certain "externalisation of evil" in order to prevent a direct association between the deity and evil.[18] As an illustration of this tendency, a fourth Bible passage where a satan appears is often mentioned, namely, 1 Chronicles 21:1. 1 Chronicles is a later adaptation of the histories of the kings of Israel, told in the second book of Samuel. 2 Samuel 24 recounts how Yahweh provoked King David to hold a census of Israel, despite the fact that this was considered a sinful action. As a consequence, Israel was stricken by a devastating plague. In 1 Chronicles 21, the same story is told, but here it is "a satan" who "provoked David to number Israel." The remarkable introduction of a third party in this text is often interpreted as an attempt by the Hebrew chronicler to exculpate Yahweh from malevolent behavior, thus signifying "the beginnings of a moral dichotomy in the celestial sphere."[19] This interpretation, however, is not undisputed. It has been suggested that the unknown author of 1 Chronicles might in fact be interested not so much in the ethics of divine action, but rather in painting a favorable picture of the relationship between Yahweh and David—especially since elsewhere in 2 Chronicles, Yahweh is unencumberedly depicted as sanctioning lies and harmful behavior (cf. 2 Chronicles 10; 14; and 18:18–22).[20]

In fact, it is considerably later—in the period between the closure of the Jewish Tenach (approximately 400 BCE) and the destruction of the second Jerusalem Temple (70 CE)—that spiritual enactors of misfortune and evil gain prominence in Jewish religious thought. The historical causes of this development are subject to debate. Biblical scholars, as we have seen, often emphasize autonomous theological developments within Judaism itself. Iranologists usually claim a strong influence from the radically dualist concept of the spirit world in Zoroastrianism.[21] After all, the tribes of Judah and Levi had been taken away in captivity to Zoroastrian Persia, and later on they could have become familiar with Zoroastrian ideas in the great cultural melting pot of Hellenistic Asia. Whatever the causes, a growing preoccupation with spiritual workers of evil becomes apparent during this period, finding expression in new cosmogonical theories, lists of demons, and eschatological concepts (ideas about the end of the world). The satan of the Tenach is caught up in this process of theological dichotomization. Although it is impossible to pinpoint the exact moment when he becomes Satan, the Evil One, there are some significant hallmarks. In the Septuagint, the Greek translation of the Hebrew Bible dating from around 200 BCE, the references in Job and Zechariah to an angel-who-is-a-satan are translated with "ho diabolos," "the Slanderer," thus marking him both as a distinct personality and as a distinctly more unpleasant one.[22]

It is not yet clear-cut that this "Slanderer" will eventually become the unchallenged lord of evil. In fact, the religious literature of contemporary Judaism mentions teems with competing candidates: rulers of wicked spirits with exotic names like Semyaza, Azazel, Semihazah, Asmodeus (probably a derivation from the Iranian *aesma-daeva*, "god of wrath"), Belial or Beliar, Mastemah, Samael, and Melkina.[23] After the destruction of the Second Temple, dominant currents within Judaism downplayed the importance of these spiritual actors, emphasizing instead the dual inclination toward good and evil within man himself.[24] The emphasis on evil spirits and eschatology was retained and elaborated, however, by Jewish religious groups outside mainstream Judaism.[25] One of these was the group that had sprung into being around an executed Jewish preacher called Jesus of Nazareth. In the selection of writings (known today as the New Testament) that this new religious movement added to the Jewish canon, the devil makes a regular appearance, while many stories tell about dramatic encounters with demons, a designation that had obtained an exclusively negative connotation in the Judeo-Christian tradition.[26] An evil kingdom of darkness opposes the kingdom of light of the true god; in most cases, Satan is pictured as the master of the former. At the moment the New Testament authors write, Earth is still dominated by these demonic forces, which bring misfortune, sickness, and temptation to sin. Jesus, however, has come to proclaim the coming victory of the kingdom of Yahweh over that of Satan, whose eventual removal from power is pictured in glowing colors in the last addition to the Christian canon, the Book of Revelation.[27]

Despite his greater prominence, the portrait of Satan in the New Testament remains rather sketchy. Older and other traditions are occasionally visible through the seams of the texts. Thus, in the synoptic Evangels (the biographical accounts of Jesus attributed to Mark, Matthew, and Luke) the Hebrew word "satan" is sometimes still used in its older, broader significance: when the apostle Peter tries to prevent Jesus from accepting his Job-like fate of suffering, he is rebuked by the latter as a "satan" (Matthew 16:23; Marc 8:33). The synoptic Gospels occasionally also refer to the ruler of evil or unclean spirits as Baalzebul, the "Great Lord" worshipped in Phoenician religion, while the apostle Paul juxtaposes Christ with Belial—and not Satan—in his second pastoral letter to the Corinthians (2 Cor. 6:14–15). Yet in most New Testament contexts the word "satan," untranslated from the Hebrew, or its Greek equivalent "devil," has clearly come to designate a distinct spiritual being that is "wholly the enemy of God and righteousness."[28]

The sketchy outlines in the New Testament were worked into a coherent topography of evil in the Christian theology of the second and third centuries. Authors like Justin Martyr (100–165), Tertullian (160–225), and Origen of Alexandria (185–254) pioneered the emergence of a systematic Christian theology modeled on the example of classic philosophy.[29] They also extended their venture into the domains of darkness, listing and classifying the hosts of evil spirits within the pages of their treatises. In their writings, Satan is firmly established as the prince of the enemy realm. His activities are also read backward into the Jewish scriptures of the Tenach, identifying him, for instance, with the Serpent who seduced Adam and Eve into original sin in the book of Genesis—an identification that had already been suggested in the New Testament Book of Revelation, where Satan is called "the Serpent of old" (Rev. 12:9).[30]

Justin, Origen, and other early theologians also tried to fill in the gaps in the devil's biography that had been left open by canonical scripture, particularly with regard to his origins (and thus, ultimately, the origin of evil), often basing their speculations on mythical accounts that eventually would not be admitted into the biblical canon.

One of these mythical accounts was that of the Watcher Angels. In the biblical book of Genesis, a remarkable passage told how the "sons of God" had observed the beauty of the "daughters of men" and "took wives for themselves" from among them. "There were giants on the earth in those days, and also afterward, when the sons of God came in to the daughters of men and they bore children to them" (Genesis 6:1–4). In the first book of Enoch (an apocryphal book dating approximately from between 300 BCE and 100 CE), this story was expanded in a myth about a class of angels who had found pleasure in mortal women and had been banished from heaven as a punishment for their cosmic downdating. On Earth, they had introduced gold, weapons, and women's cosmetics: in other words, most of the sins of civilization.[31] Although the leader of the fallen angels is called Semyaza in 1 Enoch:6–16, this myth was later applied to Satan, whose first transgression thus would have been inappropriate lust.

Yet another story identified Satan's original sin with envy. When man was created, this story maintained, the angel was not able to accept that Yahweh had selected such a lowly creature to be made into his divine image. As a consequence, he choose to revolt against his maker. This account continued to be upheld by some, particularly within Eastern Christianity, and was later also adopted by Islamic theology.[32]

The explanation that would eventually become dominant in Western Christianity, however, attributed Satan's original downfall to pride. This myth of origin was inspired by a prophecy in the biblical book of Isaiah, where it was said about the king of Babel that he had sought to set himself up as an equal to "the Most High," but instead had been humbled by Yahweh (Isaiah 14:12). From the first century CE, this oracle about the "morning star" ("Lucifer," in Latin) was associated with the devil. Being the foremost among the angels, Lucifer had wanted to assume divine power himself and had taken up the banner of rebellion, subsequently leading mankind into sin in the guise of the Serpent of Eden.[33]

By the third or fourth century CE, something resembling an official biography of Satan had evolved within Christianity. Certainly, enough problems and loose ends remained to keep Christian theologians busy for many centuries to come. Origen, for instance, still maintained that Satan would be reintegrated into creation after the final judgment as part of the "ἀποκατάστασις πάντων," the "recuperation of all things."[34] But the general contours of the Christian Satan were by now reasonably well defined. He was the archenemy, ruling a kingdom of darkness that opposed the kingdom of Christ, and he led a retinue of demons and evil spirits that mirrored the angelic hierarchy of heaven. Because of his rebellion against divine rule and his involvement in the fall of mankind, he was closely associated with the genesis and introduction of evil itself. Although he could only operate within the limits that were set for him by divine will, and although his empire would be broken in the end, as "god of this world" (John 14:30 and 16:11; cf. also I John 5:19), Satan's power in present reality was formidable. From a vaguely defined heavenly functionary with a slightly unpleasant job description, Satan had thus transformed into the principal mythological representative of evil.

CONSTRUCTING WORSHIPPERS OF SATAN

The Christian message did not stop at discerning a strong malevolent presence in the world. It also professed to be able to remedy this situation and liberate its adherents—and eventually the entire universe—from the demons that brought misfortune and evil. Jesus himself was described in the Gospels as a powerful exorcist casting out demons from the possessed and the sick.[35] In his name, his followers claimed the same power. Thus the long lists of evil spirits in theological tracts were not just frivolous speculation about inimical transcendental worlds, but a practical tool to control spiritual forces that were manifest in day-to-day reality.[36]

In their efforts to control evil spirits, the early Christians were just one group among the many rival religious specialists pertaining to do the same. What made them stand out was both the universal scope and the exclusivist character of their claims. Every person, regardless of ethnicity, social class, or gender, could become a Christian. Or, rather, everyone *should* become a Christian, because only Christ could bring true deliverance from evil. On the other side of the mirror, as we have seen, the malevolent beings that made mankind miserable were also considered to belong to one, universal antagonistic force. Whereas local specialists could offer limited succor against local malign entities, Christianity claimed to award immunity against both these local demons and the greater evil behind them all. A message like this could not fail to have appeal in the increasingly globalizing society of the Roman Empire.[37]

This totalizing discourse and its accompanying dichotomization were applied to Christianity's religious rivals as well. As the new religious movement evolved from being a Jewish sect to being a truly universal religion, its confrontation with the paganism that dominated the Roman Empire became increasingly fierce. In his first letter to the church at Corinth, the apostle Paul had already displayed an intriguing ambiguity toward the deities of paganism, calling them empty idols in the tradition of the Old Testament prophet Isaiah, yet also suggesting the presence of sinister spiritual entities behind them (1 Corinthians 10, 20a—but see also 1 Corinthians 8:4–6). The latter view came to receive increasing emphasis. For the growing numbers of heathen converts to Christianity, the pagan gods did not all of a sudden become unreal. Rather, they were *reinterpreted*: they received a new place in the order of reality. *Demons*, real supernatural powers, were the instigators and the moving force behind the worship of the pagan idols and the prodigies of the pagan religions. "These unclean spirits, or demons, as revealed to Magi and philosophers, find a lurking place under statues and consecrated images, and by their breath exercise influence as of a present god," the Christian apologist Minucius Felix wrote toward the end of the second century. "At one they inspire prophets, at another haunt temples, at another animate the fibres of entrails, govern the flight of birds, determine lots, and are the authors of oracles mostly wrapped in falsehood."[38] For Justin Martyr, even the traits in heathen religions that seemed to parallel elements of Christianity were conscious creations of demons, forged with foresight "to produce in men the idea that the things which were said with regard to Christ were mere marvellous tales, like the things which were said by the poets."[39] From the second century onward, converts to Christianity invariably had to be exorcized before they could be baptized, solemnly abjuring Satan and his works.[40] "Those whom you had presumed to be gods, you learn to be demons," Tertullian succinctly resumed in his *Apologeticus*.[41]

The religious propaganda battle that went on was not fought with words and theological treatises alone. By spectacular feats of exorcism, the gods were forced to denounce themselves. To quote Minucius Felix once again:

> All of this, as most of your people know, the demons themselves admit to be true, when they are driven out of men's bodies by words of exorcism and the fire of prayer. Saturn himself, Serapis, Jupiter, or any other demon you worship, under stress of pain, confess openly what they are; and surely they would not lie to their own disgrace, particularly with some of you standing by. When the witnesses themselves confess the truth about themselves, that they are demons, you cannot but believe; when adjured in the name of the one true God, reluctantly, in misery, they quail and quake, and either suddenly leap forth at once, or vanish gradually, according to the faith exercised by the sufferer or the grace imparted by the healer.[42]

The Antique Christian view of the gods as evil spirits, malign yet real, became the stock-in-trade with the Patristic writers and was carried on into the Middle Ages and beyond.[43] In the accounts of missionary saints, demons in the shape of "black Ethiopians" frequently make their appearance when pagan temples and shrines are destroyed or turned into Christian places of worship.[44] The polytheist and panentheist religions of the pagans had sprinkled the European landscape with spiritual hot spots, and the Christian conquest of the continent was thus as much a conquest of objects and places as of men and minds. Hallowed trees had to be felled, and sacred sources and lakes exorcised. In the rigid dualistic scheme that dominated Christianity, neutral zones all but ceased to exist: buildings, gardens, tools, animals, even the bread used in the Eucharist and the water sprinkled in baptism, all had to be freed from demonic presences through the use of officially prescribed rituals. This attitude to reality is saliently illustrated by the well-known story told by Gregorius the Great about a nun who ate a piece of lettuce but forgot to make the sign of the cross. A demon promptly took possession of her and the nun had to be exorcised before the hostile invader hidden in the leaf of lettuce evacuated her body again.[45]

The demonizing of the pagan gods and of their worship also influenced the popular conception of Satan. The well-known image of the devil as goat-footed and horned is reminiscent of the Greek god Pan and of the *fauni* and *silvani* of the Roman forests.[46] In other parts of Europe, the devil sometimes assimilated traits of native gods from other traditions. In the late medieval Dutch miracle play *Mariken van Nieumegen*, for instance, he appears as "One-Eyed Moenen" ("Moenen metter eender ooghe"), quaintly resembling the Nordic god Odin, whose worship had already been abandoned for centuries.[47]

Demon-inspired as the worship of the pagans might have been according to the *interpretatio Christiana*, the pagans were not thought of as *intentionally* worshipping the devil. The Fathers of the Church did not suggest that they were aware of the true identity of their gods and persisted in venerating them nevertheless. The pagans were simply misguided.[48] The concept that a group of people might *intentionally* be worshipping Satan or a demon—in other words, the concept of Satanism as *we* have defined it—first gained prominence in connection with enemies from within the Christian faith's own ranks: Jews who refused to recognize Jesus as Christ, and Christians whose beliefs or practices did not accord with one's own. The latter were often designated as heretics—from the Greek word αἵρεσις, which originally meant "choice."

Like other marginal groups from intertestamentary Judaism, Christianity had showed a marked tendency of ascribing a special bond with Satan to "brethren" rather than external enemies.[49] Already in the New Testament, Jews who do not convert and "false" teachers from within the Church are frequently designated as allies of Satan. "Ye are of your father the devil, and the lusts of your father you will do," Jesus retorts to his Jewish opponents in the Gospel according to John, while a pastoral letter attributed to Paul calls heretical teachers a "snare of the Devil, held captive to his will" (John 8:44a; 2 Tim. 2:26). The theme is echoed in early patristic literature: Polycarp (†165) calls the orthodox believers "the community of the first born of God," while adherents of Christianity with divergent religious views are identified as "the first born children of Satan." The Shepherd of Hermas adds the image of two cities: one is the community of those serving the god of Christianity; the other, the community of those serving Satan.[50]

From being an inhabitant of the city of Satan because of his dangerous distortion of Christian doctrine, the heretic gradually came to be conceived of as an active idolater of the devil. Early in the eighth century, the Armenina Catholicos, John of Ojun attributed such a practice to the Paulicians, a dissenting Christian group that had emerged in the Near East. According to John of Ojun's account in his 720th sermon, the Paulicians gathered at night to worship the devil. They also practiced idolatry, incest, and infanticide; mixed the host with the blood of slaughtered children; and left the bodies of their dead in the open air to decompose.[51] In Western Christianity, the first report of this kind, as far as scholarship is aware, dates from 1022, when two clerics called Stephanus and Lisoius were tried for heresy by a synod at Toulouse, in the south of France. The transactions of the synod described the practices of these alleged sectarians and their adherents in lurid detail:

> They are said to have convened on certain nights in a house agreed upon beforehand, holding a single lamp in their hand, and declaiming the name of the demon like in a litany, until suddenly the Demon could be seen descending among them in the likeness of some kind of animal. As soon as possible everyone who was able, seized the woman next to him to abuse her, without having any regard in their sins for mother or sister or nun. Such a coition they held for holy & religious. As for the children generated by this defiled coition, on the eight day they make a huge fire in their midst and then try them in the manner of the ancient Pagans, and thus burn them in the fire. . . . The diabolical fraud then enters these ashes with such force, that whoever has been imbued with the aforementioned sect & has tasted and taken even a little from these ashes, will afterwards hardly be able to direct the steps of his mind from that sect to the road of truth ever again. Enough has been said of things like these in order that the children of Christ may beware of such nefarious works and not start to imitate the things they study.[52]

Were gruesome Satanist orgies like these really taking place among the Paulicians and in medieval France? Modern historians give ample reasons to answer this question negatively. For one thing, many of the picturesque details provided by reports like these were not altogether novel. Most of them could be read with the Fathers of the Church and other early Christian authors, they recounted Roman allegations against, ironically, the early Christians themselves. This, for instance, is how a pagan Roman describes the Christian assemblies to Felix:

> They recognize one another by secret signs and marks; they fall in love almost before they are acquainted; everywhere they introduce a kind of religion of lust, a promiscuous "brotherhood" and "sisterhood" by which ordinary fornication, under cover of a hallowed name, is converted to incest. And thus their vain and foolish superstition makes an actual boast of crime. For themselves, were there not some foundation of truth, shrewd rumour would not impute gross and unmentionable forms of vice. I am told that under some idiotic impulse they consecrate and worship the head of an ass, the meanest of all beasts, a religion worthy of the morals which gave it birth. Others say that they actually reverence the private parts of their director and high-priest, and adore his organs as parent of their being. This may be false, but such suspicions naturally attach to their secret and nocturnal rites. To say that a malefactor put to death

for his crimes, and wood of the death-dealing cross, are objects of their veneration is to assign fitting altars to abandoned wretches and the kind of worship they deserve. Details of the initiation of neophytes are as revolting as they are notorious. An infant, cased in dough to deceive the unsuspecting, is placed beside the person to be initiated. The novice is thereupon induced to inflict what seem to be harmless blows upon the dough, and unintentionally the infant is killed by his unsuspecting blows; the blood—oh, horrible—they lap up greedily; the limbs they tear to pieces eagerly; and over the victim they make league and covenant, and by complicity in guilt pledge themselves to mutual silence. Such sacred rites are more foul than sacrilege. Their form of feasting is notorious; it is in everyone's mouth, as testified by the speech of our friend Cirta. On the day appointed they gather at a banquet with all their children, sisters, and mothers, people of either sex and every age. There, after full feasting, when the blood is heated and drink has inflamed the passions of incestuous lust, a dog which had been tied to a lamp is tempted by a morsel thrown beyond the range of his tether to bound forward with a rush. The tale-telling light is upset and extinguished, and in the shameless dark lustful embraces are indiscriminately exchanged; and all alike, if not in act, yet by complicity, are involved in incest, as anything that occurs by the act of individuals results from the common intention.[53]

Needless to say, this libel against early Christians had no foundation in fact. It reflected earlier rumors that had circulated in the Roman Empire with regard to "outsider groups" such as the Jews, foreign mystery cults, and "barbarians" living outside the border.[54] For pagan Romans, the Christians must have represented an extreme embodiment of such an outsider group. Secretly convening in sinister places like catacombs, the new religious movement completely reversed traditional values of citizenship and piety, worshipping an executed rebel as a god instead of the divine emperor, and adding insult to absurdity by claiming that the Empire's traditional gods were in reality evil demons.

As we have seen, Christian writers did not shrink from reapplying bogey stories of this type to their own opponents.[55] Sometimes these imputations were directed against pagan cults, but in most cases, rival factions of Christianity were targets.[56] Justin Martyr already attributes practices like this to "heretics called Christians," although he cautiously adds "whether they perpetrate those fabulous and shameful deeds—the upsetting of the lamp, and promiscuous intercourse, and eating human flesh—we know not."[57] In his writings against the Manicheans, Augustine of Hippo follows a similar strategy of subtle insinuation. Reporting allegations that the followers of Mani participated in indiscriminate orgies where male sperm was offered to the deity and consumed as Eucharist, he admits these rumors might not be true but nevertheless maintains that they were provoked by the Manichean doctrines themselves, whose logical application would indeed lead to practices like these.[58] Other writers omitted these caveats. In the *Panarion*, a fourth-century Greek catalogue of heresies, Epiphanius of Salamis describes a Christian group that he simply designates as "Gnostics." As in Roman descriptions of early Christians, they were said to recognize each other by secret hand signs and engage in group sex, presenting their semen as an offering like Augustine's Manichees and subsequently eating it, while the same procedure was applied to menstrual fluids. When a woman inadvertently became pregnant during these sacred orgies, they aborted the fetus and feasted on it in a communal meal.[59]

Again, historians have debated whether some religious groups in this period (particularly "Gnostic" ones) may indeed have performed (some of) these practices.[60] There is, after all, nothing inherently impossible in the activities described. Infanticide, cannibalism, and the ritual exchange of sexual partners all are frequently reported forms of human behavior. Marriage between close kin was considered sacred by some religions (among them ancient Zoroastrianism), and rites utilizing sexual emissions are well attested from both tribal religions and twentieth-century magical practice.[61] At the moment, it is not our concern to establish whether some Christian groups may have performed some of these actions. It must be pointed out, however, that the way these allegations fit into the pattern of prior and subsequent stereotypes should make every historian extremely wary of unhesitatingly accepting their veracity. Our only clues for their occurrence, moreover, come from polemic literature written by religious opponents.

Meanwhile, it is important to note that one crucial element seems to be conspicuously lacking from the polemics of the Antique Christian authors: that of the intentional veneration of Satan. I am not aware of one author from this period who accuses heretical groups of consciously and deliberately venerating the devil or demons. Epiphanius of Salamis, whose extensive work on heresies is nevertheless not sparing of diabolizing labels and general terms of abuse, refrains from mentioning explicit devil worship among the many evils that he detects among heretical groups—even in cases that may have particularly invited this, such as certain currents of Gnosticism that were involved in forms of extreme anti-exegesis. The Ophite Gnostics, for instance, held that the Serpent of Paradise was a divine messenger, and they worshipped actual snakes as its representatives. In a similar vein, the Cainites held that Cain and other figures vilified in the Tenach, like the Sodomites and Esau, should in reality be held in esteem because of their opposition to the evil demiurge who inspired the Jewish scriptures.[62] In neither of these cases, nor in regard to most other heresies he describes, does Epiphanius speak of direct worship of the devil.[63] The only time that he *does* mention a group that explicitly venerates Satan, it is lumped together with a group of religious movements he describes as "altogether pagan." The section Epiphanius devotes to these enigmatic "Satanians" (Σατανιανοί) is surprisingly short and largely devoid of picturesque detail:

> But others in their turn thought of something still more crafty and said, as though consulting their own intelligence in their simplicity, "Satan is great and the strongest, and does people a great deal of harm. Why not take refuge in him, worship him instead [of God], and give him honour and blessing, so that he will be appeased by our flattering service and do us no harm, but spare us because we have become his servants?" And so, again, they have called themselves Satanians.[64]

This is, as far as I know, the first time a religious group practicing Satanism is mentioned in a historical source. Epiphanius goes on to recount that they meet in the open air "and spend their time in prayer and hymns."[65] Although the group features as the last or penultimate "sect" in his work, they hardly impress one as the climax of deviance that their position in the book or their doctrine suggests they might be. It is clear from the *Panarion* that the Satanians—if they ever existed—were in all respects an extremely marginal group. Indeed, Epiphanius himself considers them "harmless" and unable to distract anybody from the Christian faith.[66]

As the bishop's work is our only source for these "Satanians," we cannot say much for or against their actual existence.[67] It might well be that some misunderstood doctrine of a peripatetic religious group is at the root of his story—Epiphanius is not exactly an author who is known for the trustworthiness of his utterances. On the other hand, at the end of the fourth century, when Epiphanius wrote his book, the concept of the Judeo-Christian Satan might have been sufficiently widespread to inspire non-Christians to seek diabolical assistance or protection. In addition, none of the classic features of the stereotype for the (religious) "other"—cannibalism, infanticide, indiscriminate sex, or secretive nightly gatherings—are attributed to these Satanians by Epiphanius. Although their appearance in the *Panarion* shows that the idea or occurrence of an intentional veneration of Satan was not inconceivable or unknown to Antique Christian authors, the latter apparently did not yet choose to include this feature in their descriptions of inner-faith dissidence.

The Middle Ages inaugurated a drastic change regarding the latter point. As we have seen, authors from that period picked up the late-Antique antiheretical discourse—it is highly suggestive in this connection, for instance, that the "sect" around Stephanus and Lisoius is designated as *novos Manicheos* ("New Manicheans") right away. Yet a new element was now added to the catalogue of alleged misdemeanor: that of veneration of Satan or of his demons. This marks the emergence of the idea of the Satanist as I have defined it in this study.

The new "Satanist" stereotype was applied to a wide array of dissenting groups throughout the Middle Ages. The seventh-century Paulicians, the Bogomils, the Cathars, the radical ascetic Fratecelli, the Waldensians, the Hussites: all were systematically or incidentally accused of worshipping the devil.[68] In many cases, this crust of attribution grew so thick that it has become all but impossible to establish the exact identity of the groups concerned, especially as most of the sources left to us were authored by their "orthodox" opponents. Even the names by which we call them have mostly come from the pen of Catholic chroniclers.[69] Wherever we are able to get some glimpses of the real practices and convictions of these groups, however, they invariably turn out to be far removed from Satanism of any kind. The Cathars, or at least some of them, were adherents to a more dualist variant of Christianity, as were the Bogomils—neither was likely to be involved in the veneration of Satan or any other evil principle.[70] The Waldensians originated as a local reform group for lay piety that eventually fell afoul of the ecclesiastical authorities.[71] If anything, these groups were more radical in their dedication to the Christian faith than their more "orthodox" coreligionists.

It will come as no surprise that the Jews, the perennial others of medieval society, were also included in the long list of religious groups accused of venerating the devil. In fact, Jews had been confronted with insinuations about their special relationship with the demon for at least as long as dissident Christians had. The Book of Revelation already referred to Jews who failed to convert as "the synagogue of Satan, which say they are Jews, and are not, but do lie" (Rev. 3:9). In the fourth century, the Greek Father of the Church, John

Chrysostom, described the synagogues of the Jews as "the homes of idolatry and devils, even though they have no images in them."[72] Medieval thought was ambiguous about the exact status of the Jewish minority. Officially, they could not be considered heretics from Christianity, because their faith clearly antedated that of the Church. But had they not repudiated Christ, although he had been so clearly foretold as the coming Messiah in their own scriptures? And had they not been responsible for his crucifixion? In many cases, views about the Jews during the Middle Ages mirrored those about heretics, and vice versa. Jews hated Christians; Jewish prayers were directed to Satan; Jews practiced demonic magic, desecrated holy objects, and slaughtered Christian children for mysterious rituals.[73] Some anti-Jewish polemicists claimed that the Jews had allied themselves collectively with the devil—or, more precisely, with the demon Ben Tamalyon, who in return for their fealty had managed to undo a Roman decree prohibiting Jewish religious observances after the destruction of the Second Temple.[74] In the sixteenth century, this tradition was continued by the reformer Martin Luther, when he claimed that the Jews venerated "216 thousand devils" instead of the true deity.[75]

The attribution of Satanism thus became part of a complex of allegations serving to demonize the religious other. This attribution did not derive from actual practiced Satanism. Rather it was yet another manifestation, adjusted to time and place, of the many forms of reversal that have been attributed to the "other" in history. In this way, the religious other came to be imagined as the photographic negative of the normal medieval Christian: transgressing accepted sexual mores, profaning what was holy, and worshipping what was evil. The fact that most dissenting Christians did not give the impression of being worshippers of Satan did not deter their Roman Catholic opponents. "How is it possible to recognize a heretic?" is a question often recurring in medieval books on heresology. The paradoxical answer frequently given is as follows: by his outstanding piety, care for those in need, and seemingly god-fearing way of life. Naturally, this apparent devotion is nothing but a mask: "speciem sanctitatis et fidei pretendunt, veritatem autem eius non habent" (holiness and faith they feign, neither of which they truly have).[76] Behind the scenes, it was maintained, horrendous things went on during their gatherings. The secretiveness alone of their goings-on already was a strong clue. How scandalous must their religion appear to themselves, that they shun the light of day like this, both Berthold von Regenburg and Bernard de Clairvaux exclaim, inadvertently echoing old accusations brought up against the early Christians.[77]

In the thirteenth century, this complex of allegations centering on devil worship and antinomian behavior attained something like a stature of independence when ecclesiastical and other authors start to mention a sect of "Luciferians." The first appearance of these Luciferians in the sources dates from around 1231, when a chronicle from Trier tells us about a religious circle led by a certain Lucardis, a woman "who was presumed to lead a most holy life," but in fact, it was discovered, deplored "with lamentations the unjust expulsion from heaven of Lucifer," whom she hoped to see restored to heavenly rule again.[78] The alleged worship of Lucifer by Lucardis's circle had been brought to light by Conrad of Marburg, one of the first papal inquisitors, who swiftly set to work to unmask more Luciferians. When he met with resistance from the local nobility, Pope Gregorius IX came to his aid by sending the bull *Vox in Rama*. This papal document (dated 1233 or 1234) contains an elaborate description of the ceremonies and customs of the Luciferians, which by now will not sound unfamiliar:

> In that pest the initiation is performed in this way. When the novice is received by them and for the first time enters the school of the damned, there appears to him some kind of animal more or less like that which we use to call a frog or a toad. Then some kiss him on the behind and some on the mouth, in a damnable way receiving the tongue and the saliva of the beast in their mouth. . . . Only then, when he goes on, does the novice come upon a man with a very pale face who has completely dark eyes, and is so very lean and skinny that of his consumed flesh only the relics of the skin are visible over his bones. The novice is kissed by him and this feels cold like ice and after this kiss all memory of the catholic faith has completely vanished from his heart. After this they sit down to their meal, and when they have finished it completely, a black cat that they keep as a statue in their schools descends to them with its back turned to them in the way of a common dog and its tail curled up. This they kiss on its behind, first the novice, then the master, and after that it is kissed in this way by every single one who is worthy of this and belongs to the *perfecti*. The imperfect however, who consider themselves not worthy to do this, receive the peace from the master, and everyone in this place chants some hymns and incline their heads to the cat. "Spare us," says the master, and the next one makes this plea also, with the third one responding to what is said: "We know you [are the] master"; the fourth one says: "And we have to obey."
>
> And when this is done like that, the candle is extinguished, and they proceed to practice the most obnoxious works of lust, without making any difference between those who are related and those who are not. When sometimes there are many more men than women, the men, swept with ignoble passions and the unquenchable fire of their desires, perform their shameful acts in men, in the same way as they would make natural use of them when they would have been women, which is against nature, and in which way they make themselves worthy of damnation.
>
> When they have finished staining themselves with this extreme wickedness, the candles are lit again and each retreats to his proper place. From a dark corner in the school, where the most damned of men are in no short supply, some man comes forth shining from above with a light clear as the sun, as they say, and from below bristly like a cat, whose splendour illuminates the whole place. Than the master takes out those in the vestment of a novice, and says to the shining one: "Master, this of mine I give to you," and the shining one responds: "You have served me well with many good slaves, I commit in your custody what you gave me." And this saying he disappears.
>
> During several years, they even received the Body of the Lord from the hand of the priest at Easter, and, bringing it home to their houses in their mouths, threw it in the latrine in insult of the Redemptor. And to this these most unhappy of all miserables, with their polluted lips add blasphemy against the heavenly order, raving that the Lord secretly violated against justice and treacherously wanted to destroy Lucifer in the inferno. And this the miserables really believe, and they affirm that the same [Lucifer] is the true founder of the heavens, who will again restore himself to glory

and throw down the Lord; and they expect to have eternal bliss with him and not earlier than him. Everything that does please God they profess not to do, and when they can they do what He hates.[79]

References to these elusive "Luciferians" continue throughout the thirteenth and four-teenth centuries, with a few new details added from time to time (Inquisition reports from fourteenth-century Germany, for instance, contain references to a Satanic paternoster and a Luciferian formula for baptism: "Lucifer, dear Lord, give this child goods and honours; he will be thine with body and soul").[80] Modern historiography agrees on their entirely ficti-tious nature.[81] Although the real identity of the groups that were branded as Luciferians is often hard to ascertain, in the descriptions of Gregorius IX, we can recognize some elements that were commonly ascribed to Catharism, particularly the worship of a cat demon. The Luciferians that were rounded up in fourteenth-century Brandenburg have been identified with some measure of confidence as Waldensians.[82]

EXORCISING THE DEVIL'S FIFTH COLUMN

The concept of Satanism, thus, sprang into existence as a polemic tool. When we call this complex of attribution *propaganda*, this is not meant to imply that the assertions it encom-passed were not earnestly believed. Although unscrupulous rulers sometimes made deliber-ate use of these allegations for their own ends (as was clearly the case with the machinations of the French King Phillip IV against the Templars and the Jews), we have no reason to doubt the sincerity of others. Devil or demon worship simply formed part of the common perception of dissident Christians and adherents of other religions during this period. Unfortunately enough, this attribution of Satanism to the religious other was not merely a rhetorical tool in a battle of words. Due to the intimate (if not always harmonious) entan-glement of Christian religion and secular power, allegations of devil worship and heresy often would invoke tangible repercussions for those involved. In many cases, the commu-nity's drive to purify society of a Satanic presence entailed the physical destruction of the accused. Exorcism thus imperceptibly evolved into persecution, and cosmic liberation into local repression.[83]

It might be worth our while to trace the outlines of this development and briefly sketch the emergence of this Christian "machinery of persecution," to use the celebrated phrase coined by R. I. Moore. Initially, as is well known, adherents to Christianity themselves had suffered periodical persecutions at the hands of the pagan emperors. As the number of Christians continued to grow, Constantine became the first Roman emperor to legal-ize the Christian faith in 313 CE. Emperor Theodosius next made Christianity the official religion of the Empire by an edict issued in the year 380. Henceforth, the old pagan reli-gions were gradually forced into illegality and oblivion. In 399 CE, the pagan cults were prohibited; in 407, an imperial edict ordered the destruction of pagan temples. By the seventh century, the Syrian monk John of Damascus triumphantly declared that "the wor-ship of demons" had all but ceased: "Altars and temples of idols have been overthrown. Knowledge of God has been implanted. . . . The demons tremble at the men who were formerly in their power."[84]

The Christian Church that had now become dominant in the Roman Empire and would continue to be so in the West for more than a millennium was in fact a specific faction within the fractioned body of the Christian faith. In large measure, it had been the creation of Emperor Constantine, who had needed a unified church to provide religious backbone to the Empire. With this attempt to establish an imperial monopoly on the "right" religion of his subjects, Constantine expanded on centralizing tendencies that had started with his pagan precursor, Diocletian.[85] In 326, Constantine issued an edict that excluded "heretics and schismatics" from the privileges that had been extended to the officially sanctioned church, in addition subjugating these outsiders to various compulsory public services.[86] His successors continued this policy, issuing legislation to confiscate the churches and property of heretics and curtail their civil rights. Manichean Christians in particular were the target of persecution. The pagan Emperor Diocletian had already taken harsh actions against this group, whom he suspected of practicing *maleficium* (malevolent sorcery) and of secretly conspiring against the Empire (due, probably, to the provenance of their religion in Persia, Rome's archenemy). The charge of malevolent sorcery probably explains why he ordered their leaders to be executed by fire, the traditional punishment for maleficium in Roman law.[87] After the declaration of Christianity as an official religion, Theodosius reinstated the death penalty for Manicheanism and a number of other heresies that were declared to be cover-ups for it. He also called a special judicial organ into being to prosecute these heretics, with its own "inquisitores" to track them down. "Orthodox" believers, moreover, were given the right to initiate pogroms against them on their own accord. With Justinian, in the sixth century CE, the stake was reestablished for Manichean ecclesiasts (and their books), while every citizen was henceforth held legally obliged to report suspected Manichees to the imperial authorities.[88]

The Christian Church (or at least the part of it that basked in official favor) did not raise many objections to the imperial repression of its competitors. Bishop Martin of Tours, it is true, protested when Priscillian of Avila was burned at the stake on trumped-up charges of maleficium and sexual misdemeanor in 383 (possibly as a Manichean, although he in fact led a lay movement of rigorous asceticism that had nothing to do with Manicheanism), and Ambrose of Milan and Pope Sicirius belatedly excommunicated Priscillian's accusers.[89] But church leaders in the West increasingly lost their reluctance to call in the strong arm of the law against unruly elements within the ranks of the faithful. When Augustine of Hippo was confronted with a particularly stubborn dissident movement in his diocese in North Africa, he did not prove averse to armed intervention by the authorities. The occasion inspired him to formulate his infamous doctrine of *compelle intrare* ("force them to enter"), the first ideological justification of religious coercion by an authoritative Christian theologian. Western Christianity, it must be noted, experienced a different development in this respect than that in the East, where the persecution of heretics remained a matter for the emperor, acting primarily in the interest of the state.[90] In the West, the cooperation of religious and secular authorities in the fight to eradicate religious deviance was much more intense. As the western part of the Roman Empire gradually collapsed, Catholic bishops frequently remained the last vestige of political order, obtaining considerable secular powers in the process. This was especially clear in Rome itself, where the last Roman emperors presented a sad spectacle of insignificance, while the Roman pope had become the real figure of power.

In the early Middle Ages, the political fragmentation of Western Christianity and the collapse of central power made other matters than routing out heresy more urgent for the Church. West European society and West European Christianity returned in great measure to being a local affair, having only limited dealings with central government, be it secular or ecclesiastical. The Germanic invaders who engulfed the West adhered to a different faction of Christianity (that of Arianism), and the Roman Catholic Church devoted most of its energies to bringing their ruling families into its fold and thus regaining its own dominance. In addition, new waves of pagan barbarians inside and outside the old Christian heartland had to be coaxed into a nominal acceptance of Christianity by way of missionary efforts, free baptismal gowns, and sheer military force. Yet when cities, commerce, international contacts, higher learning, and central government began to flourish again in the later Middle Ages, persecution also revived, and the legal and ideological constructs of Late Antiquity that had facilitated it were taken from the shelf again. Among the first victims of this revival were the above-mentioned Stephanus and Lisoius, who were condemned as "New Manichees" in 1022. With a dozen more victims, they were solemnly burned to ashes outside the city walls of Toulouse—a penalty from Roman times, inflicted on them for their alleged membership of a religious group from Roman times, on the basis of revamped antiheretical propaganda from Roman times.[91]

By the Papacy of Gregorius VII (ca. 1015–1085), the drive toward a universal and uniform Christian community had vigorously reestablished itself. Gregorius would give his name to an ambitious campaign to reorganize the church known as the Gregorian Reforms. Among the measures it proposed were compulsory celibacy for the clergy and the stamping out of simony (the buying and selling of ecclesiastical dignities and benefits). Yet the most ambitious goal of the reformers was the promotion of the Roman Papacy as the supreme authority in all matters religious and secular. Obedience to the pope, more than doctrinal position, henceforth demarcated the thin line between orthodoxy and heresy.[92] This allegiance defined the outlines of a new concept of *christianitas*, understood as "the collectivity of the *populus Christianus* as a social and temporal, as well as spiritual unity."[93] In its territorial dimension, this cultural and geographical community became roughly synonymous with "Europe" and the "Christian West," which in its turn would eventually modify and extend itself into the "Western world" as we know it today. It was a precarious bulwark of the faithful, surrounded by a sea of Islamic "heathens," Eastern Orthodox *schismatici*, and pagan barbarians.

The renewed concept of *christianitas* also led to a renewed urge to define who formed part of it, and who not, as well as a renewed effort to exclude the latter from the community. In 1215, the Fourth Lateran Council issued a famous decree that defined the community of the faithful as those who confessed to their priest and took communion at least once a year, thus consolidating, at least theoretically, the control of the clergy over ordinary believers. The council also consolidated the "machinery of persecution" of the Roman Catholic Church, issuing canons that prescribed the excommunication of heretics and their subsequent surrender to the secular power for punishment. Bishops should inspect presumed hoards of heresy at least once a year and compel the local population under oath to report any cases of religious deviance they knew. Secular rulers "ought publicly to take an oath that they will strive in good faith and to the best of their ability to exterminate in the territories subject to their jurisdiction all heretics pointed out by the Church"; if they failed to do so, their subjects had the right to withdraw their allegiance to them.[94] Anyone who sheltered, defended, or failed to take action against heretics was to be considered a heretic as well.[95]

In the 1230s, Pope Gregorius IX added a further bolt to the persecution machine when he established the Papal Inquisition. Its main purpose was to enable papal officials to bypass local episcopal authority and to allow the Papacy to act against heretics on its own initiative. One of its first activities was Konrad of Marburg's campaign against the so-called Luciferians in Germany. The contemporary *Gestorum Treverorum* depicts Konrad's operation as a veritable rampage tour that left a trail of smoldering bodies behind: out of fear for their lives and property, people started to denunciate those who had neither knowledge of nor inclination toward heresy, and many innocent people suffered.[96] The campaign was only brought to a halt when Konrad accused a prominent local nobleman of heresy after "witnesses" reported that he had attended nocturnal orgies riding on a crab: when the inquisitor traveled down a lonely road one day, he was duly assassinated by hired killers.[97] But the rising tide of persecution, inquisition, and repression was not so easily turned. Torture was increasingly applied to extract confessions of heresy by both the secular and ecclesiastical authorities; in 1252, its use by inquisitorial officers was ratified by Pope Innocent IV in his bull *Ad extirpanda*. These developments were intimately correlated with the tendency to transform dissident believers into monstrous adulators of Satan. "In the contemporary mind, the categorization of heresy as a crime deserving death was closely connected to its definition as devil worship," the German historian Alexander Patschovsky noted in this respect.[98]

The formation of a West European Christianity that aggressively sought to maintain and expand its spiritual dominance also had repercussions for the Jewish population. Since Antiquity, the Jewish community had enjoyed a certain measure of religious autonomy, the negative pendant of which was their exclusion from certain civil rights. Christian theologians had argued the legitimacy of their continuing presence because they functioned as "living witnesses" to the authenticity of the Old Testament, in addition referring to the prophecy of Paul the Apostle that "a remnant" of Jewry would be converted and saved in the last of days (Romans 9:27–28). For a long time, Jews thus remained the only legally tolerated non-Christian religious minority inside Christian Europe. With the revival of the *christianitas* ideal, however, church misgivings about a strong Jewish presence and its possible "Judaizing" influence on Christians also increased. Ecclesiastical authorities urged the maintenance of old restrictions on the Jews and the imposition of new ones, for instance, the exclusion of Jews from landownership. At the same time, old stereotypes about Jews were revived and new ones invented, such as the stories about the profanation of the host and ritual slaughter of Christian children. The latter theme resurfaced in the twelfth century and would become a staple of anti-Jewish propaganda for centuries to come.[99]

Allegations like these, and the connected attribution of demon worship, certainly functioned as legitimating and instigating factors for the violence directed against the medieval Jewish community by secular rulers and Christian mobs. The Roman Catholic Church played an ambivalent role in these developments. On the one hand, it condemned physical violence against Jews, and many ecclesiastical dignitaries tried to protect local Jewish communities from massacre. On the other hand, the Church argued for curtailment of the Jewish "other," who had to remain subjugated and "dispersed" as a punishment for his involvement in the crucifixion of Jesus. Clerical writers played a leading role in the invention and propagation of allegations against the Jews to counteract the threatening religious competition they perceived Judaism to be.[100]

The demonizing rhetoric of European Christianity in the later Middle Ages, in brief, formed part of the increasing belligerence with which this religion sought to enforce its universal claims against both inner and outer rivals. The demonization of an increasing range of (mostly self-created) "enemies of the church" is already striking in the writings of Gregorius VII and would find a preliminary zenith in the Luciferian fantasies of Gregorius IX, quoted above.[101] Significantly, Gregorius VII also was the first pope to attempt to organize a crusade against the Islamic "heathens," although this project was not materialized till over half a century later. The causes of this increasing mobilization against the enemies of the divine were manifold and complex. Yet the general mechanisms signaled by David Frankfurter could be applied here as well.[102] When local communities become involved in the turmoil of the greater world, local worldviews are often replaced or absorbed by more universal ones. This might also have occurred in Western Europe from the later Middle Ages onward, when European society began to experience an increase in economic activity, international contacts, and governmental centralization. The tendency within Western Christianity during this period toward a more centralized, uniform, and universal faith was certainly connected with this. Hand in hand with this general trend went a new (or, rather, revived) globalization and uniformization of the sources of misfortune and evil. In this way, the neighbor who practiced Judaism or some different variant of Christianity could suddenly become an agent in a global network of evil.

This also makes clear why the idea of *conspiracy* played such a prominent role in the attribution of Satanism during this period. Dissident Christians and other outsiders were not merely thought to engage in unspeakably abominable forms of worship. They were also thought to be actively involved in bringing misfortune. Jews were conspiring with Saracens; sorcerers with Jews; heretics with sorcerers and other heretics; and all were in league with the demons, or their master, the devil.[103] It is striking to see how the other is consistently perceived and described as a *threat* in the sources from this period, a worrying presence menacing the precarious safety of the religious and social community—while the reality was in most cases exactly the reverse, with the expanding power of European Roman Catholicism threatening its religious competitors. At the same time, this rhetorical demonization of the other served to demarcate and cement the community's own identity. In part, this identity was actually formed and formulated *during* this process of confrontation and exclusion.

THE SATANIST CONSPIRACY OF WITCHCRAFT

The tendency to deprecate the religious other through systematic attribution of Satanism survived the fragmentation of Western *christianitas* during the Reformation schisms in the early modern period.[104] Catholic polemicists deployed old stereotypes about Satanist heretics against Protestant Christians, while Protestants accused the Roman Catholic Church of demonic idolatry and proclaimed the Roman pope to be a servant of Satan.[105]

Indeed, it was to be exactly during this period that fears about a conspiracy of devil worshippers would reach a historical apogee. Rumors of a widespread cult of Satan increased to alarming intensity in parts of the Western world as contemporary authors started to speak about a new, ultramalicious "sectam modernum" that sought to overthrow Christendom from within. Its adherents could be found in all segments of society, but particularly among women. They allegedly used magic to inflict harm on good Christians and convened in isolated and far-away places such as mountaintops. There they performed atrocities and blasphemous rites and eventually ended up having sex with the devil and each other.

Readers familiar with the history of religion or with fairy tales will have recognized these new Satanists as witches. From the fifteenth century on, the Witch Scare moved over Europe much as the Plague had done earlier, starting in northern Italy and parts of France and reaching areas in the periphery like Scandinavia, Hungary, and North America only toward the end of the seventeenth century or later.[106] In its wake, recent research has calculated, some thirty thousand to fifty thousand people were put to death on the scaffold or at the stake.[107] Many more suffered severe repercussions. In terms of human life and loss, the early modern witch persecutions may have exceeded the earlier heresy persecutions. In fact, as we shall see, the two phenomena were intricately connected in a variety of ways; and the attribution of Satanism *avant le lettre* was one of the most important links between them.

Contrary to popular opinion, hunting witches was not the exclusive preserve of the Roman Catholic Church—and much less of the Roman and Spanish Inquisitions, which were in fact rather lenient toward those accused of witchcraft.[108] Rather, it was an activity in which the secular authorities, Protestant as well as Roman Catholic, enthusiastically shared. In fact, belief in witchcraft and maleficium had long predated Christianity. The power to ward off demons and harmful cosmic forces (by naming them properly and using apt rituals) assume the ability to exert a certain measure of control over them. This left open the possibility of its mirror image as well: directing these demons or cosmic forces to bring misfortune on those to whom one was for whatever reason unfavorably disposed. This practice, and the fear of it, has been documented from very early times.[109] The pagan Romans already considered maleficium to be an exceptionally horrendous crime for which they reserved one of their harshest legal sanctions: being burned alive.[110]

Initially, the coming of Christianity had not necessarily meant bad news for those accused of witchcraft. Charlemagne's new law for his Saxon territories, for instance, forbade the heathen Saxons to *eat* witches—apparently the customary retribution for the magic cannibalism that witches were supposed to practice.[111] Theological considerations also made ecclesiastical authorities skeptical about certain popular conceptions regarding maleficium. Although Satan and his demons were extremely powerful, official theology maintained that, as angels, they were essentially spirits and thus unable to change material reality. Their influence extended itself exclusively through manipulation of the human psyche by way of sinful suggestions, illusions, and possession. Deliberations like these seem to have formed the background for the well-known *Canon Episcopi*, a directive for tenth-century bishops that already mentions women who claim to go on night rides with Diana or Herodias. The text of the *Canon Episcopi* makes it quite clear that the nightly activities of these women were thought to be mere delusions: the real sin was to believe in the reality of these fantasies.[112]

This did not prevent belief in the danger of maleficium from being widespread in the Middle Ages. Nor was it solely the preserve of the uneducated or rural populace, as is shown by the frequent scandals evolving maleficium that erupted at the courts of Christian monarchs from the fourth up to the eighteenth centuries. The crucial step that made possible the massive witchcraft persecutions of the early modern era was the application of the Satanist stereotype that had been developed about Jews and heretics to the practice of sorcery.[113] There were some starting points for this in the earlier propaganda against the religious other. Already in Antiquity, as we have seen, the Manicheans were suspected of practicing maleficium, a suspicion sometimes extended to other heretic groups.[114] Jews enjoyed a similar reputation as sorcerers in the popular and learned imagination.[115] Toward the end of the Middle Ages, the reverse step was also made in some places: that of regarding sorcerers as members of a heretical organization. During the fourteenth century, the Papacy formally declared demonic magic heresy and veneration of Satan.[116] Toward 1400, the first trials for sectarian witchcraft—that is, witchcraft allegedly practiced in an organised sect, rather than by an individual—were held in the Savoyard Alps. Research by notable witchcraft historians has shown this occurrence to be directly related to the Inquisition persecution of Waldensians just a few decades earlier, during which the inquisitors had transformed the Waldensians into a sect of devil-worshipping sorcerers who convened at secret sabbats.[117] This demonizing effort was evidently successful. In certain parts of Europe, the designation "valdesia" or "vauderie" (Waldensianism) grew not only into a general brand name for heresy, but also into a familiar synonym for witchcraft.[118]

As the new concept of witchcraft gained ground, the age-old practitioner of witchcraft was suddenly seen in a new light and indeed was often conceived of as something entirely new. In the texts of those who combated witchcraft, the witches are commonly described as a "new sect," a *sectam modernum*, or sometimes, and equally significant, as a "synagogum diabolorum," a synagogue of devils. "In this very sect or Synagogue of bewitchers not only women assemble, but also men," wrote the Dominican inquisitor Nicolaus Jaquerius in 1458, "& what is worse, even Ecclesiastics and monks, who converse tangibly with the Demons which appear among them in various forms and under their own names. These same bewitchers venerate and adore the demons with bended knees and kisses, receiving them as Lords & Masters, abrogating God & the Catholic faith & its mysteries. In exchange, the demons promise them protection and help whenever they are invoked; upon which invocation the same demons appear to them, no matter when during the day, be it inside the Synagogue, be it in other places; and they come to their aid on demand and the Demons themselves give them poisons and substances to perpetrate crimes."[119] Significantly, Jaquerius in the very same section explicitly tried to prove that the "new sect" he described was not identical with that mentioned in the *Canon Episcopi*. In his infamous *Malleus Maleficarum* ("Hammer of the Witches") from 1487, Heinrich Kramer also devoted many words to the seeming discrepancy between the old canon and the new notions about witchcraft, vehemently defending the idea that a diabolical sect of sorcerers was trying to destroy Christendom from within.[120]

The idea of an organized Satanist witchcraft thus was neither traditional nor popular. On the contrary, it was developed by an educated elite and propagated by those who were able to participate in the most recent scholarly insights. The postulation of a heretic, devil-worshipping conspiracy behind the practice of sorcery also had important practical implications. Inquisitorial judicial procedures could now be used in the persecution of maleficium, whereas beforehand convictions of maleficium could only occur after somebody who was "damaged" by the perpetrator had laid charges against him or her and managed to prove them.[121] Because of its character as a *crimen exceptum*, torture could legally be used to extract confessions; because of the presumed collective nature of witchcraft, legal authorities tended to search for accomplices. This combination could easily lead to an epidemic of witchcraft prosecutions.

Through their sheer scale, the witchcraft persecutions also indicate the further strengthening of central, nonlocal forms of authority that had taken place in Western Europe.[122] Issues regarding maleficium, which would previously have been settled by communal justice in various brutal ways, were now brought before courts of law, where they were forced into the mold that was used by the educated judges. Secular authorities not only facilitated but also initiated these proceedings. It must be kept in mind in this respect that the sharp distinction between the religious and the secular that would characterize modern society did not exist yet. While church, monarchy, and nobility might dispute each other's exact prerogatives, the validity of Christianity as a religious framework for society was uncontested. Monarchs and secular authorities considered it their responsibility to combat heresy and witchcraft, not only out of political motivations, but also because tolerating these ungodly activities might invoke divine wrath over their realm.[123]

Nor do we need to imagine the rural or urban populace as passive and helpless providers of victims. As noted above, (fear of) witchcraft and sorcery had always been an intrinsic part of premodern community life. While the concept of witchcraft as a Satanist conspiracy was primarily a construct adopted by an educated elite, the idea that maleficium was responsible for all kinds of personal and collective misfortune certainly was not. Witchcraft was deemed responsible for impotence in marriage, milk that turned sour, beer that did not ferment, and all kinds of other natural calamities. Official campaigns to curb the activities of sorcerers might thus elicit enthusiastic support from the populace at large. Crop failure and natural calamities could arouse a demand for the extirpation of witches, as occurred in Pfalz in 1586, when the winter lasted unusually long and the bishop of Treves burned 120 people after he had made them confess that they had postponed spring through the use of magic.[124] Local government bodies sometimes requested central authorities to initiate legal procedures against witches, a request that was sometimes denied when central government had other priorities.[125]

At another level, popular conceptions also contributed to the witchcraft stereotype. Several historians have noted how folk traditions about the night witch, magical flight, the wild hunt, and the dances of the fairies were incorporated into the witchcraft stereotype.[126] These elements in turn may have reflected older cultural strata of pre-Christian origin, as Carlo Ginzburg has argued.[127] When suspects of witchcraft were interrogated, they sometimes volunteered local traditions about witches and the demonic. These might be added to the corpus of learned witchcraft lore and the checklists that judges used for examining alleged cases of sectarian witchcraft, making the new, constructed sect of witches an ever-expanding repository of folklore about the otherworld.[128] Interactions between learned judges and local experts in dealing with magical misfortune could assume various forms. In a celebrated study, Ginzburg described how the Inquisition was puzzled by the traditional antiwitchcraft specialists it met in Friuli, eventually deciding to persecute them as diabolical witches after all.[129] In contrast, Tyrolean law courts sometimes employed local soothsayers to coax confessions from Anabaptists they thought to be protected by a diabolical pact—not without some success, it seems.[130]

The roots in traditional culture of some elements of the early modern witchcraft complex have seduced some historians to propose the existence of an underground pagan cult as the origin of witchcraft rumors. The English Egyptologist Margaret Murray (1863–1963) was prominent in promoting this hypothesis, which found support among a host of authors on witchcraft and Satanism.[131] In the past three or four decades, this idea has been completely abandoned by witchcraft historians.[132] Certainly, all sorts of pagan remnants and parallel belief systems were hauled to the surface by the witch persecutions, such as the Friuli witch busters we just mentioned. In this respect, the efforts to stamp out sorcery can be regarded as a massive campaign to conclude the Christianization of the European countryside, where Christianity in many cases had never been more than a thin veneer for all kinds of folk religion.[133] In areas on the periphery, moreover, such as the Baltic or Iceland, surviving pagan religious specialists were occasionally prosecuted and executed as witches.[134] Yet there are no convincing indications that the majority of the people persecuted as witches were less (or more) Christian than their neighbors.

There is still less evidence for the existence of a secret organization of witches worshipping Satan—this at least may be clear by now. While elements from folklore were present, the early modern stereotype of the witch was primarily an amalgam and culmination of the earlier image of the religious other. The defilement of the host and killing of babies ascribed to both heretics and Jews, the incestuous orgies and perverse sex rites, the worship of demons with obscene gestures and the accompanying denial of Christianity, the magic potions that remove all memory of the Christian faith—all are present here. This catalogue of alleged blasphemy reached a new apogee in the sexual contact that witches were said to have with Satan or his demons. A dramatic reenacting of the original sin of the fallen angels in apocryphal scripture, this supernatural sex was believed to be an experience of such intensity that the participants—in the words of the inquisitor Jacquerius—"one or two days afterwards are still exhausted and bodily worn out."[135] Eventually, the Witches' Sabbath evolved into the realm of the other per se, a fantasy of total deviance where everything was the reverse of what was customary in normal society: people danced backward or back-to-back, ate inedible or rotten things, perpetrated sodomy and other "unnatural" sex acts, caressed abhorred animals as pets, and venerated Satan instead of the Christian god.[136] These improbable occurrences, it might be superfluous to add, were a strictly imaginary construct of a society that had become obsessed with the struggle to liberate itself from supernatural sources of misfortune. In fact, it can be argued that it was precisely the fact that it had *no basis* in reality that made the idea of the witches' conspiracy so potentially virulent. If nobody really was a Satanist witch, anybody *could* be.

BLACK MAGIC AND THE BLACK MASS

When witchcraft is mentioned, the idea of black magic usually is not far off in many people's minds.[137] Both concepts are frequently used as synonyms for Satanism; it thus seems apt to devote a few words to the historical phenomenon of "black magic" here as well. As with the concept of Satanism itself, a first inevitable step must be to establish what exactly we are talking about. "Magic" is a widely used and much abused term that can have different significances in different contexts. In anthropology and religious studies, it is sometimes used as a generic term for practices dealing with the supernatural that are not considered religion properly speaking. The validity of this division has been much debated.[138] This discussion, although not without relevance for our subject, will be ignored here for the moment. Instead, we will concentrate on the specific complex of magical practices that most readily came to be identified as "black magic" in the history of the Christian West.

Originally, the black arts were referred to as necromancy, or "consulting the dead." The dead gradually became spirits in general, and after the rise of Christianity, these spirits were often considered to be of a demonic, diabolic kind. During this process, scribal error or pious intent corrupted the label of necromancy into nigromancy, "the black art."[139] This medieval and early modern "nigromancy" generally belonged to the category of magic that contemporary historians of magic have called ritual, ceremonial or learned: magical practices making use of "long and complex rituals for obtaining a variety of different kinds of benefits to the operator through the conjuring of spirits."[140] Its complexity made it a genre that was closely linked with written or printed texts and literacy. Thus it can be distinguished from the spells, charms, and folk magic that also formed a common feature of the religious landscape of pre- and early modern Europe.

This distinction is sometimes reflected in contemporary texts as well: the *Malleus Maleficarum*, for instance, clearly distinguishes between necromantic magic, which is the domain of the learned, and sorcery, which "is not performed with books or by the learned but by the altogether ignorant."[141] It is safe to say, however, that the demarcation between "folkloric" and negromantic magical practices was far from watertight in real life. Nor was it given much heed by the theologians and demonologists that formulated the policy of the Roman Catholic Church on these matters. As we have already seen, Jews, pagans, and dissident Christians were frequently accused of sorcery and demonic magic. Complementary to this, Pope John XII declared negromantic magic heresy in 1326, arguing that it implied an alliance with and worship of Satan.[142] The pope's doctrinal decision was prompted by fears that attempts on his life had been prepared by practitioners of sorcery operating inside the papal court. As noted above, this official condemnation played a significant role in the legal and ideological preamble to the witch persecutions.

Pope John's negative appraisal of magic had long roots in Christian and pre-Christian history.[143] Already in the Early Church, the magic arts were considered to be incompatible with Christianity. The Acts of the Apostles told how the people of Ephesus burned their books of the "curious arts," worth fifty thousand pieces of silver, after Paul preached the Gospel in their city (Acts 19, 19), and apocryphal stories related how the apostle Peter had undone his adversary Simon the Magician.[144] From the Late Antique period on, legends associating magic with Satan proliferated. One of the earliest examples of this genre that have come down to us is the so-called Proterius legend, recorded in the *Life of Basilius* and attributed to Amphilochius of Cappadocia. The legend recounts how a young slave of the Christian senator Proterius becomes hopelessly enamored with the daughter of his master. Despairing of his love, the slave turns to "one of the detested magicians" for help. This "true poisoner" asks him if he is prepared to abrogate Christ in writing; when the young man confirms, he dictates a written declaration to him, stating that he abjures the Christian religion and wants to join the company of the devil. He then instructs him to go to "some pagan monument" at nighttime and invoke the devil, holding the written abjuration in the air. Demons duly appear and lead the young slave to the devil. Initially, the father of iniquity receives him with suspicion—there are so many Christians, he complains, who come to the devil in a time of need but return to the mercy of Christ as soon as their wishes have been granted. He would like to have some security. Could the young man give him a written pact in which he abrogates Christ and his Christian baptism and declares himself to be with him forever, even in the eternal torments that await him? The slave promptly produces the pact prepared by the magician, which is accepted by the devil.[145]

After this, the demons ignite a violent passion within the senator's daughter for her father's servant. The senator, who has pledged to make his daughter a nun, opposes their love, but the girl laments her fate with such vehemence that he eventually succumbs and agrees to their marriage. The girl and her spouse enjoy a period of married bliss. Yet, after a while, people in her environment start to voice suspicions regarding her new husband. Why does he so seldom go to church? And why does he never take communion? Is he *really* a Christian? The girl confronts the servant with these suspicions, and upon her persistent imploring, he confesses his pact with the devil.

Now Basilius enters the scene. The servant flees to him for help. Basilius asks him if he wants to convert to "the Lord our God"; the young man answers that he would like to do so but cannot. "I have abrogated Christ in writing & have made a covenant with the devil."[146] Basilius, however, urges him to trust in the benignity of the Lord, and starts to pray. A prayer battle between the saint and the demons occurs, in which the whole congregation participates with supplications and Kyrie Eleisons, while the demons try to rip the servant away from Basilius's grasp. In the end, of course, Basilius is victorious, and out of the sky a piece of paper floats into the hands of the Christian saint. The young slave at once recognizes this as the pact he made with Satan. The piece of paper is ceremoniously burned and Proterius's daughter can turn homeward with her husband saved.

Pact legends, as stories of this type are commonly called, remained hugely popular in Western Europe during the next thousand years.[147] A similar tale about a priest called Theophilus would become one of the most-cited stories from the Middle Ages, while the Renaissance would produce its own variant in the Faust legend, immortalized much later by Goethe.[148] In all these renderings, the basic theme remained the same: a man or a woman taking recourse to demonic magic ends up selling his or her soul to Satan, who in due course appears to exact his price.

The view on magic contained in these legends and hagiographies correlated with that which was formulated in theology. The great Scholastic Thomas Aquinas considered all magic in which invocations or offerings to demons took place to be an explicit or manifest pact with the devil. The offerings, he maintained, were a diabolical mirroring of the

Christian sacraments, thus constituting an alternative, Satanic form of religion. Magic with secret signs or mysterious spells, in addition, purported to a tacit or implicit pact with the devil. After all, in taking recourse to these, the practitioner of magic did not place his trust in the omnipotence of the supreme deity but gave implicit proof of a conviction that there was some other source of succor in the world. This pertained to heresy and meant in fact that the person was making a pact with the other side.[149] Thomas, it must be said, left some possibility for forms of "natural," "neutral" magic, and it must be remembered as well that the medieval category of the magical did not correspond exactly with what we currently consider as the occult or the paranormal—things like the special properties of stones and astrology, for instance, were often seen as just another form of natural science. Yet prominent theologians like Augustine of Hippo and Thomas Aquinas solidly associated demonic magic with the worship of Satan. This would become the dominant doctrine in the Roman Catholic Church and resulted in many a magician being sent to the stake.[150]

What the practitioners of magic themselves thought of all this is seldom documented. A rare glimpse of their opinions might be deduced from a preface contained in some copies of the *Liber Juratus*, a well-known medieval handbook on necromantic magic also known as the *Liber Sacer* or *Sworn Book of Honorius*.[151] In explicit reference to the ecclesiastical condemnation of magic, the preface states that the pope and his cardinals seek to eradicate magic because they are under the influence of evil spirits themselves. Magicians and necromancers, the prelates claim, sacrifice unto demons, forsake their baptism, follow the pomps and works of Satan, and drag ignorant people down to damnation by their illusions. The anonymous author of the preface emphatically denies these charges as being inspired by the devil, who wishes to keep a monopoly on such marvels. It is impossible for a wicked or impure man to work truly by the magic art, in which the spirits are compelled against their will by pure men. True magic thus is the exact reverse of Satanism: the subjection *of*, not the subjection *to*, Satan. The preface then goes on to relate that the magicians had been forewarned by their art of the measures planned against them, but after some hesitation they had decided not to summon the demons to their aid, lest these might avail themselves of the opportunity to destroy the human population altogether. Instead, an assembly of 811 masters from Naples, Athens, and Toledo chose Honorius, a master of Thebes, to reduce their magic books to one volume containing ninety-three chapters, which could be more readily concealed and preserved. Of course, this book is none other than the *Liber Juratus* itself.[152]

While the preface to the *Liber Juratus* is unique in its explicit justification of the magical arts and radical oppositional stance toward the religious authorities, the line of reasoning it contains makes its appearance in other places as well: for instance, in the late medieval Dutch miracle play *Mariken van Nieumeghen*. When Mariken, in dire straits, calls to the devil for help, he appears to her in the form of a one-eyed man and offers to teach her any art she wants. Mariken immediately asks to learn "nigremansie," "that pleasant art" by which she has witnessed her uncle the priest doing such wondrous things. The devil, however, quickly talks her out of this. "Could she perform necromancy," he muses to himself, "it would just be to force me to do whatever would suit her."[153] Meanwhile, the fact that Mariken's uncle avidly practices magic from "eenen boeck" does nothing to detract from his piety: through his ardent prayer, the "holy father" eventually saves Mariken from the dark fiend.

Who was right: the magician of the *Liber Juratus*, or the Roman Catholic Church? The answer might well be neither of the two. If we disregard angelic magic—equally condemned by the Church—and concentrate on magical practices that explicitly invoke the demonic, the picture of the magician as a noble and virtuous seeker of wisdom is not borne out.[154] The *Liber Juratus* is exceptional in this matter because the first part of the book consists of a ritual to obtain the beatific vision through a long series of sometimes rather exotic prayers.[155] Yet the other chapters of the book are taken up with "operations" that are neither particularly noble nor virtuous, but eminently practical: rituals to obtain secret knowledge, to discover hidden treasures, to gain favor with influential people, to have a girl fall in love with the operator or make her dance in the nude, or even to avenge injuries or to harm enemies, practices that venture close to the domain of maleficium.[156] This is also the picture presented by the other necromantic handbooks that have been left to us.[157] At the same time, however, the practices described do fit uneasily into the definition of Satanism adopted in this study. Demons are invoked, certainly, and occasionally even Satan himself. But this usually happens in the name of the Father, the Son, and the Holy Ghost, often accompanied by a host of saints and archangels, or by force of the secret names of the sole god, which, in the Jewish tradition, were supposed to harbor great power over all of creation, the dark denizens of the pit included.[158] The closest thing to veneration of the devil that we can detect in these texts is the offerings that they sometimes prescribe the magician to make to the demons, mostly consisting of small animals such as chickens or doves.[159] In general, however, the picture the books of demonic magic offer agrees with that presented in the *Liber Juratus* and *Mariken van Nieumeghen*. Magic is used to restrain and bind the demons, not to venerate them.

Indeed, it has been pointed out that the incantations of the books of magic display a striking resemblance to the official Roman Catholic formulae for exorcism.[160] Just as the exorcist "conjures" the demon in the name of Christ to leave the energumen—often after compelling it to disclose its true identity—so the necromancer forces the demon to do his chores for him: lifting treasures, obtaining knowledge, enticing women, harming enemies. The latter may be seen as simply an extension of the former. Nor should this continuum between liturgical practice and magical experiment surprise us unduly. Strange as it may sound, most practitioners of demonic ritual magic probably belonged to the Roman Catholic clergy. The eminent expert Richard Kiekhefer even qualifies necromancy as a "quintessentially clerical form of dark and daring entertainment" that was dominated by a lower clergy looking for thrills or extra income.[161] Although the leadership of the Church might have seen their pastime as highly dangerous and deviant, adoration of Satan it was not. Judging by their books and their occupations, most medieval magicians probably saw themselves as ordinary or even devout Christians.[162]

This may be an appropriate moment for a brief discussion of that other phenomenon that is inextricably bound up with the lore and legend of Satanism and black magic: the so-called Black Mass, or Missa Negra. In the *Dictionary of Gnosis and Western Esotericism*, Massimo Introvigne defines the Black Mass as "an "inverted" Roman Catholic Mass in which, by appropriately changing the formulae, Satan is worshipped and Jesus Christ is cursed."[163] If we accept this definition, it might be clear by now that medieval and early modern necromancy is not the most obvious place to expect it. None of the surviving manuals on necromantic magic—and we have quite a few—contain anything even faintly resembling a Black Mass. Yet it is certainly true that the host and the Eucharistic ritual receive a great deal of intense attention in both learned and folk magic. Realist views about the host being the embodiment of the divine on Earth "in its essence" had gained ascendancy early in the history of the Church and had been codified by the Fourth Lateran Council in 1215. Consequently, miraculous powers were thought to pertain to both the Eucharist and the ceremony of consecration. This belief was sometimes translated into practical forms that had not been intended by the learned doctors of the Church.[164] Substances laid upon the altar or under the host when consecration took place were believed to share in the divine radiance surrounding this powerful rite. The custom of placing herbs on the altar on certain feast days to enhance their medical properties may go back to the sixth century.[165] Similar practical applications of Eucharistic devotion can be found in magical rites. A late fifteenth-century magical manual, for example, records a recipe for becoming invisible that requires the tongue of a raven and the tongue of a kite over which nine Masses have been read.[166] In fact, the necromantic manuals themselves were often required to be consecrated to render them more efficacious.[167]

These practices evidently have nothing to do with "inverted" liturgy or blasphemy. Rather they attest to an intense awe for the power that the divine presence in the Eucharist was presumed to have. For magician and ordinary believer alike, magical practice and Christian religion often were perceived as part of a continuum. This could, by the way, also apply the other way around. Heinrich Cornelius Agrippa von Nettesheim, a famous Renaissance proponent of natural magic, described the Mass itself as a form of magic, in which a specific ritual conjures the divine to appear in bread and wine.[168]

For the real origin of the Black Mass, we have to look to a by now already-familiar domain: that of imaginary constructs regarding the religious other. Accusations of desecration of the host were a continuing refrain in the litany of horrors recited about the religiously divergent in society. We have already encountered numerous examples of this, such as the Luciferians, who were rumored to keep the holy bread in their toilets so that they could defecate on it. Stories like this functioned as corroborative evidence for the dogma of transubstantiation promulgated by the Fourth Lateran Council and experienced a revival when Protestant Christians started to contest sacramental realism after the Reformation.[169] Groups that did not have the least interest in the corporal manifestations of Jesus, like the Jews, or did not hold Roman Catholic views about transubstantiation, like some heretics, were nevertheless assumed to foster an intensely malicious interest in the Body of Christ. The same views were held about witches.[170] The most common way the enemies of the faith were supposed to maltreat the Sacrament was by trampling it or spitting on it, but more creative methods for desecration were also recorded. In 1643, Madeleine Bavent, a nun who claimed to have been possessed by demons, maintained that her confessors had used the host as a cock ring while enjoying her sexually, with further picturesque detail being added by the other nuns, who declared that this had happened in church, on the altar.[171]

These fantasies about the desecration of the host could easily be elaborated to produce more intricate travesties of liturgy. We have already noted the allegations against Manichean and Gnostic Christians, who were said to celebrate a perverse form of Eucharist in which they partook of each other's sexual fluids. In the fourteenth century, the elusive Luciferians were believed to baptize their children in the name of Lucifer and to pray diabolic parodies of the paternoster. It is again the Witches' Sabbath, however, that proved to be the most fertile breeding ground for such fantasies. In the descriptions of this phantasmagorial realm of inversion supplied by the reports of judges, the treatises of demonologists, and the confessions of exorcised nuns, the contours of a veritable antiliturgy become visible. Thus we can read of parodies of the Mass with black candles and a black host in a black chalice; of aspersions using the Devil's or witches' urine instead of holy water; of a Satanic book of liturgy bound in black leather; even of Satan preaching like a priest on the virtues of vice.[172] Louis Gaufridy, the French priest accused of sorcery in 1610, even claimed to remember how during the Sabbath "they consecrated the body of Our Lord in honour of Lucifer."[173] If we want to find the first rough outlines of the blaspheming pseudo liturgy that would later be called the Black Mass, it is here we must go looking.[174]

The Black Mass thus originated, like the concept of Satanism in general, as a construct of attribution. Despite the assertions of some historians to the contrary, I am not familiar with any positive indication that a Black Mass according to the definition of Introvigne was ever performed before the onset of modernity.[175] The seventeenth century, however, might present us with some historical exceptions to this rule. These we will scrutinize more closely in the next section.

THE AFFAIR OF THE POISONS

Demonic magic, so much is clear by now, does not equate with Satanism. Yet it is hard to deny that some practices of necromancy take us into the shadiest back lanes of the "City of God," close to where the nightclubs of the Beast begin. Even for the modern historian of religions, for instance, the notion of making small offerings to the demons invites the interpretation that they function as deities, however minor and subsidiary. It is evident we are entering a gray area here, where the dividing line between Christianity and Satanism is not as clear-cut as the textbook definitions of theologians or historians might suggest it is.

The "gray zone" character of some necromantic magic becomes especially clear when we consider the best-known instance of possible early modern Satanism, the so-called affaire des poisons (Affair of the Poisons).[176] This scandal came into the open in 1679, after a Paris soothsayer indiscreetly bragged about the profits she was making from poisoning people on behalf of her clients. This reached the ear of Nicolas de la Reynie, the Parisian chief of police, and his subsequent inquiries brought to light a vast commercial network of occult entrepreneurs in the city that allegedly counted a considerable number of people of rank among its clientele. What was worse, suggestions were put forward that a plot had been brewing in this underground circuit to assassinate the French king with poison or magic (two things that tended to blend into each other for many contemporaries).[177] Apparently thoroughly alarmed by the disclosures of his chief of police, Louis XIV, the reigning king, installed a special inquisitorial and judicial court of justice on April 7, 1679. It was soon nicknamed "Chambre Ardente," in ominous reference to the special tribunal for cases of heresy, which in the sixteenth century had convened at the Arsenal, in a room hung with black cloth and lit with torches.[178]

The new Chambre Ardente brought some colorful subjects before the bar. Among them were the divineress "La Trianon," who "lived together as man and wife" with a female colleague and had a human skeleton hanging from the ceiling in her consulting room (according to her own statement to "find out how many bones a human creature possessed"), and Catherine Montvoisin, known as "La Voisin," a beautician, soothsayer, and abortionist.[179] La Voisin was to play an important role in the erupting scandal. A bevy of smaller occultist entrepreneurs surrounded this intrepid woman, including several Roman Catholic priests who were prepared to employ their sacerdotal powers in dubious ways to generate extra income. The most squalid of these was probably Étienne Guibourg, a hideous, squinting man of seventy who had been living with a concubine for the previous twenty years and had fathered several children by her. La Voisin's practice had reputedly been frequented by some high-ranking clients, and as the gallery of rogues employed by it was brought in for questioning, allegations soon started to touch Versailles' highest circles. To their dismay, several members of the aristocracy found themselves summoned to appear before the tribunal, including one of France's foremost generals, the Maréchal de Luxembourg, who was accused of attempts to invocate the devil by an obscure adventurer-cum-magician-cum-astrologer called Lesage.[180]

Luxembourg's presumed dealings with the devil were only the tip of the iceberg of demonic traffic that was described by the arrested caterers of magic to their interrogators. La Voisin and her circle in particular seemed to have been involved in lurid practices that closely resembled diabolism, at least according to the declarations of some witnesses. These practices, of course, make the Affair of the Poisons so interesting for the historian of Satanism. We are in the particularly fortunate circumstance that the original interrogation records used in the investigation have survived, enabling us to trace in detail how notions about sacrilegious rituals of demonic magic arose during the judicial investigation. Because of the exceeding interest of these matters for our subject, I will present a brief chronological overview of the most important material here.

On November 18, 1679, while being interrogated in the royal prison of Vincennes, Martine Bergerot, "one of the most famous palmists of Paris," declared that she had been approached by a woman called Filastre to ask if she would be interested in making her fortune by selling herself to Satan. Filastre had done so herself and read to Bergerot from a pact on parchment, in which she had given herself body and soul to the devil; in return, she would receive the ability "to bring death or harm on anyone she liked," as well as the power to fulfill the requests listed in the pact of "several persons of quality."[181]

On November 28, 1679, Lesage (the same character who got the Maréchal de Luxembourg in trouble) made several highly incriminating statements regarding La Voisin and a priest of her circle called Davot. The latter, he maintained, had performed Mass on the womb or abdomen of a girl or a woman "whose name he [Lesage] might remember later on"; this had occurred in the house where La Voisin plied her trade. In addition, Davot had copulated with the anonymous girl or woman and had kissed her "shameful parts" while saying Mass. The priests had frequently celebrated Mass clandestinely at La Voisin's.[182]

On May 26, 1680, La Filastre described how she had given birth to her lover's child within a circle of burning candles while reciting incantations renouncing the holy sacrament and her own baptism. Afterward, the child had been taken away, and she feared that it had been offered to the devil. She also told how her own pact with the devil had been ratified by a priest called Cotton, who had said Mass to this purpose, during which he invoked "the three princes of demons" with unintelligible words. As had already been suggested in the earlier declaration of Bergerot, Filastre had agreed to give herself to the devil on behalf of third parties as well, so she could fulfill the demands of "all the others."[183]

The priest, Jacques-Joseph Cotton, when brought into custody, only admitted that he had put "figures" to bring about love or death under the chalice for the wine during Mass in church and that he had once said Mass over an afterbirth (presumably so it could be used in magic). He more or less stuck with his story till the end, only adding further details regarding the procedure he followed: La Filastre would give him a piece of paper with the demands to be made to the devil, as well as a conjuration; Mass was read over this for nine days "in order to make the spirit appear by the tangible presence of Our Lord."[184]

Meanwhile, La Voisin had already been burned at the stake. Her twenty-one-year-old daughter, Marie Marguerite Montvoisin, was brought in for questioning as well, and she blew the whistle on Étienne Guibourg, the squinting old priest. Together with the indefatigable Lesage, they initiated a series of divulgences that were even more sensational than those that had been disclosed before.

On June 26, 1680, Guibourg said he had celebrated Mass once over the abdomen of a woman, in the chapel of an unknown castle; on a later occasion, he performed a similar ceremony in a hovel in Saint-Denis, on the naked body of yet another unknown woman whom he thought to be a prostitute.[185] On July 15, Lesage added further elaborations: in 1660, twenty years earlier, Guibourg had said several Masses over women, "all completely nude, without chemise, on a table that served as altar; having their arms spread, they held a burning candle in each of them during the whole time the Masses lasted."[186] Three days later, he supplied more details about the case of Filastre as well: the woman had most certainly given her child to be "killed in holocaust" as an offering to the devil; another child had been aborted as a sacrifice; in addition, a girl of fourteen or fifteen had been taken away outside Paris to be given to the devil as well, by a priest who had "said three Masses over the abdomen of the girl, during one of which he had known her carnally."[187]

On August 20, 1680, La Voisin's daughter confirmed Lesage's allegations concerning Guibourg and added new ones to them. Guibourg had said Mass "on the womb, over ladies," several times at her mother's place; the first time, to her knowledge, had been some six years ago. At that time, her mother had only allowed her to arrange the mattresses and candles for the ritual; when she became older, she had been permitted to witness "that kind of Mass" and had seen how a woman had lain down naked on the mattress, "her head hanging down, supported by a cushion on a reversed chair, her legs hanging down, a piece of cloth on her abdomen, with a cross on it at the place of the womb and the chalice on it."[188] Even more spectacularly, she disclosed that one of these naked women had been Madame de Montespan, the titular mistress of the king; she had come to La Voisin to have Mass said over her some three years earlier, about ten in the evening, and had only left at midnight.[189]

Filastre next disclosed that the unknown woman who had been the altar piece during Guibourg's "nude Mass" in Saint-Denis had also been none other than Montespan. The old priest himself initially denied knowing anything about this, but later he remembered having performed four Masses on a naked lady he was given to understand was Madame de Montespan, her face hidden by a black veil.[190] On at least one occasion, a stranger had conducted him blindfolded to the place where the Mass was held.[191]

More gruesome detail was added to the story by Marie Montvoisin. On October 9, 1680, she told her interrogators how the entrails of aborted children had been used in magical ceremonies; on one occasion, Guibourg had slit the throat of a child that had been born prematurely, "pouring the blood in the chalice, and consecrating it with the host."[192] Guibourg, this time, readily acknowledged the deed; on October 10, he recounted how he had sacrificed the child over the abdomen of a woman, draining the baby with a "canif" in the neck. During the rite, he called upon the demons with the following words: "Astaroth, Asmodeus, princes of affection, I conjure you to accept the sacrifice that I present you of this child for the things that I demand of you." Afterward, the dead child had been brought to another room, where the entrails and heart were also taken out and offered in sacrifice.[193] He also disclosed how Mademoiselle des Œillets—a chambermaid for Montespan, and a former bed partner of the king as well—had performed a peculiar ceremony with an anonymous but titled Englishman. She had provided a sample of her menstrual blood in a chalice in which the Englishman masturbated; bats' blood and flour were then added. This concoction was intended as a means to kill the king.[194]

Meanwhile, Lesage confided that Guibourg had also been implicated in the sacrifice of Filastre's child, as well as in various other sacrifices to the devil of recently born children— the magician even maintained that the priest had once offered the body of a hanged man to the demons.[195] On October 1, Filastre admitted under torture that she had handed over her child for diabolic sacrifice; she was executed later, although she retracted her admission in her final confession.[196]

After the final disclosures of Guibourg and Marie Montvoisin, minor suspects continued to reveal extra details. These amounted to little more than variations of the earlier stories—a Mass said over the nude bodies of a mother and daughter at the same time, for instance—and added no substantial information.[197] Eventually, the investigations were brought to a sudden halt, like an abruptly extinguished candle, and the Chambre Ardente was suspended. The tribunal issued arrest warrants for a total of 319 persons, of whom 194 were taken into custody. Of these, 104 were tried; 36 received death sentences.[198]

In the historiographical literature on Satanism, insofar as it can be said to exist, the Affair of the Poisons is commonly considered to be the first well-established case of Satanism.[199] Massimo Introvigne speaks of the affair as being "construed on a solid base of historical facts": "the documents kept at the Bibliothèque Nationale and in other Parisian libraries are from the hand of professional policemen who do not abandon themselves to fantasies."[200] He does not doubt a veritable "list of duchesses, countesses and marquises" attended the alternative Masses of La Voisin *cum suis*, and he compares the case favorably with the earlier witchcraft persecutions and the famous French possession scandals at Loudon and

Louviers.[201] With the Affair of the Poisons, Introvigne argues, we are not confronted with "imaginary tales of pious sisters or overly zealous confessors": the investigation and prosecution were initiated in a "completely non-religious context" and by "secular police forces" rather than "ecclesiastical authority."[202]

Certainly it is vital to point out the historical context of the Affair of the Poisons: a late seventeenth-century Paris for which the early modern Witch Scare was already a thing of the past. The last witch burning in the French capital had occurred in 1625; while witchcraft prosecutions continued in the rural provinces, the Paris Parlement invariably nullified the convictions for sorcery that had been issued by subordinate courts.[203] The reports of the investigations that are left to us, moreover, are strikingly devoid of the more colorful elements that featured prominently in the stereotype of the Satanist witch: diabolical apparitions, supernatural flight, nightly revels, demonic animals. We read of rituals held and invocations uttered, but the texts remain silent about how successful these actions were in achieving their intended magical effect. To the modern reader, this attitude feels comfortably familiar.

In some measure, however, this comfortable feeling is deceptive. The contrast suggested by Introvigne between the clerical fanaticism that had dominated earlier decades, and the cool, rational police work during the Affair of the Poisons is in important ways a false one. It is based both on misconceptions about the witch trials and a mischaracterization of some of the scandal's principal players. Far from being monopolized by clerical fanaticism, as we have seen, the witch trials had been in the main a secular affair, carried out and propagated by the educated people of the day. And the "professional policeman" La Reynie stood more deeply in this tradition than some writers have cared to notice. It was not unusual for La Reynie to ask defendants if they had seen the devil, and these questions were evidently based on real concern.[204] In one instance, he cited Jean Bodin, the well-known legal apologist of the reality of witchcraft, as an authority on the possibility of such supernatural incursions.[205] The British historian Anne Somerset is probably right when she states that "residual fear of witchcraft" had been partly responsible for the scale and escalation of the affair.[206] One member of the Chambre Ardente bitterly complained that the tribunal seemed to occupy itself exclusively with accusations of sorcery, a crime long deemed defunct.[207]

Even more fundamental than La Reynie's demonic preoccupations, however, is the fact that the legal mechanisms that were brought into play during the affair were virtually identical to those used during the witchcraft trials. The nickname "Chambre Ardente" for the royal committee in charge of the proceedings was well earned: in many aspects, its practices were reminiscent of earlier heresy persecutions. Torture and threats were applied to suspects of more humble social status. The distorted testimonies that may have been the result of this are easily imagined.[208] With some of the principal suspects—Lesage, Guibourg, La Voisin's daughter—foot screws did not prove necessary. They seem to have sensed from early on what their interrogators expected to hear from them and how they could use this to their advantage. By carefully dosing their divulgences, and gradually revealing more and more spectacular "secrets" that required further investigation, they were able to postpone their inevitable fate. This may explain the strange interplay that the depositions of these suspects sometimes seem to display, as well as the readiness of some to volunteer the most horrible facts. It was a desperate gamble to escape death by people who were used to earning their living through make-believe anyway.[209]

Both modern scholars and contemporary observers have remarked upon the fundamental unreliability of the evidence uncovered in this way. In the most thorough examination of the affair to date, Somerset has thrown doubt on the involvement of Madame de Montespan, as well as the existence of a plot to kill the king.[210] Her scathing analysis of the trustworthiness of some of the principal witnesses is confirmed by the utterances of prominent contemporaries.[211] In a memorandum to the king, the French Minister Colbert wrote that "it is a common occurrence during the public investigations of magicians, soothsayers and suppliers of secrets, magic and poisons, that these wretched hawkers get the liberty and the opportunity to name whoever they like as their accomplices; because, although most of the time there is nothing solid against these persons, and although one finds almost never any hard and certain indications for these crimes which one can investigate more deeply but only mere talk, it is always very difficult to verify their calumnies. That is why these indefinite investigations have always been considered as most dangerous and adversary to the tranquillity of the people."[212] Even La Reynie, in a similar memorandum, was forced to admit that the testimony that was poured out by his prisoners could not be trusted, "neither in its entirety nor in part," that the principal facts they had divulged were probably not reliable, and that there was "no certitude whatsoever regarding what was true and what was false" in their assertions. He concluded, however, that it was nevertheless evident that "impieties, sacrileges, and abominations are practiced, both in Paris, in the countryside, and in the provinces."[213]

The "scoundrels" and "monsters" that were staking their lives on their tall stories were not the only ones whose principal interests were not necessarily congruent with those of the truth. Unknown to them, and unknown perhaps to La Reynie, bigger games were being played behind the scenes. Rather than consider it a late addendum to the Witch Scare, it may be more appropriate to place the Affair of the Poisons in the even older "tradition" of court scandals involving sorcery. Like other court scandals involving sorcery, the Affair of the Poisons functioned as yet another episode in the ceaseless "competition for power which surrounds the thrones of arbitrary rulers."[214] Louvois (1641–1691), a ruthless minister of the king and La Reynie's direct superior, clearly had his own purposes with the affair, among which the political destruction of his former pal Luxembourg was prominent. It clearly follows from the records that he manipulated the evidence and suggested to witnesses that they might come off lightly if they told "the whole truth" about their connections with Luxembourg and other people to whom he did not bear a kind heart.[215] His own estimation of the truth of their declarations and the unscrupulous way in which he had used them as his pawns are clear from a short note he wrote in 1683 regarding the astrologer Lesage, who had begun to boast of new "secrets" he could unveil from his cell. "You cannot be too harsh toward that rascal who, all the time he was at Vincennes, could never say a truthful word," Louvois declared on this occasion to the director of the fortress of Besançon—despite the fact that this same "rascal" had served as his principal incriminating witness against the Maréchal de Luxembourg.[216]

Behind Louvois appears the even more redoubtable figure of the French king. It was at his royal behest that a special committee of investigation had been installed shortly after the first indications of what was to become the Affair of the Poisons had been brought to light. It is hard to imagine that pious indignation had been his primary motivation in this. The court of the Sun King was not exactly a place associated with piety: indeed, it was probably one of the most libertine spots of its day.[217] The affair, however, fitted only too nicely into the king's tireless schemes to subdue his own nobility.[218] The Chambre Ardente had power of attorney to summon and judge even the highest members of the aristocracy, who normally held the privilege of being judged by their own peers. The insult was keenly felt by the nobility.[219]

Louis's plans backfired when the tribunal uncovered "facts" that touched his own intimate circle. It cannot have pleased the king that the French and European public were being entertained by stories in which his official mistress featured as a naked altar to invoke demons and her maid of honor mixed her menstrual fluids with the ejaculation of an Englishman. This signified the end of the Chambre Ardente. As soon as the name of Montespan popped up, Louis demanded that all official reports regarding her involvement would henceforth be directed to him personally, and to him alone. He took care to keep all sensitive documents concerning Montespan under lock and key in his personal quarters, and he burned them with his own hands in 1709. The only reason we know about them at all, in fact, is because La Reynie, his zealous chief of police, had kept separate minutes of the proceedings, which were discovered two centuries later and published by Ravaisson in his enormous collection of records of the Bastille.

Similar reasons of discretion ensured that Lesage, Guibourg, Marie Montvoisin, and several lesser suspects were never subjected to a public trial and consequently escaped the death penalty. Their gamble had worked, one might say—although their eventual fate was hardly better than execution, as they were chained to the wall in remote fortress dungeons until their deaths.[220] The Maréchal de Luxembourg had more luck: he was "released without being unambiguously absolved" after a few miserable months in the Bastille, to continue a prestigious military career. Stories about his pact with the devil, however, circulated for the rest of his life and grew into a kind of Faust-like legend after his death.[221]

So what can we conclude from all this? It may be evident by now that we cannot consider the historical material concerning the Affair of the Poisons as a priori more reliable than the trial reports that are left to us from the witchcraft prosecutions. The "solid base of historical facts" that some historians have perceived behind the affair on closer inspection turns out to be a quicksand of distortion and manipulation. Nevertheless, while we cannot be sure of the reality of the practices recounted by La Reynie's suspects, we can still be sure that they disclose actual conceptions existing at the time about what Satanism and "black magic" were supposed to be. Moreover, some of the modi operandi they describe, as we shall see below, are confirmed by what we know from other sources regarding the practice of demonic magic. In this respect, the investigation records of the affair may provide us with intriguing glimpses from the inside of the magical subculture. Consequently, it might be worth our while to take a closer look at the source material.[222]

We begin our exploration with some descriptions of magic that we have no reason to doubt and that provide a good starting point for tracing the possible evolution of "ordinary" necromancy into practices that were a great deal more deviant. All kinds of minor personages who had on occasion dabbled with magic were dragged up in the trail net of the Affair of the Poisons. One of them was a certain Father Barthélemy Lemeignan, who was questioned on July 31, 1680, regarding the conjurations he was reputed to have made to recover hidden treasures. The subsequent interrogation is recorded almost verbatim:

- Whether, while making the conjurations, he was not dressed in his surplice and his stole?
- Yes, one cannot perform them without this.
- Whether he did not perform the conjurations in cellars?
- Yes.
- Who were present at the conjurations?
- It happened five or six years ago, he does not remember who.
- Whether the conjurations had not been handwritten?
- Yes, and it had been the conjurations of Saint Cyprianus and Saint Ambrosius, and he did nothing but change a few words; instead of conjuring the demon to depart from the body, he commanded [them] to depart from that place. This was in order to lift treasures.[223]

These few lines of conversation are a perfect illustration of the organic link between Christian exorcism and necromantic magic that some historians have surmised: the "conjurations of Saint Cyprianus and Saint Ambrosius" are approved rites of exorcism; by changing a few words, they can be used to exorcise a demon from a place where a treasure is hidden instead of from a human body, thus bringing the buried riches to light.

Other practices that are reported in the records of the interrogation rooms also comply with what we know from other sources. Mention is made several times of magic "figures," books of conjurations, and pieces of paper with demands or entreaties to demons that are to be put under the chalice or under the host during consecration, preferably for three or nine times.[224] This concurs with similar practices from both learned and folk magic. It is possible that the remarkable custom of celebrating Mass over the naked belly of a woman is derived from similar ideas. This singular procedure was first disclosed by the astrologer Lesage and thus may well be entirely fictitious.[225] If there was anything real in it at all, it may be that an analogous logic was behind it: in reciting Mass over the body of the woman, the magical operation by which the demons increased her sex appeal was further enhanced, in the same way that the power of the medicinal herbs and amulets put underneath the altar or the chalice was increased during consecration.[226] The records invariably state that the Masses were said over the "ventre" of the women, a word that may simply mean "abdomen" but was also used as a polite term for the womb or the female genitalia.[227] The Mass that would have to be held for such a ceremony would evidently be clandestine: it was hardly feasible to put a naked woman on the altar during services.

Another hypothesis might be that the nude woman was meant as an offering. As the witches at the Sabbath sealed their pact with Satan by giving themselves sexually to him, so the nude lady, her legs dangling to the side, might be understood to offer herself to the demon. As was the case with witches, she could expect certain favors in return, and she could also ask for favors for others, as is reported several times during the interrogations.[228] If it is suggested that high-ranking ladies "made recite themselves . . . a Mass of this kind," this does not necessarily mean that they functioned as naked altars themselves. Rather, some of the earlier testimonies suggest that another woman would be used in a rite performed on their behalf.[229] It is tempting, in addition, to interpret the "carnal knowledge" the priest is sometimes said to have had of this female altar as a kind of diabolical sexual union by proxy.

Of course, this may be reading too much into what may simply have been a sexual fantasy. The same may hold true for the strange magical concoction of male and female sexual fluids described in the records. Introvigne retraces this practice to the sexual magic of Indian Tantra and Chinese Taoism, unfortunately without telling how the knowledge of these exotic erotic techniques had arrived in the murky underground of seventeenth-century Paris.[230] If a source must be suggested for these practices, as well as the other instances of illicit sexual behavior that have been recounted, the earlier attribution of similar activities to heretics and sorcerers might be a much better option. We have already quoted copious examples of this. In addition to Augustine of Hippo and other Patristic authors with regard to the Manicheans, the fifteenth-century inquisitor Nicolaus Jaquerius also told about oblations of human sperm. "And what a horrible thing was heard of a few years ago," he recounts. "A certain priest and a women secretly had carnal intercourse in church, so that their seed became mixed with the sacramental Crisma."[231] More or less similar "recipes" for love magic involving sexual effluvia are mentioned in medieval penitentiary manuals.[232]

What the ceremonies described above also do *not* embody—contrary to what Introvigne and others maintain—is an early example of the Black Mass.[233] That is, not if we follow the definition given by Introvigne himself for the Black Mass: an inverted Roman Catholic Mass in which, by appropriately changing the formulae, Satan is worshipped and Jesus Christ is cursed. A case could be made for the fact that demons are worshipped in these "nude" Masses (although one could equally well argue that they are "bound"). But there is no indication in the texts of an "inverted" Mass of any kind. On the contrary, it is said at least once that the ritual used is that of a perfectly normal Mass, the only difference being that the priest invokes the demons after consecration, while mentioning the names of those on whose behest he conjures them.[234] Much as in exorcism and in classic demonic magic, the consecration and the host here serve as loci of power that can be used to force the demons to appear and fulfill one's request.[235] As only a proper ritual could ensure the desired manifestation of the divine, an inverted Mass would indeed be strangely inappropriate. It would be equally surprising if this Mass was used to curse Jesus, as it was precisely his powerful bodily presence that enabled the officiating priest to deal with the demons. Indeed, there is no trace of such a practice in the records regarding the Affair of the Poisons. In the accounts recorded during the interrogations, the host is always treated with respect; the only time a host is "cut up," this is mentioned almost in passing and seems to serve a purely practical purpose.[236]

What we are looking at, in brief, can probably be best described as an odd mixture of classic necromancy, alternative Eucharistic devotion, and sexual magic of unclear origin.[237] Although the descriptions of these ceremonies furnished an important contribution to the later lore of the Missa Negra, there is nothing to suggest that they were meant to be anti-Christian or blasphemous. Labeling them as Black Masses would thus be incorrect. As a matter of fact, the term "messe noir" (Black Mass) is never used in the interrogation records, in stark contrast to Introvigne's contention that the expression originated with the "case La Voisin."[238]

As mentioned above, the peculiar female altars that we encounter in the Affair of the Poisons might be regarded either as a magical tool receiving divine blessing or as an offering to the demons (or, alternatively, as both at the same time). The notion of offering, however, gives us the best entry point to understand the other, sometimes patently gruesome practices that feature in the interrogation records. We encounter descriptions, first, of several people who are portrayed as having given themselves to the devil "body and soul."[239] We will deal with the probability of these matters more thoroughly later on. Here, it suffices to remark that concluding a pact with the devil does not always seem to have been a straightforward matter, as far as the records show. In order to amount to anything, it was clearly expected that the pact be signed by the devil or the demon himself, and this was evidently not an easy thing to arrange. Thus we hear of great magical exertions to ensure the agreement is "ratified." At one time, we even read about plans for a voyage to the Caribbean, where "by the method of the savages one would be able to converse and make a pact with Maboya, who is the devil."[240] Of course, the devil can also be conjured by harnessing the supreme divine power. This leads to paradoxical situations in which Masses are read over pacts with the devil, or invocations in the name of the Trinity serve as a prelude to ceremonies in which a person abrogates baptism and church.[241] As one suspect attested: "A consecrated host renders conjurations more powerful, and has the power to make the spirit emerge."[242]

Another, less comical way to enlist the services of Satan is to offer *somebody else* to him. The sometimes vague descriptions in the interrogation records seem to describe two ways to do this. The first is to give the soul of a child, preferably one's own, to the devil or one of his demons. The best manner to do this, apparently, is before and/or instead of ordinary, Christian baptism. This explains some of the awkward ceremonies involving women giving birth that we find described. In large parts of Europe, it was believed that children could become possessed by demons if baptism was not administered as soon as possible.[243] The archival records regarding the Affair of the Poisons describe at least one occasion on which this mechanism is deliberately reversed. In a cellar where a treasure may have been buried, rituals are performed on a women who was at the point of giving birth, during which she promised her child to the demon, "adding that she even would renounce to baptise the child of which she was pregnant; and on another piece of parchment [she] wrote another pact by which she gave her child to Astaroth, and consented that he would take possession of it on the moment that it would come to birth."[244] Apparently, however, not only recently born, unbaptized children could be offered in this way: in another interrogation, La Filastre is accused of having given her daughter of fourteen or fifteen to the devil "in order to obligate the spirits to appear." To accomplish this, a priest recited three Masses over the womb of the girl, during one of which he had sex with her—and that seems to have been everything that happened with her, for a later declaration speaks of her as being alive and presumably well.[245]

These examples of a kind of "spiritual offering" are exceptions; as we have already seen, the type of infant sacrifice most frequently noted in the records of the Chambre Ardente is the simple slaughter of a newborn child. Here we are indeed far removed from the offering of a dove or cockerel that the classic manuals of necromancy prescribe to "allure" the spirits.[246] As far as the literature shows, there is no mention of infant sacrifice in the traditions of European demonic magic. For the source of this idea, we must turn once again to the tradition of attribution regarding the religious other. By now, it is probably unnecessary to repeat how allegations of ritual infanticide and similar atrocities formed part and parcel of the stereotype of dissident Christians, sorcerers, and Jews. Witches in particular were depicted as preying on young or unbaptized children, which they presented to their master the devil at the Sabbath or slaughtered to use as a component in their magical unguents.[247] More specifically, ecclesiastical authors like Isodore of Seville and Hugo of St. Victor attested to the fact that "the demons love human blood" and that the offering of the blood of humans was an essential part of the routines of demonic magic.[248] In 1680 in Paris, these ideas must still have been very much in people's minds. Even as recently as 1675, there had been public uproar in the city about rumors that children were being sacrificed to prepare a ritual "bath of blood."[249]

The macabre practices we find in the records of the Affair of the Poisons may well derive from such attributed constructs about "reversed" diabolical worship. The next question, however, would be *in what way*? Are we dealing with mere rumors here that reflect "residual fears of witchcraft" and broader conceptions about what practitioners of diabolic magic might do? Or are they descriptions of real practices by people who adopted iconic and stereotypical forms of devil worship because they thought this the proper way to appease the princes of darkness? In other words, are we still dealing with *attribution*, or is it rather an example of *appropriation* and *identification* that the texts are showing us here?

The answer to this question depends on the actual occurrence of the macabre practices described. Modern scholarship shies away from rendering an unequivocal verdict on this point. Introvigne, for instance, writes that "in certain cases at least . . . children could have been slaughtered and sacrificed"; Mollenauer maintains that "the ring of probability adheres to the richly sacrilegious details"; and Somerset concludes that it is "impossible to know whether children had really been sacrificed."[250] Was La Voisin really a relentless organizer of horrors? One can imagine how the combination of her secret practice as an *aborteuse* with dabbling in magic may have easily evolved into more macabre practices; one can also imagine, however, how this combination could have given occasion to some grisly rumors. As a matter of fact, La Voisin steadfastly denied any knowledge of improper Masses or child sacrifices up to the moment of her death at the stake.[251] In addition, a remark from the sources tells how during one abortion, she wept tears of joy when the midwife who performed it baptized the fetus.[252] Nor were any bodily remains of the sacrifice victims ever recovered, contrary to the assertions of some historians.[253] We have no conclusive evidence that we are not dealing with pure fabrications here.

By now, the shrewd reader may have noticed that we have gradually slid from perfectly feasible practices of demonic magic into a complex of allegations that is almost identical to that traditionally ascribed to the "Satanist" other—including aberrant sexual behavior, infanticide, and even a hint of conspiracy (the plot to kill the king). We cannot be sure at what point we cross the border between events that actually occurred and the realm of imagination. As already suggested at the beginning of this section, the Affair of the Poisons resembles a gray zone where fact indiscernibly melts into fiction, attribution into identification, "Christian" magic into possible forms of Satanism. Given the inherent uncertainties the source material presents, it seems inappropriate to make overly bold assertions regarding the question of whether this is an early historical instance of Satanism or not. There is simply too much we do not know, and with the evidence available, we may never be able to resolve this matter with absolute certainty. In the next section, however, we present some interesting facts that may shed more light on what was really going on in the gray zone.

SATANISTS BEFORE THE MODERN AGE?

The Affair of the Poisons was not without consequences. In the wake of the scandalous affair, the French king issued a royal edict restricting the sale of arsenics and other harmful substances. It also stipulated penalties for every person *pretending* to be a diviner, magician, or sorcerer. These persons were to be banished; in the case of flagrant sacrilege of the Christian religion, death sentences were to be meted out. The word "pretended" in particular made this edict revolutionary. Here was an official statement of legal skepticism regarding the reality of sorcery, issued in the name of the king.[254]

It was in the context of enforcing this decree that René Voyer, Comte d'Argenson, reported on some unusual suspects in a memorandum that he submitted to his superior in October 1702. This memorandum lay buried in the archives until it was dug up and published by the French historian Robert Mandrou in 1979.[255] The count, who had succeeded La Reynie as chief of the Parisian police, had compiled his *mémoire* to urge immediate action against the guild of "false sorcerers" that had become of late, he complained, more numerous than some of the genuine guilds of honest artisans. He illustrated his discourse with descriptions of nineteen of the most important bands that plied this trade in Paris, of the false sorcerers that led them and their principal accomplices, and sometimes also of the "dupes" whose credulity they abused. Many of these descriptions are of great interest to anyone wishing to unravel the protohistory of Satanism. We learn, for instance, that right at the beginning of the eighteenth century, among the throngs of fortune-tellers, matchmakers, palm readers, treasure seekers, and people who sold waters to restore lost virginities, the French capital counted at least ten persons who occupied themselves commercially with furnishing "pacts with the devil."[256]

Apart from many practices belonging to "ordinary" necromancy, this remarkable document contains several scenes that seem directly reminiscent of the Affair of the Poisons. We can read about improper Masses celebrated by derelict clergy—for instance, by the renegade Capuchin monk Abbé Le Fevre, who lived with a woman named La Mariette in the house of her husband, "where he has recited Mass at midnight several times, in sacerdotal habits that La Mariette borrowed from a priest of Saint Séverin; a big beer jug serving as chalice.

The purpose of all these Masses had been to conclude a pact with the infernal Spirit, in order to obtain a million, a pension of two thousand *écus* a month, and the gift of making oneself beloved with persons of rank."[257] Later, Le Fevre "carried his impiety so far that he celebrated the Holy Mass and consecrated the host on the womb of La Mariette."[258] In addition, the memorandum recounts some other instances of Masses without nudity "in order to attract the infernal spirits and compel them to ratify the pacts which have been written on virginal parchment."[259] Twice, mention is made of women who give up their children to the devil, although the exact proceedings and the precise fate of these infants remain misty. (In one case, we merely read that the newborn child was "immediately taken away"; in another case, the as yet unborn child is marked by a demon, but we do not get to know what happened with it after it was born—although the demon suggested the child would be a page of Lucifer, who "passionately loves children.")[260]

Again, it becomes evident that making a pact with Satan was not a simple operation. D'Argenson tells us about a gentleman who ruined himself in fruitless attempts to seal a pact with the infernal powers, and of an old maid who tried to interest Satan in a pact with her for ten or twelve years but did not succeed, "the devil not wanting anything of her."[261] In fact, most of the pacts we read about in the memorandum fail to be concluded. Often, sacrifices have to be made and complicated operations are required; in this limbo where people desperately entreat diabolical favor, a minor industry of fraud seems to have developed, with mediums and magicians claiming to know the secret of obtaining Satan's signature.

This underworld of small-time crooks closely resembles the underground occult circuit that had been brought to light during the Affair of the Poisons. D'Argenson's memorandum, however, is clearly far more reliable as a historical source. Despite a faint hint of political intrigue, his report is not part of a political *Spiel* with predetermined objectives.[262] And despite his pious concern that the practices he describes "may lead to the destruction of religion in all its principles," his account is balanced, sober, and matter of fact, with a tone of polished skepticism that at times only half conceals his amusement.[263] In addition, his information does not derive from the interrogation of suspects, but from informers from inside the occult underworld who had opted for respectability. This does not mean D'Argenson's memorandum can be trusted in all its particulars—it is obvious to anyone who reads it that some rather tall stories have managed to creep in. But in its general outlines, the picture it presents seems true enough. There is no reason to doubt that there was indeed a group of people active in the French capital that sought to make money by negotiating "pacts with the spirits."

What exactly can we understand by these pacts? Naturally, the practices we learn about through D'Argenson's memorandum are mediated to us by his words; his terms of description might not be the ones that people who were actually involved would have used. They might have understood their relations with the otherworld as a partial agreement with spirits that they bound . We must remain wary of the sweeping terminology of the times, which also affected D'Argenson's account; he evidently did not write with the sensibilities of a modern scholar of religion. Yet throughout his long *mémoire*, we encounter more or less unambiguous descriptions of people who want to give themselves to the devil "body and soul."[264]

Evidently, D'Argenson's informers had told him that there were numerous people in Paris who were eager to become vassals of Satan. Nor do we need to have a priori doubts about the veracity of these reports. Scattered throughout the early modern period, we can find a good number of cases of genuine, solidly documented pacts with the devil. One of the most famous is the one attempted in 1596 by David Lipsius or Leipzig, a freshman theology student at the university in Tübingen. His pact is still extant, the full text of which is as follows:

> I, David Leipzig from Erfurt in Thüringen, write and inform you, Auerhahn in Hell, that I want to make a pact with you and be yours, when you will presently, when I come home again, leave three golden guilders next to this letter, and afterwards will give me what I covet. In anticipation of your answer.[265]

David's venture in Satanism was duly discovered when his roommate walked into his room and noticed the piece of paper and money Lipsius had left for the demon. In 1698, yet another Tübinger theology student tried to enlist with the devil, selling his soul for a "thousand pair of guilders, and a moneymaking homunculus" in a pact written with his own blood and signed "Georg Friederich Haim, formerly a Christian, henceforth your serf in exchange for money."[266] In 1639, local authorities in the west of Holland apprehended Jan Hartman Oosterdagh, a former Protestant preacher who had ended up as a tramp, and they were dumbfounded when they discovered a written pact on his body in which Oosterdagh surrendered himself to Satan, again in exchange for money.[267] Other examples have been uncovered from archives in Holland, Sweden, and Spanish America.[268] Although some of the stories mentioned impress one as rather frivolous or pubertal, these are all cases where we have reasonable indications of a personal, deliberate choice for the devil. They exclude instances of obvious insanity and cases where people pretended to (have) be(en) a follower of Satan as part of a public spectacle (as with the possessed nuns of Louviers and Loudun) or to attract the attention of the religious authorities (as some harshly treated slaves in Spanish South America seem to have done in order to end up in the comparatively lenient hands of the Inquisition).[269]

Clearly, opting to serve Satan was not an impossible choice in early modern Europe. The assertions of D'Argenson consequently may well have a solid foundation in truth. So here, at last, we may have a clear historical example of people we can define as Satanists. For we are certainly witnessing forms of intentional veneration of Satan here. If selling your soul to Satan does not qualify as Satanism, probably not much else will. Rituals were held for his appeasement; body and soul surrendered to him. We can certainly call this veneration religious, in an obvious sort of way. The question is: what kind of religion exactly? Although D'Argenson liked to brand them "sectateurs" and sometimes called their gatherings "assemblies," these early modern venerators of Satan were not organized into a creedal community that explicitly offered an alternative religious interpretation of the cosmos. The sources are not very eloquent about their worldview, but with few exceptions, we do not encounter proof of a complete rejection of the Christian worldview or of a religious rebellion against a dominant Christianity. Even the practices that most scandalized their contemporaries, such as holding Mass on the naked belly of a woman, do not seem to have been meant as intentional provocations or profanations of Christian religion.

Rather, rituals like these seem to encompass a *syncretism* of Christianity and Satanism, however unlikely this may sound.[270] Obviously, taking recourse to Satanic powers contains an implicit criticism of some of the central tenets of "traditional" Christianity. But as far as we can tell from our meager sources, this was not what most early modern practitioners of Satanism were interested in. Their Satanism did not focus on doctrinal issues or an explanation of the universe. Rather, it was eminently practical and pragmatic in orientation, with the supernatural, be it "good" or "evil," primarily conceived of as a possible source of power, wealth, and prosperity. Like the Late Antique Satanians described by Ephipanius of Salamis, they merely took refuge with Satan because he was powerful and strong and consequently might be capable of fulfilling their wishes.

Hard as it may be to grasp for many modern readers, such pragmatism was not at all unusual in the religious practices of the early modern period or before.[271] Those who sold their soul to Satan only drew the extreme conclusion of this attitude. Introvigne's concluding words about the Affair of the Poisons apply almost verbatim here. "None of the protagonists . . . [were] battling to combat Christianity or to glorify Satan. More prosaically, their objectives consisted in submitting, with the help of the Demon, some rival for love who was ungraceful enough to be younger in years . . . , or to earn enough money for a retirement on a nice property in Italy. . . . It [is] these particularly sordid aspects that prevent us from speaking of Satanism—in the sense of veneration of the Demon—here already."[272] This seems a fair characterization to me. I only beg to differ on Introvigne's final conclusion. I think we would do well not to apply stern post-Christian notions about what religion should be and what not to a popular and underground belief system from the early modern era. A lot of tribal and ancient religions operate on a quid pro quo basis as well; that does not prevent them from being religions.[273] Fragmented as they may be, or as they have been left to us in our sources, the incidents of "Satanist" practices we encountered in the present and preceding sections certainly imply a worldview related to "ultimate grounds of being." In all cases, veneration for Satan played a certain role, whether as a minor yet powerful god subordinate to the Christian Trinity or as an apparently equal religious alternative. Sure enough, many of the "Satanist" practitioners described by D'Argenson seem to have stopped believing in their own magic as soon as they managed to run away with their clients' money.[274] But that still leaves intact the fact that their *clients* evidently trusted in their assertions and were often prepared to invest huge sums of money out of this conviction. That they expected to reap the profits of their beliefs already in this earthly existence, and not only after death, does not strike me as the greatest of their follies.

The quotation from Introvigne brings us back to the Affair of the Poisons and the questions formulated at the end of the preceding section. Many of the practices found in D'Argenson's memo are remarkably similar to those described in the interrogation records of the Chambre Ardente. To recapitulate our conclusions from the last section: we established that our sources regarding the affair are not to be trusted at face value and that the practices they describe, although reflecting many well-attested elements of necromantic magic, tend to devolve into the realm of stereotype and attribution. Here, however, we see many of them reappear—especially the "Satanist" core element of the diabolical pact—and this time in a much more reliable document. What are the repercussions of this on our understanding of the Affair of the Poisons?

The answer to this question depends to a large extent on the exact nature of the relation between the facts described in the 1702 memorandum and those reported during the earlier affair. It is possible that the form of Satanism described by the count had only arisen in the twenty years following the Affair of the Poisons and was directly stimulated by it, in imitation perhaps of the alleged practice of La Voisin and her consorts. Religion and magic are perfectly capable of innovation, and the intense publicity surrounding the affair may well have given some people fresh ideas. That the affair still had much notoriety in 1702 is indicated by the veiled references D'Argenson made to it in the introduction to his memorandum and by the fact that one of the soothsayers mentioned by D'Argenson claimed to keep an office in the former quarters of La Voisin—apparently in the expectation that this fact would impress customers.[275]

Another—and in my eyes more plausible—hypothesis would be that the Satanism described in 1702 was a continuation of practices already surfacing during the Affair of the Poisons and only temporarily—and probably very temporarily—suppressed by the Chambre Ardente. That means that beneath the poison conspiracy, the naked participation of royal mistresses, and the weekly infanticide, there could have been some real Satanist or proto-Satanist activities going on in the 1670s. *Some* of the accused during the affair might actually have done *some* of the things they were accused of. There is nothing implausible about people making pacts with evil spirits or celebrating Mass in unusual ways—especially when we see the same things happen only twenty years later, in a roughly similar milieu of occult peddlers. What is more, we have occasional attestations of practices like these predating the affair. Anne Somerset cites a case from 1677, when a priest called Bernard Tournet was burned at the stake for "sacrileges and profanation of the holy sacrifice of Mass itself, invocation of the devil and the seduction of several persons whom he abused under false pretexts of making them find treasure by means of evil spirits."[276] Unfortunately, these transgressions are not described in more detail, but they sound intriguingly similar to those mentioned during the Affair of the Poisons and by D'Argenson. As we have seen, more general evidence for genuine attempts to conclude a pact with the devil can be found in relative profusion in earlier sources.

All these indications combined, I think, give ample occasion to speak of a marginal "tradition" of Satanism during the early modern age, and maybe before. I put the word tradition between quotation marks because this Satanism certainly is not an underground community of adherents who transmit their precepts or practices from generation to generation. In other words, we are not dealing here with a continuously organized form of secret, alternative religion standing in continuous opposition to Christianity over time, as the Christian tradition of attribution and some of its later continuators imagined to be extant. As a matter of fact, the origins of many of these practices may be found, I believe, in precisely this same tradition of attribution. Massimo Introvigne is probably right when he suggests that Satanist concepts were mainly transmitted through books during this period, discovered again and again in the pages of reports and pamphlets on famed and famous devil worshippers.[277] From very early Christian times, magicians were *attributed* to derive their powers from Satan, implicitly or explicitly requiring subjugation to him by way of a (written) pact. The methods and notions of pact making thus did not need to be invented. They had been preached from the pulpits and expounded in popular lore and literature for centuries; each time yet another variant of the Protinus or Theophilus story was recounted. For some audiences, these could easily have had an advertisement effect. After all, Protinus's servant *did* get the girl in the end, did he not?

Occasionally, the sources give a glimpse of evidence for this. In the case of David Lipsius, for instance, the authorities discovered that he found the inspiration for his pact in a popular booklet about "Christophor Wagner's Pact with the Devil called Auerhan," a fictional story in the Faust tradition.[278] This was all the more evident because Lipsius had addressed his pact to "Auerhahn," in normal life the German designation for a kind of forest bird (capercaillie in English) and an unusual name for a demon. These indications suggest that we can consider these sixteenth- and seventeenth-century instances of Satanism to be early forms of *identification*, or at least *appropriation*. Practices attributed by Christian authors to Jews, heretics, and witches, but especially to magicians, were partially adopted by these early modern Satanists, apparently because they thought this was the proper way to become a follower of the devil or to practice magic.[279] Incidentally, this also indicates once more how strongly embedded this early modern Satanism remained in the framework of Christian cosmology and theology. Rarely do we encounter traces of innovation that signal a process of autonomous religious creativity, be it in doctrine or ritual. One exceptional example of the latter may be the Satanism we find described in connection with the Affair of the Poisons, where ideas from educated and popular magic and notions from Roman Catholic liturgy seem to have blended into new rites with which to manipulate the otherworld.[280]

Another aspect of these early traces of Satanist identification and innovation must be emphasized here as well: their extreme marginality, both sociologically and historically, vis-à-vis the dominating forces of attribution. The rare instances of Satanism we encounter during this period are mostly isolated, individual cases of people who are in extremely dire straits or who can be located on the very margins of society.[281] The only exceptions, in a way, to this general rule are the "Satanists" whose presence is attested in France during the late seventeenth century and the early eighteenth century. Here we can discern the vague outlines of an underground and clandestine subculture partially involved in Satanist religious practices, with even a faint hint of something of a living tradition of ritual knowledge transmitted from one practitioner to another. But despite the fact that a few of the religious specialists in this field evidently enjoyed some measure of commercial success, the overall impression we get of this Satanism is that it was a relatively insignificant affair hidden away in the back alleys of the more sordid parts of town. D'Argenson paints an entertaining but also rather disheartening picture of a world of crooks, swindlers, and desperate clients, who mostly end their lives either in prison or in the Hôpital de Dieu, Paris's infamous relief center for paupers.

Thus, if one conclusion can be drawn from the historical findings presented in this chapter, than it must be the overwhelming preponderance of *attribution* in the history of Satanism before the onset of modernity. Although many points in this history remain uncertain or disputed, we can clearly observe how the *concept* of Satanism predated the practice of venerating Satan itself. This concept of Satanism arose in the confrontation of Christianity with divergent religious groups within and outside the Christian community. Its primary function was to serve as a tool for categorization or, perhaps more accurately, vilification. Early Christian notions about pagan polytheism as the veneration of demons, and rumors about the antinomian and blasphemous activities of heterodox groups, merged in the early Middle Ages into the concept of a counterreligion whose adherents actively and willingly venerated Satan and/or his demons in licentious rites. It was this *stereotype* of the Satanist that would prove to be the most important contribution to the later development of an actually practiced Satanism.

In this respect, what can be said to have mattered most about the Satanism of the Affair of the Poisons was not its alleged or actual ritual practice, however colorful or gruesome. Rather, it was the way this Satanism was described by the very official agencies that set out to crush it, as well as the tendency this reflects in the further development of the Satanist stereotype. Compared with earlier times, references to the actions or actual presence of Satan are conspicuous by their absence in the interrogation records regarding the affair.[282] Instead, the focus has shifted to the activities of the Satanists themselves, a group of persons who dedicate themselves completely to the Evil One, stage obscene rites for devious ends, and are suspected to have a dangerously asocial or even antisocial inclination. It was a stereotype well suited to a new, more skeptical era— one that would outlast the millennium.

For Hell and the foul fiend that rules

God's everlasting fiery jails

(Devised by rogues, dreaded by fools),

With his grim, grisly dog that keeps the door,

Are senseless stories, idle tales,

Dreams, whimsey's, and no more.

JOHN WILMOTT, Earl of Rochester,

Seneca. Troas. Act. 2. Choir. Thus English'd

Intermezzo 1

The Eighteenth Century: Death of Satan?

WHILE THE AFFAIR of the Poisons was erupting, a comical play by the playwrights Thomas Corneille and Donneau de Visé had premiered in the Paris theater. Entitled "La Devineresse" ("The Divineress"), it told the story of a female soothsayer and magician. Given the real-life scandal that had already become the talk of the town, it is not surprising that the play proved a box office hit, with spectators crowding the theater to attend its performance. What might be more of a surprise is the strikingly skeptical depiction the play gives of the magical practices of its eponymous protagonist. The divineress herself is heard to declare that "luck is the most important ingredient of success in this line of work." "All you need is presence of mind, a bit of guts, a talent for intrigue, some trusted people in the right places, and keeping track of the incidents that happen and the course of love affairs. But above all: say a lot of things when someone comes to consult you. There is always a thing among them that happens to be true; and sometimes all it takes to gain renown, is to say the right thing two or three times by coincidence."[1]

Corneille and Visé's play accurately reflected the shifting attitude toward "supernatural" crime and the involvement of Satan and his demons that had begun to surface in Western Europe. In the hundred years that followed, mass persecutions for witchcraft or religious dissidence effectively came to an end in most Western nations. Historians have suggested a variety of causes and motives for this change in attitude. Initial criticism of the witchcraft trials, most assert, was not motivated by a stance of rational criticism vis-à-vis the reality of the supernatural. Rather, most authors objecting to the persecution of witches criticized the faulty judicial procedure involved or argued for the nonexistence of diabolical witchcraft with recourse to older theological notions that denied Satan, as a spiritual being, the ability to exert direct influence on physical reality.[2] Gary K. Waite has suggested that in some regions, local societies simply grew tired of the legal bloodshed that was the consequence of the quest for a unitary

religious state, while in other places, the realities of post-Reformation religious plural-
ity made people skeptical about rumors of Satanist conspiracy.[3] More and more, people
accused of being witches and heretics came to be considered victims of slander, misunderstanding, or psychiatric disorders, instead of malicious followers of Satan.

At the same time, the playground of the devil was being correspondingly reduced.
In 1691, the Dutch protestant minister Balthasar Bekker published *The Enchanted
World*, in which he combined old providential theology and new Cartesian philosophy to argue that it was logically impossible for a spiritual entity like the angel of evil to
exert any tangible influence on the kingdom of this world.[4] Confronting Christianity's
hidden dualism, Bekker designated those believing in a powerful Satan "ditheists." "If
anyone wants to give *me* a new name because of my opinions, I may suffer it to be that
of monotheist," he provocatively exclaimed. "This Book will bear witness to my effort
to return to the Most High as much of his Power and Wisdom as those that gave it to
the Devil had taken away. I exorcise him from the world and bind him in Hell, in order
that King Jesus will reign the more supreme."[5]

Bekker's grand exorcism of Satan was picked up and intensified by the upcoming
Enlightenment. In 1773, Voltaire roundly declared that "we know well enough that
Satan, Beelzebuth, and Astaroth do not exist any more than Tisiphone, Alector, and
Megæra."[6] The French *philosophe* might also have been among the first to suggest that
the Jews had adopted their Satan in imitation of the Ahreman of the Persians while
in Babylonian captivity, and preceded modern biblical scholarship by many decades
in doubting the assertion that the "Lucifer" described in the prophecies of Isaiah
had anything to do with the devil.[7] The lemma of the devil in the *Encyclopédie* of
Diderot, that monument of Enlightenment learning, consisted mainly of Scripture
quotations, with the caustic remark thrown in that Europeans tended to think of
the devil as black, while Ethiopians pictured him as white; "The view of the former
has as much validity as that of the latter."[8] This criticism was comparatively mild,
probably with an eye to avoiding censorship.[9] Other authors were more strident in
their dismissal of Satan. In his 1696 dissertation, *De origine ac progressu Idolatriae
et Superstitionum*, Anton van Dale (an early proponent of the Dutch Radical
Enlightenment) had already voiced a reproach that would become a classic trope in
later discussions of the subject: priests and rulers had deliberately sustained fear of
the devil in the common people, he maintained, in order to secure their own power
and dominance.[10]

For the Enlightenment, in brief, Satan and sorcery were part of the dead weight that
had to be thrown off if the balloon of humanity was to reach its natural zenith. Belief
in the devil became an object of derision or ridicule.[11] This deconstruction of Satan was
part of a much more ambitious attempt to exorcise the Christian god from European
society and put an end to the doctrinal monopoly and secular influence of institutional Christianity. This does not imply that the Enlightenment, on the whole, was
areligious. It certainly wasn't. But the "god of the philosophers," as Pascal aptly called
him, was a different deity from that of the Christianity of the past. In Enlightenment
deism, the deity was seen as a wise creator who had put together the world as a flawless
machine and had subsequently left it to run by itself according to the laws of nature.

Man should use his god-given gift of rationality to understand the divine laws governing the cosmos and make sure to live in harmony with them.

The "natural" religion of Enlightenment thinking was succinctly summarized by Daniel Defoe as "Heaven resolved with Nature, Religion with Reason, and all Gods into Philosophy."[12] According to some, this had in fact been the original faith of humanity, which in present-day religions had become occluded by superstition and the manipulations of priesthood. The Enlightenment thus saw a flourishing of "scientific" theories about a primeval, universal religion, and the sketches some *philosophes* made for a new religion to replace Christianity can not only be understood as a reflection of the new height of rationality and civilization that (European) mankind had now achieved, but also as an attempt to return to a pristine, unaccreted form of religiosity.[13]

The Enlightenment was also influential in the propagation of freedom of conscience and freedom of religion. Indeed, part of the hostility of the Enlightenment to "traditional" Christianity derived from a moral distaste for its ongoing history of religious persecution.[14] Pierre Bayle (1647–1706), a Protestant who had fled from France and had become a prominent spokesman of the early Radical Enlightenment, pioneered the protest against any form of state-endorsed doctrinal coercion with his eloquent arguments for complete legal equality for all forms of religion.[15] The Dutch Republic, where he had found refuge, had been one of the first countries in Western Europe to stipulate that "nobody shall be persecuted or examined for religious matters" and to grant some measure of liberty to the religious varieties contained within its borders.[16] After the Dutch Statholder William III had ascended the English throne, the Toleration Act of 1689 brought similar freedoms to England, while in other places, rulers who had embraced the Enlightenment instated de facto religious lenience.

Even in these havens of tolerance, however, complete legal emancipation for religious minorities was still centuries away. Elsewhere, old patterns of persecution persisted. Especially in areas on the margins, the process of attributing Satanism and subsequent judicial repression continued as before. Scotland burned its last witch in 1722; Hungary and Poland experienced waves of witchcraft persecution in the early eighteenth century.[17] As late as during the final decades of the eighteenth century, the area of what is now Dutch and Belgian Limburg came under the grip of a collective terror for bands of supernatural, Satanist brigands. Known as *Bockeryders* ("Riders of the Goat"), they allegedly displaced themselves riding on demons in the form of he-goats. They were said to have abrogated Christianity and sworn loyalty to Satan, with the total overthrow of church and state as their ultimate aim. Hundreds of people died at the stake and the scaffold because of this specter, and only the arrival of the French revolutionary forces put an end to the executions.[18]

Occasional shreds of evidence tell us that older forms of Satanist identification also continued during the eighteenth century (and probably beyond). Introvigne cites the case of an Italian priest who convinced a nun and her sister to participate in "Satanist" rites of a highly sexual nature, promising they would attain the mystical "satisfaction" talked about by the Catholic Quietists of the day.[19] In a somewhat different vein, a band of robbers in the Dutch Republic made oaths binding themselves to Satan.[20] The age-old practice of soldiers giving themselves to the devil in order to remain unscathed during battle probably went on as well; even on nineteenth-century battlefields, little letters with a dedication to Satan could occasionally be found on the bodies of dead soldiers.[21] In eighteenth-century Halle, a cook was found to have written a pact with Satan while drunk. The would-be Satanist only received a mild punishment for blasphemy because, as his judges declared, "no such pact can exist according to the facts of nature" ("per rerum natura kein solch pactum seyn kan"). The judicial faculty of Halle was eminently aware of the fact that only a few generations previously, punishment would have been much more harsh, but nevertheless stood by their verdict, "since we have now adopted more reasonable principles."[22] Significantly, the German men of law held it to be self-evident that the cook had found his ideas within some cheap booklet or broadsheet.[23]

These scarce cases of devil worship in a more or less traditional mold all stem from judicial archives, where they have gathered dust for centuries. History has reserved more posthumous notoriety for the so-called Hell-Fire Clubs, a phenomenon that experienced something of a vogue in Britain during the eighteenth century. Social clubs had become highly popular in eighteenth-century Britain, with clubs formed for gambling, eating beefsteaks, patronizing art, and masturbating collectively, to mention just a few.[24] The Hell-Fire Clubs were among the most notorious and most elusive manifestations of this rage for clubbing. First reported in 1720s London and 1730s Dublin, the gutter press described them as gatherings of atheist rakes drinking to the devil and mocking the Christian religion. Later legend added further picturesque detail, such as Satanic visitations, pacts with the infernal spirit, and a chair that was always kept empty for the visiting Prince of Darkness.[25]

In order to suppress the "shocking impieties" of these assemblies, King George I proposed an "Act for the More Effectual Suppressing of Blasphemy and Profaness" to the House of Lords on April 29, 1721. The House, however, rejected the bill with sixty "noes" against thirty-four "ayes," fearing that the new law was a potential tool for persecution instead of a simple measure against blasphemy. These fears may not have been altogether unfounded, as the bill was ghost-drafted by Archbishop Wake of Canterbury, whose primary concern was the protection of Anglican "orthodoxy" against the upcoming tide of dissent, especially the "Unitarianism" of Enlightenment deism.[26] Enlightenment skepticism was probably also at the root of the Hell-Fire Clubs themselves. Although not much is known about the precise proceedings at their meetings—unless we count ghost stories and sensationalist newspaper reports as accurate historic sources—recent historiography agrees that they were certainly not the devil worshippers of popular belief.[27] The English expert Evelyn Lord suggests that they were "essentially a group of young gentlemen who met together to toast to the Devil and indulge in other sacrilegious actions," while some of them may have had "the serious intent of discussing the existence of the Trinity."[28]

The most famous of all Hell-Fire Clubs was never a Hell-Fire Club at all. The so-called Order of the Knights of Saint Francis (also known as the Medmenham Friars) was founded around 1750 by Sir Francis Dashwood, an English nobleman from a respected family of landed gentry. Dashwood was already cofounder of the Dilettanti Club, which fostered interest in Italian art, as well as the short-lived Divan Club, an assembly of persons who had visited Turkey at least once. Apparently, he felt the need for an even more intimate kind of gathering, and he began to organize regular meetings of a small circle of "knights," first at his estate at West Wycombe, afterward at Medmenham Abbey, an old Cistercian monastery he redecorated and fitted out with a stylish garden filled with playful references to the act of procreation. Here "sisters" were invited or imported from London whorehouses, and each member could use his own cell for his private devotions. In the chapter room, the holy of holies inside the abbey, more serious religious practices may have been going on (one former member spoke elusively of "English Eleusian rites"), but there is nothing to suggest that veneration of Satan was among them. Drinking and wenching seem to have been the main occupation of the Friars of Saint Francis.[29]

During its fifteen-year-long existence, the Order of Saint Francis counted some notable figures from British public life among its members. In addition to Sir Dashwood himself and John Montagu, Fourth Earl of Sandwich (famous for the well-known lunch snack and Captain Cook's voyages), Charles Churchill, George Walpole, and John Wilkes were sometime members. The American Founding Father Benjamin Franklin was on good terms with Dashwood and may have attended some of the "ceremonies." The "order" briefly sprang into the history books when some of its most prominent members took seats in British government, with Sir Francis Dashwood becoming Chancellor of the Exchequer. This so-called Hell-Fire Cabinet did not last very long, and for the rest of his life, Sir Francis betook himself to less taxing occupations. He was a dutiful member of the House of Lords, erected a church of singular design on his domains, and made a revision of the Anglican Book of Common Prayer, together with Benjamin Franklin.[30] The fame of his Brotherhood inspired a new wave of Hell-Fire Clubs, but none of these derivates came ever close to Satanism in any formal sense of the word.

Another eighteenth-century household name that frequently crops up in histories of Satanism is that of Donatien Alphonse François, the Marquise de Sade (1740–1814). Indeed it is abundantly clear that this notorious pornographer-cum-philosopher was not particularly fond of the Christian religion. After De Sade, every literary invention of sacrilege must look pale. In *Justine ou les malheurs de la vertu* (1788), for instance, the misadventurous heroine stumbles into a monastery where the inhabitants hold blasphemous, Guibourg-like Masses upon the buttocks of young virgins. Afterward, the monks use the host in a way even the nuns of Louviers would not have been able to imagine. Justine herself is forced to partake of this experience: "They take hold of me and place me at the same place as Florette; the sacrifice is consummated, and the Host . . . that sacred symbol of our august religion . . . Severino takes it in his hands, he forces it into the obscene place of his sodomizing enjoyments . . . he pounds it with curses . . . presses it with outrage under the redoubled strokes of his monstrous spear, and then spoils, while blaspheming, the impure spurts of the torrent of his lust over the holy body of his Saviour."[31]

Despite the rampant anti-Christianity that passages like these suggest, however, the traditional opponent of the Christian god is almost absent in De Sade's work. Satan makes only one brief appearance, in *La philosophie dans le boudoir* ("Philosophy in the Bedroom," 1795), where Madame Saint-Ange exclaims during orgasm: "O Lucifer! one and only god of my soul, give me the inspiration for something that goes further, offer to my heart a new outrage, and you will see how I will plunge myself into it."[32] Compared with the frequent invocations of the traditional deity (mostly in phrases like "damned name of a god with whom I wipe my ass! . . ."), this is positively meager. In fact, De Sade has no room for a Satan in his world, believing as he does in only one reigning principle, Nature with a capital N.[33] In a dark mirror image of the optimist deism of Enlightenment theology, his god is completely indifferent to the fate of humans, distributing life and destruction in a wanton and amoral way. The best one can do is harmonize oneself with Nature, leave behind all morality, and find delight in the infliction of cruelty. In this ruthless and uncompromising reflection on a world without a god, De Sade's philosophy was doubtlessly groundbreaking. But Satanism it was not.

Qu'est-ce qu'un dogme, un culte, un rite? Un Objet d'art.
VICTOR HUGO, "Les quatre vents de l'esprit"

2

The Romantic Rehabilitation of Satan

AT ABOUT THE same time that De Sade was penning down his blasphemous fantasies, a select group of authors and artists in Britain began to turn their attention toward the figure of Satan. Their portrayal of the devil would surely have surprised a medieval or early modern reader. In literary works by Romantic poets like Shelley and Byron or artworks by Fuseli and Blake, the great adversary of yore was frequently depicted in a strangely benevolent, even heroic manner. The contrast with the age-old Christian image of Satan as prime mythological representative of evil could hardly be starker. While earlier "profane" literature had occasionally featured more or less ambivalent portraits of the devil, never before had he thus openly been shown as an object of identification, edification, and even downright adulation.[1]

This new view of Satan encompassed a rehabilitation in two respects. First, and most obvious, while Christian mythology had blamed Satan for evil and banished him to hell, a select number of authors and artists now professed their sympathy with the fallen angel and endeavored to rehabilitate him in some form or another, at least in the artistic domain. Second, and not less significantly, they resurrected him from the burial he had been given by Enlightenment rationalism, which had ridiculed or ignored Satan as an obsolete relic of superstition that was certainly not fit as object of veneration. This double rehabilitation, I like to argue, represents an essential step in the historical emergence of modern Satanism. In this chapter, we will trace the genesis and development of this remarkable reversal of the image of Satan. We will try to find out why this reversal occurred at precisely this moment of history and how we can understand the specific way in which it manifested itself. Finally, we will examine the question whether this reshaping of Satan can be described as a *religious* Satanism—which would make it the first instance of modern religious Satanism in western history.

THE SATANIC SCHOOL OF POETRY

The historical genesis of the new image of Satan can be traced with some precision. During the 1780s and 1790s, a circle of Radical artists, poets, and thinkers associated with the

Dissenting publisher Joseph Johnson became intrigued with the figure of the fallen arch-angel. Their source of inspiration was unexpected: the seventeenth-century epic poem *Paradise Lost* (1663) by John Milton, which Johnson planned to publish in a new, lavishly illustrated edition. Milton's long didactic poem, now almost exclusively read by literary scholars and historians, was widely read in the eighteenth century, not only in England but also abroad, where it had been translated by Voltaire, admired by Schiller, and even found its way to the bookshelves of the Russian Old Believers.[2] *Paradise Lost* retold the Christian myth of Satan's insurrection and the subsequent fall of Man in verse, and although Milton had explicitly stated in the first book of his poem that it was written to "justifie the wayes of God to men," critics had long noted the dramatic imbalance of the work.[3] Instead of Adam or Christ, it was Satan who formed the focus of Milton's story.

Most eighteenth-century readers of *Paradise Lost* had considered this rather a weakness in Milton's poem.[4] For the circle of friends and radicals that centered around Johnson (comprising, among others, the Swiss *Sturm und Drang* painter Henry Fuseli, the etcher James Barry, Mary Wollstonecraft, William Godwin, and Thomas Paine), this was a rather different matter. For them, Satan was not the willful usurper that was eventually reduced to a groveling worm, but rather a personage of heroic grandeur. Johnson's sumptuous new edition of *Paradise Lost* and the accompanying Milton Gallery he planned would have been the primary venues for this new vision of Satan. Both projects, however, failed to materialize. Among the few traces that remained of Johnson's plans are a handful of drawings and etchings by Fuseli and Barry that depict Milton's Satan as a classical hero who makes his Thermopylean stance against his creator in a Greek battle outfit, defiantly raising his shield and spear toward the heavens.[5] Another trace might be a remarkable passage in *An Enquiry into Political Justice* by William Godwin, a classic work of political philosophy published in 1793 and often considered as the first ideological articulation of modern anarchism. Godwin's comments upon the Miltonic Satan squarely fit the latter in a new heroic mold:

> It must be admitted that his energies are centred too much on personal regards. But why did he rebel against his maker? It was, as he himself informs us, because he saw no sufficient reason, for that extreme inequality of rank and power, which the cre-ator assumed. It was because prescription and precedent form no adequate ground for implicit faith. After his fall, why did he still cherish the spirit of opposition? From a persuasion that he was hardly and injuriously treated. He was not discouraged by the apparent inequality of the contest: because a sense of reason and justice was stronger in his mind, than a sense of brute force; because he had much of the feelings of an Epictetus or a Cato, and little of those of a slave. He bore his torments with fortitude, because he disdained to be subdued by despotic power. He sought revenge, because he could not think with tameness of the unexpostulating authority that sought to dispose of him.[6]

Seen in retrospect, these lines from Godwin already give the nucleus of what was to become the Romantic Satan. The small flickers of diabolical rehabilitation connected to Johnson's Milton project set in motion a chain of authors and imaginative works that together would prove decisive in the redefinition of Satan. To start with, they might have provided inspiration to William Blake (1757–1827), a young etcher somewhat on the fringe of the Johnson circle who had been commissioned by Johnson to do some etchings for the latter's failed Milton edition.[7] Blake considered himself not only an etcher, but also an author and even a visionary. In the time remaining after finishing his etching assignments, he composed his own pamphlets and illuminated books, which he printed privately in his workplace by using a complicated procedure of relief engraving. In or around 1790—the experts do not agree on the exact date—he thus published a slim booklet called *The Marriage of Heaven and Hell*. In this highly original work brimming with idiosyncratic thought, Blake completely reversed the customary evaluation of good and evil, devil and angel. "Good is the passive that obeys reason," he wrote. "Evil is the active springing from energy. Good is Heaven. Evil is Hell. . . . Energy is the only life and is from the Body and reason is the bound or outward circumference of Energy. Energy is Eternal Delight."[8] *The Marriage of Heaven and Hell* proceeded to offer a collection of "Proverbs from Hell" and gave diabolical reversed readings of theology, history, and philosophy in a series of "Memorable Fancies," as well as three pages of statements by "the voice of the Devil." The marriage in the title, as a matter of fact, was described as the dissolving of a "good" angel into the "flame of fire" of a devil. "This Angel, who is now become a Devil, is my particular friend," Blake added in a concluding note. "We often read the Bible together in its infernal or diabolical sense which the world shall have if they behave well. I have also: The Bible of Hell: which the world shall have whether they will or no."[9]

It was not through direct contact with the Johnson circle, but probably by reading Godwin's *Enquiry into Political Justice* that Percy Bysshe Shelley (1792–1822), some twenty years later, first stumbled upon the theme of the heroic Satan. The unruly son of a British peer, Shelley was described by one of his contemporaries as a man with "a fire in his eye, a fever in his blood, a maggot in his brain, a hectic flutter in his speech, which mark out the philosophic fanatic."[10] As a young student, he had been expelled from Oxford after composing a provocative essay in defense of atheism. Irrevocably alienated from his sturdy Anglican father, he decided to devote his life to the pursuit of poetry and political activism. He was much surprised when he learned that Godwin, one of the radical authors he had devoured, was still alive and in Britain. He promptly decided to contact the philosopher.

Godwin, in the meantime, had fallen into dire straits and was eking out a meager living for his family by trying to sell progressive children's literature. He consequently was not averse to the unexpected overtures of his young but well-to-do aristocratic admirer. He was somewhat abashed, however, when Shelley invariably expressed glowing support for the most radical ideas in his *Enquiry into Political Justice*, many of which the philosopher had subsequently retracted. He was even more appalled when Shelley proceeded to bring about Godwin's earlier ideas about free love in practice with Godwin's daughter Mary, eventually eloping with the sixteen-year-old girl to Europe. This permanently damaged the relationship between the pioneering anarchist thinker and the radical young poet.[11]

The rupture did nothing, however, to reduce Shelley's admiration for Godwin's portrait of the Miltonic Satan. He echoed Godwin almost verbatim regarding this subject in his celebrated essay *A Defence of Poetry* (1820).

Nothing can exceed the energy and magnificence of the character of Satan as expressed in "Paradise Lost."

Shelley mused here,

It is a mistake to suppose that he could ever have been intended for the popular personification of evil. Implacable hate, patient cunning, and a sleepless refinement of device to inflict the extremest anguish on an enemy, these things are evil; and, although venial in a slave, are not to be forgiven in a tyrant; although redeemed by much that ennobles his defeat in one subdued, are marked by all that dishonours his conquest in the victor. Milton's Devil as a moral being is as far superior to his God, as one who perseveres in some purpose which he has conceived to be excellent in spite of adversity and torture, is to one who in the cold security of undoubted triumph inflicts the most horrible revenge upon his enemy, not from any mistaken notion of inducing him to repent of a perseverance in enmity, but with the alleged design of exasperating him to deserve new torments.[12]

Earlier, Shelley had attempted a radically reversed reading of the traditional representatives of good and evil in the prologue of a narrative poem with the long-winded title *Laon and Cythna; or, The Revolution of the Golden City: A Vision of the Nineteenth Century* (1817).[13] Here he described a primordial struggle between "a blood-red Comet and the Morning Star." The former is victorious and establishes a reign of evil and violence, transforming the "fair star" into "a dire Snake, with men and beast unreconciled":[14]

And the great Spirit of Good did creep among
The nations of mankind, and every tongue
Cursed, and blasphemed him as he passed; for none
Knew good from evil[15]

Shelley and Blake, of course, were destined to be numbered among Britain's most celebrated poets. This destiny, however, was far from apparent at the time. By the beginning of the 1820s, Godwin was all but forgotten, Blake was writing down his prophecies in utter obscurity, and Shelley's musings on Satan were virtually unnoticed or stacked away in as-yet-unpublished notebooks. The new Satan might have remained a minor footnote in literary history, had it not been for two almost diametrically opposed factors: Lord Byron, and conservative literary criticism.

Like Shelley, George Gordon Byron, Sixth Baron Byron (1788–1824), was a very British and very aristocratic rebel. He was also a man that attracted scandal like fresh horse dung attracts flies. His marriage ended in scandalous divorce because of his even more scandalous affair with his half-sister.[16] The first cantos of his poetic travelogue *Childe Harold's Pilgrimage* (1812) had already made Byron into a celebrity poet by then, and the growing hue and cry about his divorce prompted him into self-declared exile to the Continent. There he teamed up with the Shelleys for a while, who likewise roamed Europe in voluntary exile, eventually ending up in Venice, the capital of Carnival. From this safe haven under the Italian sun, he kept sending poetry out to Britain that became more and more daring.

His literary opponents replied in kind. It was they, paradoxically, who would give the new "Romantic Satanism" public renown. The *Fortnight Quarterly* had already accused Byron of showing a "strange predilection for the worser half of Manichaeism." "One of the mightiest spirits of the age," the conservative periodical had remarked, "has, apparently, devoted himself and his genius to the adornment and extension of evil."[17] Even sterner language was to be found in Robert Southey's *A Vision of Judgement* (1821). Southey had been Shelley's mentor and one of the pioneering poets of Romanticism in England, together with Wordsworth and Coleridge. All three had started out as Radicals, and all three had turned sane or soft in later years and had in greater or lesser degree "gone over" to the establishment. Yet none had done so more drastically than Southey, who had managed to become poet laureate, "a scribbling, self-sold, soul-hired, scorn'd Iscariot," according to the scathing lines of Byron.[18] In the introduction to *A Vision of Judgement*, the poet laureate complained about the "flood of lascivious books" that had recently swept English literature.

> Men of diseased hearts and depraved imagination, who, forming a system of opinions to suit their own unhappy course of conduct, have rebelled against the holiest ordinances of human society, and hating that revealed religion which, with all their efforts and bravadoes, they are unable entirely to disbelieve, labour to make others as miserable as themselves, by infecting them with a moral virus that eats into the soul! The School which they have set up may properly be called the Satanic School; for though their productions breathe the spirit of Belial in their lascivious parts, and the spirit of Moloch in those loathsome images of atrocities and horrors which they delight to represent, they are more especially characterized by a Satanic spirit of pride and audacious impiety, which still betrays the wretched feeling of hopelessness wherewith it is allied.[19]

This passage can be considered the official birth certificate of the Satanic School of Poetry. Southey's indictment is the original source for the designation "Romantic Satanism" or "Literary Satanism," still used by scholars of literature today. (We will delve more deeply into the exact significance of these terms later.) With his diatribe, the poet laureate obviously targeted Byron and Shelley; primarily the former, who was perceived to be the evil genius of the two (of Shelley's "Satanic" utterances the majority of critics were as yet unaware).[20]

Paradoxically enough, the constant harangues of his enemies on the theme of Satan may have inspired Byron to write his most "Satanic" work to date. As Peter A. Schock has argued, it was only in reaction to, and in parodying identification with, the "Satanism" attributed to him by his critics that Byron ventured into diabolical territory.[21] In the latter half of 1821, he wrote the "Mystery" *Cain*, according to his own statement in only three weeks and while being continuously drunk.[22] In the play (which would seldom see a stage performance), Byron reconstructs the biblical account of the first murder. At the root of what happened, he sees Cain's revolt against the "politics of Paradise," the exclusion of humanity from carefree happiness.[23] Cain is stimulated in this rebellious attitude by his conversations with Lucifer, who neglects no opportunity to insinuate the malignity of the creator. "You may suppose the small talk which takes place between him and Lucifer upon these matters is not quite canonical," Byron gleefully wrote to a friend after finishing the play.[24] In the play's original preface, he had written defiantly: "I am prepared to be accused of Manicheism or some other hard name ending in *ism*, which makes a formidable figure and awful sound in the eyes and ears of those who would be as much puzzled to explain the terms so bandied about as the liberal and pious indulgers in such epithets."[25]

While conservative criticism may have provided the direct stimulus to pick up the Satanic theme, Byron could draw from two specific literary sources as well. The first of these was the tragedy *Faust* by Johann Wolfgang von Goethe (1749–1833), an extensive, highly philosophical poetic work of which the first part had been published in 1808. Altogether unconnected with the developments that had spawned Romantic Satanism in Britain, Goethe's tragedy recounted the early modern saga of Faust's pact with the devil, featuring a visit to the Sabbath on Brocken Mountain and a disturbingly witty and clever devil called Mephistopheles. Byron greatly admired Goethe's poem, and we will see later in which measure the latter's Mephistopheles may have influenced the former's Lucifer. The second literary influence on Byron's *Cain* can surely be found in the person of Shelley. It is through him that Byron can be connected to the slender chain of sympathy for the devil that we have described in the preceding pages. Shelley had visited Byron several times in his Italian haunt and had urged him to retaliate against his critics within the literary establishment. It is more than likely that Shelley—who was nicknamed "the Snake" by Byron—brought the heroic, rebellious Satan of Godwin and his own writings to Byron's attention during their long discussions on politics, literature, and philosophy.[26]

Cain fell like a bombshell when published. More is said to be printed about the 1,800-line play between 1821 and 1839 than about the 20,000 lines of Byron's magnum opus *Don Juan* (and *Don Juan*, as a matter of fact, had already been something of a scandal in itself).[27] Conservative reviewers at once declared it "Hideous Blasphemy," and Byron noted with evident relish that "the parsons are all preaching at it, from Kentish Town and Oxford to Pisa."[28] More serious for the publisher John Murray, a court of law also declared *Cain* blasphemous in 1822 and refused to uphold its copyright protection. This had the unintended consequence that the play gained even wider distribution, because of both the stimulus to its notoriety that the verdict provided and the fact that it enabled pirate publishers to issue cheap editions without legal consequences.[29]

Being an internationally celebrated poet, and notorious as a somewhat diabolical impersonator on the side, Byron gave the new Satan wide international dissemination.[30] Most conspicuously, the new Satan crossed the Channel to France, where it was introduced to the public with the release of *Eloa* (1823), an epic poem by the young aristocrat Alfred de Vigny (1797–1863).[31] The original title of the work had simply been *Satan*, and its further designation as "Mystère" clearly bespoke its Byronic inspiration.[32] Whereas the Lucifer of Byron had been somewhat lonely and inhuman, Vigny rightly concluded that no superhero can do without an enticing female companion, and he duly provided Satan with one, the beautiful and virtuous female angel Eloa, who succumbs in typical nineteenth-century fashion to the melancholic but irresistible charm of her infernal seducer.[33] Masked as a pale, attractive adolescent, Satan takes on the role of Eros in the soothing words he addresses to the innocent angel:

Sur l'homme j'ai fondé mon empire de flamme
Dans les désirs du cœur, dans les rêves de l'âme,
Dans les liens des corps, attraits mystérieux,

Dans les trésors du sang, dans les regards des yeux.
C'est moi qui fais parler l'épouse dans ses songes;
La jeune fille heureuse apprend d'heureux mensonges;
Je leur donne des nuits qui consolent des jours,
Je suis le Roi secret des secrètes amours.[34]

[Over Man I have founded my empire of fire
In the desires of the heart, the dreams of the soul,
In the bonds of the body, mysterious attractions,
In the treasure of his blood, the glance of his eyes.
It is me who makes the husband speak in his dreams;
The happy young girl hears pleasing lies;
I give them nights to comfort for their days,
I am the secret Lord of secret loves.]

Eloa enjoyed considerable popularity with the French public.[35] Fashionable would-be Eloas wrote love letters comparing their beloved to Satan, and Théophile Gautier remarked in a satirical sketch that he considered himself extraordinarily lucky to be blessed with a natural pale and olive-colored complexion, as this assured him of favor with the ladies because of his likeness to the archdemon.[36] In an article commemorating the demise of Lord Byron in *La Muse Française*, a young poet who signed as "Victor-M. Hugo" presented the state of French literature in the following terms: "Two schools have formed themselves within its breast, representing the double situation in which our political troubles have left thinking people: resignation or despair.... The first sees everything from up in heaven; the other, from the bottom of the pit.... The first, in sum, resembles Immanuel, mild and strong, coursing over his kingdom on a chariot of lightning and light; the other is that superb Satan who swept with him such a number of stars when he was thrown out of heaven."[37] Although the editors of the *Muse Française* took care to distance themselves from any notion of an "École Satanique" *à la* Southey in a note appended to precisely this sentence, others were less bashful. In words closely resembling those of the British poet laureate, the influential conservative critic Auger warned against the school of Byron and consorts "which seems to [have] received its mission from Satan himself."[38] "All this comes from Byron," a French writer noted in 1833, "like smoking cigars, doing orgies, and a good many other things."[39]

De Vigny may also have initiated another trend that seemed particularly popular in France: that of Satan's eventual redemption. In a never-to-be-written sequel to *Eloa*, Vigny had planned for Satan to repent and reconcile with his creator. In the decades that followed, countless epigones set out to write the poem that Vigny never completed. The "larme rédemptrice de Satan," the single tear of remorse that would reconcile Satan to the universe, almost became a literary commonplace.[40] One of the most curious excesses of this wave of cosmic epic poems may have been *La Divine Epopée* by Alexandre Soumet (1788–1845). In this poem, which purports to describe the state of the universe after the Final Judgment, one of the beatified souls in heaven, Sémida, is unable to find happiness because she misses her lost love Idaméel. This eternal rebel has been thrown in hell and even there has succeeded to take over power from Lucifer, who has grown somewhat meek with time. To bring happiness to Sémida and reconciliation of all to everything, Jesus descends into hell and ends up crucified a second time. Amazingly enough, Soumet's poem seems to have been written in complete earnestness, although few traditional Christians can have been pleased with his soteriologic acrobatics.[41]

When Victor Hugo (1802–1885) took up the theme of Satan's redemption, the French tradition of transcendental reconciliation reached its apogee.[42] We are already in the 1850s then, and the virtually unknown Victor-M. Hugo who had written the commemorative article for Byron had meanwhile grown into the grand patriarch of French literature. While in exile on the Channel Islands, the French poet and novelist began to compose an epic poem called *Fin de Satan*. Like Vigny's original design, the immense work planned to follow the devil in his career through history, culminating in his return to the open arms of the deity amid choruses singing the praise of all-conquering love. Hugo's project was never to be finished: he continued to add new material to the poem until 1860 and then seemed to have stored it away in his archives.[43] By that time, however, the Romantic Satan had grown into a well-established trope in Western culture, leaving his footprints, either distinct or faintly, in the art and literature of Russia, Germany, Belgium, the Netherlands, Italy, Spain, Scandinavia, and America.[44]

GOD, SATAN, AND REVOLUTION

Why did some of the most important Romantics in the nineteenth century suddenly start to sing praises to Satan? What ignited this remarkable new appraisal of the fallen angel, who after all had been the prime mythological representation of evil in Western civilization for more than a millennium? We cannot understand this surprising occurrence unless we take into account the wider changes that were taking place in Western society. Two groundbreaking historical developments in particular, I would like to argue, were of paramount importance among these wider changes: first, revolution and, second, secularization. Both phenomena would bring profound changes to the face of the West and also create new opportunities for the appreciation of Satan.

On July 14, 1789, crowds had stormed the Bastille, the well-known fortress in Paris that served as the royal prison. This sparked a sequence of events in which the citizens of Paris dethroned and eventually executed their king and henceforth proceeded to govern themselves. This radical change in the political structure of one of Europe's foremost national powers became known as the French Revolution. It sent shock waves through the whole of the Western world, and eventually beyond, and can rightly be considered a turning point in modern history.

Momentous as it was, the French Revolution was no isolated event. Rather it was both the culmination of an ideological movement that had been building for many decades and the spark that ignited a whole new phase in Western culture. This chain of revolution and political renewal in Europe and the Americas has been labeled as the Western Revolution by some historians.[45] Starting with the American Revolution (1763–1783), earlier stirrings of revolutionary political upheaval had surfaced in Geneva in 1766 and 1788, in Ireland from 1782 to 1787, in the Dutch Republic from 1783 to 1787, and in the Austrian Netherlands and the prince-bishopric of Liège from 1787 to 1790. After the French Revolution (the first rumblings of which had started in 1787), revolutionary struggles for independence began to erupt in South America as well. A further series of failed or successful revolutions shook the political establishment of France and other European countries in 1831, 1848, and 1871.

All these political revolts were to a lesser or greater degree motivated by a program that was rooted in Enlightenment notions: more democratic and rational ways of government, freedom for ethnic communities from "foreign" government, freedom of press and thought, and freedom of religion, sometimes coupled with radical projects for social reform. Although this movement for democracy and liberty was in large part a vehicle of empowerment for the educated and well-to-do bourgeoisie, the tide of revolution would give rise to a series of movements demanding emancipation and equal rights for all underprivileged groups in society, including women, the poor and working classes, and a broad scope of national, religious, and sexual minorities: a process that was to continue well into the twentieth century and even, one might argue, up to today. Interlocked with these political upheavals, often in mutual empowerment, was a complex of ideological, social, demographic, and economic revolutions that together eventually would bring forth the specific Western form of civilization that is sometimes branded with the loose, slightly vague designation of "modernity."[46]

Of all the Western revolutions that made up the Western Revolution, the French Revolution undoubtedly was (in the words of the French historian Jacques Godechot) "the most important, the most profound, the most radical."[47] Whatever the significance of the events of 1789 in themselves, they certainly *became* significant in their reception afterward, dichotomizing European opinion and European culture for at least a century to come. For friend and foe, the Revolution came to signify the advent of a new spirit in European man that affirmed his right to shape his own political, cultural, and religious destiny, if necessary in opposition to the "divinely ordained" structures of tradition. Deeply internally divided as both camps might have been, the European intelligentsia would henceforth be split in "Left" and "Right," into those in favor of radical or "progressive" change and those opposed to it. (As a matter of fact, the terms "Left" and "Right" themselves originate with the French Revolution, when the more radical members of parliament had been seated to the left of the president.)

This new dichotomy was also fundamental in revolutionizing the perception of Satan. Not that a political reading of the Prince of Darkness was entirely new. Milton's *Paradise Lost*, and comparable works like the tragedy *Lucifer* (1654) by the Dutch playwright Joost van den Vondel, had already given an account of the fall of the archangel that had had obvious bearing on the political turmoil their countries were experiencing during the seventeenth century. Yet despite the ambiguity they gave their insurrectionary protagonist for dramatic purposes, their works in the end defended the claims of "divine" authority against its Satanic opponent.[48] In the century that followed, however, the *philosophes* and the French Revolution had proceeded to give "insurrection" a wholly new, positive meaning for substantial parts of Europe's intellectual elite. This re-valuation reflected on the myth of Satan as well. For radical sympathizers with the Revolution like Godwin and Shelley, Satan was no longer an evil insurgent against righteousness and cosmic order, but the mirror image and mythological embodiment of the revolutionary standing up against arbitrary and despotic power. Thus it is not surprising that the Romantic poets who lauded Satan can invariably be located somewhere on the Leftists' side of the political spectrum.

Indeed, up to the fin de siècle one can safely reverse this formula and confidently suspect Radical inclinations as soon as an author starts to speak in a positive way about the former angel of evil.

The political setting of Romantic Satanism has already been pointed out by Max Miller with regard to French literature and by Peter A. Schock for the English context. I will summarize and occasionally elaborate their findings.[49] Right from its beginning with the Johnson circle, the link between Romantic Satanism and political radicalism had been evident. All the members of Johnson's coterie could be described as political radicals of one kind or another. Godwin was an anarchist philosopher; his wife Mary Wollstonecraft one of the first proponents of women's liberation; Thomas Paine (a later member) would participate in the French Revolution in person. The first stirrings of revolution became manifest on the other side of the Channel at exactly the same time their Milton project was conceived; this circumstance may have been a potent factor in their reinterpretation of Satan.[50] "Better to reign in Hell, then serve in Heav'n," had been the brazen declaration uttered by Milton's Satan from the bottom of the pit, and these words must have closely echoed the state of mind of many Radicals during these specific historical circumstances.

Blake participated in these pro-revolutionary sentiments. His *Marriage of Heaven and Hell*, obtuse and esoteric as it may seem, makes this quite clear. It was concluded by "A Song to Liberty," which exhorted France to "rend down thy dungeon" and invoked how the "new born fire" of liberty was cast out of heaven and now dispersed (as a sort of new Holy Spirit) over the nations of the Earth. When morning would come, Blake prophesied, "The son of fire . . . spurning the clouds written with curses, stamps the stony law to dust . . . crying Empire is no More!"[51] In fact, Blake had planned to make his thoughts on liberty even more explicit in a long epic poem on the French Revolution that was to be published by Johnson. By that time, however, British mobs had started to loot the houses of suspected Jacobin sympathizers and curtailing legislature against those stirring sedition had come in force. The publication of the poem was canceled, and some authors have suggested that it was exactly in order to avoid repercussions of this kind that Blake henceforth choose to express himself in intricate, self-created mythologies that still puzzle scholars today.[52]

Reaction had set in full force when Shelley and Byron appeared on the scene, two or three decades later. The Revolution had ushered in the Terror, and after that Napoleonic autocracy; this in turn had been crushed by the combined forces of European monarchy. In England, the Pitt repression had stamped out the early flickers of Jacobinism; worse was to come with the retraction of habeas corpus and the measures against blasphemous and seditious literature by the Peel Acts.[53] All over Europe, radicalism seemed to have been reduced to a powerless, persecuted minority. These circumstances made the Satanic metaphor even more apt. Satan as Milton had painted him—the great Pariah and Exile, defeated in his objects, but even from his position of abject misery defiantly continuing his opposition because of sheer inner conviction—could now be perceived as an even more adequate role model by the Romantic Radicals, marginalized as they were in their struggle against the seemingly triumphant powers of establishment.

Shelley could certainly be called such a Romantic Radical. He was an ardent proponent of vegetarianism, free love, women's liberation, and revolutionary political reform.[54] Before eloping with Godwin's daughter Mary, he had embarked on a short-term experiment in communal living with his first wife Harriet and a school mistress, while also engaging in quixotic schemes to spread the revolutionary message, for instance by attaching pamphlets to hot air balloons let loose on the winds.[55] In Dublin, he had distributed inflammatory pamphlets on the streets with a giggling Harriet in tow, one of which ended with Milton's line "Awake!—arise!—or be forever fallen!"—Satan's famous exhortation from the bottom of hell to the other angels thrown with him into the pit.[56] Shelley's musings on the devil only receive their full sting against a background of failed revolution and brewing social unrest, for instance when he praises Milton's Satan as morally far superior to his divine master, "as one who perseveres in some purpose which he has conceived to be excellent in spite of adversity and torture, is to one who in the cold security of undoubted triumph inflicts the most horrible revenge upon his enemy."[57] *Laon and Cythna* opened up with a quite explicit evocation of the smothered French Revolution ("When the last hope of trampled France had failed/ like a brief dream of unremaining glory,/ From visions of despair I rose") and ended with the death of its protagonists as martyrs against oppression.[58] As a matter of fact, all of Shelley's works featuring Satan or related symbolic beings are permeated with political ideology and with millennialist expectations of the "broad sunrise" of a future in which

Thrones, altars, judgment-seats, and prisons—wherein,
And besides which, by wretched men were borne
Sceptres, tiaras, swords, and chains, and tomes
Of reasoned wrongs glozed on by ignorance –
Were like those monstrous and barbaric shapes,
The ghosts of a no more remembered fame.[59]

Byron is often thought of as an opponent of democracy, which he once characterized as an "Aristocracy of Blackguards."[60] Nonetheless the "diabolical lord" was, if anything, firmly sided with the cause of radical change. Even more than his friend Shelley the "philosophical fanatic," he managed to give his convictions practical implication. As a member of the peerage, he could take a seat in the British House of Lords, and during the short spell he did so, he voted for Catholic emancipation (according to his own statement to defend the liberty of "five millions of the primitive") and spoke in favor of the insurrectionary working-class movement of the Luddites.[61] While in Italy, he sheltered weapons for the rebellious Carbonari, and in the end, he would die while fighting for Greek independence. Saturated with skepticism as he was, Byron never was lured by grand ideological doctrines; rather he seems to have been motivated by a more general concern with "liberty," empathically including his own, personal liberty.

Byron's political concerns are also evident in his work. Not many scholars seem to have remarked upon the political subtext of *Cain*, Byron's most "Satanist" poem.[62] Cain's explicitly stated dissatisfaction with "the politics of Paradise," however, already suggests the possibility to translate the play's biblical subject matter to contemporary society, with god functioning as a glyph for human oppression. "Because He is all pow'rful, must all-good, too, follow?" Cain asks himself about the divine powers-that-be.

More specific political commentary may be read into the play's interhuman relations, particularly in the account of the murder of Abel. This dramatic event occurs when Abel talks the reluctant Cain into making a sacrifice unto Jehovah together. As in the biblical account of the first murder, Cain prepares an offering of the fruits of the Earth, while Abel slaughters some of the "firstling of the flock." Cain, emboldened by his preceding talks with Lucifer, then offers a "prayer" to Jehovah in which he invites the latter to choose between the two offerings:

> If thou lov'st blood, the shepherd's shrine, which smokes
> On my right hand, hath shed it for thy service
> In the first of the flock, whose limbs now reek
> In sanguinary incense to thy skies.
> Or if the sweet and blooming fruits of earth
> And milder seasons, which the unstained turf
> I spread them on now offers in the face
> Of the broad sun which ripened them, may seem
> Good to thee, inasmuch as they have not
> Suffered in limb or life and rather form
> A sample of thy works than supplication
> To look on ours; if a shrine without victim
> And altar without gore may win thy favour,
> Look on it.[63]

When Cain's offering is scattered by a sudden whirlwind, while Abel's is consumed by flames of fire, Cain erupts in anger and declares he will build no more altars and destroy that of Abel: "This bloody record/Shall not stand in the sun to shame creation."[64] His pious brother steps in to defend his place of sacrifice, "hallowed now by the immortal pleasure of Jehovah."[65] In a fit of rage, Cain then kills his brother with a stone from the latter's altar.

Apart from the obvious religious bearing of this scene—we will return to this aspect later on—Byron's narration here can also be interpreted as an extended gloss on the French Revolution. The two themes are in fact inextricably intertwined. Cain's initial opposition is motivated by arguments that reflect the Enlightenment critique on traditional Christian religion, and his impulse to level the structures and strictures of tradition must to Byron's readers have been a clear pointer to the similar attempts of the French Revolution. Abel, on the other hand, can be seen as a representative of the defenders of the ancien régime, sincere in his convictions yet in opposition of the cause of change and freedom. The French Revolution, as is well known, had indeed ushered in bloodshed and persecution against those that had sought to hold to the religious and political structures of the past. The question why human brother slew human brother is inevitably one of the important themes of Byron's play, and his account of how this violence came about can also be read as an account of why the revolutionary endeavor, despite its programmatic drive for human brotherhood and human liberation, had nevertheless devolved into ever more bloody cycles of fratricide.

Another aspect of *Cain* also must be mentioned here: the fact that it gives a kind of myth of origin for the Byronic hero. This is the term used for the type of protagonist that appears in a good deal of Byron's works and that grew into a stock figure of Romanticism: a melancholy, isolated, yet proudly independent exile burdened by some nameless crime in his past (e.g., incestuous love, or murder, or both). This personage was at the same time, of course, an archetypical portrait of Byron himself, cut loose as he was from the moral values of establishment and more or less forced to adopt a wandering existence abroad after the éclat of his relationship with his half-sister (we may note in this respect the obvious glee with which Byron points to the perfect innocence of Cain's "incestuous" union with his sister). Cain clearly has all the outlines of another avatar of this Byronic hero. He is an outsider from the start by the "fatum" of his skeptical, brooding temperament (another favorite theme with Byron) and ends up in the last act as a wanderer despairing whether he will ever find peace of mind. Seen in this light, *Cain* recounts the genesis of the demi-mythological Byronic hero and of his "original sin" and if our reading of the play has some validity, this original sin is, partially at least, brought about by religious and political revolt. Certainly this was the way Byron was read by his conservative critics, who tended to place his work firmly in a context of political rebellion.[66] "This evil is political as well as moral," Southey had already said about the new "Satanic School" in *Vision of Judgement*; far from a mere poetic diatribe, the lashing sentences in the poet laureate's preface had actually been intended as a veiled call for legal intervention against Byron and his partners in poetic crime.[67]

The political overtones of Romantic Satanism were not less evident in the case of France, the land of revolution itself. The legacy of the 1789 Revolution, the various projects to retrieve (parts of) the revolutionary endeavor, and the subsequent reactions to these attempts at radical reform would dominate the French political and cultural landscape in the nineteenth century. In the 1820s, when the new Satan had crossed the Channel, the nation was torn between those that wanted to resume the revolutionary project in one form or another and those that wanted to restore the pre-revolutionary status quo. The latter had the ascendancy at the time. Foreign military power had brought the Bourbons back to the throne; in their wake the exiled aristocratic and ecclesiastic retainers of the ancien régime had returned to positions of power. The reactionary regime actively (and, in the end, vainly) sought to resuscitate an already mythical pre-revolutionary France. Re-evangelization of the population was forcefully stimulated; Leftist political agitation was repressed; and those that propagated the values of the Western Revolution had to sit low.

This was the immediate background against which one may read the contemporary French preoccupation with Satan, as the young Victor Hugo had accurately detected when he had suggested that "our political troubles" were at the root of the fascination.[68] The deep dichotomy that split French society may also be part of the explanation for the already-mentioned popularity of poetic scenarios of cosmic reconciliation—in which, it should be noted, Satan almost invariably plays the part of intransigent revolutionary and is never wholly negatively portrayed. The coming together of the "superb Satan" and "mild and strong" Immanuel clearly reflected the wish of many French intellectuals to overcome the ideological divide that the Revolution had brought about within their nation. Not infrequently, moreover, the Revolution makes an even more obvious appearance. This is the case, for instance, in Hugo's unfinished *Fin de Satan*, in which the revolutionary values of liberty and human autonomy are celebrated as the essence of human existence.[69] Although at first glance the poem displays an almost traditional dualism, with God as the source of love and Satan as the material principle opposed to this, closer reading reveals a more complex agenda. Thus the real force of evil in the universe is not Satan, but the specter Lilith-Isis-Ananké, the embodiment of

Fate, or rather of the illusion of Fate. This specter is only dissolved by the angel of Liberty, who is born from a feather from the wings of Satan left behind in heaven and brought to life by God.[70] "The feather of Liberty falls/from the wing of Rebellion," Hugo wrote in one of the text fragments meant for *Fin de Satan*.[71] The remaining drafts of the poem show that Hugo meant this cosmic event to coincide with the fall of the Bastille in 1789. For Hugo, it seems that 1789 meant liberation from cosmic prison, not only for France, but for humanity as a whole: "the dungeon's destruction abolishes hell."[72]

It may be clear by now that the political and ideological situation of the nineteenth century is essential to understand the fascination with Satan within certain circles in this period. The extent to which the work of the Romantic Satanists is permeated with politics can hardly be overestimated. Yet it would be a misrepresentation to reduce their use of the Satanic theme to merely a thinly coded political allegory. There was also, and not just as a mere by-the-by, an unambiguous religious aspect to their artistic employment of Satan. The metaphysical entity that was really at the focus of this religious concern, however, was not Satan at all, but rather his dualistic opponent, the god of Christian tradition.

This autonomous religious component, we should observe, was for most Romantic Satanists inseparably intertwined with their political stance. The political developments in nineteenth-century society had been an important factor in nurturing their antipathy toward Christianity and toward the Christian god. The established churches in Western Europe had generally taken a stance against the Western Revolution, most particularly against its most radical manifestation, the French Revolution. After the demise of the latter, the entanglement of established religion and reaction had become even more intimate, especially in France, where royalist restoration and the Roman Catholic Church had embraced each other in an ideological alliance that proclaimed the inseparable union of "throne and altar." For the supporters of the revolutionary program, in one form or another, this made choosing a position against a religion that overtly supported law and order a logical option. But the political and religious dimensions of Romantic Satanism were linked in a much more profound way, down to the very words chosen by its proponents to describe Satan and his antagonist. Styling the deity as the "Tyrant-god" and the "prototype of human misrule" (to borrow a phrase from Shelley) does not only indicate that he served as a metaphor for the political oppressors on Earth; it also implied that the human oppressors of nineteenth-century political reality provided the frame of reference with which they approached (and discarded) the traditional theological concept of the deity.[73] As we have seen amply demonstrated, it was this assignment of roles that enabled Satan to display his new face as the noble champion of freedom against "despotic power" and "unexpostulating authority."[74]

It is worth pointing out the even more fundamental theological rift that formed the background to this development, and without which the Romantic conception of Satan would have been impossible. Charles Taylor has described how the early modern *moralization* of society, which had been fostered by Christianity itself, eventually came to be extended toward the divine realm as well. Not only man was to be judged according to moral standards of good and evil, but the deity itself could be subjected to such scrutiny as well. Although such discussions were not entirely novel (one only needs to leaf through the biblical book of Job to see this), they implied a departure, according to Taylor, from the more implicit religious mentality that had been prevalent in premodern society. In the traditional mindset, the deity had been primarily conceived as a savior from or protector against misfortune. To judge the way in which he governed the world was beyond the pale of humanity. Now, however, the creator was increasingly called to answer when misfortune occurred.[75]

This was not something that had started with the Romantic Satanists. In fact, we can already detect considerations like these in Milton. In *Paradise Lost*, Milton had intended to "justifie the wayes of God to man," and although he evidently considered the divine ways as justifiable, his statement implicitly admits that this justice *could* be doubted. In the eighteenth century, the *philosophes*, and their readership in coffeehouses and salons, had indeed set out to place the biblical god in the dock, usually ending up with declaring him guilty. In the days of the Romantic Satanists, this verdict had been repeated with considerable verbal force by Thomas Paine, author of the *Rights of Man* (1791) and paragon of Enlightenment rationalism. "Whenever we read the obscene stories, the voluptuous debaucheries, the cruel and torturous executions, the unrelenting vindictiveness, with which more than half the Bible is filled," he wrote in *The Age of Reason* (1795), "it would be more consistent that we called it the word of a demon than the word of God."[76] More or less in passing, this disengaged, morally superior stance toward the godhead enabled the Romantic Satanists to adopt a new attitude toward the devil as well. From a threatening presence that was dreaded as bringer of misfortune par excellence, he became, quite literally, a personage playing a more or less noble role in a cosmic moral drama.

The deep Enlightenment antipathy against the "omnipotent tyrant" of (a certain) Christian tradition can be found with all the Romantic Satanists.[77] Already in 1811, Shelley had avowed his explicit intention to combat Christianity with all his intellectual vigor. "Oh how I wish I *were* the Antichrist," he wrote to his friend Thomas Hogg, "that it were *mine* to crush the Demon, to hurl him back to his native Hell never to rise again. I expect to gratify some of this insatiable feeling in Poetry."[78] The poetry he was alluding to may have been *Queen Mab* (1812–1813), Shelley's first poem on an epic scale. In this poem, a young girl is visited in her sleep by the eponymous fairy queen, who, after invoking her soul with the familiar Miltonic exhortation "Awake! Arise!," tours her in the spirit through a fast digest of human and natural history.[79] This allows for several fierce diatribes against religion in general and the Christian faith and the Christian god in particular. The latter is denounced as a logical absurdity and a fiend who feasts on sacrifice of blood (among which that of his own son), but above all as a priestly tool for tyranny:

> They have three words:—well tyrants know their use,
> Well pay them for the loan, with usury
> Torn form a bleeding world!—God, Hell, and Heaven.[80]

Although Shelley would later disavow *Queen Mab* as written "at the age of eighteen, I daresay in a sufficiently intemperate spirit," anti-Christianity would remain a vital part of his poetic program throughout his life.[81] *Laon and Cythna* contains copious examples of similar sentiments; the same applies to *Prometheus Unbound* (1820), Shelley's last major poetical publication during his lifetime.[82] Jupiter, who may be read in this context as a simple stand-in for the Judeo-Christian deity, is depicted here in no uncertain terms as "Foul Tyrant of

Gods and humankind," one "who does not suffers wrong," and whose empire is founded on "Hell's coeval, Fear."[83] In typical Romantic fashion, Shelley is considerably milder with regard to the figure of Jesus, who is shown to Prometheus in a vision as "a youth with patient looks nailed to a crucifix."[84] Prometheus, however, refrains from uttering his name ("It hath become a curse") and goes on to relate the many misdeeds done by his later adherents.

Shelley's influence on Byron's anti-Christian rhetoric can be easily made probable—one only needs to point out the similarities in this respect between *Queen Mab* and *Cain*. Cain is taken on a similar tour of cosmic sightseeing by Lucifer as the one featured in Shelley's *pêche de jeunesse*, and the Christian idea of the father-god sacrificing his own son is dismissed in similar fashion.[85] Yet Byron did not need Shelley to develop a marked aversion for traditional faith: the awkward combination of zealous Calvinism and sexual abuse that he had been subjected to by his nurse as a child would have been quite sufficient in this respect. In tandem with his libertarian tendencies, this had instilled him with a deeply rooted skepticism toward organized religion of every description.[86] In 1811, the same year that Shelley had expressed his wish to become the Antichrist, Byron had given voice to his own profession of antifaith in a letter to his friend Francis Hodgson. "I am no Platonist, I am nothing at all," he wrote Hodgson. "But I would sooner be a Paulician, Manichean, Spinozist, Gentile, Pyrrhonian, Zoroastrian, than one of the seventy-two villainous sects who are tearing each other to pieces for the love of the Lord and the hatred of each other. Talk of Galileeism? Show me the effects—are you better, wiser, kinder by your precepts?"[87]

It is not hard to find echoes of the moral condemnation of the deity throughout the pages of *Cain*. We already quoted Cain's not-so-pious prayer implicitly demonizing a god that asks for sacrifice of life—the lines we quoted form in fact only a small portion of an extensive set of poetic variations on this theme. As could be expected, Lucifer is even more vocal in his criticism of his divine antagonist, declaring his solidarity with all those "who dare look the omnipotent tyrant in/his everlasting face and tell him that/his evil is not good!"[88] The main thrust of the play's antireligious sarcasm is reserved for the idea of a deity who "makes but to destroy," in which we may safely recognize the Calvinist god of Byron's childhood: an "indissoluble tyrant" who elects his helpless creatures seemingly at random to misery or happiness and who only endows them with immortality so that their torment may be eternal.[89] "Could he but crush himself," Lucifer sarcastically remarks, " 'twere the best boon/he ever granted."[90]

Blake and Hugo, the other two most important Romantic Satanists, display a more complex attitude toward metaphysical religion and Christianity (although we shall take note later of considerable complexities even with Byron and Shelley). Blake, as a matter of fact, considered himself a true Christian—possibly the only true Christian left. Yet even with him there was no love lost for the certain god of a certain Christian tradition that was flagellated by Shelley and Byron and whom Blake invokes in *The Marriage of Heaven and Hell* as the "jealous king" whose "stony law" is stamped to dust by the son of fire.[91] Blake was particularly adverse to the condemnation of sensuous enjoyment that had been a prominent feature of the traditions of Latin and Western Christianity. "As the caterpillar chooses the fairest leaves to lay her eggs on, so the priest lays his curse on the fairest joys," one of the Proverbs from Hell proclaims.[92] One of the first "errors" that are corrected by his diabolical revelation is the idea "that God will torment Man in Eternity for following his Energies."

Instead, the Voice of the Devil declares, "Energy is the only life," and "Energy is Eternal Delight."[93] Blake's tone of voice is even more militant in his later "prophecy" *America* (1793), where "Boston's Angel," the spirit of the American Revolution, cries out his indignation against the god of conformity and hypocrisy:

> What God is he, writes laws of peace, & clothes him in a tempest
> What pitying Angel lusts for tears, and fans himself with sighs
> What crawling villain preaches abstinence & wraps himself
> In fat of lambs? no more I follow, no more obedience pay.[94]

With slight mutation, much the same may be said of Victor Hugo. Although the deity retains his central place as the source of good in *Fin de Satan*, this deity was not the "Jehovah" of traditional Christianity, whom Hugo had come to consider a false god. The Christian dogma of eternal damnation in particular increasingly provoked the poet's repulsion. This repulsion grew into an obsession when his daughter Léopoldine fell into the Seine and drowned. *Fin de Satan*, thus, was ultimately intended as a rebuttal of certain Christian notions about the deity and a momentous evocation of the ἀποκατάστασις πάντων, the reconciliation of all things, even of Satan. God is appropriately described as the "heart" and "loving centre" of the cosmos, radiating love with "as many sunbeams as the Universe contains beings."[95] Like Shelley before him, Hugo was not altogether negative about Jesus, the "supreme Man" who incarnates the suffering of humanity. But toward the religion that took his name, he was similarly unfavorably inclined. From the wood of Jesus' cross, *Fin de Satan* tells, the papal tiara grew, and "of the murdered one, murderers were born."[96] Indeed, Hugo points out, it was "sinister religion" that had killed Jesus on Golgotha in the first place; its impious priests only exploit and blaspheme the eternal name of the god of love.[97]

The four most prominent Romantic Satanists, in brief, all expressed fierce animosity toward established Christianity. In their poetry, they sought to liberate themselves and society from a religious heritage they had come to reject. With this rejection, they did not stand alone. An increasing number of people in the West had grown disaffected with the perceptions and moral strictures of "traditional" Christianity. "The suspicion that the theory of what is called the Christian Church is fabulous is becoming very extensive in all countries," Thomas Paine had already remarked in 1794.[98] While the eighteenth century had witnessed the beginning of this development among the educated elite, in the century after the French Revolution, this trend would assume the proportions of a mass movement.[99]

This broader sociological process is commonly referred to as secularization. As a scholarly term, this designation is prone to different interpretations. Originally signifying the expropriation of church property by secular authorities (especially in the aftermath of the French Revolution and Napoleonic conquests), secularization has come to denote, first, the general disentanglement of the religious and the secular in the public sphere, and, second, a gradual decline in adherence to established Christianity throughout the Western world.[100] We shall use both interpretations throughout this study.

Secularization has become a somewhat contested term within scholarship.[101] As a historical phenomenon, secularization can *not* be simply equated with the disappearance of faith. Rather, recent scholarship maintains, it amounted to a *pluralization* of religious options available in society.[102] Explicit atheism or unbelief was just one of these options, and as such certainly became increasingly vocal and visible in the nineteenth century. For most of the Western population, however, and for Western culture at large, religious options that fell firmly or loosely within the pale of the Christian faith remained the preferred choice. Neither must we think of secularization as an older generation of sociologists and historians tend to do, as a deterministic process in which an atavistic Christianity inevitably gives way to the onset of science or a vaguely defined "modernity." In practical reality, even the established churches often found ways to adapt to the changing conditions of society. The increasing pluralization and the demise of traditional faith as a default option sometimes instigated them into massive campaigns for the mobilization of their adherents. In some regions, this would actually lead to a more intense practical participation in the Christian faith than before. We will have occasion to encounter some of these movements of mobilization in later chapters.

Nevertheless, few scholars will contest the appearance or intensification of three major processes in the West during the last two to three centuries: the conscious demarcation and strengthening of a secular sphere in society; the increasing pluralization of available religious (and/or ideological) options; and an increasing number of people, as a percentage of the population, adopting explicitly non-Christian religious or ideological positions (with a corresponding relative decline in people adhering to Christianity). The most common understood epithet for these developments is still secularization.

Secularization and revolution, it is worth pointing out, were by no means unconnected phenomena. The French Revolution had not only been the harbinger of the first major wave of dechristianization, but also of the first grand attempt to replace Christianity with a religious alternative, the cult of Reason.[103] The Revolutionary armies and the Napoleonic Civil Code subsequently exported legal freedom for religious dissidence and the separation of church and state to large parts of Europe. In fact, the values propounded by the Western Revolution virtually *demanded* secularization. The freedoms of conscience, of religion, and of expression that were essential parts of its program implied secularization in the first sense of the word—the disentanglement of the religious and the secular in public life in order to create a religiously "neutral" state. Its emphasis, moreover, on human autonomy and individual liberty could hardly lead to anything else than increasing pluriformity in the religious landscape.[104] Thus there is some logic to the fact that "traditional" religion and revolution were almost invariably at loggerheads with each other during the eighteenth and nineteenth centuries.

Theoretically, it was perfectly possible to be supportive of the Western Revolution and retain one's allegiance to Christianity. In practice, this position often made one a dissident in one's religious community. In Europe at least, most established churches positioned themselves against the Western Revolution and what it stood for. Naturally there was many a gray area in the ever-unschematic picture of historical reality. Christianity itself was in many parts a "contested territory" in which proponents and opponents of "revolutionary" values fought for supremacy. This fight could have different outcomes in different places or denominations.[105] Yet, seen overall, nineteenth-century European society showed a clear fault line between old faith and new values.[106]

Seen against this canvas, the fact that prominent Romantic poets suddenly began to sing the praises of Satan can hardly be regarded as coincidence. To the contrary: it was a major cultural signpost of the profound shifts that were taking place in the European consciousness. Stated baldly like this, however, this conclusion still might not do full justice to the significance of the Romantic Satanists. As the British historian Hugh McLeod remarks in his seminal work on secularization: "Secularisation happened at least in part because there were large numbers of people who were trying their hardest to bring it about."[107] And among those who were trying their hardest, the Romantic Satanists certainly deserve pride of place. The importance of their anti-Christian poetry in this respect should not be dismissed out of hand. Hugo, Shelley, and particularly Byron were all figures of public notoriety in their days who were quite widely read.[108] Their popularity, of course, will partly have been due to the fact that they sang the song of their time. But their poetry was certainly instrumental in defining the tune of the song.

POETRY, MYTH, AND MAN'S ULTIMATE GROUNDS OF BEING

Revolution and secularization were the two interlinked historical developments behind the sudden popularity of Satan with certain Romantics (and, presumably, their public).[109] Yet by itself, this historical framework is not sufficient to explain why they choose to adopt the figure of the fallen angel in their works of poetry and art. Appreciation of liberty and the revolutionary ethos could (and would) be expressed in other ways. The Romantic criticism of traditional religion, moreover, was largely a recuperation of earlier anti-Christian tropes of the Enlightenment. Few of the Enlightenment authors, however, had felt inclined to take recourse to "that miserable tale of the devil" (to quote Shelley once more) in order to make their point.[110]

In addition, it needs to be remembered that the Romantic Satanists did not appeal to Satan as a real-life, personal entity that could support them against the despised traditional deity. It is quite clear that Shelley and Byron believed as much in the existence of a real Lucifer as they believed in the existence of the Christian god. Hugo obviously did not think that the "angel of Liberty" had really been born from a feather from the wings of Satan. And while Blake might be a more complex case, the evident symbolism of his angelic and diabolical figures and the creative liberty with which he deployed them suggests a similar suspension of literal belief. This puts them in sharp contrast, for instance, to the early modern Satanists we encountered in the previous chapter, who had appealed to the devil as a tangible cosmic presence. In this attitude of practical unbelief as well, the Romantic Satanists were true children of the Enlightenment.

Peter Schock, as a matter of fact, has argued that the demise of literal belief in Satan was an essential prerequisite for the emergence of the Romantic Satan. The fact that he was no longer linked to a tangible (and threatening) cosmic force but had evolved into a kind of "free-floating symbol" enabled the Romantic Satanists to put him to novel and quite unaccustomed use.[111] Yet this still does not tell us why they *wanted* to do so and choose to return to an obsolete mythological figure derived from the "childish mummeries" (Shelley again) of biblical religion.[112] To find out why these prominent Romantic authors chose to resurrect the devil, we have to look deeper into their attitudes toward myth, poetry, and, ultimately, the finding or creation of meaning—three themes that were, in fact, intricately interwoven to them. These attitudes, I hasten to add, were not unique to the Romantic Satanists. We can see them reflected by many of the other Romantics as well, even by those who held completely antipodal religious or ideological positions. The more extreme religious views of Blake, Shelley, Byron, and Hugo, however, make the novelty of the Romantic approach stand out more clearly. We will explore this approach in the following pages and subsequently try to discover how it implicated the work of the four major "Satanist" poets, particularly with regard to their treatment of Satan. As we will see, the Romantic Satanists might have been even more revolutionary than their mere fondness of Satan suggests.

References to the old concept of the poet as "priest" or "prophet" abound in the work of the Romantics. The poet, Victor Hugo wrote for instance, "speaks as a priest to heaven and as a prophet to the earth."[113] Today, we tend to read utterances like these as poetic hyperbole, like many of the Romantics' contemporaries already did. The Romantic poets themselves, however, were quite serious about their claims. And they might have had some justification for this. For hidden underneath this seemingly ephemeral change in the appreciation of poetry was a fundamental rift in the understanding of reality.

To make this clear, we have to return to the Enlightenment once more. The Enlightenment thinkers, speaking in general, had sought to change the world by demystifying it, propagating Reason as their guiding principle. Only Reason was able to unveil the falsehood of "superstition" and "prejudice" on the one hand, and disclose the genuine nature of the universe on the other hand. The Romantics, however, held mere "Analytics" to be unable to create value or find meaning. Science might be able to discover how the world worked on a mechanical level, but not why it was there at all, and what it was all about, and what man should or should not do within it. Value and meaning, the Romantics claimed, could only be disclosed or created by the human faculty they often called Imagination.[114] This word had a less frivolous connotation for the Romantics than for us today, and it carried important associations with earlier neo-Platonic and Hermetic thinking. Imagination, roughly speaking, gave men access to the world of Ideas, which is, in its original Platonic signification, ultimate truth. Imagination is also, according to conventional usage, the human ability to be truly creative, to "imagine" things that are not present in ordinary reality (yet). The ambiguity that could be read into this concept—the fluctuation, so to say, between "inspiration" and "creation"—can be recognized in the work of many of the Romantics, with some considering the truly inspired poet as a mouthpiece of transcendental revelation and others moving toward an almost postmodern conception of value and meaning as constructs of human creativity.[115] In contrast to what the Enlightenment thinkers would have thought, however, the latter position did not necessarily diminish the value of the poetic imagination for the Romantics. On the contrary, it enhanced its status as the only possible source of value and meaning.

This epistemological background allows us to comprehend why "poetry" (in its widest possible sense, including all imaginative literature, and ultimately all the arts) was the preferred vehicle of communication for the Romantics. The super-rational truths they sought to convey could never be transmitted through rational discourse. Only the language of poetry could evoke them.[116] We are now already halfway to understanding how myth and the idiom of myth could become such a favored mode of expression for poets like Blake, Shelley, Byron, and Victor Hugo.[117] Both were a form of poetic and symbolic communication. There was, however, another dimension to this tendency to "talk myth," closely related to the Romantic notions of the poet as "priest" and "prophet" as well. If "poetry" was the only genuine way to find or create meaning, it must also be the original source of religion.

In making this claim, Romanticism was in fact building on a premise regarding the origin of religion that had been wielded by Enlightenment thinking as a tool in its deconstruction of traditional faith. Once again, however, the Romantics drew unexpected conclusions from this Enlightenment deconstruction. We can follow this clearly in Blake's *Marriage of Heaven and Hell*. In plate 11, Blake gives the following digest of the origin of religion: "The ancient Poets animated all sensible objects with Gods or Geniuses, . . . Till a System was formed, which some took advantage of & enslaved the vulgar by attempting to realize or abstract the mental deities from their objects; Thus began Priesthood, Choosing forms of worship from poetic tales. And at length they pronounced that the Gods had order'd such things." Most Enlightenment thinkers would have agreed upon this standard account of the origin of religion, and they would probably also have agreed with Blake's further statement: "Thus men forgot that All deities reside in the human breast." Yet whereas the Enlightenment had used the poetic origins of myth and religion to *disqualify* both, Blake drew a radically different conclusion. In the following plate of *The Marriage of Heaven and Hell*, he went on to describe a conversation between the narrator and the prophet Ezekiel. After implicitly describing himself as a poet, Ezekiel declares that "we of Israel thought that the Poetic Genius (as you now call it) was the first principle and all others merely derivative." All gods and philosophies, the prophet continues, are only "Tributaries" of this Poetic Genius.[118]

"I heard this with some wonder, and must confess my own conviction," the narrator of *Marriage of Heaven and Hell* adds. Indeed, there is ample reason for some wonder here, for Blake embarks on a complete reversal of the purport of the original Enlightenment theory. The thing that "animates" all things and creates even the gods is the Poetic Genius—that is to say, the Imagination, as Blake and the other Romantics also choose to call it; or the human faculty to find or construct value and meaning and truth beyond empirically given facts, as we may call it. We might also say the power to formulate *religion*, to formulate conceptions about man's ultimate ground of being and general order of existence. There is a fundamental difference with the Antique conception of the poet here as well. While the ancients believed the gods animated and "created" the poet, the Romantics came to believe that the poet animated and created the gods.[119] Stripped from its usurpers, the (Christian) priests, this power now returned to those to whom it originally belonged: the (Romantic) poets.

I propose to designate this U-turn the Romantic Reversal. In their effort to provide mythic accounts of the ultimate grounds of human existence, the Romantic Satanists parted with Enlightenment rationalism, both by the form of their work and in the underlying assumptions on which it was built. "I must Create a System or be enslav'd by another Mans/I will not Reason & Compare: my business is to Create," Blake wrote in one of his prophecies.[120] One needs only to read the work of an antipodal representative of rationalism as Thomas Paine to savor the revolutionary change in atmosphere. Speaking of the Old Testament prophets in *The Age of Reason*, Paine points out the old Hebrew word for "prophet" simply signifies "poet"—an etymology that for him needs no further elucidation as a disqualifying circumstance.[121] Reminiscing about his own youth, he subsequently remarks: "I had some turn, and I believe some talent, for poetry; but this I rather repressed than encouraged, as leading too much into the field of imagination."[122] No Romantic would ever have dreamed of making such a statement.

Of course, generalities like these tend to fade off into distortion. The Enlightenment had also displayed considerable fascination with myth. But its proponents had mostly approached myth as a code that needed to be cracked, and retold in rational language, or as a way to disparage the Christian "superstition" by highlighting the "original wisdom" of the ancient pagans (or, alternatively, by "unmasking" Christianity as just another thinly veneered form of pagan mythology).[123] The Romantics, however, embraced myths not as a code to be cracked but as an adequate language to express ultimate things.

This appreciation of myth as an autonomous medium of expression was certainly a breach with the Enlightenment past.[124] Naturally, their implicit or explicit faith in the nonrational language of poetry as a vehicle of truth did place the Romantic Satanists at loggerheads with the tenets of classic Enlightenment positivism. But not with Enlightenment positivism only. The reason the poet could be a priest or a prophet was that he mediated between humanity and the divine—or the sublime, or ideal, or whatever we call it—by means of his poetry. This made the Romantic poet an implicit or explicit competitor with other "spiritual mediators" in society: predominantly, of course, the Christian Church. With the priesthood of the old churches in discredit, the Romantics set out to demand a place of spiritual prominence for the poet, for the creative artist—in other words, for themselves.

In a series of thorough studies, one of them carrying the apt title *Le sacre de l'écrivain* ("The Sacralisation of the Literary Author"), the French historian of literature Paul Bénichou has argued that this is what the Romantics were indeed trying, and at times succeeded, to do: to become the new spiritual guides of a society that was moving toward a state of religious power vacuum.[125] The poet—he who has been endowed with "poetic genius"— had been of yore the creator of myths of ultimate concern, accounts of first and last things and man's place in the universe. In practice or theory, or both, the Romantic Satanists were reclaiming this function.[126] Naturally enough, the grand epic poem of cosmic scale was their great project, the work planned by all, begun by many, and finished by few. *The Marriage of Heaven and Hell* (a "Bible from Hell" in miniature), Blake's later "prophecies," *Faust, Cain*, the epic poems of Shelley, Hugo's *Fin de Satan*: they are all works that seek to give new, comprehensive views of the cosmos by way of myth or mythical personages.[127] In this, they represent conscious or spontaneous efforts to furnish new "grand narratives" for a secularizing European civilization by creating new mythologies or redefining the old ones.

Despite this overt or implicit competition with established Christianity, however, we should not forget that important differences marked the employment of myth by the Romantic Satanists from that in Christian tradition. In the first place, like we already saw, the Romantic myths were not meant to be literally true or factual accounts, as the biblical myths were held to be in Christian tradition (e.g., the incarnation and sacrificial crucifixion of Christ). Instead, they were what Northrop Frye has called "open myths": consciously designed systems of symbolism that used the figures of old and new mythologies as symbols or metaphors to tell a story about mankind's ultimate grounds of existence. In this respect, I'd like to emphasize once more, the Romantic Satanists were firmly post-Enlightenment. Their faith in the literal truth of the old religious language was irrevocably lost. This was the reason—Schock has certainly been right on this point—that they could adopt a traditional mythic entity like Satan and at the same time give him a radical novel interpretation.

On the other hand, however, the myths of the Romantic Satanists were meant to be more than mere allegories, or mythic codes that had to be cracked to find a hard kernel of rational truth.[128] Their poetic myths, I would like to suggest, were intended as *texts of identification*, in which the reader made his own mythic voyage in the imagination and thus discovered his place in the cosmos. In other words, reading them is to be a spiritual *experience*, evoking a spiritual response. Here we can discern another important difference with the traditional Christianity that Romantic Satanism sought to override. Although most of the Romantics surely held individual and collective assumptions that we might fairly designate as dogmas, they did not offer their poetry as dogmatic texts invoking unconditional faith. Neither did they tend to form their own religious organizations—there was no Romantic church—or to join existing ones.[129] The days of a "Priesthood" declaring that "the Gods had order'd such things" were to be overcome. What the Romantics implicitly or explicitly propagated was in fact a return to the original source of human meaning: the spiritual experience itself. In their poetry, they sought to transmit this spiritual experience, which the reader could relive by reading and re-imagining their poems.

SATAN'S NEW MYTHS: BLAKE AND SHELLEY

Although most of the Romantic Satanists were militantly anti-Christian, the foregoing will have made clear that this did by no means imply that their thinking was also nonreligious. Their poetic neo-mythologies were a symbolic form in which they tried to relate to what they thought to be the ultimate grounds of existence. How did this new spiritual investiture take form in the "Satanist" myths of Blake, Shelley, Byron, and Hugo? What message about mankind's general order of existence did they try to convey? In the following pages, we will consider the major "Satanist" works of these four authors in greater detail, giving special attention to the specific role played in them by Satan.

Of the four major Romantic Satanists, Blake might be the most complex case. Originating from a family of Dissenting stock, Blake remained in many ways a dissenting Christian all his life.[130] As previously noted, the "journeyman engraver of eccentric views" considered himself an adherent of true Christianity, and he would die singing hymns in joyful expectation of his entrance into the spiritual realm. This background is also detectable in his work, including *The Marriage of Heaven and Hell*. A few years before he published this idiosyncratic booklet, Blake had become engrossed in the works of Emanuel Swedenborg (1688–1772), a Swedish scientist and visionary. For a while, he had been so enthusiastic about the Swede's visionary works that he joined the local Swedenborgian Church of the New Jerusalem (the last religious denomination, in fact, of which we know he was a member). Swedenborgianism must have attracted him in part because he perceived it as a religious option that was far removed from traditional curtailments of freedom and "sensuous enjoyment." "Now it is Allowable," had been inscribed in capitals on the portal above the entrance of the Swedenborgian chapel that he visited.[131] When the English Swedenborgians began to return to moral conservatism, however, Blake grew disillusioned with the new religious movement. Subsequently, he would take a critical stance toward the ideas of Swedenborg himself as well.

The Marriage of Heaven and Hell was, in part, a direct reflection of this disillusion-ment. In structure and content, the book was clearly intended as a satirical counterpart of *Heaven and Hell* (1758), Swedenborg's well-known account of his visionary voyages into the spiritual realm.[132] Swedenborg had not been traditional any more than Blake in his theol-ogy: the main drift of his work had been devoted to disclaim the idea of a god that sends human beings to eternal damnation and to propound a deity that is all love. It was man's own inclination to virtue, Swedenborg taught, that allows him to find heaven or that casts him into hell. The fire of hell was really the love of self; the biblical "gnashing of teeth" the continual strife and combat that this egoism generates. This he contrasted with the spiritual fire of divine love.[133]

Despite all his doctrinal innovation, however, Swedenborg's definition of virtue had remained rather traditional. In *The Marriage of Heaven and Hell*, Blake radically reversed the scales on the Swedish visionary. Moral and religious judgments were systematically reversed, and the "hellish" fire of revolution was to be preferred above the sterile peace of a Swedenborgian heaven. "Infernal fire" now became the essence of life and of god; heaven is just a portion of this energy stolen from the abyss. Other puns on Swedenborg included the "Memorable Fancies" strewn throughout *The Marriage of Heaven and Hell*, which are humorous reversals of the "Memorable Relations" that can be found in Swedenborg's com-mentary on the biblical Apocalypse.[134] In addition, Swedenborg was on several occasions explicitly reprimanded in Blake's little book: the narrator depicts him as someone who had propounded "all the old falsehoods," and his writing as "the linen cloths folded up" in the empty tomb of resurrected Hell.[135]

Blake's most important objection against Swedenborg, nevertheless, was not so much the latter's moral conservatism, but the fact that the Swedish mystic was still too much "confined" by rationalism or that, in the words of *The Marriage of Heaven and Hell*, he had only conversed with the "religious" Angels of Reason and not with the Devils of Genius.[136] Shortly before he produced *The Marriage of Heaven and Hell*, Blake had already expressed his objections to Enlightenment rationalism and its religious derivate, deism, in two short pamphlets published circa 1788—*There Is No Natural Religion* and *All Religions Are One*. These two self-printed leaflets contain much of the argument of his later diabolical epitha-lamion. "As none by travelling over known lands can find out the unknown," principle four of the latter pamphlet read, "so from already acquired knowledge Man could not acquire more. Therefore an universal Poetic Genius exists."[137] In *There Is No Natural Religion*, Blake had drawn the same conclusion about the deficiency of rational, atomistic philosophy: "He who sees the Infinite in all things sees God. He who sees the ratio sees himself only."[138]

In his subsequent works, Blake would elaborate these ideas in a poetic, mythic, and artistic form more fitting to his Poetic Genius. We already quoted the "Memorable Fancy" on plates 11–13 of *Marriage of Heaven and Hell*, in which Blake postulated the Poetic Genius as the origin of all religion—a poetic recapitulation, in fact, of the seven princi-ples of *All Religions Are One*.[139] The prophetic mission of the inspired poet (representa-tive of the Poetic Genius par excellence) was also the subject of Blake's later epic poem *Milton* (1804–1810). This remarkable work presents both an alternative cosmogony for that described by Milton in *Paradise Lost* and an account of the prophetic investiture of Blake himself, who is possessed by the spirit of prophecy and grows into a towering figure of "fury & strength."[140] It also tells about Milton's return to Earth in order to cleanse himself of the Puritan errors in his poetry. Already in *The Marriage of Heaven and Hell*, Blake had famously portrayed the seventeenth-century author as "a true Poet and of the Devils party without knowing it"—that is, unconsciously belonging to the "party" representing life and imagination. In the poetic work that bears his name, Blake presents a redeemed Milton who solemnly pledges

> To cast off Bacon, Locke & Newton from Albion's covering.
> To cast off his filthy garments & clothe him with Imagination,
> To cast aside from Poetry all that is not Inspiration,
> That it no longer shall dare to mock with the aspersion of Madness.
> . . .
> To cast off the idiot Questioner who is always questioning
> But never capable of answering, who sits with a sly grin
> Silent plotting when to question, like a thief in a cave,
> Who publishes doubt & calls it knowledge, whose Science is Despair.[141]

Blake accompanied his verses with a full-page figure of a reborn Milton resembling the risen Christ.[142] This was no coincidence or mere artistic license. To Blake, the true poet, exemplified by Milton, *is* the risen Christ, while the risen Christ himself was, again, the imagination. The Imagination, after all, is what gives man access to the divine and forms the intermediary between mankind "caverned" in its five senses and the "real and eternal World."[143] Without this faculty, there is no salvation for humanity. In fact, Blake claimed, the Imagination is not only what brings us to the divinity, but also the divinity itself.[144] If we remind ourselves of the fact that art and the artist for Blake served as the supreme vehicle of the Imagination, this makes more sense of his seemingly hyperbolic utterances such as "Christianity is art" and "A Poet, a Painter, a Musician, an Architect: The Man Or Woman who is not one of these is not a Christian."[145]

In Blake's case, incidentally, the notion of the inspired poet as vehicle of the eternal world could be taken quite literally as well. While the narrator in *Marriage of Heaven and Hell* had poetically claimed that parts of the book were disclosed to him by a devil, and Blake had presented another book as dictated to him by a fairy, the poet-artist reported experiencing paranormal guidance in real life as well.[146] "I am under the direction of Messengers from Heaven, Daily & Nightly," he wrote to one of his patrons in 1802.[147] This does not imply that *Marriage of Heaven and Hell* and Blake's other illustrated poems were mere products of "mechanical revelation." Clearly, they are carefully crafted and composed works of art. Yet for Blake, there would have been no contradiction here: one way or another, it would have been the imagination, that is, the divine, that would have spoken.[148]

If we read *Marriage of Heaven and Hell* once more after delving deeper into Blake's theology, there are two things that are striking. First, there is the deep feeling of eschatology, of the dawning of a "new earth" that permeates the book. In one of its first pages, Blake speaks of a "new heaven" that has begun and "the Eternal Hell" that revives. "And lo!" Blake's text continues, "Swedenborg is the Angel sitting at the tomb; his writings are the linen clothes folded up."[149] We can now more fully understand what is meant here. Swedenborg's writings stand for the codes of "Reason" in general, whether Newtonian science, rational philosophy, or "systematized" theology; these are the linen clothes, the "bound or outward circumference," around the martyred body of Energy/Life/Desire/the Imagination—all terms that form rough equivalents for Blake. The vital force, however, has now burst out of its bounds and has left its tomb.

From the context, it follows that it is "Eternal Hell" that has experienced this Christ-like resurrection; but if we remember what Blake said about Christ, we can see that here, again, there is no real contradiction, because Christ = the Imagination = the devil. Both are also Jehovah ("Know that after Christ's death, he became Jehovah," Blake writes a few pages later).[150] At least, they are for those who consider them with the vision of the infinite; those who only can see with reason or ratio experience them as demonic, true to what Blake wrote in *There Is No Natural Religion*: "God becomes as we are."[151] The "god of reason" (later designated by Blake with the rather transparent homonym Urizen) is thus the true "satan," the usurper who (vainly) tries to replace the true deity.[152] Yet his semblance of power will soon be over, *Marriage of Heaven and Hell* prophesies. The "cherub with his flaming sword" will leave his post with the Tree of Life and Adam will return to Paradise. At the same time the world will "be consumed in fire"—a metaphor, Blake himself explains, for the purifying of our perception—and appear to mankind as it is, "infinite and holy." The false gods of reason will then dissolve again into the real deity of Energy/Life/Imagination, etc., as the angel at the end of *Marriage of Heaven and Hell* dissolves into a devil.

For the time being, "Mental war" must continue to be waged. But it is clear that Blake considered the "New Age" to be at hand.[153] It remains slightly ambiguous what made the moment *Marriage of Heaven and Hell* was published so propitious for this disclosure of life energy. Was it the rising tide of Revolution? This is suggested by the extension of the fire metaphor to the Revolution in Blake's concluding "Song of Liberty" ("The fire, the fire is falling!" line 11 of the poem reads).[154] Or was it Blake's own revelation that was to set humanity free?[155]

The second thing that marks Blake's mythic construct is his strong holistic views. In contrast to the traditional Christian concept of a kingdom of good opposed to a kingdom of evil, in Blake's world, everything is interrelated, and good and evil are not only relative to the speaker's vantage point ("One Law for the Lion and the Ox is Oppression"), but also necessary conditions for existence, for "without Contraries is no progression."[156] Here, Blake departs from the Christian tradition that sees good and evil as moral absolutes. Much more important for him is the opposition between creativity and noncreativity. From primeval times, Blake argues elsewhere in *Marriage of Heaven and Hell*, there have been two classes of beings: "the Prolific," those who create, and "the Devouring," those "of tame minds" that chain creativity. Both seem to be needed to keep the world going, because "the Prolific would cease to be Prolific unless the Devourer as a sea received [*sic*] the excess of his delights."[157] Seen from this angle, the *coniunctio oppositorum* to which the title of the book alludes is rather one of continual strife than blissful merger. Yet despite the apparent necessity of both sides of the cosmic medal, it is clear with what "class" Blake's sympathies must be sought. In his subsequent works, a new duality starts to manifest itself. In *Milton*, Blake speaks of a "Negation," which is something different from a "Contrary": the latter are opposing "Positives," while the Negation is "the Reasoning Power in Man . . . which must be put off and annihilated away."[158] Once more we see outlines appear of Blake's most detested enemies, the "Newtonian Phantasm" of rationalism (which is identified as "Antichrist" and "Tree of Death" in later works), as well as its appendage, the "Mathematic Holiness" of moral religion.[159]

With these holistic and postdualistic ideas, Blake foreshadows later, sometimes much later, currents in Western thinking and esotericism, among them important strands of modern religious Satanism. Blake himself, it must be added, found much of these highly heterodox points of view in the writings of earlier visionaries and mystics like Paracelsus, Jakob Böhme, and even Swedenborg.[160] He recombined these elements, however, in a new way, on the one hand connecting them with the struggle for human emancipation that characterized the Western Revolution, while on the other hand placing them in a radically post-Enlightenment, postrational discourse. In this context, the devil could transform into god, and god into devil. But most essential was the fact that the true source of divinity was redefined as the human faculty to be creative.

The contrast between William Blake and Percy Bysshe Shelley—self-declared deicide and author of *The Necessity of Atheism*—could at first glance not be greater. When looking closer, however, the contrast begins to appear less extreme. To begin with, Shelley's disgust for traditional Christianity and most other organized forms of religion cannot be translated into simple antireligiosity or nonreligiosity. Already in a note to *Queen Mab*, Shelley had stated that his antitheism "must be understood solely to affect a creative Deity," and he professed his continuing belief in a "pervading Spirit co-eternal with the Universe."[161] This pantheism, or rather panentheism, would remain with him throughout his life, and his later years showed a marked inclination toward a personal form of neo-Platonism.

All this, nevertheless, is not what strikes one as most salient when reading Shelley's major poetical works. Rather it is the spirit of prophetic eschatology in which they are drenched, evoking with great expectation the dawn of a new age without kings, priests, and gods. For Shelley, the disappearance of the traditional concept of the deity seemed to be the most important condition for human happiness, and his belief in the imminence of this disappearance seems at least as intense as Blake's end-time expectations in *The Marriage of Heaven and Hell*. In another note to *Queen Mab*, he had already looked forward with confidence toward the final demise of Christian faith:

> Analogy seems to favour the opinion that as, like other systems, Christianity has arisen and augmented, so like them it will decay and perish; that as violence, darkness, and deceit, not reasoning and persuasion, have procured its admission among mankind, so, when enthusiasm has subsided, and time, that infallible controverter of false opinions, has involved its pretended evidences in the darkness of antiquity, it will become obsolete; that Milton's poem alone will give permanency to the remembrance of its absurdities; and that men will laugh as heartily at grace, faith, redemption, and original sin, as they now do at the metamorphoses of Jupiter, the miracles of Romish saints, the efficacy of witchcraft, and the appearance of departed spirits.[162]

In the last part of *Queen Mab*, a visionary dream shows how the world will enter into paradisiacal splendor after priesthood and fear of the gods have dissolved: even the Earth's climate, Shelley seems to suggest, will return to the conditions of the Golden Age.[163] *Laon and Cythna*, although gloomier and more resigned in tone, is also prolific with references to the "broad sunrise" of the godless future that will replace the present "winter of the world," while the two final acts of *Prometheus Unbound* are almost entirely devoted to an ecstatic description of the future harmony of Man.[164] With some paradox, one could call this belief a *religion of secularism*: a millennial faith in the fact that final happiness will alight upon mankind when all vestiges of old religions have been erased.[165]

Despite the fact that the phrasing might be more exalted, Shelley here voices sentiments that had already been expressed by the more radical strand of the eighteenth-century Enlightenment. The Enlightenment had certainly not been free of its own millennial expectations, and we know that some of its poetical effluvia had been a direct source of inspiration for Shelley.[166] The latter's critique on religion and the power structures it supports is essentially an elaboration of the ethical and rational arguments of the eighteenth century. The point where Shelley departs from his Enlightenment mentors and approaches Blake is in his strong convictions regarding the role of poetry and the Imagination. These convictions are stated quite unambiguously in his posthumously published *A Defence of Poetry* (1820). This iconic essay has become a classic of English literature and a favorite provider of stock quotes on poetry ("a poet is a nightingale, who sits in darkness and sings to cheer its own solitude with sweet sounds," etc.). To experience once more the revolutionary nature of Shelley's claims in this text, we have to remove the mental dust from his words and read them with fresh eyes again—for it is here that the inherently religious character of Shelley's poetical project becomes most clear.

Already on one of the first pages of the essay, we encounter a description of the office of the poet and the function of poetry that, despite a somewhat more sober wording, almost verbatim reflects the ideas of Blake on this subject:

> Poets, according to the circumstances of the age and the nation in which they appeared, were called, in the earliest epochs of the world, legislators or prophets: a poet essentially comprises and unites both these characters. For he not only beholds intensely the present as it is, and discovers those laws according to which present things ought to be ordered, but he beholds the future in the present, and his thoughts are the germs of the flower and the fruit of latest time. Not that I assert poets to be prophets in the gross sense of the word, or that they can foretell the form as surely as they foreknow the spirit of events: such is the pretence of superstition, which would make poetry an attribute of prophecy, rather than prophecy an attribute of poetry. A poet participates in the eternal, the infinite, and the one; as far as relates to his conceptions, time and place and number are not.[167]

The family resemblance with Blake is especially made clear by the last line, where the poet is characterized as participating in "the eternal, the infinite, and the one"—in other words, in the divine. Here we see Shelley's panentheistic deity silently stealing in, the "Spirit of activity and life,/ That knows no term, cessation, or decay."[168] According to Shelley, the poet is in direct contact with the spiritual breath of the universe; it is, as with Blake, the Imagination that allows him or her to do so. Without imagination, there can be no transcendence, no "going out of our nature," and thus no love or moral feeling. In Shelley's words:

> A man, to be greatly good, must imagine intensely and comprehensively; he must put himself in the place of another and of many others; the pains and pleasures of his species must become his own. The great instrument of moral good is the imagination; and poetry administers to the effect by acting upon the cause.[169]

In this way, inspired poets can be the "unacknowledged legislators of the world," as one of the most celebrated phrases from the essay goes.[170] Elsewhere in his apology, Shelley upholds the supremacy of poetry over the "grosser sciences" of the "calculating faculty" with much the same arguments as Blake. Pointing to the social misery that seemed to accompany the technical progress of his own days, he points out that it is poetry and imagination that must lead the way for science, not only by imagining the creations which scientists afterward copy into "the book of common life," but also by demonstrating the moral principles without which technology will become a mere tool for exploitation and oppression.[171] "Poetry is indeed something divine. It is at once the centre and circumference of knowledge; it is that which comprehends all science and to which all science must be referred. . . . What were virtue, love patriotism, friendship—what were the scenery of this beautiful universe which we inhabit; what were our consolations on this side of the grave—and what were our aspirations beyond it, if poetry did not ascend to bring light and fire from those eternal regions where the owl-winged faculty of calculation dare not ever soar?"[172] In the end, Shelley does not hesitate to draw the same conclusion from his presuppositions as Blake had done: "Poetry, and the principle of Self, of which money is the most visible incarnation, are the God and Mammon of the world."[173] As we can see now, this is more than just "poetic" hyperbole. There is consistent philosophy involved here.

Shelley's *Defence of Poetry* also contains the long passage on the "magnificence" of Milton's Satan that we quoted earlier in this chapter. The most radical manifestation of Shelley's Romantic Satanism, however, can be found in *Laon and Cythna*, and particularly in the first "canto" of this poem, where he sings praises of the "Serpent," who is in reality the Morning Star—in short, Lucifer, although his name is never mentioned. This "Great Spirit of Good" is the aspirator—or we may also say the symbol—of all human efforts for liberty and good. Its genesis dates back to the time "when life and thought/sprang forth . . . of inessential Nought"; furthermore, he is described as speaking with the voice of nature.[174] All in all, Shelley's Serpent-god is almost indistinguishable from his panentheistic "pervading Spirit coeternal with the Universe." If this is indeed the case and the two are identical, Shelley here approaches a virtual deification of Satan that is every bit as radical as that in Blake's *Marriage of Heaven and Hell*.

The question that must immediately arise after this is where, then, does evil come from? How is it possible that the world is not a vale of happiness under the aegis of this eternal spirit? Shelley gives a paradoxical answer to this question in *Laon and Cythna*: it is because the Spirit of Good is opposed by a Fiend who came into being together with his benign adversary, as "Twin Genii, equal Gods," both "immortal" and "all-pervading."[175] In *Laon and Cythna*, it is true, this "spirit of evil" can be interpreted in an exclusively metaphorical way, as a tendency in the human mind or in human society (Shelley seems to identify this opposing power with "Custom" at some point).[176] But Shelley at this time also appears to have pondered the option of an ontologically independent force of evil. He discussed this possibility in another posthumously published essay, the *Essay on Christianity*, which was probably composed in 1817. "According to Jesus Christ, and according to the indisputable facts of the case," Shelley wrote, "Some evil spirit has dominion in this perfect world. But there will come a time when the human mind shall be visited exclusively by the influences of the benignant Power."[177] These words suggest that Shelley, at this moment, was postulating the existence of a "satan" who had much the same function as the Christian devil: that of blanket explanation of evil and misfortune. The stark moral framework in which he appraised the world, with a clear division between the camps of evil and of good, of liberty and of oppression, may have prompted him in this direction.

Of course, this Shelleyan satan is not the same as the Christian one. On the contrary, while the Serpent is equated with the Spirit of Good, *Laon and Cythna* depicts the spirit of evil in the form of an eagle, the traditional attribute of Zeus. Behind the Greek "father of the gods," we can immediately discern the shape of the "Demon-God" whom Shelley had wished to destroy and whose most potent manifestation in his own society was of course the "Jehovah" of established Christendom. Shelley's reversal of Christian cosmology here is complete. But this also entangles him in his own ideological propositions, for the god of Christianity, which he had sought to unmask as an illusion during most of his public career, now suddenly does gain ontological reality after all, be it as an evil entity. This may be the reason why Shelley does not seem to have pursued this line of thinking any further.

Let us return to Shelley's ideas about poetry once more. The thoughts on this subject already quoted make it easy to understand why Shelley might have considered his poetical and political activities as a continuum. In *A Defence of Poetry*, he had already characterized poetry as "the most unfailing herald, companion, and follower of the awakening of a great people to work a beneficial change in opinion or institution."[178] In the preface for *Laon and Cythna*, he wrote that his poem had as purpose "kindling within the bosoms of my readers a virtuous enthusiasm for those doctrines of liberty and justice, that faith and hope in something good, which neither violence nor misrepresentation nor prejudice can ever totally extinguish among mankind."[179]

This idea that the world could be changed with verse will have seemed less ludicrous in Shelley's days, when poetry still enjoyed a comparatively wide readership. The historical developments during Shelley's lifetime, moreover, seemed to promise new and exciting opportunities for the promotion of change through words. The Enlightenment had taught, and the French Revolution had proven, the crucial importance of the ideological superstructure in defining the substructure of society. Kings and priests eventually only wielded power by the condescension of the people; this condescension could be withdrawn if the people could be brought to "change its mind."

Myth was Shelley's favorite tool for doing so. His life project has been described by one scholar as an attempt "to free people's minds by rewriting the world's myths and religions."[180] Shelley's new or rewritten myths, moreover, give us some of the most striking examples of the Romantic use of myths as texts of identification. This is explicitly stated in the preface to *Laon and Cythna*, where Shelley writes that his epic poem does not attempt to offer "methodological or systematic argument" but only seeks to "awaken the feelings," and to this purpose will tell "a story of human passion in its most universal character," meant to appeal "to the common sympathies of every human breast."[181] Yet Shelley's most magnificent attempt in this direction was without doubt *Prometheus Unbound*, his last grand effort to eliminate the Christian deity from European consciousness and bring together the themes that were essential to his thinking. In this work, Prometheus has replaced the fallen angel as noble rebel against the tyrannous divinity, functioning as a sort of cross between Satan and Jesus, obstinate in his resistance like the former, patient in his suffering like the latter. Above all, however, he is portrayed by Shelley as great in love, due to his tremendous capability of imaginative identification with his fellow beings. Thus in Shelley's alternative version of the Greek myth, Prometheus is unbound, not because he perseveres in his aversion to Jupiter (which would be an implicit acknowledgment of the god's power, and also a continuation of the mental state of hate that characterizes the "Foul Tyrant both of Gods and humankind"), but when expressing pity even for the old god and retracting his curse.[182] Then all of a sudden, Demogorgon appears—a demonic entity that may stand here for eternity, history, or "the terrible people"—and leads Jupiter and his entourage into oblivion. The "painted veil" is torn, oppressive power structures all over the world collapse, and mankind enters into a stage of universal, anarchic happiness. In entering this narrative, the reader is expected to engage imaginatively with Prometheus, reenacting the process in the titan's psyche by which the tyrant-god is eventually dissolved and the Golden Age of Liberty begun. In doing so (Shelley hoped), the reader will also dissolve the deity from his own mind, thus starting society's march toward a future without spiritual or political oppression. The poem is thus a prophecy that brings about its own fulfillment, an "unfailing herald, companion, and follower of the awakening of a great people to work a beneficial change in opinion or institution."[183] This is certainly what Shelley hoped his poetic productions would be. "We want the creative faculty to imagine what we know," he wrote elsewhere. "We want the generous impulse to act that which we imagine; we want the poetry of life."[184]

SATAN'S NEW MYTHS: BYRON AND HUGO

When we open the pages of Byron, we seem to enter an atmosphere completely different from that which we encounter with Blake and Shelley. We are not greeted with exalted visions of future global harmony or enthusiastic utterances about the prophetic role of art. Byron considered it his destiny to be a "great statesman" similar to Napoleon and anxiously tried to avoid the impression that writing—or "scribbling," as he liked to call it—was anything more than a mere pastime for him. Significantly, his debut volume of poetry had been titled *Hours of Idleness*, and hence his statement that *Cain* had been written in three weeks of drunkenness and had never been corrected but in the proofs.[185]

Of course, we need not be deceived by this carefully constructed façade. Intoxicated writing with astonishing results also cleverly suggests the guiding hand of genius. And Byron's personal notes and letters abundantly attest to the toil that writing was for him, while the sheer extent of his œuvre indicates that he was quite serious about his business.[186] Given his ironic attitude toward his work, however, we do not need to expect extensive theoretical meditations upon the spiritual significance of poetry and art from his pen. Byron considered poetry—as far as his remaining writings tell—to be a "reflection of life," and he asserted his right to describe life as he saw and experienced it, without giving in "to all the Cant of Christendom."[187]

Notwithstanding this pragmatism, it is obvious that *Cain* fits squarely into the mytho-poetic effort to (re)write sacred history that we have encountered with Blake and Shelley.[188] As such, however, it is also one of the most ambiguous works of Romantic Satanism. For one, it is not as clear as sometimes suggested that the biblical god is the villain of the play and Lucifer its hero, despite the fact that this was the common assumption of friend and foe as soon as *Cain* hit the bookshelves (thus adding to the ongoing diabolization of its author). Byron himself often claimed that the play was as canonical as *Paradise Lost* and that the opinions uttered by its protagonists should not be confused with those of its author.[189]

What then was Byron really trying to say with his play? Much of this depends on how we should interpret the role Byron assigns to Lucifer. *Cain*'s demonic interlocutor certainly does display key features of the rebellious Satan from the tradition of Godwin and Shelley *cum suis*. Witness his Miltonic self-affirmation "I have a victor, true, but no superior"; witness his contempt for those who chose to be slaves, while he himself proudly prefers "an independency of torture/To the smooth agonies of adulation."[190] But another influence might be at least as tangible in *Cain*, namely that of Goethe, and especially Goethe's famous tragedy *Faust*. The first part of this monumental work had been published in 1808. Although Byron spoke German only rudimentarily, he had been introduced to *Faust* in 1816 by his fellow author Mathew Lewis, who had translated the German poem viva voce while staying with Byron as a guest.[191] The work had left a deep impression upon the diabolical lord, and his Lucifer is clearly indebted to Goethe's Mephistopheles. The sardonic comments on the human condition and general ironic aloofness that Byron attributes to the fallen angel are altogether alien to Blake and Shelley but form a conspicuous feature of Goethe's depiction of the demon that tempts Faust. This is not to say that Byron's Lucifer is simply an imitation of Mephistopheles. Goethe's devil has dimensions that are alien to Byron's creation—not only is he linked to the cosmic principle of negation and destruction, but also to the material world, for which *Cain*'s Lucifer only expresses utter contempt, deriding human beings as "reptiles engendered out of the subsiding slime of a mighty universe" whose wants are "gross and petty" and whose best enjoyments are no more than "a sweet degradation" and "a filthy cheat" (we will return to this soon).[192] Both in tone and subject matter, nevertheless, Byron seems closer to Goethe than to English Romantic Radicals such as Blake and Shelley.[193]

If there is something that really stands out with Byron's Lucifer, however, it is his intimate association with the spirit of inquiry. "Knowledge," and the discussion of its merits, is a recurring theme in *Cain*. Lucifer "tempts" Cain by offering him knowledge; the tour that he gives the latter through past and present worlds includes the latest scientific findings of Byron's days, for instance Cuvier's theses of prehuman extinct forms of life. "I tempt none, save with the truth," Lucifer remarks, and he places himself in explicit contrast to his divine opponent when he does not ask Cain for implicit faith, but only promises him to show him "what thou dar'st not deny."[194]

In historical terms, we might say that Lucifer here represents the scientific and philosophical rationalism of the Enlightenment.[195] The logical arguments wielded by him (and

Cain) against a benevolent biblical creator are also those that had been brought forward by Voltaire and Percy Bysshe Shelley: the existence of seemingly purposeless suffering; the relativity of "good" and "evil"; the ethical absurdity of atonement through the sacrifice of the innocent.[196] The spirit of the Enlightenment seems to waft with magnificence in the final words of Lucifer to Cain, which could serve as a poetical paraphrase of Thomas Paine's "My own mind is my own church":

One good gift has the fatal apple giv'n –
Your reason; let it not be over-swayed
By tyrannous threats to force you into faith
'Gainst all external sense and inward feelings.
Think and endure and form an inner world
In your own bosom, where the outward fails.
So shall you nearer be the spiritual
Nature, and war triumphant with your own.[197]

Nowhere in *Cain* does Byron deny the validity of these arguments, which are presented as rather irrefutable. His personal notes and correspondence show that these points of query were solidly his own.[198] Yet these premises lead to a radically different conclusion with Byron than with the Enlightenment optimists or their Romantic progeny like Shelley. As we remarked already, we find no exalted visions of a paradisiacal future with Byron. Rather, the net result of all this analysis and doubt is the despair Blake attributed to the "idiot Questioner" of science. Science, in *Cain*, is nowhere creative, only destructive. The disclosures of Lucifer only aggravate Cain's state of existential discontentment, leading eventually to the dissolution of the primeval human community (which, whatever its faults, was at least a community) and the murder of brother by brother. Cain is left disinherited and bereft of hope and inner peace. This is, literally, the point where the text of *Cain* ends.

Nowhere does Byron, neither in *Cain* nor in his other work, suggest that this demise of traditional faith, however miserable in its psychological and social effects, should be avoided or reverted. Rather, it is presented as something inevitable, a "fatum." It is inevitable for Western man to lose his old faith after he has eaten from the tree of philosophical and scientific knowledge; it is inevitable for him to kill his pious "inner" brother (for Abel, of course, can also be read as a lost part of the poet himself); it is inevitable that he will end up spiritually homeless.

A contemporary critic aptly characterized this attitude as "philosophy sitting on the ruins, weeping over its unbelief and the sad results of its science."[199] Morse Peckham proposed the term "negative Romanticism" for this outlook. As opposed to "positive Romanticism," which overcomes the spiritual vacuum created by Enlightenment's destruction of faith by creating new holistic systems of meaning, negative Romanticism merely expresses the spiritual "homelessness" brought about by the demise of traditional belief and the inadequacy of Enlightenment philosophy to fill this gap.[200] This label is certainly helpful, especially for placing Romanticism and Byron in their proper religio-historical context. Its wider applicability, however, can be debated. First, of course, the terms "positive" and "negative" imply a value judgment that seems to me *mal à propos*. We will return to this point later. Second, and more important, if formulated in terms of mere historical position, we are in danger of missing a crucial point where Byron is on common ground with the other great Romantics and also parts ways with most of them. In Byron's eyes, the condition of metaphysical despair he invoked was not simply due to his position at a certain point of human history. Instead, it was a veritable *condition humaine*, a common cosmic predicament. It is for a reason that he attributes this attitude, in *Cain*, to the first-born post-paradisiacal human being.

It is not just the alienation that may result from doubt—or science, or rationalism—that is at issue here. The troubles of Cain arise because he fails to submit himself to his mother's admonition: "Content thee with what is."[201] His issue with the deity is not so much the hypothetical absurdity of the latter's existence, but the limitations of his "politics of Paradise." This defiance has an ethical character, roughly paraphrasable as "what kind of god would let his creatures live in an imperfect world?" But it goes well beyond this. It is not so certain that even readmittance into "barren Paradise" would satisfy Cain. It is, in Byron's own words, "the inadequacy of his state to his Conceptions" that embitters Cain, and these "Conceptions," Byron's Mystery suggests, are inherently limitless. Even when Lucifer leads Cain to unfathomable scenes of astronomical grandeur, the latter readily acknowledges their majesty but nevertheless goes on to describe them as "inferior still to my desires and my conceptions."[202]

The thing that haunts Cain is, of course, the faculty that Blake had called the Imagination, the ability that allows man to perceive "more than sense (tho' ever so acute) can discover." To this definition, Blake had already appended the conclusion that "less than All cannot satisfy Man."[203] Byron will not have found this idea with Blake, of whom he can have had no more than the very slightest acquaintance.[204] There are many other Romantic authors, however, who may have transmitted this central Romantic tenet to him: Wordsworth, for instance, or Goethe.[205] The inherent transcendence of all human aspirations forms a central theme of the latter's *Faust*; according to Goethe, even the most elementary desires—for riches, for a beautiful girl, for power—only awaken a craving for the *more* and the *greater*, and thus eventually for the divine. That is why Faust forfeits his soul to the devil as soon as he utters the famous dictum with regard to the present moment, "Verweile doch, du bist so schön" ("Please stay; you are so beautiful"), because it means he has given up the quest for the greater and wants instead to cling to the lower.[206] However, while the path of unquenchable desire for Goethe eventually ends up in unity with the divine, for Byron, its destination is unending despair. And it is Lucifer who is turned into the mouthpiece par excellence of this inner urge *ad sursum*.

Byron surely will have found additional inspiration for this choice in that other famous declaration of Milton's Satan:

> The mind is its own place, and in itself
> Can make a Heaven of Hell, a Hell of Heaven.[207]

The advice to "form an inner world in your own bosom, where the outward fails" is repeated by Byron's Lucifer on more than one occasion. "Nothing can/Quench the mind if the mind will be itself/And centre of surrounding things."[208] It is this faculty, Lucifer tells, that allows intelligent beings to determine what is good and what is evil; it is this, moreover, that forms the "immortal part," the "spiritual nature" of man.[209] And it is Cain's conspicuous bent toward the transcendental, his structural unease with his earthly existence, that made him fit for the companionship of Lucifer in the first place, so the latter declares.[210]

Byron's "Master of spirits," it appears, is eminently spiritual in character.[211] In juxtaposition, it seems that we can tentatively identify the biblical deity in *Cain* as the representative of physical reality. That may be why they both "reign together" but dwell "asunder," although both their dwelling is "here and o'er all space"; that may be why they battle "through all eternity," disputing each other's reign.[212] And because physical reality will never live up to the boundless aspirations of the spirit, the latter's eternity must be one of suffering. "If any could desire what he is incapable of possessing, despair must be his eternal lot," Blake had already said.[213] *Cain* seems to conclude that despair *is* indeed our eternal lot, *precisely because* of our immortal faculty of imagination. This reversal of his own doctrine of redemptive imagination was acutely detected by Blake. He reacted to *Cain* with a short work entitled *The Ghost of Abel: A Revelation in the Visions of Jehovah Seen by William Blake* (1822).[214] In its dedication to "Lord Byron in the Wilderness," he apostrophied his fellow prophet about his lack of faith in the power of Genius and the false dichotomy between spirit and nature he postulated. "Can a Poet doubt the Visions of Jehovah? Nature has no Outline, but Imagination has. Nature has no Tune, but Imagination has. Nature has no Supernatural, & dissolves: Imagination is Eternity."[215]

Is the voice of Lucifer the voice of Byron? The fallen angel undeniably represents a part of its author, at least if we can say as much of Cain or earlier Byronic characters like Manfred. Lucifer seems much like a superhuman double of Cain at times, similar in their spiritual adversity, their isolation from other members of their species, and their intrinsic *tristesse* ("Sorrow seems half of his immortality," Cain remarks about Lucifer).[216] In earlier works, Byron's protagonists express similar feelings about the inherent impossibility of happiness for human beings—at least for those human beings that have taken the road of independent thought. As we have noted before, there is much autobiography in Byron's heroes, and the sentiments of Cain and Lucifer were certainly a reflection of his own.

We should be reluctant, however, to label this spirituality without hope as "negative." The melancholia that accompanies the Byronic hero who bows to neither god nor devil also contains an undeniable element of pride—it is brought about at least in part because he speaks from a more courageous, a more "knowing," less naïve vantage point than ordinary humanity. "I will have nought to do with happiness/Which humbles me and mine," Cain declares. Lucifer's proudly chosen "independency of torture" can also be interpreted along these lines. Byron here masterfully extends the old *topos* of Satan as the rebel against all odds, which had been given a simple political reading by Godwin, into a much deeper symbol of our state of being. The spiritual discontent that makes us melancholic, Byron seems to tell us through Lucifer, is also the part of us that makes us eminently human. As human beings, we must bear our burden like men. Byron's philosophical inclinations here veer closely to the "religion of honour" that was proposed by Alfred de Vigny, his French disciple, as the only viable spiritual path left to man in a post-Christian age.[217]

Yet this may not exhaust the possibilities of interpretation in *Cain*. As a matter of fact, some scholars have argued that *Cain* gives us the first intimations that Byron was growing more critical of his own "Byronic" type of heroics.[218] It is evidently true, to begin with, that the play articulates many voices, and even the voice of traditional religion is not rendered altogether without sympathy (in practical reality, Byron certainly did a much better job at imaginative identification than Shelley, whose villains always remain unremittingly villainous). Traditional religion, however, is not presented as a viable alternative to the fearless spirit of independence and inquiry that Lucifer advocates. Only in the person of Adah, the sister-love of Cain, Byron seems to propose a genuine third path besides Lucifer's sterile intellectualism and Adam's primitive faith. Like Cain, Adah is a first-born post-paradisiacal human (Byron here picks up a Jewish tradition according to which Cain and Abel were married to their twin sisters).[219] And despite the fact that Cain presents her as not understanding "the mind that overwhelms" him, she, too, confesses to "dissatisfied and curious thoughts" and a heart that is not tranquil ("Alas, no").[220] But her driving passion is love, an altruistic yet earthly and personal love. "What else can joy be, but the spreading joy?" is her credo.[221]

In his conversation with Cain and Adah, Lucifer explicitly demands Cain to choose between "love and knowledge," and although the latter initially chooses knowledge, he is certainly not in every way of one accord with his diabolic guide. In some of the most moving passages of Byron's "Mystery," he defends the preference of his love for Adah, physical and perishable as she may be, over the lofty but disengaged individuality that Lucifer proposes.[222] Even Lucifer, at one point, declares in a Shelleyan twist that the one thing that makes him and his fellows in rebellion more happy than the solitary creator-god is the companionship they can experience in their suffering, "the unbounded sympathy of all with all."[223]

Byron here seems to champion the cause of physical, earthbound, human love versus the lifeless absolutes of idealism, whether religious, philosophical, or "Romantic" in nature. Eventually, his play ends with the remorse of its protagonist, not for his revolt against Jehovah, but because he has irrevocably severed the bond of life and love with his brother. And it ends, moreover, with Adah's decision to follow Cain into exile and share his burden out of love. *Cain* even displays some sympathy for the idea of sacrificial atonement in this context, albeit as a voluntary act of love rather than the demand of a ruthless deity.[224] This, apparently, is the mode of being that Byron proposes for post-Christian, post-Revolutionary, and post-paradisiacal humans: a life made worthwhile by personal, earthbound love between free and equivalent individuals (and not out of social custom or propriety, as is the root, Byron emphasizes, of Cain's affection for his father).

Byron seems to have planned to accentuate this element even more in a subsequent "mystery" that explicitly deals with the Satanic, the unfinished closet play *Heaven and Earth* (1821). As a sort of sequel to *Cain*, it tells the story of the love between the "daughters of men" and the "sons of god," which served as the occasion for the fall of the angels in some apocryphal accounts (see chapter 1) and was followed, according to biblical myth, by a divinely ordained flood that destroyed most of mankind. We see Byron once again struggle with the Calvinism of his childhood in this play when he questions the humanity of a deity that destroys millions of human beings in order that "a remnant shall be saved." But the main theme of the three scenes that have been left to us rather appears to be the question of what can make life worthwhile if death is eventually to engulf us all. Yet again one of Byron's answers seems to be that it is earthly love, especially between men and women, that makes even our short mortal existence preferable to "a dead eternity."[225] Thus Japheth, the wandering, brooding son of Noah, considers to give up his place in the saving Ark in order to die with the girl he loves; thus the seraphs Samiasa and Azaziel brave "sin and fear" for the love of the mortals Anah and Aholibamah. In appropriate mythical garb, the latter instance seems to exemplify the view that our affection for the "human animal" (to quote Joost van den Vondel) should always overcome spiritual or ideological considerations; or at least that the spiritual and the earthly should be balanced in an equal and harmonious love affair.

With Victor Hugo's *Fin de Satan*, we witness the last of Romantic Satanism's titanic attempts to rewrite the sacred history of the West. Hugo was a Romantic from the same mold as Blake and Shelley, and he had played a central role in the breakthrough of the new artistic movement in France. His work swarmed with allusions to the "papacy of genius," the poet as "sacred dreamer" or "mysterious Sinai" (carrying "a complete God" on his forehead), as well as to literature as a "spiritual power."[226] The new generation that had sprung up after the Revolution, he had written as early as 1823, demanded from the poet more than it had ever before: "It asks him for a faith to believe in."[227] In those days, he still had put his poetic-prophetic gifts to the cause of monarchy and restoration; but in subsequent years, he had moved ever further toward the Left and toward an explicitly pro-revolutionary position. Consequently, Hugo decided to leave the country in protest when Napoleon's nephew Louis-Napoléon Bonaparte, in one of the stranger twists of nineteenth-century history, declared himself Emperor Napoleon III after a swift coupe d'état in 1851. As place of exile, Hugo selected the English Channel Islands, where he and his family moved into a majestic house looking out over the sea.

Banished to the wilderness like a modern Isaiah or Elijah, the dim outlines of his homeland barely visible on the horizon, Hugo once more pondered his role as prophet-poet.[228] His strong urge to proclaim a new Gospel to France and the human race is already evident in a poem that he wrote in 1854, which contains in nucleus most of the crucial elements of *Fin de Satan*:

> Écoute-moi. La loi change.
> Je vois poindre aux cieux l'archange!
>   L'Esprit du ciel
> M'a crié sur la montagne:
> "Tout enfer s'éteint, nul bagne
>   N'est éternel."
>
> Je ne hais plus, mer profonde.
> J'aime. J'enseigne, je fonde.
>   Laisse passer.
> Satan meurt, un autre empire
> Naît, et la morsure expire
>   Dans un baiser.[229]
>
> [Listen to me. The law is changing.
> I saw the archangel appear in the heavens!
>   The Spirit of heaven

Cried to me upon the mountain:
"Every hell will be extinguished, no prison
    Is eternal."

I do not hate anymore, deep sea.
I love. I teach, I lay new foundations.
    Let it all pass.
Satan dies, a different empire
Is born, and the biting teeth expire
    Into a kiss.]

For his new prophetic mission, Hugo did not have to rely on his poetic ability alone. Although he had parted ways with Christianity, he had retained a strong interest in esotericism and other forms of alternative religiosity. When spiritism—group invocations of the spirits of the dead—became popular in the 1850s, the Hugo family was one of the first on the Continent to embrace this form of otherworldly communication. In some measure, Hugo's interest in spiritism was probably due to the personal tragedy that had befallen him. The tragic death of his beloved eldest daughter had intensified his yearning for an answer to life's great questions, especially those regarding the existence of suffering, death, and the afterlife. He became particularly convinced of the reliability of the turning tables when, during one of the sessions, he experienced the sensation that he had made contact with his drowned daughter. For almost two years, he and his family convened with the spirits at regular intervals, communicating with famous dead persons such as Aeschylus, Moses, Galileo, Jesus, Rousseau, Aristotle, Voltaire, Cain, and the Wandering Jew (*sic*).[230]

The spirits he invoked greatly stimulated Hugo in his ambitious endeavor to rewrite the history of God and Satan. In October 1854, the "spirit of death" urged the "Ocean-Poet" (as the spirits liked to call him) to write an "Advice to God," a myth so forceful in its exposition of universal redemption through love that it would be capable to impress the deity itself. Hugo interpreted this message as a reference to his newly started *Fin de Satan*.[231] This was also his conclusion when, on March 8, 1855, Jesus Christ began to speak in glowing terms about a "new Gospel" that was coming soon and that would efface the old one, proclaiming the final salvation of mankind.[232] It was clear, thus, that Hugo was not to be a simple transmitter of messages from the beyond, but that it would be his own imaginative, creative undertaking that was to topple the balance and change heaven and Earth. The spirits, when consulted, confirmed many of Hugo's insights in this respect and occasionally added new ones. "Hell does not exist," the netherworld unanimously reported.[233] On December 8, 1853, after he had been queried about the future fate of evildoers, Moses had already declared: "All those criminals are slowly transfigured and become just ones. . . . Their crimes flow away as avalanches into the abyss of divine mercy."[234] Jesus Christ himself reproached Christianity for preaching hatred "under the name of hell" on February 11, 1855, repeating his disapproval of the doctrine of the "eternal flames" on February 18. On March 15 and 22 of the same year, Jesus returned and gave a long description of Satan that prefigures many aspects of the fallen angel in *Fin de Satan*. "He was the traveller of the twilight; he was the walker in the shadows; he was the explorer of the abyss . . . he was the great interrogator of God, the speaker of negations of truth, the questioner, the one that revolted, the combatant; he was the one wounded by the celestial barricade, the shining one and the bleeding one, the sublime bearer of the wounds of doubt and the scars of the idea . . . redoubtable and splendid griffon, he has Danton as wing and Robespierre as claw."[235]

There can be no doubt, then, that Hugo's project was religious in nature; in fact, it seemed to have been intended more or less as the proclamation of a new religion. What exactly was this religion, and what role did Satan play in it? In complete form, *Fin de Satan* was meant to outline a complete cosmogony. The poem starts with a description of Satan's long fall through the heavens, descending deeper and deeper into the darkness till even the last star has become invisible. Here, already, Hugo begins to give new symbolic meaning to the old myth. His Satan, in complete contrast to Byron's Lucifer, is symbolic for matter viz. the material. Matter is the cause of evil because it exists separately from the deity and the love of the deity. The source of evil, of the eclipse of the divine, is thus the creation of the material universe; the story of the fall can also be told as the withdrawal of the deity from the cosmos to make possible the existence of creation. Satan is the most absolute manifestation of this:

> God does except me. He ends with me. I am his outer limit.
> God would be infinite if I would not exist.[236]

At one point, Satan becomes aware of his solitude and of his love for the divine, but though he asks for mercy, he is unable to return to the deity. In heaven, however, the angel Liberty is born from a feather left behind by Satan and is animated into a fierce maiden by the deity. Like Vigny's Eloa, she descends to Earth to save Satan. Her appearance dissolves the specter of Isis-Lilith, the veil "that men call Fate." By her intermediary as daughter both of the deity and of Satan, of spiritual love and extra-centrifugal matter, she brings about the reconciliation of the latter with the former. God "wipes away the infamous night" and Satan is reborn as a sanctified Lucifer.

This cosmic devolution and evolution runs parallel with, or rather fulfills itself in, the historical development of mankind. Thus Satan's first anguish of solitude and cry for mercy is coincidental with Jesus' suffering on the cross, which is a symbol for the suffering of humanity as a whole. Jesus, however, is not mankind's Savior: that is the revolutionary spirit of Liberty, which for Hugo is incarnated in France:

> Ce peuple étrange est plus qu'un peuple, c'est une âme;
> Ce peuple est l'Homme même; il brave avec dédain
> L'enfer, et, dans la nuit, cherche à tâtons l'Eden;
> Ce peuple, c'est Adam; mais Adam qui se venge,
> Adam ayant volé le glaive ardent de l'ange,
> Et chassant devant lui la Nuit et le Trépas.[237]

> [This remarkable nation is more than a nation, it is a soul;
> This nation is Man itself; it braves hell with contempt,

And searches on hands and feet for Eden in the night;
This nation is Adam, but Adam with a vengeance,
An Adam that has stolen the burning sword from the angel
And chases before him both Night and Death.]

It is the French Revolution, according to Hugo, that establishes the victory of Liberty and allows man to be free, united in love. As the deity says to Satan at the end of the poem: "Man, who was enchained by you, is liberated by her. . . . Come: the dungeon's destruction abolishes hell!"[238] The new era of happiness and oneness with the divine that the events of 1789 had inaugurated was to be described by Hugo in another epic poem, provisionally entitled "God." It is small wonder, one cannot help to remark, that the Ocean-Poet only succeeded in finishing some scattered fragments of this work.

HOW SATANIST WERE THE ROMANTIC SATANISTS?

After reviewing these new or restyled Satanic myths, it is time that we address a question that by now may be pressing. Can we consider the Romantic Satanists "genuine" Satanists? Can we describe them as early adepts of a *religious* Satanism, engaging in a *religious* veneration of Satan? This would make them the first-known religious Satanists of the modern era: thus, the matter evidently merits closer scrutiny.

Before I can give a meaningful answer to this question, however, there need to be some clarifications regarding terms. With historians of literature, the terms "Romantic Satanism" or "literary Satanists" can sometimes designate a wide variety of authors. Some of these only use the devil as a traditional bogey man in spooky stories, while others merely show a marked predilection for "things wicked" (as was the older signification of the word "Satanism"; see the etymological discussion in the introduction).[239] For the purposes of my research, I narrowed down this bewildering variety to those Romantic authors who, in some measure or another, display a positive identification with Satan in their works. Even narrowed down to this, however, Romantic Satanism cannot be described as a coherent movement with a single voice, but rather as a post factum identified group of sometimes widely divergent authors among whom a similar theme is found.[240] As such, the term is still useful, particularly for localizing and analyzing shifting attitudes to Satan, as is our present aim. In addition, we have seen how the authors we have thus set apart possess some clear common denominators that unmistakably inform their treatment of Satan: a "revolutionary" or "Radical" attitude in political and religious matters, for instance, and a new, Romantic approach toward the finding or creation of meaning.

Were the authors we have thus declared Romantic Satanists also *religious* Satanists? This simple question requires a complex answer. It should be remembered, first of all, that Romantic Satanism is a term of literary history, not of religious studies. Despite sometimes persistent rumors to the contrary, there are no indications that any of the Romantic Satanists ever held religious rites to worship Satan. It is true that Byron writes about holding nightly revels dressed in monks' garbs while drinking claret from a skull; and it might be equally true that we can find a faint reference here to the practices of Sir Francis Dashwood's so-called Hell-Fire Club.[241] But this does not amount to intentional, explicit veneration of the fallen angel, let alone to the Black Masses Byron was sometimes accused of—none of which are attested for in our sources or in Byron's more sober biographies. In the same vein, Victor Hugo's immersion in spiritism is not equal to Satanism. It is certainly true that he had in part been inspired by the turning tables to compose his poem on Satan, but it had been predominantly the spirits of Jesus and Moses who had instructed him to do so.[242] Only once did a spiritual entity that was identified as Satan make his appearance during the séances on Jersey. But after more thorough deliberation, Hugo and his companions unmasked this visitor as something far worse, namely the spirit of Emperor Napoleon III![243]

Among the other major Romantic Satanists, the only instance in which we find anything resembling ritual religious practices is with Shelley, who wrote in one of his letters that he had ascended a mountain behind his Italian house "& suspended a garland & raised a small turf altar."[244] Yet these "rites of the true religion" had been intended for the worship of "the mountain-walking Pan" and, although this may have been a highly significant occurrence in itself, it hardly amounts to Satanism.

We can thus safely discard any intimations that the Romantic Satanists practiced Satanism in the stereotypical way in which it was conceived by centuries of attribution that had preceded them, and which still is the most common association with the term today—that is, by staging sinister rites for the veneration of the devil of preferably nocturnal and obscene nature. This, however, by no means exhausts the possibilities of our inquiry. As I have already stated in the introduction and in the previous chapter, I do not think we need to limit the religious to ritual or collective actions only. If we apply our slightly adjusted version of Bellah's definition to Romantic Satanism—religion being a set of symbolic forms and acts that relate man to what he thinks to be the ultimate conditions of his existence—it seems quite valid to consider the mythical poetic projects we studied in the preceding sections as *religious ventures*. It has become quite clear in the previous pages, I hope, that the Romantic Satanists strove to express conceptions about ultimate grounds of being and a general order of existence in their major "Satanist" works. They were also, sometimes quite consciously, staking claims on what had formerly been considered the territory of the church. It is true that they may not always have termed their creative construction of myths and meaning as religious themselves—Byron and Shelley would certainly not have felt inclined to do so. But when we apply our own understanding of the term, there is ample reason to consider its application valid. In the mythic works we have analyzed, Satan, or other mythological figures traditionally associated or identified with him, clearly serves as a dominant or at least important symbol to express man's relations to what are perceived to be his ultimate conditions of existence. It is inadequate to contest that these appearances of Satan were merely a matter of literature. Literature *was* a matter of religion for the Romantic Satanists, the place where they gave symbolic form to their deepest convictions. I think thus that we might be justified to describe these utterances as forms of bona fide religious Satanism.

Nevertheless I want to complicate this picture right away. Even though I hold the conclusions above to be valid, I still do not think we can speak of the Romantic Satanists as religious Satanists. Bellah had a reason to define religion as a "*set* of symbolic forms and acts which relate man to the ultimate conditions of his existence." This implies a certain consistency in practice or perception, a life stance that informs one's life in significant ways. Although such a consistent life stance might certainly have been present among the

Romantic Satanists, it did not necessarily involve the figure of Satan. In their work, the metaphoric meaning of the Romantic Satan could and would be expressed by other mythological figures, such as the Wandering Jew, Prometheus, or Frankenstein's monster.[245] And when Satan makes his appearance, his presence in different works by the same author often has widely divergent and even contradictory significances.

When considered individually, even the icons of Romantic Satanism often turn out to be not *that* Satanist at all. This is very obvious with Byron, whose Lucifer is, as we have seen, open to different, less panegyric interpretations. Byron made it quite clear, moreover, that Satan, albeit symbolizing certain abstract human tendencies in *Cain*, was not his primary object of identification. Already in his earlier play *Manfred*, the eponymous protagonist proudly rejects all mediation by organized religion, but also refuses to bow before "Arimanes" (who is quite clearly an avatar of the Christian Satan via Goethe's *Faust*) or any of his mortal or spiritual servants ("my past power/Was purchased by no compact with thy crew").[246] Cain likewise declines to bend his knee to deity or devil.[247] Given the probability that we can consider both Manfred and Cain as alter egos of their author, as well as the fact that Byron wrote *Cain* in reaction to allegations about his preference for the "worser half" of dualism, we can regard these passages as a clear rejection of the epithet of Satanist.

A similar conspicuous lack of consistent Satanism can be found with Victor Hugo. In *Fin de Satan*, the fallen angel was already an ambivalent symbol: in the rest of Hugo's work, he uses the devil as he pleases, as representative of evil or of man's better strivings.[248] Nor do we find an exclusive deployment of the Satan trope with Shelley. In *Queen Mab*, the legendary figure of the Wandering Jew has much the same role as the Romantic Satan. In *Prometheus Unbound*, Shelley abandoned the fallen angel for the morally less ambiguous character of Prometheus, whom he judged to be "a more poetical character than Satan, because, in addition to courage, and majesty, and firm and patient opposition to omnipotent force, he is susceptible of being described as exempt from the taints of ambition, envy, revenge, and a desire for personal aggrandisement, which, in the hero of *Paradise Lost*, interfere with the interest."[249]

Even greater ambiguity we find with Blake. *Marriage of Heaven and Hell* provides us with theological somersaults that even now may surprise because of their daring. Blake's subsequent work, however, at first sight seems to retract many of the work's paradoxical statements about the diabolic. A careful reader may have noted that *Marriage of Heaven and Hell* only speaks of devils and hell, never of Satan. In other poems and prophecies by Blake, Satan appears in his more or less traditional role of representative of evil and misfortune. Blake would not be Blake, however, if he would not radically redefine this evil. In *Milton*, for instance, Satan is first equated with "Newton's Pantocrator, weaving the Woof of Locke"; the fact that he is also called "Eternal Death" suggests that he might also be identified as the "devourer" of *The Marriage of Heaven and Hell*.[250] Reproached by more spiritual powers, *Milton* recounts, this Satan set himself up as deity, "drawing out his infernal scroll/Of Moral laws and cruel punishments upon the clouds of Jehovah/To pervert the Divine voice in its entrance to the earth." As a consequence, he grows "Opake," blocking the infinite and the eternal from view by his darkness.[251]

The devil stands here for the same things that Milton's Jehovah symbolized in *Marriage of Heaven and Hell*: first, "Newtonian" philosophy, and, second, the "Mathematic Holiness" and "Cruel Goodnesses" of the institutional churches, whose adherents "in his synagogues worship Satan under the Unutterable Name."[252] In the last plates of the poem, moreover, this Satan is identified as a specter and equated with Negation, which is the "Reasoning Power in Man."[253] While Jehovah is still an ambiguous lower divinity in *Milton* (he is described as a leper at one time[254]), in *The Ghost of Abel*, the reversion (or re-reversion) seems complete, with Jehovah representing the Imagination/the Eternal/the supernatural and Satan appearing as the accuser demanding human blood. At the end of the short play, he is sent to eternal death by the deity, "even till Satan Self-subdu'd/Put off Satan."[255] It might have been this Satan that Blake reported to have met on the staircase of his house during the last years of his life, a creature with large eyes like burning coals and long teeth and claws that was described by him as "the gothic fiend of our legends—the true devil."[256]

The absence of a consistent and consequential employment of the Satan symbol in and outside their work is the most important reason, in my opinion, that prevents us from categorizing the Romantic Satanists as religious Satanists. They were simply "not all that." Going back to our earlier point, I would rather say that some of the *works* of the Romantic Satanists present us with *moments* of religious Satanism. With still much ambivalence in Byron's *Cain* and Hugo's *Fin de Satan*, quite evidently in Shelley's *Laon and Cythna* and Blake's *Marriage of Heaven and Hell*, and to varying degrees in other Satanist works of these authors or of less well-known Romantic Satanists, Satan functions as a symbol expressing man's relations to the ultimate and as an object of identification, imitation, and veneration. Even though none of these authors, as far as our sources show, implemented these instances of religious creativity into a full-fledged Satanist religion, we can still say that these works confront us with a new, modern form of religious Satanism in embryo. In that sense, and in that sense only, Romantic Satanism can indeed be called a religious Satanism.

As with early modern Satanism featured in the preceding chapter, we might describe the emergence of this embryonic Satanism as a process of identification. Yet this was not so much an identification with the old medieval and early modern stereotype of the Satanist. In a later section, we will signal some Romantic utterances that indicate a faint tendency in this direction, but none of these were of decisive significance for the emergence of Romantic Satanism. Of more importance were the assertions of diabolic allegiance that were sometimes directed against the Romantic Satanists themselves by their contemporaries. We have already seen how the attribution of Satanism to some of the Romantic Satanists by conservative critics (amply documented by Schock) may have prompted them to a kind of parodying identification. (Byron is a case in point.) In fact, as we have also noted, the creation of our hermeneutic category of Romantic Satanism originates with these allegations by conservative critics. But we can also take into account the much broader demonization of the partisans of radical change and the values of the Western Revolution that occurred in the wake of the French Revolution and would continue throughout the nineteenth century. The deflection or reflection of this attribution was certainly an important creative spark for the conflagration of Romantic Satanism, working in tandem, and in mutual enhancement, with an autonomous discovery of Satan as an adequate and provocative symbol to express discontent with the old conceptions regarding the social and cosmic order. The oppressive presence in past and present of dominant forms of Christianity was an important motivating factor in this.

In brief, if we can speak of identification here, it is not so much with an earlier stereo-type of the Satanist, but rather with the symbolic character of Satan himself. Despite the difference in voices that we encounter in the major texts of Romantic Satanism, this is a clear common denominator. This fact may not be an insignificant coincidence. I would rather postulate that it marks an essential point in which Romantic Satanism departs from the marginal Satanism of earlier centuries and becomes a manifestation as well as start-ing point of something fundamentally new and different. Charles Taylor designated the life stance that came to characterize post-Christian worldviews in the West as "exclusive humanism"—a life stance in which humanity forms the ultimate horizon and anchor point for understanding the universe—while Northrop Frye described the Romantic myth as "the form in which the Romantic poet expresses the recovery, for man, of what he formerly ascribed to gods, heroes, or the forces of nature."[257] These broader historical characteriza-tions do fit well with the Romantic myths we have examined, and also with the role they ascribe to Satan. In essence, the fallen angel almost always serves as an expression for the human, for humanity as a whole, for the portion of humanity that strives for emancipa-tion, or for a certain faculty that is common to all human beings. Thus Blake, in *Marriage of Heaven and Hell*, uses the diabolic as an expression of Desire, Poetic Genius, and the Imagination, all essentially features that "reside in the human breast."[258] Shelley, in the tra-dition of Godwin, makes Satan a symbol for the struggle of humanity to free itself from political and ideological oppression. With Byron, Lucifer becomes the manifestation of the human drive for knowledge, but also for the human tendency to the ideal and transcen-dent, which we might designate with the term imagination as well, at least in the sense the Romantics used this word. Hugo's Satan, in conclusion, is a microcosm of humanity again, showing the (projected) history of humankind from the darkness of material oppression toward the realm of freedom and love.

This does not mean that the myths and worldviews of the Romantic Satanists were always limited to the purely human. Blake's idea of the imagination obtains genuinely cos-mic dimensions, with every object in the natural world containing its own "Genius." Yet, as he explains quite clearly in a text from 1809, "These Gods are visions of eternal attributes, or divine names, which, when erected into gods, become destructive to humanity. They ought to be servants, and not the masters of man, or of society."[259] Much the same might be said about Shelley's Serpent-Spirit in *Laon and Cythna* and Hugo's Satan in *Fin de Satan*. The cosmic drama they describe fundamentally unfolds itself in human history or in the human psyche. "God only acts and is in existing beings or men," Blake had already remarked in *The Marriage of Heaven and Hell*.[260] Hence he could conclude that worshipping the divine meant "honouring His gifts in other men each according to their Genius." Or, as he more succinctly phrased it in a later work: "Thou art a Man: God is no more: Thy own Humanity learn to adore."[261] We can state with some confidence that Blake was speaking here for the other Romantic Satanists as well.

Ces nouveautés, toutes, ont été Satan. Nul progrès qui ne fût son crime.

JULES MICHELET, *La Sorcière*

3

Satan in Nineteenth-Century Counterculture

ALTHOUGH THE ROMANTIC Satanists may not have been Satanists in the religious sense, this does not diminish the historical significance of their reinvention of Satan. Whatever their personal convictions or intentions, the later perception and reception of their work was to prove decisive, I would like to argue, for the emergence of new attitudes toward Satan in (certain sections of) Western culture. We can now determine the character of this influence with more precision. In three crucial ways, I believe, Romantic Satanism contributed to the later rise of modern religious Satanism.

1. They mark the first historical appearance in Western civilization of an influential cultural current that positively revaluated Satan. Their radical reappraisals of the fallen angel remained available as a potential source of inspiration in later times through their works—Byron's and Shelley's writings were widely accessible from early on; Hugo's *Fin de Satan* and Blake's works would be rediscovered in the final decades of the nineteenth century—but also sent ripples of influence through Western culture that would be transmitted into the twentieth century.

2. They show a new, post-Christian, and post-Enlightenment way of dealing with myth and meaning, rooted in a revolutionary rethinking of human creativity and human imagination as a source for the religious truth. This allowed for a resurrection and reconstruction of Satan as a cosmic symbol with which modern man could sympathize and even identify.

3. Romantic Satanism exerted a decisive influence on the shape of the rehabilitated Satan that would continue to haunt nineteenth-century counterculture and eventually emerge in modern religious Satanism. By revaluating certain traditional features of the Christian Satan, the Romantic Satanists brought together a number of elements that would be passed on into later thinking about the devil.

SEX, SCIENCE, AND LIBERTY

In the previous chapter, we have amply (perhaps too amply) discussed the first two points. To introduce this chapter, I will shortly discuss the third point. The three most important elements that would be combined in the new nineteenth-century Satan, I propose, can be summarized in shorthand as *sex, science*, and *liberty*.[1]

By now, it would be tedious to mention once more the importance of the association with *liberty* that Romantic Satanism had connected to Satan. We can see this element return with all Romantic Satanists. In traditional Christian mythology, Satan's fall had been associated with proud, unlawful insurrection against divine authority. Giving new meaning to this old theme, the Romantic Satanists transformed the fallen angel into a noble champion of political and individual freedom against arbitrary power. From a political perspective, as we have seen, the nineteenth-century poets singing paeans to Satan were almost invariably "Leftist" or "Radical," combining a progressive belief in social and political reform with strongly anti-Christian or anticlerical attitudes. The devil, in the most important of their new myths, became strongly associated with the emancipating and liberating tendencies of the Western Revolution.

A second, and perhaps more surprising feature connected with Satan that appears with Romantic Satanism was his association with *science*. "Science" in this context could take on a variety of meanings, including scientific and technical progress, "modern" critical thought, and "reason," but also the secret, esoteric knowledge of magic, or combinations of some of these elements. Ever since Satan's identification with the Serpent of Genesis, the lure of forbidden knowledge had been one of his classical attributes in Christian cosmology. In a nineteenth century that would see the birth of a scientism with sometimes plainly religious overtones, the search for knowledge could hardly be considered evil any longer. Thus Satan, in his aspect of Lucifer the light-bringer, became a paragon of those pursuing scientific inquiry and critical thinking regardless of the boundaries set by faith or tradition. "Science, and her sister Poesy,/Shall clothe in light the fields and cities of the free!" was how Shelley described the coming reign of the Serpent/Lucifer/Liberty in *Laon and Cythna*.[2] Byron's *Cain*, however, is the most eloquent testimony of this tendency. "Knowledge is good, And life is good, and how can both be evil?" wonders Cain; and it is Lucifer who discloses to him the knowledge of the stars and of other worlds past and present.[3] (That Byron, on closer reading, might not be all that lyrical about Lucifer's spirit of inquiry was something that tended to be forgotten in the reception of his play.)[4]

Finally, a third complex of meaning linked Satan with Earth, nature, and "the flesh," particularly in its manifestations of *passionate love* and *sex*. Already from the time of the apocryphal story of the Watcher Angels, the fallen angels had been brought into connection with lust, temptation, and the "works of the flesh." This "pornification" of Satan found ample continuation in later Christian lore and probably reached its apogee in the demonological fantasies of the early modern era.[5] In this respect as well, Romantic Satanism implemented a reversal of appraisal. The Romantics accorded an almost divine status to passionate love, which transcended human and godly laws; the Romantic Satanists, moreover, mostly supported notions about free love and female liberation of one kind of another. If all this was the territory of Satan, the Dark Angel might be preferable to the stern, lawgiving god of Christianity.

This reversal of sympathy is almost ubiquitous in Romantic Satanism; it can be detected in Blake's *Marriage of Heaven and Hell*, in the work of Shelley, in the beautiful lines from Alfred de Vigny's *Eloa* that we already quoted, in Byron's *Heaven and Hell*, and with a host of other authors. We should be careful, however, of rashly projecting contemporary attitudes toward "carnality" onto early nineteenth-century authors like the Romantic Satanists. A strong trait of neo-Platonism permeated Romanticism. While "Sin" was considered by Blake as an invention of "Mathematical Morality," his attitude toward nature and the body was fraught with ambivalence: on the one hand, it is the way in which the Eternal Imagination expresses itself; on the other hand, it is a mere trapping or even impediment of the true reality of imaginary forms. Hugo's *Fin de Satan* can be read as an account of the man's fall into materiality and his subsequent return to the spiritual essence of love from which he emanated. Byron's Lucifer even expresses open disdain for the corporal in *Cain* and suggests that it is only man's spirit and his faculty to conceive the ideal that makes him stand out among his fellow animals.[6] It is only among later authors that this ambivalence shifts into a full-blown rehabilitation of the body.

Despite these ambiguities, we can see clear preludes to a more profound identification of Satan with nature and carnality in some of the authors we discussed. Vigny's Satan, for instance, presents himself as the voice of the natural world in *Eloa*:

La Nature, attentive aux lois de mon empire,
M'accueille avec amour, m'écoute et me respire;
Je redeviens son âme, et pour mes doux projets
Du fond des éléments j'évoque mes sujets.[7]

[Nature, listening to the laws of my reign,
Receives me lovingly, hears me, makes me her breath;
I become its soul again, and for my sweet designs
Evoke my subjects from deep within the elements.]

A few years earlier, Shelley had expressed himself in much the same way about the presence of the Serpent-Spirit in *Laon and Cythna*:

the tempest-shaken wood,
The waves, the fountains, and the hush of night—
These were his voice, and well I understood
His smile divine, when the calm sea was bright
With silent stars, and Heaven was breathless with delight.[8]

The Satanic connection with sex and carnality gained further complexity because of Satan's historic association with the pagan gods and spirits of the natural world. This theme was already prefigured by Shelley in *On the Devil, and Devils* (ca. 1820), a witty essay enclosed in one of his notebooks that would only be published decades after his death. Commenting upon the devil's historic link with the "Antient [*sic*] Gods of the Woods," the English poet went on to suggest a stark contrast between the guiltless mirth of the pagans and Christian hypocrisy:

> The Sylvans & Fauns with their leaders the Great Pan were most poetical personages, & were connected in the imagination of the Pagans with all that could enliven & delight. They were supposed to be innocent beings not greatly different in habits & manners from the shepherds & herdsmen of which they were the patron saints. But the Xtians contrived to turn the wrecks of the Greek mythology as well as the little they understood of their philosophy to purposes of deformity & falsehood.[9]

The threefold association of the Dark Angel with sex, science, and liberty, already hesitantly present among the Romantic Satanists, would increasingly manifest itself with other authors in the century that followed. One only has to read Gisouè Carducci's *Inno a Satana* (1863)—more on that later—or Anatole France's delightful *La révolte des Anges* (1914) to see these three elements appear again and again.[10] Potentially, Satan could thus become a universal earth god that functioned as a positive mirror image of the negatively perceived god of Christian tradition. Thus the Romantic Satanists, although they never established a form of religious Satanism themselves, already provided all the necessary preliminaries for such a religious Satanism to arise. For the first time, Satan was seen not as the embodiment of evil, but as a positive force heralding the liberation of body and mind. After this fundamental reversion was made, the only thing needed, one could say, was somebody to give this idea religious bedding.

In the next sections, we will follow the legacy of the Romantic Satanists through nineteenth-century (counter)culture. Three cultural domains present themselves as particularly interesting for further examination: political ideology, historical reflections on earlier "Satanisms," and occultism and other forms of alternative religiosity. These fields of investigation not only present themselves when we browse through existing scholarly literature, but also flow more or less logically from the questions and answers that we have formulated above. Earlier, we presented the Christian invention of the Satanist stereotype as the origin of the concept of Satanism. Consequently, it might be of interest to see how the Romantic identification with Satan influenced ideas about earlier "Satanists." The paramount importance of the political context for the emergence of Romantic Satanism more than justifies a further exploration of this field. And last but not least we are still on the lookout for possible cases of genuine religious Satanism: and the place we are most likely to find these would evidently be the burgeoning domain of nineteenth-century alternative religiosity.[11]

SATAN THE ANARCHIST

Politics, as we have seen, had been the matrix of the nineteenth-century resurrection of Satan, and his role as symbolic representative of values of the Western Revolution like liberation and emancipation had been essential in this process. This connection between Satan and revolution is probably nowhere more eloquently illustrated than on the Place de la Bastille in Paris, where the French revolutionary élan is honored by an immense brass column that was erected after the July Revolution of 1830. It is topped by a gilded statue four meters high that was designed by Auguste Dumont and is officially called the "Génie de la Liberté." Anyone familiar with the nineteenth-century iconography of Satan, however, immediately will recognize yet another avatar of Lucifer, the angel of light and liberty, in this figure of a nude winged youth with a star shining above his head and a flaming torch in his hand.[12]

Given this widespread celebration of the devil as arch-revolutionary, we should not be unduly surprised to encounter the Romantic Satan among real-life revolutionaries as well. For the most vivid echoes of the Romantic fascination with Satan, we have to direct our attention to anarchism, that most radical and most individualistic of Leftist political philosophies.[13] One of the most interesting personalities in this regard is Pierre-Joseph Proudhon (1809–1865), the godfather of French anarchism. Proudhon is impossible to describe in a few phrases and seems to have embodied most of the contradictions of his century within one person. He came from a humble, rural background; his family had been so poor that he had been sent to school in wooden shoes, much to his schoolboy embarrassment. Despite this fact, the combination of unsophisticated piety and resolute republicanism that his mother had displayed would always remain an ideal shimmering before Proudhon's eyes. During his youth, he had even planned to become a Catholic apologist, and he had spent his days as a printing apprentice preparing a lavish in-quarto Bible, furnished with extensive annotations that he compiled himself.

All this radically changed after his conversion to the cause of anarchism. In 1832, when the Restoration fervor had ushered in the July Revolution, he wrote the following in his private notebook:

CLERICAL INFLUENCE

		Human Dignity
Incompatible with	{	Civil Liberty
		Economy

Delenda Carthago.[14]

This concise remark already set the theme that Proudhon would pursue for the rest of his revolutionary career. In 1846, he received a ten-year prison sentence for the publication of his *Système des contradictions économiques, ou philosophie de la misère* ("A System of Economic Contradictions, or the Philosophy of Misery"), a work purportedly on economics but doubling up in rather awkward fashion as a treatise on the existence of the divinity. Here we can encounter much of the familiar music we already heard with Romantic Satanists like Shelley and Hugo. "And I, I say," wrote Proudhon, for instance, "that the first duty of an intelligent and free man is to drive away ceaselessly the idea of God from his mind and his conscience. Because God, when he exists, is in his essence hostile to our nature, and in no way do we progress from his authority. We attain our knowledge and science despite of him, our well-being despite of him, our society despite of him; each of our progressions is a victory in which we crush Divinity."[15] This diatribe against the "lying spirit" and "tyrant of Prometheus" is continued with one of the outbursts that would gain Proudhon renown, his famous declaration that God is evil: "The faults from which we ask forgiveness, it is you who has made us commit them; the temptation from which we conjure you to deliver us, it is you who has set them against us; and the satan who besieges us, that satan, that is you. . . . God is hypocrisy and deception; God is tyranny and misery; God is evil. . . . God, back off! Because delivered from fear and having become wise, I swear today, my hand outstretched against the heavens, that you are nothing more than the hangman of my reason, the ghost of my conscience."[16]

With the old god declared tyrant, Satan cannot be far away. The archangel would make a spectacular appearance on the pages of Proudhon's chef d'œuvre, *De la Justice dans la Révolution et dans l'Église* ("On Justice in Revolution and Church"), published in 1858. In this behemoth-like work, dedicated to Monsignor Mathieu, the bishop of Besançon, Proudhon addresses virtually every social and political question of his days, interspersing his political theorizing with nostalgic reminiscences about his boyhood years. The book centers, however, around the topic that was most dear to his heart: the "clerical question," and matters concerning religion and church in general. Proudhon highlights the "betrayal" of the Revolution by the Church, as well as the destruction (in words that have a remarkably modern feel about them) of the healthy relationship man originally was supposed to have had with his environment—"the Christian sirocco, passing through our souls, has dissicated them."[17] Above all, however, it is the curbing of liberty brought about by historical Christianity that incenses the anarchist Proudhon. "Oh! I understand, Monsignor," he exclaims at the end of the second volume (addressing once again the bishop of Besançon), "that you do not love liberty, that you have never loved her."

> Liberty, who you cannot deny without destroying yourself, who you cannot affirm without destroying yourself as well, you fear her like the Sphinx feared Œdipus: when she will arrive, the Church will be exposed: Christianity is no more than an episode in the mythology of the human species. Liberty, symbolized in the history of Original Sin, is your Antichrist; Liberty, for you, is the devil.
>
> Come to me, Satan, come to me, you who are calumnated by priests and kings, that I may embrace you, that I may close you to my bossom! I have known you since long, and you know me as well. Your works, o blessed one of my heart, are not always beautiful or good; but they alone give meaning to the universe and prevent it from becoming absurd. What would justice be without you? An instinct. Reason? A habit. Man? An animal. Only you animate and fecondate our labor; you ennoble wealth; you serve as an excuse for authority; you give the seal to virtue. Don't give up hope yet, great outlaw! I have nothing but my pen to put at your service; but she is worth a million ballots.[18]

While Proudhon had already exorcised the old Christian god as the satan (with small *s*) in *Philosophie de la misère*, here the reversal is completed, and Satan (with capital *S*) provides the ultimate meaning of human existence.

It is probably hardly necessary to point out, as many critics have already done, that Proudhon's exclamation is not to be interpreted as a creedal statement of religious Satanism.[19] By now, it might be clear that the French anarchist was much given to grand outcries and less to sober philosophy: one of the things that attracted the scorn of Marx, who, with his typical wry humor, reacted to *Philosophie de la misère* with a publication entitled *The Misery of Philosophy*.[20] Proudhon's Satan is nothing more or less than Liberty, as the context of the text makes abundantly clear. Earlier, at the end of the first volume of *De la Justice dans la Révolution et dans l'Église*, he had addressed Death in a similar vein, and in much the same way at the end of the third volume, Proudhon grandiloquently offers to receive the Roman Catholic sacraments from Mathieu himself—provided the Church adopted revolutionary principles first.

This is not to say, however, that Proudhon's work is devoid of religiosity, even when it is of a religiosity of its own peculiar kind. "Proudhon is no atheist, he is an enemy of God," the bishop of Besançon is said to have remarked when he was confronted with the fierce book that was dedicated to him.[21] This comment seems remarkably apt to me. When one reads his writings, it is obvious that Proudhon never ceased to struggle with his own religious inclinations. The anguish that can be experienced when saying one's farewell to faith is well expressed in a passage from a booklet he wrote on Jesus, where he elaborates upon his axiom "God is evil": "Because of this decisive prescription, which saves his dignity, man undoubtedly loses something. He loses his immortal hopes; he loses his relation with the infinite that gave such ample satisfaction to his pride and to his most intimate consciousness. He sacrifices his own eternity, in order to be something for one moment, in order to affirm himself."[22] Satan was just a way station in this lifelong confrontation with religion, and probably not a very significant one. In *De la Justice dans la Révolution et dans l'Église*, Proudhon attempted to resolve his inner conflicts with a highly original proposal: the deification of the principle of Justice. This was not altogether devoid of inner logic. Philosophers and poets had been placing the deity in the dock for more than a century now; it was almost logical to take the next step and recognize that the one thing that superseded the deity was thus the idea of justice itself.[23] Although it may be doubted whether this newly deified Justice was ever more than a paper god to Proudhon, it may be recounted here as a fitting illustration of the spirit of the times that, in the eyes of the French anarchist, the French Revolution had been the most perfect manifestation of this deity, while in another passage, he proceeded to identify this divine justice with "Humanity," that other prominent god of nineteenth-century thinking.[24]

Proudhon, it may be remarked, probably was not altogether oblivious to these subsurface currents in his own thinking. Toward the end of *De la Justice dans la Révolution et dans l'Église*, he described himself as "every bit as religious" as the Roman Catholic bishop he addresses.[25] Such sentiments would have been far removed from the mind of Mikhail Bakunin (1814–1876), the exiled Russian nobleman who would manage to turn up on almost every barricade of revolutionary Europe in the nineteenth century. Insurgent by profession, anarchist by vocation, Bakunin was a convinced materialist, allowing no room for the existence of a deity.[26] "God being master, man is the slave," he summarized his anarchist stance in two crisp sentences: "If God is, man is a slave; now, man can and must be free; then, God does not exist."[27] Just like Proudhon, however, Bakunin proved unable to resist the temptation of the Romantic Satan. In *God and the State*, a fragment he wrote on the eve of the Paris Commune of 1871, Bakunin retells the story of Genesis from an anarchist point of view:

> Jehovah, who of all the good gods adored by men was certainly the most jealous, the most vain, the most ferocious, the most unjust, the most bloodthirsty, the most

despotic, and the most hostile to human dignity and liberty . . . expressly forbade them from touching the tree of knowledge. He wished, therefore, that man, destitute of all understanding of himself, should remain an eternal beast, ever on all-fours before the eternal God, his creator and his master. But here steps in Satan, the eternal rebel, the first freethinker and the emancipator of worlds. He makes man ashamed of his bestial ignorance and obedience; he emancipates him, stamps upon his brow the seal of liberty and humanity, in urging him to disobey and eat of the fruit of knowledge.[28]

Of course, Bakunin was quick to point out the "fabulous portion of this myth" and move on to its essence: the emancipation of Man, who "has begun his distinctively human history and development by an act of disobedience and science—that is, by *rebellion* and by *thought*." It is this, "*the power to think* and *the desire to rebel*," that makes humans human.[29] Or, as Bakunin put it, "Man, a wild beast, cousin of the gorilla, . . . has gone out from animal slavery, and passing through divine slavery, a temporary condition between his animality and his humanity, he is now marching on to the conquest and realization of human liberty."[30] Here again, Satan functions as the guardian angel of liberty and as the symbolic incorporation of a humanity struggling to be free.

It is almost impossible to trace the exact lines of influence by which the Satanic theme reached these anarchist thinkers. Theoretically, Proudhon could have picked up his ideas on Satan from William Godwin, but it is more probable that he derived them from the writings of the Satanic School, with which he was obviously familiar.[31] Bakunin did certainly read Proudhon (whom he deeply despised), but he, too, could have stumbled upon the revolutionary Satan in many ways. Satan simply seemed to be in the air at this time. By the middle of the century, he had become a familiar topos that could be picked from the shelf at will by radical or freethinking writers. Romantic Satanism will have been the most important source from which they derived their utterances. The interplay between literature and ideology, however, was mutual. As we saw earlier, Godwin's exposé of anarchist ideology had provided one of the links in the chain of textual and personal influences that had engendered Romantic Satanism. In a way, we have described a nice full circle here, in which an isolated fragment from an anarchist philosopher managed to strike a spark into literature, and literature in its turn managed to leave behind Satan's claw marks in the writings of the later anarchist tradition.

During the nineteenth century, minor anarchist writers like Elisée Reclus and Paul Lafargue would occasionally echo Proudhon's and Bakunin's rhetorical appeals to the devil.[32] Similar motives may have inspired the radical communard and feminist activist Paule Minck (1839–1901) to name her child "Lucifer-Blanqui-Vercingetorix-Révolution" and the American women's rights' activist Moses Hartman (1830–1910) to name his periodical *Lucifer the Light-Bearer*.[33] Additional appearances of the Leftist Satan occurred among Swedish socialists during the late nineteenth and early twentieth centuries.[34] Not much of this minor Left-wing tradition seems to have survived into the twentieth century and the postideological world of today. Faint traces may be discerned in the dogmatic interpretation of Milton's Satan as "cosmic revolutionary" that was de rigeur in Soviet literary studies, and in the "over-the-shoulder acknowledgment" to Lucifer as "first radical known to man" that graces the first pages of Saul Alinsky's *Rules for Radicals* (1971), a classic of American Left-wing activism that provided inspiration to the future American president Barack Obama.[35]

(RE)CONSTRUCTING HISTORICAL SATANISM

Paradoxically enough, the influence of Romantic Satanism on the perception of the West's religious past would prove to have a more tenacious afterlife. Although it may be true that identification with earlier attributed images of Satanism had not noticeably affected the rise of Romantic Satanism, this certainly did not preclude an influence the other way around. Good and bad had changed sides, and this inevitably affected the writing of history, in particular regarding those historical groups to whom Satanism had been attributed in earlier times. In this respect, too, the belles lettres led the way. Shelley had already planned to picture a heretic group of serpent-worshipping Gnostics as an ideal society in his unfinished novel *The Assassins*, and the French Romantic Alphonse Esquiros had described medieval and early modern magic as a precursor for the French Revolution in his picturesque fiction *Le magicien* (1837).[36] In 1842, the French writer George Sand did the same for the medieval Luciferians in her immensely popular novel *Consuelo*. Sand (1804–1876), now mostly remembered as the lover of the young Chopin (among others), was a devoted follower of the socialist humanism of the French philosopher Pierre Leroux; the influence of the latter's ideas is also manifest in *Consuelo*. Written in typical nineteenth-century feuilleton style, it is not easy to sum up the meandering plotline of this work in a few lines. The main story revolves around the fictitious eighteenth-century opera singer Consuelo. Arriving at a Bohemian castle to be a music teacher, she is introduced to Albert, the mysterious young heir of the noble family living there. Albert is commonly considered mad or possessed by his relations because he identifies himself with the Hussite heretics of yore—and this is where it gets interesting. Sand clearly sees the Hussite rebellion as a counterpart to the Revolution in her native France; she also mixes the Hussites with another set of medieval heretics, the Lollards, one of the many groups accused of devil worship in the Middle Ages.[37] What is more, a small remnant of the Hussite movement turns out to be still extant in the countryside surrounding the castle, hailing each other with the Satanist greeting "May he to whom injustice has been done, salute you" (referring, of course, to Satan).[38]

Albert also belongs to this group. The Satanist Hussites, however, are anything but evil fiends lurking in the shadows, as Consuelo finds out after she manages to penetrate Albert's underground hide-about. "A mysterious and extraordinary sect dreamt, with many others, to rehabilitate the flesh," he explains to her. "She wanted to sanction love, equality, universal communality, all the elements of happiness. This was a righteous and sacred idea, whatever the abuses and excesses that occured."[39] Shortly after this, Satan himself appears to Consuelo in a vision, "grand, pale and beautiful," and tells her that he has been tragically misunderstood. "I am not the demon, I am the archangel of legitimate revolt and the patron of the great struggles. Like Christ, I am the God of the poor, the weak, and the oppressed. . . . O people! Don't you recognize him who has spoken to you in the secrecy of your heart since you have existed, he who has given you solace in all your distress, telling you: seek happiness, don't give up on it! You have a right to happiness: demand it, and you will have it!"[40]

Consuelo was conceived by Sand as a deliberate alternative history from a Leftist point of view. It was especially meant to counter antirevolutionary conspiracy theories that had been circulating in conservative circles since the events of 1789. These purported that the

Revolution had been the result of an evil plot by anti-Christian forces dating back to the Manicheans through a long line of heretic groups and secret societies. (We will return to these theories in more detail in later chapters.) In *La Comtesse de Rudolstadt* (the sequel to *Consuelo*, with even more twisted and improbable plotlines), this conspiracy turns out to exist indeed, as Consuelo is introduced to a secret society of "Invisibles," whom even a superficially educated reader will easily recognize as the Illuminati. With Sand, however, their secret venture is wholly dedicated to the doing of justice. "*Liberty, Brotherhood, Equality*: that is the mysterious and profound formula of the work of the Invisible Ones."[41] Their route through history is followed through to the French Revolution, which the reader is to understand as the true culmination point of Sand's story.

The new reading of European religious history propounded in works like *Consuelo* also penetrated into the works of professional historians. Its deepest imprint would be left in the historiography of witchcraft. The eighteenth-century Enlightenment had generally considered early modern witchcraft as a construct by the Church and the Inquisition, with no basis whatsoever in reality. In contrast to this view, a few late eighteenth and early nineteenth-century authors had raised the intriguing hypothesis that witchcraft might have been a surviving nucleus of pagan cults. In most cases, they had pursued a reactionary agenda with this suggestion. After all, if there *had* been real witchcraft, the authorities had been right to defend society against this danger.[42] Their hypothesis, however, was adapted and given a completely new twist by the French historian Jules Michelet (1798–1874) in his groundbreaking book *La Sorcière* ("The Sorceress"). First published in 1862, this work can be regarded as the most prominent manifestation of the new, postrevolutionary Satan in nineteenth-century historiography.

Like Victor Hugo, whom he befriended, Michelet had started out as a royalist with a Romantic longing for the Middle Ages, and like Victor Hugo, he had gradually drifted into the radical and republican camp.[43] Two things would be of special importance for Michelet's development: his awakening to a Romantic way to practice history and his experience of the July Revolution of 1830. The first provided him with a theoretical framework in which to write history in a revolutionary and mythological way: the idea of "humanity creating itself" from then on informed Michelet's activities as a historian in the broadest sense of the word.[44] The second would prove a watershed in Michelet's political stance. "During those memorable days a great light appeared," he would write in retrospective, "And I perceived France."[45] In his *Introduction à l'histoire universelle* (1831), which he had composed "on the burning pavements of Paris" during the summer of 1830, he expounded a conception of the history of civilization as an ongoing process of human liberation. "With the world began a war which will end only with the world: the war of man against nature, of spirit against matter, of liberty against fatality. History is nothing other than the record of this interminable struggle."[46]

This new outlook also changed his perception of Christianity. In his royalist days, he had described the medieval Church as the embodiment par excellence of the people, and the Christian faith as an essential evolutionary step in humanity's development toward the ideal. Now, he began to grow more critical of the Christian religion, initially envisioning its transformation along humanist lines and, eventually, its complete removal.[47] Satan's face began to change accordingly. In Michelet's personal diary, he occasionally equated the fallen angel with Liberty and with the figure of Prometheus as early as 1825. In *Introduction à l'histoire universelle*, he stated: "The heroic principle of the world, Liberty, for long confused and confounded with fatality under the name of *Satan*, has finally appeared under her true name."[48] As with most other Romantics, these sentiments did not refrain him from maintaining a positive appraisal of Jesus, whose Passion in reality is the plight of the oppressed.[49] (The many similarities we can detect here with Victor Hugo's ideas in *Fin de Satan* will hardly have been a coincidence.)

Michelet's growing radicalism eventually estranged him from the academic establishment. When he refused to sign a declaration of loyalty to Napoleon III, he lost his position at the Collège de France and at the national archives. After his dismissal, he continued to work as an independent historian, rewriting the volumes of his *Histoire de la France* into one great panegyric of progress and revolution, with the French people as its central character. In 1849, moreover, he married his second wife, Athénaïs Mialaret, and this would set Michelet on the track that would eventually result in *La Sorcière*. His first marriage had not been very happy, but with the much younger Athénaïs, the veteran historian at last experienced marital bliss. He became interested in nature, in human physiology (particularly of the female body), in the social position of women, and in the physical processes of love and digestion. These new interests led to new writings, some of which were rather unusual for a sixty-year-old historian. In 1860, for example, he began a lesbian erotic novel entitled *Sylvine, mémoires d'une femme de chambre* ("Sylvine, Memoirs of a Chambermaid") and a biography of his wife's maiden years, *Mémoires d'une jeune fille honnête* ("Memoirs of an Honest Young Girl")—both of which his young wife dissuaded him from publishing.[50]

In the history of witchcraft, Michelet found a subject that allowed him to place his new discoveries in life on a historical canvas. In 1837, Michelet had still described witchcraft as the "disgusting abortion of vanquished old religions." In 1840, this was changed to the more neutral "left-over of vanquished old religions."[51] *La Sorcière* would take this process a step further and expound a completely new theory on the origins of historical witchcraft. Initially, Michelet related in the book, the witches' Sabbath indeed had been nothing but a "frivolous relict of paganism . . . an innocent carnival of serfs" that had survived the coming of "anti-natural" Christianity.[52] Only when the misery of the serfs reached unprecedented heights and issued in the great rural rebellions of the later Middle Ages, had the Sabbath, properly speaking, come into being.[53] This Sabbath functioned as a rallying point against the oppression by the Church and by feudalism, obtaining a more and more explicitly anti-Christian character. "Human brotherhood, defiance towards the Christian heaven, denatured cult of divine nature—that is the meaning of the *Black Mass*."[54]

Women had served as initiators of this new development, Michelet argued. Taking a decidedly feminist turn, he pictured how medieval woman in her misery found solace with the genii of the house: remnants of the friendly pagan gods of yore who helped her with her chores and transmitted the knowledge of the old ways. During the upheavals of the thirteenth century, and only then, these homestead spirits finally evolved into Satan, the "great serf Revolt, *him to whom injustice has been done*, the old Outlaw."[55]

Michelet's description of the cult of Satan is of singular interest. In *La Sorcière*, the celebrations of the Sabbath are led by a female high priest, the "fiancée of the Devil," a woman with the beauty of sorrow and a flood of serpentlike black curls, "I mean a torrent of black, indomitable hair."[56] During the apogee of the Sabbath, a priapic statue is unveiled, and the black-curled priestess mounts this. "The wooden god receives her like Pan and Priapus in the past had done. In accordance to pagan custom, she gives herself to him, seats herself over him for a moment, like the *Delphica* over the tripod of Apollo. Thus she receives breath, soul, life, simulated fecundity."[57] After this, an offering is made, with "Woman herself" serving as an altar. "On her loins, a demon officiated, said the Credo, made the offering. . . . Grain was given to the *Spirit of Earth* who made the wheat grow. Birds were released (undoubtedly from the bossom of the woman) to carry to the *God of Liberty* the sighs and the wishes of the serfs."[58] In a note, the historian adds that this "charming offering" seemed to be specific for France—through all his ideological wanderings, Michelet would never cease to be a fervent French nationalist.

Modern historians mostly adopt an ironic view on the qualities of *La Sorcière* as serious, factual history. Although it features a fairly extensive bibliography (unusual for the time), it might be better to see the book as a deliberate countermyth, an attempt to uncover an antihistory that had remained hidden or unnoticed for centuries. It is also at times a hardly veiled pornographic novel. A hostile critic described Michelet's book as a deification of the flesh, "almost a provocation to debauchery," and even one of his disciples compared the work to a cantharid.[59] Not surprisingly, *La Sorcière* was almost immediately placed on the Roman Index.[60] By then, the censors of Napoleon III had also stepped in and forbidden the sale of the book, eliciting letters of support from Victor Hugo and George Sand.[61]

The authorities were keenly aware that something more than mere immorality was at stake, as is shown by a comment in an internal government report about Michelet's publication: "Depicting in some way God as evil and the Demon as the renewer of life, imputing the moral and material miseries of man and woman during the Middle Ages to one of the main sources of modern civilisation, to Christianity: that is an idea that already contains its own refutation."[62] Of course, this was exactly the point *La Sorcière* wanted to make. Despite the copious references the book contains, it is clear that Michelet's work in this regard was not inspired by a calm new look at the sources. In fact, it is perfectly valid to consider *La Sorcière* as another example of Romantic Satanism. At least, this is where Michelet's inspiration must have come from. One of the few contemporary works explicitly mentioned in his text is George Sand's *Consuelo*. Although Michelet objected to Sand's ideas about reconciliation between Christ and Satan (which are, by the way, slightly misrepresented by him), it is unmistakable that he was highly indebted to Sand for his treatment of "him to whom injustice has been done."[63]

Even setting aside Sand's obvious influence, all the classic themes of Romantic Satanism can be seen to reappear in *La Sorcière*. To start with, the political significance of Michelet's medieval cult of the "great serf Revolt" is hard to miss. "Under the vague shadow of Satan, the people did venerate nothing else but the people," Michelet commented.[64] His efforts here amount to little more than reading the nineteenth-century revolutionary Satan into medieval history. Also very prominent in Michelet is the connection between Satan and the reappraisal of nature, especially in its sexual aspects. One of the most salient features of the medieval cult of Satan is for Michelet "the rehabilitation of the womb; . . . that worshipped womb thrice holy from which man eternally is born and reborn."[65] Medieval Satanism to him was one great revolt against the "anti-nature" of Christianity. To conclude the list, the Satanic association with science makes its appearance as well. In an ingenious way, Michelet connects the folk medicine of the witch with the rise of the medical profession and the empiricism of modern science. Science has always been revolt, argues Michelet; magic, medicine, astrology, biology, "all . . . have been Satan."[66] It is only after discerning this political, ideological, and spiritual agenda that we can understand why *La Sorcière* ends with a grand vision of coming cosmic unity, in which Michelet envisions the final triumph of science and the reunion of Satan with God, of the "Fairy-Woman" with the "Medicine-Man," and of humanity with nature.[67] "The Anti-Natural will fade away, and the day is not far away anymore on which her fortunate eclipse will bring a new day to the world."[68]

Although the influence of his literary precursors is hard to deny, we should take care not to dispose of Michelet as a mere epigone altogether. He deserves credit for being the first modern author to actually design a cult for Satan, placed in the misty medieval past as it may be. The elements of which he assembled this tableau of Satanist ritual were derived from widely different times and sources. In the first place, of course, early modern concepts about Satanist witchcraft were reworked and reinterpreted by him into a new picture. The mounting of the priapic statue, on the other hand, is evidently based on similar rituals in Antiquity, while the application of the female body as an altar must have been inspired by the practices of Voisin and consorts during the Affair of the Poisons. At the time Michelet wrote *La Sorcière*, the original documents concerning the latter event were still unpublished. But Michelet had probably been in contact with Ravaisson, the archivist who shortly was to include them in his monumental collection of Bastille archives.[69] Michelet is rather vague, it must be said, about the question of how a ritual located by him in the High Middle Ages could suddenly resurface in late seventeenth-century Paris. Neither does he explain why his female altar is positioned *face down*, with her loins serving as an offering place, while the women in the Voisin affair had most certainly had *their* clandestine Eucharist celebrated above their "thrice holy" wombs. For this remarkable choice of posture, one suspects, Michelet must have consulted a different source, albeit a rather nonacademic one: namely the indecent scenes from the work of De Sade already cited in our first intermezzo. (The Marquis de Sade, of course, had had his own, rather practical reasons for preferring this reversal.)[70]

There is one other curious element of Michelet's reinvention of medieval Satanism that might be worth relating because of the curious consequences it would have. In a note at the end of *La Sorcière*, Michelet had hinted that the witch cult might not have disappeared completely after the end of the Middle Ages, but could well have survived into the present time in the remoter parts of the countryside.[71] Already in 1899, this hint was picked up by the American folklorist Charles Godfrey Leland, with the publication of *Aradia, or the Gospel of the Witches*. According to Leland, this work presented "a veritable Gospel of the Witches, apparently of extreme antiquity, embodying the belief in a strange counter-religion which had held its own from pre-historic times to the present day." The "gospel," he recounted, had been delivered to him in manuscript form by a wandering Italian wise woman called Maddalena.[72] It told how Aradia (Herodias), daughter of Lucifer, god of light, and of Diana, goddess of darkness, was sent to Earth in human form to help the poor and oppressed by teaching them the art of sorcery. Through this art, they would be able to strike back against their oppressors.[73] Before she departed again, Aradia had instructed her followers to convene with every full moon in a lonely part of the woods in order to hold a sort of alternative Supper of the Lord and receive further instruction in the art of witchcraft.

> And ye shall all be freed from slavery,
> And so ye shall be free in everything;
> And as the sign that ye are truly free,
> Ye shall be naked in your rites, both men
> And women: this shall last until
> The last of your oppressors shall be dead.[74]

This celebration, of course, is the Witches' Sabbath, for which these instructions are given: "And thus it shall be done: all shall sit down to the supper all naked, men and women, and, the feast over, they shall dance, sing, make music, and then love in the darkness, with all lights extinguished; for it is the Spirit of *Diana* who extinguishes them, and so they will dance and make music in her praise."[75]

The salient resemblances of all this to Michelet's picture of medieval witchcraft are hard to miss. They were pointed out in passing by Leland himself, ironically enough as proof that the text of his "gospel" conformed to the historical realities of witchcraft. New was only the fact, he declared, that he had uncovered the original scripture of the witch cult, which was presented to him partly in the original (mangled) Italian and partly in English translation, supplemented with fragments from his own folkloristic researches.[76] Moreover, Leland maintained that the "Old Religion" was still alive as "a fragmentary secret society or sect" in the Italian countryside, where entire villages could be found in which people were "completely heathen."[77] Like its rival, Roman Catholicism, however, the ancient faith would quickly be reduced to oblivion by the relentless onset of modernity. "A few more years of newspapers and bicycles (Heaven knows what it will be when flying-machines appear!) will probably cause an evanishment of all."[78] Leland furthermore disclosed that the traditional nude banquets of Aradia were "not much, if at all, kept up by the now few and far between old or young witches." With his tongue firmly in cheek, he added that such practices were nevertheless not altogether uncommon among the "*roués, viveurs*, and fast women of Florence and Milan." "They are indeed far from being unknown in any of the great cities of the world. A few years ago a Sunday newspaper in an American city published a detailed account of them in the 'dance-houses' of the town, declaring that they were of very frequent occurrence, which was further verified to me by men familiar with them."[79]

SATAN IN NINETEENTH-CENTURY OCCULTISM

For Left-wing ideologists, Satan had primarily been a rhetorical tool to spice up their antireligious agitation, while the Satanist fantasies of Sand, Michelet, and Leland had been projected upon the distant past or its supposed relics in picturesque rural areas. For possible instances of *actual* Satanism provoked by the new Romantic attitude toward the devil, we have to venture into the colorful landscape of alternative religiosity that took on an increasing presence in nineteenth-century society.[80] The most popular manifestation of this new field of religious expression during the nineteenth century was without doubt spiritism: establishing contact with the dead by way of séances with mediums or by turning tables. Of course, the practice of consulting the dead—the original form of necromancy— was not at all an innovation of the nineteenth century, but something as old as the hills. It was rediscovered by the general public after the Fox sisters, three teenage girls in America, had started to communicate with a dead traveler by way of knocking sounds in 1848. They became celebrities, and the publicity surrounding them brought on a wave of séance making and spirit rapping that soon crossed the ocean to conquer the salons of Europe—with Victor Hugo and his circle among its first practitioners, as we have noted. Invoking the dead was now suddenly something one could do in civilized society, instead of in the backyards of rustic soothsayers.

The rapid onset of spiritualism was not coincidental. It came like a godsend at a time when many people were drifting away from Christianity but did not want to do without the solace of the transcendental and the prospect of life after death. In itself, spiritism was not necessarily anti-Christian. In the discrepancy of everyday practice, the spirits could take on every political and religious color. In at least one instance, a man was converted to the belief in the triune deity by the spirits, while Victor Hugo had been encouraged by messages from Moses and Jesus to write his long poem on Satan.[81] By its more systematic propagators, however, spiritism was often presented as a more democratic and a more scientific alternative to the Christian faith and, what was more important, also as a more *humane* one. There was no hell and no judging deity in spiritualism. The beloved departed lived on in an undefined but usually not unpleasant spiritual sphere; the godhead was mostly perceived in friendly pan(en)theistic terms.

Consequently, there was little need for Satan as well. While spiritist theology sometimes acknowledged the existence of minor malevolent spiritual beings (usually the wandering spirits of evildoers who had to be brought to repent), it had no room for the Christian devil. The Fox sisters still had anxiously asked if they were not exchanging knocks with "Mr. Splitfoot" during their earliest sessions, but their interlocutor had confidently replied that such was not the case.[82] Of course, this did not stop some conservative Christian critics from decrying the hand of Satan in the new faith and alleging that its practitioners were really communicating with demons, much as their precursors of centuries before had done with regard to necromancy.[83] Spiritists, however, were primarily interested in socializing with fellow human beings from beyond the grave, not in initiating contact with any evil entity of traditional religion.[84]

In the wake of the great rage of spiritualism, new, sophisticated forms of occultism arose. In common with spiritism, they promoted ways of transcendent knowledge that were presented as empirical or scientific findings, allowing access to spiritual power outside or alongside institutional Christianity. An important difference with spiritism, however, was the strong emphasis in occultism on "ancient traditions" (real or imagined) as a foundation for its teachings.[85]

One of the most important pioneers of this form of alternative religiosity was Éliphas Lévi (1810–1875), the great French theoretician of occultism, who, if not the actual inventor of the term "occultism," certainly was responsible for making it popular.[86] Lévi had been born as Alphonse-Louis Constant and had initially wanted to become a Roman Catholic priest. Enrolled in a strictly disciplined seminary, he had already taken vows as a deacon when he fell in love with one of his catechumens, a young girl "still almost a child."[87] This made him decide that he was not fit for priesthood and that priesthood was not a vocation that was fit for man. In the following years, he would continually drift in and out of the orbit of the Church, at one time staying as a guest in the restored Benedictine Abbey of Solesmes, at other times living in cheap lodgings in the more squalid parts of Paris, scraping together a meager living as a publicist, etcher, and painter of biblical scenes. Influenced by his reading of George Sand and the seventeenth-century mystic Jeanne Guyon, he began to tend toward a Christianity redefined along strongly panentheist lines, which he combined with radical Leftist views on social reform. His public endeavors in this respect would land him in jail twice.[88] Also during this period, he became amorously involved with a female teacher at the *pensionnat* where he was teaching, while at the same time exchanging tender letters with one of her pupils, an eighteen-year-old girl named Noémi Cadet. Although Constant's colleague became pregnant and eventually bore him a son, her pupil set the situation to her hand by climbing into his room one evening and staying the night. Her enraged father demanded marriage to avoid a scandal, and on July 13, 1846, Constant took the young girl for his wife.[89]

Given the radical circles he frequented, it would be surprising if we did not find any traces of the new, revolutionary concept of Satan with Constant. In a private poem he wrote to Cadet, the atmosphere of Romantic Satanism is already tangible:

Si tu veux être à moi, sois morte, sois damnée;
Sois sans parents, sans Dieu, sans loi, sans souvenir.
Quand je te dirai: viens, que ton orgueil affronte
Non la faim, non la mort; ce serait peu: la honte!
Et tu viendras, superbe enfant au cœur de fer,
Lever ton front vers Dieu du fond de notre enfer.

[If you want to be mine, be dead, be damned;
Be without parents, without God, without law, without past memories.
When I say to you: come, let your pride confront
Not hunger, not death; that would be a small thing: but shame!
And you will arrive, superb child with heart of steel,
To lift your head against God from the bottom of our hell.][90]

It was probably another woman, however, who introduced Constant to the Romantic Satan. In 1838, he had become acquainted with Flora Tristan (1803–1844), a woman of partly Peruvian descent who was active in France and England as a socialist and feminist agitator.[91] A great deal of the highly idiosyncratic, socialism-flavored theology that Constant propagated in his publications during these years almost certainly derived from her influence, including some of his more unusual ideas about Satan. To what extent he was indebted to Tristan remains an open question. While most of Lévi's biographers agree that she was an essential source of inspiration for him during this period, they also mention the strong ascendancy Constant had over this flamboyant woman, for whom he functioned as a sort of spiritual advisor.[92] The similar theologies they espoused can thus have been the result of their mutual interaction. Another problem is the fact that we only know about Tristan's theological ideas through one posthumous publication, a book that was completed and published by Constant. Although the latter declared that he had faithfully reproduced Tristan's ideas, it is without doubt that he changed and expanded the original text, at least in matters of style.[93] Because it is impossible for us to untie this intricate knot, I will treat the esoteric œuvre of Constant and Tristan as part of one evolving body of work here, giving a short chronological overview of their relevant publications and the notions they contain with regard to Satan.

A restyled devil makes its first appearance with Constant in his *Bible de la Liberté* ("The Bible of Liberty") from 1841, an esoteric and socialist rereading of the Bible that would earn him a prison term of eleven months.[94] During the same year, Constant expanded on the teachings of *La Bible de la Liberté* in two other publications, *Doctrines religieuses et sociales* and *L'assomption de la femme*. The three works are all characterized by similar radical visions of society and spirituality, featuring the familiar set of religious humanism, Communism, feminism, pantheism, anticlericalism, sexual liberation, French messianism, and religious universalism that we have already encountered in bits and pieces in works by earlier Romantic Satanists. Most remarkable, however, is the strong millennialism in which these books are drenched. Drawing on Roman Catholic speculations that date back at least to the heretic medieval mystic Joachim of Fiore, Constant predicted the arrival of the Age of the Holy Spirit in which mankind would be free and live in direct contact with the divine. This Age of the Holy Spirit was also going to be the Age of Woman. In the words of Constant:

> The six thousand years that our world has already lasted are the great week of divine creation.
>
> Christ has been the heavenly Adam who God has made in his image upon the sixth day.
>
> At this moment of time, this man is tired of being alone, and he has fallen into a profound lethargy.
>
> And God is going to draw the female from his side that has been opened by the lance; and this woman will be the mother of the living, and Heaven and Earth shall adore her.
>
> She will appear from the side of Christ, of whom she is already the mother; and she will become his bride, and their first kiss will have as its fruit a happiness that shall have no ending anymore.[95]

In the slightly incestuous variation on Joachim of Fiore that Constant propounded, the latter's theories were consistently reinterpreted from a viewpoint of humanism and Christian Communism, with the Son identified with the people: "Behold the second coming of Christ incarnated in humanity; behold the Man-People and God revealing himself."[96] In addition to this, we encounter a very Romantic Lucifer on the pages of *La Bible de la Liberté*. The ruler of darkness is presented as the Angel of Liberty, Light, and Science, a "generous spirit of revolt and noble pride."[97] Lucifer's revolt against the deity, Constant maintains, was a necessary act of freedom and love.[98] Elsewhere, this restyled Lucifer is contrasted with Satan, who is treated as a separate entity and retains his function as the representative of evil, although this evil is defined along new ideological lines:

> The spirit of evil is not Lucifer, the glorious rebel; it is Satan, the angel of domination and slavery.
>
> It is Satan who tempts the world, and it is Lucifer who saves it by raising it up against Satan!
>
> Satan is the father of law; Lucifer is the father of grace.
>
> Despotism is death; liberty is life.
>
> Despotism is the flesh; liberty is the spirit.
>
> Despotism is hell; liberty is heaven.[99]

The mythological potpourri that characterizes the book is given additional complexity in a chapter at the end, where Constant addresses the adherents of Islam, announcing that at the nearby end of times, Christ is going to marry "the most beautiful of *houris*: Holy Liberty," while earlier he equated this very same Liberty to the deity tout court, who was now sleeping but would soon awaken.[100]

In *La Mère de Dieu*, published in 1844, the same themes reappear, but with different mythological accents. As its title suggests, the star of this work is Mary, Mother of God. Even more peculiar than his earlier publications, the book purports to recount the vision of an angel experienced by Constant while in prison in 1841. This vision, he writes, inspired him to return to the fold of the Church; in accordance with this intention, the book is preceded by a notice in which Constant declares his "complete submission to the holy Catholic church," to whose judgments he surrenders his work.[101] Although containing much the same notions as his earlier works, the myth of Satan is reworked in a different way in *Mère de Dieu*. In his vision, Constant witnesses how "Satan the rebel" presents himself before Christ at the Last Judgment. The devil declares that he cannot surrender to the godhead because he cannot love, and he starts to battle with the heavenly hosts, every blow expressing a thought of revolt or desperation. Eventually, he defeats the angels and approaches the throne of Mary and Jesus, but the light of love they radiate renders him impotent. He kneels for Mary, transforms into a serpent, and lays his head at the feet of "Regenerated Eve": "and as soon as that delicate foot had touched his forehead, he closed his eyes and seemed to expire; a last sigh of fire escaped from his half-open jaws, and that flame took the form of a star that ascended and set itself on the right hand of Christ. Then a voice was heard from heaven that cried: Evil in its death has borne light; Satan has died and Lucifer is delivered."[102]

The reborn Morning Star is placed upon the forehead of Mary, and Mary and the "Man-God" (Christ) become the divine couple, with a new child to form a new trinity (or so it seems at least).[103] The Holy Mother next reveals that human progress will go on forever, in different shapes, and a utopian picture of a new, matriarchal society is given, in which, among other things, all women will be virgins and mothers at the same time, and if a man lives under their roof, he will be "nothing more in the eyes of the world than their Joseph and the guardian of their children."[104] (One cannot help to wonder what the ecclesiastical authorities may have thought of all this, but unfortunately enough, their official reaction seems not to have been left behind.)

Similar theological creativity may be found in *L'Emancipation de la Femme, ou le testament de la paria* ("The Emancipation of Woman, or the Testament of the Pariah"), the posthumous tome by Flora Tristan that appeared in 1846, "completed after her notes and published by A. Constant." Starting out with a bitter complaint about the social position of women and the poor, and especially of poor women, Tristan in this book gradually drifts into esoteric discourse. Although man may be superior in intelligence, she maintains, woman surpasses man in feeling, faith, and love, and therefore the coming Age of the Holy Spirit will be reigned by the maternal "genius" of woman. In order to attain this happy state, the male and female principles must come together. Intelligence must fuse with love, liberty with life. And the proper symbol for this new age is, somewhat surprisingly, not the traditional dove, but the light-bearing angel Lucifer. In Tristan's words:

> Lucifer, the angel of genius and science whom the superstitions of the Middle Ages have relegated to the throne of hell, now finally set free together with the human conscience, ascends in triumph towards heaven again, with his star on his forehead, and in his right hand the torch that will not be extinguished.
>
> The Holy Spirit, too, has now, like the Father and the Son, received a human form to be invoked in by men, and the symbolic dove has folded its white wings again.
>
> The spirit of intelligence and of love now must show itself to the world in the young and smiling features of Lucifer![105]

The resemblance of Tristan's portrait of the fallen angel with the Genius of Liberty at the Place de la Bastille is intentional, by the way: a "sacred instinct" has led the French people to erect this monument to the "young and glorious Lucifer."[106]

Apart from Satan, Christ also has a role to play in Tristan's scheme for the final days. But it is not the powerless Christ who is nailed to the cross; the radical feminist rather has need of a triumphant Christ. "I want the marriage of Christ with the bride of the Song of Songs. . . . I want to see him ascend to heaven in triumph again after shattering the gates of antique Tartaros, to free the beautiful angel Lucifer, the genius of light and liberty. Then Mary, the regenerated woman, will extend her arms to both of them and bury them under her caresses; the new Eve will pride herself upon the martial conquests of Jesus, her divine Abel, and she will weep when seeing the sweetness of Lucifer, Cain's angel, repentant and regenerated in his turn!"[107]

In his postscript to this incongruous feast of blurred symbolisms, Constant distances himself somewhat from his erstwhile mentor, who had thought of herself as the "female Messiah," he insinuates.[108] Her beliefs are not his anymore, he writes; he has changed. But Tristan has changed even more; she now is dead. To Constant, this fact seems the most eloquent rejoinder against the utopianisms of those that dream of attaining perfection on this Earth. Man's only hope, he continues, is Christ, "the man-God," and the true keeper of his legacy is the hierarchical Church, which will adopt "French ideas" soon, Constant foresees.

It must be said, however, that this reluctance regarding utopian speculation does not become apparent right away, because Constant's subsequent publication, *La dernière incarnation: Légendes évangéliques du XIXe siècle* ("The Last Incarnation: Evangelical

Legends of the Nineteenth Century"), once again is rich with dreams of millennialism. In this charming collection of stories, published in 1846, Constant attempts to "complement" the Gospels by describing a second coming of the "proletarian from Galilee" to nineteenth-century Europe. Most interesting for this study is the penultimate legend, in which Jesus—accompanied, of course, by his mother Mary—encounters Satan sitting on a rock near Calvary.[109] The fallen angel, bored with his work of petty corruption, makes a rather feeble attempt to tempt Jesus once again and criticizes the deity in terms that closely resemble the acrid monologues by Byron's Lucifer in *Cain*. Jesus, however, unmasks his remarks as mere human disfigurements of the divinity, and he rejoins the devil to become Lucifer again, "a star on your forehead and a torch in your hand." Moved by the love of Jesus and Mary, Satan sheds his one decisive tear and transforms into the angel of light again. Jesus, Mary, and Satan—who, incidentally, turn out to be one single spirit of "intelligence and love" and "liberty and life"—ascend to heaven together. Midway up, the gigantic form of Prometheus, freed from his vultures, also arises. "Thus the great divine and human symbols came together and greeted each other under the same heaven; after which they disappeared to make place for God himself who came to live among mankind forever."[110]

Even more explicit reminiscences of Tristan's ideas can be found in *Le Testament de la Liberté* from 1848. Immediately on page 1, Constant starts out with an alternative version of the fall of Satan that comes straight out of *L'Emancipation de la Femme*, with a few minor changes and some new material added. In this new myth, Lucifer is depicted as the original Intelligence that has sprung into being from the very breath of the creator's "Let there be light," created by the divine Word in order to express itself and be seen. The newly born angel of light and its divine maker next engage in the following dialogue:

- I will not be Servitude!
- Then you will be Grief, the uncreated voice spoke to him.
- I will be Liberty! answered the light.
- Pride will seduce you, continued the supreme voice; and you will give birth to Death.
- I need to struggle against Death to conquer Life, responded the created light.[111]

Lucifer subsequently descends to Earth, and in an undeniably original twist, Constant lets him become the mother (*sic*) of two daughters: Liberty, who springs from his forehead, and Poetry, who escapes with a sigh from his heart. While Liberty is hidden by Lucifer, his daughter Poetry may roam free. She remains close to her sister, however, and thus "youthful Poetry . . . will always serve as a guide for those who carry to the future that sacred depository [e.g., freedom] sent by the angel of Intelligence."[112] In the end, Love will come to liberate and marry Lucifer, and Liberty will be released to rejoin her sister Poetry: "Both will then cross the globe and submit the world through the magic of their beauty and the irresistible seduction of their voice."[113]

Although all this may strike the average reader as unintentionally verging on the comical, this digest of Constant's earliest works shows clearly how squarely his treatment of Satan is rooted in the tradition of Romantic Satanism—especially in its manifestation *à la française*, with its great love for reconciliation scenarios between deity and devil. One only has to point out the identification of Lucifer with Liberty (implicitly or explicitly linked to "the great, the holy, the sublime French revolution"), and his strong association with Intelligence, science, and poetry. That Constant, as an ordained deacon, continued to see himself as a Catholic does not change this basic fact. It may be evident, moreover, that we have to consider his Christianity as Blake's: a highly personal construct that did not necessarily comply with traditional dogma. Nor is Constant to be considered as merely epigenous in his Romantic Satanism: his creations, for one thing, might have been a source of inspiration for Victor Hugo's *Fin de Satan*, whose author was demonstrably familiar with Constant's work.[114]

A more complicated question concerns the exact spiritual status of Constant's texts. We have already seen the ambiguous and complicated relation of the major Romantic Satanists to myth. This ambiguity is also present with Constant, and in a more intense form. The tone of his works definitely gives the impression that they are doctrinal. This is especially true of *Mère de Dieu*, which is presented as a direct revelation by an angel, but it is present also in his other publications from this period. They are presented as expositions of theology or dogma, not as myths of identification that primarily serve to engage the reader on an imaginary psychological voyage. Yet at the same time, a relativist awareness of myth as a human creation is also visible with Constant. This tension becomes most evident in *La Dernière Incarnation*, a set of "new evangelic legends" that was unambiguously introduced as a fiction by Constant, but at the same time it does not differ in its presentation from his visionary works in any noticeably way. Jesus, Mary, and Satan are here clearly described as "symbolic forms," and heaven is "the region of the ideal" and "the spiritual world of poetry and vision"; Aeschylus, Moses, and John the Evangelist have all derived their inspiration from here.[115] In *Testament de la Liberté*, the Book of Revelation is likewise described as a glimpse into "the abstract regions of thought and poetry."[116] One may surmise that Constant's own latter-day visions in *Mère de Dieu* can also be interpreted along these lines: in apocalyptic times like these, he claims at the beginning of this book, "men of desire" are "easily visionary."

With Constant, we thus encounter a Romantic author formulating religious revelation in the apparent consciousness that he is doing so through his imagination. The idea that allows this to make sense, and forms another *traîte d'union* with the (other) Romantic Satanists, is the oneness of the divine and the human. This notion is present in almost all of Constant's works, and also in that of Tristan. God, in fact, is the "synthesis of humanity" for Constant. In accordance with humanity's stage in its march to progress, the ideas about the godhead change as well, moving closer and closer to the complete "incarnation" of the divine.[117] The Christian socialist poet showed he was acutely aware of the vital importance of religious concepts for social and political questions: in *Doctrines religieuses et sociales*, for instance, he argues that a transcendent idea of the divine will necessarily mirror itself in autocratic or oppressive forms of government. This music will by now sound familiar to the reader. Although we can assume he was unaware of the work of these English poets, Constant's project at this stage was basically the same as that of Blake and Shelley: changing the religious and ideological outlook of society by creatively reworking its old myths.

The 1850s brought a set of landmark changes to the life of Constant. Already during the 1840s, Constant had started to immerse himself in the "occult sciences." His interest in this subject had been awakened by books (particularly Knorr von Rosenroth's *Kabbala Denudata* from 1684) and by his acquaintance with the mathematician, visionary, and esoteric Józef Hoëne-Wroński (1776–1853).[118] An archetypical "mad scientist," Hoëne-Wroński is mainly remembered in occult literature for his "prognometer," an intricate machine that he claimed could foretell the future.[119] But what inspired Constant most about Wroński was probably the latter's claim to have found a mystic-mathematic "theory of everything."[120] References to a similar project of synthesis between science and faith start to appear in Constant's last two books of the 1840s and would turn out to be programmatic for his later occult publications.

In the same period, Constant gradually drifted away from his former political convictions, while on the personal plane, his young wife, Noémi, eloped with a befriended progressive publisher.[121] Abandoned, heartbroken, and poor, Alphonse-Louis Constant the Radical now became Éliphas Lévi the Magician. It was under this pen name that *Dogme et Rituel de la Haute Magie* ("Dogma and Ritual of High Magic," 1854–1856) was published, a book that would prove to be the cornerstone for modern ceremonial magic and leave a lasting imprint on occultism in general. Other works on magic and the Kabbalah would follow, among which especially *Histoire de la magie* ("The History of Magic," 1860) and *La Clef des grands mystères* ("The Key of the Great Mysteries," 1861) must be mentioned.

A different world of thought and a different tone of voice are found in these works. For one, references to the "religion" of socialism or Communism are conspicuously absent. Although Lévi probably retained his faith in the future "millennium" all his life (his last recorded words express his hopes for the advent of the Comforter), allusion to the coming Age of the Holy Spirit have been considerably toned down as well.[122] We will get to this aspect later on. Even more fundamental may be the wholly different way in which Constant (which we will call henceforth by his more famous pseudonym Lévi) proceeds to legitimize his philosophical and theological assertions. In contrast to his appeal to vision, poetry, and revelation in earlier works, and in contrast also to the otherworldly sources invoked by spiritism (with which he had experimented briefly), Lévi now claims to base his findings on science.[123] This science does not consist of physics or mathematics, but of the systematic examination and interpretation of the old religious and esoteric traditions of the world to rediscover their hidden meaning—the "key" to the great mysteries. *Dogme et rituel de la haute magie* and Lévi's other works occasionally contain indications for preparing and performing rituals, yet they are clearly not meant as practical manuals. Rather, they provide an exposition of an alternative view on the world, in which elements of Lévi's radical past, a new conservatism, and a human-centered, Romantic panentheism merge together uneasily with elements of older esoteric traditions. Nowhere does this become clearer than in Lévi's treatment of Satan.

Three, maybe four, different components can be distinguished in Lévi's representation of Satan. First, traces of the Romantic Satan remain present in *Dogme et rituel* and its sequels. Lévi was an avid recycler of his own texts, and, among other examples, the myth of origin of Lucifer we cited from *Le Testament de la Liberté* appears again in the pages of *Dogme et rituel de la haute magie*. Typically, Lévi now attributes this to a "Gnostic evangel" recently unearthed in the Orient "by a learned traveller among our friends."[124] Although he seems to range this myth among the errors of the "heresiarchs of the first centuries," in later works, he reconfirms his old Romantic conception of Lucifer as the angel of liberty and of intelligence.[125] These terms, however, have not the same exact meaning anymore, as we shall see presently.

With respect to the traditional concept of the devil as the supernatural representative of evil, Lévi is quite clear: "Satan as a supernatural personality and as a power does not exist."[126] Absolute evil can only exist as a negation and a nonentity: the idea that such an ontological void can take a personal, individual form is dismissed by Lévi as part "of the relicts of Manichaeism that still manifest themselves among our Christians time and again."[127] Intriguingly enough, this does not mean that this Satan has no presence in reality at all. "Within its circle of operation, every word creates what it affirms," argues Lévi elsewhere. Consequently, "he who affirms the devil creates or constructs the devil."[128] The traditional devil thus becomes "real" because he is made real in the imagination of its believers. "That black giant that extends his wings from the east to the west to hide the light from the world, that soul-devouring monster, that terrifying deity of ignorance and fear, in one word, the devil, is yet for an immense mass of children of all ages a terrible reality."[129]

Here we see reappear the Romantic idea of the human imagination as creator, albeit in a decidedly harmful application. Lévi was not afraid to apply this idea to biblical scripture as well. In *La Clef des grands mystères*, he gives a daring "occult" reading of Genesis in which the creation myth is retold as the story of the creation of the deity by man:

> Eternally the immensity of the heavens and the expansion of the earth have created in man the idea of God.
>
> But this idea remained indeterminate and vague, it was a mask of darkness over an immense phantom; and the spirit of man floated over these conceptions as over the face of the waters.
>
> Man then said: Let there be a supreme intelligence! And there was a supreme intelligence. And man saw this idea, that it was good; and he divided the spirit of light from the spirit of darkness. He called the spirit of light: God, and the spirit of darkness: the devil, and he created to himself a kingdom of good and a kingdom of evil. This was the first night.[130]

It therefore makes sense for Lévi to conclude that "the devil is nothing but the shadow of the phantom of God."[131] And because the image of the devil consists of all kind of debris from the "rebutted gods" of yore, it is only to be expected, he writes, "to see the god of our barbaric fathers become the devil of our more enlightened children."[132]

Alongside these two types of Satan, a third and completely novel definition of the devil appears in *Dogme et rituel de la haute magie* and Lévi's other works. On about every third page, Satan is presented as an impersonal cosmic force, a morally neutral "blind agency" that is indispensable for the preservation of a heterogeneous reality. "In nature, there exists a force that does not die," Lévi claims. "And that force incessantly transforms all beings in order to preserve them."[133] By identifying this "blind agency" as "astral light," Lévi was able to connect his older account of Lucifer as an angel of light created on the first day with his new idea of Satan as a morally neutral cosmic force of life.

This novel understanding of Satan seems to have been an original innovation of Lévi. We cannot delve into all the possible sources of inspiration for his invention. However, one deserves a brief mention.[134] In various works from the early decades of the nineteenth century, the French esoteric Fabre d'Olivet (1767–1825) had proposed a different reading of the Hebrew text of Genesis. His insights had prompted him to make a translation of Byron's *Cain* (the very first in the French language, as a matter of fact), accompanied by extensive notes in which he sought to refute the British poet's pernicious suggestions. One of the points on which D'Olivet disputed Byron was the nature of the Serpent of Paradise. A naïve and incorrect translation of the original Hebrew had been responsible for the appearance of this animal in the first books of Genesis, Fabre d'Olivet maintained. In reality, the Hebrew word that the authors of the Bible had used should be rendered more or less like "innate attraction." The Serpent thus was "not a distinct, independent being, as you [Byron] have painted Lucifer according to the system that Manes has lent from the Chaldeans and the Persians, but rather a central mobilizing force given to matter, a hidden energy, a yeast that acts in the inner deep of things and that God has placed in corporal nature to put the elements in motion."[135]

Lévi was familiar with D'Olivet's work and cites this theory in *Dogme et rituel de la haute magie*. But he goes on to criticize it, and his criticism is very revealing regarding the accents he wants to place. According to the "great keys of the Kabbalah" and the "symbolic letters of the Tarot," Lévi argues, the Hebrew word for serpent used in Genesis actually consists of two radicals—one signifying "the passive receiver and producer of forms," and the other "the force that produces mixtures." Especially the latter element is significant, because for Lévi, the cosmic force that is used by the deity to create the world is not only creative, but also destructive. "The terrible and just force that eternally destroys the abortions [of life] has been named, by the Hebrews: Samael; by the Orientals, Satan; and by the Latins, Lucifer."[136] This destructiveness does not make Satan evil. The process of regeneration "by burning" is the work of the divine, and the antagonism associated with Satan is an essential requirement for the existence of the world as we know it. "Satan" and "Michael" have a mutual need of each other, and it is their ongoing and perpetually undecided struggle that constitutes the universe. Lévi here extends the myth of origin he had recounted in *Le Testament de la Liberté* and that he did cite again as a "Gnostic evangel" in *Dogme et rituel de la haute magie*. In this myth, he had already depicted Satan as a kind of dialectic necessity, an indispensable counterforce without which the universe in all its multitude of forms cannot exist: "If the light was not repulsed by shadow, there would have been no visible forms. . . . The negation of the angel who, at his birth, refused to become a slave, established the equilibrium of the world, and the movement of the spheres began."[137]

This idea is greatly expanded in prominence in Lévi's magical works. "Equilibrium," balance, is over and over again the refrain in *Dogme et rituel de la haute magie* and also in its sequel *Histoire de la magie*.[138] Further elucidation of this concept is provided by Lévi's illustrations for *Dogme et rituel de la haute magie*, particularly the plate he designed for the frontispiece of the second volume: the famous "he-goat of the Sabbath" who is also the Baphomet of the Templars and at the same time the "pantheist and magic image of the absolute."[139] This sinister-looking figure is in fact an intricate symbol for the unity of contraries, inspired, as Lévi readily acknowledges, by the representation from the Tarot that is called "very frankly and very naïvely: THE DEVIL."[140] However, he immediately goes on to say that it is in reality not at all the devil, but rather the great god Pan, "the god of our modern schools of philosophy, the god of the theurgists of the Alexandrian school and of today's neoplatonic mystics, the god of Lamartine and of Mr. Victor Cousin, the god of Spinoza and of Plato, the god of the ancient schools of Gnosticism; the Christ himself of the dissident priest."[141] This would suggest that Lévi's image is a representation of the all-encompassing Absolute of which Satan forms only a part: but elsewhere, Lévi identifies this "hieroglyphic sign of Baphomet" with his cosmic "universal agency"—which is also called Satan in *Dogme et rituel de la haute magie*. Lévi comes very close here to declaring Satan the pantheist godhead; in fact, he does title his Baphomet "pan-theos" somewhere.[142]

Given this muddle of terms, it is not surprising some readers read dark things in Lévi's works. But although it's perfectly possible to distill passages from Lévi that lead to the conclusion that he was just a stepping stone away from religious Satanism, it would be far too rash to categorize him thus. His sometimes rather careless indulgence in contradictions admitted, the totality of his pages clearly bespeak his belief in a higher deity *above* the pantheist Baphomet, although this deity tends to remain a rather vague, abstract entity. This is only to be expected in a system of Kabbalist magic, of course, because this supreme godhead will correspond with the *Ein Sof* from the Kabbalah, the indescribable, totally transcendent original deity of whom all other manifestations of the divine (like Lévi's Baphomet/Lucifer) are emanations.

In addition, Lévi thought of himself as a *Catholic* magician. The French esoteric, who retained an ambiguous relationship with the Church all of his life, considered Christianity as one of the dual pillars of his Kabbalistic temple of wisdom.[143] His books were for an important part an apology against those Christian polemicists who indiscriminately considered all magic the work of the Evil One, as, for instance, his former mentors at the seminary had done. His line of defense in this respect was certainly daring. Magic, he claimed, was indeed only possible by the compliance of Satan. But this Satan was subsequently reinterpreted by Lévi in such a way that the meaning of this statement was fundamentally changed. In reality, Lévi maintained, his "High Magic" was not in opposition to Christianity at all: "far from it, we want to explain it and fulfil it."[144]

Just as in his earlier existence as Constant, it must be added, Lévi held very particular ideas about what the essence of Catholicism or Christianity amounted to. "The Christian-Catholic cult is a form of High Magic organised and regularised by symbolism and hierarchy," he once wrote to one of his pupils.[145] Lévi's true religion most certainly was that of "magism," perceived by him as an age-old philosophical and theological system embodying the core of all "respectable" great religions, including Christianity. This religious system, he claimed, united and encompassed religion, philosophy, and the empiricism of science and practical magic. "Our magic is at the same time a science and a perfect religion, that must not destroy or absorb, but regenerate and direct all opinions and all cults, by reconstituting the circle of the initiates in order to give wise and clear-sighted leaders to the blind masses."[146] With this idea, Lévi continued a long tradition of attempts to determine the hidden symbolic key behind or inside all religions, a project dating back to at least the eighteenth century. Because he believed he had discovered the key to what Christianity and its symbolism *really* was about, one suspects, he saw no bone in calling himself Catholic.[147]

Even if we put aside the question of his Christianity, however, Lévi would still have empathically denied that his practice of magic involved a veneration of the "blind agency" that he sometimes identified as Satan. Magic, at least the good, "white" magic Lévi propagated, was nothing else than the subduing of this Luciferian "agency of magic" by the magician, who, like the woman of biblical prophecy, must put his foot on the head of the serpent by utilizing his will and intelligence.[148] Lévi here echoes a line of apology that can already be found in some books of magic from the medieval and early modern period: the magician is actually subduing the spirits, not the other way around (see chapter 1). It is instructive, however, to point out the salient differences between these earlier practices and those propagated by Lévi. While the medieval and early modern necromancer claimed to be able to control the demons by enlisting the aid of the divine, be it by fasting, by uttering the divine names, or by using the power of the Host, Lévi's magician dominates the "agency of magic" solely by the power of his own will and intelligence. Rituals, even the most colorful ones, are only a means to concentrate the will of the magician. Consequently, the ancient mysteries of magic were nothing but a form of science. This is what makes Lévi's "magism" so eminently modern, notwithstanding all the "Christian" dogmas and "ancient" rituals he scavenged from old books or constructed himself.[149] That does not change the fact, however, that he presented his relation to the "cosmic force" of Lucifer as one of domination rather than veneration.

Meanwhile, Lévi did not deny the existence of a kind of magic that was truly evil and "Satanist" in the traditional sense of the word. Time and again, he contrasts his "white church" of "High Magic" with this "black church" of "Negromancers" and "Goetian magicians." His characterization of this black magic is not devoid, it must be said, of ambiguity and confusion of terms. It seems that there are three not mutually exclusive ways in which one can fall into this practice. First, if the magician does not succeed in retaining mastery over the vital force, he is mastered by it, leading to sensual inebriation, dementia, and destruction.[150] This is the case with both spiritist mediums and the adepts of black magic. Therefore, Lévi can write that "the devil gives himself to the magician and the sorcerer gives himself to the devil."[151] Second, all magic done for evil purposes is by definition black magic.[152] Because it is morally neutral, "indifferent in itself in some way," the "agency of magic," though created for good, can be made to serve for evil.[153] Third, and most interesting, there are those who explicitly invoke the "impossible idol" of Satan in his nonexistent shape of the god of evil.[154] This implies, Lévi argues in an ironic under-the-belt sting against conservative Roman Catholicism, that they "belong to the religion that admits a devil that is capable of creating and becoming a rival of God."[155] Because in magical operations the will of the practitioner ensures the impact of the ritual, as we have seen, the invocation of the devil can make this "pseudo-god" real for the invocator.[156] Thus, both the "black" magicians who seek to invoke the devil *and* the Christian polemicists who affirm his existence are involved in magic that *creates* the Evil One as a reality.[157]

Regarding the "criminal and insane assemblies" of the worshippers of this diabolic devil, Lévi repeats a good deal of the allegations that centuries of attribution had brought into circulation. He also added to the repertoire himself, and some of his inventions would enjoy a tenacious afterlife in folklore and pseudoscience. The idea of the "inverted" pentagram as a diabolic emblem, for instance, is first found in Éliphas Lévi: the two upward points, he claimed, signified the horns of the goat thrusting against heaven, while the "white" pentagram with two points down was a symbol for Christ.[158] With considerable sangfroid, Lévi did not hesitate to put this invention to polemic use: it was impossible, he asserted, that the Baphomet that was depicted in his book was "one of the fabulous images of Satan," for the pentagram on his forehead was pointing upward![159] (In fact, this was a piece of double daring, for the portrait of Baphomet in *Dogme et rituel* had been the product of Lévi's own creativity as well.)

This dual tradition of white and black magic was not a matter of mere theory for Lévi. In a distant echo of Sand's *Consuelo*, he maintained that his religion of magic had always had its adepts in secret, organized in invisible philanthropic societies. This was the background of the Witches' Sabbath, which came into being when the various mystery cults of paganism were driven underground by Christian persecution and subsequently amalgamated into one universal orthodoxy of magic (resembling somehow, one supposes, the great magical synthesis by Lévi himself). "In this manner, the mysteries of Isis, of the Eulisian Ceres, and of Bacchus united themselves to those of the good goddess and ancient druidism," Lévi recounted.[160] At the same time, however, Lévi also recognized the continuing reality of a counterconspiracy of black magic. Although no more than a "gathering of evildoers exploiting idiots and fools," this malevolent conspiracy degenerating the real Sabbath had its roots in Antiquity as well.[161] In a remark he did not elucidate, Lévi disclosed that this double line of hidden magic activity was not a thing of the past: "even today, there still exist secret and nocturnal assemblies where the rites of the old world were and are practiced, and of those assemblies, some have a religious nature and a social purpose, while the others consist of conspiracies and orgies."[162]

How did Éliphas Lévi the Magician relate to Alphonse Constant the Romantic Satanist? This question, which is of crucial importance for our study, can be answered in two ways: by emphasizing the continuity between the two personae of the French esotericist, or by underlining the differences between them. Starting with the continuity between Constant and his subsequent alter ego, it is evident that underneath the colorful varnish of magical lore and esoteric nomenclature, much of Lévi's older ideas remained. This is especially clear in his utterances regarding the divinity. *Dogme et rituel* and its sequels retain essentially the same panentheist and (for want of a better word) *humanist* god as his premagical works. In the first pages of *Dogme et rituel de la haute magie*, Lévi comments on the "esoteric" use of traditional theological terms and the "communication of idioms" that his magism allows. "Which also brings about that one can attribute to God the sufferings of man and to man the glories of God. In one word, the *communication of idioms* is the solidarity of divine and human nature in Jesus Christ; a solidarity in which name it is possible to say that God is man and that man is God."[163] This is, it must be noted, a perfectly "orthodox" idea. But in the context of the totality of Lévi's work, the notion it expresses is less than traditional. The

Romantic idea of the identity of god and man can be seen in more naked form in *La Clef des grands mystères*, where it appears without the camouflage of Roman Catholic Christology:

> Man is the form assumed by divine thought, and God is the ideal synthesis of human thought.
> Thus the Word of God is the revelator of man, and the Word of man is the revelator of God.
> Man is the God of the world, and God is the heavenly man.[164]

This understanding of the deity also underlies Lévi's theory about magic. Here ideas return that are at least affiliated with his earlier beliefs about poetry and vision. For Lévi, as we have seen, magic depended essentially on the power of will and intelligence. Primarily and specifically, this means asserting mastery over oneself—for the vitalizing force that sustains the universe is also the vitalizing force within man himself. "Before anything else, the Great Work is the creation of man by himself, that is to say: the full and complete conquest he makes of his faculties and his future; it is above all the perfect emancipation of his will, which assures him the total dominance over the Azoth and the domain of Magnetism, that is to say: full power over the universal agency of magic."[165] Yet it is not will and intelligence alone that allow us to do so, according to Lévi.

> Will and intelligence have as their auxiliary and instrument a faculty not sufficiently known, the power of which belongs exclusively to the domain of magic: I intend the imagination, which the Kabbalists call the *diaphanous* or the *translucent*.
> The imagination, in fact, is like the eye of the soul: it is in her that all forms make themselves visible and retain themselves, and it is through her that we see the reflections of the invisible world. She is the mirror of vision and the device of magic: it is through her that we heal diseases, that we influence the seasons, that we ward off death from the living and that we resuscitate the dead, because it is she who exalts our will and gives it grip on the universal agency.[166]

We see a familiar term return here, and we begin to understand how Levi's magic is linked to Romantic notions regarding the creative power of the imaginative artist in particular and of mankind in general. This is not to say that Lévi's ideas about imagination and will are necessarily a direct import from Romanticism. It is as probable that they derive partly from common, older sources—Paracelsus especially comes to mind, and he is indeed mentioned by Lévi on the subsequent pages.[167] But there is a clear affinity of concepts here that suggests why, for Lévi, the transition from Romantic poet to modern magician might not have been such a radical one. The magician is basically a Romantic poet in a new, slightly more exotic guise. The parallel might indeed not be too far-fetched. As the "universal agency" of magic is the same "natural and divine agency" (a.k.a. Lucifer, a.k.a. Baphomet, etc.) that serves as the "intermediary force" by which the deity creates and regenerates the world, the magician, by the application of his imagination, in fact assumes the role of the creator.[168] By logically combining the things Lévi wrote (a dubious exercise, I admit), one suspects that the magician could even, by expressing his "Word," create or give form to the deity. It is not surprising, in this light, that Lévi says elsewhere that the magician who takes a "sovereign empire" over his "inner phosphor" may gain his own immortality.[169] Blake would have agreed.

While we can discern a clear continuity here between Constant and Lévi, on another point the new apostle of magic plainly parted ways with his former self. We have already alluded to the unmistakably different political and ideological color of Lévi's works on magic. One of the places where this becomes visible, is, significantly, at the point where he discusses poetry in *Dogme et rituel de la haute magie*.[170] Being a poet is creating, Lévi writes; the deity himself was a poet when he created the world. But being a poet does not mean propounding falsehoods or dreams. "The poetry that does not accept the world as God has made it and seeks to invent another one is nothing but the delirium of spirits of darkness: it is this poetry that loves mystery and denies the progressions of the human intelligence."[171] This is the poetry of anarchism, the "personification of idealism without authority," "the impotent rage of Prometheus." The "poetry submitted to order," meanwhile, does not transcend the bounds of authority and reason: it "will march sometimes in front of science, sometimes in her traces, but always near to her."[172]

This is a different melody than we have encountered with the early Constant, and one that would have repulsed Blake, Shelley, and Byron. At the same time, we must not exaggerate or misunderstand this change. Lévi had not become a reactionary in the original sense of the word. The pages of his magical works are replete with assertions that suggest a continuing presence of many of the revolutionary and Romantic ideas of the old Constant: allusions to liberty and "fierce and audacious" intelligence, anticlerical utterances against the "Pharisees of all the synagogues and all the churches," assertions of the freedom of scientific inquiry, over and against the persecuting church of the past ("we no longer live, thanks to God, in the time of the inquisition and the stake"), and reappearances of messianic or millennialist concepts.[173] The context and meaning of these terms, however, have changed. "Liberty," for instance, can now be called "the guardian of duty"; Lucifer's conquest of Liberty will only bear fruit when he will use it "to submit himself to the eternal order" out of "voluntary obedience."[174] Lévi still prophesies the approach of a millennial era of harmony, but now this harmony consists of the embrace of liberty and authority (as well as science and religion) and is stripped of its Communist implications.[175]

Lévi's new attitude becomes very clear in his appraisal of the French Revolution, an unfailing litmus test for ideological positions during the nineteenth century. Yes, he declares in *Dogme et rituel*, the Revolution *was* a "divine experience," but *only* in the sense that it was a necessary excess leading to a new equilibrium, a "debauch of the prodigal son whose only future is a definitive return and a solemn feast in the house of the father."[176] The new *pris de position* of the Kabbalist magician can be summarized by the little catechism he published in *La Clef des grands mystères*:

Q: What is good?
R: Order.
Q: What is evil?
R: Disorder.
Q: What pleasure is permitted?
R: The enjoyment of order.[177]

What did prompt this conspicuous change in attitude? Biographers have suggested that the elopement of his wife had much to do with the emergence of the new Constant.[178] This is perfectly feasible: Lévi would not have been the only person whose wider outlook on life was fundamentally changed after a personal setback in his intimate life. One can imagine that the experience may have sorely diminished his enthusiasm for the feminist messianism propagated by Tristan and his own earlier publications. In the books he wrote as Éliphas Lévi, one sees indeed a very different attitude toward women and love. The harmful surrender of Adam to the "astral light," for instance, is depicted in terms of "erotic drunkenness"; physical love is described as "the most perverse of all fatal passions" and the "anarchist par excellence"; and at the end of *Dogme et rituel de la haute magie*, Lévi gives some rather amusing courtship tips that boil down to the fact that you have to play the devil or the indifferent to conquer the heart of woman.[179]

Still, I do not think that it was his unhappy marital experience that occasioned Constant/ Lévi's ideological paradigm shift. Noémi left him in the second half of 1853, and *Dogme et rituel* already started to roll from the printing press in the beginning of 1854; moreover, his first biographer explicitly attests that Lévi was already working on the book when his wife walked out on him. In my opinion, we have to trace Lévi's change of attitude to *political* developments: in particular, the political developments connected to the Revolution of 1848 and the years that immediately followed it.

The Revolution of 1848 had known two stages in France. In February, a Parisian uprising of the bourgeoisie and working classes had led to the flight of the French king and the establishment of a provisional government. After attempts to provide universal employment were abandoned, the Paris working classes took the streets again during the June Days, but this revolt was ruthlessly smashed by government troops. The sparse facts that we can glean from his biographers clearly indicate Lévi's enthusiasm for the initial phase of the Revolution. In February 1848, Constant was just six months out of prison after being condemned for publishing a pamphlet entitled *La Voix de la Famine* ("The Voice of Famine"), in which he had drawn attention to the appalling living conditions of the proletariat.[180] The new political climate brought about by the Revolution seems to have suited him well. Together with his editor Gallois and his boyhood friend Alphonse Esquiros (the author of *Le Magicien*), he launched a political club with a predominantly worker following. Furthermore, he attempted to present himself as a candidate for parliament with a program "of the most radical socialism," demanding an end to economic exploitation, complete freedom of thought, and liberty for "religion, love, and other legitimate enticements."[181]

The bloody events of the June Days ended all this. It appears that Constant narrowly escaped death himself: government troops apprehended a wine merchant under the impression that they were dealing with the socialist agitator; the poor man was summarily executed on the corner of a street.[182] Although this story, when true, implies that the authorities thought the future magician to be involved in the workers' insurrection, this impression does not seem to have been correct. Constant, who had always condemned violent action, seems to have been horrified with the development of things. It is probable that his political reorientation dates back to these events. We do not have a direct statement from Constant to prove this, but a strong clue can be found in a poem he published in the *Dictionnaire de littérature chrétienne* ("Dictionary of Christian Literature") from 1851. This publication, in fact, would be the last that he published under his own name. It had been commissioned by the ultra-catholic editor Jacques Paul Migne, the famed publisher of patristic and theological works—a fact that may not be deemed without significance itself. Typically, Constant profited from the occasion to include a copious amount of literary texts from his own hand as anonymous examples of Christian literature. One of these examples was a poem with the title "La chute de Lucifer" ("The Fall of Lucifer"), in which he recounted how God offers his beautiful daughter Liberty as a bride to his angels. Lucifer at once abducts her, but when he has taken her down to his infernal residence, he discovers that she has died. The enraged angel proceeds to promenade her corpse over the Earth, where the splendor of even her dead body incites the nations to revolution. The political application of the brief poem, hard to miss as it is, is made explicit by the last strophe:

O peuple, ô Lucifer! ton bras est impuissant,
Egaré par la haine et souillé dans la sang!
Ton épouse vivra, quand, déposant tes armes,
Dans tes yeux attendris tu sentiras des larmes;
Ton épouse vivra lorsque, libre en tout lieux,
Tu seras assez grand pour te soumettre à Dieu![183]

[O People, o Lucifer! Your arm is powerless,
Led astray by hate and defiled by blood!
Your bride shall live when, laying down your arms,
You will feel tears welling up in your softened eyes.
Your bride shall live when, free in every place,
You will be great enough to submit yourself to God!]

In appropriate mythological garb, this poem signals Constant's growing attachment to order, a word that would appear ever more frequently in his subsequent works on magic and that, incidentally, had also been the rallying cry of the conservative opposition during the events of 1848. Lévi's ardent admiration for both Napoleons, on whom his first magic manual contains some rather peculiar passages of panegyric, fits perfectly into this development.[184] In *Doctrines religieuses et sociales*, Constant had already praised Napoleon I, who as a tragic historic character had exerted a great attraction on many of the Romantics.[185] But there he had hailed the Corsican as a "Revolutionary Messiah." Now he lauded both Napoleons as messianic saviors because they had established a perfect balance between liberty and authority, "two contraries that are basically the same thing, because one cannot exist without the other."[186] This notion was less absurd than it may seem, because Louis Napoleon, for all his authoritarianism, had also espoused social-utopist and populist ideas, favoring direct democracy by plebiscite. Nor was Constant exceptional in his preferences: after Louis Napoleon had declared himself emperor, 90 percent of the French electorate expressed its approval of the new monarchy.[187]

Lévi's redefinition of Satan, which at first glance may seem a matter of obscure theological and esoteric theory, is actually quite consistent with this political background. As a vehicle for propagating radical change, Lévi now had no need for Satan anymore, and his new

Lucifer is in essence a symbol of status quo. Light and darkness, liberty and authority, spirit and matter, destruction and creation are all necessary constituents of the vitalizing universal force: they must balance, not replace each other. This puts Lévi's Baphomet in contrast to the redeemed Lucifer of earlier French Romantic Satanism, out of which he had grown, and who still made occasional appearances in *Dogme et rituel de la haute magie* and its sequels, uneasily combined with the French magician's new creation. The old Lucifer had been a temporary counterforce, antagonistic but emancipatory, which was to be reunited with the godhead into an ideal world. In Lévi's new concept of Satan, this Lucifer was so to say only one arm of Baphomet: to redeem the latter from his internal antagonism would cause the universe to stand still and autodestruct. Despite the fact that it preserved characteristics of the Romantic Satan—its pantheist nature, its association with intelligence (symbolized by the torch on his head) and with the material and the sexual (symbolized by the female breasts and the caducean in his lap)—this new image of Satan expressed a wholly different ideological agenda.

That this new ideological agenda was not simply a form of Catholic Reactionism is indicated by the distinctly unchristian ethos that sometimes shimmers through the pages of *Dogme et rituel de la haute magie*. Prompted by his Bonapartism and the emphasis he laid on willpower, the French master of magic formulated some remarkable ethical ideas, especially in his laudations for the Napoleons. "The man who does not succeed is always wrong," Lévi proclaimed in a "preliminary discourse" he added to the second edition of *Dogme et rituel*, "be it in literature, be it in morals, be it in politics. . . . And if we ascend into the eternal domain of dogma, two spirits could be found there once upon a time, each of them wanting divinity for himself alone: one of them succeeded, and it is he who is God; the other one failed, and became the demon!"[188] In Lévi's publications, to be sure, these serpentine whispers were drowned in choirs singing the praise of agape, duty, and devotion. But we will see this insinuating thread picked up at a later point.

Lévi's shadow would loom large over Western occultism and esotericism. This was not due to the institutional legacy he left behind. Although the "professor of magic" took on some (paying) pupils whom he instructed personally (mainly by custom-made correspondence courses), he never instituted an organized body of adherents to propagate his system of "magism." Perhaps he considered the Roman Catholic Church as the proper place to participate in the rituals of his universal religion. Rather, his fame among later occultists would be ensured by his books. Their influence is clearly discernible, for instance, in the doctrines of the Theosophical Society, one of the most important organizations within the spectrum of alternative religiosity in the later nineteenth century.

The dominant personality in the pioneering years of this esoteric movement was without doubt Madame H. P. Blavatsky (1831–1891), a woman of Russian descent who after much international wandering had settled down in New York to establish a new, "universal" religion.[189] Although she claimed to owe her enlightenment to mysterious Tibetan Masters, the impact of Éliphas Lévi upon her work is unmistakable.[190] This becomes especially apparent in her views on Satan. In her first major work, *Isis Unveiled* of 1877, a long chapter entitled "The Devil Myth" is dedicated to the mythological fallen angel. After disposing of the Christian Satan as the "prop and mainstay of sacerdotism," she goes on to paraphrase Lévi on the real nature of the devil as "an antagonistic blind force—the dark side of nature," a sort of primal energy "not *malum in se*, but only the Shadow of Light, so to say."[191] This line of thinking is continued in even more explicit Lévian terms in *The Secret Doctrine* (1888), Blavatsky's second book of esoteric teachings. Supposing a source of evil outside the all-encompassing divinity is an error, she argues here, "the first Karmic effect of abandoning a philosophical and logical Pantheism."[192] However, "as an 'adversary,' the opposing Power required by the equilibrium and harmony of things in Nature— like Shadow to throw off still brighter the Light, like Night to bring into greater *relief* the Day, and like cold to make one appreciate the more the comfort of heat—SATAN has ever existed."[193] Blavatsky showed herself keenly aware of the intricacies of Lévi's concept, for although the latter's "astral light" emanates from the absolute godhead, she maintains, it cannot be equated with the "Ain-Soph" or "Father-Æther." As a "Spirit of the earth," its soul is divine, but its body belongs to a lower, "infernal" plane, forming so to speak a "negative" reflection of the divinity in the dark waters of matter—"Demon est Deus Inversus."[194]

Theosophy also adopted the notion of Lucifer as bringer of light that had already made its hesitant appearance with the Romantic Satanists and had been prominently expounded on the pages of Lévi's earlier and later work. In Blavatsky's interpretation of Genesis, the myth of Lucifer and the Fallen Angels really signified the "hypostasizing" of divine beings into the material world to bring rationality and knowledge and thus make humans human.[195] Against this background, it becomes clear why one of the earliest Theosophical periodicals carried *Lucifer* as its title. Its front page depicted the Morning Angel as a seminude boy holding aloft the shining star of enlightenment: a short notice explained that Lucifer was "no profane or satanic title" but "the name of the pure, pale herald of daylight."[196]

For Blavatsky and many of her fellow Theosophists, the real evil was not Satan, but the hated "P.G.," the Personal God of monotheism. Or rather: the idea of the Personal God, as this godhead itself had no base in reality. Here Blavatsky diverged from Lévi the Christian magician, who might possibly have agreed with the gist of her ideas, given his strong panentheism, but never would have expressed himself in such crassly antagonistic terms on the doctrines of the "Catholic religion." Blavatsky's utterances, however, were perfectly in tune with the older anti-Christian tendencies current among Romantic Satanists like Shelley and Hugo. Volume II of *Isis Unveiled* already had been "in particular directed against theological Christianity, the chief opponent of free thought," although it contained "not one word against the pure teachings of Jesus."[197] In *The Secret Doctrine*, the roles of Satan and "the so-called Creator" were totally reversed. "Who the great 'Deceiver' really is, one can ascertain by searching for him *with open eyes* and an unprejudiced mind, in every old cosmogony and Scripture. It is the anthropomorphised *Demiurge*, the Creator of Heaven and Earth, when separated from the collective Hosts of his fellow-Creators, whom, so to speak, he represents and synthesizes. . . . Once upon a time, a philosophical symbol left to perverse human fancy; afterwards fashioned into a fiendish, deceiving, cunning, and jealous God."[198]

Eventually, Blavatsky would claim to have found the "philosophical and logical Pantheism" she was looking for in the religions of the East. Theosophical doctrine was gradually permeated with complicated Indian cosmogonies, and in 1878, Blavatsky *cum suis* sailed off to India to resettle in Adyar. This shift to the East, both spiritual and physical, was not greeted with enthusiasm by all members of the Theosophical Society. Prominent among the opponents of Easternization was Rudolf Steiner (1861–1925), head of the German branch of the Society and editor of a German Theosophical periodical that was called *Luzifer* as well (after 1903, it merged with the Vienna Theosophical bulletin and received the even more appropriate name *Lucifer Gnosis*).[199] In contrast with the autodidact Blavatsky, Steiner held a doctorate in philosophy, and he used the accompanying verbosity to emphasize the intrinsic value of the Western esoteric and spiritual legacy. When the Adyar leadership put forward a young Indian boy named Jiddhu Krishnamurti as the coming Great World Teacher, Steiner initiated a schism in the Theosophical ranks and founded a rival organization, which he dubbed the Anthroposophical Society.[200]

The European orientation of the Anthroposophical Society manifested itself in a renewed affinity with Christ and Christianity, although in a highly specific anthroposophist framework.[201] Satan, that other central mythological figure of Christianity, was also not forgotten. In the cosmology of Steiner, two different tendencies manifest themselves: that of Lucifer, which tends to spiritual and intellectual knowledge, and that of Ahriman, which represents the material, the physical, the mechanical, and even the financial.[202] (Steiner here adopted the Manichean view on Ahriman as presiding in matter, which had not been the case in original Zoroastrianism. Earlier, he had contrasted the "Lucifer-Principle" with a more or less materialistic "Jehovah-Principle.")[203] None of these two tendencies are evil in themselves, but when unchecked, one of them may gain undue prominence and cause a disastrous imbalance. The balancing force that is between these two principles and also incorporates them is the "Christ Being," who embodies the divine principle of altruism and sacrifice.

It is not hard to see that the Luciferian and Ahrimanic principles in Steiner's cosmology correspond to the nineteenth-century Satan in two of its classic roles, that of patron angel of the human pursuit of knowledge, and of metaphorical representation of the material, the carnal, and the sexual. In contrast to the Romantic Satanists, however, both principles were perceived by Steiner to have objective reality, both within the psyche of man, in the world outside him, and in the spiritual sphere. With a somewhat disturbing fondness for typologies, Steiner saw his ruling principles also represented in the various nations of the globe. Thus, the Eastern nations were predominantly Luciferian, while Western Europeans and Americans were more Ahrimanically inclined. Central Europe and Germany occupied a kind of middle ground in this scheme, in accordance with the special mission and position Steiner reserved for these territories.[204]

Steiner's cosmic hierarchy was given visible outlines by the huge wooden sculpture group in the Dornach cultic center that Steiner started to craft in 1914 with the help of the sculptor Edith Maryon.[205] Its most important component is a human figure that rises up from the ground with one arm stretched downward and the other raised to the sky, the hands clenched as if holding on to something. Steiner had originally intended this to be a depiction of the Christ, but he later changed his mind and called it the "Representative of Mankind," which also became the title of the sculpture. To the left of this figure, Ahriman and Lucifer appear, symbolizing both the vital role they play in the evolution of humanity and the threat they pose to proper human development when one of them succeeds to gain dominance. Underneath, in a kind of subterranean grotto, Ahriman reappears, chained to the ground by tree roots; another figure floating over him may represent Lucifer again. According to one of his disciples, Steiner claimed that Lucifer and Ahriman had personally posed for him to make the sculpture: and while the former had more or less willingly complied, the latter had to be forced into submission by Steiner's psychic power. (The unruly sprite, it was said, later took revenge by smashing one of the stained-glass windows in the cult room.)[206]

CHILDREN OF LUCIFER

Comme tu es triste et comme tu es beau,
ô mon Génie, mon Dieu, mon Lucifer!

[How sad you are and how beautiful,
O my Genius, my God, my Lucifer!]

This exclamation of adoration occurs in the play *Les Enfants de Lucifer* ("Children of Lucifer") by Edouard Schuré (1841–1929), which he published in 1900, exactly at the turn of the century.[207] Schuré was no obscure figure at the time; earlier, he had created a furore with his book *Les Grands Initiés* (1889), a nineteenth-century New Age bestseller (if this slight anachronism is allowable) that traced the historical path of secret esoteric wisdom through Rama, Krishna, Plato, and Jesus. His play would not earn him as much fame as his book, but it is well worth a look, as it gives a perfect digest of the alternative myth of Satan that had evolved during the nineteenth century.

Les Enfants de Lucifer is situated somewhere in the first centuries of the Christian Era and opens with Théokles, a young Greek from the city of Dionysia, seeking shelter during a journey in a mysterious "Temple of the Unknown God."[208] When this unknown god is invoked, he turns out to be no one else but Lucifer, who gives Théokles the new name of Phosphoros (which is, significantly, the Greek synonym for the angel's own name). Asked by his disciple what he must do to be like him, the god answers: "Believe in yourself, and struggle with the Eternal with all the force of your being."[209]

Armed with this advice, Théokles/Phosphoros sets out to retrieve his childhood love Cléonice, who has become a nun in a Christian monastery. After some initial resistance, the young girl in due course succumbs to the "diabolical" charms of her long-lost friend. Together they return to their native city, Dionysia, where they uproot the power of the emperor and the bishop. When the populace fills the street with cheers to "Lucifer Liberator," Théokles/Phosphoros addresses them in a stirring speech.[210] "For what purpose the last-born of the gods has been giving to you?" he asks the crowds, and the answer he gives is this: "For being a free people that does bend its knee neither to Ceasar nor before the cross; for realising that Beauty, Truth, and Justice are within yourself; for concluding a pact with them that makes you masters of yourself and of others. If each one of you does not feel himself a Lucifer to defy both Ceasar and Church, you are not worthy to die with me for Dionysia, the mother of heroes and the city of free souls!"[211]

However, all ends in tragedy when the expelled bishop returns, accompanied by an overwhelming force of imperial troops. Théokles seeks refuge once again in the Temple of the Unknown God, where together with Cléonice he invokes Lucifer anew. The fallen angel appears but proclaims he cannot help them. The times of trial have come: the

Christian spirit of submission will now rule on Earth. "But I shall arise again from my darkness," he assures them. "I shall break my chains, I shall stir up my torch. There will come a time when we will rule together over earth."[212] After these words, he disappears from view with a last, fading "Per . . . se . . . ver! . . ." In the meantime, the soldiers arrive, led by the bishop who enters crying "Death to the children of Lucifer!" Rather than falling into his hands, the two lovers prefer to die the *mors romana*, committing suicide before the altar of Lucifer.

We need not doubt which time it was Schuré was thinking of as the time that Lucifer would reappear. It was, of course, his own, and he had good reason for doing so. The nineteenth century, we have seen, witnessed an unprecedented effort in Western civilization to rehabilitate Satan. The background to this rehabilitation was a deeply felt dissatisfaction with the Christian religion and/or its institutional manifestations. Rooted in Enlightenment critique on the Christian faith, this opposition against Christianity had been catalyzed by the French Revolution and had found mythological expression in the figure of Satan with a number of prominent Romantic poets. It was within the framework of the struggle against throne and altar (dramatically personified in Schuré's play by the Roman Emperor and the Christian bishop) that Satan could take on a new role. From a supernatural personage responsible for cosmic misfortune, he had become a symbol for freedom and liberation: liberation from political and religious oppression; liberation from repressive sexual morals and a "Christian" contempt of the body; liberation from the religious shackles of the mind that hindered the glorious advance of science or esoteric knowledge. The old mythological associations of Satan with pride, rebellion, lust, and the lure of knowledge now came to be viewed in a different light. Suddenly, the fallen angel could be seen as the "Genius of Science, Liberty and Human Individuality," as Schuré described him in his introduction to *Les Enfants de Lucifer*.[213]

It must again be emphasized that this was a minority position in the nineteenth century, held by a small part of the cultural elite. In other parts of society, old, time-honored views on Satan and Satanism continued to flourish, and we will meet some of their representatives in the next two chapters. Nonetheless, the new pro-Satanic minority was a significant one. An impressive catalogue of nineteenth-century cultural icons has appeared on the preceding pages. Some of them envisioned an ultimate reconciliation between Satan and Christianity, or the deity, or Christ, however radically redefined. This had been the theme of the majority of the French Satanist poets and would be a prominent feature of the new religious movement of anthroposophy. Edouard Schuré was also devoted to this conviction. "Lucifer, Genius of Science, Liberty and Human Individuality, is the unbending enemy of the Church in its present form," he stated, "but he is not the adversary of the Christ; although he develops himself in a reversed direction, he forms his completion."[214] In the final scene of his play, Théokles is told he can find truth "where the star of Lucifer shines through the cross of Christ."[215] As a matter of fact, Schuré and Steiner were personal friends: Steiner would direct performances of *Les Enfants de Lucifer* at his cultic center in 1909 and 1910.[216]

Other sympathizers with Satan took a less conciliatory stance toward Christian religion. To them, Christianity had been the bad dream of Western civilization, a monstrous structure of oppression that had to be demolished as soon as possible. It had brought an end to the glorious sanity of the Classical world (often perceived by them as one great Dionysia), had made thousands of innocents perish at the stake, and had humiliated men of genius like Galileo. For people like Percy Bysshe Shelley, Pierre-Joseph Proudhon, Jules Michelet, or H. P. Blavatsky, Jehovah and Satan virtually changed places, the first becoming the "demon-god" of biblical cruelty, the latter a deity-like mythological representative for all that was good.

We have seen in the preceding pages how this Satan penetrated important domains of nineteenth-century (counter)culture. Satan became a political icon among some extreme fringes of the revolutionary movement. The rehabilitation of the angel of evil inspired some authors to a similar rehabilitation of groups that had been accused of worshipping the devil in the past. Variants of the Romantic Satan even gained ontological, metaphysical stature in the new religious movements of anthroposophy and Theosophy, where they enjoyed a certain measure of veneration. Starting out as a Romantic Satanist himself, the French occultist Éliphas Lévi brought radical adaptations to this new Satan to fit a new political and social agenda—prefiguring and preparing a fundamental change in the perception of Satan in the religious Satanism of the next century.

In none of these religious movements and in none of the domains we studied, however, do we encounter something like an independent religious Satanism—notwithstanding the fact, as we have argued at the beginning of this chapter, that the essential preparatory steps for such a Satanism had already been taken in the early decades of the nineteenth century. Anarchist ideologues like Proudhon and Bakunin did merely use Satan as a provocative rhetorical tool to express their anticlerical and antireligious tendencies. Historians and writers of historical romance like Sand, Michelet, and Leland described religious Satanism as something of the past or fast on its way to become so. Although they considered it as a valuable prefiguration of the Western Revolution, embodying programmatic themes that remained highly significant, none of them suggested actually resuscitating the historical cults they purported to portray. Neither, for that matter, would it be accurate to designate the pioneers of nineteenth-century alternative religion who we discussed as religious Satanists. Lévi saw himself as a Catholic Kabbalist, Blavatsky found truth in Eastern religion, and Steiner considered the Christ as the embodiment of the divine principle. Satan formed just a part of their doctrines, not its principal object of veneration. Although we can say that elements of religious Satanism appear with them, we are definitely not witnessing the emergence of a full-fledged religious Satanism.

I would like to end this chapter by noting a last significant aspect that the historical characters and groups we portrayed share with the Romantic Satanists. All their religious or ideological outlooks center in essence on Humanity or humankind as points of reference. This applies to Blavatsky's Theosophy, for instance: "The 'Fallen Angels', so-called, are *Humanity itself*," the Russian esoteric author wrote in *The Secret Doctrine*. "The whole personnel" of the old myths is in fact nothing but "the *Seed* of Humanity" around whom "our physical frames have grown and developed to what they are now."[217] But it is equally valid as a description of Steiner's anthroposophy and Lévi's "magism," as well as the various anarchist and historiographical authors we discussed. Satan, for all of them, represented in essence man's tendencies, or mankind itself—even though he may have had an independent ontological existence aside from this, as was the case with the Lucifer of Lévi, Blavatsky, and Steiner. As Schuré put it, "There is a point where man who wants to become god meets god who has become man."[218] Although he was actually referring to Christ here, the same rapprochement was attributed in his "theatre of the soul" to Lucifer, that semidivine personage who is in fact mankind itself, while man, in his turn, gropes to fashion his own destiny like a rebel angel—"each one a Lucifer."

Se livrer à Satan, qu'est-ce que c'est?

BAUDELAIRE, *Fusées*, XIV, I

Intermezzo 2

Charles Baudelaire: Litanies to Satan

READERS FAMILIAR WITH our subject will probably have missed one name in these pages up to now: that of Charles Baudelaire (1821–1867), the French poet who acquired literary fame and instant notoriety with an iniquitous collection of poetry entitled *Les Fleurs du Mal* ("The Flowers of Evil," 1857). This omission has a tactical reason. I think Baudelaire is much better understood when we see him as a transitional figure between Romantic Satanism and the somewhat different attitude toward Satan that would become en vogue in the fin de siècle. It might even be said, as I will attempt to show in this intermezzo, that the great poet of the Decadent movement exemplifies and inaugurates this transition in person, both in his life and in his work.

Baudelaire's frequent appearance in discussions of Satanism is primarily due to one poem published in *Les Fleurs du Mal*, the "Litanies de Satan" ("Litany of Satan").[1] With its opening lines,

> O toi, le plus savant, et le plus beau des Anges,
> Dieu trahi par le sort et privé de louanges,
> [O you, most wise and most beautiful of Angels,
> God betrayed by fate and bereft of praises,]

this song of praise to the archangel "to whom injustice has been done" would attain iconic status in the history of Satanism.[2] Modeled on the Roman Catholic *Miserere*, the poem sings of Satan as the protector of the drunkard and the convict, the support of the inventor and the revolutionary, the instigator of love and hope, and the "great king of subterranean things," interspersed with the continuously repeated refrain "O Satan, prends pitié de ma longue misère!" ("O Satan, take pity on my long misery!").

The long litany ends with a "prayer" that expresses the wish to find eternal peace in Satan's Paradise:

> Gloire et louange à toi, Satan, dans les hauteurs
> Du Ciel, où tu régnas, et dans les profondeurs
> De l'Enfer, où, vaincu, tu rêves en silence!
> Fais que mon âme un jour, sous l'Arbre de Science,
> Près de toi se repose, à l'heure où sur ton front
> Comme un Temple nouveau ses rameaux s'épandront!

> [Satan, to thee be praise upon the Height
> Where thou wast king of old, and in the night
> Of Hell, where thou dost dream on silently.
> Grant that one day beneath the Knowledge-tree,
> When it shoots forth to grace thy royal brow,
> My soul may sit, that cries upon thee now.[3]]

Even a cursory reading of this poem allows us to understand why it could be perceived as such a shocking statement of pro-Satanic proclivity. The "classic" Romantic Satanists had portrayed Satan as a more or less admirable mythological character, but none of them had addressed him in such a direct way, in a form that is explicitly presented by the poet as religious. While they undeniably had, in some cases, voiced admiration for the devil, Baudelaire's litany, at first sight, expresses plain adoration. As such, the poem can certainly be understood as a radical new evolvement of earlier Romantic Satanism, to which it clearly is indebted—the fact alone that "Litany of Satan" was included in the section "Revolt" of *Les Fleurs du Mal* speaks volumes here. Reminiscences of Sand, Vigny, and even Byron can be pointed out in its lines, and we can see the three classic Satanic attributes of sex, science, and liberty return once more, as well as Satan's archetypical Romantic role as shield and support of the spurned, the marginalized, and the rebellious.[4] Thus it does not surprise when Baudelaire, in one of his notes, remarks that the apotheosis of tragic beauty for him is incorporated by Satan "after the manner of Milton."[5] At the same time, however, "Litanies de Satan" exhales a markedly different atmosphere than we found in most examples of "classic" Romantic Satanism. It is, for want of a better word, more "dark," more ambiguous also; we do not encounter a Satan here that is heroically stepping into the light in order to emancipate and liberate humanity.

We will delve into Baudelaire's possible motives for this shift in presentation later. First, however, something must be told about the developments in literary history that preceded and partially clarify this more radical, darker, and more ambiguous Satan. For Baudelaire's style was not without its precursors. In the years around the July Revolution of 1830, a loose group of young French artists designated as Bouzingos ("Noise Makers"), and also known as the "Pétit Cénacle," or Jeunes France, had propounded a more ferocious and more pessimistic form of Romantic protest.[6] Apart from a few architects and painters (including Delacroix), the group consisted exclusively of minor poets, among whom only the names of Pétrus Borel, Philothée O'Neddy (a pseudonym for Théophile Dondey de Santeny), Gérard de Nerval, and Théophile Gautier have retained a marginal yet enduring place in the annals of literary history. Exceedingly Byronic, decidedly anti-establishment, and evidently juvenile, this gang of artistic rowdies had taken Romanticism to a new and feverish pitch. Although politically speaking, mostly radically inclined, they had grown pessimistic about the prospects for fundamental social and political change and disillusioned about the power of art and literature to make a change in wider society. Turning away from a France that was dominated by church, nobility, and monarchy, and after the 1830 Revolution by the even more despised bourgeoisie, they chanted the status of the artist as a social outcast and celebrated the domain of the artistic and the imagination as the only place where someone could really be free and, thus, in some sense, be real. "Being more creative than God," as O'Neddy put it in an appropriate line of poetry, was an adequate summary of their artistic intentions.[7]

The Bouzingos in this respect pioneered later ideas about "l'art pour l'art" and the autonomy of the artistic domain. They also can be considered as early examples of bohemians: for a short while, for instance, they lived aside from society in an impromptu commune in Montmartre, until the neighbors started to complain about their drunken parties and nudist practices.[8] Moreover, their anti-establishment and antibourgeois attitude translated itself into a certain penchant for gothic destruction in poetics and in the occasional act of rhetorical violence against the (Christian) deity—both as a religious entity in his own right, and in his capacity as a symbolic representative of the seemingly immutable political and social status quo. Their corresponding sympathy for Satan was put in equally uncompromising terms, for instance, by O'Neddy, who in *Feu et Flamme* ("Fire and Flame," 1833) raised his fist to heaven with the following exclamation:

> Je m'en irais, la nuit, par des sites incultes;
> Et là, me raillant du Seigneur,
> Je tourbillonnerais dans la magie infâme,
> J'évoquerais le Diable. . . et je vendrais mon âme
> Pour quelques mille ans de bonheur![9]

> [I will go, at night, to unholy places,
> And there, mocking the Lord,
> I will wallow myself in infamous magic;
> I will evoke the Devil . . . and I will sell my soul
> For a few chance millennia of happiness!]

Baudelaire was born too late to participate in the original (and very brief) heydays of the Bouzingos. When he appeared upon the cultural scene, O'Neddy had sunk into oblivion, whiling out his days as (of all things) a civil servant; Borel was living in a toolshed in the countryside and would soon exile himself to Algeria, while a destitute Nerval would eventually hang himself in desperation in a morose Parisian alleyway. Baudelaire, however, avidly went through their scattered work and met some of the principal Bouzingots personally, becoming particularly acquainted with Théophile Gautier, to whom he dedicated *Les Fleurs du Mal*.[10] The Jeunes France influenced him in several respects: in a way, the "Litanies de Satan" and its two accompanying ungodly poems in the section "Revolt" can be regarded as late fruits of the extreme Romantic Satanism of some of the Bouzingos.

Given the liturgical character of "Litanies de Satan," it is not surprising that a number of authors have claimed that Baudelaire had not stopped at mere Bouzingo provocation and had gone further, crossing the line into actual devil worship.[11] This idea will have found additional stimulus in the brooding look of the poet on some photographs and his original intent to include exactly 66 poems in *Les Fleurs du Mal*—a number that could well be pushed up, he declared, "to the Kabalistic 666 or even 6666."[12] Some scholars have been more specific and assert that Baudelaire belonged to a "Satanic chapel" of Romantic poets that is said to have flourished in the years around 1846. According to their story, this circle of poets convened every Sunday morning to "invoke Satan" with the most "anti-bourgeois" and "diabolical" poetry they could think of. In February 1846, for instance, they celebrated the seven deadly sins in verse, dedicating their works to Satan in words that, according to a modern historian, "might better have been left unspoken":

A toi, Satan, bel archange déchu,
A qui le périlleux honneur échut
De guerroyer contre un pouvoir injuste,
Je m'offre tout entier et sans retour,
Mon esprit, mon sens, mon cœur, mon amour,
Et mes sombres vers dans leur beauté fruste.[13]

[To you, Satan, beautiful fallen angel
To whom the perilous honour pertains
To battle against an unjust power
Do I offer myself completely and irreversible;
My spirit, my senses, my heart, my love,
And my sombre verses of frustrated beauty.]

There are a number of problems with this story, however. The one and only source we have for the existence of this "Satanic chapel" is a quaint book by Louis Maigron entitled *Le Romantisme et les mœurs* ("Romanticism and Morals"), in which the author, although writing more than sixty years after the events, attempts to prove the nefarious influence exerted by Romanticism on French morals. Maigron does not give any sources either for his description of the "satanic cult" or for the excerpts of poetry he cites. In other words, he could just as well have fabricated the whole thing.[14] While I do not think this probable, it is highly doubtful that actual Satanist rites were practiced by this circle. Maigron seems to mean a lot of things when he uses the word "Satanism," ranging from simple wickedness over writing bad verse dedicated to the devil to full-fledged necromantic rituals, but nothing in his description gives occasion to presume that this diabolical "chapel" was anything else than a group of unruly poets coming together to share their "sombre verses of frustrated beauty."[15] The whole thing sounds rather like some late Bouzingo offshoot, and if Baudelaire had been a member, the group might thus have formed a further *traite-d'union* between him and the Jeunes France. But as a matter of fact, Maigron does not mention him as a participant; he only remarks upon the "Baudelarian perfume" of some of their poems. To put it briefly: there is no indication at all that Baudelaire was a member of this circle, no indication that these poets did anything other than compose provocative poetry, and no indication, in fact, that this circle ever existed, except for the seven-odd pages in Maigron's rather obscure study.

Even more creative is the identification made by the German scholar Karl Frick between Maigron's elusive group of "Satanists" and the "Club des Hachichins," an informal group of nineteenth-century Parisian gentlemen who experimented with soft drugs. Because Baudelaire was a member of the latter group, Frick implies, his involvement in ritual Satanism is plausible.[16] The Club des Hachichins, so much is certain, *did* indeed exist. It was founded by a physician and psychiatrist called Jacques-Joseph Moreau de Tours (1804–1884), who distributed a homemade concoction of sugar, orange juice, hashish, and various other spices during its sessions. Apart from this, however, the club was as harmless as the average Dutch coffee shop, of which it was a kind of exclusive nineteenth-century precursor. The rumors about the Satanic character of its activities may have sprung into existence because of a witty report written by Gautier about his visit to the club, in which he describes being pestered by an impish, diabolic figure during his narcotic delirium. It was probably this drug-induced fantasy that brought about the link between the Club des Hachichins and Satanism.[17]

Not all authors who declare Baudelaire a Satanist, however, understand this term in the gross sense of staging macabre ceremonies of diabolic worship. As our prior discussions of Romantic Satanism have made abundantly clear, literature by itself can already provide ample space for the unfolding of the religious.[18] Was Baudelaire, then, such a Satanist? First of all, in order to answer this question, we have to determine *which* Baudelaire we are talking about. Over time, the poet had several personae. The first Baudelaire, for all his dandyism, was a political radical. A contemporary acquaintance remembered him as "yet another new disciple of Proudhon."[19] During the revolution of February 1848, this Baudelaire could be found on the barricades, gun in hand and bandana in his hair. Like Constant, he even launched his own political periodical in the aftermath of the revolt, *Le Salut du Peuple* ("The Welfare of the People"), although only two issues of this ephemeral publication would appear. More than one biographer dates his poems of revolt, including the "Litanies de Satan," to this period, and presupposes a strong Proudhonian inspiration for them.[20]

The revolutionary Baudelaire of 1848 who might have written the "Litanies de Satan," however, was no longer the Baudelaire of 1857 who chose to include them in *Les Fleurs du Mal*. As had happened to Constant, the events that followed the 1848 revolution had estranged him from his former revolutionary fervor. The massive popular support for autocracy that manifested itself at the plebiscites of 1851 and 1852 disgusted him with "the people" for whose welfare he had earlier striven.[21] He adopted the French reactionary writer Joseph de Maistre as one of his *maîtres à penser*, and under the inspiration of this author, and in a far echo of Plato's *Republic*, the thoughts he now begun to formulate seemed to take an increasingly reactionary turn. "There is no other reasonable and reliable form of government but an aristocracy," he wrote in his intimate cahiers, adding somewhat later: "Among men only the poet, the priest and the soldier are great. The man who sings, the man who blesses, the man who sacrifices others and himself. The others are made for the whip."[22]

This new political orientation did not translate itself in a renewed political activism, however, but rather in an apolitical retreat into art. Art for the sake of art and the creation of an autonomous domain of personalized aesthetics became the sole means with which he confronted society. "A dandy does nothing," he noted. "Can you imagine a dandy addressing the people, except to deride it?"[23] When he was forced to leave France for Belgium in 1864, this had nothing to do with his marked antipathy to Napoleon III, but with his desperate need to elude his clamoring creditors. His new host country, arguably the first industrialized mass society on the continent, only deepened his aversion for *demos* and democracy, while at the same time his declarations of sympathy for Christianity grew more frequent. "I am Catholic and Roman, and I have reflected a great deal on that," he stated.[24] In one of his last works, *Pauvre Belgique!* ("Poor Belgium!"), he combined his new anti-egalitarianism and rekindled Roman Catholicism to rail at the way in which the Belgians, according to his perception, were engrossed in shallow, boorish pleasures and the philosophical vulgarity of optimistic materialism (termed by him the "paganism of imbeciles"). "The Christian idea (the God invisible, creator, omniscient, conscious, omni-provident)," he wrote with disgust, "can not enter into a Belgian brain."[25]

These and similar utterances have inclined some critics to the other extreme: namely that Baudelaire was not a Satanist, but rather a devout if troubled Roman-Catholic.[26] Can we describe the Baudelaire who published *Les Fleurs du Mal* as a Roman Catholic reactionary? Although the poet himself jokingly defended the Catholicity of the work—even if it were to be diabolical, he wrote in a letter, there surely did not exist anyone more Catholic than the devil?—this nevertheless would amount to a misrepresentation.[27] In fact, Baudelaire's partial rejection of the Western Revolution had been preceded by the Bouzingos, whose inspiration in turn derived in part from Byron. Although republican in outlook, this did not necessarily imply *democracy* for them: being ruled by the detested bourgeoisie or the sullen masses would be as unsavory as the reign of king and church.[28] "Mon républicanisme, c'est de la lycantrophie," Borel had famously written, explaining he was a republican "because that word represents to me the greatest independence possible that society and civilisation can afford."[29] What he and his *partennaires* had dreamed about foremost was a vaguely defined "Reign of Art."[30] It may be noted that Baudelaire also mentioned the poet as the first and foremost of the ruling classes he envisioned—in the position, thus, where Plato had placed the philosopher in *The Republic*. Furthermore, in 1861 Baudelaire still maintained that he had always remained a republican as well as a "fervent Catholic."[31]

With this political position and with his spiritual attitude, Baudelaire thus set forth on the tracks of Romanticism in its most extreme manifestation. Of course, the Bouzingos, anticlerical to the core as they had been, would have found issue with his ever more intense flirtation with Catholicism. Yet underneath this apparent rift a basic unity in outlook can be detected. Crucial keywords of Romanticism reappear in Baudelaire, prominent among them "imagination," called "the queen of [human] faculties" by the poet. "The imagination is the queen of what is truly real, and the *possible* is one of the provinces of the real," Baudelaire wrote in his review of the Salon of 1859. "She is quite positively in parentage with the infinite. . . . As she has created the world (one can say so, I believe, even in a religious sense), it is only just for her to govern it."[32] In *Les Fleurs du Mal*, greeted by Flaubert as a rejuvenation of Romanticism, the same theme reappears. Although this collection of poetry is rich in subthemes and literary motifs—risqué eroticism, (pseudo)Christian obsession with suffering and guilt, dandylike spleen, to name but a few—one of the most important elements is certainly the quest for the ideal that man and especially the poet must undertake. Only in the domain of the ideal, in the domain of "dreams," of the imagination, can man find his essence and his freedom—freedom, in particular, from the "ennui" that is caused by a material world that can only repeat itself in the "dull round of a mill with complicated wheels," as Blake had already said some seventy years before.[33] In a well-known poem from *Fleurs du Mal*, "La Voix" ("The Voice"), the poet-narrator is spoken to by two voices during his childhood: one offering him a material appetite as big as the world, the other asking him not to stop there but to "come wander in dreams,/Beyond the possible, beyond that what is known!"[34] The infant chooses the latter option, and thereby its calling as a poet.

It is in this context—as a religious expression of a cherished tendency for the ideal—that we have to understand Baudelaire's Catholicism, at least during the period in which *Les Fleurs du Mal* appeared. In his notebooks, he talks of faith as "supremacy of the pure idea, with Christians as with the communistic babouvist," while he calls priests "the servants and sectarians of the Imagination."[35] Baudelaire's religion, in brief, is essentially that of Romanticism. This is made explicit by the poem "Le Coucher de Soleil Romantique" ("The Sunset of Romanticism") that appeared at the start of a supplement of *Les Fleurs du Mal* published in 1861.[36] Here the decline of Romanticism (the setting sun of the poem's title) is equated with the disappearance of the divine presence that the poet experiences.

The Romantic essence of Baudelaire's religious views becomes especially clear in his ideas about the devil and the deity.[37] We can get an impression of these from *Mon cœur mis à nu* ("My Heart Laid Bare"), a notebook in which Baudelaire jotted down sketches and keywords for a book of philosophical and personal "confessions" intended to rival those of Rousseau. "What is the fall?" Baudelaire noted under the heading "Theology": "If it is unity become duality, it is God who has fallen. In other words, would not the creation be the fall of God?"[38] This quasi-Manichean tendency to equate the natural or material world with the emergence of imperfection is translated into his remarks about Satan as well. "There are in every man, at every moment, two simultaneous postulations, one towards God, the other towards Satan. The invocation to God, or spirituality, is a desire to rise in dignity; that of Satan or animalism is a joy of descending. It is to the latter that one must ascribe the love for women and the intimate conversation with animals, dogs, cats, etcetera."[39] As Baudelaire already makes clear here himself, this "joy of descending" that degrades man to an animal becomes especially manifest in the domain of the sexual. Moreover, in "fallen" (i.e. "dualized") man, this tendency is particularly represented by woman. "Woman is hungry and she wants to eat. Thirsty and she wants to drink. She is in heat and she wants to be fucked. Big deal! Woman is *natural*, that is to say, abominable."[40]

Baudelaire here outlines a misogynist conception of the "fatal woman" that would become very popular in the fin de siècle, as we will see. For now, we can observe that the theology sketched here cannot, in any way, be called Satanist. Neither, for that matter, is it "Roman Catholic" or "Christian" in any of the accepted meanings of these terms. Despite the misleading similarity of the idiom Baudelaire sometimes uses, Christian ideas about moral good or redemption are of minor importance in all this. It is not so much "good" and "evil" in a moral sense that interests the poet, but man's capacity for the "spiritual" and the "ideal," for the "super-natural" in the literal significance of the word, versus his inclination toward "animalism" in which he is ruled by the laws of nature. Although our spiritual nature enables us to transcend our "animality" by "dreaming" and "imagining" the ideal, we are all, as "fallen," material human beings, inevitably bound to sin in this respect. Only death will release us from our animal form: as living human beings, the ultimate to which we can strive, according to Baudelaire's paradoxical conclusion, is to *do good and evil consciously*. That realization may be the background of Baudelaire's much-quoted dictum that the best trick of the devil is to make people believe he does not exist.[41] It also makes understandable other paradoxical statements of Baudelaire, such as this one about the dominance of "Satanism" in the present world: "In reality, Satanism has won, Satan has made himself innocent. Evil that knows itself is less detestable and closer to healing than evil that is ignorant about itself. G. Sand inferior to De Sade."[42] George Sand, according to Baudelaire, was nothing but a "big animal" that remained *unaware* that it was doing evil, while De Sade had at least attained a superior level of human development by doing evil *knowingly*.[43]

When this recapitulation of Baudelaire's philosophy is accepted as valid, the similarities with the ideas of Romantic Satanism become obvious. At about the same time Hugo was struggling with similar questions in his *Fin de Satan*, while Byron had discussed comparable concepts in *Cain* three decades before. It is enlightening, however, to point out the differences between Baudelaire and the latter. Byron, if our reading of his texts is correct, had associated Lucifer with the spiritual and the deity with the natural; his *Cain* can be read as a criticism of (his own) Romanticism, with its tendency to emphasize the "spiritual" world and spurn the humanity of "common," "physical" existence. Baudelaire, on the other hand (at least in his notes for *Mon cœur mis à nu*), identifies Satan with the natural and "God" with the spiritual and ideal. In addition, he wholeheartedly embraces the Romantic notions of spirituality and imaginative creativity as the essence of our humanity (while drawing conclusions from this premise, it must be noted, that certainly exhibit originality).

With this background information, we can approach *Les Fleurs du Mal* and the "Litanies de Satan" again, and see whether we can put Baudelaire's "Satanist" utterances in their proper perspective. First of all, it has to be kept in mind that *Fleurs du*

Mal is a *collection* of poetry that brought together poems written over years. Practically speaking, Baudelaire intended to gather the best of his poetic works in order to reap a financial profit; in a more substantive way, *Fleurs du Mal* was compiled to form a reflection of the poet's intellectual, artistic, and spiritual road through life, starting with his birth and ending in death. We do not necessarily have to bend over backward, like some Baudelaire scholars have done, to construct absolute coherence between Baudelaire's notes and his earlier poems. "Litanies de Satan" is the expression of a certain state and/ or stage of human existence, probably also of a certain stage in Baudelaire's existence. This has given the poem its place in Baudelaire's final selection; it would be overly rash as well as inexact to read it as a final statement of faith.

This does not mean that Baudelaire will not have written the poem, or an earlier version of it, without sincerity. One can easily imagine the Proudhonian Baudelaire of around 1848 producing a piece of radical Romantic Satanism like this. And even if the poem does not reflect Baudelaire's genuine convictions at an earlier point in time, it will have reflected a genuine *feeling* that he was able to experience. As he would write in his 1859 Salon review: "The artist, the true artist, the true poet, must not paint otherwise than according to what he sees and what he feels. He must *truly* be true to his own nature."[44] That does not mean, once again, that we can interpret the "Litanies de Satan" as a factual pronouncement of a theological dogma (once) held by its author—it is exactly against such a narrow idea of "photographic" realism that Baudelaire was arguing in his review. But it does mean that he was able to partake in the sentiments it expressed. Much the same could probably be said about "Le reniement de saint Pierre" ("The Denial of Saint Peter"), another poem in the section "Revolt" reeking of Bouzingo defiance and Romantic Satanism. In this poem, Peter denies Jesus for the second time because the latter let himself be executed passively in obedience to his father—a "tyrant gorged on meat and wines"—instead of taking action to realize a better world. The narrator applauds the apostle's decision and confesses that he himself would gladly part from a world "where action is not the sister of dream," be it through the sword or by using the sword.[45] Here it is hard not to think of Baudelaire's erstwhile revolutionary enthusiasm, given the place of the poem in the section devoted to revolt. Similarly, "Litanies de Satan" may reflect the inclinations of a more youthful Baudelaire, while simultaneously portraying a general halting place in the spiritual development of the psyche.

With regard to "Litanies de Satan," moreover, a certain distancing from the position that the poem expresses on its surface may well be detectable with a closer reading of its text. If one compares the poem with "Satanist" expressions of, say, Shelley, or Baudelaire's presumed inspirator Proudhon, it is striking how ambiguous, almost ironic, the litany sometimes is. That Satan supports mining and inspires violent and sorrowful visions of love in young girls may more or less fit the bill. But his special protection of somnambulists and drunkards seems almost comical or at least peculiar for a Satan that was usually perceived as a noble Classical hero. That the fallen angel "consoles frail man that suffers" by teaching him the art of making gunpowder might be a reference to revolutionary struggle, but it also sounds more than a bit sarcastic. And what is meant exactly by the exclamation "Toi qui poses ta marque, ô complice subtil,/Sur le front du Crésus impitoyable et vil" ("You who pose your mark, o subtle accomplice,/On the forehead of the vile Croesus without pity")? Is this mark meant to point out the rich man (to have him shot, for instance) or to indicate that he is a true "child of Satan"?

Even more interesting are the possible interpretations that arise when these ambiguities are compared to the function of Satan as inclined toward the animal and the subconscious in Baudelaire's private notes. Many of the activities that Baudelaire associates with Satan in his litany are connected with the "subconscious" in one form or another (drunkenness, sleepwalking, sexual desire) or with material, "lower" gains (as is, quite literally, the case with mining). The remarkable "prayer" at the end of the poem also allows different readings. What does it mean exactly when one requests to "repose" with Satan "beneath" the Tree of Knowledge? Could it be that we must read this "beneath" not only literally, but also symbolically; e.g., that the prayer expresses the wish to *descend* with Satan into subconscious animalism? Because there *is* another way in which the lost unity of human being can be restored in Baudelaire's scheme: not by moving upward and painfully approaching the ideal by becoming ever more *conscious* of evil, but by *going down* and stripping oneself of one's dignity in order to become an animal. Baudelaire did not deny that this descent could be joyful; numerous poems in *Les Fleurs du Mal* eloquently evoke this joy.[46] It would not be without consistency, of course, when the "Litanies de Satan" could be ranged among their number.[47]

A singular ambiguity and complexity of meaning also characterize another, less notorious poem in which Baudelaire seems to make an explicit statement of adoration to the devil. Entitled "Le Possédé" ("The Possessed"), it first appeared in the second edition of *Fleurs du Mal*, published in 1861. I quote the poem and its accompanying translation in full:

Le Possédé

Le soleil s'est couvert d'un crêpe. Comme lui,
Ô Lune de ma vie! emmitoufle-toi d'ombre
Dors ou fume à ton gré; sois muette, sois sombre,
Et plonge tout entière au gouffre de l'Ennui;

Je t'aime ainsi! Pourtant, si tu veux aujourd'hui,
Comme un astre éclipsé qui sort de la pénombre,
Te pavaner aux lieux que la Folie encombre
C'est bien! Charmant poignard, jaillis de ton étui!

Allume ta prunelle à la flamme des lustres!
Allume le désir dans les regards des rustres!
Tout de toi m'est plaisir, morbide ou pétulant;

Sois ce que tu voudras, nuit noire, rouge aurore;
Il n'est pas une fibre en tout mon corps tremblant
Qui ne crie: *Ô mon cher Belzébuth, je t'adore!*[48]

[*The Possessed*

The sun is covered in a shroud. Like him,
O Moon of my life, enwrap yourself in shadow
Sleep or smoke as you will; be mute, be sombre,
And lose yourself completely in the abyss of Ennui.

I love you thus! Nevertheless, if you would today,
Like an eclipsed star appearing out of semi-darkness,
Wish to parade yourself in places where Lunacy abounds,
That is fine to me! Charming dagger, leave your sheath!

Light up your pupils with the light of chandeliers!
Light up the fire of desire in the glances of the boorish!
All of you is pleasure to me, morbid or exultant;

Be whatever you want to be: black night, red dawn:
There is no fibre in my trembling body that does not cry out:
"O my dear Beelzebuth, I do adore you!"]

Many layers of meaning can be uncovered in this poem. The last exclamation—"*Ô mon cher Belzébuth, je t'adore!*"—is not from Baudelaire himself, but quoted from Jacques Cazotte's *Le Diable amoureux* (1772), a picardic novel in which a young man invokes the devil in jest during a necromantic ceremony but flees the scene when the latter appears in all his dark hideousness. The devil then takes on the shape of an androgynous maiden, and when the young man has fallen in love with him/her, he/she discloses her real identity and asks him to pronounce, "as tender as are my feelings for you," the following statement of love: "My dear Beelzebuth, I do adore you."[49] In addition, she proclaims that it is essential that her fiancé will know her true appearance, and she transforms into the shape of a demon with a grotesque camel head, laughs frighteningly, and sticks out an enormous tongue to the young man, who in terror seeks shelter underneath the bed.

The narrator of Baudelaire's poem, however, does not flee in terror: instead, he cries out "with every fibre in his trembling body" that he adores Beelzebuth, whether he shows himself as a charming maiden or a camel-headed demon. And the poem does indeed feature some indications that this double-faced demon *is* the devil: the enflamed looks he provokes in the eyes of the boorish, his association with night and darkness and the "abyss of Ennui." Is this another poem like "Litanies de Satan," and is the possessed of the title possessed by Satan, by the craving to descend to the lower, animal stage of life? It might be. On the other hand, however, the sun is consistently used as a symbol for the divine in *Fleurs du Mal* (for instance in "Le Soleil," or in the already-mentioned "Le Coucher de Soleil Romantique"), while the moon, in this poem, is the poet's soul or the inner reflection of the divine. The poem might then describe (and I think it does) the poet's ultimate, complete love for the divinity, or more precisely for his inner "demon" who oscillates with the appearance and disappearance of the

Sun-god, now steeped in the gloom of *Gottesfinsternis*, then again exulting in the spiritual sunbeams of divine ecstasy. It is this demonic/divine spark in man, this poetic
genius that is adored here by the name of Beelzebuth. However, we can also say, with a
slight Blakean twist, that it is the deity who is thus called, the ultimate source of both
the inner light itself and of its absence. It is this god who gives, in other poems in *Les
Fleurs du Mal*, the suffering to the poet that oppresses him but at the same time sancti-
fies him like Jesus (see, e.g., "Bénédiction"). It could therefore well be that it is this god,
and not Satan, who is called a demon here and is at the same time worthy of adoration.

Which conclusions can we draw after this concise review of Baudelaire's work? What
is probably most striking in his "Satanist" texts, in the first place, is the utter ambiguity they exhibit. When read thoroughly, they allow ever deeper layers of interpretation,
and it is not evident which one of them is the only or even most valid. Taking into
account the totality of Baudelaire's writings, his literary and personal development,
and his historical background, particularly in Romanticism, we can formulate hypotheses that go beyond the often contradicting surfaces of his texts. But to a much greater
extent than with his Romantic predecessors, finding meaning with Baudelaire depends
on the particular savor of his words, the *color* that his choice of expression conveys. With
Baudelaire, in other words, we move inevitably from a strictly historical interpretation
to a more personal, re-imaginative reading, and the border between what we can make
probable as a historian and what we infer from his texts as a person becomes increasingly
porous. In addition and in connection to this, we cannot simply interpret his utterances
as statements of personal conviction. While Baudelaire emphasized that poetry should
be veritable (i.e., a true reflection of personally experienced psychological realities), this
does not necessarily imply that they constitute their author's dictum about the cosmos.
This may be a truism for every literary scholar, but in fact we can see a marked difference
here with earlier Romantic Satanists like Blake, Shelley, Hugo, and even Byron, whose
work, however rich in complexity and difficulties of interpretation, can be read with
some confidence as an expression of their personal views at the moment of writing.

This does not mean that we are left completely in the sand drifts of the personal.
A few distinct tendencies can be marked out in Baudelaire's treatment of Satan and
his divine rival. In the first place, the *sexual* is explicitly connected to the Satanic by
Baudelaire, and this is not meant as a compliment. While the Romantic Satanists and
their successors had embarked, as we have shown, upon a hesitant revaluation of the
sexual, the bodily, and the natural, using Satan in this context as a positive symbol
of emancipation, Baudelaire, although starting out from the same Romantic roots,
completely reverses this appreciation. The "natural" is negative for him, and sex is ultimately degradation. Satan, at least in the personal notes the poet left, thus becomes a
symbol for the human tendency to degrade itself. Baudelaire here prefigures attitudes
that would appear with many fin de siècle authors, as we will see in the next chapter. At
the same time, he closely approaches the "traditional" Christian association of Satan
with lust, at least on the surface, even though his trajectory to arrive here is very specific
for his own position in the history of European culture and literature.

Baudelaire's ambiguity manifests itself here as well, however, as some of his better
poems consist of a celebration of eroticism and do not exactly strike the reader as if they
were composed with repulsion. In fact, it were precisely these poems had brought down

legal repercussion upon the publication of *Les Fleurs du Mal*. Whatever their broader framework of meaning, Baudelaire was quite frank and unabashed in his evocation of the "joy of descending."

Another tendency that has become evident in the preceding pages is the apparent ease with which Baudelaire plays with the names and attributes of religious personae. The divinity is here depicted as the origin and/or *telos* of human idealism and spirituality, there as a cruel tyrant who laughs when his own son is hammered to the cross, in yet another poem adored as a double-faced Beelzebuth. Some of these contradictions resolve themselves upon closer reading. "Le reniement de saint Pierre" describes the mood of revolt against human suffering, while the narrator of "Le Possédé" understands that both sides of the deity deserve veneration—suffering only marks out the victim as a chosen one and allows him or her to transcend his animality by the acute tension it reveals between material and the ideal. Yet however pseudo-Catholic their intent, these variations eloquently illustrate Baudelaire's extremely free deployment of the hallowed names of traditional religion. In the same way, the "Satanic" is used as a reference for the "lower" part of reality that could be considered evil, while elsewhere, Satan "after the manner of Milton" is called the perfect embodiment of beauty.

It is to Romantic Satanism that we must look for earlier examples of such a creative reworking of traditional myth. Baudelaire both continues the project of the Romantic Satanists and reacts to it. He can do so because he shares—at least at the time of *Les Fleurs du Mal*—the basic outlook of the Romantics. Like them, he does not believe in the literal existence of the demons and deities of yore; like them, the true manifestation and source of the divine is located inside humanity for him, in the human self-consciousness or imagination, while the location of the anti-divine, the Satanic, must also be primarily sought within man.[50] This might be why Baudelaire could write in one of his notebooks that even "if God would not exist, religion would still be Holy and *Divine*."[51] The essential thing, in religion as well as art, is man's effort and capability to rise from the merely "natural" and "material" to the dignity of consciousness.

One of the meanings of the "flowers of evil" from the title of Baudelaire's book might be precisely this. The flowers, growing upward to the light of the divine sun, represent the human tendency to transcend itself, even though they spring from the "evil" humus of physical existence. That Baudelaire's interest might be in this, and not so much in "evil" in the traditional moral sense, is indicated by the last lines of the poem that concludes *Les Fleurs du Mal* in its second edition, "Le voyage." No matter how much one travels, the poem tells, the world here below remains essentially the same: only when one sets sail with death, there is a possibility to find something that goes beyond the "boring spectacle" of earthly existence.

Nous voulons, tant ce feu nous brûle le cerveau,
Plonger au fond du gouffre, Enfer ou Ciel, qu'importe?
Au fond de l'Inconnu pour trouver du *nouveau*![52]

[We want to plunge, so fierce this fire burns our brain,
Into the depths of the abyss – Hell or Heaven, what does it matter? –
Into the depths of the Unknown, as long we find something *new*!]

Comme il est très difficile d'être un saint . . . ,

il reste à devenir un satanique.

J.-K. HUYSMANS, *Là-Bas*

4

Huysmans and Consorts

ON AN EARLY afternoon in January 1893, six young gentlemen met on the Pré Catalan in Paris. While the winter sun shone on the lawns and ladies on horseback interrupted their cavalcade to look on, two of them removed their waistcoats, took up swords, and set out to skirmish, their blades clattering and flashing in the green tranquillity of the park. A duel was going on, so much was clear. And although dueling was by no means an unusual sight in France at this time, the *cause d'honneur* that brought the contestants to the field made this one extraordinary even to contemporary standards. The two duelists were Gérard Encausse, better known as Papus, and Jules Bois, both self-styled experts on occultism: the grievances over which they were crossing swords were allegations of practicing Satanism and murder by magical means.[1]

Two French gentlemen having a duel over the issue of Satanism may certainly be called a remarkable occurrence. In this chapter, we will uncover the story behind this bizarre duel. We will take a long roundabout route to do so, however—a route that will take us to, among others, gentlemen-magicians, schismatic Catholic gurus, ladies of doubtful reputation, and a self-proclaimed descendant of fallen angels. In the process, we will attempt to answer one essential question: were "genuine" religious Satanists active in the fin de siècle? Do we have reason to think that actually practiced Satanism formed the background to this duel? If so, what was its nature? If not, what are we looking at instead? Of key importance with regard to these questions, and with regard to our story in general, will be a man and a book that are crucial to any discussion of nineteenth-century Satanism: Joris-Karl Huysmans (1848–1907) and his novel *Là-Bas*, or "Down There."[2]

"DOWN THERE"

On February 17, 1891, roughly two years before Papus and Bois crossed swords on the Pré Catalan, the first instalment of Huysmans's feuilleton *Là-Bas* appeared in the *Écho de Paris*.[3] The work had been announced by the daily journal as the "first survey of contemporary Satanism made after nature and based on authentic documents." "However strange this account may seem, Mr. Huysmans guarantees its absolute veracity; he requests us also to declare that the information he gives about today's satanic societies, about the secrets and formulas of the succubate, and on the practices of bewitchment and the Black Mass, were given to him by a former superior of a religious congregation, one of the most erudite of priests and most mysterious of healers of our times."[4]

It was a remarkable announcement for a remarkable book. A short digest may serve to introduce this key document in the history of modern Satanism. In *Là-Bas*, we follow a writer, Durtal, who sets out to write a novel on Gilles de Rais (1404–1440), the medieval serial killer and alleged Satan worshipper, but he gradually comes to discover that Satanism is still very well and alive in his own day as well. Much of the novel is taken up by table talk between Durtal, the erudite doctor Des Hermies, the astrologer Gevingey, and the staunchly Roman Catholic bell ringer Carhaix, four very different characters who share a profound distaste for their own time of "vulgarisation" and "Americanisation," coupled with a nostalgic longing for the Middle Ages, when piety was still sincere, craftsmanship unspoiled, and even the torturers more professional and the villains more interesting.

While they are discussing Durtal's project on Rais one evening, Des Hermies suddenly asks Durtal what he knows about Satanism and black magic in the *modern* world.

"Do you mean now?" Durtal inquires.

"Yes, in the modern world where Satanism is rampant and traces itself back in a direct line to the Middle Ages."[5]

Upon Durtal's incredulous reaction, Des Hermies maintains that there are still people who invoke the devil and celebrate Black Masses, and he goes on to explain their organization and the nature of their activities. The most widespread society of organized Satanism, he discloses, is that of the "Ré-théurgistes optimates," founded in 1855 in America by the poet Henry Wadsworth Longfellow, who styles himself the High Priest of Evocative Magic. "It is split, despite an appearance of unity, into two camps: one aspiring to destroy the universe and reign over the ruins, and the other dreaming simply of imposing a demonic cult on the world, of which it would be the high priest." At the moment, however, this society is "pretty much on the wane and perhaps defunct altogether," although a successor "is on the way of being formed."[6]

Apart from these rather shadowy societies, numerous other Satanic circles are active, both great and small, all of which practice the three core elements of the Satanic cult: (1) the casting of spells, (2) incubate and succubate, and (3) the Black Mass, which has as its sole point the consecrating of the host "to put it to unspeakable use."[7] The adherents of these Satanist circles are recruited from the richer classes ("that explains why these scandals are hushed up if ever the police do discover them"). As only a properly invested priest can enact the transubstantiation necessary for the blasphemous ritual, its celebrants necessarily derive from the clergy, once again mainly from the higher echelons of the hierarchy: "missionary superintendents, convent confessors, prelates and abbesses, and in Rome, from the highest dignitaries."[8]

Without doubt the most redoubtable of these sacrilegious clerics, so Durtal hears from Des Hermies and Gevingey, is the mysterious Canon Docre, the master of Satanism who feeds consecrated hosts to white mice and has an image of the crucified tattooed on the sole of his feet, "so he can walk over the Saviour all the time."[9] "He celebrates [the Black

Mass] with despicable men and women; he's also openly accused of obtaining inheritances by insidious means and of causing inexplicable deaths."[10] Gevingey recounts how he once spent the night in a room belonging to Docre and was "attacked" by a succubus in broad daylight. Although he could ward off the danger by a "spell of deliverance," he suffered from aftereffects of such intensity that he had to take recourse to "Dr. Johannès," an erudite exorcist unjustly banned by the Church, and the only one in France who is spiritually able to deal with Docre.

The story of the book reaches its culmination with Durtal's final personal encounter with Canon Docre and contemporary Satanism. He comes into contact with these worshippers of Satan through his love affair with a woman. Since the beginning of his probing into Satanism, he had started to receive letters from an unknown lady. Although initially reluctant (woman being the "breeding-ground of unhappiness and boredom"), he eventually succumbs to her advances.[11] The unknown lady turns out to be Madame Chantelouve, wife of a well-known Catholic historian, and although at first glance she seems to be just another lonely woman looking for some love and tenderness, Durtal soon begins to notice some strange things about her. At their first meeting, for instance, Madame Chantelouve confesses that she has already made love to him on numerous occasions—by way of an incubus that looks like him and that can be summoned at will by her. When Durtal, by now much intrigued, finds out by chance that she is in contact with Canon Docre, he asks her to take him to a Black Mass. After much hesitation, Madame Chantelouve agrees. Durtal has to sign a written declaration that everything he will say and write on the subject of the Black Mass is "pure invention" and the product of his imagination. After this preliminary precaution, he is allowed to witness a Satanic Mass.[12]

The ceremony is held in the chapel of an old Ursuline convent. A short man with rouged cheeks and painted lips opens the door, causing Durtal to wonder if he has fallen into a "den of Sodomites."[13] In the dimly lit chapel behind, nothing suggests anything out of the ordinary, except for the fact that the church altar is topped by an obscene figure of the Christ, showing an erect male member thrusting out from a tuft of horsehair. Male and female attendants are hidden in the shadows, talking to each other in low, murmuring voices. Then, black tapers are lit, and Canon Docre enters the room. He is wearing a scarlet headdress with two bison horns on top of it, as well as a red chasuble on which a red triangle is depicted, with a black ram in its center "thrusting out its horns." Burning censers are distributed, which exhale a mixture of "fragrances pleasing to Satan": rue, henbane, thorn-apple, myrtle, and dried nightshade. The women envelop themselves in the odorous smoke: as they breathe in the perfume, they start to unfasten their dresses and "heave lascivious sighs."

At that moment, Canon Docre, who is naked underneath his vestments, kneels down and starts a lengthy prayer to Satan:

Master of disorder, Bestower of Crime's Blessings, Lord of magnificent sins and noble vices, Satan, it is you we worship, God of reason, God of Justice.

Superadmirable legate of false fears, you welcome the beggarliness of our tears. You save family honour by aborting wombs impregnated through the thoughtlessness of a good orgasm, you incite expectant mothers to miscarry, and your obstetrics spare those children who die before they are born, the sufferings of age and the pains of failure!

Sustainer of the exasperated poor, Restorer of the vanquished, it is you who endows them with hypocrisy, with ingratitude and with pride, in order that they can defend themselves against the attacks of God's children, the Rich!

Sovereign of contempt, Reckoner of humiliations, Treasurer of long-standing hatreds, you alone fertilise the mind of the man crushed by injustice, you breathe into him ideas of premeditated vengeance, of deliberate wrong-doing, you incite him to murder, you grant him an exuberant joy in the reprisals he carries out, a righteous intoxication in the tortures he inflicts and the tears of which he is the cause!

The Hope of virile members and the Anguish of barren wombs, Satan, you never demand useless proofs of chaste loins or extol the madness of fasts and siestas, you alone grant the carnal supplications and petitions of poor, greedy families. You convince mothers to prostitute their daughters, to sell their sons, you encourage sterile and forbidden loves, you are the Support of shrill Neuroses, the Founder of Hysterias, the blood-stained Vessel of Rape![14]

After this invocation of the dark god, Docre addresses the Christ, roaring out in a "clear voice full of hate": "And you, you, who, in my capacity as Priest, I compel, whether you will it or not, to descend into this host, to incarnate yourself in this bread, Jesus, Worker of Deceit, Thief of Respect, Usurper of Affection, listen! Since the day you emerged from the prophetic womb of the Virgin, you have broken all your commitments, lied about your promises; centuries have wept, waiting for you, a fugitive God, a dumb God. . . . You have forgotten the Vow of Poverty you preached and became a Vassal in thrall to the Banks. You have seen the weak squeezed dry by the Press of Profit, you have heard the death rattle of the timid wasted by famine and of women disembowelled for a piece of bread, and you have replied, through your Chancery of Simoniacs, through your representatives in commerce and through your Popes, you sacristy shyster, you God of big business! . . . We want to drive in your nails, to press down on your crown of thorns, to draw the blood of suffering from your dry wounds. And this we can and will do, by violating the peace of your Body, you Profaner of bountiful vices, you Epitome of idiotic purities, accursed Nazarene, a do-nothing King, a coward of a God!"[15]

Women now fall into hysterics as altar bells are rung to announce that the ceremony is nearing its apotheosis. "One of the altar boys kneeled in front of [Docre], his back to the altar. A shiver ran down the priest's spine. Solemnly, but with a quivering voice, he recited: *Hoc est enim corpus meum.* Then, after the consecration, instead of kneeling before the Sacred Body, he turned to face his congregation and showed himself, haggard, with full erection, dripping with sweat."[16] The soaked fragments of the host are thrown into the room by the Canon, where the women fling themselves upon it, tearing off wet fragments and writhing over each other in their attempts to violate it. Meanwhile a raging Docre keeps distributing more hosts, chewing on them and spewing them out, wiping himself with them, while the altar boys continue "to pay homage to the nudity of the Pontiff." "It was like a padded cell in a lunatic asylum, a monstrous steam-room of prostitutes and mad-women. Then, while the altar boys coupled with the men, the mistress of the house, skirts tucked up, got up unto the altar, grabbing Christ's naked member in one hand, and directing the chalice between her legs with the other. In the depth of the chapel, in the shadows, a little girl, who up until then had not stirred, suddenly bent over and howled like a bitch in heat."[17]

At this point, Durtal can no longer contain himself and flees the scene. He finds Madame Chantelouve sniffing up the smell of sex and Satanic incense close to the priest, and he drags her out into the street. Under the pretext that she needs a glass of water, however, she succeeds in luring him into the squalid rooms of a café nearby, where she "took him by treason and obliged him to desire her."[18] After they have had sex, Durtal discovers fragments of mutilated hosts on the sheets. Although he is not at all sure about the doctrine of the Bodily Presence, he realizes that in the end, he as well has taken part in the defilement of the host. Disgusted, he takes his leave, with the firm intention of breaking off with his "Satanizing" mistress forever.

HUYSMANS DISCOVERS SATANISM

This, in short, was the story that *Là-Bas* had to tell about Satanism. Partly because of the way it was announced, the novel is and was widely understood as an authentic piece of thinly veiled autobiography. Durtal, so much is clear, can surely be understood as an alter ego of Huysmans himself. Yet what was fiction in Huysmans's book and what fact? Does *Là-Bas* really present us with a genuine description of nineteenth-century religious Satanism? Where did Huysmans's information on this subject originate? Answering these questions will teach us a lot about nineteenth-century Satanism—and might also clarify the circumstances that incited two gentlemen occultists to have a swordfight in a Parisian park on matters concerning devil worship.

Là-Bas opened with an extensive discussion of contemporary literature. We will start our trajectory here as well. Much had changed in the domain of literature since the Romantics had rediscovered Satan. Romanticism and its offshoots had fallen in discredit and had been replaced by a new kind of literature, with Émile Zola (1840–1902) as its most famous representative. Called naturalism, or sometimes realism, it did not wander into vast cosmologies or ascend the winding staircases of the mysterious and the ideal, but sought to describe the life of ordinary, mostly lower-class people, and demonstrate how their behavior was determined by scientifically verifiable facts like heredity and *milieu*.[19] Literature in this respect merely reflected what was going on in society at large. The latter half of the nineteenth century saw the rise of a positivism that preached an almost religious belief in the accomplishments of science. This also included the domain of the psychological and the spiritual. Had the experiments of Dr. Charcot, and others, not pointed out that physiological factors were the ultimate cause for psychopathological and parapsychological states?[20] Man was an animal ruled by instinct, only slightly more complicated than the beasts in the fields.

When George-Charles Huysmans took the pen name of Joris-Karl Huysmans (in commemoration of his Dutch origin) and began to publish his first ventures into literature, he was widely regarded as a follower of Zola. His debut as a novelist, *Marthe, histoire d'une fille* (1876), had told the story of a prostitute; in subsequent novels, he had explored the life of bachelors and working girls. In addition, he had participated in *Les soirées de Médan* (1880), the most famous collective creative outburst of the *groupe Zola*, contributing a short novella that told the story of the Franco-Prussian War from the perspective of a dysentery-stricken soldier desperately seeking the peace and comfort of a private closet.[21]

Huysmans's latent dissatisfaction with the massive reductionism of naturalism became apparent, however, when he published *À Rebours* ("Against Nature") in 1884. Described as a "manual for onanism of the imagination" by a contemporary author, this book would become one of the founding works of the Decadent Movement in late nineteenth-century literature, ensuring its author a certain amount of international renown.[22] The hero of the novel, Jean des Esseintes, is in every aspect the inversion of the standard naturalistic protagonist. Instead of a butcher apprentice or a factory worker, he is an affluent nobleman; instead of slavishly following his instincts according to the laws of hereditary disposition and animal society, he is someone who consciously strives for the exceptional, the artificial, and the unusual—in short, the cultural. Disgusted by modern society in all its aspects, he withdraws into the solitude of his own house, stocked with carefully selected objects of art, precious books (none of them by Zola), and natural flowers purposely chosen for their artificial look. In the end, Des Esseintes's effort at splendid isolation fails: he becomes ill, and the doctor prescribes, to his unspeakable horror, the distraction of society life in the city. Yet the point Huysmans wished to make with *À Rebours* did not fail to get across: to emphasize the value of the exceptional, and to underline the fact that human life was not intrinsically confined to the "natural," let alone the naturalistic.

For Huysmans, this clearly was more than merely a matter of literature. Naturalism and materialism, with their tendency to explain everything away as a result of animalistic urges "below the belt," dissatisfied him not only as a literary modus but also as a philosophy of life. Who could really explain the mysteries of coincidence, of love, even of money? Who could tell what caused the hysteric fits of the women in Dr. Charcot's clinic? Were they possessed because they were hysterical or hysterical because they were possessed?[23] Posing these questions already signaled the inadequacy of naturalism and positivism. Where could answers be found? Huysmans was looking not only for a new literary program, but also for a new metaphysical outlook that would do justice to the mystery of life as he experienced it. He dabbled a bit in spiritualism, but found the pseudo-religious theorizing of its advocates and the vulgarity of its adherents not to his taste. The experiences he witnessed, however, strengthened his belief in the reality of the supernatural.[24]

Huysmans was also looking for a way out from his own times, the opulent Belle Epoque that he found shallow, vulgar, and depressing. Like many of the Romantics before him, it was to the Middle Ages that he turned for solace. In France, this predilection for the Middle Ages had had its origins with Romantic authors of an antirevolutionary and royalist disposition. For these authors, the Middle Ages had symbolized a time of sacred kingship and popular faith unsoiled by the revolutionizing and secularizing tendencies that had arisen with the Enlightenment. This medievalism subsequently had been adopted by other Romantics, who used it as a vehicle for Romantic nationalism and as a kind of inverted mirror image to express their dissatisfaction with (Enlightenment) rationalism and a society dominated by the "computing faculty."[25] This "discomfort with modernity" had lost none of its poignancy in Huysmans's days, when the impact of industrialization, secularization, and political emancipation had only increased.[26] In these circumstances, an idealized version of the Middle Ages could continue to serve as a mythical counterpoint to the bleak realities of the present. In *À Rebours*, Esseintes had already found himself irresistibly attracted to Roman Catholicism and the medieval flavor of its art and old music: the book even ended with a not entirely ironic prayer asking for pity upon "an unbeliever who wants to believe."[27] Yet it would take a child's faith, *À Rebours* maintained, to be able to believe the absurdities of Roman Catholic dogma or follow its strict moral precepts: a faith neither Esseintes nor Huysmans possessed. Apart from that, the contemporary Church was only the diluted and corrupted shadow of its predecessor during the glorious Middle Ages. As Huysmans claimed in a rather peculiar aside in *À Rebours*, even the Eucharistic bread itself was not the same anymore—virtually everywhere, the old corn meal had been replaced with potato flour. Thus, even the holiest of the holy had quite literally fallen victim to the "Americanisation" of the times.

In *À Rebours*, however, the first dim outlines appeared of an *alternative path*: a path "as old as the Church" that also acknowledged the existence of the unexplainable yet did not demand "useless proofs of chaste loins." In the daydreams of Esseintes, this alternative presented itself under the name of Sadism, which for him had a very specific significance: "the forbidden pleasure of transferring to Satan the homage and the prayers due to God." Its practice implied an intentional inversion of the precepts of Roman Catholicism, in particular by committing the two sins that form the apogee of wickedness: pollution of the liturgy and sexual orgy. The most complete embodiment of his tendency "à rebours" could be found in the Witches' Sabbath à la Michelet, which comprised "all obscene practices and all blasphemies of Sadism."[28]

Huysmans's fascination with medieval "Satanism" is also attested in another of his publications from this period, a long essay he wrote on erotic art.[29] The major part of this piece was devoted to Félicien Rops (1833–1898), the Belgian artist whose work Huysmans had recently discovered, and especially to Rops's series of pornographic engravings entitled "Les Sataniques." Huysmans described Rops as a "Primitif à rebours" who had completely "penetrated and summarized Satanism" in his works.[30] Several pages of the essay concerned Rops's depiction of the Black Mass, sprinkled with references to classic demonologists such as Jean Bodin, Martin Delrio, Jacobus Sprengerus, and Joseph Görres.[31] Huysmans waxed lyrical, however, when describing an engraving entitled "Le Calvaire" that showed Mary Magdalene in ecstatic stupor before a crucified, satyr-like Satan with an enormous erection. "Far from this century, in a time where the materialist arts see nothing but hysterics who are eaten by their ovaries or nymphomaniacs whose brains are beating below their belly, he [Rops] has celebrated, not the woman of today, not the Parisienne, whose coaxing graces and suspect outfitting escapes his expertise—but Woman in her essence and of all times, the venomous and naked Beast, the mercenary of Darkness, the complete slave of the Devil. He has, in a word, celebrated the spirituality of lasciviousness that is Satanism, painted in unsurpassable pages the supernatural of perversity, the netherworld of Evil."[32]

While his fascination with Satanism was slowly taking form, Huysmans also started to develop a new vision on literature, the outlines of which he would expound on within the first pages of *Là-Bas*. Naturalism was dead, certainly, but it would do no good to "deny the unforgettable services the Naturalists have rendered to Art" and return to "the inflated nonsense of the Romantics." What was needed, he maintained, was to preserve "the documentary truthfulness, the precision of detail, the rich, sinewy language of Realism," but utilize it to "drive a well-shaft into the soul" and chant the "super-natural," the mystical: "in one word, a spiritual Naturalism that would be noble, more complete, and more formidable."[33]

This was the project Huysmans set out to realize with *Là-Bas*. As a fitting subject for his novel, he first considered Naundorffism, the informal movement smacking of right-wing Catholicism and occultism that had formed itself around an adventurer pretending to be a descendant of Louis XVI.[34] He soon dropped this, however, in favor of Satanism. Just like Durtal, the protagonist in his novel, Huysmans set out to discover whether any remnants of medieval Satanism still survived into his own day.

PÉLADAN, GUAITA, AND PAPUS

For an outsider, the first and most logical place to look for Satanism was the world of occultism and "modern" magic. This Huysmans proceeded to do. And while he primarily may have intended to "document" himself for his next book, clearly something more was at stake for him as well. A letter Huysmans sent to his friend Gustav Guiches attested to the personal aspect his explorations may have had. "I don't want anything of that pigsty of naturalism anymore!" he wrote. "Now what? What is left? Maybe occultism. Not spiritism! The clownery of the mediums, the wackedness of old ladies that turn tables! No: occultism! Not the 'up above,' but the 'underneath,' or the 'aside from,' or the 'beyond' of reality! Lacking the faith of the Primitive and the first communicant that I would like to have, there still is a mystery that 'demands' me, and that occupies my thoughts."[35]

Occultism was flourishing in fin-de-siècle Paris. A new generation of occultists had arisen, young men who, in the words of a contemporary observer, busied themselves with "studying Hermes-Trismegistos through an autographed fragment of some Éliphas Lévi and drawing pentacles in the public toilets."[36] Among its most important representatives were three men who will play an important role in this chapter: Joséphin Péladan, Stanislas de Guaita, and Gérard Encausse, better known as Papus.

Joséphin Péladan (1858–1918) was born in an ultra-Catholic, staunchly royalist family in the French provincial town of Lyons. His father published accounts of Roman Catholic visionaries and propagated the veneration of the seventh wound of Christ (that is, until the ecclesiastical authorities declared this devotion unorthodox); his brother practiced as a homeopathic therapist and unsuccessfully tried to obtain a doctor's degree with a thesis on the dangerous effects of voluntary and involuntary loss of semen. It was an environment that nurtured the promise of eccentricity, and Joséphin Péladan would more than live up to this promise.[37] Young Péladan soon moved to Paris, where he wrote his first novel, *La Vice suprême* ("The Supreme Vice"). Published in 1886 (the same year *À Rebours* saw light), this book can be characterized as an exposition of Lévian doctrines in the form of a novel. It featured a magician hero, Merodack, who obtained mastery over the fluidic forces by a series of sometimes bizarre trials of will ("He even quitted smoking, which proved to be a tough job").[38] This Kabbalist superhero was flanked by an impeccable, alluring priest, both striving in unison to combat the immorality and decadence of the times. The book proved a considerable success, doubtlessly because of its heady mixture of occultism, fin de siècle eroticism, and stinging criticism on the flaws of its time—a set of themes Péladan would continue to exploit in an endless series of follow-ups.

After *La Vice suprême* had brought him fame, esotericism became a life project for Péladan. When someone discovered for him that the name Péladan was mentioned in the

Bible as Baladan, an Assyrian king, he promptly declared himself to be a descendant of Assyrian royalty, adopted the kingly title "Sâr Merodack," and donned an appropriate attire of flowing robes and patriarchal beard.[39] This made him a well-known figure, and a grateful object of public attention, on the avenues of Paris. Behind this operatic façade, however, Péladan entertained an ambitious project. Inspired by Wagner's operas and the composer's quest for a "Gesamtkunstwerk," he aspired to form a Roman Catholic esoteric order in which artists of all disciplines cooperated to offer the corrupted Belle Epoque a spiritual antidote. For Péladan, the great Romantic notion of the artist as the builder of a new and more spiritual society still retained undiluted validity. "Artist, you are Priest," he wrote in a publication justifying his artistic program. "Art is the great Mystery. . . . Artist, you are King; Art is the real Empire. . . . Artist, you are Magician: Art is the great Miracle, she alone provides proof for our immortality."[40] In the years 1892 to 1897, he succeeded in organizing a series of successful art "Salons" in which influential Symbolist and Decadent artists like Redon, Rops, Delacroix, and Ogier participated, while a young Erik Satie composed a special music score for the first session.[41]

Péladan's Assyrian kingship did not prevent him from styling himself a "loyal son of the Church." Catholicism and esotericism had mingled easily in the Lyons milieu from which he sprang, and their complementary nature was never a question for him. In the prologue to *Comment on devient Mage* ("How to Become a Magician," 1892), he declared himself perfectly prepared to burn the work with his own hands if "Peter the infallible" would deem it improper or heterodox.[42] The defense of Catholicism remained his official goal throughout his life—although one wonders whether the Catholic Church was much pleased with this eccentric defender, who, in his self-assumed dignity of cardinal extraordinaire, proceeded to excommunicate the wife of Rothschild because she had demolished the former living quarters of Balzac, and in addition urged the ecclesiastical authorities to take immediate action against bullfights (primarily while it was well known, he claimed, that Spanish women in the audience experienced "several complete orgasms in a row" while watching the cruel spectacle).[43] In a handbook for female occultists, he induced ladies from the *beau monde* to use their sexual charms to further the cause of Art and Catholicism; in another book, he envisioned "curing" a club of staunch lesbians by dousing them with the highly aphrodisiacal "plante attractive" of Abraham van Helsing, thus igniting a massive but healthily heterosexual orgy.[44] For the Sâr, there was no contradiction here. He did not wish to question the role of the Church as upholder of strict morality; he simply claimed that his writings targeted a different, "decadent" audience that could not be reached by the clergy anymore. Moreover, he maintained, prudishness in prose was something for Protestant Puritans: Catholicism had always favored firm expression.[45]

For all these pious assurances, it is a safe bet that *La Vice suprême* did more to stimulate interest in occultism than in Catholicism. This was the effect, in any case, that the novel had on the marquis Stanislas de Guaita (1861–1897). Guaita sprang from a family of wealthy French nobility in Lorraine and had come to Paris under the pretext of studying chemistry. Initially, he had considered poetry as a career, and he published two volumes of verse in the neo-Romantic tradition of Baudelaire, *La Muse noire* (1883) and *Rosa Mystica* (1885).[46] Best characterized as "neither excellent nor too mediocre," his poems clearly attested to the same aversion to the prevailing spirit of positivism and spiritual materialism that Huysmans had also come to feel.[47] In between the lines, however, they also contained indications that

Guaita's belief in the Romantic Gospel of Art was wavering. In the eponymous opening poem of *Rosa Mystica*, for instance, he called the "mystical rose" of poetry a "splendid illusion" and the Ideal a deception: and while he declared his continuing devotion to the "lying charms of my mystic Dream" as the only option to make life worthwhile, the reader gets the distinct impression that these rhetorics mask a certain faintness of conviction.[48]

In these circumstances, *La Vice suprême* struck him like a thunderbolt. Here he was presented with a path that did not oblige him to live with his "eyes closed," as he had written in *Rosa Mystica*. Also, the mysticism and magic he had attributed to poetry in the preface to this work—the ability "to divinate the unknown, to penetrate into the impenetrable, and to fill up emptiness"—could now suddenly be given practical and tangible form.[49] Péladan's novel prompted Guaita to reread Éliphas Lévi, whose works henceforth became the lodestone of his thought. It also prompted him to contact Péladan personally, which resulted in a lively correspondence and a close friendship.[50] The marquis abandoned his career in letters—which up to then had not seemed promising anyhow—and embarked on a full-time study of the occult. Stacking his ancestral chateau in Lorraine with an impressive and expensive collection of occult rarities, he immersed himself in books during the night, keeping himself afoot with caffeine, cocaine, morphine, and, last but not least, his excellent wine cellar.[51] These nocturnal studies would result in his magnum opus *Le Serpent de la Génese* ("The Serpent of Genesis"), a mammoth work intending to dissolve the mystery of cosmic evil once and for all.[52]

When visiting the capital, Guaita mingled extensively in esoteric circles. Thus he met Gérard Encausse (1865–1916), a medical student who had likewise grown impatient with the all-too-arrogant positivism of the time, had discovered Éliphas Lévi, and had subsequently started to publish about occultism under the pen name "Papus" (the genius of medicine in the *Nuctemeron*, a book on magic attributed to Apollonius of Tyana and edited in French by Lévi).[53] The two men had met at a meeting of Isis, the recently founded French branch of Blavatsky's Theosophical Society.[54] Both Guaita and Papus, however, soon grew discontented with the esotericism that was *de rigueur* at Isis, which in the wake of Madame Blavatsky was taking an ever more "Eastern" coloration. Like Rudolf Steiner later on, they wanted to honor the distinct esoteric development of the Christian West and continue the pure Lévian tradition of occultism.[55] At the time, the two young disciples of Lévi had still been only students. Papus, however, was an organizer by nature. He broke away from Isis and the Theosophical Society and set up a study center for occultism at Rue de Trévisse 29 with a fellow student, Lucien Chamuel. The center was equipped with a bookshop, a library, a lecture room, and a practice room for magical experiments. In addition to this, Papus resuscitated the all-but-defunct order of Martinism, a school of Catholic-esoteric mysticism that had fallen into disarray. He used its name to give an aura of antiquity to what was in essence a thoroughly modern organization, aiming to give its members a solid education in esotericism that could stand on a par with "secular" science. It soon sprang branches all over France and the rest of the world.[56] Last but not least, Guaita and Papus resurrected—not for the first or the last time—the legendary Order of the Rosicrucians.[57] In 1888, they called into life the "Ordre Cabbalistique de la Rose + Croix." Papus, Guaita, and Chamuel all took seats in the "Supreme Council" of the new order; they were soon joined by Péladan, who claimed to have had some sort of Rosicrucian initiation (possibly with some right).[58]

Clearly, occultism in Paris was experiencing a flurry of activity. Huysmans was not alto-gether unfamiliar with the main characters of this new, blooming subculture. He had met Péladan in the salon circuit and had sent the Sâr a not unappreciative note after reading *La Vice suprême*.[59] In addition, he had had an affair with Péladan's former mistress, Henriette Maillat—it was this affair, as a matter of fact, that Huysmans would describe in *Là-Bas*, quoting Maillat's love letters verbatim.[60] By frequenting the bookstore on Rue de Trévisse, Huysmans soon became acquainted with most of the other major characters of Parisian occultism. Yet for Satanism, "pollution of liturgy," and reenactments of the medieval Witches' Sabbath, he was on the wrong track here. With regard to the complex of the mythological figures that can be captioned under the name of Satan, the new Rosicrucians strictly adhered to the triple scheme of Éliphas Lévi. Guaita can be regarded as speaking for all of them when he propounds the classic Lévian interpretation of the devil in *Le Serpent de la Gènese*, distin-guishing three levels: symbol of evil in a vulgar sense, astral light or life force in an esoteric sense, and the "mysterious attraction of the Self to the Self" on yet another esoteric level.[61] If anything, Satan was placed slightly more "on the bad side" by the marquis. Although lip service is paid to his role as "universal dispenser of elementary life," Satan-Pantheos is almost exclusively mentioned in a negative way, as a "formidable and multifarious" force that "spec-ifies itself under a thousand faces to defile every altar." Significantly, Lévi's Baphomet had suddenly become the "He-Goat of Goetia" (or Black Magic) with Guaita.[62]

Surprisingly, the only member of the trio who gave some indication of Satanist lean-ings was Péladan, the valiant champion of Catholicism. While visiting Palestine at a later date, he would scandalize the guests of a Franciscan guesthouse by pledging his love for Satan, describing him as "the most perfect creature on the spiritual plane" and "Jesus-Prometheus."[63] In *Comment on devient artiste* ("How to Become an Artist," 1894), the Sâr would even declare himself a descendant of the angels of Genesis 6:2, who had fallen from grace because of their love for the daughters of man. Apparently, he meant the latter not solely in a metaphorical sense, with Satan as the symbolic ancestor of all artists and mys-tics who strive to the ideal, but also in a quite literal one, the true artist being an "arist," a descendant of a race of supermen engendered by the fallen angels and still among us as men of special inspiration.[64] Here, as elsewhere, Péladan clearly was indebted to the ideas of the Romantic Satanists, and it is not surprising when one sees "Satan-Prometheus" appear in one of his novels as a "beautiful Androgyne chained to a rock" that could have walked in straight from a George Sand novel.[65]

Despite all this, however, the ultra-Catholic Sâr, who subjected his manuals of magic to papal scrutiny, remained an unlikely candidate for Satanism. Worship of Satan was not something Huysmans was going to find with these fin de siècle occultists. Even less were his chances of discovering Sabbath-like sexual orgies in the esoteric subculture. Péladan might describe with obvious relish a wide variety of perversions in his novels, but his magician heroes always walked through the sexual carnage with unflinching minds. In *Comment on devient Mage*, he advised, before anything, self-control.[66] Guaita took the same line in *Serpent de la Gènese*. While celibacy was an unnatural and undesirable condition for a magician (except for certain specific ritual purposes), it was essential to command the flesh instead of being commanded by it. In this manner, the magician might be able to "free himself of the sexual yoke."[67] Only in a small footnote to his enormous work does Guaita acknowledge the possibility of using sex in ritual, while prudently leaving these "Arcanæ" under the "triple veil" of esoteric secrecy.[68] Of foremost importance to Péladan, Papus, and Guaita was the control of will they adopted from Lévi. This was what enabled the adept to control the elementary universal force, which is the essence of magic. In words that seem to foreshadow Freud and Jung and harken back to Baudelaire and Lévi, Guaita stated that "Satan-Pantheos" continually proposes a "retrogression to instinct," which leads ultimately to "the apotheosis of the Unconscious."[69] The Witches' Sabbath was a prominent example of this and clearly belonged to the domain of black magic, a "perversion of the occult" that consisted of putting to action the vital force of the Serpent for purposes of evil. This was the true religion of Satan, a religion of abandon and "astral drunkenness."[70] In their description of this dark cult, the three occultists closely followed the Lévian example and repeated most of the latter's descriptions, including the famous inverted pentagram as a presumed emblem of Satanism.[71]

Huysmans does not seem to have been particularly impressed by this wealth of theorizing. "I am plunged in work in search of a demonical and sodomizing priest who says black Masses," he wrote to his Dutch friend Arij Prins on February 6, 1890. "I need him for my book. I had to penetrate the world of the occultists for all that—such a bunch of simpletons and swindlers!"[72] He would vent his scorn for the neo-Lévians uninhibitedly on the pages of *Là-Bas*, calling them "complete ignoramuses" and "unquestionable imbeciles."[73] One wonders what caused this profound irritation with a group of people that in many respects was dealing with the same issues as he did. Obviously it could be hard to take somebody like Péladan *au sérieux*, but this may not have been the root of Huysmans's irritation. In the end, the problem might have been *precisely* that the modern magicians were too much like himself, too easy to understand: "insignificant young men looking to exploit the whims of a public fed up with Positivism."[74] They did not play up to the part that Huysmans was looking for. He was seeking something more extreme, more alien, something from another time. And at roughly the same moment that he was expressing his disappointment with the occultists to Prins, he was already on the trace of somebody just like that—a man truly Satanic, truly demonic, with more than a whiff of the Middle Ages about him. It is at this point that the ex-priest Joseph-Antoine Boullan (1824–1893) enters our story.

JOSEPH BOULLAN

Time and again while exploring the occultist subculture of Paris, Huysmans had heard rumors about an excommunicated priest in Lyons practicing black magic. None of the leading occultists were prepared to bring him into contact with this man: but by another route, he had managed to obtain his address. On February 6, 1890 (the same day he heaped scorn upon the occultists to Arij Prins), Huysmans dispatched a long letter to Lyons. In it, he told about his fruitless efforts to document himself on Satanism among the occultists of Paris— "incontestable imbeciles" who had wearied him with "idiotic theories wrapped up in the most appalling verbiage"—and went on to write:

> Several times I heard your name pronounced in tones of horror—and this in itself predisposed me in your favour. Then I heard rumours that you were the only initiate in the ancient mysteries who had obtained practical as well as theoretical results, and

I was told that if anyone could produce undeniable phenomena, it was you, and you alone. . . . This I should like to believe, because it would mean that I had found a rare personality in these drab times—and I could give you some excellent publicity if you needed it. I could set you as the Superman, the Satanist, the only one in existence, far removed from the infantile spiritualism of the occultists. Allow me then, Monsieur, to put these questions to you—quite bluntly, for I prefer a straightforward approach. Are you a Satanist? And can you give me any information about succubae—Del Rio, Bodin, Sinistrari and Görres being quite inadequate on this subject? You will note that I ask for no initiation, no secret lore—only for reliable documents, for results you have obtained in your experiments.[75]

An answer from Lyons arrived by return of post. It contained a polite refusal of Huysmans's publicity offer and a formal denial that its sender was a Satanist: instead, he was "an Adept who had declared war on all demoniacal cults." It was true that he was an expert on incubi and succubae, but he did not want to give any detailed information until Huysmans had made the purpose of his inquiry more clear. The letter was signed "Dr. Johannès—and was headed with the motto *Quis ut Deus?* ("Who is like God?")—the Latin translation of Michael, the name of the archangel subduing Satan.[76]

Huysmans replied again the next day, tactically changing his tone and claiming that he did not want to glorify Satanism, but merely to prove its continuing existence.

I am weary of the theories of my friend Zola, whose absolute positivism disgusts me. I am not less weary of the systems of Charcot, who did want to convince me that demonianism and Satanism is just an atavism that he can check or develop with the women treated at La Salpétiere by pressing their ovaries. I am even wearier, if this is possible, of occultists and spiritualists: the phenomena they practise, although very real, are too identical. I want to shake up all these people, create a work of art of *supernatural realism*, of *spiritual naturalism*.[77]

This answer seemed to please the priest from Lyons. He promised his full cooperation, and confirmed Huysmans's supposition that devil worship still existed—indeed, he wrote, it was flourishing more than ever. "I can tell you things that will certainly make your book interesting. I can put at your disposal documents that will enable you to prove that Satanism is still active in our time, and in what form and in what circumstances. Your work will thus endure as a monumental history of Satanism in the nineteenth century."[78] In the weeks that followed, "documents" started to pour in. Huysmans was delighted. "I am in constant correspondence with the sacrilegious priest who invokes succubae at Lyons," he wrote his friend Arij Prins. "He sends me the most curious documents about Satanism in the present age. . . . I expect to make a little book with all this that will shake up the pork faces of our time—because incontestable documents show that from the Middle Ages on, the Black Mass has still been said. In the seventeenth century, an *abbé* called Guibourt [*sic*] celebrated it upon the naked womb of Montespan—and at this moment, the practice continues; there are adepts throughout the whole of Europe and even in America, where Longfellow, the poet, is the leader of the sect that devotes itself to sacrilege."[79] Clearly, Huysmans believed to have struck a gold mine: he had found the one person who could instruct him freely and extensively on the hidden world of contemporary Satanism.

Who was this former priest Boullan? Joseph-Antoine Boullan was born in 1824 and was ordained a priest in the revolutionary year of 1848. Gifted with undeniable intellectual capacities, he developed into a prolific writer of spiritual books and tracts, and he may (or may not) have obtained a theological doctorate in Rome. After spending some time as a missionary of the recently founded Congregation of the Precious Blood, he soon became involved with the world of Reparationist and apocalyptic piety that was flourishing in France at the time.[80] Within certain Roman Catholic circles, the Revolution had given great credence to the notion that spiritual reparation was needed: the faithful were called upon to perform substitutionary penance for the sins that the nation had committed in overthrowing the king, persecuting the Church, and profaning the holy days and the divine name. By doing this, France might be restored to its former glory as a Christian nation, and the tides of revolution and secularization turned. In the margins of the Church, this idea was often coupled to other elements of fringe spirituality, such as new apparitions of the Holy Virgin, Naundorffism, and a resurgence of the medieval belief in the imminent coming of the Age of the Holy Ghost.

Boullan was evidently attracted to this milieu and saw a place for himself in it. During a pilgrimage to La Salette (where the Virgin had appeared to two children in 1846), he met Adèle Chevalier, a Belgian nun from Soissons who experienced visions on a regular basis. He became her confessor, and together they proceeded to establish a religious order at Sèvres, near Versailles, intended for both male and female believers who wanted to devote themselves to the "Work of Reparation for Blasphemies and Sunday Violations."[81]

By this time, he and Adèle had become lovers. In 1860, Adèle became pregnant, and according to a personal confession he later wrote (the famous "Cahier rose"), Boullan believed he had to "destroy" the new- or stillborn child, after first baptizing it "by way of precaution." Apparently he thought—or intended to claim—that the child was a "monster" engendered by a demon.[82] Boullan also engaged in sexual contact with other members of the convent, the populace of which was predominantly female—sometimes ordering the pious women to insert the host into their vagina.[83] These unusual devotional practices were justified by an extreme extension of the doctrine of spiritual reparation, according to which the believer could not only take on penance for the sins of other people, but on occasion even for their sins themselves.[84]

Boullan drew attention to himself by the exorcisms he practiced on possessed nuns—according to some sources, he spit into their mouths, gave them hosts mixed with his own excrement or Adèle's urine, and taught them how they could have spiritual sex with Jesus and the saints.[85] The bishop of Versailles suspended his sacerdotal dignity, his convent was disbanded by the police, and Boullan was put on trial and spent three years in prison for swindling. After this, he departed for Rome, where he seems to have confessed himself to the Holy Office and apparently was restored to the priesthood.[86] It is improbable, however, that Boullan ever really mended his ways. An indication for this may be found in the already mentioned "Cahier rose," which contains some rather peculiar drafts of what seem to be demon-binding rites somewhere halfway between exorcisms and magical evocations. In these rites, Boullan orders the "cornus"—"horned ones"—which are attached to the priests and ecclesiastical dignitaries judging his case to do him no harm; otherwise they will be condemned to "perpetual hell" in case of very grave offences, or to 99 years of hell or "50 years in the tower of Babel" in case of lighter infringements.[87] In a rite dated June 16, 1867, he even attempted to replace all the "horned ones who are delegated to and found with the inquisitorial judges" with new ones. These texts were clearly sketches, meant to be written out on other pieces of paper for ritual purposes. In several cases, Boullan noted that he had burned them on specific dates, probably with some kind of ceremony; in one case, the "horned ones" were told to depart with the (posted?) piece of writing itself, "but without being attached to it"—a precautionary addendum that may have been meant to prevent the letter from becoming demon-infested.[88]

After his return to France, Boullan became editor of *Les Annales de la Sainteté* ("The Annals of Saintliness"), a periodical devoted to apparitions of saints and visions of Catholic mystics. Once again, he used this publication to propagate Reparationist and Restorationist views: in an article in the issue of July 1874, for instance, he urged the Papacy to hallow the executed Louis XVI as a Catholic martyr and thus repair the "social crime" of the Revolution.[89] The doctrinal views he uttered in this publication and his renewed activities as an exorcist, however, earned him another, and this time final, suspension, followed by official excommunication.

Stripped from his sacerdotal dignity, Boullan did not have to look far to find a suitable job vacancy. Already before his excommunication, he had been in contact with Eugène Vintras (1807–1875), the leader of a neo-Catholic religious movement centered on the "Work of Mercy." In 1839, Vintras had started to receive visitations of the archangel Michael, announcing the speedy arrival of the "Third Kingdom," the reign of the Holy Spirit.[90] At that moment, Vintras had still been a factory superintendent in the small town of Tilly, but he soon became the official prophet of a fairly numerous religious movement, with congregations or "septaines" sprinkled within France, Spain, Italy, and even England. Except from the familiar mixture of millennialism and Naundorffism, Vintrasism was characterized by specific points of doctrine. Some of them will be recounted later on, but prominent among them was the belief that for the faithful, the reign of the Spirit has already begun: bodily and spiritually, they had already entered perfection. To underscore this point, all Vintras's disciples received new angelic names divinely revealed to him. Another consequence was the fact that in Vintrasism, women could also officiate: a special ritual called the Provictimal Sacrifice of Mary had been instated for them, while Vintras and the other male Vintrasian priests celebrated the Ritual of Melchisedec. The traditional Mass, with its reenactment of Christ's suffering, was destined to become obsolete, since it belonged to the era of the Son that was now passing away. This was symbolized in the sacerdotal vestments of Vintras, the stole of which featured an inverted cross, signifying that the age of suffering was over. Precepts like these were obviously ill at ease with official Roman Catholic dogma; in 1851, the group of Vintras had been declared a "criminal association" and "repugnant sect" by Papal brief.[91]

Vintras died in 1875, the same year Boullan was defrocked a second time. The latter immediately went to Lyons and declared himself the official successor of Vintras.[92] Although the majority of the Vintrasians refused to recognize him as such, Boullan managed to assemble a small group of followers around him. In Lyons, he lived in the house of the architect

Pascal Misme and his family; close by were two young sisters, the Mademoiselles Gay, who earned their living as seamstresses and had been given the angelic names of Sahaël and Anandhaël. In addition, Boullan was assisted by a female "somnambulist," who functioned as a medium, and by Julie Thibault, a woman of some fifty years old who was something of a mystic in her own right. She had left her husband when still young in order to wander the roads as a pilgrim, receiving visions and prophetic dreams on a regular base. Boullan had granted her the honorary title of "Female Melchisedec." His own person he designated as "Jean-Baptiste" ("John the Baptist"), in logical imitation of Vintras, who had styled himself "the new Elijah."

At about this time, Boullan seems to have sought contact with esoteric and occult circles in Paris. As we have seen in the case of Lévi and Péladan, Catholicism and occultism were not necessarily felt to be at odds at the time, and Boullan's interest in occultism was long-standing and evidently genuine. Even in his later correspondence, he made frequent references to Kabbalah and Tarot, and one witness recalled he had a pentagram tattooed above his left eyelid.[93] There was some exchange of letters with Parisian occultists, and Boullan was visited in Lyons by the Canon Roca, a priest who had been excommunicated because of his esoteric and socialist sympathies and who later became a member of the Rosicrucian Supreme Council.[94] The Canon, in his turn, invited Stanislas de Guaita to come over. Although Péladan warned him to be wary of the old exorcist, Guaita accepted the invitation. In Lyons, he was welcomed with open arms by the two abbés and participated freely in the Vintrasian rites, even receiving some kind of consecration, it seems, from the hands of Boullan himself. Just a short time later, however, he left in all haste, apparently taking Roca with him.

Two different versions of the events that surrounded Guaita's subsequent break-up with the Lyons Carmel exist. Boullan would later confide his recollections of what had happened to Huysmans. "The Parisian Occultists," he wrote, "and Guaita in particular, came here to trick me out of the secrets of my power. Guaita even prostrated himself before Madame Thibault and tricked her into giving him her blessing: 'I am nothing but a child that wants to be taught,' he said. For twelve days, we were like a family to him."[95] Soon after his brusque departure, Boullan reported, the treacherous marquis had assaulted him by way of magic during the night; Boullan had only barely saved his life by performing the Sacrifice of Glory and receiving communion.[96] Guaita, in his turn, reported being astrally attacked by Boullan after he had left Lyons. In an undated letter to his friend Péladan, he wrote, "The other night, I was attacked fluidically with enormous force, and returned the poisoned current to its centre or pole of emission, in such a way that the conjurer in question must have sincerely regretted his encroachments.—Nergal has been paralysed in his bed and was about to submit to the outrages of a succubus without being able to move. He only managed to save himself by the name of *Jodhévauhé.*—Caillé however has succumbed to a succubus." In another letter to Péladan, he alluded to the reasons that had made him break off relations with his host. "The Abbé B. is a learned and first-rate theologian, but he lives too much with the Spirits, and falls into a fatal error with regard to the Spiritual Marriage; I will tell you about that under four eyes."[97]

What was this "fatal error" that Guaita would not put upon paper? It seems Boullan had elaborated somewhat on the doctrines he had taken over from Vintras. To the Vintrasian idea of "celestified" believers, he added the notion of "celestified" marriages between the faithful. These "unions of life," he claimed, created a "Ferment of Life" that was highly beneficial on the spiritual plane, fortified prayer, and, when performed in their name, helped deceased persons who were still wandering through the lower spheres to enter heaven and take on their final spiritual form. To further one's spiritual growth, one could contract such marriages with somebody spiritually superior, while people of great personal merit could engage in spiritual marriage with beings of a lower order, such as elementary spirits, thus helping them on in their ontological development. What Guaita had found out, was the fact that these "celestified" marriages did not merely involve the spirit of the faithful, but their body as well.[98] Boullan was "spiritually" involved with almost all women in his small group of followers, and most notably with the two seamstress sisters, with whom he shared the bed together or separately, under the maternal blessing of their pious mother. As a matter of fact, the "union of life" Boullan had concluded with one of the Gay sisters is described in an undated manuscript from his private archives. "After praying," the old abbé writes in the elevated tone of the mystics, "the heart of the Elected had been enflamed with the fires of Pure Love. The only thing that remained was to rise into Eden. . . . She told me: 'Jean-Baptiste, take me; embrace me in your fire and let me fly into Eden, into the bridal chamber of the spiritual spouses.' This was accomplished. . . . The Bridegroom came; the communion of life took place in a beatific ecstasy. 'Oh!' the Celestial Fiancé exclaimed, 'My heart is communing with Life itself!' "[99]

From other documents in Boullan's personal archives, it becomes clear that these practices had been going on for some time. In a "General Confession" to his congregation from February 6, 1881, Boullan had already made reference to these "unions of life." "The problem that has to be solved is this: one does not possess a state [of life] that entails prerogatives, and one must begin to exercise these prerogatives to acquire this state. . . . The Chosen Ones of the Carmel freely and voluntary consent to trample the laws of the Reign that is dying, to enter into the freedom of the children of God, regenerated, transfigured. The first difficulties will be followed by even greater ones with regard to the putting in practice of the holy unions of life."[100] In a manuscript from 1884, Boullan noted down the "Mission of Moses and Aaron." The "First Initiation to the third degree of the Henochite Tarot," we learn from this, consisted of the blessing of the "organ of love," including the laying on of hands. "The fall has made the organ of love the Gate of Animality: that is the reason why this organ hides itself, from shame for the state to which it has been reduced on earth. But Elijah has brought us [tidings] from heaven that this organ is also the Gate of transformation and of glory, and thus we regard it with joy, while blessing it, and for us, there is no shame anymore."[101] The first initiation to the first degree was more profound: "The chosen one asks to prove her love; she opens her organ of love which is well constituted, as it has to be with the woman that aspires to give love. With joy she receives the organ of love in its full force within her; she brushes it with her most tender caresses; she excites it, but without effort on her part, solely by the fluids with which it is surrounded."[102] In a document entitled "Doctrine of Life from the Zohar concerning the holy laws of the live-giving unions of the Virginal Bride and the ever-virginal Bridegroom," Boullan added: "And let him penetrate into the holy of holies that is the organ of love and let the Woman Bride receive the union of life, and let the organ that is the holy of holies obtain the blessing of the fluids of life, in that part which is called

Sion. . . . And these fluids of life, in the organ where they come together, and which are transmitted, in celestial and terrestrial forms, by that most holy organ, are of the whiteness of light, and it is for this reason that they are called [of] life."[103] The "Ferments of Life," this text suggests, may have consisted of a mixture of male and female sexual effluvia.

It had been these practices of sexual mysticism that had scandalized Guaita. After all, Boullan posed as a magician, and he thus brought disrepute to the adepts of the Holy Kabbalah, such as Guaita himself. He decided to take action against Boullan. By coincidence, he had just made the acquaintance of a young occultist by the name of Oswald Wirth who happened to be engaged in correspondence with Boullan. Together, they planned to trick Boullan into a written statement regarding the true nature of his "unions of life." For months, the defrocked priest was hazy about the subject, shrouding the mystery in clouds of mystical language. But then Wirth decided to write to him and say that divine inspiration had revealed to him what the rite was all about. Boullan answered that God had disclosed him the true answer by special grace; shortly afterward, the sisters Gay sent Wirth a letter (doubtlessly dictated by Boullan), which said they were ardently praying for Wirth to come to Lyons and join them in a union of life.[104]

These epistolary confessions would have been sufficiently incriminating in themselves, but the two occultists took the time to collect some more damaging material from a former member of Boullan's group, particularly in regard to the abbé's sexual endeavors.[105] After this, Guaita convened the Supreme Council of the Rosicrucian Order, whose duties included "combating black magic wherever it was encountered." This improvised court of honor, consisting of Guaita, Papus, Péladan, and a few of the marquis' other occultist friends, duly condemned Boullan in 1887.[106] Wirth notified the Lyons prophet of the verdict in a letter dated May 24 of that year, urging him to stop his "sacrilegious manoeuvres" because the "initiatory tribunal" would not tolerate to see the Kabbalah profaned for very long. "For you are condemned. As yet more overcome by Christian charity rather than strict justice, however, the initiatory tribunal wishes to wait: the sentence remains suspended over your head, until the day that by default of more merciful ways, its application will have become inevitable."[107]

Huysmans—to whom we shall now return—was certainly aware of the controversy between Boullan and the Paris occultists. Just a few days after he had exchanged his first letters with Boullan, he had had an interview with Oswald Wirth, who had warned him in plain terms about the abbé. On a later occasion, the occultists went to see Huysmans at his desk in the Ministry of the Interior to tell him what they had discovered about Boullan. But the Decadent writer only smiled wryly, telling them that if the old man "had found a mystical dodge for obtaining a little carnal satisfaction," so much the better for him.[108] Huysmans's indifference might have been related to the fact that at this date he still seems to have thought that Boullan was essentially a Satanist—despite Boullan's own assurances to the contrary, and despite Wirth's qualified statement that the former priest was surely profaning Christianity's most holy rites, but not worshipping Satan in the formal sense of the word.[109]

Boullan, for his part, did all that was in his power to recruit this promising new neophyte from Paris to his cause. In his letters, he gave Huysmans his own personal accounts of his conflict with the Roman Catholic ecclesiastical authorities (which would be included almost word for word in *Là-Bas*), as well as of his dispute with the occultists; he also actively tried to involve the writer in his semiperpetual spiritual warfare with the neo-Rosicrucians.[110] Already in his second reply, he had given Huysmans a "word of warning": the occultists, although only superficially initiated in the secrets of magic, were certainly capable of "small results." "I presume you have armed yourself for your defence," Boullan went on, "for when you will do what you say you will do in your letter, you will certainly incite them against you."[111] On July 24, 1890, Huysmans notified Prins of the fact that he was condemned to death by the Rose+Croix, "one of the recently-founded sects of Satanism in France." "In Magic, a secret disclosed is a secret lost, and for them, the point at issue is to prevent the realisation of my book."[112] We can be pretty sure that the information about this death warrant, and the whole death warrant itself, stemmed from Lyons and not from the gentlemen of the Rosicrucian Order.

Huysmans only definitely chose sides, so it seems, after he visited Boullan and his circle in September 1890. Wary because of his prior experiences with the Parisian occultists, Boullan had first sent out his trusted assistant Julie Thibault to check the state of mind of the Decadent writer. Huysmans was very impressed by this remarkable woman and the almost medieval life she led, pilgrimaging from one Holy Virgin shrine to another and living on milk, honey, and Eucharistic bread all the while. Still, he did not seem to have been totally convinced of her holiness. In his private notebook, at any rate, he jotted down that the night after she left, he was visited by a succubus who exhausted him with erotic variations that would have been impossible in real life. He felt sure that the old woman had set this sex demon upon him.[113] (The thought that the pious Thibault might have entertained this kind of desire for the writer of *Là-Bas* may not be as absurd as it seems. Julie continued to correspond separately with Huysmans for years, and Boullan told Huysmans in one of his letters that she "nourished the design" to serve him "Ferments of Life" to assist in his spiritual transformation: "Ah, dearest friend, this is not to be despised, for this rejuvenates and vitalizes one's forces."[114])

When Huysmans was duly invited to Lyons, he wrote excitedly to Prins that he would surely see some memorable sights there. "Those people are without a shadow of a doubt diabolical creatures. . . . I have only three more chapters to write now—but I cannot start with the first of them without going down there, where I ought to see some special Masses."[115] Did he refer to the "Mozarabic" Masses of Vintras, or did he expect to witness a Black Mass at Lyons? It is difficult to say, but it is clear that, at this time, he still regarded Boullan *cum suis* as candidates for Satanism. What Huysmans eventually *did* see at Boullan's Carmel is also hard to tell. Huysmans does not seem to have left us any accounts of his first visit to Lyons. He certainly would not have seen any "messe noire" but probably witnessed the "Sacrifice of Melchisedec," and possibly also the ceremonies that Boullan staged to counter the magic attacks of Guaita, Péladan, Papus, and their ilk. During his second visit almost a year later, Huysmans gave an impressed account of these "Wagrams in the air." "I am a bit afraid that I have ended up in a lunatic house. Boullan jumps around like a tiger cat, holding his hosts. He calls upon Saint Michael and the eternal judges of eternal justice, then at the altar cries three times: Bring down Péladan, Bring down Péladan, Bring down Péladan! *It is done*, says Madame Thibault, her hands in her lap."[116] Instead of the Black Mass he might have expected, Huysmans ended up attending a ceremony of long-distance exorcism.

With respect to the "angelic" marriage rites that had appalled the Parisian Rosicrucians, all circumstances indicate that Boullan did not divulge their secret to Huysmans. Indeed, even as late as 1900, Huysmans would express his disbelief in what was said to be going on in the inner circle around the abbé—although by then he had had ample opportunity to conclude that Boullan was a rather peculiar character.[117] Be it as it may, it was somewhere in 1890 and around the time of his first visit to Lyons that the gradual process began that would transform Huysmans into a de facto sympathizer of Boullan and his combat against "Satanism." As Dr. Johannès, Boullan would make a star appearance in *Là-Bas*, while the Rosicrucians would be portrayed as rather clumsy yet willing Satanists. The colorful atmosphere that surrounded Boullan and his group will certainly have played its part in enchanting the weary Decadent writer. "It's all so completely medieval," he wrote to Prins shortly before his Lyons visit. "It's like a dream come true, in days like these."[118]

Before we continue, a few words about the mysterious "documents" concerning Satanism that Huysmans reported to have received from Boullan in great numbers. Satanism, it must be noted, played an important role in the theology of Boullan. The congregation he had formed during the earlier days of his activity was meant to practice "the Work of Reparation of blaspheming and violation of the Sunday."[119] In keeping with general "Reparationist" thinking, the "blasphemies" intended were probably those perpetrated during the Revolution, or by the French secularized State, or by the French people, the most dechristianized nation of its day. Gradually, however, Boullan had come to give this concept of blasphemy a more specific meaning. In small groups all over Europe, he maintained, devil-worshipping priests and their followers were systematically profaning the host to please Satan and his demons. The involvement of a properly ordained priest was essential, because, as Boullan wrote to Huysmans, only a priest could enact the consecration that was needed to ensure the presence of Christ in the host. "To celebrate the Black Mass, that is to say, the Satanic Mass, there is more needed than just sacrilege. The priest of the Black Mass has to have crossed what is called in magic the *threshold of Mystery*. This means, in good French, that this priest has to be *consecrated to Satan*."[120] Groups that practiced Satanism without a priest were forced to steal consecrated wafers from churches; whole criminal networks, predominantly consisting of women who attended Mass under pretense of piety, existed to supply them with the object of their sacrileges.

Boullan probably had found these ideas in Vintrasianism, for whose doctrines it likewise was of great importance. In this, as we shall see in the next chapter, they were part of a wider current in the substratum of Roman Catholicism. In Vintrasianism, the concept of Satanism was not merely a device to point out the great iniquity of the times, but a lived and enacted element of religious ritual. In highly dramatic sessions that greatly resembled the "Wagrams in the air" performed by Boullan, Vintras would do battle "in the spirit" against the Satanists, disturbing their rites and rescuing the threatened body of Christ. The hosts that were maltreated by the Satanists miraculously materialized in the hands of the new Elijah, often bleeding from the wounds that had been inflicted upon them. The blood sometimes formed wondrous patterns of esoteric symbols.[121]

One of Vintras's own reports of these titanic battles has been left to us.[122] In this remarkable document, Vintras tells how a secret occult council met in "a small town near Paris" in order to annihilate him. A letter written by Vintras serves to conduct his fluidic presence to the place where the Satanists convene, whose numbers are made up out of "politicians, Dominicans and clergy." They invoke the "Omnipotent Intelligence," who reveals himself as the Egyptian god Amun-Ra. He tells them that he needs the sacrifice of the "great God of the Christians," and of a virgin waiting in the next room, in order to be able to destroy the "last prophet" of Christianity. The virgin is brought in, of course naked, and strangely enough attached to metal wires that enable the Satanists to control her in her state of catalepsy. An old priest is called in to accomplish the consecration of the host. He divests himself of his clothes as well and rises on an altar that has been prepared beforehand. Yet before he can speak the essential words, he suddenly petrifies, while the somnambular young girl is twisting and turning like a serpent. Urged on by the Satanists to perform the consecration, the priest tells them that he feels the presence of an invisible stranger in the room who prevents him from celebrating Mass. This invisible intruder is, of course, Vintras himself, spiritually intervening from his place of exile in London. The Satanists join forces to do battle against him and bring in a young man to serve as their medium, but the young man only falls on his knees to do homage to Vintras, the prophet "who precedes the Great Justice," and turns himself like "a new Balaam" against the Satanists, announcing that their magical operation has failed: "Listen, princes and depositaries of the Church of Rome, and you malicious brutes who are in league with them, hypocrites who preach pity, prayer and faith from the moment that you rise from your bed till the moment that you go to sleep, hiding all the while the pressed oils of prostitution and decomposing corpses underneath your honorary vestments—shame on you, and glory to your enemy, the Great Prophet!"[123]

Vintrasian anti-Satanism had almost certainly been the source of inspiration for Boullan's own ideas in this regard: the "documents" that the latter was sending to Huysmans mainly consisted of accounts like these from the old Vintrasian archives, as well as articles from his own hand from his former periodical *Les Annales de la Sainteté*.[124] If we unravel this thread farther back in time, we can also trace the source where Vintras picked up *his* notion of a host-abusing network of Satanists. In 1835, in the small French town of Agen, a thirty-five-year-old woman known only as "Virginie" had claimed to be possessed by the devil.[125] After being abused by a priest—so she disclosed—she had sold her soul to the devil when she had been fifteen years old, amid a Satanist congregation consisting of the "most eminent citizens" of Agen. From that time at least, the society of Satanists had been continuously deploying its blasphemous practices in Agen, with another circle active in Bordeaux. The devil regularly appeared in person at these assemblies, where sacred hosts were being abused on a massive scale.

When a priest started to exorcise Virginie, she began to vomit up hosts that had been abused by Satanists. Soon, a circle of pious women formed around the woman, who continued to vomit up an endless quantity of hosts, to the amazing total of three thousand, of which one hundred and forty were bleeding. In or around 1840, this circle of pious women had come in contact with the Vintrasists (who were still not officially excommunicated at that date), eventually forming a Vintrasian "septaine" or congregation. Vintras was keenly interested in procuring one of the bleeding hosts, and soon after this started to "receive" hosts harrowed by Satanists himself, keeping them in special boxes for the devotion of his followers. In a way, one can say that it had been this single episode that sparked the Vintrasian discourse on Satanism, and thus also spawned the avalanche of documents from Boullan that eventually resulted in *Là-Bas*.

The upheaval in Agen had also drawn the attention of the Church during the 1840s, and the bishop of Agen had ordered an investigation into the matter. In the report that ensued, it was pointed out that Virginie tended to remain vague when asked for the exact location of the "temple of the demon" or the names of the "eminent citizens" that frequented it: moreover, none of the facts that were pretended to be supernatural "could survive five minutes of the most benign scrutiny."[126] The bishop duly condemned the woman in an ordinance of July 6, 1846, closing the book on the story of the Satanist congregations. The Vintrasians, however, retained their own account of the occurrences in Agen, which they articulated in their periodical *Voix de la Septaine*. Boullan transmitted the relevant articles to Huysmans, and in this way, the story eventually ended up in *Là-Bas*. Referring explicitly to *La Voix de la Septaine*, Huysmans recounted on the pages of his book that a Satanic association celebrated Black Masses, committed murders, and polluted hosts for fifteen years without cease in Agen. "And Monsignor the Bishop of Agen, who was a good, earnest prelate, never even attempted to deny that these monstrosities were committed in his diocese!"[127]

THE REMARKABLE CASE OF CHAPLAIN VAN HAECKE AND CANON DOCRE

For one particular Satanist, Huysmans did not rely on Boullan's documentation. This was the real-life counterpart of the infamous Canon Docre. It was not the prophet from Lyons who supplied him with the information on this essential character, but a woman called Berthe de Courrière (1852–1916). Huysmans had met this colorful lady at the place of her lover Remy de Gourmont (1858–1915), a much younger Symbolist writer whose face was weirdly disfigured by lupus vulgaris. Huysmans frequented the couple, and it had been Courrière who had organized the spiritism séances that had impressed him so much. It had also been she who had brought him into contact with Boullan, although it is unclear how she had come to know the latter.[128]

Not much is known with certainty about this central character to our story. Apparently she originated from Lille, in Northern France, and had come to Paris to be a model for the famous sculptor Auguste Clésinger, adding the aristocratically sounding suffix "de" to her name. To these sparse biographical data, rumor added some salient facts. It was said she was "into priests" (meaning she wanted them to be into her) and that her apartment was furnished exclusively with ecclesiastical items—including a real pulpit topped by a De Sade volume bound like a Bible.[129] A later story claims that she always carried one or more hallowed hosts in her handbag when she went out, to feed to the dogs when the occasion occurred.[130] Courrière certainly was fascinated with occultism, and she showed keen interest in Huysmans's quest for real-life Satanism. Huysmans kept her closely informed of his visits to Boullan's Carmel in Lyons. When he expressed his surprise over the fact that he had seen rituals performed by members of the "regenerated sex" there, Courrière mischievously urged him to take advantage of the "proximity of celestified female organs": "It would be regrettable if you would return without knowing more about the fine points of the doctrine of spiritual marriage."[131]

Perhaps it had been her predilection for priests that had brought Courrière into contact with Lodewijk Van Haecke, the chaplain of the Chapel of the Precious Blood at Bruges,

Belgium. According to one story, she had sought him out after seeing his photograph in a Paris shop window.[132] A more plausible reading tells us she met him at the 1889 World Exposition in Paris, which featured, among others, the inauguration of the Eiffel Tower.[133] In 1890 she decided, or was invited, to visit the chaplain in his town of residence, taking the minor Decadent poet and major morphine addict Edouard Dubus (1863–1895) along as a companion.[134]

It is unclear what happened exactly during this fateful visit. On September 23, 1890, Gourmont sent a short message to Huysmans, telling him that he had received "disturbing news" regarding Madame Courrière from Bruges; two days later, he added that she had undergone a "very violent crisis" but was already recuperating and planning to go home. Gourmont had decided to go to Bruges to pick up his mistress and was busy making preparations for the trip. "The chaplain has conducted himself extremely well in all this," Gourmont commented; on October 2, he reported the reception of a letter from Van Haecke specifying further details.

Apparently, Berthe had experienced some kind of nervous breakdown during her visit to the priest. She had fled his house and was found nearby by two policemen: according to most narrators of the tale, she was in a state of near nakedness, but the only contemporary report on the incident merely tells us that she was displaying "signs of insanity" and "performing all kinds of crazy antics." She was committed to the local psychiatric ward, where she was registered as being apprehended in a "state of delirium" and diagnosed with "grave hysterics."[135] The medical report did not specify what had caused Courrière to succumb to mental collapse and flee the house in disarray. On this, however, Courrière would have her own, highly extraordinary tale to tell. On October 9, Gourmont arrived in Bruges and wrote "from this town so deliciously dead" to tell Huysmans that he "would have strange stories to listen to" when they would return: "There are infamous priests other than in Paris or Châlons!"[136] The exact content of the "strange stories" Gourmont promised has not been left to us, but evidently, they convinced Huysmans of the fact that Van Haecke was a redoubtable Satanist who had maliciously lured Courrière into his den of iniquity, from which the horrified lady had only barely managed to escape.

Huysmans wrote about Van Haecke to Boullan, this time furnishing Boullan with information on Satanism, instead of the other way around.[137] Boullan was hesitant at first, although by strange coincidence he had already mentioned Bruges as one of the focal points of European Satanism in his earliest letters. In a letter written on October 15, he suggested that "the chaplain Van Eyck" might have been the victim of a magical operation instead of its perpetrator; apart from that, some simple sexual misstep might have been involved. As more information became available, he quickly changed his mind. In early November, the doctor seemed to be completely convinced of Van Haecke's Satanism, adding his own hypothesis about why the Belgian chaplain would have lured Courrière into his house: "One evening, this man was trembling, saying: I am afraid, I am afraid. This was because he knew that the measure of his iniquities was about to be filled. . . . In making an *innocent person* his accomplice, he created a lightning-conductor for himself. The innocence of the lady covers the crimes of the pervert."[138] In the same letter in which he depicted a trembling Van Haecke, Boullan also told about a new evil force he had encountered during his spiritual battles. One night, he had been attacked by two gatherings of magicians at the same time, one presided by Guaita, another by Papus, when suddenly Madame Thibault had discerned a dark spirit coming from yet another direction. "It was a messenger from Bruges. That reminded me of the satanizing Chaplain." Later on, Péladan had also joined the battle, which had taken two hours. On December 10, 1890, Boullan also claimed to have prevented Van Haecke from offering a Black Mass.[139]

Van Haecke, Huysmans would later claim, had been the real-life model for Canon Docre. Nevertheless, the canon from *Là-Bas* and the chaplain from Bruges do not seem to be completely identical. The former, for instance, is described as a confessor of a Spanish queen in exile, something Van Haecke had never been. Huysmans, it might be remembered, already had been looking for a "demonizing and sodomitical priest" in February 1890, and the detailed description of Docre's activities in the novel are not paralleled by the rather meager facts Huysmans collected on Van Haecke. It is probable that Huysmans had already finished the portrait of Docre in its main outlines when the incident with Van Haecke presented itself. He then applied Docre's attributes to the Belgian chaplain instead of the other way around. Yet in a letter to a magazine written shortly after the publication of *Là-Bas*, Huysmans would unambiguously identify "a priest who still exercises his sacerdotal dignity in Belgium, in a town not far from Gand," as one of the principal models for Docre.[140]

In 1895, he added further detail in the preface he wrote for Jules Bois's book on Satanism. Here he proclaimed to possess "renewed, incessant, undisputable verifications" that there were "certain priests" who had formed diabolical circles to celebrate the Black Mass. "Such is that Canon Docre whose portrait appeared from time to time in the shop window of a photographer on the corner of the Rue de Sèvres and the Place de Croix-Rouge. This man has assembled, in Belgium, a demonical clan of young people. He attracts them by their curiosity for experiences that aim to discover 'the unknown forces in nature'—for that is the eternal excuse of those who are caught in *delictu flagrante* of Satanism—then he retains them by the attraction of women whom he hypnotizes and by sumptuous meals, and little by little corrupts and unsettles them with aphrodisiacs that they absorb under the guise of nut *confiture*. Finally, when the neophyte is ripe, he throws them into the Sabbath and mingles them with his herd of horrible sheep." He went on to tell how "one of the victims" of Docre had told him how he was trembling at night, crying "I am afraid, I am afraid"[141]—the story Boullan had written him in one of his letters.

Meanwhile, in Bruges, nobody seemed to have noticed that Satanist orgies were being held within the confines of their city, and what was worse, by the keeper of the town's most famous holy shrine. Van Haecke was generally loved by his townsmen, among which he enjoyed a reputation of being not only a saintly priest, but also a bit of a prankster. Several booklets appeared during and after his lifetime in which his numerous merry tricks were recounted. "He has gotten many a wise guy into heaven with a joke, when they were already grinning at the gates of Hell," a Flemish periodical remarked in its obituary article about the priest.[142] Huysmans visited Bruges in 1897 and was confronted with Van Haecke's special reputation when he asked around for the chaplain. "Everybody smiles when Van Haecke is mentioned," the French writer noted in his personal travel log. "He is so funny, says a bookseller with ribbons in her hair. He says Mass from time to time, says the sacristan of Saint Jacques. He is called extravagant, jocose; fun incarnated."[143] Huysmans failed to encounter his nemesis and contented himself with a brief glimpse at Van Haecke's living quarters: "31 Rue de Marécage—close to that Saint Jacques Church, at a little square—a sealed house, with yellow window-panes, the colour of houses that were shunned during the Middle Ages."

By then, Huysmans had taken formal action against Van Haecke as well. For some years, he had been in contact with a Belgian nobleman, Baron Firmin Vanden Bosch, and a Flemish priest called Henry Mœller. To the baron, Vanden Bosch would later assert, Huysmans told a story about how he had seen Van Haecke once during a Black Mass that he had witnessed. He had not known who the priest was at that moment, but later, by coincidence, he stumbled upon his photograph in a Paris bookshop. Because the woman that attended to the bookshop had refused to sell him the picture, Huysmans had gone back later and apparently stolen the photograph. In this way, he had found out that the priest at the Black Mass had been Van Haecke. At some later date, Huysmans claimed, he had confronted Van Haecke with his presence at such a blasphemous ceremony. The priest, who "seemed to distrust" Huysmans, reacted evasive but eventually responded with "Don't I have the right to be curious? And who can say that I wasn't there as a spy?"[144]

Firmin Vanden Bosch did some research on the affair, and concluded that Huysmans's allegations were "at the very least *plausible*" and that nothing did invalidate them. Nevertheless he advised him to keep silent on the matter for the time being. "It would be regrettable to be compromised in a campaign that, at the moment, cannot be crowned with a formal and proven accusation," he wrote in January 1896.[145] At the request of Vanden Bosch, Huysmans compiled a twelve-page memorandum on Van Haecke that was passed on to the Belgian ecclesiastical authorities by the Belgian baron. Although a high-ranking member of the Belgian clergy contacted Vanden Bosch to ask questions about its contents, nothing further was heard from this. The memorandum itself disappeared completely: covered up, according to Huysmans, by a corrupt or cowardly hierarchy that did not want Van Haecke's double life as a Satanist to become public knowledge.[146]

INTERMEDIARY CONCLUSIONS

Was Huysmans's discovery of Satanism fact or fiction? In the historiography of this episode, this is still a matter of debate. While some historians blankly deny that Huysmans ever had anything to do with real Satanism (not always with a wealth of evidence), others think that his depiction may contain a kernel of truth.[147] This is not merely a matter of detail. Most of the authors propounding the existence of a practiced fin de siècle Satanism flesh up their accounts with references to Huysmans. This circumstance alone more than justifies a closer look at the material Huysmans presents us. A lot has already been suggested in the preceding sections: now it is time to draw some explicit conclusions.

Huysmans himself was ambiguous about his possible firsthand knowledge of Satanist practices. When asked about it, he sometimes declared that Durtal had confessed in *En Route*—referring to the sequel to *Là-Bas* in which Durtal converts to Catholicism and tells a priest about his attendance of the Black Mass, as well as his subsequent defilement of the host with Chantelouve.[148] Huysmans's friends and relations recorded highly divergent assertions on the subject from the writer's mouth. His friend Léon Hennique would remember forty years after the event how Huysmans told him that he had attended a Black

Mass and been horrified by what he saw.[149] We already quoted Firmin Vanden Bosch's reminiscences, also recorded forty years later by the Belgian journalist Herman Bossier. The baron's account was spiced up with some remarkable details: for instance, the fact that the Satanist gathering had been divided in two rows, one for women and one for men. Arthur Mugnier, on the other hand, the priest who played a significant role in Huysmans's eventual conversion to Catholicism, maintained that the writer had categorically denied that he had ever attended a Black Mass: the description in *Là-Bas* was entirely based on documents provided by Boullan.[150]

It is probable that Huysmans remained deliberately vague on the factual background of *Là-Bas*, both to retain the mystery that was one of the novel's major selling points, and to mask the lack of precisely such a factual background. If we look at the evidence that is preserved to us from the period that Huysmans actually composed *Là-Bas*, we do not find the slightest indication that he ever had firsthand acquaintance with any kind of Satanism. When he discovered "Satanist priest" Boullan—who in the end turned out to be not so Satanist after all—he wrote enthusiastic reports to several of his correspondents. Yet to no one did he send any enthusiastic reports of a visit to a Satanist congregation. Even to Arij Prins he did not utter one word about this, although Huysmans kept his Dutch friend informed about every stage of the composition of *Là-Bas* and wrote to him about virtually every occurrence in his life, including venereal disease and brothel adventures. It is unlikely that Huysmans would not have told Prins immediately if he had actually witnessed a Black Mass.

Of the sources upon which Huysmans *did* base himself, much has already been said in the preceding sections. We will recapitulate once more in a more systematic way. Among the "documentation" utilized by Huysmans, we must mention in the very first place, once again, the primacy of literary sources. Even the most superficial reader will have recognized an adaptation in prose of Baudelaire's famous "Litanies de Satan" in Canon Docre's speech during the Black Mass—although, it must be admitted, Baudelaire could well have been a source of inspiration for any real-life Satanists, too.[151] Even more crucial is Michelet, whose shadow looms large over Huysmans's entire project. Huysmans reread *La Sorcière* shortly before he started to write *Là-Bas*, and although he expressed himself critically on the historian (particularly with regard to the latter's "sentimental" democratic tendencies), the influence of the nestor's work is undeniable.[152] In many respects, the Black Mass in *Là-Bas* is a modern reenactment of Michelet's Witches' Sabbath, with the "priestess" mounting a virile Jesus out of a Felix Rops engraving instead of a phallic statue of Pan. More in general, the whole concept of an ecstatic antireligion of the flesh is taken straight from Michelet and transplanted by Huysmans to the present time.

Except from secondary literature, Huysmans could dispose of a great abundance of more specialized works from the vaults of the French Bibliothèque nationale. His friend Remy Gourmont held a desk job at the library and provided Huysmans with relevant references: for instance, the demonological treatises that are quoted at length in *Là-Bas*, as well works about the Affair of the Poisons, on which Huysmans was well informed. We do not need to have too grand an idea about Huysmans's erudition in these matters, though: most of the quotations from the demonologies could have been derived just as easily from popular digests as that of the "Bibliophile Jacob."[153] All in all, Huysmans's literary and historic sources alone could have provided more than enough material for his romanesque construction of Satanism and the Black Mass. "It was me who searched for details concerning that fantastic ceremony," Gourmont later claimed. "I did not find them, because they are not there. Finally, Huysmans arranged into a black Mass the famous scene of conjuration . . . for which Montespan lent her body to the obscene role-playing act of an infamous sorcerer."[154]

Gourmont's statement needs qualifying, however. As we have seen, another important source for Huysmans was Joseph Boullan and the documents the former priest provided from what he rather pompously called his "archives." In Boullan, we easily recognize the "most mysterious of healers" that Huysmans had mentioned as the principal source for his revelations on Satanism when the first installment of *Là-Bas* had been published. While the information from Gourmont would by its nature refer to the past, the prophet from Lyons furnished Huysmans with the documentation on contemporary Satanism that was essential for the project of *Là-Bas*.

Boullan classified the documents he sent to Huysmans in three categories. In the first place, he distinguished "documents from the first order," with which he meant texts deriving "from he who preceded me in the path" (i.e., Vintras). These consisted almost exclusively of accounts of visions by the "New Elijah." Documents from the second order contained information originating from Boullan himself, mostly "visionary" in nature as well, while the third order stemmed from a variety of third-party sources.[155] Some of these original documents are left to us, allowing us to retrace many of the more salient elements in Huysmans's description of Satanism to their original source with Boullan or even Vintras.[156] The strange idea of an international organization called "Ré-théurgistes optimates" and led by the American poet Longfellow was copied by Huysmans straight from a letter by Boullan from February 1890.[157] Boullan, in turn, had lifted it from a vision reported by Vintras and dated June 26, 1855. Vintras here already formulated the idea of a "Rétheurgie absolue" with ramifications in France, Italy, Germany, Turkey, Austria, and Russia and its center in "the heart of America" (the peculiar notion that it was headed by Longfellow [1807–1882], author of *The Song of Hiawatha*, seems to have been a creative addition by Boullan himself).[158] In the same vision, Vintras also told about two competing societies: "one striving to dominate the universe by limitless destruction; the other wanting to maintain its universal omnipotence by leading back the world to a purely philosophical cult of which they will be the Doctors and High Priests," as well as the fact that they had selected a young girl to become the mother of the Antichrist in a special ceremony, an event that was predicted by Vintras for the "tenth of the next month," that is, July 10, 1855.[159] All these elements would eventually find their way into *Là-Bas* by the intermediation of Boullan. The fidelity of the ex-priest's renderings was actually surprisingly high, but he did not hesitate to add extra color or information to Vintras's stories once in a while. Although Vintras's accounts do feature Satan and Satanists on occasion, the secret organizations he is fighting against look more like a strange assembly of spiritism and neopaganism invoking ancient gods like Amun-Ra and Juno: the unusual designation "Ré-théurgistes optimates" probably means something like "High Theurgists of Ra."[160] Boullan "satanized" the sect a bit and also provided Huysmans with updated information on its current activities. In a letter from July 16, 1890, for instance, he informed Huysmans that *Holland* was another major power center of the Réthéurgistes optimates; on July 23, he added, somewhat surprisingly, that the secret society had all but dispersed since the death of Longfellow in 1882—the "Centre of the Grand Masters" was now located in Rome.[161] To other material of Vintras, Boullan occasionally also gave a touch of his own, usually by adding details of a sexual nature.[162]

In addition to the (slightly retouched) accounts of Vintras, Boullan's own descriptions of the practices of the Satanists were of great importance as a source for Huysmans. On September 4, 1890, Boullan had sent the French writer a piece entitled "Documents on the Black Mass of Our Days."[163] All elements that Huysmans would use in his depiction of Docre's Black Mass can already be found in this letter: the "diabolical" incense, the glorification of Satan by a long series of blasphemies, the priest who is naked underneath his robes, the practice of sodomy and incest, the mixing of semen and menstrual fluid with wine, the sacrilege of the host "by every impure contact." Boullan had come to know all these secret facts, he had disclosed in an earlier letter, because many years ago (in 1863, in Rouen), he had seen a "Ritual of the Grand Masters in Satanic Magic," written on parchment consecrated to Satan and bound in the skin of an unbaptized baby, with a profaned host glued to its first page.[164] Huysmans did not only faithfully reconstruct Boullan's ritual specifications for the Black Mass in his novel, but he included this improbable story as well. And this was just one of the many instances in which he inserted Boullan's texts in *Là-Bas*, sometimes almost to the letter.[165]

As his third category suggests, Boullan also provided Huysmans with references to other sources. Some of them were again his own: he made frequent references to his own articles in *Annales de la Sainteté au XIXe siècle*, which provided information on magic attacks and Satanist thefts of hosts.[166] But he also referred to other authors, mostly from the deep backwaters of French Roman Catholicism from which he originated himself. An interesting example is M. J. C. Thorey's *Rapports merveilleux de Mme Cantianille B . . . avec le monde surnaturel* ("The Miraculous Contacts of Miss Cantianille B . . . with the Supernatural World," 1866), which had been recommended by Boullan as a reliable account of "what is in our days the Mass of the Sabbath."[167] The two-volume work gave an account of the tribulation of the young congregation member Cantianille B, as reported to her confessor, Charles Thorey. At a tender age, Miss Cantianille recounted, she had fallen into the evil hands of an "association of possessed" that dated back to the French Revolution, to be precise to 1793, when it had been founded on the exact day that Louis XVI had been guillotined. Robespierre had been its first president, and other prominent revolutionaries like Marat and Danton had been members. Surprisingly enough, the society did not mix with politics: God would not allow this, Cantianille assured, as their ability to render themselves invisible would make its members invulnerable plotters.[168] Instead, they influenced society by way of nefarious literature and "impious novels." In addition, they performed rites of sacrilege involving stolen or surreptitiously collected hosts. On these occasions, they convened at places like grottos, ruins of castles and churches, and lonely mountain tops, as well as in the Roman Coliseum (to mock the martyrs) and at Bethlehem (to mock the Nativity).[169] Her own career in this clandestine world, Cantianille asserted, had begun when a corrupted, devious priest had brought her into contact with a demon named Ossian. When she became sixteen, the young girl had made a pact with Lucifer in person; she subsequently had descended into hell, where Lucifer had nominated her as the new president of the secret society, in which capacity she had commanded "several thousand" followers.[170] In a postscript, Charles Thorey added some impressive facts about his own activities, one of the most remarkable being his successful conversion of the demon Beelzebuth, who had adopted the Christian name Charles.[171] Despite the colorful character of this account, it inspired at least one element of *Là-Bas*: the tattooed cross on the foot soles of Docre originates with Cantianille/Thorey, who ascribe it to the members of their "association of possessed."[172]

It seems hardly necessary to comment on the trustworthiness of this kind of source.[173] In the preceding sections, most of the essential has already been said about the nature of the "documentation" provided by Boullan. The core of the material consisted of information of a "visionary" origin: observations and encounters "in the spirit" by Vintras and Boullan. While every reader must decide for him- or herself what weight he or she will lend to para-normal evidence, there is no further indication that the Satanism they described had any foundation in reality. Huysmans nevertheless considered Boullan evidently a major and trustworthy source, incorporating passages from Boullan's letters in about twenty places in his novel.[174] The correspondence between the writer and the spiritual leader, moreover, clearly indicates that Huysmans sent his finished chapters to Boullan for further scrutiny. The latter especially lauded Huysmans's portrayal of Dr. Johannès and at one point had even suggested entire dialogues for his book.[175]

Boullan and books provided the bulk of Huysmans's raw material for *Là-Bas*. "My priest continues to send me documents with a dedication that baffles me," he wrote to Prins on May 17, 1890. "And on the other side, the National Library is combed out for me with fury."[176] Apart from these, there was the case of Van Haecke, the Satanist chaplain from Belgium. Yet the evidence for Van Haecke's Satanism is slim at best and entirely dependent on the testimony of Berthe de Courrière. The latter was a personage whose eccentricity might well have crossed the border into psychopathology. She would be committed to a mental asylum once more in 1906, and the French writer Guillaume Apollinaire remembered how she once startled him when they were riding the omnibus by declaring she could control the people around them by her mental faculties.[177] In short, it is probable that the lady was somewhat mad.

The two facts that gave the Van Haecke story its enduring afterlife, both in popular and academic literature, were the tenacity with which Huysmans did stick to it and the reaction or nonreaction upon his allegation by the Belgian Roman Catholic Church.[178] Huysmans, it is often recounted, stood by his accusations against Van Haecke until the end of his life, even after he had become an ardent Catholic who played an important role in the Catholic Renouveau of the decennia directly before World War I. This circumstance and the almost saintly stature the converted writer enjoyed in certain Catholic circles have convinced a number of (mostly Catholic) authors that his allegations must have had some truth in them. While one may wonder whether Catholics are less prone to lying than non-Catholics, or vice versa, the dilemma does not really present itself, for Huysmans was obvi-ously completely convinced of Courrière's truthfulness. He did not seem to possess any other evidence—even Firmin Vanden Bosch admitted that Huysmans did not present any facts based on firsthand knowledge in his legendary lost memorandum.[179] This makes it all the more understandable why the ecclesiastical authorities did not take any action against Van Haecke. It is highly improbable that a chaplain of a prominent pilgrimage shrine could regularly organize orgies with hypnotized women and aphrodisiacal nut *confiture* with-out drawing public attention to himself. If anything, it is more likely that something of a sexual nature occurred between Van Haecke and Courrière—with or without the priest's active participation—and that Courrière later added some spice to the story by making Van Haecke a lurking Satanist.

To the catalogue of source material utilized by Huysmans, some historians also add Jules Bois (1868–1943), the writer on occultism and Satanism we encountered—sword in hand— at the beginning of this chapter. Bois was working on a book about Satanism and magic at the time Huysmans wrote *Là-Bas*, and the two authors exchanged views on the subject intensively. Their cooperation was of such a nature that Huysmans would furnish the preface for Bois's book when it was finally finished in 1895. In 1894, Bois had already published *Les petites religions de Paris* ("Little Religions of Paris"), which features two chapters devoted to Satanism and Luciferianism as well. These books are remarkable by the ambivalence they display toward their subject. In fact, Bois had set out on his literary career with a play called *Les Noces de Sathan* ("The Wedding of Sathan," 1890), in which he had managed to push almost every theme and personage of Romantic Satanism into just fourteen pages of effective text—without excluding a suitable whiff of Baudelaire for good measure.[180] With Bois as well, the influence of *La Sorcière* was tangible, particularly in the connection he made between Satanism and women's liberation, a cause that enjoyed his warm support.[181] With regard to contemporary Satanism, however, he did not uncover a single new fact. Although Introvigne, for instance, presents Bois as doing journalistic research on Satanism in the vaults of the Parisian religious underground, uncovering information that eventually found its way into *Là-Bas*, the truth of the matter was, in fact, exactly the other way round.[182] As Bois graciously admitted in a footnote in one of his books, it had been Huysmans who had provided *him* with the information he needed: in general, by forwarding him relevant letters he received from Boullan.[183] Thus the description of Eugène Vintras's battle with Amun-Ra found its way into Bois's treatise, while he also quoted copiously from *Là-Bas* itself.[184] While Bois did interview some people for the other "petites religions" he described (and did not refrain from adding a prayer to Isis written by himself), his pages on Satanism and Luciferianism are based completely on secondary sources.

By now, I think we may allow ourselves to conclude that the Satanists from *Là-Bas*, however complicated their genesis may have been, were an exclusively literary creation. Huysmans never succeeded in finding the Satan-worshipping cult he was looking for. There is no evidence that he ever witnessed a Satanist ceremony himself and indeed there is every indication to the contrary. The sources we know he *did* use do not inspire a great amount of confidence: two neo-Catholic gurus recounting their visions, as well as an eccentric lady who might have been slightly confused. Huysmans's description "after nature" of Satanism was fiction, not fact.

Huysmans himself, it must be noted, clearly believed in this fiction. Of course he must have been aware of the way his own novel was constructed. Yet for him, *Là-Bas* presented a real, or at least *realistic,* picture of practices that he believed were going on secretly. He trusted his sources, and, most importantly, he believed that the people he described were "true to type," in the same way as a prostitute or a factory worker in a naturalist novel had to be "true to type" without necessarily involving a factually accurate biographical description of an individual prostitute or an individual factory worker.[185] Thus he was able to present his book as a "documented" portrait of contemporary Satanism. "Documented" did not mean that he had made a critical comparison of available sources, as a professional historian might be expected to do. It meant simply what it said: that he had utilized *documents*, written or oral texts from real life rather than the world of literature. In this respect, it is clarifying to read the musings Huysmans put into the mouth of Durtal in *Là-Bas* with regard to the French historian Michelet, that "doddering old maid" who was nevertheless "the most intimate and the most artistic" of all historians. "Historical events," Durtal meditates, "are to a man of talent simply a springboard for his ideas and his style, seeing that all facts are played up or played down according to the demands of a particular case, or according to the disposition of the writer who handles them. As for the documents propping them up, it's worse still, because none of them are irrefutable, and all are subject to revision."[186] This is certainly a conclusion that could be applied to Huysmans's own book as well.

COMPETING CONCEPTS OF SATANISM

Having answered the question whether Huysmans's Satanists were real (with a definite no), we may now turn to the ideas that prompted Huysmans to use the concept of Satanism as his "springboard." What attracted him (as well as his readers) to the concept of Satanism? Why this obsession with worshipping the devil? As we saw before, Huysmans had already crossed two different conceptions of Satanism while conducting research for *Là-Bas*. The first of them was proposed by the neo-Lévian occultists. For Guaita, Papus, and Péladan, the real followers of Satan were the practitioners of "black magic": those that used the astral force for evil purposes and/or let themselves become inebriated with it. In this, they continued in the tracks of Éliphas Lévi. Satanism was something they implicitly or explicitly attributed to others, mostly to competitors in the sphere of esotericism, with a prominent place reserved for Joseph Boullan, that "modern avatar of the sorcerer."

It is not hard to see why the Paris Rosicrucians were so interested in propagating this stereotype of the adversary. Occultism still had a very doubtful reputation among the general populace, and the Rosicrucians were at pains to emphasize the respectability of their pursuits, which they conceived as being on a par with regular science and regular religion. What better way to do this than to contrast oneself as the good magician with the evil workers of black magic? It is important to note, however, that their concept of Satanism was purely "theological." They did not necessarily maintain that their opponents were *intentionally* worshipping Satan, but rather that their practices *implicitly* amounted to a veneration of the devil—much as the pagan Romans had *really* worshipped demons instead of gods according to the early Christians. Real, militant, "avowed" Satanism mercifully was "an evil of exception," according to Stanislas de Guaita.[187]

Boullan and his followers presented another concept of Satanism, originating in the tradition of Vintrasism. Satanism also implied black magic for Boullan, but its most important element was a deliberate anti-Christian attitude that became particularly manifest in the ritual defilement of the host. In many respects, this was merely a continuation of the old, premodern tradition of attribution regarding heretics, witches, and Jews that we described in the first chapter.[188] Although Vintras and Boullan sometimes gave their Satanists futuristic trappings (one may remember the strange metal wires used during the invocation of Amun-Ra), fundamentally they held on to the same basic scheme as the old demonologists.[189] They applied this attribution to new enemies, however. The Roman Catholic

Church in particular was depicted as a hoard of Satanism by the two heresiarchs. Time and again Boullan underlined the status of Rome as a center of Satanists, who surround the Papal Chair and control the highest ecclesiastical dignitaries. "Pius IX and Leo XIII have both been slaves, and they could not break their chains."[190] While the indispensability of ordained priests to magical practice was an idea of some antiquity, the great stress that both Vintras and Boullan placed on Satanism among priests and Roman Catholic dignitaries clearly served their agitation against a church that had evicted them. Particularly with Boullan, Satanism increasingly seems to have functioned as a mechanism that could be applied to any opponent—a mechanism to which he took recourse ever more frequently as his small religious group became more and more isolated. The intensely dramatic spiritual fisticuffs he had with the practitioners of Satanism enhanced his prestige among his followers and must have given a sense of cosmic mission to the small schismatic assembly that seemed so insignificant in real life.

Huysmans's own ideas of Satanism were more complex and more ambiguous. As we have seen, he had started out on his quest for Satanism in the hope of finding a real-life relict of the Middle Ages, an era at the same time more splendid and more terrible than the one in which he lived. Apart from common curiosity and professional interest, it was his personal thirst for genuine manifestations of the supernatural and the spiritual, whether "black" or "white," that had set him on this trail. In this context, the term "Satanism" could have a wide variety of meanings for him, which were not always identical to the definition applied in the present publication. Often, for instance, he utilized the word to designate demonic possession, even when involuntary.[191]

It is not unlikely that initially, to some degree, Huysmans had been positively inclined toward Satanism.[192] Like Baudelaire's traveler, he had been prepared to jump into the abyss of heaven *or* hell, as long as he would find something truly new and truly real in its depths. Although there are no unambiguous utterances of him to support this, he may well have been looking for a Satanist group so urgently with the dimly considered idea of joining one in the back of his mind. Some traces of this initial attitude can possibly be detected on the pages of *Là-Bas*, particularly in Canon Docre's remarkable invocation of Satan during the Black Mass. Over the top and brimming with irony as it may be, the speech contains an undeniable element of social criticism, strangely inappropriate in a congregation said to be consisting of high-ranking church officials and wealthy notables. As a contemporary observer remarked, "Many similar speeches might be discovered by anyone who would take the pains to wade through the back numbers of certain Anarchist and ultra-Socialist publications."[193] A faint remnant of "old style" Left-wing Romantic Satanism surfaces here. Huysmans's antidemocratic tendencies were matched by an equally vehement anticapitalism at this date, and, if anything, his overall political affiliation could still be described as Leftist. Relevant excerpts from *Là-Bas* were indeed published in periodicals of anarchist signature, with full compliance with their author.[194]

There is more than just the political aspect, however. Already in *À Rebours*, Esseintes had coupled an almost involuntary attraction to the Christian religion with an equally strong inclination toward darker, blasphemous forms of spirituality. This clearly reflected Huysmans's own state of mind. For a while, he found himself in roughly the same predicament as the early Romantic Satanists: rejecting the overly rationalistic outlook of his precursors and contemporaries, yet unable to "return" to the unconditional faith of traditional

Christianity. In the 1880s, Huysmans had considered occultism as a possible way out of the
naturalist lockdown. In early 1890, he dismissed the occultists as incompetent posers and
started to search for Satanism, which he expected to be a more "real," more powerful, more
medieval form of dissident spirituality. There is something in this sequence of events that
strongly suggests he was looking for more than just "documentation."

After 1890, when his correspondence and contact with Boullan gradually brought him
over to an ever more fiercely anti-Satanism, Huysmans's attitude toward Satanism shifted
from tentative identification to outspoken attribution. In April 1891 he wrote to his friend,
the artist Jean Lorrain: "Personally, I renounce all Satanism. . . . I will take a bath and give
myself a rough grooming—I will purge myself and, my body cleansed, I will confess myself—
after which, I think, I will be in such a candid state that I will be able to enter in the proper
hysteria for a reverse of *Là-Bas*!"[195] Yet even then, the concept of Satanism remained an essential ingredient of his spiritual worldview. Its existence and the supernatural facts that produced themselves in the clash between the Satanists and the faithful were irrefutable proof
that naturalism and positivism did not have the last word in describing the universe. The
world contained drama and mystery far beyond the banality of everyday life and the run-of-
the-mill of nature and its laws. This explains in part why a nineteenth-century "man of the
world" and pioneering avant-garde author like Huysmans could adopt convictions that often
strike one as completely premodern. Huysmans needed Satanism for the *Wiederbezauberung*
of the world he longed for.[196] Its existence had become an essential component in his program
of reenchantment: so when he set out to look for it, he was bound to find it.

Notwithstanding the plausibility of this reconstruction, the unexpected volte face by
Huysmans keeps presenting us with tantalizing questions. Discerning readers may have
noted that the writer's predicament mirrored in many respects that of the early nineteenth-
century Romantic Satanists. Huysmans shared their dissatisfaction with the reductionist
rationalism that confronted them and him, as well as their disgust for the dominating
forms of institutional religion. Why then did Huysmans choose to abjure "the devil and
all his pomp" and convert to Roman Catholicism and, what is more, to a Catholicity that
seemed to be more conservative than that of the pope?

Without reducing Huysmans's spiritual path to a mere contextual product, we can nevertheless point out certain historical developments that make his decision more understandable. In the first place, it is essential to remember that not all Romantics had supported
revolutionary change or expressed sympathy for Satan. Romanticism had always had its proponents of "old-time" religiosity and "traditional Christianity," especially in France. In the
early nineteenth century, this position could be interpreted—correctly or incorrectly—as
signifying one's compliance with the hegemony of conservatism and the moral majority. In
the decades that followed, however, secularizing and democratizing tendencies had gradually attained an even greater ascendancy, especially in France, and certainly among the
cultural elite.[197] In these circumstances, embracing traditional forms of Christianity could
become a *countercultural* statement. As one of the protagonists of *Là-Bas* explained, neatly
reversing one of the favorite ideas of Romantic Satanism, "At the present time, it is very
clear that the good Lord has gotten the losing part and that the Evil one rules the world as
its master. Well . . . , as for me, I am for the Vanquished! That seems a generous idea to me,
and a proper kind of opinion."[198]

We can, in retrospective, fairly precisely point out when the balance had begun to tilt: somewhere in the 1850s, under the Second Napoleonic Empire, when Baudelaire, who had lost nothing of his keen instincts for dandyism, began to move toward a more and more conservative Roman Catholicism. This does not imply that extreme versions of political and religious rebellion like anarchism and Satanism had become stripped of their shock value. It simply meant that a new, paradoxical option had presented itself to the cultural avant-garde as a way to express countercultural dissent: that of *radical reaction*. Baudelaire may have anticipated this attitude when he called the archconservative doctrine of throne and altar a "revolutionary maxim" in his personal notes.[199]

In this and other respects, Huysmans merely followed in the tracks that the French poet had set out some three decades before. The importance of this countercultural element in Huysmans can be clearly discerned from his reaction to the occultism of his day. This he dismissed in a surprisingly off-hand manner, not because he had found fault with its doctrines, but because he considered it too much a product of his own times, as something *modern*. The French writer was looking for something that really went against the grain of his own culture. This attitude may help to explain the comparative ease with which Huysmans changed from a vanguard exponent of modernity into a reactionary Roman Catholic gladly immersing himself into a world of premodern beliefs, (neo)medieval monasticism, and physical asceticism.

Huysmans's gullibility for the premodern, meanwhile, was not without its limits, at least in the period that he was writing *Là-Bas*. He did not incorporate every bit of information provided by Boullan directly into his novel. Some of the points on which he decided to deviate from Boullan concern minor issues—he disinclined to mention Holland as a center of the Ré-Théurgists, for instance, perhaps out of respect for his Dutch roots, and he probably thought it imprudent to repeat Boullan's assertion that the Rosicrucians had sent him a venereal disease by astral waves (which the old thaumaturg boasted to have cured himself, however).[200] Yet one crucial difference between Huysmans's and Boullan's descriptions of Satanism that certainly deserves to be mentioned concerns the appearance of the devil during Satanist ceremonies. Boullan, in his letters, again and again emphasized the actual presence of Satan during the Black Mass.[201] This was also the reason for all the "diabolical" incense that Huysmans would describe with loving detail. "The purpose of that <u>dense Cloud of perfumes</u>," Boullan had stipulated, "is to furnish the Princes of Satan the means to <u>materialize themselves</u> . . . in the natural order. The black Mass does not start unless Satan, or his Princes, Beelzebuth, Astaroth, Asmodeaus, Belial, Moloch, Baal-Shegor, and others, have made themselves visible."[202]

Apparently Huysmans did not found it credible or feasible to include a real-life appearance of the devil into the Satanism scenes featured in his novel. Although he did not hesitate to suggest the involvement of supernatural actors, Huysmans proceeded along the lines that had already become visible during the Affair of the Poisons: his Satanism is essentially a *human* affair, an activity *about* Satan, and not *by* Satan. This may have been a key to the success of *Là-Bas*. Despite its recuperation of premodern religious elements, Huysmans's Satanism remained eminently suited for a public that had lost the "faith of the Primitive." The presence of the otherworld was tantalizingly suggested but limited itself to phenomena on the border of the psychological and the physical that were open to different interpretations. If this adequately reflects the attitude of Huysmans himself, he had remained more a child of his time than he would have liked.

An analysis of the motives that attracted Huysmans to Satanism would be widely off the mark if another element is not given its full dues: namely that of sexuality. For Huysmans, Satanism clearly implied a lot of sex. In *Là-Bas*, the anecdotes concerning historical Satanism can almost always be grouped around this theme. Canon Docre's speech is mainly a paean of sexual license; the host at the Black Mass is consecrated by him by ejaculating upon it; and the way the women afterward "bury" the hallowed bread underneath their bodies also suggests sexual abuse.

Here we may come to the core of both Huysmans's attraction to and his revulsion of Satanism as he saw it. Huysmans had a troubled relationship with the other sex and his own sexuality. In his works, he generally described the sexual act as degrading and ultimately unsatisfying. Sexuality meant surrender, a capitulation to woman who wielded the instincts of the male as her tool; woman remained, after all was said and done, the more primitive and pettier part of mankind. In these sentiments as well, Huysmans was a child of his time. This was the era in which the femme fatale—the woman who entices and dominates man by his own sexuality—enjoyed its greatest flourishing in poetry and fiction.[203] Decadents, Naturalists, and Symbolists all devoted many pages to eroticism, preferably in its more deviant forms. Yet they seldom described the sexual encounter as a joyful or even gratifying experience. We can see a reflection of these fin de siècle attitudes even in the works of the Parisian occultists we discussed, with their repeated emphasis of the magician's control of his own and other's sexuality—turning the tables, as it were, on femininity and its spell of attraction. At the same time, they wrote at length on the debaucheries of witches, "black magicians," and spiritualists. The "flowers of evil" clearly retained their fascination—it was no coincidence that Baudelaire was celebrated as their forerunner by the fin de siècle Decadents.

For Huysmans, this alteration between attraction and repulsion was a lived experience. A frequent visitor of the brothel, he felt unable and disinclined to live up to the rigorous moral standards of Christianity. His struggle to come to terms with the sexual force forms the implicit and often explicit subtext of his wavering between Satanism and Roman Catholicism. He translated his inner conflict to the spiritual plane by juxtaposing Christianity and Satanism. Already before 1886, in a review of Wagner's *Tannhäuser*, Huysmans identified Venus with Satan, and both Venus and Satan with a name that only was to be whispered: "Sodomitica Libido."[204] While Christianity was the religion of chastity, of "purity," and of sexual abstinence, Satanism was the "spirituality of lasciviousness," giving free rein to the subconscious and the instinctive: a spiritual alternative that did not demand "useless proofs of chaste loins." "As it's very difficult to be a Saint, ... it only remained to become a Satanist," Huysmans wrote about Gilles de Rais in *Là-Bas*. It is more than probable that he was also talking about a part of himself here.[205]

At the very same time, however, the sexual emphasis Huysmans placed on Satanism devaluated it in his eyes to something ultimately banal. It is worthwhile to note the significant resemblances between Huysmans and Baudelaire once more here, but this time specifically with respect to their treatment of the "Satanic." Baudelaire had already associated the diabolical with the feminine, the sexual, and the material, which all occluded the human perception and reception of the transcendent. Huysmans shared these attributions.[206] His repugnance of the sexual was partly brought about by a Baudelarian contempt for the "natural," which had only been intensified by his weariness with literary naturalism, scientific materialism, and the vulgar this-worldliness that he perceived around him. From the viewpoint of this tradition, it was certainly no compliment when he made Satanism into a *sexual* religion in *Là-Bas*. While Christianity lifted the bodily into the spiritual—in the Eucharist, for instance, or in its sanctification of bodily suffering—Satanism degraded the spiritual into the animal—most conspicuously by turning the host into an object of sexual abuse. *Là-Bas* was, before anything, an imprecation of a time and a people only living to indulge into their urges "down there," below the belt: the women who were only interested in being bedded while pretending not to; the "realist" writers who always wrote the same stories about adultery; the common people who just wanted "to stuff their guts and excrete their souls through their backsides," as the famous last lines of the novel proclaimed. In this respect, Satanism was perfectly in vogue with its time. And with that, it was also dismissed.

The association between Satanism and deviant sexuality dated back to at least the Middle Ages, as we have noted in previous chapters. *Là-Bas*, however, did much to give this notion a new poignancy and a modern restatement. It also gave a basic ambivalence to Huysmans's picture of Satanism, an ambivalence reflecting his own inner duality. On the one hand, Satanism was a religion of "gothic" mystery and intense perversion; on the other hand, it was surrounded by a certain sordidness that made it almost commonplace, a mere celebration of the "baser" instincts of man.

This ambivalence also helps to understand what happens in the apotheosis of Durtal's visit to the Black Mass, when Madame Chantelouve seduces him in a shabby room above a pub. This scene, sometimes felt to be an anticlimax, and dismissed by one author as badly written soft pornography, in fact marks the final descent of Durtal into the "down there" of Satanic sexuality. It is also the moment that Durtal himself commits Missa Negra–style sacrilege. The crumbs of the host he discovers on the bed after having sex with Madame Chantelouve are clearly implied to have arrived there in a blatantly blasphemous way. The implication is made explicit in *En Route*, the sequel to *Là-Bas*, where Durtal confesses his attendance of the Black Mass and his subsequent defilement of a host that Chantelouve had hidden "en elle"—"inside of her."[207] The episode forms a shocking counterpart to the description earlier in *Là-Bas* (cited from Joseph Görres and ultimately deriving from Madeleine Bavent) of the sacrilegious priests who placed the host around their member before proceeding to abuse their female victims. "Divine Sodomy, in other words?" Durtal jokingly remarks after this anecdote. Even to non-Catholic ears, this joke has a definite ring of impropriety.[208]

Few commentators elaborate on what exactly happens in this crucial scene with Chantelouve. Only Ellis Hanson frankly tells us that she hid the host in her vagina.[209] It may be wondered, however, whether he really hit the right spot here. We have already noticed Huysmans's association of Satan with "Sodomitica Libida"; in the prolegomenon to their final act, one can read that Chantelouve showed Durtal "the practices of convicts, depravities that he not even had suspected to exist, giving them extra spice by ghoulish frenzies."[210] Would mere vaginal abuse not be rather tame for a writer like J.-K. Huysmans? Huysmans had certainly read De Sade, and it may well be that the terrible tribulation inflicted upon poor Juliette by the impious monks makes yet another camouflaged appearance here.

AFTERMATH

Sex and Satanism proved to be a powerful selling combination in fin de siècle Paris. *Là-Bas* was a huge commercial success, especially after the national railroads forbade its sale at station bookstalls because of the novel's immoral content.[211] In his letters to Prins, Huysmans rejoiced about the continuing sales of his book, remarking with unmistakable delight that he had brought into light, and even into vogue, the Satanism that had been abolished since the Middle Ages. "There are lots of people asking me to take them to a Black Mass," he added.[212]

In truth we can say that Huysmans, for once, was not boasting vainly here. *Là-Bas* was very well the work that introduced the idea of a living, flourishing Satanism to the general public of the late nineteenth century. Fashionable Parisians traveled to Bruges to see Mass said by Van Haecke, the unholy priest with the crucifix tattooed on his foot soles, or made excursions to a disused chapel that rumor had pointed out as the location of the book's Black Mass.[213] Writers and journalists all over France and Europe copied Huysmans's format and "discovered" Satanism—usually with a comparable carelessness about fact and fiction.[214] The respected English occultist Arthur Waite, observing from the other side of the Channel, saw things clearly when he claimed Huysmans as the originator of the Satanism obsession of his days. "A distinguished man of letters, M. Huysman [*sic*], who has passed out of Zolaism in the direction of transcendental religion, is, in a certain sense, the discoverer of modern Satanism," he wrote. "Under the thinnest disguise of fiction, he gives in his romance of La Bas [*sic*], an incredible and untranslatable picture of sorcery, sacrilege, black magic, and nameless abominations, secretly practiced in Paris. Possessing a brilliant reputation, commanding a wide audience, and with a psychological interest attaching to his own personality, he has given currency to the Question of Lucifer, has promoted it from obscurity into prominence, and has made it the vogue of the moment."[215] We can safely say that the "flourishing" of Satanism that some historians tend to discern at the end of the nineteenth century was to a great degree due to J.-K. Huysmans.

Not everybody was pleased with *Là-Bas*. Papus, Guaita, and Pèladan were understandably not amused with the way they were represented in Huysmans's novel. Papus suggested in his journal *L'Initation* that Huysmans got his list of old demonologies from Larousse and that his ideas about bewitchment, succubi, and the Black Mass were hopelessly out of date (or, in other words, not in accord with the latest insights of the Lévian school). Huysmans, Papus concluded, had been "the victim of a mystification" deployed by a certain ex-abbé in Lyons. Papus also argued that a real Black Mass would need an "effusion of blood" and the inversion of holy symbols like the cross or the pentagram. Neither of those could be found in Huysmans's description of the Black Mass, but both elements were present in the "Masses of Blood" that had been practiced in this century by "a deranged person": Eugène Vintras. Again, it was Vintras's "successor" Boullan who was implicated.[216]

Péladan adopted a similar line of defense, also pointing out the maleficent influence of Boullan, whose misdeeds, the Sâr claimed, had already been well known to Péladan père.

Furthermore he stipulated that Huysmans should have gone straight to the police if he had really witnessed a Black Mass, as such a ceremony always included the sacrifice of a newborn child—since Huysmans obviously had not done this, it might be concluded that he was either a liar or an accomplice to murder. In addition, Péladan took revenge in fiction by including a "Dr. Johannès" in one of his later novels, a "music teacher" who lives in Lyons and stages improper ceremonies "without positive blasphemy" in his apartments, involving ritual flagellation as well as a "phallomime" performed by a young woman to the "banal tones" of a harmonium.[217]

Là-Bas may also have prompted Stanislas de Guaita to make haste with the exposure of Boullan he had been planning for years. In 1891, he published the first part of his magnum opus *Le Serpent de la Genèse*. A considerable part of this volume was taken up by a long chapter on "modern avatars of the sorcerer": most of this chapter was devoted to Vintras and Boullan, indicated here with the name "Dr. Baptiste." In it, Guaita presented the material he and Wirth had collected on the sexual activities of the prophet, with the most salacious parts rendered in prude Latin. Apart from "celestifying himself every night in the embraces of angels of light like Sahäel, Anandhäel, and others," Boullan also regularly practiced black magic, Guaita claimed. The Rosicrucian even maintained (although he had only the word of one of Boullan's ex-followers for it) that Dr. Baptiste was in the habit of feeding the hallowed host to white mice he kept for use in his magical experiments—just as *Là-Bas* said of Canon Docre.[218]

Guaita's allegations, and the similar statements of Papus and Péladan, have been at the root of the idea uttered by a number of historians that it was Joseph Boullan who was the real Satanist in the whole story, attributing his own practices to Docre/Van Haecke and the Rosicrucians.[219] This scheme, although temptingly simple, is highly implausible. The fact that he frequently indulged in religious rites of a sexual nature does not make Boullan a Satanist, and everything suggests that he saw his own practices (including the more unusual ones) as of the loftiest nature, certainly not on a par with the evil doings of the Satanists against whom he was waging war almost daily in the astral sphere. Naturally, the infamous "child sacrifice" mentioned in Boullan's "Cahier rose" is frequently referred to in this context as well.[220] But here again, there is not the slightest indication that elements of Satanism were involved, however insalubrious the priest's activities may have been.

In *Le Serpent de la Genèse*, Guaita dealt with Huysmans in a long footnote, repeating Papus's opinion that the writer had been misled by a third party, the "horrible joker" he had depicted under the name of "Dr. Baptiste." Huysmans, Guaita knew "from an extremely certain source," had lightly put his trust in this impostor and the documents he provided, copying the abbé's notes without even bothering to verify them. Guaita did not doubt, however, that Huysmans would admit his error as soon as he set eyes on the revelations in *Le Serpent de la Genèse*.[221]

Nothing could be farther from the truth. In fact, Huysmans only seemed to get more involved with Boullan and his group after *Là-Bas* appeared. His latent sympathy for Satanism was by now a thing of the past, and the polite skepticism with which he had initially approached the eccentric mysticism and dramatic thaumaturgy of the new Johannès was gradually crumbling away as well. Already during the preparation of *Là-Bas*, Boullan had warned him that his novel would attract "a host of evil spirits" and had sent the Decadent writer a variety of objects to ward off supernatural misfortune, such as a talisman containing one of Vintras's original blood-stained hosts, and a "tephilim" (a blue cord containing a parchment covered with benedictions) that the writer had to pin to his cushion at night.[222] Huysmans apparently utilized these items, and as time passed by, his customary wink of irony could no longer hide the seriousness of his involvement in this spiritual warfare. In late 1890, he startled a visiting journalist by demonstrating for him the use of an exorcist paste made of "myrrh, incense, camphor, and dried cloves, the plant of Saint John the Baptist."[223]

When the tremendous impact of *Là-Bas* began to be felt, Boullan wrote Huysmans a long letter to congratulate him on the success of his novel, for which the whole Lyons Carmel had been ardently praying. He warned him, however, that now the attacks of his enemies would also intensify.[224] Indeed extraordinary occurrences started to happen over the next months, and Huysmans began to experience strange afflictions in the still of the night: a strange recurring feeling on his breast, like the fists of an invisible creature thumping him. In the summer of 1891, he took a train to Lyons, were Boullan enacted the ritual we described before to protect him, with the threefold declamation "Bring down Péladan, bring down Péladan, bring down Péladan!" Similar precautions were taken against Guaita, whom Madame Thibault subsequently reported cloistered to his bed, stricken with illness as a result of Boullan's powerful counterstrike.[225] (It seems that Péladan did got wind of these proceedings, because in *Comment on devient Mage* he commented upon the ceremony, remarking that as a High Magician, he was invulnerable to this kind of low magic: "One can only bewitch his inferiors, not the just nor the magician; but a failed incantation returns to the one that has unleashed it; and I fear greatly that Vintras II and Mr. Huysmans have given themselves nothing but a bad headache in my honour; the first in his vain efforts to startle and to make himself believed, the second in obedience to a secret law that he incited, as slanderer of occult pretensions against the novelist that, in 1882, restored into literature the pure Pythagorean ideal of the magician of light in the shape of Merodack."[226])

By going to Lyons, Huysmans was fleeing not only the astral encroachments of the occultists, but also his own inner demons. Foremost among these was, as ever, the "spirit of lasciviousness." To friends and relations, the Decadent writer frequently testified of his desire "to whiten his soul" at this time. Boullan admonished him as if he was an ascetic monk himself, transmitting to Huysmans a special message from Jesus that exhorted him to retain the purity of loins expected of a "Knight extirpating Satanism."[227] The ex-abbé harbored his own designs with Huysmans, whose newly found prominence made him an attractive potential propagator of the Boullanist doctrine. After his "black book," he urged the novelist, his next step should be to write a "white book," a *Là-Haut* ("Up There") in which Durtal's subsequent conversion would be told and the miraculous powers of good extolled. To entice the former Decadent writer, Boullan promised him "the spectacle" of persons "giving themselves over to all kinds of satanic obscenities while experiencing at the same time the illumination of divine life," as well as startling revelations regarding the "sanctification of the generative act."[228]

It is not known if Huysmans ever bothered to react to these offers. Things would not go the way Boullan planned them to, anyway. Huysmans was much impressed by the pilgrimage he and Boullan made to La Salette, but he gradually started to drift away to more regular forms of Roman Catholicism. In 1891, he was introduced to the priest Arthur Mugnier (again by the ubiquitous Berthe de Courrière), who gradually took over Boullan's role as spiritual guardian. In 1892, he visited a Trappist monastery and at last encountered the "medieval" Catholic faith he had been unable to find earlier. When he finally wrote his "white book" (*En Route*, published 1893), it told about his conversion to Roman Catholicism and was destined to become one of the landmarks of the *renouveau catholique*, the literary revival within French Catholicism at the end of the nineteenth century.

Huysmans would remain in contact with the Boullanists for many years to come, however. In 1895, Julie Thibault herself moved in at Huysmans's quarters at Rue de Sèvres, number 11, to serve as the writer's housekeeper and spiritual protector. She took her small, homemade altar with her, on which she performed the "Provictimal Sacrifice of Mary" every morning before attending to her chores. Huysmans only sent her away in 1899, when he moved to Ligugé to live near the Benedictine monastery where he was to become an oblate. "I want no more diabolism in my new home!" he wrote to an old friend on this occasion.[229]

By that time, Boullan himself had long been dead. The old abbé had died in 1893; with his sudden death, the conflict between Rosicrucians and "Boullanists" had also been brought to its climax. On January 2, Boullan had written to Huysmans that the new year opened with "ominous presentiments." On January 3, he had continued his letter to report "a terrible incident" that had occurred during the night. "At three in the morning, I awoke with a feeling of suffocation and called out twice: Madame Thibault, I'm choking! She heard, and came to my room, where she found me lying unconscious. From three till three thirty I was between life and death. At Saint-Maximin, Madame Thibault had dreamt of Guaita, and the next morning a bird of death had called to her—prophesying this attack." The danger had passed at four, Boullan wrote, but this was too rashly spoken. The next day, Dr. Johannès died.[230]

Heart failure was the most probable cause of death, but his followers suspected evil machinations behind his unexpected death. "1893 must be a terrible year if it can begin with the triumph of Black Magic," Huysmans wrote in his letter of condolence to Madame Thibault.[231] At the Lyons cemetery, he bought a grave for the Lyons prophet with an inscription that read "Joseph Boullan (Dr. Johannès), noble victim."[232] He also shared his suspicions and Boullan's strangely prophetic letter with Jules Bois. The latter, reacting with "the spontaneous zeal of recent converts" (as he would later recall), published an article in the Parisian tabloid *Gil Blas* in which he implicitly but unmistakably accused the Rosicrucians of being responsible for Boullan's demise.

> I consider it my duty to relate these facts: the strange presentiments of Joseph Boullan, the prophetic visions of Mme Thibault and M. Misme, and the seemingly indisputable attacks by the Rosicrucians Wirth, Péladan, and Guaita on this man who has died. I am informed that M. le Marquis de Guaita lives a lonely and secluded life; that he handles poisons with great skill and marvellous sureness; that he can volatilize them and direct them into space; that he even has a familiar spirit—M. Paul Adam, M. Dubus, and M. Gary de Lacroze have seen it—locked up in a cupboard at his home, which comes out in visible form at his command. . . . What I now ask, without accusing anyone at all, is that some explanation may be given of the causes of Boullan's death. For the liver and the heart—the organs through which death struck at Boullan—are the very points where the astral forces normally penetrate.[233]

Bois repeated his allegations two days later, again in *Gil Blas*, while *Figaro* published an interview with Huysmans, in which the writer of *Là-Bas* was quoted as declaring it to be "indisputable that Guaita and Péladan practice Black Magic everyday": "Poor Boullan was engaged in perpetual conflict with the evil spirits which for two years they continually sent him from Paris. Nothing is more vague and indefinite than these questions of magic, but it is quite possible that my poor friend Boullan has succumbed to a supremely powerful spell."[234]

By now, the Paris Rosicrucians were no longer a house undivided. In 1891, Papus and Guaita had ousted Péladan from their organization—ostensibly because they deemed that the eccentric behavior of the Sâr made the discipline of magic look ridiculous, but Péladan's outspoken ultramontanism may have been an equally significant factor. The Sâr founded his own esoteric society, the Rose + Croix Catholique, which he claimed to be the original Rosicrucian society. This led to endless bickering between the two factions, an episode that is known as the "War of the Roses" among historians of esotericism.[235] Neither Guaita cum Papus, nor Péladan, however, were pleased to see themselves accused of practicing voodoo murder in all the Paris popular press. Papus compiled a booklet and Péladan an article in which both argued the absurdity of these accusations in the light of recent insights in magic.[236] Guaita, characteristically, reacted more strongly. He retorted with an exasperated public letter that was published in *Gil Blas* on January 15, 1893. "Everybody knows," he wrote sarcastically, "that I surrender myself to the most detestable practices of sorcery; that I stand at the head of a school of Rosicrucians compiled of fervent Satanists devoting their free time to the evocation of the Dark Spirit: . . . I play Gilles de Rais on the threshold of the twentieth century; I maintain (like Pipelot with Cabrion) *relations of friendly and other nature* with the redoubtable Docre, the beloved chaplain of Mr. Huysmans; finally, I keep imprisoned in my cupboard a familiar spirit who appears in visible form on my order!" Guaita singled out Huysmans as the main culprit behind this campaign of slander, as it was he who had—deliberately—furnished Bois with the documents that had prompted the latter to go public with his allegations. The marquis concluded as his noblesse obliged him to: "I am being asked for explanations with loud voices. . . . The best explanations in a case like this are given on the field. This at least is my opinion."[237]

With all this upheaval around his death, the verdict issued over Boullan by the Rosicrucian court of honor many years ago suddenly appeared in a wholly different light. Guaita, Papus, and Wirth maintained that the "execution" implied in this sentence had been the disclosure of Boullan's practices of sex magic to the public—and that this sentence had in fact been executed with the publication of Guaita's *Serpent de la Genèse*.[238] Some of Guaita's phrases in this work support this reading.[239] Yet part of the public sought to read a more obvious meaning in the verdict, and the thought may not be as absurd as one may think. While the Paris Rosicrucians, on the whole, could be characterized as a discussion group giving conferences and issuing publications on the subject of magic, they did not altogether refrain from practicing what they preached. In the "Center of Esoteric Studies" led by Papus, fearless experimenters armed with blessed swords and prepared by vegetarian fasts regularly ventured into the realm of "elementary beings" and "fluidic larvæ," sometimes feeling mysterious drafts of cold air or seeing columns of gray vapor rise before them.[240] Péladan and Guaita, too, had certainly not shunned more practical experiments in their younger years, predominantly involving the famed "plante attractive" of Van Helmont. Even later on, Péladan once indiscreetly declared to the Reverend Arthur Mugnier that he did not understand why the bishop of Paris did not use the spiritual powers invested in him to eliminate the enemies of the Church by astral means.[241]

More in general, the great similarities in worldview that bound Guaita, Péladan, Papus, Boullan, Huysmans, and Bois together are striking, in spite of their differences of opinion and their animosity. All were living in a common postmaterialistic world where succubae made regular appearances, fluidic forces could transport death and destruction over vast distances, and incantations and colorful rituals dispensed great powers. While it is wildly implausible that the Rosicrucians had been "continuously" staging ritual murder attempts on Boullan for the past two years, it is not impossible that they had lost count somewhere in the succession of "choc" and "choc de retour."[242] Whether this was likely to have caused Boullan's demise is a question I would like to leave to the reader's own discernment.

While talking of the spirit world, we might as well pursue another entertaining side-line over which much ink would be spilled: that of the "familiar spirit" assisting Stanislas de Guaita. According to Oswald Wirth—ever defendant of his master—this rumor had entered the world because Guaita had told the story to his housekeeper in order to scare her away from the closet where he kept his dangerous chemicals.[243] (Wirth refrained to mention that these "dangerous chemicals" would probably have been cocaine and morphine.) Guaita, however, thought the rumor had its origin in the fact that his Parisian apartment was *indeed* haunted: from time to time, a white, female shape appeared in his living quarters, presumably of some unknown girl that had once died a foul death in the house.[244] Huysmans seemed to have been firmly convinced of the truth of the story: when the marquis suddenly died in 1898, he declared that the occultist must have been strangled, in true Faustian manner, by his familiar spirit.[245] More sober observers thought it probable that Guaita had succumbed to the ravages of long-term morphine abuse, while some of his admirers had still another explanation—they suggested that he had been eliminated by the Higher Powers before he could finish the third and final volume of *Le Serpent de la Genèse*, in which the last veil would have been lifted from the cosmic mysteries of Good and Evil.[246]

Let us return to our story. Following Guaita's public challenge, Huysmans had published a letter that may or may not have been intended to be conciliatory. While there was no material proof that Guaita had attempted to eliminate Boullan by way of magic, he stated, the verdict published by the occultists in *Le Serpent de la Genèse* hardly left room for another interpretation; whether or not Boullan's death had been the result of these attempts, they at least demonstrated that the Rosicrucians practiced Satanism. Naturally, this did nothing to assuage Guaita. "Mr Huysmans persists in addressing to me the hateful and ridiculous accusation of Satanism," he wrote in a letter of challenge. "And I consider this allegation a grave insult, for which he owes me satisfaction."[247] He duly proceeded to send his seconds to both Huysmans and Bois. Papus followed his example, while Péladan "played dumb as he was wont to do"—the Sâr never engaged in dueling because (so he once claimed) his great magical powers would render him invincible, thus reducing the whole duel to simple murder.[248]

Huysmans, however, was not inclined to risk his life or position over the matter, and when the aides located him at his office, he signed a protocol stating he had never intended to put into doubt Guaita's "character of perfect gentleman."[249] Bois initially retracted as well, but, being young, from the south, and rashly tempered as he was, he soon repeated his mistake. Publishing another fierce article, he defiantly declared that Guaita defended himself rather awkwardly: "When his defence against this suspicion of Satanism is at stake, he retreats and tries a diversion. He changes from terrain, he withdraws from the discussion; he drops the pen and takes up the sword, of which he feels himself more sure." After appealing to the examples of Jesus, Buddha, Pythagoras, and Plato, "your masters and our masters," the journalist continued brazenly, "I will stand before him, Stanislas de Guaita, on the field, with the same tranquil courage."[250]

A settlement by gentlemanly display of courage had now become inevitable. Pistols were chosen as a weapon, and an appointment for a duel was set for January 14, close to the Tour de Villebon. Not surprisingly, ominous incidents preceded the engagement. "You will see that something remarkable will happen," Bois had already predicted to one of his seconds beforehand. "From two sides, people are praying for us and busying themselves with incantations." On their way to Versailles, one of the horses of their carriage suddenly stopped, trembling over his whole body "as if it was seeing the demon in person."[251] This unexplainable phenomenon lasted for twenty minutes, causing Bois and his party to arrive on the field of honor barely in time and much shaken. The two contestants took their places and shots were fired, but when the smoke cleared, both men were still standing in their places unharmed. A protocol was duly made, containing a declaration of Bois's seconds that their friend "had only meant to express an appreciation of a philosophical and esoteric order on Mr. de Guaita, but that his criticism did not extend to Mr. de Guaita's character of perfect gentleman, and never would be able to attain to this."[252] Guaita, sometime later, declared that he returned his estimation to his adversary while the latter had "stood his ground on the field."[253] A further note of mystery attached itself to the story when the pistols were returned to the armorer, who subsequently discovered—if we are to believe one of the witnesses—that one of the weapons had misfired, the bullet never having left its barrel.[254]

A few days later, Papus and Bois met on the Pré Catalan to fight over the same dispute. Again, strange events occurred before the Bois party reached its designated destination: their horse stumbled twice, overturning the carriage and causing Bois to arrive at the place of battle with preliminary injuries. Papus had some reason to look forward to the encounter with confidence, as he was an expert swordsman. Still, his worried mother had had an armored vest specially prepared for him that looked more like a cuirass than a jacket.[255] These precautions proved unnecessary, however, for the inexperienced Bois was no match for the Rosicrucian. While "elegant amazons" looked on in wonder, Bois was wounded twice, once in the outer triceps of his left arm, and once in the left forearm.[256] Fortunately, his wounds were only slight. But blood had been drawn, so to the relief of all those involved, the hostilities could now cease. In the shade of a tree, the appropriate documents were composed, signed, and countersigned; after that, both adversaries shook hands and went their separate ways. And in this manner ended one of the most bizarre episodes in the history of Satanism, involving an all-too-credulous novelist, charismatic Roman Catholic schismatics, eccentric occultists, and at least one slightly shady lady—but not a single actual Satanist.

La Révolution sociale, c'est les *Gesta Satanæ per massones.*
PAUL ROSEN, *L'Ennemie Sociale*

5

Unmasking the Synagogue of Satan

THE SWORD FIGHT between Bois and Papus was not to be the last word on Satanism during the fin de siècle. Just two years after the much-disputed demise of Boullan, Paris had another world premiere in the history of Satanism. On the first day of the month Pharmuthi in the year 000895, or March 21, 1895, according to the "Vulgar Era," a periodical called *Le Palladium régénéré et libre* ("The Free and Regenerated Palladium") saw the light of day. It was subtitled *Lien des groupes lucifériens indépendants* ("Bulletin of Independent Luciferian Groups") and claimed to be the public organ of an inner-Masonic group devoted to Satanism—or, rather, devoted to the worship of *Lucifer*, a distinction that seemed to carry great weight for the organization behind the periodical. We shall hear more about the reasons behind this distinction in the next section of this chapter. For now it suffices to note the absolute novelty of this occurrence. For the first time in modern history, a religious group affiliated to the angel that had forfeited divine favor presented itself openly to the public.

The organization behind this unprecedented publication called itself the "Independent Palladist Convention." It appeared to be a splinter faction split off from the greater body of Palladism, a mysterious association of inner-circle Freemasons that venerated the fallen angel. On 2 mékir 000894 (January 21, 1895, Vulgar Era), the convention had decided to undertake "an attempt at public propaganda of the Luciferian principles"—for the time being only by way of experiment and for a period of a year.[1] As a first step, *Le Palladium régénéré et libre* had been set up to serve both as a vehicle for evangelization and as a link between existing gatherings or "family groups" of independent Luciferians. The editor in charge was Miss Diana Vaughan, Grand Mistress of Independent Palladism, who mostly filled the pages of her periodical with articles in a strongly polemic vein, directed either against the "Adonaïtes" (as the publication was wont to style adherents of the Christian religion) or against her former brethren of the Palladium proper. In a gesture of missionary zeal and defiance, sample copies of the bulletin's first issue had been sent to all major Roman Catholic convents in France.

THE UNVEILING OF FREEMASONRY

For a reader who had been vigilantly following the literature on Freemasonry, the fact that an organization of Lucifer worshippers was apparently active in Paris would not have been a cause for surprise. For years, a select body of predominantly Roman Catholic authors had been raising the storm flag about what was going on in the hidden vaults of the Masonic world. In the previous ten years, their suspicions had been spectacularly confirmed by a steady influx of information from within the secret brotherhood, often brought to light by former Masons who had left the lodge. In 1885, for instance, Léo Taxil, renowned free-thinker, onetime Freemason, and founder of France's most infamous anticlerical publishing house, suddenly revoked his former way of life and returned to the Roman Catholic faith of his forefathers. He promptly set out to publish a series of volumes that contained salient disclosures about what went on in the inner circles of Masonry. The first of these, *Les Frères Trois-Points* ("The Three-Point Brothers"), sought to demonstrate that Freemasonry's true philosophy was "nothing but gross pantheism, to which the adept is gradually brought through a series of ridiculous masquerades, starting with the glorification of the Material and ending with the adoration of Satan."[2]

Ordinary Masons were unaware of this; only to initiates of the higher grades was the truth disclosed, step by step. Taxil described this process in detail. In the twentieth degree of Masonry, he wrote, the neophyte received the exhortation to shine like the morning star: "in the sacred name of Lucifer, uproot obscurantism!"[3] In the twenty-fifth degree, the true key to reading biblical history was unveiled: it was not Adonaï, the unjust creator, who had helped mankind throughout the ages, but his opponent, the Angel of Light, known throughout history by different names like Ormuzd, Osiris, or Lucifer.[4] In the twenty-eighth degree, the initiate was introduced to the adoration of Baphomet, whom the Freemasons, like their precursors the Templars, venerated as the "pantheistic and magic symbol of the Absolute."[5] Bit by bit, it became clear to the adherent that the true God in Freemasonry was none other than Lucifer. The full extent of this secret, Taxil claimed, was only revealed in the thirty-third and final degree, that of Knight Kadosh. The Knights Kadosh could be seen as the true "Holy Congregation of the Church of the Grand Architect." Unbeknown to Freemasons of the lower grades, they controlled the lodges by their resolutions. "And who inspires those resolutions," Taxil asked, "when it is not the Spirit of Evil, Lucifer; this so-called Iblis whom they pretend to be the angel of Light, and . . . with whom they stand, by way of their execrable occult practices, in direct communication?"[6]

In the sequel to his first book, *Le culte du Grande Architecte*, Taxil further supported his central thesis by citing a wealth of Masonic documents. The third book of the trilogy, *Les sœurs maçonnes* ("Sister Masons"), concentrated on the existence of secret Masonic lodges for women. This was certainly astonishing news, for Freemasonry officially was and is an exclusively male reserve. Taxil, however, presented indications for the existence of a top-secret network of women's lodges that had the phallus as their central object of adoration and served as a reservoir of sex partners for high-grade Masons during the highly libidinous Masonic festivities.[7] "Mothers of France, hide your daughters; here come the Freemasons!" the author exclaimed. In addition to these salient facts, the book furnished further details on the Satanist nature of Masonic ritual. Nothing was what it seemed in Freemasonry,

Taxil wrote. The frequent use, for instance, of biblical psalms and other Christian elements in ritual suggested a modicum of Christian piety. The god addressed in this way, however, was the so-called Grand Architect, who was in reality none other than Lucifer himself. "Thus, through sacrilegious parodies that remind one of the sorceries of the Middle Ages, the sect uses the prayers of the Catholic Church itself to invoke Satan, right in the nineteenth century!"[8]

After this first wave of divulgences, a comparative lull set in, but in 1891 Huysmans's novel *Là-Bas* burst upon the scene and led to fresh interest in all things Satanic. Taxil reacted with a reprint of *Les sœurs maçonnes*, under the title *Y a-t-il des Femmes dans la Franc-Maçonnerie?* ("Are There Women in Freemasonry?"). Not only did he give the book a new title, however, he also grasped the opportunity to present some new, recently disclosed facts on Freemasonry. The most important of these pertained to a secret order within Freemasonry called the Palladium. *Les sœurs maçonnes*, it is true, had already devoted a few pages to the "Palladic Rite," mentioning that the Order pretended to have been founded in 1637, but in reality dated from 1737, and used the word "Megapan" as its secret password.[9] References to the Palladium could be found in a few old Masonic handbooks as well, but most experts held the Order to be defunct. In 1891, however, Taxil disclosed the fact that a "New and Reformed Palladium" had been established in America. This new Palladic Order was completely devoted to "Luciferianism" and had surreptitiously managed to find its way into France. "In a work that appeared in May 1891 and that has attracted much notice," Taxil explained,

> Mr. Huysmans has made numerous allusions to these assemblies, which are even more secret than those of ordinary Masonic Ateliers. But when he talks about them, the author (I can hardly imagine why) takes care never to pronounce the word 'Freemason.' Every time, he writes 'Rosicrucian' to designate the initiates who practice this kind of Satanism. Now, every Rosicrucian is a Freemason. On the other hand, the term which Mr. Huysmans uses is not of absolute exactness, as the sacrileges that he attributes to them are in reality not imputable to the Chapters of the Rosy Cross, but rather to certain Areopagi of the Kadosh. It is true, one cannot be Kadosh without being at the same time a Rosicrucian; nevertheless, not all Rosicrucians are Kadosh, and not even all Kadosh indulge in Palladism. I hasten to add to this that Mr. Huysmans' unfortunate choice of terms to describe Luciferian Freemasonry is of no further consequence.[10]

The newly discovered order, Taxil took care to point out, had nothing to do with the "hysterics" whose rituals Huysmans had witnessed in a derelict Paris convent. On the contrary, the Freemasons of the New Palladium operated in an extremely cool and collected way; furthermore, they did not worship Lucifer as evil, but "consider him as the Principle of Good and the equal of the God of the Christians, called by them the Principle of Evil."[11] In France, the secret association already had three lodges, the most important of these being the Mother-Lodge "Lotus," named after the delicious fruit of the Lotus-Eaters "that makes one forget fatherland and religion."[12] This lodge had originally been established in the 1850s by Knights Kadosh who devoted themselves to black magic under the guidance of Brother

C***, "better known in literature under an Israelite pseudonym."[13] After his demise, however, it had fallen into disarray, to be resurrected in 1881 by an emissary of the new American Palladium. Now the new rite was spreading across Europe, eclipsing the slightly older Rite of the Old-Fellows [*sic*], who were also purely Luciferian and could be identified with Huysmans's waning Order of the Re-Theurgists Optimate.[14]

The rituals of the new order were not exactly an afternoon tea party. In the true spirit of modern tolerance, the Palladium was open to both men and women. The latter were led to the worship of Lucifer in only five stages, culminating in their initiation to "Templar Mistress." Taxil gave a vivid depiction of the trials the aspirant sisters had to brave during this rite of initiation. In the "Trial of Lazarus," for instance, the female postulant was led to a plateau, the "Pastos," where a motionless male waited in a recumbent pose. "You see before you a dead man," the initiatress explains. "Ecce homo! It is to you to transform him into a living god." With a huge depiction of Baphomet approvingly looking on and the congregation raising a general acclamation of "Cain, Cain!," the neophyte then was expected to bring the "dead man" back to life by performing the sexual act with him. After this part of the ritual, the aspirant Templar Mistress was given a host that she had to pierce with a small ceremonial dagger to the cry "Nekam, Adonaï, Nekam!"—"Vengeance, Adonaï, vengeance!" Subsequently, a Luciferian prayer was offered and the Templar Mistress was taught the duties of her new position, which could be summarized as "execrating Jesus, insulting Adonaï, adorating Lucifer." She then solemnly vowed herself to Lucifer: "To you, Genius of Liberty, I swear to devote myself, by all means at my disposal, whatever they may be, to the annihilation of political despotism and sacerdotal tyranny. And now, o Lucifer, I am your daughter forever."[15]

Y a-t-il des Femmes dans la Franc-Maçonnerie? received some public attention—although the reactions of those sections of the press with Masonic affiliations were rather derogatory, with headlines that spoke sarcastically of "Masonic Harems."[16] Amand-Joseph Fava, the bishop of Grenoble, sent Taxil an approving letter; Léon Meurin, the bishop of Port Louis in Mauritius, personally visited the author to consult him for his own book, *La Franc-Maçonnerie, Synagogue de Satan*, which would appear in 1893 and confirm most of Taxil's revelations.[17] Taxil's claims, however unbelievable some of them may have seemed, found further corroboration in a book by an obscure author called Adolphe Ricoux, published in 1891 as well. The main significance of this book lay in the fact that it quoted the full text of Albert Pike's "Compilation of Secret Instructions to the Supreme Counsels, Grand Lodges, and Grand Orients," dated Charleston 1890.[18] Albert Pike (1809–1891) had been Grand Commander of the Scottish Rite in the southern states of the United States and had already been pinpointed as the leading figure of the Palladium by Taxil.[19] Taxil had quoted a few lines from this secret briefing, but Ricoux had somehow managed to obtain the full text of the document, which provided interesting insight into the hidden agenda of Freemasonry. Freemasonry's mission, Pike specified, was to combat wherever and however it could the temple of intolerance that is Roman Catholicism. Special instructions were given to the Palladium's Political Directorate at Rome to monitor the Vatican's activities and do all that was in its power to undo them.

Even more intriguing were the hints that could be gleaned from Pike's instructions with regard to dissent simmering within the powerful machinery of Palladism. With solemn ire, the Grand Master orated against the tendency in certain Palladist lodges, predominantly in Italy, to extend their worship to *Satan* instead of Lucifer. "It has been brought to our attention that a Lodge in Genoa has pushed its ignorance so far as to even raise a banner saying 'Glory to Satan!' during a public manifestation. In Milan, Mason Brothers staged a declamation and chanted a Hymn to Satan during a feast."[20] In contrast to this, the document stressed a strict Luciferian orthodoxy: Satan was a name invented by the priests of Adonaï and an insult to the Good God.

The enormous extent of worldwide Luciferianism was only made fully clear when the startling revelations of Dr. Bataille started to appear. This author was no converted Freemason or Palladist; his case was far more extraordinary. Bataille was the pen name of a medical officer who had sailed with the French nautical company Messageries Maritimes. One day, he was called to attend to a dying Italian who declared himself to be damned. The Italian told him that he had been a Freemason and, what was worse, a member of the New and Reformed Palladium. Dying now, and repentant of his involvement in Luciferianism, he handed Bataille the highly confidential passwords and signs that gave entrance to the secret meetings of the Palladium. After duly consulting his confessor, Bataille decided to use these to investigate the dangerous underworld of Palladism. "I shall be, I said, the explorer, and not the accomplice, of modern Satanism."[21] What followed was a wild ride into the hidden recesses of Freemasonry that brought to light facts that sometimes verged on the improbable and baffled even the most seasoned experts on Masonry.

The printed reportage of this Verne-esque "voyage extraordinaire" into occultism started to appear in separate issues from 1892, under the improbably long title *Le Diable au XIXᵉ siècle. La Franc-Maçonnerie luciférienne ou les mystères du spiritisme. Révélations complètes sur le Palladisme, la théurgie, la goétie et tout le satanisme moderne. Récits d'un témoin* (which the reader may translate for himself). It is impossible to do justice in a few paragraphs to the enormous range of topics and 2,000-plus pages of *Le Diable au XIXᵉ siècle* (as we will call it henceforth for brevity's sake). His possession of the secret signs had given Bataille free access to centers of Lucifer worship all over the world; to his astonishment, the worship of Lucifer turned out to be the secret core of virtually every non-Christian religious tradition. Bataille visited Hindu fakirs in Indian temples, where he witnessed parodies of the Roman Mass interspersed with liturgical chants to "Lucif" and gruesome rituals that involved dead bodies. In China, he penetrated the abode of a secret brotherhood that specialized in the massacre of missionaries. In Gibraltar, he was introduced to underground caverns where fiendish-looking, dwarfish outcasts produced chemical and biological weapons for the Palladium. In between these accounts of travel adventures, long, documentary digressions told about the Luciferian conspiracy that lurked behind spiritism, magnetism, anarchism, feminism, occultism, and modern capitalism.

Most important for our story, however, is the wealth of new information that Bataille offered on Palladism, the "organised cult of Lucifer the Good God." Bataille greatly extended the facts brought to light by Taxil and Ricoux; his words had the added value of being those of an eyewitness. As a religion, Bataille stressed once more, Palladism was strictly Luciferian and not to be confused with Satanism pure and simple.[22] It had its own sacraments (among which the "Eternal Pact" figured prominently, as well as exorcism rituals to cleanse deserted monasteries and other places of Christian worship of "adonaïte impregnation"), its own credo, and its own religious orders.[23] Among the latter, the "Godlike enchantresses" deserve special mention, who were like a type of Luciferian nuns who devoted themselves to sex with demons in the "Nuptorium," where, according to Bataille, "indescribable scenes of orgy" took place.[24] Also of particular interest are the "Rosy Serpents," an elite corps of Palladist spies who infiltrated Catholic convents. "The leaders of the Re-Theurgists Optimate do not shrink from anything, and imagine and act out the most improbable enterprises," Bataille noted. "A few years ago, their maliciousness pushed them so far as to found a Palladic Lodge of little girls in a boarding school run by Catholic sisters. These wretched children, inspired by their criminal parents, concerted to steal the consecrated hosts and experienced an infernal joy in burying these and in feeding them to worms or ants."[25]

While the political center of the sect was located in Rome (facing the Vatican), and the administrative directory could be found in Berlin, its "Supreme Dogmatic Directory" had been established in Charleston, South Carolina, the "Luciferian Rome."[26] It is here that the original Baphomet of the Templars was kept—although Bataille, after inspecting it, expressed doubts about the authenticity of the object. A splendid sanctuary had been erected around it. In the heart of this holy of holies, Bataille reported, Lucifer in person appeared every Friday as the clock struck three in order to give face-to-face instructions to the highest dignitaries of Palladism.

In the course of his fact-finding journey, Bataille had the opportunity to become personally acquainted with a great number of high-ranking Luciferians. Foremost among them was Albert Pike himself, the "Pope of Satanism," whom the exploring doctor described as a "living enigma." On the one hand, the Luciferian pope was an enthusiastic keeper of birds; on the other hand, he was a fearsome practitioner of occultism and the great man behind the global centralization of occult Masonry. The manuscript of his "Book of Revelations," a true "Satanic Bible" with diabolical autographs on every page, was conserved in Charleston with devotional care.[27] A "diabolical telephone" operated by demons enabled Pike to keep in close touch with the other Supreme Directors of High Masonry across the globe, foreshadowing in a way the presidential hotlines of later centuries.[28] Bataille also met two high priestesses of Lucifer who are to play a prominent part in the rest of our story: Sophia "Sapho" Walder and Diana Vaughan. As Sophie W***, Miss Walder had already been introduced in Taxil's *Y a-t-il des Femmes dans la Franc-Maçonnerie?*, where Taxil described her as an "ardent Lesbian" (hardly surprising, given her byname), whose sole passion was sacrilege. "Not content with spitting on the host and having others spit upon it, it has occurred several times that she demanded a recently received Female Knight of the Palladium to lay herself down on the Pastos outside the regular initiations and submit to sexual intercourse with a host in her vagina."[29] While staying in Charleston, Bataille took an afternoon stroll with this fiery lady, during which she disclosed to him, inter alia, that she was destined by diabolical prophecy to be the great-grandmother of the Antichrist. She then burst into the declamation of a hymn to Satan, even though Pike, as we have seen, had strictly forbidden the use of "Satan" for the "Good God."[30]

Even more bizarre was the life story of Diana Vaughan, at least as it was told to Bataille by various members of the Palladium. She was said to be the daughter of a Presbyterian minister who descended from a liaison of the famous occultist Thomas Vaughan with Venus-Astarte. Diana herself was betrothed to the demon Asmodeus, who jealously guarded his future spouse. Due to this high protection, she had been able to dispense with the sexual initiation rite normally required for the grade of Templar Mistress. On this occasion, she had also refrained from stabbing the host, claiming that her staunch Protestant upbringing had impressed upon her the utter absurdity of the notion that a piece of wafer could embody the divine presence. This had earned her the enmity of Sophia Walder, who had sought to prevent her graduation to Templar Mistress; but yet again, the divine diabolic intervention of Asmodeus had made sure that Vaughan prevailed.[31]

Unsurprisingly, the rather romanesque revelations of *Le Diable au XIXe siècle* met with skepticism from certain critics. This attitude became hard to maintain, however, when some of the principal personages of the book took the stage themselves. In 1893, Sophia Walder took pen in hand to address several newspaper editors. Some of her internal Palladic correspondence was intercepted as well.[32] Her rival Diana Vaughan proved even more media-happy and seemed to be engaged in regular correspondence with several anti-Masonic writers.

The background to the increased public profiling of certain Palladists was the internal strife that had broken out within the Palladium after the demise of Albert Pike in 1891. After a brief interregnum, the Italian Grand Master, Adriano Lemmi, had taken over control of the Palladic world organization. Pike had always opposed the "Satanist" element in Italian Palladism, but with Lemmi coming to power, the Palladium moved from Luciferianism into Satanism *sensu strictu*. As a staunchly orthodox Luciferian, Vaughan was vehemently opposed to this change of doctrine. She also claimed that Lemmi had secured his election with swindle and bribery and that Lemmi himself was a convicted thief, unworthy of his office. In 1893, she declared herself an "Independent Luciferian" and formed her own body of Luciferians, the "Free and Regenerated Palladium."[33] This renewed Palladium stood for a return to the orthodox worship of Lucifer the "Good God," and the cleansing of ritual of atavistic, nonrational, or distasteful aspects, like the sexual initiation rites described by Taxil. Luciferianism had to become a respectable public religion. To that end, Vaughan was mandated by the London-based Convent of Independent Palladists to engage in public propaganda. She duly published a compendium of (prudently pruned) Luciferian rituals and prayers and set up an official press organ, the above-mentioned *Palladium régénéré et libre*.[34] It was in the pursuit of this activity that we encountered Miss Diana Vaughan at the beginning of this chapter, editing the first public utterance of what we can surely call religious Satanism, according to the definition applied in this study.

As is often the sad lot of people who uncompromisingly follow their own principles, Miss Vaughan was soon at loggerheads with her Luciferian coworkers, who seemed strangely attached to their old, somewhat risqué rites. More important, however, Diana herself had started to experience a radical change in spiritual orientation. The Luciferian camp had already incurred a serious defection earlier that year, when Domenico Margiotta, "Former Sovereign Grand General Inspector of the 33rd Degree of the Accepted Scottish Rite; Former Souvereign Prince of the Order of the Rite of Memphis and Misraim (33e∴, 90e∴, 95e∴), Former Inspector of the Misraimite Lodges of the Calabrias and of Sicily; Former Honorary Member of the National Grand Orient National of Haiti," and so forth, announced his conversion to the Adonaïte faith. He promptly published a book called *Souvenirs d'un Trente-Troisième: Adriano Lemmi, chef suprême des Franc-Maçons*

("Remembrances of a 33:.: Adriano Lemmi, Supreme Head of Freemasonry"), which was a three-hundred-page denouncement of the Italian Grand Master, and followed this up a year later with another volume on his former coreligionists.[35] In June 1895, Diana Vaughan herself converted to Roman Catholicism. As had happened with Léo Taxil some ten years earlier, it had been the study of Joan of Arc that had led her to have doubts about the Luciferian creed. Although Palladism considered Joan a sort of proto-Luciferian, burned at the stake for her communication with Lucifer's spiritual messengers, a close reading of the sources did not support this interpretation. Moreover, Vaughan started to receive personal visions of the Maid of Orléans, and she discovered that the mere mention of her name caused her fiancé Asmodeus and his fellow demons to flee in disarray. "Lucifer is Satan," she wrote in her diary on the fourteenth of July. "Indeed, Lord, there is but one God: and you are this God."[36]

Vaughan now took the name of Jeanne-Raphaëlle, announced her intention to live a life of Catholic piety, and reinforced the ranks of anti-Masonic writers. *Le Palladium régénéré et libre* ceased to appear and was replaced by a new periodical publication, the *Mémoires d'une ex-Palladiste Parfaite Initiée, Indépendante* ("Memoirs of an Independent and Completely Initiated Ex-Palladist"). She also published a "Eucharistic Novena for Penance," containing prayers to compensate for profaned communions and other sacrileges by the Masonic sects; a hymn to Joan of Arc; and a volume with further insights into Freemasonry, particularly regarding the Italian Prime Minister Crispi, who was unmasked as a pawn and active member of the Palladium.[37]

Like the reader may well be, some followers of Masonic developments were rather startled by this fast succession of dramatic events. Doubts about the veracity of the whole story soon arose. Certain sections of the French and German Catholic press, although traditionally in the anti-Masonic camp, even expressed the opinion that the mysterious former Grand Mistress of Lucifer did not exist at all. Vaughan herself was unable to refute these allegations. She remained hidden in a convent for the time being, as she was now a fair target for Masonic assassins sent out to enact the traditional vengeance reserved by the sect for those that betrayed its secrets. Denying her existence and drowning her voice, however, was precisely what Freemasonry wanted, she declared from her place of hiding. In addition, she pointed out, a fair number of witnesses had spoken to her in person, including Léo Taxil, Domenico Margiotta, and her editor, Alfred Pierret, whom she had visited at his office to arrange for the publication of *Le Palladium régénéré et libre*. ("She impressed me as a charming person," Pierret remembered later. "Fairly tall, slim, simply dressed, and although her mantle of black wool made a great deal of hustle, she sat herself down with ease."[38]) In her pre-Christian days, moreover, the worthy Pierre Lautier, president of the Order of the Advocates of Saint Peter, had met her in a hotel in Paris, where she had held a long discourse about the state of Freemasonry. Particularly striking to him had been her refusal to partake of a glass of Chartreuse, which according to the adamant Luciferian was an "adonaïte beverage," since it was produced by a Roman Catholic monastery.[39] In addition to these eyewitness accounts, photographs of Miss Vaughan were in circulation; there were also the letters she had sent, posted from London, New York, and other places.[40]

In September 1896, Roman Catholic experts on Freemasonry from all over the world met in Trent for the first International Antimasonic Congress. A special session of the Congress was devoted to the Diana Vaughan question, which had by now become a hotly debated issue in the field of Masonic studies. The session convened on Tuesday, September 29, 1896, at three o'clock in the afternoon. Léo Taxil had traveled to the Italian city to plead the cause of Miss Vaughan, who purportedly was still hiding in a convent to escape Masonic hitmen. Taxil again emphasized that casting doubt on Diana Vaughan's revelations was exactly what High Masonry wanted. Two German members of the audience, Canon Berchmann and Reverend Baumgarten, assaulted him with tenacious questions, asking for Miss Vaughan's birth certificate, the name of the priest who had taken her confession, the place where she had received her first communion. Taxil responded with much bravado that he had these documents "in his pocket" but could not disclose these facts because of fears for Diana's personal safety.[41] He was prepared, however, to divulge the requested information in a personal meeting with the Cardinal Lazzareschi the following day.[42] The special session was only brought to a conclusion when a resolution was adopted that left the decision about Miss Vaughan's existence to a special committee of church notables. This committee deliberated endlessly, and in January 1897 the verdict came that neither Diana Vaughan's existence nor her nonexistence could be sufficiently proven.[43]

In the meantime, Vaughan herself had not remained inactive. While she continued to pour out revelations in her *Mémoires* (telling how Asmodeus had taken her to the Garden of Eden and the planet Oolis, for instance, or breaking the disturbing news that Sophia Walder had recently given birth to the grandmother of the Antichrist in Jerusalem), she also proclaimed her firm intention to put a definitive end to the controversy about her existence. To this purpose, she announced a grand tour of public readings for the coming spring, with a planned itinerary from Paris by way of Cherbourg, Rotterdam, London, Edinburgh, various places in France, and Brussels, to Turin and Genoa, ending in Rome itself. In the issue of March 31, 1897, she furnished the curious reader with the program of the announced readings as well. Photographic slides would be included, mainly with reproductions of official documents, but also including the engagement picture of Diana with her demonic lover, Asmodeus.[44] "Come what may, I will make my public appearance," the ex-Mistress of Luciferianism assured.[45]

The final revelation of Vaughan's existence turned out to be a spectacular occurrence indeed. On April 19, 1897, a large crowd assembled in the Hall of the French Geographical Society, where the event was to take place. This first installment of Miss Vaughan's European tour was reserved for invitees and members of the press only, with representatives of both anti-Masonic and nonspecialized periodicals present. First, a new American typing machine was raffled among the journalists present: Ali Kemal, the correspondent for the Istanbul-based *Ikdam*, held the lucky number. After this, a technician prepared the projector, projecting a gravure of Saint Catherine and Joan of Arc onto the wall. Instead of Diana Vaughan, however, Léo Taxil appeared on stage to address the public and reveal the shattering truth about Diana Vaughan and the Palladium. *It had all been a grand joke.* Not only was Diana Vaughan his personal creation, he declared, but the revelations of Dr. Bataille and Margiotta had been dictated by him as well. A secret Masonic organization of Luciferians and Satanists *did not exist* and *never had existed*.

While the public started to cheer or shout angry interjections, Taxil sketched the trajectory by which he had set up his phenomenal prank. His own conversion, more than twelve years previously, had already been a fake, partly by way of experiment, partly by way of practical joke. The idea of setting up the grand canard of Palladism and its High Priestess had by then already dawned upon him. Dr. Hacks (on whom more later) and Mr. Margiotta had all been in on the plot, and the part of Diana Vaughan had been played by Taxil's personal secretary, "a rather freethinking French protestant, typist by profession and representative of an American typing machine company."[46] With this performance, the curtain had irrevocably fallen on Miss Vaughan and Palladism. "I have committed infanticide," Taxil confessed. "The Palladium is dead now, dead as a doornail. Its father has come to kill it."[47]

Upheaval followed this shocking disclosure. Freethinking members of the public intoned satirical antireligious songs; more religiously inclined attendants heaped insults upon the speaker. The audience nearly came to blows—it was a good thing that everyone had been asked to hand over their walking canes when entering the hall—and Taxil had to leave the building under police protection. With a small band of supporters (among whom onlookers noticed a mysterious woman in black), he retreated to the second floor of a nearby restaurant, where they celebrated what could well be styled, for its scope and daring, the hoax of the century. A sudden downpour swiftly cleared the shouting mob from the streets, but other guests still had not left the hall of the Geographical Society. They could not believe the presentation was over and were waiting for the slide show to begin.[48]

TAXIL BEFORE PALLADISM

Thus ended this spectacular fairy tale from the history of Satanism. Although I do not believe I have deceived any reader who has read more than a few odd pages on the history of Satanism, I deliberately chose to present the story of Palladism as I did. With the exception perhaps of the two volumes by Bataille, the Taxil hoax was presented to the public in seemingly quite serious publications that included semi-academic annotation and copious references to both Catholic and external sources, the latter in many cases (allegedly) stemming from within Freemasonry. This crafty edifice may have looked quite convincing for the unaware reader in Taxil's day.[49]

I will not, I promise, test the reader's vigilance in such a devious way again and henceforth will restrict my narrative once again to the sober realities of historical fact. This is not something to regret. The true story of Taxil's life and of the setup of his giant hoax might be at least as romanesque as his stories of mystification. In the following sections, we look behind the scenes of Taxil's masquerade, investigate the trajectory he followed to build up his Palladist palace of deception, explore the sources that he may have used and the personal motivations he may have had, and ask ourselves how it was possible that his improbable inventions were believed for so long by such an extensive readership. Trying to answer these questions will give rise to other questions, some of which will lead us into unexpected territory.

Léo Taxil, the future inventor of Palladism, had been born Marie-Joseph-Antoine-Gabriel Jogand-Pagès in 1854 in a wealthy Marseille merchant family. His staunchly Catholic and monarchist parents sent him to the best Catholic private schools in Marseille that money could buy. This education, however, did not have the desired effect, and at a surprisingly young age, Gabriel Jogand developed into a political radical and a freethinker with fierce anticlerical inclinations. In 1868, when Jogand was only fourteen years old, he was apprehended by the French police during an attempt to reach Belgium to join the exiled political activist Henri Rochefort. He was subsequently sent to a juvenile correctional institute at Mettray, near Tours. In a later, doubtlessly thoroughly romanticized account, Taxil imputed his anticlericalism to a visit he received during his detention from a Roman Catholic priest who had rebuked the self-declared "materialist" for his stubborn refusal to attend Mass. After this confrontation, Taxil solemnly swore vengeance on the man who had mocked him in his cell, and on all other ecclesiastics, those men who "victimize children under the pretext of belief and faith, and turn fathers into bullies."[50] When his father retrieved him from his detention to send him to another school, his revolutionary political stance and his total lack of discipline soon got him expelled once more.

Jogand's great gift for journalism and publicity soon became apparent as well. At only sixteen, he founded a satirical journal called *La Marotte*, solidly anticlerical in content. It was at this point that he adopted the pseudonym Léo Taxil. *La Marotte* was banned in 1872 but was soon replaced by another journal, *La Jeune République*. Taxil henceforth led the life of a "petit journaliste": "lawsuits, duels, legal fines, expedients of every description."[51] The journals he issued were forbidden one after another by the authorities, and in 1876, Taxil fled to Geneva to escape an eight-year prison sentence. In the Swiss town, he tried to set up a Garibaldian revolutionary cell. In the meantime, he also married a working-class woman who already had several children by other men.

In addition, Taxil's great gusto for mystification, sometimes bordering on downright fraud, was already becoming noticeable in this period. According to the French dictum, a person from Marseille is prone to be a liar and a prankster; and in his long speech of April 19, 1897, Taxil sketched a whole career of practical jokes. In 1873, he claimed, he had convinced the population of Marseille that giant sharks were roaming the sea before the Mediterranean town; and while in Switzerland, he had launched the rumor that the ruins of an old Roman city had been discovered on the bottom of Lake Geneva.[52] Not all his hoaxes, however, were of this glorious kind. He was eventually expulsed from Switzerland because of his "immoral advertisements" for a product called "Harem Sweets"—aphrodisiacal pills of harmless but presumably ineffective content.[53]

Profiting from the general amnesty for political prisoners that the new Republican government had proclaimed, Taxil returned to France in 1878 and took up domicile in Paris. He now decided to devote himself fully to anticlerical propaganda. Together with his wife, he established an "anticlerical bookshop" and started to publish the "Anticlerical Library," a series of cheap popular publications and leaflets "energetically directed against superstition and sectarians" and mostly written by himself.[54] The quotes from Voltaire ("Crush the infamous!") and Gambetta ("Clericalism, that is the enemy!") adorning the series frontispiece accurately reflected the library's program. Browsing the titles in its prospectus gives a fair impression of their character, which ranged from the simply irreverent (*The Life of Jesus*, "a satirical and instructive parody of the Evangels") by way of the blatant (like *No More Cockroaches!*, or *Down with the Calotte!*, which featured a diatribe against the sexual abuse of minors by clerics) to the downright pornographic (for instance, *The Secret Loves of Pius IX, by a former valet of the Pope*, which told how Vatican henchmen abducted innocent maidens to pleasure His Holiness, who was, however, only able to find sexual gratification in the hands of an experienced Jewish prostitute).[55] Taxil also produced an *Anticlerical*

Marseillaise; issued a journal, the *Anti-Clérical*; and had a small assortment of merchandise that included "anticlerical envelops" with anti-Catholic comic drawings.[56] He was also one of the instigators of the Anticlerical League, an independent organization of freethinkers that sought to combat "clerical oppression."

This was, in brief, the story of the man who almost singlehandedly invented the most infamous organization of Satanists of the nineteenth century. What follows is slightly more controversial. On April 23, 1885, Taxil announced his conversion to Roman Catholicism. It was the study of the life of Joan of Arc for yet another anti-Catholic work that had brought him into the orbit of grace, he claimed, as well as the continuous prayer of some pious relatives. He retracted all his antireligious writings and liquidated his publishing house. The Church, at first, was rather suspicious of this unexpected convert. The old country vicar initially chosen by Taxil to be the Ananias on his road to Damascus was replaced by an experienced Jesuit Father who submitted the former freethinker to intensive soul searching. Taxil finally managed to convince him of his sincerity, he claimed in later reminiscences, by confessing a fictional murder.[57]

Taxil's return into the fold of the Church was greeted by many French Catholics as a miracle in itself, and in 1887, the ancient pamphleteer-cum-pornographer was even granted an audience by Pope Leo XIII. His former brethren against Christ, in contrast, were thoroughly shaken by his lapse into faith. In a tumultuous meeting on July 27, 1885, the Anticlerical League deplored his "betrayal of the cause of Free Thought and of his co-antireligionists." Bewildered, some insisted that he must have been bought by Rome. Others raised the hypothesis that he had been a clerical infiltrator all the time, while a few of his friends seriously considered the possibility that he had gone mad. Taxil, who surprisingly attended the meeting, declared emphatically that he was not mad at all. "One day, I hope, you will come to see this, if you cannot understand it now."[58] Inevitably, the league went on to oust him as a traitor and renegade. Taxil only protested against the accusation of treason, stating that they might not be able to grasp what he was doing at the moment but would understand it later on.[59]

Although it has been suggested by some that Taxil's conversion was initially sincere, utterances like these prove that his entrance into Roman Catholicism was part of a game of double play all along.[60] Regarding his personal motives for setting up such a gargantuan practical joke, different ideas have been proposed. Pecuniary gain usually figures prominently among them. The French police, which had kept Taxil under close surveillance since his early revolutionary ventures, noted in a report of May 19, 1884, that he had run into extreme money trouble. The print number of his anticlerical journal had dropped from 67,000 exemplars to a mere 10,000, and continuous legal bickering had exacted a heavy toll on his financial resources.[61] In *Confessions d'un ex-libre-penseur* ("Confession of a Former Freethinker"), his "Catholic" autobiography, Taxil gainsaid these allegations, proving that they were already in circulation as early as 1887; but while he here presents the liquidation of his Anticlerical Bookshop as a token of his radical conversion, other sources simply call it a bankruptcy.[62] Undeniably, the Catholic publishing market allowed for considerable profits to be made—Huysmans also gained his largest readership with his later, Catholic novels. It is unclear how much money Taxil actually made with his Luciferian saga, but *Le Diable au XIXe siècle* undoubtedly was a bookstall success, netting its editors as much as 300,000 francs. Taxil's coworker Karl (or Charles) Hacks purchased a restaurant in Montmartre from his share of the revenues, while Taxil seems to have laid hands on a modest chateau for his wife and family in this same period.[63]

It is hard to believe, however, that need or lust for money could have been the sole motive that sustained Taxil in putting up with twelve years of what must have been at times an enormously strenuous double life. Behind his façade of jocosity, he was probably sincere in his antireligious zeal. The two motivations are not, of course, mutually exclusive. And a third motivation must certainly be taken into account as well: the pure pleasure of pulling it all off. In his April 19 speech, Taxil frequently referred to "the intimate joy that one experiences when neatly fooling one's adversary, without malice, just to amuse oneself and have a bit of a laugh."[64]

While there can be little doubt that Taxil was bent on sabotage from the beginning, it would be a fallacy to think that he had meticulously planned his setup of Luciferian Freemasonry beforehand. The evidence, at least, strongly indicates otherwise. Taxil himself told his audience on April 19 that he had entered into his adventure "a bit at a venture," planning to withdraw himself "as soon as the experience had been made." "But then, the sweet pleasure of the joke getting the better of me and dominating everything completely, I lingered longer and longer in the Catholic camp, more and more extending my plan for an amusing as well as instructive mystification and allowing it to obtain ever grander proportions, as dictated by the events that rolled on."[65] Even the theme of Freemasonry, while certainly already prominent, had not been overriding from the start. Taxil tried his hand at several other issues as well, and he published books on the corruption of the French Republic and on the hidden goals of progressive politicians.[66] His new journal *La petite Guerre* ("The Small War") initially devoted as much space to anarchists and freethinkers as to Freemasons on its pages, and it only obtained the subtitle *Popular Organ of the Struggle against Freemasonry* in July 1888. Nor was the Satanist (or Luciferian) character of Freemasonry such a domineering feature from the start. While the formal worship of Lucifer in Masonry is already mentioned in Taxil's first books on the subject, much more emphasis is laid on the political machinations of the organization and its propensity for moral corruption.

Taxil himself claimed that it was his visit to the Pope that had finally convinced him to pursue the Satanism trail for real. At the Vatican, he continued, Cardinal Rampolla, Leo XIII's secretary of state, had praised his first three books on Freemasonry, although the ecclesiastical had added that the facts they described had long been familiar to the Vatican, even the most improbable ones. Cardinal Parocchi had taken the same line, while showing particular interest in the question of female Freemasonry; but Leo XIII had been particularly adamant where the devil was concerned, insisting on the Satanically led nature of Freemasonry and muttering the ominous phrase "the devil is there" with a peculiar intonation on the word "devil."[67] This portrait clearly has the traits of a caricature, although it may contain, as we shall see, more than a grain of truth. Yet it seems strange in this respect that it took Taxil three years after this audience to publish his first description of Luciferian Palladism in *Y a-t-il des Femmes dans la Franc-Maçonnerie?*, a book that was, moreover, not much more than a slightly reworked version of his earlier book *Les sœurs maçonnes*. Evidently, the direct spark for the Palladic undertaking was provided by Huysmans's novel, which had been published earlier that year and had proved the potential of "Satanic" themes to gain large audiences.[68]

The decision to use Freemasonry as the institutional background for this Luciferianism certainly owed much to the public and private mutterings of the Papacy, as we will see more clearly later on. Taxil, however, also had his own history with the lodge. In the days before his conversion, his anticlerical activities had gained him some approval among the more radical elements within French Freemasonry. In 1878, he was guest of honor at a lodge in Béziers, and in 1880, he affiliated himself with the Paris lodge "Les Amis de l'Honneur Français." His initiation to the degree of apprentice took place on February 7, 1881. Even on this occasion, if we are to believe Taxil's later reminiscences, his indomitable spirit of irreverent mockery did not fail to show. When he noted a spelling mistake in the inscriptions of the Chamber of Reflection, he took the skull that was given to the initiate to reflect upon and jotted down on it with pencil: "The Grand Architect of the Universe is kindly asked to correct the mistake in orthography on the 3rd panel from the left."[69] Not surprisingly, he was soon at odds with the other members of the lodge. Already on April 28, he was forbidden to hold conferences at lodge meetings, and in January 1882, he was declared "expulsed for indignity."[70] Some rather muddy episodes with a distinctly Taxilian flavor provoked this expulsion: an affair of plagiarism, in which Taxil was accused of faking letters from Victor Hugo and Louis Blanc, and the fact that he chose to run as a candidate in a local election *against* an official Masonic candidate. For his part, Taxil would maintain in his "Catholic" memoirs that his persistent refusal to put his Anticlerical League under the umbrella of French Freemasonry had earned him the hostility of the Grand Orient.[71]

In his final disclosure in 1897, Taxil would style these differences as "rows over nothing" and deny that he had any intention of taking revenge on his former three-pointed brothers. He also showed himself rather laconic about the consequences of his hoax for Freemasonry. Apart from the fact that his mystifications had held Catholic anti-Masonism up to total ridicule, he claimed that his publications would have a sanitary effect on the internal affairs of the lodge, contributing to reforms that suppressed "superannuated practices."[72] It might be wise, however, not to accept Taxil's utterances in this (or any) matter at face value. While the Church was undoubtedly his main target, he may well have considered Freemasonry a legitimate secondary one. After all, even in France, Freemasonry remained in essence a semi-esoteric group, with many religious or pseudo-religious "superannuated practices." Taxil could surely be considered a devoted antireligionist, and nothing suggests that he deplored having made Freemasonry the temporary butt end of his gigantic joke. In fact, his earliest anti-Masonic publication, a comical novel completely devoid of any specific Catholic content, may well predate his so-called conversion.[73] And how are we to explain otherwise his publication of Masonic membership lists, gleaned by assiduous labor from the lodge's internal publications? It is hard to see the joke in this potentially harmful practice, which seems to have been inaugurated by Taxil and subsequently taken over by other organs of the Catholic Press.[74] Whether out of personal or ideological motives, these facts suggest that Taxil did not fail to grasp the opportunity to settle some old accounts with the Ancient Brotherhood.

EXCURSUS: TAXIL'S SOURCES

For the construction of his Palladic universe, Taxil pillaged a wide variety of sources. Firstly, he used authentic Masonic publications and catechisms, works that were not particularly secret but often fairly hard to find: these he would cite at length, stressing a few odd sentences that could be interpreted at their most devious, and adding his own comments and some carefully selected historical facts taken completely out of context. He also took great avail of earlier anti-Masonic literature and of the work of some of his contemporaries who pursued similar careers, particularly one Paul Rosen, a mysterious character of whom not much is known with certainty—he seems to have been born in Warsaw and to have lived in Istanbul before coming to Paris, and he claimed to have been both a Jewish rabbi and a thirty-three-degree Freemason before converting to Catholicism.[75] The idea of portraying Albert Pike as the Black Pope of Satanism was almost certainly picked up by Taxil from Rosen's books, and he also seems to have purchased some rare Masonic works from the former rabbi.[76]

Thus far, Taxil's methods did not differ much from those of a rather one-sided academic historian, and his first three books on Freemasonry were a correspondingly dreary read. From 1891 on, Taxil's material became increasingly colorful. Yet here as well, he mostly did not bother himself with originality. We have already noted the importance of J. K. Huysmans's epoch-making novel. *Là-Bas* not only inspired Taxil to relaunch the Satanism theme, but also furnished many elements for Taxil's descriptions. Thus we see the recurrence of the famous Re-Theurgists Optimate, a designation that is used for the Odd-Fellows in *Are There Women in Freemasonry?* and for the Palladists proper in *Le Diable au XIXe siècle*.[77] The peculiar name first had been uttered by Vintras in a visionary trance several decades previously, then had been penned down by his followers in privately circulated notebooks, and subsequently had been conveyed by Boullan to Huysmans, who eventually inserted it in his novel. There was no other place where Taxil could have reasonably found it.[78] More subtle Huysmaniana include the figure of Sophie "Sapho" Walder in *Y a-t-il des Femmes dans la Franc-Maçonnerie?*, the "ardent lesbian" delighting in sacrilege, who is an evident spin-off from Hyacinthe Chantelouve; her habit of vaginally introducing the host is another clear reminder of *Là-Bas* (Taxil either did not pick up Huysmans's anal undertones, or considered them unsuitable to copy). In *Le Diable au XIXe siècle*, Huysmans himself would make a brief appearance in the chapter on "Non-organised Satanists," as "an occultist [who is] more of a researcher and an investigator than a practitioner." Like Bataille himself, the text noted, Huysmans has gone undercover to study the devil worshippers close by, "but in another milieu."[79] An accompanying engraving showed him side by side with Papus, his sworn enemy. It appears from his correspondence that Huysmans had submitted the photograph that was used to make this portrait himself, after the engraver of the illustration had requested this.[80]

Huysmans was not the only author that furnished Taxil with inspiration and raw material. Alphonse Constant (a.k.a Éliphas Lévi) also deserves pride of place in this list. The father of occultism was featured as a real person in Taxil's works, first as "brother C***" with the Jewish pseudonym in *Y a-t-il des Femmes dans la Franc-Maçonnerie?* and then in *Le Diable au XIXe siècle* with his full name. In both publications, he was portrayed as the founder of the first Satanist lodge in France.[81] Far more important, however, was the rich mine of ritual paraphernalia and occult terminology that Taxil found in Lévi. In his first trilogy on Freemasonry, Lévi's esoteric hand gesture is reproduced as the secret recognition sign of the Palladists; the inverted pentagram (the "signature of the devil") made its inevitable appearance; and in the Palladic nomenclature, Taxil with some creative ingenuity replaced the Masonic three points with the inverted triangle, a further symbol of "Satanic" inclination originating with Lévi.[82] Taxil's Luciferians and Satanists frequently quote Lévi verbatim in their discourses, and they afterward bend down to worship a Baphomet idol that is copied directly from Lévi's original engraving.[83] Lévi's books may also have transmitted much of the lore from older demonology that can be found in Taxil's works, for instance, the picturesque diabolical signatures that adorn the pages of the *Palladium régénéré et libre* and ultimately derive from the presumed demonic pact of Urbain Grandier.[84]

It is difficult to say what other or later occultists were utilized by Taxil, who had been personally interested in esotericism during his youth.[85] Nor are his other sources always easy to pinpoint. Like virtually every progressive intellectual in nineteenth-century France, Taxil was evidently familiar with the traditions of Romantic Satanism; the utterances and descriptions of his Luciferians, with their frequent invocations of the "genius of liberty" and the "generative principle" against the "god of superstition," often read as a persiflage of the discourse on Satan that had emerged from the greenhouse of Romanticism. In fact, works like *Le Diable au XIXᵉ siècle* and Margiotta's *Le Palladisme* are a veritable *Fundgrube* of obscure references to Satan in nineteenth-century counterculture.[86] In the highest degrees of Freemasonry, for instance, the Freemasons call on Lucifer with a prayer that is a compilation of infamous passages from Proudhon, the radical anarchist encountered in chapter 3. This time, however, Proudhon is honestly mentioned as their author, but only because he was a prominent Luciferian Freemason anyway, as the reader might have guessed by now.[87]

While copycatting was without doubt Taxil's most important tool in constructing his imaginary Luciferian universe, it cannot be denied that he displayed a good deal of virtuosity in arranging his material and inventing additional elements. What to think of the *male-aks*, the evil supernatural agents that oppose the demons of the Good God and are venerated as saints and angels by the deceived Adonaïtes? Or the *Gennaïth Menngog*, the Litany to the Demons sung at Palladic gatherings, and written in a ritual language apparently invented by Taxil or his cooperators?[88] As the success of his mystification grew, Taxil increased in boldness, fabricating complete doctrinal statements said to be from Albert Pike, detailed plans of the sect's headquarters at Charleston and other Palladic complexes, a separate Palladic calendar, and an intricate international Palladic hierarchy that freely mixed real-life personages with fictional characters. The printed material that has come down to us, although spanning thousands of pages, probably does not represent the full output of Taxil's fabrication factory. Alfred Pierret, Diana Vaughan's publisher, remembered having received a voluminous manuscript version of the "Book Apadno," the Palladic Holy Scripture. The mysterious book remained in his hands for six weeks, but it was retrieved by letter by Diana shortly after her alleged conversion and has never been seen or mentioned since.[89]

Taxil's most important addendum to the lore of Satanism was probably the doctrinal distinction between Luciferians and Satanists that he invented. Huysmans had merely echoed Vintras in *Là-Bas* with his rather vague statement about two factions within Satanism, "one aspiring to destroy the universe and reign over the ruins, and the other dreaming simply of imposing a demonic cult on the world."[90] Taxil's distinction between Luciferians and Satanists was much more ingenious and much more believable. He may have found inspiration for this in contemporary esotericism, where ideas that stressed a distinction between Lucifer and Satan had already been present in embryonic form. Lévi's polyvalent statements on the devil could be read in this way, and Theosophy explicitly emphasized the special character of Lucifer as opposed to the Christian Satan. Yet Taxil reworked these notions into a totally fictional but dogmatically rational schism with international and even literary ramifications that apparently sounded so plausible that it would continue to haunt the literature on Satanism for many decades after Taxil's eventual self-exposure.[91]

THE RISE AND FALL OF PALLADISM

The opposition of Luciferians and Satanists had a clear purpose for Taxil. It allowed him to differentiate between bad and better devil worshippers. For however helter-skelter his venture might have been at the outset, at a later stage the outlines of planned progression are undeniably present in Taxil's deception. With all its amusing sidelines and miniature controversies, the whole construction was essentially meant to introduce Taxil's masterpiece of mystification, the fictive Grand Mistress of Palladism, Diana Vaughan.[92] Diana's personal profile—Luciferian yet virtuous, attractive yet virginal, pious in her own way, but sadly misled—was clearly designed to evoke the sympathy of Catholic audiences, and all stages of her career, including her later defection and conversion, give the impression of being carefully planned. The execution of this plan involved some most hazardous steps, for instance, that of setting up the short-lived Luciferian bulletin that Vaughan was to direct without giving away Taxil's own involvement. Taxil put out some feelers to the small Roman Catholic publisher Alfred Pierret by way of a middle man, and he then visited the publisher himself to arrange the publication in the name of Miss Vaughan. When Pierret expressed his bewilderment about the fact that Taxil, converted Catholic and fierce anti-Mason, lent his support to the publication of a Luciferian journal, the latter declared that it was all part of a bigger plan that would bring back twenty thousand Luciferians to the fold of the Church and result in his own sanctification. Astonished, the publisher swore himself to secrecy, but he refused indignantly when Taxil offered him a thousand francs to paint his shop front flaming red and adorn it with small golden triangles.[93]

By now, Taxil had also found accomplices for his magnificent fraud. The first of these was Karl Hacks, a medical officer of German descent who had been living in Paris for a long time and had displayed some propensity for writing in French. His earlier efforts in this direction had resulted in a small volume of dilettante anthropology of religion entitled *La Geste* ("The Gesture"). Although a convinced freethinker, Hacks found nothing inherently implausible in the notion of a devil-worshipping core organization operating within Freemasonry—at least according to Taxil, who would later give a mildly improbable account of the way that he recruited the future Doctor Bataille. Taxil's story was that he had told Hacks that he was trying to discredit both Christian gullibility and Masonic Luciferian superstition by telling improbable tales on the latter. He even went so far as to send a letter signed by Sophie Walder to his coworker, in which the Grand Mistress indignantly protested against the distorted picture of Palladism that had been given in *Le Diable au XIXe siècle*. The good doctor was intensely looking forward to meeting the vicious Luciferian, and great was his disappointment when Taxil eventually told him that Miss Walder did not exist. This story, of course, sounds a bit too delicious to be true. Hacks's importance to Taxil's venture was, at any rate, limited. He mainly provided the travel descriptions that formed the narrative core of *Le Diable au XIXe siècle*: Taxil then embroidered these with tales of Palladism.[94] After volume 1, Hacks's activities as coauthor seem to have practically ceased, at least if we can believe the subsequent declarations of the doctor himself.[95]

Another contributor that Taxil recruited was Diana Vaughan herself. Taxil would always maintain that his assistant was indeed called Diana Vaughan and that this was the sole reason the Grand Mistress had been provided with this name—although others claimed that Taxil had found the name in a Sir Walter Scott novel.[96] However this may be, Taxil certainly used a female assistant to play the part of Miss Vaughan once in a while, and as the historians have not yet managed or bothered to uncover her real identity, we have only Taxil's post factum avowals to inform us of who or what she was.[97] Taxil had met her, he said, in the course of his professional activities; she was a typist, and a European representative of an American typing-machine company. Her English name went back to an American great-grandfather; her parents had been French Protestants, although she herself was "rather more of a freethinker." Taxil gradually interested her in his "devilries," which amused her greatly; for 150 francs a month, plus expenses, she agreed to play her part in the fabrication. For this salary, she copied Taxil's manuscripts on a typing machine (then still a comparative novelty) and wrote the Grand Mistress's letters by hand. The latter would then be delivered to a specialized agency, the "Alibi Office," which enabled its clients to have their letters posted from various locations in the world. She probably also impersonated the Grand Mistress on the one or two occasions that Taxil found this necessary, although some suspected that he had hired a *demimondaine* to play the part. If so, she is probably the woman who posed for the photographs that Taxil put into circulation of his central character. If we are to believe Taxil, his typist grew to enjoy her part in the hoax ever more; "corresponding with bishops and cardinals, receiving letters from the Pope's private secretary, telling them tales too strange to be true, informing the Vatican of the black conspiracies of the Luciferians: all this brought her into a mood of inexpressible cheerfulness."[98] These sparse facts are about all we know about the real Diana Vaughan.[99]

Even more questions surround a third accomplice who later joined the Taxil team, the Italian "Souvereign General Grand Inspector" Domenico Margiotta. Margiotta had been featured in an engraving in *Le Diable au XIXe siècle* and had received a short mention in the text of this work as the founder of a lodge in Florence, but this had probably not been done with any special purpose.[100] Rather, it seems that the Italian gentleman with the flossy beard had come out of his own accord as an informer on Palladism, reporting himself as such to Bishop Fava in Grenoble. Although he may have been a Freemason, he certainly had not been in possession of all the ranks and titles he mentioned in his first book; his main occupation seems to have been that of an adventurer, with some occasional ventures into literature on the side, and even wilder assumptions about his real profession have been made, as we shall see in a later section.[101] How he was harnessed into Taxil's schemes is not altogether clear. Taxil would later claim that Margiotta had initially considered Palladism to be true and had been effectively blackmailed into cooperation out of shame over his naivete. Margiotta, who blew the whistle on Palladism shortly before Taxil did so himself, simply spoke of a "barbarous contract" that bound him to Taxil. Whatever the truth in this, Taxil made effective use of the Italian, both as a third voice for his revelations about Diana Vaughan and as an "inside expert" on Italian Masonry. Letters from him that Margiotta showed to a Catholic journalist in December 1896 show how Taxil dictated the Italian adventurer's themes, revised his proofs, and told him which members of the press to approach and with what material.[102] This accounts for the strange circumstance that Margiotta's books were first published in French and only then translated into Italian; and also for the perfect pace they keep with the disclosures in Taxil's other publications.[103]

Taxil's most essential contributors, however, were mostly sincere in their convictions and entirely unaware of the role they played in his scheme. These were the Catholic publicists, journalists, and anti-Masonic activists that adopted his fabrications. The Palladium would have died an early and silent death had it not been enthusiastically maintained by large sections of the Catholic media, especially in France itself. A few key figures played a central role in the acceptance of Taxil's Luciferian inventions. In Grenoble, Bishop Fava, appropriately nicknamed "the Scourge of Freemasonry," propagated the Taxilian premises on Freemasonry from beginning to end. *Le Franc-Maçonnerie demasqué*, the journal founded by Fava, followed suit, and its editor, Gabriel Bessonies, would prove to be one of Diana Vaughan and Taxil's most tenacious apologists. Important in this respect was also Abel Clarin de la Rive, a journalist who, for rather mysterious reasons, enjoyed great prestige as a learned and unimpeachable expert on Freemasonry in Catholic circles. His adoption of Taxil's stories on sexual rites, devil worship, and Palladism in his extensively footnoted work *La Femme et l'Enfant dans la Franc-Maçonnerie* ("Woman and Child in Freemasonry"), greatly contributed to the acceptance of these notions among more serious Catholic authors dealing with Freemasonry.[104] Bishop Meurin, as we have seen before, also lent his assistance to the mystifications of Taxil: the false convert was consulted several times by the bishop while the latter prepared his book *La Franc-Maçonnerie, Synagogue de Satan*. In his wake followed J.-K. Huysmans, whom the popular press was eager to style an "expert on Satanism" following the publication of *Là-Bas*. The novelist devoted several pages to the Palladium in his preface to *La Satanisme et la magie* by Jules Bois, quoting extensively from Vaughan's *Palladium régénéré et libre*, and once again lashing out at the judicial authorities who neglected the criminal investigation of these sacrilegious activities.[105] Taxil stimulated and exploited these expressions of support with care. He was wont to send his books to bishops and other ecclesiastical dignitaries, subsequently citing their letters of appreciation or recommendation on the opening pages of his works.

Support from experts and ecclesiastics like these paved the way for the acceptance of Taxil's stories in parochial journals and the Catholic mass press. Thus the *Revue Bénédictine* from Maredsous lauded Bataille's ludicrous *Le Diable au XIXe siècle*, remarking that the gravures sometimes displayed "an unsettling fantasy" and that its author was clearly "a man of imagination," but chiefly deploring the fact that the two volumes were not brought out in a cheap edition for the general populace: "That would be a work of apostolate."[106] The Assumptionist daily *Le Croix*, the *Revue Catholique de Coutances* of L.-M. Mustel, the Quebeçois newspaper *La Vérité* of J. P. Tardivel: all reported extensively and unskeptically on Palladism and Diana Vaughan. Taxil made grateful use of these channels for propagation. Under his own name, or under those of Bataille, Vaughan, and Margiotta, he fed them with interesting news items and proofs of upcoming publications; the newspaper articles that would result from this he then quoted in his subsequent publications, thereby creating a deceivingly realistic tissue of seemingly reliable references and a carefully built-up illusion that his own inventions were in fact independent discoveries by a vigilant Catholic press.

The gullibility of Catholic opinion should not be exaggerated. Taxil's inventions were by no means universally accepted by all of Catholicity. In Germany, the Jesuit Hermann Gruber of the *Kölnische Volkszeitung*, an anti-Masonic author of some renown, turned skeptical after initially believing Taxil, and the German Jesuit started to publish articles that meticulously demolished Taxil's creations. In this, he seems to have had the support of the bishop of Cologne.[107] Even in France, important sections of Catholic publicity did not take the Palladic bait. The ultraconservative *L'Univers* mostly ignored Taxil's fabrications, and in the even more conservative *La Vérité*, Georges Bois heaped scorn upon Taxil and his inventions, despite the fact that both he and his journal were militantly anti-Masonic.[108]

What is most striking in retrospect, nevertheless, is the improbable amount of credibility that Taxil was able to muster for his wild inventions among the Catholic public. These inventions included wondrous feats like voyages to other planets, visits to the Garden of Eden, children engendered by (or with) demons, the capturing of the tail of the Lion of Marcus by demonic hosts, the birth of the grandmother of the Antichrist in Jerusalem, Luciferians passing through walls, and Satan giving regular conferences at the "Sanctum Regnum" in Charleston, South Carolina. Sometimes one can almost sense the pleasure that Taxil and his team must have had in pushing the boundaries of credibility just a bit farther: for example, in the delightful story of a spiritist séance during which Moloch suddenly appeared in the shape of a winged crocodile. The demon drank all the liquors on the table, played a short tune on the piano "in the most strange notes," and disappeared again without inflicting further harm because, it seems, he was not "in one of his cruel days."[109]

Taxil's most successful invention was without doubt Diana Vaughan. Reading their utterances with regard to this young lady, it seems that many Catholic publicists were positively in love with this "angelic creature living in an inferno of Palladism by the hazard of birth" (as Taxil aptly put it).[110] For the twenty-first-century reader, it is hard to believe that somebody like, say, Abel de la Rive was not actually in league with Taxil and his consorts when he burst out in laudatives for Miss Vaughan toward the end of his book. Exclaiming how much "this strange personality is above the other members of Palladism and the two million seven hundred fifty-five thousand five hundred fifty-six Sisters Masons in the rest of the world," Rive quotes a prayer from Corneille's play *Polyeucte*, where the hero asks the divinity to convert the beautiful pagan girl Pauline with whom he is in love: "She has too many virtues not to be a Christian."[111]

After Miss Vaughan's "conversion," this Catholic adulation only increased. Her publisher Pierret reported receiving six thousand letters for the former Luciferian Grand Mistress after she announced her religious shift; the already quoted *Revue Bénédictine* expressed its admiration of the divine mercy that displayed itself in this wondrous occurrence.[112] Cardinal Parocchi, Vicar of Leo XIII, sent Vaughan a letter on December 16, 1896, to transmit "a most special blessing" from His Holiness and tell her that she would not be forgotten in his prayers, especially at Mass. "You have won my sympathy since a long time past," the cardinal added. "Your conversion is one of the most magnificent triumphs of grace that I know of."[113] Women were not immune to the seductive power of Taxil's fantasy either. The Carmelite nun Theresa de Lisieux corresponded with the converted Luciferian and wrote a little piece of theater for her fellow nuns in which Asmodeus, Lucifer, and Beelzebub grievously deplored the loss of Diana for their infernal cause. The future saint was greatly dismayed when it turned out the former Grand Mistress had never existed, and she personally burned the letters she had received from her.[114]

The Catholic eagerness to embrace Taxil's fantasies contrasts strongly with the attitude of the nonconfessional press, who either took no notice of Palladism until the very end or reported on it with studied amusement.[115] In general, the spokesmen and –women of fin de siècle occultism and esotericism showed more critical acumen as well, although some did not manage to avoid stumbling in Taxil's trap. With an official journal called *Lucifer*, the Theosophists were obliged to react to Taxil's allegations sooner or later. In January 1896, George Robert Stowe Mead, the influential personal secretary of the late Blavatsky, commented on the Palladism revelations in an editorial in *Lucifer*, stating that Theosophy's Lucifer, being a benign spiritual being helping mankind in its intellectual evolution, had nothing to do with Palladism or Satanism. He did not, however, seem to doubt the existence of a large organization of Lucifer-worshipping Freemasons, and he expressed the presumption that this apparent vogue of Satanism might be caused by a sudden mass reincarnation of souls that had debauched themselves in orgies during the final decades of the Roman Empire.[116]

In the spiritist periodical *Light* ("A Journal of Psychical, Occult, and Mystical Research"), excerpts from *Le Diable au XIXe siècle* started to appear in English translation from the fall of 1895 onward. The translator (who hid behind the initials C. C. M.) deplored Bataille's "violent prejudice against this country, a prejudice which he indulges by statements, not less shameful because ridiculously false," but asserted that the publications should nevertheless not be neglected by students of occultism. "From several quarters, of late years, there have been rumours, becoming more and more assured and definite, of the actual existence and spread of the 'Luciferian' cult, of its connection with the highest degrees of Masonry, and practical influence in political and revolutionary organisations. Perhaps the obvious and inevitable re-action [*sic*] from materialism is to the nature-worship (the 'natural divinity') in which the spiritual is reinstated as the consecration of sensuous spontaneity."[117] In the subsequent issues of the journal, a lively controversy over the new divulgences ensued. One correspondent discerned dark astral forces behind the writings of Bataille, "who is probably an active member of the 'Black' party, *as they call themselves*, those intransigents who have but one object in view, the reestablishment of the temporal power founded on the basis of Fear and Awe, instead of Love and Mercy"; a female letter writer saw the recrudescence of Satanism as a typical example of the eschatological battle between evil and good of "these days of the Kali Jug" and added a reference to George Sand ("doubtless the old Hussite password, 'May he who is wronged salute thee,' is not abrogated"); a third contributor, who presented himself as "Past Master and Holy Arch-Mason," ventured that the whole thing was a plot of "Popish Priests and Jesuits" and expressed his conviction that Diana Vaughan was "under the hypnotic power" of Dr. Hacks "or possibly some wily member of the Order of Jesus."[118] Even after Papus had been asked for his expert opinion and two reactions of the French occultist had been published, the debate continued to flare up.

In France, Jules Bois displayed slightly more skepticism in his treatment of the Palladic revelations. The journalist-cum-esotericist interviewed Hacks/Bataille for *Figaro* and devoted a short chapter to "The Luciferians" in his *Petits Religions de Paris*, where he voiced the suspicion that the whole thing might very well turn out to be "the dream of a will-o'-the-wisp."

But true or false, the whole story was surely a sign of the times. "Certainly it takes all the fatigues of our century to imagine or re-establish such a cult of the fallen Archangel."[119]

Those with real inside knowledge of the world of alternative religion and esoteric societies made short shrift of the Taxilian charade. Guaita, who had predictably been portrayed in *Le Diable au XIXe siècle* as a practicing Satanist with a familiar spirit hiding in a cupboard, declared once more that true devil worship was an extremely uncommon phenomenon.[120] Papus (whom Bataille had declared to be possessed by the demon that had furnished his pseudonym) reacted with another brochure, in which he pointed out how liberally Bataille and consorts had stolen from the works of Éliphas Lévi.[121] One of his fellow occultists did what the complete Catholic press apparently failed to do: he took a coach to the Parisian address of the publisher of *Le Palladium régénéré et libre*, where he found not a shop painted red and sprinkled with diabolical symbols, but a perfectly Catholic establishment where the Luciferian journal was on display in the rather uneasy company of rosaries and Catholic books of devotion.[122] Across the Channel, the English Freemason and follower of Lévi, Arthur Edward Waite, also took up the defense of his late spiritual mentor and published a sharp-witted and critical overview of the Palladism literature that left no doubt about the utter nonsense of it all.[123] It must be noted, however, that neither occultist seems to have grasped the full extent of the deception right away. In his earlier contributions to the debate in *Light*, Waite was not altogether dismissive of some of the disinformation that had been produced by the Taxil factory, and although Papus, in his letters to the same periodical, denounced *Le Diable au XIXe siècle* as a "financial speculation" by its Catholic publishers, he added, surprisingly enough, that Hacks had inside knowledge about Palladism nevertheless: "It is true that Dr. Hacke [*sic*] was a member of an almost unknown Italian lodge, and that he was invited to assist at a Palladic *initiation*, which included no occult ceremonials, and this was at a small lodge of no importance, now extinct (and who really held the cultus of Lucifer, star of the morning, not the spirit of darkness as represented)."[124] With regard to Diana Vaughan, he declared that neither he nor any of the "about one hundred and fifty" leaders or officers of initiated groups in France with whom he was familiar had ever seen her—but she might have frequented "atheistic Masonic lodges," where most of the members of the Palladium were assumed to be located as well.[125]

Meanwhile, Taxil did not altogether hide his own person from view. He toured the country to give conferences accompanied with oxhydric slides, the latest in visual technology.[126] With Doctor Bataille, Diana Vaughan, and Margiotta, he was an important contributor to the *Revue mensuelle religieuse, politique, scientifique*, a journal that accompanied and succeeded the feuilletons of *Le Diable au XIXe siècle*. Merchandise opportunities were apparently not neglected either. If we are to believe Papus, a medical and dental practice was annexed to the Taxilian publishing establishment, "with special reduction for gentlemen from the clergy."[127] The most bizarre of Taxil's Catholic projects was probably the foundation of an anti-Masonic lay order, the "Antimasonic Labarum." This "militant Catholic Order" declared itself inspired by Pope Leo XIII, in whose footsteps it was to follow in undertaking "a war without quarter, defensive and offensive, against the infernal sect, which it will not cease till the day of the final triumph of Religion, that is to say: till the day of the establishment of the kingdom of Jesus Christ over society, and his recognition as King of France by the public authorities."[128]

Taxil had found a remarkable collaborator for this remarkable venture. This was Jules Doinel (1842–1903), who had cooperated intimately with Papus, Guaita, and Péladan and who had been founder and first "Archont" of the Gnostic Church, an esoteric group that sought to resurrect Catharism. In 1895, Doinel had suddenly converted to Catholicism and published a book entitled *Satan démasqué* ("Satan Unmasked"), in which he pointed out the hand of Lucifer behind all forms of esotericism and occultism, supporting his thesis with his personal experiences in Masonic and esoteric groups.[129] (These amounted mainly to "psychic manifestations" of the Prince of Evil he had sensed during meetings and rituals.) Although Doinel seems to have reverted to Gnosticism later in life, his conversion was probably sincere. On November 19, 1895, after Mass, he convened with Taxil and six other militants in the Paris Sacre Cœur to found the Antimasonic Labarum, Doinel taking on the "religious" name of Br⁺ [*sic*] Kostka de Borgia (reminiscent of Jean Kostka, the pseudonym he had used in publishing *Satan Unmasked*) and Taxil that of Br⁺ Paul de Règis (after a distant relative noted for his piety).[130]

The new order was an audacious endeavor to establish a Catholic parallel for Freemasonry, with its own colorful uniforms and sashes, its own banners and rituals, and its own system of degrees: one for women (that of "Sister of Joan of Arc") and three for men (Legionnaire of Constantine, Soldier of Saint Michael, and Knight of the Sacred Heart). The Labarum also had a youth organization, its own journal (*L'Anti-Maçon, Revue spéciale du mouvement anti-maçonnique, organe officiel de la ligue du Labarum*), and a nationwide web of subdivisions that assembled from time to time to parade in ceremonial apparel. Men and women of the highest degree could offer their life to Christ in voluntary sacrifice to perform expiatory penance for the sacrileges committed by Freemasonry. The movement seems to have obtained some measure of success. In 1896, eleven "companies" were already in the process of formation in various places all over France, with foreign units operating in Canada and Scotland. Hundreds flocked to the annual "Grand" Garde" of the Paris division on February 22, 1896.[131]

The zenith and at the same time turning point of Taxil's career as a Roman Catholic anti-Masonist may well have been the International Antimasonic Congress of 1896. The idea of organizing this congress had not been Taxil's, but he had been closely involved in the initial stages of its preparation, and his creations and personality were at the center of interest during its proceedings. During the opening procession, Taxil made his entrance as a conquering hero, decked out with the red sash and ritual regalia of Honorary Grand Master of the Labarum and surrounded by his self-created anti-Masonic knighthood carrying banners and standards. He frequently made confession and took communion. At official religious ceremonies, he invariably entered the Church when it was already filled; and as he slowly walked down the aisle with an air of utmost humility, churchgoers broke out in spontaneous approval, shouting "Long live the great Convert!" and "Un santo, un santo!"[132] His interjections on behalf of Diana Vaughan during the congress earned him rounds of frenetic applause.

Regarding the popular esteem in which he was held, Trent certainly was a triumph for Taxil. Yet in a "political" respect, it could be considered a failure. Prior to the congress, Taxil had sought to get himself appointed as official representative of the French anti-Masonists at the conference; but word had arrived from the Italian organizational committee that his nomination would not be accepted.[133] At Trent itself, he tried, in rather devious ways, to get himself elected into the commission that would be charged with drawing up the statutes of the nascent International Antimasonic Union. In this way he would place himself right at the heart of the emerging global anti-Masonic movement. In the nick of time, however, his election was prevented by whispered instructions from a prominent member of the board.[134] Taxil's evasiveness in furnishing proof of Diana Vaughan's existence, moreover, could not possibly have left a favorable impression with the hierarchy. In order to protect the safety of Miss Vaughan, Taxil had claimed, he could only give the name of her confessor and other proofs of her conversion in a private tête-à-tête with a bishop, who could then transmit it to the Pope. However, Taxil failed to appear at the arranged meeting with Bishop Lazzareschi. When the bishop and he met later that evening, he assured the bishop that even the slightest revelation could endanger the converted Grand Mistress, and he drew a revolver from his pocket in front of the ecclesiastical dignitary, remarking that he never went out without a weapon because he was continually in danger.[135]

Evidently, suspicions had been raised in high places about Taxil. Even before the Antimasonic Congress, in fact, cracks had started to appear in his Palladic edifice. As early as April 22, 1894, Rosen had denounced Taxil in an article entitled "The Key of the Mystification," mainly by consulting a Masonic encyclopedia to show that most of Bataille's soi-disant confidants were already dead.[136] In January 1896, while touring Roman Catholic institutes in the Netherlands, the former rabbi had once again declared Taxil to be a fraud. Diana Vaughan was a mere fabrication, he maintained, impersonated by Taxil's wife. Taxil effectively shut the mouth of his competitor by spreading the rumor that Rosen was a secret agent of Adriano Lemmi operating under the code name Moses Lid-Nazareth.[137] But he was not able to keep the lid on the box forever. The Parisian newspaper *L'Éclair* divulged the existence of the Alibi Office in December 1896 and advised Taxil to confess his imposture "in a peal of laughter."[138] The cracks in his construction became chasms when Taxil's own contributors started to defect. Karl Hacks, alias Doctor Bataille, more or less opened the books to an English journalist shortly before the Antimasonic Congress; in November 1896, he gave an interview to *L'Univers* and wrote letters to *La Vérité*, the *Kölnische Volkszeitung*, and *La Libre Parole* in which he disclosed the real story behind *Le Diable au XIXe siè-cle*.[139] "One can permit oneself everything with those Catholics; they are nothing but imbeciles!" a shocked journalist from *La Vérité* recorded from his mouth.[140] In December 1896, Margiotta also threw off his mask and told *La Libre Parole* how he had been dancing to Taxil's strings. He also maintained, although certainly incorrectly, that Diana Vaughan was in reality Taxil's wife.

It was clear that the tenability of Taxil's grand hoax was nearing its end. Taxil himself also appears to have been creaking under the strain of continuous masquerade by now. He was seen by an anonymous source in a Parisian cabaret, dead drunk, loudly singing anticlerical songs that he had written himself during his earlier career, and proudly boasting of the fact.[141] In his April 19 speech, Taxil once again tried to create the impression that his final self-exposure had been contrived long before, purposely terminating an activity of almost exactly twelve years as a self-appointed undercover agent. He even claimed that Hacks's defection had occurred in close accord with himself, with the intention of drawing the attention of the "grande presse" to the Vaughan story.[142] In the intricate web of fabrications that Taxil wove, it is at times all but impossible to ascertain the truth of some of his claims, but a number of circumstances indicate that he might not have been merely venting wind in this particular case: for instance, Hacks's seemingly deliberate vagueness about Diana Vaughan's actual existence and true identity. Planned or not, the end of his charade could not be postponed much longer if it was not to be ended by others, as Taxil acknowledged with as many words in his final discourse.[143]

The April 19 press conference formed a fitting finale to Taxil's almost unbelievable feat of infiltration and sabotage. Notwithstanding the fact that he certainly had not neglected his own material interests, Taxil had in some sense indeed sacrificed himself for his cause, spending twelve years of his life living in his own bizarre experiment and effectively eliminating, as he noted himself, his chances of any further public career. No newspaper whatsoever, whether Icelandic or Patagonian, would henceforth accept a news story from his hands.[144] Taxil's remaining years would be spent in reissuing his old anticlerical publications and publishing pornography and cooking books. He died in 1907, virtually forgotten.[145]

THE GREAT MASONIC CONSPIRACY

It is not hard to allocate the Taxil saga a place in the history of Satanism.[146] Palladism is a crystal-clear case of attribution: a case of attribution made extraordinary because it had been consciously invented from the beginning, with the explicit purpose of exposing the very mechanics of attribution itself. As noted above, all serious historians accept Taxil's statements about its wholly fictive nature. What is much more intriguing and difficult to explain is the tremendous success of Taxil's hoax among the contemporary Catholic public. How is it possible that his improbable inventions were believed by so many, up to the highest echelons of Roman Catholicism? For the Taxilian inventions found credence not only among pious parishioners in rural backwaters, but also among leaders of Catholic opinion of quite evident intellectual capacity.

For an answer, some historians have simply blamed the immense credulity nineteenth-century Roman Catholic believers seemed to possess.[147] Yet this is at best half an explanation and involves some questionable assumptions about Roman Catholic believers. Humanity's great willingness to be deceived is certainly a striking fact. But there were some historical circumstances that facilitated Taxil's endeavor, without which we cannot understand why substantial parts of Europe's Catholic population eagerly embraced dark fictions about worldwide networks of devious Lucifer worshippers. To begin with: Taxil did not build on virginal grounds. A long tradition of anti-Masonic literature, predominantly stemming from within the orbits of conservative Christianity, provided the foundations on which his construction rested.

There had been precedents for this long tradition in the eighteenth century and even in the seventeenth century.[148] But it was the Western Revolution, and especially its emblematic highpoint, the French Revolution, that gave the theme its enormous proliferation and its new political significance. The Revolution had been a thorough and totally unexpected shock for those who had deemed the old order indestructible. Suddenly (so it seemed) the people of France, eldest daughter of the Church, had deposed and eventually decapitated their divinely anointed king; had declared that they would rule themselves according to their own natural lights and without recourse to divinity, tradition, or precedent; and had proceeded to worship the Goddess of Reason instead of the god of Christianity, whose churches they had disowned and whose clergy they had persecuted with violence.[149] And although the combined forces of the old order had eventually succeeded in crushing the French insurgence and restoring royal rule in France, the ghost of Revolution would not lie down and die. Instead, it engendered other ghosts in all parts of Europe. Liberalism, socialism, Communism, and anarchism clamored for radical change in wild succession. All shook their menacing fists at the Christian Church. Even where their revolutions failed, governments adopted measures that curbed religious influence on society and legalized the practice of other religions, while revolutionary tenets such as parliamentary control and universal suffrage were gradually becoming a political reality in many West European countries. At the same time, an increasing number of Europeans and Americans abandoned Christianity to adopt metaphysical notions that had formerly been the domain of a handful of infidel *philosophes*. The rule of man had indeed begun.

From the perspective of those that represented the "outraged traditions," these changes were incomprehensible.[150] They almost seemed to be part of an evil scheme. Already during the Revolution years itself, publications started to appear that proclaimed Freemasonry to be the secret motor behind the recent political turmoil.[151] Was not the famous slogan "Liberté, Egalité, Fraternité" an invention of Freemasonry? Had religious tolerance not been propagated for centuries in the secrecy of the lodges? And could Freemasons not be found among the most prominent revolutionaries? In 1797, these rumors found their codification in the four-volume *Mémoires pour servir à l'histoire du jacobinisme* ("Memoirs for a History of Jacobinism") by father Augustin Barruel, a French priest who had fled to England when the revolutionary regime had started its religious persecutions. The vast historical panorama painted by Barruel in his *Mémoires* would dominate the discourse on Freemasonry for the following century and longer. Evidently, Barruel maintained, the French Revolution had been the work of Freemasons, led on by their radical vanguard, the Illuminati, and banding together with the "Conspiracy of the Philosophers." But this event was only the most recent and most dramatic eruption of a long campaign against "the crucified God and the crowned kings."[152] During the Middle Ages, its precursor in conspiracy had been the Templar Order, as some Freemasons claimed themselves, a military religious order that had been disbanded on accusations of heresy and conspiracy against the King of France. The Templar heresy, in its turn, stemmed from the Albigensi and the other heretic "sects of the South," and these, eventually, were all offshoots from Catharism. "Everything is connected," Barruel wrote, "from the Cathars to the Albigenzi, on to the Templars, & from them on to the Jacobin Masons; everything indicates a common father." This common father, the Catholic author went on, was Manicheism, the heresy that had already been scourged by the fathers of the Church.[153] What had seemed thoroughly modern was thus in fact the latest upsurge of an age-old conspiracy that had consistently pursued its anti-Christian and anti-authoritarian objectives since the early days of Christianity. "It is always royalty & Christianity that has to be destroyed, Empires and Altars that have to be reversed, to establish *equality & liberty* for the human race."[154]

Barruel's book became a classic in its genre, was translated into virtually every European language, and set the pattern for the rich anti-Masonic literature that bloomed in the decades that followed.[155] Its popularity was due in large part to the fact that it made comprehensible what was otherwise incomprehensible. Now the unprecedented events of 1789 and the seemingly spontaneous defection of many Europeans from a faith that was so evidently true could be given a place in the historical framework of what had come before. Now it was clear that nothing new had happened in the first place. The Revolution had been organized by a secret anti-Christian network that had reared its head under a different disguise in every epoch; there had been nothing spontaneous in it. This network was not vaguely invisible but tangibly present in virtually every town and city; although Barruel held the rank-and-file of Freemasonry to be ignorant of the sect's dark devices, and its Anglo-Saxon branches completely exempt, it was in the secret recesses of the lodge that the plot against the Christian faith and Christian society was hatched.[156] This refreshingly simple explanation found wide acceptance, and not just among hillbillies or bigots. Joseph de Maistre (1753–1821), the sharp-witted Roman Catholic intellectual who had been active in fringe esotericism himself, initially wrote a refutation of Barruel's thesis but later "converted" to Barruelism.[157] And, bizarrely, the Comte Ferdinand de Bertier (1782–1864), impressed by Barruel, allowed himself to be initiated in Loge de la Parfaite Estime in order to bring to light its occult machinations, subsequently founding the Chevaliers de la Foi ("Knights of the Faith") to conduct a clandestine counteraction against the dark workings of Freemasonry.[158]

No one who skims through a bibliography of anti-Masonic literature can fail to notice that many of its authors were Catholic or Protestant clergy, with Barruel himself a prominent example. This was no coincidence. In the dichotomy that the French Revolution had engendered, as we have seen, the Roman Catholic Church had, after some initial wavering, chosen the side of the forces of reaction; important parts of Protestant Christianity, especially in its more "fundamentalist" manifestations, had joined in this antirevolutionary stance.[159] Some aspects of the French Revolution—the disowning of church property, the persecution of priests who did not want to swear loyalty to the republic—made this understandable. The aversion called forth by these occurrences soon formed itself into an ideology. Barruel's work repeatedly attested to a notion that was rapidly becoming an article of faith for many antirevolutionaries: that of the "traditional" alliance between throne and altar. In fact, the absolute monarchs of the ancien régime had often been far from kind or protective to the Church and its dignitaries. Yet in the common cause of "outraged traditions" against the swelling tide of Revolution, this part of recent history was swiftly forgotten. For much of the nineteenth century, the Catholic Church would strive to restore the "Christian" monarchy and the official Christian character of the state, obstinately opposing the most important legal consequences of the Western Revolution, such as freedom of the press, freedom of religion, and separation of church and state.

By its very nature, the Papacy itself was the most striking embodiment of the alliance between throne and altar. The Pope was the spiritual head of the most powerful church of Christianity, but he was also de facto monarchical ruler of the Papal States, a strip of territory that had been granted to the Roman Pope by the first of the Carolingians in the remote days of the Dark Ages. For both friend and foe, this strip of territory became the symbol of the claim of the Church to dominate both the spiritual and the secular sphere in a world that was entering into a phase of radical secularization. Not surprisingly, its status would be a source of constant dispute in the aftermath of the French Revolution. In 1799, Rome had been "liberated" by French Revolutionary troops; the city had been declared a Republic and the "citoyen-pape" taken away in captivity. After Napoleonic France had been defeated, the European monarchs had restored the temporal rule of the Pope. But the spirit of revolt now threatened the Papacy from within the boundaries of its own territories, as Italian radicals clamored for democratic and constitutional government and a united Italy. In 1848, when a new wave of revolutionary fervor spread over Europe, rebels led by the Italian revolutionary Giuseppe Mazzini (1805–1872) captured Rome and reestablished a republic. Pope Pius IX had to flee the eternal city in the habit of an ordinary priest. Mazzini's republic proved short-lived, and Pius IX was once again restored to his throne, protected (ironically) by French troops sent by Napoleon III. Yet the Papal autocracy was now increasingly becoming an anomaly in the European political landscape. When the Franco-Prussian War broke out in 1870 and the French soldiers were withdrawn, the unified Italian state that had taken shape in the meantime reacted immediately. In September 1870, Italian troops marched into Rome. Pius IX commanded his soldiers to put up symbolic resistance to the invading force and then locked himself in the Papal palaces, henceforth spending his life as the "prisoner of the Vatican."

These experiences had formed the attitudes of the popes and confirmed their suspicion of the new ideological winds that blew over Europe. In their own home base, they had radically rejected the overtures of modernity. In the 1820s, when most of Western Europe had groaned under the repression of reaction, the Papal States had distinguished themselves by their ultra-reactionary regime. When the French had left in 1814, the Holy Inquisition was restored immediately; Pope Leo XII, who was elected to the See of Peter in 1823, stepped up the persecution of non-Catholic "sects" (resulting in seven death penalties) and found occasion to castigate the French monarch Louis XVIII for his tolerant religious laws that would "permit everyone to think and believe as he thinks most fit." He even banned encores and ovations in theaters, as they might give occasion to vent political discontent.[160] These excesses were somewhat mitigated under his successors, but the fundamental attitude of staunch antimodernism remained. In 1832, Leo's successor Gregorius XVI issued the encyclical *Mirari Vos*, in which he condemned every attempt to revolt against legitimate rulers and called the notion of freedom of conscience a "delirium."[161] With Pius IX, the condemnation of modern tenets and ideologies accumulated into a veritable Syllable of Errors, solemnly proclaimed in December 1864 and condemning pantheism, rationalism, socialism, liberalism, and a host of other -isms.

Unsurprisingly, Freemasonry could and would not remain absent from these lists. The nineteenth-century popes found precedent for this in their eighteenth-century predecessors. Already in 1738, Pope Clemens XII had condemned the new society of "liberi Muratori seu Francs Massons" that had started to become something of a craze in continental Europe. Drawing on the favorite *topoi* of medieval and early modern heresology, the Pope had declared that the secret proceedings of the lodges must have been the scene of evil deeds, "because if they would not do wrong, they would not hate the light so much."[162] His main allegation against Freemasonry, however, had been that the society promoted religious relativism, because Masons of different religious affiliation could be admitted, and that they might foment revolt against their rightful kings. Although shrouded in the usual theology, the purport of Clemens's Bull was probably predominantly practical and local.

The Pope seems merely to have followed other European rulers who already had outlawed Freemasonry because they suspected it would undermine absolutist control over their subjects. He was likewise unsuccessful, and although the Roman and Spanish Inquisitions apprehended and executed a few Masons, the various reprises of Clemens's condemnation of Masonry by his eighteenth-century successors mostly attest to its ineffectivity. Lodge membership of clergy had been quite common in the eighteenth century; in one instance, there had even been a monastery with its own Masonic lodge.[163]

A totally different atmosphere breathed from the Papacy's inveighing against Freemasonry in the nineteenth century. The new atmosphere was that of Father Barruel. Behind the Masonic associations, there now lurked the spectre of Revolution and an age-old network of antichristian conspirators bent on the destruction of Christianity. Again, local experiences had helped to shape this attitude. Freemasonry had played a certain role in the organisation of the Italian movement for liberation; and an even greater role had been played by the so-called Carbonari, the secret association of charcoal burners that displayed some similarity with Freemasonry and had grown into a popular guerrilla organisation after the 1820s. Mazzini had been both Mason and member of the Carbonari, and his revolutionary organisation *Young Europe* had been modelled upon these secret societies.[164] It was hardly surprising that the Papacy did not look kindly upon these associations of initiates that had raised rebellion in the Papal States twice and had managed to chase the Pope from the Vatican in 1848. But behind its local political *malheurs*, it discerned the hand of greater forces. Pius VII, Leo XII, Pius VIII, and Gregorius XVI all issued excommunications of members of Freemasonry and secret societies that betrayed an increasing preoccupation with Barruelian conspiracy ideas. Masonry now was more than just a potentially uproarious spiritual rival: it had become the hidden actor and symbolic representative of the Western Revolution.

Pius IX's *Syllabus Errorum* would, for the time being, be the crown on this development. At first sight, "secret societies" were only mentioned in passing on the list of errors, together with socialism, Communism, "biblical societies," and clerico-liberal societies (section IV). Apart from a series of faulty doctrines, most of the errors in the syllabus concerned issues of a political nature: the conviction, for example, that "every man is free to embrace that religion which, guided by the light of reason, he shall consider true" (15); the idea that the Church "has not the power of using force" (error 24); the idea that education should be free from ecclesiastical authority (error 47); the right to refuse obedience to "legitimate princes" (error 63); the institution of civil marriage (error 74); the abolition of Roman Catholicism as state religion (error 77); and a multitude of other faulty opinions that could be placed under the supreme falsehood: "The Church ought to be separated from the State, and the State from the Church" (error 55). In many respects, the Syllabus was an incomplete but extensive catalogue of the political and social changes that the Western Revolution had brought about; and the continuing resistance of the Popes to the mental transformation of Europe was defiantly flung in the face of the world by the eightieth and last error that Pius IX rejected: "The Roman Pontiff can, and ought to, reconcile himself, and come to terms with progress, liberalism and modern civilization." But the real sting, with regard to Freemasonry, sat in the tail of the document. In an almost offhand manner, Pius here declared that "the present misfortune" of the Church could "mainly" be ascribed to "the frauds and machinations" of Freemasonry and comparable "sects":

> Venerable Brothers, it is surprising that in our time such a great war is being waged against the Catholic Church. But anyone who knows the nature, desires and intentions of the sects, whether they be called masonic or bear another name, and compares them with the nature of the systems and the vastness of the obstacles by which the Church has been assailed almost everywhere, cannot doubt that the present misfortune must mainly be imputed to the frauds and machinations of these sects. It is from them that the synagogue of Satan, which gathers its troops against the Church of Christ, takes its strength. In the past Our predecessors, vigilant even from the beginning in Israel, had already denounced them to the kings and the nations, and had condemned them time and time again, and even We have not failed in this duty. If those who would have been able to avert such a deadly scourge had only had more faith in the supreme Pastors of the Church! But this scourge, winding through sinuous caverns, . . . deceiving many with astute frauds, finally has arrived at the point where it comes forth impetuously from its hiding places and triumphs as a powerful master. Since the throng of its propagandists has grown enormously, these wicked groups think that they have already become masters of the world and that they have almost reached their pre-established goal. Having sometimes obtained what they desired, and that is power, in several countries, they boldly turn the help of powers and authorities which they have secured to trying to submit the Church of God to the most cruel servitude, to undermine the foundations on which it rests, to contaminate its splendid qualities; and, moreover, to strike it with frequent blows, to shake it, to overthrow it, and, if possible, to make it disappear completely from the earth.[165]

The "several countries" where Freemasonry, according to Pius IX, had managed to obtain dominion were a clear reference to the anticlerical governments that had come to power in a number of European countries. Here we come to the immediate prelude to Léo Taxil's appearance. The history of the *Risorgimento* had left the Italian electorate in a prevalent anticlerical mood; in Germany and Switzerland, the *Kulturkampf* sought to reduce the position of the Roman Catholic Church; in the Netherlands and Belgium, the conflict over confessional education dominated the political debate; in Spain, liberal regimes had cautiously started to propose secularizing measures from 1868 on. To a large extent, the conflict between church and state dominated the political agenda of Western Europe. Extremist Christians demanded that the church should control the state; liberals asked for a strict separation between the public and spiritual spheres; secular nationalists pleaded for state control over the church in the name of national security. The political struggle that ensued was often concentrated on those aspects where the role of the Church had traditionally been vital: the education of children, the solemnization of marriage, the care for the sick, the burial of the dead.

France, the heartland of revolution, was the exemplary arena for this struggle of European consciousness. For part of the French population, the Revolution had become an essential component of national identity, and the emancipatory struggle that it represented, the pride of their nation. For most French Catholics, on the other hand, the Revolution represented memories of religious persecution, the apogee of an anti-Christian nightmare that dissonated shrilly in the proud Catholic history of the "eldest daughter of the Church." The fifteen years of Bourbon restoration after the fall of Napoleon had brought a traumatized, militantly antirevolutionary, and militantly royalist clergy back from exile; the shifting political tides in the ensuing decades had done nothing to change the basically antimodern attitude of French Catholicism. Two nations were living in France, both claiming to be its genuine embodiment; one raised statues of Marat and Voltaire, the other of Joan of Arc; one made monuments to commemorate the destruction of the Bastille, the other provocatively built a cathedral in honor of the Holy Heart of Jesus on a hill overlooking Paris, in order to reclaim the city for Christ.

After the fall of the pragmatically pro-Papal regime of Napoleon III in 1870, those who raised statues of Marat increasingly got the upper hand at the ballot box. A constant stream of legislation that sought to curb ecclesiastical influence began to stream from French parliament: laws concerning the legal status of religious congregations; laws concerning the installment of secular education and secular care for the sick; laws concerning the regulation of Catholic processions. The large and increasingly self-conscious Catholic population felt more and more like a persecuted minority and, unable to understand the logic of the secularizers, suspected itself to be the victim of a devious plot set up behind the scenes.

In this context, the time was ripe for a revival of the Barruelian thesis. Not that the Masonic conspiracy theory had ever been dead. On the contrary: in Catholic and conservative circles, it had remained as credible as in the days that Joseph de Maistre had adopted "Barruellism." The complex of ideas stemming from Barruel had been popularized by Bishop Louis Gaston Adrien de Ségur in a booklet from 1862 (significantly entitled *La Révolution*) and its sequel from 1867, *Les Francs-Maçons: Ce qu'ils sont, ce qu'ils font, ce qu'ils veulent* ("The Freemasons: What They Are, What They Do, What They Want"), on which more later.[166] Another bishop that we have already encountered, Monseigneur Amand-Joseph Fava from Grenoble, the "Scourge of Freemasonry," continued in this track by publishing a series of letters in Catholic magazines that reprised Barruel with some slight updates, for instance, by quoting Bakunin's Revolutionary Catechism as an illustration of the Masonic agenda.[167] Freemasonry, the bishop argued, pursued the combined goals of total dechristianization and the destruction of Western civilization. Its tools were anti-Christian agitation, laicization of education, corruption of women, and political revolution. The protection of church and civilization was clearly close to the French bishop's heart, because a few years later, he founded the first French anti-Masonic periodical, called (without much fantasy) *La Franc-Maçonnerie*, which started publication on March 19, 1884.[168]

The decisive impetus for the Catholic anti-Masonic movement came just a few months later, and again from the Vatican, when the Encyclical *Humanum Genus* was issued by Pope Leo XIII, successor of Pius IX. Since the *Syllabum errorum*, secular troops had overrun the Vatican, and this had not exactly helped to make the tone of the Pontiff milder. In many respects, *Humanum Genus* was the most resounding Papal condemnation of Freemasonry yet. It opened with a stark Augustinian picture of the "race of man" that had been polarized since original sin in two opposite parts: the kingdom of God ("namely, the true Church of Christ") and "the kingdom of Satan," or those who refuse to obey divine law. These two kingdoms had been perpetually at war with each other, although not always with equal intensity. "At this period, however," the pope went on, "The partisans of evil seem to be combining together, and to be struggling with united vehemence, led on or assisted by that strongly organised and widespread association called the Freemasons. No longer making any secret of their purposes, they are now boldly rising up against God Himself."[169] The ultimate aim of their activities was, of course, the destruction of the Church and Christendom, as had been proven abundantly by their outrages against the Roman Pontiff himself: "The Pontiff was first, for specious reasons, thrust out from the bulwark of his liberty and of his right, the civil princedom; soon, he was unjustly driven into a condition which was unbearable because of the difficulties raised on all sides; and now the time has come when the partisans of the sects openly declare, what in secret among themselves they have for a long time plotted, that the sacred power of the Pontiffs must be abolished, and that the papacy itself, founded by divine right, must be utterly destroyed."[170] As his predecessor had done, Leo went on to ascribe most of modernity's bitter fruits to the Freemasons and the "naturalism" that they promoted: religious indifference and religious relativism, the separation between church and state, "journals and pamphlets with neither moderation nor shame," immoral stage plays and artworks, civil marriage and legal divorce, and "doctrines of politics" that supposed every man to be by nature free and governments to be bound to the will of their subjects. "Moresque et instituta ethnicorum duodeviginti saeculorum intervallo revocare, insignis stultitiae est impietatisque audacissimae." the Pope concluded. ("To bring back after a lapse of eighteen centuries the manners and customs of the pagans, is signal folly and audacious impiety.")[171]

As a remedy against the encroachments of "the sect," Leo XIII urged, first of all, "to tear away the mask of Freemasonry, and let it be seen as it really is."[172] This advice was followed with great enthusiasm, not just by the Catholic bishops to whom it formally had been directed, but also by Catholic publicists of every description. Among them was Taxil himself, who cited Leo's call "to tear away the mask of Freemasonry" on the frontispiece of virtually all his anti-Masonic works and always claimed that *Humanus Genus* had provided the original inspiration for his Masonic venture. (And there is nothing in the chronology of his publications to make this improbable.) But Taxil was just one voice among many. Leo's Encyclical functioned as a catalyst for conservative Catholic opinion, legitimizing long-held convictions about Masonic machinations and stimulating the overall acceptance of such ideas within the Catholic community. The former rabbi Paul Rosen, for example, only started to pour out his revelations after the Pope had lashed out against the Freemasons, dedicating his second book to Leo XIII, for which he had obtained the latter's explicit permission.[173] In Grenoble, Bishop Fava promptly changed the name of his recently founded periodical *La Franc-Maçonnerie* to *La Franc-Maçonnerie démasqué*; he also founded a "Crusade of Free-Catholics" that was meant to function as a Catholic mirror organization to powerful Freemasonry. The enthusiastic bishop was also the man behind the handbook for anti-Masonists that appeared in Grenoble in 1887, signed "un franc-catholique."[174]

This flurry of organizational activity was reflected on a wider scale. *Humanum Genus* had suggested the Third Order of Saint Francis as a suitable organization to lead the struggle against Freemasonry; but when this order proved reluctant to fulfil its Papal assignment, lay initiative soon filled up the gap. In 1885, the Pope gave his blessing to a Belgian project to found an Antimasonic League. Characteristically, this initiative had its origin in the National Union for the Rectification of Injustices, a Belgian organization of lay Catholics that sought to redress ecclesial losses brought about by legal secularization in Belgium.[175] Control over the movement was soon taken over by Italian straw men of the Vatican. At the same time, local organizations under the patronage of the archangel Saint Michael had been founded in the north of France, and in 1893, representatives of the French Catholic press created a nationwide Antimasonic Committee. This eventually merged with the Antimasonic League to form a Universal Antimasonic Union with branches in places as far away as Ecuador in South America.

These organizations were indicative of the atmosphere of the "cold" civil war that characterized those European countries where secularizing governments confronted a Catholic population that was increasingly vocal in its demands. In France, an otherwise ludicrous incident served to reveal the radical antagonistic attitudes of French Catholics and French Republicans vis-à-vis each other and the role that was assigned to Freemasonry in this. When a group of young Roman Catholic pilgrims wrote "Long live the Pope" in the guest book of the Roman Pantheon, the Italian government filed a formal complaint with its French counterpart. French pilgrimages to Rome were banned for a certain period of time. Fierce protests of Catholics followed; and in 1892, Monsignor Gouthe-Soulard, the archbishop of Aix-en-Provence, wrote an angry letter of protest to the French Minister of Public Worship, in which he summed up the impression of many of his coreligionists in a single infamous sentence: "We are not living under a Republic, we are living under Freemasonry."[176] The bishop faced severe legal repercussions for this *faux mot*, resulting in a three thousand franc fine and temporary suspension of his salary. This only served to make him a hero to many Catholics, and it increased their perception of being a persecuted minority in a state dominated by the machinations of Freemasonry. When the first crusade was festively commemorated in 1895, French Catholicism used the occasion to issue a thinly veiled declaration of war against the secular republic. Thousands of hard-line Catholics gathered at Clermond-Ferrand to hear the celebrated Dominican preacher Father Monsabre (for whom nomen was certainly omen) proclaim a new crusade "against an enemy for whom the Turk was nothing but an instrument, and who threatens to destroy the sacred reign of Jesus Christ." This enemy was Satan himself, who had taken control of the public powers by way of political leaders that "despicably receive their orders from impious and hateful sectarians."[177] Although he did not explicitly name these "sectarians," every person in his audience understood who he had in mind.

HOW FREEMASONS BECAME SATANISTS

It was this atmosphere of paranoia and persecution that provided the hotbed in which Taxil's mystification could flourish, while at the same time a long pedigree of anti-Masonic literature had prepared his readership to believe almost everything that was wicked concerning Freemasonry. The bulk of Taxil's "revelations" about the lodges had simply been gleaned from this long tradition of lore and literature. He also added to it, however. His most important contribution—and an essential one for our present subject—was the introduction of *Satanism* in Freemasonry.

Even here, Taxil's allegations were not completely without precedent. Already in 1698, shortly after the lodge had gained prominence in England, an anonymous brochure had appeared in London that denounced Freemasonry as the precursor of the Antichrist and a den of devil worship.[178] This, however, had occurred in the wake of the Wars of Religion and amid the last embers of the witchcraft persecutions. Since then, accusations of Satanism had gone out of vogue, and the anti-Masonic literature of the eighteenth century mainly reproached Freemasons for spreading religious indifference through their tolerant admittance policy and for conspiring against the state in their secret assemblies. With slight modifications, these themes remained paramount in the nineteenth century. For all its talk about the "kingdom of Satan," *Humanum Genus* accused the Freemasons of being pantheists, rationalists, and naturalists—not Satanists. And even though the very titles of their books sometimes suggest otherwise, Catholic writers on Freemasonry prior to Taxil generally did not describe Freemasons as self-consciously venerating the devil. In 1825, for instance, an anonymous "Letter from Satan to the Freemasons" appeared in France. Clearly intended as a fictive construction, it quoted Satan himself praising the Freemasons for their promotion of the "reign of the philosophers," the "progress of the Enlightenment," and the "triumph and glory of Reason." The Catholic author of the booklet took the trouble to write a letter of response to the devil, in which he characteristically argued that legal religious tolerance was a device to "inoculate atheism" into the nation of France (a statement that ensured him one month in prison and a one hundred franc fine for attacking "civic tolerance" and the "liberty of cults").[179] Nowhere, however, did the author suggest that Freemasons were invoking Satan or otherwise paying homage to him.

Whenever "Satan," "Satanic," or even "Satanism" was mentioned in connection with Freemasonry during this period, generally one of the "older" significations of the word was implied. Either it was simply a way to indicate the extremely nefarious nature of the sect and its conspiracy or it pointed to the role the lodge was said to play in the advance of the Antichrist (by plotting revolution and by spreading atheism, "naturalism," and anarchism). Alternatively, the term "Satanism" denoted the diabolical essence of Masonic ideology, without Freemasons being thought to be aware of this.[180] Frequently, these significations were used simultaneously, mishmashed together with the vehemence of alarmist rhetoric. But even Paul Rosen's books, sporting lurid titles like *Satan & Co* and filled to the brim with demonizing metaphors, did not claim that freemasons were involved in *intentional* devil worship. It was the anti-Christian ideology and the secret direction of global anti-Christian politics that made Freemasonry a genuine Company of Satan. "La Révolution sociale, c'est les *Gesta Satanæ per massones*," Rosen summarized. ("The Revolution of society is the work of Satan by the Freemasons.") The former rabbi sometimes played with the suggestion that more was going on. But only among the Freemasons of Italy, who publicly glorified their "satanic filiations," did he find sufficient indications to point out the existence of a veritable "infernal cult."[181]

It is not hard to see, however, that the consistent Satanic rhetoric of anti-Masonism invited literal interpretations. Pius IX had already called the freemasons "children of the Demon" in one of his pontifical statements, and although Leo XIII had refrained from completely identifying the lodge with the "Synagogue of Satan" in *Humanum Genus*, lesser Catholic publicists soon forgot about these kinds of subtleties.[182] It was a relatively small step, from here, to hold that Freemasons engaged in formal worship of the devil. In addition, we can only speculate what conceptions of Freemasonry were flourishing among the "general populace" at this period of time. Behind the allegations of Virginie, for instance, the possessed and host-vomiting woman from Agen that we encountered in the previous chapter, the contours of the lodge are almost tangibly present. Although Freemasonry is not mentioned by name in the accounts of her case, her story of a temple for the demon where the notables of the town gather to desecrate the host and venerate the devil conspicuously mirrors later Taxilian allegations against Freemasons, while at the same time faithfully reflecting the practices commonly attributed to heretics and non-Christians in premodern and early modern times. Old patterns of attribution had survived in many places during the eighteenth century, as we saw above. Among the "uneducated classes," the conceptions that supported them may well have remained present during the nineteenth century, particularly in areas that had been only superficially touched by modernity.[183]

Prior to Taxil, these old prejudices and new rumors seldom surfaced in the printed anti-Masonic literature. A prominent exception had been *Les Francs-Maçons: Ce qu'ils sont, ce qu'ils font, ce qu'ils veulent*, the above-mentioned popular booklet by Bishop Ségur. After repeating the familiar ideas of Barruel and insisting that the Masonic "sectarians" did not shrink from assassination or sacrilege, the bishop recounted how during the revolutionary year of 1848, nocturnal gatherings had been discovered in Rome where male and female Freemasons celebrated "that which they call the Mass of the Devil." During this ceremony, the attendants spat and stepped on crucifixes and profaned hosts brought from the Church "or sold to them for money by some evil and poor old woman, like Judas." The Masons would end the ceremony by stabbing Christ's bodily manifestation with daggers, after which all lights would be extinguished (Ségur prudently refrained from telling what happened next). From Italy, the alarmed bishop claimed, these practices had spread to France: "and very recently, the existence has been discovered of a kind of under-masonry, already completely organised, with the exclusive purpose of making common cause regarding the surest and most efficient way to destroy the Faith." This society was organized in small cells of twelve to fifteen persons and recruited predominantly among educated or at least influential people; its center was in Paris, with branches in many other cities in France. "One has named to me, with absolutely certainty, Paris, Marseille, Aix, Avignon, Châlons-sur-Marne, Laval."[184]

We can only guess what real facts lay behind these wild assumptions: possibly some confusion with the Carbonari, who featured some sinister although not necessarily Satanist initiation rituals. Important elements of Taxil's constructions are already present in embryonic form here: the existence of hidden "backdoor lodges," which had already been proposed by Barruel; the sacrilegious initiation rites including violation of the host; the suggestion of promiscuous festivities. Publications like Ségur's, and Catholic theories about a Masonic plot in general, were also a definite source of inspiration for Vintras and Boullan in their conception of a network of secret Satanist cells.[185] Yet the urban legend recounted by Ségur was an exception in the landscape of Catholic anti-Masonic literature of his day, which maintained its emphasis on the political nature of Freemasonry's plot against Christianity. Wilder ideas about Masonic worship of Satan would remain a marginal phenomenon until the colorful accounts of Doctor Bataille and Diana Vaughan appeared on the scene.

6

Unmasking the Synagogue of Satan: Continued and Concluded

ANOTHER RICH CURRENT of Catholic literature may have been even more important in preparing the Satanist theme of Taxil's writings: that of polemic publications against occultism and esotericism.[1] In this field as well, the particular circumstances of the nineteenth century had provided new bottles for old wine. As the eighteenth century had progressed, even Roman Catholic theologians had tended to frown upon the old demonologies. Publications that endorsed traditional practices of attribution had dwindled to a mere trickle, represented by eccentrics like the abbé Fiard, who had defended the reality of witchcraft with some virtuosity against the scorn of the *philosophes* and had maintained the duty of the state to combat this pest by force of arms.[2] Fiard survived the French Revolution with his conviction unshaken, and after the revolutionary storm subsided, he published a work in which he blamed its devilish work on the tolerated presence of magicians, ventriloquists, and "demonolâtres," idolaters of demons. In a passage that was clearly inspired by the recently published work of Barruel, Fiard insisted that the political plots of "illuminates, Jacobins, and Backlodge Masons" provided insufficient explanation for the overwhelming success of their conjuration against the religious and profane order. Only the involvement of supernatural powers could explain the cataclysm of the Revolution. "If Jacobins, Freemasons, illuminates do not in fact communicate with demons, if they are not initiated in their mysteries of damnation, however numerous they might be, their wrath would be impotent against the whole of the human race. But if they partake in this commerce, if they have in truth made their pact with hell, a pact they transmit to their progenitors (and this is in fact the secret of most of them)—then here we have found our genuine conspirators, then here we have our slaughterers."[3]

Even in his own day, Fiard was considered a "fou littèraire" by all but his most sympathetic readers, and his thesis of supernatural conspiracy would remain buried, for all practical purposes, until the time of Taxil. Yet even before that, Satan had already made his reappearance on the pages of Catholic authors on occultism. The rising tide of Romanticism had also had an impact on Roman Catholicism, where it had stimulated a heightened interest in practices of popular devotion, in the "pure" religious expression of the Middle Ages, and in the supernatural and miraculous, be it of divine or demonic origin.[4] From the middle of the century, moreover, the spread of spiritism had once again transformed the occult into a table-talk subject for educated people. Catholic authors like Jules Eudes de Mirville (1802–1873) and, particularly, Henri-Roger Gougenot des Mousseaux (1805–1876) reacted to this trend with great agility. They applauded the renewed thirst for the transcendental that could be discerned behind the increasing popularity of "table rapping" and occultism, and they commended the disgust with prevailing doctrines of "materialism" that occultist writers often expressed. The Catholic Church, they maintained, had upheld the reality of the supernatural for centuries against all adverse ideological winds. She had also taught, however, that not all encounters of the third kind were necessarily beneficial. In his first book on occultism, *La magie au dix-neuvième siècle* ("Magic in the Nineteenth Century"), Gougenot des Mousseaux devoted many pages to refute the idea promoted by occultists like Éliphas Lévi (whom he quoted extensively), according to which the "fluidic agent" acting in magic was a neutral, seminatural force that could be operated at will by the magician.[5] Ultimately, he argued, all supernatural manifestations were either of divine or diabolic origin, and only the Church was able to determine with certainty which superhuman power was working when. Gougenot des Mousseaux prudently warned against an overly enthusiastic attribution to the fallen angel of every extraordinary occurrence. Yet this prudence did not notably affect the pages of his own publications, where he did not shrink from dragging the whole supernatural bestiary of early modern demonology out of the closet again, including lycanthropes, vampires, succubae, and incubi.[6]

In contrast with Fiard, Gougenot des Mousseaux was no lone eccentric writing in isolation. As an expert on the occult, he was taken seriously in Catholic circles. At the important Catholic Congress of Malines in 1863, for instance, he was invited to expound his ideas during a session behind closed doors.[7] Among the educated Catholic public, the intervention of the supernatural was increasingly thought plausible, be it in its demonic or divine variant. This was reflected in the apparitions of the Virgin Mary in La Salette in 1846; it was also reflected in the *Annales du surnaturel au 19ᵉ siècle* compiled by Péladan père; even the activities of Eugène Vintras and Joseph Boullan on the fringes of the Catholic world were a manifestation of this general trend. These examples could easily be multiplied. In 1888, when *Blackwood's Magazine* published a fictitious story that described how the devil had made acte de présence during a spiritist séance in Paris, many French readers took this account at face value. Much speculation occurred regarding the true identity of its characters, and for years to come, the apparition of Satan as a young man of immense melancholy but fashionably attire would be recounted in quite serious Catholic publications on the occult.[8]

It is clear that Taxil only continued an already existing trend when he recounted tales of weekly apparitions of Lucifer in Charleston, South Carolina. Sheer cosmological coherence required some kind of fusion between the increasing insistence on a diabolical presence by Catholic anti-occultism and the Barruelian thesis of the Masonic world conspiracy. Anti-Masonic literature contained some openings for such a fusion. Barruel had already accused the "Kabbalist" branch of Rosicrucian Freemasonry of having regular commerce with spirits and of honoring the firm conviction "that the *worst of them,* the worst of those beings that the vulgar people call *demons, never is to be considered bad company for a human*

being."[9] Allegations like this were occasionally repeated in subsequent literature to provide picturesque detail: the veritable Satanic character of Freemasonry still lay in the part
it played in Satan's plan for world domination through its sinister political ploys and its
diabolic humanist ideology. It is to Taxil that the—somewhat debatable—credit must be
given for performing the fusion of a politically oriented Barruelian anti-Masonism and a
demonological antispiritism.[10] It was no coincidence that *Le Diable au XIX*ᵉ *siècle* spoke of
"Luciferian Freemasonry, or: the Mysteries of Spiritism" in its subtitle.[11] Taxil's Palladism
was the crown and logical outcome of a trajectory that had started with Barruel and Fiard,
the final blending of two traditions of Catholic polemic.

This partially accounts for its surprising credibility among the Catholic public. From
about 1892 until Taxil's final self-exposure, the Satanism thesis dominated the Catholic
discourse on Freemasonry, and the existence of secret Satan worship and hidden Luciferian
superlodges was embraced as the official master code for interpreting the political and religious realities of the fin de siècle. Palladism seeped into the catechisms that were used to
teach the children of the faithful; when Father Monsabre preached his crusade at Clermond-
Ferrand, he did not just speak about "impious and hateful sectarians," but about "impious
and hateful sectarians of whom Satan is the Sovereign Grand Master and the dark idol."[12]
At Trent, in 1896, the crème de la crème of Catholic anti-Masonism formally ratified the
idea of a cult of Satan operating within Freemasonry. Their final conclusions did not mince
words about this, and the first four points of these deserve to be quoted at length:

> The first international antimasonic Congress declares itself to be fully convinced:
> First, that Freemasonry is a religious and Manichean sect; that the final key of its
> secrets and mysteries is the cult of Lucifer or Satan, worshipped in the back-lodges in
> opposition to the God of the Catholics;
> Second, that the Demon (inspirer of the Masonic sects), knowing that he will never
> succeed in obtaining the direct adoration of mankind in general, seeks to sow in its souls,
> by way of Freemasonry, the seeds of naturalism, which is nothing else than the complete
> emancipation of Man in juxtaposition to God;
> Third, that in order to implant this impious naturalism in the world, Freemasonry
> strives to familiarise mankind with the idea of the equality of all religions, the only true
> one and the false ones, and to substitute the Catholic atmosphere with a Masonic atmo-
> sphere, by way of a press without God and a school without God.
> Fourth, that one particular method used by Freemasonry to lead to perdition those
> famishing for the supernatural but not yet ripe for Luciferian Manicheism, is to coax
> them into surrendering themselves to the evil practices of Spiritism.[13]

Taxil can be held almost singlehandedly responsible for the insertion of "the cult of Satan,
worshipped in the back-lodges" in this marvelous concoction of more than a century of
Roman Catholic conspiracy thinking.[14] We may well say that this was no mean achievement.

FIGHTING DEMOCRACY BY DEMOCRATIC MEANS

We can see now why Taxil was believed not only by simple, uneducated Catholic believers, but also by erudite Catholics like the reviewer of the *Revue Bénédictine* or the bishop

of Grenoble. His revelations confirmed suspicions that had already been raised in Catholic publications for decades and that had gained further urgency in the polarized atmosphere of fin de siècle France. "You wanted someone to tell you this," Taxil had quipped to a Catholic journalist scolding him after his April 1897 press conference. "So, very well, I've told."[15] In fact, Taxil's Catholic publications read like a grotesque catalogue of the apprehensions of ultramontane French Catholicism. Satanism was attributed to almost every incarnation of the other: the "Americanisation" that Huysmans had already flagellated (with Palladism itself as the supremely Satanic American export product); archenemy Germany (where one of Satanism's international headquarters was located and where chancellor Otto Bismarck was receiving his orders directly from Satan); Great Britain (also rife with Satanism and hosting a Palladist underground weapon factory in its imperial stronghold, Gibraltar); Protestants of all denominations (to meet a Protestant was to meet a criminal; and "often a criminal doubling up as a Satanist"); non-Christian and non-Western religions (mere cover-ups for Satanism); and socialists, feminists, biologists promoting evolution, and so on. The bankers of aggressive capitalism and the terrorists of radical anarchism were both at the service of Satanic Freemasonry. This improbable syllabus of Satanists tends to look rather comical from today's vantage point. But for Taxil's Catholic audience, part of its seduction lay precisely in this comprehensiveness. "All that is modern, is from the Devil," said fin de siècle writer Léon Bloy, who effectively summarized the intuition of many Catholics.[16] Taxil made this intuition inevitably simple and refreshingly literal. All that was modern, was worshipping Satan.

Catholic antimodernity, however, was just one side of the picture that explained the prolific success of Taxil's pseudo-revelations. At the same time, paradoxically, Taxil's massive mystification was only possible because, in much of its practical methods, fin de siècle Catholicism had become highly modern. When intransigent Catholics pleaded for restrictions on the freedom of the press, they usually did so on the pages of their own very developed network of press organs. These periodicals sometimes carried strangely liberal-sounding names such as "The Public Good" or "Liberty"; these, however, referred strictly to the liberty they demanded for the Catholic Church against secular "persecution."[17] Catholic mass organizations mobilized and directed Catholic opinion in a way that rivaled and at the same time closely resembled the socialist movement. In several European countries, Catholic political parties had taken seats in parliament, brought to political prominence by the "revolutionary" democratic system they abhorred. Remarkably, it was seldom the more liberal Catholics who took the fore in the creation of this Catholic mass movement, but mostly their ultramontane and ultraconservative coreligionists. It was the existence of this national and international net of Catholic organizations and press organs that enabled Taxil to find such a wide audience, sell so many of his books, and tell his tall tales of Palladism to Catholic farmers in remote provincial villages. In retrospect, it is striking how closely his activities as an anti-Masonic agitator mirrored his earlier methods as an anticlerical publicist—not excepting the occasional dash into pornography. Reactionary Roman Catholics, it seems, were pursuing their goals by methods of modern mass mobilization similar to those of their radical opponents.

Although its first sparks had been spontaneous, there was deliberate policy behind this Roman Catholic organizational activity. The dissolution of the Papal State in 1870 had been a vital moment in the shaping of this policy. Before the Italian troops marched into the Eternal City, the popes had mostly relied on diplomacy to pursue their political goals, parleying with the European powers as a head of state with other heads of state. The events of 1870 effectively ended this. Although popes would never cease to cling to the regalia of temporal sovereignty, there was now in fact only one effective power base left to them: the spiritual authority of the Papacy over millions and millions of Catholic believers in Europe and the rest of the world. The pressure these Catholics could and did exert on the governments in their countries now became the weapon the popes held against the political leaders of Europe.[18]

Pius IX, for all his thundering against the Western Revolution, had been a pioneer in this respect. He had greatly stimulated the Catholic press and made untiring appearances before Catholic mass audiences, and he had also proved himself well disposed to the Catholic lay organizations that had mushroomed all over Europe. The shock of 1870 had stimulated the Curia further down this line. The anti-Christian movement that was conquering Europe had now swept over the stronghold of the apostolic successor of Peter himself. The rulers of Christendom had deserted the Pope. In this atmosphere of war with the world, the Curia pondered radical options. "The princes have abandoned us: so let Catholic democracy take form," the leading *zelanti* Cardinal, Filippo De Angelis, commented, "Let us go to school by the children of darkness. . . . We'll do some Mazzinism on our own."[19] Ultramontane lay radicals even considered calling a "Catholic strike" to paralyze Europe and force it to abandon its collision course with the Church.[20] This extremist idea was not adopted, but political agitation by the Catholic populations of Europe increasingly became an essential and consciously wielded weapon in the arsenal of the Papacy.

Leo XIII had inherited Pius's intense involvement with the press but was hesitant at first about Catholic lay organizations. Lay organizations inevitably led to lay influence, and he favored strong sacerdotalism: divinity had appointed priests and their bishops to herd the sheep.[21] He changed his opinion, however, after his first years in office. The Catholic organizations had become too important for Vatican policy, serving as a tool to control the faithful, organize political resistance, and reclaim terrains of society that had been wrested from the Church by secularizing governments. In fact, Leo eventually would go further than his predecessor in playing the card of modern mass politics. In 1891, in the Encyclical *Rerum Novarum*, he expressed his worries about the situation of the "labouring poor" in terms that sounded almost like socialism, describing their plight as "a yoke little better than that of slavery itself."[22] And in 1892, he shook French Catholicism to its foundations when he enjoined the French bishops to acknowledge the French Republic as a legitimate form of government and to work together with its rulers. This so-called *ralliement* swept away the holy alliance of throne and altar that had been the cornerstone of Catholic political thinking for almost a century and that was practically part of their profession of faith for many French Catholics. The Catholic Church, the Vatican now claimed, had no preference for any particular form of government, as long as the prerogatives of the Church and the principles of Christianity were honored.

Naive observers may have believed that the Pope had turned liberal. Nothing could be further from the truth, however. Leo had been the driving spirit behind the *Syllabum Errorum* before he became pope. Behind the smiling mask of a frail old man, his conviction that the nature of Europe's prevailing ideological winds was utterly anti-Christian was as firm as that of Pius IX. Yet he was also a fundamentally *political* pope. His overtures to workers' demands—however genuine his concern about their plight—were certainly meant to retain the Catholic masses in the lower social strata for the Catholic political program, an increasingly urgent matter with universal suffrage under way in more and more European countries. (And on this point, Leo's course of action would prove prophetic, ensuring the rise of Catholic popular parties as a determining factor in the political spectrum of many European countries.) Considerations of political realism had also been prevalent in the *ralliement*. After the French defeat at the hand of the Prussians in 1870, the Vatican had briefly hoped that the Bourbon monarchy would return to power in France. Instead, the provisional Third Republic that had installed itself in Paris proved to be a lasting phenomenon, and after 1873, restoration of the French throne was fast becoming a political chimera. The alliance between throne and altar, which had proved fruitful in the years of the Reaction, when the Holy Alliance had reinstated monarchical rule in most of Europe, now had become an ideological deadlock that only hindered the Holy See in pursuing its political objectives.

These political objectives were twofold: a short-term one and a long-term one. The short-term objective, as it had been under Pius IX, was the restoration of the Papal States in order to secure the temporal sovereignty and autonomy of the Papacy. To accomplish this, the Vatican hoped to coax the Great Powers of Europe into forcing Italy to restore the Patrimony of Peter. For a short while, Leo had put his hope for this in Germany, where Bismarck gradually abandoned the *Kulturkampf* when it became clear that his aggressive secularization only fortified Catholic political resistance. When Leo's German hopes proved deceptive, he turned his eyes on France. The primary aim of the *ralliement* was to enable French Catholics to enter into the political life of the Republic, so they could use their influence, possibly in tandem with other conservatives, to turn France into an ally of the Holy See once more. [23] "When you follow my advice," Leo had told the skeptical bishop of Montpellier, "you will have 400 Catholic parliament members and you will be able to reinstall the monarchy. I am a monarchist myself." [24] In its diplomatic power play to ensure the restitution of temporal power, the Vatican frequently employed Catholic opinion as a tool in the most literal sense of the word: something that could be used at will to put the fear of the Lord in local governments, then laid aside again in accordance with the unpredictable twists of international politics (although, in reality, Catholic indignation often proved not so easy to hush up). [25]

In its long-term objective, the Vatican under Leo XIII also continued the policy of Pius IX. Stemming the swell tide of dechristianization was the goal toward which its grand effort was directed, and dechristianization in this context did refer not only to the desertion of the faith by a growing number of individual Europeans and Americans, but also, and primarily, to the demolition of the traditional presence of the Church in the public sphere. This amounted to a virtual reversion of the Western Revolution, and the pontiffs were only too well aware of this fact, as they made abundantly clear in their Encyclicals again and again. Time and again this thoroughly antimodern undercurrent reveals itself in seemingly progressive Papal utterances. *Rerum Novarum*, for instance, did call attention to social injustices but blamed these principally on the abandonment of "Christian religion and Christian institutions." Although the Pope did encourage the organization of workmen, he emphasized that this organization should be, above anything else, a *Catholic* organization. In fact, Catholic criticism of modern social conditions was to a great extent the domain of radical ultramontanes, for whom it formed part of their broader rejection of the new political and social order. The solution they proposed for the ills of modern society was corporatism, a social doctrine that envisaged a return to the guild system from an idealized medieval past and a corresponding revival of an idealized hierarchical community.

In the same manner, the de facto acceptance of the French Republic by the Papacy did not mean that it accepted what the Republic stood for. Instead of striving for the restoration of a Bourbon king, the Catholic Church would now strive for recognition of the "règne social du Christ," as it was often expressed in sermons or contemporary publications. This sounded deceptively progressive, but what was meant with this concept was in fact the reign of Christ *over* society. The restitution of "Christ as King of France" would herald the establishment of a political order that accepted directions from the Church and the subsequent retraction of revolutionary achievements like freedom of the press, freedom of religion, and nonconfessional public education. What the *ralliement* did signify, however, was a radical confirmation of the Papacy's change in outlook regarding the means by which this could be accomplished. The main thrust of the Catholic political effort would henceforth be directed at recatholization of the public sphere by deploying the Catholic masses to attain political influence via the channels of democracy. Leo XIII, in other words, hoped to destroy democracy by using its means, to revert the Western Revolution by adopting her methods. (Eventually, things would not go quite the way he imagined. The growing entanglement of Catholics in the mechanics of modern politics would bring forth a Catholic political movement that became increasingly committed to the tenets of Western democracy. But that is another story.)

Freemasonry retained its by now traditional role in all this: as a representative par excellence of the Western Revolution, standing for secularization in all its various manifestations. This role had not become obsolete in the new era of mass mobilization and mass communication: on the contrary, it had become more important than ever. As one historian has aptly remarked, the struggle over secularization was in many respects a "war of symbols" that translated an almost abstract long-term development involving complex sociological and cultural processes into terms that could be grasped by the masses.[26] The rhetorical barrage against the "encroachments" of Freemasonry was a prime example of this kind of symbolic warfare. Identifying an enemy made things clear and simple. To a great extent, the anticlerical enemy was employing its image of the Christian church in the same manner, and the ideological pressure this helped to build up would unleash itself bloodily against both clergy and believers in later European revolutions.

It is remarkable to see how, in contemporary Catholic publications, the struggle against Freemasonry was tied up with the exertions to build up a modern organization of mass mobilization. Apart from prayer and the above-mentioned deployment of the Third Order of Saint Francis, the recommendations in *Humanum Genus* to combat Freemasonry encompass all the main features of Catholic organization: propaganda, especially by way of the "Good Press" (included by implication in the Pontiff's appeal to "those among the laity in whom a love of religion and of country is joined to learning and goodness of life" to assist the episcopate in unmasking Freemasonry); corporate organization for workmen ("for the protection, under the guidance of religion, both of their temporal interests and of their morality"); and, last but not least, Catholic education for the young.[27] Father Monsabre had echoed these words in his speech in Clermond-Ferrand a decade later, particularly emphasizing the work of a Catholic press that was always and everywhere on its guard to expose "the hypocrite sectarians and the sinister exploiters of the passions of the multitude."[28] It was only the incorporation of the Catholic faithful of all ages and social strata in the Catholic hierarchical and organizational framework that could protect them against an all but invisible enemy that was waging total war against Christian truth.

From the distant vantage point of the historian, it is not hard to see that, in reality, it was probably as much the other way around. The danger of Freemasonry gave urgency and legitimacy to the Catholic organizational effort and served to keep Catholic opinion in a state of constant mobilization. It also served as a handy pretext to keep the ranks of the faithful closed. This explains why Catholic anti-Masonic agitation was not alleviated but only became more intense after the *ralliement* was launched. There was a need for a common enemy to reunite a French Catholicism that was hopelessly divided and, in part, utterly dismayed at the sudden turnabout of its hierarchical leaders.[29] In this specific case, the effort to use the Masonic fraud as a unifying factor failed; in this, Taxil played a (presumably unwitting) part, as we will see later on. Yet in general, the cold war against Freemasonry proved an excellent instrument to give the rank and file of the *Ecclesia militans* a sense of unity and purpose. The importance of this factor sometimes shimmered through the texts of official declarations. In *Inimica vis* ("The Enemy Forces"), for instance, an Encyclical from December 8, 1892, in which the bishops of Italy were exhorted to remain firm in their war against Freemasonry, Leo XIII stated significantly that "there can be no middle ground" for those who fought to repel the attack on religion. "Therefore, in the case of the weak and sluggish, courage must be stirred up through your efforts; in the case of the strong, it must be kept active; with all trace of dissent wiped out, under your leadership and command, the result will be that all alike, with united minds and common discipline, may undertake the battle in a spiritual manner."[30]

HIDDEN TEMPLES, SECRET GROTTOS, AND INTERNATIONAL MEN OF MYSTERY

Another feature of the work of Taxil and his mouthpieces that stands out in retrospect is the vast international scope of his constructions. By "international scope," I do not refer primarily to his descriptions of the Palladic headquarters in South Carolina or Satanic rituals in India, all of which clearly belong to the realm of fantasy, but rather to the publicity offensive against real-life European politicians he deployed in both his books and the often extensive newspaper controversies that he fed, predominantly in the Catholic press.[31] In Germany, as we have already seen, the *Kulturkampf* was denounced as a maneuver of Palladism, and Bismarck as a willing pawn of demonic forces. In Belgium, the prominent liberal politician and Masonic Grand Master Goblet d'Alviella was a special target of the books and articles of Domenico Margiotta, in which he was branded as a convinced Palladist.[32] Anti-Masonic agitation was indeed instrumental in preventing his reelection as a member of Belgian parliament.[33]

It was Italy, however, that played the leading role in these ventures into European politics. In Bataille's *Diable au XIXe siècle*, Palladism's foundation coincided exactly with the breach of Rome's Porta Pia by Italian troops on September 20, 1870; and the destruction of the Papacy was listed as a prime objective in Albert Pike's secret (and apocryphal) instructions to international Freemasonry. Nor can it be deemed coincidental that Italian Grand Master Adriano Lemmi was pinpointed as Pike's successor. In fact, Lemmi can be considered the principal target of many of Taxil's publications in the 1890s. In *Le Diable au XIXe siècle*, Lemmi already figured as a convert to Judaism and, even more surprisingly, as the second identity assumed by the Marseillais revolutionary Gaston Crémieux, who was presumed to have been executed after the Commune of 1870.[34] No mention was made of this story in Margiotta's first book, but in other respects the work, which was entirely devoted to the Italian Grand Master, represented a crescendo in the offensive against Lemmi. "If I was not born Italian, I would have liked to be a Prussian," Margiotta (falsely) quotes Lemmi. "There are two things I hate with all my heart: God and France."[35] Nothing could be more damning for Margiotta's French Catholic readership. The allegations vented by Margiotta, however, were not all in the realm of comical fantasy, but included disclosures about Lemmi's supposed apprehension fifteen years previously for theft and swindle in Marseilles—including a photographic reproduction of his judicial file—and a detailed discussion of his involvement in illegal tobacco import, which had given rise to something of a scandal in the Italian political arena just at that moment. Other prominent representatives of the new Italy also received bad press in the Taxilian corpus: Mazzini and Garibaldi feature, of course, as founding fathers of Italian Masonic Satanism; Giambattista Pessina, the Grand Hierophant of the Rite of Memphis and Misraim in Italy, is depicted as a sorcerer sporting a familiar demon with the peculiar name of Beffabuc; and the Italian Prime Minister Crispi also ranks as a member of Palladic Satanism.[36]

The campaign against Lemmi culminated in the story about the secret Palladic temple in the Palazzo Borghese: a story that had such a tenacious afterlife that it can virtually be called a legend. Its immediate instigation was provided by the transference of the Italian Grand Orient to the first floor of the splendid palace of the Borghese family in Rome. In his first book on Lemmi, Margiotta already provided some picturesque details about the changes the Grand Master had made to the interior decoration of the palace. "He ordered the latrines of the Supreme Council to be constructed above the private chapel, directing the discharge of the excrements to the altar itself. This furnishes abundant proof of his loathsome soul: for to commit this abomination, he was obliged to stink out the place. Protests followed, and for hygienic reasons, the architect had to choose another disposition of the latrines. But Lemmi then imagined something new: he gave order to place a crucifix in the water closets, with its head downwards; and on it was pasted, by his command, a sign saying: *Before you leave, spit on the traitor. Glory to Satan!*"[37]

In 1895, the Borghese family ended the lease of the Palazzo to the Italian Freemasons. Soon after the Grand Orient had evacuated the building, wild rumors started to circulate. On May 15, 1895, Margiotta telegraphed to the Catholic daily *Croix du Dauphiné* that the agents of the Borghese house "had discovered, in a room which was categorically refused to be opened to them, a Palladic temple where a horrible statue of Satan was sitting enthroned on an altar, surrounded by other horrible and monstrous figurines and symbols."

The breaking news, which had been placed in an inconspicuous place in the newspaper "due to a typographical error," was reproduced on the front page the following day, under the headline "Temple of Satan."[38] On May 18, Margiotta returned with some more details.[39] By then, other Catholic newspapers had also commented on the discovery of "Lemmi's Temple of Satan," quoting Italian sources.[40] Of course, Taxil's *Revue mensuelle religieuse, politique, scientifique* ("Complement to the Publication *Le Diable au XIXe Siècle*") followed suit in its May number, quoting the story from the Italian Catholic newspaper *Unione* from Bologna of May 15, which in its turn gave as its source the "accredited correspondent in Rome" of another Catholic newspaper, the *Corriere Nazionale* from Turin. In its main points, this report was identical to that of Margiotta, telling also how the plenipotentiaries of the Borghese prince had inspected the palace and had been freely admitted to all rooms except one, which was only opened to them after they threatened to call in the assistance of the police. "In this hall," the report continued,

> there was a temple named thus: Palladic Temple. And here is its description: The walls, adorned with damask of red and black silk, displayed in the back of the room a huge tapestry, on which stood out, in colossal form, the effigy of Lucifer. Very close by, a sort of altar or burner was placed. Strewn around here and there, one could still remark the triangles, the angle brackets, and the other symbols of the satanic sect, as well as their books and rituals. Everywhere around magnificent gilded seats were placed, all having up in their back a kind of big transparent eye lighted by electricity. Finally, in the midst of this vile temple, there was something resembling a throne. The horrified visitors took good care, in view of the mental state this unexpected sight brought them in, not to remain any longer in this place where, evidently, an abominable cult had been rendered to the demon; so they did not examine the interior in detail. They left the room with as much haste as they could.[41]

This story circulated in roughly similar wording through the Catholic press, betraying a single source that may indeed have been Italian. Margiotta, evidently not trusting in the power of suggestion, added that the throne in the middle of the room had been that of the "Satanist Grand Pontiff" Adriano Lemmi, who had thus been officiating as a high priest of Satan practically in front of the Saint Peter itself.[42]

The Temple of Lucifer inside the Borghese Palazzo was just one of the many lesser stories at the fringes of the great Palladism hoax. Another of these stories that is simply too good not to tell is that of Miss Lucie Claraz, the High Priestess of Lucifer in Fribourg, Switzerland. That Fribourg had to be the scene of this tale was probably not entirely coincidental. The Swiss town was the epicenter of Catholic organization in francophone Switzerland; as such, it was also a place where the secularization struggle and the Swiss *Kulturkampf* were most keenly felt. The Masonic presence in this regional Catholic capital was spurious. In 1848, a lodge called "La Régénérée" had been founded, but this had collapsed into virtual oblivion after a few decades.[43] In the 1860s, only a few disorganized Masons were left, when the barrister, journalist, and newspaper editor Ernest Stoecklin initiated a renewal of the local lodge. Stoecklin had been involved in the revolutions of 1848, had turned conservative for a while, and then turned radical again. Anticlerical motives were surely involved in his initiative, which must be situated against the background of the Swiss *Kulturkampf* and the backlash that was engendered by the growing Catholic influence in the Fribourg area.[44] In addition, Stoecklin seems to have had a notable inclination for the picturesque, for he chose as the location for the renewed lodge the grotto of Pertuis, a cavern that was situated in a granite cliff on the outskirts of Fribourg and had been used as a public bath in the Middle Ages. [45] Works to make the place suitable for Masonic ritual commenced in 1877.

The battle lines of ideological strife during this time sometimes ran right through families. This at least was the case in Ernest Stoecklin's family. His sister Julie was a Sister within the ultra-Catholic Congregation of Saint Paul; his wife Marie Claraz was also a devout Catholic.[46] His wife's brother had been superficially involved in Freemasonry, but her sister, Lucie Claraz, more than matched the other female family members in Catholic activism. To redress her brother-in-law's un-Christian activities, or maybe her own trespassing in younger days, she had founded a Catholic "Work" that sought to obtain the cave of Pertuis, in order to transform it into an expiatory chapel for the "Fraternity of the Union in Jesus-Maria of the Servants of the Holy Family."[47] The chance to obtain victory in this intrafamilial war of religion came when Stoecklin ran into money trouble because his Mason brethren were reluctant to finance his extravagant building schemes. Lucie succeeded in obtaining the support of the internationally famous missionary bishop of Geneva, Monsignor Mermillod, and flooded Catholic France, Belgium, and Italy with leaflets aiming to muster financial support.[48] On March 16, 1885, the Paris-based Catholic periodical *Le Pèlerin* broke the news that, by the grace of God, the temple had been "snatched from the Demon" and sold to the Congregation of the Holy Family.[49] The grotto was transformed into a chapel, with a triumphal statue of Saint Michael subduing the Dragon at the entrance.[50]

It is not clear when Satanism entered the Fribourg story. Was it already with *Le Pèlerin*'s mention of the "temple snatched from the Demon," just half a year after *Humanum Genus*? Or had this just been metaphor? There is some suggestion that the Catholics who visited the lodge directly after its dismantling were already extraordinarily impressed by "the peculiarities of the place."[51] Among these Catholics, the chaplain Joseph Schorderet (1845–1893), a charismatic priest who was very active in Catholic organizations in Fribourg and beyond, is mentioned by name. We know he was acquainted with Lucie Claraz, that he was not particularly well inclined toward Freemasons, and that he corresponded with Léo Taxil.[52] The latter, in his final declaration on April 12, 1897, gave a highly satirical description of a "good chaplain from Fribourg" in which we can without much doubt recognize Schorderet. According to Taxil, one fine day the Swiss ecclesiastical burst into his quarters "like a bomb," hailing him as a saint and demanding a miracle. When Taxil politely refused, the chaplain went back to Fribourg, convinced that the great convert had abstained from miracles out of humility; from Switzerland, he sent Taxil an enormous Gruyere cheese engraved with pious inscriptions.[53] There is also some indication that the French Antimasonic Committee had been actively involved in the affair of the grotto—yet another group of people who were prepared to believe the worst about Freemasons.[54] In one way or another, the rumor surfaced that Black Masses had been held in Fribourg's Masonic cave. It is hardly necessary to add that these rumors had no foundation whatsoever in facts. Except for its picturesque location, there is nothing to suggest that there was anything out of the ordinary about the Fribourg lodge. A short work on Masonic ritual that Stoecklin published in 1882 only attests that he was a dedicated follower of the nineteenth century "cult of Humanity," which he considered to be the essence of Freemasonry. In an aside on the initials INRI (also used in Masonic ritual and iconography), he even regretted the new significance of "Igne natura renovatur integra" that had been given to this acronym by some lodges. Instead, Stoecklin defended the old meaning of "Iesus nazarenus rex Iudæorum"—for had not Jesus been the first to realize a devotion to humanity as a whole?[55]

After Schorderet's demise in 1893, the story of the Satanist grotto took an unexpected twist. Suspicions suddenly fell on devout Miss Claraz. Her pious activities were only a cover-up, it was said, to hide the fact that she secretly participated in the Satanist rituals of her brother-in-law. This rumor may have originated from the fact that the curate of nearby Gruyere had refused her communion—although this happened, it seems, because of some wild saturnalia Miss Claraz had held in her garden in a moment of slackened devotion.[56] In addition, it was said that her takeover of the Masonic grotto had been a sham and that the money she had raised with her religious foundation had in reality been used to pay off her brother-in-law's debts.

An appearance on the scene was then made by none other than the writer J.-K. Huysmans, recently converted and widely considered an expert on the occult by the media. It is he who first seems to have made the connection between the refusal of communion and the presumed activities of Lucie Claraz as a Satanist Priestess. He did so in an interview that was printed in both *La Semaine de Fribourg* and *Le Matin*, stating that his information was based on an eyewitness account.[57] Like so much in this affair, it is unclear how the former Decadent writer managed to become mixed up in the story; neither the literature on Huysmans nor the historiographic references to Lucie Claraz offer any clarification on this point.

In the wake of Huysmans, the Catholic journalist Abel Clarin de la Rive appeared on the scene. We have met this character as a faithful echo of Taxil, and there is a strong possibility Léo Taxil also gave him the cue on Claraz: but Clarin de la Rive evidently went on to make the story his personal project.[58] In February 1894, he published an article entitled "The Black Mass at Fribourg" in Taxil's *Revue mensuelle religieuse, politique, scientifique.*[59] Dark ceremonies had taken place in the grotto, the article claimed. In the orchard that lay before it, prefatory rites had taken place involving naked Masonic Sisters. The actual Black Mass was celebrated in the grotto itself, using specially prepared black hosts, while at the same time consecrated hosts were abused and "Luciferian psalms and hymns" intoned to the accompaniment of a harmonium. Clarin de la Rive mentioned Lucie Claraz by name as the Grand Mistress of this infernal cult. With admirable creativity, he proceeded to counter the objections raised against his thesis. Why were there no altars and no Baphomet statue in the grotto when the Freemasons evacuated it? Evidently, they had first removed the evidence of their secret cult. The neighbors did not recall seeing any women entering the premises? Quite possible: for could the women not have entered by way of a secret tunnel from the nearby tavern, a local establishment considered "of ill repute from a moral point of view"?[60]

Clarin de La Rive's article did not go unnoticed. It was taken over by the *Nouveau Moniteur de Rome*, Pope Leo XII's international news organ that was headed by the fierce Monsignor Bœglin. In an editorial, the periodical lauded the firm stand of the local curate. He had steadfastly refused the Body of Christ to a woman who planned to abuse it in deicidal rites, even when she had appealed to secular courts to exact the administration of the hallowed bread. In reality, according to the *Moniteur*, her secret design in this had been to "legalize by judicial precedent the right to celebrate sacrilegious Communion."[61]

Another person who was alerted was Lucie Claraz herself, whose first name and surname had been mentioned in De la Rive's article. She sent an angry letter to the *Revue mensuelle*, demanding instant rectification. This only served to increase Clarin de la Rive's conviction. When he saw that the exasperated woman had signed her letter with "Lucie," he read this as short for Deodata-Lucif, her religious name as the High Priestess of Lucifer.[62] Lucie Claraz then decided to sue the *Revue*'s publisher for infamy. The French and foreign tabloid press, already warmed by Huysmans's" interview, now leaped on the story, repeatedly comparing the Fribourg grotto to the subterranean temple of Albert de Rudolstadt in George Sand's *Consuelo* and looking forward with great relish to the "curious details" and "extraordinary aberrations of religious sentiment" regarding Luciferians and Satanists that would be unveiled by the process. Had Catholic Fribourg been the scene of Luciferian ceremonies? Was Lucie Claraz, who looked "more fit to be the servant of a curate," in reality a priestess of Lucifer, officiating at the orgiastic rites of the "God of Joy and Pleasure"?[63]

The Paris court sat on January 15, 1896. Lucie Claraz entered the courtroom dressed in the full regalia of the Knighthood of the Holy Sepulchre; her lawyer demanded five thousand francs indemnity.[64] The counsel for the defense argued, surprisingly, that it was an evident absurdity to admit to the actual occurrence of devil worship and that to accuse a person of an impossible offense could hardly be called libel.[65] But the judge thought otherwise and condemned the *Revue* to a one hundred franc fine and required it to provide an official rectification for putting a stain on the plaintiff's honor as a woman and Catholic.[66] Bœglin and the *Nouveau Moniteur de Rome*, against whom Claraz had also pressed charges, were less lucky. The Italians had already expulsed the troublesome ecclesiastic some time before. They profited from the opportunity the trial gave them to make sure he would stay away for good, sentencing him to two years of prison *in absentio* and the payment of an eight thousand franc indemnity.[67] The grotto, meanwhile, had been turned into a convent for the Franciscan Missionaries of Mary, who would maintain their presence there until 1973. Today, it is a cultural center featuring expositions and electronic music concerts.[68]

The sheer scope and the enormous volume of Taxil's corpus have led some historians to suppose that greater forces were at work in the shadows behind him. Massimo Introvigne, the Italian expert on Satanism, does not think it unlikely that a small group of freethinkers or even Freemasons was secretly supporting Taxil's operation.[69] He also considers "not improbable" the thesis of his fellow Italian Aldo Mola, a renowned expert on the history of Italian Freemasonry, who suspects the hand of the French secret services in some of Taxil's schemes, particularly those involving the Italian "Grand Master" Domenico Margiotta.[70] Their aim in this would have been to influence Italian public opinion, with the ultimate intention of toppling Italian Prime Minister Crispi and breaking up the Triple Entente between Italy, Germany, and the Habsburg Empire. Mingled with grotesque fantasies of diabolism, politically explosive documents had indeed appeared in the pages of Margiotta's books. What to think, for instance, of the photographically reproduced condemnation of young Adriano Lemmi for theft and financial malversation in Marseilles? It is as yet unclear how this ended up in the hands of Taxil or Margiotta—in fact, the latter claimed to have

received it from the hands of Diana Vaughan![71] Taxil, moreover, is known to have occasionally informed on his corevolutionaries to the French police during his freethinking days.[72]

Hard evidence for the presumed involvement of government agencies in the Taxil fraud,
or part of it, can only be given when hitherto undisclosed documents come to light. But
I personally hold the hypothesis to be improbable. Eugen Weber, who utilized police
archives for his work on Taxil, does not seem to have come across any indications pointing
in this direction. Margiotta's book on Lemmi, moreover, was not primarily directed at an
Italian readership—its Italian translation was only published after the French version and
was probably intended primarily to boost Margiotta's plausibility with the French public
(with the additional effect of extracting some extra revenue from the Italian market). We
have already seen that Margiotta was in reality a pawn of Taxil (at least, this is what they
both declared), so to assume covert secret service manipulations behind Margiotta is to
assume the same behind Léo Taxil. It is hard to imagine that the French *Sureté* would set
up an infiltration operation lasting twelve years and causing considerable damage to the
nation's political cohesion in the meantime. This argument has double force when it comes
to a possible Masonic involvement in Taxil's operations. The sheer bulk of Taxil's output—
final point—ought not to surprise us unduly. Taxil had always been a prolific writer; he had
been publishing about Freemasonry for some five years already; and much of his work, as
we have seen, consisted of rehashed excerpts of old stories, Masonic manuals, and previous
anti-Masonic literature. He was also a master in the art of multiple uses of texts, publishing
them first as magazine or newspaper articles, then reassembling them in his books, and
subsequently quoting them once more in the books of his other persona. While his output
certainly was impressive, there is nothing ipso facto impossible in the idea that Taxil could
have accounted for it more or less singlehandedly, with the help of an occasional Dr. Hacks
or Margiotta, as well as an able typist with modern office equipment.[73]

If one would wish to uncover hidden operators behind Taxil's anti-Masonic activities,
I think it would be much more fruitful to search for them in quite another direction.
A wealth of indications but a dearth of serious research exists concerning the possibility
of a systematic Roman Catholic involvement in Taxil's anti-Masonic campaign. And with
systematic involvement, I do not refer merely to the obvious cooperation of Catholic anti-
Masonic organizations. I mean the possibility that Taxil was covertly provided with funds
and/or information and/or instructions by ultramontane, possibly even Vatican, agencies.

To make this suggestion credible, a small excursion into the back alleys of Vatican history might be useful. As we have seen, the loss of temporal sovereignty in 1870 brought
about a shift in Vatican policy, which henceforth increasingly relied on the manipulation
of Catholic opinion to support its international politics. Recent historical research has
brought to light that the Papacy did not shrink from using covert channels for the surrep-
titious direction of Catholic opinion. Directly after the taking of Rome, an international
group of ultramontane aristocrats and notables spontaneously sprang into being in order to
organize an efficient Catholic reaction to the crisis. Styling itself the "Black International"
(in conscious emulation of the Communist International), the group had put itself at the
unconditional disposal of the Papacy; and a secret liaison had been established with Pius
IX by way of the "innominato," a high-ranking ecclesiastical who had direct access to the
Pope but whose identity was to remain secret. While the group initially prepared for armed

resistance (setting up secret weapon stockpiles and organizing clandestine networks of ex-zouaves), the Papacy used it primarily as a tool for the manipulation of the Catholic press.[74] In 1872, the Vatican took over the funding of the organization, ensuring its control over the operation. By way of the innominato, articles and drafts for articles approved or even written by Pius IX were sent to the central bureau of the Black International in Geneva. From there, they were sent on as handwritten briefings known as "Conferences de Genève" to the permanent members of the Black International in various Catholic countries, who in turn distributed them to Catholic press organs and key Catholic opinion makers. In this way, informal Papal instructions could be transmitted to the Press, especially regarding the Roman Question. At the same time, the Permanents served as kinds of intelligence officers to the Papacy, reporting on the political and ecclesiastical situation in their homeland. Secrecy was an essential ingredient of the whole operation. Thus, its deniability was guaranteed: in this way, the Black International served as a tool not only for propaganda, but also for diplomacy. Through the Geneva channel, the Pope was able to fan up indignation in the Catholic press to intimidate European governments, while simultaneously extending an open hand through diplomatic channels. When the desired concessions had been obtained, the Catholic press could be instructed to cool down in the same way.[75]

Leo XIII was even more passionate about the press than Pius IX; it was even rumored that he personally wrote articles for the *Osservatore Romano* on occasion.[76] But he also preferred to keep press policy in his own hands and those of his confidants, employing a range of Vatican newspapers to play the organ of Catholic opinion. The Black International was rather abruptly disbanded when their Vatican Mr. X (a Polish prelate named Wladimir Czacki) was promoted to a different position within the Papal hierarchy. This did not mean the end of covert Papal press activities, however. In June 1878, a secret *Ufficio stampa* was established, doing much the same as the Black International had done, and with much of the same people, too; virtually all former Black International Permanents functioned as its correspondents. The Ufficio was so secret that even most of the Cardinals were not aware of its existence; those who knew about it mostly referred to it as the "House Salmini," one of the cover addresses the agency used. After 1881, the Ufficio came under the responsibility of the secretary of state, Cardinal Rampolla; renamed "Cassa di stampa," it assumed a more modest role, mainly supplying handouts to Italian newspapers and journalists. At the same time, Leo XIII relied more heavily on local bishops and papal nuncios to direct Europe's Catholic press.[77]

This brings us right up to the time that Taxil started to divulge his revelations on Freemasonry. How does he fit into this picture? There are some suggestive facts that might enable us to sketch the outlines of a hypothesis.

First, directly after his so-called conversion, a few potentially significant personages were involved in setting Taxil up as an anti-Masonic author. Among them was the papal nuncio in Paris, who did not deign to extend formal invitations to the former freethinker.[78] Another of these highly significant personages was Joseph Schorderet, the "good chaplain from Fribourg" that we encountered in the grotto at Pertuis. Notwithstanding the merciless ridicule Taxil heaped upon him in his memoir, Schorderet was in fact a key figure in international ultramontane Catholicism.[79] He was part of, or at least worked in close concord with, the Black International, corresponding with several of its Permanents; he was an important organizer of Swiss counter-secularization agitation; he was a driving force behind the establishment of Switzerland's first Catholic University, which in turn played an essential role in the so-called Union of Fribourg, an ultramontane think tank that helped to formulate the anticapitalist corporatism of Leo XIII's *Rerum Novarum*.[80] Yet Schorderet's most important work was in the domain of the press. As a young priest, he had founded his own newspaper, called *Liberté*, which soon grew to be the most important Catholic newspaper of francophone Switzerland; in addition, he had established a nationwide Catholic press network. He also founded the Sisters of Saint Paul, which counted Julie Stoecklin among its members. The official name of this sisterhood was "Congregation of Saint Paul for the Apostolate of the Press," and far from being a merely devotional order, it was a powerful tool in Schorderet's press activities. He had called the congregation into life when the workplace employees of his printing establishment had threatened to go on strike; its aim was to furnish a reliable and cheap body of young female workers to the printing presses of the Catholic press.[81] This proved to be a master stroke, and the work of Saint Paul gradually extended from Switzerland into France. It was probably as a result of this initiative that Taxil and Schorderet crossed paths. Relations between the two men were much more intricate than Taxil's story of the elated chaplain sending him Swiss cheese might suggest. Right after his "conversion," and still deep in debt, Taxil had held a job at the Librarie Saint-Paul, the Paris bookshop of Schorderet's congregation.[82] In a way, it may not be far off the mark to say that Schorderet's Apostolate of the Press had paid Taxil to write his first book against Freemasonry.

Second, if we look at the *reception* of Taxil's Palladism project, something tentatively suggesting a pattern becomes visible. Not all conservative Catholic press organs accepted Taxil's inflated revelations. Some of the most virulent critics of Taxil—Veuillot's *L'Univers*, Georges Bois's *Vérité*, Gruber's *Kölnischer Volkszeitung*—were radically intransigent and firmly convinced of the existence of a Masonic plot of the "philosophical," Barruelian kind. What these Catholic newspapers all had in common was that the Vatican had failed to attain an effective grip on them. In the French case, they moreover represented an anti-*ralliement* stance—*La Vérité* had explicitly been founded as a voice for Catholic anti-*ralliement* sentiments.[83] If we examine, on the other hand, the sections of the Catholic press that gave positive coverage to Taxil's output, we see that newspapers and periodicals closely allied to the Papacy are overrepresented. This applies to the press organs linked to Bishop Fava (a loyal proponent of the *ralliement*, surprising as it may seem); it applies to the Jesuit *Civittà Catolica*; it also applies to the *Nouveau Moniteur de Rome* of Monsignor Bœglin, set up to serve as a semi-official international press organ of the Vatican by Cardinal Rampolla.[84] Given the things we know about Vatican press policy, this at least makes abundantly clear that there was never a whisper of disapproval regarding Taxil through the various confidential channels that the Papacy had at its disposal to brief the Catholic press. One is tempted to suppose, on the contrary, that somebody somewhere gave a slight nod of encouragement.[85]

Third, and lastly, there is the *content* of Taxil's Palladic publications. If we look beyond the piano-playing crocodiles and demonic telephone lines, a picture emerges that perfectly complies with the objectives of Vatican policy. The *ralliement*, it might be remembered, was intended to further a pro-Papal French intervention in the Roman Question, both by enabling better diplomatic relations between the Vatican and the current French government and by bringing French Catholicism into the field as a proper political force by enticing it to operate within the Republican framework. These complicated maneuvers may have been reflected in Taxil's Palladism saga. Certainly, the secular Republic is brought under fire in a roundabout way, with the suggestion that an important part of its political elite was in fact acting as unknowing pawns for a diabolical sect. But the enormous corpus of Bataille and Vaughan is conspicuously bare of personal allegations against prominent French politicians, in stark contrast with the vitriolic attacks against foreign, and especially Italian, politicians. Behind these attacks, the contours of the Roman Question are clearly visible. Is it a mere coincidence, in this respect, that the Vatican started a renewed "all-out offensive" on the Roman Question after 1887?[86] Or that the *ralliement* had been in opera-tion for only two years when *Le Diable au XIXe siècle* started to appear?

For those for whom this is all a bit too abstract, a brief look at the latest Catholic pro-duction that left the Taxil factory might suffice. It was called *Le 33e:. Crispi: Un Palladiste Homme d'état démasqué* ("Crispi of the 33th Degree: A Palladist Politician Unmasked") and was published in June 1896. The book was clearly meant to be the third title in the series of "Italian books" that had appeared under the name of Margiotta (and which might have been the occasion for his recruitment). But because the former "Grand Master" had already deserted the Taxilian enterprise, the name of the nonexistent and ever-compliant Diana Vaughan was put upon the cover. Sure enough, the book contains many new rev-elations on the perfidious nature of Palladism. Who would want to miss, for instance, the official Masonic charter in which the demon Bitru solemnly vouches to make Sophie "Sapho" Walder the grandmother of the Antichrist, signed by the demon himself, and countersigned by Crispi and the ubiquitous Adriano Lemmi?[87] Even more surprising in a book on Satanism, however, is a two-page map illustrating the imperialistic ambitions of the "Masonic" Italy of the "Brothers Lemmi and Crispi."[88] In fact, most of the book's five hundred pages are devoted to Italian politics. The conclusion of *Le 33[e]:. Crispi* sheds light on what are probably the book's intentions: to agitate against the Italian "Republic of the Devil, . . . where Satan will have his statue of massive gold under the dome of the Saint Peter," and in favor of a Federal Italian state with the restored Patrimony of Peter at its cen-ter and the Pope as President! "Salute to the Pope-King, President of the Italian Republic!'" Diana Vaughan alias Léo Taxil cheers on the last page, leaving the historian in a state of mild bewilderment.[89] Was this still part of Taxil's giant practical joke? Or was it all meant to be taken seriously, and was he advised to write this, even furnished with material maybe, by people he could not afford to refuse?

A suggestive picture emerges from the three points that I listed. Taxil had been in contact with two clerics who served as covert liaisons between the Papacy and the press; Catholic press organs allied to the Papacy ranked high among the periodicals that spread his anti-Masonic tales of horror; and the content of these tales closely corresponds to the Papal political agenda and sometimes amounts to undiluted Papal propaganda. Was Pope Leo XIII, would-be president of the Italian Republic, the secret employer of Léo Taxil? Did he use the former freethinker as franc-tireur to manipulate Catholic opinion in France? It would not have been the first time that the Vatican used questionable mercenaries in its efforts to influence public opinion. In Germany, the Papacy had employed the shady Protestant publicist Wallgreen Schuman to incite anti-Italian feelings in the Protestant press.[90] In practice, Taxil was fulfilling the same role in France. Was this a coincidence? Or was Taxil funded and briefed by the Papacy as well, through some as-yet-unidentified middleman?

In this respect, it might be interesting to have a closer look at the attitude the Papacy adopted toward Taxil and his Palladium hoax. This has been the object of differing interpretations, among both contemporary and current historians. The central question here is usually did the pontiff and his retinue fall for Taxil's tales? That Leo XIII believed in a Masonic conspiracy of some kind hardly needs corroboration. His encyclicals attest to this, and we will have occasion to cite further proof below. Nor does this need to surprise us unduly in an age in which even great statesmen like Joseph de Maistre and Benjamin Disraeli embraced conspiracy theories centering on Masonic secret societies.[91] Within the Roman Catholic hierarchy, belief in a great Masonic conspiracy must have been even more virulent. Schorderet died in the firm conviction that Mason assassins were after his life, and even a Realpolitiker *pur sang* as Wladimir Czacky—the *innominato* of the Black International—was motivated in his covert activities by the idea that the Papacy must be upheld as a last theocratic banner in a world dominated by secret Masonic machinations.[92]

That the Pope believed in the reality of the Masonic plot hence is hardly a matter of doubt. But did he also adhere to the particular Taxilian variant of the Masonic conspiracy theory, with its secret sex rites, its inner circle of Lucifer-worshipping Palladists, its diabolic apparitions, and its hidden subterranean temples? It seems utterly incredible. But, again, we should not consider the Pope a priori any wiser than his coreligionists. Taxil was believed to a greater or lesser degree by many in the hierarchy: Bishop Meurin and Bishop Fava may be cited as two particularly flagrant cases. In his official encyclicals, Leo XIII never adopted the explicit diabolical schemes propagated in Taxil's writings: for all its demonizing rhetoric, *Humanum Genus* speaks of Freemasons as adherents to "naturalism" and rationalism, not Satanism. Yet the Pope certainly was not disinclined to accept the possibility of active intervention by Satan in the earthly battle between the city of God and the kingdom of the devil. He reintroduced, for example, a special exorcism of Satan in the official rituals of exorcism, and he added a prayer to Saint Michael to the Mass ordinarium that beseeched the archangel's protection against the forces of evil.[93] These innovations must have been the reflection of some kind of inner conviction, and the depiction Taxil gave of Leo XIII as an old man darkly muttering about the devil might have had a core of truth in it. They suggest a mindset in which Palladic constructions might well fit.

If we look at the official and semiofficial utterances of the Vatican regarding Taxil, no clear image emerges. It is true, as we have seen, that Taxil obtained an audience with the Holy Father in 1887. But although Taxil was able to list nineteen short or long letters of recommendation from various French bishops in his book on female Freemasonry of 1891, the Holy See remained silent. This contrasts starkly with a no less shady figure than Paul Rosen, who cited a long personal letter from Pope Leo XIII at the front of his second book.[94] Diana Vaughan, it is true, did correspond with various members of the Papal hierarchy. Taxil quoted extensively from these letters in both Miss Vaughan's publications and his own final declaration in 1897. We already cited a letter by Cardinal Parocchi, the Papal Vicar, transmitting a "most special benediction" of the Pope; Parocchi added to this that Leo XIII had been reading Vaughan's memoirs, which he considered of "palpitating interest."[95]

When Diana Vaughan's book on Crispi was sent to the Pope, the response was a short letter written by Monsignor Vincenzo Sardi, one of Leo's private secretaries. It contained a formal expression of gratitude for the volume and an appeal to continue the good work: "Go on, Miss, go on to write and to unmask the iniquitous sect! To this purpose, Providence has allowed you to be part of it for such a long time."[96] However significant this may be, the Pope never deigned to respond in person to Taxil's overtures. Only "Grand Master" Domenico Margiotta could boast of having received a note from His Holiness himself. Its laconic nature and three single lines of text, however, hardly amounted to a spectacular Papal avowal of support.[97]

In the controversy that arose about the question of whether Diana existed, the Papacy also remained aloof. Yet one can detect some cautious expressions in acceptance of the Grand Mistress's reality. On May 27, 1896, Rodolfo Verzichi, the secretary of the Universal Antimasonic Union at Rome, addressed the following official letter to the converted Grand Mistress:

> Miss,
> Monsignor Vincenzo Sardi, one of the private secretaries of the Holy Father, has given me charge to write to you, by order of His Holiness himself.
> I must tell you also that His Holiness has read with great pleasure your *Eucharistic Novena.*
> The Commander Mr. Alliata [the president of the Antimasonic Union] has had an interview with the Cardinal-Vicar [Parocchi] with regard to the veracity of your conversion. His Eminence is convinced; but He has made clear to our president that He can not give a public testimony. "I can not betray the secrets of the Holy Office"; that is what His eminence has responded to the Commander Mr. Alliata.
>
> Yours truly in Our Lord.[98]

This and other indications imply that the Vatican was actively occupied with the Diana Vaughan Question. When the Congress at Trent deferred the case to a special Vatican committee, this special committee turned out to exist already. Other sources allude to the existence of a dossier entitled "Vaughan, Taxil, and Company" in the files of the Holy Office (which is certainly something a historian of Satanism would like to read).[99] In the months preceding and following the congress in Trent, a flurry of correspondence left Rome in order to establish the truth of the matter. Bishop Lazzareschi, president of the Antimasonic Congress, and Commandeur Alliata, president of the Universal Antimasonic Committee, both addressed Father Bessonies, president of the French Antimasonic Committee, asking for "documents that are able to prove that Palladism, as it is revealed in the works signed by Doctor Bataille, Domenico Margiotta and Diana Vaughan, really exists."[100] On November 15, 1896, Monseigneur A. Villard, the secretary of Cardinal Parocchi, followed suit, writing on behalf of the special committee of investigation that was presided over by the latter. In his epistle, Villard assured the addressee that the question of Diana Vaughan's existence could only be decided with authority at Rome, "but Rome, I repeat to you, needs more information": "It is an error to think that Rome is completely informed at her regard." He added "in complete confidentiality" that Taxil had gravely compromised her cause, and he underlined it to be "extremely important" that she disengage herself from her "pretended defender."[101] Villard repeated his requests in several letters during the subsequent months, addressing Vaughan directly as well.[102] Also in 1896, Abel Clarin de la Rive, the shrewd expert on Masonic tunneling, was sent on a mission to Gibraltar with the official sanctification of Cardinal Parocchi to find out if Freemasonry was really operating hidden workplaces in the Cliff of Tarik. In America, the ultramontane Quebeçois journalist Tardivel was commissioned with a similar mission.[103]

If these indications adequately reflect the attitude of the Papacy, it is evident that the Vatican already knew or had decided that Taxil was unreliable but was completely at a loss with regard to the actual nature of his creation, Diana Vaughan.[104] Meanwhile, the official attitude of the Holy See remained cautiously noncommitted. After endless deliberations, as we have seen, the special committee issued a neutral verdict on the Vaughan Question, at the same time using the occasion to castigate the troublesome German press for its sin of hypercriticism. The impression one gets is that it was one of the two. Either the Vatican was genuinely in doubt and did not a priori wish to discard the possibility that a High Priestess of a secret inner-Masonic organization devoted to the worship of Lucifer had indeed defected to the Church. Or it was deliberately holding its hand over a setup that it suspected or knew to be rotten but that it considered useful anyway—giving just enough encouragement to keep it afloat but not enough to compromise itself.

Léo Taxil, for one, was firmly convinced of the latter, and he squarely accused the Papacy of this policy during his final press conference. In Rome, where "all indications come together," people would surely have been aware that there were no female Freemasons who surrendered themselves to sexual rites of initiation.[105] Moreover, local ecclesiastical dignitaries who had denied some of his revelations had been deliberately hushed by the Vatican at several occasions.[106] Taxil's utterances, however, need to be treated with extreme caution. For Taxil was pursuing his own plot in this respect. It is evident that he wanted to crown his operation of deceit by trapping the Papacy into implicating itself in his fraud. This might have been his prime reason for continuing to impersonate a Catholic author for twelve years, and this might have been the reason he sent his books to the Holy See time after time. The letters he received in return were compromising enough. But Taxil was fishing for some more official token of approbation.[107] Taxil's last book on Crispi can also be interpreted as a last desperate bid for overt Papal approval, a dance of courtship to entice Leo XIII into some blatantly compromising mating posture. This might account for its blunt Papal propaganda with regard to the Roman Question, and also for the somewhat embarrassing poem about Leo XIII on its opening pages. The Pope did not really fall for the bait, however, and the short message of encouragement by Monsignor Sardi that we cited earlier was the only thing Taxil got.

Although Taxil liked to paint the Vatican as a prey to helpless confusion, it is clear that he entertained a high, possibly inflated notion of the powers wielded by Rome. In a way, it was the Papacy that had incited him to come out in the open in the first place. The Congress at Trent had voted for the essentially Satanist nature of Freemasonry; but simultaneously, its predominantly Italian organizers had prevented Taxil from assuming any important official functions. We may safely assume the hand of the Vatican behind this. Taxil, for his part, clearly understood the hint and feared the effects that a whispered word from the Papacy could have. "The peril that threatened was silence; it was the strangling of the mystification in the backrooms of a Roman committee; it was an interdict to the Catholic papers to whisper another word upon it."[108]

This last sentence almost suggests that Taxil knew something of the way the Papacy operated to direct the Catholic press behind the scenes. If the Vatican had also been covertly employing or exploiting Taxil, however, he himself was clearly not aware of this. Otherwise he certainly would have thrown this compromising information into the open when he decided to raise his Catholic mask. Instead, he tried to row with the oars he had and compromise the Papacy as much as he could during his press conference anyhow. But although he might have had more of a point than he suspected himself, it is clear Taxil did not really convince most of his contemporaries. He was missing the spectacular piece of evidence that incontestably implicated Leo XIII. In the end, the noncommittal approach of the Papacy bore fruit, and the Pontiff's reputation escaped relatively unharmed from the collapse of the Palladium.

It is time to draw this section to a conclusion. What can we salvage from the wreckage of historical suggestions? Was the Vatican involved in the Taxil hoax? Or have we fallen prey to the temptation of conspiracy thinking ourselves? Whatever the truth may be, it is evident that simple options do not apply. The Holy See did *not* control Taxil as a sort of enlisted secret agent. The outcome of the whole affair makes this abundantly clear; and all Taxil's utterances suggest that he was working pretty much on his own. The Vatican, moreover, seems to have been as bewildered about the Diana Vaughan story as a good many other Catholics were. Yet there is much to suggest, at the very least, that the Vatican was not averse to riding the Taxilian bandwagon, and there are some tantalizing shreds of information that could imply that it had been actively involved in setting Taxil up as an anti-Masonic writer and that it continued to give him at least tacit support in his later career. This would probably make Taxil the greatest failure in the history of Vatican press policy. Although it must be remembered that Taxil was intently courting the Papacy, the remarkable accuracy with which his work sometimes follows the fault lines of Vatican international policy is hard to ascribe to the shrewd political instincts of a hackney writer alone.

The only firm conclusion we can draw is that more research is necessary. The seemingly peripheral stories we recounted earlier in this section might present a good starting point for this. Interesting facts might emerge, for instance, with closer study of Taxil's relations with the apostolic nunciature and with Schorderet. For the latter, the strange history of the Fribourg grotto might offer an interesting start. Pinpointing the exact source of the persistent rumor about the Palladic temple in the Palazzo Borghese could also produce some interesting insights. The evidence we surmised suggests that this story was already circulating in Italy before it was published in France; this, in turn, might indicate that for at least this particular piece of misinformation, Taxil was not responsible.[109] Who was the "accredited correspondent at Rome" that brought it into circulation? And could it have been the Vatican *Cassa di stampa* that supplied it to him? This would furnish clear proof that the Vatican was much more actively involved in the exploitation of the Taxil fraud than it would have liked to disclose. In the meantime, it remains an exciting idea to imagine Léo Taxil and Leo XIII locked in a strange kind of duel without knowing it, each trying to manipulate the other for his own designs, and each sliding out of the other's embrace at exactly the critical moment.

A FEW WORDS ON SATAN IN FREEMASONRY, AND ON NEO-PALLADISM

An apology to the reader might be due by now. I spent many pages discussing Roman Catholicism within a historical account that professes to be about Satanism. As in the case of J.-K. Huysmans, the realities of Satanism only played a small role in the story of Taxil and the Palladism hoax. Except as a product of human fantasy, the religious Satanism within Freemasonry that its Catholic opponents and Taxil described never existed. Nevertheless, for the sake of comprehensiveness, it seems appropriate to take a look at the reality of Freemasonry as well. This may eventually lead to the question that I have not yet properly addressed and that is largely unexplored by modern historiography: if we dismiss the obvious constructions of fantasy, was something going on with Satan in Freemasonry after all?[110]

A lot remains unclear about the early history of Freemasonry. Latest research has indicated Scotland as the country of origin of the Masonic fraternity as it exists today.[111] Toward the end of the sixteenth and the beginning of the seventeenth century, the medieval guild of masons here was transformed into a semi-esoteric lodge also admitting those not practicing the craft of masonry. Spreading to England, the new association fell under the influence of the Latitudinarian deism of Isaac Newton and consorts, and it soon became a popular pastime for gentlemen. From the United Kingdom, Freemasonry spread to the Americas and continental Europe. In these regions, the Craft identified itself increasingly with the values of the Enlightenment, such as religious tolerance and rationalism. Most of the Founding Fathers of the American Revolution were active lodge members.

This identification with the Enlightenment was never complete. The eighteenth century also saw the emergence of a wide variety of rites and disciplines within Masonry, most of them strongly esoteric in nature. According to the fashion of the times, wild theories about the origin of the Craft were proposed that linked Freemasonry to the Templars, the druids, the Essenes, or the Kabbalah—many of which would be gratefully recycled by later anti-Masonic conspiracy theorists.[112] In Germany, real conspirators sought to control Freemasonry for their own political purposes: the famous Illuminati for their agenda of radical Enlightenment; the Rosicrucian brotherhood for the defense of traditional values. In France, the first lodge was strictly Catholic, consisting of Englishmen who had followed the Catholic King James II into French exile. Native lodges soon sprang up and became major dissemination centers of the ideas of the *philosophes*. Yet the French Revolution, when it came, cut right through the ranks of Freemasonry. Because *tout le monde*, so to say, had been a Mason brother, many Freemasons could be found among the Revolutionaries; many others, however, found themselves on the opposite side of the line.

It was only in the aftermath of the French Revolution that Freemasonry in France (and in other Roman Catholic countries such as Belgium, Italy, and Spain) came to identify itself fully with the values of the Western Revolution. Before the Revolution, it had not been particularly uncommon for priests or clerics to be lodge members; afterward, this became unthinkable—not just because the Roman Catholic interdict was now upheld with maximum severity, but also because French Freemasonry took a definite anticlerical turn and increasingly frowned on the idea of a priest being a Freemason.[113] In the decades that followed, French Freemasonry grew into a sort of unofficial "Church of the Republic" and embarked on a secularization process of its own. The traditional requirement of belief in a deity for neophytes was dropped in 1877; in 1879, the references to the "Grand Architect of the Universe" were removed from the Grand Orient; in 1887, less religiously tinged rituals were introduced. From 1895 on, high-ranking Masons were obliged to be buried civilly.[114]

These measures indicate how both sides increasingly dug themselves into holes as the secularization struggle continued. They also prompted a sort of secularization struggle within Freemasonry itself. The more traditionally inclined lodges of the Anglo-Saxon world objected strongly when the French Grand Orient removed the requirement to believe in a deity in 1877, and they eventually broke off relations of amity with their French brethren. Continental or Liberal Freemasonry, as it often came to be called, became the dominant style of Freemasonry in the Latin countries of Europe and South America. Within France, a "Grand Loge de France" separated itself from the Grand Orient in 1894, reuniting lodges that disagreed with the agnostic and anticlerical stance of the latter.

Curiously, Albert Pike (1809–1891), the alleged Pope of Luciferianism, had been particularly vocal in persuading the United Grand Lodge of England and its many affiliated Grand Lodges to oust the infidel French from traditional Masonry. Pike, a former Confederate brigadier general, had been "Sovereign Grand Commander of the Southern Jurisdiction of the Ancient and Accepted Scottish Rite of Freemasonry" until his death at age eighty-one. Although a towering figure in American Freemasonry, he was certainly not the titular head of international Masonry. No such figure existed anyhow in the federal structure of Freemasonry. Pike had been avidly interested in occultism all his life, and his antagonism toward a secular Freemasonry was inspired not so much by Christian affiliation as by a desire to defend the place within Freemasonry of what we would now call spirituality. In this, the Sovereign Grand Master was clearly inspired by Éliphas Lévi, the father of occultism. The influence of Lévi was also tangible in the few scattered passages on the fallen angel that can be found in his Masonic writings. In his explanation of the third degree in *Morals and Dogmas of Freemasonry*, for instance, Pike wrote with typical Lévian ambiguity: "The true name of Satan, the Kabalists say, is that of Yahveh reversed; for Satan is not a black god, but the negation of God. The Devil is the personification of Atheism or Idolatry. For the Initiates, this is not a Person, but a Force, created for good, but which may serve for evil. It is the instrument of Liberty or Free Will. They represent this Force, which presides over the physical generation, under the mythologic and horned form of the God PAN; thence came the he-goat of the Sabbat, brother of the Ancient Serpent, and the Light-bearer or Phosphor, of which the poets have made the false Lucifer of the legend."[115]

It was not because of these scattered passages, however, that Pike earned the doubtful honor of being proclaimed the earthly representative of Satan. It was Paul Rosen who first awarded the American Sovereign Commander this prerogative; his inspiration had been Pike's response to the encyclical *Humanum Genus* of Pope Leo XIII. In this "Reply of Freemasonry on behalf of the Human Race to the Encyclical Letter 'Humanum Genus' of the Pope Leo XIII," and in the "praelocution" that preceded it, Pike gave the Pope an eloquent *quid pro quo*, pointing to the Roman Catholic Church as the real conspirator against lawful governments, calling the encyclical "a declaration of war against the human race," and its widest possible publication the best service Freemasonry could do itself.[116] "With such a Past as that of the Church of Rome has, it would have been wise not to provoke comment upon its real crimes by accusing others of having committed imaginary ones," the Sovereign Grand Commander pointedly concluded.[117] Whether willfully or out of sincere conviction, Rosen misinterpreted this gesture as a proclamation by Pike as head of all Freemasonry.[118] Once Pike's status as commander of Satan's auxiliary forces had been established, it was not hard to find dark allusions in Pike's esoteric writings. Rosen stumbled upon a little book by Pike called *Sephar H'Debarim, The Book of the Words,* which in eighteenth-century fashion proposed the "generative principle" as the origin of all godhead, and which, according to Rosen, contained "horrors that only the Devil could have dictated to him."[119] Taxil, who adopted Rosen's notion of Pike as Anti-Pope, showed even more ingenuity in this respect. When he discovered some juvenile poetry of Pike in an age-old issue of *Blackwood's Magazine* (a cycle of poems called "Hymns to the Gods"), he reissued these under the name of Diana Vaughan as the official hymnal of the pagan religion that Pike sought to reinstate.[120]

Were all claims against Freemasonry then mere grotesques? This would be too simple as well. Historical reality, which may look black or white from afar, usually dissolves into tints of gray when examined up close; this is also the case with fin de siècle Freemasonry. Particularly within French, Belgian, and (it seems) Italian Freemasonry, internal currents had become dominant that promoted an explicitly political course, using the influence of the Craft for the pursuit of "liberal" political objectives.[121] Opposing the "obscurantism" of the Roman Catholic Church was an important aim and motive of this program. While the French government was not "guided" by Freemasonry, Freemasons certainly were prominent among the Republican elite. In a reflection of the practices of confessional factions, the lodge put forth or supported its own selected candidates in elections, rallying its members to give these their vote. (It was this practice, one may remember, to which Taxil had attributed his expulsion from the lodge when he had put himself up for election in opposition to the "official" Masonic candidate.) In 1892, in reaction to the increasingly aggressive tone of Catholic and right-wing agitators, the Grand Orient made Freemasons who stood as candidates for parliament sign a convention that compelled them to vote in favor of the separation of state and church and in favor of the suppression of the French embassy by the Vatican.[122] In the aftermath of the Taxil affair and the Dreyfus hysteria, the Grand Orient took recourse to means of action that were even more at odds with its liberal principles. Convinced of the necessity to "purify" the French armed forces of reactionary elements, it started to monitor the religious allegiance of French army officers in a vast inventory. This inventory was put at the disposal of the fiercely anticlerical Combes government (1902–1905), who saw to it that Catholic officers received no promotions. The "Affaire des Fiches" came to light in 1904, thanks to a Catholic infiltrator who had declared himself "converted" to freethinking more than twelve years previously and had succeeded in becoming vice secretary of the Grand Orient.[123]

There were also occasional kernels of reality in the material that anti-Masonic crusaders brought to the surface regarding Satan. Although fully ripped out of context, some of their citations from Masonic periodicals were doubtlessly genuine. As Paul Rosen had already suggested, it was predominantly Italian Freemasonry that distinguished itself by "glorifying their Satanic affiliation with remarkable compliance."[124] Their strong committal to the *Risorgimento,* the Italian struggle for reunification, had placed the Freemasons there in direct opposition to the Roman Catholic Church and the Papacy. It had imbued them with a fierce anticlericalism that was sometimes reflected in radical utterances about the fallen angel. In 1880, for instance, a certain Brother G.-G. Seraffini published an article in Italy's official Masonic bulletin that eulogized Satan as "the Spirit of the Future": "Salute the Genius of renewal, all you who suffer. Lift up your heads, my Brothers: for he will arrive, He, Satan the Great!"[125] It is hard to establish the veracity of other not a priori improbable assertions of this kind, for instance the claim that Freemasons in Genoa had carried a banner saying "Glory to Satan" through the streets in solemn procession.[126] The future concentration camp victim Maximilian Kolbe recounted how he decided to become a priest in 1917 while in Rome and seeing Italian Freemasons hoist a banner on which Lucifer subdued Michael, with the motto "Satan will reign in the Vatican and the Pope will be his slave."[127]

These utterances do not prove the existence of a hidden cult of Satan within Italian Freemasonry. But they do suggest the existence of a metaphoric "Satanism" treading in the footsteps of the Romantic Satanists. Nowhere is this clearer than in the most well-known pro-Satanic declaration of an Italian Freemason, the famous "Inno a Satana" by Giosuè Carducci.[128] Carducci was the only Romantic Satanist to win a Nobel Prize (in 1906), and his hymn can be considered a résumé of classic Romantic Satanism in fifty stanzas. It represents Satan as the embodiment of nature, the origin of *eros*, the inspiring force of poetry, and the divine presence in the gods of Antiquity. Although driven underground by Christianity, he has gradually been regaining territory ever since, first during the Renaissance and the Reformation (even Martin Luther was inspired by the devil, according to Carducci's poem), and more clearly in the triumphs of science and the stirrings of revolution in recent times. Embracing an unequivocal faith in positivism and progress, the poem ends in a mood of ringing optimism. With the steam machine already heralding his coming reign, the victory of Satan is at hand and will spell final dissolution for "the god of the greedy popes and cruel kings."[129]

Salute, o Satana,
O ribellione
O forza vindice
De la ragione!

Sacri a te salgano
Gl'incensi e i voti!
Hai vinto il Geova
De i sacerdoti.[130]

[Be greeted, O Satan,
O rebellion
O avenging force
Of reason!

Sacred to you may rise
Incense and vows!
You that have triumphed over
The priest's Jehovah.]

Carducci was already a Freemason but still an unknown man of letters when he wrote this poem in 1863. It appeared under a pseudonym and without his permission in several Masonic periodicals in Italy before its "official" publication in *Il Popolo* on December 8, 1869, the day the First Vatican Concilium opened.[131] This fact alone, of course, was welcome fodder to anti-Masonists of the calibre of Taxil and company. Carducci and his hymn appear fairly regularly in the Palladism saga. It was this "Hymn of Satan" whose use Pike criticized in his faked Secret Instructions; it was this poem that Sophie "Sapho" Walder recited in the presence of Dr. Bataille; and when Lemmi became Grand Master of Palladism, he promoted the "Inno a Satana" to the status of official anthem by an encyclical letter dated September 21, 1893.[132] On this occasion, Taxil even claimed that the poem had been expressly composed at the behest of the Italian Grand Master.[133] As a real-life personage, the Italian poet also played a role of some prominence in the Taxilian œuvre. Through the pen of Margiotta, Taxil suggested that Carducci, who was known within Freemasonry as "Br∴ 675," had been a rival candidate to Adriano Lemmi when the new Satanist Pope was elected in Rome on September 20, 1893; after he got only thirteen votes against Lemmi's forty-six, however, he voluntarily withdrew his candidacy.[134] Carducci was quite right when he qualified these allegations as "halfway between delirium and imposture" in a letter to Lemmi.[135] Yet behind this utter nonsense was the bare fact that the "Inno a Satana" indeed seems to have functioned as a kind of battle hymn against the Roman Catholic Church for Italian Freemasons. Several anti-Masonic authors and at least one modern historian maintain that it was regularly sung at official Masonic banquets, which would probably made this the closest that regular Freemasonry ever came to anything resembling the religious veneration of Satan.[136]

Another work of Italian poetry brought into connection with Freemasonry and Palladism by Taxil is the epic poem *Lucifero* (1877), composed by the freethinking poet Mario Rapisardi (1844–1912). This by now largely forgotten work may be considered a late reprise of earlier Romantic Satanism as well, with mythical figures as Lucifer, Liberty, Reason, Christ, and Prometheus all making an appearance, together with various historical figures. The book is presented as a grand poetic monologue by Lucifer to Prometheus, who is finally addressed by the angel of light with the words "Lèvati, il gran tiranno è spento!" ("Arise; the grand tyrant is no more!").[137] This tyrant, of course, is the Christian deity, and the battle of Lucifer is the battle of Thought, Reason, and Liberty against the forces of inertia, obscurantism, and oppression, which is recounted in a series of *tableaux* that reflect the history of humanity in its long struggle for emancipation. Lucifer finds love, is persecuted by the angry deity, fights a jaguar, and assists various scenes of history, prominent among which is, again, the French Revolution. A few episodes of recent Italian history are also alluded to: for instance, the breaching of the Porta Pia during the capture of Rome in 1870 ("crowning deed of the Italian people"), and the deathbed of Pope Pius IX, who in his final moments implores Lucifer to grant him forgiveness.[138] The poem ends in an over-the-top apotheosis in which Lucifer conquers the heavens, with most of the angels and saints defecting to his cause and only Ignatius of Loyola, Domenico di Guzman, Torquemada, and a few popes keeping their posts to defend the deity. Although I am unaware of any indications that Rapisardi was a Freemason, Taxil did not hesitate to make full use of this poetic curiosity, claiming that it was composed at the personal bequest of Albert Pike to serve as a poetic counterstroke against Carducci's "Inno a Satana."[139]

This pretty much sums up the allusions to Masonic "Satanism" in Taxil's body of work that may have some ground in historical reality in one form or another. A detailed search of Masonic archives might render some more instances, but I doubt this will change the overall picture. Keeping in mind that a dedicated corps of nineteenth-century anti-Masonic authors was scanning Mason publications for clues to the secret worship of Satan, the few examples they managed to come up with make a decidedly meager impression. It seems safe to assume that true "veneration of Satan" never occurred within Freemasonry. The rare and often questionable instances that have been brought forward, originating from the furnace of heated Masonic-clerical conflict, point to an exclusively metaphoric use of the fallen angel, along the lines already set out by the Romantic Satanists.[140]

Behind this symbolic usage of Satan, as one historian has aptly noted, we can discern an almost complete reversion of association between anticlerical Freemasons and anti-Masonic Roman Catholics. In the wake of Romantic Satanism, Satan could be perceived as a positive metaphor by some Freemasons; while for most Roman Catholics, such metaphorical use could only indicate the worst of horrors. The ensuing attribution of devil worship by the latter only fortified the tendency toward identification by the former, particularly in Italy. "In the end, all agreed, because what for the one was a crime, for the other was a motive for pride."[141] While there is nothing to suggest that these occasional instances of identification ever grew into a properly *religious* Satanism, it eloquently shows how the Romantic rehabilitation of Satan retained its ideological value throughout the nineteenth century.

This may also be the right moment to discuss another subject related to Palladism, a subject that will take us beyond the limits of the nineteenth century: to wit, the presumed existence of neo-Palladism. For although it is evident that Palladism proper was an invention altogether lacking reality, this construction evidently held appeal for some people. Alfred Pierret described how personages of all rank and form visited his printing establishment at the time that he published the Luciferian periodical *Le Palladium Régénérée*. Apart from the countess who sprinkled him with holy water, most of these visitors had seemed avid to join the new Luciferian creed.[142] In addition, Taxil gleefully recounted in his final memoir how his revelations had been taken seriously by some Freemasons themselves: those from the south of Italy had been particularly vexed, according to him, when learning from his writings that Lemmi had surreptitiously taken control over worldwide Palladism without asking them in. They convened in protest at a congress in Palermo and proceeded to found three independent Supreme Councils, those of Sicily, Naples, and Florence, naming Diana Vaughan as their protector and honorary member.[143] Taxil's statements, however, obviously need to be treated with proper distrust. The same principle applies to the probable apocryphal story told by Massimo Introvigne, according to which Italian Masons spontaneously sent a "tiara of Lucifer" to Lemmi on September 20, 1894, to honor his ascension to the position of head of Palladism the year before.[144]

Introvigne also tells us about two groups of neo-Palladists that operated in Paris during the Interbellum and sought to "reproduce as much as possible" the rites of Palladism.[145] The Italian historian bases his claims on the works of Pierre Geyraud, a pseudonym for the "ancien ecclésiastique" Raoul Guyader, a French journalist who wrote reportage in the style of Jules Bois about the colorful religious groups that he found in Paris during the

1930s. The neo-Palladists were first described in his third volume on this subject.[146] After a short introduction to Luciferianism (in which he uncritically repeats a range of Taxilian inventions), Geyraud provided a vivid description of a "Palladic initiation." He hastened to explain that he had not witnessed this ceremony himself: instead, in his publication he reproduced the written account of an initiate "with whom I am already acquainted a long time."[147]

In this account, the anonymous initiate had told how he received, one day, a mysterious letter of invitation to attend an unusual ceremony. He was instructed to wait at a given hour on the quays close to the Notre Dame. As he walked on the quay, a limousine stopped beside him, and he was asked to step in the car and blindfold his eyes. After arriving at an unknown destination and descending several staircases, he was told to remove his blindfold and found himself in an oval room clad in black velour and ornamented with inverted pentagrams and "ritual daggers." He was dressed in a white robe and subjected to some pseudo-Masonic trials in the presence of forty-odd fellow Palladists. When he had proved himself worthy, the whole congregation gave him the kiss of peace on his behind, while the Master, a man in a black robe and a blood-red cap nicknamed the "Black Pope," transmitted "the breath of the Order" to him by kissing him on the mouth.

After this, a pretty hefty ritual began. A statue was revealed of a figure "half he-goat, half ox, half man, half woman, with two splendid horns of silver, between which shone a small circle of brilliant green." It is, of course, Baphomet. An inverted crucifix was attached nearby. A woman now appeared and started to dance, baring her left breast. The Grand Master solemnly asked her: "Quid velis? [What do you want?]," to which she replied: "Ad sacrificium offere corpus meum [To offer my body in sacrifice]." She was then stretched out on the altar, the Grand Master intoning a kind of offertory with a black host in his hands, and the audience responding with repeated cries of *Laus Satani!*" The officiate placed a number of profaned hosts on the woman's vagina, after which the Palladists, "excited to the heights of antique orgies" by the "heavy and suffocating odour of the perfumes of rut, henbane leaves, and datura," launched themselves onto the eagerly awaiting "living altar."[148] The inevitable orgy ensued, during which the Black Pope endeavored to absorb the psychic energy of the collective coitus. The ritual ended rather abruptly when the bats that hung from the ceiling to serve as lanterns suddenly started to "detonate." The initiate, who had not been allowed to join the orgy, was now led to a corner of the room where his personal "shakti" awaited him, a beautiful woman "of Nordic race and the most perfect lunar type."

Although Geyraud insisted that he personally knew several of the persons that had been present at these ceremonies, his account sounds rather fantastic, to say the least. For these fantastic elements, however, only partial credit is due to Geyraud or his anonymous informer. At least half the story, in fact, is copied from an article by Serge Basset, which was published in May 1899 in the French newspaper *Le Matin*, and republished in 1927 in a book on occultism by a certain Frédéric Boutet.[149] After he had expressed doubts about whether the Black Mass was still celebrated in modern Paris, Basset tells in this article, he had received two letters and a personal visit from a mysterious woman who offered to show him "things." After this familiar introduction, the story develops along practically identical lines to that of Geyraud, including the blindfold, guards, and Latin questioning, with the difference that Basset flees the scene of the Satanist gathering when the orgy commences and is thus unable to describe exploding bats or personal shaktis. Basset, moreover, did not give his assembly the appendage "neo-Palladist," but claimed that they called themselves "the Brothers and Sisters of the Observance of the Evil One."

Basset's story sounds a bit too much like a J.-K. Huysmans persiflage to be true. Apparently, this is also what Geyraud himself eventually concluded, for in the selection from his reportage that he published in 1954, he retained his introduction to Luciferianism and Palladism but omitted the story of the catacomb orgy with the exploding bats.[150] Instead, he inserted another of his earlier reports, namely that on the T.H.L. or "Très-Haut Lunaire" ("Most High Lunary").[151] Geyraud became acquainted with this group, he claimed, when he was walking on a midsummer night in a forest near Paris and chanced upon a group of sixty men and women dancing around some ancient megaliths. These midsummer night dancers turned out to be an occult society called T.H.L., based on rue Chapon, Paris. The only thing that gives this group a vague resemblance to Palladism, however, is the fact that they venerate Baphomet (which could be found just as well on the pages of Éliphas Lévi) and that their leader is called "the black Pope" (by Geyraud). If they really existed at all, they seem to have been, as far as one can gather from Geyraud's description, some sort of Crowleyan proto-Wiccans.[152] And with that, Geyraud's neo-Palladism dissolves into the mists of myth and mystification once again, just like its original model.[153]

THE JEWISH QUESTION

"Antisemitism in the nineteenth century was as French as the baguette," a historian of fin de siècle France has remarked.[154] Anti-Jewish attitudes were rife during the Third Republic, and the years in which the Taxil hoax reached its apogee were also those in which the Dreyfus affair burst into the open, splitting the French nation into two opposite camps. This section will delve into the relation between Taxil's mystification and the "Jewish Question." If this subject seems dragged in by the hair to the unprepared reader, this is far from being the case. From very early on, anti-Masonism and antisemitism were like twin brothers: where the former appeared, the latter was usually not far away.[155] Right after Barruel published his four-volume anti-Masonic classic, for instance, he received a mysterious letter from a person who described himself as an Italian officer from Florence called Jean-Baptiste Simonini, asking why Barruel had not made any mention of the involvement of Jews in the Great Masonic Plot he described. The letter disclosed that Mani and the Old Man on the Mountain had both been Jews and that Jews had founded Freemasonry and the Illuminati. It also described a remarkable adventure the author claimed to have had with regard to this matter. While pretending to be Jewish, he had been approached by a Piedmontese Jew who offered him great sums of money and the position of an army general, if only he would become a Freemason. Barruel, it was said, had sent this letter to the Vatican in 1806 for its official opinion on the matter: Testa, the Papal secretary, had allegedly responded that the epistle was certainly trustworthy. Although the letter was not published in print until 1879, it circulated in manuscript form before that date, influencing, among others, Joseph de Maistre.[156]

Barruel had indeed planned a fifth volume to treat the Jewish aspect of the Masonic conspiracy, but he had deliberately chosen to maintain a "profound silence" on the involvement of Jews in the anti-Christian conspiracy. "If they were to believe me, I could occasion a massacre of the Jews," he jotted down in his private papers.[157] This deficit, however, had since then been profusely compensated for. Virtually every Catholic anti-Masonic author of significance— Gougenot des Mousseaux, Fava, Meurin, Kostka, De la Rive—published works on the nefarious maneuvers of international Jewry as well. In these works, a few standard elements linked Judaism with Freemasonry. The first of these was the *religious* element. The worship of Satan and the anti-Christian ideology of Freemasonry ultimately derived from Jewish sources, according to these writers. The ancient stereotype of the Jew as "prince of black magic" was clearly an influence in this. Frequently mentioned in this respect was the Kabbalah, the esoteric system of Jewish origin that had been an important source of inspiration for nineteenth-century occultism. It also inspired authors of the Catholic reaction, but in an inverted sense. For them, it was the "metaphysics of Lucifer," a pagan deviation that had crept into Judaism from Canaanite or Chamite sources and had spawned the Talmud and the denial of Christ by today's Jewry.[158] Various readings were given of how Freemasonry had become infected with this religion of the devil. Some authors, following Freemasonry's own origin myth, held that Freemasonry had been imbued with it from its earliest beginnings with the temple builders of Solomon; others speculated that the Templars might have adopted the Kabbalah during their campaigns in the Holy Land or that the Jews and their nefarious system had only started to infiltrate Freemasonry after the Revolution.[159]

The second theme that linked Judaism and Freemasonry was the *political* element. For the authors we mentioned, Freemasonry was the tool, or one of the tools, that the Jews utilized to seek world domination, the "covert organisation" of "militant Judaism."[160] It had been the Jews who had animated the conjuration of the *philosophes* in the eighteenth century; it had been they who had organized the French Revolution through their Masonic ground troops; it was they who were still spreading liberalism and secularization throughout Europe. Their purpose in this, according to some, was bringing about the legal emancipation of the Jews. Had it not indeed been the armies of the French Revolution and Napoleon who first brought liberty and equality to Jews throughout Europe?[161] For most authors, however, the ultimate aim of the Jewish conspiracy was not this limited. Rather, its ultimate purpose was the complete dechristianization of Europe and the dismantling of Europe's Christian civilization. For those defending "outraged tradition," the Jews thus came to hold hands with Freemasons as archetypical representatives of the Western Revolution.[162]

One of the first authors to bring together these elements was Gougenot des Mousseaux, whom we encountered earlier as a prominent Catholic antagonist of spiritism and occultism. In 1869, he published *Le Juif, le judaïsme et la judaïsation des peuples chrétiens* ("The Jew, Judaism, and the Judaization of the Christian Nations"), a book that has been called "the Bible of modern antisemitism."[163] In its six hundred pages, Gougenot des Mousseaux denounced the Jew as "the representative of the spirit of darkness on earth" and "the true Grand Master of Freemasonry," which had reserved six of the nine places in its secret Supreme Council for Jews. Éliphas Lévi, "the perfidious Kabbalist foe of the Church" with his "Judaic nom de guerre," was again frequently cited to support this thesis.[164] Using the Enlightenment philosophers to pave the way and the Freemasons as their pawns, the Jews had organized the French Revolution, and they continued to organize new revolutions, in order to prepare for the coming of the Jewish Messiah, the Antichrist. "Therefore, and according to important confessions that numerous enemies of the Church have made, those antique Jews who Éliphas [Lévi] calls our fathers in science, and who Christ calls the prodigy of the Demon (*vos ex patre diabolo*)—that is to say: the fathers of the demonic church—have as offspring the elect of Judah in which we are obliged to recognize the philosophers, the learned doctors, and the mysterious superiors of 'the great Kabbalist association known in Europe under the name of Freemasonry,' which has as its aim the ruin of the Christian Church and of Christian civilization."[165]

In other respects as well, Gougenot des Mousseaux was epoch-making in antisemitism. While retaining age-old accusations of human sacrifice and cannibalism, at the same time, he brought nineteenth-century antisemitism up to date, coupling the Jewish peril with the disturbing new realities of modernization and industrialization. The new steam transportation, for example, was part of Judaism's plan for world domination, making the fast movement of Jewish people possible. But their instruments of control par excellence were money, banking, and the press.[166] This amalgam would have a sad and sinister future on the European continent. Increasingly, Jews would be designated as a symbol for capitalism, globalization, and modernity.[167]

As the Masonic conspiracy theory itself had been, the introduction of the Jewish element in the great plot was a concoction of Christian, and primarily Roman Catholic, authors. After Gougenot des Mousseaux's book, it became a near-permanent feature in the repertoire of Catholic anti-Masonism. Bishop Fava, who maintained that Freemasonry and other secret societies were governed by perhaps "half a dozen individuals," mentioned the Jewish hypothesis in passing, declaring it "plausible."[168] The indefatigable Clarin de la Rive devoted a whole book to the question, meant "to demonstrate the intimate and secular rapports that exist between Jews and Freemasons and to establish with what ingenuity the former serve themselves of the latter to accomplish their base works that are as Kabbalistic as they are Satanic."[169] The overall spirit of this literature can perhaps best be tasted by partaking of *La Franc-Maçonnerie, Synagogue de Satan*, the book by Léon Meurin, the bishop of Saint Louis, who had gathered much of his wisdom on the true nature of Freemasonry while sitting at the feet of Taxil. The title of his book—"Freemasonry, the Synagogue of Satan"—was meant to be taken literally. The work was a dense volume on the Jewish, antisocietal, and Satanic character of Freemasonry, illustrated with diagrams and schemata that gave it a semblance of sober science, with as a central theme the bishop's conviction that the "Jewish Kabbalah" was the true philosophical basis of the Masonic edifice. Meurin expressed the pious hope that as a result of his exposure of their slavery to the "Pharisees," non-Jewish Masons would open their eyes and renounce their allegiance to the Masonic organization.[170] Toward the end of the book, his tone becomes more apocalyptic and grim. Looking into the future, Meurin writes:

It would not be the first time that we will see the wrath of the people, too long restrained, erupt and fall to regrettable acts of violence against the Jews. The Governments who are not yet completely taken hostage by the Sect, should take precautions against this menacing danger. It would be wrong not to envisage this with all required foresight.

But what to do?

The expulsion of the Jews of one country means a lack of charity and justice towards the neighbouring countries, on which one lets loose this voracious vermin. It is also too hard a measure against those among the Jews who are not to blame for the crimes of the daring handful that exploits the nations by way of Freemasonry. It would be enough, we think, to forbid to Jews the profession of banker, merchant, journalist, teacher, doctor, and apothecary. It does seem just, moreover, to proclaim the gigantic riches of certain bankers national property, because it cannot be allowed that a single man can amass by financial manoeuvres in a whiff of time, a fortune that exceeds that of kings, a truly *national* amount of capital, and thus deplete the country and the nation that offer him their hospitality.[171]

In conclusion, Meurin also addressed the Jews directly, offering some undoubtedly well-meaning advice to the members of this stubborn nation who continued to close their eyes to the evident truth of Christianity. "Do not expect, o Jews, that you can escape the calamity that threatens you once more! Your deicide nation has at this moment reached one of its apogees of power and prosperity that repeat themselves oft in your history, and that has to end, as always, in a great national tragedy. The day that crushes you, will see the dawn of a vital expansion of the Church, your victim, such as history has never seen before."[172]

Sentiments like these were not merely the domain of abstruse writers in obscure books. They were increasingly becoming a matter of mass politics in fin de siècle Europe. Some of the proponents of antisemite ideology used (or rather misapplied) the newest insights in biology and Darwinism to argue that the Jews were representatives of a different racial group that surreptitiously endangered the purity and supremacy of the superior nations of the West. All of them held to variants of conspiracy thinking that attributed an important and devious role to "the Jews" (or a select inner core among their number) as hidden actors behind the scenes of European or global politics.[173] In France, the vitriolic publicist Édouard Drumont (1844–1917) played an important role in this respect with his untiring and eloquent advocacy of the opinion that his country was secretly governed by Jews. Although Drumont was a Catholic by faith, politically and ideologically he can more properly be considered a nationalist.

While the Roman Catholic Church steadfastly rejected the racial variant of antisemitism as incompatible with official dogma, ultramontane and intransigent Catholics were certainly not reluctant to sing their own versions of the great antisemitic song. *La Croix*, France's largest Catholic newspaper, proudly declared itself to be "the most anti-Jewish paper of France, the periodical that carries the Cross, sign of horror to the Jews." It had no inhibitions about sporting front-page headlines saying "Do Not Buy from Jews."[174] As with the Catholic authors we quoted, alarmist theories against Jews were almost invariably coupled with allegations against that other powerful enemy, Freemasonry, with both merging into one giant conspiracy "of Masonic Judaism or of Judaic Masonry (ad libitum)," to quote the words of yet another Catholic journalist.[175]

The new, antimodernist, and anticapitalist variant of antisemitism was also wholeheart-edly embraced by the Catholic social and corporatist movement.[176] This had been the other side of the coin to the new Catholic commitment to the social question that had found expression in *Rerum Novarum* and the Catholic worker organizations. Catholic mass organizations tried to mobilize Catholic workers by promising social justice, on the one hand, and pointing out the enemy, on the other hand, appealing to the age-old prejudices against Jews held by many of the lower class. This was by no means a phenomenon restricted to France. In Austria (another prominent motherland of antisemitism), the "Christian Socialists" under Karl Lueger (1844–1910) willfully and successfully exploited antisemitic sentiments to win lower- and middle-class votes. In Italy, the Jesuit *Civiltà cattolica* took the lead in spreading the idea of the Jewish-Masonic Plot and the secret Jewish World Government.[177]

A few celebrity cases were indicative of the antisemite tensions that were rampant in fin de siècle Western Europe. The German Rhineland saw ritual murder allegations brought to court in Xanten in 1891 and 1892. In France, the nation was brought virtually to the brink of civil war because of the Dreyfus affair, the most notorious eruption of antisemitism during the fin de siècle. Albert Dreyfus (1859–1935) had been the first Jewish officer to become a member of the French general staff, when he was arrested in 1894 on charges of espionage and high treason, condemned on trumped-up evidence, and whisked away to infamous Devil Island. This cause célèbre caused great upheaval, especially when the naturalist writer Émile Zola took up his pen in defense of Dreyfus in 1898 with a famous open letter to the French presidency entitled "J'accuse." While Republicans and Left-wing politicians gradu-ally rallied in favor of the banished officer, royalists, clericals, and right-wing nationalists made common cause in denouncing Dreyfus. Here again, antisemitism and anti-Masonism found each other in an inextricable embrace, helped by the fact that Dreyfus was not only a Jew but also a Freemason.[178]

What was Léo Taxil's position in all this? Taxil had certainly not been an antisemite before his "conversion" to Roman Catholicism. From his time in juvenile detention, there exists a manuscript he wrote on religion in which he concluded that for those who could not do without some system of belief, Judaism might be the best option: "You will be clos-est to the truth."[179] Even after his transition to Catholicism, Jews remained conspicuously absent among the groups Taxil targeted with his publications. His reluctance in this might have been enhanced by his confrontation with Édouard Drumont, the prima donna of French antisemitism. In 1890, both authors stood as candidates for a place in the Municipal Council for the Parisian district Gros Caillou: Drumont as an antisemite candidate, Taxil as a representative for the clerical party.[180] Unsurprisingly, Taxil was swept from the field by his immensely popular opponent, and he retorted by writing and publishing an insulting "psychological study" of Drumont. The latter responded in kind with a long article in which he rhetorically asked how the Church could possibly ally itself with a former blasphemer and pornographer like Taxil, citing extensively from Taxil's semipornographic novel *The Secret Loves of Pope Pius IX*. Sarcastically, he added: "I hope the Jews, reduced to employing such a defender, have paid that wretch what is due to him."[181]

Drumont also accused Taxil of hypocrisy. Before the elections, he argued, the "Catholic" publicist had proved himself significantly less philosemitic. He cited an article from *Le*

France chrétienne, where Taxil had spoken about "Masonic Jewry," and some more instances from Taxil's own periodical *La Petite Guerre* containing derogatory phrases about the Jews of Vienna.[182] These citations were doubtlessly genuine, and *La Petite Guerre* had included some mildly antisemitic utterances by other authors as well. Yet they had remained the exception rather than the rule. In general, Taxil held himself strangely silent on the Jewish Question.[183] That at least was the opinion of a large part of his readers. Drumont and Taxil themselves might be mortal enemies, but their readership was roughly identical. The correspondence of Taxil that is left to us contains numerous letters from parish priests and other Catholics imploring him to provide more elucidation on the Jewish share in the great anti-Christian plot. In another tone of voice, Taxil's friend Father R. Fesch urged him to tone down his attacks on Drumont. "Considering Drumont," the priest wrote, "do not write against him. The French clergy, who hold him in high esteem, will turn their back on you. You should consider this, believe me. There are still a lot of people out there who have not come back on their false ideas on your account: could this not be the way to convince them? I'll say it again, it is a friend who is talking to you, after having thoroughly reflected on the matter."[184]

This supplication suggests a firm opinion concerning the Jewish Question on the part of Taxil. In his publication contra Drumont, he had written that the greatest enemies of the Church (Luther, Voltaire) had also been the greatest antisemites, and he proceeded to express his compassion for the victims of the Russian pogroms in terms that have stricken at least one historian as sincere.[185] Nevertheless, somewhere around 1892, Taxil evidently ceded to the pressure put upon him. In one of the most grotesque turns of an already sufficiently grotesque history, "Docteur Bataille" sternly admonished Taxil from the pages of *Le Diable au XIXᵉ siècle* on the subject of the Jews:

> A great fault of Mr. Léo Taxil, of whom I am far from sharing certain points of view, has been that he never carried his investigations to the field of Masonic Jewry. He would have discovered salient facts on the Lemmis, the Bleichroeders, the Cornelius Hertzs, and the other Israelite Freemasons who have succeeded in obtaining an important role in the leadership of the sect. Mr. Drumont, for his part, has been more astute, and it is probable that a false pseudo-brother, in whom he would quickly have scanned the Jew, would not be able to fool him.
>
> The secret agents of Lemmi, for the rest, are easy to recognise: in no matter what country, they possess, I repeat it, one distinctive mark that exposes them, for those that pay a bit of attention or keep themselves informed: *there is not one of them who isn't a Jew.*[186]

The second volume of *Le Diable au XIXᵉ siècle* included a complete chapter of almost a hundred pages on "The Jews in Freemasonry."[187] Taxil's later publications under the names of Margiotta and Vaughan also featured occasional rallies on the Jewish theme, mostly centered on the figure of Lemmi, whom Taxil graced with the ultimate insult of being a *convert* to Judaism.[188] When Paul Rosen started to denounce his creations, Taxil did not shrink from sidetracking his competitor by consistently calling attention to his Jewish origins.

The most probable explication of this volte-face is simply that Taxil was afraid he would lose his readers when he refused to meet their expectations about Jewish involvement in the Masonic plot. But in the strange world of Taxil, where every phrase is open to reversed interpretation, and vice versa, another explanation might also be valid. Perhaps Taxil was trying to make a virtue of a necessity and did plan to entangle Drumont and other apostles of antisemitism in his mystification so that they would be ridiculed as well on the moment of his final exposure. A letter that Margiotta showed to a journalist after his desertion of Taxil suggests this. It contained detailed instructions on how to lure Drumont into the trap of the Taxil mystification by using Margiotta as a decoy. "Yesterday, I received pages 161 to 224 [of *Le Palladisme*], in well-printed quires," Taxil wrote to Margiotta on 19 September 1895. "I have immediately sent them, with express post, to Drumont, in Brussels: but I have indicated as sender 'Dispatch from Delhomme and Briguet, publishers at Paris.' In this way, you can write to him that you have let them be sent to him, and call his attention to the question of the role of the Jews in Masonry, on which he'll find some initial explications in the pages that he receives today."[189] This plan to set up Drumont failed, but it might give us a glimpse of Taxil's personal attitude in the matter. The master impostor, it seems, was hoping to get his revenge on his antisemite rival after all, if not through the front door, then through the back.

Léo Taxil was not the only one walking the tightrope concerning the Jewish Question. The Papacy, in a different way, was busy trying to do the same. Pius IX had not refrained from openly insulting Jews on occasion.[190] Leo XIII, who was anxious to establish the position of the Papacy as a moral power and global arbiter, showed considerably more circumspection in public. While he continued, as we have seen, his predecessor's hard-line stance against Freemasonry, he did not issue any official or semi-official statements against Jews. On the contrary, his rare public utterances on the "Jewish Question" suggested a break with the attitudes of his predecessor. On August 3, 1892, the pope granted an interview to the socialist and feminist journalist Sévérine, which the popular French daily *Le Figaro* published the following day under the title "Pope Leo XIII and Antisemitism." In the interview—which came to be known as the "Encyclical for a Pence"—he expressed strong disapproval of any "war of religion" or "war of the races." All people, regardless of ethnicity, Leo XIII argued, had a common descent from Adam and were equal to the grace of God. The pope solemnly vowed to provide the protection of the Papacy to the Jews should popular violence erupt against them. Meanwhile, however, the Church could not help to prefer its own children over those that obstinately preferred to remain in a state of impiety, and it also had a duty to protect the defenseless sheep of its flock against those that sought to oppress them—especially through the "scourge of money." "They want to defeat the Church and dominate the people by way of money!" Leo XIII lashed out, "Neither the Church nor the people will let this happen!" When his interviewer asked him if he was referring to the "grand Jews" with this remark, the Pope skillfully evaded the question.[191]

There was more than a whiff of Meurin and Gougenot des Mousseaux in this. Notwithstanding the fact that we cannot be certain of the personal opinion of Leo XIII, and that the official representatives of the Church maintained a prudent silence on the matter in public, the utterances of the Vatican behind the scenes suggest a certain picture. They make clear that the line of Pius IX was maintained regarding the Jews, especially in connection with the Masonic conspiracy—and also that the Papacy, by the final decade of the nineteenth century, had firmly chosen to place its bets on the popular Catholic movement, including the antisemitism that was an inevitable ingredient of it.[192] Some even expressed the conviction that this would bring many a lost sheep back into the fold of the Church and considered it the best card to play "if one wants the Catholic movement, and thus the Church, to regain her lost hegemony over society."[193] Thus, in Austria, the Vatican came out in support of the antisemite Christian Socialists, and it was only due to the personal intervention of Leo XIII that their leader Karl Lueger was eventually allowed to become mayor of Vienna.

Although the innermost convictions of people will always remain beyond the pale of the historian, these silent nods in favor of anti-Jewish demagogy were clearly not just a matter of cold-blooded political maneuvering. They also reflected sincere beliefs that could be found up to the highest echelons of the Church. In his missives to Rome, the Papal nuncio in Paris, Monsignor Lorenzelli, often spoke of the "judeo-masonic war" against Christianity; Cardinal Rampolla's answers testified a tacit acknowledgment of its existence. Vatican attitudes become especially clear in its reaction to a scandal in Austria-Hungary, where the Papal nuncio had praised a Jewish benefactor of Catholic workers, raising a considerable brouhaha from the ranks of the Catholic antisemites. The Vatican responded by sending an official reprimand to its nuncio from the hand of Monsignor Boccali, the secretary of Leo XIII. "It is too well known that the Masonic sect is nowadays intimately linked to the Jewish sect, to the detriment of the Catholic Church," Boccali wrote. "Knowing this, it would have been more prudent for the official representative of the Holy See to have abstained from these words of eulogy."[194] Even in 1900, when the Cardinal of Westminster asked the Pope for an official rebuttal of the ritual murder allegations against Jews, the Vatican answer was a staunch refusal. The existence of these facts was held to be "historically certain": moreover, it would be absurd to expect the Papacy to defend the Jews, the dominators of Europe![195]

By analogy, Vatican politics regarding antisemitism might teach us much about the Holy See's possible involvement with Taxil's anti-Masonic campaign. In both cases, we are confronted with a Papacy that kept its distance in its official manifestations, but seemed keenly interested to profit from "spontaneous" eruptions of antisemitic or anti-Masonic sentiments in the background. Most clearly in the case of Catholic antisemitism, but probably also in the case of Taxil, the Vatican was not afraid to give a discreet hint to key people in the hierarchy and in lay organizations every once in a while in order to point them in the right direction. In both cases, there is nothing to suggest that the inner convictions of the Vatican were widely different from those of its flock; yet in both cases, political objectives were prominently involved as well. The mechanics of attribution and ostracism served to enhance the morale, cohesion, and popular appeal of the Catholic movement.

In France, more particularly, warlike rhetoric against Freemasons and Jews can be placed within a wider effort to paste together a Catholic community that was chronically divided as a result of the Papal policy of *ralliement*. Here, the designation of a minority enemy might also function as a bridge to other conservative forces in the country's political spectrum, which, in turn, might bring about the alliance between Catholics and conservatives the Vatican hoped for, and thus the transformation of France into a political ally of the Holy See. With regard to these last-mentioned objectives, the Vatican proved to have placed its bets on a pair of Trojan horses. Taxil first radicalized the Catholic allegations against Freemasons until they became ridiculous and then turned the tables on the Catholics, inflicting severe damage on their public reputation. The Dreyfus affair—initially hailed by the nunciature as a god-given opportunity that would make clear to France the real extent of the Jewish conspiracy—eventually backfired against Vatican interests even more dramatically.[196] Dreyfus's ultimate acquittal in 1898 was a triumph for Republican and Left-wing France, and the upheaval created by the scandal was instrumental in bringing the fiercely anticlerical Combes government to power, which broke off relations with the Vatican and continued the French secularization drive with even more vigor than its predecessors.

BY WAY OF CONCLUSION

What was the net result of Taxil's imposture? A definite answer to this question is hard to give. We can, however, tentatively discern a few sets of repercussions that followed the end of Taxil's adventure in 1897 like ripples in a pond. The first ripple was probably exactly what Taxil had intended with his deconstruction of Catholic attribution. The international press had a field day dwelling on the gullibility and paranoia of Catholicism. Liberal representatives of the German Reichstag invoked the affair to point out once again the dangers of confessional education.[197] Ultramontane anti-Masonism itself fell prey to disarray and utter disorientation in the immediate aftermath of Taxil's self-exposure. Rightly considering himself too deeply implicated, Amand-Joseph Fava, bishop of Grenoble, submitted his resignation to Rome (which was refused).[198] The second international congress of Catholic anti-Masonism, originally planned for 1898, would never take place.

This first ripple of discomfiture, however, proved of extremely temporary nature. Although Taxil had confidently stated at the end of his press conference that he had effectively murdered his own creation of Palladism, this statement immediately turned out to be premature. A number of Catholic anti-Masonists found themselves unable to accept the nonexistence of their beloved Diana Vaughan, the converted Grand Mistress of Luciferianism. They took resort to the first reflex of any believer in conspiracy theories: to explain the unacceptable by designing a new conspiracy. Miss Vaughan, they suggested, had certainly existed, but had been—physically—assassinated by Taxil.[199] Diana's former publisher, Alfred Pierret, was of this opinion, suspecting behind this foul deed the hand of the past subscribers to *Le Palladium régénérée et libre*, who had wanted to prevent her from revealing more damaging facts on their secret activities.[200] Others maintained that Miss Vaughan was still alive but had returned to the religion of her fathers and disappeared once more into the mysterious netherworld of international Luciferianism. Abel Clarin de la Rive—who had been so disoriented by the collapse of the Taxilian edifice that he had sought guidance from a clairvoyant—eventually adopted this view. In October 1897, he even reported that Vaughan had been sighted in England.[201] Up to the 1930s, certain circles of Catholic anti-Masonism were still discussing the possible existence of the elusive Grand Mistress.[202]

Many more were confident that, once again, the machinations of Freemasonry were behind the whole affair. Already in the immediate aftermath of Taxil's press conferences,

Catholic journalists had remarked on the "strong atmosphere of the lodge and the secret police" that had hung around the final episode of the mystification.[203] Why, for example, had the metropolitan police appeared instantly on the scene to protect Taxil when he left the building? The whole thing had been set up by Freemasonry from the beginning, with the express purpose of holding Catholicism up to ridicule. In this way, even Taxil's deconstruction of Catholic conspiracy thinking could be incorporated into the Grand Masonic Plot. But this was not all. Freemasonry, it was speculated, had also used Taxil to divert public attention from genuine diabolical practices that were going on within the fraternity. By mixing real facts with patent absurdities, Taxil had raised a smoke screen to cover up the former and make sure that every serious discussion about them was predestined to falter into hilarity.[204] For Catholic investigators not deceived by this ploy, this meant that many facts about Satanism could be salvaged from the wreckage of Taxil's constructions.

Amongst the adherents of this thesis was J.-K. Huysmans. In an interview immediately after the explosion of the Taxil affair, he declared that a "swindle of somebody from the south of France" by no means proved the nonexistence of Satanism and Luciferianism, and he referred to the publication of Bishop Meurin (obviously unaware of the origin of the latter's information).[205] In his last substantial work of literature, a pseudo-hagiography of Lydwine of Schiedam that appeared in 1901, Huysmans painted a sinister picture of the Europe he was living in, with most of its countries dominated by the "Jewish vermin" and the "crocodiles of the lodges." These in turn were under the command of the "cult of Lucifer," whose existence, "notwithstanding interested denials," was "an undeniable, absolute, certain fact."[206] In this opinion, Huysmans was followed like a shadow by his protégé Jules Bois, that other self-styled expert on occultism, who incidentally converted to Roman Catholicism a few years later. In *Le monde invisible* ("The Invisible World"), Bois boasted that he had seen through the setup of "Taxil and doctor Hachs [*sic*], also known as Bataille" from the very start, but that among the "unbelievable and seemingly crazy legends" of the duo, true facts had been mingled in. These facts apparently included the existence of both Satanism and Luciferianism; the worship of Baphomet by adherents of the latter; and also, "according to documents considerably less reliable," the existence of a statue of Lucifer in the shape of a winged young man subduing the crocodile of monarchy and papacy; the location of Charleston as seat of Lucifer's most important sanctuary; and the position of Albert Pike as the "most recent reformer" of the Luciferian sect.[207]

Both Huysmans and Bois were undoubtedly instrumental in keeping many elements of Taxil's mystification in circulation. Other authors would continue in their tracks, some of whom we will meet in the next chapter.[208] But the rumor of Palladism, one suspects, was to a great degree liable to survive on its own. While the newspaper clippings on Taxil's final confession disappeared into the archives, the anti-Masonic books written by him and his epigones remained on the shelves of libraries and Catholic institutions. Even today, Taxilian inventions sometimes surface in the ultraconservative milieu of sedevacantist Catholics, and also, more surprisingly perhaps, in anti-Masonic publications against Freemasonry by extremist evangelical and Islamic groups.[209] Thus one can suddenly see Lévi's Baphomet and Pike's "secret instructions" reappear in a Christian comic book warning against the demonic danger of Freemasonry, with a footnote to

Clarin de la Rive's *La Femme et l'Enfant dans la Franc-Maçonnerie Universelle* at the bottom of the page.[210]

There can be no doubt, however, that these were and are minority views, held only by tiny groups of extremists. The majority of Catholic anti-Masonists silently abandoned the explicit Satanist hypothesis after Taxil's deceit came to light. The notion of devil worship by Freemasons was henceforth reduced to suggestive asides, as it had been before Taxil came on the scene. Yet this by no means signified the end of the idea of the Great Masonic Plot. After Taxil, Catholic anti-Masonism returned to its original hypothesis of a secret political and ideological conspiracy of Masons against "Christian society" through the triple means of secularizing governments, big money, and revolutionary agitation. The first four decades of the twentieth century would see the heyday of a Catholic anti-Masonism propagating the idea of a global Judeo-Masonic plot.[211]

Nor would this concept remain the exclusive prerogative of Catholics for long. The mobilization of the masses by anticapitalist and corporatist ideas, hierarchical authoritarianism, and attribution of societal ills to minority groups proved a combination that could also be put to work by other political movements that fed on discontent with the Western Revolution. The only thing they needed to do was to replace the explicit Roman Catholic and ultramontane framework of their Catholic predecessors with other, usually nationalist allegiances. Already at the fin de siècle, as we have seen, the anti-Masonic theme was taken up by nonconfessional politicians like Drumont and later by the nationalist Action Française.[212] And it was from Catholic antisemite propagators in Vienna that a commercially unsuccessful painter named Adolf Hitler adopted the idea of a Judeo-Masonic-Marxist conspiracy in the years before the First World War. An occasional turn of phrase in Hitler's autobiographical *Mein Kampf* still betrays the religious roots of his conspiracy theories: for instance, when he claimed he was "defending the handiwork of the Lord" by sending the Jew "back to Lucifer."[213]

Seen from this perspective, it appears possible that the overall result of Taxil's venture was the opposite of what he intended. As a result of causing Catholic anti-Masonists to strip their allegations of extreme religious elements such as Satan worship and diabolic apparitions, the adoption of their ideas by nonconfessional movements was facilitated. At the same time, the anti-Masonic propaganda he successfully disseminated during the previous twelve years must necessarily have left some residue in the minds of ordinary Catholics, preparing them to believe the worst of Freemasons and their allies.[214] In this way, Taxil may unintentionally have cooperated in laying a few of the sleepers for the ideological railroad tracks that would eventually lead to the great genocide of the twentieth century. "They will end up by cutting our throats," the Jewish banker Rothschild had already predicted during the antisemitic commotions of the fin de siècle.[215] These words would prove to be prophetic.

Es ist etwas Wahres daran, daß wir alle Satans Kinder sind.

STANISLAW PRZYBYSZEWSKI, *Satans Kinder*, Abs. I, Kap. II

Intermezzo 3

Nineteenth-Century Religious Satanism: Fact or Fiction?

WERE RELIGIOUS SATANISTS active during the nineteenth century? In a broad variety of publications—ranging from personal memoirs to academic works, from pulp books to monographs on Satanism—the firm conviction can be found that underground groups of Satanists were operating during this period; and even, in the words of one historian, "that this perversion seems to have flourished."[1] On closer inspection, all these statements, if provided with supporting evidence at all, turn out to derive eventually from the publications of Huysmans, or from those of Taxil and the wider repertory of anti-Masonic propaganda. In chapter 4, we saw that Huysmans did not have any first-person knowledge of actually existing Satanist groups. In the extensive personal correspondence that the French writer left to us, nowhere is a hint of evidence in this direction found. For his ideas regarding a widespread practice of religious Satanism, Huysmans relied mostly on Boullan, who can be summarily dismissed as a reliable witness; Boullan, in his turn, retrieved much of his information from the equally unreliable Vintras. The fabricated stories spread by Taxil and comparable artists of misinformation can obviously not be admitted as evidence either. Up to now, other proof for a substantial movement of religious Satanism in the nineteenth century has not been forthcoming. The idea that such an underground movement existed can thus be referred to the domain of legend.

This does not exclude the possibility that isolated individuals or groups were practicing religious Satanism during the nineteenth century. It is impossible, for all practical purposes, to prove that something did *not* exist. All we can say with certainty, is that the assertions in the available literature regarding the actual existence of religious Satanism during this period do not stand up to critical scrutiny.[2] It is very well possible, however, that new evidence may be uncovered in the future for hitherto unknown or undetected religious Satanists.

As a matter of fact, two possible cases of exactly such an isolated religious Satanism, both dating from the very end of the nineteenth and the threshold of the twentieth century, have recently been presented to the scholarly community by the Swedish historian Per Faxneld. The first of these is the Polish author Stanislaw Przybyszewski (1868–1927), a now largely forgotten Decadent and Expressionist writer who had been a figure of some note in Polish, German, and Scandinavian avant-garde circles of the fin de siècle (he befriended August Strindberg and Edvard Munch).[3] Przybyszewski was a prolific writer of novels, essays, and prose poems, mostly in German, and in many of these works, Satanism played a substantial role. As had been the case with many of his contemporaries, Przybyszewski's source of inspiration in this had been his reading of Huysmans, as he freely admitted.[4] One of the first works of the Polish author in which Satan played a prominent part was the novel *Satans Kinder* ("Satan's Children"), which appeared in 1897, the same year in which Taxil unmasked his Palladism hoax. In the vein of Dostoyevsky's *Demons*, it tells about a small group of nihilist anarchists who plot to overthrow the established order in a German town by burning down vital edifices like the town hall and a factory. The central character in the plot is a young man named Gordon, the most radical of the conspirators, who is not interested in building a better world, but rather promulgates destruction for its own sake. In a significant scene in the book, he seems to confess his belief in Satan, "because Satan is older than God"; although he denies that he is a "Palladist," he declares to know "the sect very well" and to agree with its "essential principles."[5]

In Gordon and his love for wanton destruction, Przybyszewski seems to have attempted to give a description of Huysmans's secret Satanists "aspiring to destroy the universe and reign over the ruins"—but this time, significantly, from the inside out. In his description of these nihilist Satanists, he is not unambiguously negative. Classic elements from Romantic Satanism reappear: the "children of Satan" from the title, for instance, are defined in compassionate terms as "everyone who has fear, everyone who is desperate, who gnashes his teeth in powerless fury, everyone who is on the way to prison, everyone who is hungry and is humiliated, the slave and the syphilis-stricken gentleman, the whore and the pregnant maiden left by her lover, the convict and the thief, the writer without fame and the actor who is whistled from the stage."[6] Elsewhere, Gordon makes the ultimate Romantic equation and defines his deity simply as one's self—which is understood by him, in contrast to the more collective Romantic concept of "Humanity," in a strictly individualist way.[7] Nor does it suffice to draw a sharp dividing line between characters like Gordon and their author. Przybyszewski was decidedly Left-wing himself: as Faxneld argues, many ideas that he put into the mouth of Satanists like Gordon were repeated as his own in his nonfiction works, which seem to form a continuum with his novels.[8]

One of these nonfiction works appeared in 1900 and was entitled *Die Synagoge Satans* ("The Synagogue of Satan").[9] It was clearly inspired by and partly based on Jules Bois's *Le Satanisme et la Magie*, and it shared a similar ambiguity toward its subject.[10] It opened with a discussion of Satan that closely followed Bois in distinguishing several manifestations of the fallen angel. As "Satan-Thot," he was the origin of (esoteric) knowledge and the "Father of Science"; as "Satan-Pan," he was the embodiment of nature and "earthly beauty"; as "Satan-Satyr" or "Satan-Phallus," he was the god of sexuality.[11] Like Lévi had argued about the "magical agency," Przybyszewski claimed that Satan's powerful force could only be "beschwören" (a German word that means both to invoke and to control or subdue) by a disciplined elite of the intellectually advanced. When the masses tried to do this, the result was only free play for the lower instincts.[12] A particular example of the latter could be seen in early modern witchcraft, which was described by Przybyszewski as "horrid up to bestiality," with added graphic details to match. The witch persecutions, he maintained, had been a legitimate form of self-defense on the part of society: although Przybyszewski admitted that innocent people had died, the majority of his estimate of eight million executed witches had not been put to death without reason.[13]

Information about these practices in his own days was scarce, the Polish writer continued. His most important source for contemporary forms of Satanism was once again Huysmans; Przybyszewski explicitly referred to "his immortal *Là-Bas*" and to Huysmans's introduction to the book of "Jules Blois." After making cursory mention of the Taxil hoax, Przybyszewski followed the latter in his assertion that the "sect of Satan-worshippers" was divided in two factions nowadays: first, the Luciferians or Palladists, whose doctrine amounted to a simple reversal of Roman Catholicism, with Lucifer replacing "Adonai" as the good god ("it must remain an open question in which relation exactly they stand to Italian Freemasonry," Przybyszewski added); second, Satanism proper, or the veneration of the fallen angel as a representative of evil.[14] "Leaving aside purely artistic additions," *Là-Bas* remained, of course, "a first class document" for the practices of the latter group.[15]

It is evident from this description that Przybyszewski did not consider himself part of or attracted to these Satanist movements. Nevertheless he and his circle styled themselves on occasion as Satanists—we will return to this in the next paragraph—and this is one of the most important reasons for Faxneld to consider him as such as well. In addition, Faxneld argues, Przybyszewski developed a more or less coherent philosophy or spirituality in which Satan played a major symbolic role, amounting to "what is likely the first attempt ever to construct a more or less systematic Satanism."[16] Interestingly enough, moreover, Przybyszewski was probably the first to connect Satanism with both the philosophy of Nietzsche and social Darwinism, two strands of thought that would come to play a prominent role in later religious Satanism. Although he professes his contempt for Nietzsche as ultimately bourgeois, Gordon in *Satans Kinder* can be seen as a living example of Nietzsche's *Übermensch* such as Przybyszewski might have understood him: somebody who is free from all traditional morality and, by the time the novel ends, also liberated from the restraints of pity or petty love for the human "canary birds" of this world. In *Die Synagoge Satans*, Nietzsche is explicitly connected with Satan as part of a catalogue of those who bring liberty under the aegis of the fallen angel: "In Satan's name did Nietzsche teach the revaluation of all values; in his name the anarchist dreams of reshaping the world of laws; in his name, the artist creates."[17] This panegyric reflects Przybyszewski's real-life opinion about the "Philosopher with the Hammer," of whom he was an ardent and early admirer.[18]

Like many intellectuals of his day, Przybyszewski was also deeply influenced by evolutionism and social Darwinism. But whereas most of his contemporaries used these
scientific or pseudo-scientific theories to express fashionable apprehensions regarding
"degeneration" and loss of racial strength, Przybyszewski adopted an undeniably original take on the subject. For him, it was the evolution of the mind that was most important, and in this evolution, it was precisely the mad, the neurotic, and the hypersensitive
artist that might provide the genetic variations that would lead to the new human
being of tomorrow.[19] Przybyszewski had already described his ideas regarding human
evolution in one of his first works of literature, the prose poem *Totenmesse* ("Requiem
Mass") from 1893. This publication told in a semibiblical manner how the world had
originated with "das Geslecht," a German word best translated in this context with sex
drive or libido in its broadest possible sense. "In the beginning was the libido. Nothing
outside it—everything within it."[20] In its desire to propagate and copulate, the libido
evolved into myriad life forms, until it finally spawned the brain, and within the brain,
the human soul. Although the soul, according to Przybyszewski, is the apotheosis of its
evolution, it also means a kind of suicide for the libido. Because it is self-conscious, the
soul can rise above and cut itself off from the libido, thereby creating a sphere of being
not dominated by the libido. In this way, however, the soul also spells its own end,
because biologically, life can only persist by the libido. This is the human predicament,
which is at the same time the crowning achievement and the swan song of the libidinous life-creating force. Because the soul sustains itself on the libido and the physical, and at the same time rises above it and seeks to detach itself from its limitations,
conflict between man's different drives is inevitable, and the fate of human beings,
Przybyszewski suggested, is intrinsically bound to suffering.

How systematically this complex of ideas was connected to Satan by Przybyszewski
is still insufficiently explored. The Polish author's continuing sympathy for Satan, however, is well attested. His openly declared tendencies in this direction may even have
resulted in the formation of a rudimentary group of like-minded "Satanists." After
1898, when Przybyszewski had returned to Poland, a circle of disciples gathered around
him that took on the name "Children of Satan," after his eponymous novel.[21]

As Faxneld already notes, it was Romantic, literary Satanism that provided the core
of the Satan that Przybyszewski venerated.[22] This veneration, however, was not without deep ambiguities. If we follow our earlier dissection of the Romantic Satan, it could
be said that Przybyszewski the Left-wing poet was unabashed in his enthusiasm for
Satan as the patron of liberty and as champion of the oppressed—sentiments that he,
unencumbered, managed to combine with Nietzschean elitism and social Darwinist
ethics. (The "oppressed" he chiefly talked about, in fact, were the writer and artist who
are now marginalized but contain the seed of the "new human" of tomorrow.) He was
also uninhibited in his admiration for "Satan-Thot," the father of science and of the
human drive for knowledge. More complex, however, was his relationship with Satan
as a symbol of sex and nature. This had everything to do with his ambiguous attitude
toward "das Geslecht," and, by extension, to the natural world that was dominated
by it. In some passages in *Totenmesse* and *Die Synagoge Satans*, Przybyszewski seemed
to express a positive appreciation of man's and nature's instinctive drives, and thus

of Satan's patronage of them. The libido was, after all, what sustained life and made humanity's spiritual accomplishments possible. More dominant in his works, nevertheless, was a typical fin de siècle attitude of disgust and apprehension toward the life of the instinct. In *Die Synagoge Satans*, the gruesome excesses of historical and contemporary Satanism are invariably coupled to "das Geslecht." "The libido alone is responsible for all these manifestations"; "In the abysses of the libido, everything is possible."[23] Echoing Lévi, Baudelaire, Huysmans, Bois, and many more, Przybyszewski argued that Satanism offered only one remedy for "desperate Humanity": the "delirium" of a total abandon to the libido. "That is the only Satan Paraclet: *énivrez-vous*."[24] It is clear, however, that it was in his spiritual development that Przybyszewski saw man's most important sphere of activity: the Satan of human instinct must be subdued or at least controlled by the Michael of his intellect.

Our analysis is borne out by the most explicit articulation by Przybyszewski of his Satanism, in the personal memoirs he wrote many years later during the 1920s. "To what amounted my cult of Satan?" the Polish author asked in this publication. "The spirit of refusal, the Promethean spirit, the patron and emblem of all free spirits who refuse to be subdued to the yoke of what is useful for society and allowed by lawful norm; the spirit that refuses to be enchained by a narrow, rachitic dogmatism, but strives to ever greater perfection—naturally at the expense of the ethics of officialdom—and would like to lead the spirit of humanity into the festal day of freedom; this spirit the established churches call Satan, Lucifer, Baphomet. . . . Well, it is this symbol that is adopted by artists when they crush dogmas or penetrate into the tremendously wide expanses of the human soul over which dogmatism has pronounced its strictest anathemas and interdicts."[25] In the subsequent pages, Przybyszewski mentioned or quoted a great number of classic "diabolical" authors as representatives of his Satanism, including Byron, Baudelaire, Carducci, Huysmans, and the Polish poets Juliusz Słowacki and Adam Mickiewicz. "My Satanism—that is the belief of Slowacki," he declared, "that not God, but only the human spirit can work wonders."[26] On the same page, he approvingly cited a text by Mickiewicz in which the fallen angel is represented as the first one to separate himself from the "All-Unity" of the divine and thus establish his own individuality and independence.

This suggests that the Satan Przybyszewski admired roughly corresponded to the Lucifer of Byron, that is, the human capacity to transcend the merely natural by the boundless aspirations of his spirit. In other places, however, the Polish author seems to have propagated a kind of synthesis or balance between man's dual inclinations, a marriage between libido and mind, between the natural and the spiritual. One of the domains where this marriage was possible for Przybyszewski might be that of art, which is also a seemingly redundant excretum of the libido, but in contrast to the pure world of the spirit not thought of as sterile or suicidal, "while in her the mighty pulse of the living libido, the fever-hot sperm-wave of light, the will to personal immortality quivers."[27] Przybyszewski's own Satanism, it might be superfluous to add, was also exclusively a matter of literature and art. In his memoirs, he spoke scathingly of reviewers and literati who were only able to conceive Satanism on the lines of the "stupid and rascally swindle of a Léo Taxil and his illusionary, probably completely inexistent assistant Miss Diana Vaughan."[28] His own cult of Satan, he remarked ironically, was a cult without Black Masses, mysterious rites, sadistic outrages, theft of sacramental wafers, or blood of premature babies. "What a poor, boring and prosaic Satanism!"[29] Characteristically enough, however, Przybyszewski added in an aside that he somewhat regretted to destroy the "interesting legend" of his Satanism and that he would gladly have joined a "sect" that would have put Satan, "the most glorious of God's angels," on the throne of the divinity.[30] It is hard to establish to what extent he was speaking ironically or rhetorically here and to what extent he was serious.

Much less complex and more clear-cut is the case of Carl William Hansen (1872–1936), alias Ben Kadosh. Hansen was a Danish dairy salesman from a humble background who devoted most of his time to esotericism and alchemy. An avid collector of post-order charters, he became a member of various international esoteric societies, among them Papus's Martinist Order, as well as an enthusiastic participant within a number of marginal spiritual groups in Denmark. In 1906, he published a twenty-some-page pamphlet entitled *Den ny morgens gry: erdensbygmesterens genkomst* ("The Dawn of a New Morning: The Return of the World's Master Builder"), in which he announced the establishment of a cult of Satan/Lucifer and proposed the formation of a Masonic Luciferian organization. Interested would-be Luciferians were to inquire at his home at Hjørringgade 29 in Copenhagen.[31] During the Danish census of the same year, Hansen declared himself a Luciferian by religion, making himself without doubt the first officially registered Satanist in history. A newspaper article from about the same time described how he celebrated Christmas in the Luciferian manner, honoring Baphomet rather than the "white Christ."[32]

Den ny morgens gry was written in an extremely muddled and deliberately obscure Danish, which does not really help to determine the exact nature of its author's Luciferian creed. Faxneld nevertheless has attempted a reconstruction. The central tenet of Ben Kadosh's system, as the title of his pamphlet already indicates, was the assertion that the Grand Architect of the Universe venerated in traditional Freemasonry was in reality none other than Lucifer. Judging by the way he defined this Lucifer, Kadosh appears to have been quite familiar with the ideas of Lévi. I quote part of Faxneld's paraphrase:

> The source of all life is, according to Kadosh, Lucifer's father, "that which language does not have any understandable pronounceable word for." Lucifer himself is "the expression of the unpronounceable," i.e. his father, and the Luciferian cult should be viewed as centred on "the worship and adoration of [an] eternal, hidden, mighty or omnipotent force in nature." Satan, in other words, is the vehicle of the hidden, unknowable God, and the appropriate path for man to approach this mystery beyond words. God can only be known through his vessel, Lucifer.[33]

Reading this, it seems as if Kadosh had taken Lévi's ideas to its logical conclusion. It is not hard to recognize the Kabbalist Ein-Sof in Hansen's "unpronounceable god," and Lévi's "magical agent" in his Lucifer—although Lévi, of course, had emphasized that this Luciferian agent should be mastered rather than worshipped. Unsurprisingly,

Kadosh also equates Lucifer with Pan, "the 'Sum'—or Ego—of the material nature, the creating Logon and Force!"[34] Kadosh claimed that this divinity, which was both impersonal and personal, could be invoked or evoked by proper ritual, and he seems to have performed alchemist experiments to this purpose.[35]

Both these isolated and exceptional instances of early Satanism are found exactly at the point where we would expect them: Przybyszewski's in the wake of Romantic Satanism and its later nineteenth-century successors; that of Ben Kadosh within the world of occultism, as an outgrowth of Lévian esotericism. In retrospect, it is almost surprising that it took an eccentric Dane operating as late as 1906 to bring the heterodox potential of Lévi's system to full bloom. In both cases, identification played a role of some importance. Although Kadosh distanced himself from traditional images of the Satanist as a fetus-devouring, orgy-celebrating fiend, Faxneld tentatively suggests that he derived his idea for a Masonic organization worshipping Lucifer indirectly from the publications of Taxil.[36] This hypothesis seems more than plausible to me. As a further clue, Hansen's esoteric alias of Ben Kadosh might be mentioned—the Scottish degree of Knight Kadosh was, according to Taxil's fabrications, the degree that initiated the adept to the true and secret core of Masonry, that is, the worship of Lucifer. Kadosh will have known about the fictitious character of Taxil's Palladium: this might have been the reason, one may speculate, that he proceeded to form a religious organization himself. Perhaps with Ben Kadosh, then, we have at long last found a genuine example of neo-Palladism of some sort.[37]

With Przybyszewski, matters are less unequivocal. Like the earlier Romantic Satanists, he adopted Satan as a positive symbol in a general sense, but his attitude toward Satan, as we have noted, was never free from ambiguities (as, for that matter, had been the case with the Romantic Satanists as well). The alleged practices of historic and contemporary Satanists were described by him in lurid and uncomplimentary terms. His self-designation as a Satanist may have been initially inspired by the fact that others had attributed Satanism to him because of the content of his fiction. In his memoirs, he mentions the "masses for Satan" that were rumored to be held in the bohemian circles which he frequented, and his definition of his own Satanism is introduced by a long remark about the personal stigma of Satanist that seemed attached to his person since the publication of *Die Synagoge Satans*.[38] Przybyszewski's utterances about his diabolical image were not devoid of reality: a contemporary author even published a novel that featured him as ideological instigator and real-life participant of a sect of Satanists involved in blasphemous and orgiastic rites.[39] We can recognize the familiar process of attribution and identification at work in miniature here. But the Polish author also strikes one as someone with a keen eye for nineteenth-century countercultural trends. Donning the dark mantle of the Satanist certainly was not without *chic* in the fin de siècle, just as Nietzscheanism, anarchism, and Darwinism enjoyed a certain vogue. The possibility remains that Przybyszewski's Satanism originated as a rather resilient whim of fashion that was only given a more or less sophisticated philosophical shape by the Polish author many years later because his personality had become inseparably linked to his identification as a Satanist.[40] Further research is needed to establish how complete his identification with the cause of Satan really was, and to what measure the fallen angel is systematically evoked in his publications and personal texts.

However this may be, it is clear that these lonely examples of Satanist inclinations do not amount to the significant movement of Satanism that many contemporary and later authors thought to detect in the last decades of the nineteenth century. The Luciferianism of Ben Kadosh seems to have remained a one-man affair: even his wife and two daughters declared themselves Lutherans during the Danish census of 1906.[41] Przybyszewski exerted a slightly wider influence in Polish, Scandinavian, and German avant-garde circles; but after the turn of the century, he seems to have foundered into oblivion. Faxneld does not recount what became of his "Children of Satan." The existence of these two exceptional characters thus does not notably affect our general picture of a nineteenth century that was devoid of actual Satanists. As we have already remarked in an earlier chapter, the alleged "flourishing" of Satanism in the fin de siècle primarily was a flourishing of people *talking about* Satanism.

This observation, of course, logically gives rise to the question of *why* so many people concerned themselves with Satanism in this period. What caused this peculiar obsession with the worship of Satan? A proper response to this question exceeds the bounds of this study. But a few remarks may be made, which will conveniently serve to sum up much of what I have argued in the preceding chapters.

To start with, from early in the nineteenth century, Satan had been given political, ideological, and spiritual significance as a symbolic reference point by important members of nineteenth-century counterculture. The Romantic Satanists had used Satan to propose or discuss political and religious transformation in mythological form; anarchist thinkers had employed him as a metaphor to express anticlerical or antireligious sentiments; historians like Michelet had attempted to root these positions in a reconstructed pedigree of past Satanism. In the slipstream of Romantic Satanism, occultists like Lévi had displayed attitudes toward the fallen angel that were at least partly positive. This Satanic rehabilitation remained present as a significant cultural substratum during the whole of the nineteenth century. In addition, the ideological program to which it was linked—the political, social, and religious conflicts brought about by the Western Revolution—remained relevant as well throughout this period. As a consequence, a portion of the population will certainly have been interested in, or at least not a priori dismissive of, the idea of a religious Satanism. One can detect this benevolent attitude in certain contributions to the secular and occult press, in which it was argued that a decent form of Satanism or Luciferianism should be perfectly allowable in this "age of general toleration."[42] A stronger manner of adhesion was manifested by the individuals who sought to join the Palladism fabricated by Taxil. Pierret, the publisher of the movement's bulletin, reported several such cases; perhaps a similar attempt had been made by the "few members recruited from among atheistic Masons" reported by Papus to the correspondent of *Light*, the most notable of whom, according to the occultist, was "a senator, who is a leading manufacturing chemist and Professor at the *Ecole de Medecine* of Paris."[43] More than one observer assumed that there would soon be "a large and fashionable congregation" when the worship of Lucifer would finally come out in the open.[44]

This assumption, it is true, may have been linked to a more general perception of fin de siècle society as profoundly decadent. But all the same, one gets the distinct impression that at the end of the nineteenth century a certain number of souls were ripe for a religious venture into Satanism. Apart from that, there remained the more traditional type of would-be devil worshipper who was willing to turn to Satan out of desperation because of personal misfortune—as is attested by a delightfully naïve letter sent to a Masonic lodge in Momberg, Germany, in which the writer declared himself prepared to become a Mason in order to gain riches. "I reckon one will have to give oneself to the devil (and I want to do that) and he will provide all the other things, money etc. Please write me immediately where and how I must proceed to become a member."[45]

Second, but not less important, was the continuation of the practice of attribution in the nineteenth century. In fact, the two phenomena were not altogether unconnected. As we have seen, the polemic attribution of their presumed preference for the diabolic had been a major incitement for some of the Romantic Satanists to identify themselves with Satan, and the intense preoccupation with the devil of an occultist like Lévi can doubtlessly be partly ascribed to the same factor. On the other side of the spectrum, the sympathy for the devil expressed by several proponents of the Western Revolution was construed by some (Christian) opponents as a confirmation of their worst fears. While a substratum of attribution had probably always persisted, the nineteenth century saw an unexpected resurgence of this phenomenon, particularly when the Roman Catholic Church increasingly came to organize itself as a modern political and ideological force. Although traditional suspects like Jews, "heterodox" Christians, pagan believers, (modern) magicians, and Freemasons remained the most important targets for allegations of devil worship, these allegations were now packaged in and part of a new ideological program that centered on the anxieties caused by the Western Revolution. The preoccupation with Satan was thus linked to very modern and very relevant political and social issues. First among these were the entwined processes of liberalization and secularization. More in the background, broader, equally anxiety-ridden developments were sometimes included in the discussion, such as the rise of industrialization, capitalism, and mass society.[46] Individuals or movements that promoted or were thought to promote these political and social tendencies belonged to the most explicit targets for allegations of Satanism. Toward the end of the nineteenth century, comparatively moderate, "theological" forms of attribution (e.g., Freemasons were the tools of Satan without being aware of it) were increasingly replaced by more blatant accusations of intentional adoration of the devil—a process that was partly instigated, partly exploited by "double agent" Taxil, as we saw in the previous chapters. The result of this was an apprehensive interest in the subject of Satanism among conservative Christians, particularly within ultramontane Roman Catholicism. This apprehension must have reached its peak in the years of the Diana Vaughan affair, when all the latent fears of the faithful seemed to be corroborated.

When studying the public utterances about Satanism in the fin de siècle, however, one gets the marked feeling that, for many people, fascination with the subject of Satanism did not derive from either of these crisp, ideologically motivated positions of sympathy or antipathy. Both camps, after all, encompassed only a minority of the population, especially in their more extreme variations. The keen interest in things Satanic displayed by the general public thus must have had additional grounds. Some of them may be easily surmised from the narrative in the preceding chapters. First of all, the (misguided) idea of an "ancient" cult surviving into modern times obviously gave people a thrill of gothic horror and gothic marvel. This idea of Satanism as a mysterious relict of a nebulous past was especially manifest in its depiction by Huysmans (who had become interested in Satanism as a possible escape from the "inauthenticity" of his own days, as we have seen), as well as in the different accounts given by occultist writers (a subculture displaying great fondness for secretly transmitted ancient traditions anyway). In contrast to texts from confessional sources, the actual involvement of Satan in his cult was often rationalized or skillfully left in suspense by these authors, making the descriptions much more plausible for a more or less secularized public.

In this respect, the fin de siècle attention for Satanism continued, generally speaking, the tendency that we have already discerned in the late seventeenth-century reports during or after the Affair of the Poisons: that of "demystifying" the worship of Satan into an undertaking that was, at bottom, merely human. There was a difference, though. While the seventeenth-century reports had been fact-finding missions that sought to shine unprejudiced light on a subject that was still widely considered the terrain of very real supernatural incursions, the late nineteenth-century accounts, to the contrary, meant to tickle a readership living in a world that was thoroughly *entzaubert* by offering a choice sniff of magic. In this respect, the fin de siècle Satanist obsessions obviously fitted into a wider resurgence of interest in things "spiritual" and "mysterious," which in many ways resembled the similar reaction that had become visible in Romanticism earlier in the nineteenth century.

At least as prominent in the appeal of fin de siècle stories about Satanism was the element of sex. Regardless of whether one reads the personal notes of a poet like Baudelaire, the "supernaturalist" novels of Huysmans, the occult treatises of Lévi and Guaita, the historical reconstructions of Michelet, or the publications of (pseudo)Catholic agitators like Rosen, Taxil, and Clarin de la Rive, Satanism is invariably associated with sex. This association, as we have noted several times, was no novelty. Sexually "inverted" practices had been a major ingredient of the Satanism stereotype in medieval and early modern times, and the lore and literature of this period were gratefully employed by authors like Huysmans or Guaita as a source for lurid sexual descriptions. Nevertheless one gets the impression that this element has a much more deliberate, almost autonomous role in the fin de siècle literature about Satanism. Sacrilege and Satan worship almost seem to become instruments for new varieties of sexual "perversion," instead of the other way around.

This is not to say that this sexual element is generally treated as positively in the texts from this era. Far from it. Even a writer like Michelet, who closely approaches attitudes toward carnality that have become de rigueur in Western Europe after the Sexual Revolution, sometimes betrays great anxiety about the dangers of a full unleashing of the sexual instincts. With other authors, this anxiety can be described as a downright obsession. In the depictions of women—commonly conceived as more instinctual and "animalistic" and less capable of controlling their natural urges—this fear of the incontrollable and unsettling empire of the instincts becomes particularly evident. In most cases, the association between the "lower" drives "down there," and the world of Satan and Satanism is thus not meant as a compliment, in contrast to the more bucolic treatments of this theme by some of the earlier Romantic Satanists and by other authors that continued more fully in this tradition. At the same time, the Satanist association with dark, perverse sexuality was not without its own allure, and the texts that describe Satanism invariably seem to hesitate between repulsion and attraction, sometimes ending up on one, sometimes on the other side, but always fraught with ambiguity. Of course, as any good psychologist might remark, this ambiguity had always been inherent in premodern and early modern depictions of Satanism and similar "monstrous" cults. Yet during the final decades of the nineteenth century, this ambiguity impresses one as being much more consciously evoked and much more consciously employed by authors writing about Satanism. The "joy of descending" is explicitly described as such (i.e., as a joy, but also as a descent). The fantasy of sexual fulfillment without limits and the horror of a world of moral anarchy sliding into "horrid bestiality" formed a combination that flavored much of the fin de siècle descriptions of Satanism and provided a large part of their appeal.[47]

This interest and anxiety regarding sex—although quite sufficient in itself as an explanation—were part of a broader anxiety about the moral state of society. Concern about the decline of moral vigor was a common feature of both the Left and the Right, as one historian of the fin de siècle has noted.[48] The idea of a widespread practice of Satanism was perfectly suited to this perception of degeneration—as a presumed social phenomenon, Satanism was "vintage fin de siècle, my dear," as a Dutch novel about the subject remarked.[49] In itself, the Satanist stereotype was a forceful reflection of the moral uncertainty experienced by living in a society that was more and more losing its traditional moorings in established religion. It vividly illustrated a range of questions that gained increasing urgency as the century went by. What forms of human behavior would appear when all morality had disappeared? Would a civilization that was absolutely free spawn monstrous inversions of normal morality, such as Huysmans's Satanists? And would a society devoid of authentic spirituality and only venerating the fulfillment of sensual desires still be worthwhile to live in? (This last question was answered by Huysmans in *Là-Bas* in a way that was masterful in its sordidness.)

The trope of Satanism as the embodiment of complete antinomianism, as an incorporation of the *reversed world* where every moral rule is turned into its opposite, was, of course, practically as old as the concept of Satanism itself. In the nineteenth century, however, the poignancy of this age-old trope increased considerably as a growing number of philosophers, ideologues, and revolutionaries clamored for exactly such a reversal of the established moral order, in a wild variety of ways. These were the days when Nietzsche started to raise his philosophical hammer, and it was no coincidence that Satanism was linked to anarchism and nihilism in many publications.[50] For a small number of people rejecting the accepted values of nineteenth-century society, the specter of Satanism might not have looked completely unattractive in this respect. Huysmans himself may have been among their number at some moment. He was probably not unique in this regard: an inherent ambiguity between horrified indignation and peculiar fascination seems to have been typical for the attitude toward Satanism in his days. By its haunting vision of Satanism, nineteenth-century society was looking at itself in the mirror, projecting mostly its fears and anxieties, but sometimes also its secret or not-so-secret dreams.

As the nineteenth century flowed over into the twentieth, an inevitable backlash of Satanism commercialization and ridicule seems to have set in. The *déconfiture* of the Taxil hoax may have played its part in this. In 1903, the French illustrated magazine *L'Assiette au beurre* ("Plate of Butter") dedicated an entire issue to the theme of Satanism and "black Masses." One of the illustrations that it contained, drawn by the Italian artist Manuel Orazi (1860–1934), showed a row of somewhat smug and sordid-looking young men in black coats standing behind a naked woman stretched out on her belly, with a human skull positioned in the hollow of her back. The accompanying poem was entitled "Deception" and told of frustrated adolescents vainly invoking the devil in their desperate quest for sexual thrills.[51] Interestingly enough, Orazi had used a similar design just eight years ago to illustrate the sumptuous *Calendrier Magique*, an extravagant but not altogether jocular item of luxury that sought to cater for the then-flourishing market for occult paraphernalia.[52]

This dual tendency for commercialization and ridicule is also exemplified by a curious and risqué "dramatic reconstruction" of the Black Mass throughout the ages that was staged at the Parisian Théâtre de la Bodinière on 17 February 1904. The text of the spectacle was published in a small brochure that included four black-and-white photographs of the tableaux vivants interspersing its performance.[53] Huysmans, Michelet, and Lévi clearly served as direct or indirect sources of inspiration and information for its author, one Roland Brevannes. The first scene enacted the Black Mass of Gilles de Rais, celebrated on the back of a nude woman (played by an actress wearing a flesh-colored body suit, as the accompanying photograph clearly shows) with fragments of consecrated hosts mixed with the blood of two children, the last one who died and the last one born; the chalice was supposed to be the skull of a parricide, footed by the horn of a buck that had copulated with a country girl. This was followed by the improper rites of Voisin *cum suis*, with nothing much new offered except for the audacious suggestion of lesbian love between Voisin and Trianon (while the possibility was also hinted at that the latter had in fact been a hermaphrodite). The third and final scene reconstructed a Black Mass "in Paris, in our own days." The modern Black Mass, if we are to believe the play, is in fact a strictly homosexual affair and meant to confront "Love" and "Death." It is performed for a company of jaded upper-class gentlemen, giving occasion to conversations like this:

> PARNOIS: What special treat do you offer us tonight?
> KARL: We celebrate a black Mass.
> PARNOIS: That is not *that* special, they are celebrated from time to time in Paris.
> AXEL: Have you ever seen one?
> PARNOIS: Quite recently—down there, near to the Pantheon.

THE MARQUIS: I know what you intend to talk about. These are base debaucheries that have nothing in common with the magnificent sacrileges of our forefathers. I have said "magnificent," and I maintain: atheism can only be truly
grand in times of faith. Today, one does not even know what a proper orgy
is anymore. The followers of Satan make me laugh, even when they write his
name with an h.[54]

The scene descends into the burlesque when two women enter incognito, later followed
by the police. When the latter are told by the attendants that they are in the process
of celebrating a "modernized black Mass," the inspector of police responds that in
the Middle Ages, this would have earned them the stake, and under Louis XIV, the
Bastille. But now, he will simply say: "montrez-moi ça"—"show me that thing."

Blessed are those that believe what is best for them, for never shall their minds be terrorized.

ANTON SZANDOR LaVey, *The Satanic Bible*, Book of Satan, V, 9

7

Paths into the Twentieth Century

⌒

THE CLOCK OF history has jumped forward for more than half a century. We are in an old house, painted black. The date: somewhere in the late 1960s. The place: 6114 California Street, San Francisco, California. In an eerily lit room, three dozen men and women have assembled, some of them wearing black robes with large hoods. On a large slab of stone—actually the protruding mantle of the fireplace—a naked young woman lies supine, her long hair cascading around her head. Above her, painted on the black wall, sprawls an enormous pentagram, pointed upward, from which the mocking outlines of the face of Baphomet, the Goat of Mendes, leer at the congregation. On the other side of the room stands a pale-faced man dressed in the black garb of a Roman Catholic priest, his head shaved bald except for a carefully trimmed beard around his mouth. In addition, he sports a long black cape and a tight skullcap with two horns protruding from it, giving him the overall appearance of a carnival devil.

A bell is tolled, and an organ moans sinister melodies. The horned High Priest draws a ceremonial sword and extends it over the naked altar, uttering the words: "In nomine Dei nostri Satanas Luciferi excelsi. In the name of our exalted God, Satan, Lucifer, Ruler of the Earth, King of the World, I command you to come forth from the Gates of Hell and bestow the blessings of the Power of Darkness upon us. Come forth." Invocations of Belial, Leviathan, Asmodeus, Balaam, Beelzebub, Hecate, Ishtar, Mammon, Pan, and Shaitan follow, and the Lord's Prayer is recited backward. Next, a parody of Roman Catholic Mass is enacted. A hostlike wafer is inserted between the labia of the naked woman on the chimney mantle and is subsequently distributed among the spectators; a man dressed in bishop's robes is ritually humiliated; another man impersonating Jesus (with a cross on his back) is flogged with a cat-o'-nine-tail as he crawls across the room; a plastic figurine of a saint is smashed and urinated upon by the High Priest and several female acolytes. Among cheers from the spectators, a woman dressed as a nun divests herself of her habit, letting loose her long blond hair and dancing suggestively in the tight miniskirt she wears underneath while the other women in the room join hands with the hooded men and dance for a few minutes back to back in naked revelry. "The sagging spirit of guilt and repression is cast off!" the High Priest solemnly declares. "The carnal nature of the beast is bared. Heaven shakes and Hell laughs. Ecstasy triumphs over the decadent self-denial preached by milksops and eunuchs. The way of the flesh encompasses humanity in its folds of pleasure. Satan rules the Earth. Hail Satan!"

"Hail Satan!" the congregation shouts in response.[1]

THE CHURCH OF SATAN

The description above is not a specimen of church propaganda or Decadent literary fiction, but an authentic account of a Black Mass as celebrated at the headquarters of the first "Church of Satan," a California group of Satanists that had been officially founded in 1966 by Anton Szandor LaVey, the High Priest officiating at the ceremony.[2] Although the ceremony was concluded with coffee and cake rather than a general orgy, here at last we witness a clear and quite conscious instance of identification and appropriation.[3] For the first time in our quest through history, the age-old fiction of Satanism had become fact and a religious group unabashedly identifying itself as Satanist had arisen.

To construct his Satanism, LaVey purposefully appropriated an array of elements that had been attributed to followers of Satan at various times in history. Even in the short description that opened this chapter, many of these elements can already be discerned. The upward pentagram that the Church had adopted as its sigil had been designated by Éliphas Lévi as an emblem of black magic.[4] The backward dancing is of course a clear reminder of the descriptions of the Witches' Sabbath in early modern demonology, and the naked female body that served as an altar derived from the magical rituals ascribed to Voisin and company during the Affair of the Poisons, the account of which may have reached California via Legué, Huysmans, or sundry popular paperbacks.[5] Huysmans's Black Mass, however, clearly had been the principal model for the ceremony, with the High Priest in his devilish outfit quaintly reminiscent of Canon Docre with his buffalo horns. Indeed, in the official liturgy for the Black Mass published by LaVey in 1972, the long harangue against Christ uttered by Canon Docre in *Là-Bas* was integrally incorporated, both in its original French and English translation.[6]

These trappings of ritual and indoor decoration indicate the more profound historical influences that converged in the construction of modern religious Satanism. Later, we shall explore in depth in what way LaVey's religious Satanism was indebted to the traditions and tendencies described in the previous chapters of this book. We also will have learned by then by which historical trails these elements might have trickled into 1960s California. Before we delve into these matters, however, it is proper to tell something about the genesis of the Californian Church of Satan and its immediate historical context.

Telling the story of the Church of Satan is in large measure telling the story of its founder, Anton Szandor LaVey. LaVey himself liked to shroud his ancestry and pre-Satanist years in mystery. After he had assumed his priesthood for Satan, he claimed to have a Transylvanian grandmother, as well as having Mongolian, Jewish, and gypsy blood flowing through his veins. After running away from home at the age of seventeen, he had subsequently been a lion tamer, calliope player, police photographer, ghost buster, and night-club organist. In the course of the latter occupation, he had also, he claimed, been the lover of Marilyn

Monroe, then on the brink of her rise to fame. In addition, LaVey would later suggest that he suffered from pathologic sensibility to daylight and an allergy to garlic, and in his authorized biography, he related how he had been born with a tail-like caudal appendage that had been surgically removed in his early teens.[7]

Most of these claims would eventually be proven false or highly dubious, although they had graced the pages of popular as well as academic treatments of modern Satanism for decades by then.[8] What is certain is that LaVey had been born April 11, 1930, as Howard Stanton LeVey in Chicago, Illinois.[9] His father may indeed have been partly Jewish, but did not practice his religion; young Howard had indeed enrolled with the circus, although probably as a general handyman, not as a lion tamer. Certain as well is the fact that LaVey developed some musical skills, playing the calliope (a steam-driven keyboard instrument) in his circus days and afterward playing Hammond organs and Wurlitzers on the carnival circuit and at San Francisco entertainment venues. Neither is there reason to doubt LaVey's claim that he became fascinated at an early date with the occult, or rather, more generally, with the bizarre and sinister.[10] Photographs from the late 1940s show him dressed as a movie gangster holding a cigarette and sporting a ring formed like a skull, a thin moustache, and a long, faked scar on his right cheek. LaVey's interest in the *ars sinistrae*, so much is clear as well, was no mere fad. In the 1960s, he would be able to display an extensive library on the occult that could not have been collected overnight. In the first half of the same decade, he started to give lectures on the weird and the wonderful: "freaks of nature," extrasensory perception, cannibalism, spiritualism, historical torture methods, and so forth. These talks were usually concluded by some sort of practical demonstration. Legend has it, for instance, that after LaVey's lecture on cannibalism, grilled portions were passed around of a female human thigh that had been procured from the hospital mortuary. Likewise the lecture on the Black Mass had included a demonstration of this ritual, reconstructed by LaVey "from a number of sources"—the forerunner, we may assume, of the Black Mass described at the opening of this chapter.[11]

Meanwhile, LaVey had started to practice his own magic—on which more in later sections—and had assembled a number of similarly inclined people in a small group that was dubbed the "Magic Circle." Divesting himself of his "gangster" outfit, he began to wear attire roughly resembling Count Dracula's. The Magic Circle already convened in the Black House, the house on Los Angeles Street that would remain LaVey's lifelong place of residence. LaVey told improbable stories about how he had miraculously acquired this building, claiming it to have been the former speakeasy of an infamous San Francisco madam who had riddled it with secret passageways to facilitate her illegal undertakings.[12] (In reality, the house had been from his parents, who had bought it in 1956; LaVey probably constructed the secret passageways himself.[13]) To contrast with the lightly colored dwellings of his neighbors, LaVey and his consort, Diane Hegarthy, painted the house black. The future High Priest obtained further neighborhood notoriety by keeping a range of unusual pets, such as a lion cub named Togare, which eventually was removed to the San Francisco Zoo on municipal orders, after neighbors complained about the deafening roars that arose from LaVey's unkept garden.

Such was LaVey's station in life when one of his acquaintances suggested to him that all this magic and philosophy sufficed for the establishment of a new faith. Why didn't he found a church? LaVey picked up the proposition, and in 1966, the first Church of Satan was registered within the state of California. This, we might claim with some reason, was the actual beginning of Satanism as a religion such as it is practiced in the world today. LaVey styled himself High Priest of Satan and Exarch of Hell, and he declared 1966 to be Year One of the new Satanic Era.[14]

Why did LaVey choose to dedicate his "church" to Satan? This seemingly simple question actually still awaits a definite answer. LaVey's involvement in magic and his apparent predilection for the sinister may have pointed the way. But there is nothing to suggest that he had undergone any religious experience involving the mythological adversary. More important were probably the philosophical premises that he wanted to espouse with his new organization. Satan was for him the most suitable symbol to express these. The main line of LaVey's philosophy was that man should live according to his natural desires, without encumbrance of "white light religions," of which Christianity was by no means the only but certainly the most prominent example. "For two thousand years man has done penance for something he never should have to feel guilty about in the first place," LaVey would write a few years later in his principal doctrinal digest, *The Satanic Bible* (1969). "We are tired of denying ourselves the pleasures of life which we deserve. . . . Satan represents opposition to all religions which serve to frustrate and condemn men for his natural instincts. He has been given an evil role simply because he represents the carnal, earthly, and mundane aspects of life."[15] What Satan stood for was summarized by LaVey in his "Nine Satanic Statements," a sort of creedal abstract that has become traditional to quote in studies on LaVeyan Satanism:

1. Satan represents indulgence instead of abstinence!
2. Satan represents vital existence instead of spiritual pipe dreams!
3. Satan represents undefiled wisdom instead of hypocritical self-deceit!
4. Satan represents kindness to those who deserve it instead of love wasted on ingrates!
5. Satan represents vengeance instead of turning the other cheek!
6. Satan represents responsibility to the responsible instead of concern for psychic vampires!
7. Satan represents man as just another animal, sometimes better, more often worse than those that walk on all-fours, who, because of his "divine spiritual and intellectual development," has become the most vicious animal of all!
8. Satan represents all of the so-called sins, as they all lead to physical, mental, or emotional gratification!
9. Satan has been the best friend the Church has ever had, as He has kept it in business all these years![16]

LaVey's new religious organization gained public notoriety by a series of clever publicity stunts. In 1967, the Church performed its first Satanist marriage; its official status as a church entitled it to carry out this privilege. The ceremony attracted a lot of curiosity from the press and the general public, as did the "Satanic" military funeral of one of the church members a few months later. On May 23, 1967, LaVey baptized his three-year-old daughter, Zeena, in a rite he had composed specifically for the purpose. A recording of the baptism and other Satanist liturgy was issued on a long-playing record. In 1969, Avon books published *The Satanic Bible*, a compilation of doctrinal texts and rituals based on material that had circulated within the Church of Satan on loose leaflets. LaVey's anti-Bible proved a popular title and was translated into Spanish, German, Russian, Swedish, and Czech.[17] It was followed in 1972 by *The Satanic Rituals*, a title that featured various ceremonies that could be used by Satanist assemblies—among them a mildly revised version of the Black Mass that I described at the beginning of this chapter.

That the Church of Satan came into being at precisely this moment in time and succeeded in attracting such media attention can hardly be called a coincidence. Profound changes had started to become manifest in the religious landscape of North America. As the first-born child of the Western Revolution, the United States had been exceptional in its early legal enshrinement of "freedom of religion" and the official separation between Christian church and state that had been codified by law. Notwithstanding this legal secularization, America had always been a de facto Christian nation. Shortly after World War II, polls revealed that 94 percent of the population believed in the existence of a deity, a substantially larger share than in most Western European countries; furthermore, 83 percent of the American public regarded the Bible as "the revealed word of God" and 80 percent subscribed to the divinity of Christ.[18] In the 1960s, however, both church membership and church attendance began to decline dramatically. While in a random American city like Detroit, 68 percent of the population had felt certain of God's existence just prior to the 1960s, in 1971, this had dwindled to less than half of the Detroit public.[19] Higher levels of social and geographical mobility and of education had induced or enabled an increasing number of predominantly younger people to break away from the faith of their forefathers and turn to alternative or personal forms of religiosity.

The most dramatic manifestation of this new wave of dechristianization had occurred precisely in 1966, the founding year of the Church of Satan, and in San Francisco, its place of birth, as young people from all over America started to "wear flowers in their hair" (as the Scott McKenzie song had it) and converged on the Frisco borough Haight Ashbury during the Summer of Love, igniting a wave of countercultural activity in the entire Western world. In their demonstrative rejection of established values, the hippies epitomized broader currents in society. Eastern spiritualities and psychedelica, and also various species of the occult, featured prominently among the alternatives to traditional forms of Christianity they embraced. The 1960s saw a great upsurge of interest in and participation with occultism in America, and in the West in general, initiating the wide proliferation of "occulture" in today's society.[20] Parallel with this occult revival, the Sexual Revolution was changing Western morals with regard to sexuality, proposing fewer restrictions to varieties of sexual practice that had hitherto been considered improper, and emphasizing enjoyment as the principal function and purpose of sex.

Clearly, the new Church of Satan fitted neatly into these trends of anti-Christianity, occult attraction, sexual liberalization, and general rebelliousness. "We are experiencing one of those unique periods in history when the villain consistently becomes heroic," LaVey himself noted. "The opposite has become desirable, hence this becomes the Age of Satan."[21] Not insignificantly, the Black House was only a few blocks away from the permanent hippie camping grounds in Haight Ashbury. Modern religious Satanism could thus be described as a child of the 1960s counterculture. Yet the relation between the new religion of Satan and the emerging counterculture was not as straightforward as it may seem. Anton Szandor

LaVey was certainly not the type of person to put flowers in his hair. In fact, he had ritually shaven his head bald when he established the Church of Satan on Walpurgisnacht 1966. LaVey belonged to an earlier generation than most members of the new counterculture; despite his flamboyant personal style and ideological unconventionality, his aesthetic preferences were firmly entrenched in the 1940s and 1950s. This set him at loggerheads with the long-haired, loosely clothed, guitar-plucking youths who swarmed over his home city. Most of his congregation also was considerably older than the high school dropouts and college students in the hippie movement.[22]

Apart from matters of taste, considerable ideological differences separated LaVey's Satanic church from the young counterculture. While hippies and protesting students were propounding more or less articulated programs for social and political revolution, the Church of Satan's "might is right" philosophy made it paradoxically pro-establishment (as well as, presumably, the close ties of its founder with the San Francisco police force). While more than a few counterculture groups propagated sexual liberation by way of communal sex and radical back-to-nature egalitarianism, LaVeyan Satanism preached sexual differentiation, personal deviance, and fetishism. ("The Satanist realizes that if he is to be a sexual connoisseur (and truly free from sexual guilt)," LaVey wrote in the *Satanic Bible*, "he cannot be stifled by the so-called sexual revolutionists any more than he can by the prudery of a guilt-ridden society."[23]) While the counterculture made "peace" its goals and catchword, the *Satanic Bible* declared man to be a predatory animal and eulogized the "iron-handed," the "victorious," and the "bold."[24] While the counterculture sought to free its mind with drug-induced transcendent experiences, LaVey was fiercely anti-drugs, even suggesting the celebration of an alternative Black Mass that would not ridicule Christianity but the god of the day, psychedelic drugs, with components such as a portrait of drugs guru Timothy Leary hung upside down and an LSD tablet crushed underfoot.[25] While the Haight Ashbury hippies dabbled heavily in mysticism and the irrational, the Church of Satan officially propagated a religion of rationality.

LaVey would later recount how he had held a ritual in the early years of the Church to curse the hippie movement and "drive the slaves back into their pens."[26] Although this story may be apocryphal, it succinctly captures the vast rift in attitude between his Church of Satan and hippiekind. Some of the differences between emerging Satanism and wider counterculture can be ascribed to the personal inclinations of Anton LaVey. Others were rooted in the specific brand of anti-Christian discourse and alternative spirituality from which LaVey's Satanism drew, which we will explore in more depth shortly. Yet however this may be, LaVey's attitude toward the "love generation" would prove indicative of the peculiar course that modern Satanism was to take.

PRECURSORS AND INSPIRATIONS

LaVey presented his Church of Satan as "the first above ground organisation of Satanism."[27] He probably did so in good faith. Yet his Satanic church was not the first religious group venerating Satan in the twentieth century, not even the first above-ground one. Even if we pass over rumors and newspaper reports that lack further corroboration, there are a few well-documented cases of Satanist organizations that antedate or are contemporary with LaVey's.[28] Principal among these is the "Temple de Satan" that had sprung into being in the permissive atmosphere of Interbellum Paris. Founded in 1930 by Maria de Naglowska, a Russian noblewoman who had fallen on hard times after her morganatic marriage to a Jewish violin player, it featured colorful sex rites, a touch of millennialism, and strident feminism. The "Order of the Knights of the Golden Arrow," as it was officially called, unabashedly operated in the open.[29] Its founder held regular audience in La Coupole and gave weekly conferences in Studio Raspail, rue Vavin 36, while the movement issued a periodical entitled *La Flèche: Organe d'Action Magique* ("The Arrow: Bulletin for Magical Action").

In its curious assembly of doctrines, Naglowska's Temple of Satan was a clear heir to nineteenth-century esotericism. Not at all anti-Christian in its outlook, the Order of the Golden Arrow professed to propagate the reign of the "Third Term of the Trinity," the Holy Spirit. For Naglowska, however, "Holy Spirit" was synonymous with "Woman." She also liked to refer to the "Esprit Saint" as "Esprit Sain"—the Wholesome Spirit instead of the Holy Spirit—pointing to the more benevolent attitude toward the human body that the new era would bring.[30] The idea that the coming Age of the Holy Ghost was to be a feminine era had already been propagated by esotericists like Flora Tristan, Éliphas Lévi, and Jules Bois, and before them by several medieval mystics. Women, Naglowska held, sought to "organize" life instead of trying to dominate it, as the male impulse was; only the end of male domination and the establishment of matriarchy would bring harmony to the world. The Third Term of the Trinity would establish the "right to be different" for women, so they would be able to concentrate on those functions that they alone were capable of fulfilling.[31]

Naglowska spoke of herself as "Priestess of Satan" and did not hesitate to describe the first stage of her ritual system as a "satanic initiation" that gave access to the "Truth of the Wholesome Satanic Doctrine."[32] In this sense, her order was undoubtedly Satanist. But Satanism was only one component of her religious system, which could probably best be described as an intricate semi-Hegelian compound of Christian, occultist, and Satanist elements. God, Naglowska held, was Life, and Life, God, ever changing, ever becoming, never static.[33] Against this eternal "Yes" of God, Satan positioned itself. Not to be understood as something "living outside of us," he represented the co-eternal "No," which stood for destruction and, by application, human reason—the Goethean spirit "der stets verneint" and that unceasingly tries to deconstruct creation.[34] This deconstructive force was not to be considered as something inherently "evil," but rather as necessary to the continuous becoming of the universe. Only when old things were destroyed, could new things come into being.

Reality as we know it was a complicated interplay between these two forces. From the struggle between the Will to Live (God) and the Will to Die (Satan) sprang the Son, symbol of the victory of the father in its visible manifestation, creation. When Satan battles against the Son, a second victory of God occurs, the reconfirmation of life by the Holy (or Wholesome) Spirit. These victories are only temporal, however, because if the eternal "No" would fall silent, the eternal "Yes" would also cease.[35] In Naglowska's system, these complicated trinitarian (or quartarian) notions were also reflected in other levels of creation, most importantly the human microcosm. Satanic reason was, according to Naglowska, the domain par excellence of the Male, while the Female represents the generative and intuitive force of life. Both of them, however, also contain this bipolarity in themselves. The male mind is Satan, but his genitals represent life. In contrast, the female sexual organs are of Satan, because it is here that Satan in the shape of the Serpent introduced himself to initiate woman into lust, which is the attraction to death.[36]

The teachings of the Order of the Golden Arrow encompassed symbolic and practical sex magic that utilized these positive and negative poles. The male initiate was to strengthen his Satanic essence by various trials, the culmination of which involved ritual intercourse with a naked woman without allowing his "sacred force to crystallize in mortal liquid" (i.e., without ejaculating).[37] The grand finale of the initiation process was the surrender of the male to the female, who embodied the New Era, which was to occur through self-immolation of his Satanic self in sacred coitus with a purified woman while the man was hung from a gallows. This ritual brought about the banishment of Satan to the underworld (i.e., the male genitals) and the unbalancing of reason, transforming him into the Sublime Fool of which the "Secret Writings" spoke. When he came to himself—the hanging was not intended to be lethal—he would have become a New Man, the vanguard of the coming age of the Holy or Wholesome Spirit. The beginning of this period was imminent. Naglowska intimated that it would be heralded by the celebration of a "Golden Mass" involving three men and four women. Unfortunately, perhaps, she never performed this magnificent ceremony—only a chiefly symbolic "Providential Golden Mass" during a public ceremony that was witnessed, among others, by the journalist of esotericism Pierre Geyraud.[38]

Naglowska's Order of the Golden Arrow, with its intricate and highly nineteenth-century complex of ideas, can arguably be considered the first known organized body of religious Satanism. It disappeared as abruptly as it had manifested itself. In early 1936, Maria de Naglowska suddenly left Paris. Rumor had it the Paris police had become wary of the Temple of Satan after one of its hanging rites had almost resulted in getting a male celebrant killed. The self-styled Satanic priestess departed to her daughter in Zürich, where she died a few months later (a fact that only became known decades later, spawning wild stories about her fate in the intermediate period).[39]

Even before Naglowska, sympathy for the other site of the traditional duality had been expressed in a more muffled way by the German magical lodge Fraternitas Saturni. Founded in 1926 by the bookseller Eugen Grosche (1888–1964), the Fraternitas Saturni was an elitist and eclectic esoteric order that busied itself with astrology, tantric sex magic, and drug-induced trance experiments, among other things. Central to its mythology was the opposition and interaction of light and darkness. During primordial times, darkness had been the stronger element, but the light had been contained in it. In our planetary system it had been the Logos of the sun (Chrestos) that had brought light and, along with it, life. Lucifer, however, grabbed the torch of light from God and retreated with the divine secrets to the farthest reaches of the spheres. His planetary form is therefore Saturn, which in ancient cosmology lies farthest from the sun, the place where the last light passes over into darkness. He is therefore considered the Guardian of the Threshold who opens the door to transcendence and salvation, and who guards the realm of the dead.[40]

This Lucifer is not to be considered evil, the Fraternitas maintained. Although Saturn/Lucifer, as representative of the forces of darkness, battles with the principle of Chrestos, this does make him an exclusively negative figure. Both light and darkness are necessary for life, Grosche argued in the brotherhood's periodical, and they indeed form its basic condition.

> Thus the negative Luciferian principle is not only of divine origin, but as an element of balance it is just as necessary as the Chrestos principle. For people who have a [*sic*] understanding of him, Lucifer, the great Light-Bearer for mankind, who of his own will shattered the egocentric power of the sun's Logos, can function just as well as a figure of salvation as does the Chrestos-principle of the sun. . . . God has a bright and a dark face.[41]

For human beings, following the demiurge of Saturn meant a path of austerity, asceticism, and suffering. The magician had to transform the darkness or "lead" in Saturn into "gold" by a "polarity reversal of the lights." In this union of opposites Saturn finally would become the sun, the original Luciferian core of the Saturn principle. For the initiate, therefore, serving Saturn was actually giving spiritual service to the Sun and contributing to the return of the "dark brother." In practical life, the path from Saturn to the Sun corresponded to overcoming the obstacles of jealousy, hate, laziness, doubt, and inconstancy, which must be repolarized into longing, love, energy, faith, and perseverance. "To follow a cult of Saturn thus means to comprehend the higher octaves of this demiurge, to recognize the Luciferian principle as a divine spiritual power, and to organize this consciously in the service of the sun's Logos."[42]

As in the case of Naglowska, these ideas seem clearly rooted in Romantic Satanism and Lévian occultism, while the Fraternitas Saturni was also influenced by Crowley's Thelema (on which later more).[43] In contrast to Naglowska, however, the Brotherhood did not describe itself as Satanist. Indeed, a sharp distinction was drawn in its theology between Lucifer, who represents the "higher octaves" of Saturn, and Satan, who embodies the deity's "lower octaves." It is also an open question if we can call them Satanist according to the criteria adopted in this study. While Lucifer obviously plays a central role in their mythology, he receives scarce mention in their literature and rituals. In the pseudo-Masonic Saturnic Mass, the most important order rite, only Saturn is invoked and praised (although it must be admitted that he is also called *Ophis ho archaios*, "the ancient Serpent").[44] Pending a deeper study of the order's immense production of German-language esoteric publications, I would rather describe them as an esoteric current with a strong element of Satanism, like Lévi's Magism and Blavatsky's Theosophy.

The Brothers of Saturn were suppressed during the Nazi era but resuscitated by Grosche after the war. Following Grosche's demise in 1964, Luciferian elements seem to have further diminished in importance, while the already small organization was fragmented by feuds and schisms.[45] Nevertheless the Fraternitas persists to this day and continues its veneration for the Luciferian Saturn.

Another pre-1966 Satanist group mentioned in scholarly literature is the Ophite Cultus of Sathanas in Toledo, Ohio, a concoction of one Dr. Herbert Sloane, a former barber, cardologist (card reader), and tasseographist (tea reader).[46] As the name of his cult suggests, Sloane had found inspiration for his cults in reading books on ancient Gnosticism. In classic Gnostic mode, the Toledo "Sathanists" regarded the creation of the material world as evil, while above and beyond this, there is the good god of the realm of pure spirit. Sathanas, according to the neo-Ophites, was the messenger of this ultimate god, and Sloane claimed that this messenger had manifested himself to him on two or three occasions during his life. His modest circle of followers met in his Toledo barbershop, which Sloane had baptised into the "Coven of Our Lady of Endor." It seems probable the group was in existence before 1966, although I have not found any traces of it in literature prior to that date. Sloane himself suggested that he was already operating in the 1940s, but given the many parallels with Wicca the group displayed, it is more likely its date of origin must be located sometime after 1953, the year Gerald Gardner's neopagan cult of witchcraft came into the open.

In addition to Sloane's Cultus of Sathanas, the 1960s did produce at least one group of genuine counterculture Satanists—although they also extended veneration toward Jehovah, Christ, and Lucifer (whom they considered as an identity clearly separated from Satan, like the Fraternitas Saturni). This was the Process Church of the Final Judgement, the remarkable history of which deserves to be told in full.[47] The Process, as the movement was commonly called, had come into existence as a London therapy group. In the early years of the decade, Robert de Grimston (then still just Robert Moor and a student of architecture) met call girl Mary Anne Maclean at a Scientology therapy session. The two soon become lovers and afterward spouses, and they started to work on their own with Scientology therapy methods. After they were evicted from Scientology, their close-knit analysis circle moved increasingly into spiritual waters, renaming itself The Process in 1965, and its members started to live communally in a house at 2 Balfour Street in London. The Process also began to develop marked eschatological tendencies, expecting the imminent end of the world—a not-uncommon sentiment in the years of the nuclear armament race and Cuban missile crisis. In 1966 the entire group of Processeans—approximately thirty individuals, plus six German shepherd dogs—moved to the Caribbean, in search of an island where they could live off the land and await the imminent collapse of civilization. Eventually, the group settled on the Yucatán Peninsula, in a deserted salt factory called Xtul, living off fish, cacao nuts, and a local fruit called prickly pear.

It was during this adventure that the gods seem to have made their first appearance. During group meditations in the Caribbean, some Process group members became aware of contact with noncorporeal intelligences. Initially, the Processeans simply called them "Beings."[48] It had been the Beings who had guided them to the ruined salt mine in Mexico. There, amidst the awesome natural scenery of Yucatán, the first god emerged, Jehovah. In his Xtul Dialogues, which became part of the groups' scripture, Robert de Grimston wrote:

1. Is there more than one universe?

Yes. On various levels there are many universes, but they are all only part of the One True Universe, which exists on all levels. That is to say, there are many Gods; but only One True GOD who embodies all of them.

2. Is each God, then, a universe?

Or an aspect of a Universe. Jehovah, for example, is the knowledge of the Physical Universe.[49]

After a hurricane struck Yucatán and the Process returned to civilization, other gods embodying other aspects of the universe began to be described by Grimston, culminating in an intricate theology and an impressive corpus of holy writ. In 1967, the community founded an American "Chapter House" in New Orleans and registered itself officially as the Process Church of the Final Judgement, probably to obtain the legal tax exemption that religious organizations receive in the United States. As the movement spread over the United States—gaining a presence in San Francisco, Los Angeles, and New York City—the four gods of the Process pantheon consolidated themselves in their definite forms. Jehovah, female god of the Earth, represented austerity, authoritarianism, and strength. He was soon joined by Satan, female god of fire, representing separation, conflict, and fierceness, and by Lucifer, male god of the air, who stood for sensuousness, liberality, and intellectual light.[50] When the American Process community moved to New York in 1968, these gods were already firmly in place, and the Processeans wandered the streets to solicit donations while clad in black uniforms ornamented both with large silver crosses and a triangular "badge of Mendes" that displayed a goat head indicating their acceptance of the power of Satan.[51] Finally, Christ was added to this inventory, initially as prophet or messenger bringing unity between the gods, later as a deity in his own right.

None of these gods or semideities were considered evil. They simply were representative of "basic human patterns of reality," as Grimston put it.[52] The real "devil," he maintained, was humanity, or more precisely, the "Grey Forces," the powers of compromise and conformity that made the mass of humanity march mindlessly to its future destruction. The most important thing was not to be "grey." This understanding also extended to the political spectrum: the Process joined Leftist student manifestations as well as Right-wing political rallies, causing hilarious confusion on either side. In the end, however, all opposites would be reconciled, not into blandness, but in love, through the unity of Satan and Jehovah brought about by Christ.[53] Had not Christ said to love your enemies? And was not Christ's enemy Satan? Until the "reuniting of the Gods," Grimston maintained, the deity would remain no more than a scattered, fragmented mirror of human concepts.[54]

This theology was given expression at ritual assemblies called "Sabbaths," which blended Judeo-Christian, occult, and Satanist imagery. Solemn hymns were sung to Jehovah, Satan, Lucifer, and Christ:

> Jehovah is Strength
> Lucifer is Light
> Satan is Separation
> Christ is Unification
> They are the Great Powers of the Universe
> And all mankind is subject to Their Will[55]

For the Process, the gods were not only a philosophical equation describing the universe. They first and foremost reflected social and psychological realities—not in the least within the Process itself. Every person, Process doctrine held, tended to one of the gods in particular. Later, this was slightly modified into the idea that everyone formed a psychological combination of two god types. In particular, Mary Anne represented the female gods Jehovah and Satan, while her consort Robert de Grimston was the incorporation of Lucifer and Christ. His eerie resemblance to the traditional image of Jesus was meticulously exploited, with pictures showing him in Christ-like poses, his waving blond locks haloed around his head.

At an early stage, the two founders had begun to keep aloof from the rank and file of their followers, living in separate and usually rather luxurious quarters while their congregation hovered on the brink of poverty. By the time they had moved to the United States, the couple only had contact with a small number of deputies within the Process Church, becoming the elusive, mysterious "Omega" that ruled unseen. While Grimston was pushed to the fore as the oracle and prophet of the Church, pouring out scripture upon scripture in his characteristic semibiblical, dialectic prose, the real power in the background was Mary Anne. On one level, the theology of the Process could be understood as an extensive therapy session and mythological power play between the two spouses. The free, pleasure-loving Lucifer, for instance, had been introduced by Grimston as a counterweight to the strict, authoritarian Jehovah of stern Mary Anne. Although all gods received their share of homage, the attitude of the Process Church initially had been mainly Jehovan, with emphasis on abnegation, discipline, and celibacy. At some time, however, Grimston succeeded in replacing "Jehovah's Game" with that of Lucifer, which brought more room for personal enjoyment for the members of the Church.[56]

It was also the hidden personality-related theological battle within the Omega that proved to be the undoing of the Process. The system of the four gods collapsed when Robert began an extramarital liaison. This had happened with the initial permission and even stimulation of Mary Anne, but along the way, she changed her mind and proceeded to throw her husband out of the Omega. The couple divorced in 1973. Along with the departure of Robert de Grimston, Satan and Christ were also formally exorcised from the movement, while Lucifer was silently dropped from the pantheon. Process priests went around with bell, book, and candle to cast out the negative spirits of Satan and Christ from each chapter house.[57]

With only staunch Jehovah left, the church renamed itself into the Foundation Church of the Millennium, becoming a quasi-Judaic congregation concentrating on faith healing. Grimston made some feeble attempts to restore the original Process with a few dissident Processeans, conceiving them as a Luciferian Order that would counterbalance the Jehovian Order of the Foundation.[58] These attempts all failed, and with them, the Process adventure with Satanism came to a definitive end. The Foundation's Jehovah, meanwhile, grew ever more transcendent and distant, as did the Foundation's true leader, Mary Anne de Grimston. Her very existence was hidden from outsiders, and she was tacitly accepted as a goddess by inner-circle members. In the 1980s, the Church underwent a last surprising metamorphosis and became the Best Friend Animal Society, moving to Utah and establishing an animal sanctuary of some note. Although the organization had divested itself of all religious trimmings by now, Mary Anne kept living on the Best Friends premises, her further life shrouded in mystery. Reports claim that the goddess passed away in 2006.

The histories of Naglowska, Grosche, Sloane, and the Process clearly show that LaVey was not the first or the only one to bring Satanism "into the open." Yet there was a kernel of truth in his claim. None of his twentieth-century precursors had been able to instigate an enduring tradition of Satanism; except for the marginal Fraternitas Saturni, all of them ultimately disappeared more or less without a trace. Genealogically speaking, every known Satanist group or organization in the world today derives directly or indirectly from LaVey's 1966 Church of Satan, even if they are dismissive of LaVey or choose to emphasize other real or alleged forerunners of Satanism.[59]

There is no indication, furthermore, that LaVey and his circle were influenced by or even aware of their precursors. LaVey makes no mention whatsoever of Naglowska and the Fraternitas Saturni. It is probable that he had simply never heard of them, especially as the literature from and about both groups was and is mainly written in French and German. Neither is there anything to suggest that LaVey knew about the obscure Ophite Cult of Sathanas prior to 1966—while Mr. Sloane, on the other hand, became a card-carrying member of the Church of Satan after its foundation.[60]

In the case of the Process Church of the Final Judgement, the direction of influence may well have been in the reverse. It is not altogether clear when precisely Satan and Lucifer made their appearance in Process theology. But in December 1967, the movement opened a short-lived chapter in San Francisco, close to the Haight Ashbury district, and in this environment, the Processeans would have been bound to stumble upon LaVey's Satanist venture.[61] Also in December 1967, the first written attestation of the "Three Gods of the Universe" appeared in Grimston's writings, in an essay entitled *The Hierarchy*.[62] Not much later, after the group's headquarters had moved to New York, Processeans started to wear badges displaying the "Goat of Mendes." These coincidences do not conclusively prove LaVeyan influence and could simply be the result of separate, parallel developments. Yet a possible influence will almost certainly have been one-way, as it is not to be expected that the San Francisco Pope of Satanism would have been able to muster much sympathy for a Jehovah- and Christ-venerating cult of latter-day end-time prophets.[63]

ALEISTER CROWLEY, OR THE GREAT BEAST 666

If we want to find a genuinely significant influence on the emerging Satanism of LaVey, we can put these early Satanist movements aside. Instead, a single historical figure looms up: that of the English occultist Aleister Crowley (1875–1947), who would prove to be a crucial influence on many forms of modern alternative religion, particularly of the neopagan or "Left Hand Path" variety. Poet, novelist, painter, explorer, leader of the first climbing expedition to K2, chess master, classical scholar, and heir to a small family fortune accrued by his father's beer brewery, Crowley would travel a long and tortuous road that ended by his attempt to establish a new world religion meant to supersede Christianity, that of Thelema, or Will.[64] Growing up in a family of strict Plymouth Brethren, this "boyhood in Hell" (to use his own phrase) left him with a virulent anti-Christian attitude early in life. This did not deter his interest in "matters religious," however. While at Cambridge, he came into contact with the Golden Dawn, an occult order that combined elements of Theosophy and Lévian magic with inventions of its own.[65] Crowley was admitted to the Order on November 18, 1898, receiving the alias Frater Perdurabo, "I will endure till the end." He passed the lower grades rapidly, but his membership in the Golden Dawn was terminated abruptly when he became involved in a feud between its chief creative genius, Samuel Lidell Mathers, and a faction of discontented adepts.[66]

The termination of his membership did not prevent Crowley from advancing on the scale of grades by himself, using the rituals he had obtained from Mathers. In addition, he experimented with psychedelics and sex magic and eventually decided, like Blavatsky, to depart for the mystic East, where he initiated the first attempt to climb K2 and immersed himself in yoga and Buddhism. Back in Europe, he founded a new, highly individualistic magical order with his former Golden Dawn initiator, the A∴ A∴, or Astrum Argenteum. It mixed Golden Dawn material with mystic techniques he had picked up in India.[67] In 1912, moreover, he was contacted by a German occultist called Theodor Reuss, founder of the OTO (Ordo Templi Orientis), a small neo-Masonic occult order that busied itself explicitly with sex magic.[68] Crowley became "Summum Rex Sanctissimus X°" of the order for "Ireland, Iona, and all the Britons that are in the Sanctuary of the Gnosis," and he assumed the leadership of the whole order in the 1920s, although a number of members refused to accept the wild British occultist as their new Outer Head.[69]

Arguably the most important event in Crowley's spiritual career, however, had occurred some years before, when he was returning from the East with his wife, Rose, in 1904. Crowley had turned one of the rooms of his Cairo hotel suite into an impromptu magical temple where he continued to perform ceremonies. According to his own account, his wife began to utter strange announcements during these ceremonies, intimating that the ancient Egyptian god Horus was "waiting" for Frater Perdurabo and that the "Equinox of the Gods had come."[70] He was instructed (through the voice of his wife) to be ready in his temple at noon on April 8, where, after due invocation of Horus, Aiwass, the messenger of Set, would address him. Obeying these instructions, Crowley sat at his desk, a fountain pen in hand, and at noon exactly, Crowley maintained, a voice began to dictate to him. The revelation continued for an hour, and in the next two days, Aiwass spoke forth again at noon as Crowley wrote down, resulting in three chapters of biblical-sounding instructions and prophecies that Crowley would baptize as "The Book of the Law."

Biblical-sounding as the revelation may have been, its contents were far from biblical. The Book of the Law proclaimed sexual freedom, urged people to "enjoy all things of sense and rapture," and announced that the era of the old religions had ended.[71] "I am in a secret fourfold word, the blasphemy against all gods of men," the voice from the otherworld had declared the third day. "Curse them! Curse them! Curse them! With my Hawk's head I peck at the eyes of Jesus as he hangs upon the cross. I flap my wings in the face of Mohammed & blind him. With my claws I tear out the flesh of the Indian and the Buddhist, Mogul and Din. Bahlasti! Ompehda! I spit upon your crapulous creeds."[72] The "word" for the new age of mankind would be θελημα, Will: the new Golden Rule "Do What Thou Wilt Should Be the Whole of the Law." This was a variation on Dashwood's motto for his mock-order of St. Francis, which in its turn was a translation of Rabelais's dictum "Fay ce que vouldras" from Pantagruel.[73] Yet in Crowley's religious system, this motto did not retain the free-going meaning it had had with Rabelais and Dashwood.[74] Do What Thou Wilt meant following one's *True Will*, that is, to discover the purpose for which one was destined and to follow this as a star the trajectory determined for it. This explains, for instance, a paradoxical utterance in the Book of the Law as "thou hast no right but to do thy will."[75]

In retrospect, the Cairo revelation would be the turning point in Crowley's life. After an initial period of dismissal and hesitation, he discovered that his True Will was to be the Chosen Messenger of this new gospel. He began to count the years according to the Æon of Horus that had started in the year 1904 of the "vulgar era." His inheritance all but spent on travel and extravagance, he began to drift through Europe, America, and North Africa, using every publicity opportunity to spread the Thelema. To prove that the principles of the Book of the Law could form a viable guide for society, Crowley founded a small religious community in Cefalú, Sicily, which he appropriately called the Abbey of Thelema. In the 1930s, when totalitarian regimes swept Europe, he tried to contact both Stalin and Hitler in the hope of interesting them to adopt Thelema, or part thereof, as the new official religion for their states.[76] These efforts, not surprisingly, came to naught. When Crowley died in 1947 as an exhausted and impoverished old man, only a smattering of disciples dispersed throughout the world had embraced the new religion. "I am perplexed" were the last words recorded from the prophet's mouth.

Both before and after his death, Crowley was frequently accused of worshipping the devil, especially by the popular press and by authors with a Christian bias.[77] Did these allegations contain a kernel of truth and had Crowley been a Satanist? The answer to this question is both yes and no. Crowley certainly had been a Satanist *at some point* of his life, at least if we can trust his own assurances to this purport in his *Confessions*. In this "autohagiography," he describes how he tried to live a life of holiness as a schoolboy, until his father died. He then willingly decided to enlist with the enemy of the Christian god and desperately sought to commit the mysterious "sin against the Holy Ghost" for which no forgiveness was possible according to Christian scripture, in order to ensure that he would not be predestined to grace after all.[78] Reading Milton, Crowley came to the same conclusions regarding Satan as Blake, Godwin, and Shelley before him.[79]

His passionate antagonism to Christianity was also the spark that had ignited his interest in magic. The first work he acquired on this subject was *The Book of Black Magic and Pacts*, a popular digest compiled by A. E. Waite, which disappointed him sorely, because, in his own words, it was clear that the writers of the old *grimoires* had been "sincere Christians in spirit, and inferior Christians at that," with "no conception of the Satan hymned by Milton and Huysmans."[80] In his Golden Dawn years, when he seriously embarked upon the study of magic, he furnished two temple rooms in his quarters: one for the practice of white magic and one for the practice of black magic; the latter he provided with a human skeleton and an altar supported by a statue of a Negro standing on his head.[81]

An additional aspect drawing attention in this respect is Crowley's consistent identification with another biblical figure from the "other side": the "Great Beast" that opposes the Lamb and precedes the Antichrist in the biblical book of Revelation. According to his own recollections, Crowley's deeply religious mother had started to call her son "the Beast" from early in his youth.[82] Crowley adopted the title as a *nom de geux* and had the custom to sign with "To Megatherion 666" (The Great Beast 666), "Master Therion" (Master Beast), or simply "the Beast" or "666" later in his career.[83] An anti-Christian attitude that verged on the pathologic remained a salient feature of his thought throughout his life. In 1910, he lashed out in Shelleyan fashion against Christianity in an epic poem called *The World's Tragedy*; the tragedy of the title was, of course, the Christian faith, particularly its Protestant variety, as he elucidated in the poem's introduction: "That religion they call Christianity; the devil they honour they call God. I accept their definitions, as a poet must do, if he is to be at all intelligible to his age, and it is their God and their religion that I hate and will destroy."[84] Even as late as 1916, while doing a "magical retirement" in a cottage near Bristol, New Hampshire, he found himself compelled to perform a "Magical Operation to banish the "Dying God"." Baptizing a toad as "Jesus the slave-god," he crucified the poor animal in ritual mockery of the crucifixion, after solemnly confronting his captive with the misery he (Crowley) had suffered because of Christianity.[85]

With this fierce anti-Christian attitude, one could expect Crowley to have no qualms about a bit of Satanism. Yet Massimo Introvigne and a host of other scholars have argued, and to my mind convincingly, that applying the label of Satanist to Crowley is inappropriate.[86] In the short description we gave of the Great Beast's life, it has already become apparent that Crowley frequently invoked quite other deities: Horus and Aiwass, to begin with (although Aiwass is a tricky one, he being the messenger and manifestation of Set, the god that was considered as the original for Satan in Theosophy; Crowley himself designated him as "Our Lord God the Devil" at one occasion).[87] Furthermore, notwithstanding his unorthodox probing of all kind of magic, Crowley certainly considered himself a "white magician" in the Lévian sense of the term—a wizard that employed the magical force for good, altruistic purposes—and one encounters in his writings accounts of doing battle against "black magic gangs" that could as well have been written by Péladan, Guaita, or Papus.[88]

Indeed, leafing through Crowley's vast corpus of writings, Satanist elements are far from striking. Instead, one encounters a multifaceted and at times seemingly contradicting system of religious thought that has been aptly designated as "programmatic syncretism" by one scholar.[89] Encompassing virtually all the classic themes of the "Theosophical Enlightenment" and a few new ones, it features the Lévian tradition of Western esoteric magic and Kabbalah; the Theosophical interest in Hinduism and Buddhism (with some Taoism thrown in for good measure); eighteenth-century theories about the perennial core of religion (the worship of the sun, or the generative powers); a fascination with Egyptian mythology dating back at least to the time of Mozart; neopagan nostalgia to the gods of Antiquity; Romanticism and the cult of individuality; modern determinism and Nietzscheanism; and last but not least a sniff of Freud and of cocaine—adding up to a gargantuan synthesis in which the few elements that could be called Satanist are drowned into insignificance.[90] Labeling this system Satanism would be as appropriate as calling it Buddhism or Jewish mysticism.

The Satanist elements we find with the Beast mostly reflect nineteenth-century concepts that should be familiar by now. In a footnote to *Magick*, Satan is described as the great initiator who stands for life, love, and liberty, and similar ideas are prevalent in his famous "Hymn to Lucifer" and in his lesser-known "Hymn to Satan."[91] When Crowley discusses the devil more systematically, it is mostly in the context of Lévi's reinterpretation inspired by Tarot and Kabbalah. Already in one of his earliest magical writings, Crowley had extended and systematized Lévi's Kabbalism, making the symbolism of the Kabbalah the master key to interpret and test magical visions, devise new rituals, and interpret the perennial truths expressed in the world's most important mythological systems.[92] In this system, the Devil from the Tarot accordingly corresponds with the Egyptian god Set, the Hindu deities Lingam and Yoni, the human genital system, the Goat as symbolic animal, and the Antique gods Priapus and Pan.[93] This rather straightforward schema is complicated, however, because the Greek god Pan is also equated with the Kabbalist Ein Sof, the all-transcending, ineffable, indescribable original divine principle that is One and None at the same time.[94] For Crowley, the emanation of the universe from this oneness is the origin of all things; all things at the same time aspire to reunite with this original oneness. The cosmos thus is a constant flux between the One and the Many—"creation-parturition is the Bliss of the One; coition-dissolution is the Bliss of the Many."[95] Evidently. Lévi's shadow looms large here again, with his Satan/Baphomet who is also the "pan-theos." In contrast to Lévi, however, the highest divine principle is emphatically not identified with the Judeo-Christian deity by Crowley, but with Pan *tout court*.

It is this complex identification of the devil with Pan that forms the background to Crowley's most "Satanist" statements. In *The Book of Thoth*, Crowley's exposition on the Tarot, he writes that the Devil card was completely misunderstood "in the Dark Ages of Christianity," but that Lévi "at least . . . succeeded in identifying the goat portrayed upon the card with Pan."[96] This is indeed the real significance of the Devil card according to Crowley: in the rest of the chapter he is variously called "creative energy in its most material form," "Pan Pangenetor, the All-Begetter," and "the masculine energy at its most masculine." The Tarot Devil becomes the embodiment of a supreme holism: "The formula of this card is then the complete appreciation of all existing things. He rejoices in the rugged and the barren no less than in the smooth and the fertile. All things equally exalt him. He represents the finding of ecstasy in every phenomenon, however naturally repugnant; he transcends all limitations; he is Pan; he is All."[97]

Apart from Set and Saturnus, the Beast quite frankly states, another name for this godhead is Satan. As he notes himself, this identification was already made by Crowley in an earlier text, "Book Four" of *Magick*, a theoretical exposé on magic in the style of Lévi's *Dogme et Rituel*. Crowley's Satan, however, has nothing to do with evil. This crude association only arose because the original "S"-gods were associated with the South, a quarter that carried negative connotations with heat and drought in the Middle East. "But to us," Crowley continues, "aware of astronomical facts, this antagonism to the South is a silly superstition which the accidents of their local conditions suggested to our animistic ancestors." More in general, good and evil are only "an arbitrary device for representing our ideas in a pluralistic symbolism based on duality" and "must be defined in terms of human ideals and instincts." "We have therefore no scruple in restoring the 'devil-worship' of such ideas as those which the laws of sound, and the phenomena of speech and hearing, compel us to connect with the group of 'Gods' whose names are based upon *ShT*, or *D*, vocalized by the free breath *A*. For these Names imply the qualities of courage, frankness, energy, pride, power and triumph; they are the words which express the creative and paternal will."[98]

This "Devil," Crowley goes on to say, is also "the Godhead which, if it become manifest in man, makes him Aegipan, the All"; in other words, it is the ecstatic force of "coition-dissolution" that unites one again with the original oneness. This oneness is the ultimate goal of magical initiation. As Crowley considered himself the only one of his day to have reached this elevated stage (or at least its penultimate grade, that of "Ipsissimus" or god), the description that follows is also a barely veiled self-advertisement of the Great Beast:

> Thus, he is Man made God, exalted, eager; he has come consciously to his full stature, and so is ready to set out on his journey to redeem the world. But he may not appear in this true form; the Vision of Pan would drive men mad with fear. He must conceal Himself in his original guise.
>
> He therefore becomes apparently the man that he was at the beginning; he lives the life of a man; indeed, he is wholly man. But his initiation has made him master of the Event by giving him the understanding that whatever happens to him is the execution of this true will.[99]

Taken to their logical conclusion, these words imply that the supreme principle of Crowleyanity is Satan and that Crowley himself is Satan's living embodiment on earth.[100] Yet such hermeneutic acrobatics fail to do justice to the true purport of Crowley's ideas and his syncretism. During his long career, the Great Beast never presented Satan as the central character of his religion; if anyone, his favorite god was probably Pan, whom he equated in Lévian fashion with the devil and the Goat of the Sabbath. But the crux of the matter was not that Pan was really the devil, but that the devil was really Pan.[101] And even Pan was just a name from one historical religious tradition for a concept that could just as well be expressed by other names from other historical religious traditions. In a similar vein, Crowley could write in *Magick* that Satan was also "Saturn, Set, Abrasax, Adad, Adonis, Attis, Adam, Adonai, etc."[102] There was not one god whose secret worship was at the core of Crowleyanity; rather, Crowleyanity provided the true interpretation of all the gods and, ultimately, the way to master them and forge one's own destiny.

Even though he cannot be called a Satanist himself, Crowley would prove to be a major influence on the religious Satanism that eventually would form in the twentieth century.[103] In the Anglo-Saxon world, at least, Crowley was virtually the only religious teacher of some public renown that had unblinkingly identified himself with "the Satanic." It was only to be expected that LaVey would stumble upon the Great Beast in the fruitless quest for Satanist groups that he claimed to have undertaken before founding his own church. Crowley had made frequent visits to the United States, and among the traces he left behind was a particularly active Californian OTO chapter. Its guiding light had been Jack Parsons, a rocket-fuel scientist who would have a lunar crater named after him because of his contribution to the American space program. Probably Crowley's most promising pupil, he had adopted the magical alias Belarion Armiluss All Dajal Anti-Christ, claiming to be the apparition of the latter-named apocalyptic figure that was destined to lead mankind to the "Law of the Beast 666." He also enthusiastically engaged in sexual magic, at one point, curiously enough, involving a young L. Ron Hubbard (the future founder of Scientology), who eventually ran away with Parsons's female sex magic partner and a substantial part of his financial resources.[104]

LaVey was not unfamiliar with this colorful figure. According to his authorized biography, the future High Priest contacted Parsons in the late 1940s, ordering an extensive list of Crowley's works—*Equinox of the Gods, Magic without Tears, Moonchild, Diary of a Dope Fiend, Sword and Song, Tannhaeuser, The Book of Lies, Yoga for Yahoos*, and *The Book of the Law*.[105] In 1951, he visited a Berkeley OTO Lodge, but if we are to believe his reminiscences, he came back disappointed, finding "the Berkeley bunch mystically-minded card readers who emphasized the study of Eastern philosophy, Oriental languages, stars and contemplation to reach the spiritual Nirvana of Oneness."[106] When the first version of Symonds's rather hostile biography of Crowley came out in 1952, LaVey wrote off the Great Beast as "a druggy poseur whose greatest achievements were as a poet and a mountain climber."[107]

LaVey's dismissal of the Thelemites as "rather innocuous" was not entirely justified, however: in the same year, Parsons blew himself to the moon in his laboratory, according to rumor during an auto-erotic magical experiment. In fact, LaVey's offhand waving away of Crowley bears all appearances of the pose of someone who wants to mask his true spiritual origins. In the *Satanic Bible*, LaVey stamped Crowley as a "poseur par excellence," but he also qualified his religious philosophy as one of the "closest outward signs" of Satanism before 1966, describing the OTO in an accompanying note as "practising some of the principles set forth in this volume."[108] The real historical connection was of course the other way around: LaVey was practicing some of the principles that had been expounded by Crowley. Although there are important differences between LaVey's Satanism and Crowley's Thelemic religion, the similarities between both are hard to overlook. We will look into these similarities and differences in more detail in some of the sections later on. On a more mundane level, we may already remark that LaVey's styling as "Exarch of Hell" probably had much to thank from Crowley's example. LaVey's bald head, for instance—which LaVey himself suggested to be in imitation of medieval hangmen and in accordance with a, probably fictitious, *yezidi* ritual—must have been at least partly inspired by the Great Beast, who had likewise shaven his head as a token of his dedication to Aiwass (at times leaving one or two small tufts of hair in remembrance of the phallic horns of Pan).[109]

A different, much more roundabout route in which Crowley contributed to the emergence of religious Satanism, was through Wicca, or neopagan witchcraft, another religious current that had sprang from the spiritual seed he had sown. Crowley's lineage crossed or recrossed here with several other elements from European counterculture, the most important being probably the rehabilitation of the European witch that had been initiated by Michelet. As we have seen, both Michelet and Lévi had suggested in a rather vague way that remnants of the original witch cult might still be around in the wilder parts of the European countryside; as we have seen, this suggestion had been picked up already in 1899 by the American Leland who published a "Gospel of the Witches." In the period between the two world wars, Michelet's thesis of a nature-loving, feminine witch cult had been adopted and elaborated almost beyond recognition by the English Egyptologist Margaret Murray.[110] Without even mentioning the French historian, she based herself on dubious interpretations of archaeological finds to postulate the historical existence of a European fertility cult venerating a female goddess and her male consort, the "Horned God." She also argued this cult had maintained an underground presence way beyond the advent of Christianity, and, like Michelet, she hinted at the possibility that pockets of the "Old Religion" might still be extant. In the 1940s, one of these "pockets" duly resurfaced in the form of an English "coven" of "traditional" witches led by Gerald Gardner. In 1954, after the United Kingdom lifted its legal ban on witchcraft, Gardner began to seek publicity for his new/old religion, and in a perfect promotional coup, he found "expert" Murray prepared to provide an endorsing preface for his book on this subject. This was the beginning of the religious movement we now know as Wicca, which, according to some, is the fastest-growing neopagan religion in the Western world.[111]

Specific information about what had been the rites and doctrines of the Old Religion were naturally rather sparse, and Gardner had turned to the corpus of Crowleyanity to fill up this gap. In fact, Gardner had been an OTO member and had known Crowley personally, who may have given him tacit stimulation to continue his venture.[112] This may not be so strange as it seems, because Crowley certainly had a Romantic attitude toward nature: he frequently sighted sylphs during his walks in the forest and claimed to have made love once to a female tree spirit in the Burmese jungle ("It was a woman vigourous and intense, of passion and purity so marvellous that she abides with me after these many years as few indeed of her human colleagues").[113] More important, the veneration of the "generative powers" and the male-female duality had been two of the core features of Crowley's religious system, providing ready material for a primeval fertility cult. Roughly speaking, Gardner clad Crowleyanity in the pseudo-historical garb provided by Murray and others, adding a few ideas from other sources and a few elements that reflected his own predilections— including, it seems, a healthy dose of good old English flogging.[114]

At the time LaVey established his new religion, a booming subculture of neopagan witchcraft had already asserted itself on both sides of the Atlantic. Relations between the practitioners of revived witchcraft and the Black Pope *cum suis* were far from cordial, however. Already in the *Satanic Bible*, LaVey scuffed at the "guilt-ridden philosophy" held by "neo-pagan, pseudo-Christian . . . white witchcraft groups" pretending to practice "good" magic.[115] In a later article for his bulletin *Cloven Hoof*, he took the "white magicians" to task who "play the Devil's game and take the Devil's tool" yet deny "His great Infernal Name."[116] Christianity at least was consistent to itself, LaVey argued. "But those who play the Devil's Game yet cloak themselves in RIGHTEOUSNESS besmirch the names of those who bore the mark of brand and tongs and gazed upon their dead and dying with curses softly spoken."[117] In 1972, LaVey returned to the subject in *The Satanic Rituals* and with keen historical intuition pointed out that the adherents of the "safe schools of witchcraft" were playing the same game as the Christian church had done for centuries in their dismissive attitude toward "black" magic. "What is even worse, the followers of the 'Witchcraft-NOT-Satanism!' school harbor the same need to elevate themselves by denigrating others as do their Christian brethren, from whom they claim emancipation."[118]

In their turn, Wiccans were at pains to deny any connection with Satanism. For much of the past decades, their efforts had been directed at gaining "respectability" for their new religion. Sinister images of devil worship did not fit into this strategy.[119] Early Wicca, furthermore, had held its own mythology about black magic and underground circles of devil worshippers opposing the benevolent sorcery of "white" witches. Gardner himself claimed to have battled "in the spirit" against practitioners of black magic, and the British maverick Wiccan Charles Pace (1919–?) even stated to have been a "Master Satanist" before crossing over to the good side.[120] Wicca here was entirely in line with the Lévian tradition of "high magic"; we already saw similar claims and practices with Péladan, Guaita, and even Crowley.

The deliberately sinister image that LaVey adopted did not fit well with this attitude. Accordingly, most Wiccans tended to consider LaVey either as a charlatan harmful for their reputation or as someone genuinely devoted to the black arts. In addition, some neopagans mirrored LaVey's criticism and accused the Church of Satan of being too *Christian*. After all, Satan had been a creation of Judeo-Christian tradition and was thus ultimately a *Christian* deity.[121]

From a historian's vantage point, a few things might be said to put this inner-occult feud in proper perspective. If we consider the Wiccan's side of the argument, it might be remarked that a more thorough awareness of Wicca's and modern Satanism's common roots might be in place, which reach far beyond Aleister Crowley. The dual god and goddess of Murrayite witchcraft never existed as such. When we excavate the bread-crumb trail of textual references that engendered them, we find that one of the most important historical prototypes for the Horned God of Wicca was none other than the rehabilitated, Pan-like Satan of nineteenth-century counterculture.[122] In many respects, neopagan witchcraft and LaVeyan Satanism were thus two branches sprouting from the same tree of Romantic Satanism, nineteenth-century esotericism, and Crowleyanity. Some early representatives of neopagan witchcraft, moreover, displayed a much more open attitude toward the "Satanic." Australian witchcraft pioneer Rosaleen Norton (1917–1979), for instance, venerated not only Pan but also Hecate, Lilith, and Lucifer, whom she described as a trickster god exposing man to the limitations of his ego.[123]

With regard to the Church of Satan, it is hard to deny that LaVey's organization profited greatly from the 1960s occult revival, of which neopagan witchcraft formed a prominent exponent. After all is said and done, Wicca remained the most important religious movement during the 1960s that displayed overt identification with the "other side" of traditional attribution, regardless of the thorough redefining of witches and witchcraft this entailed. (And as we will see later on, LaVeyan Satanism was not above its own condescensions to public respectability.) We can only speculate to what extent this might have inspired LaVey to establish his own brand of "black magic." There is an undeniable resemblance between LaVey's visual setup and the much-photographed rites of, for instance, Alex Sanders, Gardner's self-appointed successor as "King of the Witches." The latter also featured much female nudity and the occasional goat head or human skull. However this may be, it is clear that LaVey sought to "hook on" with the popular fancy for witchcraft, calling his adepts "witches" and "warlocks" and publishing a manual called *The Satanic Witch*, a slightly corny handbook devoted to the lesser or perhaps ultimate magic of being a vamp.[124]

THE OTHER TRADITION: ATTRIBUTION

Crowleyanity and Wicca were not the only channels that may have passed on older notions about Satan and Satanism to LaVey. The "age-old" tradition of attribution was at least as vital for the formation of Satanism as we know it. The continuing transmittance of old, attributed images of devil worship was the rich stock from which people like LaVey took their main inspiration for the composition of their new identity. Huysmans had established and Taxil had exploited a certain stereotype of the Satanist—sinister, blasphemous, sexually deviant, antisocial, conspirational—that had remained in production ever since. This image, in turn, was but a variation of the stereotype of the religious other that had evolved during the Middle Ages. Reports of visits to secret Satanist groups in the style of Huysmans (and with similar reliability) continued to appear in newspapers and popular nonfiction during the entire twentieth century. Mostly, these follow the same rough mold: the inquisitive narrator is picked up in a limousine at a prearranged time and taken to a secret location where he witnesses blasphemous pseudo-medieval rites that more often than not climax in sexual orgies. When he flees in disgust or breaks off relations with the sectarians, he may suffer supernatural harassment or psychic intimidation. The alleged adventures of the American publicist William Seabrook form a classic example, but other instances abound.[125] In addition to these reports of actual encounters with Satanists, books of (usually self-styled) "experts on occultism" transmitted the myth of lurking cells of Satanists in a more general way.[126]

Both these types of reports pretend to be factual descriptions but tend to blend quite easily into the world of fiction and entertainment. As we have seen, the myth of the Satanist had already been commercially appropriated in the fin de siècle, and this process continued in the twentieth century. Horror novels, pulp comic books, movies, and other forms of popular culture passed on and exploited the image of the Satanist. In fact, there is such a wealth of publications and other sources of information transmitting the attributed image of the Satanist during the twentieth century that tracing its trajectory in detail is an all but impossible task, inducing some scholars to speak of a "contemporary legend" or even a "contemporary mythology."[127] It is correspondingly unfeasible to trace the exact channels from which LaVey and his circle picked up this well-nigh universal archetype of the adversary. Yet in order to illustrate the many-forked pathways by which the classic stereotype of Satanism filtered into twentieth-century culture, we will highlight two authors who undoubtedly played important roles in this process. These are the "Reverend" Montague Summers (1880–1948), and the English thriller writer Dennis Wheatley (1897–1977).

Montague Summers was clearly the type of man that the English call "an eccentric."[128] A Cambridge lecturer on Restoration drama, he returned from a voyage to the continent one fine day dressed in clerical garb and claiming to be vested as a Roman Catholic priest. The question of if and how he received holy orders still puzzles his biographers, but however this may be, his sacred vocation apparently made him feel entitled to raise his pen on subjects of a "spiritual" nature.[129] Among these, his preference clearly lay with the sinister and the macabre. At the instigation of publisher C. K. Ogden of Kegan Paul, he devoted several semipopular monographs on subjects like vampires, werewolves, "black magic," and "witchcraft." In 1926, he published a *History of Witchcraft and Black Magic*; in 1927, *The Geography of Witchcraft*, followed in 1937 by *A Popular History of Witchcraft*; and in 1946, *Witchcraft and Black Magic*.

The position taken by Summers in these publications was highly incongruous with his times. Proclaiming himself firmly convinced of the reality of the supernatural, he went on to say that witchcraft and magic not only had been objectively genuine phenomena, but also that Christian society had been quite right in forcefully suppressing this "dangerous cult." "All magic, all witchcraft, depends on the Devil, and is fundamentally evil."[130] Lumped together under the epithet "Satanist," virtually every historical group we encountered in the previous chapters as a victim of attribution passed through Summers's pages, which in general consist of a haberdashery of quotations from old demonologists, recent newspaper articles, and rumors that are given only vague historical coordinates.[131] Thus the affair in Agen that had inspired Vintras pops up again, but in fully "anonymized" wording. ("As early as 1818 . . . Satanists had an active branch in the department of Lot-et-Garonne, and in 1843 it was proved that during some twenty-five years of their existence they had defiled and mutilated no less than three thousand three hundred and twenty Hosts."[132]) And while Taxil is tacitly ignored, the Luciferian chapel on the Borghese Palace reappears as well, in a still more generalized vestment. ("Even more recently, about some ten years ago, another chapel arranged for diabolical worship was accidentally discovered at Rome, great scandal ensued, and this haunt of the infernal cult was speedily suppressed." [133])

Nor was this underground Satanism a thing of the past to Summers. "The Black Mass is said in London and Brighton—and I doubt not in many other towns too—under conditions of all but absolute secrecy," Summers wrote in *Geography of Witchcraft*.[134] In *Witchcraft and Black Magic*, the "many other towns" were further specified, and devil worshippers were said to be active "in London; in Brighton and Birmingham; in Oxford and Cambridge; in

Edinburgh and Glasgow, and in a hundred cities more of the British Isles."[135] And this was just the British outcrop of a vast diabolical conspiracy that sought to plunge Europe into anarchy and destruction. "It can be proved that the French Revolution was carefully planned and mapped out in detail many years before it happened," Summers claimed. "The whole upheaval was manipulated and designed by Satanists from first to last, and this not merely in its broad outlines and events, but even in detail. This can be shown beyond all dispute by the testimony of Professor Robison, Abbé Barruel, and many other solid historians. Since then the same evil forces have planned and carried out other revolutions, until at last they have involved the whole world in chaos and strife."[136] With these "other revolutions," Summers hinted primarily at the Bolshevik takeover in Russia and similar Communist and anarchist attempts in Germany, Hungary, Mexico, and Spain. Elsewhere, Summers even suggested that actual "demons under the form of men" had mingled "among the red raving mobs" to whip the incendiary crowds on to further outrages.[137] To stem this tide of Satanic upheaval, Summers, with so many words, proposed to reinitiate the persecution of witchcraft and occultism. "England has repealed the law against witchcraft," he wrote in conclusion of one of his books. "The Divine Law she cannot repeal. *Thou shalt not suffer a Witch to live.*"[138]

It is hard to say how serious Summers was in all this. For a Roman Catholic hard-liner, so much is certain, he surely displayed some strange traits. Before he had taken the cloth, Summers had been something of a Decadent, with a marked preference for faddish clothes, French poetry, and obscure erotica. The old Montague Summers sometimes shimmered through the pages of the fire-and-brimstone preacher, for instance in his repeated emphasis on the "debaucheries" of Satanism. Summers's translation of the seventeenth-century memoir of Madeleine Bavent had brought his publisher to the attention of British censorship, and when the Reverend referred to the "lewd pages" and "revolting pictures" of the Marquis de Sade, he did not fail to supply detailed bibliophilic advice on said works in an accompanying note.[139] Nor had this interest been merely bookish. Summers had been a practicing homosexual both before and after attaining priesthood, and he had published a slim volume of verse on the theme of pederasty.[140] His model and idol had been the famous Decadent poet Oscar Wilde, and in his student days, he had driven his father to madness by adopting the lisping intonation of a Wildesque dandy. Apart from being more or less openly homosexual, it may be noted that Wilde had converted to Catholicism later in life as well. Becoming Roman Catholic was apparently a very Decadent thing to do, at least in Anglican England. When he took the cloth in 1913, Summers may well have been merely indulging a Decadent fantasy.

Another obvious model for Summers, and one that has not received nearly as much attention in the (admittedly sparse) critical literature devoted to him, was J.-K. Huysmans. For many years, and as one of the few non-French nationals, Summers had held membership in the Société Huysmans, while Summers's works on Satanism are markedly similar in tone and factual content to *Là-Bas*.[141] Huysmans's "sombre romance" is mentioned two times as being "true in every detail". Summers's books repeat and extend many details that Huysmans had also recorded: for instance, the reference to host thefts as irrefutable proof for the existence of Satanist organizations.[142]

Summers's imitation of Huysmans may have extended beyond the domain of literature. As we have seen, the French writer had started out as a Decadent author as well; his original interest in Satanism might not have been entirely motivated by antipathy. Summers seems to have followed him in his traces in this regard and may even have gone a few steps further. One of his former sexual partners confided to the bibliophile Timothy D'Arch Smith that during the year 1918 he and another youth had participated in a "private" Black Mass held by Summers that consisted of a debased version of the Roman Catholic Mass interspersed with homosexual acts.[143] If this event really occurred, Summers provides us with one of the earliest known cases of an actually performed Black Mass. It is not hard to guess where he got his original inspiration for the sacrilegious ceremony. As many did and do, Summers probably took Huysmans's description from *Là-Bas* as autobiographical.[144]

If these reports are true, we may wonder once more what Summers's initial motivation for becoming a priest had been. According to *Là-Bas*, it may be remembered, only an ordained priest could perform a real Black Mass.[145] The conspicuous parallels between Huysmans and Summers also throw a different light on the latter's sudden transformation into a virulent anti-occult author a few years later. Timothy D'Arch Smith speculates that this was brought about by "some sort of psychic kick-back" provoked by his "accumulation" of blasphemies. This could well have been the case. But here again, it looks suspiciously as if Summers was once more acting as an epigone of one of his favorite authors.

Dennis Wheatley, the other author we will discuss here, also owed more than a bit of his inspiration to J.-K. Huysmans. This is particularly apparent in the first work of his hand in which Satanism is a theme, the classic supernatural pot-boiler *The Devil Rides Out*, published in 1934. One of its principal personages is the French royalist Duke, De Richleau, who could have walked straight out of the cabal of conservatives frequented by Durtal in *Là-Bas*, while the Satanist villain is a "former canon" called Mocata that reminds one quaintly of Huysmans's Docre. A close reading of Huysmans is manifest at several lesser points as well: for instance, the statement that half of the people in mental asylums are actually suffering from demonic possession "brought about by looking upon terrible things that they were never meant to see," and the story about white mice fed on holy wafers "that they [the Satanists] compel people to steal from churches for them."[146] Just like Huysmans with *Là-Bas*, Wheatley was careful to maintain the impression that there might be more fact to his fiction than readers might think. In an author's note, he took care to deny that he had ever personally "assisted at, or participated in, any ceremony connected with Magic—Black or White." Yet the book was well researched, Wheatley claimed, and he had verified his findings with "actual practitioners of the Art" and "found ample evidence that Black Magic is still practised in London, and other cities, at the present day." "Should any of my readers incline to a serious study of the subject, and thus come into contact with a man or woman of Power, I feel it is only right to urge them, most strongly, to refrain from being drawn into the practice of the Secret Art in any way. My own observations have led me to an absolute conviction that to do so would bring them into dangers of a very real and concrete nature."[147]

In *The Devil Rides Out*, these "dangers of a very real and concrete nature" include an assembly of Satanists that enact a Sabbath on the heath (complete with nude dancing, cacophonic music, and "the foulest orgy with every perversion which the human mind is capable of conceiving"); an actual apparition of the "Goat of Mendes" (whom the bold heroes of the novel eventually charge at with an automobile); and the evil, child-abusing magician

Mocata with his eerie hypnotizing powers. In Wheatley's next novel in the genre, *To the Devil a Daughter* (1953), an innocent maid is rescued from ritual defloration at the hands of a band of devil worshippers. In 1960 followed *The Satanist*, featuring a diabolical rocket scientist who plans to unleash global nuclear war in order to annihilate Christendom and establish the rule of Satan.

A few words should be devoted to the "actual practitioners of the Art" that Wheatley claimed to have consulted. This was not entirely an empty boast, for Wheatley had indeed sought out a few people who he thought could help him to unravel the mysteries of Satanism. First and foremost among them was none other than Aleister Crowley. Wheatley talked extensively with the Great Beast 666; according to some, the novel writer even may have received some minor initiation into the OTO.[148] Canon Mocata, the grand Satanist from *The Devil Rides Out*, was partly modeled on Crowley, and throughout his novels, Wheatley attributed many tenets of Crowley to Satanism: the Crowleyan system of grades, for instance, the dictum of Do What Thou Wilt, and the term "Order of the Left-Hand Path" as the proper designation for Satanism.[149] This did not prevent Wheatley from making a total mumbo jumbo from Crowley's teachings, interpreting the Word of the Law in its most coarse sense and spreading the wildest rumors about the Beast in print, such as the completely apocryphal story that Crowley had been temporarily committed to a mental asylum when an invocation of Pan had gone out of hand and had led to the demise of the Beast's "spiritual son," one "MacAleister."[150]

Apart from Crowley, Wheatley had also consulted "black magic expert" Montague Summers. The *faux* or *vrai* reverend made a distinctly unsettling impression on Wheatley and his wife, who had stayed for a weekend in Summers's cottage in the country. First, the pair had become alarmed by the enormous number of spiders that scurried over the ceiling of their bedroom. Later, Wheatley's wife stumbled upon a huge old toad in the garden, which Summers promptly declared to be the reincarnation of an old friend of his. The atmosphere grew awkward after Summers fruitlessly tried to sell Wheatley one of his old books for an exorbitant price. The reverend's normally benign face, according to Wheatley, "suddenly became positively demoniac," and the latter hurriedly arranged for an excuse to return to London with his wife.[151] The thriller writer repaid Summers's hospitality by making him the model for the Canon Copley Syle, the principal villain and chief Satanist in *To the Devil a Daughter*.

(Summers in his turn, interestingly enough, had also been in contact with Crowley regarding their mutual sphere of interest—in the twentieth century, our trail of influences crosses and recrosses into a knot of threads that is impossible to disentangle. Rather surprisingly, the two seemed to have gone on quite well, and after having dinner together on July 5, 1929, the Beast jotted down in his journal that he had had "the most amusing evening I have spent in decades."[152] Needless to say, Summers was less kind toward Crowley in print. The anonymized but unmistakable references to Crowley in his publications describe him as an all-out Satanist masking as a follower of Horus.[153] In his memoirs, Summers called the prophet of Thelema "one quarter conjuror and three-quarter charlatan" and much of what he had written "definitely and designedly evil." But he also admitted that the Great Beast had had his occasional "flashes of genius."[154])

Despite the shiver that Summers gave Wheatley, one can detect deep similarities between the attitude of both men toward Satanism. As with Summers, Wheatley's Satanists are

placed in a framework of malevolent conspiracy. While Wheatley was an arch-British sup-
porter of empire, royalty, and class, the Satanists in his novel figure as secret plotters devoted
to establish Satanic misrule. "With that as their goals they do everything they can to foment
wars, class-hatred, strikes and famine, and to foster perversions, moral laxity and the taking
of drugs," a knowing protagonist of one of his novels explains. "There is every reason to
believe that they have been behind many of the political assassinations that have robbed
the world of good rulers and honest statesmen, and naturally communism has now become
their most potent weapon."[155] In *The Satanist*, the Brotherhood of the Ram schemes similar plots, using sexual blackmail, workers' agitation, and the publishing industry. Lothar
Khune, a Satanist rocket-fuel scientist who is the novel's principal evil genius, had been a
Nazi and now was a Communist, but even that is only a front for his real ideology, which
probably can be best described as Satanic anarchism—a Satanic anarchism employing
atomic weapons yet otherwise still basically identical to the anarchism that Huysmans and
Taxil ascribed to *their* Satanists.

To Wheatley, these ideas were clearly more than merely a device of fiction. In fact, the
line between fiction and nonfiction often blurred in his life and work. The publication of
The Devil Rides Out had given him a reputation as an expert on occultism (his own "author's
note" undoubtedly will have been a factor in this), and after its publication, Kegan Paul
asked him to compile a nonfiction book on "black Magic." This he declined, proposing
instead the (equally dubious) expertise of an Egyptian Jew and "White Magician" called
Rollo Ahmed.[156] Almost forty years later, however, Wheatley succumbed after all, writing
a popular nonfiction work called *The Devil and All His Works* (1971). Only the lack of a
plot distinguishes this book from Wheatley's novels, and reading it mainly impresses one
with the wisdom of his initial refusal. But it also makes clear that Wheatley did believe that
many of the things he had presented under the guise of fiction were in fact quite real—or
at least that he had no objection to foster this impression. After suggesting that the French
and Russian Revolutions are the work of Satan, and a particularly laconic and misinformed
section on modern witchcraft and Satanism, Wheatley concluded his book with a strong
appeal to his readers to follow the "Right Hand Path."[157] He intermingled this advice with
political statements of a generally conservative type, deploring the rising tide of decoloniza-
tion, totalitarianism, and socialism. Modern witchcraft and Satanism were further agents
in this demise of civilization because, Wheatley claimed, they actively induced people to
take drugs and served as a "focus for evil." "No civilized person would dream of initiating
witch-hunts such as took place in the seventeenth century," the veteran author muttered.
"But I am most strongly of the opinion that to fight this evil, which is now a principal
breeding-ground for dope-addicts, anarchists and lawlessness, new legislation should be
introduced."[158]

It would be too quick, however, to place an equal sign between Summers and Wheatley.
Huge differences were visible between Summers's self-consciously ultra-Catholic stance
and the more general conservatism of Wheatley. One important difference that immediately strikes the eye is Wheatley's strong inclination toward alternative religiosity. While
Summers, in style with his traditional Catholic posture, rashly discounted these spiritualities as masked forms of devil worship, Wheatley's novels display a more diversified palette of
light and darkness. In *The Devil Rides Out*, for instance, the trappings of Roman Catholic

exorcism function as a potent protection against the sinister powers. Yet these are combined in a completely carefree way with elements of neo-Kabbalist magic and Theosophical theology; and the motivation Wheatley gives for their potency is far from orthodox. ("This is going to protect me," one of the novel's heroes says while holding aloft a crucifix, "because I've got faith that it will.")[159] In the apotheosis of the novel, the deus ex machina that saves the day with a last-minute intervention is not an angel or a saint, but a "Lord of Light nearing perfection after many lives" who is summoned straight from the "Hidden Valley" where he was meditating (and/or from the writings of H. P. Blavatsky, one suspects).[160] Again, this accurately reflects Wheatley's real-life convictions, which seem to have been a mixture of residual Christianity and Theosophical tenets such as reincarnation, karma, and all-wise Hidden Masters.[161] Seen in a broader historical framework, Wheatley's attitudes vis-à-vis "black" and "white" magic resemble those of Éliphas Lévi and the French neo-Kabbalists before him, and those of many adherents of occultism and New Age after him.

Another point that separates Wheatley from Summers is his much more positive attitude toward the values of what we have called the "Western Revolution." Wheatley could certainly be called a conservative. He cherished law, class, order, and tradition, and he was not above mild racism and old man's whining against, for instance, "ultramodern music" (which is disparagingly associated with Satanism in *The Satanist*).[162] Nevertheless, and in contrast to the Catholic reactionaries we discussed in the prior chapter, Wheatley had a high regard for personal and civil liberties. Much of this was undoubtedly due to the simple fact that Wheatley was British; the author probably felt he was only pursuing an English tradition dating back to the Magna Carta in championing the cause of liberty. The principal threat he discerned against the latter was the egalitarian totalitarianism espoused by Communism, to which the seemingly moderate stance of socialism was only a "half way house." That he was serious in his fears and convictions is shown by a "letter to posterity" that was discovered hidden in an urn on the estate where he had lived. In this quaint document, Wheatley urged future generations to initiate guerrilla warfare if a socialist or Communist dictatorship is established in Great Britain after his death. "All men are not equal," the letter proclaimed. "Some have imagination and abilities far above others. It is their province and their right to take upon themselves the responsibility of leading and protecting the less gifted."[163] In case this "false, pernicious doctrine" of equality has prevailed nevertheless (and Wheatley clearly expected that it would), a British patriot can only do one thing. "Therefore, if when this document is discovered, the people of Britain are bound to a state machine, my message to posterity is REBEL. . . . Your life does not matter, but your freedom does. . . . Therefore, if need be, fight for your RIGHT to live, work, and love, how and where you will. If need be die for it."[164]

Summers and Wheatley—both widely read popular authors—present two tangible stepping-stones in the much wider and much more diffuse process by which the centuries-old stereotypes of attribution were carried into the latter half of the twentieth century.[165] This provided the large storehouse of imagery, ritual, and historical association that LaVey would exploit for his venture of appropriation. The High Priest of Satan, as a matter of fact, was directly familiar with the writings of Summers and Wheatley.[166] It has even been suggested that LaVey with his Church of Satan consciously sought to re-create the organization described in Wheatley's *The Satanist*, which appeared in print just six years before LaVey declared the Age of Satan.[167] There are indeed interesting parallels between the Satanists described by Wheatley and the construct of Anton LaVey. Some of them are rather trivial perhaps: Wheatley's Satanists convene in an old Georgian house riddled with unexpected spy holes, passages, and galleries. LaVey's Black House likewise contained secret passageways and other spook-house applications, possibly constructed by LaVey himself. Other similarities are more profound. When the villainous Lothar Khune announces the dawning of a new Satanic Age in the final part of the book, one is involuntarily reminded of LaVey's corresponding venture; also, the way in which Wheatley has Khune denounce the "Christian heresy" (which has "inflicted on the world many generations of senseless self-denial" and "denied the people the joy in life which was their birthright") would be mirrored by LaVey in the *Satanic Bible*.[168] Furthermore, LaVey was definitely much attracted to the idea of Satanists as powerful conspirators scheming behind the scenes, as we will notice later on.

THE HERITAGE OF ROMANTIC SATANISM

Of course, it would be misleading to suggest that LaVey simply copycatted his idea for a Satanic church from a Wheatley thriller. The "Exarch of Hell" could employ a much wider variety of sources for this, and he clearly did. Wheatley and LaVey, it might be said, drew from the same well of historical influences and took from the same stock of images to invent their respective enactments of Satanism. The essential difference between them remains, evidently, that the former attributes Satanism to the (villainous) other, while LaVey identified with it. As stated in chapter 3, the first individuals to make this fundamental shift in modern history had been the Romantic Satanists. Their positive reversal of attributes traditionally ascribed to Satan and Satanism, I also argued, would be decisive for the shape of modern religious Satanism, and the Romantic attitude toward religion/spirituality would prove essential in enabling the emergence of modern religious Satanism. Are these presumptions borne out when we take a closer look into the Satanism of LaVey? This will be the subject of the current section and an important part of the next.[169]

The most conspicuous aspect of nineteenth-century heritage manifesting itself in modern religious Satanism is, without doubt, the threefold revaluation of "Satanic" attributes initiated by the Romantic Satanists. The trio sex, science, and liberty are prominently present in the writings and utterances of LaVey. Sex, to start with this ever-fascinating theme, fills many pages of the *Satanic Bible*; in fact, one of the longest chapters in the book is devoted to "Satanic Sex."[170] To the *Wall Street Journal*, LaVey described his congregation as simply one of "pleasure-loving individuals who want to throw off the stifling factors of denial and hypocrisy."[171] With the Sexual Revolution gaining pace, Satan's priest boldly spoke out in defense of "deviant and/or fetishistic" sexual practices. "Satanism condones any type of sexual activity which properly satisfies your individual desires—be it heterosexual, homosexual, bisexual, or even asexual, if you choose. Satanism also sanctions any fetish and deviation which will enhance your sex-life, so long as it involves no one who does not wish to be involved."[172]

Nor is the wider application of this theme to carnality/nature that we noticed in the nineteenth century absent from Church of Satan material. "Satan represents opposition to all religions which serve to frustrate and condemn man for his natural instincts," LaVey wrote. "He has been given an evil role simply because he represents the carnal, earthly, and mundane aspects of life."[173] The acknowledgment of man as a carnal being forms an essential ingredient of Satanist doctrine. This point is made several times in the *Satanic Bible*, both implicitly and explicitly: for instance, in LaVey's creative reversal of the seven deadly sins into harbingers of physical, mental, and emotional pleasure.[174] "The FLESH prevaileth," LaVey announced in his prologue to the *Satanic Bible*, "and a great Church shall be built, consecrated in its name."[175] Even the extension of Satan into a sort of Pan-like all-embracing god of Earth (as displayed by Carducci, Lévi, and Crowley) finds some reflections in LaVeyan Satanism. In an obscure passage that we will discuss more thoroughly later on, LaVey described his godhead as the "balancing force in nature" and the "powerful force which permeates and balances the universe."[176] With all his criticism of Crowley, LaVey did express great admiration for the Great Beast's famous "Hymn to Pan."[177]

Science, or the pursuit of knowledge, is less distinctive as a Satanic attribute in the corpus of LaVeyan Satanism. Certainly, a strong rationalism pervades LaVey's religious construction; but although we can now understand why, historically speaking, this element is not necessarily alien to his new religion of Satanism, it is questionable whether LaVey is reflecting a specific tradition concerning *Satan* here. Carducci's hymn to Satan, it is true, is mentioned favorably by him.[178] But LaVey's attempt to build a "rational" religion can be placed in a much more general tradition of Western alternative religiosity dating back to the nineteenth century, and probably before, as well as to the rational antireligious critique of the Enlightenment. We will come to speak about this aspect of LaVeyan Satanism in more detail in the next section.

Nevertheless, small echoes of the nineteenth-century connection between Satan and science are to be found in the pages of LaVey. In the introduction to the "Book of Lucifer" (the second part of the *Satanic Bible*), Lucifer is called the "personification of enlightenment," bringing "mental emancipation" and "truth" and unmasking "bogus values" and "clouded definitions."[179] In *Satanic Rituals*, LaVey appealed to scientists not to forget the diabolical stigma their "academic and laboratory forebears" suffered and to acknowledge that they stand in a Satanist tradition.[180] With some benevolence, a faint flicker of this thematic thread might also be discerned in LaVey's preoccupation with "artificial human companions," the creation of which he dubbed "the most Satanic activity possible."[181] "The cold and hungry of the past produced offspring to till the fields and work the mills," the High Priest of Satan mused in the epilogue of *Satanic Rituals*. "Their cold will stop and their hunger shall end, but they will produce fewer children, for the by-product of the magician's frozen seed which has been born upon the earth will perform the tasks of the human offspring of the past. . . . The existence of the man-god will be apparent to even the simplest, who will see the miracles of his creativity."[182]

As in the nineteenth-century countertradition initiated by Romantic Satanism, however, the essence of Satanist identity in the *Satanic Bible* can be summarized as *liberty*. Freedom, which for LaVey predominantly meant *personal* freedom, is the red thread that runs through most of modern Satanism's doctrine. It is, for instance, the crucial factor in LaVey's treatment of sex. According to LaVey, a person must not primarily seek to "emancipate" himself from religion-induced guilt complexes to experience sexuality as a "healthy" person "should." Rather, he is free to find sexual gratification in the way he likes as an *individual*, however perverse others might consider his preferences. In this LaVey, according to himself, reacted against the quasivoluntary "liberation" through collective sex practiced by the wilder fringes of 1960s counterculture, as well as against the surrogate priesthood of psychiatry that had established new, "scientific" standards of accepted sexual behavior.

Freedom for the individual is the hidden premise behind most of LaVey's philosophy. Yet the circumstances in which he founded the Church of Satan differed substantially from those in which the Romantic Satanists and their nineteenth-century heirs had propagated the "Satanic" cause of liberty. Autocratic monarchs and officially imposed religion had all but disappeared from the West. Many of those we encountered in the nineteenth century as in some way identifying themselves with Satan had faced or feared personal consequences for their standpoints, whether prison sentence, exile, censorship, or loss of custody of their children. In the place and time where LaVey founded his Church of Satan, these things seemed of the past. The ease and immunity with which LaVey could create his church, which called on a deity diametrically opposed to that of the majority of Americans, attest to the degree by which values of the Western Revolution like freedom for religion had become rooted in the West by the 1960s. It was therefore perhaps not altogether illogical that other issues obtained more urgency on LaVey's agenda. The Angel of Liberty that Satan had been to a segment of nineteenth-century counterculture rears its head most conspicuously in LaVey's continuous insistence on the right and the necessity to be genuinely individual and nonconformist, not heeding the conventions and fads of the "herd" (i.e., mankind's majority). LaVey's own experiences with the community-enforced conformity of the 1940s and 1950s will surely have had something to do with this.[183] Some twenty years later, LaVey would thus explain the significance of Satan: "Satan is the name used by Judeo-Christians for that force of individuality and pride within us, . . . the one who advocates free thought and rational alternative by whatever name."[184]

The recurrence of precisely these elements in modern religious Satanism can, to my mind, hardly be coincidental. But this does not yet explain the exact historical relation between Romantic Satanism and the modern Satanism that came into being with the Church of Satan. How did the poetical Satanism of some of the Romantics result in a Californian Church of Satan? Certainly this relation is not to be understood as one of direct inspiration or imitation. Anton LaVey did not pick up a volume of Shelley's verse or Byron's *Cain* and decide to start an organization to venerate Satan. Although it is hardly probable that the Black Pope was not at least superficially familiar with their "Satanic" works, neither Blake nor Shelley nor Byron are mentioned in his writings, in contrast with much less "pro-Satanic" authors like Milton, Baudelaire, and Huysmans.[185]

That is not to say that the influence of the Romantic Satanists did not reach LaVey, even if we cannot be sure whether he or anybody in his circle read them. As we have seen before, the rehabilitation of Satan had become a widespread topos toward the end of the nineteenth century and was transferred as such into the twentieth. It might be described as a sort of countertradition to that of the attributed image of the Satanist, not as near-universally spread as the latter, perhaps, but like this very much a diffuse presence among a wide range of literary authors, occultists, and others. If we are looking for concrete channels by which certain notions of Romantic Satanism may have come through to California, the lore and literature of occultism especially suggests itself. Both Lévi and Crowley repeat and re-create premises of Romantic Satanism, and LaVey was demonstrably familiar with their work.[186]

However, the relation of the Romantic Satanism of yore and the religious Satanism of today is not adequately described, I would like to argue, as that of direct or indirect influence transmitted by this or that publication. Rather, the Romantic Satanists, I think, set in motion a cultural chain process of appropriation and rehabilitation of Satan that, through a series of diverse but interconnected stages, eventually gave birth to a religious Satanism. One of these intermediate stages is the creation of neopagan witchcraft via Michelet and Crowley; another, the Romantic notions about Satan that filtered down into occultism by way of Lévi, Blavatsky, Crowley (once more), and others; yet another, the incorporation, albeit in a negative mirror image, of ideas of Romantic Satanism with authors like Huysmans and Wheatley, which were then again reappropriated and reversed positively by LaVey *cum suis*. Ultimately, the answer to our question is the story told in this book.

It would also be overtly simplistic to view religious Satanism as a bare reenactment of Romantic Satanism that had finally taken recognizable religious form. Anti-Christian discourse had evolved into new shapes in the century that separated Anton LaVey from Victor Hugo, and the form of the former's Satanism was duly affected. Darwin's account of natural history had further discredited the Christian creation myth and had unsettled dominant anthropocentric notions about the world. Freud had followed with his relentless analysis of man as a primarily libido-driven organism and his *démasqué* of religion as a projection of the father figure. The thinker who was to have the most profound influence on modern Satanism, however, was Friedrich Nietzsche (1844–1900), the "philosopher with the hammer." Famous as the man who announced the death of the Christian god, his vehement criticism of Christianity and "pseudo-Christian" Idealist philosophy would win him posthumous notoriety and make him an essential stepping-stone in the development of modern Satanism.[187]

An important feature of Nietzsche's philosophy was the radical way in which he deconstructed Christian morals. Enlightenment and earlier nineteenth-century critics of religion had attacked the oppressive and self-conflicting aspects of Christianity, but they had not called into question the fundamental premises of "good" and "evil" in Christian ethics. Thus the Romantic Satanists, although decrying some aspects of Christian morality (for instance, regarding sexuality), had generally not uttered doubt about its general framework. In a sense, they had merely applied the professed ethics of Christianity to the Christian god himself and had found him wanting: a brutal tyrant ordering the massacre of entire peoples and condoning the cruelty of kings. Likewise, they recognized, extolled, and created a Satan that sometimes was almost Christ-like in its embodiment of virtue; as a French historian has aptly stated, their portrayal of the devil basically amounted to a "canonization of Satan."[188]

Nietzsche went much further and targeted the "old delusion of good and evil" itself.[189] To the German philosopher, all ethics were relative, dependent on the vantage point of those who formulate them; what was more, all ethics were in essence an *instrument of power*. In particular, he distinguished two sets of ethics: the morality of the slaves (*Sklavenmoral*) and the morality of the masters (*Herrenmoral*). The former embodied values that were strategic to "the weak": for instance, the value of compassion with those that are defenseless or vulnerable, or the belief that one's meager existence on earth would be compensated in a glorious afterlife and that abnegation and asceticism were virtuous. The strong, according to Nietzsche, did not need these values or beliefs. They simply enjoyed existence, including the struggle it contains, and were able to face reality as it is, without the need for life-transcending compensations.

Christianity, of course, presented the apogee of slave morality. It could be described as the revolution of the weak, who had succeeded in dominating Europe through the gradual imposition of the Christian system of values. Strictly speaking, none of the two value systems were "good" or "bad." "Slave morality" was simply the natural and most fitting moral strategy for the "herd" of the weak and the unfit, while the *Herrenmoral* presented the natural morality of the strong. It was abundantly clear, however, which values Nietzsche preferred. It was the system of the strong, of the ruler, that gave voice to the human being in its most healthy, sublime, and joyful manifestation. It was this pre-Christian value system that had allowed the splendor of Greek and Roman civilization. "What is good?" Nietzsche wrote. "Everything that stimulates the perception of power, the will to power, power itself in Man. What is bad? Everything that originates from weakness."[190]

Nietzsche saw himself as the prophet of the impending counterrevolution of the strong; his work was one strident call for an "Umwertung aller Werte," a "revaluation of all values." The signs were there that this revolution was imminent. God was dead, Nietzsche had written. By this phrase, he meant that the Christian god had already been dismissed as a figure of practical consequence by most modern Europeans: he merely lived on as a pale specter in philosophical notions as the Kantian "moral imperative" and as a hollow camouflage for institutional self-interest. The "philosopher with the hammer" castigated his fellow Europeans for clinging to these hypocritical vestiges of a superseded faith and urged them to embrace a new morality. A new, better kind of man could then evolve, a kind of man that was morally free and spiritually bold, called the "*Übermensch*" by Nietzsche, literally the "Superman."

Nietzsche published his views in a series of mostly self-financed works—of which the most important were *Also sprach Zarathustra* ("Thus Spoke Zarathustra," 1883–1885), *Jenseits von Gute und Bösen* ("Beyond Good and Evil," 1885–1886), and *Zur Genealogie der Moral* ("On the Genealogy of Morals," 1887)—before slipping into madness and spending the final decade of the nineteenth century in catatonic silence. The last manuscript he finished was appropriately called *Antichris*. It ended with a "Law against Christianity" that declared "war to the death" against the "slander" of the Christian religion for its role as promoter of "anti-nature." "Every display of contempt for sexual love, and every defilement of it through the concept 'unclean' is the original sin against the holy spirit of life," he hammered in the seven-point text, which was probably intended to be reproduced and distributed as a leaflet. In conclusion, the German philosopher suggested to banish all priests and to raze to the ground all the "accursed places in which Christianity has hatched its basilisk eggs." The decree was signed with "Antichrist" and dated "on the day of salvation, on the first day of the Year One (– September 30, 1888 of the false time-chronology)."

While Nietzsche succumbed to insanity, his fame began to rise. Nietzschean concepts began to interact with social Darwinism, the nineteenth-century bastard child of Darwinism that was characterized by an often rather crude application of Darwin's theories to human society. In its simplest form, it argued that the "unfit" would and/or should be eradicated from society. As such, the doctrine served as a rationale for unbridled capitalism; moreover, it was soon coupled to older racial or ethnic prejudices, giving these a new, pseudo-scientific rationale. The 1930s and 1940s would prove the potential catastrophic nature of this ménage à trois among old prejudices, new social Darwinist theories, and Nietzschean ideas exploited at their roughest edge. Although he was undoubtedly influenced by Darwinism, Nietzsche would certainly not have condoned this perverse coupling. The philosopher had been vocal in his utter contempt for antisemitism and nationalism, considering himself first and foremost as a "European," heir to the philosophical and spiritual tradition of his continent. Yet this did not mean that he had refrained from drawing violent conclusions from his own philosophy. "The weak and the misfits must perish: first principle of our charity," he wrote in *Antichrist*. "And what's more: one should help them to do so."[191]

It is largely, if not exclusively, due to LaVey's enthusiastic absorption of Nietzschean ideas, I would venture, that modern Satanism became the religious movement that it is: that is, a religion that can broadly be placed on the "Rightist" side of the political spectrum, instead of the Leftist. This represents a clear break with the nineteenth-century "tradition" of identification with Satan, which almost always served, for better or worse, "progressive" causes. In *The Satanic Bible*, their Californian successor trumpeted a completely different tune. In the first verse of the first book of the foundation text of modern Satanism, the resounding injunction "Death to the weakling, wealth to the strong!" can be read.[192] A few pages later, the words attributed to Jesus are completely reversed:

Love your enemies and do good to them that hate and use you—is this not the despicable philosophy of the spaniel that rolls on its back when kicked?

Hate your enemies with a whole heart, and if a man smite you on one cheek, SMASH him on the other!; smite him hip and thigh, for self-preservation is the highest law![193]

These and similar sentiments are repeated, although in somewhat more measured language, throughout LaVey's bible. Number four of the Nine Satanic Statements states: "Satanism represents kindness to those who deserve it instead of love wasted on ingrates!" This is also the first sentence of the short chapter dealing with "love and hate," which continues "Therefore, the Satanist believes you should love strongly and completely those who deserve your love, but never turn the other cheek to your enemy!"[194]

Given these passages, it is not surprising that LaVey does not think it unfeasible to harm or kill others by magical curses, if the circumstances are exceptional and the receiver of the curse is a structural pest bound on the Satanist's destruction.[195] Elsewhere, LaVey gives Nietzsche a virtuoso kitchen-psychological application when he introduces the concept of the "psychic vampire": people who "practise the fine art of making others feel responsible and even indebted to them, without cause." These should be "graciously" shaken off.[196] In fact, Nietzsche's influence on *The Satanic Bible* is so pervasive that some have dubbed the book a Nietzschean travesty. LaVey was not evasive about his inspiration. He frequently named Nietzsche as the single most influential writer he read, and when he mentioned other authors, these were generally not Romantic Satanists or occultists, but American and English writers that he considered (rightly or wrongly) as expounding Nietzschean or social Darwinist ideas, such as Ayn Rand, H. L. Mencken, H. G. Wells, Ben Hecht, George Bernard Shaw, Herbert Spencer, and Jack London.[197]

For clarity's sake, this Nietzschean inspiration is purely philosophical. Apart from a few scattered and inconsequential phrases, Satan or the devil hardly come up in Nietzsche's work. Furthermore, it is clear that LaVey had dipped deeply into text material from ideological currents mixing Nietzscheanism with social Darwinism. This is made apparent by the "infernal diatribe" that makes up the bulk of the first book of *The Satanic Bible* and from which I quoted some martial injunctions just before. In reality, this part of LaVey's book was nothing but a reworked version of the blatantly social Darwinist tract *Might Is Right* that had appeared in 1896 under the pseudonym Ragnar Redbeard.[198] The text was so obscure that it took two decades before LaVey's plagiarism was discovered, although LaVey mentioned Ragnar Redbeard on the dedication page of the first edition of his *Satanic Bible*. LaVey's retouches consisted mainly of removing the many instances of misogyny, racism, and antisemitism from the text, as well as adding a few superficial allusions to the devil (e.g., the "righteously humble" shall be trodden "under cloven hoofs" instead of the original ordinary hoofs).[199] When his "loan" was discovered, LaVey was unapologetic, both for his plagiarism and for the character of the work he had plundered. Instead, he wrote an introduction to a new edition of the pamphlet, praising it for its "blasphemy."[200]

In the earliest stage of the Church of Satan, the influence of these "might is right" ideas was not yet so dominating. At least, that is not the impression one obtains from reading *The Satanic Bible*, which on the whole exhumes an atmosphere of cheerfulness and liberation and is rich with irony and not devoid of common sense (who does not know at least one "psychic vampire"?). However, LaVey's more obscure philosophical wellsprings explain some passages that would otherwise strike one as out of place, as well as some of LaVey's ideological stances, which seem surprising in the light of the "Satanist" heritage of the nineteenth century. In one passage, for instance, Nietzsche's naturally dominating *Übermensch* and the Darwinist "fittest" are implicitly equaled with those enjoying covert or overt success in society; and those in turn are identified as the genuine "Satanists" of this world. "It would be an over-simplification to say that every successful man and woman is, without knowing it, a practising Satanist," LaVey argues, "but the thirst for earthly success and its ensuing realization are certainly grounds for Saint Peter turning thumbs down. If the rich man's entry into heaven seems as difficult as the camel's attempt to go through the eye of the needle; if the love of money is the root of all evil; then we must at least assume the most powerful men on earth to be the most Satanic. This applies to financiers, industrialists, popes, poets, dictators, and all assorted opinion-makers and field marshals of the world's activities."[201]

Realizing that this definition is highly ideological or theological (for want of a better word) and not so much historical, LaVey continued to identify as the "true legacy of Satanism" a string of historical characters that exerted their influence in secret and had allegedly "dabbled in the black arts": "Names like Rasputin, Zaharoff, Cagliostro, Rosenberg and their ilk."[202] This secret "tradition," however, was bound to come into the open now that the Age of Satan had begun to bloom. Thus, LaVey elsewhere in *The Satanic Bible* describes how the true Satanist "either escapes from the cacklings and carpings of the righteous, or stands proudly in his secret places of the earth and manipulates the folly-ridden masses through his own Satanic might, until that day when he may come forth in splendor proclaiming 'I AM A SATANIST! BOW DOWN, FOR I AM THE HIGHEST EMBODIMENT OF HUMAN LIFE!' "[203]

"Might is right" ideology had also been a factor in determining LaVey's ideas regarding wider society and the attitude his newly born religious organization should adopt toward it. We will return to these in more detail in the next chapter. In interviews, LaVey repeatedly declared his Church of Satan to be a strictly law-abiding organization and emphasized that a true Satanist should work within the given parameters of society. These utterances seem surprising for a Satanist organization. Doubtlessly they were primarily inspired by pragmatic motives, but "might is right" gave the ideological rationale for this position. In the America of the 1960s, where political agitation by Leftwing groups experienced a resurgence and the civil rights struggle was still in process, this law-abiding stance was by no means a given choice. By taking the direction he did, LaVey effectively moved his religious Satanism away from the "revolutionary" tradition of Romantic Satanism that had preceded it and steered it into decidedly Right-wing waters. Indeed, Church of Satan outlooks on issues like drugs, government, social legislation, legal retribution, and even abortion were often strangely alike to those that conservatives might hold, however horrified the latter were bound to be by the religious tenets Satanism holds.[204] Wheatley and LaVey could have had a friendly coffee-table conversation, one suspects.

THE PARADOX OF ANTIRELIGIOUS RELIGION

Sex, liberty, and relentless Nietzschean philosophy go a long way to describe the essential makeup of LaVeyan Satanism. Yet there are more aspects of LaVey's religious venture that show interesting links with the European heritage that I described in earlier chapters. The component of magic is one of them—I will elaborate upon this in the next section. Another at least as interesting theme is LaVey's ambivalent and highly modern (or even postmodern) outlook upon religion. His paradoxical attempt to create an *antireligious religion* is another aspect that gives modern religious Satanism much of its specific flavor.

The Satanic Bible and LaVey's other writings abound in criticism of what he called "white light religion": the religions of revelation, abstinence, and (self-)transcendence. Implicit in LaVey's writing on all past religion is the idea that it is basically a superstition—something that had been superimposed on man's normal, "natural" comport. If this religious "superimposition" can be lifted, man can (re)start to live as he really is supposed to do. It is clearly implicated that this would be the "right" way to live, although many aspects of this "natural" behavior may seem "evil" and "savage" to "white light religionists" and their ilk, and although the Satanist may even adopt epithets like "evil" and "diabolical" for himself in conscious defiance. Ultimately, however, this is only because concepts of "good" and "evil" have become tainted by religious "superstition"—or rather because these concepts are in essence religious superstitions themselves.

There is nothing new in these suppositions, and it is not hard to detect the faraway echoes in them of the antireligious discourse of Enlightenment thinkers like Voltaire, Rousseau, and Feuerbach (as well as, of course, the ubiquitous Nietzsche, who himself continued in the footsteps of Enlightenment religious criticism as well). At times, one is also quaintly reminded of Romantic Satanists like Shelley and Blake, who adopted (part) of the Enlightenment criticism of organized religion in their own anti-Christian program: for instance, when LaVey argues that the primary instrument utilized by past religions to get dominion over man, is fear. "Without such wholesale fear religionists would have had nothing with which to wield power over their followers."[205] With fear established, the "white light religionists" could further extend their power by introducing the idea of *sin*. When as much as possible of man's natural acts are declared "sinful," people are guaranteed to transgress. Thus they will be bound to feel guilt and can easily be induced to atone for their trespassing. LaVey formulated this hypothesis most clearly in his treatment of masturbatory sex. "The Satanist," he declared, "fully realizes why religionists declare masturbation to be sinful. Like all other natural acts people *will* do it, no matter how severely reprimanded. Causing guilt is an important facet of their malicious scheme to obligate people to atone for 'sins' by paying the mortgages on temples of abstinence!"[206]

The gospel LaVey's Satanism posited against this Christian conspiracy is basically the idea that human beings are good when they "indulge in their natural desires."[207] LaVey preached, one could say, salvation from salvation, deliverance from the idea that one needs to be delivered.[208] This acceptance of the self is surely one of the principal factors that made and makes his religion attractive, even for those without a prior religious background: restriction and restraint are deep-rooted aspects of any human society and any form of social interaction. Of course, the "self" that LaVey postulates is a highly simplified, almost mythic one—man "as just another animal."[209] But this simplification probably is in itself part of the attraction. Obviously, we can see a basic assumption return here that was held by both Enlightenment and Romantic thinkers: that man should be guided by his "natural lights." Rousseau's "noble savage," one could say, thus makes his reappearance on the pages of LaVey—although this time he is allowed considerably more savagery.

The stark reductionism of LaVey's philosophy begs the question of why one would still want to have a religion at all, or at least something suspiciously like it. Why still engage in symbol-fraught rituals in the name of supernatural beings borrowed from older religions? LaVey asked this question himself in *The Satanic Bible*. Even though modern man "has become disenchanted with the nonsensical dogmas of past religions," he answered, and increasingly had come to realize his true nature, this did not mean that he had genuinely attained the new "awareness of the flesh" that *The Satanic Bible* called the highest plateau of human development.[210]

> It is one thing to accept something intellectually, but to accept the same thing emotionally is an entirely different matter. . . . Man needs ceremony and ritual, fantasy and enchantment. Psychiatry, despite all the good it has done, has robbed man of wonder and fantasy which religion, in the past, has provided. Satanism, realizing the current need of man, fills the large grey void between religion and psychiatry. The Satanic philosophy *combines* the fundamentals of psychology *and* good, honest emotionalizing, or dogma. It provides man with his much needed fantasy. There is nothing wrong with dogma, providing it is not based on ideas and actions that go completely against human nature.[211]

There is more than a streak of Romanticism in this call for "wonder and fantasy" and for the recognition of man's irrational side. In another part of *The Satanic Bible*, LaVey makes an even more fundamental shift that greatly resembles the reversion of the Enlightenment critique of religion made by some of the Romantics. I quote this passage extensively:

> All religions of a spiritual nature are inventions of man. He has created an entire system of gods with nothing more than his carnal brain. Just because he has an ego and cannot accept it, he has to externalize it into some great spiritual device which he calls "God." . . . If man needs such a god and recognizes that god, then he is worshiping an entity that a human being invented. Therefore, HE IS WORSHIPPING BY PROXY THE MAN THAT INVENTED GOD. Is it not more sensible to worship a god that he, himself, has created, in accordance with his own emotional needs—one that best represents the very carnal and physical being that has the idea-power to invent a god *in the first place*? If man insists on externalizing his true self in the form of "God," than why fear this true self, in fearing "God,"—why remain externalized from "God" IN ORDER TO ENGAGE IN RITUAL WORSHIP AND RELIGIOUS CEREMONY IN HIS NAME? . . . Could it be that when he closes the gap between himself and his "God" he sees the demon of pride creeping forth—that very embodiment of Lucifer appearing in his midst?[212]

The ultimate consequence of this is that man is a god himself "if he chooses to recognize himself as one"—something that is humorously acknowledged by LaVey when he declares the Satanist's own birthday to be the most important religious holiday of the year.[213] Satan ultimately represents the god that man is himself; and the religion of Satanism is the way a person can empower himself as such by therapeutic use of the "pageantry" of old religion. "If he accepts himself, but recognizes that ritual and ceremony are the important devices that his invented religions have utilized to sustain his faith *in a lie*, than it is the SAME FORM OF RITUAL that will sustain his faith *in the truth*—the primitive pageantry that will give his awareness of his own majestic being added substance."[214]

In passages like these, the religious core of LaVeyan Satanism becomes most clear—in essence a quest to transcend the current self of the adherent, a self that must realize an ever-elusive state of "carnal" purity by stripping itself of all that is judged unnatural or detrimental. The strong affinities with the Romantic thought we encountered in chapter 2 also become evident here. LaVey's claim that all spiritual religions are "inventions of man" is reminiscent of William Blake's "all human deities reside in the human breast," and LaVey's conclusions from this axiom are remarkably similar to those of Blake as well. If man creates the gods, then the real divine power, if any, is man's creativity: LaVey's "idea-power" and Blake's poetic Genius or Imagination. Of course, there are great differences between Blake and LaVey, stemming partly from the latter's rejection and the former's acceptance of the supernatural. But both arrive ultimately at the same conclusion: that the real god is man, or at least those men that are truly great. LaVey thus fits perfectly in the general shift from transcendent sky god to immanent "earth" deity that Northrop Frye detected as an overall pattern in Romantic thought. For Romantic Satanism, the essence of Satan or Lucifer was his symbolic embodiment of a humanity that, Prometheus-like, assumes the dignities of a deity. This tallies closely with the way LaVey presents the devil: as the symbolic deity who "closes the gap" between man and his gods. Other than most Romantics, however, LaVey proceeded to establish a "formal" religion with ritual, dogma, and hierarchy based on these tenets. "Man needs ritual and dogma, but no law states that an *externalized* god is necessary in order to engage in ritual and ceremony performed in a god's name!"[215] Thus modern religious Satanism was born.

Again we may ask: how did these Romantic notions travel to 1960s California? Once more, this question may miss the point. Romanticism may have been simply the first movement in modern European history that formulated options of self-religiosity and self-created spirituality, options that were rediscovered again and again in the two centuries that followed, particularly at times when the corrosion of traditional faiths accelerated, as in the 1960s. And they were rediscovered again and again because the conditions of Western civilization enabled them to arise and gave rise to the questions for which they were a possible answer. In fact, self-religiosity, creative reconstruction of myth, and self-created spirituality form a common part of many new religious groups and movements that have emerged since the onset of secularization—LaVeyan Satanism was just one, if certainly an extremely blatant, example of this trend.[216] Romanticism is often mentioned as one of the original well founts of these movements.[217] This, I think, is not without ground. We have just one history. There might have grown a German fascism without Versailles, but it is impossible to say how it would have looked like; likewise, Romanticism was decisive in the emergence of the religions of the self in modern history. It does not matter much whether these concepts have been adopted directly or indirectly from the Romantic authors themselves or were reinvented independently in an intellectual world that had been given its shape in part by the Romantic movement that came before.

Nevertheless, it may be worthwhile to examine the historical sources through which LaVey could have had access to this diffuse Romantic complex of ideas about spirituality—both to explore possible routes of transmittance and to gain an impression of the historical evolution that the ideas of the Romantics had experienced in the intermediate spiritual and intellectual history of the West. The first mediator that has to be mentioned in this context is, once again, the German philosopher Nietzsche. With his celebration of free human creativity as the sovereign creator of value and meaning, Nietzsche can in many respects be considered an apogee of Romantic thought. He expressed this part of his ideas most eloquently and most poetically in the famous parable of the camel, the lion, and the child from *Thus Spoke Zarathustra*:

> Three metamorphoses of the spirit do I designate to you: how the spirit becometh a camel, the camel a lion, and the lion at last a child.
>
> Many heavy things are there for the spirit, the strong load-bearing spirit in which reverence dwelleth: for the heavy and the heaviest longeth its strength. . . .
>
> All these heaviest things the load-bearing spirit taketh upon itself: and like the camel, which, when laden, hasteneth into the wilderness, so hasteneth the spirit into its wilderness.
>
> But in the loneliest wilderness happeneth the second metamorphosis: here the spirit becometh a lion; freedom will it capture, and lordship in its own wilderness.
>
> Its last Lord it here seeketh: hostile will it be to him, and to its last God; for victory will it struggle with the great dragon.
>
> What is the great dragon which the spirit is no longer inclined to call Lord and God? "Thou-shalt," is the great dragon called. But the spirit of the lion saith, "I will."

"Thou-shalt," lieth in its path, sparkling with gold—a scale-covered beast; and on every scale glittereth golden, "Thou shalt!"

The values of a thousand years glitter on those scales, and thus speaketh the mightiest of all dragons: "All the values of things—glitter on me. All values have already been created, and all created values—do I represent. Verily, there shall be no 'I will' any more." Thus speaketh the dragon.

My brethren, wherefore is there need of the lion in the spirit? Why sufficeth not the beast of burden, which renounceth and is reverent?

To create new values—that, even the lion cannot yet accomplish: but to create itself freedom for new creating—that can the might of the lion do.

To create itself freedom, and give a holy Nay even unto duty: for that, my brethren, there is need of the lion.

To assume the right to new values—that is the most formidable assumption for a load-bearing and reverent spirit. Verily, unto such a spirit it is preying, and the work of a beast of prey.

As its holiest, it once loved "Thou-shalt": now is it forced to find illusion and arbitrariness even in the holiest things, that it may capture freedom from its love: the lion is needed for this capture.

But tell me, my brethren, what the child can do, which even the lion could not do? Why hath the preying lion still to become a child?

Innocence is the child, and forgetfulness, a new beginning, a game, a self-rolling wheel, a first movement, a holy Yea.

Aye, for the game of creating, my brethren, there is needed a holy Yea unto life: ITS OWN will, willeth now the spirit; HIS OWN world winneth the world's outcast.[218]

Liberated humanity constructing in childlike creativity its own values and spirituality: that is the essence of Nietzsche's *Übermensch*. This is, I would say, nothing but a recast of the self-emancipating humanity celebrated by many of the Romantics, a humanity that would "rather be god itself" than bow for a god of tradition, a humanity that wants "the kingdom of the earth" instead of that of heaven.[219] "I guess you would call my Superman—a Devil," Nietzsche had predicted: and this is indeed what happened in LaVeyan Satanism.[220]

Apart from Nietzsche, modern occultism suggests itself as a possible channel by which the Romantic anchorage in the "divine self" may have filtered through to LaVey. We have seen in chapter 3 how Romantic attitudes of religious creativity echoed in the work of Lévi, who could be described as having started out as a minor poet in the "Satanic School" himself. In addition, Aleister Crowley once more provides a link between this tradition and LaVeyan Satanism. Incidentally, Crowley had set out on his checkered career as a Romantic and Decadent poet, and he never ceased to be one.[221] Poetry, religion, and magic were closely intertwined domains in his life, and fragments of his poetry frequently ended up in his ritual texts. In true Romantic mode, the Beast considered the author as "the hierophant or oracle of some god, and the publisher as his herald."[222] He was also very explicit as to which "school of poetry" he felt he belonged. "Baudelaire and Swinburne, at their best, succeed in celebrating the victory of the human soul over its adversaries, just as truly as Milton and Shelley. I never had a moment's doubt that I belonged to this school."[223]

Given this pedigree, it is no surprise to encounter statements like "There is no god but man" in Crowley's work.[224] Yet the application of this dictum in Crowley's system of magic and esotericism is sometimes surprising, displaying interesting similarities and differences with LaVey's utilization of the Romantic Reversal. If we can take his own word for it, Crowley had started out his explorations into magic as a thorough rationalist. At times, this Crowley is still very evident throughout his work, especially in his treatment of magic (on which more later).[225] In fact, he saw no contradiction between this initial materialist outlook and his eventual practice of magic, Kabbalah, Eastern mysticism, and invocations. "It is to be carefully observed that we unhesitatingly class as 'material' all sorts of ideas which are not directly appreciable by any of our senses," he wrote in his "autohagiography." "I was in no way apostatizing from my agnosticism in looking for a universe of beings endowed with such qualities that earlier observers, with few facts and fewer methods of investigation and criticism at their disposal, called 'gods,' 'archangels,' 'spirits' and the like." He continued almost in the same breath, however, with the arch-Romantic statement that Reason was "incompetent to create a science from nothing and restricted . . . to its evident function of criticizing facts."[226] The Kabbalah, in contrast, "asserted the existence of a faculty . . . by the use of which I could appreciate truth directly." Elsewhere, Crowley called this the "solution of the mystic," and somewhere else again, the "secret source of energy which explains the phenomenon of Genius."[227]

What is this "secret source of energy" and this "faculty of apprehension independent of reason which informs us directly of the truth"?[228] Certainly not faith, which had been proven bankrupt by reason and science. Rather, the faculty of apprehension is a kind of natural intuition in man, it seems, while the secret source of energy was the human ability to be *creative*. This concept of creativity was taken to be almost crudely literal by Crowley: it was the human potency to propagate and generate new life, the "solve et coagula" of sexuality that reflected the perpetual dissolving and evolving of the universe. The veiled or open veneration of the phallus or the sexual act is the core of much of Crowley's ritual.[229] But Crowley here also reflects more modern thought: that of Freud and Jung, for instance, whom he was familiar with. Like Freud, he saw sexuality as a manifestation of the subconscious; and this subconscious was the true motor of man, the part with which he partakes in the cosmic generative principle, often invoked under the name of Pan by Crowley.[230] In other words, his essential godhead. One is irresistibly reminded of Blake's "Desire" here. Thus, everything created in inspiration—that is, inspired by the divine subconscious—is a further expression of divinity, or divinity itself. In the end, Crowley thus takes up a position that embodies the essence of the Romantic Reversal, which is well expressed, for instance, in this poem from his *Book of Lies*:

THE BLIND WEBSTER

It is not necessary to understand; it is enough to adore.
The god may be of clay: adore him; he becomes GOD.
We ignore what created us; we adore what we create.
Let us create nothing but GOD!

That which causes us to create is our true father and mother;
we create in our own image, which is theirs.

Let us create therefore without fear;
for we can create nothing that is not GOD.[231]

Although in many ways continuing its tradition, Crowley at this point presents a break with the Lévian esotericism that came before him. Lévi implied that magic was the domination of the "wild" magical agent by conscious will. Crowley taught the surrender of conscious will to the true self, which he sometimes equated with the Freudian subconsciousness.[232] The "astral inebriation" that the adept was urged to avoid in the neo-Kabbalist tradition, becomes a thing to be coveted with the follower of Thelema, something to be pursued by drugs, sexual ecstasy, and other trance-inducing mechanisms. "Magick will show him the beauty and majesty of the Self which he has tried to suppress and disguise," Crowley wrote.[233] To accomplish this "silencing of the human intellect so one may hear the voice . . . of the divine consciousness," he appropriated Eastern meditative practices and a few inventions of his own. One of the exercises for neophytes at the Abbey of Thelema, for example, consisted in cutting the arm every time the word "I" was used.[234] In doing so one could ultimately reach the state of mind that the Buddhists called "Samadhi," which "means that they remove the inhibitions which repress the manifestations of genius, or (practically the same things in other words) enable one to tap the energy of the universe." By letting loose the natural, subconscious part of human nature, according to Crowley, a person can find his genuine self, unadulterated with the encroachments of convention or religion; in this way, he also finds his True Will. The Great Beast reversed the traditions from which he drew inspiration: the neo-Kabbalism of Lévi (that urged the magician to control his inner chthonic and chaotic forces), the Freudian (that sought to exorcise and dominate the subconscious by making it conscious through therapy), and the Buddhist (that called for the elimination of ego in order to become free from desire).

"The true God is man. In man all things are hidden," Crowley stated boldly in *Magick*.[235] Yet the complexities of Crowleyanity are not exhausted by this. The Beast also played with the idea of a true polytheism. His writings and diaries abound with references to "the Gods," and although these may sometimes be understood as forces "within man," at other times, clearly independent entities are implied.[236] Yet, as we have seen, the overarching umbrella of Crowley's theology is one of pantheism or panentheism. Pan, "the reflection of All," was for Crowley the primary representation of the generative urge in creation.[237] Here is found a further ground for the divinity of man. By being a (creative) part of the universe, man forms also a part of the divine. "There is no part of me that is not of the Gods," Crowley proclaimed in his Gnostic Mass.[238] The holism and panentheism that was conspicuous in much of Romanticism and nineteenth-century esotericism surely was one of the wellsprings from which the British occultist took his water in this respect. For the disciple of Thelema, however, a more personal road to the godhead was available. In his path of initiation, the magician can return to the original cosmic unity through the ecstasy of "coition-dissolution" and conquer his own divinity. Although Crowley claimed to be the only one to have made this conquest in his own days, the Way of Thelema was ultimately meant to lead all its followers to this lofty stage of self-deification. "I am for the Children of the Earth—for Man—against the Gods," Crowley noted in one of his magical diaries, "I don't try to dodge the Sorrow of the World: I swear to master Fate. This is the Master-Key to my poetry."[239]

An explicit religious and spiritual framework that transcends the earthly thus accompanies Crowley's magic and ritual. This even is the case with his worship of the "generative powers"—or so at least he claimed:

> The demonstration of anthropologists that all religious rites are celebrations of the reproductive energy of nature is irrefutable; but I, accepting this, can still maintain that these rites are wholly spiritual. Their form is only sexual because the phenomena of reproduction are the most universally understood and pungently appreciated of all. I believe that when this position is generally accepted, mankind will be able to go back with a good conscience to ceremonial worship. I have myself constructed numerous ceremonies where it is frankly admitted that religious enthusiasm is primarily sexual in character. I have merely refused to stop there. I have insisted that sexual excitement is merely a degraded form of divine ecstasy. I have thus harnessed the wild horses of human passion to the chariot of the Spiritual Sun.[240]

To return to the Satanism of Anton Szandor LaVey, there are obvious similarities between LaVey's deification of man and Crowley's. Both follow the "Romantic Reversal," declaring man the god-creating god. Crowley's belief in the subconscious and the generative force (in its broadest possible application) as man's essential core finds rough reflection in LaVey's emphasis on "carnality." At least as striking, however, are the differences that separate them. The theological intricacies and paradoxes from Crowley's synthesis of magical and religious traditions were summarily discarded by LaVey, who would later derisively describe the local OTO group as a bunch of "mystically-minded card readers who emphasized the study of Eastern philosophy, Oriental languages, stars and contemplation to reach the spiritual Nirvana of Oneness."[241] LaVeyan Satanism did not feature complex cosmologies, mystic guidelines, or spiritual hierarchies, and it called for the "complete gratification" of the ego in a much more roundabout and simplified way, dismissing the quasi-Buddhist meditation practices and endless grades of Kabbalist initiation that obviously delighted Crowley.[242] The individual "I," which was only a way station for Crowley, is the ultimate destination for LaVey.

This is not to say that clearly "spiritual" elements are completely lacking in LaVeyan Satanism. But when they appear, they often seem anomalous against LaVey's general framework of official materialism. A striking example of this are LaVey's musings about "life after death through fulfilment of the ego" in *The Satanic Bible*. "Satanism encourages its members to develop a good strong ego because it gives them the respect necessary for a vital existence in this life," LaVey philosophized. "If a person has been vital throughout his life and has fought to the end for his earthly existence, it is this ego which will refuse to die, even after the expiration of the flesh which housed it."[243] LaVey seems to have written here on the wings of poetical inspiration, contradicting his own professed convictions of man as "just an animal" and death as the "one great abstinence."

This is not the only fundamental ambiguity in LaVey's modest corpus of Satanist writ—we will encounter more instances in the following sections. Of particular relevance for this section is the continuous tension between "Enlightenment" rationality and "Romantic" nonrational knowledge that runs through LaVeyan Satanism as it did through

Crowleyanite philosophy. Although we have seen that LaVey combined a criticism of religion that derives from the Enlightenment with concepts about spiritual creativity that were first formulated by Romanticism, these two positions are in their essence irreconcilable. Either "creative genius" (inspiration) or rational analysis (reason) must be the ultimate source for our understanding of the world. LaVey's writings, it must be admitted, do not contain an explicit epistemology or theory of human understanding. Implicitly, however, his position is more on the "Enlightenment" side. *The Satanic Bible* is littered with phrases like "clouded definitions and bogus values," "obsolete absurdities," "unreasonable religious demands," and "hogwash" with regard to "religionists"—while Satanism is portrayed as a "sensible and humanistic new morality," "sound philosophy," and "undefiled wisdom."[244] Ultimately, LaVey bases his rejection of old religious premises and his defense of his own on "sound and logical reasons."[245] Later, LaVey would emphasize the rationalist streak of his religion even more, describing Satanism as "a secular philosophy of rationalism and self-preservation (natural law, animal state), giftwrapping these ideas in religious trappings to add to their appeal."[246]

We are not concerned here with the question of whether this claim is viable and to what extent modern Satanism is really "sound and logical." What is important now is LaVey's implicit *pris de position*. The radical reversion of epistemology that occurs with Romantics like Blake is absent from LaVeyan Satanism. Eventually, (presumed) "sound and logical reasons" remain the criterion by which the "truths" are established that subsequently can be celebrated in dogma and ceremony. LaVeyan Satanism thus presents us with the paradoxical picture of a religion that is rationally designed to fulfill man's "instinctive" need for spiritual expression in order to enable him as much as possible to "live as the beast of the fields."[247]

REVIVING "BLACK" MAGIC

Describing the Church of Satan only as a theoretical system of anthropology and theology, however, would present a grave distortion of LaVey's religious venture. An equally essential and much more visible component was the practice of magic and magical ritual. Descriptions of magic rites for individuals or groups make up the greater part of *The Satanic Bible* and fill most of the pages of *The Satanic Rituals*. Indeed, LaVey's preface presents *The Satanic Bible* as the first straight-talking book "on the subject of magic."[248] When we look at LaVey's earlier ventures into occultism, it seems plausible that it was his fascination with magic that led him onto the path that would eventually result in the Church of Satan. It was not for nothing that the Church's immediate precursor had been an informal gathering called the Magic Circle.[249]

This strong element of ritual magic is what distinguished the Church of Satan from more doctrinally oriented groups like The Process and puts it squarely into the tradition of "high magic" that had been instigated by Éliphas Lévi and continued by Guaita, the Golden Dawn, and, more recently, Crowley and Wicca. When reading the rituals in *The Satanic Bible*, however, one is reminded even more of premodern practices of magic such as we encountered in the last part of chapter 1. In their eminent practicality, LaVey's rites here seem to fit in seamlessly into the (semi)clandestine magical practices from before the nineteenth century. Their objective is roughly the same: sex or love; material gain or personal influence; the physical or psychological destruction of adversaries. *The Satanic Bible*, for instance, offers an "Invocation employed towards the conjuration of lust" and an "Invocation employed towards the conjuration of destruction" as two of its three standard magic rites.[250] This earthly orientation contrasts with the nineteenth-century Lévian tradition of magic, which generally pursued the more "lofty" goals of personal transformation and transcendence. LaVey, on the other hand, proclaimed with characteristic straightforwardness that "anyone who pretends to be interested in magic or the occult for reasons other than gaining personal power is the worst kind of hypocrite."[251]

Of course, this does not mean that an "underground" tradition of early modern magic had mysteriously resurfaced in 1960s California. LaVey constructed his magic from nonfiction books, reproduced *grimoires*, and the writings of his nineteenth- and twentieth-century precursors, as we will come to see.[252] LaVey's (re)construction of magic, in fact, gives us some of the clearest instances of invention of tradition within the LaVeyan religious construct. It also makes clear that identification and appropriation (to remain within the terminology we have adopted in this study) are always *qualified* processes, consisting of the acceptance of some elements from the attributed stereotype and the rejection of others.

Satanism scholar Jesper Petersen has distinguished a dual thrust in LaVey's attitude toward the real or alleged legacy of devil worship and black magic from the past: on the one hand, one of "satanization"; on the other hand, that of "sanitization."[253] These concepts prove particularly useful when we look at the magic practices within the Church of Satan. Satanization here is a positive designation (in contrast to "demonization"), pointing to the appropriation of non-Satanist elements into the construction of Satanism. Instances of this abound in *The Satanic Rituals*, as (presumed or invented) rites from the Knight Templars, the National-Socialist *Sicherheitsdienst*, pseudo-Slavonic paganism, and the works of horror author Lovecraft are incorporated into LaVey's Satanism. The most blatant example is probably the "translation" of John Dee's Enochian Keys at the end of *The Satanic Bible*, wherein the many pious references to the Christian deity by the Elizabethan magician were simply swapped with "Satan" by LaVey, to the great horror of some occult connoisseurs.[254] But one can say that the Satanic High Priest's treatment of magic amounted to a wholesale "satanization" of (black) magic, divesting it from "the brittle relics of frightened minds and sterile bodies."[255] Real magic, according to LaVey, unabashedly called upon "the Devils themselves," without drawing pentagrams to protect the practitioner from these "evil" forces or reciting "long incantations with the name of Jesus thrown in for good measure."[256] A dechristianization, and corresponding "satanization," is performed here on a loose body of practices that had always been highly syncretist in the centuries before.

More conspicuous in historical perspective, however, is the amount of "sanitization" LaVey undertook. The High Priest would later declare that his Satanic religion consisted of "nine parts social respectability to one part outrage."[257] This certainly applies to his system of magic. As has become copiously clear in the previous chapters, "black magic" had commonly been associated with child sacrifice and orgies in the history of the West. Although many rituals in the inventory of the Church of Satan featured some sexual element, indiscriminate orgies were not included among these. One suspects they would be ill-suited for the individualism reigning within the new Satanism. The ritual sacrifice of "small children and voluptuous maiden[s]" was rejected by LaVey (with some reason) as the substance of malevolent rumors that had been attributed by their enemies to the magicians, mere "prattling" by the "propagandists of the right hand path."[258] Less obviously, LaVey also argued vehemently against the "offering" of animals, a practice that certainly had had its place as a legitimate magical proceeding in the *grimoires* of yore. The High Priest, however, dismissed all practices that were harmful to animals, and children, for "sound and logical reasons":

> Man, the animal, is the godhead to the Satanist. The purest form of carnal existence reposes in the bodies of animals and human children who have not grown old enough to deny themselves their natural desires. . . . Therefore, the Satanist holds these beings in a sacred regard, knowing he can learn much from these natural magicians of the world.[259]

This passage is remarkable because it is one of the few in which LaVey uses the word "sacred" in a positive sense. Without putting any doubt on the sincerity of his love for animals and children (which does not mean he always knew how to take care of them), it seems safe to say that sanitization considerations had been prominent in his motivation for this doctrinal statement. It is, in retrospect, striking how LaVey here anticipated the sensibilities of the next decades. Without these moderations, his movement would have been doomed to obscurity as an illegal or underground group.

In the same vein, LaVey stipulated that true "Satanic" sex did not include "child molesting" or "sexual defilement of animals," but was only to be engaged upon by "mature adults who willingly take full responsibility for their actions."[260] But the sanitization effort did extend to the core values of LaVeyan Satanism as well. Although presented as a religion and deification of the ego, LaVey moderated the potential extremism of these convictions by explaining that Satanism advocated "a modified form of the Golden Rule": "Do unto others as they do unto you."[261] Indulgence had to be balanced by responsibility.[262] Doing something for somebody you care for also could be a form of personal gratification, LaVey maintained, while reserving the right for the Satanist to treat others who maltreat him "with the wrath they deserve." At a later moment, he would even formulate a set of "Satanic Sins" and "Satanic Rules of the Earth."[263]

Sanitization and "Satanization" were important factors in LaVey's attitude toward earlier forms of magic and his partial identification with them. Much more fundamental differences, however, distinguish the magic propounded by him from the premodern magic that seems so near to it in its practical outlook. A crucial difference was the fact that LaVey's practical magic was embedded in a distinctly modern ideological framework. While the urge to "indulgence" and "gratification of the ego" is probably as old as mankind, the Californian High Priest had incorporated them in an explicitly formulated philosophy of life. Premodern magic in many cases certainly had had the same objectives. But it had usually refrained, as far as we know, to make its motivations explicit in ideological terms; in the rare cases that it did, it had rather underscored the altruistic and "pious" aspects of its practices.

Partly as a result of this ideological framework, LaVeyan magic also entertained completely different ideas about how it worked. In contrast to its premodern precursors, LaVey's practice of magic did not involve a belief in the reality of the supernatural entities invoked. LaVeyan Satanism, on its most practical level, was characterized by an immanent and not a transcendent outlook on the world. The main function of magical rites, in LaVey's view, was "to isolate the otherwise dissipated andrenal and other emotionally induced energy, and convert it into a dynamically transmittable force."[264] How this worked exactly was not explained in detail by LaVey, but great stress was laid by him on the fact that it was a "purely emotional" and not an intellectual act. Hence his comparison of the "Satanic Temple" and its rites and ceremonies to an "intellectual decompression chamber":

> The formalized beginning and end of the ceremony acts as a dogmatic, anti-intellectual device, the purpose of which is to disassociate the activities and frame of reference of the outside world from that of the ritual chamber, where the whole will must be employed. This facet of the ceremony is *most* important to the intellectual, as he *especially* requires the "decompression chamber" effect of the chants, bells, candles, and other trappings, before he can put his pure and willful desires to work for himself, in the projection and utilization of his imagery.[265]

Time and again LaVey stressed the fact that the Satanist enters into this "honest emotionalizing" in full knowledge of its man-created nature. All religious services, according to the High Priest of Satan, were essentially courses in temporary ignorance. "The difference is that the Satanist knows he is practising a form of contrived ignorance in order to expand his will, whereas another religionist doesn't."[266] As LaVey put it in *The Satanic Rituals*, "The essence of Satanic ritual, and Satanism itself, if taken up out of logic rather than desperation, is to objectively enter into a subjective state."[267]

Both the fact that it operated within an explicitly formulated ideological and theological framework, and the immanent nature of the mechanisms it supposed to be involved, clearly demarcated LaVey's magic as belonging to the tradition of "high magic" that had been propounded by Éliphas Lévi in the nineteenth century and continued by Aleister Crowley in the twentieth. The influence of Lévi and Crowley is also visible in many details of LaVey's magical edifice. The High Priest's insistence on the "discharge of bioelectrical energy" by masturbation as a form of magical sacrifice, for instance, seems directly reminiscent of similar practices developed by Crowley, who jokingly remarked in a footnote in *Magick* that he had made "this particular sacrifice on an average about 150 times every year between 1912 e.v. and 1928 e.v.."[268] More in depth, the whole idea to use orgasmic energy to make magical contact with the "suppressed" godhead in the human subconscious had been central to Thelemic magic. While LaVey's Satanism discarded the elaborate metaphysical superstructure that Crowley had built around this, it added other "primal emotions" like anger and grief as possible sources of magical energy.

A further reminiscence of Lévi and Crowley (and other occult authors in their tradition) is the frequent mention of "will" and "fantasy" ("imagination") as principal ingredients of Satanist magic. Although LaVey predominantly appealed to psychological and (pseudo-) biological mechanisms to explain the efficacy of his magic, terms like "pure will," "pure and willful desires," and "projection of imagery" betray the way his magical system is rooted in the Lévian and Crowleyan traditions.[269] The overall procedure of LaVey's rites in this respect was still the same as that of Lévi: by strongly imagining what he wished for in a symbolic setting, the magician fortified his will and could make his projected imagination true. As with both of his precursors, control, especially *self*-control, was the key word here. Although Crowley (and LaVey) might take recourse in their magic to various forms of ecstasy that would have been branded by Lévi as "astral drunkenness," there was no fundamental difference between them in this regard. Toward the end of his life, the Great Beast could confidently claim that "about 90% of Thelema, at a guess, is nothing *but* self-discipline."[270] LaVey can be seen to make similar statements. In a 1969 newspaper column, he simply stated that the "prime requisite in ceremonial magic is CONTROL."[271] Even when one uses emotional surrender as a magic method, this must always be done within a carefully controlled setting and for a predetermined goal. Thus one could "objectively enter into a subjective state."

This attitude becomes especially clear in LaVey's treatment of "Lesser Magic" (another term he borrowed from Crowley), which is essentially the craft to manipulate others (and oneself) to obtain what one wants in love and life. Most of this consists of rather common-sense or sometimes even blunt methods for controlling others to do what you want them to do, some of which seem directly taken from the slightly ludicrous "magical" dating tips Lévi had given a century before. Here again, the "self-control" and "self-knowledge" of the magician is the recurring theme. This attitude was even extended by LaVey to the sexual, despite his stress on the freedom and right of self-gratification of human beings in this area. "The true Satanist is not mastered by sex any more than he is mastered by any of his other desires."[272]

Exactly the same attitude, as we have seen, could be found with Lévi and many of his occult descendants. But for Lévi, Crowley, and their ilk, this self-discipline had a clear and unambiguous goal: attaining the unity between man and the divine—a pantheist divine, to be exact, that was already present in man. In LaVey's system, a paradox becomes manifest in this regard. If Satanism is a religion of gratification, why postpone or restrict this gratification by controlling it? What is this gratification exactly? Is it experiencing pleasure itself, which always entails a form of surrender? Or is it the act of "cunningly" obtaining the *objects* that give gratification, be it a man or a woman, a position of power, or material possessions of one kind or another? Here again, the fundamental tension permeating LeVeyan Satanism becomes visible between two conflicting ideals of human transcendence: that of "animal," "childlike" carnal man that should be allowed to fulfill its natural urges uninhibitedly, and that of the rational human being that is somehow elevated above the self and the environment it seeks to control.[273] Of course, this tension only becomes visible if you look at LaVey's utterances from a philosophical or theological point of view. For the practitioner, his magic may just seem a shrewd way to get what you want.

Some of the tensions running through LaVey's system of magic may have been purposefully created. One of them was probably the friction between free and freely admitted neo-Romantic creativity and the aura of historical legitimacy with which LaVey liked to shroud his magical rites, particularly in *The Satanic Rituals*. "Satanic Ritual is a blend of Gnostic, Cabbalistic, Hermetic and Masonic elements, incorporating nomenclature and words of power from virtually every mythos," LaVey declared in this compendium, and he stressed the creativity and "avowed fantasy" the Satanist could deploy in crafting his own rituals.[274] He also gave a practical demonstration of this principle by incorporating fragments and fictional figures from the work of American horror writer H. P. Lovecraft into full-blood rites.[275]

In a way, these notions had already surfaced during Romanticism and had already been put in practice by Lévi; but LaVey was certainly pioneering in the brazenly explicit application he gave them in the domain of occultism. Yet despite this theoretical farewell to tradition as a legitimatization strategy, many rites in *The Satanic Rituals* were furnished with textual clues suggesting historical authenticity and age-old tradition. The ritual for the "Messe Noir" that was described earlier, for instance, was said to be based upon the version used by the (nonexisting) "Societé des Luciferiens"; to bolster its authentic look, it featured extensive French quotation from *Là-Bas*.[276] Likewise, "Die elektrischen Vorspiele" were claimed to have been performed in the 1930s "by the intellectual element of the budding *Sicherheitsdienst*," the "Homage to Tchort" was presented as an old Slavonic rite made available by "oral communication and fraternal legacy," and a rite called "Al-Jilwah" was presented as an original ceremony from Yezidi scripture.[277] This mixture of carefree invention and pretended historical authenticity sometimes led to tortuous constructions that leave one wondering what effect LaVey exactly wanted to achieve. The ceremony called "L'Air Epais," for example, was claimed by him to be the rite for the sixth degree of the Order of the Knights Templar. This chivalrous order had adopted Satanism through contacts with the Yezidi in the Middle East, LaVey went on, a fact that was demonstrated by the pride and affirmation of life they displayed. At the same time, however, LaVey freely admitted that his actual text was taken from James Thompson's atheist dirge *The City of Dreadful Night* (1873) and from "Raynouards drama of 1806, *Les Templiers*."[278]

It is obvious, here as at other places, that LaVey is purposely using the presumed historical origins of his bricolated rites as "emotion producing devices" just like candles and bells. As he had written himself, "Inasmuch as ritual magic is dependent upon emotional intensity for success, all manner of emotion producing devices must be employed in its practice."[279] A tension remains, however, which does not reside solely in the eyes of the beholder. One wonders, on the one hand, why LaVey has not been more rigorous in the presentation of his rites as genuine historical relicts, and on the other hand, if some of his "emotion producing devices" in this respect are not rather the reflection of sincere convictions from his part regarding the history of Satanism, for instance the assertion that the Templars were secret worshippers of the devil.[280] Of course, given the state of historical research on Satanism at the moment he wrote, LaVey may be excused in detecting more historical Satanism than there had really been.

Another tension that may have been intended by LaVey is that between the supposedly "materialist" character of his magic and its mythic, supernaturalistic shell. Indeed, LaVey seems at pains to retain the "mysterious" character of magic, especially when we compare him with his immediate precursor, Aleister Crowley.[281] The Great Beast had given a very straightforward definition of his "Magick": "Magick is the Science and Art of causing Change to occur in conformity with Will."[282] He illustrated his conception with an example that had already been used by Lévi: "It is my Will to inform the World of certain facts within my knowledge. I therefore take 'magickal weapons,' pen, ink, and paper; I write 'incantations'—these sentences—in the 'magickal language' i.e, that which is understood by the people I wish to instruct; I call forth 'spirits,' such as printers, publishers, booksellers and so forth and constrain them to convey my message to those people. The composition and distribution of this book is thus an act of Magick by which I cause Changes to take place in conformity with my Will."[283] Although it must remembered that the word "Will" held special meaning for Crowley, he did not hesitate to draw extremely "disenchanting" conclusions from his own tenets. Elsewhere in *Magick*, he wrote that "every intentional act is a Magickal act" and that "in one sense Magick may be defined as the name given to Science by the vulgar."[284]

This did not mean that Magick could be reduced to physics and chemistry: neither could the Universe, and the rituals prescribed by Crowley were meant as tools for "discovering and employing hitherto unknown forces in nature."[285] Yet even breathing might be an intentional, and thus magickal, act.[286] The main purpose of Crowley's system was to make man *conscious* of his innate powers and make him use them according to his Will. "Remember that Magick includes all acts soever. Anything may serve as a Magical weapon. To impose one's Will on a nation, for instance, one's talisman may be a newspaper, one's triangle a church, or one's circle a Club. To win a woman, one's pantacle may be a necklace; to discover a treasure, one's wand may be a dramatist's pen, or one's incantation a popular song."[287]

LaVey was in many ways indebted to Crowley's theories. He adopted many of the practical considerations of his precursor, particularly the principle he called the "balancing factor," which meant that one should not aspire to obtain by way of magic what one cannot reasonably expect to have (i.e., somebody who knows no music at all should not think that a magic ceremony can make him a master violinist, and a "gross, lumpy, lewd-mouthed, snaggle-toothed loafer" should not expect to conquer a "luscious young stripper").[288] "Magic requires working in harmony with nature," the High Priest of Satan would declare later in life.[289] Yet LaVey probably recognized that a completely reductionist approach would kill the magic in magic, so to speak. Thus he maintained in *The Satanic Bible* that, while many of his instructions and procedures were nothing more than "applied psychology, or scientific fact," magic was "never totally scientifically explainable." Accordingly, modifying Crowley's definition, he defined magic as "the change in situations or events in accordance with one's will, which would, using normally accepted methods, be unchangeable."[290]

With regard to his own person, LaVey also meticulously fostered an image of paranormal prowess. Part of his personal legend, for instance, was the story that a curse he had placed was responsible for the death of Jayne Mansfield, the Hollywood actress famous for her buxom looks. Mansfield had been one of the most famous celebrity adepts of the Church of Satan, openly displaying her sympathy for the new religion, which she allegedly called "Khalil Gibran with balls."[291] When her agent/paramour Sam Brody tried to dissuade her from associating with LaVey, the latter threw a curse over the man. Although the High Priest warned Mansfield not to do so, she foolishly stepped into the car with Brody, which subsequently got involved in an accident, killing both. LaVey rather ruthlessly exploited this tragic happening to bolster his own magical record. But he also claimed more mundane magical powers, such as an unfailing ability to find a parking space in crowded San Francisco.[292]

It is hard to assess what exactly LaVey's and the early Church of Satan's real stance was in this matter. On the one hand, LaVey seemed to have entertained some ideas that seem to belong solidly in the domain of the occult—for instance, his insistence on the hidden powers of triangles and trapezoids. On the other hand, the many ambiguities he displayed in this field may have been deliberate. "The fascination of the occult itself is what makes it so popular," LaVey stated once, and his whole edifice of magical mystery might be another example of his own method of utilizing "fantasy" as a "magical weapon."[293] Still, there remains much paradox, if not contradiction, in the fact that LaVey's materialist, rationalist religion borrowed much of its appeal from the sinister and the unexplained and from colorful rites that invoked the names of old gods and old demons. Like the present-day historian, not every observer or participant may have found it easy to find out what exactly was supposed to be objective fact and what subjective fantasy. Some proved to have a hard time doing so indeed, as we will see in the next chapter.

The sign of the horns shall appear to many now, rather than the few;

and the magician will stand forth that he may be recognized.

ANTON SZANDOR LaVey, *The Satanic Bible*,

The Book of Lucifer, chapter XII

8

Tribulations of the Early Church

᠔ ──

THE MILLENNIUM-OLD TRADITION of Christian attribution deeply imprinted in popular culture, the anti-Christian reaction in European thought from the Enlightenment up to Nietzsche, the rehabilitation of the fallen angel by Romantic Satanism, the human-centered attitude on religiosity of the Romantic Reversal, the Sexual Revolution and occult revival of the 1960s, and a thoroughly modernized medieval and early modern magic had all contributed to the emergence of the Church of Satan, a surprising new religion that adopted the mythical embodiment of evil from Christianity as its prime object of veneration and dispended with the Judeo-Christian deity altogether. The inventiveness and daring of its founder, former circus handyman and organ player Anton LaVey, also was decisive in shaping this unusual religious venture. Apart perhaps from Naglowska's short-lived Temple, never before had a religious group thus openly and explicitly claimed its allegiance to the devil. In this final chapter, we explore the earliest history of the new religion of Satan up to approximately the end of the millennium, focusing especially on the Church of Satan and the biography of its founder. How did the Church of Satan fare in the last three decades of the twentieth century? What was the reaction of the wider society to this new antireligious religion? Would Satanism grow into a new world religion, as LaVey seemed to foresee with such confidence?

SATAN AND SET; LAVEY AND AQUINO

As the 1960s turned into the 1970s, the young Church of Satan seemed to be flourishing in an organizational respect. Spokesmen of the Church claimed it had 10,000 adherents nationwide, although more conservative observers thought the real number to be in reality about half of this, and later defectors would speak of only a few hundred active members.[1] Geographically, the new religion was spreading its tentacles. LaVey established a chain of local chapters throughout the United States, which he called "grottos," probably to avoid the Wicca-infected term "coven." In 1972, the new religion was reimported into Europe, its intellectual homeland, when a young Dutch businessman called Maarten Lamers established an official grotto in the Netherlands.[2] In the same year, LaVey ceased the weekly rituals in his own house. Church services would henceforth be conducted by local grottos, while the Black House was to become the cult's international headquarters.

Optimism was soaring, but the Church was not without its problems. Competitors eager to cash in on Satan appeared on the scene, but more serious were the problems within the ecclesiastical organization itself. It was bound to be difficult to retain cohesion in an institution officially devoted toward individualism and self-indulgence, and internal schisms soon arose. In Detroit, the head of the local Babylon Grotto, a former Catholic priest from Britain, was defrocked for the second time by LaVey when members accused him of raising fees for his own benefit and transforming the grotto's rites into an arena for personal fantasies of bondage and homosexuality. The priest proceeded to form a schismatic "Universal Church of Man," which he described as "Satanism without Satan"; but this venture soon dwindled away.[3] In 1973, a number of Chicago members founded "Thee Satanic Orthodox Church of the Nethilum Rite," a splinter group that was splintered in its own turn in 1974, when a number of adherents split off to establish an even smaller denomination simply called "Thee Satanic Church."[4] In February 1973, Central Grotto revoked the charter of the Stygian Grotto in Dayton because some of its leaders allegedly had dealt in stolen goods. They duly went on to form their own organization as well, the Church of Satanic Brotherhood, which met a dramatic end when one of its principal instigators, John DeHaven, announced his conversion to Christianity.[5]

These schismatic groups were short-lived and generally insignificant, but they caused their inevitable amount of disruption and pointed to a wider discontent among some of the Church's members that would eventually erupt into a much more serious schism. This discontent had two principal causes that are interesting enough to explore further. The first of these was the personality and leadership style of Anton LaVey. The second had to do with the doctrinal content of his Satanism.

To start with LaVey himself: the charismatic High Priest was running the Church he had begun like it was his own private enterprise. Although he had appointed (or claimed to have appointed) a Council of Nine to assist him with the management of the Church, true authority rested solidly with the "Exarch of Hell." LaVey's approach, moreover, was not devoid of commercial aspects, and these aspects seemed to become increasingly prominent in the early 1970s. The question could be asked about how serious LaVey actually was with his antireligious religion. After all, LaVey *had* been in show business, and his whole setup was disturbingly reminiscent of a carnival act, with the High Priest running around in a slightly ridiculous devil suit. In the legend of his life that he designed for himself, he even claimed to have been a carnival and circus employee. What if the Church of Satan was basically a religious carnival show meant for the personal aggrandizement and financial benefit of its High Priest?

With respect to the use of Satanism for commercial and titillating purposes, LaVey hardly would have been a pioneer. Although this subject has been somewhat neglected by serious historical research, the exploitation of "Satanic" themes certainly had antecedents in the adult entertainment industry. In *The Satanic Bible*, LaVey already described "sex clubs using Satanism as a rationale" as a phenomenon that was "perennially concurrent" with more serious forms of "dark" esotericism: "that persists today, for which tabloid newspaper

writers may give thanks."[6] Reports in pulp literature, moreover, maintain that paying customers could attend "real" Black Masses in the rougher parts of the red-light districts of
Paris and Rome during the 1940s and 1950s: even Princess Irene of Greece once told the
press that she had witnessed such a ceremony in a Paris cellar.[7] We may speculate that the
"base debaucheries" practiced "near the Capitol" mentioned in Brevannes's *Messes Noires*
also belong into this category—indeed, the 1904 play itself had been more or less a live soft-
porn show. In some cases, the border between sexual role playing, commercial venture, and
genuine religious ceremony is hard to discern. What to think, for instance, of a "Sabbath"
that a correspondent of *Beyond* claimed to have witnessed in Stockholm, and during which
a young woman ritually sacrificed her purported virginity as a tribute to the suffering people of Vietnam?[8]

LaVeyan Satanism in its early phase undeniably had some affinities with this "peep
show Satanism." In Amsterdam, Dutch grotto leader Lamers had a sex club annexed to his
church called "Walpurgis Abbey," in which professional "Sisters" performed acts involving
bananas.[9] The Black Pope himself had not been above such things either. In the earliest
days of the Church, he staged a "Topless Witches Review" in one of the nightclubs in San
Francisco's Night Beach, during which bare-breasted witches seduced a "Grand Inquisitor"
(played by a former divinity counselor for Billy Graham dressed in "the bottom half of a
light-blue bikini"), and a likewise bare-breasted female vampire appeared from a coffin—
all this very much to the dismay of his advisor Edward Webber, who feared the state of
California would refuse to grant its charter to the new church if it found out it was running a topless show.[10] Although LaVey discontinued this operation, female nudity played a
conspicuous role in the public profiling of the Church, and the High Priest frequently gave
interviews and granted photo shoots to men's magazines.[11] Correspondingly, a lot of people
coming to the Church were there to find a more fulfilling sex life, although LaVey tried
to dissuade attendants hoping for a free orgy.[12] Because of its permissive attitude toward
most variations of human sexuality, the Church seemed to have had particular attraction to
homosexuals and practitioners of S&M.[13]

From the beginning, moreover, there had also been a commercial streak in LaVey's religious undertaking. A lifelong membership of the Church could be bought by mail for $20,
later $13.[14] For this investment, the new adept received a scarlet membership card, printed in
black and embossed with a silver Baphomet symbol. (This type of membership, by the way,
may have been the source of the 10,000 adherents the Church claimed it had.[15]) Members
could also buy Baphomet pendants and special amulets for prices ranging from $4 to $10.[16]
Satanists belonging to the various grottos contributed $15 annually to "Central Grotto" in
San Francisco. These prices were rather modest, however, and although LaVey was probably
making a living out of his Satanism venture at this date, he did so largely through meetings,
lectures, and the output of his literary endeavors.[17]

In the 1970s, LaVey and his consort, Diane Hegartey, started to grow tired of the
institutional framework they had called into being. Not only did it take a lot of time
and correspondence to administer the network of followers, the net return was a barrage
of troubles and a meager revenue. Moreover, the type of person attracted to organized
Satanism generally failed to comply with the superior kind of men LaVey had had in mind
for his new religion. "Membership inquiries continue to increase, but brain surgeons and

Congressmen are still in short supply," LaVey wrote in a letter to one of his lieutenants dated 6 March A.S. VII/1972.[18] In the same letter, he suggested a new approach. Instead of painstakingly building up a network of congregations, more energy was to be invested in raising a mass following for Satanism as a movement. This mass following could then be exploited for the time being, it seems, primarily in a commercial sense, by "marketing Satanic goodies to low-level gadflies." Amulets should be sold on a mass-market scale, and the *Cloven Hoof,* the Church's internal bulletin, should become a glossy magazine on a par with *Playboy.*[19] Followers who wished to convene with other Satanists should organize themselves in grottos on their own, using the soon-to-be-published *Satanic Rituals* as their guide, while the Church of Satan properly speaking should become an organization for an elite of leaders. "In due time, after conditioning has been achieved and the movement (not the Church) has grown vast, human potential can be categorized into shouters, money-donors, leaders, legitimacy-providers, menial volunteers, etc.—just as past religions which have dealt with human animals have done. Each person's respective value can then be extracted, and the Temples and Pleasure Domes can be built . . . according to our plans."[20]

In the next years, LaVey wavered in his attitude toward his organization, but in September 1974, he announced "Phase IV" of his "Masterplan" to his increasingly startled followers. Group activity had had its purpose in establishing Satanism as "a force with which to be reckoned," but had taken on "a dimension of ducklings huddling together to keep warm."[21] Satanists were supposed to be strong-willed individuals, it said, and "strong-willed individuals do not tend to mix well with other strong-willed individuals."[22] Therefore, all regional organization should cease and individual members and grottos should henceforth report to Central Grotto only, minimizing contact between them. In the future, every Satanist would serve as a "unique agent" for the movement, operating on an individual basis. The degrees of priest and magister would be conferred upon "observable achievements and influence outside the Church of Satan."[23] The membership of the Church was further incensed when LaVey awarded the degree of "Magister IV°" to his personal driver; an honor that had been awarded to only one of the official priests, who had generally obtained their priesthood through a strenuous examination process.[24]

The growing distrust between the High Priest and his officials came to a head in 1975, when LaVey published an edict in *Cloven Hoof* clarifying some of the criteria for "observable achievements and influence outside the Church of Satan," which could made one fit for Satanic priesthood. Among other conditions, the text bluntly stated that those who made "material contributions" to the Church could be ordained as priests. "The frankly materialistic concept of Satanism can always use a little bread or its equivalent," LaVey added.[25] In a way, indeed, LaVey was only drawing the logical consequence of his own philosophy here. Already in *The Satanic Bible,* he had stated: "If the rich man's entry into heaven seems as difficult as the camel's attempt to go through the eye of a needle; if the love of money is the root of all evil; then we must at least assume the most powerful men on earth to be the most Satanic."[26] With a decidedly carnal, this-worldly, and practical approach to magic as the Church of Satan propagated, a successful magician would need to be a wealthy or powerful person. The older hierarchy of the Church did not look kindly upon this line of reasoning, however, and concluded, perhaps not without reason, that LaVey was offering the Satanic

priesthood for sale in order to enrich himself. A schism broke out that would almost eliminate the Church as an effective physical organization.

The schism was also a result of what one could call, for want of a better word, a theological or diabological dispute: the growing divergence among LaVey and some of his followers about the ontological status of Satan.[27] From the beginning, the Church of Satan had
attracted adherents who believed in the existence of Satan as a real, independent personality. Despite LaVey's official stance on Satan as a metaphor, some passages in his writings
seemed to leave room for other interpretations. In *The Satanic Bible*, for instance, LaVey
had written that it was a "popular misconception" that a Satanist did not believe in a deity.
"To the Satanist 'God'—by whatever name he is called, or by no name at all—is seen as the
balancing factor in nature, and not as being concerned with suffering. This powerful force
that permeates and balances the universe is far too impersonal to care about the happiness
or misery of flesh-and-blood creatures on this ball of dirt upon which we live."[28] It is unclear
from this passage if "God" here is the same as "Satan," but the suggestion that they are to
be thought of as identical is reinforced by another passage, where LaVey distances himself
from the anthropomorphic image of Satan and declares instead that the fallen angel "represents a force of nature—the powers of darkness which have been named just that because
no religion has taken these forces *out* of darkness."[29] In both cases, LaVey's terminology
was taken directly from Lévi, with whom he was certainly familiar. If we remember that
for Éliphas Lévi, "the powerful force that balances and permeates the universe" was indeed
Satan in his manifestation as "pantheos," and at the same time the "magical agent" that was
employed by the magician, it is hard to avoid the impression that the Satanic High Priest
was entertaining a notion of Satan as an impersonal yet divine cosmic principle at the time
of writing these lines.[30]

One of the earlier schismatic split-offs of the Church of Satan, Thee Satanic Orthodox
Church of Nethilum Rite, had already "returned" to traditional notions of a creator-god
with Satan as its opposing force (preferring, of course, the latter). Within the Church of
Satan, however, the most prominent articulator of a theist view on Satan would be Michael
A. Aquino, one of LaVey's most trusted deputies and editor of the Church's bulletin, *Cloven
Hoof*. Aquino, then a lieutenant in the U.S. Army employed with conducting psychological
warfare in Vietnam, visited one of LaVey's ceremonies out of curiosity when on leave in
San Francisco in March 1966. He was immediately taken in with the charisma of the flamboyant High Priest.[31] According to his later recollections, Aquino had been experiencing
a major spiritual crisis at the time. After immersing himself in existentialist philosophy,
he had come to the conclusion that life had no purpose, and for a while, he had even been
contemplating suicide. "At this point," he would later recount in a letter, "Anton LaVey
said, 'Where there is no meaning, we *ourselves* can *create* it. Thus we are not creatures, but
creators: we are gods.' "[32] In the following years, the young army officer would invest much
of his energy into building up the administrative and regional base of the Church of Satan
for LaVey, whom he clearly saw as a kind of spiritual father.

Despite his loyalty, however, Aquino soon started to depart from LaVeyan orthodoxy
where the figure of Satan was concerned. The process seems to have been gradual. The clues
dispersed through the memoirs he later wrote about his occult experiences suggest that it were
the magic rituals invoking Satan that first set him on the theistic trail. "Satanists participating
in rituals of Black Magic quickly became aware of an 'interest' or 'influence' in the atmosphere

of the chamber that felt somehow alien to their own personalities. The pageantry and the oratory would fade into the background, and the participants would find themselves gripped in a sensory empathy so piercing, so powerful that it would leave them exhausted, drained, and shaken at the conclusion of the rite. It was not a chance occurrence, but an inevitable, recurring one. After such experiences participants were subdued, introspective, and disinclined to exchange comments on their feelings. There was even perhaps a slight feeling of embarrassment, as though one had somehow 'slipped' from being a proper psychodramatic atheist."[33] This sequence from bare ritual invocation into actual belief is not necessarily improbable. In her celebrated study on modern neopagan magicians, T. M. Luhrmann reported the same "interpretive drift" from "imaginative, emotional involvement" into a more rationalized commitment to doctrinal assertions.[34] Aquino himself later preferred to cite a famous line by Éliphas Lévi: "When he is called, the devil comes and is seen."[35]

Except the almost inevitable confusion between a devil that was defined as a symbol in doctrinal texts and invoked as an actual being in the "intellectual decompression chamber" of ritual, Anton LaVey's own comportment might have given some of his followers further reason for theistic inclinations. The High Priest tossed about his shouts of "In the name of Satan!" and "Satan shall reign!" with great liberality and obvious relish, and was not above suggesting that the devil had officially mandated the Church of Satan during conflicts with defectors and rival groups.[36] Aquino at least seems to have been convinced at an early date that the Church was dealing with the real entity after which it was named.[37] It did not take long before he began to speak as a prophet in its name. When Aquino returned to active duty in Vietnam in June 1969, he took a copy of Milton's *Paradise Lost* along. Much like the Romantic Satanists before him, the epic poem inspired him to produce his own retelling of the biblical myth of origin. Writing "in old bombed-out buildings dating from the French occupation, in helicopters, in tents, in the midst of underbrush" while incoming fire forced him at times to duck for cover, Aquino came to feel that his text was inspired in a deeper sense as well.[38] "It was as though the text had a life of its own; and even when it was done, I felt myself unable to type it as I had originally intended to do. Instead I took another month to copy it into a finished book of two volumes in an odd calligraphic script of mine that, once more, 'imposed itself' on the project."[39]

The result was a "Satanic" myth of creation in a semibiblical prose style that he dubbed *The Diabolicon*, containing statements by Satan, Beelzebub, Asmodeus, and other demons. It told how from the chaos of primordial times an order had arisen "which is now called by name God."[40] This order, however, aspired to a state of universal stasis. Only Satan was exempt from this stagnation, because he had "through unknown celestial fusion" assumed life with a "mind and identity" undefined by the divine order. For a long time he had remained unaware of this special gift, Satan recounted in *The Diabolicon*. "But finally my Will flamed to life, and I thought—and I perceived my Self, and I knew that I was alone in mind and a being in essence unique. And through the power of my new mind, I reached out to others who had been formed with me, and I touched them and gave them identity."[41] Recognizing that the deity would in the end not allow any other "Will" than his own, Satan rose against him. War ensued between the angels who sided with Satan and those who defended order, led by a powerful angel called "Messiah."

Because this conflict threatened to destroy the cosmos, the angels of order withdrew to Heaven and the angels "of the new Mind" to a place beyond the confines of the universe, where they created a "riotous pandemonium" where all wills would be equal.[42] The battle-field shifted to Earth, where the forces of order had set up a new world peopled by a mankind living in "the idiocy of innocence."[43] By way of counterstroke, Satan infiltrated their domain and bestowed the "Black Flame" of will and individuality upon them. Ever since, Messiah and his angels have tried to subdue this spark in man, establishing "God-churches" that brought fear and religious terror and filled Earth with "the screams of men whose friendship to Lucifer brought them only the horrors of intolerance, inquisition, and death." Step by step, however, and against all odds, man is growing in the "creation, perpetuation, and exercise of the Satanic marvel that is free and unbounded Will."[44]

In its philosophy and presentation, *The Diabolicon* immediately reminds one of Blake and of the Lucifer in Byron's *Cain*, although Aquino would never mention these authors as a source of inspiration. With the official ideological line of the Church of Satan, in contrast, this personal revelation from Satan seemed ill at ease. LaVey, however, displayed remarkable tolerance toward the theist inclinations of his follower. When Aquino sent him his text, he responded with a brief but courteous letter of thanks. "I received the *Diabolicon* safely. It is indeed a work which will have a lasting impact. It is done in an ageless manner and with complete awareness. So impressed am I that I have selected passages from it for my own personal reading in this evening's ceremony, which pays homage to the writings of the Satanic Masters of the past, such as Machiavelli, Nietzsche, Twain, Hobbes, etc., who will be portrayed by members of my Council reading their respective works."[45]

LaVey also did not intervene when Aquino formulated an initiation oath for his Kentucky grotto, which included theological and philosophical elements from *The Diabolicon*.[46] Instead, he incorporated the oath in a somewhat modified form in the adult baptism rite from *The Satanic Rituals*, which exhorted the candidate Satanist to foreswear "divine mindlessness" and "oblivion of self" and to accept "the pleasure and pain of unique existence" and declare his "friendship with Lucifer, Lord of Light, who is exalted as Satan."[47] In his column in the *National Insider*, LaVey would likewise cite letters from Satanists that were frankly theistic in content, "to give my readers an idea how dedicated some people are to the concept of the Devil," while in other columns he would represent Satan unencumbered as "nothing more than a symbolic entity": "Man himself is the God; Satan is merely the symbolic representation of the WHOLE man and is given a place in Satanic ritual as a strengthening device to affirm one's own convictions."[48]

This, however, was most certainly not what Aquino had come to believe by this date. In letters to other Satanists, the young intelligence officer described Satan in ways indistinguishable from a traditional deity.[49] To a fellow priest of Satan, he proclaimed that the "mandato" for the Church of Satan came "directly from the Prince of Darkness himself": "If we were not convinced of this, it would be hypocritical to call ourselves by the name we do."[50] In the *Cloven Hoof* of July–August 1974, Aquino, with implied compliance of the High Priest, boldly insisted on the factual existence of the devil, which had only been disavowed by the Church for tactical reasons that were no longer valid. "Indeed Satan exists. Not just as a myth, nor as a mere psychological archetype, nor as only a colourful figure of speech, but as an *essential, intelligent entity*."[51]

For the time being, Aquino remained a loyal lieutenant to LaVey. When a new message from Satan came through to him in the summer of 1974, it was staunchly supportive of LaVey's policies with the Church. In it, the archdemon declared to have looked upon his

Church "with pleasure and the pride that is our nectar."[52] He predicted a time, however, when the name of Satan would again be shunned and his Church would "vanish in fiction" to "survive in fact." In order to attain the latter, the institutions of the Church had to be discarded and its companionship reserved to "the Elect."[53] This was of course exactly what LaVey was proposing at this moment, and Satan consequently loaded his Magus with praise: he was ordered to burn the pact that he had made with Satan, as he now was "in [his] Self a Demon" and "a true god."[54]

The tone of this prophecy strikes the reader as almost too shrill, however, as if Aquino was trying to silence a different voice within him. He had worked hard to build up a nationwide organization for LaVey's new American Satanism, and his post facto written memoirs clearly attest to his exasperation with the callous way LaVey sometimes dealt with his most loyal followers. His memoirs also show him as a man attached to ritual grades and degrees. In addition, he genuinely considered the Church of Satan as hallowed by His Infernal Majesty, and its priesthood as sacred. Consequently, when LaVey awarded a master grade to his driver, he was much taken aback, and when the High Priest announced that the Satanic priesthood would henceforth also be granted to those who gave extraordinary donations in material form, he was aghast. He sent Diane and Anton LaVey a long letter that he ended by notifying them that the "Infernal Mandate" was now withdrawn from "The Church of Satan, Inc." and that they were no longer empowered to execute their offices.[55] As letters of resignation began to pour in from grotto leaders all over the country, Aquino sent a message to the whole membership, telling them that the Church of Satan no longer carried "the true sanction of the Prince of Darkness," encouraging them to contact him.[56]

With the circle of discontented Satanists that had gathered around him, Aquino pondered what to do next. For a short while, they deliberated about the formation of a "New" or "Reformed" Church of Satan, but this idea was eventually rejected. Exasperated, Aquino decided to ask Satan himself for his guidance regarding his Church. He shut himself into his home, put on a Ralph Vaughan Williams recording on endless repeat, and spoke aloud the first Enochian Key. Immediately he felt inclined to enter his study and sit down to write. As he would later recall:

> The experience was neither one of "dictation" . . . or of "automatic writing" after the spiritualist fashion. The thoughts, words, phrases seemed to me indistinct from my own, yet impressed me as both unique and necessary, as though no other sequence would do. Frequently I paused for a time, waiting for what might occur next. Three times I got up from the desk entirely—once to find a small book by Wallis Budge, *Egyptian Language*, and leaf through it until I found the sentence that had gnawed at me, copying its hieroglyphs in my writing; once to trace an exact copy of a scrawled passage from *The Book of the Law* into the narrative; and finally, at its apparent end, to place a small piece of my own artwork (which I had done some time previously, merely on a meditative whim) as a "seal."[57]

The resulting text, subsequently titled *The Book of Coming Forth by Night* by Aquino, contained some remarkable messages from the angel of darkness.[58] In the first place the fact that he wished no longer to be called by the "Moorish" name of Satan: "Reconsecrate my Temple and my Order in the true name of Set. No longer will I accept the bastard title of a

Hebrew fiend."[59] He further described himself as the "ageless Intelligence of the Universe," who had been venerated in "Khem" (Egypt) in times of yore but had long been forgotten there and had since roamed the earth, looking for those who sought him. In 1904, he had appeared as his "Opposite Self" to Aleister Crowley to bring purification and "end the horrors of the stasis of the death-gods of men." The establishment of the Church of Satan had fused Set and this Opposite Self together. But now the time had come for Set to appear again in his pure, uncorrupted form, to be invoked directly, in his own name. "The Satanist thought to approach Satan through ritual. Now let the Setian shun all recitation, for the text of another is an affront to the Self. Speak rather to me as a friend, gently and without fear. Do not bend your knee nor drop your eye, for such things were not done in my house at PaMat-et. But speak to me at night, because the sky then becomes an entrance and not a barrier. And those who call me the Prince of Darkness do me no dishonor."[60]

Thus invested with a divine mission, Aquino officially registered the Temple of Set as a nonprofit religious corporation on October 23, 1975.[61] A substantial part of the Church of Satan hierarchy joined the new religious venture and took high positions in its leadership. In practical as well as ideological respect, the new Setian church sought to resolve many of the tensions and inconsistencies that had characterized LaVey's Church of Satan and replace them with less ambivalent positions. First, of course, Satan/Set was now unambiguously elevated to the status of a genuine, transcendent deity. Aquino was at pains to make clear that he was not a "death-god" in the traditional mold, a projection of humanity that required unconditional surrender or slavelike obeisance. Instead, Set had to be seen as a friend or companion who could help one in attaining a higher level of humanity. But Aquino clearly saw him as an independent, personal, and superior being, the creator, moreover, of the human (and angelic) consciousness of autonomy and individuality.[62]

In addition, the revelation of Set as the real identity of the entity known as Satan neutralized the problematic genealogy of the latter. Instead of being a Judeo-Christian creation, the Temple's object of veneration now turned out to be one of the oldest gods known to mankind. Aquino professed to be quite surprised by the sudden disclosure of the fact that he was really worshipping an "Egyptian god." In reality, he had already become interested in Egyptian mythology and the figure of Set some years before his break with LaVey.[63] In nineteenth-century esotericism, moreover, there had already been suggestions that the Egyptian god Set had been the original source of the Hebrew designation Satan, an ingenious but utterly incorrect etymology that had already been propounded by both Blavatsky and Crowley.[64]

Historically, the new Temple explicitly restored the link with the Western occult tradition, and particularly with Crowley, that LaVey had consciously tried to mask. *The Book of Coming Forth by Night* even quoted directly from the *Book of the Law*, decoding a ciphered fragment from the manuscript as a direct reference to LaVey and Aquino.[65] On the organizational level, Aquino took care to prevent the perceived abuses that had occurred in LaVey's organization. Although Set had conveniently declared him a "Magus V°" in the *Book of Coming Forth by Night*, formal power was given to a Council of Nine. The Temple was also formatted as a respectable nonprofit organization in order to prevent any future deviation into commercialism. In practice, the Temple of Set soon evolved into an esoteric study group organized in local "pylons" modeled on LaVey's grottos and a multitude of inner-Temple Orders. Aquino retained the elitism that LaVey had espoused, but intellectual accomplishments were now the most important criterion for promotion in the organization's intricate system of grades. Later, members would sometimes complain of the extensive reading lists containing rare and often costly books they had to peruse in order to qualify for esoteric promotion.[66]

Arguably the most profound disambiguation with respect to LaVeyan Satanism concerned the Temple's anthropology. Like LaVey, Aquino also saw man as a "true, complete, ultimate divinity," at least in potentiality.[67] But in stark contrast to LaVey's view of man as "just another animal," this divine potential was to be found in the creative and conscious essence of the human being.[68] Along the lines already set out in *The Diabolicon*, the ultimate object of the Temple of Set was and is the emancipation of its adepts vis-à-vis the material, physical universe, with Set functioning both as the source and representation of this ability to attain a truly individual existence. The tentative and somewhat inconsistent suggestions regarding the possibility of personal immortality made by LaVey in *The Satanic Bible* were elaborated into a comprehensive theory about life after death. While "undeveloped wills" would probably dissolve "into non-existence" after the demise of their physical body, a Setian argued in the Temple's bulletin in 1977, "stronger and more developed wills" might last beyond the grave. This could occur in the realm of "astral projection" and "subjective reality," the "personal and private universe" of "dreams and fantasies."

> "God's" laws need not apply in our universe if we so choose. Our universe can be filled with whatever creatures or beings we wish. In it, one day we can be hunters, the next day we can be kings. There are no holds barred. We are supreme in it. In our subjective universe *we* are "God," and only *we* rule. . . . Now when a person dies, perhaps all that is left is the astral universe. . . . Perhaps when a person dies, that person enters into his own completely subjective universe, completely detached from objective existence.[69]

Ultimately, it was this view of man as a spiritual, creative entity that lay at the base of the Temple's theology and much of its practical outlook. Needless to say, this view was neither ancient nor Egyptian, but eminently modern. We might also add that it was thoroughly Romantic—Aquino had been an avid reader of German Romantic philosophy—much more so, in fact, than LaVey's Satanism had been.[70] In the Temple of Set, one could say, Byron's Lucifer eventually found its adherents after all, albeit masked as a cult to an Egyptian deity.[71]

What had become of Anton LaVey and his Church of Satan in the meantime? There are certainly indications that LaVey was considerably shaken by the defection of some of his most trusted coworkers. For the rest of his life, he would practically never utter the name of the Temple of Set in his publications, disparagingly referring to Aquino *cum suis* as "Egyptoids who'd be better off as Shriners or in Laurel and Hardy's *Sons of the Desert*."[72] In later years, he would deny the rumors spread by "one group in particular" that the Church had been crippled "beyond recovery" by a "non-existent schism or mass defection of high-ranking officials."[73] Instead, the 1975 events had all been part of his five-phase master plan for Satanism, "a diabolical way to "clean house" and phase out members more interested in 'Phase One Satanism' (i.e., group rituals, blaspheming Christianity in a rigidly-structured, limited way)."[74]

I could see that many people were joining our ranks simply because it was a guarantee of friends, or because they wanted the glory of passing tests to earn degrees, much like the "Grand Poobahs" who take off their robes and vestments and become another local nobody again outside their lodge. . . . Groups encourage dependence on beliefs and delusions to reinforce their omnipotence. Instead of fostering self-sufficiency and honest scepticism, I saw my group lapsing into blind belief and unhealthy anthropomorphism.[75]

It was now time for the fifth phase of the master plan, "Application," which would entail the breakthrough of Satanism as an overt or covert influence in society and the reorganization of his organization into a "loosely-structured cabal for the productive aliens, not misfits who need to depend on a group."[76] In addition, he also distanced himself from theist tendencies, unambiguously describing Satan as a metaphor and his own "religion" as "a secular philosophy of rationalism and self-preservation (natural law, animal state), giftwrapping these ideas in religious trappings to add to their appeal."[77]

Aquino, for his part, has doubted if such a master plan ever existed.[78] LaVey had certainly been referring to a plan with phases and stages long before the rift with his lieutenant, but it is, of course, impossible to say if the actual schism was also part of it—although some of his actions preceding it reek of deliberate provocation, particularly the elevation of his personal driver into a fourth-grade magister.[79] In addition, Aquino maintained that LaVey's view of Satan presented a departure from the earlier theology of the Church of Satan. Prior to 1975, according to the Setian Magus, LaVey and the inner core of the Church had always believed in the devil as a genuine, personal deity, while the presentation of the Prince of Darkness as a symbol had just been a front to assuage contemporary sensibilities. He quoted an early coworker of LaVey in support of this assertion, as well as the personal talks he and his partner Lilith Sinclair had had with the High Priest.[80] His crowning piece of evidence was the "formal, written pact" that he claimed LaVey had concluded with Satan.[81] To quote Aquino:

What I did not know for many years was that coincidental with the forming of the Church in 1966, Anton LaVey had privately handwritten and signed a personal Pact with Satan (titled simply "My Pact"). He never mentioned it nor displayed it to others, but on one evening in 1974, during a visit of mine to 6114, we happened to be discussing Robert W. Chambers' *The King in Yellow*. He left the Purple Room, then returned with a locked metal strongbox, which he opened, revealing his personal copy of the then-quite-rare book. The only other item in the strongbox was his Pact—which I was unable to read beyond seeing its title and noting that it was completely handwritten on a single sheet of paper.[82]

LaVey's alleged pact has not surfaced since Aquino saw it, and thus we cannot know what it contained and if it would have constituted proof for a theist belief in the devil. Neither can we ever hope to prove or disprove whether the inner core of the original Church of Satan covertly worshipped Satan as a real entity. It may be noted that on the one hand, LaVey was remarkably consistent in his public utterances about this and other subjects, both before and after 1975; on the other hand, he undeniably tolerated theist leanings among his followers before that date.[83] But except from secret theist convictions (which are by no means outside the range of possibilities), alternative explanations for these incongruities might be hypothesized. The first explanation might be that LaVey was tactically motivated to maintain a certain ambivalence on the matter, in order to retain theist followers for the Church. The High Priest was certainly not above a bit of a foil now and then, as this chapter makes abundantly clear. In 1975, when he decided to shrink down the organization to a "cabal" of select, like-minded members, the necessity to retain these "Phase One Satanists" might have ceased to exist. The second explanation is more profound and touches the very core of LaVey's religious venture. We noted before how LaVey conceived magic and ritual as the domain of fantasy, where deities and demons were invoked *as if* they were genuine super-natural personalities. It was in this world of "honest emotionalizing" that the Satanist could indeed address Satan as his personal god. Most of the texts where LaVey speaks of (or rather to) the devil in this way are ritual in content; quite obviously, for instance, in *The Satanic Rituals*, or in the invocations included in *The Satanic Bible*. We may remark in passing that when LaVey wrote in approval of *The Diabolicon*, Aquino's personal revelation from Satan, he told the latter that he was going to employ it in his Sunday ceremony: that was apparently the occasion he considered it fit for.

When explaining "rational" dogma, LaVey consistently adopted a much more sober tone, emphasizing the man-made nature of religion of which the Satanist was eminently aware, not excluding his own. Satanism, in its nonrational, ritual part, was "avowed fantasy," he wrote quite clearly in *The Satanic Rituals*. "The Satanist can easily invent fairy tales to match anything contained in holy writ, for his background is the very childhood of fiction—the myths immemorial of all peoples and all nations. And he admits they are fairy tales."[84]

Like we suggested before, however, it must not always have been easy to keep the two domains apart. In a way, the Church of Satan *in itself* was a construction of fantasy, not only by virtue of the obvious fact that LaVey had made it up, but also because its primary aim, as a "temple," had been to create a sphere, a zone of fantasy, in which Satanist rites could be performed. It was not called Church of Indulgence or Church of Individualism, but it was named after the symbol that was invoked in its rites *as if* it was a deity. We could also say that LaVey's whole setup was a work of imaginative art (although art of a rather kitschy kind, one feels tempted to add). Just like with the Romantic Satanists, who had treated Satan as if he was real within the context of their poems to make the reader experience certain notions they considered meaningful, so Satan had a certain reality within the structure of the Church of Satan. In this context, the "Hail Satans," diabolically themed stationery, and freaky paraphernalia of the Black House all had their place. Even LaVey's imaginary biography, without doubt initially devised by him to foster his "magical" entrepreneurship, played its role in this construct.

I do not think it probable that this construct was "masterminded" by LaVey from the beginning. Rather, it will have been something that evolved naturally out of the Church's original precepts and ambiguities. In these circumstances, it was small wonder that many members grew confused about the real core beliefs of the Church concerning Satan. Even LaVey must on occasion have had trouble to demarcate the boundaries between fact and "magical" fiction; with his chameleonlike ability to be a different person to different people, he probably added deliberately to the confusion at other times. But the words he had written in his preface to *The Satanic Bible* may also have been applicable to the Church of

Satan in its completeness: "Herein you will find truth—and fantasy. Each is necessary for the other to exist; but each must be recognized for what it is."[85]

The theological dispute that erupted in 1975 also confronts us with some rather ironic complications of definition. If LaVey was indeed only considering Satan as a metaphor, this may raise the question whether we can still consider his Church of Satan as a form of religious Satanism. Can we call a body of thought and practice religion when it presents itself as a rationally based philosophy that only adopts gods and rituals as tools and symbols in a form of consciously devised psychodrama? My answer, obviously, would be yes. LaVeyan Satanism still presents a "set of symbolic acts and forms" that function to relate the Satanist to what it considers the ultimate conditions of his existence. Whether he or she believes Satan to be an independently existing personage or a symbol for his or her own deeper divinity or fierce independence ultimately does not matter according to the definition of religion that we adopted, as long as this set of symbolic acts and forms is present and displays a modicum of consistency.

Even later, more radical offshoots of LaVeyan Satanism, which discard ritual altogether and manifest themselves as a completely rational, antireligious philosophy and lifestyle, can still be termed as forms of religious Satanism under this definition. All retain the systematic use of Satan or related demons and deities as a symbol for values that are deemed essential in their worldview (e.g., pride, carnality, indulgence, critical thinking).[86] As with the Romantic Satanists, the "symbolic forms and acts" that qualify them as religious are here reduced to oral and written speech acts. This may seem a precarious basis on which to consider them religious. But if we perform a small thought experiment and replace the name of "Satan" with that of "God" or "Jesus," the issue may become somewhat clearer for the more puzzled reader. One is then immediately reminded of radical forms of liberal theology that portray "God" or "Jesus" as representing human values like compassion, agapic love, or social emancipation. Although more conservative Christians may disagree, few scholars will refuse to call these variants of Christianity religion.

Quite another problem for our definition is presented by the Temple of Set, Aquino's schismatic restyling of LaVey's Satanism. Here, the religious nature of this movement will not be a matter of dispute, although ceremony and ritual actually play a much less prominent role within the Temple. Nominally, however, the organization had ceased to venerate Satan and adopted the Egyptian deity Set instead. For at least one scholar of Satanism, this was ample reason to declassify the Temple as a form of Satanism.[87] Formally speaking, I must say I agree with this view. In analogy with Wicca, and in a much more obvious way, the Temple of Set can be considered as a form of neopaganism that evolved out of an older form of Satanism. Yet from a historian's point of view, I must add, it is quite evident that the Temple of Set's Set has much more to do with the conception of Satan as it arose in the Western occult tradition and the Church of Satan than with the pre-Christian Egyptian deity. Aquino himself considered Satanism and Setianism as a continuum, and even in later years, he occasionally referred to Black Magic and Satanism in positive ways.[88]

THE SATANISM SCARE, OR, THE VIRULENCE OF OLD LEGENDS

While schism rocked the young Church of Satan, in wider society, developments began to become visible that would have a far bigger impact on the popular perception of Satanism.[89]

The most important of these was the unexpected resurgence of American Christianity. When compiling *The Satanic Bible* in the 1960s, LaVey had made light sport of the Christian religion. Christianity was certainly most prominent among the "white light religions" castigated by Satan's High Priest, but LaVey seemed primarily anxious to point out the nefarious historical role played by the faith in estranging modern man from his authentic self. In its current form, he considered it on the way to inevitable extinction, and he made fun of it in a lighthearted, almost mild way—particularly of the more amusing manifestations of the liberalizing tendency, which at the time was taking center stage in most major Christian denominations, such as "Christian Atheism," "Beat Masses," and shorter habits for nuns. "Is it possible we will soon see 'topless' nuns sensually throwing their bodies about to the 'Miss Solemnis Rock'?" LaVey gleefully fantasized. "Satan smiles and says he would like that fine—many nuns are very pretty girls with nice legs."[90] If the Christian god was not dead altogether, he sardonically continued, he certainly needed Medicare.[91] LaVey's strong belief in the imminent disappearance of Christianity formed the official motivation for his decision to cease the celebration of the Black Mass and similar Christianity-mocking ceremonies in the early 1970s—it was no use beating a dead horse, he would later declare.[92]

Evidently, these predictions proved premature. In the 1970s, there was a steady decline of American church membership and related figures as the sale of religious books came to a standstill; the 1980s witnessed a modest rise.[93] What was more, this increase did not favor liberal Christianity but mainly fundamentalist, evangelical, and charismatic denominations or groups. These groups were generally characterized by the great stress they placed on the (presumed) supernatural aspects of the faith, like speaking in tongues, prophetic visions, and deliverance from demons. This almost inevitably was accompanied by a fierce animosity against occultism.[94] While liberal theology had said goodbye to these elements of traditional Christianity, charismatic Christians considered the demonic very real and Satan an adversary still prowling the world like a roaring lion.[95] In addition, their theology usually displayed a strong eschatological tendency. The return of Christ was near but would be preceded by increasing persecution of Christians and the reign of the Antichrist. The innovations that the 1960s had introduced in Western culture—sexual freedom, greater religious pluralism, alternative modes of living—were interpreted as threatening signs of these imminent events. As had happened before in the history of Christianity, these ingredients proved a perfect breeding ground for a resurgence of old patterns of attribution.

One of the first announcements of this resurgence was a publication by the Christian author Hal Lindsey, who had won fame with his 1970 bestseller *The Late Great Planet Earth,* an apocalyptic book of popular theology suggesting that the rise of the Antichrist and the final battle of Armageddon were at hand. In his second book, *Satan Is Alive and Well on Planet Earth* (1972), Lindsey had shifted his attention to the increase of Satanic manifestations he perceived in contemporary society. "Witches and Satanists, spirits and demons have surfaced in our generation," the popular theologian wrote.[96] The establishment of Anton LaVey's Church of Satan was cited as a prime indicator of this trend.[97] Lindsey did not make much distinction in this respect between Satanism, neopagan witchcraft, and other popular manifestations of occultism—they were all essentially Satanic. More important to Lindsey, however, were the deeper intellectual forces that had shaped Western civilization: the "Thought Bombs" of Kant, Hegel, Kierkegaard, Marx, Darwin, and Freud. The "contamination" of their "explosive ideas" had been an important tool for the devil to shape twentieth-century thinking in the West.[98] The new, demon-inspired outlook was spread through television, movies, popular music, modern art, liberal theology, secular education, international banking, and "innocent" occult games like the ouija board; its consequences were visible in the rising homicide rate in the United States and the "disarray" of the American family.[99] "We are reaping the fruits of permissiveness," Lindsey proclaimed. "Real spiritual beings are beginning to come out in the open to such an extent that people are willing to worship Satan!"[100]

More concrete illustrations of Lindsey's Satanism angst were already in press at the very moment that *Satan Is Alive and Well on Planet Earth* was being published. In 1972, *The Satan Seller* saw print, a purportedly autobiographical account in which former hippie Mike Warnke described how he had descended into the maelstrom of drugs and free sex of 1960s counterculture and eventually stumbled upon a powerful sect of Satanists, "a deep and widespread organization, operating not only in the U.S., but all over the world." Warnke had managed to become a high priest in the sect with fifteen hundred followers in three cities and unlimited wealth at his disposal, a position that put him directly underneath the top level of leaders, the elusive Illuminati.[101] As his book recounted, however, he had eventually converted to Christianity and stepped out of Satanism. The former Satanist priest now toured America as an evangelist with his "Witchmobile," a colorfully painted trailer filled with bric-a-brac vaguely connected with occultism: he would subsequently engage upon a successful career as a Christian comedian before being exposed as a fraud by two Christian reporters in the early 1990s.[102] His counterpart in Britain was Doreen Irvine, a former prostitute and drug addict with a psychiatric past who had been converted to Christianity during an evangelization campaign and according to her own account had been exorcised of forty-seven demons. In her 1972 testimonial, *From Witchcraft to Christ*, she described how she had been both lover of England's top Satanist and "Queen of Black Witches." Satanists, she divulged, were numerous and spread throughout all layers of society: nevertheless, they succeeded in maintaining utmost secrecy. As Queen of Black Witches, Irvine had witnessed Satan himself appear during gatherings of devil worshippers, and she herself had once prevented the discovery of a group of a hundred witches holding a nude ritual on the Dartmoor heath by magically raising a sudden mist.[103] This supernatural mist, by the way, was only the most conspicuous detail among many which curiously remind one of a Dennis Wheatley novel, the place where Doreen Irvine most likely had found her Satanists and "black witches."

It was also during the 1970s that the first rumor panics connected with Satanism began to appear. Even before the emergence of Wicca and LaVey, pulp authors and newspaper reporters had written about dangerous Satanist cults once in a while.[104] But now, these thrilling stories on the border between fact and fiction could evoke genuine local panics. In 1970, a concerned or thrill-seeking multitude had assembled before the decrepit Highgate Cemetery in London after rumors had surfaced that Satanists were planning to resurrect a "King Vampire."[105] More substantial panics swept the American Midwest from about 1973 onward as farmers and townspeople became increasingly concerned over allegedly "mutilated" cattle they found on their premises. Among the diverse explanations suggested for this phenomenon—lone psychopaths, government experiments, alien abductions—"blood rites" by secret Satanist groups loomed prominently. In many cases, it was assumed that

cattle were only the beginning of their sacrificial practice and that human beings would follow suit. Alarmed by these rumors of roaming Satanists, ranchers formed armed vigilante
groups that patrolled pastures, parents were warned to keep their children home after dark
(especially during Halloween), and several official investigations were ordered.[106] These
investigations, by the way, invariably pointed out natural predators and normal decompo-
sition processes as the culprits for the "mutilated" animal carcasses. The rumors reflected
allegations that had surfaced earlier in California about Satanist "Hippie Blood Cults" that
skinned live dogs and held cannibalistic rites.[107]

A wider aversion for cults had already asserted itself in American society by that date.
In 1969, the dream of "Peace and Love" of 1960s counterculture had been overshadowed
in the public mind by the brutal murder of actress Sharon Tate and several other people
by Charles Manson's Family, a violent hippie group that combined drugs and communal
sex with racism and eschatology. Manson had identified himself at times with Lucifer—
although far more frequently with Jesus—and two of his followers had been in contact
with LaVey's Church of Satan.[108] These sparse and completely insufficient indications were
enough to brand Manson a Satanist in the media and to link him to the Church of Satan
and The Process—in case of the latter group, it seems, only because of its equally eschatological nature and the probability that Manson's group may have bumped into them in San
Francisco.[109]

The flood of publicity surrounding the Manson group constituted both a response and a
stimulant to the unease many Americans felt concerning new alternative forms of religiosity. In addition, it promoted the emergence of an anticult movement of informal groups that
united conservative Christians, mental health professionals, and local law enforcement officers.[110] This movement maintained that "cults" used brainwashing techniques to transform
young people into unquestioning, unconditionally obedient disciples. In reaction, anticult
activists extracted followers from these groups, sometimes by force, and submitted them to
a "deprogramming" therapy that amounted to a reverse brainwashing, with the objective to
make them "normal" (and, in most cases, Christian) society members once again.[111]

A similar teaming up of religious organizations and secular officials would allow the
Satanism Scare of the 1980s and 1990s to arise. From the late 1980s, conservative Christians
had begun to organize in interdenominational pressure groups in order to procure political influence. This obviously made it easier to put religion-related issues like abortion on
the national agenda. Yet it may be doubted if Right-wing Christian lobbying could ever
have brought an obscure theme like that of Satanism to such prominence without secular
allies.[112] Some of these allies were unexpected. Radical feminists, child protection workers,
and professional therapists would all contribute to the spread of the Satanism Scare.

The winding way that led to their involvement began with the heightened interest by psychiatry for patients with multiple personality disorder (MPD)—a controversial psychiatric
disorder in which patients manifested different, often totally dissociated identities (awkwardly resembling, one might add, classic patterns of demonic possession).[113] Severe physical or psychological trauma was seen as the most likely cause for affliction. In the late 1970s,
therapists began to experiment with hypnosis to question a patient's alternate personalities
and bring out "repressed memories" about the traumatic event that had triggered their disorder. In many cases, patients recounted sexual abuse as a child during sinister, seemingly

religious rites, often by close family members. This was not exactly new. Freud, during his own experiments with hypnotism, had already found that almost all his female patients described stories like these, and for a short while, he had postulated a quasi-universal occurrence of paternal incest as the cause of a wide range of psychiatric disorders. Thinking better about this, he eventually classed them as fantasies and developed his famous theory of the Oedipus complex. In the 1970s, however, women liberation and child protection activists campaigning to break the code of silence regarding inner-family sexual abuse had begun to criticize Freudian theorizing as a patriarchal blanket for real cases of child abuse.[114] As a result, some therapists were inclined to look upon the utterances of their patients as factual descriptions.

Trendsetting in this respect would be the book *Michelle Remembers* (1980) by the Canadian psychiatrist Lawrence Pazder. It narrated the memories that his client Michelle Smith had "recovered" of her earliest youth during therapy. Gruesome in nature, they included regular physical and sexual assault during Satan-worshipping ceremonies by a coven of witches who each had their left middle finger amputated; in the persona of a five-year-old child, Smith also described how she was forced to witness animal and human sacrifices, at one time involving a heap of murdered babies.[115]

Michelle Remembers effectively introduced the theme of Satanism to the therapeutic community. The book was linked in various ways to the earlier ideas about devil-worshipping cults that had been developed within American Right-wing Christianity. The American folklorist Bill Ellis made it plausible that Michelle's account was influenced by the charismatic discourse on exorcism and hidden Satanic cults.[116] Pazder himself was a devout old-style Roman Catholic who had even sought official permission from the Vatican for his investigation of Michelle's case.[117] Indeed, Smith and Pazder's book ended in a typical apocalyptic note, with a long, rhyming "Master Plan" transmitted by Satan in 1955 that suggested that the archfiend would reveal himself in his full power during the 1980s.[118]

Despite its clear religious overtones, *Michelle Remembers* proved a very influential book with secular therapists. The close-knit community of MPD therapists and their clients adopted "ritual abuse" or "satanic abuse" as its dominant causal narrative; "occult survivors" with ever more spectacular stories of Satanist outrages came forward during therapy.[119] A flood of lawsuits against parents ensued that reached such proportions that some lawyers began to hand out preprinted forms on which their clients could select options like rape, torture, sodomy, and ritual abuse.[120] Although these stories were located in the past—mostly, given the patients' ages, in the 1940s or early 1950s—it made sense, of course, that the activities of such a widespread and powerful underground group were still being continued. The first assertions that such was indeed the case soon came into the open. In 1983, seven workers at the McMartin preschool in Los Angeles were indicted on charges of abusing 360 children during rites involving blood sacrifices.[121] The case had been brought in motion by one of the toddler's mothers who was later diagnosed as paranoid schizophrenic; however, the accusations were picked up by other parents, who soon became convinced that their children had fallen victim to a communitywide cult of child-abusing Satanists.

The widely published and long-drawn-out court case inaugurated a wave of other instances in which daycare centers were linked to child sex rings and/or Satanism by police investigators and social workers still inexperienced in matters concerning child abuse and eager to protect alleged victims.[122] In the Los Angeles area alone, sixty-three other daycare centers became involved in cases of alleged ritual abuse.[123] By then, the idea of a underground cult of criminal Satanists that had spread throughout America had gained a firm foothold, disseminated by the mass media and by networks of religious specialists, "occult survivors," therapists, child workers, and "cult cops."[124] Some accounts told about one million Satanists secretly practicing their blood rites and 50,000 children being sacrificed to Satan on a yearly basis (some of the latter produced especially for this purpose with "breeders," young girls kept in captivity in order to give birth to sacrificial babies).[125] Local rumor panics about Satanists out to kidnap blue-eyed, blond virgins ensued in several smaller towns throughout the United States, and a Satanist conspiracy was constructed that combined organized child molestation, pornography, extreme forms of popular music, adolescent Satanism (on which later more), "occult" graffiti, and local legends about the supernatural.[126] When asked in a poll during the early 1990s, 63 percent of Texans confirmed they thought Satanism a "very serious" problem to society.[127]

More than one commentator has drawn attention to the salient similarity between this late twentieth-century Satanism Scare and the witchcraft scare from roughly three centuries before.[128] Basically it was the same trope of a secret and threatening "otherworld" of reversed morality and devil worship that was reactivated here. In some cases, there was more than a morphological link, for instance when "cult experts" cited indicators of Satanist activity taken from demonologies from the early modern era.[129] As with the witchcraft persecutions, this phantasm could only have social and political impact because it was adopted and implemented by representatives of secular authority—notwithstanding the obvious religious origins of its contents. And it could only have this impact because it provided a distorted reflection of anxieties that were shared by larger portions of the population. At the root of these anxieties, many scholars have pointed to insecurities about parenting in the changing social and economic landscape of twentieth-century America.[130] It was no coincidence that daycare centers were among the most frequent targets for rumors and investigations of Satanist abuse. But it seems probable that a wider unease regarding gender roles and sexual mores was at stake, an unease triggered by the new "permissiveness" in these fields that the 1960s and 1970s had brought.[131]

There were, of course, also differences between the early modern Witch Scare and the twentieth-century Satanism Scare. One was the much less prominent role for Satan as a direct participant in the latter. It is true that the devil regularly made an earthly appearance in many accounts of "occult survivors," for instance, in those of Mike Warnke and Doreen Irvine, to begin with; it is also true that his continuing menacing presence was accepted by many secular "experts" with a Christian background. But Satan was absent in the officially accepted discourse about the Satanist Scare. In court proceedings or government publications, veiled terms like "ritual abuse" or "multivictim, multi-offender abuse" were used in order to avoid an overly religious coloring, even when the cases they discussed clearly originated from the matrix of Satanism conspiracy thinking.[132] In this, they fitted into a trend to "secularize" Satanism that went back to the end of the seventeenth century and that interpreted Satanism primarily as a *human* activity that could be perceived as dangerous or harmful to society. In fact, only this transformation of the old attributed stereotype made it possible that public authorities in a modern secular society like the late twentieth-century United States occupied themselves with this complex of allegations at all.

Another difference, and a fortunate one, was the much smaller toll on human life taken by the Satanism Scare. This was mainly due to the judicial system, which was only shortly swept along with the moral panic and with few exceptions eventually maintained adequate evidentiary standards. In 1990, all defendants in the McMartin trial (reputedly the longest and most expensive in Californian legal history) were finally acquitted when the proceedings resulted in a hung jury for the second time; after that, the number of court cases involving "satanic ritual abuse" dwindled.[133] By that time, noted scholars within the academic community had begun to demolish the mythology of the Satanism Scare, while the FBI, in an official report on the matter, declared it had been unable to find convincing indications for even one genuine case of Satanist ritual abuse. At the end of the decade, the stereotype of the dangerous Satanist had retreated in the United States to where it came from: to the subcultures of fundamentalist Christians and conspiracy buffs.

Still, considerable harm had been done in the meantime. To begin with, an unknown number of small children had been sexually harassed and psychologically traumatized—not by Satanists, but by well-meaning child workers who had probed their genitals in order to test whether they had been abused, intimidated them with prolonged and intense questioning, and in some cases had them taken away from their families for a period of time.[134] By 1989, some fifty people had been put on trial on charges stemming from ritual abuse cases, which usually meant permanent damage to their personal reputations. Of these, approximately half were convicted and received often very harsh penalties.[135] The majority of them eventually were released after going into appeal, but this usually meant that they had already spent several years in custody. A few individuals were even more hapless. One of the most tragic stories is that of Californian deputy sheriff Paul Ingram, who was accused of sexual abuse by his teenage daughters after one of them, while at a summer bible camp, had recovered memories about Satanist rituals in the family home.[136] Ingram, who was a pious Pentecostal Christian himself and the county Republican Party chairman, did not remember anything: but after much prayer and intensive questioning, he eventually "recovered" memories of the Satanist abuse of his daughters he had never committed. In accordance, he pleaded guilty at his trial and was convicted to twenty years in prison on May 1, 1989. Once behind bars, the former sheriff thought better of his confession, but an appeal against his verdict was pointless because he had already pled guilty himself. He was eventually released in 2003.[137]

The Satanism Scare, in addition, did not remain constrained to America and Canada only. Christian "experts" and literature exported the moral panic about the secret Satanist conspiracy abroad, where it spread like ripples in a pond, much as had been the case with the early modern Witch Scare some three centuries before. The United Kingdom was one of the earliest countries that was affected. The moral panic probably reached its peak there with the abduction of nine children in a predawn police raid with helicopters on a remote Orkney island in February 1991, after other children from the island had been coaxed into declarations about Satanist ritual abuse by social workers.[138] Moral panics connected with Satanism and ritual abuse then flared up in New Zealand, Australia, South Africa, the Netherlands, Scandinavia, Italy, and Israel.[139] While the impact of the Satanism Scare on these countries proved limited and short-lived, more tragic consequences ensued when the Satanic conspiracy model reached African countries like Nigeria and Kenya. In these areas, American and British evangelical ideas about the dangers of Satanism tended to fuse with local fears of traditional witchcraft in a way that seemed not just to reflect, but actually reenact, the early modern witchcraft persecutions.[140] Approximately sixty people died in lynching campaigns, and the Kenyan President Daniel arap Moi even established an official "Commission of Inquiry into the Cult of Devil Worship."[141] In its 2000 report, this commission concluded that Satanist cults were seducing the educated youth and causing trainwrecks and other accidents in Kenya, repeating traditionl allegations of human sacrifice, cannibalism, and ritual abuse.[142] The report also disclosed that many minority religions were infiltrated by Satanists, including, of course, the Freemasons. Even Albert Pike was mentioned once more as "Supreme Pontiff of Freemasonry."[143]

What had been the fate, in the meantime, of the select group of self-declared Satanists who had organized themselves into the Church of Satan and the Temple of Set? Surprisingly enough, they remained largely unscathed by the Satanism Scare. To be sure, LaVey and his family already had rich experience of the enmity that the concept of Satanism could evoke before the moral panic about Satanic ritual abuse erupted. Their daughter Zeena, for instance, had returned from school one day to find a murderous lunatic with a knife at her doorstep, and in a letter from 1973, Diane LaVey reported that the Black House had been "bombarded with bricks, bullets, one bomb, eggs, and spray paint."[144] Already in 1971, Anton LaVey had surrounded "Central Grotto" with barbed wire, while he also kept a pop gun at the ready to scare off hooligans. In 1975, the LaVeys even painted 6114 beige to make it more inconspicuous: in addition, they also spread the rumor that they did not live on the premises anymore, using mail addresses as far apart as Beverly Hills and Amsterdam to mask their geographical whereabouts.[145] But that was still during the 1970s, and nothing suggests that this small-scale violence intensified during the Satanism Scare. The existence of the Church of Satan, strange as it may seem, generally did not play a major role in the conspiracy scenarios propounded by the moral entrepreneurs that propagated the Scare. Some "occult survivors" mentioned that they had met or seen LaVey at meetings of Satanist blood cults or that they knew he was a pawn in the bigger game; more general theorizers, like Lindsey, invoked him as a symptom of the times or a nefarious influence on society's morals.[146] Few of them seem to have known exactly what to do with a carnival church and a buffoonish Black Pope who firmly declared his support for law and order and denied he believed in the personal existence of Satan.[147]

This may be one of the reasons why the Church of Satan was generally left in the lurch during the Satanism Scare. The wave of moral panic failed to produce serious legal repercussions for Satanist organizations. Although ultraconservative senator Jesse Helms tried to pass a bill revoking tax exemptions for groups that were involved in "the worship of Satan or the powers of evil," this proposal was not approved and freedom for religion remained intact.[148] The only prominent (former) Satanist directly affected by the Satanism Scare was, in fact, LaVey's erstwhile disciple Michael Aquino, and this was largely due to a coincidence. The army officer was stationed at Presidio, California, in 1987, when the daycare center at the army base also became swept up in the epidemic of ritual abuse allegations. After the customary questioning, one of the small children identified Aquino and his wife as participants in alleged gruesome rites. No formal charges were filed against them, however, and an official spokesman at the Presidio base declared to the press that Aquino was a good soldier who "did his job."[149]

What the Satanism Scare did change was LaVey's mild, condescending attitude toward Christianity. With understandable repulsion, he saw the revival of forms of Christian religion that seemed to date from at least the nineteenth century. In his church bulletin, he voiced his bewilderment. How was it possible that adult victims were loudly proclaiming that they had been abused by powerful Satanists as a child, when he had not been able to find one single Satanist in the 1940s and 1950s? Why were the personal and psychological histories of these "survivors" not investigated by the media? Their family members queried? How believable was a Satanist conspiracy that was said to be simultaneously responsible for complicated international legal coverups and kids spray-painting pentagrams beneath freeways? "Where was Freudian wisdom when psychiatry like *Michelle Remembers* was validated by the media?" [150]

> In its senescence, Christianity seems to be pulling all its old chestnuts out of the fire and creating the most irrational witch hunt ever. Hysteria is not only heeded, but encouraged. Indeed, one wonders about the unquestioning gullibility of not only the general public but specifically those in positions of authority. Children are enticed— not by Satanists, but by authorities, to concoct damaging lies about their own parents. Any star, circle, triangle, hexagram or octagon becomes a "Satanic" symbol. The list of accursed objects grows: stained glass, ceramic cats, a solid color bathrobe, leather clothes, rock recordings (especially if played backwards). If a *Satanic Bible* is discovered, it becomes proof that its reader perpetrates every crime known to man.[151]

As the Satanism Scare raged, the High Priest's tone of speech regarding Christianity grew markedly more bitter. "Christianity, as always, is the only thing standing in the way of progress," he declared. "We don't need to show any tolerance or good fellowship to these sheep now that we're calling the shots. Have Christians ever shown Satanists any mercy?"[152] As LaVey did more often in times of particular affliction, he eventually vented his feelings in song. Behind the keyboards, the Exarch of Satan improvised a "Hymn of the Satanic Empire" (or "Battle Hymn of the Apocalyps") that told in no uncertain terms of his bitterness toward the Christian hordes:

> Let the lions and tigers rip them up
> The arena shouts for Christian blood.[153]

NAZISM, THE WESTERN REVOLUTION, AND GENUINE SATANIST CONSPIRACIES

However scathing LaVey could be about the conspirational paranoias of fundamentalist Christians, he did not object to the basic notion that Satanism was a kind of secret force covertly and overtly influencing the evolution of society.[154] His own Church of Satan was increasingly conceived by him as a conspirational organization, a "cabal of creative misfits."[155] Society would evolve to a higher, more sane level when the Satanic Empire would burst forth in all its splendor, and the Church of Satan was to be a prime instrument in bringing about this evolution.

Initially, as we saw earlier in this chapter, LaVey had considered his Church as the nucleus of a future mass movement. But LaVeyan Satanism had failed grievously in becoming a mass movement, and the intermediate nuisance of running an organization to enroll the inevitable foot soldiers needed to become one had made the High Priest tired of the whole business of playing church. The two other options for being a Satanist had already been outlined by LaVey in *The Satanic Bible*: "he either escapes from the cacklings and carpings of the righteous, or stands proudly in his secret places of the earth and manipulates the folly-ridden masses through his own satanic might, until that day when he may come forth in splendor."[156] These two options, presented almost as a by the by in *The Satanic Bible*, would dominate the rest of LaVey's career. And it primarily would be the last option—the Satanist as "secret manipulator of folly-ridden masses"—that informed the course he set out for the Church of Satan in the two decades after 1975.

It might be needless to say by now that the concept of the Satanist as a conspirator was almost as old as the concept of Satanism itself. Here again, LaVey appropriated the old image of the Satanist and gave it a new, positive twist. "The first time I read the Protocols of the Elders of Zion," he declared sardonically, "my instinctive reaction was, 'So what's wrong with THAT? Isn't that the way any master plan should work? Doesn't the public deserve—nay, demand—such despotism?' "[157] This concept of the Satanist as a secret conspirator explains the appearance in *The Satanic Bible* of "de facto Satanists" Rasputin and arms dealer Basil Zaharoff (1849–1936).[158] Both stand for the Satanist as powerful hidden manipulator. The Black Pope clearly liked to see himself as such a shadowy manipulator and preferably presented his decisions concerning his Church as steps in a great "Master Plan." Already during the early 1970s, as we have seen, he had talked in his letters to Aquino about the different "phases" Satanism would have to go through, suggesting he was working according to a carefully planned strategy. This "Master Plan" was only published in the Church's newsletter *after* the schism of 1975, which gave it all the trappings of a post factum fiction, as Aquino rightly remarked.[159]

According to this final plan, the first three phases had entailed the establishment and propagation of a "Satanic body politic." The conflict with Aquino and the hierarchy had been part of the fourth phase, that of "dispersion" and "de-institutionalism" to separate "the builders from the dwellers."[160] Where LaVey had first seen the Church of Satan as the Satanist mass movement itself, and later as the select core of Satanists that would lead the mass movement, he now adopted a plan of action that was even more within the conspirational mold. The church would henceforth be a "loose cabal" of people who influenced society in whatever field and who would, independently, and if need be secretly, exert their influence to insert society with Satanist principles. For this, the church needed "superior people," men and women of genuine capacity or power, and not social misfits looking for a "Satan pen pal club."[161] The Church of Satan, as an organization, only needed to stay around to function as a sort of public beacon for Satanists like this, and to ascertain the proliferation of the Satanist philosophy, particularly through the writings of Anton Szandor LaVey himself. In fact, LaVey declared, it was not even necessary for true Satanists to join. A true Satanist could operate independently, without the psychological support of a miniature herd. If they felt the need to do so, groups could perform rituals on their own.[162] The elusiveness this might bring about suited LaVey very well. "Trying to discover Satanists, real Satanists, is like nailing custard to the wall," he gloated in 1990. "One of our strengths is that we don't have to have big buildings. We have cells of activity all around the world. . . . The Church of Satan doesn't need to be governed or dictated by anything other than the guidelines of the Satanic Bible. That's one of the dangers of our religion."[163]

Phase five of the LaVeyan master plan was simply designated as "Application," and described by the High Priest as "tangible fruition, the beginning of the harvest, so to speak." What was this next and final stage of Satanic evolution meant to be? LaVey would only publish his ideas on this point in 1988, at the height of the Satanism Scare, which may have radicalized his views considerably. Yet this does not mean that there was no consistency with his earlier ideas. To the contrary, themes he had been talking about since the late 1960s and early 1970s make their reappearance in his sketch for the Age of Satan. Under the title "Pentagonal Revisionism," LaVey proposed a five-point program of "goals":

1) stratification
2) strict taxation of churches
3) re-establishing Lex Talionis
4) development and production of artificial human companions
5) the opportunity for anyone to live within a total environment of his or her choice.[164]

In many respects, this program shaded off into science fiction, but some of its points were crisply concrete. The proposal to tax churches, of course, reflected LaVey's antireligiosity, which was only intensified by the Satanism Scare. At the tender beginnings of his own Church, he may have planned to profit from tax exemption himself; now, he expressed confidence that churches would "crumble overnight of their own obsolescence" as soon as their income and property were taxed.[165] The introduction of "Lex Talionis"—an eye for an eye and a tooth for a tooth—was also presented as a measure against "religious beliefs secularised and incorporated into law and order issues." With this proposal for "a complete overturning of the present in-justice system based on Judeo-Christian ideals, where the victim/defender has been made the criminal," and for the establishment of a "Satanic society" in which "everyone must experience the consequences of his own actions, for good or ill," LaVey reflected his earlier ideas in *The Satanic Bible* about "responsibility to the responsible," as he himself was quick to point out.[166]

The crucial point, however, "the point on which all others ultimately rest," as LaVey acknowledged himself, was stratification. This term in fact signified his radical goodbye of the notion of equality as it had developed during the Western Revolution—both as an *anthropology*, a philosophical principle about common humanity, and as an *ideal* for the shaping of society. "There can be no myth of equality for all," LaVey elucidated in no uncertain terms. "It only translates to mediocrity and supports the weak at the expense of the strong. Water must be allowed to seek its own level without interference from apologists for incompetence. No one should be protected from the effects of his own stupidity."[167] Instead of the myth of equality, he saw humanity as stratified in a hierarchy of inferior and superior people: a creative and intellectual elite "that must be sanctioned at any cost," and the rest of humanity, which was categorized as "locusts."[168] In his more extreme "ramblings," LaVey did not hesitate to propound police state measures to curtail the "herd" and "sanction" the elite: ghettoization, eugenics, forced sterilization.[169]

LaVey did not develop these radical ideas *ex nihilio*. We have already encountered one probable source of inspiration for them in the previous chapter: the philosophy of Friedrich Nietzsche. LaVey's plans look like a crude but not necessarily incorrect implication of Nietzsche's plea for a creative elite that would reshape Western values and reign like the philosopher kings from Plato's Republic.[170] Until now, we have considered Nietzsche's (and LaVey's) ideas only as an extreme evolution of the critique on Christian ethics that had originated with the Western Revolution. But it can also be placed within a different framework, in a loose "tradition" that is eminently political and embodies a reaction *against* the Western Revolution. Labeling this tradition as "reactionary" or "conservative" might be slightly misleading. Rather, it is best understood as a critique that developed out of the Western Revolution itself and continuously accompanied it. And from the three core terms of the Western Revolution—liberty, equality, and brotherhood—it was primarily the notion of human equality that drew its criticism. Equality and egalitarian democracies, this criticism maintained, fostered the rule of mediocrity and created societies in which excellency in any field would be wielded out. LaVey's Satanism can be considered another manifestation of this school of thinking. Significantly enough, the intellectual progenitors most often mentioned by LaVey were authors belonging (or thought by LaVey to belong) to the American branch of this tradition—names like Ben Hecht, H. L. Mencken, and Ayn Rand. Most of them had not written a single line on Satan: they simply had espoused freethinking and anti-egalitarian ideas similar to those of LaVey.

In the occultist tradition LaVey sprang from, might-is-right ideas and (proto-)Nietzschean notions were not altogether unfamiliar as well. Like we saw in chapter 3, Éliphas Lévi, after he had become an admirer of the Napoleons, had already voiced similar ideas in his works. These had filtered through in later occultism.[171] Aleister Crowley had been directly inspired by reading Nietzsche, whom he considered "almost an avatar of Thoth, god of wisdom," and whose echoes we may detect in passages of the *Book of the Law* like "the slaves shall serve," "the law of the strong," and "damn them who pity!"[172] In the commentary on the *Book of the Law* that he wrote later, the Beast elucidated:

> Nature's way is to weed out the weak. This is the most merciful way, too. At present all the strong are damaged, and their process hindered by the dead weight of the weak limbs and the missing limbs, the diseased limbs and the atrophied limbs. The Christians to the lions!
>
> We must go back to Spartan ideas of education; and the worst enemies of humanity are those who wish, under pretext of compassion, to continue its ills through the generations. The Christians to the lions![173]

LaVey's adoption of Nietzsche, social Darwinism, and "might is right" philosophies was thus not completely lacking in precedent with the strands of occultism that will have influenced him most. From occultism, LaVeyan Satanism also inherited an outlook that can be called elitist, for want of a better word. Those to whom "occult knowledge" is disclosed are, by this fact alone, set apart and made more "knowing" and "powerful." The system of grades that is common to many occult organizations creates differentiation by its very nature; the real and ritual trials one has to overcome suggest that only exceptional individuals may attain the higher grounds of wisdom and power. When Marie Naglowska, for instance, stated that her doctrines were not meant for the "blind masses," not much else was implied other than the self-complimentary notion that she and her followers were the true elite (an elite composed, in her case, of "those that neither rule nor are ruled").[174] Even Nietzsche's ideas on the *Übermensch* and the born ruler had some correlation to this. It is clear, at least, that the German philosopher never envisioned his new and higher type of man as a sort of blond, muscular Nazi athlete. Rather, in a sense, he is one of the initiated: a member of a *spiritual* elite consisting of those who can dispose of old prejudices and embrace a new, radical, nontranscendent, and this-worldly life-view.

LaVey's ideological direction was thus not without pedigree in Western occultism. But with regard to Satanism, as we have already remarked, he here embarked on a reinvention of tradition and a political repositioning that was without precedent. Sympathy for the devil had up to then been predominantly a Left-wing affair, as previous chapters have shown. In the early beginnings of the Church of Satan, this had caused some confusion about which side of the political spectrum LaVey belonged to. Given the long history of Leftist "Satanism" and the countercultural origins of his Church, some had assumed LaVey to pursue a Leftist-oriented political agenda. This had been the conclusion, for instance, of the John Birch Society, a civil watchdog organization of extreme conservatives who sought to continue McCartney's anti-Communist crusade by "unmasking" alleged Communists. A representative of the society visiting the Black House in 1970 had noted "a well-thumbed copy of the *Communist Manifesto*" as well as several other works by "identified communists" on LaVey's bookshelves: in addition, the good man "caught a glimpse of something red hanging on the wall" in the cellar, which he assumed to be a Soviet Union flag.[175]

Isaac Bonewits, a seventeen-year-old Berkeley student who later grew into a prominent member of the neopagan community, had joined the Church of Satan with opposite motives but upon similar assumptions. Bonewits had been invited into the Church after LaVey had noticed the pro-Satanic street-corner sermons he had given on the campus to mock the evangelization campaigns of the "Jesus People" descending upon San Francisco University. For a time, he participated with much gusto in the Church's rites.[176] But as he was moving to the Left and protesting the Vietnam War, it became increasingly evident that LaVey and his followers espoused quite different principles. "Some were bringing authentic Klu Klux Klan robes and Nazi uniforms for the ceremonies," Bonewits would later recall. "I was assured that the clothes were merely for 'Satanic shock value' to jar people from their usual staid patterns of thinking. Then I would talk to the men wearing these clothes and realize they were not pretending anything. I noticed that there were no black members of the Church and only one Asian, and began to ask why."[177] Bonewits's suspicions were not without ground. In the decades that followed, LaVey would at several times retain friendly contacts with neo-Nazi and Right-wing organizations.[178] The High Priest of Satan, when asked, mostly replied that the affinity between modern Satanism and National Socialism was primarily a matter of aesthetics. "The aesthetics of Satanism are those of National Socialism," he once declared.[179] But it seems plausible that more was at stake than mere aesthetic attraction to black uniforms and invigorating marching tunes. Fascism was, of course, another historical manifestation of the same current of anti-egalitarian critique that had been embraced by LaVey.

In fact, various motives can be discerned in the fascination by LaVey and many of his disciples for the Third Reich and its later scions. First, seldom made explicit but always present, was the obvious provocative potential of Nazism in the post-1945 West, which without doubt equaled or superseded that of Satan himself. Second, the National Socialists, and particularly the "Black Order" of the SS, were perceived by LaVey *cum suis* as powerful black magicians. Thus LaVey included a rite in his *Satanic Rituals* that was presented as originating with "the intellectual element of the budding *Sicherheitsdienst*"; in addition, he pretended in his authorized biography that he had been introduced firsthand to the esoteric secrets of Nazism during a visit to Germany directly after the end of the war.[180] Aquino, likewise, went to the former ceremonial center of the SS at Wewelsburg to do a magical "working" that revealed to him that the human spirit was in fact "anti-natural"— and although he knew and condemned the concentration-camp labor involved in constructing the SS castle, this did not prevent him from considering Himmler and consorts as genuine and powerful magicians.[181] In the third place, the National Socialists were often brought up by LaVey and Aquino as prime examples of political manipulators, masterful architects of a movement that had gained immense political power by effectively playing the darker chords of the human psyche. Thus *The Satanic Bible* spoke of the "madness of the Hitlerian concept" but expressed admiration for Hitler's idea to gain German loyalty through a program of "strength through joy."[182] This, one suspects, is where LaVey located the true magical prowess of the Nazis. It is also the point at which they could serve as a model for himself and his Church as powerful "movers" behind the scenes. For this reason, probably, LaVey included Nazi ideologue Alfred Rosenberg among his list of "Satanist conspirators."[183]

Yet the most important reason for LaVey's affinity with the National Socialists remains without doubt the ideological resemblance they displayed on many points. Both criticized the equality concept of the Western Revolution; both propagated a radical form of (pseudo-)Nietzschean and social Darwinist ethics; both envisioned a society that moved beyond Christianity. This was where LaVeyan Satanism and (neo)Nazism could find common ground in a more fundamental way, and this forms the background of the persistent flirtations of LaVey with Nazism—a flirting that never evolved into unqualified identification, but went beyond mere provocative posing or "tongue-in-cheek cultural critique," as some apologetic scholars have suggested.[184]

Meanwhile, it must be emphasized that this affinity with the radical Right did not mean that LaVey also accepted the racist agenda of Nazism. Given his Jewish roots, it would have been an extraordinary thing indeed for him to adopt Nazi antisemitism. Instead, he half-jokingly proposed a Satanist form of Jewish Nazism to provide a "tough identity" for secularized Jews and "the vast number of children of mixed Jewish/Gentile origins": "a rational amalgam of proud, admitted, Zionist Odinist Bolshevik Nazi Imperialist Socialist Fascism."[185] Already in *The Satanic Bible*, LaVey had stated that true Satanism "transcends ethnic, racial and economic differences," and he would repeat this message until the end of his days.[186] And notwithstanding Bonewits's remark quoted earlier, the Church of Satan *had* known nonwhite members, the most famous of whom had been the singer Sammy Davis Jr., of mixed Jewish, black, and Puerto Rican descent.[187] It was true as well, however, that Sammy Davis Jr. was rather an exception. LaVey naturally had not failed to notice this.

In the "official" church history published in 1990, he ventured a bit of improvistu sociolog-ical analysis in this regard:

> One of the more astute law enforcement occult investigators asked me recently why she seemed to notice a preponderance of young white middle-to-upper class males getting involved in Satanism now. I offered the possibility that it's because they're the only group without a racial identity anymore. Young black men can be African Americans, young Mexicans can be Chicanos, Homeboys and identify with various gangs. There's all kind of attention given to minority rights and interests. White kids grow up feeling angry and resentful that there doesn't seem to be an identity of power for them anymore. So—there are the Skinhead factions, there's white-oriented heavy metal, and beyond those elements—there's Satanism.[188]

This long quotation gives already a clue for a further motive for LaVey's friendly face toward some neopagan strands of neo-Nazism. He considered them as a potential recruiting ground for his church and a reservoir of future allies. Already in 1974, in a secret letter to Aquino, he had given precisely this kind of tactical reasoning as an explanation for his con-tacts with the neo-Nazi National Renaissance Party, commenting that they could easily be propagandized into becoming Satanists. "Their racist ideals are also worn on their sleeves, and, I believe, are as removable as their armbands. . . . As it stands, there is only a handful of them. But if they revamp their approach, their ranks would grow."[189]

The direct context of this remark reveals an even more ambitious agenda behind LaVey's small-scale political scheming. In various letters to fellow Satanists at this time, Aquino had predicted "a tremendous right-wing political backlash" in America. "No jackboots and swastikas, of course. American flags, Sousa marches, hard-hats, Minutemen-type paramil-itary groups, and so forth."[190] It was with regard to this scenario that LaVey had revealed his strategic alliance with a neo-Nazi group. Judging from their correspondence, one gets the impression that both he and Aquino looked rather forward to an imminent Right-wing regime. Indeed, it seems that the inevitability of its ascension was identical to that of the coming of the Age of Satan itself and that both were somehow connected or even the same. This would not be entirely illogical, given LaVey's own Right-wing tendencies and the fact that he liked to present his Satanism as quintessentially American as well. Saliently enough, for instance, in 1990 LaVey restated Aquino's ideas about the way this "right-wing political backlash" would take place as a "directive" that Satanism should follow. "When Satanism becomes the major religion in the United States, it will be complete with red, white and blue banners flying, accompanied by the blaring trombones of John Phillip Sousa."[191] Nor does this seem to have been a later afterthought with "the Doctor." "Satanism IS Americanism in its purest form," LaVey had already written in a tabloid column from 1971. "We do not advo-cate or even approve of denial or desecration of such sacred American traditions as home, family, patriotism, personal pride, etc. but instead champion these things."[192] In rubbing shoulders with Rightist activists, he may have hoped to secure a position of power for his organization with the ruling party of the future.

Adding it all up, I think it is not impossible that LaVey envisioned more or less the same role for him and his Church of Satan under a new Right-wing regime as he thought the "Black Order" had held under the Third Reich: that of a "spiritual" elite organization that was covertly at the heart of power. Thus there really was some kind of would-be conspiracy at the heart of LaVeyan Satanism, although it looked a bit different than the feverish fantasies of fundamental Christians. Nor was there much ground for panic in this matter, for there was a huge gulf between LaVey's grandiose conceptions of his and Satanism's role and the real-life significance (or insignificance) of both his person and his movement. In the 1980s and 1990s, the Church of Satan sometimes seemed close to complete disappearance.[193] Its bulletin was reduced to one page in 1981 and dissolved in 1988 "due to the rapid expansion of the Church of Satan," while a regional agent of his organization claimed he had not heard of his High Priest for ages and was unaware whether he still participated in anything at all.[194]

LaVey himself, naturally, liked to present a different picture. Time and again, he would point out new indications of the coming Age of Satan. Until his final days, he would uphold an image of his Church and his person as powerful forces hidden behind major social developments, at one point even suggesting that he had masterminded the Satanism Scare himself to draw more attention to Satanism.[195] As one author has remarked, LaVey here rather resembled the mouse marching beside the elephant and boasting of the mighty noise it makes. The stark contrast between imagined importance and actual reality may in fact have provided an additional motive for LaVey's openness to neo-Nazi courting. His attitude in this regard was in flagrant contradiction with the analysis to which he subscribed of Americanism as the future of fascism and of the evident ineptitude of the current neo-Nazi movement. He acidly described the latter as "acned and bucolic types" who "spend their time getting jeered at in street demonstrations," and he was acutely aware of the fact that any group brandishing swastikas would never be able to attain the proportions of a mass movement in America. The overtures he nevertheless made to elements from this sordid subculture may have been motivated by the simple need to feel significant, to do some actual "plotting" and establish "strategic alliances" with those few groups that showed any interest. "They would do anything for us," he had written to Aquino in 1974. "So would Klan, for that matter. I do not endorse either, but acknowledge camaraderie from any source."[196]

By thus minimizing the impact of LaVey's Satanism as a social and political force, I do not mean to suggest that the cocktail of social Darwinism, elitism, and anti-egalitarianism it propagated was altogether harmless. The consequences of a LaVeyan Satanism that is taken to its logical extremes are well illustrated by the history of the Order of the Nine Angles.[197] This elusive Satanist organization is or was largely the brain child of Anton Long, pseudonym for the British fascist David Wulstan Myatt (born 1950 or 1952). In its own writings, the Order claims to derive from a thousands-year-old secret tradition in which Long/Myatt was initiated in 1968 by the female leader of a Wicca coven. There is no outside corroboration for this myth of origin, however. The only thing that is known is the fact that David Myatt joined the British National Socialist movement in 1968 as a bodyguard for one of its leaders and started to publish texts as Anton Long outlining the philosophies and methods of the Order of the Nine Angles in the late 1970s and early 1980s. The name of his order suggests direct inspiration from the Church of Satan—a "Ceremony of the Nine Angles" is included in *The Satanic Rituals*.[198] In fact, the Satanism propagated by Long/Myatt can in many ways be described as an extreme extrapolation of tendencies already present in LaVeyan Satanism.

As Myatt's political activities indicate, the Order of the Nine Angles (ONA) took LaVey's modest trysts with Right-wing extremism to full-blown identification with National Socialism and antisemitism. Among other things, this radical orientation is expressed by a strict avoidance of any concepts or entities from Judeo-Christian religious and occult traditions, with the one exception, of course, of the figure of Satan himself, who is conceived as a real supernatural being.[199] The ultimate purpose of the Order is to create a new species in the human evolution, a species of Satanic god-men that look a lot like an aryanized version of LaVey's Satanist as the "highest embodiment of human life." The advent of this new form of humanity will mark a new era in history, the "Galactic Aeon" in which man will conquer the cosmos by interstellar travel. The adept of the ONA is to further the advance of the coming Galactic Empire, both by training to become a god-man himself and by disrupting present society as much as possible to bring about its collapse.

To become a true Homo Galactica, the adept has to pass through a rigorous sevenfold set of initiation trials, with each trial giving access to a higher grade. This strict initiation process is explicitly contrasted with that of the Church of Satan, which had started to award grades to influential people who had bestowed favor upon the Church; neither is it a kind of academic exam of the candidate's esoteric knowledge, as with the Temple of Set. Instead, it is meant to prepare the adept and test his fitness both physically and psychologically. Thus the first grade requires one to stay a night out in the open without sleeping, and other levels include ordeals like running long distances with a heavy load and surviving for three months in the wilderness without the benefits of civilization. Other practices are intended to ascertain that the ONA member has thoroughly cleansed himself of Judeo-Christian ethics and has embraced a truly Satanist "warrior ethos." The most notorious of these is the practice of "human culling," which requires the member to murder someone considered useless or harmful to society and remain undetected—an extreme appliance, one could say, of the Church of Satan's curse ritual, giving practical application to what LaVey had kept safely magical. In addition to this, the initiate is required to start his own "magickal" temple and to play out so-called insight roles, for instance by joining a Leftist or Right-wing insurrectionary organization in order to wreak havoc on the status quo and transgress one's own ethical and mental boundaries. The latter practice is very reminiscent of a rite performed by LaVey in the early Church of Satan, which consisted of people taking on the role of someone whom they most hated—their boss, for instance, or a Nazi villain—in order to gain "magical" insight into their adversary (this, it may be remembered, was the reason stated by LaVey to Bonewits for the presence of people dressed in SS uniforms in his house). It seems that here, once again, the ONA translated into action what LaVey had restricted to the ceremonial realm. Absurdly enough, the ONA initiate is also required to do board games: to be exact, to build and play the "Star Game," which was designed by Anton Long and enables the player to magically enact the history of human civilizations.

The Order offers no assistance to its initiates through all these ordeals. Like later LaVeyan Satanism, it is largely a virtual cult spreading the lore of its path by way of its literature, which each adept subsequently must follow by himself. This also makes the Order an extremely shadowy organization. It is unclear whether any "human culling" has actually taken place and whether someone ever actually made it through all the grades of the initiation system. It might be that the only one to have put them all into practice is David Myatt, whose career seems to have been informed by the methods and aims of the ONA. He has been active, as already mentioned, in various militant fascist organizations in Britain, at one point even establishing a group of his own that was simply called the National Socialist movement. The latter group attained notoriety in 1999, after one of its members, David Copeland, conducted a campaign of nail-bomb attacks at venues frequented by gay, black, and Asian people, killing three and injuring more than a hundred. Copeland was said to have been guided by Myatt's pamphlet, "A Practical Guide to Aryan Revolution," which included detailed instructions for the manufacture of explosives and the incitement of racial war.

Myatt himself, by then, had made a surprising move and converted to Islam. He established contact with various jihadist organizations and wrote an English-language theological tract defending the lawfulness of martyrdom operations, "according to Quran and Sunnah," which was offered as a reference text on the Hamas website for a time. While his acceptance of Radical Islam actually allowed him to pursue many of the themes that had been dear to him before—antisemitism/antizionism, revolt against Western materialism, space travel (this time under the sign of the crescent)—after 2010, Myatt underwent an even more abrupt change of heart. This change may have been portended by the unexpected fact that the ONA suddenly began to accept "sinister tribes" into its fold that used "Semitic" and "Right Hand Path" notions in their esotericism and propounded a Left-wing, "progressive" form of Satanism.[200] Myatt announced his apostasy of Islam and declared he would henceforth follow his own personal philosophy, which he first called the "Numinous way" and later "pathei-mathos." This included a farewell to dehumanizing abstractions about the other as "race," "clan," and "tribe," and embracing a way of life dominated by compassion for other beings.[201] Whether this new conversion is sincere or just another "insight role" is, for the time being, impossible to ascertain. To this day, however, Myatt denies that he is Anton Long: so if scholarship has correctly identified him as the mastermind behind the Order of the Nine Angles, this does not bode well for his sincerity.

Of course, Anton LaVey cannot be held responsible for the way his philosophy evolved with Long/Myatt and other extremists. Nor would it be correct to designate him or his movement as fascist or National Socialist, notwithstanding his and its leanings in this direction on certain points. LaVey's relationship to the Western Revolution was not simply one of negative reaction. As we saw in the previous chapter, liberty might rightly be considered the most important theme in LaVeyan Satanism, or, more precisely: the liberation of the autonomous individual from religious, ideological, and social restraints. In this respect, the ideological program of the Church of Satan remained very much within the emancipatory framework of the Western Revolution and the Western reaction against Christianity.

LaVey's elitist anti-egalitarianism might also be approached this way; it is also, in a way, a defense of the privilege and value of being different. The Western Revolution had, of course, insisted not only on collective, but also on individual freedom. Modern Satanism presented an obvious extension of this insistence, with its emphasis on hyper-individualism, anti-egalitarianism, and the right to be *unequal*. This anti-egalitarianism is the background even of LaVey's later, more extreme utterances, and although it could lead sometimes, paradoxically, into the same practical positions, its formative premises are radically opposed to those of the movements of reaction. Thus the subjugation to the leader and the submersion of the individual in the masses of the "People" that is an essential feature of fascism were completely anathema to LaVeyan Satanism, which in many respects could more aptly be described as a form of "anarchism of the Right."

In LaVey's later writings, this adherence to the liberating agenda of the Western Revolution found a different expression than with the "Satanist" tradition that had come before him. In twentieth-century San Francisco, LaVey felt his right to nonconformity threatened in ways that were different from 1820s Europe: not by oppressive governments or repressive legislation, but by hippie egalitarianism, the general conformity of the "herd," and, increasingly, by the dictates of mass-market production and consumption. With tacit compliance, he could paraphrase Ragnar Redbeard's words in *The Satanic Bible*: "Theories and ideas that may have meant life and hope and freedom for our ancestors, may now mean destruction, slavery, and dishonor to us! As environments change, no human ideal standeth sure!"[202] LaVey consequently turned his pen against other, less tangible enemies of liberty, in particular against the alleged influence of mass media and the resulting mass consumer culture. In one of his later essays, the Black Pope succinctly stated his position on this point:

> A Satanist should not allow himself to be programmed by others. He should fight tooth and nail against it, for that is the greatest enemy to his freedom of spirit. It is the very denial of life itself, which was given to him for a wondrous, unique experience— not for imitation of the colorless existence of others. . . . The very essence of Satanism is described by its semantic designation, The Other. A person who comfortably accepts the dictates of popular culture might be sympathetic or even enthused about Satanism, but he cannot be termed a Satanist.[203]

In other articles, LaVey warned against the "subliminal suggestion" exercised by the media, especially television, the "new god" and "a major religion for the masses," and against the "death cult" of fashion, which he considered on a par with Judeo-Christianity as an enemy of progress.[204] All were instruments for the creation of "herd mentality." Even ethnic cultural differences, LaVey complained, had ceased to be meaningful in the global village of consumerism. "What an Asian wants, is what a Latino wants, is what an Anglo wants, is what a Native American and African American . . . *all* want. As seen on TV. In other words: talk about your roots, dwell upon your heritage, study your ancestry, but live like everybody else. That, in turn, translates to: buy the same products, discard them at the appointed time, and then buy new ones."[205]

As an antidote against this, LaVey again hammered upon one essential feature: nonconformity, "Satanism's Greatest Weapon."[206] His advice in this regard was simple: "Stop and consider if whatever you buy, see, listen to, or do is popular. If it is, it is programmed, and like it or not, so are you."[207] A Satanist should consciously develop his own identity. Paradoxically, this was not done by "escaping" or criticizing consumer society, but rather by making a deliberate stylistic choice for what is neglected, forgotten, or repudiated by the mainstream. For LaVey, this meant selecting the "questionable, if not unacceptable," and the "archetypical," but above all allowing oneself "to go out of style."[208] In his essays and articles, he persistently propagated or prognosticated a return to the music, art, and dress style of decades gone by, especially the 1930s, 1940s, and 1950s—roughly the period, predictably enough, when the High

Priest himself had been young. "I believe our culture reached its apex in 1939," he once declared in an interview.[209] "Satanic aesthetics," hence, did not oppose popular culture per se but favored elements of it that had gone "out of fashion" or existed on the margin. This even applied to buying a car. A Satanist should preferably purchase an "orphan" brand like a Studebaker or Hudson, which could serve as an "instant badge of non-conformity" and would also end up as a more profitable investment in the long run.[210] Naturally, LaVey had nothing but contempt for the "planned or put-on nonconformity" one could acquire by buying into a commercially offered subculture of rebellion.[211] Contemporary Satanism was not exempt from the peril of its own conformist form of nonconformity, he warned. "The predictable antics of heavy-handed 'Satanists' are quite profitably exploited by non-Satanists."[212]

When compared, for instance, to certain neo-Marxist critiques of the market society, these suggestions sound rather shallow. And in a way, they probably were. But what was at stake here was clearly no trivial matter for LaVey. For him, real nonconformity embodied true "Satanic" magic, perhaps even the core or essence of magic. "If the definition of magic is 'the change in situation or events in accordance with one's will, which would, using normally accepted methods, be unchangeable,' it would seem that any successful magical working is an act of nonconformity. The greater one's natural degree of nonconformity, the greater are one's magical powers."[213] Successful nonconformity was not only, in its essence, the true way to "create one's self," but also to change one's environment according to one's will; in other words, to work magic.[214] Ultimately, this meant changing the world. Hence the rather peculiar fifth point of LaVey's program of "Pentagonal Revisionism," "the opportunity to live within a total environment of his or her choice." LaVey envisaged these communities as "privately owned, operated and controlled environments as an alternative to homogenized and polyglot ones," safe retreats that would offer both "the freedom to insularize oneself within a social milieu of personal well-being" and "an opportunity to feel, see and hear that which is most aesthetically pleasing, without interference from those who would pollute or detract from that option."[215] Although LaVey's own proposals for such a total environment were rather Disney-like, what was basically at stake here were total freedom and total autonomy through total control over one's living conditions.[216] As the Black Pope put it himself, "An individualist must always live in his own world, not one created by other's standards."[217]

Presented like this, LaVey's adherence to the agenda of human autonomy of the Western Revolution seems evident. Indeed, he might be considered an extreme representative of it. But here as well, a snake is hiding underneath the bushes. For LaVey's total freedom is not meant for all. It is only intended, according to LaVey's plans, for a small elite of nonconformists, those who are true "Satanists" in deed rather than word. The rest of society, the much-despised "herd," should be siphoned off to ghettos, he suggested quite literally (although this term was to be avoided in public communication)—preferably, in fact, "space ghettos" on other planets. In other words, they should be launched into outer space. "The herd has been softened up to it by the media since the days of Buck Rogers and Flash Gordon," the High Priest joked.[218] The only segment of the human population really worthwhile was, ultimately, the small group of genuinely creative people. As LaVey had already written in *The Satanic Rituals*: "One cherished child who can *create* will be more important than ten who produce—or fifty who can *believe*!"[219]

In line with this, LaVeyan Satanism should not be understood, according to the Black Pope, as a proselytizing movement for nonconformity and independent thinking among the populace at large. The swarms of unthinking locusts are a fact of life; Satanism, by its essence as an elitist movement, is not meant as a vehicle to emancipate "the people," but rather to "prey" upon it. LaVey's attitude in this and also his conspirational leanings become especially clear in his articles about television. On the one hand, TV is described by him as a medium "dictating fashions, thoughts, attitudes" and as an agent of the "Demoralization Process." On the other hand, he heralded the device as the "major mainstream infiltration of the New Satanic Religion" and important evidence of the dawning of a "New Satanic Age."[220] Television had effectively replaced Christianity as a daily religious practice; it was an excellent tool, moreover, to manipulate and pacify the masses. The Satanist, thus, should *use* television and avoid being used by it. "Once it's been resolved in a Satanist's mind that TV is a very workable proponent of Satanism in its most practical form, then he may want to remove himself from the firing line, much like the Jesuit priest or Rabbi or minister who doesn't, in his secret life, go along with every rule that he admonishes his parishioners to adhere to."[221] The stratification LaVey advocated could now further crystallize by categorizing people according to their "TV lifestyle": "TV junkies"; "ordinary believers"; or the hidden manipulators operating on or behind the scenes, the "High Priests" of the new, secular religion. It will come as no surprise that a genuine Satanist could only be part of the third stratum of this hierarchy. This could have been one of the reasons, one may speculate, why LaVey awarded so many figures from the entertainment industry with a priesthood in his later years.

The crucial question arising from all this, is, of course, what determines who becomes a Satanist? LaVey's answer is surprising: "Satanists are born, not made."[222] Apparently, this "Satanism" is hereditary, and LaVey actually suggested using eugenic techniques to "breed" a Satanist elite.[223] But this hereditariness is not based upon racial descent or aristocratic bloodlines. Rather, it is the inclination to be creative, nonconformist, "alien," which LaVey apparently considered inborn.[224] At first sight, this seems to contradict his statement that a Satanist "creates" himself. But that is only on first sight. Those who stand out by a genetically determined inclination toward creativity and originality, and only those, may later mold themselves into nonconforming, truly individual persons. Time and again, LaVey emphasized the "otherness" and outsiderness during youth of creative individuals and genuine Satanists—himself included.[225] In dire contrast to this, the majority of people are genetically destined to be part of a herd. "Herd behavior suits them, and they thrive on it. Through chromosomal and conditional cloning, they cannot be otherwise."[226] And if Satanists are "superior people," ordinary, herdlike humanity can only be classed as inferior. In the end, the nonconformity of LaVeyan Satanism was not simply about freedom, but also a mark to distinguish the "alien elite" and establish their superiority. "Thus, Satanism serves as the Great Separation Process," LaVey aptly remarked.[227]

With this ambiguous relation to the legacy of the Western Revolution, it should be added, LaVey once again followed in the footsteps of Aleister Crowley. The British occultist had displayed a similar ambivalence in this regard, an ambivalence that was highlighted by an episode in the final years of his life. On November 6, 1941—with the Battle of Britain still raging and Luftwaffe air raids sowing terror around him—Crowley published a one-sheet pamphlet in magical support of the Allied war efforts. The five points it contained can justly be called a clarion call for the values of the Western Revolution:

1. Man has the right to live by his own law—
   to live in the way that he wills to do:
   to work as he will:
   to play as he will:
   to rest as he will:
   to die when and how he will.
2. Man has the right to eat what he will:
   to drink what he will:
   to dwell where he will:
   to move as he will on the face of the earth.
3. Man has the right to think what he will:
   to speak what he will:
   to write what he will:
   to draw, paint, carve, etch, mould, build as he will:
   to dress as he will.
4. Man has the right to love as he will: –
   "take your fill and will of love as ye will,
   when, where, and with whom ye will."
5. Man has the right to kill those who would thwart these rights.

Directly underneath this proclamation of human rights, the Great Beast, unperturbed, quoted chapter 2, verse 58, of the *Book of the Law*: "the slaves shall serve."[228]

LAVEY'S LAST YEARS

As the 1990s progressed, LaVey seemed to have turned himself away from humanity in ever greater measure. The tendency to back away from the more unpleasant aspects of his self-sought notoriety had been present from at least the early 1970s, as we have seen, but it became more marked as the years advanced. By now, it was clear he had been unable to assemble a Satanist "elite"—there are at least no indications to suggest otherwise. Of the two alternatives for the Satanist he had sketched in *The Satanic Bible*—to manipulate the "folly-ridden masses through his satanic might" in secret, or to escape "from the cacklings and carpings of the righteous"—the High Priest seemed increasingly inclined toward the latter option. In contrast to his nemesis Aquino, for instance, LaVey remained conspicuously absent from television to comment on the rising hysteria during the Satanism Scare. He left this task to his youngest daughter Zeena, who in the intermediate period had grown into a "tantalizingly curvaceous blonde."[229] The Black Pope himself now granted interviews only rarely, while his own publications remained restricted to crisp and increasingly misanthropic contributions to the Church's newsletter *Cloven Hoof* and its later successor *The Black Flame*.[230]

This reclusiveness may partly have been prompted by a series of setbacks in LaVey's personal life. His partner, Diane, who had been an invaluable support in "running" the Church from its earliest beginnings, initiated a palimony suit against him in 1986 and left the Black House for good in 1988. Endless legal bickering followed, during which she claimed to have been "periodically subjected to physical and verbal abuse" by her common-law husband, although only two cases of actual abuse were substantiated.[231] Additional reasons for her departure could have been Anton's promiscuous sexual contacts with "student witches" in the earlier decades of the Church and his more and more malodorous presence in later years—because of his lack of dental hygiene and his publicly stated proclivity to bathe as little as possible, the High Priest of Satan increasingly came to smell like the Goat of Mendes itself.[232] The judge eventually rewarded half of LaVey's property to Diane, which forced Anton to file for bankruptcy. To pay the amount due to his former partner, 6114 San Francisco Street was sold to Don Werby, a real estate millionaire who befriended LaVey and generously allowed him to remain in the house for the rest of his life.

A further personal blow struck LaVey in 1990, when a dramatic breach occurred with his daughter Zeena. It is unclear what exactly provoked this event. According to LaVey biographer Burton Wolfe, father and daughter had already become estranged since the latter had entered into a relationship with one Barry Dubin, a Nazi sympathizer who had changed his name to Nicolas Schreck and publicly declared his intention to take humanity to a place where "Nazism will look like kindergarten stuff."[233] Together, they had organized an event to commemorate the Manson murders on August 8, 1988. LaVey had not been askew from fascist leanings himself, as we have seen, but he had struggled hard in the 1960s to dissociate Satanism from the Manson case, and in contrast to many other prominent Church of Satan members, he did not attend the Manson rally.[234] Thus it might be that LaVey indeed expelled Zeena and Schreck from the priesthood in 1990 out of displeasure with their extremist leanings, as Wolfe claims; it might also be true that Zeena broke off relations with her father on her own accord, as she herself asserts. However this may be, her eventual exit was drastic and dramatic. Zeena even proceeded to renounce her surname and embarked on a virtual defamation campaign against LaVey, whom she henceforth referred to as her "unfather." To add further insult, she and Schreck joined the Temple of Set, where she was promptly appointed High Priestess.[235]

The legal proceedings against LaVey also revealed the health problems he was struggling with. Already in 1970, a doctor had diagnosed hypertension and heart murmurs. According to Diane and Zeena, the Satanic High Priest had been worrying constantly about his health ever since, occasionally asking them to check his blood pressure as often as fifteen times a day. They also alleged that he systematically used his medical condition as an excuse to escape pressing engagements.[236] Whatever the truth of this picture of LaVey as an ailing armchair hypochondriac, the medical records handed over during the alimony trial evidenced genuine health problems. The Black Pope had been hospitalized several times with cardiac complications, sometimes under a false name, probably in order to avoid publicity.

In these circumstances, LaVey inclined more and more to nostalgia. His own house seemed a small-scale experiment in a total controlled environment, and the environment he liked most to recreate was the film noir décor from the time of his youth, the 1940s. Back in the 1970s, he had already constructed a replica of an old-fashioned seedy bar in his cellar, which he had baptized the "Den of Iniquity," complete with a drunken woman sprawled on the floor and a prostitute soliciting a sailor who exposed an enormous male member. Even in the way he dressed, the High Priest of Satan seemed to return more and more to the film noir gangster style that he had sported before turning toward magic. In several articles, he propounded his personal pet theory of "Erotic Crystallization Inertia": a man surrounded by the things that had given him joy in his youthful prime would remain vital and fresh.[237] "Most people die from newness," he assured. "The only way you can get old is by exposure to the new."[238] He advised to "immunise" oneself as much as possible by creating a "genuine time warp" and recreating an era that "represents one's best interests and most vital responses."[239] Half-joking as this may have been, LaVey seemed to have heeded his own advice.

Soon after Diane had left him, LaVey found a new consort, a plump young woman named Sharon Densley whom LaVey renamed as "Blanche Barton." In 1993, she bore his only son, who was given the unlikely name of Satan Xerxes Canacki: everybody, mercifully enough, called him by his second name.[240] Barton did much to revive the withering Church of Satan, particularly by resuscitating the Church's news bulletin, and her devotion to "the Doctor" was unremitting. Yet it may be doubted whether she really succeeded to assuage the Black Pope, whose derision for the rest of humanity only seemed to be growing. He became more and more engrossed in an old obsession, the creation of "artificial human companions." In 1988, as the reader may remember, he had even made this an item on his five-point program of "Pentagonal Revisionism." "They are ideal companions," the High Priest cheerfully commented in a later essay. "They require no energy-consuming interaction in order to salve a non-existent ego. . . . They can be shelved when they grow tiresome, brought back out when needed, modified in appearance, and destroyed without moral conscience."[241] In his basement, LaVey undertook his own experiments with this "forbidden industry" and tried to construct his perfect female companion, but precisely at the moment he was about to enter her for his "great test run," he told a reporter, an earthquake had shook the house.[242]

Journalists who visited the Black House during this period were struck by the way it had come to resemble a fortress where LaVey lived "a life more circumscribed and reclusive than a Benedictine monk's," playing nostalgic tunes on his battery of synthesizers or assembling "artificial human companions" in the basement.[243] They pitied his dog, who was kept in a dark entranceway inside the house. And they noticed his growing paranoia: for instance when he insisted that secret warfare by satellites or Earth-grounded microwave dishes had given his consort Barton a cold.[244] A picture in his authorized biography showed him with his hands wringed together in a strange yoga-like gesture of protection that served to counter "the forces of the Invisible War."[245]

At the same time, LaVey remained unshaken in his belief that the "Age of Satan" would be coming, observing ever new indications that the time was nigh that would bring a generation ruled by Satanist principles to power. "It's approaching D-Day and the apocalypse is at hand," he declared in a late interview. "God help the Christians then!"[246] Although he once is said to have described his strange priesthood as just "a living," utterances like these suggest otherwise. The undeniable consistency of his most important ideas over the years and the very stubbornness with which he kept impersonating the Devil's Exarch make clear that he had long become one with his role as Satanist, whatever his intentions had been when he started his daring religious venture.

In 1997, LaVey died of cardiac arrest, at the age of sixty-seven. Friends and foes attempted to launch some minor mystifications in the aftermath of his demise—LaVey's daughter Karla tried to register October 31 (Halloween) as his dying day, which was later corrected to October 29; Christian fundamentalists launched the rumor that the High Priest had repented on his deathbed.[247] Obituaries appeared in major American newspapers.

After LaVey's death, the Church of Satan became a marginal organization, even in the already marginal milieu of Satanism. Squabbling arose almost immediately over who would succeed him as High Priest. Karla LaVey, who had remained aloof from the Church for years and had spent much of her time undergoing plastic surgery in Brazil, presented herself as her father's lawful heir and let herself be photographed in a somewhat awkward pose with a statue of LaVey borrowed from a wax museum. When she lost the battle for the throne to Blanche Barton, she founded the First Satanic Church, a Satanist organization that seems to exist mainly as a web page.[248] Barton, in her turn, abdicated in 2001 as High Priestess in favor of Peter Gilmore, a patriarchally looking figure who had been cofounder of *Black Flame* in 1989, the first genuinely public Satanist magazine. The Church of Satan, meanwhile, grew into a dogmatic group that presented itself as the sole legitimate representative of religious Satanism and considered LaVey's writings as holy writ.[249]

Even sadder was the fate that befell the Black House. The place had already begun to fall apart before LaVey's death. A professional appraisal at the time of his bankruptcy plea had stated that boards were rotting, plaster was in disrepair, and the heating system was inexistent or malfunctioning.[250] Blanche Barton had tried to keep the property out of the hands of Diane by warning her that "some people" could become "blindly zealous" when the "Mecca" of Satanism would be attacked.[251] After LaVey's death, however, there was nothing to indicate any blind zeal among his followers to save the house. Although Barton sent out an appeal to Church of Satan members for funds to restore the place where their religion had been born, reactions were disappointing, and the house was left to further decay. Tramps were breaking in and sleeping in the building, while a newspaper report described how "some blasphemous graffiti artist" had scrawled the words "Jesus Rulz" over the mail slot.[252] In October 2001, finally, a real estate investor had the house torn down in order to build a rather bland condominium worth $890,000 in its place. Even the original address was scrapped, and replaced with 6118 California Street.[253] Thus the birthplace of one of the world's most remarkable religions disappeared under the gray concrete of mass-produced conformism.

I am Your Disciple
And therefore my own.
DARKTHRONE, "To Walk the Infernal Fields,"
Under a Funeral Moon (1993)

Intermezzo 4

Adolescent Satanism, Metal Satanism, Cyber-Satanism

BECAUSE OF HIS self-chosen policy of "isolation and abdication," LaVey remained aloof of two developments that would prove to be of great importance for religious Satanism in the first decades of the next millennium: the rise of the Internet and of "Satanic" metal music. Rock music's flirtation with Satan (to start with the latter phenomenon) started with the famous 1968 song "Sympathy for the Devil" by the Rolling Stones, then in their "occult" period. During the heyday of the 1960s occult revival, a number of other groups adopted Satanist themes in a playful manner. This flirtation with Satan became more intense in heavy metal, a subgenre of rock appearing in the 1970s, and reached its apogee with the subsubgenres of death metal and Black Metal that evolved in the 1980s and 1990s. Bands dressed in black sang lyrics praising Satan or exploring the macabre that could vie with the most extreme texts of the Bousingos and accompanied these with noise that was considerably louder. At their concerts, fans en masse raised their hands to make the sign of the horns. Not since the Romantic Satanists had there been a subculture that had thus openly identified itself with the Satanic.[1]

Not all metal bands, it must be emphasized, sang about Satanism; of those who did, most were simply exploiting a theme they had come to find artistically and commercially interesting. Likewise, their mostly very youthful audience clearly was not always aware of the full purport of the symbology in which they indulged or couldn't care less if they were. Yet for some musicians and fans, this artistic dalliance with the fallen angel was more than a frivolous matter. In the Norwegian Black Metal subculture, for instance, a particular grim and serious form of Satanism developed. Deriding LaVeyan Satanism as too humanistic, its adherents insisted on being truly "evil."[2] This could lead to almost hilarious consequences, for instance in the care with which some of them retained a solemn or gloomy attitude (as mirth was something "good" and thus to be shunned). The more purist members of the subculture even avoided saying that they had had a "good dinner" but preferred to describe it as "tasty."[3]

It is an open question, scholarly speaking, to what measure the existence of groups of "metalheads" with Satanist proclivities coincided with the phenomenon of "adolescent Satanism," which came to public and scholarly notice in the latter decades of the twentieth century.[4] In fact, parental and social unease regarding actual or alleged practices of juvenile Satanism had been one of the major factors in the rise of the Satanism Scare and remained a source of anxiety after the moral panic subsided.[5] As a social phenomenon, it seems, "adolescent Satanism" had already existed before the emergence of the metal subculture properly speaking: there are occasional indications that it had first manifested itself in the "psychedelic scene" of the late 1960s and early 1970s, as the designation "Acid Satanism" sometimes found in older literature seems to suggest.[6] But notwithstanding individual cases of youths that developed forms of Satanism from other sources (literature, for instance), one gets the distinct impression that by the 1980s and 1990s, adolescent Satanism as a collective trend had become firmly entrenched in the "metal" subculture.

The reason for my uncertain vocabulary on this point is not just to be found in the by nature fleeting and ephemeral character of adolescent Satanism, but also by the lack of attention for this subject from scholars studying religious Satanism, who tend to consider it as a psychological or social problem instead of a genuine articulation of religiosity.[7] This attitude is shared by many established Satanist groups, who often take care to dissociate themselves as much as possible from the antics of their more immature younger brethren. Of course, youthful Satanisms are often crude and short-lived expressions of juvenile rebelliousness, as most elements of adolescent culture tend to be. Surveys suggest, however, that most practicing Satanists today are in their late twenties or thirties and developed their interest in their religion in their late teens—that is, as adolescent Satanists.[8] And although statistical data on this question are altogether lacking, even a rough observation of the milieu of Satanism leaves one with the impression that musicians and fans of more "dark" forms of rock music are much more strongly represented among Satanists than among other religionists. My guess would be that "metal" subcultures have played a crucial role in providing new blood and vitality to the diverse forms of religious Satanism in the past three to four decades.

Both adolescent Satanism and Black Metal primarily came to the attention of the general public because of incidents involving criminal activities. Most of these involved small-scale vandalism and graffiti, but some were more shocking. In 2000, for instance, three Italian girls of sixteen and seventeen killed a nun as a "sacrifice to Satan."[9] Much more systematic was the rampage campaign that was inaugurated by members of the Norwegian Black Metal scene, where in-group rivalry, ferocious anti-Christian rhetoric, and a cult of violence had instigated an escalating cycle of depredations, including several murders that were at least partially linked to their extreme ideology and the burning down of a series of churches—among which were priceless medieval monuments—in a symbolic effort to purify their homeland of the "alien oppression" of Christianity. It must be underlined, however, that such incidents were and are exceptional. Thousands of youths have "dabbled" in adolescent Satanism or continue to do so without reverting to extreme acts of violence or destruction; and many more must have made the sign of the horns during rock concerts and grew up to be perfectly respectable citizens.[10]

In many respects, the history of adolescent and metal Satanism can be considered as a miniature version of the history of Satanism as a whole, at least as it is portrayed in this study. Scholar after scholar has argued that attributed images of Satanism spread by the media, particularly during the Satanism Scare, were the most important inspiration for the construction of Satanist identity in both adolescent and early Black Metal Satanism.[11] Although the mere existence of LaVey's Church of Satan and other forms of Satanism has had a certain inspirational value, and *The Satanic Bible* was read by some in the subculture, sensational newspaper reports and television programs that voiced anti-Satanist rumors were often the primary source of information regarding what Satanism should look like. "In fact, anti-Satanism workshops and lectures may do much more to network directions on how to carry out a 'Satanic' ritual than any underground group of networkers," one scholar asserts.[12] This strange interaction between attribution and identification repeated itself in an endless cycle with regard to heavy metal and its progeny, as Christian fundamentalists and concerned citizens took metal bands to court for inciting violence or accused them of forming part of a Satanist conspiracy to corrupt youth, thus adding to the music's popularity among a certain segment of the juvenile public and provoking bands to increasingly outspoken utterances of Satanism.[13]

The emergence of metal Satanism also looks much like a small-scale replay of the way Romantic Satanism may have evolved into religious Satanism. As in Romantic Satanism, metal music's involvement with Satan started as poetry that evoked Satan or Satanism in a symbolic and artistic way.[14] As may have happened in the larger history of Satanism, for a small minority, artistic sympathy for the devil gradually evolved into identification and genuine religious involvement. While the music and its performance remained its main form of enactment, this Satanism also found its expressions in texts, dress codes, life styles, and sometimes even terrorist actions.

With metal Satanism, this process only took a few decades. The different historical circumstances also gave a different Satanism than had been the case with the Romantics. Especially within the more extreme fringe of the Black Metal scene, Satan was and is often conceived as a genuine supernatural entity who is revered as a brutal god of vengeance and punishment. By contrast, the Christian god, at least in the shape he had been given by more moderate and liberal denominations, is scorned as a soft deity embodying love and forgiveness. In an ironic twist of history, Black Metal thus confronts us with the emergence of a Satan who displays a remarkable resemblance to the grim "Jehovah" against whom the Romantic Satanists had written their accusing lines of poetry and positioned their rebel angel as a herald of liberation. The odd and tangled implications to which this ideology of martial fierceness could lead are well expressed by the statements made by a prominent member of the Norwegian Black Metal scene in a 1992 interview:

> There are of course tons of black metal bands all over the world. The problem is that they are calling themselves Satanists but they are actually into Christianity.

This is because they think Christianity is corrupt and evil, it represses people. But we think this is great! When bands are talking about how all Christianity is evil and should be stopped, these bands are preaching goodness and freedom and therefore I don't accept them as Satanic. . . . We think it's important to take care of our enemies in a certain way. These enemies are mostly Christians, but when I speak of Christians I don't mean extreme or fundamentalist Christians—we support them 100 per cent because they are spreading so much sorrow and oppression. . . . What we hate is Christian moderates and those Christians who use their lives to help others, like Mother Theresa. That's the enemy, not the religious leaders who oppress others.[15]

As I already hinted, these juvenile forms of Satanism evoked mostly disparaging reactions from more "established" Satanisms such as the Church of Satan. Needless to say almost, metal music was not exactly Anton LaVey's cup of tea. The Black Pope liked bombastic classical music and old-fashioned popular tunes; he even developed a quaint magical theory according to which long-buried hits of yore released their magic power when played anew. True Satanic music, he explained, was melodic and lyrical and mind-opening, citing the song "Yes, We Have No Bananas" as an example.[16] Heavy metal, in contrast, was no more than another niche in the conformist world of consumerism and converted its listeners into "unthinking zombies."[17] In a particularly unflattering essay, he described heavy metal as a product of Christianity and its sound as an imitation of the kind of noises possessed people made according to Christian lore.[18]

Later, as the propaganda benefit of the new musical subculture became more apparent to him, his utterances about metal became more tolerant. "If a car passes with a bunch of long-haired kids in it and they recognise me and make the sign of the horns at me, I'm very flattered," he confided to an interviewer. "I consider it a compliment—these are, in a way, my children."[19] He awarded priesthoods to Danish metal musician King Diamond and industrial shockrocker Marilyn Manson, and to other people from the scene whose philosophies conformed to his own. Before long, he suggested that the whole thing was part of the Church's strategy. "Instead of holding our rituals in chambers designed for a few dozen people, we are moving into auditoriums crowded with ecstatic Satanists thrusting their fists forward in the sign of the horns."[20] Yet despite all this, LaVey never really grew to like the music. He welcomed the fervent Satanism that part of the scene displayed but liked to fantasize what would happen when the "wash of omnipresent sound" of their music was suddenly interrupted by genuinely Satanic music that had "the sound of Wagner or Liszt or Beethoven" and the same impact as the Horst Wessel-Lied had had in the thirties. "That will be like putting guns in the savages' hands, like giving them AK-47's!"[21]

Neither did the High Priest of Satan have much interest in the Internet. Although he was still present to witness its first boom in the 1990s, the Church of Satan would only obtain substantial web presence in the post-LaVey era.[22] In contrast to his malicious interest in television, the Black Pope's attitude toward the new medium would remain derisive. "New information technology has bred a lot of desktop Satanists," an ageing LaVey scoffed contemptuously in a late interview. "And bulletin boards mean that cyberspace seem to be just full of Satanists. There are a lot of armies of one out there."[23]

All the same, Internet would revolutionize the modes of contact and presentation of modern Satanism.[24] As with many other interest groups of extreme marginality, cyberspace proved to provide a safe haven for Satanists. In pre-Internet Satanism, fellow religionists had established or retained contact with each other through courses, group ceremonies, publications, and letters delivered by post. Around 1990, when the institutional structure of the Church of Satan had been all but dismantled, LaVey had advised Satanists who craved for contact with likeminded people to wear a Baphomet medallion or black outfit in order to be recognizable as a follower of Satan or (for the more timid) to place an ad on a (physical!) bulletin board or in a local newspaper.[25] Now Satanists could hook up and express their convictions on or via the Internet, if need be anonymously. The ultra-individualist expression that the new medium enabled seemed a natural venue for the adherents of an anti-authoritarian and anti-institutional religion like modern Satanism.[26] A recent survey suggests that for a substantial part, current adherents of Satanism exclusively speak to other Satanists online. Virtually all of them use the Internet as their main channel of communication.[27] It has probably also been the Internet that has made Satanism truly global. Organized and unorganized Satanists can now be found in almost every Western country.[28]

The Internet is a habitat, it has been argued, that fits current Satanism as a glove.[29] The relativist and ironic stance of many modern Satanisms does nothing to encourage the formation of a solid organization in the traditional sense. With such an attitude, websites, webforums, and webcommunities offer some of the few viable venues to claim a minimal objective presence in reality.

In all his grumpiness, nevertheless, LaVey may have touched a certain point with his disparaging remark about online Satanism. Already before the rise of the Internet, Satanism had become a highly fragmentized religion; but with only a (free) website or forum needed, new groups ranging from marijuana-loving Rastafarian Satanists to Leftist Satanic Reds sprang up like desert flowers after the rain.[30] Today, shadowy Satanist "churches" consisting of only a few individuals (or less) abound, their members sometimes only known by juvenile pen names and their activities often limited to their presence on the web or the discussions on their message boards. Finally, as William Blake had hoped for, everybody could be a prophet. Or at least act like one.

Le histoire prodigieuse qui est évoquée ici est l'histoire de l'orgueil européen.

ALBERT CAMUS, *L'homme révolté*

Conclusion

○—————————————————————————————————————

IN THE STEAMING jungles around the Markham River in Papua New Guinea, tribal people had been living in a Stone Age way since times immemorial, when in the nineteenth and early twentieth centuries the Europeans gradually started to infiltrate the region. They arrived in giant canoes, carrying superior weapons and unloading unknown commodities, and started telling people that they had to change their way of living and of worship. The Papuans were naturally much taken aback. Their traditional gods and the spirits of their ancestors seemed powerless against this sudden invasion. In the spiritual turmoil that ensued, all kinds of new religious cults sprang up among the Papuan population.

One example of such a cult occurred in the villages along the Erop and Lower Lehron tributaries of the Markham River, in the Morobi District in Southeastern New Guinea. It was led by a man named Marafi from Bunki village and first manifested itself in 1933 or 1934. Marafi was not well inclined to the European invaders and their new god. This at least is suggested by the fact that he sought to contact the spirit opposing the god of the whites, "the devil, Satan." The devil, he claimed, had taken him into the bowels of the earth, where the dead ancestors were living, and had disclosed to him that the Golden Age would dawn when all the villagers would convert to belief in Satan as the Supreme Being. Large houses had to be built to shelter the community; then an earthquake would shake the earth, the sky would turn black, and a rain of burning kerosene would destroy everything outside these places of refuge. After this apocalypse, the dead would return to earth, bringing all kinds of gifts and weapons more powerful than those of the Europeans. There would be no need to garden anymore.

The good tidings of Satan's coming kingdom provoked much enthusiasm in the district of Morobi. Marafi toured the area, performed wondrous feats, and appointed deputies whom he instructed in cult songs and dances. These men then spread the cult of Satan to other villages. When some of the villagers suggested that there would be trouble with the white invaders when they heard about the movement, they were told that there were not going to be any more visits by colonial officials, "and even if there were, Satan would cause the ground to open beneath their feet and bury them."[1] Because of the coming apocalypse, gardens were neglected; deserters from colonial employment hid in the villages. This in the end drew the attention of the colonial administration to the new religious movement. District officers stepped in and arrested the principal instigators of the movement.[2] As the chosen prophet of the black god, it turned out, Marafi had taken good care of himself. At his eventual arrest, he was found to have in possession £2.9s. in cash, a blanket, twenty-six loincloths, three women's blouses, two knives, and an axe; in addition, he had commandeered two women as his wives.

I wanted to tell the story of Marafi the Papuan Satanist because I think it summarizes half the story of Satanism in the Western world. When you, for any reason, dislike the Christian god, or think he does dislike you, one of the things you can do is turn to his traditional opponent, the devil. A small number of people in history have indeed drawn this conclusion and opted for Satan. The story of these Western Marafis has been told in this study. Although only a minority of today's Satanists derive from an active Christian background or have embraced their new creed because of personal traumatic experiences with the Christian religion, in a historical sense, the genesis of Western Satanism is only understandable as a reaction to Christianity.[3]

The emergence of Western Satanism, however, was a far more complicated process than a simple analogy with Papuan Satanism suggests. When I wrote that the case of Marafi represents half the story of Western Satanism, I meant exactly that. There is another half, a half that went before. In the West, both the concept of Satan and the concept of Satanism had a much longer history. Here, the Christian tradition introduced Satan roughly two thousand years ago, and the millennia-long dominance of this tradition had solidly established an interpretation of the devil as the prime mythological representation of evil. Biblical and apocryphal myth attached further associations to Satan: with rebelliousness, for instance, with pride, and with sexual lust. Although Marafi's ultimate source for his knowledge of the devil must have been Christian missionaries or at least Christian Europeans, nothing in the report on his cult indicates a genuine confrontation with this tradition. Satan was simply described by him as a fierce and powerful figure with a finger "which was very long and like a pig spear."[4] No discussion of the good or evil character of his nature is mentioned, and in most respects, Marafi's Satanism seems more deeply rooted in traditional Papuan religiosity, in which the ancestors played an important role.

The dominant interpretation of Satan as evil made opting for the devil in the Christian West evidently a very different and much more radical thing to do. But that was not all. In addition, the Christian tradition had also impressed its own concept about what Satanism entailed into Western culture. During a period of more than a millennium, ecclesiastical and secular authorities had attributed the practice of worshipping Satan to a long line of religious and social outsider groups. As a consequence, a predefined set of ideas had evolved about what it meant to be a Satanist. Within the cultural setting of the Western world, a choice to adopt Satanism thus meant identification or at least coming to terms with this preceding image of the Satanist. Without keeping in mind these mechanisms of *attribution* on the one hand, and *identification* or *appropriation* on the other, the history of Western Satanism cannot be properly understood.

ATTRIBUTION

The historical genesis and development of the complex of attribution has been extensively sketched in this study, particularly in the first chapter. For early Christianity, other religions were essentially the domain of the devil: albeit unwittingly, adherents of other religions in reality worshipped evil spirits. In the Middle Ages, the first accusations of *intentional* veneration of Satan or his demons appeared. During this period, Satanism was primarily attributed to dissident inner-Christian groups, although other groups—pagans, Jews, practitioners of folk magic—were also accused of covert devil worship. The early modern Witch Scare represented in many respects a culmination of this practice of attributing Satanism. But the application of attribution continued well into the nineteenth and twentieth centuries—and in fact continues today. In the nineteenth century, the Satanist stereotype was actively deployed by Christian polemicists against competing religions or ideologies, while some proponents of occultism likewise used it to blacken the reputation of their rivals and emphasize their own legitimacy. Prime examples of such Satanism polemics include the conflict between Boullan/Huysmans and the Paris Rosicrucians, as well as, on a much larger scale, the Roman Catholic campaign against Freemasonry that was so masterfully hijacked and exposed by Léo Taxil. In the last decades of the twentieth century, fundamentalist Christians succeeded in unleashing a wave of mass hysteria in the United States by revamping this age-old complex of attribution. As might be needless to add by now, this long line of allegations usually was devoid of all basis in reality. During most of its history, Satanism thus functioned as a mythical religion, a ghost sect with no actual adherents that was used to demonize rival religious or ideological groups.

The basic elements of this Satanist stereotype are remarkably consistent from early on. In a Christian tradition that defined the devil as a mythological representative of evil and arch opponent of the deity, intentional veneration of Satan was practically synonymous with intentional veneration of evil. Or rather, it was the other way around: veneration of Satan was part of the presumed cult of evil that the enemies of the true faith adhered to. "Everything that does not please God, they profess not to do," Pope Gregorius IX claimed about the elusive sect of Luciferians in the thirteenth century: "And when they can, they do what He hates."[5] From this general premise, all kinds of antinomian behavior could be associated with Satanism. In their secret gatherings, devil worshippers were said to perform sacrilege, engage in forbidden sexual practices, and commit infanticide, human sacrifice, or even cannibalism. In addition to this immorality, Satanism was usually conceived of as a conspiracy to bring about the collapse of (Christian) civilization and crumble the precarious edifice of society into chaos. These rumors of reversed morality and conspiracy reflect calumnies told since Antiquity about various manifestations of "the other" (including at one point, ironically enough, the early Christians). The addition of worship of Satan to this cocktail, however, was an innovation particular to Christianity. With this addition, the concept of Satanism—the intentional religious veneration of Satan—had de facto sprung into existence.

Throughout the centuries, only minor changes were made to this stereotype. Most amounted to a shift of emphasis on alleged transgressions, according to what was considered most sacrilegious or horrifying in a particular society or period of time: profanation of the host in a Roman Catholic context, for instance; child abuse in the late twentieth-century. Details of ascribed rites also were elaborated over time, often with fiction as a source. Huysmans's depiction of the Black Mass in *Là-Bas* offers a striking example, as well as Lévi's invention of the inverted pentagram as a Satanist symbol. The most profound modification may be the fact that the stereotype of the Satanist became subject to "secularizing" tendencies, along or even before society at large. While during the Witch Scare, the tangible and intimate involvement of Satan and other malevolent supernatural entities still formed an integral part of the concept of Satanism, from the late seventeenth century onward, veneration of Satan was increasingly described as an exclusively human affair. Actual Satanic interference continued and continues to be featured in descriptions from religious sources, and more vague suggestions that "dark forces" may be called forth by Satanist practices remain a well-worn cliché in descriptions of Satanism up to this day. But since the onset of the scientific worldview, most accounts pretending to factuality refrain from mentioning an actual appearance of Old Nick.

The sheer persistence of the trope of the nefarious and menacing Satanist—and of the more general and much older practice to ascribe all kinds of monstrosity and malice to "the other"—suggests that this tendency to demonize is something firmly rooted in the human psyche. In this book, we have not delved into the possible nonhistorical causes for this phenomenon. A wealth of scholarship has pointed out the seductiveness of the idea of an alien and secret conspiracy for people who are confronted with sudden and seemingly inexplicable misfortune. Naming the indistinct demons that afflict us apparently offers comfort in such circumstances. Other scholars have argued that concepts of the monstrous other take their strength from universal childhood fears deeply anchored in our mind. Recent research among primates suggests that our very morality may be based on intraspecies and intercommunity conflict between "us" and "the other."[6]

On a more specific historical level, this study may offer some tentative clues as to why the attribution of Satanism has proved such a recurring phenomenon in Western history. In the first place, Christianity, the West's dominant religion, has shown itself to be fertile ground for the extreme form of demonization that the concept of Satanism represents. Christianity's claim to universal, exclusive truth and its semidualist nature reduced rival religions or rival religious factions to diabolical deceptions. From there, it was a comparatively small and seductive step to conceive of their adherents as willing and active followers of Satan. Adherents of profoundly different religions could be forced into this mold, but also, and by preference, those belonging to dissident groups or closely related faiths with whom the struggle to demarcate the boundaries of truth was much more intense and much more insecure. Not for nothing, Christian "heretics" were among the first to be accused of devil worship, while Jews were a popular target as well.

While this tendency for demonization is always present in Christianity at large, there are periods when it becomes more active and acute. In accordance with more general research on conspiracy thinking, taking recourse to the idea of a Satanist plot seems especially attractive when large-scale but impersonalized developments of disruption confront Christian communities or Christian society. This becomes apparent in the nineteenth and twentieth centuries, when massive recurrences of Satanism attribution seem to coincide with intensifications of the secularization process. In such circumstances, the idea of Satanism proved a potent tool to disqualify competitors on the spiritual market and to provide easy-to-grasp answers and remedies in hard-to-comprehend and confusing situations of collective misfortune. In addition, it also could function as an instrument to mobilize, unite, and discipline one's own divided flock. We have seen this happen with Roman Catholicism in the later nineteenth century. Other scholars have noted how raising the specter of a sinister external adversary may have served to close the ranks and reignite the faithful with a sense of urgency during the Satanism Scare.[7]

These factors elucidate the persistent evocation and perception of being under threat that we encounter with those who raise the alarm about Satanism. Historically speaking, we must underline, the other who is thus described as a threat is in reality almost invariably the one who is being threatened. As Miri Rubin has written about medieval anti-Jewish polemics, words are never only words. "Once violent intolerant language is about, increasingly heard, spoken with impunity, then violent action is almost sure to follow."[8] This certainly holds true with regard to the attribution of Satanism, which time and again has served as an incitement or ideological excuse for violence. The legal violence against those accused of heresy or witchcraft during the Middle Ages and the early modern era provides the most dramatic example of this development. But even in the last decades of the twentieth century, parents and daycare-center employees suffered indictment, prison sentences, and social ostracism after being accused of involvement in secret Satanist organizations. In this respect, it made good sense that nineteenth-century occultists like Guaita and Papus decided to challenge their calumniators to a duel when faced with allegations of Satanism.

Up to the twentieth century, to sum up, the history of Satanism can adequately be resumed as a continuum of attribution: practically no real, and an abundance of alleged Satanists. Yet it would be too rash to conclude that there had been no actual Satanism at all during this period. Particularly during the early modern era, scattered archival records testify of genuine cases of people opting for Satan. From German theology faculties and lonely Scandinavian woods to Latin American prisons, we find individuals prepared to vow their souls to the devil. Many of them might be mentally deranged, or drunk, or in extremely dire straits. But this does not account for all cases. Evidently, opting for the other side was not altogether an impossible choice in the Christian West.

Although without doubt a very marginal phenomenon, isolated cases like these occurred, and probably more frequently than we are currently aware of. They mostly remained just that: isolated cases of people engaging in metaphysical petty crimes in the hope of material gain. Our only indications for a more organized form of early modern Satanism come from the Parisian black magic underground that flourished during the last decades of the seventeenth century. Magic—especially "black" or necromantic magic—had been branded as covert or overt devil worship by the Christian Church since Antiquity. This view was not necessarily shared by the necromancers themselves; as far as we know, they mostly claimed to *bind* the demons rather than venerate them. Yet in some exceptional instances, invocation could come very close to ritual worship. This seems to have been the case with the organized magical practices attested during the so-called Affair of the Poisons in the 1680s, allegedly involving the use of nude women as altars, ritual sex acts, consecrated hosts, and even the sacrifice of infants. Given the ever-looming possibility of attribution and the fact that most of our sources are tainted by thumbscrews, it is extremely difficult to separate fact from fiction in the reports that are left to us regarding this affair. But a slightly later, more

reliable source confirms that there was at this time indeed a small-scale commercial industry of magical specialists (or swindlers) active in Paris mediating for people who wanted to
conclude pacts of various kinds with the "infernal spirit" or his demons. Apparently, there
was some demand for people to whom one could turn for help in selling one's soul to Satan.
It is evident from these reports, moreover, that making a pact with the devil—or rather,
inducing the devil to *ratify* one's pact—was not always a simple matter. Complicated rituals
were involved, and the result was not given beforehand. We are told of an old maid, for
instance, who tried to conclude a pact for ten or twelve years but did not succeed, "the devil
not wanting anything of her."[9]

On a modest scale, these cases can be regarded as early examples of identification or appropriation. This is particularly evident with the isolated instances of individuals concluding
a pact with Satan. The idea of the diabolical pact had been a construction of Christian theology and hagiography that had grown into a common trope in popular lore and literature.
It is clear that this attributed concept was the source from which people during this period
derived their cue about how to get in league with the devil, and not some independent,
secret tradition of pact making. In this unexpected way, the Christian construct of diabolical magic occasionally gained some measure of reality after all.

Although we can consider these unglamorous real-life Fausts as the West's first Satanists,
we have to keep in mind that their Satanism was a very different thing than its contemporary manifestation. Our sources tell us little about the state of mind of these people, but
there are almost no indications that they explicitly sympathized with Satan or positioned
themselves in conscious opposition against Christianity. On the whole, their Satanism was
a highly practical affair focused on obtaining love, riches, or a prosperous career. Making a
pact could be considered as concluding a (supernatural) business agreement, not as an act of
faith. Seldom do we encounter suggestions that Satanism or "devil worship" was adopted as
(part of) a conscious religious identity. Even when we find descriptions of rituals that seem
highly anti-Christian in content, a closer view often yields a different picture. The "Amatory
Masses" organized by Voisin, for instance, which featured nude women and consecrated
hosts in order to conclude a demonic pact, were certainly not intended as sacrilege. The
hosts were included not in order to ridicule or deride Christianity but because the superior power of Christ was believed to "force" the devils to manifest themselves and accept
the pact. An explicit theological or ideological rejection of Christianity is not involved in
these practices. Rather, we can speak of a peculiar "syncretism" between Christianity and
Satanism. This fact was even recognized by the Spanish Inquisition. A manual for inquisitors published in Barcelona in 1503 was careful not to categorize invocation of Satan as
heresy, except when he was treated as a creator.[10]

REHABILITATION

Its attitude of practical "syncretism" and lack of explicit theology sharply distinguishes this
early diabolism from current religious Satanism, which can primarily be understood as an
ideological reaction against the Western Christian heritage. And even with the Papuan
Satanists of Marafi, we can reasonably postulate that their embracing of "Satan, the devil,"
was part of a conscious opposition against the invading Christian Europeans. The first

significant instances of such a self-conscious Satanism developed comparatively late in the West—in fact, roughly at the same time as that of Marafi, if we take Maria de Naglowska's Temple de Satan as its first uncontested example. But it did sprout from a fertile cultural compost prepared long before. As I have said, the story of Marafi reflects only half of that of Western Satanism. The preceding pages have only told a part of the missing half. Not only had there been a strong tradition in the Christian West of extremely negative associations with Satan and Satanism but there had also been another, more recent tradition that sought to *rehabilitate* both Satan and, to a lesser extent, Satanism.

(Romantic) poets and (anarchist) philosophers inaugurated this movement of rehabilitation. Drawing inspiration from John Milton's seventeenth-century epic poem *Paradise Lost*, they proposed a rereading of Satan as a tragic hero standing up against a tyrannous deity.[11] First appearing with the anarchist philosopher William Godwin and the eccentric artist/author William Blake, the new Satan was picked up by renowned Romantic poets like Percy Bysshe Shelley, Lord Byron, and, in France, Alfred de Vigny and Victor Hugo. Although they did not form a self-designated and coherent group, scholars of literature have given these authors the name of Romantic Satanists. In three ways, I have argued, the Romantic Satanists laid the foundation for a later religious Satanism.

- First, and most obviously, they formed the first culturally significant movement in the West that positively redefined the mythological figure of Satan. Their redefinition enabled the fallen angel to transform into a symbolical personage who was potentially attractive to adopt as an object of identification and veneration.
- Second, the attributes that the Romantic Satanists gave their redefined Satan would prove to be of lasting influence. I summarized these elements as sex, science, and liberty. With each of them, attributes that had been negatively associated with Satan in Christian myth were reversed in a positive way. The devil had traditionally been associated with illicit sexuality and sinful lust; now, some of the Romantics reinterpreted him as a symbolic patron of passionate love and unrepressed, natural sexuality. Although this development was still largely embryonic with the Romantic Satanists, this reversal of association would eventually enable the devil to grow into a kind of Earth god, a Pan-like symbol for the world of nature and the flesh that Christianity was thought to have disdained. In addition, ever since his identification with the Serpent of Paradise, the devil had been linked to the lure of forbidden knowledge. Somewhat hesitatingly at times, some of the Romantic Satanists inversed this attribute from a negative one into a positive, paving the way for Satan to become a symbolic representative of scientific inquiry and free thought. But most important, Satan's classic depiction as a proud and spiteful rebel against the life-affirming divine order was now reinterpreted as that of a courageous champion of human liberty, human dignity, and human emancipation. *Freedom* was the central tenet that the new, Romantic Satan came to represent, and this value was at the core of his other two metaphorical attributes.
- The third point that makes the Romantic Satanists important is more complex: their attitudes toward myth and religion prefigure attitudes that would later manifest themselves in modern religious Satanism (and in other forms of new religiosity, for

that matter). The Romantic Satanists did not believe in biblical or other myths as stories conveying literal truths, as the traditional attitude toward myth had been. But neither did they dismiss myths as mere old wives' tales, as Enlightenment rationalism had tended to do. Instead, they embraced myth as a vehicle that allowed them to express notions of truth and value, which could not be adequately expressed in mere rational discourse. Poets like Blake, Shelley, and Hugo held that the human imagination, which manifested itself most strongly in poets and other artists, was the channel by which knowledge of divine or cosmic truth was transmitted to humanity. Some of the Romantics even claimed that the human imagination ultimately *created* these notions of divine or cosmic truth. Whereas traditionally, the gods had been thought to inspire the poets to create their poetry, the poets were now thought to create the gods with their inspired poetry.

I have called this shift in viewpoint the Romantic Reversal. We can see this reversal explicitly or implicitly reflected with most of the Romantic Satanists, and with other Romantics as well, although they varied in the radicalism of their position, with some holding on to a more classic notion of the poet as divinely inspired prophet, and others adopting an almost postmodern attitude that proclaimed human creativity as the sole source for value, meaning, and truth. The latter position, it must be added, did not imply a denigration of the human endeavor to find value, meaning, and truth. To the contrary, it emphasized the crucial importance of creativity and the creative artist in constructing a meaningful universe.

As we have seen, this new attitude to myth and religion enabled the Romantic Satanists to resurrect Satan. They did so in a twofold way. In the first place, of course, they rehabilitated him from the degradation to hell and vileness that Christianity had allotted to the fallen angel. But in the second place, and not less importantly, they resurrected him from the burial the Enlightenment had given him. Although most Romantic Satanists shared the Enlightened disbelief in the literal, personal existence of Satan, they were fascinated with him as a potent symbolic figure to express essential metaphysical truths. Accidentally, this is the role Satan would play in most forms of modern, post-Enlightenment Satanism.

As the scholar of literature Peter Schock has pointed out, miniature processes of attribution and identification attributed to the emergence of Romantic Satanism. Conservative critics had accused Byron and Shelley, two of its most prominent representatives, of propounding a "Satanic school of poetry." These in turn had responded by identifying themselves with this stigma, in a way that was partly mockery, partly provocation, and partly serious insurgency. Yet as we have seen, far bigger issues than mere literary squabbles were at stake in the Romantic attempts to rehabilitate Satan. Two historical developments that have been crucial to the formation of Western society as we know it today nurtured the appearance of a new attitude toward the former angel of darkness. These were the interrelated processes of emancipation that we have designated as secularization and the Western Revolution.

Political revolutions marked the history of the West from 1776 to well into the twentieth century, with the French Revolution as the most epoch-making and most inspiring of them all. This monumental event and the political developments in its wake can be pinpointed as the direct spur for most of the pro-Satanic works of Romantic Satanism. On a deeper level, it was the slow tectonic movement for democratization, liberalization, and emancipation of which the Western revolutions were the volcanic eruptions that made the Romantic Satan such an urgent symbol at this period of time. While the Christian deity came to be perceived by many as the symbolic representative of the old order of autocratic and traditional rule, the rebel angel was heralded by a number of progressive intellectuals as the mythological embodiment of the new spirit of liberation and insubmission. Pro-Satanic utterances during the nineteenth century thus almost invariably indicate Leftist, radical tendencies by their authors. In general, the political character of the discourse on Satan in this period is striking, with both sides of the conflict employing him as a powerful symbolic weapon of ideological warfare.

Revolution formed one decisive factor in the emergence of the new Satan; secularization was the other. As we have already suggested, both historical processes were intimately intertwined. While the deity could function as a cipher for the autocratic or traditional regimes that the revolutionary political movements sought to replace, on a purely religious level, the new ideologies of human emancipation and liberation also tended to be unfavorably inclined to a god and a religion that was perceived to derive its legitimization from "brute force" and "unexpostulating authority" (to quote William Godwin). In accordance with recent scholarly definitions, secularization must not be understood as a simple decline of religiosity. Instead, it was both a movement reducing the direct influence of religious institutions (read: the Christian churches) in the social and political sphere and an increase of religious and ideological pluralism that would eventually give rise to a "supernova" of new spiritual options. In the particular situation of Western society, both aspects meant in practice that the age-old political and social dominance of Christianity was ended or severely weakened.

This evolution had already started during the earliest Enlightenment, or arguably during the Renaissance and the Reformation; but in the nineteenth century, it intensified into a mass movement that began to have increasing social and political repercussions. Romantic Satanism can be seen as an acute reflection and augmentation of this struggle. Virtually every author we have classified as Romantic Satanist criticized the social domination by Christianity in past or present; some of them (Shelley in particular) actively promoted secularism as the key to human or even cosmic liberation. All of them promoted religious or ideological options in their work that formed an alternative to both traditional Christianity and the more blatant positivist and demystifying tendencies of the Enlightenment. Some of them proposed radically redefined (and largely self-defined) forms of Christianity (Blake, Constant); others embraced pantheist and/or deist theologies (Shelley, Hugo); others again formulated exclusively human-centered notions of value and meaning that seem to foreshadow later existentialism (Byron, Vigny). All of them exemplify a tendency that was at the core of the surging tide of secularization and also linked directly to the ideological turmoil of the Western Revolution: that of making religion into an autonomously chosen or devised option that was predominantly humanist and predominantly immanent in orientation. This is accurately reflected in the Romantic Satan, who transformed from a real supernatural being into a figure who primarily represented a variety of human tendencies— almost invariably tendencies related to man's autonomy vis-à-vis the natural, the spiritual, the social, or the political.

It was without doubt this double anchorage in the Western Revolution and the secularization struggle—two issues that dominated political and ideological discussion during the "long" nineteenth century—that ensured the popularity of the new Romantic Satan in the counterculture of this period. His traces can be found in art and literature, in anarchist and socialist publications, and last but not least with some of the most seminal forms of alternative religiosity that manifested themselves during the nineteenth century. Lévi's occultism, Blavatsky's Theosophy, and Steiner's anthroposophy all retain influences of Romantic Satanism. On a much more modest scale, Romantic Satanism also brought the first attempts to rehabilitate the Satanist and identify oneself with him. Shelley made an unfinished attempt to portray the Ophite Gnostics as an ideal human community; George Sand featured "Satanist" Hussites as early revolutionaries; and the French historian Michelet portrayed the "Satanic" witch as a proponent of proletarian revolution, female emancipation, and rehabilitation of the natural and the carnal.

APPROPRIATION

In many respects, Romantic Satanism already provided the essential groundwork for the emergence of a new religious Satanism. Yet as this study shows, it took quite some time before examples of the latter actually evolved. There are no reliable indications for the existence of a significant religious Satanism during the nineteenth century, notwithstanding the persistent buzz proclaiming the opposite. Even those esoteric currents that adopted elements of the Romantic Satan retained the attributed stereotype of Satanism and "black magic" as a horrifying image of "the other" to contrast with their own respectability. Isolated instances of genuine religious Satanism only start to appear at the very end of the nineteenth century (Ben Kadosh; Przybyszewski, perhaps) and the first decades of the twentieth (Naglowska's Temple de Satan; the Fraternitas Saturni). From a certain angle, Wicca—neopagan witchcraft—might be considered the first major manifestation of a modern religious movement that identified itself with the "other side" of attribution, rehabilitating the "Satanist" figure of the witch and occasionally featuring veneration for Lucifer or other "diabolical" mythological figures. Despite its partial roots in Romantic Satanism, however, explicit religious veneration of Satan has been absent from mainstream Wicca, while its adepts adamantly denied the presumed Satanist character of historical witchcraft, describing it instead as a relict of ancient paganism. In addition, Wicca continued the tradition of nineteenth-century occultism in ascribing a negative Satanism stereotype to dangerous "others" operating in nebulous black magic rings.

It was only in the 1960s that a significant religious Satanism became visible in the West. During this decade, Anton Szandor LaVey established the Church of Satan in California, and the English Process Church of the Final Judgement adopted Lucifer and Satan as major gods in its pantheon. This point in history, of course, was far from random. It coincided with a new wave of secularization in Western society, which showed itself both in an enhanced aversion of "mainstream" Christianity among certain segments of the population and a boom of alternative forms of religiosity. The new Satanism neatly agreed with both these elements. While The Process eventually lost its Satanist aspect and disappeared from the scene without leaving behind notable spiritual offspring, the Church of Satan succeeded in engendering a marginal but continuing tradition of Satanism in the religious landscape of the West. Notwithstanding the small size of the present Church as an organization, all groups and currents of Satanism still in existence today have their genealogical origin in LaVey's religious venture, while his Satanism also directly or indirectly stimulated Satanist tendencies in certain musical subcultures. With an estimated number of adherents of 10,000 to 100,000 worldwide, religious Satanism remains a small and extremely fragmentized religious minority.[12] Yet its presence has endured for more than half a century and does not seem prone to disappear anytime soon.

Without the prior "traditions" of both attribution and rehabilitation, the shape of this modern religious Satanism would certainly not have been what it is now.[13] We have concentrated our study of these influences on LaVeyan Satanism, which not only merits our attention as the fount from which all current forms of Satanism spring, but also because it is, to my opinion, its most interesting manifestation, particularly with respect to the uncompromising manner in which it embraces the secular, individualist, and science-dominated nature of Western society and yet seeks to offer meaning and purpose in a religious way. Especially in its earliest phase, the Church of Satan displayed copious examples of appropriation of elements from the earlier complex of attribution in its imagery and ritual, many of which would prove defining for the iconography of subsequent Satanisms. The nude women on the altar; the inverted pentagram; the "sinister" ceremonies pillaged from *grimoires*, horror literature, and Huysmans; the black robes and dark outfits: they were all part of a deliberate reenactment of the Satanist stereotype. This reenactment was at the same time an ironic criticism. With some reason, David Frankfurter speaks of "direct mimetic parody" in this respect, although this element of parody, it must be noted, does not exclude serious religious involvement.[14]

As this study and earlier literature has convincingly shown, LaVey's knowledge about (presumed) Satanist practices had not been transmitted by some secret tradition, despite the fact that he sometimes winkingly liked to suggest otherwise. Rather, it had been collected and reconstructed from books, movies, and art. Of course, this could hardly be expected to be otherwise with a religion that did not yet exist. As original sources for his magical lore, LaVey claimed a wide array of alleged Satanists and demonized groups—Templars, Freemasons, Illuminati, "Luciferians," "occult" Nazis. On a deeper level, LaVey, and other Satanists after him, explicitly presented Satanism as a religion of "otherness," transgression, and inverted (Christian) morality.

Appropriation and identification are fitting terms to describe this process of construction. But they also risk to mask the profound way in which LaVey sought to modify the Satanist stereotype for his own use. Although he sometimes toyed with slogans as "evil spelled backwards is live," LaVeyan Satanism was not a religious pursuit of evil. Instead, the Church of Satan propounded to offer a thoroughly sanitized Satanism for slightly wicked ladies and gentlemen. Thus the starker elements of inversion, such as cannibalism, human sacrifice, and ritual orgies, were silently dropped by LaVey. Even animal sacrifice, a practice that for millennia had enjoyed perfect respectability in religious and magical traditions, was abandoned to accord with the more animal-friendly spirit of the times. Instead of a vehicle for sedition, LaVey posited his church as a law-abiding organization that supported the established order. The transgressive potential of his movement was mostly limited to issues of ideology and personal sexuality. In the latter aspect, LaVey also marched with the music of his days, although it has to be admitted that he was certainly in the front rows of the band.

His attempt to make his Satanism respectable placed LaVey—and much of later Satanism—in a paradoxical and potentially self-defeating position. By intentionally identifying himself with the older stereotype of the Satanist, he ensured himself and his movement considerable provocative and titillating appeal. In addition, the deliberately adopted stigma that this entailed may have provided him and his followers a measure of mental freedom to shrug off the moral straitjackets that every society incurs. Yet the same age-old stereotype ensured his Satanism the perennial stamp of incarnated evil and monstrosity. LaVey preached endlessly against this preconception, and other modern Satanists continue to preach. Among a more well-informed public, this campaign was not altogether without success, and as a result, contemporary Satanism is now seen by many in the West as a somewhat eccentric but basically harmless religious variant. This image of harmlessness, however, in its turn threatens to destroy the provocative and transgressive appeal that undeniably forms a part of the attractiveness of Satanism as a religious or ideological option. Hence the self-contradicting attitudes that we can often detect with LaVey: maintaining the respectability of his Satanism on the one hand, prone to insinuate dark and sinister things on the other hand.

In some ways, LaVey's Satanism remarkably resembled the earlier forms of "Satanism" that had been marginally present before the nineteenth century. Like early modern "Satanism," it presented itself primarily as a form of magic; and like early modern Satanism, the purpose of LaVey's magic was primarily practical—prosperity, love, lust, misfortune for enemies. Some of its ritual forms and paraphernalia also resembled those of premodern magic, arriving with LaVey through the intermediating agencies of Lévian/Thelemian magic or through reprints of old *grimoires*.

These resemblances are slightly deceptive, however. LaVeyan magic functioned in a completely different historical and ideological context and was based on completely different religious and philosophical preconceptions. While its early modern precursors had still been part of a world in which the reality of magic and the supernatural had been accepted as a given fact, LaVeyan magic appeared in a society in which empirical science had become a dominant determinant of the collective worldview. Whereas the proponents of scientific, rational, or empirical ways of thinking had first needed to defend their assertions against a dominant and largely implicit magical and religious worldview, the same now applied to those who sought to reintroduce magic. In this respect, magic after the Enlightenment could never be the same as before, at least in the *entzauberte* world of the West.[15] It henceforth needed a declaration or explanation, however limpid, of why it could work.

We can find such explanations with virtually every modern system of magic. With LaVey, two of them were most important: the general assumption that there were hidden, unexplored forces in nature as yet untapped by science, and the more practical idea that magic was a powerful form of "psychodrama" that could help to change a person's psychic outlook and release untapped forces within himself. Such a rationalist framework was alien to premodern or early modern "Satanist" magic. Although LaVey drew inspiration from older modes of "black" magic for props or routines, the similar emphasis on practical magic was largely coincidental. It resulted from a deliberate and partly ideologically motivated attempt by LaVey to bring more rationalism, simplicity, and *diesseitigkeit* to the highly arcane systems of nineteenth- and twentieth-century magic out of which his Satanism had grown.

Thus, when we see ancient magical practices reappear in this context, they do not attest to the age-old roots of modern Satanism but are the result of an appropriation process in which they have first been disembedded from their original context and subsequently re-embedded in that of modern Satanism.[16]

In line with this historical gap, the underlying motive and the practical manifestation of the mechanics of appropriation and identification were also profoundly dissimilar. Early modern Satanists had appropriated practices attributed to devil worshippers because they thought them to be the right way to approach supernatural presences whose reality they assumed. They did not adopt these practices in order to define an alternative identity. It is probable that most of them would happily have remained within the confines of accepted religion if they had thought it could offer them the same practical benefits; many, in fact, evidently kept considering themselves as Christians. With LaVeyan Satanism and its successors, this situation was completely reversed. The appropriation of elements of the Satanist stereotype and the self-identification as Satanist primarily served to construct an identity around an ideological core that was quite recent, quite modern, and explicitly oppositional and anti-Christian. In this way, modern Satanism's identification with the old image of the Satanist was indeed in great measure a veneer. But without this veneer and without this identification, modern Satanism would not have been Satanism at all.

The other tradition we have identified, that of the Romantic rehabilitation of Satan, is also much in evidence with LaVeyan Satanism. Even a cursory reading will reveal the preponderance of the three classic themes of sex, science, and liberty in *The Satanic Bible* and LaVey's other writings. While Lévi's post-Romantic holistic Satan is also easy to spot in *The Satanic Bible*, the main function of the LaVeyan Satan is being a symbolic representative for human emancipation and personal liberation, just as with the Romantic Satanists and their epigones. It is hard to think of this as a coincidence. However, the precise historical trails by which the Romantic Satan reached LaVey's Californian Church are not so easy to excavate. We can trust that LaVey, with his wide reading of the "Satanic," was at least superficially familiar with the major English representatives of the "Satanic school of poetry" and with translations of classic foreign-language works like Michelet's *La Sorcière*. Another channel by which he may have picked up bits and pieces of the nineteenth-century rehabilitated devil was occultism: Lévi and Crowley were profound influences on the gestation of LaVey's Satanism. Yet the three-faced Satan of Romanticism had only been diffusely present in nineteenth-century counterculture, and English-language publications that extracted this symbolic complex from the hoards of literature and art were only sparsely available when LaVey founded his Church of Satan. We cannot rule out the possibility that similar anti-Christian sentiments and similar cultural trends led to a certain measure of independent invention in this respect.

The latter point is especially apt with regard to the third strand of historical significance that we allotted to the Romantic Satanists. The attitude toward myth and religion that we have distilled from Romantic Satanism is strikingly similar to that which can be found in LaVeyan Satanism and much of its progeny. We see the same perception of religion as a product of human creativity that is nonetheless vital to our humanity; the same perception of myth, poetry, and "fantasy" as indispensable modes of human expression; the same perception of man as the divine creator of the divine. Satan is used in the same symbolic way as a "free-floating signifier" (to lend Schock's phrase), and LaVeyan Satanism allows the same creative liberty, at least in theory, to adopt other symbolic signifiers (although the "demonic" deities incorporated by LaVey in his pantheon are all subject to "Satanization," i.e., redefined to fulfill roughly the same symbolic function as the LaVeyan, post-Christian Satan).[17] LaVeyan magical rites and ceremonies, one can argue, play the same role as territories of human imagination as literature and art in Romanticism; one of the ultimate aims of modern religious Satanism, one can argue as well, is to make one's life an artwork of individual creativity. All this makes LaVeyan Satanism a particularly outlined example of what Robert Bellah in the 1960s predicted to be the upcoming manifestation of Western religiosity: a religiosity capable of remaking "the very symbolic forms . . . that state the unalterable conditions of [man's] own existence . . . but with a growing awareness that it is symbolism and that man in the last analysis is responsible for the choice of his symbolism."[18]

Modern religious Satanism, in this respect, is part of a much broader development evident in many new religious movements, occultural manifestations, and refashioned forms of traditional religion. Noted scholars have singled out Romanticism, particularly Romantic philosophy, as one of the most important sources for this development.[19] This assertion seems certainly valid to me. But if we try to trace the actual route of transference of these Romantic ideas to present-day religious movements, the picture we find is much more blurry and doubtful than a simple analysis of similarities suggests. This at least is the case with LaVeyan Satanism. There is no evidence that a simple reading of either Romantic philosophers or Romantic Satanists provided the direct inspiration for LaVey's blatantly Romantic attitudes in this respect. Indeed, this seems unlikely: the full purport of the Romantic Reversal remains implicit with many Romantic Satanists or only partially expressed in dispersed passages. Although their language may have been more readily understood in their own days, today only a painstaking analysis (such as this study has hoped to provide) can decode its implications to the average reader. The same may apply to many Romantic philosophers. Of course, here again, modern occultism presents itself as a possible missing link; as I have demonstrated in this volume, the influence of Romanticism and Romantic Satanism on noted occultists like Lévi is salient in this respect. Nevertheless we are in danger here that a post factum analysis, however valuable and careful, magnifies into momentous stepping stones what in reality had been only pebbles in the river of history.

In reality, again, we cannot exclude the possibility that Romantic Satanism and LaVeyan Satanism *autonomously* developed similar answers to a similar historical predicament. This predicament was the challenge to redesign religion in a post-Christian and post-Enlightenment context. The Romantics, and the Romantic Satanists, can be considered as an early manifestation of a new religious attitude that had been made possible by Enlightenment demystification and secularization and that would spark a "supernova" of religious innovation in later Western society. They also undoubtedly were a direct contributing factor to the emergence of certain forms of this new religiosity. LaVey made his attempt to create a "secularized" religion more than a century later than his Romantic precursors, picking up inspirational vibes from Lévian-Crowleyan occultism, Nietzschean philosophy, counterculture ideology, and a wide personal reading. The Romantic Satanists, so much we can say, will certainly have contributed to the great spiritual stew from which he sipped his spoonful of inspiration, be it directly or indirectly.

In addition to the striking similarities between Romantic and modern religious Satanism, there are also significant ideological differences to point out. To start with, LaVeyan Satanism never did go as far along with the Romantic Reversal as Romantic Satanists like Blake or even Shelley did. For them, human imagination and human creativity—which expressed themselves in the language of myth, poetry, and art—had been the key to essential truths that (Enlightenment) rationalism could never attain. LaVey did recognize the value of both truth and "fantasy," but he considered them as distinct categories. In the end, it was human ratio (or common sense) that had the last word, both regarding the practical life of everyday and our cosmological framework of existence. In this respect, LaVeyan Satanism was very much an Enlightenment religion, comparable to other attempts to create a rational conduit for man's religious instincts like the revolutionary cult of Reason and Comte's religion of positivism. LaVey's anti-Christianity (like that of the Romantic Satanists themselves, by the way) also harkened back to Enlightenment discourse about religion as obscurantism and a priestly tool of domination.

To LaVey, man was "just another animal" living in an indifferent universe. By rationally (or cleverly) recognizing and exploiting his own and others' instinctual drives, the Satanist could hope to live an existence as gratifying as possible. Myth, ritual, and other forms of "fantasy" had their place in this, but only because man, as an instinctual animal, could not live without a decent dose of "honest emotionalizing." By rationally defining the content and forms of his religion, the Satanist could manipulate his own and others' psyche to attain a maximum of personal happiness. Satan only had his place as a mythological symbol in this "intellectual decompression chamber" of rite and fantasy. Thus LaVey could both claim to disbelieve in the actual existence of the devil and invoke him like a traditional deity during weekly ceremonies in his church.

Of course, this epistemological dividing line was hard to keep clear in everyday practice. LaVey himself may have been swept along with his "honest emotionalizing" at times. Many of his followers came to believe in the real presence of the entity they venerated, if they had not already done so beforehand. This resulted in several split-offs by Satanist groups reverting to more or less traditional theist notions, with the Temple of Set as the most prominent example. In contrast to this, LaVey himself, and some Satanist groups inspired by him, increasingly emphasized the rational component of their ideology, sometimes evolving into vehicles for purely atheist or humanist discourse with only the bare mention of Satan reminding us of the fact that we are still dealing with manifestations of religious Satanism.

An equally salient difference between Romantic Satanism and modern religious Satanism is the political orientation of the latter. Whereas Romantic Satanism was generally speaking a "Left-wing" affair, and conspicuously so, LaVeyan Satanism and most of its later offshoots were clearly situated on the right in most matters of political ideology, sometimes even leaning toward neofascism or neo-Nazism. On important points, as we have seen, LaVeyan Satanism was still very much a religious vehicle for the values of the Western Revolution. Issues of freedom, personal autonomy, and individualism were at the core of almost everything LaVey wrote and defined the essential symbolic significance of his Satan. The marked individualist and nonsocial character of his Satanism, moreover, can partly be explained as a logical evolution of the emancipation effort of the Western Revolution. In twentieth-century America, where important values of the Western Revolution had been legally enshrined at a very early date, other challenges could take the fore, such as the conformism enhanced by implicit group morality and consumerism.

Yet we can also discern a reaction *against* the Western Revolution in LaVeyan Satanism. This ideological rift or shift, which determines much of the flavor of current Satanism, partly derived from the development of anti-Christian discourse since the early nineteenth century. While the Romantic Satanist had canonized Satan, so to speak, into the humane deity that the Christian god had failed to be, more radical critics like Nietzsche had started to hammer at the moral foundations of Christian religion and Christian society themselves, disparaging Christian altruism as a hidden tool of domination by "weak" people. Combined with crude social Darwinism, this could nurture "might is right" ideas such as can be found in both fascism and LaVeyan Satanism.

Equally important for the political reorientation of modern Satanism may have been the ideological backlash engendered by the Western Revolution itself. From the three classic themes of the French Revolution—liberty, equality, and brotherhood—it was especially the concept of equality that had fallen under criticism. Although this catchword had initially implied the modest objective of establishing equality before the law, it was interpreted and eschewed by currents critical toward the Western Revolution as a program for egalitarianism. In response, some of them came to emphasize the difference between human beings, not just in personality, but also in intrinsic worth. Some humans were thought more fit to rule, and others were to be ruled. This antidemocratic tendency, later supplemented with notions imported from biological Darwinism, could lead to the hailing of interhuman struggle as the only means to establish who was worthy to rule.

It is slightly misleading to call this attitude reactionary or conservative. Rather, it was something new that manifested itself only as a result of the Western Revolution itself. Occasional manifestations of this tendency already had appeared in Western esotericism with Lévi and Crowley; we have also found its traces with Baudelaire and Huysmans. Nietzsche, and his American disciples, like Ayn Rand, can also be considered as representatives of this ideological reaction, and their influence on LaVey had been considerable. Whereas a modern esoteric current like Wicca, which had had a common hatching ground in "conservative" European occultism, went into a more Left-wing direction during the 1960s and 1970s, LaVey, to the contrary, chose to emphasize the anti-egalitarian attitudes that had already been present in Western esotericism. We can speculate, by the way, whether LaVey's almost total silence on obvious "proto-Satanists" like Blake and Shelley, or Bakunin and Proudhon, might also have been informed by his critical stance toward their "Left-wing" political ideas. They were, one suspects, heroes in the wrong kind of tradition for him.

As the Church of Satan evolved, LaVey increasingly conceived his Satanism as an organizational and ideological vehicle enabling an elite of superior personalities to dominate or at least escape the "herd" of ordinary citizens. Fascism and Nazism shared this anti-egalitarian attitude. This may in large measure account for the fact that the Black Pope could on occasion rub shoulders with these ideological currents, notwithstanding their antithetical position on issues of individualism and personal liberty. Other post-LaVeyan forms of Satanism, such as the Order of the Nine Angles, went even further and adopted neo-Nazism or antisemitism as integral parts of their religion. A Right-wing emphasis on power, struggle, and elitism penetrated Satanist theology as well and led at times to the imple-mentation of a more "fierce" Satan. We can see this prominently displayed in Black Metal Satanism, where violence and vengeance were frequently celebrated as noble virtues. As a Surinam Black Metal fan at one occassion declared to a reporter: "God is a weakling, . . . Satan however is a powerful figure. If you venerate and serve him as a loyal follower, you will find yourself in paradise. But if you disappoint him, you will burn in hell."[20] Extreme ideas like these, it should be emphasized, are only held by a very marginal fringe within the current Satanism scene. Yet it is highly ironic that we can see a Satan appear here as an object of veneration who strikingly resembles the stereotypical Judeo-Christian Jehovah so intensely abhorred by the Romantic Satanists.

APPLICATION

With modern religious Satanism, we thus make a full circle in the history of religion. Satan, of yore the evil opponent of the true god, becomes a representative for all that is considered good or praiseworthy, while the god of Christianity transforms into a symbol for evil or is totally eclipsed. As far as I know, this is a unique occurrence in religious history. In the past, physical or ideological warfare had sometimes reduced venerated spiritual beings into objects of abhorrence, especially if they belonged to different cultural communities. But never had a society, or at least part of it, by its own will chosen to renounce its original deity and adopt its mythological opponent in its place.[21] The comparatively recent character of this peculiar religion has allowed us to describe its emergence in some detail, and it is striking how *human* an affair this turned out to be. Poetic fiction, invented tradition, and downright falsification provided the building stones for its formation; skillful profiteers, passionate reformers, and charismatic prophets all played their role in its genesis. In fact, these categories frequently overlap or appear indissolvably united. Most poignant, however, is the fact that divine names turn out to be virtually interchangeable labels, even when such starkly contrasting characters as the devil and the deity are involved.

So where does this all lead to? Can we quote Shakespeare on the rose that smells as sweetly when it would be called otherwise and consider the history of Satanism a simple swap of nomenclature? Seen from some other galaxy, this may indeed be the case. But if we zoom in more closely, a different picture becomes visible. The god that is called Satan in modern religious Satanism is not the god that is called God or Christ in (traditional) Christianity. For Romantic as well as LaVeyan Satanism, to start with, Satan is not a real supernatural personage, such as the Christian deity was to Christianity, but a symbolic rep-resentation for metaphysical forces that are for all intents and purposes located in earthly reality. For LaVey, for instance, Satan was a representation of the life force pulsing in the universe and an archetypical manifestation of this life force in the individual. And even with Satanist groups who hold to a more traditional concept of Satan as a personal, onto-logically real deity, he seldom adopts the features of the omnipotent Judeo-Christian god. For the Temple of Set, for example, Satan/Set has basically the character of an otherworldly helper and companion, while the essential task for the adherent is his own emancipation into godhood. Northrop Frye's analysis of Romanticism as a movement of "recovery, for man, of what he formerly ascribed to gods, heroes, or the forces of nature" is thus eminently applicable to modern religious Satanism.[22] Ever since the Romantic Satanists, it has sought to allocate the divine to this side of the cosmos and/or to place it within humanity. LaVeyan Satanism, and most of its later derivates, have taken this premise a step further and hallowed the individual *itself* as godhead, at least in potentiality. As Anton LaVey's consort Blanche Barton stated: "We needed a representative for that revolutionary, creative, irrepressible spirit within us—not a Holy Father but perhaps a rebellious brother."[23] This is the exact opposite of the original Judeo-Christian conception of a transcendent deity who is unapproachable to human beings except when he chooses to present himself.

An observer from another galaxy might also remain unaware of another thing that our terminology tends to hide: namely, the extreme diversity of human phenomena that I described as religion in this study. The historical forms of Satanism we have encountered in this study display profound differences. With many of them, applying the term "religion" evokes a distinct intuitional unease. Premodern pacts to coax supernatural diabolical entities, for instance, may strike many of us as magical techniques rather than an exercise of religion. They seem miles apart from the purely symbolical use of Satan that we find in Romantic Satanism and which only expresses itself in the domain of art: expressions we might tend to consider as "mere" poetry or literature. A somewhat similar reluctance arises when dealing with LaVeyan Satanism, which uses myth and ritual as a form of psychological therapy in an ideological system that proclaims itself explicitly atheist and even antireligious, and in its later stages even divests itself of ritual "trappings" altogether. Here again, we see scholarly authors (including the present one) struggle with synonyms and terms, and words like "philosophy of life," "lifestyle," or "ideology" pop up as frequently as "religion." Yet if we apply Bellah's extended definition of religion as "a set of symbolic forms and acts which relate man to what he perceives to be the ultimate conditions of his existence," all these diverse phenomena can rightfully be categorized as religious.

Inevitably, the question arises whether it is still meaningful to do so. Are we not rather dealing with phenomena that are not just profoundly different, but from another category altogether? This question, obviously, cannot be resolved by one author. Its answer ultimately depends on conventions in scholarly and nonscholarly parlance. But a few remarks may be ventured. In the first place, if thoroughly scrutinized, all these areas of unease indicate that we are faced with forms of religion that deviate from a certain image of "normal" religion that is seldom made explicit. This image is that of a human activity that regards the supernatural; more specific, the variant of this activity which is institutionalized or at least communal, oriented toward the transcendental in the traditional sense, and involves an explicit inner *pris de position*. In other words, conventional Judeo-Christian religion.[24] I think it might be constructive as well as (fruitfully) confusing to broaden our thinking of religion and make it include all attempts to create value, meaning, and mythological models of life; the domains in life, in brief, where the "mere Analytics" of empirical science are unable to provide answers, as Blake already postulated.

With the majority of people still holding on to more traditional notions of religion, or even considering the term as an epithet of opprobrium, such a wider appliance of the word seems far off from broad acceptance. Yet such an extension might certainly be a worthwhile endeavor. It might provide a potent and delightfully provocative tool to locate attempts to formulate meaning, value, and myth in secularized society that are yet more masked than modern religious Satanism. In addition, it may restore a vital human link between "us," inhabitants of a secular world, and religionists of past and present. When seen as the ever-present and eminently human form in which we manifest our attempt to create forms of "macromeaning," religion ceases to appear as a mere relict from a past that most educated Westerners, in their heart of hearts, can only consider obsolete and alien. Instead, it can be seen as a logical consequence of our extended consciousness and the ability this human attribute brings about to ask questions about the "why" and "whereto" of existence that we are in no position to answer empirically.

This does not mean, to be sure, that religions or religious convictions are always or equally valid and sensible. In the last half century, there seems to have arisen a strange reluctance to acknowledge this basic fact within the humanities, inspired in part by our growing aware-ness of the limitations of our knowledge and our thinking, and of the inevitable way both are anchored in our own specific cultural and historical position. Yet let us not forget that this desire to listen to others and to question ourselves is made possible by a framework of exploration that was established in reaction to a tradition that sought to silence the other and that refused to question itself. Even if we, as academic scholars, or as human beings, are prepared to explore other worldviews in past and present that are alien or antagonistic to our own, it must be remembered that this compliment would not be and is not always returned. It is this willingness to listen, to question and be questioned, that marks our cur-rent position in human thinking. I do not hesitate to call this position superior. Like the Romantic Satanists before us, we can acknowledge the fact that our questioning may not bring us all the answers we desire; like them, we may acknowledge other ways in which human understanding can be found. But like the Romantic Satanists, we should and do not wish to revert to a tradition that does not allow us to question. The fact that we engage in academic research at all (or consume its results, as you, resolute reader, at present are doing) already attests to this conviction.

It may be clear from this, but should be brought to mind explicitly once more, that reli-gions or religious convictions are not automatically good things. Naturally, in the muddy world of history—which is our only world—there is seldom or never a thing that can be called "good" or "evil" in a wholesale way. Humanity's religions, in their almost infinite variety, are prime examples of this. As a way to formulate meaning and purpose, they can exert tremendous power over human beings and human societies; as this study has abun-dantly shown, this influence is not always beneficial. Posing these questions of "good" and "evil," however, brings us back in the religious realm ourselves, at least if we adopt the broad significance of the term proposed in this study. Every attempt to write a history of religion that transcends mere specialist fact-finding cannot escape from articulating or implying a certain amount of religious and/or ideological convictions. Thus there is a certain point at which even the academic historian, if he wants his work to be meaningful, inevitably finds himself engaged in the religious endeavor.

This bring us to a third historical question that might be more central and more inter-esting than issues of theological or scholarly nomenclature—namely, the question of what modern Satanism tells or tries to tell about definitions of good and evil, and the way this may reflect shifting conceptions regarding both in the Western world. As I already remarked in the introduction, veneration of Satan is not necessarily the same as veneration of evil.

The few attempts to establish a Satanism that was meant as a cult to evil were crude and short-lived, and even a superficial analysis will show that these groups in fact very well held their own ideas about what is "good," be it only martial prowess or sincere commitment to the cause. Yet opting to venerate a figure like Satan in a society that predominantly considers him the representation par excellence of evil almost automatically means that one assumes a position that challenges commonly accepted ethic conceptions.[25] All Satanisms we encountered in this volume involve implicit or explicit forms of ethical positioning. If we listen to the utterances of their adherents, it is clear that they were not primarily concerned with matters of theology or diabology, but rather with transgressing, evading, or invalidating the practical and moral limitations forced upon them by church or society (or, in some cases, by human nature itself). At the heart of the mobilization of Satan by the Romantic Satanists, for instance, were issues of what was right or wrong; issues about the legitimacy of insubmission and the illegitimacy of repressive forms of government; issues regarding the freedom to experience love or sexuality outside the bounds of convention; issues regarding the freedom to confess to other religious convictions than the Christian ones, or maybe to no explicit religious conviction at all. These values, which are mostly taken for granted in Western societies today, were still highly controversial in their days. By raising Satan, as a former representative of evil, on their banners, they not only underlined in a vivid way that Christianity's evil was not good (to paraphrase Byron's Lucifer), but also that much of what Christianity had considered evil was for them quite legitimate. LaVey's Satanism provided a more extreme continuation of this tendency and adopted Nietzschean premises to call into question the viability of basic ethical values from the heritage of Christianity, such as the laudability of altruism and the reprehensibility of egoism or aggression.

Although pure antinominianism is absent in LaVeyan Satanism (and in all current forms of Satanism, for that matter), most modern Satanisms tend to question the "evilness" of evil, proposing instead a more holistic approach in which "light" and "darkness" both have their rightful place and have to balance instead of supersede each other. This represents a clear break with a Christian past. While the ontological status of evil in the Christian tradition is not always completely clear-cut (witness Augustinus of Hippo's famous definition of evil as absence of good), the boundary lines between the divine and the Satanic are liable to be much more crisp. As an ontological category, "evil"—a word that LaVey, like Crowley, tends to write between quotation marks—is mostly described in Satanist "tradition" as delusion, religious superstition, or a lack of balance between contraries that are in themselves neither good nor bad: a position that derives directly from the nineteenth-century esotericism of Lévi and Crowley and reflects similar attitudes with Romantic Satanists as Blake and Hugo.[26]

Satanism does not operate in a cultural vacuum in this respect. Like Massimo Introvigne has stated, modern religious Satanism is indeed a "mirror image of modernity."[27] It is so historically speaking: as this study has demonstrated, it evolved as a complement to the processes of secularization and Western Revolution, which proved to be defining for modern Western society. But it also mirrors our common predicament in the questions it seeks to answer. Can we still define moral standards when we have repudiated their age-old basis in tradition or revelation? What kind of morality would this be? What balance can we strike, if any, between individual freedom and the demands of the social? Can we have a society at all without a focus of dedication beyond the individual (be it in religion, ideology, nationality, or ethnicity) to activate our instincts for mutual care? To what measure must society protect its members from the consequences of their own actions? Can one affirm one's individuality in a society that seems increasingly massified and in which identity has become a prepackaged commercial commodity? And what meaning does life offer if we have to find it ourselves within the horizon of the human? These are questions that are acute to all secularized societies, questions on which definite answers are still to be found.

Despite the fact that their mask of cult for Satan will probably deter people from joining them in large numbers, many of the answers given by Satanist groups like LaVey's reflect attitudes that can be commonly found in wider society. In fact, many of LaVey's social and ethical ideas amount to little more than "ancient street-smart egocentric cynicism," as one historian of Satanism has aptly put it.[28] Many will agree with the advice not to "turn the other cheek," but to "smash" your enemy twice as hard as he did you. For many, personal gratification and the demarcation of individuality are among the highest values in life, even if they would not put this in theological terms of deification, as the Church of Satan does. Individual autonomy in sexual and religious choices is now a matter of common agreement, and LaVey's demand for a Lex Talionis in which criminals receive severe retribution resembles ideas that can be heard during many a conservative political rally or late-night barstool conversation. His thoughts about a society that allows the "strong" to flourish, moreover, are perfectly consistent with values that have been enshrined into the "American way of life"; they tend to pale besides the measures promoted by some of the apostles of neoliberalism (who share with LaVey, by the way, a common source of inspiration in the neo-Nietzschean thought of Ayn Rand).[29]

Modern Satanisms are at most more radical or more loud in the way they formulate these answers. Their answers themselves are not always so unusual. And their more mature articulations, such as that developed by LaVey, cannot be denied a certain measure of inventiveness. Personally I have doubts, however, if adopting the extreme individualist answers proposed by current Satanism will really make our world a more enjoyable place. While modern religious Satanism is far removed from the "unspeakable acts" that have traditionally been ascribed to it, and only in exceptional cases dangerous in a criminal sense, one can doubt if society would profit if, say, LaVeyan Satanism became its dominant voice. Without doubt, LaVey's religious thought offers its fair share of sound logic and undefiled wisdom. But it may be most valuable, like LaVey himself suggested, as a *correction* on older values, not as an intrinsically solid base for building a new and presumably saner ethical and social edifice.[30]

It may sound rather ironic given its strong emphasis on "otherness," but what may be missing most in much of modern Satanism is a genuine place for the other. I do not refer to a lack of altruism here, a concept on which LaVey and company uttered some not altogether unjust criticism, or to the small place most modern Satanism reserves for social questions in the traditional sense of the word. I mean that there is no significant place for the other in a theological or philosophical sense. LaVey was certainly no proponent of inhumanity, and the practical prescriptions of his Satanism attest to a liberal amount of decency in the treatment of fellow creatures and a great deal of sympathy for the "freaky" and deviant sides of humanity. But on a more fundamental level, there is no real role to play in most modern Satanisms for other people facing you. By radically identifying with the "other," it almost seems, the Satanist usurps this position for himself. Everything turns around being and becoming the other, around nurturing one's otherness, without leaving much place for the real-life others who confront the I—other beings, other humans. The experience of life might nonetheless be essentially the experience of our encounter with the other, in whatever form. And only by acknowledging the other and ceding him his place, in whatever way, can human society and human community become possible.

History shows that every religious or ideological system that gains a monopoly over society deteriorates sooner or later (and mostly sooner) into a system of intolerance and exploitation. Until now, Satanism has been granted the mercy of failure in this respect, and it is utterly unlikely that it will ever attain a position of dominance in Western society. As a practiced religion, it remains exceedingly marginal; as a cultural force, its impact is negligible. Despite the fact that LaVey was and is a towering figure in the history of modern religious Satanism, his influence on wider society probably has been limited to the mediamatic spectacle of his early appearance as spokesman of Satan and his authorship of *The Satanic Bible*, that hasty compilation of mimeographed membership tracts that landed a confused but potentially disruptive mixture of occultism, rationalism, Romanticism, anti-Christianity and social Darwinism on many a doorstep.

From a historical perspective, one could argue, Satan played a much more important role in the nineteenth century, when he was given a tiny but fascinating part in the unique adventure of a civilization that spontaneously decided to renounce its old gods and enter into a permanent state of religious indecision. During this period, he was mobilized by a small but influential segment of the cultural elite in its struggle against repression and exploitation and celebrated as a symbolic champion for values such as the freedom to worship whom we like and how we like, the freedom to love whom we like and how we like, and the freedom to express ourselves how we like and to live how we like. These values have made Western society as it is: that is, for better or worse, a place of unprecedented liberty. In that respect we are all, in a way, children of Lucifer.

INTRODUCTION

1. Martin Ebon (ed.), *The World's Weirdest Cults* (New York: Signet, 1979); chapters (partly) concerned with Satanist "cults" are B. J. Baronitis, "Beheadings in West Virginia," 39–48; Jerome Clark, "Cattle Mutilations: Sex and Satanism?," 115–126; "Pity the Drug-Cult Witch!" ("by Ruth Pauli, as told to Daphne Lamb"), 127–139; Jean Molina, "Black Pope of San Francisco," 140–151; Michael Ballantino, "The Man Who Called Himself 'The Beast,'" 152–161; William R. Atkins, "Hell-Fire Club," 162–175; and Stephan A. Hoeller, "The Real Black Mass," 176–186.

2. Robert Ambelain, *Adam Dieu Rouge: L'ésotérisme judéo-chrétien, la gnose et les Ophites lucifériens et rose + croix* (Paris: Éditions Niclaus, 1941), 161, where Ambelain calls their doctrines "nettement luciférienne."

3. "Docteur" Bataille, *Le Diable au XIXᵉ siècle: La Franc-Maçonnerie luciférienne ou les mystères du spiritisme. Révélations complètes sur le Palladisme, la théurgie, la goétie et tout le satanisme moderne. Récits d'un témoin*, 2 vols. (Paris: Delhomme & Briguet, [1892–1893]), 1:37.

4. Bataille, *Le Diable au XIXᵉ siècle*, 1:37.

5. Cf. chapters 1 and 4.

6. Cf. Alain Boureau, *Satan the Heretic: The Birth of Demonology in the Medieval West* (Chicago: University of Chicago Press, 2006), 38. Also Jules Bois, *Le Satanisme et la Magie: Avec une étude de J.K. Huysmans* (Paris: Ernest Flammarion, 1895), 47n; Anton Szandor LaVey, *The Satanic Rituals* (New York: Avon, 1972), 55.

7. Elliot Rose, *A Razor for a Goat: A Discussion of Certain Problems in the History of Witchcraft and Diabolism* (Toronto: University of Toronto Press, 1989), 160–170.

8. Cf. Karl R. H. Frick, *Satan und Die Satanisten: Ideengeschichtliche Untersuchungen zur Herkunft der komplexen Gestalt "Luzifer/Satan/Teufel," ihrer weiblichen Entsprechungen und*

ihrer Anhängerschaft, 3 vols. (Graz: Akademische Druck- u. Verlagsanstalt, 1982–1985), 2:57–62, who mentions that rumors of allegiance to the Devil circulated about Pope John XIII, Sylvester II, John XVIII, Benedictus VIII and IX, John XIX and XXI, Gregorian VII and XI, Paul II, and Alexander VI.

9. Among others, see Laurent Kilger, O.S.B., "Le diable et la conversion des païens," in *Satan: Les Études Carmélitaines* 27 (Paris: Desclée De Brouwer, 1948), 122–129.

10. Cf. further on in this introduction and in chapter 1.

11. Anton Szandor LaVey includes him among his "de facto Satanists" in Blanche Barton, *The Secret Life of a Satanist: The Authorized Biography of Anton LaVey* (London: Mondo, 1992), 4.

12. Cf. Anton Kippenberg, *Die Sage vom Herzog von Luxemburg und die historische Persönlichkeit ihres Trägers* (Niederwalluf bei Wiesbaden: Dr. Martin Sändig oHG, 1970).

13. Among others, see Hoeller, "The Real Black Mass," 186; see also chapter 1.

14. Cf. Mike Hertenstein and Jon Trott, *Selling Satan: The Evangelical Media and the Mike Warnke Scandal* (Chicago: Cornerstone, 1993), 102–106, citing William Guy Carr's *Pawns in the Game* (1958) and Mike Warnke's *The Satan Seller* (1972).

15. Bataille, *Le Diable au XIXe siècle*, 1:95, 1:184.

16. M. J. C. Thorey, *Rapports merveilleux de Mme Cantianille B . . . avec le monde surnaturel*, 2 vols. (Paris: Louis Hervé, 1866), 1:40n.

17. Cf. Massimo Introvigne, "The Beast and the Prophet: Aleister Crowley's Fascination with Joseph Smith," in *Aleister Crowley and Western Esotericism*, ed. Henrik Bogdan and Martin P. Starr (New York: Oxford University Press, 2012), 255–284, 259–260.

18. See chapters 3 and 4.

19. Cf., e.g., Max Milner, *Le diable dans la littérature française: De Cazotte à Baudelaire 1772–1861*, 2 vols. (Paris: Librairie José Corti, 1960), 2:348–355.

20. See chapter 4.

21. Bataille, *Le Diable au XIXe siècle*, 1:730.

22. Gerhard Zacharias, *Satanskult und Schwarze Messe: Die Nachtseite des Christentums. Eine Beitrag zur Phänomenologie der Religion* (München: F. A. Herbig, 1990), 132, where his unfinished hymn "Ad Arimane" is described as "satanistischer Kultmystik."

23. See intermezzo 2.

24. Anton Szandor LaVey includes him among his "de facto Satanists," in Barton, *The Secret Life of a Satanist*, 4.

25. Bataille, *Le Diable au XIXe siècle*, 1:37.

26. Richard Wurmbrand, *Was Karl Marx a Satanist?* (s.l.: Diane Books, 1979).

27. Anton Szandor LaVey includes him among his "de facto Satanists," in Barton, *The Secret Life of a Satanist*, 4.

28. Brad Steiger, *Sex and Satanism* (New York: Ace, 1969), 147–162, basing himself on Helen Holdredge's *The House of the Strange Woman* (1961).

29. Joseph Boullan to Joris-Karl Huysmans, 27 February 1890, Bibliothèque National de France, Bibliothèque de l'Arsenal, Fonds Lambert 76 (Lettres et Documents adressées par l'abbé Boullan à J. K. Huysmans), ff. 69–73, here f. 69.

30. On the legend regarding Rampolla, see http://www.cfnews.org/ch-ramp.htm and http://fr.wikipedia.org/wiki/Discussion:Mariano_Rampolla_del_Tindaro, accessed 16 September 2011.

31. Among others by Robert Muchembled, *A History of the Devil: From the Middle Ages to the Present* (Cambridge, UK: Polity, 2003), 217. Cf. also Marco Pasi, *Aleister Crowley und die Versuchung der Politik*, trans. Fredinand Leopold (Graz: Ares Verlag, 2006), 243.

32. Cf. Peter Paul Schnierer, *Entdämonisierung und Verteufelung: Studien zur Darstellungs- und Funktionsgeschichte des Diabolischen in der englischen Literatur seit der Renaissance* (Tübingen: Max Niemeyer, 2005), 183.

33. For an interesting perspective on this stubborn blues myth, cf. http://www.luckymojo.com/crossroads.html, accessed 16 September 2011.

34. Cf. Josef Dvorak, *Satanismus: Schwarze Rituale, Teufelswahn und Exorzismus. Geschichte und Gegenwart* (München: Wilhelm Heyne Verlag, 1993), 188.

35. Cf. Gareth J. Medway, *Lure of the Sinister: The Unnatural History of Satanism* (New York: New York University Press, 2001), 261.

36. Cf. Pasi, *Aleister Crowley*, 246.

37. Cf. Wouter J. Hanegraaff, *New Age Religion and Western Culture: Esotericism in the Mirror of Secular Thought* (Leiden: E. J. Brill, 1996), 2.

38. Zacharias, *Satanskult und Schwarze Messe*.

39. See http://www.jesus-is-savior.com/Evils%20in%20America/Rock-n-Roll/imagine.htm, accessed 16 September 2011.

40. Jeffrey Burton Russell, *Mephistofeles: The Devil in the Modern World* (Ithaca, NY: Cornell University Press, 1986), 253.

41. Wurmbrand, *Was Karl Marx a Satanist?*, 67, where it is suggested that "Communist movements are . . . front organizations for occult Satanism." See also 73–75, where Wurmbrand discloses that Lenin's tomb has been deliberately modeled on the Hellenistic altar of the "Satanist temple at Pergamos."

42. Cf. Medway, *Lure of the Sinister*, 272.

43. Cf. Medway, *Lure of the Sinister*, 272; James R. Lewis, *Satanism Today: An Encyclopedia of Religion, Folklore, and Popular Culture* (Santa Barbara, CA: ABC-CLIO, 2001), 216–218. In 1982, it was rumored that three 6s were discernible in the curls of the beard of the man in the Procter & Gamble trademark; the company had to assign fifteen telephone operators to answer all the calls it received about this.

44. See http://pinballking.blogspot.com/2010/06/christina-aguilera-exposed.html, accessed 16 September 2011: "Disney is presented as a 'wholesome' company but it is really an illuminati training camp for 'preachers of immorality.' "

45. As well as among extreme Protestant Christians, this idea frequently surfaces among sedevacantist Catholics; see, e.g., http://sedevacantisme.wordpress.com/2010/09/16/ratzinger-accomplit-le-plan-du-cardinal-sataniste-rampolla, accessed 16 September 2011.

46. Among many websites, see, e.g., http://www.apfn.org/apfn/hijacking.htm, as well as the Hon. James David Manning of Atlah World Ministries preaching on President Barack Obama on 31 January 2009, http://www.youtube.com/watch?v=qzxtH15A_Do (both accessed 16 September 2011).

47. J. A. Simpson and A. S. C Weiner, *Oxford English Dictionary*, 2nd ed. (Oxford: Clarendon, 1989), 14:494–495; Walther von Wartburg (ed.), *Französische Etymologischen Wörterbuch*, 25 vols. (Basel: Zbinden, 1964), 11:238.

48. Paul Imbs and Bernard Quemada (eds.), *Trésor de la Langue Française*, 16 vols. (Paris: Gallimard, 1992), 15:78–79: "Je vous voir faire des progrès bien rapides en satanisme. . . .

Vous devenez ironique, sarcastique et même diabolique." Merimée, *Lettres à une inconnue* I, 1842, p. 77. Of course, Merimée was being ironic himself as well.

In some historiography, even of recent date, an even wider and highly confusing application of the terms "Satanism" and "diabolism" is encountered, namely, as designating *any* intense preoccupation with Satan and the devil, even when resulting from intense antipathy. See, for instance, Muchembled, *History of the Devil*, 16 ["theological satanism"], 31, 108.

49. Imbs and Quemada give Huysmans as the first reference for this new significance of Satanism (*Trésor de la Langue Française*, 15:78–79; for Huysmans, see chapter 4); in English, the *Oxford English Dictionary* notes the first instance of this modern significance with Arthur Lillie's 1896 *Worship of Satan in Modern France*, a publication in the wake of the Léo Taxil affair (see Simpson and Weiner, *Oxford English Dictionary*, 14:494; for Taxil, see chapters 5 and 6). The French Larousse encyclopedia of 1875 still defined Satanism as "caractère de ce qui est satanique"; in the 1933 edition, this had become "culte de Satan" (cf. Von Wartburg, *Französische Etymologischen Wörterbuch*, 11:238).

50. Aloïs Mager explicitly identifies National Socialism and Satanism in his article "Satan de nos jours," in *Satan: Les Études Carmélitaines* 27 (Paris: Desclée De Brouwer, 1948): 635–643.

51. A useful introduction to the academic discussion can be found in Fiona Bowie, *The Anthropology of Religion: An Introduction* (Malden, MA: Blackwell, 2006).

52. Cf. Daniel L. Pals, *Seven Theories of Religion* (Oxford: Oxford University Press, 1996), 16–53.

53. The same problem occurs with the temptingly simple definition of religion by the Dutch scholar of religion Jan van Baal: "All explicit and implicit notions and ideas, accepted as true, which relate to a reality which cannot be verified empirically" (J. van Baal, "Magic as a Religious Phenomenon," *Higher Education and Research in the Netherlands* 7 [1963] 3/4: 10–21). In many ways, this is a mirror image of Tylor's definition, making religion, on the one hand, too narrow ("survivals" relating to that ever-shrinking part of "reality" that is "left over" by empirical science), and on the other hand, too broad (not all notions that cannot be verified empirically are necessarily religious).

54. This critique was already expressed by Mircea Eliade, among others, who wrote in 1969 that "religion may still be a useful term provided we keep in mind that it does not necessarily imply belief in God, gods, or ghosts, but refers to the experience of the sacred, and, consequently, is related to the ideas of *being, meaning*, and *truth*" (cf. Mircea Eliade, *The Quest: History and Meaning in Religion* [Chicago: University of Chicago Press, 1969], i). I have not adopted Eliade's category of "the sacred" in this study.

55. Massimo Introvigne, "Satanism," in *Dictionary of Gnosis and Western Esotericism*, ed. Wouter J. Hanegraaff, 2 vols. (Leiden: Brill, 2005), 2:1035.

56. Massimo Introvigne, *Enquête sur le satanisme: Satanistes et antisatanistes du XVIIe siècle à nos jours*, trans. Philipp Baillet (Paris: Éditions Dervy, 1997), 10.

57. This is not a purely theoretical point: the French scholar Olivier Bobineau refuses to class modern Satanism as a religion, precisely on the grounds of Durkheimian denominators like these. See his "Le satanisme ou le 'religieusement incorrect,' " *Social Compass* 56 (December 2009) 4: 503–514.

58. Robert Bellah, "Religious Evolution," in *Reader in Comparative Religion: An Anthropological Approach*, ed. W. A. Lessa and E. Z. Vogt (New York: Grune and Stratton, 1965),

73–87, here 74. Bellah's definition, by the way, is based on that of Clifford Geertz: "religion is (1) a system of symbols which acts to (2) establish powerful, pervasive, and long-lasting moods and motivations in men by (3) formulating conceptions of a general order of existence and (4) clothing these conceptions with such an aura of factuality that (5) the moods and motivations seem uniquely realistic" (cited in Bowie, *Anthropology of Religion*, 20). I prefer Bellah's reformulation, not only because of its superior terseness, but also because Geertz's definition seems to contain an inherent value judgment about the truth of religious statements that seems inappropriate for an academic study on religion.

59. Cited in Bowie, *Anthropology of Religion*, 20.

60. This point was forcefully made by Talal Assad in his essay "The Construction of Religion as an Anthropological Category," in Talal Assad, *Genealogies of Religion: Discipline and Reasons of Power in Christianity and Islam* (Baltimore, MD: Johns Hopkins University Press, 1993), 27–54. As is obvious from what follows, I do not share his conclusion that it would therefore be better to do away with definitions of religion altogether.

61. A tendency to do so may be partly behind the present vogue of the concept of "spirituality" in certain academic circles. I see no real ground for why most of the phenomena that some scholars of religion now categorize under "spirituality" should not be considered religion, keeping in mind that the manifold varieties of human religion may show important differences. Spirituality, to me, is the (collective or individual) *experience* of religion. This also closely concurs with the original significance of the term. I must admit, however, that the broad definition of religion I have adopted makes it easier to do so; with a narrower definition of religion, the range of phenomena between the religious and the secular widens considerably, thus allowing for some kind of third category.

62. One problematic aspect of Bellah's definition is the demarcation between religion and philosophy, both of which attempt to formulate statements pertaining to man's "ultimate conditions of existence." These categories may indeed overlap, if we distinguish between philosophy as the rigorous application of logic to certain propositions, and the building of a systematic philosophical system about a "general order of existence." The latter indeed often takes on the shape of religion, with Hegel and Nietzsche as particularly striking examples. Still, areas of unease remain, for instance, with ideologies that relate man to the ultimate conditions of his existence but are extremely secular, such as Communism.

63. Without a proper realization of this fact, it is hard to make sense of Satanism. This is made clear, for instance, by the confusion of the noted historian of Satan, Jeffrey Burton Russell, in the face of modern religious Satanism. Because Russell assigns only one valid meaning to Satan (that of the Christian symbol for evil), there can be only one genuine form of Satanism for him. "The term Satanist is properly applied only to the tiny number who believe Satan is a personal principle to true evil, selfishness, and suffering, and who worship him as such" (cf. Russell, *Mephistopheles*, 205). Thus, he writes, "The few eccentrics who took the view that only Satan exists and not God, or that both exist but that Satan is good and God evil, are not real Satanists . . ., for they were merely reversing terms emptily" (205; see also 175). On the other hand, clearly non-Satanist groups like the "Jim Jones cult" can be included by him as Satanists, assumedly because they are evil, albeit under the pretence of holiness (253). In this way, we are confronted by the amusing paradox of the Roman Catholic Russell establishing orthodoxy in Satanism. This is all the more surprising, given that his three volume history of the devil must

have made Russell eminently aware of how the character and attributes of Satan constantly change throughout history.

64. Set, Loki, Kali, and Marduk are all invoked in Anton LaVey's *The Satanic Bible* (New York: Avon, 1969), 145–146.

65. Kennet Granholm, "The Left-Hand Path and Post-Satanism: The Temple of Set and the Evolution of Satanism," in *The Devil's Party: Satanism in Modernity*, ed. Per Faxneld and Jesper Petersen (Oxford: Oxford University Press, 2012), 209–228, here 225. Granholm already expressed similar views in "Embracing Others Than Satan: The Multiple Princes of Darkness in the Left-Hand Milieu," in *Contemporary Religious Satanism: A Critical Anthology*, ed. Jesper Aagaard Petersen (Farnham, UK: Ashgate, 2009), 85–101.

66. Granholm, "The Left-Hand Path and Post-Satanism," 225.

67. Jesper Aagaard Petersen, "Introduction: Embracing Satan," in *Contemporary Religious Satanism: A Critical Anthology*, ed. Jesper Aagaard Petersen (Farnham, UK: Ashgate, 2009), 1–24, here 5.

68. Per Faxneld, *Satanic Feminism: Lucifer as the Liberator of Woman in Nineteenth-Century Culture* (Stockholm: Molin & Sorgfrei, 2014), 23.

69. Petersen, "Introduction: Embracing Satan," 7.

70. We will have occasion to encounter some of this theologically flavored literature in chapters 6 and 8. A mild but nevertheless illustrative example is Bernhard Wenisch, *Satanismus: Schwarze Messen—Dämonenglauben—Hexenkulte* (Mainz: Matthias-Grünewald Verlag, 1988), issued in the Lutheran-Catholic series "Unterscheidung: Christliche Orientierung im religiösen Pluralismus," intended to give practical information to believers in the labyrinth of multireligiosity. The book is based on cursory reading, magazine articles, and bad source material; the author, for instance, reproduces without questioning the claim of Satnic Ritual Abuse alarmists that "thousands of children become a victim to cults of Satan every year," while giving as reference only the article of "ein Beobachter der amerikanische Szene" in a regional church periodical (29–30). Such instances of overly rash conclusions based on dubious literature from "expert" coreligionists are unfortunately rather typical of this type of literature.

Histories of Satanism from Satanists' points of view are rare, given the marginality of this religious subculture. One example that might be mentioned is Gavin Baddely, *Lucifer Rising: Sin, Devil Worship & Rock 'n'Roll* (London: Plexus, 1999), which is insufficiently annotated for scholarly use but invaluable for its interviews with prominent contemporary Satanists.

71. Zacharias, *Satanskult und Schwarze Messe.*

72. Biographical facts on Zacharias are from Josef Dvorak, *Satanismus: Schwarze Rituale, Teufelswahn und Exorzismus. Geschichte und Gegenwart* (München: Wilhelm Heyne Verlag, 1993), 83–85.

73. Frick, *Satan und Die Satanisten.* I did not manage to locate the third volume of this work.

74. Frick, *Satan und Die Satanisten*, 1:19–29; 1:210–233, 1:306–309, 1:303.

75. Frick, *Satan und Die Satanisten*, 2:229–231; Joachim Schmidt, *Satanismus: Mythos und Wirklichkeit* (Marburg: Diagonal-Verlag, 1992), 5.

76. http://en.wikipedia.org/wiki/Josef_Dvorak, accessed 29 September 2011.

77. With "articles of note," I refer in the first place to the excellent article by Jean La Fontaine, "Satanism and Satanic Mythology," in *Witchcraft and Magic in Europe, Volume 6: The Twentieth Century*, ed. Willem de Blécourt, R. Hutton, and J. La Fontaine (London: Athlone,

1999), 81–140, which still serves as the best short introduction to the subject currently available in the English language (although the author unfortunately reproduces many of LaVey's autobiographical fabulations). Also recommended is Per Faxneld and Jesper Aagaard Petersen, "Introduction: At the Devil's Crossroads," in *The Devil's Party: Satanism in Modernity*, ed. Per Faxneld and Jesper Petersen (Oxford: Oxford University Press, 2012), 3–18.

78. Arthur Lyons, *The Second Coming: Satanism in America* (New York: Dodd, Mead and Company, 1970).

79. Arthur Lyons, *Satan Wants You: The Cult of Devil Worship in America* (New York: Mysterious Press, 1988).

80. See Chris Mathews, *Modern Satanism: Anatomy of a Radical Subculture* (Westport, CT: Praeger, 2009), 173–174. Matthews correctly claims that Lyons was a member of Anton LaVey's Church of Satan. LaVey himself strongly endorsed Lyons's book as "concise and perceptive" in his column in *The Exploiter* on 31 January 1971, reprinted in Anton Szandor LaVey, *Letters from the Devil* (s.l.: Underworld Amusements, 2010), [18].

81. Gareth J. Medway, *Lure of the Sinister: The Unnatural History of Satanism* (New York: New York University Press, 2001).

82. Medway, *Lure of the Sinister*, 12.

83. I have consulted the French translation for Introvigne, *Enquête sur le satanisme*.

84. Introvigne, *Enquête sur le satanisme*, 11.

85. Introvigne, *Enquête sur le satanisme*, 11.

86. Introvigne, *Enquête sur le satanisme*, 11.

87. Introvigne does discuss various works of literature in *Enquête sur le satanisme*, but only insofar as they might offer any clues about actually practiced, ritual Satanism, with the exception of a brief paragraph on pages 213–214.

88. Introvigne, *Enquête sur le satanisme*, 16, 394.

89. Introvigne is involved in the ultra-conservative Roman Catholic organization Alleanza Cattolica and in various Italian neoconservative endeavors. See the extensive Wikipedia page on him at http://en.wikipedia.org/wiki/Massimo_Introvigne, accessed 11 October 2011.

90. Per Faxneld, *Mörkrets apostlar: Satanism i äldre tid* (Ouroboros: Sundbyberg, 2006).

91. For a theoretical framework relating to "attribution" and "identification," see Wolfgang Lipp, "Außenseiter, Häretiker, Revolutionäre: Gesichtspunkte zur systematischer Analyse," in *Reliogiöse Devianz in christlich geprägten Gesellschaften: Vom hohen Mittelalter bis zur Frühaufklärung*, ed. Dieter Fauth and Daniela Müller (Würzburg: Religion & Kultur Verlag, 1999), 12–26.

92. Cf. Eric Hobsbawm and Terence Ranger (eds.), *The Invention of Tradition* (Cambridge, UK: Cambridge University Press 1983), 1–14. Hobsbawm's concept of "invented tradition" has not remained uncriticized—see Joseph Mali, *Mythistory: The Making of Modern Historiography* (Chicago: University of Chicago Press, 2003), 7–8, for a résumé of some of the most important criticism. For our present exploration, however, it remains a good starting point, without obliging us to accept Hobsbawm's more reductionist ideas. In addition, while Hobsbawm's concept may strike veteran historians as comparatively "old bread," there is still much terrain to be gained in the history of (alternative) religion and esotericism in this respect. Cf. the remarks on this matter in Egil Asprem and Kennet Granholm, "Constructing Esotericisms: Sociological, Historical and Critical Approaches to the Invention of Tradition," in *Contemporary Esotericism*, ed. Egil Asprem and Kennet Granholm (Sheffield, UK: Equinox, 2013), 25–48, there 32–33.

93. This way of looking at the history of modern religious Satanism has some antecedents in the prior literature. Despite the differences already indicated, it has obvious affinities with Introvigne's model of Satanism and anti-Satanism. Jean La Fontaine also suggested a similar approach in her long article on Satanism, distinguishing between alleged and self-styled Satanists, although she does not elaborate on the connection between these two categories (see especially "Satanism and Satanic Mythology," 81). Schmidt, *Satanismus*, 10, also makes useful suggestions about the interactions among "theologische Satanslehre," "projizierte Satanismus," and "positiver expliziter Satanismus," again without giving these much application in his book. Titus Hjelm, "Introduction," *Social Compass* 56 (December 2009) 4: 499–502, ventures some poignant thoughts on "the interaction between the public image of Satanism and the actual practise of Satanism" (499–500), while J. Gordon Melton wrote in his lemma "Satanism and the Church of Satan," in *Encyclopedic Handbook of Cults in America*, ed. J. Gordon Melton (New York: Garland, 1986), 76–80: "The Satanic tradition has been carried almost totally by the imaginative literature of non-Satanists, primarily conservative Christians, who describe the practices in vivid detail in the process of denouncing them. That is to say, the Satanic tradition has been created by generation after generation of anti-Satan writers. Sporadically, groups and individuals have tried to create groups which more or less conform to the Satanism portrayed in Christian literature" (76).

94. Islam adopted an earlier Christian apocryphal account according to which Satan was cast out of heaven because he refused to bow before the newly created Adam when Allah ordered him to do so. Some medieval Sufi mystics developed remarkable theories about this occurrence, which may be said to contain an element of Satanism, describing Satan as the perfect monotheist (because he refused to kneel before any being other than Allah) and/or a model for the faithful striving for unity with the divine (who is similarly cut off from Allah because of the paradoxes of the latter's commands). On this intriguing subject, see Peter J. Awn, *Satan's Tragedy and Redemption: Iblīs in Sufi Psychology*, Studies in the History of Religions no. 44 (Leiden: E. J. Brill, 1983); and Annemarie Schimmel, *Mystical Dimensions of Islam* (Chapel Hill: University of North Carolina Press, 1975), particularly 62–77, 193–199.

Also interesting with respect to Satanism are the *yezidi*, a religious group from Kurdistan that numbers between 150,000 and 300,000 adherents and that venerates Melek Tawus, the "Peacock Angel." Scholarship is still divided on the question of whether this angel can be identified as Satan. There is also divergence about the origins of their religion: Awn, for instance, maintains that they essentially present a local outgrowth of Sufi theology (*Satan's Tragedy and Redemption*, 196–917), while the Iranist Kreyenbroek claims they are rooted in Iranian Zoroastrian and pre-Zoroastrian beliefs that antedate Islam (cf. Philip G. Kreyenbroek, *Yezidism—Its Background, Observances and Textual Tradition* [Lewiston, NY: Edwin Mellen, 1995], especially 58–61, 94–95). Both these examples of possible "Satanisms" within the Islamic world represent autonomous religious developments that have no real connection with Western early modern or modern religious Satanisms—despite the fact that some modern religious Satanists may make occasional references to the *yezidi* (see, for instance, the alleged *yezidi* rite in LaVey's *Satanic Rituals*, 151–172, while a rather spurious link between Aleister Crowley and the *yezidi* is explored in Tobias Churton, "Aleister Crowley and the Yezidis," in *Aleister Crowley and Western Esotericism*, ed. Henrik Bogdan and Martin P. Starr [New York: Oxford University Press, 2012], 181–207).

95. For the same practical reasons, the role of popular culture has not received proper attention in this study, a lacuna I hope other researchers will fill.

96. Penelope J. Corfield argues for a similar "temporal turn" and a return to "big history" in her "Historians and the Return to the Diachronic," in *The New Ways of History: Developments in Historiography*, ed. Gelina Harlaftis, Nikos Karapidakis, Kostas Sbonias, and Vaios Vaiopoulos (London: Tauris Academic Studies, 2010), 13–34. The 1980s and 1990s—the great decades of postmodernism—saw a certain vogue of narrativism in historical thinking, with Frank Ankersmit, *Narrative Logic: A Semantic Analysis of the Historian's Language* (Den Haag: Nijhoff, 1983), as one of the founding texts of this school. While I like to emphasize the place of narrative as a proper method of historical reconstruction, I do not think it necessary to subscribe to the postmodern epistemology endorsed in this book. (Incidentally, Ankersmit himself has in the meantime also moved on to new, even more radical points of view.)

97. Mali, *Mythistory*, makes a valiant case for the reevaluation of meaning and myth in historiography.

98. Mircea Eliade, "Crisis and Renewal," in *The Quest: History and Meaning in Religion* (Chicago: University of Chicago Press, 1969), 54–71, there 62. This article is a revised version of "Crisis and Renewal in History of Religions," *History of Religions* 5 (1965): 1–17.

CHAPTER 1: THE CHRISTIAN INVENTION OF SATANISM

1. It is impossible to write a general history without writing generalizations, but, of course, a sweeping statement such as this immediately calls for qualification. Clearly, there has never existed one monolithic "Christian" institution or identity, but rather a wide variety of religious manifestations in time and space that can be brought together under the umbrella term "Christianity." For some problems regarding the scholarly use of the terms "Christian" and "Christianity," see Wouter J. Hanegraaff, "The Dreams of Theology and the Realities of Christianity," in *Theology and Conversation: Towards a Relational Theology*, ed. J. Haers and P. De Mey (Leuven: Peeters/Leuven University Press, 2003), 709–733. Even more problematic for the historian are the demarcations and historical relations between "heterodoxy" and "orthodoxy"; the latter, in current scholarship, is usually regarded as being formulated only in reaction to the former. For this point, see Daniela Müller, "Aspekte der Ketzerverfolgung unter den römischen Kaisern bis Justinian," *Journal of Eastern Christian Studies* 60 (2008) 1–4:175–193, there 175–176.

2. For its general outlines, this section mostly draws from Henry Ansgar Kelly, *Satan: A Biography* (Cambridge, UK: Cambridge University Press, 2006), and the relevant entries in *Dictionary of Deities and Demons in the Bible*, ed. Karel van der Toorn, Bob Becking, and Pieter W. van der Horst (Leiden: Brill, 1999): C. Breytenbach and P. L. Day, "Satan," 726–732; G. J. Riley, "Devil," 244–249. Also consulted were the three volumes about the devil by Jeffrey Burton Russell: *The Devil: Perceptions of Evil from Antiquity to Primitive Christianity* (Ithaca, NY: Cornell University Press, 1977); *Lucifer: The Devil in the Middle Ages* (Ithaca, NY: Cornell University Press, 1984); and *Mephistofeles: The Devil in the Modern World* (Ithaca, NY: Cornell University Press, 1986), digested by the author himself in *The Prince of Darkness: Radical Evil and the Power of Good in History* (Ithaca, NY: Cornell University Press, 1988).

For broader insights regarding these sections, and indeed for this entire chapter and entire book, I am greatly indebted to the monograph by David Frankfurter, *Evil Incarnate: Rumors of Demonic Conspiracy and Ritual Abuse in History* (Princeton, NJ: Princeton University Press, 2006).

3. Frankfurter, *Evil Incarnate*, 21. The American folklorist Bill Ellis, in *Raising the Devil: Satanism, New Religions, and the Media* (Lexington: University Press of Kentucky, 2000), xvii, called this mechanism of gaining control the "Rumpelstiltzkin Principle." For a concise overview of spiritual beings in various religious traditions, the article "Demons and Spirits" by L. H. Gray and others is still worthwhile to consult, in the *Encyclopaedia of Religion and Ethics*, ed. J. Hastings, 12 vols. (Edinburgh: T&T Clark, 1911), 4:565–635.

4. Frankfurter, *Evil Incarnate*, 18, citing an Egyptian amulet; cf. 16–22 for more examples.

5. Cf. Riley, "Demon," 235–240; Keimpe Algra, "Stoics on Souls and Demons: Reconstructing Stoic Demonology," in *Demons and the Devil in Ancient and Medieval Christianity*, ed. Nienke Vos and Willemien Otten, Supplements to Vigiliae Christianae: Texts and Studies of Early Christian Life and Language, no. 108 (Leiden: Brill, 2011), 71–96, there 74.

6. Wash Edward Hale, *Ásura—in Early Vedic Religion* (Delhi: Motilal Banarsidass, 1986), especially 180–181, 193.

7. See, for this point with regard to the Meso-American gods, Michael T. Taussig, *The Devil and Commodity Fetishism in South America* (Chapel Hill: University of North Carolina Press, 1984), 169–181, especially 177–179. For similar notions in Hindu religion, see John Chethimattam, "The Concept and the Role of the Demon in Indian Thought," in *Le Défi Magique II: Satanisme, sorcellerie*, ed. Jean-Baptiste Martin and Massimo Introvigne (Lyon: Presses Universitaires de Lyon, 1994), 311–320.

8. H. te Velde, *Seth, God of Confusion: A Study of His Role in Egyptian Mythology and Religion*, Probleme der Ägyptologie, no. 6 (Leiden: Brill, 1977), 25, 59. Although he was ritually deprecated for it in the cult of Osiris, even Seth's murder of his brother eventually served to assign Osiris his rightful place as ruler of the dead.

9. Velde, *Seth*, 99–108.

10. Velde, *Seth*, 138.

11. Velde, *Seth*, 148–151; the hymn is cited on 151.

12. Velde, *Seth*, 116.

13. Albert de Jong, *Traditions of the Magi: Zoroastrianism in Greek and Latin Literature*, Religions in the Graeco-Roman World, no. 133 (Leiden: Brill, 1997), 312n.

14. Jong, *Traditions of the Magi*, 338–347.

15. Jong, *Traditions of the Magi*, 178–180. Some scholars hold these stories to be a distorted echo of secret cultic practices within pre-Zoroastrian religion; cf. Kris Kershaw, *The One-eyed God: Odin and the (Indo-)Germanic Männerbünde*, Journal of Indo-European Studies Monograph, no. 36 (Washington, DC: Institute for the Study of Man, 2000), 207–208n.

16. Breytenbach and Day, "Satan," 726; Kelly, *Satan*, 30; "Satan," in *Encyclopaedia Judaica* (Jerusalem: Keter, 1972), 14:901–903.

17. Kelly, *Satan*; Breytenbach and Day, "Satan," 727–728.

18. Cf. Russell, *The Devil*, 57, and Gerd Theißen, "Monotheismus und Teufelsglaube: Entstehung und Psychologie des biblischen Satansmythos," in Vos and Otten, *Demons and the Devil in Ancient and Medieval Christianity*, 37–69, especially 43, 50.

19. Breytenbach and Day, "Satan," 730.

20. Breytenbach and Day, "Satan," 729–730.

21. Riley, "Devil," 245, and Russell, *Prince of Darkness*, 19, both propound the "Iranian hypothesis." Authors more skeptical about Iranian influence include James Barr, "The Question of Religious Influence: The Case of Zoroastrianism, Judaism, and Christianity," *Journal of the*

American Academy of Religion 53 (June 1985) 2:201–235; Kelly, *Satan*, 5, 31; P. de Menasce O.P., "Note sur le dualisme mazdéen," *Satan: Les Études Carmélitaines* 27 (1948): 130–135; Theißen, "Monotheismus und Teufelsglaube," 49–50. Herbert Haag and Bernard Lang conclude in Herbert Haag, *Teufelsglaube* (Tübingen: Katzmann Verlag, 1974), 267–268, that "Zurückhaltung geboten" is concerning the early postexilic period, but they argue for a "tiefgreifenden iranischen Einfluß" in the late postexilic period. For a more general discussion of the influence of Zoroastrianism on Judaism and Christianity, see Mary Boyce, *Zoroastrianism: A Shadowy but Powerful Presence in the Judaeo-Christian World* (London: Dr. William's Trust, 1987).

22. Riley, "Devil," 244. Kelly, *Satan*, 31, even writes, "We have thus witnessed the Birth of Satan."

23. Riley, "Devil," 246; Russell, *The Devil*, 189; Victor P. Hamilton, "Satan," in *The Anchor Bible Dictionary*, ed. David Noel Freedman (New York: Doubleday, 1992), 5:985–989; B. Janowski, "Azazel," in Van der Toorn et al., *Dictionary of Deities and Demons*, 128–130; S. D. Sperlinger, "Belial," in Van der Toorn et al., *Dictionary of Deities and Demons*, 169–171.

24. See, among others, the entry "Satan," in *Encyclopaedia Judaica*.

25. For a discussion of dualistic tendencies and references to demons with the Jewish group whose writings were recovered at Qumran, see Michael Mach, "Demons," in *Encyclopedia of the Dead Sea Scrolls*, ed. Lawrence H. Schiffman and James C. VanderKam (Oxford: Oxford University Press, 2000), 1:189–192; and Jean Duhaime, "Dualism," in Schiffman and VanderKam, *Encyclopedia*, 1:215–220.

26. Cf. Riley, "Demon." The negative Judeo-Christian attitude toward the *daemones* may be an intensification of an already existing trend in the Greco-Roman world; see Russell, *The Devil*, 142, and Algra, "Stoics on Souls and Demons."

27. Riley, "Devil," 247–249, and Geert van Oyen, "Demons and Exorcism in the Gospel of Mark," in Vos and Otten, *Demons and the Devil in Ancient and Medieval Christianity*, 99–116.

28. Riley, "Devil," 247.

29. Cf. Jaroslav Pelikan, *The Emergence of the Catholic Tradition*, The Christian Tradition: A History of the Development of Doctrine, vol. 6 (Chicago: University of Chicago Press, 1971), 135–170.

30. Kelly, *Satan*, 177, 191–195.

31. Elaine Pagels, "The Social History of Satan, the 'Intimate Enemy': A Preliminary Sketch," *Harvard Theological Review* 84 (1991) 2:105–128; there 117.

32. M. J. Kister, "Ādam: A Study of Some Legends in *Tafsīr* and *Hadīt* Literature," *Israel Oriental Studies* 13 (1993): 113–174.

33. Riley, "Devil," 246–247.

34. Pelikan, *Emergence of the Catholic Tradition*, 151; Theißen, "Monotheismus und Teufelsglaube," 57.

35. Oyen, "Demons and Exorcism in the Gospel of Mark."

36. Frankfurter, *Evil Incarnate*, 21–24.

37. Frankfurter, *Evil Incarnate*, 7, 13–37.

38. Minucius Felix, *Octavius*, xxvii.1, English translation by G. Rendall and W. Kerr in Tertullian, *Apology. De Spectaculis*, ed. T. R. Glover, Loeb Classical Library, no. 250 (1933; repr., London: William Heinemann, 1960), 397. Significantly, the Vulgate, following the Septuagint, translated Psalm 95:5 as "Omnes dii gentium daemones": "All the gods of the nation are demons."

39. Justin Martyr, *First Apology*, liv, English translation by Alexander Roberts and James Donaldson in *The Ante-Nicene Fathers: The Writings of the Fathers down to A.D. 325* (1885; repr., Peabody, MA: Hendrickson, 1994), vol. 1. For Justin's attitude toward demons, see Theodoor Korteweg, "Justin Martyr and His Demon-ridden Universe," in Vos and Otten, *Demons and the Devil in Ancient and Medieval Christianity*, 145–158.

40. Cf. Arnold Angenendt, "Die Liturgie und die Organisation des Kirchlichen Lebens auf dem Lande," in *Cristianizzazione ed organizzazione ecclesiastica delle campagne nell'alto medioevo: espansione e resistenze* (Spoleto: Centro Italiano di Studi sull'Alto Medioevo, 1982), 1:169–226. The reference to "satanae et omnibus operibus ejus" is still preserved in the baptismal rite of many Western Christian denominations, for instance that of the Roman Catholic Church—see the "Ordo initiationis christianae adultorum" and the "Ordo baptismi parvulorum" from the *Rituale Romanum*, which I consulted in *Rituale Romanum Pauli V Pontificus Maximi jussu editum, aliorumque pontificum cura recognitum atque auctoritate ssmi. d. n. Pii Papæ XI ad norman codicis juris canonici accommodatum* (Ratisbonæ: Friderici Pustet, 1925), 38, 45.

41. Tertullian, *Apology*, xxiii.11, English translation by T. R. Glover in Tertullian, *Apology. De Spectaculis*, 127.

42. Felix, *Octavius* xxvii.5–7, English translation by G. Rendall and W. Kerr in Tertullian, *Apology. De Spectaculis*, 399. See also Tertullian's challenging reference to the Christian exorcism of the gods in his *Apologeticum*: "Produce someone before your tribunals, who is admittedly demon-possessed. Let any Christian you please bid him speak, and the spirit in the man will own himself a demon—and truly—just as he will elsewhere call himself a god, falsely. Similarly bring forward some one or other of those persons who are supposed to be god-possessed, who by sniffing at altars inhale a divine power in the smell, who cure themselves by belching, who declaim panting. Let us take your Great Virgin of Heaven herself, promiser of rain, your great Aesculapius, discoverer of medical arts, giver of life to Socordius, Thanatius, Asclepiodotus (who will die some other day all the same)—if they do not confess they are demons, not daring to lie to a Christian, then shed the impudent Christian's blood on the spot!" Tertullian, *Apology. De Spectaculis*, 125 (*Apology*, xxiii.4–6). A similar reference from the fifth century can be found in Norman Cohn, *Europe's Inner Demons: An Enquiry Inspired by the Great Witch-Hunt* (London: Sussex University Press, 1975), 67.

43. Cf. Augustine of Hippo's *City of God*, viii, 24, and Thomas Aquinas, *Summa Theologica*, II, ii, 94. The Patristic view of other gods as demons was also a decisive influence in the confrontation of Western Christianity with the non-Western world in the colonial era, and it continues to be upheld by some strands of Christianity today. For some illustrative situations from Spanish America, see Fernando Cervantes, *The Devil in the New World: The Impact of Diabolism in New Spain* (New Haven, CT: Yale University Press, 1994), 5–39; and Iris Gareis, "Wie Engel und Teufel in die Neue welt kamen. Imaginationen von Gut und Böse in kolonialen Amerika," *Paideuma: Mitteilungen ur Kulturkunde* 45 (1999): 257–273.

44. Kelly, *Satan*, 217, 226–227. For other examples, see the episode with the statue of Apollo when Benedictus establishes Monte Casino, and St. Gall's struggle with the demon of a Swiss lake, both quoted in Edward Peters (ed.), *Monks, Bishops and Pagans: Christian Culture in Gaul and Italy, 500–700* (Philadelphia: University of Pennsylvania Press, 1975), 64, 115–116; see also Nienke Vos, "The Saint as Icon: Transformation of Biblical Imagery in Early Medieval Hagiography," in *Iconoclasm and Iconoclash: Struggle for Religious Identity*,

ed. Willem van Asselt, Paul van Geest, et al. (Leiden: Brill, 2007), 201–216; and Kerstin Zech, "Heidenvorstellung und Heidendarstellung: Begrifflichkeit und ihre Deutung im Kontext von Bedas *Historia Ecclesiastica*," in *Die wahrnehmun anderer Religionen in früheren Mittelalter: Terminologische Probleme und methodische Ansätze*, ed. Anna Aurast and Hans-Werner Goetz, Hamburger geistwissenschaftliche Studien zu Religion und Gesellschaft no. 1 (Berlin: Lit Verlag, 2012), 15–45.

45. The story of the nun and the lettuce was reported by Gregorius the Great in his *Dialogues*, I, 4.7; paraphrases can be found in Angenendt, "Liturgie und Organisation des Kirchlichen Lebens," 189–190, and Alain Boureau, *Satan the Heretic: The Birth of Demonology in the Medieval West*, trans. Teresa Lavender Fagan (Chicago: University of Chicago Press, 2006), 94.

46. Cohn, *Europe's Inner Demons*, 234; according to Françoise Lavocat, "L'Arcadie diabolique: La fiction poétique dans le débat sur la sorcellerie (XVIe–XVIIe siècles)," in *Fictions du Diable: Démonologie et littérature de saint Augustin à Léo Taxil*, ed. Françoise Lavocat, Pierre Kapitaniak, and Marianne Closson (Geneva: Librairie Droz, 2007), 57–84, there 62–67. Augustine of Hippo was the first author to identify Pan and the satyrs with incubi and succubi.

47. *Mariken van Nieumegen: Ingeleid en toegelicht door Dirk Coigneau* ('s-Gravenhage: Martinus Nijhoff, 1982), 71, line 212; see also 67 and 153. On the eye of Odin, see Kershaw, *One-eyed God*.

48. Richard Kieckhefer, *European Witch Trials: Their Foundations in Popular and Learned Culture, 1300–1500* (Berkeley: University of California Press, 1976), 39.

49. The Essenes, in particular, adhered to a stark demonization of other Jews; see Pagels, "The Social History of Satan," 127. In this article, and her later monograph, *The Origin of Satan* (London: Penguin, 1996), Pagels makes the intriguing suggestion that the concept of Satan *itself* owed its flourishing in Judeo-Christian religion to this application to the "intimate enemies" within the own creedal community.

50. Russell, *Prince of Darkness*, 55.

51. I owe the reference to the Paulicians to Carlo Ginzburg, *Ecstasies: Deciphering the Witches' Sabbath*, trans. Raymond Rosenthal (London: Hutchinson Radius, 1990), 75.

52. "Gesta Synodi Aurelianensis an. MXXII, adversus novus Manicheos," in Bénédictins de la Congrégation de S. Maur (eds.), *Recueil des Historiens des Gaules et de la France* X (Paris: Gabriel Martin, H. L. Guerin & L. F. Delatour, Antoine Boudet, 1760), 536–539, there 538. See also M. Guérard, *Cartulaire de l'abbaye de St.-Père de Chartres*, Collection des Cartulaires de France, no. 1 (Paris: Imprimerie de Crapelet, 1840), 1:108–115 and 1:cciv-ccvi. A German translation of the text can be found in Zacharias, *Satanskult und Schwarze Messe*, 49–50.

53. Felix, *Octavius*, ix.2–7, quoted in Tertullian, *Apology. De Spectaculis*, 337–339. See also Tertullian's sarcastic refutation of these accusations in his *Apology*: Tertullian, *Apology. De Spectaculis*, 10–11, 36–38, 42–47 (*Apology*, II.5, VII.1–5, VIII).

54. Frankfurter, *Evil Incarnate*, 107–128.

55. Cohn, *Europe's Inner Demons*, 1–17, 56, covers the background of the pagan accusations and their Christian reapplication in some depth. Already in 1760, the Benedictines who edited the *Recueil des Historiens des Gaules et de la France* noticed these great resemblances, remarking in a footnote: "Hæc narratio, & calumniæ quibus appebantur primi Christiani, quamdam similitudinem inter se habent. Imitando numquid unum ad altero expressum?" Bénédictins de la Congrégation de S. Maur, *Recueil des Historiens des Gaules* X, 538n.

56. Frankfurter, *Evil Incarnate*, 107.

57. Martyr, *First Apology*, xxvi, English translation by Roberts and Donaldson. The passage refers to the followers of Simon Magus, probably a Gnostic group.

58. Augustine of Hippo, *On the Morals of the Manichæans* and *Concerning the Nature of Good, against the Manichæans*, in *Nicene and Post-Nicene Fathers*, ed. Phillip Schaff, transl. Richard Stothert and Albert H. Newman (Edinburgh: T&T Clark, 1887), first series, 4:86–89, 4:364.

59. Epiphanius of Salamis, *The Panarion: Book I (Sects 1-46)*, trans. Frank Williams, Nag Hammadi Studies, no. 35 (Leiden: Brill, 1987), 85–86 [26, 4, 2–5, 7].

60. Frank Williams, in his introduction to Epiphanius of Salamis's *Panarion*, xxi, considers the idea that all Gnostics were "sexual libertines" a "judgement of unlikely accuracy," but he does not exclude the possibility that there may be some kernel of truth in Epiphanius's description: "In all probability libertine Gnostics were a minority." Stephen Benko, in "The Libertine Gnostic Sect of the Phibionites According to Epiphanus," *Vigilæ Christianæ* 21 (1967): 103–119, there 114, is also inclined to put faith in these rumors, while Christoph Markschies, *Die Gnosis* (München: Beck, 2001), 110–112, remains skeptical. Roelof van den Broek, in "Sexuality and Sexual Symbolism in Hermetic and Gnostic Thought and Practice (Second–Fourth Centuries)," in *Hidden Intercourse: Eros and Sexuality in the History of Western Esotericism*, ed. Wouter J. Hanegraaff and Jeffrey J. Kripal (Leiden: Brill, 2008), 1–21, there 16–17, believes sexual rites may indeed have been going on but that the more gory details with Epiphanius result from "the same mixture of truth, hearsay, misunderstanding and sheer slander that so often characterizes his anti-heretical polemics."

61. Jong, *Traditions of the Magi*, 424–432; Bruce M. Knauft, "Bodily Images in Melanesia: Cultural Substances and Natural Metaphors," in *Fragments for a History of the Human Body*, ed. Michel Feher (New York: Urzone, 1989) 3:198–279; Hugh B. Urban, "Magia Sexualis: Sex, Secrecy, and Liberation in Modern Western Esotericism," *Journal of the American Academy of Religion* 72 (September 2004) 3:695–731.

62. On the Ophites, see Jean-Daniel Kaestli, "L'interprétation du serpent de Genèse 3 dans quelques textes gnostiques et la question de la gnose 'Ophite,' " in *Gnosticisme et monde hellénistique: Actes du colloque de Louvain-la-Neuve (11–14 mars 1980)*, ed. Julien Ries, Publications de l'Institut Orientaliste de Louvain, no. 27 (Louvain: Université Catholique de Louvain, Institut Orientaliste, 1982), 116–130.

63. Schmidt, *Satanismus*, 32 ("Tatsächlich spielt Satan in den gnostischen Lehren keine Rolle, ja in den meisten Systemen wird er nich einmal erwähnt"), and Faxneld, *Satanic Feminism*, 65–66, reach similar conclusions.

64. Epiphanius of Salamis, *The Panarion: Book II and III (Sects 47–80, De Fide)*, trans. Frank Williams, Nag Hammadi Studies, no. 36 (Leiden: Brill, 1994), 630–631 [80, 3, 1]. The Greek text uses the designation "Σατανιανοί" for these people (Epiphanius of Salamis, *S.P.N. Epiphanii, Constantiae in Cypro episcope, opera quae repriri potuera omnia*, 3 vols., Patrologiae Cursus Completus. Patrologiae Graecae no. 41–43 [Paris: J.-P. Migne, 1863], 1:164), with the variant "Σατανιανους" later on (ibid., 2:760). Frank Williams translated this as "Satanists" in *Panarion: Book I*, 5 [Proem I, 4,8], and as "Satanians" in the sections quoted. The Latin translation in the Patrologiae Graecae shows a similar confusion, using "Satanici" in the Proem (Epiphanius of Salamis, *Epiphanii opera omnia*, 1:163) and "Satanianos" in Epiphanius's description in book III (ibid., 2:759).

65. Epiphanius of Salamis, *Panarion: Book II and III*, 631 [80, 3, 2].

66. Epiphanius of Salamis, *Panarion: Book II and III*, 631 [80, 3, 3].

67. Epiphanius of Salamis, *Panarion: Book I*, 5 [Proem I, 4,8].

68. Cf. Alexander Patschovsky, "Der Ketzer als Teufelsdiener," in *Papsttum, Kirche und Recht im Mittelalter: Festschrift für Horst Fuhrmann zum 65. Geburtstag*, ed. Hubert Mordek (Tübingen: Max Niemeyer Verlag, 1991), 317–334; Cohn, *Europe's Inner Demons*, 18–31; Ginzburg, *Ecstasies*, 73–78. The whole complex of accusations could also appear without the Satanist element, as would be the case with the persecutions of the lepers in 1321; see Ginzburg, *Ecstasies*, 33–63.

69. For a glimpse of the historiographic problems that confront the historian here, see the articles in the volume edited by Monique Zerner, *Inventer l'hérésie? Discours polémiques et pouvoirs avant l'Inquisition* (Nice: Z'éditions, 1998), as well as Daniela Müller, "Les historiens et la question de la vérité historique: L'église cathare a-t-elle existé?," in *1209–2009, Cathares: Une histoire à pacifier? Actes du colloque international tenue à Mazamet les 15, 16 et 17 mai 2009*, ed. Anne Brenon (Portet-sur-Garonne: Nouvelles Éditions Loubatières, 2010), 139–154.

70. Daniela Müller, "Gott und seine zwei Frauen: Der Teufel bei den Katharern," *@KIH-eSkript. Interdisziplinäre Hexenforschung online* 3 (2011) 1:69–76, at http://www.historicum. net/no_cache/persistent/artikel/9107 (accessed 14 December 2011).

71. Michel Rubellin, "Au temps où Valdès n'était pas hérétique: Hypothèse sur le rôle de Valdès à Lyon (1170–1183)," in *Inventer l'hérésie? Discours polémiques et pouvoirs avant l'Inquisition*, ed. Monique Zerner (Nice: Z'éditions, 1998), 193–218.

72. Cf. Joshua Trachtenberg, *The Devil and the Jews: The Medieval Conception of the Jew and Its Relation to Modern Anti-Semitism* (Philadelphia: Jewish Publication Society of America, 1961), 21.

73. Léon Poliakov, *Histoire de l'antisémitisme: Du Christ aux Juifs de cour* (Paris: Calmann-Lévy, 1955), 140–171; Trachtenberg, *Devil and the Jews*, 26, 64–71, 115, 125–139, 181.

74. Raymond Martin, *Pugio Fidei*, XIV.19, cited in Syds Wiersma's forthcoming dissertation on this Spanish priest.

75. Cited in Haag, *Teufelsglaube*, 482.

76. Stephan de Bourbon, cited in Herbert Grundmann, "Der Typus des Ketzers in Mittelalterlicher Anschauung," in *Kultur- und Universalgeschichte. Walter Goetz zu seinem 60. Geburtstage dargebracht von Fachgenossen, Freunden und Schülern* (Leipzig: B. G. Teubner 1927), 91–107, there 97; see also 102. Grundmann's groundbreaking article, though already old, is still highly illuminating in many ways. For a more recent treatment, see Daniela Müller, "Our Image of 'Others' and Our Own Identity," in van Asselt et al., *Iconoclasm and Iconoclash*, 107–123, and Hans-Werner Goetz, "Was wird im frühen Mittelalter unter 'Häresie' verstanden? Zur Häresiewahrnehmung des Hrabanus Maurus," in Aurast and Goetz, *Die Wahrnehmung anderer Religionen in früheren Mittelalter*, 47–88.

77. Grundmann, "Typus des Ketzers," 98.

78. "Gestorum Treverorum Continuatio IV," in *Monumenta Germaniae Historica inde ab Anno Christi quingentesimo usque ad annum millesimum et quintegentesimum. Scriptorum* (Hannoverae: Impensis Bibliopolii Hahniani, 1879), 24:401 and 24:401n. On Lucardis, see Daniela Müller, *Frauen vor der Inquisition: Lebensform, Glaubenszeugnis und Aburteilung der deutschen und französischen Katharerinnen*, Veröffentlichungen des Instituts für Europäische Geschichte Mainz, no. 166 (Mainz: Von Zabern, 1996), 46–47 and 219–222.

79. Pope Gregorius IX, "Vox in Rama," in *Monumenta Germaniae Historica inde ab Anno Christi quingentesimo usque ad annum millesimum et quintegentesimum. Epistolae Saeculi XIII e Regestis Pontifcum Romanorum selectae*, ed. G. H. Pertz and Carolus Rodenberg (Berolini: Apud Weidmannos, 1883), 1:432–434, there 1:433, ll. 8–44. Gregorius's description of the practices of the Luciferians, it must be noted, is derived almost verbatim from a letter sent to him by Conrad of Marburg.

80. Dietrich Kurze, "Zur Ketzergeschichte der Mark Brandenburg und Pommerns vornehm-lich im 14. Jahrhundert," *Jahrbuch für die Geschichte Mittel- und Ostdeutschlands* 16–17 (1968): 50–94, there 93. The formula is transmitted in the German vernacular: "Lucifer, leve herre, gyf ime gut vnde ere, dyt kynt daz sal ewek dyn wessen mit libe vnde sele."

81. Cohn, *Europe's Inner Demons*, 31–33, 56; Kieckhefer, *European Witch Trials*, 15. Some historians (Grundmann, "Typus des Ketzers," 105n) maintain that the whole heresy of Luciferianism was an invention suggested by the Late-Antique Luciferians. These had nothing to do with the devil, but were followers of Lucifer of Cagliari, a fourth-century bishop declared heterodox because of his extreme hardline views on the reacceptance of former Arians into the Catholic Church. An in-depth modern coverage of the (medieval) Luciferians is still lacking.

82. Kurze, "Zur Ketzergeschichte der Mark Brandenburg," 50–94.

83. The historical interaction between demonizing rhetorics and (institutional) violence still deserves further study: see Miri Rubin, *Gentile Tales: The Narrative Assault on Late-Medieval Jews* (New Haven, CT: Yale University Press, 1999), for an exemplary treatment of this question with regard to the late medieval rumors of Jewish host desecration.

84. John of Damascus, *Writings*, trans. Frederic H. Chase, Jr. (New York: Fathers of the Church, 1958), 338. Augustine of Hippo already spoke of the "few pagans that remain" in his later sermons and described them as convening clandestinely in secret hideouts, continuously in fear of police infiltrators in civil disguise. Cited in Anne-Isabelle Bouton-Toubolic, "Le *De diuinatione daemonum* de Saint Augustin," in Lavocat et al., *Fictions du Diable*, 15–34, there 15–21(n). On the persecution and assimilation of paganism in the Christian Empire, see Ramsay MacMullen, *Christianity and Paganism in the Fourth and Eight Centuries* (New Haven, CT: Yale University Press, 1997), who notes that by 450 "the legal system became wholly an instrument of persecution" against pagans (30).

85. On this subject, see Marie Theres Fögen, *Die Enteignung des Wahrsager: Studien zum kaiserlichen Wissensmonopol in der Spätantike* (Frankfurt am Main: Suhrkamp, 1997). This monopolization attempt was also the background of Diocletian's persecution of Manicheans and Christians and his legislature against astrologers and magicians.

86. R. I. Moore, *The Formation of a Persecuting Society: Power and Deviance in Western Europe, 950–1250* (Oxford: Basil Blackwell, 1987), 12; Daniela Müller, "Aspekte der Ketzerverfolgung unter den römischen Kaisern bis Justinian," *Journal of Eastern Christian Studies* 60 (2008) 1–4:175–193, there 182.

87. Müller, "Aspekte der Ketzerverfolgung," 181(n), 182–183.

88. Müller, "Aspekte der Ketzerverfolgung," 186–190.

89. Moore, *Formation of a Persecuting Society*, 12–13; Müller, "Aspekte der Ketzerverfolgung," 187–188.

90. Müller, "Aspekte der Ketzerverfolgung," 191, citing Beck, *Actus Fidei*, 43. Ecclesiastical authorities in the East proved significantly less inclined to legitimize the use of force against

religious opponents. When, in the ninth century, the Byzantine emperor issued an edict sentencing the Paulicians to death, Abbot Theodore of the Studiu monastery protested vehemently and successfully, arguing that execution made it impossible for heretics to convert; rather, one should admonish them and pray for them.

91. Moore, *Formation of a Persecuting Society*, 15–16; Müller, "Aspekte der Ketzerverfolgung," 188–189; Patschovsky, "Ketzer als Teufelsdiener," 319–320. It is clear that their identification as Manichees was mere pretext. In reality, they probably adhered to a neo-Platonic form of Christian asceticism; this was only a subsidiary circumstance anyway, as the true ground for their conviction lay in a conflict between local rulers regarding the control of the bishopric.

92. Müller, "Our Image of 'Others,'" 13.

93. Nora Berend, *At the Gate of Christendom: Jews, Muslims and "Pagans" in Medieval Hungary, c. 1000–c. 1300* (Cambridge, UK: Cambridge University Press, 2001), 43. Cf. pages 42–53 of this publication for more information regarding the *christianitas* concept.

94. Moore, *Formation of a Persecuting Society*, 7.

95. Moore, *Formation of a Persecuting Society*, 7–8.

96. "Gestorum Treverorum," in *Monumenta Germaniae Historica. Scriptorum*, 24:400–401. In a typical medieval twist, the chronicle also adds that many real heretics gave themselves up to the inquisitors by pretending to be penitent and then falsely reporting "Catholics and innocents."

97. Cohn, *Europe's Inner Demons*, 24–29.

98. Patschovsky, "Der Ketzer als Teufelsdiener," 326.

99. Moore, *Formation of a Persecuting Society*, 36–37.

100. Moore, *Formation of a Persecuting Society*, 27–45; Wiersma, forthcoming.

101. On Gregorius VII, see Müller, "Our Image of 'Others,'" 111.

102. Frankfurter, *Evil Incarnate*, 7.

103. A striking illustration of this idea can be found in Gary K. Waite, *Eradicating the Devil's Minions: Anabaptists and Witches in Reformation Europe, 1525–1600* (Toronto: University of Toronto Press, 2007), 257n, who mentions a stained-glass window commissioned in Nuremberg in 1598 that depicted a Jew about to stab a child while a witch assists him.

104. Scholarly publications about witchcraft could currently fill a small library. For my treatment of witchcraft, I have particularly drawn on the following authors: Cohn, *Europe's Inner Demons*, and Kieckhefer, *European Witch Trials*, as well as articles in the volumes *Early Modern European Witchcraft: Center and Peripheries*, ed. Bengt Ankarloo and Gustav Hennigsen (Oxford: Clarendon, 1990), and *Palgrave Advances in Witchcraft Historiography*, ed. Jonathan Barry and Owen Davies (Houndmills, UK: Palgrave Macmillan, 2007). For additional insights, Boureau, *Satan the Heretic*, and Waite, *Eradicating the Devil's Minions*, proved invaluable. Also useful was the concise overview by Michaela Valente, "Witchcraft (15th–17th Centuries)," in *Dictionary of Gnosis and Western Esotericism*, ed. Wouter J. Hanegraaff, 2 vols. (Leiden: Brill, 2005), 2:1174–1177.

105. See, among others, Waite, *Eradicating the Devil's Minions*, 17, 34–35.

106. Bengt Ankarloo, "Introduction," in Ankarloo and Hennigsen, *Early Modern European Witchcraft*, 1–15, there 12; Robert Muchembled, *A History of the Devil: From the Middle Ages to the Present* (Cambridge, UK: Polity, 2003), 148.

107. Waite, *Eradicating the Devil's Minions*, 15. For some glimpses of the harsh realities of the witch persecutions, see Cohn, *Europe's Inner Demons*, 90; Robert Muchembled, "Satanic

Myths and Cultural Reality," in Ankarloo and Hennigsen, *Early Modern European Witchcraft*, 139–160, 143. Thousands of cats were burned at the stake as diabolical agents as well (cf. Müller, "Our Image of 'Others,' " 114).

108. Julio Caro Baroja, "Witchcraft and Catholic Theology," in Ankarloo and Hennigsen, *Early Modern European Witchcraft*, 19–43, particularly 34–35. John Tedeschi has devoted much of his scholarly career to rehabilitating the Roman Inquisition from the Black Legend that surrounds it; see, for instance, his article in the same volume, "Inquisitorial Law and the Witch," 83–118.

109. Frankfurter, *Evil Incarnate*, 21.

110. But see Fögen, *Die Enteignung des Wahrsager*, for the specific background behind this.

111. Cohn, *Europe's Inner Demons*, 208. Incidentally, Charlemagne also decreed that those found guilty of sorcery "should be turned over to the Church as slaves, while those who sacrificed to the Devil (i.e., the Germanic gods) should be killed"; Richard Kieckhefer, *Magic in the Middle Ages* (Cambridge, UK: Cambridge University Press, 1990), 179.

112. Boureau, *Satan the Heretic*, 12; Kieckhefer, *European Witch Trials*, 39. These ideas can be found with many earlier Christian authors, for instance, Epiphanius of Salamis, *Panarion: Book I*, 94.

113. Kieckhefer, *European Witch Trials*, 20–22.

114. Epiphanius of Salamis, *Panarion: Book I*, 101, regarding the Carpocratians.

115. Poliakov, *Histoire de l'antisémitisme*, 166.

116. Boureau, *Satan the Heretic*, especially 14–15, 54–67, 203.

117. Waite, *Eradicating the Devil's Minions*, 11–12; Wolfgang Behringer, "How Waldensians Became Witches: Heretics and Their Journey to the Other World," in *Communicating with the Spirits*, ed. Gabor Klaniczay, Eva Pócs, et al. (Budapest: Central European University Press, 2005), 155–192.

118. Kurze, "Zur Ketzergeschichte der Mark Brandenburg," 60.

119. Nicolaus Jaquerius, *Flagellum Haereticorum Fascinariorum* (Francofurti ad Moenum: [Nic. Bassaeus], 1581), 41 [chapter 7].

120. Jaquerius, *Flagellum Haereticorum Fascinariorum*, 36–51; Henricus Institoris and Jacobus Sprengerus, *Malleus Maleficarum*, ed. and trans. Christopher S. Mackay, 2 vols. (Cambridge, UK: Cambridge University Press, 2006), 2:44–54 (I Qu. I). Cf. 2:71–72 (I Qu. 2).

121. An extensive discussion of this transformation can be found in Boureau, *Satan the Heretic*. See also Kieckhefer, *European Witch Trials*, 18–19.

122. Muchembled, "Satanic Myths and Cultural Reality"; Marko Nenonen, "Culture Wars: State, Religion and Popular Culture in Europe, 1400–1800," in Barry and Davies, *Palgrave Advances in Witchcraft Historiography*, 108–124. Compare Frankfurter, *Evil Incarnate*, 211.

123. Waite, *Eradicating the Devil's Minions*, 19, 63, 199–202.

124. Trachtenberg, *Devil and the Jews*, 201.

125. Waite, *Eradicating the Devil's Minions*, 187–189. On "spontaneous" violence against sorcerers, see also Kieckhefer, *Magic in the Middle Ages*, 188.

126. Waite, *Eradicating the Devil's Minions*, 196–197. See also Gustav Henningsen, " 'The Ladies from Outside': An Archaic Pattern of the Witches' Sabbath," in Ankarloo and Hennigsen, *Early Modern European Witchcraft*, 191–215; and Cohn, *Europe's Inner Demons*, xii, 209–216.

127. Ginzburg, *Ecstasies*. Peter Burke, "The Comparative Approach to European Witchcraft," in Ankarloo and Hennigsen, *Early Modern European Witchcraft*, 435–441 (there 441), summarizes the matter with exceeding clarity: "Behind the diabolical witchcraft of the witch-hunters has been discovered a more traditional, neighbourly witchcraft. Behind this in turn we are seeing glimpses of a still more archaic, shamanistic witchcraft."

128. On the standard interrogatories that were sometimes used by the judicial authorities, see Kieckhefer, *European Witch Trials*, 91.

129. Carlo Ginzburg, *The Night Battles: Witchcraft and Agrarian Cults in the Sixteenth and Seventeenth Centuries* (Baltimore, MD: Johns Hopkins University Press, 1983).

130. Waite, *Eradicating the Devil's Minions*, 180.

131. Margaret Alice Murray, *The Witch Cult in Western Europe* (Oxford: Clarendon, 1962), and *The God of the Witches* (London: Faber and Faber, 1956). Cf. Cohn, *Europe's Inner Demons*, 103–125, for an overview of the roots in earlier historiography of her theories.

132. Cf. Carlo Ginzburg, "Deciphering the Sabbath," in Ankarloo and Hennigsen, *Early Modern European Witchcraft*, 121–137, especially 131.

133. Muchembled, *History of the Devil*, 35. Cf. Ankarloo, "Introduction," 13; his description of the Church's demonology as "the other side of the missionary message" seems to me particularly well chosen.

134. See, for instance, Juhan Kahk, "Estonia II: The Crusade against Idolatry," in Ankarloo and Hennigsen, *Early Modern European Witchcraft*, 273–284; Antero Heikkinen and Timo Kervinen, "Finland: The Male Domination," in ibid., 319–338; and Kirsten Hastrup, "Iceland: Sorcerers and Paganism," in ibid., 383–401. In the case of the Swedish Saami, it was precisely the equation of paganism with sorcery that seemed to have spared them for witchcraft persecutions. Saami were frequently employed by Swedish farmers as magical specialists, and their reputation in this profession was such that local authorities seldom dared to prosecute them for sorcery. Cf. Gunlög Fur, *Colonialism in the Margins: Cultural Encounters in New Sweden and Lapland* (Leiden: Brill, 2006), 85.

135. Jaquerius, *Flagellum Haereticorum Fascinariorum*, 36. For medieval ideas about Satan and demons, see Peter Dinzelbacher, "Die Realität des Teufels im Mittelalter," in *Der Hexenhammer: Entstehung und Umfeld des Malleus maleficarum von 1487*, ed. Peter Segl (Köln: Böhlau, 1988), 151–175.

136. Robert Lowland, " 'Fantasticall and Devilishe Persons': European Witch-beliefs in Comparative Perspective," in Ankarloo and Hennigsen, *Early Modern European Witchcraft*, 161–190, especially 166; Richard van Dülmen, "Imaginationen des Teuflischen. Nächtliche Zusammenkunfte, Hexentänze, Teufelssabbate," in *Hexenwelten: Magie und Imagination*, ed. Richard van Dülmen (Frankfurt am Main: Fischer Taschenbuch Verlag, 1987), 94–130. The "reversed" nature of the Sabbath is illustrated in a particularly vivid way by the seventeenth-century demonologist Pierre de Lancre in his *Tableau de l'inconstance des mauvais anges et démons, où il est amplement tracté des Sorciers, & de la Sorcellerie* (Paris: Nicolas Buon, 1613); see particularly the "Advertissement." Further contemporary accounts of the Sabbath, along with a German translation, can be found in Zacharias, *Satanskult und Schwarze Messe*, 56–62, 61–82, 95–96.

137. Scholarship on the history of medieval and early modern "black arts" is still in a pioneering phase. For this section, I mainly relied on the two books by Richard Kieckhefer, *Magic in the*

Middle Ages, and *Forbidden Rites: A Necromancer's Manual of the Fifteenth Century* (University Park: Pennsylvania State University Press, 1998), as well as on the articles and texts in *Conjuring Spirits: Texts and Traditions of Medieval Ritual Magic*, ed. Claire Fanger, Magic in History, no. 4 (Thrupp, UK: Sutton, 1998). Still useful as well is the classic book by Lynn Thorndike, *A History of Magic and Experimental Science during the First Thirteen Centuries of Our Era* (1932; repr., New York: Columbia University Press, 1964). For the evolution of Roman Catholic views on magic during the Middle Ages, Boureau, *Satan the Heretic*, again proved valuable.

On the subject of the Black Mass, serious historiography is even scarcer. Henry T. F. Rhodes, *The Satanic Mass: A Sociological and Criminological Study* (London: Rider, 1955), is still often quoted as an authoritative work on the matter, but the scholarship in this book is seriously outdated and inaccurate. Massimo Introvigne gives much information on this legendary ritual strewn through the pages of his *Enquête sur le Satanisme*; however, I disagree with his assertions on several important points, as will be made clear presently. The best introduction on the subject might be the eight-page appendix that Gareth J. Medway devotes to the Black Mass in *Lure of the Sinister*, 380–388; his conclusions here are largely congruent with those that I have reached in this section.

138. On this discussion, see Wouter J. Hanegraaff, *New Age Religion and Western Culture: Esotericism in the Mirror of Secular Thought* (Leiden: Brill, 1996), 79–85. Hanegraaff himself dismisses the juxtaposition of magic and religion, concurring instead with the views expressed on this subject by the Dutch scholar of religions J. van Baal (see the latter's "Magic as a Religious Phenomenon," *Higher Education and Research in the Netherlands* 7 [1963]: 3–4, 10–21).

139. Kieckhefer, *Magic in the Middle Ages*, 152.

140. Claire Fanger, "Medieval Ritual Magic: What It Is and Why We Need to Know More about It," in Fanger, *Conjuring Spirits*, vii–xviii, there vi.

141. Institoris, *Malleus Maleficarum*, 2:225 [II, Introd. Qu.].

142. Cf. Boureau, *Satan the Heretic*, in particular, 14–15, 54–67.

143. On pre-Christian campaigns against magic by the Roman emperors, see again Fögen, *Die Enteignung des Wahrsager*.

144. See Hagit Amirav, "The Application of Magical Formulas of Invocation in Christian Contexts," in Vos and Otten, *Demons and the Devil in Ancient and Medieval Christianity*, 117–127, who extensively discusses this passage and also highlights magical elements within early Christianity itself.

145. I have consulted Amphiliochos of Cappadocia's *Life of Basilius* in the Latin translation from Herbert Rosweyde, *Vitae Patrum: De Vita et Verbis Seniorvm sive Historiæ Eremiticæ Libri X. Avctoribus fuis et Nitori pristino restituti, ac Notationibvs illustrati, Operâ et studio Heriberti Ros-Weydi Vltraiectini, e Soc. Iesu Theologi* (Antverpiæ: Ex officina Platiniana, 1628), 156.

146. Rosweyde, *Vitae Patrum*, 157.

147. An overview can be found in Frick, *Satan und Die Satanisten*, 2:52–81, and Michael Siefener, "Der Teufel als Vertragspartner," *@KIH-eSkript: Interdisziplinäre Hexenforschung online* 3 (2011) 1:61–68, at https://www.historicum.net/themen/hexenforschung/akih-eskript/heft-3-2011/artikel/Der_Teufel_als_Vertragspartner/ (accessed 14 January 2012). Medway, *Lure of the Sinister*, 58, suggests that the idea of the pact could have been derived from oaths to the pagan gods, which were sometimes also written out on parchment.

148. On the profilation and original text places of the Theophilus story, see George Webbe Dasent, *Theophilus in Icelandic, Low German and other tongues: From M.S.S. in The Royal Library, Stockholm* (London: William Pickering, 1895).

149. Boureau, *Satan the Heretic*, 68–92. The views of Thomas Aquinas on magic can be found, among other places, in his *Summa Theologica*, 2, 2.95.3, as well as in his *Commentary on Pronouncements*, 2, 7. Aquinas partly based his views on similar ideas by Augustine of Hippo; see the latter's *Christian Doctrine*, 2.19–21 and 2.23.

150. Robert Mathiesen, "A Thirteenth-Century Ritual to Attain the Beatific Vision from the *Sworn Book* of Honorius of Thebes," in Fanger, *Conjuring Spirits*, 143–162, there 147; Russell, *Lucifer*, 80–84, 293.

151. Thorndike, *History of Magic*, 2:283–285; Mathiesen, "A Thirteenth-Century Ritual to Attain the Beatific Vision"; Richard Kiekhefer, "The Devil's Contemplatives: The Liber Iuratus, the Liber Visionum and the Christian Appropriation of Jewish Occultism," in Fanger, *Conjuring Spirits*, 250–265. Mathiesen dates the *Liber Juratus* to the thirteenth century, probably during the pontificate of Gregory IX, while Thorndike, Cohn, and Kiekhefer assign it to the fourteenth century (145–147).

152. Mathiesen, "A Thirteenth-Century Ritual to Attain the Beatific Vision," 147–150; Thorndike, *History of Magic*, 283–285.

153. *Mariken van Nieumegen*, 73–74 [lines 254–256]: "Cost si nighermancie . . . , tware om mi te bedwinghen alst haer paste." A medieval English edition of this play was republished in 1932: Harry Morgan Ayres and Adriaan Jacob Barnouw (eds.), *Mary of Nimmegen: A Facsimile Reproduction of the Copy of the English Version in the Huntington Library* (Cambridge, MA: Harvard University Press, 1932). For a modern English translation, see E. Colledge, *Mediaeval Netherlands Religious Literature* (Leiden: Sythoff, 1965).

154. For a specimen of angelic magic, see Nicholas Watson, "John the Monk's *Book of Visions of The Blessed and Undefiled Virgin Mary, Mother of God*: Two Versions of a Newly Discovered Ritual Magic Text," in Fanger, *Conjuring Spirits*, 163–249.

155. This was precisely the reason, it has been suggested, that the book was considered one of the most abject of its kind by ecclesiastical dignitaries: see Mathiesen, "A Thirteenth-Century Ritual to Attain the Beatific Vision," 158.

156. Kieckhefer, "Devil's Contemplatives," 255.

157. See particularly Kieckhefer, *Forbidden Rites*; W. Braekman, *Magische experimenten en toverpraktijken uit een middelnederlands handschrift* (Ghent: Seminarie voor Volkskunde, 1966); Juris G. Lidaka, "*The Book of Angels, Rings, Characters and Images of the Planets*: Attributed to Osbern Bokinham," in Fanger, *Conjuring Spirits*, 32–63—all of which contain complete transcriptions and/or translations of medieval necromantic texts.

158. An instance of invoking Satan is cited from a fifteenth-century *grimoire* in Kieckhefer, *Forbidden Rites*, 276–286, and in Lidaka, "*The Book of Angels*," 54–55. Later necromantic handbooks also confirm the picture sketched above: for instance, the anonymous *Gremoire du Pape Honorius: Avec un recueil des plus rares secrets* from 1670 (repr., Paris: Éditions Bussière, 2012), which contains amidst much general piety a rather matter-of-fact conjuration of Lucifer "par le Dieu vivant, par le Dieu vrai, par le Dieu saint par le Dieu qui a dit, et tout a été fait" (34–35). This grimoire was still reprinted during the eighteenth century as *Grimoire du Pape Honorius, avec un recueil des plus rares secrets* (Rome [Lille]: Imprimerie Du Blocquel, 1760). Norman

Cohn was of a similar opinion—cf. his *Europe's Inner Demons*, 193 and 169: "Nowhere, in the surviving books of magic, is there a hint of Satanism."

159. See, for instance, Lidaka, "*The Book of Angels*," 54–55, 61–63.

160. Kieckhefer, *Forbidden Rites*, 3.

161. Kieckhefer, *Forbidden Rites*, 35, also 4.

162. Kieckhefer, *Forbidden Rites*, 15, 26, 131, 157. Frank Klaassen, "English Manuscripts of Magic, 1300–1500: A Preliminary Survey," in Fanger, *Conjuring Spirits*, 3–31, there 20, cites a medieval magical manuscript that claims that Christians are better magicians than pagans and Jews because the operators of the latter groups "are nott signed with the sign of god, that is to saye with the signe of the crosse therefore they spirites will nott answere them trewly."

163. Introvigne, "Satanism," 1035. It must be pointed out that there is also a Roman Catholic liturgy called Missa Negra, which is a private Mass for a deceased person, with the ministering priest wearing black vestments. It is seldom celebrated and obviously must not be confused with the other type of Missa Negra we are discussing here (see Elliot Rose, *A Razor for a Goat: A Discussion of Certain Problems in the History of Witchcraft and Diabolism* [Toronto: University of Toronto Press, 1989], 35).

164. Piero Camporesi, "The Consecrated Host: A Wondrous Excess," in *Fragments for a History of the Human Body*, ed. Michel Feher (New York: Urzone, 1990), 1:220–237.

165. Braekman, *Magische experimenten en toverpraktijken*, 14. Similar practices are mentioned in Kieckhefer, *Magic in the Middle Ages*, 58; Robert Mandrou, *Magistrats et sorciers en France au XVIIe siècle: Une analyse de psychologie historique* (Paris: Éditions du Seuil, 1980), 497; and Dieter Harmening. *Superstitio: Überlieferungs- und theoriegeschichtliche Untersuchungen zur kirchlich-theologischen Aberglaubensliteratur des Mittelalters* (Berlin: Erich Schmidt Verlag, 1979), 22–24.

166. Braekman, *Magische experimenten en toverpraktijken*, 14–15.

167. Kieckhefer, "Devil's Contemplatives," 261.

168. Cf. D. P. Walker, *Spiritual and Demonic Magic from Ficino to Campanella* (London: Warburg Institute, 1958), 90–95, 151. Playful forms of inverted liturgy, it must be noted, were not unknown in the Middle Ages. In some churches, carnivalesque parodies of normal religious services were performed each year on New Year's Eve. Priests and clergy would dress up, dance, sing scurrilous songs, play at celebrating Mass, incense the building with fetid fumes from an old shoe, jump around, and make obscene gestures and jokes. Although this behavior was greatly deplored by the Paris Faculty of Theology, to whose indignation we owe much of our knowledge of these revelries, it is nowhere suggested that this parody of liturgy encompasses the abrogation of Jesus and the adoration of Satan. (The description of the Paris Faculty of Theology, dating from 1444, can be found in J. P. Migne [ed.], *Patrologiae cursus completus* [Paris: Siroune, 1800–1875], Series Latina 207:1169–1176; see especially 207:1171.)

169. Waite, *Eradicating the Devil's Minions*, 168–169. There are some historical cases in which Anabaptist Christians trampled or dispersed the host, the adoration of which they considered as demonic idolatry.

170. Institoris, *Malleus Maleficarum*, 117. See also the translator Montague Summers on this subject in his introduction, xxvi.

171. Madeleine Bavent, *The Confessions of Madeleine Bavent*, trans. Montague Summers (London: Fortune, 1933), 18, 48–49, 103–104.

172. Cf., for instance, Robert Mandrou, *Possession et sorcellerie au XVIIe siècle: Textes inédits* (Paris: Librairie Arthème Fayard, 1979), 24–25; Rhodes, *Satanic Mass*, 61–63; Zacharias, *Satanskult und Schwarze Messe*, 56–62. According to Mandrou, *Magistrats et sorciers*, 79, "tout sabbat . . . comporte quelque cérémonie de messe inversée."

173. Mandrou, *Magistrats et sorciers*, 202. Lancre, *Tableau de l'inconstance des mauvais anges*, "Advertissement," also mentions priests who were accused of having said Mass at the Sabbath.

174. Medway, *Lure of the Sinister*, 380–388, is of the same opinion.

175. Among these historians we find Rhodes, *Satanic Mass*, 15, 51–57. Rhodes's book is not striking for its critical appraisal of historical sources, however, and his claims about medieval Missae Negrae are entirely based on the work of the nineteenth-century French historian Jules Michelet, whose creative reconstruction of history is discussed more fully in chapter 3. Rose, in *A Razor for a Goat*, 160–170, propounds the theory that wandering scholars during the High Middle Ages took over surviving nuclei of paganism and introduced the Black Mass "as an improvement," while organizing their followers in covens "partly in mockery" of the model of the friars. This is also supposed to be the origin of the witch cult. Unfortunately this interesting hypothesis is presented without a shred of evidence. The opinions of Massimo Introvigne and Karl Frick on this subject are discussed more extensively in the next section.

176. For the historical facts concerning the Affair of the Poisons, I have relied primarily on Lynn Wood Mollenauer, *Strange Revelations: Magic, Poison and Sacrilege in Louis XIV's France* (University Park: Pennsylvania State University Press, 2006), and Anne Somerset, *The Affair of the Poisons: Murder, Infanticide and Satanism at the Court of Louis XIV* (London: Weidenfeld and Nicolson, 2003), the most recent scholarly monographs available on the subject. Additional information was derived from Anton Kippenberg, *Die Sage vom Herzog von Luxemburg und die historische Persönlichkeit ihres Trägers* (1901; repr., Niederwalluf bei Wiesbaden: Dr. Martin Sändig oHG, 1970), and Mandrou, *Magistrats et sorciers*, 466–472. In addition, I consulted the interrogation records that still serve as our main source for the affair and that have been published in volumes 6 and 7 of *Archives de la Bastille*, ed. François Ravaisson, 19 vols. (Paris: A. Durand & Pedone-Lauriel, 1866–1904).

177. On the difficulty during the early modern period of drawing a demarcation between "natural" poisoning and poisonous magic, see Giovanna Fiume, "The Old Vinegar Lady, or the Judicial Modernization of the Crime of Witchcraft," in *History from Crime*, ed. Edward Muir and Guido Ruggiero, Selections from *Quaderni Storici*, no. 3 (Baltimore, MD: John Hopkins University Press, 1994), 65–87.

178. Somerset, *Affair of the Poisons*, 151.

179. Ravaisson, *Archives de la Bastille*, 5:373; Mollenauer, *Strange Revelations*, 29, 74; contrary to most literature, Mollenauer claims that La Voisin only incinerated aborted fetuses, not performed abortions herself.

180. Kippenberg, *Die Sage vom Herzog von Luxemburg*, 63–64. Luxembourg had been implicated earlier by a woman named Marie Bosse, a soothsayer who was burned on 10 May 1679 (with her daughter of fourteen being forced to witness the spectacle, presumably on educational grounds)—see Somerset, *Affair of the Poisons*, 160.

181. Ravaisson, *Archives de la Bastille*, 6:46–47; Somerset, *Affair of the Poisons*, 243.

182. Ravaisson, *Archives de la Bastille*, 6:56–57, Somerset, *Affair of the Poisons*, 194.

183. Ravaisson, *Archives de la Bastille*, 6:211–213.

184. Ravaisson, *Archives de la Bastille*, 6:220–221, 6:283–284.

185. Ravaisson, *Archives de la Bastille*, 6:232; Somerset, *Affair of the Poisons*, 246–247.

186. Ravaisson, *Archives de la Bastille*, 6:252.

187. Ravaisson, *Archives de la Bastille*, 6:258–259.

188. Ravaisson, *Archives de la Bastille*, 6:294–295.

189. Ravaisson, *Archives de la Bastille*, 6:294–295.

190. Somerset, *Affair of the Poisons*, 264–271.

191. Ravaisson, *Archives de la Bastille*, 6:327.

192. Ravaisson, *Archives de la Bastille*, 6:333–334.

193. Ravaisson, *Archives de la Bastille*, 6:335.

194. Ravaisson, *Archives de la Bastille*, 6:336. The masturbating Englishman has been iden-tified on rather doubtful grounds as George Villiers, Duke of Buckingham. See Montague Summers in his introduction to Institoris, *Malleus Maleficarum*, xxii; Summers is followed by Rhodes, *Satanic Mass*, 212.

195. Ravaisson, *Archives de la Bastille*, 6:390.

196. Ravaisson, *Archives de la Bastille*, 6:324; Somerset, *Affair of the Poisons*, 267.

197. Ravaisson, *Archives de la Bastille*, 7:5.

198. Somerset, *Affair of the Poisons*, 306. Two imprisoned suspects had already died under torture, while a few more died of other causes while in prison.

199. Introvigne, *Enquête sur le satanisme*, 34, 38; Frick, *Satan und Die Satanisten*, 2:119–131; Zacharias, *Satanskult und Schwarze Messe*, 123. Kippenberg, *Die Sage vom Herzog von Luxemburg*, 48–50, denies the complicity of Luxembourg but seems to believe in the veracity of the Black Mass stories and the participation of Montespan. Medway, *Lure of the Sinister*, 79, seems undecided. A whole host of more or less popular authors hold similar opinions, such as R. Lowe Thompson, *The History of the Devil: The Horned God of the West* (London: Kegan Paul, Trench, Trubner, 1929), 146; Martin Koomen, *Het ijzige zaad van de duivel: Geschiedenis van heksen en demonen* (Amsterdam: Wetenschappelijke Uitgeverij, 1973), 132–134; and Wenisch, *Satanismus*, 22, to name just a few.

200. Introvigne, *Enquête sur le satanisme*, 35. The criminologist and self-styled Black Mass expert Henry T. F. Rhodes calls La Reynie "one of the great detectives of all time"; Rhodes, *Satanic Mass*, 86.

201. Introvigne, *Enquête sur le satanisme*, 37, 34.

202. Introvigne, *Enquête sur le satanisme*, 34–35.

203. Somerset, *Affair of the Poisons*, 143; Mandrou, *Magistrats et sorciers*, 313–368. See also Mollenauer, *Strange Revelations*, 5–7, for the judicial context.

204. Somerset, *Affair of the Poisons*, 221. "Yes, I have seen him, and he looked just like you," the Duchesse de Bouillon was said to have answered La Reynie, according to a probably apocry-phal anecdote; cf. Mollenauer, *Strange Revelations*, 39.

205. Somerset, *Affair of the Poisons*, 249.

206. Somerset, *Affair of the Poisons*, 144.

207. Somerset, *Affair of the Poisons*, 229.

208. It must be noted, however, that judicial torture in late seventeenth-century France was subject to strict regulations and produced few confessions; on this, see Mollenauer, *Strange Revelations*, 26.

209. Cf. Mollenauer, *Strange Revelations*, 5. The use of divulgences of alleged magical plots against royalty as "a mean of negotiation" is not unknown from other historical instances; see particularly Sabina Loriga, "A Secret to Kill the King: Magic and Protection in Piedmont in the Early Eighteenth Century," in Muir and Ruggiero, *History from Crime*, 88–109, there 95.

210. Somerset, *Affair of the Poisons*, 319–302; see also her general conclusions about the affair on pp. 326 and 339. Mollenauer is more inclined to accept the involvement of Montespan and the veracity of many of their allegations; see Mollenauer, *Strange Revelations*, 48–49.

211. Somerset characterized Lesage as "a practised and polished liar who was accustomed to live on his wits" (*Affair of the Poisons*, 174), Marie Marguerite Montvoisin "relished being in the centre of attention" (252), and Guibourg was probably on the brink of senility (247).

212. "Mémoire contre les faits calomnieux imputés à Madame de Montespan," 415, cited in Mandrou, *Magistrats et sorciers*, 470.

213. "Mémoire de M. de La Reynie sur le fait touchant les abominations, le sacrifice de l'enfant pour la Des Œilletes et pour l'étranger prétendu milord anglais" [ca. Dec 1680], in Ravaisson, *Archives de la Bastille*, 6:395–399. The memorandum was actually written by the lawyer Claude Duplessis and commissioned by Colbert, who had his own reasons to support Montespan—cf. Mollenauer, *Strange Revelations*, 49.

214. Moore, *Formation of a Persecuting Society*, 141. For a similar affair in early eighteenth-century Piedmont, see Loriga, "Secret to Kill the King."

215. Ravaisson, *Archives de la Bastille*, 6:18–19; Somerset, *Affair of the Poisons*, 186; Kippenberg, *Die Sage vom Herzog von Luxemburg*, 62, citing Ravaisson, *Archives de la Bastille*, 5:501.

216. Somerset, *Affair of the Poisons*, 324; Ravaisson, *Archives de la Bastille*, 7:125 ("Louvois à M. De Moncault, commandant citadelle Besançon, Versailles 6 april 1683").

217. Cf. Somerset, *Affair of the Poisons*, 58–62.

218. Somerset, *Affair of the Poisons*, 337–338.

219. The Duchesse de Bouillon explicitly stated that she had no regard for the tribunal and had only appeared at its hearing out of respect for the king; Somerset, *Affair of the Poisons*, 221.

220. Mollenauer, *Strange Revelations*, 51; Somerset, *Affair of the Poisons*, 301.

221. Kippenberg, *Die Sage vom Herzog von Luxemburg*, 67, citing Ravaisson, *Archives de la Bastille*, 6:210. Particularly in German-speaking countries, the Maréchal was turned into a Faust-like figure of folklore. Kippenberg gives an extensive inventory of pamphlets dealing with Luxembourg's relations with the devil (93, 117ff.).

222. Unbeknownst to me at the time of writing, a similar analysis of the interrogation records from the vantage point of modern insights into demonic magic is made by Mollenauer, *Strange Revelations*, 71–110, where she reaches more or less similar conclusions.

223. Ravaisson, *Archives de la Bastille*, 6:272–273. An exorcism that was (falsely) attributed to Ambrosius did indeed circulate in the medieval and early modern ages, while Cyprian, in one of his letters, gives an exorcism formula to be used during baptism that involves threatening the demons with eternal punishment. See Adolph Franz, *Die kirchliche Benediktionen im Mittelalter*, 2 vols. (Freiburg im Breisgau: Herdersche Verlagshandlung, 1909), 2:578–579 and 2:534n.

224. Ravaisson, *Archives de la Bastille*, 6:57, 6:81, 6:213, 6:220–221, 6:238 (where Guibourg recounts how he consecrated a "book of conjurations" by reading Mass over it on nine consecutive

days), 6:283–284. Mollenauer, *Strange Revelations*, 78, 100, also emphasizes the continuity with medieval practices of "Eucharistic" and other magic.

225. Ravaisson, *Archives de la Bastille*, 6:56–57. References to this practice prior to the Affair of the Poisons seem scarce. I am only aware of one earlier occurrence of a roughly similar nature, described by Reginald Scot in his *Discoverie of Witchcraft* from 1584 (cited in Medway, *Lure of the Sinister*, 382): "In Gelderland a priest persuaded a sicke woman that she was bewitched; and except he might sing a masse upon her bellie, she could not be holpen. Whereunto se consented, and laie naked on the altar whilest he sang masse, to the satisfieng of his lust; but not to the release of hir greefe."

226. It must be remarked that Lesage, in his interrogation of 28 November 1679, also describes how ceremony and conjuration were used by a priest to convince a girl he had seduced that she did not need to be afraid of becoming pregnant: Ravaisson, *Archives de la Bastille*, 6:56.

227. Mollenauer, *Strange Revelations*, 174n.

228. Ravaisson, *Archives de la Bastille*, 6:300, 6:328.

229. Cf. Ravaisson, *Archives de la Bastille*, 6:295, where it is said that "Madame de Montespan s'est fait dire une de ces sortes de messes"; in Ravaisson, *Archives de la Bastille*, 6:328, Guibourg gives the formula of conjuration used during these masses as such: "I invoke you, spirits whose names are written on this paper, to accomplish the will and wishes of the person for which this Mass is celebrated." The possibility of having Masses celebrated "by procuration" (i.e., on the body of another female) is clearly indicated in Marie Montvoisin's deposition regarding Madame de Montespan—although it is made equally clear that Montespan had had Masses read over her own body, too. See Ravaisson, *Archives de la Bastille*, 6:295.

230. Introvigne, *Enquête sur le satanisme*, 37.

231. Jaquerius, *Flagellum Haereticorum Fascinariorum*, 57–58.

232. Harmening, *Superstitio*, 230–231.

233. Introvigne, *Enquête sur le satanisme*, 34; Introvigne, "Satanism," 1035 ("La Voisin invented the 'black Mass'"); Schmidt, *Satanismus*, 61, 63.

234. Ravaisson, *Archives de la Bastille*, 6:300, 6:327.

235. Cf. Ravaisson, *Archives de la Bastille*, 6:221–22, 6:238–284.

236. Ravaisson, *Archives de la Bastille*, 6:275, 6:277; 6:336, where the host is "cut in little pieces" to be kept in vases with consecrated blood. On analogous popular practices of magical use of the Eucharist by French shepherds in roughly the same period, see Mollenauer, *Strange Revelations*, 100.

237. Mollenauer, *Strange Revelations*, 106, explicitly cites these practices as testimony for the success of the Catholic Reformation.

238. Introvigne, *Enquête sur le satanisme*, 34. Scanning the records, I only encountered one faint allusion to a "reversed Mass" ("messe à l'envers"), but this testimony is clearly only hearsay, with the accused explicitly stating that she did not witness the ceremony (deposition of La Filastre in Ravaisson, *Archives de la Bastille*, 6:221).

239. Ravaisson, *Archives de la Bastille*, 6:46–47; 6:167; 6:438. My objections are shared by Mollenauer, *Strange Revelations*, 106, who accordingly calls them "amatory Masses."

240. Ravaisson, *Archives de la Bastille*, 6:73.

241. Ravaisson, *Archives de la Bastille*, 6:221–22, 6:283–284.

242. Ravaisson, *Archives de la Bastille*, 6:225.

243. Waite, *Eradicating the Devil's Minions*, 100–102.

244. Ravaisson, *Archives de la Bastille*, 6:438.

245. Ravaisson, *Archives de la Bastille*, 6:258–259; 6:309.

246. Kieckhefer, *Forbidden Rites*, 157. The use of fetuses or parts thereof was not uncommon in magic, however; cf. Mollenauer, *Strange Revelations*, 108.

247. Waite, *Eradicating the Devil's Minions*, 100–102.

248. Harmening, *Superstitio*, 205–206.

249. Ravaisson, *Archives de la Bastille*, 6:288n.

250. Introvigne, *Enquête sur le satanisme*, 36–37; Mollenauer, *Strange Revelations*, 108; Somerset, *Affair of the Poisons*, 326, 339. Medway, *Lure of the Sinister*, 79, seems inclined to believe La Reynie's account.

251. Somerset, *Affair of the Poisons*, 232–233.

252. Somerset, *Affair of the Poisons*, 152.

253. Anne Somerset at least could find no mention of such a search for human remains: cf. *Affair of the Poisons*, 162. Introvigne, *Enquête sur le satanisme*, 36, claims that the police discovered a crematory at the premises of La Voisin with the charred fragments of burned bodies still in it, but unfortunately he does not refer to any sources for these statements. Even if the bodies of children had been recovered, however, this would not prove that they had been sacrificed to demons rather than being the remains of abortions.

254. Mandrou, *Magistrats et sorciers*, 482; Mollenauer, *Strange Revelations*, 130–131.

255. "Mémoire de M. d'Argenson sur les associations de faux sorciers à Paris en 1702," in Mandrou, *Possession et sorcellerie au XVIIe siècle*, 275–328.

256. D'Argenson mentions the following characters as being involved in "negotiating contracts with the devil" (page numbers from Mandrou, *Possession et sorcellerie au XVIIe siècle*, added between parentheses): Jemme (286), Abbé Touzard (290), Bendrode (291), D'amour and his wife (292), Louvet (294), Lion (296), Abbé Le Fevre (300), Rouillon (306), Père Robert (309), Marotte la Jardinière (309).

257. Mandrou, *Possession et sorcellerie au XVIIe siècle*, 296–297.

258. Mandrou, *Possession et sorcellerie au XVIIe siècle*, 299. In 1695, D'Argenson had already reported a similar case of Mass being said on the naked body of a women in order to conclude a pact; see Ravaisson, *Archives de la Bastille*, 7:172–173.

259. Mandrou, *Possession et sorcellerie au XVIIe siècle*, 290, 297–298.

260. Mandrou, *Possession et sorcellerie au XVIIe siècle*, 286–287, 319–321.

261. Mandrou, *Possession et sorcellerie au XVIIe siècle*, 292, 300.

262. At one point, D'Argenson suggests interrogating certain suspects in the Bastille, "parce qu'on a lieu de croire qu'ils ont été consultez par des personnes d'un rang distingué dont il sera peut être du service du Roy de savoir les visions et les folies"; Mandrou, *Possession et sorcellerie au XVIIe siècle*, 281.

263. Mandrou, *Possession et sorcellerie au XVIIe siècle*, 279. I fail to understand where Muchembled detected a lingering fear of the devil in D'Argenson's text, as he claims in his *History of the Devil*, 172.

264. Mandrou, *Possession et sorcellerie au XVIIe siècle*, 315, 299, and 308 (Boyar wants to engage himself with the devil in a "perpetual pact").

265. Quoted in Volker Schäfer, "Tübinger Teufelspakte," in ". . helfen zu graben den Brunnen des Lebens": Historische Jubiläumsausstellung des Universitätsarchivs Tübingen, ed. Uwe Jens Wandel, et al., 72–77 (Tübingen: Universitätsbibliothek Tübingen, 1977), 77.

266. Schäfer, "Tübinger Teufelspakte," 74. Both students had been motivated by money problems, and both were only punished lightly. Lipsius was banished from Tübingen; he later became a respected medical practitioner. Haim joined the army and may have ended up as a mayor.

267. Hans de Waardt, "Met bloed ondertekend," *Sociologische Gids* 36 (1989): 224–244 and 288–289; there 233.

268. Mikael Häll, " 'God Is Caught in Hell, so It Is Better to Believe in the Devil': Conceptions of Satanists and Sympathies for the Devil in Early Modern Sweden," in *The Devil's Party: Satanism in Modernity*, ed. Per Faxneld and Jesper Petersen (Oxford: Oxford University Press, 2012), 23–40; Cervantes, *Devil in the New World*, 49, 80–81, 85–87, 90–97; Iris Gareis, "Feind oder Freund? Der Teufel in Spanien und in der Neuen Welt im 16.-18. Jahrhundert," @ *KIH-eSkript: Interdisziplinäre Hexenforschung online* 3 (2011) 1:77–84, at http://www.historicum.net/no_cache/persistent/artikel/9107/, there 83–84 (accessed 14 December 2011). If somebody were to shake the box of European archival evidence really well, many more cases might tumble out.

269. For "Satanists" with evident psychic problems, see De Waardt, "Met bloed ondertekend," 233–234. A more well-known example is the Austrian painter Christoph Haitzmann (1651–1700), whose case attracted the attention of Sigmund Freud in 1923—see Sigmund Freud, "Eine Teufelsneurose im siebzehnten Jahrhundert," in *Gesammelte Werke*, ed. Anne Freud, et al., 15 vols. (1940; repr., London: Imago, 1947), 13:315–353. For the famous affairs of Louviers and Loudun, see, among many others, Mandrou, *Magistrats et sorciers*, 263–312; on the mechanisms involved with "voluntary" Satanist impersonators, here and at other times, see Frankfurter, *Evil Incarnate*, 181–184. South American slaves who sought the refuge of the Inquisition by pretending to have made a pact with Satan are mentioned in Cervantes, *Devil in the New World*, 79–81.

270. D'Argenson gives another illustration of such syncretism when he describes the practices of Picot, "grand mareschal des magicians," who heals by making nine signs of the cross and nine "soufflets a nom de Lucifer." Mandrou, *Possession et sorcellerie au XVIIe siècle*, 287. Syncretism had a long history in the practice of magic, which tended to function as a storehouse for potential useful spiritual knowledge that functioned independently from official theology. For examples from Late Antiquity, see MacMullen, *Christianity and Paganism*, 140. One is reminded here of Hutton's words about the practices of British "cunning folk": "It was not a counter-religion to Christianity; rather, the two coexisted and complemented each other" (Ronald Hutton, *The Triumph of the Moon: A History of Modern Pagan Witchcraft* [Oxford: Oxford University Press, 1999], 101).

271. Waite, *Eradicating the Devil's Minions*, 24, gives an example from rural communities where blessed weather bells that failed to avert storms would be blessed anew, this time in the name of the devil.

272. Introvigne, *Enquête sur le satanisme*, 39.

273. Kieckhefer, *European Witch Trials*, 6, also makes this distinction, calling magic involving a pact "contractual" and separating it from religious veneration of the devil. The same objections apply here. See the introduction for a more extensive theoretical discussion of these matters.

274. See the delightful story about the Abbé Pinel, his consort Marie Anne, and their dealings with a certain Divot in Mandrou, *Possession et sorcellerie au XVIIe siècle*, 309–324.

275. Mandrou, *Possession et sorcellerie au XVIIe siècle*, 281, 303.

276. Somerset, *Affair of the Poisons*, 141.

277. Introvigne, *Enquête sur le satanisme*, 46.

278. Schäfer, "Tübinger Teufelspakte," 73. Subsequently, the magister who had read the book to Lipsius was also arrested, as was one of his relatives who owned a copy of the book. All were soon released, however. An example of a similar mechanism of appropriation is provided by an anonymous sixteenth-century author who scavenged Reginald Scot's antisorcery diatribe *Discovery of Witchcraft* for useful magic charms; see Frank Klaassen and Christopher Phillips, "The Return of Stolen Goods: Reginald Scot, Religious Controversy, and Magic in Bodleian Library, Additional B. 1.," *Magic, Ritual, and Witchcraft* 1 (Winter 2006) 2:135–175.

279. In a more general way, Dieter Harmening already suggested the unintentional side effects that churchly propaganda could have had; see Harmening, *Superstitio*, 73: "Verordnungen über Superstitionen stehen in einem doppelten Verhältnis zur Wirklichkeit: sie können sie abbilden, können sie aber auch erst schaffen."

280. Rudimentary forms of early modern Satanist "theology" or ideology are also recorded by Häll, " 'God Is Caught in Hell,' " and Cervantes, *Devil in the New World*, 84–85.

281. The marginality of early modern Satanists is emphasized by all authors that speak about them; see De Waardt, "Met bloed ondertekend," 239; Gareis, "Feind oder Freund?" 84; and Häll, " 'God Is Caught in Hell,' " 38–39.

282. Cf. Mollenauer, *Strange Revelations*, 6–7.

INTERMEZZO I

1. Thomas Corneille and Donneau de Visé, *La Devineresse: Comédie. Introduction et Notes par P.J. Yarrow* (s.l.: University of Exeter, 1971), 42.

2. Peter Maxwell-Stuart, "The Contemporary Historical Debate, 1400–1750," in *Palgrave Advances in Witchcraft Historiography*, ed. Jonathan Barry and Owen Davies (Houndmills, UK: Palgrave Macmillan, 2007), 11–32; Mollenauer, *Strange Revelations*, 5–7, 130–131.

3. Waite, *Eradicating the Devil's Minions*, 128, 197–205.

4. On Bekker's debt to earlier providential theology, especially that of the spiritualists, see Waite, *Eradicating the Devil's Minions*, 29.

5. Baltasar Bekker, *De Betooverde Weereld, zynde een grondig onsoek van 't gemeen gevoelen aangaande de geesten, derselver Aart en vermogen, Bewind en Bedryf: als ook 't gene de Menschen door derselver kragt en gemeenschap doen* (Amsterdam: Daniel van den Dalen, 1691), "Aan den Leser." For Bekker, see G. Stronks, "The Significance of Bathasar Bekker's The Enchanted World," in *Witchcraft in the Netherlands from the Fourteenth to the Twentieth Century*, ed. M. Gijswijt-Hofstra and W. Frijhoff (Rotterdam: Universitaire Pers, 1991), 149–156. Although the Calvinist church authorities proceeded to expel Bekker from the pulpit, they could not prevent his book from being translated into virtually every major European language and provoking intense debate.

6. *La Pucelle*, Chant Vingtième, note 2, cited in Milner, *Le diable dans la littérature française*, 1:33.

7. Voltaire, *Essai sur les mœurs et l'esprit des nations et sur les principaux faits de l'histoire depuis Charlemagne jusqu'à Louis XIII*, 2 vols (Paris: Éditions Garnier Frères, 1963), 173–174, 177 (section 48).

8. Dennis Diderot and Jean le Rond D'Alembert, *L'Encyclopédie ou Dictionnaire raisonné des sciences, des arts et des métiers*, 17 vols. (Paris: Briasson, David l'Ainée, Le Breton and Durand, 1751–1772), 4:927.

9. In their treatment of "sorcellerie," the *philosophes* could be more explicit. "One only hears about feats of magic & malefice in places & times of ignorance," the *Encyclopédie* stated (Diderot and D'Alembert, *Encyclopédie ou Dictionnaire raisonné*, 15:36). Voltaire voices similar opinions in his *Essai sur les mœurs*, 125–126 (section 35).

10. Reference from -Stuart, "Contemporary Historical Debate," 30. For the disappearance of Satan in Enlightenment thought, see also Ernst Osterkamp, *Lucifer: Stationen eines Motivs* (Berlin: Walter de Gruyter, 1979), 154–156; Peter A. Schock, *Romantic Satanism: Myth and the Historical Moment in Blake, Shelley, and Byron* (Houndmills, UK: Palgrave Macmillan, 2003), 13–17; and Muchembled, *History of the Devil*, 161–186.

11. Compare the long list of eighteenth-century works featuring an ironic view on the devil or the demonic in Milner, *Le diable dans la littérature française*, 1:73–90.

12. Daniel Defoe, *A System of Magic* (1728), quoted in Evelyn Lord, *The Hell-Fire Clubs: Sex, Satanism and Secret Societies* (New Haven, CT: Yale University Press, 2010), 8.

13. Charles Taylor, *A Secular Age* (Cambridge, MA: Belknap Press of Harvard University Press, 2007), 292–293. See also Joscelyn Godwin, *The Theosophical Enlightenment* (Albany: State University of New York Press, 1994), particularly 1–26, for an overview of Enlightenment theories on original religion. On the roots of the Enlightenment in earlier Christian dissent, see the still insightful chapter by H. R. Trevor-Roper, "The Religious Origins of the Enlightenment," in *The European Witch-Craze of the Sixteenth and Seventeenth Centuries and Other Essays* (New York: Harper and Row, 1969), 193–236.

14. Taylor, *Secular Age*, 262.

15. Pierre Bayle, *Commentaire philosophique sur ces paroles de Jésus-Christ "Contrain-les d'entrer," ou Traité de la tolérance universelle*, in *Oeuvres diverses*, 6 vols. (La Haye: P. Husson, 1727–1731), 377–420.

16. Waite, *Eradicating the Devil's Minions*, 92.

17. Hungarian witch persecutions were at their height from 1710 to 1750, while in Poland, 55 percent of known witch prosecutions date to the period between 1676 and 1725; see Muchembled, *History of the Devil*, 148.

18. There does not seem to exist any recent publication on the *Bockereyders* in a non-Dutch language. Anton Blok, *The Bokkerijders Bands 1726–1776: Preliminary Notes on Brigandage in the Southern Netherlands*, Papers on European and Mediterranean Societies, no. 7 (Amsterdam: Antropologisch-Sociologisch Centrum Universiteit van Amsterdam, 1976), does not stand out for a critical treatment of its sources. For those who understand Dutch, François Van Gehuchten, *Bokkenrijders: Late heksenprocessen in Limburg. Het proces van vier bokkenrijdersgroepen in Limburg* (1773–1795) (s.l.: s.i., 2002) is as good an introduction as any. On the Nachleben of the Bockeryders in anti-Satanism literature, cf. Medway, *Lure of the Sinister*, 86–87 (who does not seem to be aware of the real historical core of these stories).

19. Introvigne, *Enquête sur le satanisme*, 40–46, citing Giuseppe Orlandi, *La fede al vaglio: Quietisme, satanismo e massoneria nel Ducato di Modena tra Sette e Ottocento* (Modena: Aedes Muratoriana, 1988). Rumors about "Messes d'Amour" of a sexual but not necessarily Satanist character would prevail well into the nineteenth century. Cf. Philippe Martin, *Le théâtre divin: Une histoire de la messe du XIVème au XXème siècle* (Paris: CNSR Éditions, 2010), 38–41.

20. In the Rabonus band of gypsies and Christians that roamed the Dutch countryside in the late eighteenth century, new members had to swear an oath featuring the words "now we part from Our Lord and go alive to the Devil. And now we accept the Devil as our Lord." Cf. Florike Egmond, *Underworlds: Organized Crime in the Netherlands 1650–1800* (Cambridge, UK: Polity, 1993), 136.

21. Kippenberg, *Die Sage vom Herzog von Luxemburg*, 156–162; Kippenberg cites an incident dating from the Prussian-Austrian War of 1866. "Devil, help me: body and soul I give to thee" was the common expression on these so-called Passauer Zettel. Practices like these are already mentioned in the *Malleus Maleficarum*; cf. Institoris and Sprenger, *Malleus Maleficarum*, 2:339–342.

22. Kippenberg, *Die Sage vom Herzog von Luxemburg*, 149.

23. Kippenberg, *Die Sage vom Herzog von Luxemburg*, 171: "So kan er das formular von einem andern abgeschmiehrt haben und sind ja leyder solche gedruckt zu finden ... obgleich inquisit sagt, er hätte dergleichen formular weder jemahls gehöret noch gelesen, so ist solches nicht zu glauben, denn wie hätte er sonst die requisita dieses pacti wissen können."

24. Lord, *Hell-Fire Clubs*, 19–24, 75–95, 157–201.

25. Lord, *Hell-Fire Clubs*, 66.

26. Lord, *Hell-Fire Clubs*, 45–49.

27. The historiography of the Hell-Fire Clubs is comparatively well developed. Lord's recent *Hell-Fire Clubs* can be considered the best monograph on the subject. Geoffrey Ashe's *The Hell-Fire Clubs: A History of Anti-Morality* (Stroud: Sutton, 2001) is a book any author would dream to write, but alas it is rather meager in annotation and sometimes faulty in details. Gerald Suster, *The Hell-Fire Friars: Sex, Politics and Religion* (London: Robson, 2000), is mainly a rerun of Ashe with some Crowleyan numerology and less-than-profound philosophy thrown in. These authors basically agree on the nonexistence or utter triviality of the Hell-Fire Clubs' Satanism, as do most authors writing about the history of Satanism in general (see, for instance, Introvigne, *Enquête sur le satanisme*, 54–55, Medway, *Lure of the Sinister*, 79–86; Schmidt, *Satanismus*, 69–71, seems less skeptical, but still designates the clubs as "essentially pseudo-Satanist").

28. Lord, *Hell-Fire Clubs*, 51, 72.

29. For the background of Dashwood's Order in contemporary English erotic culture, see Randolph Trumbach, "Erotic Fantasy and Male Libertinism in Enlightenment England," in *The Invention of Pornography: Obscenity and the Origins of Modernity, 1500–1800*, ed. Lynn Hunt (New York: Zone, 1993), 253–282.

30. According to Ashe, *Hell-Fire Clubs*, 178–181, Dashwood and Franklin's version of the Book of Common Prayer is still in use in American Episcopal churches today, although Dashwood is not mentioned as an author.

31. D. A. F. de Sade, *Justine ou les malheurs de la vertu* (Paris: Jean-Jacques Pauvert, 1955), 232. De Sade apparently liked this scene, because he used it again in chapter 10 of *Nouvelle Justine*; in the fifth book of *Juliette*, the willing protagonist is introduced to similar pastimes by the Pope himself.

32. D. A. F. de Sade, *La philosophie dans le boudoir* (Paris: Jean-Jacques Pauvert, 1968), 154.

33. "Es fehlt die Bezugperson des Satans," Frick already remarks on De Sade (Frick, *Satan und Die Satanisten* 2:133). See also Russell, *Mephistopheles*, 147–149.

CHAPTER 2: THE ROMANTIC REHABILITATION OF SATAN

1. The Romantic Satanists are somewhat neglected by historians of religious Satanism. They are either ignored (Introvigne, *Enquête sur le satanisme*), spoken about as though they had virtually no connection with the history of "real" religious Satanism at all (Schmidt, *Satanismus*, 80–101; Frick, *Satan und die Satanisten*, 2:131–155; Medway, *Lure of the Sinister*, 12), or discussed mainly with regard to the question of whether or not they participated in Black Masses (Frick and Medway again). It is true that Schmidt (p. 84) and Medway (p. 12) present Byron and Baudelaire, respectively, as the first modern Satanist, but this does not noticeably affect their historical accounts of Satanism (compare Schmidt's significant conclusion about "literarischen Satanismus" [*Satanismus*, 101]: "Mit dem Satanismuskonzepten des 20. Jahrhunderts hat dies allerdings nicht mehr allzuviel zu tun"). Bernd U. Schipper has been one of the few authors to present a more elaborate analysis of the connection between "literary Satanism" and modern religious Satanism in his article "From Milton to Modern Satanism: The History of the Devil and the Dynamics between Religion and Literature," *Journal of Religion in Europe* 3 (2010) 1:103–124. See the notes to chapter 7 for a discussion of this article. Per Faxneld gives a fine analysis of Romantic Satanism in *Satanic Feminism*, 113–143. The Romantic Satanists are also prominently mentioned in Petersen, "Introduction," 11–13 (together with personages we'll meet in the next chapters like Lévi, Blavatsky, and Crowley); in Lewis, *Satanism Today*, xiii; and by Katherina Elliger in Haag, *Teufelsglaube*, 492 ("Die Wiederentdeckung der Teufelsfigur in der Romantik mag unter anderem die Voraussetzung dafür gewesen sein, daß der Satanskult im 19. Jahrhundert ganz andere Formen annahm"; see also p. 495). The synthesis presented in this chapter, however, is my own. I have presented important segments of this material in an earlier article, "God, Satan, Poetry and Revolution: Literary Satanism in the Nineteenth Century," *Religion and Theology* (2016): 1.

For separate sections in this chapter, I have profusely profited from earlier scholarship; appropriate references will be given at appropriate places. Among the works dealing with the "Satanic School of Poetry" in general, the most important for this chapter have been Schock, *Romantic Satanism*, and Max Milner's two-volume *Le diable dans la littérature française*. In addition I learned a lot from the articles by Karl S. Guthke, "Der Mythos des Bösen in der westeuropäischen Romantik," *Colloquia Germanica. Internationale Zeitschrift für germanische Sprach- und Literaturwissenschaft* (1968): 1–36, and Marilyn Butler, "Romantic Manichaeism: Shelley's 'On the Devil, and Devils' and Byron's Mythological Dramas," in *The Sun Is God: Painting, Literature and Mythology in the Nineteenth Century*, ed. J. B. Bullen (Oxford: Clarendon, 1989), 13–37. Also useful has been Peter Paul Schnierer's *Entdämonisierung und Verteufelung: Studien zur Darstellungs- und Funktionsgeschichte des Diabolischen in der englischen Literatur seit der Renaissance* (Tübingen: Max Niemeyer, 2005), particularly 87–106, as well as the three impressive books on French Romanticism by Paul Bénichou, which will be quoted in later notes.

2. Milner, *Le diable dans la littérature française*, 1:211–222. On Russian vernacular editions of *Paradise Lost*, see Valentin Boss, *Milton and the Rise of Russian Satanism* (Toronto: University of Toronto Press, 1991), xi–xii.

3. *Paradise Lost*, Book I, line 26 (1667 edition). The majority of Miltonists maintain that this was indeed what Milton wished to do. Schipper, "From Milton to Modern Satanism," 114–115, postulates that Milton's *Paradise Lost* in itself already provided the essential "paradigm shift"

to allow a new appraisal of Satan. In contrast to this view, and in accordance with most of the authors cited earlier, I hold that it was the Romantic *reinterpretation* of Milton that was crucial in this respect. For some troubling questions about Milton's own "subconscious" subversions of his message, see John Leonard's introduction to Milton's *Paradise Lost* (London: Penguin, 2000), xxiii–xxiv, and Schnierer, *Entdämonisierung und Verteufelung*, 75–87.

4. Schock, *Romantic Satanism*, 26; Peter Ackroyd, *Blake* (London: Sinclair-Stevenson, 1995), 88. In this context it might be interesting to note that Rousseau, godfather of Romanticism and the French Revolution, expressed his admiration for Milton's "blasphemies de Satan," while also, unsurprisingly, approving Milton's paradisiacal picture of the first human couple. Cf. Robert Sharrock, "Godwin on Milton's Satan," *Notes and Queries for Readers and Writers, Collectors and Librarians* 9 (December 1962) 12:463–465, there 464.

5. Gert Schiff, "Füssli, Luzifer und die Medusa," in *Johann Heinrich Füssli 1741–1825*, ed. Werner Hofmann (München: Prestel-Verlag, 1974), 9–22; Schock, *Romantic Satanism*, 31–33.

6. Godwin, *An Enquiry into Political Justice*, 1:261–262 (Book IV, Appendix 1); quoted from *Political and Philosophical Writings of William Godwin*, ed. Mark Philp, 7 vols. (London: Pickering, 1993), 3:146. See also Schock, *Romantic Satanism*, 34–35.

7. Ackroyd, *Blake*, 134, 159.

8. William Blake, *The Marriage of Heaven and Hell: With an Introduction and Commentary by Sir Geoffrey Keynes* (Oxford: Oxford University Press, 1975), plates 3–4. I will henceforth refer to the original plate numbers of *The Marriage of Heaven and Hell*, enabling the reader to find the appropriate text place in his or her own particular edition of Blake.

9. Blake, *Marriage of Heaven and Hell*, plate 24. The narrator here can clearly be understood as Blake himself. This had been the original ending of *The Marriage of Heaven and Hell* in its earliest edition; Blake later added a "Song of Liberty."

10. Janet Todd, *Death and the Maidens: Fanny Wollstonecraft and the Shelley Circle* (London: Profile, 2007), 247, quoting William Hazlitt.

11. This episode is masterfully retold in Janet Todd's *Death and the Maidens*. On Godwin, Shelley, and free love, see especially pp. 8, 91, and 198.

12. Percy Bysshe Shelley, *Essays and Letters by Percy Bysshe Shelley*, ed. Ernest Rhys (London: Walter Scott, 1905), 26–27.

13. Percy Bysshe Shelley, *The Complete Poetical Works of Percy Bysshe Shelley*, ed. Neville Rogers, 4 vols. (Oxford: Clarendon, 1972–1975), 2:97–273. The poem is more generally known as *The Revolt of Islam*, a fairly deceptive title that I will consequently not adopt.

14. Shelley, *Complete Poetical Works*, 2:119 (*Laon and Cythna*, Canto 1,26–27).

15. Shelley, *Complete Poetical Works*, 2:119 (*Laon and Cythna*, Canto 1,28).

16. Cf. Fiona MacCarthy, *Byron: Life and Legend* (London: John Murray, 2002), particularly 243.

17. The Reverend Reginald Heber in the *Quarterly Review* of May 1820, quoted in Schock, *Romantic Satanism*, 101.

18. Byron, *Don Juan*, Dedication, ix. "I doubt if 'Laureate' and 'Iscariot' be good rhymes," Byron added in a note, "but must say, as Ben Jonson did to Sylvester, who challenged him to rhyme with—

I, John Sylvester,
Lay with your sister.

Jonson answered—'I, Ben Jonson, lay with your wife.' Sylvester answered,—'That is not rhyme.'—'No,' said Ben Jonson; 'but it is *true.'*" [George Gordon] Lord Byron, *The Poetical Works of Lord Byron* (Oxford: Oxford University Press, 1961), 301.

19. Robert Southey, *A Vision of Judgement* (London: Longman, Hurst, Rees, Orme & Brown, 1821), xix–xxi.

20. Schock, *Romantic Satanism*, 78.

21. Schock, *Romantic Satanism*, 25.

22. [George Gordon] Lord Byron and Truman Guy Steffan, *Lord Byron's Cain: Twelve Essays and a Text with Variants and Annotations* (Austin: University of Texas Press, 1968), 4n.

23. Byron to Thomas Moore, 19 September 1821, quoted in Byron and Steffan, *Cain*, 8–9.

24. Byron to Thomas Moore, 19 September 1821, quoted in Byron and Steffan, *Cain*, 8–9.

25. Byron and Steffan, *Cain*, 156. These lines from the manuscript were suppressed by Byron's publisher John Murray in the first edition of the play.

26. Schock, *Romantic Satanism*, 25, 101. Shelley himself denied this influence and, in a letter to Horatio Smith from 11 April 1822, claimed that *Cain* had been conceived by Byron many years before (Shelley, *Essays and Letters*, 372).

27. At least according to Truman Guy Steffan, in Byron and Steffan, *Cain*, 307.

28. *The Gentleman's Magazine*, December 1821, quoted from Osterkamp, *Lucifer*, 184, and Byron and Steffan, *Cain*, 339. For more about the contemporary critical reaction on *Cain*, see Byron and Steffan, *Cain*, 335–381; and Schock, *Romantic Satanism*, 78.

29. Byron and Steffan, *Cain*, 13–18.

30. On Byron's international literary influence in general, see MacCarthy, *Byron*, 544–554; for Russia, see also Boss, *Milton and the Rise of Russian Satanism*, xxv, 84. French literary historians tend to be laconic about Byronic inspiration—see, for example, Paul Bénichou, *Le temps des prophètes: Doctrines de l'âge romantique* (Paris: Éditions Gallimard, 1977), 461—but a short résumé can be found in Milner, *Le diable dans la littérature française*, 1:298–308.

31. On Vigny, see Milner, *Le diable dans la littérature française*, 1:373–401; Paul Bénichou, *Les mages romantiques* (Paris: Éditions Gallimard, 1988), 112–270. There were some sporadic precursors of Romantic Satanism in French literature, for instance, in the obscure work *Le Mort d'Azaël ou le Rapt de Dina* (1799) by P. D. Dugat, in which Satan challenges the creator that he has done a better job with mankind: "Tu exigeas de lui une obéissance servile, et moi seul ai dirigé le premier acte de sa volonté; Adam prévariqua du moment qu'à ma voix il fut libre" (Milner, *Le diable dans la littérature française*, 1:232). An even earlier example can be found in *Voyage autour de mon chambre* by Xavier de Maistre (émigré officer and brother to the more famous Joseph de Maistre). In this charming little book that first saw print in 1795, Maistre declared his "admiration malgré moi" for Milton's Satan, despite the fact that the latter is "un vrai démocrate, non de ceux d'Athènes, mais de ceux de Paris" (Xavier de Maistre, *Voyage autour de ma chambre* (Paris: Librairie Arthème Fayard, 2000), 59–60). The contra-revolutionary poet René Chateaubriand, whose heroes share similar traits with those of Byron, is sometimes also ranged with the Romantic Satanists. His Satan, however, is a more or less traditional representative of evil (Milner, *Le diable dans la littérature française*, 1:233–246, particularly 244). Maximilian Rudwin, *Supernaturalism and Satanism in Chateaubriand* (Chicago: Open Court, 1922), totally seems to miss this point.

32. For further Byronic themes in *Eloa* or its sketches, see Milner, *Le diable dans la littérature française*, 1:380–382, 390, 400.

33. There were some hints for this in *Cain*, particularly in the strange magnetic attraction Lucifer seems to exert on Cain's sister Adah (Byron and Steffan, *Cain*, 182 [Act I, lines 406–414]).

34. A[lfred] de Vigny, *Œuvres Complètes*, ed. F. Baldensperger, 2 vols. (Paris: Librairie Gallimard 1950), 1:73–75. "There you have before your eyes the work of the Malefactor/The evil one, accused by all, in truth is a Comforter," Satan continues ("La voilà sous tes yeux l'œuvre du Malfaiteur;/Ce méchant qu'on accuse est un Consolateur.") Several authors have argued that *Eloa* had been severely pruned by its author to prevent public outrage; see Paul Bénichou, *Le sacre de l'écrivain, 1750–1830: Essai sur l'avènement d'un pouvoir laïque dans la France moderne* (Paris: Éditions Gallimard, 1996), 360, 371–374. Milner, *Le diable dans la littérature française*, 1:373–401, does throw doubt on this fear of censorship, but earlier sketches of *Eloa* certainly show a considerably more grim antitheism.

35. Claudius Grillet, *Le Diable dans la littérature au XIXe Siècle* (Lyon: Emmanuel Vitte, 1935), 163–164.

36. Louis Maigron, *Le Romantisme et les mœurs: Essai d'étude historique et sociale d'après des documents inédits* (Paris: Librairie Ancienne, 1910), 231–232; Grillet, *Le Diable dans la littérature au XIXe Siècle*, 93. "Il a les yeux de Satan. J'aime Satan" was the way Romantic women talked about the man of their dreams in the 1830s, according to the satirical magazine *Figaro* (quoted in Milner, *Le diable dans la littérature française*, 1:518). On French Romantic Satanism in general during this period, see Armand Hoog, "La révolte métaphysique et religieuse des petits romantiques," in *Les petits romantiques français*, ed. Francis Dumont (Paris: Les Cahiers du Sud, 1949), 13–28, here 27; and Milner, *Le diable dans la littérature française*, 1:516–562.

37. Victor Hugo, "Sur George Gordon, Lord Byron," in *La Muse française 1823–1824*, ed. Jules Marsan, 2 vols. (Paris: Édouard Correly, 1907) 2:297–309, here 302–303.

38. Mario Praz, *The Romantic Agony*, trans. Angus Davidson (Oxford: Oxford University Press, 1951), 80.

39. Maigron, *Le Romantisme et les mœurs*, 373, citing an anonymous diary: "Tout cela vient de Byron, comme l'usage du cigare, la pratique de l'orgie, et bien d'autres choses."

40. This tear could also be shed by Jesus, as in Pierre-Jean de Béranger's poem *La Fille du Diable* (1840–1841); Eloa also sprang into existence from one of Jesus' tears of pity.

41. On Soumet, see Milner, *Le diable dans la littérature française*, 2:116–145; Grillet, *Le Diable dans la littérature au XIXe Siècle*, 167–176.

42. On Hugo and *Fin de Satan*, see Milner, *Le diable dans la littérature française*, 2:358–422; Paul Zumthor, *Victor Hugo, poète de Satan* (Paris: Robert Laffont, 1946). Hugo was without doubt influenced by Vigny's earlier plans: he wrote a review of *Eloa* for the *Muse française* of May 1824 (Victor Hugo, "Eloa ou la Sœur des Anges, mystère par le comte Alfred de Vigny," in Marsan, *La Muse française*, 2:247–258), while Vigny himself informed him about his idea for a sequel in a letter (Milner, *Le diable dans la littérature française*, 1:397). A sketch left of this project gives an ending greatly resembling that which Hugo planned for *Fin de Satan*, with the deity pardoning the devil with these words: "Tu as été puni pendant le temps; tu as assez souffert, puisque tu fus l'ange du mal. Tu as aimé une fois: entre dans mon éternité: le mal n'existe plus" (Milner, *Le diable dans la littérature française*, 1:398).

43. Victor Hugo, *Le texte de "La Fin de Satan" dans le manuscrit B.N. n.a.fr. 24.754*, ed. René Journet and Guy Robert, Contribution aux études sur Victor Hugo, no. 2, Annales Littéraires de l'Université de Besançon, no. 232 (Paris: Les Belles-Lettres, 1979), 11–27.

44. Schnierer, *Entdämonisierung und Verteufelung*, 106–160, gives much information on Satan's career in later English-language literature. For German literature, see Osterkamp, *Lucifer*, 213–248; for the case of Russia, see again Boss, *Milton and the Rise of Russian Satanism*. The very early work of the Portuguese poet Fernando Pessoa is also strongly influenced by Romantic Satanism: see, for instance, his *A Hora de Diabo*, in which Satan represents the (poetic) imagination (consulted by me in a Dutch translation: Fernando Pessoa, *Het uur van de Duivel*, trans. August Willemsen [Amsterdam: Uitgeverij De Arbeiderspers, 2000]; see also Willemsen's accompanying text on 33–53). Romantic Satanism seems to have passed by Dutch literature almost completely, but faint traces of it can be found in an early and unpublished narrative poem by the young Herman Gorter—cf. Herman de Liagre Böll, *Herman Gorter 1864–1927: Met al mijn bloed heb ik voor U geleefd* (Amsterdam: Olympus, 2000), 47–49. We will read about Italian literary Satanism later. Feminist literary Satanism in all its deliciously obscure byways is treated by Per Faxneld in his indispensable monograph, *Satanic Feminism*; see also Adriana Craciun, "Romantic Satanism and the Rise of Nineteenth-Century Women's Poetry," *New Literary History* 34 (2004) 4:699–721.

45. Jacques Godechot, *La Grande Nation: L'expansion révolutionnaire de la France dans le monde de 1789 à 1799* (Paris: Aubier Montaigne, 1983), 23–41.

46. Godechot, *La Grande Nation*, 23–41.

47. Godechot, *La Grande Nation*, 37.

48. This is especially clear in the case of Vondel, a Roman-Catholic living in the Protestant-dominated Dutch Republic. His Lucifer is a disguised portrait of the statholders of Orange, who had become the de facto leaders of the Dutch insurrection against Habsburg (i.e., Spanish) rule. The work was dedicated to Ferdinand III, the Habsburg Emperor Elect of the Holy Roman Empire, whose governance Vondel wished to see restored. (Osterkamp, *Lucifer*, 93–94, dismisses this obvious political relevance much too quick, I think, although this does not invalidate his more general social and economical analysis.)

49. See, apart from the works already cited, also Max Milner's essay "Signification politique de la figure de Satan dans le romantisme français," in *Romantisme et politique 1815–1851: Colloque de l'Ecole Normale Supérieure de Saint-Cloud (1966)*, ed. Louis Girard (Paris: Librarie Armand Colin, 1969), 157–163. Russell, *Mephistopheles*, 169, also pointed out the significance of the French Revolution.

50. Ackroyd, *Blake*, 158.

51. Blake, *Marriage of Heaven and Hell*, plates 24–25. That Blake adhered, generally speaking, to the ideals of the Western Revolution cannot be doubted; see, for instance, the short poem "An Ancient Proverb" from the 1793 "Rossetti Manuscript" (William Blake, *Poems and Prophecies* [London: J. M. Dent and Sons, 1924], 381): "Remove away that black'ning church,/Remove away that marriage hearse,/Remove away that man of blood,/You'll quite remove the ancient curse."

52. J. Bronowski, *William Blake and the Age of Revolution* (London: Routledge and Kegan Paul, 1972), 71.

53. Bronowski, *William Blake*, 105; Schock, *Romantic Satanism*, 88; Michael Henry Scrivener, *Radical Shelley: The Philosophical Anarchism and Utopian Thought of Percy Bysshe Shelley* (Princeton, NJ: Princeton University Press, 1982), 33–34.

54. Cf. Scrivener, *Radical Shelley*, 44–45. For expressions on free love and women's liberation by Shelley, see Shelley, *Complete Poetical Works*, 1:301–304 (*Queen Mab*, note 9), 2:140–143

(*Laon and Cythna*, Canto 2,37–43), for instance, 141 (Canto 2,43): "Can man be free if woman be a slave?" Faxneld, *Satanic Feminism*, 158, calls *Laon and Cynthia* "the earliest specimen of . . . Satanic feminism"; see his analysis of the poem on pp. 123–128.

55. Todd, *Death and the Maidens*, 92.

56. Todd, *Death and the Maidens*, 90; Shelley, *Essays and Letters*, 383–384.

57. Shelley, *Essays and Letters*, 26–27.

58. Shelley, *Complete Poetical Works*, 2:111 (*Laon and Cythna*, Canto 1,1). See also Scrivener, *Radical Shelley*, 119–133.

59. Percy Bysshe Shelley, *Shelley's "Prometheus Unbound": The Text and the Drafts* (New Haven, CT: Yale University Press, 1968), 185 (Act III, Scene 2, lines 164–169); "broad sunrise" from Shelley, *Complete Poetical Works*, 2:227 (*Laon and Cythna*, Canto 9,25).

60. Quoted in Osterkamp, *Lucifer*, 198.

61. MacCarthy, *Byron*, 155–157; Schock, *Romantic Satanism*, 160.

62. I am unconvinced by Osterkamp's analysis of *Cain* as a dirge for the loss of power of European aristocracy (Osterkamp, *Lucifer*, 179).

63. Byron and Steffan, *Cain*, 241 (Act III, lines 255–268).

64. Byron and Steffan, *Cain*, 244 (Act III, lines 303–304).

65. Byron and Steffan, *Cain*, 243 (Act III, lines 295–296).

66. Byron and Steffan, *Cain*, 335–337. The *Quarterly Review* (quoted in Byron and Steffan, *Cain*, 381) noted that cheap editions of *Cain* were circulated "among the populace" by "atheists and Jacobins."

67. Southey, *Vision of Judgement*, xxi; significantly, except from being a "tribute to the sacred memory of our late reverend Sovereign," *Vision of Judgement* is primarily a long condemnation of the French Revolution. On Southey's agenda, see Schock, *Romantic Satanism*, 101.

68. Compare Milner, "Signification politique de Satan dans le romantisme français"; Hoog, "La révolte métaphysique et religieuse des petits romantiques."

69. For the more specific ideological background of *Fin de Satan*, see Bénichou, *Les mages romantiques*, 278.

70. Hugo, *Fin de Satan*, 86–88 (lines 1305–1372).

71. Milner, *Le diable dans la littérature française*, 2:411.

72. Hugo, *Fin de Satan*, 240: "la prison détruite abolit le géhenne."

73. Shelley, *Complete Poetical Works*, 1:271 (*Queen Mab*, Book VI, line 105).

74. Godwin, *Political and Philosophical*, 3:146.

75. Taylor, *Secular Age*, 225, 232–233, 294.

76. Thomas Paine, *The Age of Reason* (1794/1795; repr., New York: Prometheus, 1984), 20.

77. Byron and Steffan, *Cain*, 167 (Act I, lines 138–140).

78. Schock, *Romantic Satanism*, 80.

79. Shelley, *Complete Poetical Works*, 1:235 (*Queen Mab*, Book I, line 129).

80. Shelley, *Complete Poetical Works*, 1:259 (*Queen Mab*, Book IV, lines 208–210). See also Shelley, *Complete Poetical Works*, 1:244 (Book II, 149–161), where the Hebrew deity is called a "Demon-God"; 1:269–271 (Book VI, 64–65); 1:277–278 (Book VII, 106–152); and 1:269 (*Queen Mab*, note 2), 1:309–316 (note 13), and 1:308–325 (note 15).

81. Shelley, *Essays and Letters*, 339–340 (letter to *The Examiner*, 22 July 1821). Shelley's public statement was prompted by the publication of a pirate edition of *Queen Mab*. In a private letter

to John Gisborne of 16 June 1821, Shelley declared that he had only written this disavowal "for the sake of a dignified appearance . . . and really because I wish to protest against all the bad poetry in it," admitting to be "much amused" by the "droll circumstance" of the poem's reappearance (ibid., 339). As a matter of fact, in his very letter to *The Examiner*, Shelley took care to emphasize that he retained his position as "a devoted enemy to religious, political, and domestic oppression."

82. See, for instance, Canto 8,6 of *Laon and Cythna* in Shelley, *Complete Poetical Works*, 2:213.

83. Shelley, *Prometheus Unbound*, 65 (Act I, line 265), 63 (Act I, 239), 157 (Act III, scene i, 10).

84. Shelley, *Prometheus Unbound*, 89 (Act I, lines 584–585). In other writings, Shelley portrayed Jesus as a noble teacher and martyr for truth and justice: see particularly his "Essay on Christianity," written in 1816–1817 but only posthumously published (Shelley, *Essays and Letters*, 83–113).

85. Byron and Steffan, *Cain*, 168–169 (Act I, lines 168–169), where Lucifer remarks about his cosmic rival:

> Perhaps he'll make
> One day a Son unto himself, as he
> Gave you a father, and if he so doth
> Mark me! that son will be a sacrifice.

These lines were suppressed in the first printing of the play.

86. MacCarthy, *Byron*, 23.

87. Letter to Francis Hodgson, 3 September 1811, in Lord Byron, *Selected Letters and Journals*, ed. Leslie A. Marchand (Cambridge, MA: Belknap Press of Harvard University Press, 1982), 53.

88. Byron and Steffan, *Cain*, 167 (Act I, lines 138–140).

89. Byron and Steffan, *Cain*, 174 (Act I, line 267), 168 (Act I, 143–144).

90. Byron and Steffan, *Cain*, 168 (Act I, lines 154–155). These lines were suppressed in the first printing of the play.

91. Blake, *Marriage of Heaven and Hell*, plates 26–27: it is clear from the rest of the text that Blake is alluding to the Ten Commandments here.

92. Blake, *Marriage of Heaven and Hell*, plate 9. See also plate 27: "Let the Priests of the Raven of dawn no longer in deadly black, with hoarse note, curse the sons of joy. . . . Nor pale religious letchery [*sic*] call that virginity, that wishes but acts not!" Several other poems also attest to Blake's preoccupation with this theme: for instance, the famous poem "The Garden of Love" from *Songs of Experience* (*Poems and Prophecies*, 30). On Blake and "sexual liberation," see Ackroyd, *Blake*, 81–82, 154.

93. Blake, *Marriage of Heaven and Hell*, plate 4.

94. Blake, *Poems and Prophecies*, 67 (plate 11). In *Europe*, Blake called the deity "a tyrant crowned" (Blake, *Poems and Prophecies*, 371), while to the end of his life, he wrote, "God is the Ghost of the Priest & King who exist whereas God exists not except from their effluvia" (quoted in Ackroyd, *Blake*, 365).

95. ". . . autant de rayons que l'univers a d'êtres": Hugo, *Fin de Satan*, 210 (line 4876). Bénichou, *Sacre de l'écrivain*, 373–374, has rightly remarked that the French epodes of "reconciliation of Satan" implicitly encompassed a rehabilitation not only of the devil, but also of the deity, "le Réprobateur avec son Réprouvé," in which the "somber side" of Christianity was placed under critique and replaced by a euphoric, millennial panentheistic theology.

96. Hugo, *Fin de Satan*, 175 (line 3894).

97. Hugo, *Fin de Satan*, 175 (line 4014); 175 (3896–3902); 210 (4875).

98. Paine, *Age of Reason*, 18.

99. Taylor, *Age of Secularisation*, 437; Owen Chadwick, *The Secularization of the European Mind in the Nineteenth Century: The Gifford Lectures in the University of Edinburgh for 1973–4* (Cambridge: Cambridge University Press, 1975), 9; Paulus Lenz-Medoc, "Le mort de Dieu," *Satan. Les Études Carmélitaines* 27 (1948): 611–634.

100. Taylor, *Age of Secularisation*, 423.

101. Concepts like "desecularization" and "the postsecular" seem to have become *en vogue* within recent scholarship. See Kocku von Stuckrad, "Discursive Transfers and Reconfigurations: Tracing the Religious and the Esoteric in Secular Culture," in *Contemporary Esotericism*, ed. Egil Asprem and Kennet Granholm (Sheffield, UK: Equinox, 2013), 226–243, there 227–229; and Kennet Granholm, "The Secular, the Post-Secular and the Esoteric in the Public Sphere," in ibid., 309–329. Granholm's suggestion "to reserve the use of the term [secularization] to official Christianity and its institutions" (313) would be fine with me with regard to this study, where secularization is only used to designate the particular historical evolution with regard to religion in the West. It remains to be seen, however, if similar processes will not occur in other societies with a dominant social and political role for one religion (e.g., in the Islamic world).

102. Hugh McLeod, *Secularisation in Western Europe, 1848–1914* (Houndmills, UK: Macmillan, 2000), 28–29, 287; Taylor, *Age of Secularisation*, 300 (et alia).

103. McLeod, *Secularisation in Western Europe*, 175, 287.

104. Cf. Chadwick, *Secularization of the European Mind*, 26.

105. Cf. McLeod, *Secularisation in Western Europe*, 50, from which I also borrowed the phrase "contested territory." An exemplary exception is Roman Catholicism in the Netherlands, which embraced parliamentary democracy in order to gain legal emancipation, but apparently not altogether without genuine conviction. See Theo Salemink, "Politischer Katholizismus in den Niederlanden," in *Die Rolle des politischen Katholizismus in Europa im 20. Jahrhundert: Band 1*, ed. Heiner Timmermann (Münster: Lit Verlag, 2009), 161–175.

106. McLeod, *Secularisation in Western Europe*, 31–51.

107. McLeod, *Secularisation in Western Europe*, 29. Taylor likewise gives a brilliant apology of the importance of ideas as a historical factor on pp. 212–213 of *Age of Secularisation*.

108. Of course, no statistical data are available, but compare Scrivener, *Radical Shelley*, 7, 67–68. Blake would only be really discovered far after his death.

109. There is a wealth of literature regarding the theoretical questions connected with Romanticism. Particularly helpful for this section have been the three books by Paul Bénichou: *Le sacre de l'écrivain; Le temps des prophètes*; and *Les mages romantiques*. Regarding the Romantics and myth, Northrop Frye's seminal work *A Study of English Romanticism* (New York: Random House, 1968) and Isaiah Berlin's *The Roots of Romanticism* (Princeton, NJ: Princeton University Press, 2001) have provided essential insights, while an article by Isaiah Berlin, "The Romantic Revolution: A Crisis in the History of Modern Thought," in *The Sense of Reality: Studies in Ideas and Their History* (London: Pimlico, 1996), 168–193, has proved particularly valuable for my understanding of Romantic philosophy.

110. Shelley, *Complete Poetical Works*, 1:296 (*Queen Mab*, note 2). See also his tongue-in-cheek treatment of the devil in his posthumously published essay *On the Devil, and Devils*: Percy Bysshe Shelley, *Shelley's "Devils' Notebook: Bodleian MS. Shelley Adds. E.9. A Facsimile*

Edition with Full Transcription and Textual Notes, ed. P. M. S. Dawson and Timothy Webb (New York: Garland, 1993), 40–101.

111. Schock, *Romantic Satanism*, 16–17.

112. Shelley, *Complete Poetical Works*, 1:296 (*Queen Mab*, note 2).

113. From "À M. Alphonse de Lamartine," *Odes* III, 1, cited in Bénichou, *Sacre de l'écrivain*, 385. For the roots in Antiquity and Renaissance of the idea of the poet as a divine medium, see ibid., 11–15, and Leslie A. Wilson, "Dichter-Priester: Bestandteil der Romantik," *Colloquia Germanica: Internationale Zeitschrift für germanische Sprach- und Literaturwissenschaft* (1968): 127–136.

114. On the Imagination with the Romantics, see also Morse Peckham, "Toward a Theory of Romanticism," in *Romanticism: Points of View*, ed. Robert F. Gleckner and Gerald E. Enscoe (Englewood Cliffs, NJ: Prentice-Hall, 1970), 231–257, there 254, and Charles Larmore, *The Romantic Legacy* (New York: Columbia University Press, 1996), 1–30.

115. Berlin, "Romantic Revolution," 178–184, and *Roots of Romanticism*, 87; H. W. Piper, *The Active Universe: Pantheism and the Concept of Imagination in the English Romantic Poets* (London: Athlone, 1962), 82–181; René Wellek, "The Concept of 'Romanticism' in Literary History," *Comparative Literature* 1 (1949) 1:1–23, 2:147–172, there 147, 157(n), 160, 171.

116. The paradox of writing academic prose on Romantic poetry has been pointedly expressed by Bénichou, *Les mages romantiques*, 14: "On est conduite, dans un travail comme celui-ci, à employer tour à tour, selon la circonstance, les mots ou expressions 'pensée', 'philosophie', 'religion', 'credo', 'profession de foi', 'vue des choses', 'distribution des valeurs', 'figuration', 'idéologie' même, ou tout autre terme qui convienne à l'occasion, et à tenir pour sous-entendu que le poète, quoi qu'il pense, le pense en poète."

117. Berlin, *Roots of Romanticism*, 120–121.

118. Max Plowman already drew attention to this passage in his introduction to Blake, *Poems and Prophecies*, xvi. For similar ideas with Wordsworth, compare Piper, *Active Universe*, 149.

119. Wilson, "Dichter-Priester," 129.

120. Blake, *Poems and Prophecies*, 171 (*Jerusalem*, plate 10); I owe this reference to Ackroyd, *Blake*, 113.

121. Paine, *Age of Reason*, 22: "The case is, that the word *prophet*, to which latter times have affixed a new meaning, was the Bible word for poet, and the word *prophesying* meant the art of making poetry."

122. Paine, *Age of Reason*, 49.

123. Butler, "Romantic Manichaeism," 15–16; Godwin, *Theosophical Enlightenment*, 1–26. Compare Paine, *Age of Reason*, 12: "The Christian theory is little else than the idolatry of the ancient Mythologists, accommodated to the purposes of power and revenue; and it yet remains to reason and philosophy to abolish this amphibious fraud," and also C.-F. Volney, *Les Ruines* (1822; repr., Paris: Slatkine, 1979), 183 (chapter 22).

124. There had been a few precedents for this attitude, one of the most notable exceptions being Giambattista Vico (1668–1744), an Italian historian and political philosopher who in many respects foreshadowed Romanticism. In his *Scienza Nova* (1725), Vico had remarked that ancient myth and poetry represented a metaphysical knowing that was "felt and imagined" instead of "rational and abstract like that of learned men now." In it, he discerned "a sublimity such and so great that it excessively perturbed the very persons who by imagining did the

creating, for which they were called 'poets,' which is Greek for 'creators.' For this is the threefold labour of great poetry: (1) to invent sublime fables suited to the popular understanding; (2) to perturb to excess, with a view to the end proposed; (3) to teach the vulgar to act virtuously, as the poets have taught themselves." Giambattista Vico, *Principles of a New Science concerning the Nature of the Nations*, par. 376, quoted from Mali, *Mythistory*, 72. See pp. 70–72 (paragraphs 375–376) for similar notions. See also Berlin, *Roots of Romanticism*, 40–51, on Hamann, Vico, and others.

125. Bénichou, *Sacre de l'écrivain*, 275, 469–470; Bénichou, *Le temps des prophètes*, 566 (on p. 423 of this older book, Bénichou is still considerably more skeptical about the religiosity of Romanticism); Bénichou, *Les mages romantiques*, 12–15, 533. See also the utterances of Novalis and Schelling quoted in Wilson, "Dichter-Priester," 135. Even with the Romantic poets who couched their attempts to fill the post-Enlightenment religious vacuum in terms of a return to traditional religion or a nostalgic yearning for a premodern Christian past (in France, for instance, the idea of the "priest-poet" was first brought forward in contra-revolutionary literary circles—cf. Bénichou, *Le sacre de l'écrivain*, 111–192, 333), there was an implicit power conflict with the traditional mediators of meaning: the clergy or hierarchy. This conflict becomes blatantly obvious with poets, like the Romantic Satanists, who propounded radical different systems of meaning.

126. Wellek, "Concept of Romanticism," 165; Bénichou, *Le sacre de l'écrivain*, 361; Frye, *Study of English Romanticism*, 16; Isaiah Berlin, *Roots of Romanticism*, 122.

127. Anyone doubting the appropriateness of the term "myth" here should compare the scholarly definitions for myth in Mali, *Mythistory*, 4–6, or Irving Hexham and Karla Poewe, *New Religions as Global Culture: Making the Human Sacred* (Boulder, CO: Westview, 1997), 70: "A creative mythmaker is the example par excellence of someone who is confident that he or she has sapped the source of sacred power and, through the creation of a mythological map, can show followers, too, how to find it."

128. In his notebook, Blake wrote that his work did not consist of "Fable or Allegory" but of "Vision": "Vision or Imagination is a Representation of what Eternally Exists, Really and Unchangeably" (Blake, *Poems and Prophecies*, 357; notes to The Last Judgment, about 1818).

129. Bénichou, *Le sacre de l'écrivain*, 473–474; Bénichou, *Temps des prophètes*, 423–424; Bénichou, *Les mages romantiques*, 12.

130. Ackroyd, *Blake*, 18. On Blake's background in Dissenting Christianity, see also Mark Knight and Emma Mason, *Nineteenth-Century Religion and Literature: An Introduction* (Oxford: Oxford University Press, 2006), 17, 42–51.

131. Ackroyd, *Blake*, 104.

132. Schock, *Romantic Satanism*, 45; Jos van Meurs, "William Blake and His Gnostic Myths," in *Gnosis and Hermeticism: From Antiquity to Modern Times*, ed. Roelof van den Broek and Wouter J. Hanegraaff (Albany: State University of New York Press, 1998), 269–309, here 284. Kathleen Raine, *Blake and Tradition*, 2 vols. (Princeton, NJ: Princeton University Press, 1968), 1:335–371, downplays Blake's satire of Swedenborg and emphasizes instead the latter's positive influence.

133. Emanuel Swedenborg, *Heaven and Hell*, chapter 59, consulted on http://www.theistic-science.org/books/hh/hh59.html, accessed 5 April 2012. Swedenborg's book was originally published in Latin as *De Coelo et Ejus Mirabilibus, et de Inferno, ex Auditis et Visis* (London, 1758).

134. Emanuel Swedenborg, *The Apocalypse Revealed, Wherein Are Disclosed the Arcana There Foretold, Which Have Hitherto Remained Concealed*, 3 vols. (Boston: Otis Clapp, 1836), 2:76–81 (Chapter 10.484).

135. Blake, *Marriage of Heaven and Hell*, plates 22 and 3. See also plate 19, where the narrator uses "Swedenborgs volumes" as dead weight to sink back to Earth from "the glorious clime."

136. Blake, *Marriage of Heaven and Hell*, plate 22; see also plate 5. While the visionary content of his work placed Swedenborg, of course, well outside the pale of strict rationalism, his "Memorable Relations" depict him indeed as a sort of philosopher traveling through the netherworld and debating with its denizens, intent on showing the compatibility of the divine truths with the precepts of reason. Blake's "Memorable Fancies" adopt a totally different tone, with a narrator that "drives" his spiritual conversation partner before him and "imposes" upon him with his "fantasy," "perturbing him to excess," Vico would have said.

137. Blake, *Poems and Prophecies*, 5–6. Blake remarked upon the idea of "Poetic Genius" for the first time in an annotation on a book by Swedenborg (Ackroyd, *Blake*, 103).

138. Blake, *Poems and Prophecies*, 4.

139. Blake, *Poems and Prophecies*, 5–6.

140. Blake, *Poems and Prophecies*, 133 (*Milton. A Prophecy*, plate 24). The spirit of prophecy is called Los in Blake's mythology, a figure that also stands for time; cf. Blake, *Poems and Prophecies*, 134 (plate 26).

141. Blake, *Poems and Prophecies*, 159–160 (*Milton*, plate 48); I owe this reference to Raine, *Blake and Tradition*, 2:248.

142. Blake, *Milton*, plate 16.

143. Blake, *Poems and Prophecies*, 255 (*Jerusalem* [1804–1820], plate 77).

144. "The Eternal Body of Man is the Imagination: that is God himself/The Divine Body"—letterpress to *Laocoön* (ca. 1820), in Blake, *Poems and Prophecies*, 288. On plate 77 of *Jerusalem*, Blake had stated that the Imagination was the "real and eternal World" tout court.

145. Letterpress to *Laocoön* (ca. 1840), in Blake, *Poems and Prophecies*, 290. Cf. p. 289: "Jesus & his apostles & Disciples were all Artists," as well as p. 290: "Prayer is the Study of Art. Praise is the Practise of Art" and "You must leave Fathers & Mothers & Houses & Lands if they stay in the way of Art."

146. Ackroyd, *Blake*, 18, 111, 330. The work that was dictated by a fairy is *Europe, A Prophecy* (1794); cf. Blake, *Poems and Prophecies*, 70.

147. Letter to Thomas Butts, quoted in Bronowski, *Blake and the Age of Revolution*, 28–29. "I have written this poem from immediate dictation," he stated in a letter about *Vala, Or the Four Zoas* (1797): "I may praise it, since I dare not pretend to be any other than the Secretary, the Authors are in Eternity" (quoted in Ackroyd, *Blake*, 238).

148. See Blake, *Poems and Prophecies*, 357, where Blake protests against the idea of Plato that "Poets & Prophets do not Know or Understand what they write or Utter." On this point, consult also Bronowski, *William Blake*, 28–29.

149. Blake, *Marriage of Heaven and Hell*, plate 3.

150. Blake, *Marriage of Heaven and Hell*, plate 6.

151. Blake, *Poems and Prophecies*, 4.

152. Compare *Marriage of Heaven and Hell*, plates 5–6.

153. Blake, *Poems and Prophecies*, 109 (*Milton*, preface).

154. Blake, *Marriage of Heaven and Hell*, plate 26.

155. This is suggested by *Marriage of Heaven and Hell*, plate 14, and also more clearly in *Milton*, plate 24, where Blake-who-has-become-Los introduces himself as the "Shadowy Prophet" who returns after six thousand years, which is also the time for which the "Great Harvest & Vintage of the Nations" is announced (Blake, *Poems and Prophecies*, 133, 161 [*Milton*, plate 24 and 50]. As noted, Los stands for Time as well as the "Spirit of Prophecy"; see ibid., 137 [plate 26]).

156. Blake, *Marriage of Heaven and Hell*, plates 24 and 3. Concerning moral relativity, see also *Milton*, plate 4 (Blake, *Poems and Prophecies*, 112): "Every Man's Wisdom is peculiar to his own Individuality."

157. Blake, *Marriage of Heaven and Hell*, plate 16. Blake here seems to contradict the millennialist expectation of a return to paradise that erupts at other places within *Marriage of Heaven and Hell*.

158. Blake, *Poems and Prophecies*, 146 (*Milton*, plate 33), 159 (46).

159. Blake, *Poems and Prophecies*, 159 (*Milton*, plate 46), 289, 149 (*Milton*, 35).

160. Raine, *Blake and Tradition*, 1:335–371, particularly 363 and 367; Ackroyd, *Blake*, 146–149. One may also detect, however, the influence of contemporary scientific literature, for example, Joseph Priestley's hypothesis of matter as energy. Compare Piper, *Active Universe*, 31.

161. Shelley, *Complete Poetical Works*, 1:309 (*Queen Mab*, note 13).

162. Shelley, *Complete Poetical Works*, 1:320 (*Queen Mab*, note 15). See also earlier in the poem, where Shelley wrote about Jehovah and his followers (*Complete Poetical Works*, 1:244; Book I, lines 158–161):

> His name and their are fading, and the tales
> Of this barbarian nation, which imposture
> Recites till terror credits, are pursuing
> Itself into forgetfulness.

163. Cf. Piper, *Active Universe*, 166, on Shelley's scientific sources of inspiration here.

164. Shelley, *Complete Poetical Works*, 2:227 (*Laon and Cythna*, Canto 9,25).

165. This notion might be less paradoxical than one would tend to suppose. Owen Chadwick, in his Gifford Lectures on secularization, was also struck by the many indications he had found "that secularization was a religious process, not an irreligious." Chadwick, *Secularization of the European Mind*, 156.

166. In particular Volney, *Les Ruins*, that displays many similarities with *Queen Mab*. Cf. Butler, "Romantic Manichaeism," 17.

167. Shelley, *Essays and Letters*, 5–6.

168. Shelley, *Complete Poetical Works*, 1:272 (*Queen Mab*, Book VI, lines 148–149).

169. Shelley, *Essays and Letters*, 12.

170. Shelley, *Essays and Letters*, 41. Shelley may have been inspired for this phrase by Godwin, as well as for some of his other ideas regarding imagination: see Todd, *Death and the Maidens*, 116.

171. Shelley, *Essays and Letters*, 30–33.

172. Shelley, *Essays and Letters*, 33–34.

173. Shelley, *Essays and Letters*, 33; compare Blake's "Christianity is Art & not Money," *Lacoön*, in *Poems and Prophecies*, 290. There is no indication that Shelley and Blake were familiar

with each other's work, although Shelley's friend John Hunt devoted a few lines to Blake in *The Examiner*, in which he characterized him as an "unfortunate lunatic, whose inoffensiveness secures him from confinement" (Ackroyd, *Blake*, 288).

174. *Laon and Cythna*, Canto 1,25.

175. *Laon and Cythna*, Canto 1,25.

176. *Laon and Cythna*, Canto 1,33.

177. Shelley, *Essays and Letters*, 91–92.

178. Shelley, *Essays and Letters*, 40.

179. Shelley, *Complete Poetical Works*, 2:99.

180. Butler, "Romantic Manichaeism," 14.

181. Shelley, *Complete Poetical Works*, 2:99–100.

182. Frye, *Study of English Romanticism*, 110–112.

183. Shelley's words about poetry in *Defence of Poetry*: Shelley, *Essays and Letters*, 40.

184. Shelley, *Defence of Poetry*: Shelley, *Essays and Letters*, 32–33.

185. Byron and Steffan, *Cain*, 10(n).

186. See, for example, Byron and Steffan, *Cain*, 4n.

187. Byron in letters to James Hogg, 24 March [1814] and to Hobhouse and Kinnaird, 19 January 1819, in *Selected Letters*, 100, 185.

188. This was keenly acknowledged by his French translator and critic, Fabre d'Olivet, who wrote, "Ce ne sont plus des individus humains que vous avez mis en scène, mais des principes cosmogoniques; ce ne sont plus des actions particulières, des opinions quelconque que vous avez exposées, mais des actes universels." Fabre d'Olivet, *Caïn, mystère dramatique en trois actes de Lord Byron, traduit en vers français et réfuté dans une suite de remarques philosophiques et critiques* (1823; repr., Geneva: Éditions Slatkine, 1981), 7.

189. Letter to John Murray, 2 November 1821, in Byron, *Selected Letters*, 280–281. Cf. Byron and Steffan, *Cain*, 11 (n).

190. Byron and Steffan, *Cain*, 226 (Act II, scene ii, line 429) and 181 (Act I, lines 385–386).

191. Fred Parker, "Between Satan and Mephistopheles: Byron and the Devil," *Cambridge Quarterly* 35 (2006) 1:1–29, there 3–4.

192. Byron and Steffan, *Cain*, 208 (Act II, scene ii, lines 97–98) and 194 (Act II, scene i, lines 54, 56–57).

193. Byron's *The Deformed Transformed: A Drama* (1824) also features a figure called "The Stranger" who has all the characteristics of a Mephistophelian devil, displaying the same sarcasm toward mankind. Byron, *Poetical Works*, 605–623: see especially 616 (Part I, scene ii, lines 320–332).

194. Byron and Steffan, *Cain*, 170 (Act I, lines 196–197) and 192 (Act II, scene ii, 24).

195. Parker, "Between Satan and Mephistopheles," 11, also suggests this.

196. Guthke, "Der Mythos des Bösen," 17 ; Byron and Steffan, *Cain*, 203–227 (Act II, scene ii); see also Cain's story of the lamb bit by a snake, where the idea that evil is only a road to good is criticized, in *Cain*, 218 (Act II, scene ii, lines 285–305). Incidentally, many of these arguments would be equally valid against the providential watchmaker-god of deism, and some of them almost seem to be selected with this purpose by Byron. When Cain remains in awe before the beauty of creation, for instance, Lucifer takes him to Hades to show the mighty beings that inhabited Earth in prehistory and of whom humanity is but a lesser relict—thus implicitly dispelling the notion that the universe is a perfectly made biotope for human happiness.

197. Byron and Steffan, *Cain*, 227 (Act II, scene ii, lines 459–466). Paine's dictum is from *Age of Reason*, 8.

198. Cf. his letters to Francis Hodgson of 3 and 13 September 1811, in Byron, *Selected Letters*, 52–55; "Detached thoughts," No. 96 (1821/1822), in Byron, *Selected Letters*, 277–278. James Kennedy wrote that Byron had confided similar sentiments to him toward the end of his life: Byron and Steffan, *Cain*, 168.

199. ". . . philosophie assise sur des ruines, pleurant son incrédulité et les tristes résultats de sa science," cited in Bénichou, *Sacre de l'écrivain*, 334.

200. Peckham, "Toward a Theory of Romanticism," 241.

201. Byron and Steffan, *Cain*, 162 (Act I, line 44).

202. Byron and Steffan, *Cain*, 195 (Act II, scene i, lines 82–83).

203. Blake, *There Is No Natural Religion*, in *Poems and Prophecies*, 3–4.

204. Blake attended a dinner party of Lady Caroline Lamb, one of Byron's lovers, in 1818; Ackroyd, *Blake*, 232.

205. On Wordsworth, compare M. H. Abrams, "English Romanticism: The Spirit of the Age," in *Romanticism: Points of View*, ed. Robert F. Gleckner and Gerald E. Enscoe (Englewood Cliffs, NJ: Prentice-Hall, 1970), 314–330, there 327.

206. [Johann Wolfgang] Goethe, *Faust: Eine Tragoedie* (München: Droemersche Verlaganstalt, 1949), 73. The second part of *Faust*, which contains the apotheosis of the story, only appeared in 1832, nine years after Byron's death. But the central theme is clear enough from part I. It was, at least, to Shelley, who read part I in 1822 and remarked in a letter to his friend John Gisborne on exactly this motive. "Perhaps all discontent with the *less* (to use a Platonic sophism), supposes the sense of a just claim to the *greater*, and that we admirers of Faust are on the right road to Paradise." Shelley to John Gisborne, 10 April 1822, in *Essays and Letters*, 368–369.

207. Milton, *Paradise Lost*, I, lines 254–255.

208. Byron and Steffan, *Cain*, 171 (Act I, lines 213–215).

209. Byron and Steffan, *Cain*, 186 (Act I, lines 492–496); 165 (Act I, 103).

210. Byron and Steffan, *Cain*, 170 (Act I, lines 192–193).

211. Schock, *Romantic Satanism*, 110–111, seems to miss this point when he reduces *Cain*'s Lucifer to the voice of Reason only.

212. Byron and Steffan, *Cain*, 222–223 (Act II, scene ii, lines 365–442). Likewise, Cain's violence against Abel is, in the end, according to Byron, a misguided attempt at cosmic revolt, directed "rather against Life—and the author of Life—than the mere Living." Byron, *Selected Letters*, 281.

213. Blake, *There Is No Natural Religion*, in *Poems and Prophecies*, 3–4.

214. Blake, *Poems and Prophecies*, 312–315.

215. Blake, *Poems and Prophecies*, 312.

216. Byron and Steffan, *Cain*, 165 (Act I, lines 95–96).

217. Vigny, *Œuvres Complètes*, 2:942, 2:1011. On Vigny's "spiritualisme du séparation," which displays salient resemblances to that of Byronism, cf. Bénichou, *Sacre de l'écrivain*, 371, and also Vigny, *Œuvres Complètes*, 2:1001.

218. Butler, "Romantic Manichaeism," 36–37; Parker, "Between Satan and Mephistopheles," 13–15.

219. On this tradition, see Byron and Steffan, *Cain*, 271, and Lieve M. Teugels, "The Twin Sisters of Cain and Abel: A Survey of the Rabbinic Sources," in *Eve's Children: The Biblical Stories Retold and Interpreted in Jewish and Christian Traditions*, ed. Gerard P. Luttikhuizen (Leiden: Brill, 2003), 47–56.

220. Byron and Steffan, *Cain*, 170 (Act I, line 189); 181 (Act I, 404, 484).

221. Byron and Steffan, *Cain*, 185 (Act I, line 481).

222. Byron and Steffan, *Cain*, 216–217 (Act II, scene ii, lines 255–269); 335 (Act II, scene ii, 337–338). In addition, when Lucifer's disclosures make him ever more despondent, Cain protests that he sought knowledge only "as road to happiness": *Cain*, 215 (II, ii, 231).

223. Byron and Steffan, *Cain*, 168 (Act I, lines 160–166). We should be careful before we enlist Lucifer on the side of human love here, however, because his "unbounded love" has all the characteristics of an abstract philosophy, reminding one of Shelley's depiction of Prometheus. Byron might be covertly criticizing Shelley here. Indeed, if any living person may have functioned as the model for Byron's Lucifer, I would venture it was Shelley. See the intriguing parallels and Shelley's discontent with Byron's insufficient unchristianity mentioned by Parker, "Between Satan and Mephistopheles," 11n. Shelley praised *Cain* as "apocalyptic" and "a revelation not before communicated to man" (letter to John Gisborne, 10 April 1822, in *Essays and Letters*, 370), but he also denied that he had had "the smallest influence" over Byron with regard to its composition, "and if I had, I certainly should employ it to eradicate from his great mind the delusions of Christianity, which, in spite of his reason, seems perpetually to recur, and to lay in ambush for the hours of sickness and distress" (letter to Horatio Smith, 11 April 1822, in *Essays and Letters*, 372).

224. Byron and Steffan, *Cain*, 232 (Act III, lines 79–86); 255 (Act III, 510–515).

225. Byron, *Heaven and Earth*, Part I, scene iii, line 635, in *Poetical Works*, 559.

226. Letter to Lamennais, 1 September 1823—Bénichou, *Les mages romantiques*, 283; "Fonction du poète" (1839)—Bénichou, *Les mages romantiques*, 309; "La Poète" (1823)—Bénichou, *Sacre de l'écrivain*, 391; "Discours de réception à l'Académie Française," 3 June 1841—Bénichou, *Les mages romantiques*, 307.

227. ". . . elle lui demande des croyances" : Hugo in *La Muse française*, August 1823—quoted in Bénichou, *Sacre de l'écrivain*, 387.

228. Zumthor, *Victor Hugo, poète de Satan*, 1–61.

229. Victor Hugo, "Océan," quoted from Milner, *Le diable dans la littérature française*, 2:378.

230. Bénichou, *Les mages romantiques*, 503–507.

231. Zumthor, *Victor Hugo, poète de Satan*, 35, 48–50.

232. Zumthor, *Victor Hugo, poète de Satan*, 50–51.

233. Zumthor, *Victor Hugo, poète de Satan*, 52.

234. Grillet, *Le Diable dans la littérature au XIXe Siècle*, 158–159.

235. Zumthor, *Victor Hugo, poète de Satan*, 256.

236. Hugo, *Fin de Satan*, 210 (lines 4884–4885): "Dieu m'excepte. Il finit à moi. Je suis sa borne./Dieu serait infini si je n'existais pas."

237. Hugo, *Fin de Satan*, 221 (lines 5180–5185). In a guidebook, Hugo would describe Paris as "the place of revolutionary revelation" and "the Jerusalem of mankind"—see Zumthor, *Victor Hugo, poète de Satan*, 157.

238. Hugo, *Fin de Satan*, 240 (fragment).

239. Cf., for instance, Praz, *Romantic Agony*, 53–91. In the Gothic literature of the Romantic era, the devil is mostly used as a traditional representative of evil and terror, although a deeper reading may sometimes reveal other subconscious messages. See the article by Per Faxneld, "Woman Liberated by the Devil in Four Gothic Novels: William Beckford's *Vathek* (1786), Matthew Lewis' *The Monk* (1796), Charlotte Dacre's *Zofloya, or The Moor* (1806), and Charles Maturin's *Melmoth the Wanderer* (1820)," in *Grotesque Femininities: Evil, Women and the Feminine*, ed. M. Barrett (Oxford: Inter-Disciplinary Press, 2010), 29–43, as well as the corresponding section in his monograph *Satanic Feminism*, 205–276.

240. Schock, *Romantic Satanism*, 6, already remarks that Romantic Satanism was not "monolithic or univocal."

241. Byron to John Murray, 19 September 1820, in Byron, *Selected Letters*, 234. The skull cup is also mentioned in a letter to Lady Melbourne from 17 October 1813, in ibid., 76.

242. Zumthor, *Victor Hugo, poète de Satan*, 1–62.

243. Milner, *Le diable dans la littérature française*, 2:361.

244. Shelley to Thomas Jefferson Hogg, 22 October 1821, in Percy Bysshe Shelley, *The Letters of Percy Bysshe Shelley*, ed. Frederic L. Jones, 2 vols. (Oxford: Clarendon, 1964), 2:359–362 (Letter 667), there 2:361. Shelley's letter was a reaction to an epistle from Hogg dated 15 June 1821 in which the latter speaks of "propitiating" Pan with an inscription and a garland in Bisham Wood while taking a walk with Thomas Love Peacock (Shelley, *Letters*, 359–360n). I owe this reference to Hutton, *Triumph of the Moon*, 25.

245. Mary Wollstonecraft Shelley, *Frankenstein; or the Modern Prometheus* (1912; repr., London: J. M. Dent and Sons, 1927), particularly the scene on pp. 135–136, where Dr. Frankenstein's creature reads *Paradise Lost* and compares his own situation with that of Milton's Satan.

246. Quote from *Manfred: A Dramatic Poem*, Act III, scene iv, lines 374–375; cf. Act II, scene ii, 252–255; Act II, scene iv, 405–406; Act III, scene i, 52–56.

247. Byron and Steffan, *Cain*, 176 (Act I, lines 310–317). In the next line, Lucifer declares "Ne'er the less/Thou art my worshipper; not worshipping/Him [the creator] makes thee mine the same." Does Byron make Lucifer here simply into the echo of Christian theology, as the subsequent allusions to the eternal punishment of hell suggest? Or is he making a deeper point, and is he referring to the irredeemable loss of naive faith that eating of the Tree of Knowledge occasions, or the irrevocable loss of primal unity that individual consciousness brings about?

248. Grillet, *Le Diable dans la littérature*, 153: "C'est ainsi que le progresse s'accomplit par Satan, contre Satan, pour Satan." At other occasions, Hugo did adopt the archangel Michael, the traditional mythological antagonist of Satan, as the heroic embodiment of Liberty, France, "or quite simply the Spirit of Modernity" (ibid., 156).

249. Shelley, *Shelley's "Prometheus Unbound,"* 36–37 (preface, lines 11–50). In *The Devil's Walk*, a poem from 1812, Satan also appears as a representative of evil, although this evil is, once again, described as oppression and the exploitation of the poor by the rich. Cf. Schock, *Romantic Satanism*, 81–82.

250. Blake, *Poems and Prophecies*, 112 (*Milton*, plate 4).

251. Blake, *Poems and Prophecies*, 118 (*Milton*, plate 9); compare also 122 (plate 14), where Blake writes that this opacity is one of the (self-set) limits of the infinite.

252. Blake, *Poems and Prophecies*, 149 (*Milton*, plate 35); 123 (plate 14); 120 (plate 12). Compare 118 (plate 9), where Blake describes how Satan creates the seven deadly sins, "drawing out his infernal scroll/of Moral laws and cruel punishments upon the clouds of Jehovah,/ To pervert the Divine voice in its entrance to the earth/With thunder of war & trumpet's sound," and 156–157 (plates 43–44), where Milton derides "Satan's holiness," with Satan responding: "But I alone am God, & I alone in Heav'n & Earth,/Of all that live and dare utter this, others tremble & bow,/'Till All Things become One Great Satan, in Holiness/Oppos'd to Mercy."

253. Blake, *Poems and Prophecies*, 159 (*Milton*, plate 46). Lucifer is depicted with more sympathy in *Milton*, as a "Combination of Individuals" forced by Satan to appear in human form but nevertheless "combined in Freedom & holy Brotherhood"; ibid., 148–149 (plate 35).

254. Blake, *Poems and Prophecies*, 122 (*Milton*, plate 14).

255. Blake, *Poems and Prophecies*, 315.

256. Ackroyd, *Blake*, 332.

257. Taylor, *Age of Secularisation*, 17; Frye, *Study of English Romanticism*, 125–126. Cf. McLeod, *Secularisation in Western Europe*, 281, on the nineteenth-century emergence of "Religions of Humanity."

258. See also *Milton*, plate 2 (in *Poems and Prophecies*, 110), where Blake tells how "The Eternal Great Humanity Divine" planted its paradise in the "Portals of my Brain" by the ministry of the Muses.

259. Blake, "A Descriptive Catalogue" (1809), quoted in Schock, *Romantic Satanism*, 63–64.

260. Blake, *Marriage of Heaven and Hell*, plate 28.

261. Blake, *Marriage of Heaven and Hell*, plate 39; *Poems and Prophecies*, 350 (from *The Everlasting Gospel*, written circa 1818). A friend quoted Blake thus: "Christ he said—he is the Only God—But then he added—And so am I and so are you" (Ackroyd, *Blake*, 325).

CHAPTER 3 : SATAN IN NINETEENTH-CENTURY COUNTERCULTURE

1. The idea of the threefold emphasis in the Romantic Satan was put forward earlier in my article "Sex, Science & Liberty: The Resurrection of Satan in 19th Century (Counter) Culture," in *The Devil's Party: Satanism in Modernity*, ed. Per Faxneld and Jesper Petersen (Oxford: Oxford University Press, 2012), 41–52. The nineteenth-century author Jules Bois, when he analyzes his century's obsession with the fallen angel in *Le Satanisme et la Magie* (1895), also distinguishes these three Satans: Satan "le plus désolé des Anarchistes," Satan as "intelligence lucide," and Satan-Pan. See his *Le Satanisme et la Magie: Avec une étude de J. K. Huysmans* (Paris: Ernest Flammarion, 1895), 27–35 (on Jules Bois, see chapters 4 and 5).

2. Shelley, *Complete Poetical Works*, 181 (*Laon and Cythna*, Canto 5,51).

3. Byron and Steffan, *Cain*, 162 (Act I, lines 37–38).

4. Blake, of course, is quite another story in this respect: when he identifies Satan with science, both terms are usually unambiguously negative. This negative attitude toward science, however, only applied to its current, perverted form: in its original state, it was an intrinsic part of human nature. See, for instance, *Jerusalem*, "To the Public" (*Poems and Prophecies*, 163): "The Primeval State of Man was Wisdom, Art and Science," and also *Milton*, plate 29 (ibid., 141): "But in eternity the Four Arts, Poetry, Painting, Music/And Architecture, which is Science, are the Four Faces of Man."

5. For this aspect in particular, see Günther Jerouschek, "'Diabolus habitat in eis' Wo der Teufel zu Hause ist: Geslechtigkeit in rechtstheologischen Diskurs des ausgehenden Mittelalters und der frühen Neuzeit," *Rechtshistorischer Journal* 9 (1990): 301–329.

6. Likewise, while Goethe made Satan the representative of nature and sexuality in a repressed scene for *Faust* (1808–1832), this also marks him as ambivalent: it is the human striving for the ideal, Goethe tells us in his play, that is to be considered the better part of our nature (see Albrecht Schöne, *Götterzeichen, Liebeszauber, Satanskult: Neue Einblicke in alte Goethetexte* [München: C. H. Beck, 1982], 107–230, for Goethe's repressed Brocken Mountain scene).

7. Vigny, *Œuvres Complètes*, 1:74.

8. Shelley, *Complete Poetical Works*, 2:125 (*Laon and Cythna*, Canto 1,45).

9. Shelley, *Shelley's "Devils" Notebook*, 97–99. A late manifestation of "Satan-Pan" can be found in Sylvia Townsend Warner's *Lolly Willowes or the Loving Huntsman* (1926; repr., London: Women's Press, 1978); see Faxneld's analysis of this work in *Satanic Feminism*, 617–656.

10. Anatole France, *La révolte des Anges: Préface de Pierre Boulle* (Paris: Calmann-Lévy, 1980). This book about a new insurrection by some of the "good" angels reads like a half-ironic commentary on Romantic Satanism, ending with Satan's refusal to lead the conquest of heaven because it would only transform him into a new tyrant-god: "Dieu vaincu deviendra Satan, Satan vaincu deviendra Dieu" (162). Also prominently present is the Romantic association of Satan with science (cf. 141), with nature (cf. 110–111), and with classic paganism—"le sainte antiquité, le temps où les dieux étaient bons" and Satan roamed the Earth as Dionysus (cf. 49, 135–169).

11. Categorizing references or longer analyses of key figures in these three domains appear in Russell, *Mephistopheles*, 201 (Lévi), 204 (Proudhon), 219 (Blavatsky); Milner, *Le diable dans la littérature française*, 2:249–258 (Constant/Lévi), 2:260–262 (Proudhon); Dvorak, *Satanismus*, 321 (Proudhon and Bakunin); Frick, *Satan und die Satanisten*, 2:151–155 (Lévi); Schmidt, *Satanismus*, 92–96 (Lévi), 120–124 (Theosophy and anthroposophy). Russell, Milner, and Schmidt explicitly or implicitly place these personages in the framework of Romantic Satanism, as will be my main thesis in the subsequent sections. Schmidt, moreover, categorizes Lévi, Blavatsky, and Steiner as proponents of an "integrativen Satanismus." These references remain sketchy, however, and mostly do not supersede the level of description or simple allusion. Per Faxneld has been the only one to make a systematic inventory of "Satanist" themes in these domains; see especially his *Satanic Feminism*, 140–157 ("Red Satanism"), 161–204 (Theosophy), 277–348 (Michelet, Leland).

12. In the 1794 Gothic novel *The Monk* by Matthew Lewis, Lucifer in his appearance as the angel of light is already described thus: "It was a Youth seemingly scarce eighteen, the perfection of whose form and face was unrivalled. He was perfectly naked: A bright Star sparkled upon his forehead; Two crimson wings extended themselves from his shoulders; and his silken locks were confined by a band of many-coloured fires, which played round his head, formed themselves into a variety of figures, and shone with a brilliance far surpassing that of precious Stones." See Matthew Gregory Lewis, *The Monk: A Romance* (London: Brentano's, 1924), 2:184 (Volume II, chapter 4). Maurice Agulhon notes the unusualness of Dumont's masculine genius in his article "Paris: A Traversal from East to West," in *Realms of Memory: The Construction of the French Past. Volume III: Symbols*, ed. Pierre Nora and Lawrence D. Kritzman, trans. Arthur Goldhammer (New York: Columbia University Press, 1998), 523–553, there 692n. In his standard work on the French republican imagery, *Marianne au combat: L'imagerie et la symbolique*

républicaines de 1789 à 1880 (Paris: Flammarion, 1979), 62, he writes that the statue in its features and postures evokes "plutôt un Mercure," which evidently misses the point.

An interesting article could be written about the traces of the Romantic Satan that remain in statues sprinkled across the European continent, and sometimes beyond. Prominent examples include Constantino Corti's *Lucifero* (1867), present whereabouts unknown, and the *Monumento al Traforo del Frejus* (1879) by Marcello Panissera di Veglio, at the Piazza Statuto in Turin. Another interesting example is Guillaume Geefs's *Génie du Mal* (1848) at the back of the pulpit in the Cathedral of Liège, perfectly Catholic except for the telltale tear of repentance it displays; it replaced the *Ange du Mal* (1842, now in the Bruxelles Musée des Beaux Arts) by Guillaume's brother Jozef Geefs, which was said to be too distracting to the female faithful because of its unsettling beauty (cf. Jacques van Lennep, *De 19e-eeuwse Belgische beeldhouwkunst* [Brussels: General Bank, 1990], 57–58, 421–422). Clearly inspired by the Romantic Satan, although not unorthodox per se, is Ricardo Bellver's *El Angel Caído* (1877), now in the Parque del Buen Retiro, Madrid (cf. Muchembled, *History of the Devil*, 200). A statue of Eloa carried away by Satan from the hand of Joseph-Michel Pollet can (or could) be found in Oued Zenati in Algeria; a bronze version of the same statue dating from 1862 is kept in the collection of the Musée des Beaux-Arts in Rouen. Faxneld, *Satanic Feminism*, 332, 334, mentions an 1897 *Lucifer* by the sculptress Teresa Fedorowna Ries, which was destroyed in the 1940s.

13. Karl Marx, the most famous and most influential of revolutionary thinkers, has been depicted as a secret worshipper of the devil by Richard Wurmbrand, in a somewhat obscure publication entitled *Was Karl Marx a Satanist?* (s.l.: Diane Books, 1979). Wurmbrand was a Protestant minister who had fled Communist persecution in his native Rumania; his book, which appeared under different titles in a number of editions and translations, found a ready reception among Christian audiences in Cold War America, just a few years before President Ronald Reagan would declare the Soviet Union an "empire of evil." While it is true, however, that Marx wrote some antitheist Promethean poetry in his Romantic days of youth, and while it might also be true that he liked to sign letters with "Old Nick" (English slang for the devil) and told his children stories about a diabolical toy-shop owner, this hardly accounts to proof for practicing Satanism. (Cf. A. N. Wilson, *God's Funeral: The Decline of Faith in Western Civilization* [London: John Murray, 1999], 90.)

14. Pierre Haubtmann, *P.-J. Proudhon, genèse d'un antithéiste* ([Tours]: Mame, 1969), 118. I owe most of the autobiographical details about Proudhon to Haubtmann's book.

15. Pierre-Joseph Proudhon, *Système des contradictions économiques, ou philosophie de la misère*, 2 vols. (Paris: Guillaumin et Cie, 1846), 1:414. See also 1:416: "Tant que l'humanité s'inclinera devant un autel, l'humanité, esclave des rois et des prêtres, sera réprouvée; tant qu'un homme, au nom de Dieu, recevra le serment d'un autre homme, la société sera fondée sur le parjure, e paix et l'amour seront bannis d'entre les mortels." On p. 2:529, Proudhon likewise declares that true human virtue, "celle qui nous rend dignes de la vie éternelle," consists of combating the idea of the deity with all means possible.

16. Proudhon, *Philosophie de la misère*, 1:416. See also 1:425ff.

17. Pierre-Joseph Proudhon, *De la Justice dans la Révolution et dans l'Église: Études de philosophie pratique*, 3 vols. (Paris: Garnier Frères, 1858), 2:84.

18. Proudhon, *De la Justice dans la Révolution et dans l'Église*, 2:540. In 1851, Proudhon had written in a similar vein in *Idée génerale de la Révolution au dix-neuvième siècle*, p. 290: "A moi,

Lucifer, Satan, qui que tu sois! Démon que la foi de mes pères oppose à Dieu et à l'Eglise! Je porte-rai ta parole et je te demande rien" (quoted in Milner, *Le diable dans la literature française*, 2:260).

19. Milner, *Le diable dans la literature française*, 2:262; Russell, *Mephistopheles*, 204.

20. Giving quite unsuspectingly more ammunition to the Rev. Richard Wurmbrand in the process, who notes in his book that such reversals are "one of the peculiarities of black magic." Wurmbrand, *Was Marx a Satanist?*, 21.

21. Quoted in Haubtmann, *P.-J. Proudhon*, 217n.

22. Quoted in Haubtmann, *P.-J. Proudhon*, 226–227.

23. "La théologie a beau vouloir renverser cet ordre," writes Proudhon in the second edition of *De la Justice dans la Révolution et dans l'Église*, "donner à Dieu le souveraineté et lui subordon-ner la Justice: le sens intime proteste, et, dans l'enseignement populaire, dans la prière, c'est la Justice qui sert de témoin à la Divinité et gage à la religion. La Justice est le Dieu suprême, elle est le Dieu vivant, le Dieu tout-puissant, le seul Dieu qui ose se montrer intolérant vis-à-vis de ceux qui le blasphèment, au-dessous duquel il n'y a que des idéalités pures et des hypothèses." Pierre-Joseph Proudhon, *De la Justice dans la Révolution et dans l'Église. Études de philosophie pratique*, 2 vols. (Paris: Arthème Fayard, 1988), 1:53.

24. Proudhon, *De la Justice dans la Révolution et dans l'Église* (1858 edition), 1:85.

25. "Chrétien, déiste, anti-théiste, je suis tout aussi religieux et presque dans les mêmes termes que vous": *De la Justice dans la Révolution et dans l'Église* (1858 edition), 2:607–608.

26. It must be remarked that his materialism sometimes takes on almost religious over-tones: cf. Mikhail Bakunin, *God and the State* (New York: Dover, 1970), 13, 76.

27. Bakunin, *God and the State*, 24, 25.

28. Bakunin, *God and the State*, 10. *God and the State* was first published in French as *Dieu et l'état* in 1882, six years after Bakunin's death.

29. Bakunin, *God and the State*, 12, 9.

30. Bakunin, *God and the State*, 21.

31. Proudhon, *De la Justice dans la Révolution et dans l'Église* (1858 edition), 1:33. Godwin's *Enquiry* was not yet translated in French at this date.

32. Dvorak, *Satanismus*, 266–267.

33. For Mincke, see Richard E. Burton, *Baudelaire and the Second Republic: Writing and Revolution* (Oxford: Clarendon, 1991), 198. For *Lucifer the Light-Bearer*, see Faxneld, *Satanic Feminism*, 152–156, and http://en.wikipedia.org/wiki/Lucifer_the_Lightbearer (accessed 9 May 2012). Some poorly scanned issues are available on http://libertarian-labyrinth.org/lucifer/ (accessed 9 May 2012). The issues are dated "E.M," or "Era of Man," which began in 1600, when the Italian freethinker Bruno was executed for heresy. The periodical appeared from 1883 to 1907 (CE), gaining notoriety and legal harassment because of its frank discussion of sexual issues: it eventually eclipsed into the *American Journal for Eugenics*. According to the editor's colophon, "The name Lucifer means Light-Bringing or Light-Bearing and the paper that has adopted this name stands for Light against Darkness—for Reason against Superstition—for Science against Tradition—for Investigation and Enlightenment against Credulity and Ignorance—for Liberty against Slavery—for Justice against Privilege" (taken from *Lucifer the Light-Bearer* [27 July EM 301/CE 1901]: 875, 220).

It is to be noted that nineteenth-century France had already known a short-lived radical peri-odical called *Satan*, which saw print from 1843 to 1844 and was initially directed by Francisque

Borel and afterward by his more famous younger brother, the *Bousingo* poet Pétrus Borel (see Enid Starkie, *Petrus Borel, the Lycanthrope: His Life and Times* [New York: New Directions, 1954], 146–147). According to http://ngnm.vrahokipos.net/index.php/translations/149-anarchist-giannis-magkanaras (accessed 4 February 2013), there was also a Greek anarchist satirical with the name *Satanas*, published during July–September 1897, probably on initiative of the well-known Greek anarchist Gianis Magkanaras.

34. Faxneld, *Satanic Feminism*, 144–150, and in his article "The Devil Is Red: Socialist Satanism in Nineteenth and Early Twentieth Century Europe," *Numen: International Review for the History of Religions* 60 (2013) 5, which also mentions some faint reflections of a similar sympathy for the devil with West German anarchists.

35. Boss, *Milton and the Rise of Russian Satanism*, 140; Saul D. Alinsky, *Rules for Radicals: A Practical Primer for Realistic Radicals* (New York: Random House, 1971), ix. Alinsky seems to cite one of his own earlier works here; I have been unable to find out which. My attention to Alinsky was drawn by the Hon. James David Manning of Atlah World Ministries.

36. Shelley, *Essays and Letters*, 159–179; Alphonse Esquiros, *Le Magicien* (Lausanne: L'Age d'Homme, 1978), 132–133. Esquiros's novel may be considered as belonging at least in part to the tradition of Romantic Satanism; compare p. 121 ("Satan c'est le génie") and pp. 131–132 ("voilà le but rayonnant vers lequel nous marchons en dehors de l'Église et de l'État: nous voulons être libres et dieux"). On Esquiros, compare Bénichou, *Le temps des prophètes*, 446–453, particularly 452–453.

37. For her historical information, Sand relied mainly on an obscure book by Jacques Lenfant, *Histoire de la Guerre des Hussites et du Concile de Basle*, 2 vols. (Amsterdam: Pierre Humbert, 1731), especially 1:29–20. On Sand's sources of inspiration, see also the article by Léon Guichard, "L'occultisme dans Consuelo et la Comtesse de Rudolstadt," in George Sand, *Consuelo. La Comtesse de Rudolstad*, 3 vols. (Paris: Éditions Garnier Frères, 1959), 1:xlvii–lxxviii, as well as Milner, *Le diable dans la littérature française*, 2:164–170.

38. Also derived from Lenfant, *Histoire de la Guerre des Hussites*, 1:29: "Que celui à qui on a fait tort te salute."

39. Sand, *Consuelo*, 2:19.

40. Sand, *Consuelo*, 2:28, 29. It is to be noted that Sand, like most of the Romantics, is not anti-Christian here, in the sense of opposed to Christ.

41. Sand, *Consuelo*, 3:371: "*Liberté, fraternité, égalité*: voilà la formule mystérieuse et profonde de l'œuvre des Invisibles."

42. Cohn, *Europe's Inner Demons*, 103–125; Milner, *Le diable dans la littérature française*, 1:62; Hutton, *Triumph of the Moon*, 136–137; Christa Tuczay, "The Nineteenth Century: Medievalism and Witchcraft," in Barry and Davies, *Palgrave Advances in Witchcraft Historiography*, 52–68. Heinrich Heine also supported this idea (from an opposite ideological position) in his famous essay from 1834, *De l'Allemagne depuis Luther*, and its 1853 sequel *Les dieux en exil*.

43. On Michelet's *Werdegang*, see Chadwick, *Secularization of the European Mind*, 154, 198–202, and Bénichou, *Le temps des prophètes*, 497–564. According to Faxneld, *Satanic Feminism*, 140, Proudhon had been a student of Michelet.

44. Michelet marked these two experiences as decisive himself; his new take on historiography was inspired by his discovery of Vico. See Mali, *Mythistory*, 86.

45. Quoted in Mali, *Mythistory*, 86.

46. Both quotes are from Mali, *Mythistory*, 86.

47. Bénichou, *Le temps des prophètes*, 517. On Michelet's changing view of the Middle Ages, see Barbara G. Keller, *The Middle Ages Reconsidered: Attitudes in France from the Eighteenth Century through the Romantic Movement* (New York: Peter Lang, 1994), 151–157.

48. *Introduction à l'histoire universelle*, 27, quoted in Bénichou, *Le temps des prophètes*, 518. For the 1825 diary entry, see ibid., 559.

49. See *Histoire de France* (1833 edition), 2:637–638: "Oui, le Christ est encore sur la croix, et il n'en descendra point. La Passion dure et durera. Le monde a le sienne, et l'humanité dans sa longue vie historique, et chaque cœur de homme dans ce peu d'instants qu'il bat. A chacun sa croix et ses stigmates. Les miennes datent du jour où mon âme tomba dans ce corps misérable, que j'achève d'user en écrivant ceci. Ma Passion commença avec mon Incarnation. . . . Vivre, c'est déjà un degré dans la Passion" (quoted in Bénichou, *Le temps des prophètes*, 521).

50. Wouter Kusters, *La Sorcière: Nouvelle édition critique avec introduction, variantes et examen du manuscrit* (Nijmegen: s.i., 1989), 20–21.

51. Kusters, *La Sorcière*, 92.

52. Jules Michelet, *La Sorcière: Nouvelle édition* (Bruxelles: A. Lacroix, Verboeckhoven & Cie, 1867), 141.

53. Michelet, *La Sorcière*, 142–146.

54. Michelet, *La Sorcière*, 146. Esquiros had already described the Witches' Sabbath as an antiroyalist conspiracy in *Le magicien*, 195–203.

55. Michelet, *La Sorcière*, 146.

56. Michelet, *La Sorcière*, 148.

57. Michelet, *La Sorcière*, 149.

58. Michelet, *La Sorcière*, 150, 151. The "demon" in the ceremony was a dressed-up peasant, Michelet explains on the same pages.

59. Kusters, *La Sorcière*, 74, 72.

60. Kusters, *La Sorcière*, 109n.

61. Kusters, *La Sorcière*, 68, 110n.

62. Kusters, *La Sorcière*, 60.

63. Michelet erroneously supposes that Sand wanted to reconcile the Church with Satan, while she only speaks of Christ and the fallen angel. This misinterpretation has already been noted by Philippe Règnier, "Le chaudron idéologique de *La Sorcière*: Féminisme, homéopathie te saint-simonisme," in *La Sorcière de Jules Michelet: L'envers de l'histoire*, ed. Paule Petitier, 127–148 (Paris: Honoré Champion, 2004), 129n; Michelet's remark in *La Sorcière*, 379–380.

64. Michelet, *La Sorcière*, 152: "Sous l'ombre vague de Satan, le peuple n'adorait que le peuple."

65. Michelet, *La Sorcière*, 125, 127.

66. Michelet, *La Sorcière*, 389.

67. Règnier, "Le chaudron idéologique de *La Sorcière*," 145.

68. Michelet, *La Sorcière*, 383.

69. As Michelet acknowledges in a footnote: *La Sorcière*, 150n.

70. The altar position described by Michelet would find its reflection in the iconography of later decades; see, for instance, the Martin van Maele illustrations for the 1911 edition of *La Sorcière*, or Manuel Orazi's lithos for Augustin de Croze's *Calendrier magique* from 1895, and for the "messes noires" theme number of *L'Asiette au beurre* (12 December 1903): 144, 15–16.

71. Michelet, *La Sorcière*, 408n: "mais il subsiste dans les campagnes." It is unclear to what time frame Michelet is referring.

72. Charles G. Leland, *Aradia, or the Gospel of the Witches* (London: David Nutt, 1899), x. Leland's explanations about his procurement of the manuscript and its nature can be found on pp. vi–vii, 101–102, and 116–117.

73. Leland, *Aradia*, 1–5.

74. Leland, *Aradia*, 6–7.

75. Leland, *Aradia*, 14.

76. Leland, *Aradia*, 101–102: "Now be it observed, that every leading point which forms the plot or center of this *Vangel* . . . had been told or written out for me in fragments by Maddalena (not to speak of other authorities), even as it had been chronicled by Horst or Michelet; therefore all this is in the present document of minor importance. All of this I expected, but what I did not expect, and what was new to me, was that portion which is given as prose-poetry and which I have *rendered* in meter or verse. This being traditional, and taken down from wizards, is extremely curious and interesting, since in it are preserved many relics of lore which, as may be verified from records, have come down from the days of yore." (Horst is Georg Conrad Horst [1767–1832], a German scholar and a well-known compiler of source material concerning witchcraft.)

77. Leland, *Aradia*, 116.

78. Leland, *Aradia*, vi; compare 117 for similar sentiments.

79. Leland, *Aradia*, 114–115. To my knowledge, a thorough scholarly examination of Leland and *Aradia* is still lacking. Academic scholarship is rightly doubtful about the authenticity of Leland's book, although it is as yet undecided whether Leland was pulling his readers' leg or had his own leg pulled by his informant. Cf. Hutton, *Triumph of the Moon*, 141–148.

80. For a general introduction into the world of nineteenth-century alternative religiosity, see, among others, McLeod, *Secularisation in Western Europe*, 147–170; Godwin, *Theosophical Enlightenment*; Christopher McIntosh, *Eliphas Lévi and the French Occult Revival* (London: Rider, 1972); Daniël van Egmond, "Western Esoteric Schools in the Late Nineteenth and Early Twentieth Centuries," in *Gnosis and Hermeticism from Antiquity to Modern Times*, ed. Roelof van den Broek and Wouter J. Hanegraaff (Albany: State University of New York Press, 1998), 311–346; James Webb, *The Occult Underground* (La Salle, IL: Open Court, 1974). I have relied on these works and more specific titles referenced in other footnotes to become familiar in the landscape of nineteenth-century esotericism and to locate groups and authors that might be interesting in regard to their attitude to Satan. The limitations of this approach will be obvious. A further examination of the ideas regarding Satan within Saint-Simonism and the mystic socialism of Pierre Leroux in particular might well yield interesting results, although the existing scholarly literature on Satan and Satanism seems to have passed them by completely—including Max Milner, whose treatment of the theme of Satan in nineteenth-century French culture seems well-nigh encyclopedic to me. For further and more general deliberations concerning the problem of detecting "hidden" groups of religious Satanists, see intermezzo 3.

A connection between Romanticism and post-Enlightenment esotericism in a general sense was already proposed by Wouter J. Hanegraaff: see, for instance, his article "Romanticism and the Esoteric Connection," in van den Broek and Hanegraaff, *Gnosis and Hermeticism*, 237–268. Among other elements, Hanegraaff also emphasized the importance of imagination, but tracing a different trajectory, which gives a prominent place for the German philosophers of

Romanticism while remaining unparticular about the precise lines of historical diffusion that transmitted Romantic notions into modern esotericism. I will discuss these matters more thoroughly in chapter 7 and my conclusion.

81. Godwin, *Theosophical Enlightenment*, 172.

82. Godwin, *Theosophical Enlightenment*, 187.

83. Milner, *Le diable dans la littérature française*, 2:348–349, 2:353–355; Régis Ladous, "Le spiritisme et les démons dans les catéchismes français du XIXe siècle," in *Le Défi Magique II: Satanisme, sorcellerie*, ed. Jean-Baptiste Martin and Massimo Introvigne (Lyon: Presses Universitaires de Lyon, 1994), 203–228.

84. R. Laurence Moore, "Spiritualism," in *The Rise of Adventism: Religion and Society in Mid-Nineteenth-Century America*, ed. Edwin S. Gaustad (New York: Harper and Row, 1974), 79–103; Milner, *Le diable dans la littérature française*, 2:348–355; Nicole Edelman, "Diable et médium: Histoire d'une disparition," in Martin and Introvigne, *Le Défi Magique II*, 321–329.

85. Helmut Zander, *Anthroposophie in Deutschland: Theosophische Weltanschauung und gesellschaftliche Praxis 1884–1945*, 2 vols. (Göttingen: Vandenhoeck and Ruprecht, 2007), 1:78, 82. Zander's remarks about Theosophy here can be applied to occultism in general.

86. According to Wouter J. Hanegraaff, "Occult/Occultism," in *Dictionary of Gnosis and Western Esotericism*, ed. Wouter J. Hanegraaff, 2 vols. (Leiden: Brill, 2005), 884–889, the word "occultism" first appears in 1841; Éliphas Lévi includes the term in the 1856 volume of his *Dogme et rituel de la haute magie*, 2 vols. (Paris: Félix Alcan, 1910), 2:161. Throughout this study, I will apply Hanegraaff's wider definition of occultism as a specific form of Western esotericism developed in reaction to the Enlightenment "disenchantment" of the world.

87. Abbé Constant, *L'Assomption de la femme ou le Livre de l'Amour* (Paris: Aug. le Gallois, 1841), xv; pp. iii–xxviii of this publication contain an autobiographical sketch by Constant. A scholarly biography of Lévi is still needed. Paul Chacornac, *Éliphas Lévi: Rénovateur de l'occultisme en France (1810–1875)* (Paris: Librairie Général des Sciences Occultes Chacornac Frères, 1926), provides a wealth of details but also has the character of a hagiography; McIntosh, *Eliphas Lévi*, mostly bases himself on Chacornac, although adding much information on Lévi's subsequent influence. I have gratefully profited from Wouter J. Hanegraaff, "The Beginnings of Occultist Kabbalah: Adolphe Franck and Eliphas Lévi," in *Kabbalah and Modernity: Interpretations, Transformations, Adaptations*, ed. Boaz Huss, Marco Pasi, and Kocku von Stuckrad (Leiden: Brill, 2010), 107–128, which he gave me in digital form before publication. While finishing this text, I stumbled upon a reference to Daniel S. Larangé, "Théologie mariale et discours féministe: La foi romantique en l'avenir du pouvoir féminin selon l'abbé Alphonse-Louis Constant," *Tangence* 94 (autumn 2010): 113–134, which, unfortunately, I was unable to consult on such short notice.

88. Constant, *L'Assomption de la femme*, xix–xxi; Chacornac, *Éliphas Lévi*, 41–42. The work of Sand mentioned here by Lévi is *Spiridion*, and not *Consuelo*, contra Milner, *Le diable dans la littérature française*, 2:249.

89. Chacornac, *Éliphas Lévi*, 95–98.

90. Chacornac, *Éliphas Lévi*, 98–99; requoted in Milner, *Le diable dans la littérature française*, 2:253.

91. Chacornac, *Éliphas Lévi*, 32–33. Tristan was the maternal grandmother of the painter Paul Gauguin.

92. Chacornac, *Éliphas Lévi*, 35: "on peut dire que Flora Tristan a été l'initiatrice du futur auteur de la *Bible de la Liberté*"; 33: "sa parole exerça-t-elle sur Flora Tristan un grand ascendant." Constant's advices were not always on the mark: for instance, when he advised Tristan to be indulgent with the husband she had left: shortly afterward, her irate ex-man attempted to kill her with a pistol (ibid., 33–35).

93. Cf. Chacornac, *Éliphas Lévi*, 81.

94. Chacornac, *Éliphas Lévi*, 47–54, 59.

95. Alphonse Constant, *La Bible de la Liberté* (Paris: Le Gallois, 1841), 11. Constant was already introduced to theories about the Age of the Holy Spirit by one of his tutors on the seminary; Constant, *L'Assomption de la femme*, iv–vi.

96. Constant, *Bible de la Liberté*, "Préface": "Voilà le second avènement du Christ incarné dans l'humanité; voilà l'homme peuple et Dieu qui se révèle." Agulhon, *Marianne au combat*, 73–77, gives some more examples of the peculiar confusion of feminist messianism, millennialism, Marial devotion, and political radicalism that sometimes could be found in French radical circles during this period.

97. Constant, *Bible de la Liberté*, 17–19, 18.

98. Constant, *Bible de la Liberté*, 19.

99. Constant, *Bible de la Liberté*, 22.

100. Constant, *Bible de la Liberté*, 31, 99.

101. Alphonse Constant, *La Mère de Dieu, épopée religieuse et humanitaire* (Paris: Librairie de Charles Gosselin, 1844), 168–169, 6.

102. Constant, *Mère de Dieu*, 265.

103. Constant, *Mère de Dieu*, 266–267.

104. Constant, *Mère de Dieu*, 364, 355.

105. Flora Tristan and A. Constant, *L'Emancipation de la Femme, ou le testament de la paria* (Paris: Bureau de la direction de *La Vérité*, 1846), 37.

106. Tristan and Constant, *L'Emancipation de la Femme*, 36.

107. Tristan and Constant, *L'Emancipation de la Femme*, 44–45.

108. Constant in Tristan and Constant, *L'Emancipation de la Femme*, 116.

109. Alphonse Constant, *Le dernière incarnation: Légendes évangeliques du XXIᵉ siècle* (Paris: Libraire sociétaire, 1846), 109–114.

110. Constant, *Le dernière incarnation*, 114.

111. Alphonse Constant, *Le Testament de la Liberté* (Paris: J. Frey, 1848), 1–5, there 2–3. Compare Tristan and Constant, *L'Emancipation de la Femme*, 37–40.

112. Constant, *Testament de la Liberté*, 9.

113. Constant, *Testament de la Liberté*, 9.

114. Milner, *Le diable dans la littérature française*, 2:410; Auguste Viatte, *Victor Hugo et les Illuminés de son temps* (Montréal: Les Éditions de l'Arbre, 1942), 171–172. In 1873, Hugo and Lévi met each other personally, according to Chacornac, *Éliphas Lévi*, 278—"le grand poète connaissait, paraît-il, les ouvrages du Kabbaliste, et les avait même appréciés." On Constant's embeddedness in Romanticism, see also Bénichou, *Le temps des prophètes*, 435–446.

115. Constant, *Le dernière incarnation*, 113–114. In another legend, Constant describes the archetypical poet as being inspired by the Holy Spirit (ibid., 98).

116. Constant, *Testament de la Liberté*, 60.

117. Constant, *Mère de Dieu*, 273.

118. On Kabbalah, and other readings: Chacornac, *Éliphas Lévi*, 129–130. The trajectory of Kabbalah in nineteenth-century and early twentieth-century occultism is sketched in Egil Asprem, "*Kabbalah Recreata*: Reception and Adaptation of Kabbalah in Modern Occultism," *Pomegranate* 9 (2007) 2:132–253.

119. Chacornac, *Éliphas Lévi*, 137–139. The prognometer would later end up in the hands of Constant himself. Modern scholarly literature on Hoëne-Wroński is practically nonexistent; one of the few exceptions is an introductory article by Roman Murawski, "The Philosophy of Hœne-Wronski," *Organon* 35 (2006): 143–150.

120. McIntosh, *Eliphas Lévi*, 98.

121. Chacornac, *Éliphas Lévi*, 140–141.

122. Chacornac, *Éliphas Lévi*, 281 quoting an account by one Madame Hutchinson, in *L'Initiation*, 16 (August 1892) 11:135: "Il savait certainement qu'il allait mourir, car ses yeux prirent une expression extatique que je ne leur avais jamais vu, pour me dire, en désignant le Christ: 'Il a dit qu'il en verrait le Consolateur: l'*Esprit*, et maintenant, j'attends l'*Esprit*, l'*Esprit Saint*!'"

123. On spiritism, see Lévi, *Dogme et rituel de la haute magie*, 1:265–266.

124. Lévi, *Dogme et rituel de la haute magie*, 2:10.

125. Éliphas Lévi, *La Clef des grands mystères, suivant Hénoch, Abraham, Hermés Trismégiste et Solomon* (Paris: Félix Alcan, [1923]), 23–25, 66. There is even a spark of his old millennialism here ("Glory to the Holy Spirit who has promised the conquest of heaven and earth to the angel of liberty!").

126. Lévi, *Dogme et rituel de la haute magie*, 2:230.

127. Lévi, *Dogme et rituel de la haute magie*, 2:230–231; Éliphas Lévi, *Histoire de la magie, avec une exposition claire et précise de ses procédés, de ses rites et de ses mystères* (Paris: Germer Ballière, 1860), 200.

128. Lévi, *Dogme et rituel de la haute magie*, 2:244.

129. Lévi, *Clef des grands mystères*, 250.

130. Lévi, *Clef des grands mystères*, 337.

131. Lévi, *Clef des grands mystères*, 250.

132. Lévi, *Clef des grands mystères*, 17.

133. Lévi, *Dogme et rituel de la haute magie*, 1:136, 1:200, 2:4.

134. Among other sources of inspiration, of particular importance must have been the "spiritus mundus" of neo-Platonic Renaissance magicians, like Ficino and Agrippa, and the "magnetic fluid" from the Mesmerists deriving from it; cf. Wouter J. Hanegraaff, "How Magic Survived the Disenchantment of the World," *Religion* 33 (2003): 357–380, there 363–364, 368. None of them did identify this force with Satan, however, as Fabre d'Olivet and Lévi do. Neither Agrippa et alia, as far as I am aware, nor D'Olivet, as we shall note, ascribe to this force the fundamental dialectics between destruction and creation that Lévi attributes to his magical agent. Some Jewish Kabbalists (particularly Luria) had already suggested that both "good" and "evil" forces had been present in the divine Ein Sof. Lévi may also have found inspiration for his dialectic thinking in Hindu or Taoist thought, to which references can be found in his works. Yet the idea to equate this "mixed emanation" of the divine with Satan is original for Lévi, as far as I am aware. The origin of this idea, as this chapter suggests, will have been his earlier Romantic

Satanism, as well as a highly inventive defense strategy against the traditional attribution of magic as devil worship by identification and reversion.

135. Fabre d'Olivet, *Caïn traduit en vers français et réfuté*, 27, 34–35. D'Olivet's influence on Lévi deserves detailed scholarly attention. There are striking similarities, for instance in the description of Gnostic sects (ibid., 170), of the scientific nature of Kabbalah (14), and of the historical origin of the devil (169), while Lévi's idea about the "evil" Satan made real by its invocation seems prefigured in D'Olivet's view that Byron's Lucifer "n'est qu'une sorte de reflet magique de l'esprit de Caïn, réactionné par une puissance astrale" (169).

136. Lévi, *Dogme et rituel de la haute magie*, 2:5; Lévi, *Histoire de la magie*, 200, 197.

137. Constant, *Testament de la Liberté*, 4.

138. Lévi, *Dogme et rituel de la haute magie*, 1:1–66; 1:381. Lévi's fundamental dialectic—as opposed to dualistic—tendency is also emphasized by Hanegraaff, "The Beginnings of Occultist Kabbalah."

139. Lévi, *Dogme et rituel de la haute magie*, 1:vi; figure on frontispiece in volume 2.

140. Lévi, *Dogme et rituel de la haute magie*, 2:225.

141. Lévi, *Dogme et rituel de la haute magie*, 2:226–227.

142. Lévi, *Dogme et rituel de la haute magie*, 1:vi.

143. A well-known posthumous photograph shows Lévi on his bed with a large cross on his breast (Chacornac, *Éliphas Lévi*, facing 288), and although this obviously does not tell much about his own inclinations, it is true he made confession willingly to a priest before he died. See on this, however, Chacornac, *Éliphas Lévi*, 284, and my own subsequent remarks. Lévi's genuine attitude toward institutional Roman Catholicism is perhaps better captured by a passage from a letter he wrote in 1870, after the First Vatican Council had declared the infallibility of the papacy: "Maintenant je suis une voix de l'avenir et j'ai fait mon devoir en sortant de la Babylone condamnée à l'apostasie. Maintenant je suis du côté de Jésus-Christ et des apôtres! je suis absous! je suis réhabilité! je suis libre! hosannah!" (quoted in ibid., 260).

144. Lévi, *Dogme et rituel de la haute magie*, 1:105. Chacornac, *Éliphas Lévi*, 183n, recounts in an amusing anecdote how Lévi submitted his magical works to the "officialité de Paris" and received this response: "Nous n'approuvons ni ne désapprouvons; vos livres ne sont ni hérétiques ni impies; ils sont extravagans." Unfortunately, Chacornac fails to provide a source reference for this story.

145. Letter to his pupil Moutant, cited without date in Papus, *La Caballe: Tradition secrète de l'Occident* ([Paris]: Bibliothèque Chacornac, 1903), 49. See also Lévi's utterances cited in McIntosh, *Eliphas Lévi*, 146.

146. Lévi, *Dogme et rituel de la haute magie*, 2:48–49.

147. Lévi, *Dogme et rituel de la haute magie*, 2:242–243. Lévi's attitude is exemplified by a passage in *Dogme et rituel de la haute magie*, 1:56, where he attests that it is a "ridiculous contradiction" to say one is a Catholic but not a Roman Catholic: Catholic means universal, and Rome is in the universe!

148. Lévi, *Dogme et rituel de la haute magie*, 1:140, 200.

149. Cf. McIntosh, *Eliphas Lévi*, 150; Hutton, *Triumph of The Moon*, 82.

150. Lévi, *Histoire de la magie*, 197.

151. Lévi, *Dogme et rituel de la haute magie*, 1:288–292; see also 1:114. This is also what caused the fall of Adam: Lévi, *Histoire de la magie*, 196.

152. See in particular Lévi, *Dogme et rituel de la haute magie*, 1:306: "LE DIABLE EN MAGIE NOIRE, C'EST LE GRAND AGENT MAGIQUE EMPLOYÉ POUR LE MAL PAR UNE VOLONTÉ PERVERSE."

153. Lévi, *Dogme et rituel de la haute magie*, 1:200; Lévi, *Histoire de la magie*, 200–201.

154. Lévi, *Dogme et rituel de la haute magie*, 2:242–243.

155. Lévi, *Dogme et rituel de la haute magie*, 2:243.

156. Lévi, *Dogme et rituel de la haute magie*, 1:306: "Lorsqu'on appelle le diable avec les cérémonies voulues, le diable vient et on le voit."

157. Lévi, *Dogme et rituel de la haute magie*, 2:252–253.

158. Lévi, *Dogme et rituel de la haute magie*, 2:98–99. For older uses of the "sign of the horn" as an initial gesture devoid of diabolical implications, see Maurice Bessy, *A Pictorial History of Magic and the Supernatural*, trans. Margaret Crosland and Allan Daventry (London: Spring Books, 1964), 202, plates 649–650. The pentagram, upward or downward, is an exceedingly ancient symbol used at least since Sumerian times; it also had an important place in Pythagorean numerology.

159. Lévi, *Dogme et rituel de la haute magie*, 2:230.

160. Lévi, *Dogme et rituel de la haute magie*, 2:235.

161. Lévi, *Dogme et rituel de la haute magie*, 2:239: "assemblée de malfaiteurs qui exploitaient des idiots et des fous."

162. Lévi, *Dogme et rituel de la haute magie*, 1:235. Lévi goes on to describe the ceremonies to invoke the devil "pour qu'on les connaisse, qu'on les juge, et qu'on se préserve à jamais de semblables aberrations" (ibid., 1:307), but the ritual he describes is clearly a pastiche, requiring among other things the skull of a patricide, a bat drowned in blood, the head of a black cat fed with human flesh for five days, and the horns of a he-goat with which a girl has copulated (*Dogme et rituel de la haute magie*, 2:246).

163. Lévi, *Dogme et rituel de la haute magie*, 1:8–9.

164. Lévi, *Clef des grands mystères*, 17. Compare for similar Romantic reinterpretations of Christ and Christian dogma: Bénichou, *Temps des prophètes*, 424.

165. Lévi, *Dogme et rituel de la haute magie*, 1:267. Lévi here adapts classic notions about the relation between microcosmos and macrocosmos from neo-Platonism and hermeticism and notions about the power of will he may have picked up with the later Mesmerists. Another unexpected source may have been his old friend Alphonse Esquiros, who had already underlined the importance of will in magic in his 1837 novel *Le Magicien*, 184: "Il faut vouloir. La volonté est une main intérieure qui remue tout: *fiat lux!*" Compare Lévi's celebrated dictum from *Dogme et rituel de la haute magie*, 2:32: "Il faut SAVOIR pour OSER. Il faut OSER pour VOULOIR. Il faut VOULOIR pour avoir l'empire. Et pour régner, il faut SE TAIRE." Although Lévi dismissed *Le Magicien*, with some reason, as "un livre de haute fantaisie" in *Histoire de la magie*, 497, it seems this did not prevent him from drawing inspiration from it. Interestingly enough, Esquiros's book already drew as conclusion from this premise that the ultimate aim of the magician is to become god; see *Le Magicien*, 71, 132–133.

166. Lévi, *Dogme et rituel de la haute magie*, 1:124.

167. On Romanticism and will, compare Berlin, *Roots of Romanticism*, 119. Another field of influence that should be explored is that of contemporary philosophy, particularly the idealism of Hegel, Schopenhauer, and the earlier German *Naturphilosophe*. A possible inspiration

for both the Romantic idea of the divine human and its application in modern occultism can be found in Hermeticism: see Neville Drury, *Stealing Fire from Heaven: The Rise of Modern Western Magic* (Oxford: Oxford University Press, 2011), 122–123. Compare, however, T. M. Luhrmann, *Persuasions of the Witch's Craft: Ritual Magic and Witchcraft in Present-day England* (Oxford: Basil Blackwell, 1989), 274–279, on some essential differences between the two discourses.

168. Lévi, *Histoire de la magie*, 18, 196.

169. Lévi, *Histoire de la magie*, 196–197.

170. Lévi, *Dogme et rituel de la haute magie*, 1:53–55.

171. Lévi, *Dogme et rituel de la haute magie*, 1:54–55.

172. Lévi, *Dogme et rituel de la haute magie*, 1:55; compare 1:52.

173. Liberty and intelligence: among other places, Lévi, *Clef des grands mystères*, 23, 66 (compare 22; "La loi est une épreuve de courage."); anticlericalism: Lévi, *Clef des grands mystères*, 22; science: Lévi, *Dogme et rituel de la haute magie*, 2:62 ("Nous ne sommes pas, grâce à Dieu, au temps des inquisiteurs et des bûchers"); compare 2:242; messianism: Lévi, *Dogme et rituel de la haute magie*, 1:56; millenialism: Lévi, *Dogme et rituel de la haute magie*, 1:2, Lévi, *Clef des grands mystères*, 20–21, 23, where Constant's earlier ideas of the coming Age of the Holy Ghost and the Mother return practically intact.

174. Lévi, *Clef des grands mystères*, 24.

175. Lévi, *Dogme et rituel de la haute magie*, 1:2; Lévi, *Clef des grands mystères*, 23–25.

176. Lévi, *Dogme et rituel de la haute magie*, 1:20.

177. Lévi, *Clef des grands mystères*, 109.

178. Chacornac, *Éliphas Lévi*, 128, 141; McIntosh, *Eliphas Lévi*, 100.

179. Lévi, *Histoire de la magie*, 196; Lévi, *Clef des grands mystères*, 281 ("L'amour physique est la plus perverse de toutes les passions fatales. C'est l'anarchiste par excellence; il ne connaît ni lois, ni devoirs, ni vérité, ni justice. . . . Vaincre l'amour, c'est triompher de la nature tout entière"); Lévi, *Dogme et rituel de la haute magie*, 2:296–303. Compare also *Dogme et rituel de la haute magie*, 1:194: "Celui-là dispose de l'amour des autres qui es maître de le sien. Voulez-vous posséder, ne vous donnez pas." These utterances are counterbalanced by less misogynist statements, for instance, *Clef des grands mystères*, 19–20 ("La femme est le sourire du Créateur content de lui-même" et ff.); in contrast with *Dogme et rituel*, 1:194, see also *Clef des grands mystères*, 24–25.

180. Chacornac, *Éliphas Lévi*, 100–106.

181. Chacornac, *Éliphas Lévi*, 113–117. Together with his wife, Constant during this period was also active in "Le club des Femmes," a feminist political association. His attempts to become a political candidate failed, in contrast to those of his friend Esquiros, who was elected to the National Assembly in May 1849. Chacornac, *Éliphas Lévi*, 116, mentions a bit mysteriously that "á partir de cette époque, l'amitié qui unissait A. Constant et A. Esquiros se rompit." It seems probable that this was due to Constant's growing conservatism and especially his Bonapartism: Esquiros remained a Radical and departed in exile after Louis Napoleon's 1851 coupe.

182. Chacornac, *Éliphas Lévi*, 117. Chacornac's source for this story, it should be noted, is an article by Jules Claretie in *L'Evénement* that only appeared on 26 April 1866.

183. Alphonse Constant, *Dictionnaire de littérature chrétienne* (Paris: Migne, 1851), 557–558.

184. Lévi, *Dogme et rituel de la haute magie*, 1:8, 20–21, 25–29.

185. Alphonse Constant, *Doctrines religieuses et sociales* (Paris: Aug. Le Gallois, 1841), 76.

186. Lévi, *Dogme et rituel de la haute magie*, 1:22.

187. In later life, Lévi apparently grew more critical of Napoleon III. Chacornac, *Éliphas Lévi*, 165–168, mentions a satirical song produced by him in which he compared the French emperor to Caligula. This gained him his last term in prison, but he was soon released, according to Chacornac, after he sent Napoleon a crafty retraction in verse. Chacornac does not date this episode, but a reference in Lévi's poem to Felice Orsini makes 1858 the date non ante quem. A more detailed study of Lévi's ideological and political development in this period is greatly desired.

188. Lévi, *Dogme et rituel de la haute magie*, 1:7.

189. On the Theosophical Society and Blavatsky, see Godwin, *Theosophical Enlightenment*, 280–367; Zander, *Anthroposophie in Deutschland*, 1:78–87. The only scholarly publication that I am aware of dealing extensively with Blavatsky's Satan is Per Faxneld, "Blavatsky the Satanist: Luciferianism in Theosophy, and Its Feminist Implications," *Tenemos* 48 (2012) 2:203–230 and the chapter on her in the same author's *Satanic Feminism*, 161–204.

190. Blavatsky shared Lévi's emphasis on will and his general pantheistic cosmic model (cf. H. P. Blavatsky, *Isis Unveiled: A Master-Key to the Mysteries of Ancient and Modern Science and Theology*, 2 vols. [Pasadena, CA: Theosophical University Press, 1972], 1:57), and she also adopted from the French magician the notion that the entities appearing in spiritualist séances were not the deceased themselves, but their astral bodies—much to the indignation of the spiritualists, who rightly concluded this implied that they were only communicating with the spiritual corpses of the departed. ("Nous évoquons les souvenirs qu'ils ont laissés dans la lumière astrale," Lévi had written about the "dead" of spiritism; *Dogme et rituel de la haute magie*, 1:289.) Regarding Lévi's influence on Blavatsky, see also Zander, *Anthroposophie in Deutschland*, 1:85n.

191. Blavatsky, *Isis Unveiled*, 2:472–528; quote on 2:480. See also 1:138.

192. H. P. Blavatsky, *The Secret Doctrine: The Synthesis of Science, Religion, and Philosophy*, 2 vols. (London: Theosophical Society Publishing, 1888), 1:412.

193. Blavatsky, *Secret Doctrine*, 1:411.

194. Blavatsky, *Secret Doctrine*, 1:423–424.

195. Blavatsky, *Secret Doctrine*, 2:275.

196. Osterkamp, *Lucifer*, 225–226, 230.

197. Blavatsky, *Isis Unveiled*, 2:iv.

198. Blavatsky, *Secret Doctrine*, 1:413.

199. Zander, *Anthroposophie in Deutschland*, 1:128–129, 344. There is some confusion about the nomenclature of this periodical: for an example of a cover, see http://upload.wikimedia.org/wikipedia/commons/5/5d/Lucifer-gnosis-1904.jpg, accessed 28 May 2012, or Georg Hartmann, *Das Wirken Rudolfs Steiners von 1890–1907: Weimar und Berlin*, Vier Bildbände zu Rudolf Steiners Lebensgang 2 (Schaffhausen: Novalis Verlag, 1975), 126.

200. Zander, *Anthroposophie in Deutschland*, 1:138–181.

201. Zander, *Anthroposophie in Deutschland*, 1:781–830.

202. On Satan with Steiner, see Osterkamp, *Lucifer*, 229–234; Zander, *Anthroposophie in Deutschland*, 1:833–834. Steiner's ideas on Lucifer had antecedents in earlier Theosophy: C. G. Harrison, *Das Transcedentale Weltenall: Sechs Vorträge über Geheimwissen, Theosophie und den katholische Glauben, gehalten vor der "Berean Society,"* trans. Carl Graf zu Leiningen-Billigheim

(1897; repr., Stuttgart: Engel and Seefels, 1990), 115–119, already stated that Lucifer most certainly was "der Lichtträger" to whom mankind owed "die Fähigkeit intellektueller Unterscheidung oder der Erkenntniss von Gut oder Böse," but that he could also, because of his limited appearance as intelligence, sometimes work *against* the final revelation of the godhead of love.

203. Zander, *Anthroposophie in Deutschland*, 1:834. Steiner first thought to name his antagonistic principle Sorat, whom he planned to place in opposition to the "Christ-Lamb" as representative of "black magic."

204. Rudolf Steiner, *Christus in verhouding tot Lucifer en Ahriman: De drievoudige gestalte*, trans. J. Stolk-van Greuninge (Driebergen: Zevenster 1986), 22. On Steiner's theories in this respect, see Zander, *Anthroposophie in Deutschland*, 1:631–637.

205. Zander, *Anthroposophie in Deutschland*, 2:1111–1116.

206. Zander, *Anthroposophie in Deutschland*, 2:1114. The nine-and-a-half-meter-tall sculpture was never finished but had been meant to occupy a central place in the first Dornach Goetheanum. After this structure burned down on New Year's Eve, the "Menschheitsrepräsentant" was stored in an attic for some years; today, it can be found in a side room of the second Goetheanum that serves as columbarium (ibid., 1:1111n).

207. Édouard Schuré, *Le théâtre de l'âme* (Paris: Perrin, 1900), 1–159; quote on 51.

208. The pun on the story of Paul the Apostle on the Areopagus can of course hardly be misunderstood: see Acts of the Apostles 17, 16–34.

209. Schuré, *Le théâtre de l'âme*, 51. On Schuré and an analysis of this play, see Zander, *Anthroposophie in Deutschland*, 2:1019–1028.

210. Schuré, *Le théâtre de l'âme*, 102.

211. Schuré, *Le théâtre de l'âme*, 126.

212. Schuré, *Le théâtre de l'âme*, 140.

213. Schuré, *Le théâtre de l'âme*, xvii.

214. Schuré, *Le théâtre de l'âme*, cvii.

215. Schuré, *Le théâtre de l'âme*, 142.

216. Osterkamp, *Lucifer*, 230; Zander, *Anthroposophie in Deutschland*, 2:1018, 1025. On Steiner and Schuré, see Zander, *Anthroposophie in Deutschland*, 2:1020–1024. Schuré obviously was also inspired by Lévi's books: the account of the fall of Lucifer in the play is only a very slightly adapted version of that recounted in *Dogme et Rituel*—witness Lucifer's proclamation to the deity: "Je suis l'Intelligence et la liberté, je suis la lumière! Je ne te obéirai pas. C'est par moi-même que je veux être, savoir et conquérir!" (Schuré, *Le théâtre de l'âme*, 52).

217. Blavatsky, *Secret Doctrine*, 2:274, 2:284 (Blavatsky was talking here of Indian mythology, but the context allows for a more general interpretation of her words). My analysis here is shared by Faxneld in his authoritative analysis of Blavatsky's Satan; see his *Satanic Feminism*, 172, 175.

218. Schuré, *Théâtre de l'âme*, xvii.

INTERMEZZO 2

1. References to Baudelaire can be found in Dvorak, *Satanismus*, 327–337; Frick, *Die Satanisten*, 2:145–148; Medway, *Lure of the Sinister*, 12; Schmidt, *Satanismus*, 96–100; and Zacharias, *Satanskult und Schwarze Messe*, 126–129, as well as Baddeley, *Lucifer Rising*, 21.

2. Charles Baudelaire, *Les Fleurs du Mal: Texte de la seconde edition suivi des pieces supprimées en 1857 et des additions de 1868. Édition critique établie par Jacques Crépet et Georges Blin* (Paris: Librairie José Corti, 1968), 243–246.

3. Translation from James Elroy Flecker, *The Collected Poems of James Elroy Flecker*, ed. John Squire (New York: Doubleday, Page, 1916), 42–44. Flecker's translation of the "Litany to Satan" first appeared in his volume of verse *Forty-Two Poems* from 1911.

4. Reminiscent of Sand is in particular the line "O Prince de l'exil, à qui l'on a fait tort"; "Toi qui, même aux lépreux, aux parias maudits,/Enseignes par l'amour le goût du Paradis" reminds one strongly of Vigny's *Eloa*; Byron's Cain might have inspired the refrain "Père adoptif de ceux qu'en sa noire colère/Du paradis terrestre a chassés Dieu le Père." Some of these influences are mentioned in Crépet and Blin's critical edition of *Fleurs du Mal*, 512–515. As a more direct inspiration for the form of the "Litany," Crépet and Blin, as well as Milner, *Le diable dans la littérature française*, 2:423, point to the judicial procedures against the possessed nun Marie de Sains in 1614, during which she spoke about psalms and litanies sung for the devil at the Witches' Sabbath: "Lucifer, Miserere nobis; Belzébuth, Miserere nobis, etc." References to the litanies were widely available in publications from Baudelaire's days, for instance, in Jules Garinet, *Histoire de la magie en France, depuis le commencement de la monarchie jusqu'à nos jours* Paris: Foulon, 1818), 195–197, while Collin de Plancy also cites it in his *Dictionnaire des Sciences occultes* from 1846 (cf. Milner, *Le diable dans la littérature française*, 2:423, who also remarks that the name of Satan is missing in this seventeenth-century litany: "Ne serait-ce pas ce qui aurait donné à Baudelaire l'idée de consacrer des litanies à Satan lui-même?").

5. Charles Baudelaire, *Journaux intimes. Fusées—Mon cœur mis à nu—Carnet. Édition critique établie par Jacques Crépet et Georges Blin* (Paris: Librairie José Corti 1949) 22 (*Fusées* X, 35–39).

6. For the Bouzingos, I have mainly relied on two biographies of Pétrus Borel: Enid Starkie, *Petrus Borel, the Lycanthrope: His Life and Times* (New York: New Directions, 1954), and Jean-Luc Steinmetz, *Pétrus Borel. Vocation: Poète maudit* (Paris: Librairie Arthème Fayard, 2002).

7. "Être plus artiste que Dieu!!! ...": from "Rodemontade," in Philotée O'Neddy, *Feu et Flamme* (Paris: Librairie Orientale de Dondey-Dupré, 1833), 33.

8. Starkie, *Petrus Borel*, 89–95.

9. O'Neddy, *Feu et Flamme*, 31–32. Starkie, *Petrus Borel*, 193–194, claims that Borel did "efforts to practise Sadism and Satanism," but does not corroborate her statement with facts. Probably either she meant that he led a very wicked life or she intended to characterize his literary output. See Hoog, "La révolte métaphysique et religieuse des petits romantiques," for some more instances of Romantic Satanism by the Jeunes France.

10. In his dedication, Baudelaire called Gautier "most beloved and most venerated master" and "perfect magician in French literature." Baudelaire also published in *Satan-Corsaire*, a periodical edited by Pétrus Borel and his brother.

11. Frick, *Die Satanisten*, 2:145–148. Zacharias, *Satanskult und Schwarze Messe*, 129, calls him "vielleicht die erste voll bewußte Persönlichkeit in der Geschichte des Satanskultes" (in the copy I consulted, an anonymous reviewer had scrabbled with crayon "bull-shit" in the margins of this sentence).

12. Baudelaire, *Journaux intimes*, 132 (Carnet, XLIII): "jusqu'au cabalastique 666 et même 6666."

13. Maigron, *Le Romantisme et les mœurs*, 187. The modern historian in question is Russell, *Mephistopheles*, 204; my translation is partly based on his.

14. Maigron, *Le Romantisme et les mœurs*, 187–192. According to Milner, *Le diable dans la littérature française*, 2:431–436, the documents consulted by Maigron subsequently became lost, so we have no chance to establish the truth of the story. Both Frick and Zacharias repeat Maigron's story and link it to Baudelaire.

15. Maigron, *Le Romantisme et les mœurs*, 187–193, speaks about "groups" of Satanists but admits to knowing details about only one. The other references he gives mostly concern deviant (homo)sexual practices.

16. Frick, *Die Satanisten*, 2:141: "Baudelaire soll einer Gruppe von Satanisten nahegestanden haben, die sich Mitte der 40er Jahre in Paris etabliert hatte und angeblich auch Satansmessen abhielt. Sie dürfte mit dem Club Haschischins identisch sein. . . . Diese Gruppe soll Baudelaire zu den 'Litanies de Satan" inspiriert haben."

17. Théophile Gautier, "Le club de Hachichins," *Revue des Deux Mondes* 1 (1846): 248–259. For details on the Club des Hachichins, see also F. W. J. Hemmings, *Baudelaire the Damned: A Biography* (New York: Charles Scribner's Sons, 1982), 159–160.

18. Something like this, I presume, is meant by Medway, *Lure of the Sinister*, 12, and Schmidt, *Satanismus*, 92, 96–100, when they designate Baudelaire as a Satanist.

19. T. J. Clark, *The Absolute Bourgeois: Artists and Politics in France 1848–1851* (London: Thames and Hudson, 1973), 163, citing Jean Wallon.

20. Burton, *Baudelaire and the Second Republic*, 197; Clark, *Absolute Bourgeois*, 163–171, quoted with acquiescence by Hemmings, *Baudelaire the Damned*, 196.

21. Burton, *Baudelaire and the Second Republic*, 354. On Baudelaire's political evolution, of which our representation must of need remain very schematic, see this author, as well as Clark, *Absolute Bourgeois*.

22. Baudelaire, *Journaux intimes*, 64 (*Mon cœur mis à nu* XIII, 22); 81 (*Mon cœur mis à nu* XXVI, 47). The English translation of the last quote is cited from Pierre Emmanuel, *Baudelaire: The Paradox of Redemptive Satanism*, trans. Robert T. Cargo (Tuscaloosa: University of Alabama Press, 1970), 158–159.

23. Baudelaire, *Journaux intimes*, 64 (*Mon cœur mis à nu* XIII, 22).

24. Cited in Emmanuel, *Baudelaire*, 159.

25. Letter to Ancelle, 18 February 1866, cited in Emmanuel, *Baudelaire*, 154; *Pauvre Belgique!*, cited in Emmanuel, *Baudelaire*, 154.

26. Cf. Emmanuel, *Baudelaire*, 15–17 and 19: Russell notes that he took up confession upon his dying bed.

27. Letter to V. de Laprade, cited in Emmanuel, *Baudelaire*, 158.

28. Steinmetz, *Pétrus Borel*, 91; Starkie, *Petrus Borel*, 93. Baudelaire also drew this parallel himself in an unpublished notice he wrote about Borel (in a collection of notes entitled "Réflexions sur mes contemporains"; for the section on Borel, see [Charles] Baudelaire, *Curiosités esthétiques, L'Art romantique et autres œuvres critiques* [Paris: Éditions Garnier Frères, 1962], 757–760): "Cet esprit à la fois littéraire et républicain, à l'inverse de la passion démocratique et bourgeoise qui nous a plus tard si cruellement opprimés, était agité à la fois par une haine aristocratique sans limites, sans restrictions, sans pitié, contre les rois et contre la bourgeoisie, et d'une sympathie générale pour tout ce qui en art représentait l'excès dans la couleur et dans la forme, pour tout ce qui était

à la fois intense, pessimiste, byronien; dilettantisme d'une nature singulière, et que peuvent seules expliquer les haïssables circonstances où était renfermée une jeunesse ennuyée et turbulente."

29. Steinmetz, *Pétrus Borel*, 67.

30. "Nous rêvions le règne de l'Art," O'Neddy would declare in retrospective. "Il nous semblait qu'un jour la Religion devait, dans ses conditions d'*extériorité*, être remplacée par l'*Esthétique*." Cf. Philotée O'Neddy, *Lettre inédite de Philothée O'Neddy, auteur de Feu et Flamme, sur le groupe littéraire romantique dit des Bousingos (Théophile Gautier, Gérard de Nerval, Petrus Borel, Bouchardy, Alphonse Brot, etc.)* (Paris: P. Rouquette, 1875). For proper nuance, it must be said that O'Neddy, in this letter, goes on to say that certain members of the group certainly held visions for a "social revolution," as the preface of his own *Feu et Flamme* indeed attests.

31. Burton, *Baudelaire and the Second Republic*, 359.

32. Baudelaire, *Curiosités esthétiques*, 322, 321 (I have reversed the order of this quotation).

33. Blake, *Poems and Prophecies*, 4.

34. Baudelaire, *Fleurs du Mal*, 186: "viens voyager dans les rêves,/Au delà du possible, au delà du connu!"

35. Baudelaire, *Journaux intimes*, 84 (*Mon cœur mis à nu*, XXIX, 52): the English translation is from Emmanuel, *Baudelaire*, 158; Baudelaire, *Journaux intimes*, 9 (*Fusées*, II).

36. Baudelaire, *Fleurs du Mal*, 267–268.

37. For my treatment of Baudelaire in these paragraphs, I am particularly indebted to ideas suggested by Emmanuel, *Baudelaire*, and Milner, *Le diable dans la littérature française*, 2:423–483.

38. Baudelaire, *Journaux intimes*, 73 (*Mon cœur mis à nu*, XX, 33): English translation is from Emmanuel, *Baudelaire*, 78.

39. Emmanuel, *Baudelaire*, 106; Baudelaire, *Journaux intimes*, 62 (*Mon cœur mis à nu*, XI, 1–9).

40. Baudelaire, *Journaux intimes*, 53 (*Mon cœur mis à nu*, III, 5–10).

41. This famous quote is from Baudelaire's short prose poem "Le Joueur généreux" (cf. Charles Baudelaire, *Le spleen de Paris: Petits poèmes en prose* [Paris: Librio, 2010], 53–56) (XXIX). Baudelaire was not the first to voice this idea; some earlier sources are given by Milner, *Le diable dans la littérature française*, 2:441n.

42. "Notes sur Les liaisons dangereuses," in Baudelaire, *Curiosités esthétiques*, 828–837, there 830.

43. "Elle est surtout, et plus que tout autre chose [*sic*], une grosse bête": *Journaux intimes*, 69 (*Mon cœur mis à nu*, XVII, 27).

44. Baudelaire, *Curiosités esthétiques*, 320–321: "L'artiste, le vrai artiste, le vrai poète, ne doit peindre que selon qu'il voit et qu'il sent. Il doit être *réellement* fidèle à sa propre nature."

45. Baudelaire, *Fleurs du Mal*, 237–239.

46. Cf. "Invitation à voyage" and many of the erotic poems.

47. Two prose poems from *Le Spleen de Paris* also depict Satan as offering complete "earthly" satisfaction: "L'Étranger" and "Le Joueur généreux" (cf. Baudelaire, *Le spleen de Paris*, 7 [I] and 53–56 [XXIX]). Both are essentially variations on "La Voix" from *Les Fleurs du Mal*.

48. Baudelaire, *Les Fleurs du Mal*, 82–83. The poem was first published in 1859, in the *Revue Française* of 20 January; cf. *Les Fleurs du Mal*, 232.

49. Jacques Cazotte, *Le diable amoureux, et autres écrits fantastiques* (Paris: Flammarion 1974), 125: "Mon cher Béelzébuth, je t'adore . . ."

50. Emmanuel, *Baudelaire*, 120.

51. Baudelaire, *Journaux intimes*, 7 (Fusées, I).

52. Baudelaire, *Les Fleurs du Mal*, 263.

CHAPTER 4: HUYSMANS AND CONSORTS

1. For a description of the duel, including weather conditions, see Jules Bois, *Le monde invisible* (Paris: Ernest Flammarion, s.a.), 30. More sources can be found in the notes at the end of this chapter.

2. Huysmans and the historical figures and episodes featuring in this chapter have been the subject of numerous publications. With regard to the history of Satanism, particularly useful *comptes-rendus* can be found in Frick, *Die Satanisten*, 2:155–229 (with many original documents quoted); Introvigne, *Enquête sur le satanisme*, 100–142; McIntosh, *Éliphas Lévi*, 177–197; Webb, *Occult Underground*, 153–184; Fernande Zayed, *Huysmans: Peintre de son époque* (Paris: Nizet, 1973), 421–465; as well as the biography by Robert Baldick, *The Life of J.-K. Huysmans* (Oxford: Clarendon, 1955). During the 1950s and 1960s, Pierre Lambert did pioneering research on these matters, which still has to find an adequate reception among Anglophone authors; the dispersed articles in which he presented his findings will be referenced at the appropriate places. This chapter is in many ways indebted to his research, not in the least because I was able to verify my findings by consulting the rich collection of source material concerning Huysmans brought together by Lambert and now kept in the Bibliothèque de l'Arsenal of the Bibliothèque nationale de France (henceforth, BnF). I also consulted other primary sources available at the French Bibliothèque nationale, allowing me to present a historical synthesis supported by original source material.

3. *Echo de Paris*, 8 (17 Feb. 1891) 2465:2.

4. *Echo de Paris*, 8 (13 Feb. 1891) 2461:1.

5. J.-K. Huysmans, *Là-Bas: A Journey into the Self*, trans. Brendan King (Sawtry, UK: Dedalus, 2009), 64. All quotations from *Là-Bas* will be from this translation, unless otherwise noted.

6. Huysmans, *Là-Bas*, 75–76.

7. Huysmans, *Là-Bas*, 74.

8. This and preceding citation: Huysmans, *Là-Bas*, 73.

9. Huysmans, *Là-Bas*, 207.

10. Huysmans, *Là-Bas*, 146.

11. Huysmans, *Là-Bas*, 95.

12. Huysmans, *Là-Bas*, 241.

13. Description of the Black Mass from Huysmans, *Là-Bas*, 246–255.

14. Huysmans, *Là-Bas*, 251–252.

15. Huysmans, *Là-Bas*, 252–253.

16. Huysmans, *Là-Bas*, 253, with King's translation slightly modified.

17. Huysmans, *Là-Bas*, 255.

18. My translation, from J.-K. Huysmans, *Là-Bas* (Paris: Plon, s.a.), 381.

19. Bruno Gelas, "Le satanisme et le roman Là-Bas de Huysmans," in *Le Défi Magique II: Satanisme, sorcellerie*, ed. Jean-Baptiste Martin and Massimo Introvigne (Lyon: Presses Universitaires de Lyon, 1994), 271–277.

20. On Charcot, cf. LaChapelle, *Investigating the Supernatural*, 59–85, and Faxneld, *Satanic Feminism*, 291–294.

21. J.-K. Huysmans, *Marthe: Histoire d'une fille* (Paris: Le Cercle du Livre, 1955); Émile Zola and others, *Les Soirées de Médan* (Paris: Georges Charpentier, 1880).

22. Charles Buet, *Grands Hommes en Robe de Chambre* (Paris: Société Libre d'Édition des Gens de Lettres, 1897), 231.

23. These and foregoing examples are paraphrased from Huysmans, *Là-Bas*, 27, 149.

24. J.-K. Huysmans, *Lettres inédites à Arij Prins, 1885–1907* (Genève: Droz, 1977), 235 (letter of [24 January] 1892); Remy de Gourmont, "Souvenirs sur Huysmans," in *Promenades Littéraires: Troisième Série* (Paris: Mercvre de France, 1916), 5–18, here 16–17; Joanny Bricaud, *Huysmans, Occultiste et Magicien: Avec une Notice sur les Hosties Magiques qui servent à Huysmans pour combattre les Envoûtements* (Paris: Bibliothèque Chacornac, 1913), 10–11.

25. Barbara G. Keller, *The Middle Ages Reconsidered: Attitudes in France from the Eighteenth Century through the Romantic Movement* (New York: Peter Lang, 1994), especially 48, 199. The Middle Ages played an important role in the conflict between Romantics and Classicists in French literature and art, during which they were juxtaposed as a source for vernacular, "national" thoughts and forms, vis-à-vis the "universal" ideals of Classicism. Similar notions can be found in German and English Romanticism. This predilection for the Middle Ages was not necessarily a "Reactionary" affair. The French writer Charles Nodier (1780–1844), for example, described the first medieval knights as "quelques nobles pauvres unis par la nécessité d'une légitime défense, épouvantés par des excès que devoit entraîner la multiplicité des pouvoirs souverains, [qui] prennent en pitié les misères et les larmes du peuple"; later, this beneficial institution had become monopolized by the monarchy, who exploited it for its own devious purposes (cited in Keller, *The Middle Ages Reconsidered*, 90).

A decent English-language overview of nineteenth-century medievalism in an international perspective seems to be lacking, but two publications in Dutch on this subject deserve mention: Ronald van Kesteren, *Het verlangen naar de Middeleeuwen: De verbeelding van een historische passie* (Amsterdam: Uitgeverij Wereldbibliotheek, 2004), with pp. 333–378 exclusively devoted to Huysmans, and Peter Raedts, *De Ontdekking van de Middeleeuwen: De geschiedenis van een illusie* (Amsterdam: Uitgeverij Wereldbibliotheek, 2011).

26. I have taken the phrase "discomfort with modernity" from Otto Gerhard Oexle's article "Das Mittelalter und das Unbehagen an der Moderne: Mittelalterbeschwörungen in der Weimarer Republik und danach," in *Geschichtswissenschaft im Zeichen des Historismus: Studien zu Problemgeschichten der Moderne*, Kritische Studien zur Geschichtswissenchaft, no. 116 (Göttingen: Vandenhoeck and Ruprecht, 1996), 137–162. Although dealing with attitudes toward the Middle Ages during the Weimar Republic, Oexle's analysis in this article seems remarkably apt to Huysmans as well.

27. J.-K. Huysmans, *À Rebours* (Paris: Bibliothèque-Charpentier, 1919), 294; see also ibid., 106.

28. All quotations in Huysmans, *À Rebours*, 212–213.

29. "Félicien Rops," originally published as "L'Œuvre érotique de Félicien Rops," in *La Plume*, 15 June 1886; reprinted in *Certains* (Paris: Tresse and Stock, 1889), 76–118.

30. Huysmans, *Certains*, 92. On Rops, see also Faxneld, *Satanic Feminism*, 393–407.

31. Jean Bodin (1530–1596) was a well-known French political writer and demonologist; Martin Delrio (1551–1608) was a Spanish Jesuit author who published a work on magic and the occult. Jacobus Sprengerus was, of course, one of the authors of the *Malleus Maleficarium*,

and Johann Joseph Görres (1776–1848) was a Catholic writer who had given much attention to demonology in his *Christliche Mystik* (1836–1842).

32. Huysmans, *Certains*, 117–118.

33. Huysmans, *Là-Bas*, 18, 20.

34. Cf. Introvigne, *Enquête sur le satanisme*, 101–102.

35. Letter to Gustave Guiches, written after 1887, quoted from Zayed, *Huysmans*, 429.

36. Letter from Charles Vignier in Jules Huret, *Enquête sur l'évolution littéraire* (Vanves, France: Éditions Thot, 1982), 105. For a more general background to the new occultism, see McIntosh, *Éliphas Lévi*, 219, and LaChapelle, *Investigating the Supernatural*, 37–58.

37. Biographical details about Péladan derive almost exclusively from the excellent biography by Christophe Beaufils, *Joséphin Péladan (1858–1918): Essai sur une maladie du lyrisme* (Grenoble: Jérôme Millon, 1993).

38. Joséphin Péladan, *La vice suprême (La décadence latine: Éthopée I)* (1896; repr., Genève: Editions Slatkine, 1979), 163. The influence of Lévi permeates the whole book but is particularly explicit on pp. 160 and 240.

39. Beaufils, *Joséphin Péladan*, 143.

40. Sar Péladan, *L'Art idéaliste & mystique: Doctrine de l'Ordre et du Salon Annuel de Rose + Croix* (Paris: Chamuel, 1894), 17–18.

41. Beaufils, *Joséphin Péladan*, 213, 226–235. After the first Salon, Satie broke away from the Sâr to found his own church.

42. Sar Mérodack J. Péladan, *Comment on devient Mage* (Paris: Chamuel, 1892), xiii; see also 129: "Quiconque ne va pas à la messe, n'entrera pas au temple du mystère. . . . Sois catholique pour devenir mage, et n'oublie jamais que si tes maîtres sont parmi les morts, tu as une supérieur parmi les vivants, Sa Sainteté le Pape."

43. Beaufils, *Joséphin Péladan*, 217.

44. Joséphin Péladan, *Comment on devient Fée* (1893; repr., s.l.: Paréiasaure, 1996), 58, a.o.; the scene of sexual therapy is included in *La Gynandre* (1891): see Beaufils, *Joséphin Péladan*, 210.

45. Beaufils, *Joséphin Péladan*, 162.

46. Stanislas de Guaita, *La Muse Noire* (Paris: Alphonse Lemerre, 1883), and *Rosa Mystica* (Paris: Alphonse Lemerre, 1885).

47. Quote from Bois, *Le monde invisible*, 22. Guaita's (neo)Romantic sentiments become evident in poems as "La Disgrâce de la Lyre" (*Muse Noire*, 9–11; "l'humanité stupide a renié ses dieux . . ."), "Le Progrès" (ibid., 75–77), "Positivisme" (ibid., 137–138; "le Positivisme a triomphé du Songe"), as well as in the title poem of *Rosa Mystica* and the extensive preface of the latter publication, in which Guaita explicitly gives tribute to Hugo, Théophile Gautier, and Baudelaire. Significantly, the mysticism of the title is defined on p. 3 of this preface as "l'amour de nos cœurs pour les songes de nos cerveaux."

48. Guaita, *Rosa Mystica*, 65–66.

49. Guaita, *Rosa Mystica*, 66, 3. On the same page, Guaita had written about the poet: "Vous êtes donc magicien, et la rose mystique ira d'elle-même, pour peu que vous le vouliez, fleurir en votre jardin."

50. Stanislas de Guaita, *Lettres inédites de Stanislas de Guaita au Sâr Joséphin Péladan*, ed. Edmund Bertholet and Emile Dantinne (Neuchâtel: Éditions Rosicruciennes, 1952), 51–53. In later letters, Guaita would defend Lévi to Péladan, who was critical of Lévi's presumed pantheism; see ibid., 71–73.

51. Bois, *Le monde invisible*, 23. Guaita's addiction to morphine is also attested in his letters (see Guaita, *Lettres inédites au Sâr Joséphin Péladan*, 96, 115–116), while two of the best poems in *Rosa Mystica* deal with the "flowers of oblivion" as well (cf. "Notre-Dame d'Oubli," *Rosa Mystica*, 95–98, and "Les fleurs vénéneux," ibid., 101–105). For Guaita's library, see Guaita, *Lettres inédites au Sâr Joséphin Péladan*, 25; 2,227 works were put on sale after Guaita's death.

A scholarly biography of Guaita is still conspicuously lacking. The obituary of his friend Maurice Barrès, *Un rénovateur de l'occultisme, Stanislas de Guaita (1861–1898)* (Paris: Chamuel, 1898), does not offer much in terms of factual information; André Billy, *Stanislas de Guaita* (Paris: Mercure de France, 1971), is also unsatisfying. Oswald Wirth, *Stanislas de Guaita: Souvenirs de son Secrétaire* (Paris: Éditions du Symbolisme, 1935), is indispensable as a source text but is uncritically laudatory of the French occultist.

52. Two tomes of this work would see print: *Première Septaine (Livre I): Le Temple de Satan* and *Première Septaine (Livre II): La Clef de la Magie Noire*. I have consulted the edition published in Paris by Hector and Henri Durville, 1915–1920.

53. Biographical details on Papus are mostly taken from the biography by his son Philippe Encausse, *Sciences occultes ou 25 années d'occultisme occidental: Papus, sa vie, son œuvre* (Paris: Éditions Ocia, 1949). As with Guaita, a scholarly biography of Papus is still wanting.

54. Beaufils, *Joséphin Péladan*, 121.

55. This point is made very explicit in Papus, *Traité élémentaire de science occulte* (Paris: Albin Michel, 1926), 183–187.

56. Encausse, *Sciences occultes*, 57–107.

57. Encausse, *Sciences occultes*, 109–120. On the earlier history of the Rosicrucians, see Zander, *Anthroposophie in Deutschland*, 1:90–92, 1:838–844, and Horst Möller, "Die Gold- und Rosenkreuzer: Struktur, Zielsetzung und Wirkung einer anti-aufklärischen Geheimgesellschaft," in *Geheime Gesellschaften*, ed. Peter Christian Ludz, Wolfenbütteler Studien zur Aufklärung V/1 (Heidelberg: Verlag Lambert Schneider, 1979), 153–202.

58. Péladan claimed to have been initiated by his older brother Adrien; see Edmund Bertholet's introduction to Guaita, *Lettres inédites au Sâr Joséphin Péladan*, 39.

59. Beaufils, *Joséphin Péladan*, 134. This might be the right moment to point out the striking similarities in program between Péladan's *Vice suprême* and Huysmans's *Là-Bas*, two novels that both confront the decay of their times with an alternative world of Catholicism and occultism. The possibility must not be excluded that Huysmans had been inspired by Péladan.

60. Baldick, *Life of J.-K. Huysmans*, 139.

61. Guaita, *Le Serpent de la Genèse*, 1:24–25.

62. Guaita, *Serpent de la Genèse* 1:21, 67, 51, 572; see also 2:138, as well as Péladan, *Comment on devient Fée*, 24, and Papus, *Le Diable et l'Occultisme* (Paris: Chamuel, 1895), 34–35: "Dieu est l'Esprit dont l'antithèse dernière est la Matière. Le Diable est ce qui donne à la Matière la prééminence sur l'Esprit."

63. Beaufils, *Joséphin Péladan*, 327. The unsympathetic reactions of the other guests and the Franciscan caretaker made the Sâr fear for his life—he barricaded the door of his room and slept with his pistol under his cushion, checking out early next morning. It must be added, however, that Péladan does not seem to have been free of a slight touch of paranoia.

64. Sar Mérodack J. Péladan, *Comment on devient artiste: esthétique* (Paris: [Chamuel], 1894), 19, 43, 38–40: "Toute vision du ciel, religion, et art vient des daïmons et non de l'homme. Les fils

de l'au-delà seuls les perçoivent: eux seuls le peuvent montrer aux hommes. Mais comme Sathan leur père perdit sa gloire pour achèver son œuvre sur les hommes, ainsi les daïmons doivent enseigner tout ce qui exhausse l'être et l'accomplit." Compare Beaufils, *Joséphin Péladan*, 148, 278. Fittingly, *Comment on devient artiste* opened with a dedication to the devil, in which Péladan declared that he "felt daïmonic blood palpitating" in his veins and expressed the hope that he, too, was a descendant of the fallen angels (see xi–xiii).

65. Beaufils, *Joséphin Péladan*, 189; see also 282. The quotation originates from Péladan's novel *Cœur en peine* (1890).

66. Péladan, *Comment on devient Mage*, 42–43, 153.

67. Guaita, *Serpent de la Genèse*, 2:542.

68. Guaita, *Serpent de la Genèse*, 2:542n.

69. Guaita, *Serpent de la Genèse*, 1:532n: "D'après la tradition ésotérique, l'homme terrestre, *Conscience* individuelle, se trouve placé entre deux *Inconscients*: l'*Inconscient supérieur* ou Esprit universel, et l'*Inconscient inférieur* ou instinct collectif. Selon qu'il se met en rapport avec l'un ou l'autre, l'homme reçoit: d'en haut, l'*Inspiration divine*, ou d'en bas, l'*Intuition physique*. Libre donc à chacun de s'assimiler de l'un ou de l'autre breuvage, dans la mesure de sa capacité; mais il ne faut pas plus se noyer ou dissoudre son Moi dans l'Esprit universel que dans l'Instinct collectif.—Au demeurant, l'Esprit universel ne se nomme *Inconscient* (supérieur) que par opposition à la *Conscience* individuelle; comme on pourrait l'appeler encore *Non-Moi* (supérieur), pour le distinguer du *Moi* individuel. Est-ce à dire qu'il soit dépourvu en soi de conscience ou d'entité? Conclure de la sorte, ce serait jouer sur les mots.—Au cas particulier, il ne s'agit que de l'*Inconscient inférieur*."

70. Quotation from Péladan, *Comment on devient Mage*, 223–224; see also Guaita, *Serpent de la Genèse*, 1:171, 2:9, 2:110, and Victor-Émile Michelet, *L'Amour et la Magie* (Paris: Librairie Hermétique, 1909). An adequate summary of the typical fin de siècle misogyny of the latter work can be found on p. 49: "Or, l'œuvre de la femme, par l'amour, est aussi magie bénéfique ou magie maléfique. Elle exalte les forces de l'homme ou bien elle les détruit. Je suis bien obligé de reconnaître que le plus souvent elle les détruit."

71. Guaita, *Serpent de la Genèse*, 2:416–417; Papus, *Traité élémentaire de science occulte*, 141–142 (whose interpretation is a bit different and does not mention devil or goat; the inverted pentagram is a pictogram for a man with his legs in the air, thus signifying his subjugation to passions and evil spirits); also Michelet, *L'Amour et la Magie*, 48–49.

72. Huysmans, *Lettres inédites à Arij Prins*, 182.

73. Huysmans, *Là-Bas*, 137.

74. Huysmans, *Là-Bas*, 137.

75. Baldick, *Life of J.-K. Huysmans*, 160; Henri Jouvin, "Les Lettres de J.-K. Huysmans: Essais de Bibliographie," *Bulletin de la Société J.-K Huysmans* 28 (1953) 27:288–296, here 289. According to Baldick, this letter was sent on February 5; Jouvin gives February 6 as its date.

76. Baldick, *Life of J.-K. Huysmans*, 160–161.

77. Jouvin, "Les Lettres de J.-K. Huysmans," 289.

78. Baldick, *Life of J.-K. Huysmans*, 161; Frick, *Die Satanisten*, 2:194.

79. Letter from 19 February 1890; Huysmans, *Lettres inédites à Arij Prins*, 184; see also Huysmans's letter from the same year to Jules Destrée, quoted in J.-K. Huysmans, *Lettres inédites à Jules Destrée* (Genève: Droz, 1967), 162–163.

80. For biographical data on Boullan, Marcel Thomas, "Un aventurier de la mystique: L'abbé Boullan," *Les Cahiers de la Tour Saint-Jacques* 8 (1963): 116–161, is still authoritative. See also, in the same volume, Pierre Lambert, "Adèle Chevalier raconte . . . ," *Les Cahiers de la Tour Saint-Jacques* 8 (1963): 217–226, and Jean Jacquinot, "En marge de J.-K. Huysmans: Un Procès de l'Abbé Boullan," *Les Cahiers de la Tour Saint-Jacques* 8 (1963): 206–216.

81. "L'œuvre réparatrice des blasphèmes et de la violation des Dimanches"; Jacquinot, "En marge de J.-K. Huysmans," 26.

82. "J. A. Boullan, Confession au St. Office, ou 'cahier rose.' Copie faite d'après microfilm en possession du R.P. Bruno. Janv. 1951," BnF, Fonds Lambert, 95/39, f. 2v: "un monstre, qui n'avait rien d'humain." Boullan burned the infant body three days later. It is clear from Boullan's story that he did not "sacrifice" the child during the Eucharistic rite, as some authors have claimed; Adèle Chevalier merely gave birth (more or less) at the moment that he performed Mass but was not present at the rite. The child may have been deformed. Attribution of deformed children to demons had some precedents in premodern (informal) Roman Catholic practice. Nicolas Rémy, on p. 26 of his *Démonolâtrie* from 1582, claimed that deformed children were engendered by demons: thus the Church "considers them unfit to receive Christian baptism, and we take care to smother them to death as soon as they are born; doubtless because they carry suspicion of the hidden presence of a Demon lurking within them" (cited from Waite, *Eradicating the Devil's Minions*, 102).

That there might have been different readings of this event is indicated by Boullan on the same page of the "Cahier rose," where he recounts that two other members of the congregation may have talked about this during the judicial inquest. He regrets that he was not allowed to be present at their interrogation, "afin que le démon ne leur fit pas dire autre chose que la vérité": they might have claimed that he was the father of the child, thus making his act one of simple infanticide to cover up his own sexual practices. Boullan would hint at the occurrences in a letter to Huysmans on the Black Mass from 4 September 1890 ("Lettres de l'Abbé Boullan à Jules Bois et à Huysmans," BnF, Mss. Occ. N.a. fr. 16596, ff. 119v–°120 = BnF, Fonds Lambert, 76, ff. 219–223). Here he presents them as a personal triumph over "un démon qui voulait à tout prix me faire monter à l'échafaud," recounting that he used the power of the Consecration to vanquish the demon and heal Adèle.

83. These practices are clearly admitted by Boullan in the "Cahier rose," ff. 1v–°3v°, where he confesses to have made use of "caca" to cure skin diseases ("J'en fait mettre une fois à Mlle Zoé Legrix sur tout la figure pour l'humilier"); to have "regardé dans les parties génitales de plusieurs personnes"; to have exhibited himself several times and had the sisters touch his genitals; to have ordered them to adopt indecent postures, bath naked in his presence, and embrace each other in the bed "d'une manière indécente"; and to have had oral sex with one of the sisters, "et deux fois, je crois, elle a avalé de la semence." He also admitted having ordered "quelques personnes de la maison de mettre dans les parties génitales des hosties" to chase away incubi—although he added that these hosts were not consecrated "mais données, je crois alors d'une manière miraculeuse"—and to have asked a sister "de venir avec moi en esprit, comme si je pouvais aller charnellement avec elle." Boullan maintains, however, that he kept his practices with the sisters within certain bounds, "sans violer la virginité, ni pénétré en elles"; this happened only two times with a sister called Hortense Guerry.

84. Thomas, "Un aventurier de la mystique," 131–133, quoting Boullan, who also makes veiled references to these ideas on ff. 3v°–4v° of the "Cahier rose."

85. These allegations can be found in Charles Sauvestre, *Les congrégations religieuses dévoilées* (Paris: E. Dentu, 1870), 118; giving the confessions of Boullan we quoted earlier, their veracity must be considered probable.

86. Thomas, "Un aventurier de la mystique," 136. Bruno de Jésus-Marie, "La confession de Boullan," *Satan: Les Études Carmélitaines* 27 (Paris: Desclée De Brouwer, 1948): 420–426, here 420, maintains that Boullan was only freed when Piedmontese forces captured Rome in 1870. It is not certain that Boullan even deposited the "confession" he wrote down in his "Cahier rose"; the texts in the notebook are clearly drafts that were meant to be copied in a better hand later on (see hereafter).

87. Jésus-Marie, "La confession de Boullan," 420, identifies these "cornus" with "les prêtres romains" *tout court*, but this interpretation is not supported by a close reading of the text.

88. "Cahier rose," ff. 8v°, 11, 12v°, 13v°. The historical fate of the "Cahier rose" is a story in itself. After Boullan's demise, the notebook, together with other personal effects, was entrusted to Huysmans by Boullan's followers. Contrary to the assertion of Joanny Bricaud (*J.-K. Huysmans et le Satanisme: D'après des documents inédits* [Paris: Bibliothèque Chacornac, 1913], 76), Huysmans did not burn these documents but left them in his will to his friend Léon Leclaire, in the hope, it seems, that a "priest that is apt to study and comprehend them" would one day be able to use them for a publication, and with the stipulation that they would subsequently be destroyed (see Louis Massignon, "Huysmans devant la 'confession' de Boullan," *Bulletin de la Société J.-K Huysmans* 22 (1949) 21:40–50, here 40–41). Leclaire, in his turn, entrusted them to the Arabist and Huysmans disciple Louis Massignon, who, after searching in vain for a suitable priest, officially transmitted them to Cardinal Giovanni Mercati, Prefect of the Vatican Secret Archives, on July 14, 1930, who deposited them in the "Reserve" of the Vatican Library. When the Carmelites issued their famous 666-page volume on Satan in 1948, Bruno de Jésus-Marie obtained permission to publish from the manuscript and received a copy on microfilm of the "Cahier." In his article, however, he only included some rather general references to its contents and a hazy reproduction of a few choice pages—according to his own statement because the reader otherwise "n'en aurait supporté la lecture" (Jésus-Marie, "La confession de Boullan," 426); according to Louis Massignon's malicious suggestion because he feared "certains chocs en retour préternaturels" (Massignon, "Huysmans devant la "confession' de Boullan," 42). It was this microfilm that was consulted and typed out by the French Huysmans scholar Pierre Lambert in January 1950; his dactylographic copy can now be consulted in the Bibliothèque de l'Arsenal of the BnF, where Lambert's collection of Huysmaniana is currently kept.

Apart from the "Cahier rose," a great number of letters, mostly by Boullan to Huysmans and vice versa, must still be kept in the Vatican libraries, as well as some other personal documents from the legacy of Boullan (a raw inventory can be found in Massignon, "Huysmans devant la 'confession' de Boullan," 49). Due to limitations of time and resources, I have not been able to consult these, but I do not doubt that additional scholarly insights can be gained from them.

89. "Le martyre du Roi Louis XVI au jugement du Pape Pie VI," *Annales de la Sainteté au XIXe siècle* (July 1874) 55:45–54.

90. For Vintras, see Maurice Garçon, *Vintras: Hérésiarque et prophète* (Paris: Librairie critique Émile Nourry, 1928).

91. Introvigne, *Enquête sur le satanisme*, 100–101.

92. Boullan's own account of his meeting with and subsequent succession of Vintras can be found in one of his journals, kept in the file "J.A. Boullan. Textes, notes et lettres, après 1875," BnF, Fonds Lambert, 98/17, especially p. 1–6.

93. Even in his later letters to Huysmans, Boullan often referred to the "sublime Tarot"; see Maurice M. Belval, *Des ténèbres à la lumière: Etapes de la pensée mystique de J.K. Huysmans* (Paris: Maisonneuve and Larose, 1968), 84, 144, 117. Boullan sent Huysmans extracts from the Zohar on July 23, 1890 (BnF, Mss. Occ. N.a. fr. 16596, f. 104 = "J.A. Boullan. Textes, notes, et lettres, 1883–1893," BnF, Fonds Lambert 97/6065 = BnF, Fonds Lambert, 76, ff. 153–161), and on May 6, 1890, a document entitled "La destinée de Mr. J.K. Huysmans par les figures du Tarot et les 5 essences en Dieu" (BnF, Fonds Lambert, 76, ff. 257–278). In his personal papers, extracts on Hindu mythology and Paracelsus can be found (BnF, Fonds Lambert, 97/33; BnF, Fonds Lambert, 98/24).

The detail about the pentagram is mentioned by Jules Bois in *Les Petites Religions de Paris* (Paris: Ernest Flammarion, s.a. [1894]), 127.

94. See Boullan's journal for 1885–1886, BnF, Fonds Lambert, 98/19, p. 44. Boullan had apparently visited Roca in Paris in February 1886: the latter returned the visit in July of the same year. "J'ai fait son marriage spirituel le 26 Juillet 1886," Boullan notes on the same page, where he also mentions contacts with René Caillié and Albert Jhounet, both familiar names from the world of nineteenth-century French occultism.

95. Letter from Boullan to Huysmans, quoted without date in Bricaud, *J.-K. Huysmans et le Satanisme*, 35. Billy, *Stanislas de Guaita*, 134, maintains Guaita was ordained as a priest by Boullan. The marquis himself wrote on this in an undated letter to Péladan headed "confidentiel": "Quant aux onctions que j'ai reçues, il m'est impossible de te dire *de qui* je les ai reçues; mais je les ai *régulièrement* reçues, valablement reçues, selon le rituel catholique romain, et non le rituel Eliaque. Je suis donc *Sacerdote occulte*, comme l'ont été, *à toutes époques, tous les adeptes du 3ᵉ degré*, et j'ai tous les pouvoirs pour exercer le culte in secretis, *magiquement* et non *sacerdotalement*." (Guaita, *Lettres inédites au Sâr Joséphin Péladan*, 128; the whole letter is extremely interesting in this respect.)

96. Compare "J.A. Boullan. Journal sommaire de sa vie de 1876 au Juillet 1889," BnF, Fonds Lambert, 98/23, p. 55.

97. Undated letters from Guaita to Péladan; Guaita, *Lettres inédites au Sâr Joséphin Péladan*, 106, 126—see also ibid., 128.

98. Garçon, *Vintras*, 151, does think it improbable that Vintras had endorsed this kind of practice, despite rumors to the contrary—during one of his spells in prison, however, one of his lieutenants had briefly instated practices of communal male masturbation and female sexual license (ibid., 109–125; cf. Introvigne, *Enquête sur le satanisme*, 108(n)).

99. "Relation de la cérémonie pour la conception par Claudine Gay de corps glorieux de Madame de Raimbaud, gouvernante de Louis XVII, 14 février [1882?]," BnF, Fonds Lambert, 96/34; partly published in Pierre Lambert, "En marge de 'Là-Bas': Une Cérémonie au "Carmel de Jean-Baptiste', à Lyon, d'après une relation de Boullan," *Bulletin de la Société J.-K Huysmans* 28 (1953) 27:297–306, here 300–301. Boullan's text suggests that other believers were present at this ceremony.

100. "Confession de Jean Bᵗᵉ Elie Gabriel, pour le Pardon général, le relèvement et l'absolution plénière du 6 Février 1881, Au Sanctuaire du Trématique Eliaque," BnF, Fonds Lambert, 96/32, pp. [3], 5.

101. "Mission de Moyse et Aaron. Initiation à ce Ministère de la 1er de la 3ème degré du Tarot Henochite," BnF, Fonds Lambert, 98/11–12, f. 14–14°; quote f. 7.

102. "Mission de Moyse et Aaron," BnF, Fonds Lambert, 98/11–12, f. 20.

103. "Doctrine de vie du Sohar concernant les lois saintes dans les unions vivifiantes de l'Épouse Virginale et de l'Époux toujours vierge," BnF, Fonds Lambert, 97/47.

104. Guaita, *Serpent de la Genèse*, 1:482–487. In his personal notes, Boullan noted that this union had been enacted "in spirit and soul" on 17 Augustus 1885, 10 p.m.; autobiographical notes 1883–1884, BnF, Fonds Lambert, 98/17, p. 9.

105. Guaita, *Serpent de la Genèse*, 1:457–516; also Wirth, *Stanislas de Guaita*, 98–107.

106. Guaita, *Serpent de la Genèse*, 1:457. Indeed, it may have been that Guaita had primarily called the Rosicrucian Order into life in order to deal with the case of Boullan; this is suggested by Wirth, *Stanislas de Guaita*, 109, and by a letter from Papus in *L'Écho de Paris* 10 (13 Jan. 1893) 3162:3.

107. Letter from Oswald Wirth to Boullan, 24 May 1887, BnF, Fonds Lambert 30/5 (13), f. 2. The text of the letter of condemnation is also reproduced in Wirth, *Stanislas de Guaita*, 135–138.

108. Baldick, *Life of J.-K. Huysmans*, 162. BnF, Fonds Lambert, 30/5 contains a "feuillet de notes autographes de Huysmans" that were probably (according to Lambert) jotted down after his interview with Wirth on 7 February 1890, containing references to the earlier judicial proceedings against Boullan and to the book of Sauvestre, as well as Boullan's address. The same file contains a letter by Wirth dated 15 February 1890 that gives the precise title of the book by Sauvestre "dont je vous ai parlé" (BnF, Fonds Lambert, 30/5; the categorization of this file seems inconsistent).

109. Baldick, *Life of J.-K. Huysmans*, 159; Wirth, *Stanislas de Guaita*, 142, also 103, 107; Herman Bossier, *Un personnage de roman: Le chanoine Docre de La-Bas de J.-K. Huysmans* (Bruxelles: Les Ecrits, 1943), 100.

110. Thomas, "Un aventurier de la mystique," 143.

111. Frick, *Die Satanisten*, 2:194.

112. Huysmans, *Lettres inédites à Arij Prins*, 200. Huysmans wrote about a similar condemnation in a letter to Gustave Boucher on 19 Augustus 1891: see Zayed, *Huysmans*, 449n.

113. Pierre Lambert, "Un culte hérétique à Paris, 11, Rue de Sèvres: Avec des textes inédits de Huysmans," *Les Cahiers de la Tour Saint-Jacques* 8 (1963): 190–205, here 194. Huysmans would utilize this note in his description of an experience with a succubus in his 1895 novel *En Route*.

114. Boullan to Huysmans, letter from 14 November 1890 quoted in Belval, *Des ténèbres à la lumière*, 88; see also ibid., 89 and 120.

115. Letter from 21 September 1890; Huysmans, *Lettres inédites à Arij Prins*, 203. The context suggests that Huysmans is talking about the chapter on the Black Mass here (chapter XIX). This, however, is followed by three more short chapters in the final version of *Là-Bas*. While it is possible that Huysmans changed his chapter division after September 1890, the last three chapters also provide much information on Dr. Johannès. A final conclusion must be suspended until more material is available.

116. Undated letter (July 1891) from Huysmans to Berthe de Courrière, quoted in André du Fresnois, *Une étape de la conversion de Huysmans: D'après des lettres inédites à Mme de C . . .* (Paris: Dorbon-Aîné, s.a. [1912]), 28. In a personal note, Boullan describes a similar "spiritual battle" against the Rosicrucians on 11 Augustus 1890; see BnF, Fonds Lambert, 97/50.

117. In a letter to Adolphe Berthet from 1 May 1900, he suggested that nothing more had been going on than "succubal excesses"; "It was just a bunch of old folks for whom that game [i.e., physical sexuality] would have been unwise and without charm." See Lambert, "Un culte hérétique à Paris," 195, and Baldick, *Life of J.-K. Huysmans*, 189. Bois, *Petites Religions*, 129–130, was of the same opinion. Huysmans had inherited Boullan's personal papers in 1896, among them the infamous "Cahier rose."

118. Letter from 24 July 1890, Huysmans, *Lettres inédites à Arij Prins*, 200. In a letter published in the *Écho de Paris* 8 (18 April 1891) 2535:1, Huysmans described the entourage of Boullan in similar terms: their "bonté" and "delicatesse d'âme," he declared, "me suggèrent l'idée de créatures oubliées sur le marge des ages, des créatures d'un autre temps."

119. Jacquinot, "En marge de J.-K. Huysmans," 208.

120. Boullan to Huysmans, 10 December 1890; see Thomas, "Un aventurier de la mystique," 150–151 (italics as in original). It is possible that Boullan makes an intentional pun on Guaita here, whose first publication on occultism was entitled *Au Seuil du mystère* ("On the Threshold of Mystery"). Boullan possessed a copy of this book with a personal dedication by Guaita, according to Bricaud, *J.-K. Huysmans et le Satanisme*, 34–35n.

121. Éliphas Lévi, who met Vintras once, had seen some of these hosts and discerned an inverted pentagram on one of them, which made him decide that Vintrasism was Satanic in nature. See Lévi, *Clef des grands mystères*, 148–165, especially 161–163.

122. See the description in Jules Bois, *Le Satanisme et la Magie: Avec une étude de J.K. Huysmans* (Paris : Ernest Flammarion 1895), 201–207. Bois based himself on original documents from the Vintrasian archives, passed on to him by Huysmans, who did receive them from Boullan.

123. Bois, *Le Satanisme et la Magie*, 207.

124. An article titled "Les périls des sociétés secrètes, et le moyen donné par le ciel pour les combattre," *Annales de la Sainteté au XIXᵉ siècle* (April 1873) 39:307–310, already gives details on the way to combat secret societies by Masses said by a "trio of priests" that are strongly reminiscent of Vintras; "Un coup d'œil sur une étude importante de la science sacrée," *Annales de la Sainteté* (January 1875) 61:68–72, talks about a secret society in Paris that brings homage "to a living representation of Venus Astarte."

125. This story was unearthed by Maurice Garçon, "La société infernale d'Agen," *Mercvre de France* (15 July 1928): 271–304, who based himself on a ms. volume kept in the BnF, "L'Affaire d'Agen," Fr. Nouv. Acq. 11.053.

126. Garçon, "La société infernale d'Agen," 300–303.

127. Huysmans, *Là-Bas*, 74.

128. Biographical information about Courrière from Bossier, *Un personnage de roman*, 48— see also the second Dutch-language edition of this book, Bossier, *Geschiedenis van een roman-figuur: De "chanoine Docre" uit Là-Bas van J.-K. Huysmans* (Hasselt: Heideland, 1965), 66—as well as Justin Saget, "Notes pour servir à la Grande Histoire de la Vieille Dame," *Cahiers du Collège de Pataphysique* (1952) 5–6:17–23 (on pp. 9–16 some publications by Courrière from the *Mercvre de France* are reproduced). Clésinger eternalized Courrière in the bust of the Republic in the French Senate. For Courrière and Boullan, see Belval, *Des ténèbres à la lumière*, 73. Introvigne, *Enquête sur le satanisme*, 131, claims that Guaita provided Huysmans with the address of Boullan, while Wirth is also a not unlikely candidate.

129. Courrière's preference for clergy is hinted at in Pierre Dufay, "L'Abbé Boullan et le 'Chanoine Docre,' " *Mercvre de France* (15 March 1935) 882:509–527, here 523 ("Elle avait, paraît-il, l'obsession du prêtre"); see also Huysmans, *Là-Bas*, 207, 233. The description of Courrière's interior is from Henry de Groux, as quoted in Baldick, *Life of J.-K. Huysmans*, 138.

130. The story of the hosts in Courrière's handbag is attributed to Madame Rachilde, the wife of the director of the *Mercvre de France*, and was transmitted in a letter by Joanny Bricaud to Herman Bossier—see the latter's *Un personnage de roman*, 60. It may have been invented by Bricaud. In the chapter devoted to "Mme Berthe de C . . ." in Rachilde's *Alfred Jarry ou le sur-mâle de lettres* (Paris: Bernard Grasset, 1928), 43–66, she only tells that Courrière "procurait . . . des hosties pour messes noire, et de nouveaux fidèles aux prêtres de bonne volonté": and even this unsubstantiated allegation, published thirty years *post factum*, may originate from an overly rash backward projection of Huysmans's description of Madame Chantelouve in *Là-Bas*. The same chapter also cites a love letter from Courrière to Jarry, which, when authentic, clearly shows her to be at home in the vocabulary of neo-Lévian occultism and fin de siècle Symbolism (ibid., 61–66).

131. Courrière to Huysmans, 27 July 1891, BnF, Fonds Lambert, 30/5 (12); quoted by Lambert, "En marge de 'Là-Bas,' " 303–304.

132. Dufay, "L'Abbé Boullan et le 'Chanoine Docre,' " 524.

133. Huysmans, *Lettres inédites à Arij Prins*, 182n.

134. On Dubus, see Leon Bocquet, "Édouard Dubus (1863–1895)," *Le Nord littéraire et artistique* (19 January 1928): 10–11.

135. According to a short notice in *Burgerwelzijn* (Brugge), 10 September 1890, quoted by Herman Bossier, *Geschiedenis van een Romanfiguur: De "Chanoine Docre" uit "Là-Bas" van J.-K. Huysmans* (Brussels: De Lage Landen, 1942), 47; and in his *Un personnage de roman* on p. 51. The register of the Sint Juliaansgesticht is referred to on p. 49, respectively, pp. 53–54 of the same works. Her state of undress is remarked upon by Thomas, "Un aventurier de la mystique," 146, among others; see also Bossier, *Un personnage de roman*, 55, who cites an "anonymous priest" as source.

136. Letters from Gourmont to Huysmans deriving from "Lettres adressées pour la plupart à J.K. Huysmans," BnF, Fonds Lambert, 28/25, and quoted in Pierre Lambert, "Annexes au dossier Van Haecke-Berthe Courrière: Lettres inédites de Gourmont et de Firmin Vanden Bosch à Joris-Karl Huysmans," *Les Cahiers de la Tour Saint-Jacques* 8 (1963):180–189, here 182–184.

137. Thomas, "Un aventurier de la mystique," 146–151.

138. This and preceding letter quoted in Thomas, "Un aventurier de la mystique," 147–149.

139. Thomas, "Un aventurier de la mystique," 149–151.

140. *Echo de Paris* 8 (18 April 1891) 2535:1. The other model was, of course, the chaplain of the exiled queen, who already had committed suicide. In a private letter to Charles Buet dated 17 April 1891 (Zayed, *Huysmans*, 445), Huysmans denied that Boullan was Docre: "c'est le chanoine V.H. qui reside à Bruges, un terrible prêtre, allez!" A similar statement can be found in a letter to Prins from 30 March 1892 (Huysmans, *Lettres inédites à Arij Prins*, 237): "A Bruges, il y a un chanoine du précieux sang qui m'a, il est vrai, servi pour mon chanoine Docre, mais qui est autrement fort que le mien. Malheureusement, les meilleurs renseignements me sont venus après l'apparition de mon livre." Frédéric Boutet, *Tableau de l'au-delà* (Paris: Gallimard, 1927), 137–138, claims that Canon Roca was the principal source of inspiration for Docre, but he is alone in defending this hypothesis.

141. Huysmans in Bois, *Le Satanisme et la Magie*, xix–xxx.

142. The obituary appeared in *Biekorf: Leer- en leesblad voor alle verstandige Vlamingen* (Zaaimaand 1912); I quote from Bossier, *Geschiedenis van een Romanfiguur*, 37. For biographical information on Van Haecke, see Bossier, *Un personnage de roman*, 33–41.

143. This and following quotation from Massignon, "Huysmans devant la 'confession' de Boullan," 47. Also quoted in Baldick, *Life of J.-K. Huysmans*, 256.

144. Bossier, *Un personnage de roman*, 71–72. Michel de Lézinier, *Avec Huysmans: Promenades et souvenirs* (Paris: André Delpeuch, 1928), 207–209, recounts how Huysmans showed him a photograph of "Docre" around 1900. There is no indication that Huysmans ever met Van Haecke, although he may have glimpsed him when he spent a few days in Bruges in 1902 for an exhibition of Primitive painters. "The place is exquisite as ever," he wrote to his friend Leon Leclaire in remarkably off-hand fashion. "And in the course of my walk I caught a glimpse of Van Eycke [*sic*] with his snow-white locks" (quoted in Baldick, *Life of J.-K. Huysmans*, 312). The stories attested by Vanden Bosch may have been made up or incorrectly transmitted by either Huysmans or Vanden Bosch himself. There are some clues that Van Haecke was not unfamiliar with occultist circles, however: Péladan was quoted in a newspaper interview as claiming that he had dined a few times with the model of Docre, "un doux illuminé, incapable de vouloir du mal à une mouche" ("Chez le Sar," *Le Jour* [28 April 1891]: 1–2).

145. Vanden Bosch to Huysmans, 23 July 1895 and 30 January 1896; "Documents relatifs au satanisme," BnF, Fonds Lambert, 30/4 (3); Lambert, "Annexes au dossier Van Haecke-Berthe Courrière," 186, 189.

146. Bossier, *Un personnage de roman*, 73–74, 143–144. See also the rather hazy letter by Huysmans to Mœller from 20 February 1896; Henry Mœller, "Joris-Karl Huysmans d'après sa correspondance," *Durendal: Revue Catholique d'Art et de Littérature* 5 (1908): 444.

147. As witnesses *pro* Huysmans, we may cite, in the first place, Introvigne, *Enquête sur le satanisme*, 137: "Toutefois, sauf à considérer Huysmans comme totalement insincère et à disqual-ifier aussi un grand nombre de documents . . . , il faut admettre que la messe noire de Huysmans, que celui-ci y ait personnellement assisté ou non, est décrite, au moins dans ses grandes lignes, de façon plausible. . . ."—cf. also 142, where Introvigne argues that it is precisely the vagueness and incompleteness of his documentation that makes it plausible that Huysmans was describ-ing real Satanism: "C'est cette obscurité même qui nous laisser penser que nous sommes alors, pour de bon, en présence de satanistes." In his article "Satanism" in the *Dictionary of Gnosis and Western Esotericism*, 2:1035, Introvigne also unequivocally assumes the veracity of Huysmans's report; in his article on Huysmans in the same publication, 1:579–580, he seems more circum-spect but nevertheless designates Huysmans's novels and correspondence as "important refer-ences." Other believers include Dubois, *Jules Bois*, 52 ("[Huysmans] avait, il est vrai, fréquenté le milieu sataniste"; Lyons, *Satan Wants You*, 59 [= *Second Coming*, 82]: "It is more than likely that parts of the ceremony that Huysmans described did have a basis in reality"; Massignon, "Huysmans devant la 'confession' de Boullan" (and other publications); Rita Thiele, *Satanismus als Zeitkritik bei Joris-Karl Huysmans* (Frankfurt am Main: Verlag Peter D. Lang, 1979), 10, 101–104; Zacharias, *Satanskult und Schwarze Messe*, 140: "Huysmans wohnte aber auch unz-weifelhaft mindestens einmal einer der eigentlichen Schwarzen Messen bei, die regelmäßig in der Nähe seiner Wohnung (Rue de Sèvres) abgehalten wurden"; Zayed, *Huysmans*, 424–465 (with some ambiguity). From the nonacademic literature, copious references could be given;

see, for instance, Bricaud, *J.K. Huysmans et le satanisme*, 7; Bricaud, *Huysmans, Occultiste et Magicien*, 20 ("Husymans avait bien assisté à une des messes noires"), who is followed by Boutet, *Tableau de l'au-delà*, 173; Buet, *Grands Hommes en Robe de Chambre*, 233 ("bonnes sources"); Koomen, *Het ijzige zaad van de duivel*, 136; Wenisch, *Satanismus*, 23; Rhodes, *The Satanic Mass*, 167: "Despite his [Huysmans's] unwillingness or inability to produce documentary and direct evidence, it is difficult to doubt the essential truth of his reports even presented as they are in the guise of fiction."

Contra: Dufay, "L'Abbé Boullan et le 'Chanoine Docre,'" 524; Medway, *Lure of the Sinister*, 88–89 (yet without giving any real argumentation); Schmidt, *Satanismus*, 108–109: "Huysmans beschreibt … verschiedene Typen des Satanismus, die in die Realität so sicher nie existiert haben … ein immer wieder behauptete Augenzeugenschaft Huysmans bei einer solchen schwarzen Messe konnte indes nie nachgewiesen werden."

148. Frick, *Die Satanisten*, 2:194–195, citing the not-always-very-reliable Bricaud as his source.

149. Frédéric Lefèvre, "Une heure avec M. Léon Hennique de l'Académie Goncourt," *Les Nouvelles Littéraires, artistiques et scientifiques* 9 (10 May 1930) 395:1–2, here 2.

150. Mugnier is quoted in Paul-Antoine-Honoré Rolland, *Étude psychopathologique sur le Mysticisme de J.-K. Huysmans* (Nice: Imprimerie de l'Éclaireur du Nice, 1930), 10. Mœller, "Joris-Karl Huysmans d'après sa correspondence," 443–444, drew the same conclusions. We may also quote, for curiosity's sake, the testimony of Léon Bloy (1846–1917), Huysmans's former literary brother in arms, who claimed in an article published 1 June 1891 in *La Plume* that Huysmans owed "three quarters of his book" to him. He returned to the subject in an article entitled "L'Expiation de Jocrisse," published 24 January 1893 in *Gil Blas*; reprints in Léon Bloy, *Sur Huysmans* (Bruxelles: Éditions Complexe, 1986), 131, 144 (see also Richard Griffiths, *The Reactionary Revolution: The Catholic Revival in French Literature 1870–1914* [London: Constable, 1966], 140–143). Bloy's allegations inspired a French historian of literature to claim that Bloy was in reality a Luciferian; cf. Raymond Barbeau, *Un prophète luciférien: Léon Bloy* (Aubier: Éditions Montaigne, 1957). Although this book (to put it bluntly) seems to be that of a raving fanatic and was justly ignored by more serious Bloy critics, the citations Barbeau gives from Bloy's writings do suggest some influence of Romantic Satanism and deserve further study.

151. Huysmans, *À Rebours*, 114, refers to Baudelaire's "Litanies de Satan."

152. Huysmans to Prins, 22 November 1889: "J'ai acheté le Michelet—Au fond, ça a perd à être relu" (Huysmans, *Lettres inédites à Arij Prins*, 177). Another probable literary influence may have been Catulle Mendès's 1890 novel *Méphistophéla*, which is extensively discussed in Faxneld, *Satanic Feminism*, 455–473.

153. Garçon, "La société infernale d'Agen," 271. "Le Bibliophile Jacob" was the pseudonym of the French librarian Paul Lacroix; his *Curiosités des sciences occultes* was published in 1885 by Garnier fréres in Paris.

154. Gourmont, "Souvenirs sur Huysmans," 15–16.

155. Boullan to Huysmans, 18 February 1890, BnF, Mss. Occ. N.a. fr. 16596, f. 61–62 = Fonds Lambert 76, f. 53.

156. The bulk of the letters and "documents" that Boullan sent to Huysmans for the documentation of his novel are kept in the BnF, Mss. Occ. N.a. fr. 16596; they derive from the estate of Jules Bois, to whom Huysmans had transmitted them as documentation for his publication on Satanism (see further on for more information on this). Pierre Lambert, at some

date, had them photographed (BnF, Fonds Lambert, 97), and afterward copied them in his own hand (BnF, Fonds Lambert, 76). Whenever I have been able to retrace them, I give references to all three document collections. As already noted earlier, many more letters from Boullan must still remain in the Vatican Library; a few other autographs can be found in the collection Lambert (Fonds Lambert, 30/5). The Fonds Lambert also contains some accounts by Vintras of his visions deriving from the entourage of Boullan and copied by hand by one of his followers, Pascal Misme (BnF, Fonds Lambert, 123–126).

157. Document from Boullan to Huysmans entitled "Les Ré-Théurgistes Optimates," BnF, Mss. Occ. N.a. fr. 16596, f. 64 = BnF, Fonds Lambert 76, f. 49.

158. Eugène Vintras, "Récit des Nuits de saint Joseph, 1855," BnF, Fonds Lambert, 123, 139–176, there 140: "La France, L'Italie, L'Allemagne, la Turquie, l'Autriche et la Russie ont des ramifications qui se relient à un grand centre établi dans le cœur de l'Amérique."

159. Vintras, "Récit des Nuits de saint Joseph, 1855," 140–141.

160. This etymology was already suggested by Legge, "Devil-Worship and Freemasonry," 472n. Vintras, "Récit des Nuits de saint Joseph, 1855," 172 and 174 speaks simply of a "société des Théurgistes Optimates," but on p. 141, Vintras already used the phrase "Rétheurgie absolue" (as well as "nouveau Magisme évocateur").

161. Boullan to Huysmans, 16 July 1890, BnF, Mss. Occ. N.a. fr. 16596, ff. 97–98 = BnF, Fonds Lambert, 76, ff. 129–137; ibid., 23 July 1890, BnF, Mss. Occ. N.a. fr. 16596, ff. 100–102 = BnF, Fonds Lambert 97, ff. 60–65 = BnF, Fonds Lambert, 76, ff. 153–161.

162. Compare Vintras's account of a Black Mass dated 4 February 1842 (BnF, Fonds Lambert, 125, ff. 68–71), with Boullan's rendering in a letter to Huysmans from 15 February 1890 (BnF, Mss. Occ. N.a. fr. 16596, f. 63 = BnF, Fonds Lambert, 76, f. 55).

163. Boullan, "Documents sur la Messe Noire, de nos jours," BnF, Mss. Occ. N.a. fr. 16596, ff. 119–120 = BnF, Fonds Lambert, 76, ff. 219–223.

164. Boullan to Huysmans, 18 July 1890, BnF, Mss. Occ. N.a. fr. 16596, ff. 92–95 = BnF, Fonds Lambert, 97, ff. 51–52 = BnF, Fonds Lambert, 76, ff. 139–141.

165. Some examples: remarks about the importance of the involvement of a consecrated priest in Satanic magic, and the corresponding weakness in power of the (unconsecrated) Rosicrucians—Boullan to Huysmans, 20 February 1890, BnF, Mss. Occ. N.a. fr. 16596, f. 66 = BnF, Fonds Lambert, 76, ff. 59–61; about the involvement of certain members of the Parisian clergy in Satanism—Boullan to Huysmans, 12 July 1890 (with documents on the "question délicate"), BnF, Mss. Occ. N.a. fr. 16596, ff. 90–91 = BnF Fonds Lambert, 76, ff. 123–127; about Boullan's eviction from the Roman Catholic Church—Boullan to Huysmans, 10 July 1890, BnF, Mss. Occ. N.a. fr. 16596, ff. 85–86 = BnF, Fonds Lambert, 76, ff. 109–117; as well as some minor elements, as, for instance, the references to the "protective" chapel of Notre Dame de l'Épine—Boullan to Huysmans, 5–6 August 1890, BnF, Mss. Occ. N.a. fr. 16596, ff. 116–117—and the story about the bewitched statues given to a church by a rural nobleman—Boullan to Huysmans, BnF, Mss. Occ. N.a. fr. 16596, f. 89 = BnF, Fonds Lambert, 76, ff. 123–127.

166. Cf. Boullan, "Un coup d'œil sur une étude importante de la science sacrée" (magic attacks) and "Des crimes qui mettent en péril la société et du remède divine à y apporter," *Annales de la Sainteté* (April 1875) 64:307–311 (host thefts). Boullan referred to these articles in "Documents sur la Messe Noire, de nos jours" (BnF, Mss. Occ. N.a. fr. 16596, ff. 119–120 = BnF, Fonds Lambert, 76, ff. 219–223). A manuscript note from the Collection Lambert, probably

composed by Remy de Gourmont for Huysmans, also makes reference to the *Annales de la Sainteté* (BnF, Fonds Lambert, 30/5).

167. Letter by Boullan to Huysmans, 18 February 1890, BnF, Fonds Lambert, 76, f. 57: "ce qu'est de nos jours la Messe du Sabbat."

168. M. J. C. Thorey, *Rapports merveilleux de Mme Cantianille B . . . avec le monde surnaturel,* 2 vols. (Paris: Louis Hervé, 1866), 40n.

169. Thorey, *Rapports merveilleux de Mme Cantianille B,* 43.

170. Thorey, *Rapports merveilleux de Mme Cantianille B,* 37–39.

171. Thorey, *Rapports merveilleux de Mme Cantianille B,* 139–161.

172. Thorey, *Rapports merveilleux de Mme Cantianille B,* 42: "Quelques-uns avaient poussé l'impiété jusqu'à se tatouer, sous les pieds, l'image de la croix afin de marcher dessus constamment."

173. Amazingly, Introvigne considers *Cantianille B.* as part of a "série d'indices convergents sur l'activité, en France particulièrement, de vrais satanistes"; the veracity of Vintras's visions, he acknowledges, is more difficult to judge; "Mais ils fournissent suffisamment de détails pour être jugés souvent fiables." Introvigne, *Enquête sur le satanisme,* 141–142, 105.

174. Thomas, "Un aventurier de la mystique," 143–145.

175. Letter by Boullan to Huysmans, 10 July 1890, BnF, Mss. Occ. N.a. fr. 16596, ff. 85–86 = BnF, Fonds Lambert, ff. 109–117; ibid., (around) 30 July 1890, BnF, Mss. Occ. N.a. fr. 16596, ff. 111–114 = BnF, Fonds Lambert, 6, ff. 193–207.

176. Huysmans, *Lettres inédites à Arij Prins,* 192; see also Huysmans's letters to Jules Destrée from May–June 1890 and September 1890—Huysmans, *Lettres inédites à Jules Destrée,* 163, 166–167.

177. Bossier, *Un personnage de roman,* 48; Jean Vinchon, "Guillaume Apollinaire et Berthe Courrière, inspiratrice de 'Là-Bas,' " *Les Cahiers de la Tour Saint-Jacques* 8 (1963): 162–165. By contrast, Introvigne, *Enquête sur le satanisme,* 138, maintains that "le chanoine belge a laissé derrière lui toute une série d'indices plutôt sulfureux, qu'il paraît impossible de croire inventés par l'imagination de Berthe Courrière." I think Introvigne underestimates the human imagination here, and it is not clear to me which facts provided the "series of indications" mentioned by him, or it must be the possibility that Van Haecke did dine a few times with "Catholic Magus" Péladan.

178. Thus Baldick, *Life of J.-K. Huysmans,* 153, who refers to the suspect reaction of the Belgian Church, and the Belgian judge Paul Wouters in Bossier, *Geschiedenis van een romanfiguur* (1965), 152, who invokes Huysmans's Catholicity. See also the curious statements in Massignon, "Huysmans devant la 'confession' de Boullan." As "Van Harche," the Belgian chaplain even made it to the pages of volume 4 of the *Bilderlexikon der Erotik:* see *Ergänzungsband zum Bilder-Lexikon: Kulturgeschichte—Literatur und Kunst—Sexualwissenschaft* (Wien: Verlag für Kulturforschung, 1931), 270–271. (I owe this reference to Bossier, *Un personnage de roman,* 19–20.)

179. Bossier, *Un personnage de roman,* 73–74.

180. In this strange little work, a fierce "Sathan" marries "Psyché," who makes him understand that love is the most powerful force in the world. In a subsequent monologue, Satan presents himself as "the Jesus of another age," "more of a redemptor than the other." The "ineffable voice" of the deity then announces that he opens his heart to Satan and blesses the couple with

the words "Be united in your strivings for the beyond." See Bois, Jules, *Les noces de Sathan* (Paris: Albert Savine, 1890), 12, 14.

181. For Michelet, see Bois, *Le Satanisme et la Magie*, 36, 153–179; Bois criticized Michelet while continuing to use him in *Monde Invisible*, 200–201, 206. A proper scholarly biography of Jules Bois is still lacking, but a good introduction can be found in Dominique Dubois, *Jules Bois (1868–1943): Le reporter de l'occultisme, le poète et le féministe de la belle époque* (s.l.: Arqa, 2006). Pages 53 and 69–71 of this book tell about Bois's ventures in occultism; pages 175–186 are devoted to his feminism. Like Huysmans, Bois would convert to Roman Catholicism at a later date and move increasingly toward a position of Franco-Catholic nationalism. In 1916, he was sent to America, officially by his newspaper, but in reality probably by his friend, the French Minister Poincaré; he would remain in the United States for the rest of his life (cf. Dubois, *Jules Bois*, 26, 204, 252).

182. Introvigne devotes a section to Bois under the title "Jules Bois enquête," in *Enquête sur le satanisme*, 116–126. The Italian expert on fringe esotericism also refers to documents that Huysmans would be able to dispose of in his capacity as civil servant in the French Ministry of the Interior (cf. pp. 133–134). There is no indication at all, however, that Huysmans could have found anything on Satanist organizations in the ministerial archives; only one minor story in *Là-Bas* has been conclusively proven to be based on police reports consulted by him.

183. Bois, *Le Satanisme et la Magie*, 197n: "À lui [Huysmans] d'ailleurs je dois la documentation de l'office ténébreux et de l'office qui le combat, sans compter son exemple qui guida mon style." Bois accompanied Huysmans to the Boullanist Carmel at least once and also corresponded directly with Boullan, who urged him to write a novel on the position of women under the Reign of the Paraclet (letters by Boullan to Bois, 3 July 1892 and 6 September 1892, BnF, Mss. Occ. N.a. fr. 16596, ff. 10–12 and 30). Bois would indeed publish a book on the "female question" in 1896, under the title *L'Eve Nouvelle*; the possible influence of Boullan on this work remains to be investigated.

184. As noted before, many letters from Boullan to Huysmans ended up in the estate of Bois. The scene with Amun-Ra (Bois, *Le Satanisme et la Magie*, 201–206) was derived by Bois from one of them, a document entitled "Example du Succubat, et de la Messe pour Satan" sent by Boullan to Huysmans around 25 February 1890, BnF, Mss. Occ. N.a. fr. 16596, ff. 67–69 = BnF, Fonds Lambert, 76, ff. 63–67. I have not encountered the Vintrasian original for this story in the Collection Lambert. Another description of a Black Mass in Bois (*Le Satanisme et la Magie*, 199–201) originates with a letter from Boullan to Huysmans sent around 18 February 1890, BnF, Fonds Lambert, 76, f. 55, which in turn was copied by Boullan from a vision noted down by Vintras on 4 February 1842, "Visions de Vintras. 1851–1865," BnF, Fonds Lambert, 125, pp. 68–71. *Là-Bas* is quoted on pp. 281–286 of *Le Satanisme et la Magie*.

185. Huysmans did explicitly compare his novel with his earlier naturalist work in this way in a letter to an unidentified correspondent cited in Jouvin, "Les Lettres de J.-K. Huysmans," 290; "car *Là-Bas* est naturaliste, en effet, si par ce mot vous entendez seulement la véracité du document, la réalité des personnages."

186. Huysmans, *Là-Bas*, 32–33.

187. Guaita, *Serpent de la Genèse*, 1:520.

188. This applies to many elements of their—and Huysmans's—description of Satanism, also to some that appear eminently factual on the face of it. The allegation, for instance, that women

attended Mass to obtain hosts that could be given or sold to Satanists reflects rumors we encountered with the medieval "Luciferians" and that also formed a staple of the late medieval myth of Jewish host desecration (for examples of the latter, see Rubin, *Gentile Tales*, 73–77, 143, fig. 16a, fig. 22).

189. In a "Rapport apolostique sur Rome," dated 1 September 1864, Vintras recounts a conversation he had with "Sathan," in which the latter interestingly enough declares that he now no longer uses war, pests, and catastrophe as his arms, but instead scientific and technical progress. See "Visions de Vintras, 1848–1864," BnF, Fonds Lambert, 126/6, pp. 44–45.

190. Letter Boullan to Huysmans, 27 Feb. 1890, BnF, Mss. Occ. N.a. fr. 16596, ff. 70–71 = BnF, Fonds Lambert, 76, ff. 69–73: "Pie IX et Léon XIII ont été esclaves, et ils ne peuvent briser la chaine." Compare letter from 23 July 1890, BnF, Mss. Occ. N.a. fr. 16596, ff. 100–102 = BnF, Fonds Lambert, 97, f. 64 = BnF, Fonds Lambert, 76, f. 159.

191. Cf. Huysmans's preface to Bois, *Le Satanisme et la Magie*, vii.

192. This hypothesis was also forwarded by Remy de Gourmont, who claimed that "Huysmans, pendant qu'il écrivait *Là-Bas*, n'avait pas été sans faire quelques tentatives pour l'incliner au satanisme." Gourmont, "Souvenirs sur Huysmans," 15.

193. Legge, "Devil-Worship and Freemasonry," 469.

194. See Jean F. Desjardins, "Huysmans fut-il anarchiste? À propos des collaborations retrouvées," *Bulletin de la Société J.-K Huysmans* 37 (1959) 36:366–374.

195. Jouvin, "Les Lettres de J.-K. Huysmans," 292.

196. In a letter to Vanden Bosch, Huysmans declared that it had been through "the vision of the supernatural of evil that I have begun to have a perception of the supernatural of good"; Firmin vanden Bosch, *Impressions de littérature contemporaine* (Bruxelles: Vromant, 1905), 16.

197. Cholvy, *La religion en France*, 72–77.

198. Huysmans, *Là-Bas* (Plon, s.a.), 85. For the emergence of Roman Catholicism as a countercultural identity in the fin de siècle, and Huysmans's role in this, see Ewoud Matthijs Kieft, *Tot oorlog bekeerd: Religieuze Radicalisering in West-Europa 1870–1914* (Groningen, unpublished dissertation, 2011).

199. Baudelaire, *Journaux intimes*, 9 (Fusées, II).

200. See Boullan's letter from 16 July 1890 to Huysmans, BnF, Mss. Occ. N.a. fr. 16596, ff. 97–98 = BnF, Fonds Lambert, 76, ff. 129–137.

201. With his letter of 18 July 1890, for instance, Boullan wrote explicitly in the margin that Satan appeared visibly at the Black Mass; BnF, Mss. Occ. N.a. fr. 16596, ff. 92–95 = BnF, Fonds Lambert, 97, ff. 51–52 = BnF, Fonds Lambert, 76, ff. 139–141. He repeated this explicit assurance in his letter from 23 July 1890 (ibid., ff. 100–102/ff. 60–65/ ff. 153–161). In this, he was in accord with Vintras, who had described Satan appearing as a goat during a Black Mass (BnF, Fonds Lambert, 125, pp. 68–71, recuperated in a letter by Boullan to Huysmans d.d. 18 February 1890, BnF, Fonds Lambert, 76, f. 55).

202. Boullan, "Document sur la Messe Noire, de nos Jours," f. 119. Boullan continued on the verso of the page: "Alors Satan, ou ses Princes, qui sont là visible, répandent cette odeur du sabbat, qui excite le passion jusqu'à la fureur."

203. Cf. Ellis Hanson, *Decadence and Catholicism* (Cambridge, MA: Harvard University Press, 1997), 23; Praz, *Romantic Agony*, 187–286.

204. J. K. Huysmans, "L'ouverture de Tannhæuser"; this review was included in the second edition of his *Croquis parisiens*, published in 1886. See Joris-Karl Huysmans, *Croquis parisiens*

(Paris: Éditions Slatkine, 1996), 186–191, and especially 188–189. Incidentally, Huysmans had been preceded in his admiration for Wagner by Baudelaire, who had published a pamphlet defending the composer in 1861; see "Richard Wagner et *Tannhäuser* à Paris," in Baudelaire, *Curiosités esthétiques*, 689–728.

205. Huysmans, *Là-Bas*, 63.

206. This is exemplified in the attitude to women that Huysmans's works from this period express. In his article about Rops and erotic art, he had already declared that "la femme acquiert, elle aussi, son Dieu, un Satan" (*Certains*, 106). In a letter to Prins from 25 April 1891, he called woman "le plus puissant outil de douleurs qui nous sont donné" (*Lettres inédites à Arij Prins*, 255), a description he found apt enough to repeat in *En Route*, 80.

207. J.-K. Huysmans, *En Route* (Paris: Plon, 1955), 236: "Il raconta, en balbutiant, qu'il avait assisté, par curiosité, à une messe noire et qu'après, sans le vouloir, il avait souillé une hostie que cette femme, saturée de satanisme, cachait en elle." Frick, *Die Satanisten*, 2:213, made the remark about the motel room scene: "Jeder Pornoschriftsteller von heute würde diese 'Soft-Liebesszene' besser zu Papier brengen."

208. Huysmans, *Là-Bas*, 78. Johann Joseph (von) Görres (1776–1848) was a German Roman Catholic author who had devoted many pages of volumes three and four of his extensive work *Die Christliche Mystik* (1842) to "dämonischen Mystik."

209. Hanson, *Decadence and Catholicism*, 147.

210. Huysmans, *Là-Bas* (Plon, s.a.), 382: "Elle le saisit et elle lui révéla des mœurs de captif, des turpitudes dont il ne la soupçonnait même pas; elle les pimenta de furies de ghoule." Brendan King's translation of "mœurs de captif" with "slavish habits" seems quaintly inappropriate to me, especially given the context.

Although it would technically be something of a challenge to insert a host this way, I suspect, the sexual practice suggested here was certainly not far from Huysmans's bed. His letters to Prins dwell extensively on the pleasures of anilingus and his quest among the prostitutes of Paris for a "lilac and rose little hole" suitable for this pastime (Huysmans, *Lettres inédites à Arij Prins*, 93, 140, 141, 149, 203–204, 231). His biographer Baldick thinks it probable that Huysmans had had homosexual experiences as well (Baldick, *Life of J.-K. Huysmans*, 82). During the preparation of *Là-Bas*, Huysmans explored the underground subculture of Paris homosexuals, and while he does not seem to have found personal gratification there, he used elements of his explorations for the construction of Satanism in *Là-Bas* (cf. Huysmans, *Lettres inédites à Arij Prins*, 180, 184). On Huysmans and "sodomy," see Hanson, *Decadence and Catholicism*, 138–152.

211. Baldick, *Life of J.-K. Huysmans*, 166.

212. Huysmans to Prins, 23 May 1891 and [24 January] 1892; Huysmans, *Lettres inédites à Arij Prins*, 222, 235. For many years to come, Huysmans would continue to receive letters from occultists consulting him as an expert: the Lambert Collection of the BnF, for instance, contains such letters from the Dutch editor A. J. Riko (letter of 11 October 1895, BnF, Fonds Lambert, 31/44) and Fabre des Essarts (letter of 7 February 1902, ibid., 31/2).

213. Legge, "Devil-Worship and Freemasonry," 470; Buet, *Grands Hommes en Robe de Chambre*, 234.

214. Among the many writers inspired by *Là-Bas*, we may mention the Dutch author Frits Lapidoth, whose *Goëtia* appeared with S. C. van Doesburg in Leiden in 1893 (2 vols.) and in a German translation as *Goëtia: Die Priesterin der schwarzen Kunst* (Dresden: Heinrich

Minden, s.a. [1897]). It sought to combine some measure of Left-wing sympathy for Satan ("the Prince . . . not of Darkness, but of Individual Liberty," 1:42) with the Decadentism and sordid eroticism of Huysmans's works. Some laconic information about this book can be found in Jacqueline Bel, "Satan in Holland: Over *Goëtia*, de salon-sataniste van Frits Lapidoth," in *Teruggedaan: Eenenvijftig bijdragen voor Harry G.M. Prick ter gelegenheid van zijn afscheid als conservator van het Nederlands Letterkundig Museum en Documentatiecentrum*, ed. Th. A. P. Bijvoet, S. A. J. van Faassen, and Anton Korteweg ('s-Gravenhage: Nederlands Letterkundig Museum and Documentatiecentrum, 1988), 27–35. More prominent examples will follow in the next chapters; in addition, a long list of authors basing themselves on Huysmans can be found in Thiele, *Satanismus als Zeitkritik bei Joris-Karl Huysmans*, 103n.

215. Arthur Edward Waite, *Devil-Worship in France, or the Question of Lucifer: A Record of Things Seen and Heard in the Secret Societies according to the Evidence of Initiates* (London: George Redway, 1896), 11–12. On Waite, see the entry by Robert A. Gilbert in the *Dictionary of Gnosis and Western Esotericism*, 2:1164–1165.

216. Papus, "La-Bas. Par J.-K. Huysmans," *L'Initation: Revue philosophique indépendante des Hautes Études* 11 (May 1891): 97–114, here esp. 106–107, 109, and 112. Papus repeated these allegations in *Peut-on Envoûter? Étude historique et critique sur les plus récents travaux concernant l'envoûtement* (Paris: Chamuel, 1893), 18; on p. ii of this book, he also reproduced a "bewitchment pact from the 19th century" under the heading "Reproduction photographique d'un document arraché à un sorcier contemporain, l'ex-abbé Boullan." The (rather unclear) photograph seems to show some kind of esoteric diagram, however, rather than a demonic pact.

217. Péladan, *Comment on devient Mage*, 226–227; Péladan, *"Pereat!" (La décadence latine: Éthopée XV)* (1902; repr., Genève: Editions Slatkine, 1979), 229–236.

218. Guaita, *Serpent de la Genèse*, 1:440–416: quote from 1:516 and references to black magic on 1:497n and 1:498. On page 1:491, Guaita revealed some disgraceful details that had been confided by "Madame T." (in which we may easily recognize Julie Thibault) concerning her sexual contacts with subhuman spiritual entities—resulting in a lifelike pregnancy that ended in an enormous outburst of flatulence.

219. This hypothesis has been particularly defended by Joanny Bricaud; see Bricaud, *J.K. Huysmans et le satanisme*, 76; Bricaud, *Huysmans, Occultiste et Magicien*, 21; Joanny Bricaud, *L'abbé Boullan (Docteur Johannès de Là-Bas): Sa vie, sa doctrine et ses pratiques magiques* (Paris: Chacornac Frères, 1927), 90. His conclusion was adopted by Bossier, *Un personnage de roman*, 98–99; Ach, *Joris-Karl Huysmans und die okkulte Dekadenz*, 136 ("ein praktizierende Anhänger diabolischen Riten"); Introvigne (with more reservations), *Enquête sur le satanisme*, 116. Much later, Huysmans also would (once again) class Boullan and his group as "satanist" (cf. Baldick, *Life of J.-K. Huysmans*, 190)—but then again, Huysmans was not exactly sparing with this epithet.

220. For example Ach, *Joris-Karl Huysmans und die okkulte Dekadenz*, 137: "Bei einer Schwarzen Messe am 8. dezember 1860 habe Boullan auf dem Altar ein Kind geopfert, welche ihm Adèle Chevalier im Moment der Konsekration geboren habe."

221. Guaita, *Serpent de la Genèse*, 1:520n.

222. Frick, *Die Satanisten*, 2:194; Baldick, *Life of J.-K. Huysmans*, 170–171; Belval, *Des ténèbres à la lumière*, 90.

223. Huret, *Enquête sur l'évolution littéraire*, 165–166. Huysmans sent a letter of rectification with regard to the interview, but only to correct Huret's misquoted description of the compilation of the exorcist mixture: Huysmans to Huret, 6 April 1891; ibid., 353.

224. Boullan to Huysmans, 14 June 1891, BnF, Fonds Lambert, 30/5 (4); quoted in Pierre Lambert, "Une lettre de J.A. Boullan à Huysmans," *Bulletin de la Société J.-K Huysmans* 25 (1952) 24:203–207.

225. Fresnois, *Une étape de la conversion de Huysmans*, 21–22, 27–28. The extraordinary occurrences are described in Baldick, *Life of J.-K. Huysmans*, 170–171, 190, and in an interview with Jules Bois, "L'envoûtement et la mort du docteur Boullan," *Gil Blas* (9 Jan. 1893) 4801:2; Huysmans here complained about "coups de poing fluidiques": "mon chat lui-même en est tourmentée." Compare *Gil Blas* (11 Jan. 1893) 4803:2.

226. Péladan, *Comment on devient Mage*, 229.

227. Letter from Boullan to Huysmans, 3 March 1891: Belval, *Des ténèbres à la lumière*, 111; cf. also the letter of Boullan to Huysmans from 27 August 1892; BnF, fonds Lambert, 30/5 (9), f. 2. Huysmans wrote about his desire to whiten his soul to Jean Lorrain in a letter dated approximately 15 April 1891 (Jouvin, "Les Lettres de J.-K. Huysmans," 292); he expressed similar sentiments when he sought contact with the Reverend Mugnier. A letter to Berthe de Courrière recounts a vision of the Holy Virgin he had in a brothel, according to André du Fresnois "under an appearance and in postures that the imagination of an honest man would hardly be able to conceive" (Fresnois, *Une étape de la conversion de Huysmans*, 56–57).

228. Letters from 7 May 1891 and 28 April 1891, quoted in Thomas, "Un aventurier de la mystique," 156, 160; see also 153.

229. Baldick, *Life of J.-K. Huysmans*, 277, who translates the original French "diabolisme" with "devilry"; see Lambert, "Un culte hérétique à Paris," 200. Julie returned to her native village and would be remembered for many years after her death as a woman of great saintliness by the villagers and the local priest, even though she never relinquished her Vintrasian/Boullanist beliefs. The delightful story is recounted in Lambert, "Un culte hérétique à Paris."

230. Baldick, *Life of J.-K. Huysmans*, 208–209; the telegram from Pascal Misme to Huysmans announcing Boullan's death is kept in BnF, Fonds Lambert, 30/5 (21).

231. Letter from Huysmans to Julie Thibault, 4 January 1893, BnF, Fonds Lambert, 21/50; English translation from Baldick, *Life of J.-K. Huysmans*, 208–209.

232. Dufay, "L'Abbé Boullan et le 'Chanoine Docre,'" 520.

233. Bois in *Gil Blas* (9 January 1893), 2; translation quoted from Baldick, *Life of J.-K. Huysmans*, 209. Jules Bois talks about his spontaneous zeal in *Le monde invisible*, 229.

234. Jules Bois, "L'envoûtement et la mort du docteur Boullan," *Gil Blas* (11 Jan. 1893) 4803:2 and (13 Jan. 1893) 4805:2; English translation from Baldick, *Life of J.-K. Huysmans*, 209.

235. McIntosh, *Éliphas Lévi*, 171–176.

236. Papus, *Peut-on Envoûter*.

237. Article quoted in a compte-rendu entitled "L'envoûtement," *L'Initation. Revue philosophique indépendante des Hautes Études* 6 (XVIII, March 1893) 6:182–188, here 182–183.

238. Papus, *Peut-on Envoûter*, 17; Wirth, *Stanislas de Guaita*, 139: "Il ne nous était jamais venu à l'idée d'opérer magiquement, ce qui eût contraire à tous nos principes. La punition prévue était la publication des ignominies du Carmel, afin d'éclairer les victimes du pontife halluciné."

239. See in particular *Serpent de la Genèse*, 1:490, 1:520n.

240. Beaufils, *Joséphin Péladan*, 129.

241. Beaufils, *Joséphin Péladan*, 115, 215.

242. Bricaud, *Huysmans, Occultiste et Magicien*, 33(n), citing convincing supportive evidence.

243. Wirth, *Stanislas de Guaita*, 145.

244. Encausse, *Sciences occultes*, 114n, quoting an interview by Gaston Méry with Guaita in *Écho du Merveilleux*, 1 January 1898; also, idem. Dubus, *Gil Blas* (10 Jan. 1893) 4802:1.

245. Frick, *Die Satanisten*, 3:222, quoting Bricaud. In *Huysmans, Occultiste et Magicien*, 33, Bricaud mentions that other people proposed yet another explanation for Guaita's death: the magician had succumbed to the "choc en retour" brought about by his operations against Boullan.

246. Thus Victor-Émile Michelet, *Les compagnons de la hiérophanie: Souvenirs du mouvements hermétiste à la fin du XIXIe siècle* (Paris: Borbon-Aîné, s.a. [1938]), 20. Guaita himself had uttered similar fears in his letters to Péladan when he started to work on *Serpent de la Genèse*. In an undated letter to the Sâr, he wrote, "NOTE QUE JE POURRAIS DÉVOILER LES DERNIERS ARCANES SUR TOUS LES SUJETS QUI Y SONT ÉNONCÉS! Ah! Que Dieu m'en donne la force! . . . Je t'en supplie, Mérodack, prie pour moi. Je commence une *redoutable* gestation. Irai-je à terme?," finishing his epistle with the request: "*Brûle cette épitre*; si jamais on la trouvait, on me croirait atteint de la folie des grandeurs.—Mais Dieu m'est témoin que je dis vrai, et cela me suffit." Cf. Guaita, *Lettres inédites au Sâr Joséphin Péladan*, 134–135. Guaita would in fact never finish the third part of his *Serpent de la Genèse*, which was to be called "Le Problème du Mal." The sketches that remain (recorded in Wirth, *Stanislas de Guaita*, 173–186) suggest he envisioned an ultimate reconciliation between the deity and the demon. "La Rédemption aboutit à la Réintégration, qui est le Paradis. . . . Satan-Panthée s'évanouit en Dieu." (ibid., 178, 186).

247. Michelet, *Compagnons de la hiérophanie*, 26. Michelet (not the historian, but a fellow Rosicrucian) was initially one of Guaita's seconds, along with Maurice Barrès, who was an old study friend of the marquis. Guaita's letter of challenge to Huysmans, dated 13 January 1893, can be found in BnF, Fonds Lambert, 30/5 (19/1).

248. Quote from Bois, *Monde invisible*, 130; on Péladan's scruples against dueling, see Beaufils, *Joséphin Péladan*, 203; the remark about his invulnerability was made with regard to another personal enemy in an interview entitled "Chez le Sar," *Le Jour* (28 April 1891). Péladan here also declared that he could not spill blood as a Catholic.

249. Michelet, *Compagnons de la hiérophanie*, 27–28. See also Baldick, *Life of J.-K. Huysmans*, 210.

250. Article in *Événement*, quoted in "L'envoûtement," *Initation* 18 (March 1893) 6:186.

251. These and subsequent strange occurrences were recorded by Paul Foucher, one of Bois's seconds, in a short article he published 12 May 1894 in *SudOuest-Toulouse*. The complete text was reprinted in Bois, *Monde invisible*, 409–410; on pp. 27–30, the reader can find Bois's own account of the duels. See also Boutet, *Tableau de l'au-delà*, 199.

252. Protocol cited in "L'envoûtement," *Initation* 18 (March 1893) 6:186–187.

253. Michelet, *Compagnons de la hiérophanie*, 30.

254. Foucher in Bois, *Monde invisible*, 409–410.

255. Encausse, *Sciences occultes*, 9.

256. Frick, *Die Satanisten*, 2:225; Foucher in Bois, *Monde invisible*, 410: "Fort heureusement, et quoique les épées fussent magiques, elles ne firent que des blessures peu graves et qui sont depuis longtemps guéries."

CHAPTER 5: UNMASKING THE SYNAGOGUE OF SATAN

1. *Le Palladium régénéré et libre: Lien des groupes lucifériens indépendants* 1 (1 Pharmuthi 000895/21 March 1895) 1 (and subsequent issues), back-cover text. Introvigne, *Enquête sur le Satanisme*, 179, incorrectly gives 1894 as the year of issue of the first number.

2. Léo Taxil, *Les Frères Trois-Points*, 2 vols. (Paris: Letouzey and Ané, [1885]), 1:3–4.

3. Taxil, *Les Frères Trois-Points*, 2:236.

4. Taxil, *Les Frères Trois-Points*, 2:246.

5. Taxil, *Les Frères Trois-Points*, 2:251.

6. Taxil, *Les Frères Trois-Points*, 2:234.

7. Significantly, at about the same time, progressive Freemasons attempted to integrate women into the lodges. In 1882, the feminist Marie Deraismes was initiated in the French lodge "Les Libres-Penseurs." When she was ousted again under pressure from other French lodges, she established a schismatic lodge for women and men in 1893 named "Le Droit Humain." This lodge would be the origin of the (equally "irregular") Co-Freemasonry (cf. Introvigne, *Enquête sur le Satanisme*, 173). These have nothing to do with the lodges described by Taxil, as a simple look at the chronology makes clear. The same applies to the Dutch Orde van Weefsters ("Order of Weavers"), a women-only organization closely allied with Dutch Freemasonry; this was only founded in 1947. It must be noted, however, that a separate "Freemasonry for ladies" had existed in eighteenth-century France, which was sometimes designated with the term "Rites of Adoption"; the same term returns in *Les sœurs maçonnes*.

8. Léo Taxil, *Les sœurs maçonnes: La Franc-Maçonnerie des dames et ses mystères* (Paris: Letouzey & Ané, [1886]), 318.

9. Taxil, *Les sœurs maçonnes*, 340–349.

10. Léo Taxil, *Y a-t-il des Femmes dans la Franc-Maçonnerie?* (Paris: Delhomme and Briguet, s.a. [orig. 1891]), 209–210. Taxil here confuses the Kabbalistic Rosicrucian Order of Papus and Guaita, against which Huysmans leveled his accusation of Satanism and magical murder, with the "Knight Rose Croix," the title used to designate the eighteenth degree within Scottish Rite Freemasonry.

11. Taxil, *Y a-t-il des Femmes dans la Franc-Maçonnerie?*, 211.

12. Taxil, *Y a-t-il des Femmes dans la Franc-Maçonnerie?*, 209n.

13. Taxil, *Y a-t-il des Femmes dans la Franc-Maçonnerie?*, 235.

14. Taxil, *Y a-t-il des Femmes dans la Franc-Maçonnerie?*, 237.

15. Taxil, *Y a-t-il des Femmes dans la Franc-Maçonnerie?*, 248–267.

16. Adolphe Ricoux, *L'existence des loges de femmes affirmée par Mgr Fava, évêque de Grenoble, et par Léo Taxil: Recherches à ce sujet et réponse à M. Aug. Vacquerie, rédacteur du Rappel* (Paris: Téqui, 1891), 17.

17. Cf. Léon Meurin, *La Franc-Maçonnerie, Synagogue de Satan* (Paris: Victor Retaux and Fils, 1893).

18. Ricoux, *L'existence des loges de femmes affirmée*, 64–95.

19. Taxil, *Y a-t-il des Femmes dans la Franc-Maçonnerie?*, 208–209.

20. Ricoux, *L'existence des loges de femmes affirmée*, 90.

21. Docteur Bataille, *Le Diable au XIXᵉ siècle: La Franc-Maçonnerie luciférienne ou les mystères du spiritisme. Révélations complètes sur le Palladisme, la théurgie, la goétie et tout le satanisme moderne. Récits d'un témoin*, 2 vols. (Paris: Delhomme and Briguet, [1892–1893]), 1:20.

22. Bataille, *Le Diable au XIXᵉ siècle*, 1:170.

23. Bataille, *Le Diable au XIXᵉ siècle*, 2:889, 1:492; the Luciferian credo can be found at 1:126.

24. Bataille, *Le Diable au XIXᵉ siècle*, 1:772–726.

25. Bataille, *Le Diable au XIXᵉ siècle*, 1:779.

26. Bataille, *Le Diable au XIXᵉ siècle*, 1:379.

27. Bataille, *Le Diable au XIXe siècle*, 1:328; the term "Bible Satanique" is from *Le Diable au XIXe siècle* itself.

28. Bataille, *Le Diable au XIXe siècle*, 1:392.

29. Taxil, *Y a-t-il des Femmes dans la Franc-Maçonnerie?*, 393.

30. Bataille, *Le Diable au XIXe siècle*, 1:382, 1:386–391.

31. Bataille, *Le Diable au XIXe siècle*, 1:708–722.

32. Cf. A. C. de la Rive, *La Femme et l'Enfant dans franc-maçonnerie universelle* (Paris: Delhomme and Briguet, 1894), 637–648.

33. The "Protesting Vault" of Independent Luciferians against Lemmi's election and Diana Vaughan's letter of decommission can both be found, although in somewhat truncated English, in Domenico Margiotta, *Souvenirs d'un Trente-Troisième: Adriano Lemmi, chef suprême des Franc-Maçons* (Paris: Delhomme and Briguet, s.a.), 320–351 and 364–365.

34. Unfortunately, I was unable to track down this unique "Receuil des prières luciféri-ennes," which none of the world's major libraries seem to have preserved. Its publisher Alfred Pierret, however, later declared that a thousand exemplars had been printed (*Mémoires d'une ex-Palladiste Parfaite Initiée, Indépendante* [5 May 1897] 23:720—in another place, he suggests the number was two thousand; A. Pierret, "Chiffres des divers tirages effectués," *Mémoires d'une ex-Palladiste Parfaite Initiée, Indépendante* [10 June 1897] 24:745–747). The compendium of prayers is not to be confused with a later publication by Diana Vaughan, *La restauration du paganisme: Transition décrétée par le Sanctum Regnum pour préparer l'établissement du culte public de Lucifer. Les hymnes liturgiques de Pike. Rituel du néo-paganisme* (Paris: Librairie Antimaçonnique, [1896]), which gives the unexpurgated rituals by Pike and is listed separately by Pierret in his overview.

35. Margiotta, *Adriano Lemmi* (the impressive list of Masonic titles cited before is from the frontispiece of this work); Domenico Margiotta, *Le Palladisme: Culte de Satan-Lucifer dans les triangles maçonniques* (Grenoble: H. Falque, 1895).

36. Diana Vaughan, *Mémoires d'une ex-Palladiste Parfaite Initiée, Indépendante* (July 1895) 1:13.

37. Diana Vaughan [Jeanne-Marie-Raphaëlle], *La Neuvaine Eucharistique pour réparer* (Paris: Librairie Antimaçonnique, s.a. [1895]); Diana Vaughan [Jeanne-Marie-Raphaëlle], *Le 33e:. Crispi: Un Palladiste Homme d'état démasqué. Histoire documentée du héros depuis sa naissance jusqu'à sa deuxième mort (1819–1896)* (Paris: Librairie Antimaçonnique, [1896]). The "Hymne à Jeanne d'Arc (Contre la Franc-Maçonnerie)" was also published by the Librairie Antimaçonnique and could be purchased for three francs with piano accompaniment or for one franc in small format without accompaniment. Its text (with the stirring last sentences "Let us destroy the Temple of Satan/God wills it: no more Freemasons!") can be consulted in *Mémoires d'une ex-Palladiste Parfaite Initiée, Indépendante* (September 1895) 3:95–96.

38. Cf. *Mémoires d'une ex-Palladiste Parfaite Initiée, Indépendante* (5 May 1897) 23:717, where Vaughan cites from her diary and gives a complete account of her conversion.

39. A report by Lautier was published in the *Echo de Rome* of 1 January 1894 and reprinted in Bataille's *Revue mensuelle*; Pierre Lautier, "Une luciferienne," *Revue mensuelle religieuse, poli-tique, scientifique: Complément de la publication Le Diable au XIXe Siècle* 1 (January 1894) 1:4–6.

40. A gravure with Vaughan's portrait had already appeared in Bataille, *Le Diable au XIXe siècle*, 1:705. A somewhat different, more elegant photogravure was published in A. C. de la Rive,

La Femme et l'Enfant dans franc-maçonnerie universelle (Paris: Delhomme and Briguet, 1894), 705, after prepublication in the *Revue mensuelle religieuse, politique, scientifique* 1 (January 1894) 1:5. It was republished in *Mémoires d'une ex-Palladiste* (September 1895) 3:82–83. A completely different photograph apparently surfaced three decades later and was published in L. Fry, *Leo Taxil et La Franc-Maçonnerie: Lettres inédites publiés par les amis de Monseugneur Jouin* (Chaton: British-American-Press, 1934), facing 265; as its author, "L.B. Unterveger, Trento" is indicated.

41. See the short report in Union Antimaçonnique Universelle, *Actes du Ire Congrès antimaçonnique international, XXVI–XXX Septembre M DCCC XCVI, Trente*, 2 vols. (Tournai, France: Desclée, Lefebvre and Cie, 1897–1899), 2:94–95.

42. This meeting never took place, owing to circumstances about which the parties concerned gave differing accounts. Cf. *Diana Vaughan: Haar persoon, haar werk en haar aanstaande komst* (Leiden: J. W. van Leeuwen, 1897), 29–33, and the subsequent section of this chapter.

43. Cf. Hildebrand Gerber [= Hermann Gruber], *Betrug als Ende eines Betruges. Oder: Die Kundgebung Leo Taxil's vom 19. April 1897 under der Hereinfall, bezw. die Schwindeleien, deutscher "Kulturkämpfer" anläßlich derselben* (Berlin: Germania, 1897), 107–108.

44. Diana Vaughan, " Ma manifestation public," *Mémoires d'une ex-Palladiste* (31 March 1897) 21:670–671; and also Alfred Pierret, " Le conférence du 19 avril," *Mémoires d'une ex-Palladiste* (10 June 1897) 24:748–751, there 749–751.

45. Vaughan, "Ma manifestation public," 604. Léo Taxil would also appear at the first meeting in Paris, in order to elucidate his recent decision to abandon the anti-Masonic struggle after twelve years of continuous activity, due to the ever more vocally expressed doubts of his co-combatants regarding his personal integrity.

46. Taxil's speech was published in *Le Frondeur* of 25 April 1897; the complete text can be found in Eugen Weber, *Satan franc-maçon: La mystification de Léo Taxil* (Paris: Julliard, 1964), 155–183 (quote on p. 157).

47. Weber, *Satan franc-maçon*, 183.

48. Pierret, " Le conférence du 19 avril," *Mémoires d'une ex-Palladiste* (10 June 1897) 24:748.

49. Taxil has been a bit neglected by academic historiography, but the few modern historians who have written about him at some length generally agree on the basic facts regarding his life and Luciferian fabrications. Introvigne's chapter on Taxil in *Enquête sur le satanisme*, 143–208, is the best of his book and an excellent introduction to the subject and its current state of research. W. R. Jones, "Palladism and the Papacy: An Episode of French Anticlericalism in the Nineteenth Century," *Journal of Church and State* 12 (1970) 3:453–473, and David Allen Harvey, "Lucifer in the City of Light. The Palladium Hoax and 'Diabolical Causality" in Fin de siècle France," *Magic, Ritual, and Witchcraft* 1 (2006) 2:177–206, fail to add substantial new insights to the already extant literature in French. All three rely heavily on Eugen Weber's pioneering study *Satan franc-maçon*, which presents the historical facts and many contemporary documents. A few other articles in academic conference volumes deal with minor points of the story; references to these will be given in the appropriate notes. In addition, Fry, *Leo Taxil et La Franc-Maçonnerie*, provides important source material, although the conspirationalist views of its compiler should be treated with proper skepticism.

As a historical figure, Taxil, along with his creation Diana Vaughan, is still begging for a proper biography. A lot of questions surrounding the Palladism affair are still not satisfactorily answered, and a hoard of contemporary literature in virtually every Western language awaits the patient researcher. Due to time limitations, I only consulted the most important publications from this wealth of material. With regard to the basic historical facts, I have based my statements on Weber as well, unless otherwise noted; where I propose a reading that differs from that of the existing literature, this has been duly marked in the footnotes.

50. Léo Taxil, *À bas la calotte!* (Paris: Strauss, 1879), viii–x.

51. Weber, *Satan franc-maçon*, 193.

52. Weber, *Satan franc-maçon*, 157–159.

53. Introvigne, *Enquête sur le satanisme*, 169; Weber, *Satan franc-maçon*, 194.

54. Léo Taxil, *Pie IX devant l'histoire: Sa vie politique et pontificale, ses débauches, ses folies, ses crimes*, 3 vols. (Paris: Librairie Anti-Cléricale, [1883]), 1:214.

55. These titles can be found in the catalogue of the publishing house, consulted by me in Taxil, *Pie IX devant l'histoire*, 1:207–215. The French titles are *La Vie de Jésus, À bas la calotte!, Plus de Cafards!,* and *Les amours secrètes de Pie IX, par un ancien camérier du Pape* (Paris: Librairie anti-cléricale/Librairie populaire, [1881]). For more information on the activities of the "Bibliothèque anticléricale," cf. Weber, *Satan franc-maçon*, 195–198, and Introvigne, *Enquête sur le satanisme*, 170.

56. Taxil, *Pie IX devant l'histoire*, 1:214: "Ces enveloppes constituent la plus heureuse innovation que se puisse imaginer pour la propagande. Elles sont illustrés de dessins comiques anti-cléricaux par Pepin, ménageant la place pour le timbre-poste et l'adresse."

57. Taxil in Weber, *Satan franc-maçon*, 163.

58. Léo Taxil, *Confessions d'un ex-libre-penseur* (Paris: Letouzey & Ané, [1887]), 389.

59. Weber, *Satan franc-maçon*, 161.

60. Introvigne initially leaves the possibility open, quoting Paul Fesch (1858–1910), Catholic priest and friend of Taxil, but eventually also concludes that Taxil was never genuinely Catholic. *Enquête sur le satanisme*, 174, 206.

61. Weber, *Satan franc-maçon*, 196–198.

62. Taxil, *Confessions d'un ex-libre-penseur*, 400; Introvigne, *Enquête sur le satanisme*, 171, referring to *Figaro* 30 (2 August 1884) 215:1. "Il est permis de croire que l'exploration des œuvres ordurières que l'on décore du nom de productions anti-cléricales, n'est pas absolument ce que l'on peut appeler une bonne affaire," the newspaper noted. "Nous revelons, en effet, dans la liste des faillites du 30 juillet, cette mention: *Dame Jogand (Marie-Jeanne Besson), séparée de biens, libraire, rue des Écoles, 26 et 25*. . . . Mme Jogand, susnommée, est marié avec M. Léo Taxil, lequel a acquis une célébrité relative dans le monde des 'mangeurs de prêtres.'"

63. Weber, *Satan franc-maçon*, 207n; Introvigne, *Enquête sur le satanisme*, 176. In a letter to Father Gabriel de Bessonies from 24 April 1895, Taxil claimed to be in dire straits financially; he also claimed the chateau had been an inheritance, which he had recently been forced to sell for an inferior price—Fry, *Leo Taxil et La Franc-Maçonnerie*, 49–50.

64. Taxil in Weber, *Satan franc-maçon*, 156.

65. Taxil in Weber, *Satan franc-maçon*, 156.

66. Léo Taxil, *La République se démasque ou le vrai programme républicain exposé par les soixante-treize fédérations et groupes républicains radicaux-socialistes de Paris et expliqué avec toutes ses conséquences* (Paris: Letouzey et Ané, s.a.). I did not have a chance to consult this publication myself, but it is listed in the catalogue of the BnF, Paris, under notice number FRBNF34036105.

67. Taxil, cited in Weber, *Satan franc-maçon*, 167–168.

68. Weber agrees in *Satan franc-maçon*, 208.

69. Taxil, *Les Frères Trois-Points*, 1:39–41.

70. Introvigne, *Enquête sur le satanisme*, 171.

71. Taxil, *Confessions d'un ex-libre-penseur*, 217–218, 315–341.

72. Taxil, quoted in Weber, *Satan franc-maçon*, 165.

73. Léo Taxil and Tony Gall, *Les admirateurs de la lune à l'Orient de Marseille: Histoire Amusante d'une Loge de Francs-Maçons* (Paris: Agence Centrale des Bons Livres, s.a.). This novel was reissued several times during the period of Taxil's "Catholic" activity, and the copy I consulted in the BnF clearly dated from this time. It is unclear to me what its original year of publication was. Taxil's publications are mostly undated and were often frequently reprinted, with or without alterations. The rather buffoonish style and content of the book, however, and the total lack of the pious interspersions that characterize all of Taxil's "Catholic" works strongly suggest that it was not prepared for a specifically Catholic readership.

74. Taxil already started to publish lists of Masons in *La Petite Guerre* 1 (10 April 1887) 11, and subsequent issues. Similar lists mentioned by Michel Jarrige in other Catholic periodicals are all from later dates. Cf. Michel Jarrige, *L'église et les Francs-Maçons dans la tourmente: Croisade de la revue*, La Franc-Maçonnerie Démasquée (1894–1899) (Paris: Éditions Arguments, 1999), 191–194.

75. Cf. the sparse biographical data in Pierre Barrucand, "Quelques aspects de l'antimaçonnisme, le cas de Paul Rosen," *Politica Hermetica* 4 (1987): 91–108, which was also the source for Introvigne, *Enquête sur le satanisme*, 163–166.

76. Cf. Paul Rosen, *Satan et Cie. Association Universelle pour la destruction de l'ordre social: Révélations complètes et définitives de tous les secrets de la Franc-Maçonnerie* (Paris: Veuve H. Caterman, 1888), 317, where he calls Pike "Pope of Freemasonry" and attributes to one of his books "horrors such as Satan only could have dictated to him." In *L'Ennemie Sociale: Histoire documentée des faits et gestes de la Franc-Maçonnerie de 1717 à 1890 en France, en Belgique et en Italie* (Paris: Bloud and Barral, 1890), 260–261, Rosen would again describe "his Satanaty" Albert Pike as an anti-Pope, "the representative of Satan on earth facing the representative of God on earth."

77. Taxil, *Y a-t-il des Femmes dans la Franc-Maçonnerie?*, 237; Bataille, *Le Diable au XIXe siècle*, 1:11.

78. Meurin, *La Franc-Maçonnerie, Synagogue de Satan*, 215–216, suggests that the Re-Theurgists are already mentioned in *Les Frères Trois-Points* from 1885, but the bishop is once again sloppy in his references here.

79. Bataille, *Le Diable au XIXe siècle*, 2:754.

80. Letter from "Artiste Peintre" G. Dubouchez to J. K. Huysmans, 4 July 1894; BnF, Fonds Lambert, 31/48. The portrait can be found on p. 793 of the second volume of *Le Diable au XIXe siècle*.

81. Taxil, *Y a-t-il des Femmes dans la Franc-Maçonnerie?*, 235; Bataille, *Le Diable au XIXe siècle*, 1:39, 1:341, 2:607–726. Taxil's debt to Lévi, Huysmans, and a plethora of other authors was already suggested by Legge in his article "Devil Worship and Freemasonry," 479–480. The actual nature of Lévi's involvement with Freemasonry is described in Chacornac, *Éliphas Lévi*, 191, 200–201. Lévi was initiated on 14 March 1856 in the lodge Rose du Parfait Silence, declaring on this occasion, "au grand étonnement de l'assistance": "Je viens rapporter au milieu de vous

les traditions perdues, la connaissance exacte de vos signes et de vos emblèmes, et par suite, vous montrer le but pour lequel votre association a été constituée." He regularly attended the rites but quit the Craft on 21 August 1861, according to his own post-factum declaration "parce que les Francs-Maçons, excommuniés par le pape, ne croyaient plus devoir tolérer le catholicisme." In 1871, he would finish a work entitled *Le Gremoire Franco-latomorum*, which explained Masonic rites from an esoteric viewpoint (ibid., 268).

82. Taxil, *Les Frères Trois-Points*, 2:285, and Bataille, *Le Diable au XIXe siècle*, 1:182 feature the secret hand sign; Taxil, *Les sœurs maçonnes*, 322, mentions the "signature of Lucifer"; *Les Frères Trois-Points*, 2:255, talks about the inverted triangle (on the significance of which, Taxil writes, the reader can consult any tract on the occult sciences—"Or rather *don't*: don't open any of these horrifying books full of diabolical invocations, and apprehend that the triangle pointing down is the emblem of Satan").

83. See, for instance, Taxil, *Les Frères Trois-Points*, 2:251–252, where an allocation on Baphomet ("the magical and pantheist symbol of the Absolute") that could have been copied straight from Lévi is put into the mouth of the Masonic initiator.

84. Taxil could have found the signatures in Lévi, *Dogme et rituel de a Haute Magie*, 2:250–251. Collin de Plancy's *Dictionnaire infernale* is another possible source for these signatures and also for the numerous stories from folklore, demonology, and Roman Catholic hagiography that helped to fill the pages of *Le Diable au XIXe siècle*.

85. Introvigne, *Enquête sur le satanisme*, 168.

86. Some of these references are mighty hard to relocate for today's historian. It took me long, for instance, to find more information on the oratorio *Lucifer*, which is mentioned in *Le Diable au XIXe siècle*, 2:737–738, and which had been composed, according to Taxil, at the behest of the Duke de Camposelice by the composer Paul Benoît and performed on 7 May 1883 in the Trocadero by a choir and orchestra of no fewer than five hundred persons. The oratorio actually existed, although it was composed by *Pierre* Benoit; its text, however, was not "pro-Satanic" in any sense, at least if we are to judge by the Flemish-language version. Cf. Emanuel Hiel, *Lucifer: Oratorium* (Brussel: J. Nijs, 1866). I am still struggling to find the poem on Satan by the French anarchist Clovis Hugues, published in the first number of the (or a) *Revue anarchiste* and also mentioned in *Le Diable au XIXe siècle*.

87. Taxil, *Y a-t-il des Femmes dans la Franc-Maçonnerie?*, 264(n)–266; Bataille, *Le Diable au XIXe siècle*, 1:219n, corrects this by stating that the prayer is an *adaptation* by the Vicomte de la Jonquière *after* Proudhon. Taxil probably also borrowed from himself, putting parts of his earlier anticlerical books into the mouths of his god-defying Luciferians. A more thorough analysis of the enormous corpus of Taxilian texts might render surprising results in this respect.

88. Margiotta, *Le Palladisme*, 97–101.

89. Alfred Pierret in *Mémoires d'une ex-Palladiste* (5 May 1897) 23:721. The publication of this Bible of Lucifer had been announced by Vaughan in a letter published in Margiotta, *Le Palladisme*, 287.

90. Huysmans, *Là-Bas*, 75.

91. Copious examples can be given; one of the most recent being Marcello Truzzi, "Towards a Sociology of the Occult: Notes on Modern Witchcraft," in *Religious Movements in Contemporary America*, ed. Irving I. Zaretsky and Mark P. Leone (Princeton, NJ: Princeton University Press, 1974), 628–645, there 639, who distinguishes "Non-Stereotypical Satanists (Palladists or

Luciferians)," a group that includes "Baphometists" and LaVeyan Satanists. Elsewhere in this article (p. 635), Truzzi elucidates: "This form of Satanism has sometimes been called Palladism or Luciferianism [*sic*] to distinguish it from the Christian variety," indicating as his source an old encyclopedia from 1908.

92. Taxil seems to have found inspiration in (or exercised his operation with) the case of Barbe Bilger, another woman who was claimed to have deserted Palladism. This story, like many others connected in some way or another to the Taxil hoax, does not seem to have attracted scholarly interest yet. References to it can be found, among others, in A. C. de la Rive, *La Femme et l'Enfant dans la franc-maçonnerie universelle* (Paris: Delhomme and Briguet, 1894), 672–698. Taxil also discusses the Bilger Affair in a letter to Bessonies dated 9 Augustus 1893; cf. Fry, *Leo Taxil et La Franc-Maçonnerie*, 21.

93. Pierret in *Mémoires d'une ex-Palladiste* (5 May 1897) 23:708–710.

94. Cf. Taxil in Weber, *Satan franc-maçon*, 168–171.

95. Introvigne, *Enquête sur le satanisme*, 184–185.

96. Taxil in Weber, *Satan franc-maçon*, 173–174. In Scott's *Rob Roy*, a certain Diana Vernon is featured, whose father's name is Vaughan, as the Parisian daily *Le Matin* pointed out in an article on "Miss Diana Vaughan" that was published 23 November 1896.

97. Cf. Introvigne, *Enquête sur le satanisme*, 202.

98. Taxil in Weber, *Satan franc-maçon*, 173.

99. I am unconvinced by the rather fantastical suggestion that Vaughan was in reality a mentally deranged American woman who had fled her mental asylum and was (somehow) exploited by Taxil and company to impersonate a Palladist Grand Mistress, an idea put forward by Waite and seemingly not judged implausible by Introvigne, *Enquête sur le satanisme*, 197–199, 202.

100. Bataille, *Le Diable au XIXᵉ siècle*, 1:450; the engraving can be found on 1:433.

101. Introvigne, *Enquête sur le satanisme*, 179(n).

102. See the article by one Alphonse Lorain, " L'Entreprise Diana Vaughan," published in *La France Libre*, December 1896 (I consulted this article as a newspaper clipping by Huysmans kept in the BnF, cf. BnF, Fonds Lambert, 31/78–79: the exact date on the clipping was unfortunately unreadable).

103. Margiotta's *Souvenirs d'un Trente-Troisième* was translated into Italian as *Ricordi di un trentratré: Il Capo della Massoneria Universale* (Paris: Delhomme and Briguet, 1895); cf. p 181 of the French edition. In *Adriano Lemmi*, xv, Margiotta gives some information on his itinerary during his conversion; on pp. xiii–xv of the same book, a letter is printed in which he urges Diana Vaughan to convert as well. In a letter to Bessonies of 23 April 1895, Taxil declared that he had abandoned his work on a "volume sur le Palladisme" out of exasperation with the doubts thrown upon his integrity by certain Catholic journalists and authors, although the first two chapters were already finished; he repeats this statement in a letter to Bessonies dated 27 April 1895 (Fry, *Leo Taxil et La Franc-Maçonnerie*, 49–50, 54). Coincidentally, Margiotta's Palladism book appeared the same year.

104. Rive, *La Femme et l'Enfant dans la franc-maçonnerie*, esp. 109–141, 566–569, 610–654, 703–721.

105. Huysmans in Bois, *Le Satanisme et la Magie*, xv–xviii. "Ce qui est plus confondant c'est que le parti luciférien fait une revue de propagande, le Palladium," Huysmans wrote to Dom Besse on 5 June 1895. "C'est un tableau de blasphèmes—c'est surtout d'une incommensurable

bêtise. Ça n'a, du reste, aucun succès et personne ne s'en occupe. Diana Vaughan, qui la dirige, va fonder une chapelle luciférienne dans notre quartier, mais elle n'obtiendra pas plus de succès." See Joseph Daoust, *Les débuts bénédictins de J.-K. Huysmans: Documents inédits receuillis avec le concours de dom J. Laporte et de dom J. Mazé, Moines de Saint-Wandrille* (Abbaye Saint Wandrille: Éditions de Fontenelle, 1950), 91.

106. G., "Littérature anti-maçonnique," *Revue Bénédictine* 13 (February 1896) 2:78–84, 81.

107. This is suggested by the fact that the bishop's representative at Trent was among Taxil's most vocal critics, adopting Gruber's misgivings: Union Antimaçonnique Universelle, *Actes du Ire Congrès antimaçonnique international*, 2:94–96; Jones, "Palladism and the Papacy," 470.

108. Bois called *Le Diable au XIXe siècle* "a bad novel" and ridiculed Bataille's revelations about the preparation of biological and chemical weapons by Freemasonry in secret ateliers in (or underneath) Gibraltar. "He adds that the Freemasons have not generally employed these weapons of destruction yet," Bois wrote dryly on 19 June 1893. "This observation is apt" (quoted in Jarrige, *L'église et les Francs-Maçons dans la tourmente*, 221–222). *La Vérité*'s program expressly mentioned as one of its objectives "combating the enterprises of the sects" threatening the Church.

109. Bataille, *Le Diable au XIXe siècle*, 1:618–619.

110. Taxil in Weber, *Satan franc-maçon*, 172.

111. Rive, *La Femme et l'Enfant dans franc-maçonnerie*, 712. The prayer is from Act IV, Scene III, of Paul Corneille's *Polyeucte*, lines 1267–1272:

> Seigneur, de vos bontés il faut que je l'obtienne:
> Elle a trop de vertus pour n'être pas chrétienne;
> Avec trop de mérite il vous plut la former
> Pour ne vous pas connaître et ne pas vous aimer,
> Pour vivre des enfers esclave infortunée
> Et sous leur triste joug mourir comme elle est née!

112. Pierret in *Mémoires d'une ex-Palladiste* 23, 720; G., "Littérature anti-maçonnique II," *Revue Bénédictine* 13 (April 1896) 4:178–182, 182.

113. Taxil in Weber, *Satan franc-maçon*, 179, 180.

114. The play, entitled "Le Triomphe de l'Humilité," can be found in Sainte Thérèse de L'Enfant-Jésus et de la Sainte-Face, *Œuvres complètes (Textes et derniers paroles)* (Paris: Éditions du Cerf/Desclée De Brouwer, 2004), 915–927; cf. also Marianne Closson, "Le *Diable au XIXe Siècle* de Léo Taxil, ou les 'mille et une nuits' de la démonologie," in *Fictions du Diable*, 313–332, there 322n, as well as Introvigne, *Enquête sur le satanisme*, 203.

115. On 13 April 1895, for instance, a journalist called Émile Dehau wrote in the local newspaper *Charente* with regard to the public emergence of the New and Reformed Palladium: "Pour nous, nous n'avons pas à intervenir dans ces querelles mystiques dont la science aura raison tôt ou tard. L'État laïque n'a pas davantage à proscrire, comme certains le demandent, un culte nouveau si ses adhérents respectent les lois de la société." Émile Dehau, "Le culte de Lucifer," *Charente* (13 April 1895), consulted by me in BnF, Fonds Lambert, 26/24.

116. Quoted in Jarrige, *L'église et les Francs-Maçons dans la tourmente*, 225–226.

117. C. C. M., "Luciferian Palladism: Illustrated by the Story of Romance of a Remarkable Convert from It," *Light: A Journal of Psychical, Occult, and Mystical Research* 15 (14 September

1895) 766:435–439; both quotes derive from p. 429. In subsequent articles, "C. C. M." supplied more translated excerpts: see "Two Luciferian Seances," *Light* 15 (28 September 1895) 768:470–471; "More Luciferian Phenomena: Levitation Extraordinary," ibid., 15 (12 October 1895) 770:495–496; and "More Luciferian Phenomena: The Evocation of the Living," ibid., 15 (26 October 1895) 772:515–517.

118. "Hesperus," "The Case of Miss Vaughan," *Light* 15 (5 October 1895) 769:482–483; Isabel de Steiger, F.T.S., "Luciferianism," ibid., 15 (2 November 1895) 773:535; Africanus Theosophus, "Le Diable au XIXe Siecle," ibid., 15 (26 October 1895) 772:522, and "Luciferians and Freemasonry," ibid., 15 (16 November 1895) 775:557–58.

119. Bois, *Petites Religions de Paris*, 155–164, here 164, 163.

120. Quoted in Gerber, *Betrug als Ende eines Betruges*, 81.

121. Papus, *Le Diable et l'Occultisme* (Paris: Chamuel, 1895), 9–10, 13–23.

122. Papus, *Catholicisme, satanisme et occultisme* (Paris: Chamuel, 1897), 24, 30.

123. Waite, *Devil-Worship in France*; pp. 294–298 in particular defend Lévi against "diabolising" interpretations of his work.

124. For Waite, see *Light: A Journal of Psychical, Occult, and Mystical Research* 15 (7 December 1895) 778:593–594 and 16 (28 March 1896) 794:152–153. Papus was paraphrased in Q. V., "Le Diable au XIXme Siecle: An Interview with 'Papus,'" *Light* 16 (7 March 1896) 791:112–113. Waite referred to this interview with Papus when he mentioned the existence of "a society which was devoted to the cultus of Lucifer, star of the morning, quite distinct from Masonry, quite unimportant, and since very naturally dead"; *Devil-Worship in France*, 291.

125. Q. V., "Le Diable au XIXme Siecle," *Light* 16 (16 May 1896) 801:231–232, there 231.

126. Jarrige, *L'église et les Francs-Maçons dans la tourmente*, 45.

127. Papus, *Le Diable et l'Occultisme*, 12.

128. *Le Labarum anti-maçonnique: Statuts de l'ordre, déclaration de principes et grandes constitutions, cérémonial des grand'gardes, extraits du rituel des chevaliers du Sacré-Cœur* (Paris: Librairie Antimaçonnique, [1895]), 5.

129. Jean Kostka, *Lucifer démasqué* (Paris: Delhomme and Briguet, [1895]).

130. So Taxil said himself, but he may also have been inspired by the address of his offices with the Catholic publishing company Téqui, which was located on rue Régis, 6, Paris (Fry, *Leo Taxil et La Franc-Maçonnerie*, 17).

131. Jarrige, *L'église et les Francs-Maçons dans la tourmente*, 207–209. In-depth research on the Labarum, as well as on the official Roman Catholic reaction to this organization, remains a great scholarly desideratum.

132. Gerber, *Betrug als Ende eines Betruges*, 33–34. Gruber here cites from the (liberal) Italian newspaper *Corriere della Sera* (22 and 23 April 1897) but does not deny the picture this periodical paints, only remarking that "un santo" in Italian does not have the same significance as "ein Heiliger" in German.

133. Jarrige, *L'église et les Francs-Maçons dans la tourmente*, 214. In a letter to Father Octave, vice president of the Union Anti-Maçonnique de France and a member of the French Committee for the organization of the International Antimasonic Congress, Taxil enumerated the reasons given by Rome for this refusal; "1° personnellement je ne suis pas capable de coopérer à une œuvre sérieuse, et 2° je vis avec une femme (c'est-à-dire une concubine) d'une profonde impiété qui continue à tenir commerce de mes anciens ouvrages anti-cléricaux." Taxil also told

that rumors were circulated that his wife was actually a Palladist who celebrated Black Masses (quoted in Fry, *Leo Taxil et La Franc-Maçonnerie*, 84–86.

134. Union Antimaçonnique Universelle, *Actes du Iᵉ Congrès antimaçonnique international*, 2:92–94.

135. Letter from Monseigneur A. Villard, Secretary of Cardinal Parocchi, to Diana Vaughan, 7 January 1897; Fry, *Leo Taxil et La Franc-Maçonnerie*, 374: "Voyez, je ne sors jamais sans cela, car je suis toujours en danger."

136. Cf. Papus, *Catholicisme, satanisme et occultisme*, 24, who refers to this article as "La clef de la mystification," *Gazette du High Life*, 22 April 1894. Rive, *La Femme et l'Enfant dans la franc-maçonnerie*, 566–569, cites a letter from Rosen published in the Masonic periodical *La Chaîne d'Union*, November 1887 (*sic!*), 465–467, entitled "A propos du livre 'Les Sœurs Maçonnes' par Léo Taxil," which makes the same point.

137. *Diana Vaughan: Haar persoon, haar werk en haar aanstaande komst*, 5–7.

138. "Diana Vaughan," *L'Éclair*, 10 December 1896.

139. Introvigne, *Enquête sur le satanisme*, 184–185.

140. Jarrige, *L'église et les Francs-Maçons dans la tourmente*, 229.

141. M. Casis, "M. Taxil chez Chopinette," *La Verité* (15 April 1897): 2.

142. Taxil, in Weber, *Satan franc-maçon*, 183.

143. Taxil, in Weber, *Satan franc-maçon*, 182. Introvigne, following Waite, suggests that Taxil would *never* have disclosed his mystification if circumstances had not forced him to do so (*Enquête sur le satanisme*, 204–205). My estimation is otherwise, given the increasing pressure he was facing from the (Roman Catholic) press and the Vatican; but there is no way, of course, to determine what really could or would have happened in a different situation.

144. Taxil, in Weber, *Satan franc-maçon*, 159.

145. Introvigne, *Enquête sur le satanisme*, 189; Weber, *Satan franc-maçon*, 219–220. Weber, *Satan franc-maçon*, 219–220, mentions that Taxil started a feuilleton on his adventures in Catholicism after 19 April 1897 and returned to the affair in many of the prefaces he wrote for reissues of his old anticlerical works; these texts seem to have remained relatively unexplored by modern historiography.

146. On anti-Masonic literature in general, cf. Johannes Rogalla von Bieberstein, *Die These von der Verschwörung 1776–1945. Philosophen, Freimaurer, Juden, Liberale und Sozialisten als Verschwörer gegen die Sozialordnung* (Frankfurt am Main: Peter Lang, 1978), 20–188; Jérôme Rousse-Lacordaire, *Rome et les Franc-Maçons. Histoire d'un conflit* (Paris: Berg International Editeurs, 1996), 1–110; Introvigne, *Enquête sur le satanisme*, 156–167; Wolfgang Wippermann, *Agenten des Bösen: Verschwörungstheorien von Luther bis heute* (Berlin-Brandenburg: be.bra verlag, 2007), 47–57; and the various contributions to *Les courants antimaçonniques hier et aujourd'hui*, ed. Alain Dierkens, Problèmes d'histoire des religions 4 (Bruxelles: Éditions de l'Université de Bruxelles, 1993), mentioned in subsequent footnotes. This chapter concentrates on anti-Masonism within Roman Catholicism, where the phenomenon became most virulent and most influential, and it furthermore focuses especially on the situation in France and the role played by the Papacy. Protestantism had and has its own manifestations of anti-Masonism. In the United States, for instance, organized anti-Masonism particularly flourished in the 1820s and 1830s and briefly became a political factor of some importance: on this, see Michel L. Brodsky, "L'affaire Morgan et le parti antimaçonnique aux Etats-Unis (1826–1842)," in *Les*

courants antimaçonniques hier et aujourd'hui, ed. Alain Dierkens, Problèmes d'histoire des religions 4 (Bruxelles: Éditions de l'Université de Bruxelles, 1993), 25–37, and Lorman Ratner, *Anti-Masonry: The Crusade and the Party* (Englewood Cliffs, NJ: Prentice-Hall, 1969). For anti-Masonism in nineteenth-century Holland, see Anton van de Sande, "Antimaçonisme bij katholieken en protestanten," in *"Een stille leerschool van deugd en goede zeden": Vrijmetselarij in Nederland in de 18ᵉ en 19ᵉ eeuw*, ed. A. van de Sande and J. Roosendaal (Hilversum: Uitgeverij Verloren, 2005), 137–155.

147. Cf. Émile Poulat in his preface to Jarrige, *L'église et les Francs-Maçons dans la tourmente*, ii; Jones, "Palladism and the Papacy," 456.

148. Jacques Lemaire, "Les premières formes de l'antimaçonnisme en France: Les ouvrages de révélation (1738–1751)," in *Les courants antimaçonniques hier et aujourd'hui*, ed. Alain Dierkens, Problèmes d'histoire des religions 4 (Bruxelles: Éditions de l'Université de Bruxelles, 1993), 11–23.

149. Cf. Cholvy, *La religion en France*, 7–20.

150. "Outraged traditions" was the term employed by the British politician Benjamin Disraeli (1804–1881) to denote the surge of reactionary political forces in postrevolutionary Europe. See his *Lord George Bentinck: A Political Biography* (London: Colburn, 1852), 555: "A dynasty may be subverted, but it leaves as its successor a family of princely pretenders; a confiscated aristocracy takes the shape of factions; a plundered church acts on the tender consciences of toiling millions; corporate bodies displaced from their ancient authority no longer contribute their necessary and customary quota to the means of government; outraged traditions in multiplied forms enfeeble or excruciate the reformed commonwealth."

151. Rousse-Lacordaire, *Rome et les Franc-Maçons*, 91.

152. Augustin Barruel, *Mémoires pour servir à l'histoire du jacobinisme*, 4 vols. (London: Ph. Le Boussonnier, 1797), 2:418.

153. Barruel, *Mémoires pour servir à l'histoire du jacobinisme*, 2:397, 2:403.

154. Barruel, *Mémoires pour servir à l'histoire du jacobinisme*, 2:413.

155. Bieberstein, *These von der Verschwörung*, 110. For Barruel's place in contemporary Roman Catholic and ultramontane discourse, see also Anton van de Sande, "Freemasons against the Pope: The Role of Anti-masonry in the Ultramontane Propaganda in Rome, 1790–1900," in *The Power of Imagery: Essays on Rome, Italy & Imagination*, ed. Peter van Kessel (Sant'Oreste: Apeiron Editore, 1993), 212–230, there 216–220. George Sand's *Consuelo* novels had been an attempt to reverse the ethical significance of Barruel's narrative; cf. the essay of L. Guicard, "L'occultisme dans Consuelo et la Comtesse de Rudolstadt," in Sand, *Consuelo*, 1:xlvii–lxxviii; esp. xxii.

156. Barruel, *Mémoires pour servir à l'histoire du jacobinisme*, 2:266, 2:277–278. Barruel had briefly been an "ignorant" lodge member like this himself, as he tells on pp. 2:270–277.

157. Bieberstein, *These von der Verschwörung*, 135.

158. Rousse-Lacordaire, *Rome et les Franc-Maçons*, 84. Barrucand, "Quelques aspects de l'antimaçonnisme," 91, suggests the Chevalier de la Foi were not anti-Masonic; I have followed Rousse-Lacordaire.

159. As was to be expected because of its fragmentary nature, Protestantism proved more divided with regard to the French (and Western) Revolution. In France in particular, Protestants would rank among the staunchest supporters of the Republican heritage, to which they owed their legal emancipation. This gave some logic to the anti-Protestantism erupting in Taxil's

pseudo-Catholic publications mentioned above. On the (political) position of Protestants in France, see Cholvy, *La religion en France*, 90–92.

160. Hauptmann, *P.-J. Proudhon, genèse d'un antithéiste*, 53–56; Eamon Duffy, *Saints and Sinners: A History of the Popes* (New Haven, CT: Yale University Press, 1997), 217.

161. Duffy, *Saints and Sinners*, 220–221.

162. Pope Clemens XII, *In Eminenti*, retrieved from http://www.papalencyclicals.net/ Clem12/c152nemlt.htm; Rousse-Lacordaire, *Rome et les Franc-Maçons*, 46.

163. Rousse-Lacordaire, *Rome et les Franc-Maçons*, 74; for the context of the eighteenth-century anti-Masonic Bulls, see ibid., 57–59.

164. Cf. E. E. Y. Hales, *Mazzini and the Secret Societies: The Making of a Myth* (London: Eyre and Spottiswoode, 1956).

165. Pius IX, *The Syllabus of Errors Condemned by Pius IX*, retrieved from http://www.papalencyclicals.net/Pius09/p9syll.htm. The syllabus accompanied a more brief encyclical titled *Quanta Cura* that similarly condemned "current errors"; cf. http://www.papalencyclicals.net/ Pius09/p9quanta.htm.

166. Jarrige, *L'église et les Francs-Maçons dans la tourmente*, 30.

167. Mgr. Fava, *La Franc-Maçonnerie: Doctrine, histoire, gouvernement. Lettre à la Revue Catholique des Institutions et du Droit* (Paris: Librairie de la Société Bibliographique, 1880), 65–66.

168. Jarrige, *L'église et les Francs-Maçons dans la tourmente*, 36.

169. Pope Leo XIII, *Humanum Genus*, section 2, retrieved from www.vatican.va.

170. Pope Leo XIII, *Humanum Genus*, section 15.

171. Pope Leo XIII, *Humanum Genus*, section 24; Latin text from *Acta Sanctae Sedis*, 16:417–433, there 436.

172. Pope Leo XIII, *Humanum Genus*, section 31.

173. Paul Rosen, *L'Ennemie Sociale. Histoire documentée des faits et gestes de la Franc-Maçonnerie de 1717 à 1890 en France, en Belgique et en Italie* (Paris: Bloud and Barral 1890), i; Leo XIII's letter of permission is quoted on pp. iv–v.

174. Jarrige, *L'église et les Francs-Maçons dans la tourmente*, 128–130.

175. Aldo A. Mola, "La Ligue antimaçonnique et son influence politique et culturelle aux confines des XIXᵉ et XXᵉ siècles," in *Les courants antimaçonniques hier et aujourd'hui*, ed. Alain Dierkens, Problèmes d'histoire des religions 4 (Bruxelles: Éditions de l'Université de Bruxelles, 1993), 39–55.

176. Jarrige, *L'église et les Francs-Maçons dans la tourmente*, 69; Alexander Sedgwick, *The Ralliement in French Politics 1890–1898* (Cambridge, MA: Harvard University Press, 1965), 49. "You talk of peace, but your actions reflect hatred and persecution because Freemasonry, eldest daughter of Satan, guides them," Gouthe-Soulard additionally wrote to the French Minister of Public Worship.

177. T. R. P. Monsabre, *La Croisade au XIXe siècle: Discours prononcé à Clermont-Ferrand à l'occasion du 8ᵉ centenaire de la 1ʳᵉ Croisade, le 18 Mai 1895* (Paris: Bureaux de La Revue Thomiste, s.a.), 5, 17.

178. David Stevenson, *The Origins of Freemasonry: Scotland's Century, 1590–1710* (Cambridge: Cambridge University Press, 1988), 227. The pamphlet, entitled *Mischiefs and Evils Practised in the Sight of God by Those Called Freed Masons*, stated that Freemasonry was "the Anti-Christ which was to come leading Men from Fear of God. For how should Men meet in secret Places and with secret Signs taking Care that none observe them to do the Work of God; are these not the Ways of Evil-doers?"

179. *Lettre de Satan aux Francs-Maçons, suivi d'une réponse à Satan* (Paris: Potey, 1825), 13–14. Rousse-Lacordaire, *Rome et les Franc-Maçons*, 111, cites this title to indicate that the "Luciferian theme" was already current in the first half of the nineteenth century; but it is clear that its author does not intend to imply the existence of a literal, formal veneration of Satan by Freemasonry. For the legal repercussions, cf. *Réflexions sur le procès intenté à M. Waille, au sujet de l'écrit intitulé: « Lettre de Satan aux francs-maçons": Extrait du Mémorial Catholique (février, 1826)* ([Paris]: Impr. De Gueffier, 1826).

180. Cf. Union Antimaçonnique Universelle, *Actes du Ire Congrès antimaçonnique international*, 1:334–335, where these varying interpretations play an essential role.

181. Rosen, *L'Ennemie Sociale*, 348–349; the phrase about *Gesta Satanæ per massones* can be found on the title page and is quoted again in the last lines of the book on p. 424. In *Satan et Cie*, Rosen summarized the "Supreme Secret" of Scottish and Cabbalistic Freemasonry as "Satan is the One and Only God" (see the explicatory plate at the front of the book). But it remained somewhat unclear whether the followers of these rites were thought to be aware of this: it was only Rosen himself, it appears, who had unveiled this hidden core.

182. Mola, "La Ligue antimaçonnique," esp. 40. Pius IX qualified members of secret societies as "children of the Demon" in his pastoral letter *Singulari quadam* (issued 9 December 1854); cf. Rousse-Lacordaire, *Rome et les Franc-Maçons*, 109.

183. One of the few studies devoted to conceptions from folklore regarding Freemasonry is Karl Olbrich, *Die Freimaurer im deutschen Volksglauben: Die im Volke umlaufenden Vorstellungen und Erzählungen von den Freimauern* (Breslau: M. & H. Marcus, 1930), who argues that the belief that Masons were involved with the devil was nearly universal and far pre-dated "der berüchtigte Riesenschwindel des Schriftstellers Leo Taxil" (cf. pp. 8–9, 13). Although this could well be true, it must be noted that all material presented by Olbrich is from the early twentieth century and in some cases explicitly connected with Roman Catholic anti-Masonic agitation (see particularly pp. 26, 84).

184. Ségur, *Les Francs-Maçons*, 46–48.

185. In Boullan's *Annales de la Sainteté au XIXe siècle*, many articles on "secret societies" can be found that clearly reflect and extend current Roman Catholic attitudes in this respect. "La magie au sein des sociétés secrètes: Remède divin à ce grand mal," *Annales de la Sainteté au XIXe siècle* (February 1875) 62:138–146, for example, explicitly concerns Freemasonry. Interestingly, an idea that would be fully exploited by Taxil can already be found here, namely, the notion of the three degrees of Satanist involvement in secret societies: that of ignorant ordinary members, who are told these organizations only serve to practice charity; a second level of people who use them for their (political) ambitions; and the inner core of "adeptes de Satan." Similar articles on "les perils des sociétés secrètes" can be found in *Annales de la Sainteté au XIXe siècle* (April 1873) 39:307–310, and (January 1875) 61:68–72.

CHAPTER 6: UNMASKING THE SYNAGOGUE OF SATAN, CONTINUED

1. I made extensive use of the fine overview of this literature in Introvigne, *Enquête sur le satanisme*, 65–99, for the following paragraphs.

2. These articles were reproduced as *Lettres magiques, ou lettres sur le diable* ("En France": s.i., 1791).

3. Abbé Fiard, *La France trompée par les magiciens et démonolatres du dix-huitième siècle, fait démontré par des faits* (Paris: Grégoire and Thouvenin, 1803), 88–89.

4. Duffy, *Saints and Sinners*, 225–227; Cholvy, *La religion en France*, 21–24; Vincent Viaene, "The Roman Question. Catholic Mobilisation and Papal Diplomacy during the Pontificate of Pius IX (1846–1878)," in *The Black International/L'International noire 1870–1878*, ed. Emiel Lamberts (Leuven: Leuven University Press, 2002), 135–177, here 135–136.

5. Chevalier Gougenot des Mousseaux, *La magie au dix-neuvième siècle: Ses agents, ses vérités, ses mensognes* (Paris: Henri Plon and E. Dentu, 1860), esp. 450; Lévi is quoted on pp. 228, 225, 138, and 137.

6. Cf. Chevalier Gougenot des Mousseaux, *Les Hauts Phénomènes de la Magie, précédés du Spiritisme Antique* (Paris: Henri Plon, 1864). It is important to note, however, that Gougenot des Mousseaux did not consider the occultists to be engaged in willful and purposeful veneration of Satan: generally speaking, they were deluded about the real nature of their activities, in the same way as the pagans of Antiquity had venerated idols without suspecting them to be demons.

7. Gougenot des Mousseaux, *Les Hauts Phénomènes de la Magie*, i(n).

8. Cf. "His Interview with Satan," *New York Times*, 21 October 1888. The story originally appeared under the title "Aut Diabolus aut nihil: The True Story of a Hallucination," *Blackwood's Magazine* 1 (October 1888) 44:475–499, and was signed "X.L.," a pseudonym for the writer Julien Osgood (1852–1925). Bishop Meurin nevertheless quotes it as an "authentic apparition of the Devil" in *La Franc-Maçonnerie, Synagogue de Satan*, 218–224. The tale may also have served as inspiration for the portrait of Satan in black tie that is featured on the gravure in Bataille, *Le Diable au XIXᵉ siècle*, 1:953. (For those who have doubts: in 1895, "X.L." wrote that the episode was fictive, as were all the characters it portrayed, except for "His Satanic Majesty" himself, whose description was, "as indeed many of my readers will recognise at once—a photograph taken from life." The tale was based on a "rather meagre" anecdote told by a French Catholic nobleman regarding a priest who attended a séance and saw the devil. Cf. X.L., *Aut Diabolus Aut Nihil, and Other Tales* (London: Methuen, 1895), viii–ix.

9. Barruel, *Mémoires pour servir à l'histoire du jacobinisme*, 2:327.

10. A few isolated authors had proceeded Taxil in this. The Catholic lawyer Joseph Bizouard (1797–1870), for instance, published a "philosophical and historical essay" about "contacts between Man and Demon" in which he not only designated the ideology of the freemasons as "Satanism pure and simple" but also claimed that they, in this very century, frequently "consulted the devil" (cited in Introvigne, *Enquête sur le satanisme*, 91). Bizouard's assertions, however, remained buried in the six volumes and almost four thousand pages of his gigantic work.

11. See also Arthur Lillie, *The Worship of Satan in Modern France* (London: Swan Sonnenschein, 1896), xxi, where Palladism is characterized as "a combination of freemasonry and modern spirituality: 'Hence its great success.'"

12. Régis Ladous, "Le spiritisme et les démons dans les catéchismes français du XIXe siècle," in *Le Défi Magique II. Satanisme, sorcellerie*, ed. Jean-Baptiste Martin and Massimo Introvigne (Lyon: Presses Universitaires de Lyon, 1994), 203–228, there 219–223; Monsabre, *La Croisade au XIXe siècle*, 17.

13. Union Antimaçonnique Universelle, *Actes du Iʳᵉ Congrès antimaçonnique international*, 1:337.

14. Jarrige, *L'église et les Francs-Maçons dans la tourmente*, 162, also considers Taxil's influence determining for the adoption of the "Luciferian thesis" in Catholic anti-Masonic discourse.

15. L. Nemours Godré, "La fin de Diana," *La Vérité* (21 April 1897).

16. Quoted in Weber, *Satan franc-maçon*, 14n.

17. The Universal Antimasonic Union also featured the devise "Pro Libertas et pro Patria" in its banners: with this the liberation of Catholic countries from the Masonic stranglehold was meant.

18. Cf. Viaene, "The Roman Question," esp. 162.

19. Angelis uttered these remarkable words against the prominent Dutch ultramontane Willem Cramer, who visited Rome in October 1870: Viaene, "The Roman Question," 162.

20. Viaene, "The Roman Question," 169.

21. Emiel Lamberts, "Catholic Congresses as Amplifiers of International Catholic Opinion," in *The Papacy and the New World Order: Vatican Diplomacy, Catholic Opinion and International Politics at the Time of Leo XIII, 1878–1903 = La Papauté et le nouvel ordre mondial: Diplomatie vaticane, opinion catholique et politique internationale au temps de Léo XIII*, ed. Vincent Viaene (Bruxelles: Institut Historique Belge de Rome/Belgisch Historisch Instituut te Rome, 2005), 213–223, there 217.

22. Pope Leo XIII, *Rerum Novarum*, section 3. Retrieved from http://www.papalencyclicals. net/Leo13/l13rerum.htm.

23. Cf. Sedgwick, *The Ralliement in French Politics*.

24. Duffy, *Saints and Sinners*, 244. The Pope may primarily have thought of his own monarchical status when making this last remark.

25. Vincent Viaene, " 'Wagging the dog': An Introduction to Vatican Press Policy in an Age of Democracy and Imperialism," in Viaene, *The Papacy and the New World Order*, 323–348, esp. 329.

26. "Guerre de positions autour de plusieurs thèmes symboliques" is how Jan De Maeyer describes the secularization conflict in Belgium; cf. his article "La Belgique. Un élève modèle de l'école ultramontaine," in *The Black International/L'International noire 1870–1878*, ed. Emiel Lamberts (Leuven: Leuven University Press, 2002), 360–385, there 365. Anton van de Sande already pointed out that it was the new role of the Vatican as wielder of Catholic opinion that instigated it to engage in active anti-Masonic propaganda; cf. van de Sande, "Freemasons against the Pope," 223.

27. Pope Leo XIII, *Humanum Genus*, sections 33–36, retrieved from www.vatican.va.

28. Monsabre, *La Croisade au XIXᵉ siècle*, 29–30.

29. Jarrige, *L'église et les Francs-Maçons dans la tourmente*, 203–204.

30. Pope Leo XIII, *Inimica Vis*, section 9, retrieved from www.vatican.va.

31. On the Roman Temple of Satan and possible connections between Taxil and semicovert Vatican press operations, no substantial scholarly research has yet been done. The story of the Grotto of Pertuis is explored in the articles by Francis Python and George Andrey in *La Franc-maçonnerie à Fribourg et en Suisse du XVIIIᵉ au XXᵉ siècle*, ed. Yvonne Lehnherr (Gèneve: Slatkine and Fribourg; Musée d'Art et d'Histoire, 2001), which both are excellent yet scarcely provide more than a starting point for in-depth study. In this section, I hope to provide some additional historical clues and hypotheses, in anticipation of a more thorough historical reconstruction.

32. Margiotta, *Le Palladisme*, 243; he was echoed by De la Rive, who called Goblet d'Alviella a "Satanist patriarch"; cf. A. de la Rive, "Mensonges & menaces maçonniques," *L'Écho de Rome: Organe de la défense du Saint-Siège* 27 (1 October 1894): 1.

33. On Goblet d'Alviella, see Marc D'Hoore, "Goblet d'Alviella, un intellectuel en politique: Commentaires sur son œuvre et sa pensée," in *Eugène Goblet d'Alviella, historien et franc-maçon,* ed. Alain Dierkens, Problèmes d'histoire des Religions 4 (Bruxelles: Éditions de l'Université de Bruxelles, 1995), 19–34.

34. Bataille, *Le Diable au XIXe siècle,* 1:436–438; 2:350–391.

35. Margiotta, *Adriano Lemmi,* 316, and title page.

36. Bataille, *Le Diable au XIXe siècle,* 1:466; Margiotta, *Le Palladisme,* 120–127, 135–175; Vaughan, *Crispi.* On Pessina, see also Jarrige, *L'église et les Francs-Maçons dans la tourmente,* 173.

37. Margiotta, *Adriano Lemmi,* 250. Introvigne, *Enquête sur le satanisme,* 160n, seems to describe the presence of a depiction of Lucifer in the lodge as an authentic fact.

38. "Le Temple de Satan," *La Croix du Dauphiné* 3 (16 May 1895) 709:1.

39. Domenico Margiotta, "Le Temple de Satan à Rome," *La Croix du Dauphiné* 3 (18 May 1895) 711:1; the article from *La Croix* was reproduced in Margiotta, *Le Palladisme,* 31–34.

40. Cf. "Le Temple Palladique du Palais Borghese," *Revue mensuelle religieuse, politique, scientifique: Complément de la publication Le Diable au XIXe Siècle* 2 (May 1895) 17:300–306, there 301.

41. "Le Temple Palladique du Palais Borghese," 300–301.

42. Margiotta, *Le Palladisme,* 34n.

43. See Jean-Daniel Dessonaz, "Les débuts de la Juste et Parfaite Loge de Saint-Jean 'La Régénérée' à l'Orient de Fribourg (1848–1851),'" in *La Franc-maçonnerie à Fribourg et en Suisse du XVIIIe au XXe siècle,* ed. Yvonne Lehnherr (Gèneve: Slatkine and Fribourg; Musée d'Art et d'Histoire, 2001), 141–152.

44. Francis Python, "Diable, les Franc-Maçons sont de retour! 1877–1903," in Lehnherr, *La Franc-maçonnerie à Fribourg,* 153–175, esp. 154–155.

45. Cf. http://www.pertuis.ch/fr/history_f.html, accessed 13 November 2010.

46. Python, "Diable, les Franc-Maçons sont de retour!" 154–155; Léon Barbey, *L'âme du Chanoine Schorderet* (Fribourg: Éditions de l'Imprimerie St-Paul, 1943), 149.

47. Jean-Pierre Laurant, "Le dossier Léo Taxil du fonds Jean Baylot de la Bibliothèque Nationale," *Politica Hermetica* 4 (1990): 66–67, there 61.

48. Rive, *La Femme et l'Enfant dans franc-maçonnerie,* 678.

49. Python, "Diable, les Franc-Maçons sont de retour!" 161.

50. See the picture of the chapel in Python, "Diable, les Franc-Maçons sont de retour!" 162.

51. Rive, *La Femme et l'Enfant dans franc-maçonnerie,* 676.

52. Python, "Diable, les Franc-Maçons sont de retour!" 161–162; Georges Andrey, "La Croisade antimaçonnique (XIXe–XXe siècles)," in Lehnherr, *La Franc-maçonnerie à Fribourg,* 177–186, 183.

53. Taxil in Weber, *Satan franc-maçon,* 166; cf. Andrey, "La Croisade antimaçonnique," 183.

54. Python, "Diable, les Franc-Maçons sont de retour!" 161.

55. E. Stoecklin, *Instructions au 18me grade* (Fribourg: Chapitre L'Amitié de Lausanne, 1882), 80–81; see also p. 3.

56. Rive, *La Femme et l'Enfant dans la franc-maçonnerie,* 678.

57. Laurant, "Le dossier Léo Taxil," 61; "Les Sacrilèges Maçonniques," *Le Nouveau Moniteur de Rome,* 1:125 (20 June 1894).

58. For contacts between Taxil and De la Rive regarding Fribourg, see Laurant, "Le dossier Léo Taxil," 61.

59. A. C. de la Rive, "La Messe Noire au Fribourg," *Revue mensuelle religieuse, politique, scientifique. Complément de la publication Le Diable au XIXe Siècle* 1 (February 1894) 2:43–45. De la Rive republished the text of this article in *La Femme et l'Enfant dans franc-maçonnerie*, 674–679, replacing the name Lucie Claraz with "Mlle. X."

60. Rive, *La Femme et l'Enfant dans la franc-maçonnerie*, 679. De la Rive was clearly fond of secret subterranean constructions; on pp. 693–694, he also gives detailed information on Masonic tunnels elsewhere in Switzerland.

61. "Les Sacrilèges Maçonniques," *Le Nouveau Moniteur de Rome*, 1 (20 June 1894) 125.

62. Laurant, "Le dossier Léo Taxil," 61.

63. Lillie, *The Worship of Satan in Modern France*, xix–xxi, quoting from the *London Globe* of 30 April 1895.

64. Jarrige, *L'église et les Francs-Maçons dans la tourmente*, 199.

65. Lillie, *Worship of Satan in Modern France*, xxi.

66. "Copie du Jugement," *Revue mensuelle religieuse, politique, scientifique* 3 (May 1896) 29:297–298. Typically, this verdict was immediately interpreted by some of Taxil's supporters as judicial proof for the existence of Luciferianism—evidently, the judge had *not* considered devil worship to be nonexistent? Cf. Lillie, *Worship of Satan in Modern France*, xxi.

67. Vaughan, *Crispi*, 448–451n; Maillard de Broys, "Échos de Rome," *L'Écho de Rome: Organe de la défense du Saint-Siège* 27 (1 November 1894): 1–2.

68. Cf. http://www.pertuis.ch/fr/history_f.html, accessed 13 November 2010.

69. Introvigne, *Enquête sur le Satanisme*, 207.

70. Introvigne, *Enquête sur le Satanisme*, 180, 203, basing himself on Aldo A. Mola, "Il Diavolo in loggia," in *Diavolo, Diavoli. Torino e altrove*, ed. Filippo Barbano (Milan: Bompiani, 1988), 257–270, an article I unfortunately was unable to consult.

71. Introvigne, *Enquête sur le Satanisme*, 180; Mola, "La Ligue antimaçonnique," 46.

72. Introvigne, *Enquête sur le Satanisme*, 169.

73. Alfred Pierret, Vaughan's publisher, remembered two other collaborators visiting him on behalf of Taxil; a well-dressed man in his forties who called himself Daniel Svelti, and a young woman who called herself Dorothy Lindlay and who regularly delivered messages from "Diana," as well as the zinc printing molds for the demonic signatures used in Vaughan's Luciferian bulletin. As to office equipment, Pierret consulted some experts regarding the typescripts he received for Vaughan's publications; all assured him the texts were produced on an extremely modern machine still unavailable in France. See *Mémoires d'une ex-Palladiste Parfaite Initiée, Indépendante* 2 (5 May 1897) 23:706–708, 712, 717.

74. Viaene, "The Roman Question," 169; for the history of the Black International, see especially Emiel Lamberts, "L'internationale noire. Une organisation secrète au service du Saint-Siège," in Lamberts, *The Black International*, 15–101; Jacques Lory, "La 'Correspondance de Gènève' (1870–1873): Un organe de presse singulier," in Lamberts, *The Black International*, 102–131, and the other contributions to that volume. Emiel Lamberts published a monograph in Dutch that is largely devoted to the Black International: *Het gevecht met Leviathan: Een verhaal over de politieke ordening in Europa 1815–1965* (Amsterdam: Bert Bakker, 2011)—this publication, however, has eluded me.

75. Viaene, "A Brilliant Failure," 246.

76. Viaene, "'Wagging the dog,'" 323.

77. Cf. Viaene, "A Brilliant Failure," and Viaene, "'Wagging the dog.'"

78. We know this because it evoked the chagrin of Drumont, who lashed out against the support that ex-pornographer Taxil was receiving from the ecclesiastical hierarchy; cf. Édouard Drumont, "Léo Taxil et le Nonce du Pape," in *Le Testament d'un Antisémite* (Paris: E. Dentu, 1891), 404–437. Introvigne, *Enquête sur le Satanisme*, 172, also acknowledges the important role of the apostolic nunciature in Taxil's early days as a Catholic author.

79. On Schorderet, see Urs Altermatt, "L'engagement des intellectuels catholiques suisses au sein de l'Internationale noire," in Lamberts, *The Black International*, 409–426, esp. 416–420. Barbey, *L'âme du Chanoine Schorderet*, is a semi-hagiography but provides basic biographical facts. I was unfortunately unable to consult the extensive biography of Joseph Schorderet by Dominique Barthélémy, *Diffuser au lieu d'interdire: Le chanoine Joseph Schorderet (1840–1893)* (Fribourg: Editions universitaires, 1993).

80. Schorderet is listed as a member of the Black International by Emiel Lamberts in "L'internationale noire," 49; in "Conclusion: The Black International and Its Influence on European Catholicism (1870–1878)," in Lamberts, *The Black International*, 464–480, there 475, Lamberts says he operated "in close concert" with the Black International. Altermatt, "L'engagement des intellectuels catholiques suisses," 424, writes that the Swiss priest worked "de façon largement indépendante, mais du même esprit que le Comité international." Be this as it may, Schorderet was without doubt in regular correspondence with several Black International Permanents, among them the Dutch Permanent Cramer (Lamberts, "L'internationale noire," 77–78); his national press agency was formed precisely at the time that the Black International came into being.

81. Barbey, *L'âme du Chanoine Schorderet*, 139–168.

82. Introvigne, *Enquête sur le Satanisme*, 172. Even as late as 1893, Taxil seems to have held a job with the Catholic publishing house Téqui, which originated with "l'œuvre de Saint-Michel" a similar organization for doctrinal propaganda (cf. http://www.librairietequi.com/#PS-who-Qui-sommes-nous, accessed 20 July 2012). Taxil sent a letter to Bessonies on 9 August 1893 on paper with a letterhead of Téqui that names him (using his real name, G.-A. Jogand) as responsible for "Administration et Régie des Annonces" and in the capacity of "Administrateur-Gérant" for *Le Médecin de la Famille Chrétienne*, a periodical published by Téqui (Fry, *Leo Taxil et La Franc-Maçonnerie*, 17; later letters do not feature this letterhead). Was this a cover-up or did Taxil make ends meet with this unglamorous occupation? Just two years earlier, it must be noted, the book by his alter ego Ricoux had also been published by Téqui. In addition, Drumont revealed that Taxil's works were printed on the presses of "l'œuvre de Saint-Michel" (Drumont, "Léo Taxil et le Nonce du Pape," 434). I have not found more information on this organization; in fact, a thorough inventory of the printing and publishing logistics of Taxil remains a job to be done.

83. Viaene, "'Wagging the dog,'" 339.

84. Viaene, "'Wagging the dog,'" 343.

85. Legge, "Devil Worship and Freemasonry," 482, already noted "the part played in the affair by some of the French Episcopate": "The list of those who have given testimonials to Signor Margiotta includes nearly all the bishops who have rallied to the Republic." Likewise, Abel Clarin de la Rive enjoyed the practical support of the archbishop of Rheims and Cardinal Benoit-Marie Langénieux, a confidant of Leo XIII and a fervent anti-Mason who called Freemasonry in

a pastoral instruction from 1894 "L'église même de Satan." De la Rive was granted access to his extensive library but wrote to the Abbé Bessonies on 2 July 1894, "Ne pas parlez bien entendu de la bibliothèque du Cardinal qui désire rester absolument dans l'ombre en cette affaire; mais donner à supposer que cette bibliothèque est ma propriété" (Fry, *Leo Taxil et La Franc-Maçonnerie*, 203–204; compare 208, 219).

86. Viaene, "A Brilliant Failure," 255.

87. The charter is reproduced in Vaughan, *Crispi*, 317.

88. Vaughan, *Crispi*, 472–473.

89. Vaughan, *Crispi*, 489, 491.

90. Viaene, " 'Wagging the dog,' " 341.

91. On conspiracy theories in early nineteenth-century Europe, see J. M. Roberts, *The Mythology of the Secret Societies* (London: Secker and Warburg, 1972). See also Disraeli, *Lord George Bentinck*, 553: "The origin of the secret societies that prevail in Europe is very remote. It is probable that they were originally confederations of conquered races organized in a great measure by the abrogated hierarchies. In Italy they have never ceased, although they have at times been obliged to take various forms; sometimes it was a literary academy, sometimes a charitable brotherhood; freemasonry was always a convenient guise. . . . The two characteristics of these confederations which now cover Europe as a network, are war against property and hatred of the Semitic revelation."

92. Andrey, "La Croisade antimaçonnique," 183; Viaene, "A Brilliant Failure," 233.

93. "Exorcismus in Satanam et angelos apostaticos," in *Rituale Romanum Pauli V Pontificus Maximi jussu editum, aliorumque pontificum cura recognitum atque auctoritate ssmi. d. n. Pii Papæ XI ad norman codicis juris canonici accommodatum* (Ratisbonæ: Friderici Pustet, 1925), 354–357. The "Small Exorcism against Satan and the Fallen Angels" was promulgated 18 May 1890; cf. Dvorak, *Satanismus*, 160. The Prayer to Saint Michael was added to the Leonine Prayers in 1886; the addition was directly linked to developments in the Roman Question. A corpus of lore grew up around the prayer, which told how Leo XIII had been inspired to write it after seeing a host of demons hovering above the Eternal City in a vision; cf. http://en.wikipedia.org/wiki/ Prayer_to_Saint_Michael, accessed 14 November 2011.

94. Rosen, *L'Ennemie Sociale*, iv–v. A Belgian priest writing on Freemasonry, Auguste Onclair, also received a long approbative letter from Leo XIII for his book *La franc-maçonnerie contemporaine* from 1885, which is integrally cited by Barrucand, "Quelques aspects de l'antimaçonnisme," 98.

95. Letter by Cardinal Parocchi, 16 December 1895, quoted by Taxil; Weber, *Satan franc-maçon*, 179.

96. Letter by Vincenzo Sardi, 11 July 1896, quoted by Taxil; Weber, *Satan franc-maçon*, 180.

97. Margiotta, *Le Palladisme*, 1.

98. Weber, *Satan franc-maçon*, 179.

99. Gerber, *Betrug als Ende eines Betruges*, 111.

100. Fry, *Leo Taxil et La Franc-Maçonnerie*, 316–318.

101. Fry, *Leo Taxil et La Franc-Maçonnerie*, 369–370.

102. Letters from 16 November 1896, 30 November 1896, 29 December 1896, 7 and 8 January 1897, 25 January 1897, 6 February 1897, 21 March 1897; Fry, *Leo Taxil et La Franc-Maçonnerie*, 370–378. It is clear from this correspondence that Villard was initially convinced of the existence

of Vaughan; in a letter to Bessonies, he expressed his surprise that a private letter that he had addressed to her "dans l'unique but de lui apporter un peu de consolation et d'encouragement dans les circonstances actuelles" had been promptly rendered to the public (Fry, *Leo Taxil et La Franc-Maçonnerie*, 370). In these and other letters, moreover, he repeatedly emphasized the disorientation of Rome regarding Vaughan: "À Rome, on desire la lumière pleine et entière. Je puis vous assurer qu'en haute lieu on est encore dans le doute" (ibid., 370); "Dans une question aussi grave où l'honneur de l'Église catholique est en jeu, il n'est pas permis de laisser son Chef dans le doute et le Pape, je vous l'assure, est dans le doute" (20 November 1896; ibid., 371).

103. Laurant, "Le dossier Léo Taxil," 61; *Diana Vaughan: Haar persoon, haar werk en haar aanstaande komst*, 37. It is hard to say if the Vatican intended these ventures as serious reconnaissance undertakings or simply sent the two well-intentioned reporters away to busy themselves on some impossible errand. "La véritable enquête n'a pas été faite par les hommes dont les noms ont été livrés à la publicité," Villard assured Bessonies in a letter from 25 January 1897. "Ceux-là ont servi de couverture à l'enquête secrète, mais ils n'ont jamais pu la connaître. Je ne puis pas vous en dire davantage." At the same time, Bessonies was conducting his own private investigation through his contacts with the Catholic press in America. See Fry, *Leo Taxil et La Franc-Maçonnerie*, 376 (letter, Villard); 379–389 (investigation, Bessonies).

104. In a told-you-so letter to Bessonies from 29 April 1897, Villard claimed "À Rome, Léo Taxil était regardé depuis quelque temps comme un individu de plus mauvaise espèce, surtout pornographe et hypocrite" (Fry, *Leo Taxil et La Franc-Maçonnerie*, 378).

105. Taxil in Weber, *Satan franc-maçon*, 177.

106. According to Taxil, Mgr. Northrop, bishop of Charleston, traveled "tout exprès" to the Vatican to deny the Taxilian allegations about his town of residence; he repeated his denials in an interview while traveling to Rome but held his tongue after he returned from the Eternal City. Cf. Weber, *Satan franc-maçon*, 178.

107. In letter to Gabriel Bessonies from 25 April 1895, Taxil explicitly asked for a personal token of support from the Pope, threatening to resign from the anti-Masonic battle otherwise because of "toutes les inimitiés de mauvaise foi que ma lutte contre la secte maçonnique m'a values." "Si le Saint-Père daigne écrire personnellement un mot d'approbation, j'en serai très heureux; il me consolera ainsi du chagrin que j'éprouve pour les avanies subies depuis déjà longtemps" (Fry, *Leo Taxil et La Franc-Maçonnerie*, 50–52). This appeal to the Pope's pastoral care remained fruitless as well.

108. Taxil in Weber, *Satan franc-maçon*, 182.

109. This did not prevent him from making effective use of it as an independent corroboration of the existence of Palladism vis-à-vis his Catholic opponents; cf. *Revue mensuelle religieuse, politique, scientifique: Complément de la publication Le Diable au XIXe Siècle* 2 (May 1895) 17:300–305.

110. Only Introvigne, in his chapter on Taxil in *Enquête sur le Satanisme*, treats this question in some depth, basing his views partly on Aldo Mola's article "La Ligue antimaçonnique." As I was unable to explore primary Masonic sources, this section must remain preliminary. The use of Satanic metaphor in nineteenth-century Freemasonry, particularly in Italy, certainly deserves further historical research.

111. On the early history of Freemasonry, see Stevenson, *The Origins of Freemasonry*. Roger Dachez, "Freemasonry," in Hanegraaff, *Dictionary of Gnosis and Western Esotericism*, 1:382–388, gives a helpful introduction.

112. Rousse-Lacordaire, *Rome et les Franc-Maçons*, 69.

113. Rousse-Lacordaire, *Rome et les Franc-Maçons*, 77.

114. Rousse-Lacordaire, *Rome et les Franc-Maçons*, 114–155.

115. Albert Pike, *Morals and Dogma of the Ancient and Accepted Scottish Rite of Freemasonry, prepared for the Supreme Council of the Thirty Third Degree for the Southern Jurisdiction of the United States* (Charleston, SC: s.i., A. M. 5632 [1871]), 65. Similar ambiguous statements can be found on p. 210, where Pike describes Lucifer thus: "LUCIFER, the Light-bearer! Strange and mysterious name to give to the Spirit of Darkness! Lucifer, the Son of the Morning! Is it he who bears the Light, and with its splendors intolerable blinds feeble, sensual or selfish Souls? Doubt it not! for traditions are full of Divine Revelations and Inspirations: and Inspiration is not of one Age nor of one Creed." This passage is sometimes still referred to as a proof for Pike's "Luciferianism," but the context makes it abundantly clear that he considered Lucifer to be the embodiment of a "lesser" light, the light of the material world that blinds "feeble, sensual or selfish Souls"—the true disciple of wisdom seeks the divinity alone. Although Pike's debt to Lévi is obvious in these and other passages, Pike seldom made explicit mention of the French esoterist in his writings; an exception can be found in *The Book of the Words* (Whitefish, MO: Kessinger, 1992), 169n. See also Dachez, "Freemasonry," 387.

116. Albert Pike's reply and praelocution were reprinted in Alphonse Cerza, *Anti-Masonry: Light on the Past and Present Opponents of Freemasonry* (Fulton, MO: Ovid Bell, 1962), 253–295; see there 287–289, 293, 275, 265. The idea that Taxil may have found inspiration in Pike's spurious efforts to set up a Masonry of Adoption in the United States does not seem convincing to me: cf. Jay M. Kinney, "Shedding Light on a Possible Inspiration for Taxil's Hoax Letter: Pike's *The Masonry of Adoption*," *Heredom* 11 (2003): 149–157.

117. Pike in Cerza, *Anti-Masonry*, 287.

118. Rosen, *L'Ennemie Sociale*, 260–266.

119. Rosen, *Satan et Cie*, 317–318.

120. Albert Pike, "Hymns to the Gods," *Blackwood's Edinburgh Magazine* 45 (June 1839) 284:819–830; Diana Vaughan, *La restauration du paganisme: Transition décrétée par le Sanctum Regnum pour préparer l'établissement du culte public de Lucifer. Les hymnes liturgiques de Pike. Rituel du néo-paganisme* (Paris: Librairie Antimaçonnique, [1896]).

121. Cholvy, *La religion en France*, 87–90. For the Belgian situation, see Els Witte, "Pierre-Théodore Verhaegen et la franc-maçonnerie," in *Pierre-Théodore Verhaegen: L'homme, sa vie, sa légende. Bicentaire d'une naissance*, ed. Jean Stengers (Bruxelles: Université Libre de Bruxelles, 1996), 47–60.

122. Jarrige, *L'église et les Francs-Maçons dans la tourmente*, 102.

123. Introvigne, *Enquête sur le Satanisme*, 192–194.

124. Rosen, *L'Ennemie Sociale*, 348.

125. Rosen, *L'Ennemie Sociale*, 349; Ricoux, *L'existence des loges de femmes*, 91n; Margiotta, *Adriano Lemmi*, 269n, citing *Rivista della Massoneria Italiana* 10 (1879–1880), 265, colon 1–2.

126. This allegation is put into the mouth of Albert Pike in his faked *Secret Instructions* in Ricoux, *L'existence des loges de femmes*, 90, and is requoted in Margiotta, *Adriano Lemmi*, 268. Albéric Belliot in his *Manuel de Sociologie Catholique*, 387 (cited in E. Cahill, *Freemasonry and the Anti-Christian Movement*, 2nd revised ed. [Dublin: M. H. Gill and Son, 1930], 69–70) mentions a similar occurrence in Geneva on 20 September 1884 [*sic*]; possibly the same event is meant and the transference is due to a mistranslation by Cahill.

127. Dvorak, *Satanismus*, 256.

128. The complete text of the poem can be found in Zacharias, *Satanskult und Schwarze Messe*, 133–138.

129. "Il dio de' rei pontifici/ de' re cruenti"; Zacharias, *Satanskult und Schwarze Messe*, 134.

130. Zacharias, *Satanskult und Schwarze Messe*, 138. A similar connection between Satan and progress is also evident in the poem "Rehabilitación" (1878) by the Spanish poet Joaquín María Bartrina y de Aixemús, which associates Satan with revolution and the "triunfante carro del Progreso": Joaquín Maria Bartrina, *Obras poéticas* (Barcelona: Bosch, 1939), 56. I do not know whether this poet was in any way connected with Freemasonry, but Taxil suggests he was by having Pike quote this poem in his apocryphal *Secret Instructions* as lines that certainly attest to the generosity of spirit of "Brother Joaquin-Maria Bartina," but are nevertheless "en opposition directe à l'orthodoxie maçonnique": Ricoux, *L'existence des loges de femmes*, 91n; Margiotta, *Adriano Lemmi*, 269–270.

131. Hans Rheinfelder, "Giosuè Carducci und sein Werk," in *Carducci. Discorsi nel Cinquantenario della morte* (Bologna: Zanichelli, 1959), 501–524, there 508–511; Rosen, *L'Ennemie Sociale*, 349.

132. For Pike's allusions, see Ricoux, *L'existence des loges de femmes*, 91 (also quoted by Margiotta, *Adriano Lemmi*, 269, and others). The hymn mentioned is clearly Carducci's "Inno a Satana," as the note on page 91 makes clear, for it mentions as its author Enotrio Romano, which was the pseudonym initially used by Carducci when he published the poem. By the time he wrote his later publications, Taxil seems to have found out the real identity of the poet. The passage in which Walder re-cites Carducci may be found in Bataille, *Le Diable au XIXᵉ siècle*, 1:386–391 (where Bataille also describes it as "hymne recité à toutes les fêtes des hauts grades maçonniques"); Lemmi's solemnization of the poem is in Margiotta, *Le Palladisme*, 47–48.

133. Margiotta, *Le Palladisme*, 47–48.

134. Margiotta, *Adriano Lemmi*, 309.

135. Carducci to Lemmi, 15 December 1885, quoted in Introvigne, *Enquête sur le Satanisme*, 180.

136. F.i. Margiotta, *Adriano Lemmi*, 273; in Margiotta, *Le Palladisme*, 47–48, Taxil even claimed that Lemmi had raised the poem to the status of official hymn of Freemasonry, ordering it to be sung at all banquets in an "Encyclical" dated 21 January 1894. Belliot in Cahill, *Freemasonry and the Anti-Christian Movement*, 69–70, mentions that the hymn was "chanted in the crowded theatre" of Turin in 1882.

The modern historian is Massimo Introvigne, who maintains in his *Enquête sur le Satanisme*, 213, that the poem was chanted "souvent . . . , et dans plus d'un pays" at assemblies of nineteenth-century Freemasons. I wrote to Introvigne by email on 29 and 31 March 2010 to ask what his sources had been for this claim; he proved unable, however, to furnish me with any references and directed me to Professor Aldo Mola, who I tried in vain to contact during the better part of 2010. As I have not been in a position to search the Masonic archives in Italy myself, this puts me at a loss to establish whether the "Inno a Satana" was indeed ever sung by Freemasons or others. As the earliest texts I found to support this claim all originate with Taxil, this might be yet another tenacious mystification from his prolific pen: but to anyone who can show me an example of nineteenth-century sheet music of Carducci's hymn, I hereby solemnly pledge a signed copy of this publication.

137. Mario Rapisardi, *Lucifero: Poema* (Rome: Eduardo Perino, 1887), 317.

138. Rapisardi, *Lucifero*, 227 and also 271 ("E tardi!" Lucifer replies).

139. Margiotta, *Le Palladisme*, 47–70; Margiotta also quotes a (nonexistent) letter from Pike to Rapisardi in which the Anti-Pope declares that he kept his own translation of Rapisardi's poem always with him.

140. As we noted earlier, Papus also asserted that a small Italian lodge venerating Lucifer as the morning star had indeed existed. His description suggests that this occurred in an "atheist" (i.e., secularized) lodge that extended some form of symbolic devotion to Lucifer, as the veneration it offered, he claimed, "included no occult ceremonials." The whole story, I must add, seems extremely questionable to me.

141. Mola, "La Ligue antimaçonnique," 49.

142. *Mémoires d'une ex-Palladiste Parfaite Initiée, Indépendante* 2 (5 May 1897) 23:714. Pierret especially remembered the visit of a former prefect, who asked him, "Vous êtes luciférien, vous êtes franc-maçon?" and hastily departed when the Catholic publisher denied this.

143. Taxil in Weber, *Satan franc-maçon*, 174, 176. This is probably the source for the assertion that genuine Palladist groups arose after Taxil started to spread his allegations, primarily in Italy, as is claimed by Josef Dvorak in a note to Stanislaw Przybyszewski, *Die Synagoge Satans: Entstehung und Kult des Hexensabbats, des Satanismus und der Schwarzen Messe* (Berlin: Verlag Clemens Zerling, 1979), 140n.

144. Introvigne, *Enquête sur le Satanisme*, 204. Introvigne indicates as his source Pierre Geyraud, *Les religions nouvelles de Paris* (Paris: Éditions Émile-Paul frères, 1937 [=1939]), 161, who only mentions this fact in one single sentence: "C'est ainsi que le 20 septembre 1894, une secte palladiste confia le tiare de Lucifer à l'Antipape Lemmi." It is clear from the context that Geyraud here simply refers to the Taxilian story of the election of Lemmi as Palladic Grand Master, misspelling the date as "20 September 1894" instead of "20 September 1893."

145. Introvigne, *Enquête sur le Satanisme*, 200–201. Introvigne is the only notable historian devoting a few lines to these reports, in which he seems, to my opinion, much too uncritical toward Geyraud.

146. Geyraud, *Les religions nouvelles de Paris*, 158–171 ("Les Neo-Palladistes").

147. Geyraud, *Les religions nouvelles de Paris*, 161–162.

148. Geyraud, *Les religions nouvelles de Paris*, 169.

149. Serge Basset, "Une messe noire: Chez les adorateurs du prince des ténèbres," *Le Matin* 14 (27 May 1899) 5571:1–2; Frédéric Boutet, *Tableau de l'au-delà* (Paris: Gallimard, 1927), 173–175.

150. Pierre Geyraud, *Sectes & rites, petites églises, religions nouvelles, sociétés secrètes de Paris* (Paris: Éditions Émile-Paul frères, 1954), 119–128.

151. Pierre Geyraud, *Les sociétés secrètes de Paris* (Paris: Éditions Émile-Paul frères, 1938), 112–118.

152. Geyraud mentions Crowley with emphasis in connection with the T.H.L.; cf. Geyraud, *Sectes & Rites*, 128.

153. In his 1938 autobiography, *Shadows of Life and Thought*, 144, Arthur Edward Waite also mentioned the existence of (extremely marginal) neo-Palladist groups, at least according to Introvigne, *Enquête sur le satanisme*, 211. I have not been able to consult this publication myself.

154. "Au XIXe siècle, l'antisémitisme était aussi français que la baguette": Eugen Weber, *La France à la fin du XIXe siècle*, trans. Philippe Delamare (Paris: Fayard, 1986), 163.

155. The history of this myth and the real historical relations between Jews and Freemasons are treated in detail by Jacob Katz, *Jews and Freemasons in Europe, 1723–1939*, trans. Leonard Oschry (Cambridge, MA: Harvard University Press, 1970).

156. Norman Cohn, *Warrant for Genocide: The Myth of the Jewish World-Conspiracy and the Protocols of the Elders of Zion* (Harmondsworth, UK: Penguin, [1967]), 32; Bieberstein, *Die These von der Verschwörung*, 161–163. According to Bieberstein, the letter may have been fabricated at the instigation of Fouché, the head of Napoleon's Secret Police, in a deliberate attempt to hinder his superior's Jewish policies.

157. Bieberstein, *Die These von der Verschwörung*, 228; Wippermann, *Agenten des Bösen*, 52.

158. Roger Gougenot des Mousseaux, *Le Juif, le judaïsme et la judaïsation des peuples chrétiens* (Paris: Plon, 1869), 545. The description "métaphysique de Lucifer" is used by Jean Kostka, *Lucifer démasqué* (Paris: Delhomme and Briguet, [1895]), 70–71.

159. Meurin, *La Franc-Maçonnerie, Synagogue de Satan*, 9; Kostka, *Lucifer démasqué*, 70–71.

160. Gougenot des Mousseaux, *Le Juif*, xxiii.

161. A. de la Rive, *Le Juif dans la Franc-Maçonnerie* (Paris: Librairie Antimaçonnique, 1895), 18–20.

162. This identification of Jews with the ideologies of the Western Revolution and with modernity in general was a distorted reflection of genuine historical realities, as Steven Beller, *Antisemitism: A Very Short Introduction* (Oxford: Oxford University Press, 2007), 23–39, convincingly argues. The Jews had profited in both social and economic respects from the emancipatory legislation brought about by the advent of liberalism; in addition, important strands of Europe's Jewish population came to identify themselves with the political and social program of the Western Revolution (or its radical outshoots, like socialism) during the nineteenth century. The same mechanism applied to other minorities, such as Protestants in France (cf. Cholvy, *La religion en France*, 90–92) and, to a lesser extent, Roman Catholics in the Netherlands (cf. Salemink, "Politischer Katholizismus in den Niederlanden").

163. Cohn, *Warrant for Genocide*, 46.

164. Gougenot des Mousseaux, *Le Juif*, 525–530.

165. Gougenot des Mousseaux, *Le Juif*, 539.

166. Gougenot des Mousseaux, *Le Juif*, 491, 159–186.

167. Bieberstein, *Die These von der Verschwörung*, 156–169.

168. Fava, *La Franc-Maçonnerie*, 101.

169. Rive, *Le Juif dans la Franc-Maçonnerie*, 11.

170. Meurin, *La Franc-Maçonnerie, Synagogue de Satan*, 7.

171. Meurin, *La Franc-Maçonnerie, Synagogue de Satan*, 464.

172. Meurin, *La Franc-Maçonnerie, Synagogue de Satan*, 466.

173. The difference between the new, ideological antisemitism, and the older "theological" anti-Judaism and ethnic prejudices out of which it grew, is maintained by many authors; see, for instance, Beller, *Antisemitism*, particularly 1–21. The distinction between a "rassenbiologisch begründete Antisemitismus" and an "allgemeine gesellschaftpolitische [i.e., 'conspirationalist'] Antisemitismus," particularly useful to understand the Catholic case, I owe to Theo Salemink; see, for instance, his article "Die zwei Gesichter des katholischen Antisemitismus in den Niederlanden: Das 19. Jahrhundert und die Zeit zwischen den Weltkriegen im Vergleich," in *Katholischer Antisemitismus in 19. Jarhhundert: Ursachen und Traditionen im Internationalen Vergleich*, ed. Olaf Blaschke and Aram Mattioli (Zürich: Orell Füssli Verlag, 2000), 239–257.

174. Giovanni Miccoli, "Saint-Siège et antisémitisme durant le pontificat de Léon XIII," in Viaene, *The Papacy and the New World Order*, 413–433, there 422; "N'achetez pas chez les Juifs," *La Croix du Dauphiné* 3 (26 April 1895) 693:1.

175. P. Lautier, "Nouvelle infamie d'une magistrature sectaire et vénale, aux gages et sous la coupe des Franc-Maçons et des juifs régnants en haine de 'Dieu et de l'Église, des catholiques et du Pape,' " *L'Écho de Rome* 27 (5 February 1895) 29:1.

176. Miccoli, "Saint-Siège et antisémitisme," 413–415.

177. Cohn, *Warrant for Genocide*, 52.

178. Cf. *La Croix du Dauphiné* 3 (3 January 1895) 595.

179. Laurant, "Le dossier Léo Taxil," 58.

180. Weber, *Satan franc-maçon*, 122n; Introvigne, *Enquête sur le Satanisme*, 172.

181. Drumont, *Le Testament d'un Antisémite*, 408; quotes from *Les Amours secrètes de Pie IX*, 420–421.

182. Drumont, *Le Testament d'un Antisémite*, 405–407.

183. "Les maçons bourgeois, voltairiens et libres-penseurs iront rejoindre dans leur impopularité les juifs exploiteurs," wrote, for instance, J. des Apperts, "Le complot maçonnique," *La Petite Guerre* 2 (11 March 1888) 59:3–4, there 4.

184. Laurant, "Le dossier Léo Taxil," 59–60.

185. Closson, "Le *Diable au XIXe Siècle* de Léo Taxil," 316n.

186. Bataille, *Le Diable au XIXe siècle*, 1:475.

187. Bataille, *Le Diable au XIXe siècle*, 2:443–537.

188. Cf. Margiotta, *Adriano Lemmi*, esp. 189: "Maçonnerie et judaïsme sont en Italie la même chose; et si je dis seulement: en Italie, cela ne signifie pas qu'il en soit autrement ailleurs"; Margiotta, *Le Palladisme*, 78–81.

189. Letter from Taxil to Margiotta, 19 September 1895, quoted in Lorain, "L'Entreprise Diana Vaughan" (BnF, Fonds Lambert, 31/78–79).

190. Miccoli, "Saint-Siège et antisémitisme," 418.

191. Séverine, "Le pape et l'antisémitisme. Interview de Léon XIII," *Le Figaro* 38 (4 August 1892) 217:1. I follow here the analysis of Miccoli, "Saint-Siège et antisémitisme," 422.

192. Cf. Emiel Lamberts, "Political and Social Catholicism in Cisleithania [Austria] (1867–1889)," in Lamberts, *The Black International*, 298–317, there 315.

193. Miccoli, "Saint-Siège et antisémitisme," 425; also 415.

194. Miccoli, "Saint-Siège et antisémitisme," 419.

195. Miccoli, "Saint-Siège et antisémitisme," 432.

196. Miccoli, "Saint-Siège et antisémitisme," 430.

197. Gerber, *Betrug als Ende eines Betruges*, 60.

198. Introvigne, *Enquête sur le Satanisme*, 189.

199. The rumor seems to have surfaced first in an obscure publication by Gabriel de la Tour de Noé, *La vérité sur Miss Diana Vaughan la Sainte et Taxil Tartufe* (Toulouse: s.i., 1897), which I was unable to consult personally. This author was initially suspected by Introvigne, *Enquête sur le Satanisme*, 195, to be another pseudonym for Taxil, but the Italian scholar withdrew this hypothesis in a later article ("Diana Redux: Retour sur l'affaire Léo Taxil—Diana Vaughan," *Aries: Journal for the Study of Western Esotericism* 4 [2004] 1:91–97, there 93).

200. Pierret in *Mémoires d'une ex-Palladiste* 2 (10 June 1897), 24:739, 753.

201. Laurant, "Le dossier Léo Taxil," 61–62. In *La France Chrétienne* (30 April 1897) 163, Clarin de La Rive suggested that Taxil had eliminated the real Diana Vaughan; cf. Gerber, *Betrug als Ende eines Betruges*, 40.

202. Cf. Introvigne, *Enquête sur le Satanisme*, 195–197, 219–235. On 8 May 1897, De la Rive wrote a letter to the Abbé Bessonies, admonishing him not to retract completely on the point of Palladism. "Croyez-moi, une fois, L. T. n'a put tout inventer et imaginer. Il y a du vrai, beaucoup de vrai et surtout beaucoup de mensonges intentionnels dans la conférence du 19." Cited in Fry, *Leo Taxil et La Franc-Maçonnerie*, 250.

203. G. L. Nemours Godré, "La fin de Diana," *La Vérité* (21 April 1897), consulted by me in BnF, Fonds Lambert, 31/74.

204. Gaston Mery, *La vérité sur Diana Vaughan: Un complot maçonnique* (Paris: Librairie Blériot, s.a.); Cahill, *Freemasonry and the Anti-Christian Movement*, 70n. See also Rousse-Lacordaire, *Rome et les Franc-Maçons*, 128; Weber, *Satan franc-maçon*, 216n. The Paris police in one of their reports suspected the whole thing to be a publication stunt to sell new American typing machines, a hypothesis that has not been followed up by great numbers of historians. Cf. Weber, *Satan franc-maçon*, 214n.

205. Gerber, *Betrug als Ende eines Betruges*, 79, citing an interview with Huysmans in the periodical *XIXᵉ Siècle*. Cf. Billy, *Stanislas de Guaita*, 90, for a letter in which Huysmans stated similar convictions.

206. J.-K. Huysmans, *Sainte Lydwine de Schiedam* (Paris: Plon, 1901), 224–226. See also Huysmans's letters to Henry Mœller from 23 June 1900 and 9 November 1900; Mœller, "Joris-Karl Huysmans d'après sa correspondence," *Durendal: Revue Catholique d'Art et de Littérature* 7 (1910): 493–502, there 494.

207. Bois, *Le monde invisible*, 161–181.

208. In addition, mention must be made of a publication by Edith Starr Miller, "Baroness Lady Queenborough," *Occult Theocrasy*, 2 vols. (Abbeville: s.n., 1933), which did much to spread Taxilian notions in the Anglo-Saxon world. Geyraud, *Les religions nouvelles de Paris*, 158–161, and *Sectes & Rites*, 120–121, also uncritically reproduce much material from Taxil, referring to Jules Bois as their source.

209. Cf. http://gestadei.bb-fr.com/actualites-f1/quand-le-plan-pike-est-applique-a-la-lettre-t586.htm, accessed 30 November 2010, where Bataille's *Le Diable au XIXe Siècle* is quoted; see also Introvigne, "Diana Redux."

Evangelical references to Pike's Luciferian instructions can be found in several of the infamous Chick tracts, for instance, Jack T. Chick, *Spellbound?* (Ontario: Chick, 1978), 26, where Lady Queensborough's *Occult Theocrasy* is given as a source. See also the references in the next note.

An example of Islamist references to Taxil can be found in the documentary *The Dark History of Satanism*, spread by the organization of the Turkish fundamentalist author Harun Yahya (accessed at http://www.youtube.com/watch?v=FtpL_6zQ-K4 on 30 November 2010; see esp. 4:30–4:45).

210. Jack T. Chick, *The Curse of Baphomet* (Ontario: Chick, 1991), [8], [11]. Before 1991, this footnote referred to "*The Freemason* (The organ of English Freemasonry), 19th January 1935," where Pike's apocryphal instructions had been cited with approbation according to a tenacious (but incorrect) fundamentalist legend (cf. "Quelques erreurs des anti-maçons," http://onvousment.free.fr/antimacons.htm, accessed 19 July 2012). *The Unwelcome Guest* (Ontario: Chick,

2006) includes an identical page on Freemasonry, but here the reference in the footnote is changed to a book by Bill Schnoebelen.

211. Jarrige, *L'église et les Francs-Maçons dans la tourmente*, 261.

212. Jarrige, *L'église et les Francs-Maçons dans la tourmente*, 202. On the *Action Française*, see Eugen Weber, *Action Française. Royalism and Reaction in Twentieth Century France* (Stanford, CA: Stanford University Press, 1962), esp. 72, 200. For clarity's sake: Drumont was a believing (if troubled) Roman Catholic, and the Action Française recruited its following in large measure among Roman Catholics and pursued a Franco-Catholic agenda. Yet neither was a "confessional party" in the strict sense of the word and both operated independently from Rome or the hierarchy; Action Française, as a matter of fact, eventually incurred an interdict by the Vatican.

Another ardent believer in the Judeo-Masonic-Communist plot was the Spanish dictator Francisco Franco, who ordered Freemasons to be summarily shot during the Spanish Civil War and later wrote a series of articles on the Masonic danger that were published, under the pseudonym Jakim Boor, as *Masonería* (Madrid: Grafica Valera, 1952). See José A. Ferrer Benimeli, "L'antimaçonnisme en Espagne et en Amérique latine," in *Les courants antimaçonniques hier et aujourd'hui*, ed. Alain Dierkens, Problèmes d'histoire des religions 4 (Bruxelles: Éditions de l'Université de Bruxelles, 1993), 77–86, there 80–83; and Matthew Scanlan, "Freemasonry and the Spanish Civil War," *Freemasonry Today* (2004): 30.

213. Adolf Hitler, *Mein Kampf*, trans. James Murphy (Mumbai: Embassy Book Distributions, 2005), 58, 627. For anti-Masonism, see pp. 295–296; for Hitler's own description of how he became acquainted with antisemitic ideas, see p. 51. Hitler often mentioned Karl Lueger as an inspiration for his political program. That National Socialist ideas in this respect were rooted in the earlier conspiracy theories of reactionary Catholic authors is made plausible by both Cohn, *Warrant for Genocide*, 25–45, 230, and Bieberstein, *Die These von der Verschwörung*, 189–232. For Hitler's own theological convictions, see Rainer Bucher, *Hitlers Theologie* (Würzburg: Echter, 2008).

214. Andrey, "La Croisade antimaçonnique (XIXe–XXe siècles)," 183; Closson, "Le *Diable au XIXe Siècle* de Léo Taxil," 332.

215. Cited in Miccoli, "Saint-Siège et antisémitisme," 420.

INTERMEZZO 3

1. Griffiths, *The Reactionary Revolution*, 124–125. The most prominent example of an academic historian supporting this thesis is, once more, Massimo Introvigne, who quotes Griffiths with acquiescence in *Enquête sur le satanisme*, 100. Here again, Introvigne suggests the existence of an underground tradition of Satanism that existed long before Huysmans somehow discovered it and continued well into the twentieth century. See, for instance, his remark about Huysmans's Black Mass on p. 137 (" . . . il faut admettre . . . qu'elle est conforme à la tradition du satanisme qui la précède (depuis la procès La Voisin) et du satanisme qui la suivra"), and about Satanism after 1897 on p. 209 ("Il y a encore, cachés quelque part, des satanistes héritiers de la tradition que Huysmans avait en quelque sorte eu l'occasion de connaître"). It is clear from the substance of these statements that Huysmans (and consorts) is the only viable source for Introvigne. See also Introvigne's article "Satanism," in Hanegraaf, *Dictionary of Gnosis and Western Esotericism*, 2:1035: "The Satanists of the 1880s were not invented by Huysmans; they already existed, although they had admittedly only a few members in two or three small cults operating in France and Belgium."

For some rather random examples of contemporary reflections attesting to the deep impact of the myth of fin de siècle Satanism, see the memoirs of the Dutch actress Jeanne Schaik, who presents Huysmans's Satanism almost as a personally experienced reality (with reference, of course, to priests who have crosses tattooed on their foot soles and who feed hosts to white mice; Jeanne van Schaik-Willing, *Dwaaltocht: Een stukje eigen leven* ['s Gravenhage: Nijgh and Van Ditmar, 1977], 82–85), or the travelogue of the well-known Dutch Protestant politician Abraham Kuyper, *Om de Oude Wereldzee* (Amsterdam: Van Holkema and Warendorf, 1907), 1:26: "wat van de satanistische orgieën der zwarte en blanke Mis nu nog in Europa voortkruipt, levert voldingend bewijs voor het doodelijk gevaar, waarmee de Oostersche, en nader Babylonisch-Semitische ontaarding op dit punt telkens weer het Westen bedreigt." Cf. Bel, "Satan in Holland," 34n.

2. As is argued by Schmidt, *Satanismus*, 80–81. It may be added, however, that more sober contemporary authors do not mention Satanism in their overview of the nineteenth-century religious landscape; it is not included, for instance, in the two volumes by Alexandre Erdan, *La France mystique: Tableau des excentricités religieuse de ces temps* (Amsterdam: H. C. Meijer, 1858).

3. As mentioned, my account of Przybyszewski is mainly based on Per Faxneld, "Witches, Anarchism, and Evolutionism: Stanislaw Przybyszewski's Fin-de-siècle Satanism and the Demonic Feminine," in *The Devil's Party: Satanism in Modernity*, ed. Per Faxneld and Jesper Petersen (Oxford: Oxford University Press, 2012), 53–77, and the same author's *Satanic Feminism*, 426–436, with additional insights from Josef Dvorak's introduction to Stanislaw Przybyszewski, *Die Synagoge Satans: Entstehung und Kult des Hexensabbats, des Satanismus und der Schwarzen Messe* (Berlin: Verlag Clemens Zerling, 1979).

4. Przybyszewski describes Huysmans as "eine Zeitlang Herr über meine Seele" in his memoirs and mentions *Certains* and *Là-Bas* with emphasis; see Stanislaw Przybyszewski, *Ferne komm ich her . . . : Erinnerungen an Berlin und Krakau*, trans. Roswitha Matwin-Buschmann, Studienausgabe Werke, Aufzeichnungen und ausgewählte Briefe, 7 (Paderborn: Igel Verlag, 1994), 107, and Dvorak in Przybyszewski, *Die Synagoge Satans*, 21–22. Huysmans's influence on Przybyszewski can be made tangible in many ways: like the French writer, for instance, Przybyszewski also wrote an essay on Rops (cf. Faxneld, "Witches, Anarchism, and Evolutionism," 71–72; the quotations by Faxneld suggest that Przybyszewski was merely paraphrasing Huysmans in his treatment of the Belgian artist).

5. Stanislaw Przybyszewski, *Homo Sapiens (Unter Bord. Unterwegs. Im Malstrom). Satans Kinder*, Studienausgabe Werke, Aufzeichnungen und ausgewählte Briefe, 8 (Paderborn: Igel Verlag, 1993), 321–322.

6. Przybyszewski, *Satans Kinder*, 351. Compare also 322: "Alle, die verzweifelt sind, die Angst haben, deren Gewissen beladen ist . . ."

7. Przybyszewski, *Satans Kinder*, 322–323. Compare Gordon's fulminations against the idea of "Menschheit" on p. 339.

8. Faxneld, "Witches, Anarchism, and Evolutionism," 55; in his autobiographical memoirs, for instance, Przybyszewski explicitly attests to his love and compassion for "den armen, enterbten Kindern Satans" in similar terms as in his novel—see Przybyszewski, *Ferne komm ich her*, 75.

9. Przybyszewski, *Die Synagoge Satans*. The book was actually the compilation of a series of articles Przybyszewski had published in 1897.

10. Bois's book (or rather Huysmans's introduction to it) is mentioned explicitly on p. 118. I think that Bois's book was Przybyszewski's direct source for the composition of *Die Synagoge Satans*, and not Michelet's *Sorcière*, as Faxneld suggests. However, the difference is largely academic, as Bois extensively paraphrases Michelet; moreover, it is probable that Przybyszewski consulted both works. For some historic episodes, Przybyszewski utilized other publications as well: he mentions G. Legué's *Médecins et empoissonneurs au xviiᵉ siècle* (Paris: Bibliothèque-Charpentier, 1895), as his source of information for the Affair of the Poisons, although without adopting this author's antisemitic reading of historic Satanism.

11. Przybyszewski, *Die Synagoge Satans*, 30, 33; compare 72.

12. Przybyszewski, *Die Synagoge Satans*, 72.

13. Przybyszewski, *Die Synagoge Satans*, 83, 111. In his memoirs, Przybyszewski linked his continuing fascination with witches with traumatic experiences during his childhood in Poland involving a servant girl living in his parents' household rumored to be an "ulicka" (witch); see Przybyszewski, *Ferne komm ich her*, 188–193.

14. Przybyszewski, *Die Synagoge Satans*, 118n.

15. Przybyszewski, *Die Synagoge Satans*, 169.

16. Faxneld, "Witches, Anarchism, and Evolutionism," 74.

17. Przybyszewski, *Die Synagoge Satans*, 71. In a later work, Bois would also list Nietzsche among the authors who had prepared the way for "modern" Satanism; cf. his *Monde invisible*, 176.

18. See, for instance, his adulatory description of his visit to the old and demented Nietzsche in Przybyszewski, *Ferne komm ich her*, 149.

19. See, for instance, the preface to Stanislaw Przybyszewski, *Totenmesse* (http://gutenberg. spiegel.de/buch/2799/1, accessed 11 August 2012).

20. Przybyszewski, *Totenmesse*, chapter 1. Faxneld already points out the striking similarities between Przybyszewski's and Freud's ideas in these and other respects.

21. Faxneld, "Witches, Anarchism, and Evolutionism," 63.

22. Faxneld, "Witches, Anarchism, and Evolutionism," 59.

23. Przybyszewski, *Die Synagoge Satans*, 123, 119.

24. Przybyszewski, *Die Synagoge Satans*, 125: "Das ist der einzige Satan Paraklet: ennivrez-vous." This ambiguous but ultimately dismissive attitude toward the "natural instincts" is reflected in his attitude toward women, whom he sees, in common with most of his contemporaries, as essentially instinctive creatures and thus harmful to man's spiritual evolution. I am not convinced by Faxneld's ingenious assumption that, because of the fact that he may have been a Satanist, Przybyszewski's many misogynist utterances must be read as "semantic inversions" that are really intended as compliments. Faxneld himself also notes that "an ambivalent attitude towards women is present throughout Przybyszewski's oeuvre, and some of his descriptions of the gruesome crimes of medieval witches are hardly intended as eulogy" ("Witches, Anarchism, and Evolutionism," 75).

25. Przybyszewski, *Ferne komm ich her*, 222.

26. Przybyszewski, *Ferne komm ich her*, 223. Juliusz Słowacki (1809–1849) was a Polish Romantic poet who had become much *en vogue* in Poland among Przybyszewski's generation. Przybyszewski here is doubtlessly alluding to "The Genesis of the Spirit," a philosophical and autobiographical prose poem that had been received in a vision by the Polish bard during a stay in Bretagne in 1841 (a complete French translation by Stéphane Danysz may be found at http:// slowacki.chez.com/, accessed by me on 11 August 2012). The text told about the evolution of

the spirit or soul out of a succession of anorganic and organic modes of being. This evolution-ist aspect must have appealed to Przybyszewski; but contrary to what the latter suggests in his memoirs, Słowacki did not describe this evolution as a purely natural process; rather, the human spirit was an emanation of the deity, and the principle of sacrifice, as exemplified in Jesus, was the great lever by which humanity could return to the divine, enabling it to evolve in a still more spiritual and supernatural direction. "The Genesis of the Spirit" was the obvious model for Przybyszewski's *Totenmesse*—comparing the two texts is very instructive regarding the similar-ities and differences between the Romantics and the fin de siècle avant-garde.

27. Przybyszewski, *Totenmesse*, chapter 1.

28. Przybyszewski, *Ferne komm ich her*, 225.

29. Przybyszewski, *Ferne komm ich her*, 226.

30. Przybyszewski, *Ferne komm ich her*, 225–227.

31. Per Faxneld, "The Strange Case of Ben Kadosh: A Luciferian Pamphlet from 1906 and Its Current Renaissance," *Aries: Journal for the Study of Western Esotericism* 11 (2011) 1:1–22, there 2–3. Faxneld's article and his later, slightly more extended article " 'In communication with the powers of darkness': Satanism in Turn-of-the-Century Denmark, and Its Use as a Legitimating Device in Present-day Esotericism," in *Occultism in a Global Perspective*, ed. Henrik Bogdan and Gordan Djurdjevi (Durham, UK: Acumen, 2013), 57–77, are about the only sources of information on Kadosh in a non-Scandinavian language available, and I have thus relied almost exclusively on Faxneld's work here. According to Faxneld, an English translation of Kadosh's pamphlet appeared in the independent Satanist journal *The Fenris Wolf* in 1993 (Fr. GCLO, "Lucifer-Hiram," 72–97): unfortunately, I was unable to consult this periodical.

32. Faxneld, "Strange Case of Ben Kadosh," 9.

33. Faxneld, "Strange Case of Ben Kadosh," 5, and " 'In communication with the powers of darkness,' " 62–63.

34. Faxneld, "Strange Case of Ben Kadosh," 3.

35. Faxneld, "Strange Case of Ben Kadosh," 3, 7.

36. Faxneld, "Strange Case of Ben Kadosh," 4.

37. Curiously enough, a "neo-Luciferian Church" claiming Ben Kadosh as its predecessor was established in Denmark in 2005. This would arguably make it a form of neo-neo-Palladism. In practice, however, the ideas of Aleister Crowley seem to play a dominant role in the group's the-ology or philosophy, although spurious references to Albert Pike can be found in their creedal statements. Membership seems to be restricted to ten to twenty people. See Faxneld, "Strange Case of Ben Kadosh," 13–21.

38. Concerning rumors of "bohemian Satanism," see Przybyszewski, *Ferne komm ich her*, 100 ("sie hielten unmenschliche 'schwarze Messen' ab. Es fehlte nicht viel, und man hätte für sicher ausgegeben, daß in diesen Zirkeln armer Bohèmiens all das vorging, was Minucius Felix über die ersten Christen erzählt hat!"), 134 ("die lästerlichen 'Satansmessen' . . . welche die nämliche Boheme angeblich feierte"); regarding the rumors about his own Satanism, ibid., 221–222 ("Dieser Satanismus machte meinen Namen überall berühmt oder brachte ihn vielmehr durch unglaubliche Klatschgeschichten in Verruf. Einmal macht man mich zum Hierophanten einer satanistischen oder palladistischen Sekte, ich stand ja angeblich in engen Beziehung zu Miss Diana Vaughan und Leo Taxil"). Cf. also Faxneld, "Witches, Anarchism, and Evolutionism," 53–54.

39. The novel was Arthur Landsberger's *Wie Hilde Simon mit Gott und der Teufel kämpfte: Der Roman einer Berlinerin* (1910); I owe this information to Gabriela Matuszak, *"Der geniale Pole"? Stanislaw Przybyszewski in Deutschland (1892–1992)*, trans. Dietrich Scholze (Paderborn: Igel Verlag, 1996), 125. In his memoirs, Przybyszewski identifies this author incorrectly as [Marcus] Landau (Przybyszewski, *Ferne komm ich her*, 222).

40. A more general mechanism of attribution and identification may have been involved as well, as Decandentism as a cultural current was frequently equated with Satanism by its critics, most prominently by Max Nordau in his 1892 book *Entartung*. Cf. Faxneld, *Satanic Feminism*, 364–368, and his more general treatment of Decadentism on pp. 349–438.

41. Faxneld, "Strange Case of Ben Kadosh," 9. There is a slight possibility that three or four members of an informal occult circle that Hansen co-organized may have shared his ideas (cf. Faxneld, "Strange Case of Ben Kadosh," 11), but this remains to be proven.

42. C. C. M., "Luciferians and Freemasonry," *Light: A Journal of Psychical, Occult, and Mystical Research* 15 (2 November 1895) 773:534–535. I already cited the journalist Émile Dehau: "L'État laïque n'a pas davantage à proscrire, comme certains le demandent, un culte nouveau si ses adhérents respectent les lois de la société," he wrote in his article "Le culte de Lucifer" (*Charente* [13 April 1895], consulted by me in BnF, Fonds Lambert, 26//24).

43. Letter by Papus quoted in Q. V., "Le Diable au XIXme Siècle," *Light* 16 (16 May 1896) 801:231–232, there 231. Cf. also the suggestive research by Per Faxneld on real-life imitators of Huysmans's Chantelouve in *Satanic Feminism*, 419–426, and his section on "devilish jewelry" in ibid., 555–564.

44. C. C. M., "Luciferians and Freemasonry," 534–535. "Lucifer is another name for Light-bearer; and the world needs more light": another occultist reacted on this statement—Africanus Theosophus, "Luciferians and Freemasonry," *Light* 15 (16 November 1895) 775:557–558, there 558.

45. Quoted in Olbrich, *Die Freimaurer im deutschen Volksglauben*, 70–71, who mentions as its original source a Masonic periodical from 1914.

46. Cf. the way how Jules Bois connects Luciferianism, "cet évangile de New-York," to modern technology in *Monde invisible*, 172–173, 179: "Et nous avons le 'Dieu Bon' [Lucifer], dernier genre, c'est-à-dire le Dieu de toutes les licences, le dieu américain, qui porte dans ses bras non pas la rénovation des âmes par l'épreuve et les magnifiques devoirs du dévouement, mais les présents industriels, le téléphote, le télégraphe avec ou sans fil, le téléphone, les explosifs les plus formidables, l'automobile, le machinisme perfectionné, et jusqu'aux tables tournantes, jusqu'au la télépathie, le meilleur onguent et le meilleur fantôme! Il nous fallait le dieu compatissant à nos exigences nouvelles, le dieu du confort, le dieu de l'électricité et de la réclame."

47. This "coupling of moralization and fascination" is also noted as "a mainstay of Decadent writing" by Faxneld, *Satanic Feminism*, 469.

48. Weber, *La France à la fin du XIXe siècle*, 143.

49. Lapidoth, *Goëtia*, 2:68: "Dat is 'eind-eeuwsch,' mijn waarde."

50. See again Bois, *Monde invisible*, 174: "Une religion nouvelle est née, d'une part; c'est le Luciférisme; de l'autre un parti politique, l'Anarchie. Fruits amers d'un arbre cinéraire!"

51. *L'Assiette au beurre—messes noires* (12 December 1903) 141:[15–16]. The issue was mostly devoted to "Satanism" in a metaphorical sense, predominantly in the form of the tyranny of money. The poem and picture are also reproduced in Zacharias, *Satanskult und Schwarze Messe*, 156, Tafel 35.

The background of the issue and the drawing was a notorious affair involving the decadent nobleman Jacques d'Adelswärd-Fersen, who was arrested in 1903 by the Parisian police on suspicion of indecent conduct with minors and offending the public decency. As it turned out, he had staged homoerotic events for a selected circle of guests in his apartment at 18 Avenue Friedland, which the ever-eager press soon described as "Black Masses." This interpretation probably had no basis in fact: according to Fersen himself, these soirées consisted of a tableau of a seminude fourteen-year-old boy flanked by a flower arrangement and a human skull while the poem "La Mort des amants" from *Les Fleurs du Mal* was recited (cf. Will H. L. Ogrinc, "Frère Jacques: A Shrine to Love and Sorrow. Jacques d'Adelswärd-Fersen (1880–1923)," semgai.free. fr/doc_et_pdf?Fersen-engels.pdf, 2006, downloaded 29 July 2014, 20). Fersen's trysts with rent boys and adolescent pupils from high-class *lycées* occurred in private and involved no Satanism. Apparently the shadow of Huysmans's *Là-Bas* still loomed large over the public consciousness, although both he and Jules Bois issued statements adamantly denying that the affair had anything to do with "real" Satanism (cf. Jean-Claude Féray in his postface to M. de Fersen, *Messes Noires: Lord Lyllian*, Question de Genre 62 [Montpellier, France: GayKitchCamp, 2011], 146n, who refers to articles in *La Presse* dated 12 and 18 July 1903). Féray suggests that the misconception may also have been stimulated by the coincidence that self-styled occultism expert Gabriel Legué had been very active in the press to promote his recent book on the Black Mass, a highly sensationalist and antisemite work, to judge by an earlier title of this author on the same subject I consulted (see note 10).

After serving his prison sentence, Fersen published his own account of the affair in a thinly veiled autobiographical novel entitled *Messes Noires: Lord Lyllian*, an antihomosexual homoerotic memoir such as only the fin de siècle could produce. In a typical twist that we have seen repeated many times in our history of Satanism, this work actually contains a passage in which Satan is lauded as the embodiment of fleshly instincts and vital self, described by Faxneld as "noteworthy for fitting well with contemporary ideas about Satan as a saviour from Christian oppression of all things carnal" (Faxneld, *Satanic Feminism*, 452; cf. Fersen, *Messes Noires*, 107 [chapter XVIII]). It must be noted that this *laudatio* is put into the mouth of a minor protagonist of the novel and does not represent the views of its author. Fersen's later experiments with (homoerotic) ritual were purely in a pseudo-Classical, paganist vein.

The connection with the Fersen affair was pointed out to me by Per Faxneld, *Satanic Feminism*, 450–452, 455n. For a thorough treatment of Fersen and the "Black Mass" scandal based on primary sources, consult Ogrinc, "Frère Jacques," especially pp. 9–22.

52. Austin De Croze, *Calendrier Magique* (Paris: L'Art Nouveau, 1895), 19 [August]; consulted on http://fantastic.library.cornell.edu/imagerecord.php?record=236, accessed 17 August 2012.

53. Roland Brevannes, *Les Messes Noires: Reconstruction dramatique en III parties et IV tableaux. Donnée au Théâtre de la Bodinière, le 17 février 1904* (s.l., s.i. s.a.). According to the title page, the performance of the play had been accompanied by music composed by René Brancour.

54. Brevannes, *Les Messes Noires*, 25. Faxneld, *Satanic Feminism*, 455n, rightly points out that this depiction of the Black Mass was probably inspired by the Fersen affair as well (see note 51). The mention of the Pantheon may have been inspired by Bois, *Petits religions*, 104, who also talks about Black Masses held "non loin du Panthéon" (unfortunately without any further specification).

CHAPTER 7: PATHS INTO THE TWENTIETH CENTURY

1. For twentieth-century Satanism, Introvigne, *Enquête sur le satanisme*, 257–309, remains a valuable entrance; shorter introductions can be found in Drury, *Stealing Fire from Heaven*, 205–223, and La Fontaine, "Satanism and Satanic Mythology." Important recent scholarship on current religious Satanism has been assembled in the *Social Compass* issue of December 2009 (56/ 4) and the volumes *Contemporary Religious Satanism: A Critical Anthology*, ed. Jesper Aagaard Petersen (Farnham: Ashgate, 2009), and Faxneld and Petersen, *Devil's Party*. More detailed reference to these and other articles will be made at the appropriate places.

An impartial scholarly monograph of Anton LaVey and the Church of Satan is still lacking. Blanche Barton's *The Church of Satan: A History of the World's Most Notorious Religion* (New York: Hell's Kitchen, 1990) and *The Secret Life of a Satanist: The Authorized Biography of Anton LaVey* (London: Mondo, 1992) are openly hagiographic and follow LaVey uncritically; they are mainly interesting as a source for the image LaVey wanted to present and because of the fact the latter is quoted at length, sometimes for pages. Burton H. Wolfe's e-book *The Black Pope: The Authentic Biography of Anton Szandor LaVey* (s.l.: s.n., 2008) is very informative, but strangely partial at times, especially when the more recent history of the Church of Satan is concerned. Michael A. Aquino's behemothlike e-book *The Church of Satan* (San Francisco: s.n., 2009) is also far from an impartial account, given the history of Aquino and LaVey, which will be recounted in the next chapter. It is an invaluable source, however, for internal correspondence within the Church of Satan and hard-to-find articles from Church of Satan periodicals, and the quoted material strikes me as completely authentic. In addition, Lawrence Wright's long article "Anton LaVey: Sympathy for the Devil" must be mentioned, which was originally published in *Rolling Stone* and included in Wright's *Saints and Sinners* (New York: Vintage, 1995), 121–156, as it was the first journalistic publication to debunk a number of LaVey's mystifications. Also interesting is Marco Pasi, "Dieu du désir, dieu de la raison (Le Diable en Californie dans les années soixante)," in *Le Diable*, ed. Jean-Claude Aguerre, Jean Céard, Antoine Faivre, and others (Paris: Éditions Dervy, 1998), 87–98. Apart from these and other scholarly publications, I have reverted again and again to the published writings of LaVey himself, references to which can be found in later footnotes or the bibliography.

2. I base my description on the eyewitness account in Wolfe, *Black Pope*, 6–16. The paleness of LaVey is remarked upon by, among others, Susan Atkins (with Bob Slosser), in *Child of Satan, Child of God* (Plainfield, NJ: Logos International 1977), 51. A description of a Church of Satan ritual forms a staple ingredient, it seems, of works on modern religious Satanism: see Barton, *Church of Satan*, 1–5; Introvigne, *Enquête sur le satanisme*, 269–270; and Edward J. Moody, "Magical Therapy: An Anthropological Investigation of Contemporary Satanism," in *Religious Movements in Contemporary America*, ed. Irving I. Zaretsky and Mark P. Leone (Princeton, NJ: Princeton University Press, 1974), 355–382. I have adhered to this tradition.

3. That LaVey's identification with the "villain" was quite conscious can be surmised from passages from Anton Szandor LaVey, *The Satanic Rituals* (New York: Avon, 1972), 11, or his later essay "Ravings from Tartarus," which is included in Anton Szandor LaVey, *The Devil's Notebook* (Los Angeles: Feral House, 1992), there 38. LaVey was familiar with sociological theories about the "power of stigma" as expounded by Erving Goffman in *Stigma: Notes on the Management of Spoiled Identity* (New York: Jason Aronson, 1973). The scholar of religion Randall H. Alfred noted in 1976 that "LaVey is familiar with and admires the works of sociologist Erving Goffman,

and this, along with his comments on the Devil as a symbol, would indicate that the conversion of stigma to charisma is a deliberate undertaking. As the first of the above-ground Satanists, he has a treasure of stored stigma at his disposal, although he must share some of it with witches now publicly practicing the less-disapproved white magic." Alfred, "The Church of Satan," in *The New Religious Consciousness*, ed. Charles Y. Glock and Robert N. Bellah (Berkeley: University of California Press, 1976), 180–202, there 194. Goffman's book is mentioned in the reading list of LaVey's *The Satanic Witch* (Los Angeles: Feral House, 2003; first published as *The Compleat Witch, or What to Do When Virtue Fails* in 1970), 270.

4. The exact version of the pentagram used by the Church of Satan, with the goat head inserted and the Hebrew characters for Leviathan within its five points, was taken by LaVey from Maurice Bessy, *A Pictorial History of Magic and the Supernatural*, trans. Margaret Crosland and Allan Daventry (London: Spring, 1964), where it is featured on page 198 and in relief on the front cover. The earliest source for this particular version of the pentagram that I have encountered is in Guaita, *Le Serpent de la Genèse*, 2:417 ("Le bon et le mauvais Pentagramme").

5. Legué is mentioned in LaVey's *Satanic Rituals*, 34.

6. Lavey, *Satanic Rituals*, 48–51.

7. Barton, *Secret Life of a Satanist*, 9–10.

8. LaVey's mystifications are still reproduced in academic works like Jean La Fontaine, "Satanism and Satanic Mythology," in *Witchcraft and Magic in Europe, Volume 6: The Twentieth Century*, ed. Willem de Blécourt, R. Hutton, and J. La Fontaine (London: Athlone, 1999), 81–140, and in the entry on LaVey in Lewis, *Satanism Today*, 144–147 (however, the latter was written by Peter Gilmore, the current High Priest of the Church of Satan). Bill Ellis, *Raising the Devil: Satanism, New Religions, and the Media* (Lexington: University Press of Kentucky, 2000), 169, and James T. Richardson, Joel Best, and David Bromley, "Satanism as a Social Problem," in *The Satanism Scare*, ed. James T. Richardson, Joel Best, and David G. Bromley (New York: Aldine de Gruyter, 1991), 3–17, there 9, still mention LaVey's apocryphal role as a consultant for Roman Polanski's horror movie *Rosemary's Baby*. Not surprisingly, Arthur Lyons's books on Satanism both repeat LaVey's autobiographical fantasies as well.

9. Wolfe, *Black Pope*, 17, shows a reproduction of LaVey's original certificate of birth.

10. In a *Cloven Hoof* article from September 1971, LaVey claimed he had started to read *grimoires* "at the tender age of twelve"; see Aquino, *Church of Satan*, 143.

11. Barton, *Secret Life of a Satanist*, 66.

12. Barton, *Secret Life of a Satanist*, 54.

13. Wolfe, *Black Pope*, 52–55.

14. Anton LaVey, "Letters from the Devil," *National Insider* (15 February 1970), 15; cf. the reprint in Anton LaVey, *Letters from the Devil* (s.l.: Underworld Amusements, 2010), [13].

15. Anton Szandor LaVey, *The Satanic Bible* (New York: Avon, 1969), 54–55.

16. LaVey, *Satanic Bible*, 25.

17. James R. Lewis, "Infernal Legitimacy," in *Contemporary Religious Satanism: A Critical Anthology*, ed. Jesper Aagaard Petersen (Farnham, UK: Ashgate, 2009), 41–58, there 51. Some of these translations were pirate editions. In 1991, 618,000 copies of the English-language edition had been sold.

On the genesis of *The Satanic Bible*, see ibid., 48–50, and Anton Szandor LaVey, "To: All Doomsayers, Head-Shakers, Hand-Wringers, Worrywarts, Satanophobes, Identity Christers,

Survivor Counselors, Academia Nuts, and Assorted Tremblers," a *Cloven Hoof* editorial reprinted in LaVey's *Satan Speaks!* (Los Angeles: Feral House, 1998), 4–7, there 5.

18. Robert Wuthnow, *The Restructuring of American Religion: Society and Faith since World War II* (Princeton, NJ: Princeton University Press 1988), 17. On the contrasting paths of secularization of Western Europe and the United States, see Peter Berger, Grace Davie, and Effie Fokas, *Religious America, Secular Europe? A Theme and Variations* (Aldershot, UK: Ashgate, 2008).

19. Wuthnow, *Restructuring of American Religion*, 159.

20. The term "occulture" has been coined by Christopher Partridge to denote the increasing absorption of esoteric and/or occult elements within modern popular culture. See his book *The Re-Enchantment of the West. Volume I: Alternative Spiritualities, Sacralization, Popular Culture, and Occulture* (London: T&T Clark, 2004), and his article "Occulture Is Ordinary," in *Contemporary Esotericism*, ed. Egil Asprem and Kennet Granholm (Sheffield, UK: Equinox, 2013), 113–133.

21. LaVey, *Satanic Rituals*, 11.

22. Cf. Moody, "Magical Therapy," 355–382.

23. LaVey, *Satanic Bible*, 67.

24. LaVey, *Satanic Bible*, 33–34; Lyons, *Second Coming*, 185.

25. Susan Roberts, *Witches U.S.A.* (New York: Dell, 1971), 228.

26. Barton, *Secret Life of a Satanist*, 107, 195–199.

27. LaVey, *Letters from the Devil*, [13]; Barton, *Secret Life of a Satanist*, 74.

28. A list of cases without further corroboration or documentation could be quite extensive. Inside rumors about "diabolical" festivities in German avant-garde circles around Karl Wolfskehl circulated in the early years of the twentieth century (cf. Rose Carol Washton Long, *Kandinsky: The Development of an Abstract Style* [Oxford: Clarendon, 1980], 18–19), although their descriptions rather point to some kind of neopagan festivity. Pierre Geyraud gives an undated and unconfirmed account of a former priest ("M. G.") who celebrated Black Masses in his *Les petites églises de Paris* (Paris: Éditions Émile-Paul frères, 1937), 133–143. An obscure Dutch author claimed to have contacted a group of Interbellum German Satanists basing their doctrine upon Johann Benjamin Erhard's *Apologie des Teufels* (Marcus van Praag, *Pantheïstisch pleidooi* [Weesp, the Netherlands: s.i., 1976], 154–155. I contacted the next of kin of the late Van Praag, yet no documents remained to solidify his claims—personal message from Oliver van Praag, 4 May 2011).

29. On Naglowska and her order, cf. Introvigne, *Enquête sur le Satanisme*, 238–248; Marc Pluquet, *La Sophiale: Maria de Naglowska. Sa vie. Son œuvre* (Paris: Ordo Templi Orientalis, 1993); Geyraud, *Petites églises de Paris*, 144–153; Hans Thomas Hakl, "The Theory and Practice of Sexual Magic, Exemplified by Four Magical Groups in the Early Twentieth Century," in *Hidden Intercourse: Eros and Sexuality in the History of Western Esotericism*, ed. Wouter J. Hanegraaff and Jeffrey J. Kripal (Leiden: Brill, 2008), 445–478.

30. *La Flèche: Organe de action magique* 1 (15 October 1930), 1:1; Pluquet, *La Sophiale*, unpaginated introduction. Curiously, the painter Vincent van Gogh had already referred to the "Esprit Sain" in much the same way, at least according to an account that Gauguin published in 1894; cf. Paul Gauguin, "Natures mortes," reprinted in Paul Gauguin, *Sous deux latitudes, suivi de Natures mortes* (Paris: L'Échoppe, 2000), 17–21.

31. Pluquet, *La Sophiale*, 43–47.

32. Maria de Naglowska, *La Lumière du Sexe: Rituel d'initiation satanique, selon la doctrine du Troisième Terme de la Trinité* (Montperoux, France: Ordo Templi Orientis, Oasis Sous les Étoiles, 1993), 103.

33. Naglowska, *Lumière du Sexe*, 10.

34. Naglowska, *Lumière du Sexe*, 34.

35. Naglowska, *Lumière du Sexe*, 50–55.

36. Naglowska, *Lumière du Sexe*, 56.

37. Naglowska, *Lumière du Sexe*, 112–113.

38. Geyraud, *Petites églises de Paris*, 148–151. Despite the strong reminiscences of Christian millennialism, Naglowska did not think her new age was an everlasting finale of history. The Age of Woman would eventually make place once more for the Age of the Father, and this in turn for that of the Son, and so on in an eternal triangular cycle.

39. Medway, *Lure of the Sinister*, 20, still reproduces the rumor that Naglowska disappeared during World War II, presumably by the hands of the Nazis.

40. My account of the Fraternitas Saturni is based on Hans Thomas Hakl, "The Magical Order of the Fraternitas Saturni," in *Occultism in a Global Perspective*, ed. Henrik Bogdan and Gordan Djurdjevi (Durham, UK: Acumen, 2013), 37–55. Some scholarly and a considerable amount of unscholarly literature has been published on the order in German, which shortage of time has prevented me from consulting.

41. Grosche published these words in 1953 under his magical name Gregor A. Gregorius in the Brotherhood's *Blätter für angewandte okkulte Lebenskunst*; English translation quoted from Hakl, "Magical Order of the Fraternitas Saturni," 45–46.

42. Grosche, in Hakl, "Magical Order of the Fraternitas Saturni," 46.

43. On Crowley and de Fraternitas Saturni, cf. Richard Kaczynski, *Perdurabo: The Life of Aleister Crowley* (Berkeley, CA: North Atlantic, 2010), 419–420.

44. An English translation of the Missae Fraternitas Saturni was published by Stephen Flowers in an appendix to his book *Fire and Ice: Magical Teachings of Germany's Greatest Secret Occult Order* and can be found in various places on the Internet, for instance, on http://www.american-buddha.com/nazi.fireiceflower.app.htm, which I consulted on 11 December 2014.

45. The diminishing importance of Lucifer in the Fraternitas Saturni is postulated by Faxneld, "'In communication with the powers of darkness,'" 47; in *Satanic Feminism*, 60, Faxneld also remains undecided about the order's Satanism.

46. Roberts, *Witches U.S.A.*, 200–220, contains a mildly ironic account of ritual proceedings at the Coven of Our Lady of Endor. See also Brad Steiger, *Sex and Satanism* (New York: Ace, 1969), 16–21; Marcello Truzzi, "Towards a Sociology of the Occult: Notes on Modern Witchcraft," in Zaretsky and Leone, *Religious Movements in Contemporary America*, 628–645, here 637, 644.

47. The classic account on the Process is still William Sims Bainbridge, *Satan's Power: A Deviant Psychotherapy Cult* (Berkeley: University of California Press, 1978), in which the group is represented as the Power, with pseudonyms for its members in order to maintain anonymity. An article by Bainbridge updating his study appeared as "Social Construction from Within: Satan's Process," in Richardson et al., *Satanism Scare*, 297–310, while, recently, Timothy Wyllie published a compilation of his and other Process members' reminiscences: Timothy Wyllie, *Love, Sex, Fear, Death: The Inside Story of the Process Church of the Final Judgment*, ed. Adam Parfrey (Port Townsend: Feral House, 2009).

48. Wyllie, *Love, Sex, Fear, Death*, 38.

49. Bainbridge, *Satan's Power*, 69.

50. Bainbridge, *Satan's Power*, 4; Wyllie, *Love, Sex, Fear, Death*, 170.

51. Bainbridge, *Satan's Power*, 87.

52. Bainbridge, *Satan's Power*, 100.

53. Bainbridge, *Satan's Power*, 110.

54. Grimston, *The Gods*, 1.5–7, cited in Bainbridge, "Social Construction from Within," 303.

55. Bainbridge, *Satan's Power*, 170. A beautiful description of a Process Sabbath can be found in ibid., 16–20.

56. Although the Processeans were officially celibates, behind the scenes and in the innermost circle, sessions of group sex took place. Incidentally, these were not so much remembered by the participants as passionate orgies, but rather as further exercises in mind control by the Omega, and especially by Mary Anne de Grimston, who would direct the proceedings and sometimes order a man to have sex with her or with a woman of her choice. See Wyllie, *Love, Sex, Fear, Death*, 95–97.

57. Bainbridge, "Social Construction from Within," 300.

58. Bainbridge, *Satan's Power*, 247–286.

59. Introvigne, *Enquête sur le satanisme*, 257.

60. Roberts, *Witches U.S.A.*, 214.

61. Bainbridge, *Satan's Power*, 84

62. Bainbridge, *Satan's Power*, 176.

63. La Fontaine, "Satanism and Satanic Mythology," 105, suggests the adoption as gods of Lucifer and Satan was due to contact with LaVey, but gives no reference for this assertion. Chris Mathews claims that "at one point, Grimston's cult approached LaVey proposing an union of sorts, which LaVey dismissed immediately" (*Modern Satanism: Anatomy of a Radical Subculture* [Westport, CT: Praeger, 2009], xiv), but provides neither date nor source. Neither Bainbridge nor Wyllie mention LaVey in their histories of the Process.

64. Authoritative biographies on Crowley include John Symonds, *The King of the Shadow Realm. Aleister Crowley: His Life and Magic* (London: Duckworth, 1989), and Richard Kaczynski, *Perdurabo: The Life of Aleister Crowley* (Berkeley, CA: North Atlantic, 2010). In addition, I consulted Marco Pasi's *Aleister Crowley und die Versuchung der Politik*, trans. Ferdinand Leopold (Graz: Ares Verlag, 2006); Introvigne, *Enquête sur le satanisme*, 209–254; and Crowley's own autobiography, *The Confessions of Aleister Crowley: An Autohagiography* (London: Jonathan Cape, 1969). For Crowley's place and influence in the wider field of religious history, see especially *Aleister Crowley and Western Esotericism*, ed. Henrik Bogdan and Martin P. Starr (New York: Oxford University Press, 2012), relevant articles from which will be quoted in the notes that follow.

65. On the Golden Dawn, see Ellic Howe, *The Magicians of the Golden Dawn: A Documentary History of a Magical Order, 1887–1923* (London: Routledge and Kegan Paul, 1972), and Drury, *Stealing Fire from Heaven*, 44–75. Although limited in the number of its adepts and the time of its activity, in retrospect, the Golden Dawn can be considered a key organization in the proliferation of occult lore in the English-speaking world, especially through its publications of ceremonies and magical rites. The Golden Dawn itself claimed that it was the "Order of mystics which gave Eliphaz Levi [*sic*] his occult knowledge," but the organization undoubtedly postdated the

French occult revival. On Lévi and the Golden Dawn, see Howe, *Magicians of the Golden Dawn*, 9, 17–18, 26, 28, 46.

66. Howe, *Magicians of the Golden Dawn*, 203–232; Kaczynski, *Perdurabo*, 73–80.

67. Pasi, *Aleister Crowley und die Versuchung der Politik*, 41. The full name of the A∴ A∴ was never disclosed, but is generally assumed to be Astrum Argenteum, "Silver Star." Cf. ibid., 245n.

68. On Reuss and the early OTO, the classic account is Helmut Möller and Ellic Howe, *Merlin Peregrinus: Vom Untergrund des Abendlandes* (Würzburg: Köningshausen + Neumann, 1986). Rudolf Steiner, the future founder of anthroposophy, shortly headed the Berlin chapter of the organization. On Steiner's involvement, see ibid., 164–166, 269; Howe, *Magicians of the Golden Dawn*, 262–264; and Zander, *Anthroposophie in Deutschland*, 1:397, 1:598, 2:975–981, 2:987–988.

69. Symonds, *King of the Shadow Realm*, 162; Pasi, *Aleister Crowley*, 42–43.

70. Crowley, *Confessions*, 394.

71. Aleister Crowley, *Liber L vel Legis, given from the mouth of Aiwass to the ear of The Beast on April 8, 9 & 10, 1904*, http://www.themagickalreview.org/classics/liber_0031-transcript.php, accessed 15 May 2011, 2:22.

72. Crowley, *Liber L vel Legis*, 3:49–53.

73. Which Rabelais might, or might not, have derived from Augustine of Hippo's "Love, and do what you want." Augustine is already quoted by Tristan, *Émancipation de la Femme*, 53: "Aimez et faites ce que vous voudrez"; "en cette parole … se résume tout l'Evangile du Saint-Esprit." Another source of inspiration for Crowley, by the way, may have been the short description of "magic science" by Anatole France in Papus, *Traité élémentaire de science occulte*, 8: "Sans vouloir entrer dans un exposé méthodique de la science magique, disons qu'elle aboutit à la divinisation de la volonté: 'Le Thélème de tout le monde est la volonté,' dit le mage." For the prominence of "Will" in nineteenth-century occultism, see the section on Éliphas Lévi in chapter 3 and the discussion of the Parisian neo-Kabbalists in chapter 4. Compare also Péladan, *Vice suprême*, 180, 240.

74. Crowley remarked himself on the antecedents of "Do What Thou Wilt" in an essay entitled "The Antecedents of Thelema," which was written in 1926 and remained unpublished during his lifetime (consulted by me on 16 May 2011 at http://hermetic.com/eidolons/The_Antecedents_of_Thelema). Here he mentions Augustine and Rabelais but seems unaware of Dashwood.

75. Crowley, *Liber L vel Legis*, 1:42.

76. Pasi, *Aleister Crowley*, 163–167.

77. Douglas Hill, Pat Williams, Frank Smyth, and Tessa Clarke, *Witchcraft, Magic and the Supernatural: The Weird World of the Unknown* (London: Octopus, 1974), 36; Elliger in Haag, *Teufelsglaube*, 498; Carl A. Raschke, *Painted Black: From Drug Killing to Heavy Metal—The Alarming True Story of How Satanism Is Terrorizing Our Communities* (San Francisco: Harper and Row, 1990), ix, 36–37; cf. also Symonds, *King of the Shadow Realm*, 201, 509.

78. Crowley, *Confessions*, 66–67. On p. 73, Crowley recounts how he would still write "hymns of quite acceptable piety" as late as 1894; "My Satanism did not interfere with it at all; I was trying to take the view that the Christianity of hypocrisy and cruelty was not true Christianity."

79. Crowley, *Confessions*, 81. As Crowley wrote his memoirs in the 1920s, it is evident that his later reading might have influenced his account here.

80. Crowley, *Confessions*, 126.

81. Crowley, *Confessions*, 182.

82. Cf. Kaczynski, *Perdurabo*, 16, 133.

83. His female sexual partners were accordingly called Scarlet Whores or Scarlet Women. In an entry of 23 July 1923 in his *magical diary*, Crowley gave a distinctly Blakean explanation for his choice of epithets: "Throughout [my poetry], in every line, I imply that Energy is Delight. Thus the 'modest woman,' the mother, is to me a symbol of defeat & death: the Scarlet Whore who rides the Great Wild Beast, who drains the Blood of the Saints into Her Cup, who is 'adulterous,' demanding change, is Victory & Life." Aleister Crowley, *Magical Diaries of Aleister Crowley: Tunisia 1923*, ed. Stephen Skinner (York Beach, ME: Samuel Weiser, 1999), 95.

84. Cited in Hendrik Bogdan, "Envisioning the Birth of a New Aeon: Dispensationalism and Millenarianism in the Thelemic Tradition," in Bogdan and Starr, *Aleister Crowley and Western Esotericism*, 89–106, there 100. In the sentence immediately preceding this, Crowley stated that he held "the legendary Jesus in no wise responsible for the trouble": in the tradition of nineteenth-century esotericism and Romanticism, he occasionally exempted Jesus as a benevolent human teacher from his criticism on Christianity.

85. Crowley, *Confessions*, 808.

86. Introvigne, *Enquête sur le satanisme*, 209–219; Schmidt, *Satanismus*, 133; Kaczynski, *Perdurabo*, 556; Asbjørn Dyrendal, "Satan and the Beast: The Influence of Aleister Crowley on Modern Satanism," in Bogdan and Starr, *Aleister Crowley and Western Esotericism*, 369–394.

87. Symonds, *King of the Shadow Realm*, 67, quoting the entry for 22 July 1920 from Crowley's Magical Record. See also Aleister Crowley, *Magick*, ed. John Symonds and Kenneth Grant (London: Routledge and Kegan Paul 1973), 264n, 296n, where Crowley identifies Aiwaz [*sic*] with the "solar-phallic-hermetic 'Lucifer.'" In *Liber L*, 2:22, Aiwass describes himself as "the Snake that giveth Knowledge & Delight." Crowley would remain undecided about Aiwass's real nature for much of his life; see Kaczynski, *Perdurabo*, 126.

88. Crowley, *Confessions*, 408; Crowley, *Magick*, 248; Howe, *Magicians of the Golden Dawn*, 195; Kaczynski, *Perdurabo*, 467, 561.

89. Asprem, *"Kabbalah Recreata,"* 133, 146.

90. Some of these influences are explored in Richard Kaczynski, "Continuing Knowledge from Generation unto Generation: The Social and Literary Background of Aleister Crowley's Magic," in Bogdan and Starr, *Aleister Crowley and Western Esotericism*, 141–179. On the adoption of ideas from psychoanalysis, see Alex Owen, "The Sorcerer and His Apprentice: Aleister Crowley and the Magical Exploration of Edwardian Subjectivity," in Bogdan and Starr, *Aleister Crowley and Western Esotericism*, 15–52.

91. Crowley, *Magick*, 296n; *Equinox* 1 (An. IX/September 1913 o.s.) 10:206.

92. Asprem, *"Kabbalah Recreata,"* 137–150.

93. But, significantly, perhaps not with the Christian Satan, who is absent from Crowley's diagram; see [Aleister Crowley], *777 vel Prolegomena Symbolica ad Systemam Sceptico-Mysticæ Viæ Explicianda, fundamentum Hieroglyphicum Sanctissimorum Scientiæ Summæ* (London: Walter Scott, 1909), column XIV, XX, XXII, XXXIII, XXXIV, CLXXXII, n° 26.

94. [Crowley], *777*, column XXXIV, n° 0.

95. Aleister Crowley, *The Book of Lies, which is also falsely called Breaks: The Wanderings or Falsifications of the one thought of Frater Perdurabo (Aleister Crowley)* (Boston: Weiser, 2001), 16.

96. Aleister Crowley, *The Book of Thoth: A Short Essay on the Tarot of the Egyptians, being The Equinox Volume III No. V*, chapter "The Atu," section XV, consulted via http://hermetic.com/crowley/book-of-thoth/atu.html, accessed 23 March 2015.

97. Crowley, *Book of Thoth*, "Atu" XV.

98. Crowley, *Magick*, 172–173.

99. Crowley, *Magick*, 173. On Crowley's ascension to the grade of Ipsissimus, see Kaczynski, *Perdurabo*, 407–409.

100. Already in the introduction to his early Decadent poem *Aceldama: A Place to Bury Strangers* (1898), Crowley described his struggle with religion in the following words: "God and Satan fought for my soul. . . . God conquered—now I have only one doubt left—which of the twain was God?" Cited in Kaczynski, *Perdurabo*, 47.

101. Cf. Schmidt, *Satanismus*, 133, who also discerns much in Crowley "was sich ohne weiteres als Satanismus deuten läßt," but reaches a similar conclusion here.

102. Crowley, *Magick*, 172–173.

103. Among others, La Fontaine, "Satanism and Satanic Mythology," 89–92, already calls Crowley the "father of modern Satanism," although he does not succeed, in my view, to make this (correct) assumption plausible. Crowley's influence is more deeply analyzed in a recent article by Dyrendal, "Satan and the Beast."

104. Symonds, *King of the Shadow Realm*, 560–565; Introvigne, *Enquête sur le satanisme*, 248–254; Kaczynski, *Perdurabo*, 537–540. The connection with Hubbard is explored in Hugh B. Urban, "The Occult Roots of Scientology? L. Ron Hubbard, Aleister Crowley, and the Origins of a Controversial New Religion," in Bogdan and Starr, *Aleister Crowley and Western Esotericism*, 335–367.

105. Barton, *Secret Life of a Satanist*, 49.

106. Barton, *Secret Life of a Satanist*, 49. A letter from LaVey to Michael Aquino dated 15 July 1971 suggests a deeper involvement: "Eighteen years ago I was reciting Crowley and smearing myself with VanVan and Patchouli."—see Aquino, *Church of Satan*, 167. Some of the members of LaVey's original Magic Circle were also very much into Crowley, most notably the independent filmmaker Kenneth Anger, who had shot a documentary at the deserted Abbey of Thelema in 1955. For Crowley and LaVey, see also the interview with Anger in Baddeley, *Lucifer Rising*, 78.

107. Barton, *Secret Life of a Satanist*, 49.

108. LaVey, *Satanic Bible*, 103. LaVey explicitly denied any influence by the Californian OTO in one of his columns from 1972 in the *News Exploiter*, reprinted in LaVey, *Letters from the Devil*, [48]. Distancing himself from Crowley's legacy was probably deliberate policy with LaVey. "We *must* avoid the nomenclature of Crowley like the plague," he wrote to his lieutenant Michael Aquino in 1971 (Aquino, *Church of Satan*, 167).

109. Barton, *Secret Life of a Satanist*, 71; Symonds, *King of the Shadow Realm*, 97. Space and time constraints forbid the discussion of possible influences from Crowley on Maria de Naglowska and the Process. The influence of Crowley on Naglowska, or of Naglowska on Crowley, if any, has still to be properly studied, as far as I am aware. It seems certain, however, that Naglowska's main source for her sexual magic was the American occultist J. B. Randolph, while Crowley only published veiled references to his own practices in this respect during his lifetime. On Randolph and Naglowska, see Hugh B. Urban, "Magia Sexualis: Sex, Secrecy, and Liberation in Modern Western Esotericism," *Journal of the American Academy of Religion* 72

(September 2004) 3, 695–731; a possible influence of Péladan's ideas is proposed by Hakl, "The Theory and Practice of Sexual Magic," 473.

It is known that the Process at one moment planned to establish its headquarters in Crowley's derelict abbey in Sicily (Bainbridge, *Satan's Power*, 99). Bainbridge devotes a few paragraphs to similarities between Crowley and the Process, but those he signals are mostly of a singular superficial nature (e.g., both Crowley and Grimston were in the habit of consulting the I Ching). A much more likely source for Processean theology, it seems to me, would be Theosophy or Steiner's anthroposophy. Here as well, however, serious academic research has still to begin.

110. Margaret Alice Murray, *The Witch Cult in Western Europe* (1921; repr., Oxford: Clarendon, 1962) and *The God of the Witches* (1931; repr., London: Faber and Faber, 1956). On Murray, see Juliette Wood, "The Reality of Witch Cults Reasserted: Fertility and Satanism," in *Palgrave Advances in Witchcraft Historiography*, ed. Jonathan Barry and Owen Davies (Houndmills, UK: Palgrave Macmillan, 2007), 69–89.

111. On the history of neopagan witchcraft, Hutton, *Triumph of the Moon*, remains authoritative. Gardner himself initially presented Wicca as a "dying cult" along the lines of Leland; see his *Witchcraft Today* (London: Rider, 1954), 18.

112. On Crowley's influence, see Hutton, *Triumph of the Moon*, 49, 171–180; Kaczynski, *Perdurabo*, 543–544, as well as Hutton's article "Crowley and Wicca," in Bogdan and Starr, *Aleister Crowley and Western Esotericism*, 285–306. Gardner made veiled references to Crowley as a source for Wicca in *Witchcraft Today*, 47, 113, claiming that the British occultist had belonged to the "witch cult" in secret.

113. Crowley, *Confessions*, 268–269. For sylphs, see Symonds, *King of the Shadow Realm*, 567. See also Crowley's hilarious description of his attempt to invoke an undine in *Confessions*, 174.

114. Ronald Hutton, "Modern Pagan Witchcraft," in Blécourt et al., *Witchcraft and Magic in Europe, Volume 6: The Twentieth Century*, 1–80, there 49–50. It must be remarked that Crowley had already included ritual scourging in the neophyte initiation rite of the A.A. in 1906; see Crowley's *Liber 671* a.k.a. *Liber Pyramidos* and Kaczynski, *Perdurabo*, 160.

115. LaVey, *Satanic Bible*, 51ff.

116. LaVey, "By any other name," reprinted in LaVey, *Devil's Notebook*, 33–34.

117. LaVey, *Devil's Notebook*, 34.

118. LaVey, *Satanic Rituals*, 14; LaVey's attack on neopagan witchcraft fills pp. 12–14. See also LaVey, *Satanic Witch*, 7–9.

119. Already in the very first publication in which he had presented his "new" witchcraft, Gardner had explicitly denied that the names of the gods were "any devils' names": *Witchcraft Today*, 136. The Wicca strategy seems not to have been without success, at least with the general media; cf. Laurel Rowe and Gray Cavender, "Caldrons Bubble, Satan's Trouble, but Witches Are Okay: Media Constructions of Satanism and Witchcraft," in Richardson et al., *Satanism Scare*, 263–275.

120. Charles Pace told about his adventures in an article headed "A Witch Confesses" that appeared in *News of the World* on 29 March 1970. I owe this and other references on Pace to http://www.thewica.co.uk/Others.htm, accessed 17 May 2011. According to Baddeley, *Lucifer Rising*, 64, 75, LaVey claimed to have corresponded with Pace "after the war," a connection that certainly would merit more thorough investigation.

Alex Sanders, the self-proclaimed "King of the Witches," also claimed to have battled black magic rings after he had for a short time practiced black magic himself; he performed stage shows with his young wife and magical partner, Maxine, during which the latter would be possessed by a demon (Ellis, *Raising the Devil*, 154–155). The attitude of some Wiccans toward Satanism and the Church of Satan is vividly illustrated in Roberts, *Witches U.S.A.*, 184–185, 219–220.

121. Cf. Michael York, "Le neo-paganisme et les objections du wiccan au satanisme," in *Le Défi Magique II. Satanisme, sorcellerie*, ed. Jean-Baptiste Martin and Massimo Introvigne (Lyon: Presses Universitaires de Lyon, 1994), 174–182.

122. Hutton, *Triumph of the Moon*, 46.

123. See Drury, *Stealing Fire from Heaven*, 153–173, and his article, "An Australian Original: Rosaleen Norton and her Magical Cosmology," in Bogdan and Djurdjevi, *Occultism in a Global Perspective*, 231–243; Drury here specifically rejects labeling Norton a Satanist on pp. 246–247. Norton seems to have developed her witchcraft independently, with much influence from the writings of Crowley: see on this Keith Richmond, "Through the Witch's Looking Glass: The Magick of Aleister Crowley and the Witchcraft of Rosaleen Norton," in Bogdan and Starr, *Aleister Crowley and Western Esotericism*, 307–339. Norton's activities were described as "black Masses" and "unbridled orgies" in the popular press; some Sydney students then added to the rumors by setting up and photographing a bogus Satanist ceremony—cf. the report from the German tabloid *Quick*, cited in Zacharias, *Satanskult und Schwarze Messe*, 156 (with photos in Tafel 34), and Drury, "Australian Original," 243. On further "Satanist" ambiguities in early Wicca and current Luciferian witchcraft, see Frederik Gregorius, "Luciferian Witchcraft: At the Crossroads between Paganism and Satanism," in Faxneld and Petersen, *Devil's Party*, 229–249.

124. Even the academic literature of the 1960s and 1970s usually categorized Satanism under the general heading of witchcraft: for example, Truzzi, "Towards a Sociology of the Occult," 628–645. Moody, "Magical Therapy," 356, described the Church of Satan in 1974 as "a new group of practising witches."

125. For instance in Steiger, *Sex and Satanism*, 21–27, 53–70. Cf. Hutton, *Triumph of the Moon*, 248, 258; Masters, *Devil's Dominion*, 119; Medway, *Lure of the Sinister*, 322.

126. For instance, Boutet, *Tableau de l'au-delà*, 200–201; Ahmed Rollo, *The Black Art* (1936; repr., London: Jarrolds, 1968), esp. 276.

127. "Contemporary legend" was proposed by Jeffrey S. Victor for the body of folk narratives about Satanism that surfaced during the Satanism Scare; Ellis, *Raising the Devil*, 284, 5, suggests "contemporary mythology" as a more adequate term. Compare Melanie Möller, *Satanismus als Religion der Überschreitung: Transgression und stereotype Darstellung in Erfahrungs- und Aussteigerberichten* (Marburg: Diagonal-Verlag, 2007), 11.

128. A short introduction on Summers can be found in Wood, "Reality of Fertility Cults Reasserted," 77–85; see also Hutton, *Triumph of the Moon*, 254–255.

129. On Summers's ordination, see Brocard Sewell, "The Reverend Montague Summers," in *Montague Summers: A Bibliographical Portrait*, ed. Frederick S. Frank, The Great Bibliographers Series, no. 7 (Metuchen, NJ: Scarecrow, 1988), 3–23, there 9.

130. Montague Summers, *Witchcraft and Black Magic* (London: Rider, s.a. [1945]), 17.

131. Summers's historical instincts, it must be noted, could be remarkably shrewd when a theory did not fit his own paradigms: see, for instance, his sharp criticism of the Murrayite thesis on witchcraft in *A Popular History of Witchcraft* (London: Kegan Paul, Trench, Trubner, 1937),

101–102. "It is surely permissible to express surprise when one reads Satanism described as 'a joyous religion,'" Summers snapped.

132. Montague Summers, *The Geography of Witchcraft* (Evanston, IL: University Books, 1958), 444.

133. Summers, *Geography of Witchcraft*, 574–575.

134. Summers, *Geography of Witchcraft*, 184.

135. Summers, *Witchcraft and Black Magic*, 223. See also Summers, *Popular History of Witchcraft*, 109.

136. Summers, *Witchcraft and Black Magic*, 91. Apart from classic conspiracy authors like Robison and Barruel, Summers elsewhere makes approving references to Fiard and Ségur (Summers, *Geography of Witchcraft*, 444, 573).

137. Summers, *Popular History of Witchcraft*, 16.

138. Summers, *Witchcraft and Black Magic*, 223.

139. Summers, *Geography of Witchcraft*, 443 and 464n. De Sade was then still a below-the-counter book in England; Summers in fact published the first treatise in English on his work in 1920 (see Timothy D'Arch Smith, *The Books of the Beast: Essays on Aleister Crowley, Montague Summers and others* [s.l. (London): Mandrake, 1991], 37). For Madeleine Bavent, see also D'Arch Smith, *Books of the Beast*, 43.

140. Originally published in 1907, the volume was reprinted as Montague Summers, *Antinous and Other Poems* (London: Cecil Woolf, 1995). Significantly, it had been dedicated to Jacques d'Adelswärd-Fersen. The Anglican curacy Summers shortly held was terminated on charges on the theme of pederasty. Furthermore, Summers was a member from 1918 to 1923 of the British Society for the Study of Sex Psychology (characterized by D'Arch Smith as "little more than a cabal of homosexuals"); in the 1940s, he was living with his male "secretary" Hector. Cf. D'Arch Smith, *Books of the Beast*, 40–42; Symonds, *King of the Shadow Realm*, 159.

141. Frank, *Montague Summers*, 235. Cf. ibid., 227: "The division in Huysmans' character between the sensuous and the spiritual had made him a subject of Summers's curiosity, attention, and perhaps identification."

142. Summers, *Geography of Witchcraft*, 445; Summers, *Popular History of Witchcraft*, 194. For organized host theft, see, for instance, *Geography of Witchcraft*, ibid., and *Popular History of Witchcraft*, 15.

143. D'Arch Smith, *Books of the Beast*, 44–45. For reasons of discretion, D'Arch Smith give his informant the name of "Anatole James." At a later occasion, Anatole James claimed, Summers had also told him that his special sexual interest was in devout young Catholics, "their subsequent corruption giving him inexhaustible pleasure."

144. Cf. Summers, *Popular History of Witchcraft*, 194.

145. Something along the lines of this hypothesis is suggested in veiled terms by Devendra Varma when he writes, "Father Valentine testifies that Summers had a sincere desire to serve the Church; and if on his 'dark' side he desired to serve the Devil, that also would supply a motive, an unhallowed one, for seeking ordination."—Devendra P. Varma, "Montague Summers: A Gothic Tribute," in Frank, *Montague Summers*, 24–34, there 31–32.

146. Dennis Wheatley, *The Devil Rides Out* (London: Reed International, 1996), 134, 222.

147. Wheatley, *The Devil Rides Out*, 6.

148. Cf. Pasi, *Aleister Crowley*, 183–184.

149. Wheatley, *The Devil Rides Out*, 32, 52; Dennis Wheatley, *To the Devil a Daughter* (Ware, UK: Wordsworth, 2007), 186–188 (where Crowley is spoken about directly); Dennis Wheatley, *The Satanist* (London: Arrow, 1975), 79, 106, 355. Of course, Crowley's system of grades was not his own invention, but an almost exact copy of that used by the Hermetic Order of the Golden Dawn.

150. Dennis Wheatley, *The Devil and All His Works* (London: Book Club Associates, 1977), 259–261. On the same pages, Wheatley also discloses about the Cefalú Abbey that "Black Masses were said there and animals offered up to Satan."

151. See the introduction of Anthony Lejeune to Wheatley, *To the Devil a Daughter*, 9–10.

152. Symonds, *King of the Shadow Realm*, 159.

153. Summers, *Witchcraft and Black Magic*, 180; on pp. 16–17 of the same work, Summers refers to a public lawsuit in which Crowley appeared.

154. Montague Summers, *The Galanty Show: An Autobiography* (London: Cecil Woolf, 1980), 242.

155. Wheatley, *To the Devil a Daughter*, 79.

156. Wheatley, *The Devil and All His Works*, 257; Rollo, *Black Art*, 11–12. On Ahmed Rollo, see Medway, *Lure of the Sinister*, 147.

157. Wheatley, *The Devil and All His Works*, 267 (revolutions), 268–272 (modern witchcraft and Satanism), 275–279 (Right Hand Path). In this context the backside blurb of my 1975 edition of *The Satanist* speaks volumes: "For years Colonel Verney had suspected a link between Devil-worship and the subversive influence of Soviet Russia. When they found Teddy Morden's crucified body, he knew his grimmest fears were justified."

158. Wheatley, *The Devil and All His Works*, 277.

159. Wheatley, *The Devil Rides Out*, 134.

160. Wheatley, *The Devil Rides Out*, 315.

161. Compare *The Devil and All His Works*, 277–279, and Wheatley's "Letter to Posterity" (on which more below), http://www.bbc.co.uk/bbcfour/documentaries/features/wheatley_letter.pdf, retrieved 4 April 2011, 11. Wheatley might thus be considered an early product and proponent of the development of "occulture," as Christopher Partridge has called it.

162. Wheatley, *The Satanist*, 93. In the same novel, the female protagonist infiltrating the Satanist brotherhood particularly fears to have "to undergo sexual initiation from the hands of some of the Negroes or Orientals who had been at the meeting" (106).

163. Wheatley, "Letter to Posterity," 10.

164. Wheatley, "Letter to Posterity," 10–11.

165. Not only was Wheatley a best-selling author in his own right, his novels were also made into popular horror films, particularly by Hammer Studios. Space and time prohibits me here from dwelling deeply on the rich cinematic tradition regarding Satanism, but the interested reader might consult Ellis, *Raising the Devil*, 156–159, and Baddeley, *Lucifer Rising*, 80–88. A not altogether correct "diabolic" filmography is offered by Muchembled, *History of the Devil*, 322–331.

166. See Aquino, *Church of Satan*, 143; LaVey, *Satanic Bible*, 103; Anton Szandor LaVey, "The Church of Satan, Cosmic Joy Buzzer," in *Devil's Notebook*, 28–32, there 28.

167. Lewis, *Satanism Today*, 290.

168. Wheatley, *The Satanist*, 491.

169. The only earlier publication I know of where the link between the literary tradition on Satan and modern Satanism is treated in some detail is Schipper, "From Milton to Modern Satanism." This article compares Milton's Satan with the theology of the Temple of Set. Unfortunately, Schipper's treatment of the question remains limited to pointing out analogies, while I would argue that the Miltonian Satan he describes is essentially the Romantic interpretation of Milton. I subscribe wholeheartedly, however, to Schipper's remarks about the two-way traffic between literature and religion: "not only do religious traditions affect the secular medium of literature, but the medium itself can affect religious traditions, too—even to the point of leading to the founding of a new religion." On the place of the Romantic Satanists in the historiography of Satanism in general, see note 1 of chapter 2. A genealogical line similar to that which I propose in this chapter is already suggested in very rough lines by Petersen, "Introduction," 11–13, and Lewis, *Satanism Today*, xiii.

170. LaVey, *Satanic Bible*, 61–74.

171. Stephen J. Sansweet, "Strange Doings: Americans Show Burst of Interest in Witches, Other Occult Matters," *Wall Street Journal*, 23 October 1969, 32.

172. LaVey, *Satanic Bible*, 67.

173. LaVey, *Satanic Bible*, 55.

174. LaVey, *Satanic Bible*, 46–47. See also 25, Satanic Statements #2 and #7.

175. LaVey, *Satanic Bible*, 23.

176. LaVey, *Satanic Bible*, 40.

177. Wolfe, *Black Pope*, 47.

178. LaVey, *Satanic Rituals*, 77. Pasi, "Dieu du désir," 91, places a stronger emphasis on the nineteenth-century tradition regarding a "rational" Satan, but also points to broader influences.

179. Wolfe, *Black Pope*, 39.

180. LaVey, *Satanic Rituals*, 13.

181. LaVey, *Devil's Notebook*, 132.

182. LaVey, *Satanic Rituals*, 12.

183. Convincingly described in his small essay "The Good Old Days: A Devil's Advocacy," in LaVey, *Satan Speaks!*, 11–16.

184. LaVey in Barton, *Secret Life of a Satanist*, 207; compare also *Satanic Rituals*, 77, where LaVey approvingly describes the Satan sung by Carducci as "the spirit of revolt that leads to freedom, the embodiment of all heresies that liberate."

In differing degrees, the attributes inherited from Romantic Satanism were also present in other Satanist groups prior to, or contemporary with, the 1966 Church of Satan. With Naglowska, the relation of Satan with reason and inquiry is very clear and explicit; as is his association with sex, however ambivalent this element might be. The great "No," which is Satan's slogan, does also invite more political or social interpretations, but Naglowska—seemingly deliberately—moves away from these, emphasizing the primacy of esoteric initiation (Naglowska, *Lumière du Sexe*, 102). Lucifer and Satan in the Process displayed even more traits of the earlier literary tradition. Both were associated in Process theology with sensual delight, Lucifer with that of the more gentle and delicate variety, Satan with depraved and perverted sexual practices. Lucifer, Grimston noted in one of his books, urges us "to enjoy life to the full, to value success in human terms, to be gentle and kind and loving, and to live in peace and harmony with one another." Satan was more ambiguous, representing both the urge to rise above "common" human needs and the opposite urge "to sink beneath all human values" and live out one's mere carnality (Grimston in *The Gods on War*; Wyllie, *Love, Sex, Fear, Death*, 270; cf. Bainbridge, *Satan's Power*, 176–178). Both contrast strongly with the wrathful, ascetic, ruthless Jehovah, in a way that reminds one strongly of the similar antithesis that the Romantic Satanists propounded.

185. Baudelaire and Huysmans are not unfavorably mentioned in LaVey, *Satanic Bible*, 103. As already mentioned, in *Satanic Rituals*, 77, LaVey briefly refers to Carducci.

186. Apart from the traits from Lévi that we have noted and will note, LaVey profusely quotes the French occultist in a 1971 *Cloven Hoof* article, dismissing him as "one of the sustainers of occult unwisdom" whose work confronts one with "page after page extolling the merits of Jesus Christ as king and master": Anton Szandor LaVey, "On Occultism in the Past," *Cloven Hoof* 3 (1971) 9, consulted on http://churchofsatan.com/occultism-of-the-past.php, accessed 15 January 2015. In a recent article, Dyrendal, "Satan and the Beast," 370, also pointed out Crowley's contribution "to bridging the gap between earlier 'literary Satanism' and later actualizations of Satanism as an organized religion."

187. As an aside, it may be mentioned that Bois, *Monde Invisible*, 175, already makes prominent reference to Nietzsche as a preliminary stepping-stone leading to religious Satanism—albeit with Bois this religious Satanism is the nonexistent Palladism of Pike and consorts. "Le face fière et triste de l'Archange s'annonçait en ces prophéties inconscientes," he notes about *Also sprach Zarathustra*.

188. Max Milner, "Signification politique de la figure de Satan dans le romantisme français," in *Romantisme et politique 1815–1851: Colloque de l'Ecole Normale Supérieure de Saint-Cloud (1966)*, ed. Louis Girard (Paris: Librairie Armand Colin, 1969), 157–163, here 160.

189. Friedrich Nietzche, *Also Sprach Zarathustra: Ein Buch für Alle und Keinen* (Leipzig: Alfred Kröner Verlag, 1930), 223: "einen alten Wahn, der heißt Gut und Böse."

190. Friedrich Nietzsche, *Der Antichrist: Versuch einer Kritik des Christentums* (Berlin: Nordland Verlag, 1941), 20 (section 2).

191. Nietzsche, *Der Antichrist*, 20 (section 2).

192. LaVey, *Satanic Bible*, 30.

193. LaVey, *Satanic Bible*, 34–35. These words, as we will see, were not originally LaVey's, yet few of his readers will have been aware of this fact in the 1960s and 1970s, and he explicitly presented them as Satanist scripture. "Smite him hip and thigh," by the way, is a variation on the biblical "he smote them hip and thigh" from the Book of Judges 15:8 (King James).

194. LaVey, *Satanic Bible*, 64. See as well *Satanic Bible*, 51, where LaVey gives a modified form of the Golden Rule. The second Satanic Statement also reflects Nietzsche in a nutshell—"Satan represents vital existence, instead of spiritual pipe dreams!"

195. LaVey, *Satanic Bible*, 89–90.

196. LaVey, *Satanic Bible*, 75.

197. Nietzsche is extolled as "a realist" on the dedication page of the first edition of LaVey's *Satanic Bible*, [7]. Compare LaVey, *Devil's Notebook*, 127; Barton, *Secret Life of a Satanist*, 4; Barton, *Church of Satan*, 59; LaVey cited in Mike Hertenstein and Jon Trott, *Selling Satan: The Evangelical Media and the Mike Warnke Scandal* (Chicago: Cornerstone, 1993), 425. LaVey sometimes misinterpreted an author, for instance in the case of Jack London, who was in fact a staunch socialist (cf. Mathews, *Modern Satanism*, 211n).

198. Redbeard was probably the New Zealander Arthur Desmond, although Jack London has also been suggested as the author; cf. Mathews, *Modern Satanism*, 64–66 (some hold the tract

to be a satirical persiflage on social Darwinist discourse; hence the possibility of Jack London as its writer).

199. Some alterations LaVey made to the tract tell a lot, however. He suppressed, for instance, the line "Cursed are the unfit for they shall be righteously exterminated," and he changed Redbeard's "Blessed are they who believe in Nothing" into "Blessed are they who believe in what is best for them." Mathews, *Modern Satanism*, 65; Eugene V. Gallagher, "Sources, Sects, and Scripture: The Book of Satan in *The Satanic Bible*," in Faxneld and Petersen, *Devil's Party*, 103–122, there 108–112.

200. Mathews, *Modern Satanism*, 56.

201. LaVey, *Satanic Bible*, 104. While authentic spiritual intent could be one of the things that distinguishes the "true" Christian in many Christian traditions, LaVey, in a neat Nietzsche-derived reversal, defines the "true" Satanist by his intentional *lack* of such spiritual intent and his dedicated this-worldliness. In fact, LaVey might be going even further than Nietzsche, while for him, it is not so much pious intent as the successful practice of this this-worldliness that counts.

202. LaVey, *Satanic Bible*, 104–105.

203. LaVey, *Satanic Bible*, 45.

204. For LaVey's distaste for abortion, see his column in *the eXploiter* of 21 March 1971, p. 18, reprinted in LaVey, *Letters from the Devil*, [30], and LaVey, *Satan Speaks!*, 30.

205. LaVey, *Satanic Bible*, 61. This is an essential example of conspiracy thinking. As noted, the general idea of a conspiracy by (Christian) priests to dominate humanity was not original to LaVey, but dated back to at least the Enlightenment and had also been in evidence with the Romantic Satanists. On conspiracy thinking as a polemic tool to "other" the mainstream in marginal esoteric traditions, see Asbjørn Dyrendal, "Hidden Knowledge, Hidden Powers: Esotericism and Conspiracy Culture," in Asprem and Granholm, *Contemporary Esotericism*, 25–48.

206. LaVey, *Satanic Bible*, 73; see also 94.

207. LaVey, *Satanic Bible*, 81.

208. I owe this apt phrase to my supervisor, Professor Daniela Müller.

209. LaVey, *Satanic Bible*, 25.

210. LaVey, *Satanic Bible*, 52, 81.

211. LaVey, *Satanic Bible*, 53.

212. LaVey, *Satanic Bible*, 44–45.

213. LaVey, *Satanic Bible*, 96.

214. LaVey, *Satanic Bible*, 45; compare LaVey, *Satanic Rituals*, 15, 27.

215. LaVey, *Satanic Bible*, 44.

216. See Asbjørn Dyrendal, "Darkness Within: Satanism as a Self-Religion," in Petersen, *Contemporary Religious Satanism*, 59–73; Amina Olander Lap, "Categorizing Modern Satanism: An Analysis of LaVey's Early Writings," in Faxneld and Petersen, *Devil's Party*, 83–102; Petersen, "Introduction," 2. For similar themes within the world of (post)modern religiosity, see Hanegraaff, *New Age Religion and Western Culture*, 204–210, and Hexham and Poewe, *New Age as Global Culture*, 70.

217. Hanegraaff, *New Age Religion and Western Culture*, 415–421; Hutton, *Triumph of the Moon*, 21 (with regard to modern paganism).

218. Nietzsche, *Also Sprach Zarathustra*, 25–27, "Von der drei Verwandlungen," English translation by Thomas Common, http://www.gutenberg.org/files/1998/1998-h/1998-h.htm, accessed 30 May 2011.

219. Nietzsche, *Also Sprach Zarathustra*, 289. Nietzsche had been an ardent admirer of Byron in his younger years, it might be noted (Young, *Friedrich Nietzsche*, 26, 30, 154). Even in the form of his work, Nietzsche sometimes leaned closely to the mythopoetic projects of Romanticism. *Thus Spoke Zarathustra* particularly is a strange book for a philosopher, strongly reminiscent at times of the epic poetry and mythical recreations of Shelley, Blake, and Byron. Its playful mix of mythologized autobiography, reconstructed myth, aphorism, and lyricism shows that Nietzsche took his own ideas about "childlike creativity" seriously and chose to rely on "Poetical Genius" in addition to "Mere Analytics" for his supreme attempt to create a new ethos and a new worldview for humanity. Reading this book is more a (potentially transformative) experience than an exercise in rational thought. Compare also Nietzsche's view on the Greek gods as analyzed in Young, *Friedrich Nietzsche*, 470.

220. Nietzsche, *Also Sprach Zarathustra*, 159: "ich rate, ihr würdet meinen Übermenschen—Teufel heißen!"

221. In the epilogue and dedication to his Eleusis rite, for instance, Crowley simply declared "We are the poets!" and referred in true Baudelairian spirit to "that ever-haunting love—nay, necessity!—of the Beyond which tortures and beautifies those of us who are poets" (cited in Matthew D. Rogers, "Frenzies of the Beast: The Phaedran *Furores* in the Rites and Writings of Aleister Crowley," in Bogdan and Starr, *Aleister Crowley and Western Esotericism*, 209–225, there 212 and 220). Compare Kaczynski, "Continuing Knowledge from Generation unto Generation," 147: "he was just as much a poet as he was a magician."

222. Crowley, *Confessions*, 655.

223. Crowley, *Confessions*, 144: "To me a book is a message from the gods to mankind; or, if not, should never be published at all." As mentioned before, Crowley particularly identified with Shelley—cf. Pasi, *Aleister Crowley*, 57n.

224. Crowley, *Liber Oz*; Crowley, *Magick*, 264.

225. Pasi, *Aleister Crowley*, 18.

226. Crowley, *Confessions*, 511.

227. Crowley, *Confessions*, 509; Crowley, *Magick*, 10–11.

228. Crowley, *Confessions*, 509.

229. In this, the Great Beast continued in the footsteps of eighteenth-century writers on comparative religion like Richard Payne Knight, who had considered the veneration of the "generative principle" as the universal, original core of all human religions. See on this Godwin, *Theosophical Enlightenment*, 1–26; Marco Pasi, "Crowley, Aleister," in Hanegraaff, *Dictionary of Gnosis and Western Esotericism*, 1:281–287, there 287; and Kaczynski, "Continuing Knowledge from Generation unto Generation," 151–167.

230. Compare Symonds, *King of the Shadow Realm*, 289.

231. Crowley, *Book of Lies*, 52. Compare Crowley, *Confessions*, 661: "What, then, is the difference between the Magician and the ordinary man? This, that the Magician has demanded that nature shall be for him a phenomenal mode of expressing his spiritual reality." Drury, *Stealing Fire from Heaven*, 97, adequately describes Crowley's magic as "a technique that subjects God to the artistic intent and human will."

232. Cf. Kaczynski, *Perdurabo*, 365, 375.

233. Crowley, *Magick*, 140.

234. Crowley, *Confessions*, 510; cf. *Confessions*, 624. There was a distinct streak of asceticism in Crowleyanity, as Pasi rightly remarks in "Varieties of Magical Experience: Aleister Crowley's

Views on Occult Practice," in Bogdan and Starr, *Aleister Crowley and Western Esotericism*, 53–87, there 65.

235. Crowley, *Magick*, 264; or, as he put it more poetically on p. 326 of the same work:
Behold within, and not without
One star in sight!

236. Crowley, *Magick*, 264n. This inconsistency in Crowley's utterances is also commented on in Pasi, "Varieties of Magical Experience."

237. Crowley, *Book of Lies*, 32.

238. Crowley lifted this line from the Golden Dawn Adeptus Minor initiation ritual, which took its inspiration in turn from a line on plate 32 of the Egyptian Book of the Dead (which significantly would be more accurately translated as "there is no member of mine devoid of a god"): see Kaczynski, "Continuing Knowledge from Generation unto Generation," 167.

239. Crowley, *Magical Diaries: Tunisia 1923*, 95.

240. Crowley, *Confessions*, 554.

241. Barton, *Secret Life of a Satanist*, 49.

242. LaVey, *Satanic Bible*, 94.

243. LaVey, *Satanic Bible*, 92–94. See also LaVey's abstruse remarks on this subject in Lyons, *Second Coming*, 188; Wright, *Saints and Sinners*, 145; and in a column in the *News Exploiter* from 1972, reprinted in LaVey, *Letters from the Devil*, [51]. In Barton, *Church of Satan*, 98, on the other hand, LaVey presents a strongly reductionist interpretation of these words: "You'll live as long as there are people to talk or write about you." For an illustration of the further rationalization of these utterances in current Church of Satan theology, see Cimminnee Holt, "Death and Dying in the Satanic Worldview," *Journal of Religion and Culture* 22 (2011) 1:33–53.

244. LaVey, *Satanic Bible*, 39, 83, 74, 52, 25.

245. LaVey, *Satanic Bible*, 89.

246. Barton, *Secret Life of a Satanist*, 202–203.

247. LaVey, *Satanic Bible*, 144. After concluding this section, I discovered Jesper Aagaard Petersen's excellent article " 'We demand bedrock knowledge': Modern Satanism between Secularized Esotericism and 'Esotericized' Secularism," in *Religion and the Authority of Science*, ed. Olav Hammer and James R. Lewis (Leiden: Brill, 2011), 67–114, which treats roughly the same subject and reaches roughly the same conclusions.

248. LaVey, *Satanic Bible*, 21–22.

249. Compare Barton, *Church of Satan*, 9–10.

250. LaVey, *Satanic Bible*, 147–152.

251. LaVey, *Satanic Bible*, 51.

252. LaVey himself claimed that he had gone through "all the grimoires and all I saw was junk!"—Barton, *Secret Life of a Satanist*, 2–3.

253. Jesper Aagaard Petersen, "The Carnival of Dr. LaVey: Articulations of Transgression in Modern Satanism," in Faxneld and Petersen, *Devil's Party*, 167–188, there 181–186.

254. LaVey, *Satanic Bible*, 155–272.

255. LaVey, *Satanic Bible*, 21.

256. LaVey, *Satanic Bible*, 57, 51–52.

257. Barton, *Church of Satan*, 16. Burton Wolfe, in his introduction to the first edition of *Satanic Bible*, 17, quotes this formula reversed. I am unable to tell whether this is due to a scribal error on Wolfe's part or an evolution in LaVey's thinking.

258. LaVey, *Satanic Bible*, 89.

259. LaVey, *Satanic Bible*, 89.

260. LaVey, *Satanic Bible*, 70.

261. LaVey, *Satanic Bible*, 51.

262. Barton, *Church of Satan*, 12.

263. The "Nine Satanic Sins" were introduced in a *Cloven Hoof* article in early 1987 and can be found in Barton, *Church of Satan*, 65–67. The "Eleven Satanic Rules of the Earth" were first published, as far as I am aware, in Barton, *Church of Satan*, 85–86, although Barton claims they had already been formulated by LaVey in 1967.

264. LaVey, *Satanic Bible*, 111.

265. LaVey, *Satanic Bible*, 120.

266. LaVey, *Satanic Bible*, 120.

267. LaVey, *Satanic Rituals*, 15.

268. LaVey, *Satanic Bible*, 87–88; Crowley, *Magick*, 219n. On Crowley's sexual magic and its sources, see Hugh B. Urban, "Magia Sexualis: Sex, Secrecy, and Liberation in Modern Western Esotericism," *Journal of the American Academy of Religion* 72 (September 2004) 3:695–731.

269. LaVey's debt to Crowley regarding magic was already pointed out by Lyons, *Second Coming*, 183, among others.

270. Crowley, *Magick without Tears*, ch. LXX.

271. LaVey, "Letters from the Devil," *National Insider*, 5 October 1969, 15, reprinted in *Letters from the Devil*, [9].

272. LaVey, *Satanic Bible*, 85.

273. Toward the end of his life, LaVey would present his religion and his magical system as consciously designed to fulfill both emotional and rational tendencies in man: "We can't afford to neglect either aspect—rational or bestial—but rather integrate the two, augmenting each as much as possible. . . . That's where Satanic power comes from—the full use of both extremes, both polarities" (Barton, *Church of Satan*, 94, 96). Although these utterances form a logical extension of his original philosophy, the High Priest's earlier writings do not yet provide clues for such a conscious elaboration of the rationality-carnality tension that runs through his magic and philosophy.

274. LaVey, *Satanic Rituals*, 21, 15, 27.

275. "Ceremony of the Nine Angles" and "The Call to Cthulhu," in LaVey, *Satanic Rituals*, 173–201.

276. LaVey, *Satanic Rituals*, 34. In Barton, *Secret Life of a Satanist*, 78, it is said: "The elements were consistent with the reports of Satanic worship from the famous writings of diabolists, such as the description in Joris-Karl Huysman's *La Bas*." Repeated in Barton, *Church of Satan*, 16.

277. LaVey, *Satanic Rituals*, 106–172.

278. LaVey, *Satanic Rituals*, 55, 58. Much the same applies to "Das Tierdrama" on pp. 76–105, which is presented by LaVey as an Illuminati rite, while at the same time several literary sources of inspiration are cited.

279. LaVey, *Satanic Rituals*, 15.

280. Barton, *Secret Life of a Satanist*, 74, describes the "Sigil of Baphomet" as "the symbol of Satanism adapted from the design used by the Knights Templars in the 14th Century." I am not so sure LaVey was always making such assertions with an "ironic smile, and mischievous glint in his eyes," as Per Faxneld ("Secret Lineages and de Facto Satanists," 78) writes.

281. Dyrendal, "Satan and the Beast," 376–378, rightly describes LaVey's appropriation of Crowley's Magick as a process of "secularizing magic," but misses in my view this simultaneous reverse current of "re-enchantment."

282. Crowley, *Magick*, 131.

283. Crowley, *Magick*, 131. This passage is in fact a paraphrase of Lévi, *Dogme et rituel*, 2:175.

284. Crowley, *Magick*, 132n. On Crowley's scientific attitude regarding magic, cf. Egil Asprem, "Magic Naturalized? Negotiating Science and Occult Experience in Aleister Crowley's Scientific Illuminism," *Aries* 8 (2008): 139–165.

285. Crowley, *Magick without Tears*, ch I.

286. Crowley, *Magick without Tears*, ch In.

287. Crowley, *Magick*, 234.

288. LaVey, *Satanic Bible*, 127–128. Compare this with some of Crowley's examples in chapter I of *Magick without Tears* (e.g., "A banker may have a perfect grasp of a given situation, yet lack the quality of decision, or the assets, necessary to take advantage of it"). An earlier example of this balancing principle can be found in Péladan, *Comment on devient Mage*, 163–164: "Il faut un permission, une équité et une possibilité au début du vouloir. Sans cesse, au cours du vouloir, il te faudra rectifier ta volonté selon le triple compas des trois causes secondes."

289. Barton, *Church of Satan*, 17. See also LaVey's pragmatic 1968 statement to Truzzi, recorded in the latter's article "Towards a Sociology of the Occult," 631: "I don't believe that magic is supernatural, only that it is supernormal. That is, it works for reasons science can not yet understand. As a shaman or magician, I am concerned with obtaining *recipes*. As a scientist, you seek *formulas*. When I make a soup, I don't care about the chemical reactions between the potatoes and the carrots. I only care about how to get the flavor of the soup I seek. In the same way, when I want to hex someone, I don't care about the scientific mechanisms involved whether they be psychosomatic, psychological, or what-not. My concern is with effectively *doing* the thing not with the scientist's job of *explaining* it."

290. This and previous citations: LaVey, *Satanic Bible*, 110.

291. At least according to LaVey, cited in Wright, *Saints and Sinners*, 152.

292. On Mansfield, see Barton, *Secret Life of a Satanist*, 84–106, where LaVey also suggests that Mansfield was erotically involved with him; for the miraculously appearing parking spots, see ibid., 69. A list of effective curses is offered on pp. 193–199 of the same work. Aquino gives a more sober account of Mansfield's involvement with Satanism and LaVey; cf. his *Church of Satan*, 30–33.

293. *National Insider*, 27 April 1969, 15, reprinted in LaVey, *Letters from the Devil*, [6]; LaVey, *Satanic Rituals*, 15.

CHAPTER 8: TRIBULATIONS OF THE EARLY CHURCH

1. Lyons, *Satan Wants You*, 115. Barton, *Church of Satan*, 24, claims that the Church had "well over 10,000" members by the time *The Satanic Bible* was released, but this must be deemed improbable. See however further on.

2. Lyons, *Satan Wants You*, 120–122; Baddeley, *Lucifer Rising*, 103–105. Lamers published his own monograph on Satanism, *Vlucht in de werkelijkheid* ("Flight into Reality"), which displays quite a few personal touches, especially a much greater emphasis on more traditional occult lore as auras, astral travels, and the fifth dimension. Lamers also claimed that Satanism as a religion

was at least 20,000 years old and originated in Lemuria: Maarten Joost Lamers, *Vlucht in de Werkelijkheid: Inleiding tot het Satanisme* (Amsterdam: Satanisch Seminarium, 1983), 3, 19.

3. Lyons, *Satan Wants You*, 116.

4. Lewis, *Satanism Today*, 258–259.

5. Lyons, *Satan Wants You*, 116–117; Lewis, *Satanism Today*, 51–52. On schism within modern religious Satanism, see especially Jesper Aagaard Petersen, "Satanists and Nuts: Schisms in Modern Satanism," in *Sacred Schisms: How Religions Divide*, ed. S. Lewis and J. R. Lewis (New York: Cambridge University Press, 2009), 218–247; pp. 234–239 give a concise account of the genesis of the Temple of Set, which is the subject of this section.

6. LaVey, *Satanic Bible*, 103; compare Lyons, *Second Coming*, 164; Baddeley, *Lucifer Rising*, 106. Truzzi, "Towards a Sociology of the Occult," 643, also mentions "sexual groups and clubs involved with Satanism."

7. Rhodes, *Satanic Mass*, 212–213; Lyons, *The Second Coming*, 5, 83 (who claims these practices could still be witnessed by the Paris tourist who has "a stipulated amount of cash handy"); Gardner, *Witchcraft Today*, 28.

8. *Beyond*, October 1968, as reported in Steiger, *Sex and Satanism*, 14–16. If there is any truth in the matter, Steiger's description rather suggests a kind of live sex show.

9. For the banana act (and the ensuing vaginal rash for the performing sisters), see Karin Schaapman, *Zonder moeder* (Amsterdam: Muntinga Pockets, 2005), 192–276, the memoirs of a Dutch prostitute who worked in Lamers's club and remembers the Dutch Church of Satan mainly as a cover-up for an adult entertainment business. However, an interview with one of the "sisters" in Baddeley, *Lucifer Rising*, 109–110, suggests that some of them were genuinely religiously involved.

10. Aquino, *Church of Satan*, 34–35.

11. Barton, *Church of Satan*, 26–27.

12. LaVey, *Satanic Bible*, 66: "opportunists who have no deeper interest in Satanism than merely the sexual aspects are emphatically discouraged."

13. This also was not without precedent: see Intermezzo 3 and the delicious chapter on nineteenth-century sapphic and gay "Satanism" in Faxneld, *Satanic Feminism*, 439–524.

14. Roberts, *Witches U.S.A.*, 216–219; Aquino, *Church of Satan*, 41–42.

15. This is suggested by LaVey in Barton, *Church of Satan*, 67.

16. Roberts, *Witches U.S.A.*, 219.

17. Aquino, *Church of Satan*, 145.

18. Letter from LaVey to Aquino, 6 March 1972, cited in Aquino, *Church of Satan*, 198.

19. Aquino, *Church of Satan*, 197.

20. Aquino, *Church of Satan*, 196.

21. Aquino, *Church of Satan*, 811.

22. Aquino, *Church of Satan*, 811.

23. Aquino, *Church of Satan*, 812.

24. Aquino, *Church of Satan*, 413.

25. Article for *Cloven Hoof* by Anton LaVey, enclosed in a letter to Aquino by Diane LaVey, 20 May 1975, in Aquino, *Church of Satan*, 421–422.

26. LaVey, *Satanic Bible*, 104.

27. Cf. Pasi, "Dieu du désir," 89–90.

28. LaVey, *Satanic Bible*, 40.

29. LaVey, *Satanic Bible*, 62.

30. This possibility is reinforced by utterances by LaVey to Lawrence Wright around 1990, in which the former returns to the theme of "balance of nature." "A natural order. That's God. And that's Satan. Satan is God. He is the representation of the state of flux; he is action-reaction; he is the cause and effect; he is all the elements interwoven in what we call evolution" (Wright, *Saints and Sinners*, 145).

31. Aquino, *Church of Satan*, 42–43.

32. Letter from Michael Aquino to John Ferro, 12 March 1974, in Aquino, *Church of Satan*, 393. For similar statements by other Church members during the period, see ibid., 256.

33. Aquino, *Church of Satan*, 39–40. Aquino here nominally describes rituals taking place before he joined the Church of Satan himself, but I am convinced this passage rather reflects his own experiences. The same applies to similar descriptions on pp. 28–30; on p. 45, Aquino recounts his first ventures in Satanist ritual.

Amusingly enough, some Christian authors cite these remarks from Aquino as proof that the Church of Satan was effectively a vehicle of Satan; see, for instance, Johannes Aagaard, "Occultisme/Satanism and the Christian Faith," in *Le Défi Magique II: Satanisme, sorcellerie*, ed. Jean-Baptiste Martin and Massimo Introvigne (Lyon: Presses Universitaires de Lyon, 1994), 259–267, there 263.

34. Luhrmann, *Persuasions of the Witch's Craft*, 310, 353.

35. Michael A. Aquino, *The Temple of Set* (e-book published by the author, draft 11, San Francisco: s.n., 2002–2010), 176.

36. See his *Cloven Hoof* announcement of the excommunication of Wayne West, cited in Aquino, *Church of Satan*, 574.

37. See, for instance, his answers to the examination for the Satanic priesthood that he submitted in 1970 (Aquino, *Church of Satan*, 75).

38. Aquino, *Church of Satan*, 70.

39. Aquino, *Church of Satan*, 71.

40. Michael A. Aquino, "The Diabolicon," included in Aquino, *Church of Satan*, 512–529, there 512.

41. Aquino, *Church of Satan*, 512–513.

42. Aquino, *Church of Satan*, 519, 520.

43. Aquino, *Church of Satan*, 521.

44. Aquino, *Church of Satan*, 516.

45. LaVey to M. A. Aquino, 27 March 1970, in Aquino, *Church of Satan*, 71.

46. Aquino, *Church of Satan*, 83–84.

47. LaVey, *Satanic Rituals*, 212.

48. LaVey, "Letters from the Devil," *National Insider*, 15 March 1970, 15; LaVey, "Letters from the Devil," *the eXploiter*, 14 March 1971, 18; both reprinted in LaVey, *Letters from the Devil*, [15], [29]. A year later, in the same periodical that had been renamed in the meantime into *the eXploiter*, he answered the question "Have you ever encountered Satan?": "Only in the figurative sense, in that we daily encounter Satan in ourselves. When man has become realistic enough to recognize and accept the demon(s) within him, he shall truly become as his own godhead" (*eXploiter*, 16 May 1971, 18, in LaVey, *Letters from the Devil*, [36]).

49. Aquino, *Church of Satan*, 350.

50. M. A. Aquino to Michael Grumboski, 5 June 1974, in Aquino, *Church of Satan*, 375.

51. Michael A. Aquino, "Quo Vadis?," *Cloven Hoof* 6 (July–August 1974) 4, reproduced in Aquino, *Church of Satan*, 799–800.

52. Aquino, "The Ninth Solstice Message," reproduced in Aquino, *Church of Satan*, 801–803, there 801.

53. Aquino, *Church of Satan*, 803.

54. Aquino, *Church of Satan*, 802.

55. Aquino to Diane and Anton LaVey, 10 June 1975, in Aquino, *Church of Satan*, 848–851, there 851.

56. Michael A. Aquino, "Letter to the Church Membership," 10 June 1975, in Aquino, *Church of Satan*, 853.

57. Aquino, *Temple of Set*, 14.

58. Aquino, *Temple of Set*, 170–175.

59. Aquino, *Temple of Set*, 173, 174.

60. Aquino, *Temple of Set*, 174.

61. Aquino, *Temple of Set*, 32, 36.

62. It must be noted that the current Temple of Set membership espouses a variety of views on Set. Cf. Graham Harvey, "Satanism: Performing Alterity and Othering," in Petersen, *Contemporary Religious Satanism*, 27–39, there 33.

63. Aquino, *Church of Satan*, 387–398.

64. Blavatsky, *Isis Unveiled*, 1:554, 2:483, 2:523.

65. In Crowleyan discourse, this was doubly significant, as this passage in *Book of the Law*, 2:76, was followed by the statement that only Crowley's true successor would be able to decode the cipher. Cf. Dvorak, *Satanismus*, 137. On Crowley and the Temple of Set, see Dyrendal, "Satan and the Beast," 379–387.

66. Aquino, *Temple of Set*, 84–85.

67. Aquino, *Temple of Set*, 29.

68. This was also noted in La Fontaine, "Satanism and Satanic Mythology," 102. Compare statements on the Temple of Set website like "the individual psyche is the hidden sanctuary of something godlike," "the one difference that distinguishes man from the rest of the cosmos is the feature of . . . conscious, willful existence," and "the Temple of Set seeks above all to enshrine consciousness." http://www.xeper.org/pub/pub_hp_welcome.html and http://www.xeper.org/pub/pub_gil.html, both accessed 7 September 2011.

69. Richard D. Murad, "The Subjective Universe and Life after Death," *Scroll of Set* 3 (December 1977) 4, quoted from Aquino, *Temple of Set*, 522. These ideas, by the way, display great similarities to those pronounced by Swedenborg on the afterlife: cf. Hanegraaff, *New Age Religion and Western Culture*, 429. The Temple of Set website also describes its path as "a process for creating an individual, powerful essence that exists above and beyond animal life. It is thus the true vehicle for personal immortality." http://www.xeper.org/pub/pub_gil.html, accessed 7 September 2011.

70. Drury, *Stealing Fire from Heaven*, 216. At times, Aquino would express himself as an extreme proponent of the Romantic Reversal. In *Black Magic in Theory and Practice*, for instance, he urged the magician to create his own gods or make his own selection from existing pantheons. "Neither type is inauthentic. Gods exist as they are evoked to meaningful existence

by the individual psyche" (cited in Schmidt, *Satanismus*, 185). A statement like this suggests that the theological rift between Aquino and LaVey may not have been so profound after all.

71. The Temple of Set during the 1980s is portrayed under the name "Church of Hu" in Gini Graham Scott, *The Magicians: An Investigation of a Group Practicing Black Magic* (New York: ASJA Press, 2007). Scott is a social scientist who infiltrated the Temple as a member. Her work, however, is marked by a rather hostile tone and a strong theoretical bias.

72. LaVey, *Devil's Notebook*, 29. Barton, *Church of Satan*, 49, forms an exception, but on pp. 127–128 of this book, where LaVey is talking about the schism, the Temple of Set is never mentioned by name.

73. Barton, *Church of Satan*, 127–128.

74. Barton, *Church of Satan*, 29.

75. LaVey cited in Barton, *Church of Satan*, 30.

76. LaVey cited in Barton, *Church of Satan*, 30. According to p. 119, the fifth phase was announced in an article in *Cloven Hoof*, Second Quarter, 1976; this is the article reproduced as "The Church of Satan, Cosmic Joy Buzzer," in LaVey, *Devil's Notebook*, 28–32.

77. Barton, *Church of Satan*, 71; Barton, *Secret Life of a Satanist*, 202–203, 207 ("We don't worship Satan, we worship ourselves using the metaphorical representation of the qualities of Satan").

78. Aquino, *Church of Satan*, 369.

79. In a letter to Aquino dated 6 January 1972, for instance, LaVey already mentioned that "we are well into our Fourth Phase and we'd best toughen our hides"; cited in Aquino, *Church of Satan*, 154.

80. Aquino citing Edward M. Webber, in Aquino, *Church of Satan*, 28; Aquino, *Church of Satan*, 284.

81. Aquino, *Church of Satan*, 362.

82. Aquino, *Church of Satan*, 28. It has to be noted that Aquino gives a slightly different reading of how he found out about LaVey's pact on p. 362, suggesting the existence of the pact had already been revealed to him by Satan/Set during the Ninth Solstice Working.

83. Aquino could voice strongly theist notions in the official bulletin for Church of Satan priests as late as January 1975; see Aquino, *Church of Satan*, 834–835.

84. LaVey, *Satanic Rituals*, 27.

85. LaVey, *Satanic Bible*, 21.

86. On radical rationalist Satanism, see Petersen, "'We demand bedrock knowledge,'" 99–102.

87. Kennet Granholm, "Embracing Others Than Satan: The Multiple Princes of Darkness in the Left-Hand Milieu," in Petersen, *Contemporary Religious Satanism*, 85–101, there 96.

88. According to Granholm, however, these instances all refer to the pre-1975 period and are "rarely . . . self-designative": cf. Granholm, "Embracing Others Than Satan," 96.

89. On the Satanism Scare, a solid body of scholarship exists. The most essential publications are Ellis, *Raising the Devil*; Jeffrey S. Victor, *Satanic Panic: The Creation of a Contemporary Legend* (Chicago: Open Court, 1993); and the volume of articles edited by James T. Richardson, Joel Best, and David G. Bromley under the title *The Satanism Scare* (New York: Aldine de Gruyter, 1991). Useful overviews can also be found in Introvigne, *Enquête sur le satanisme*, 310–368, and Medway, *Lure of the Sinister*.

Although academia generally remained skeptical about the rumors spread during the Satanism Scare, there were some exceptions, the most notable being *Painted Black* (1990) by Carl A. Raschke, a Denver professor of religious studies. Raschke's book can best be described in the same terms with which he discards Lyons's publication *Satan Wants You* (p. 132): "neither serious reporting nor scholarship" but rather "cleverly worded appeals to prejudice."

90. LaVey, *Satanic Bible*, 49, 43.

91. LaVey, *Satanic Bible*, 43.

92. Barton, *Secret Life of a Satanist*, 119–120; Barton, *Church of Satan*, 29.

93. Wuthnow, *Restructuring of American Religion*, 164.

94. Ellis, *Raising the Devil*, 7–10. An additional reason for the fierce animosity of Charismatic Christians to the occult may have been the difficulty to distinguish the "gifts of the Spirit" from similar occultist practices; occultism, moreover, was a competitor on the same spiritual terrain (ibid., 47–48).

95. On modern theology's goodbye to Satan, cf. Kelly, *Satan*, 308–315.

96. Hal Lindsey and C. C. Carlson, *Satan Is Alive and Well on Planet Earth* (Grand Rapids, MI: Zondervan, 1972), 30.

97. LaVey and his proclamation of the "New Age of Satan" are explicitly revoked on pp. 20–22, using Lyons as a source (Manson and Wicca are also classed as Satanist on pp. 21–22). These utterances follow directly on an interview with "no-nonsense man" Bob Vernon, commander of the Los Angeles police force, describing the excesses of hippie "cults" and claiming a new upsurge of Satanic crime—although most of the things he describes seem not connected with religious Satanism at all, especially those concerning "cults" located on communes ("They were living in the most primitive way you can imagine—just a short distance from one of the most affluent neighborhoods in the country—indulging in acts of sexual deviation, pagan ceremonies, and rites which defy imagination"). Lindsey, *Satan Is Alive and Well*, 19.

98. Lindsey, *Satan Is Alive and Well*, 84.

99. On the ouija board, see Lindsey, *Satan Is Alive and Well*, 158. International banking and the "One World Economic System" as tool for the "Satan . . . the unifier": 109–110. Page 110: "Many other economic manipulations can be used to centralize control in the hands of a few: industry taken from the free market economy and placed under state control; destruction of individual initiative through excessive taxation; regulatory laws which strangle private enterprise; government intervention into every aspect of private affairs."

100. Lindsey, *Satan Is Alive and Well*, 94, 228. An analysis of Lindsey's book can be found in Hertenstein, *Selling Satan*, 154–156.

101. Hertenstein, *Selling Satan*, especially 3, 105. Warnke probably derived his ideas about the Illuminati from the 1958 book *Pawns in the Game* by the Canadian Roman Catholic William Guy Carr, which combined classic antisemitic and anti-Masonic conspiracy theory with charismatic theology (and thus forms yet another bridge between the Satanism attribution of the nineteenth century and the early modern era, and the Satanism Scare). Cf. Ellis, *Raising the Devil*, 125–132.

102. Hertenstein, *Selling Satan*; cf. also Ellis, *Raising the Devil*, 185–192. A similarly shady figure was John Todd, who claimed to have been a Satanist Grand Druid. His "testimony" on his past briefly circulated through the Charismatic Christian circuit in the early 1970s. He subsequently disappeared from view for a few years, during which he started a Wicca coven

and an occult bookstore in Dayton, Ohio, only to reappear in 1977 with an even more alarmist and conspirational anti-Satanism message. Todd is still referred to as a reliable source in some ultrafundamentalist publications, particularly the comic books of Jack Chick (see for instance Chick's *Spellbound?*). On Todd's story, cf. Ellis, *Raising the Devil*, 192–201; Hertenstein, *Selling Satan*, 164–165.

103. Doreen Irvine, *From Witchcraft to Christ* (Cambridge, UK: Concordia, 1973). I consulted the Dutch translation, *Van hekserij tot Christus: Mijn ware levensverhaal*, trans. Loek Visser (Den Haag: Gazon, s.a.), 122–123. Irvine may also have found inspiration with "king of the witches" Alex Sanders, who operated in London in the late 1960s. His consort Maxine would later remember that their basement home was "virtually an out-patients" clinic for drug addicts"; see Hutton, *Triumph of the Moon*, 327. On Irvine, cf. Ellis, *Raising the Devil*, 160–166.

104. For instance, the former Scotland Yard Inspector Robert Fabian and the erstwhile benefactor of Crowley, William Seabrook. Cf. Ellis, *Raising the Devil*, 146–147, 149–151; Baddeley, *Lucifer Rising*, 30.

105. Ellis, *Raising the Devil*, 221, 202–239.

106. Ellis, *Raising the Devil*, 240–278, 244–247.

107. Ellis (who is skeptical), *Raising the Devil*, 178; Lyons (who is not), *Second Coming*, 168. Although these stories are occasionally repeated in more or less serious literature on Satanism, until now no author has brought forward specific, concrete examples of these "Hippie Cults."

108. Atkins, *Child of Satan*, 51–57.

109. Counterculture author Ed Sanders and his book *The Family* (1971) was particularly influential in establishing a link between Manson and Satanism in the popular imagination (cf. Ellis, *Raising the Devil*, 173–185). Sanders's ideas about a Manson-Process link were shared by Vincent Bugliosi, the public attorney in the Manson case; see Bugliosi's book *Helter Skelter*, which I consulted in its Dutch translation (Vincent Bugliosi and Curt Gentry, *Helter Skelter: Het ware verhaal van de Manson-moorden*, transl. Frédérique van der Velde [Bussum: Van Holkema & Warendorf, 1978], there 372–374); they are also reproduced by Raschke, *Painted Black*, 111. Manson is linked to LaVey by Hill, *Witchcraft, Magic and the Supernatural*, 164.

110. David G. Bromley, "Satanism: The New Cult Scare," in Richardson et al., *Satanism Scare*, 49–72, there 49.

111. James T. Richardson, "Satanism in the Courts: From Murder to Heavy Metal," in Richardson et al., *Satanism Scare*, 205–217, there 208–210.

112. Wuthnow, *Restructuring of American Religion*, 173–214, on "Mobilization on the Right."

113. Ellis, *Raising the Devil*, 89; Sherrill Mulhern, "Satanism and Psychotherapy: A Rumor in Search of an Inquisition," in Richardson et al., *Satanism Scare*, 145–172. MPD is now officially called dissociative identity disorder in the *DSM-IV*. On influences from Christian deliverance ministry on secular MPD therapy, cf. Ellis, *Raising the Devil*, 103.

114. Philip Jenkins and Daniel Maier-Katkin, "Occult Survivors: The Making of a Myth," in Richardson et al., *Satanism Scare*, 127–144, there 140. A concise overview of Freud's ideas with regard to child abuse can be found in Lawrence Wright, *Remembering Satan*, which I consulted in its Dutch translation *In de ban van Satan: Over ritueel seksueel misbruik en de mysteries van het geheugen*, trans. Nicky de Swaan (Amsterdam: L. J. Veen, 1994), there 118–122.

115. Ellis, *Raising the Devil*, 106.

116. Ellis, *Raising the Devil*, 109–112.

117. Ellis, *Raising the Devil*, 63. Notwithstanding his devout Catholicism, by the way, Pazder eventually divorced his wife to marry his client, a fact that suggests a certain lack of critical distance.

118. Ellis, *Raising the Devil*, 111.

119. Jenkins and Maier-Katkin, "Occult Survivors." The rise of the "occult survivor" fitted into a trend: various categories of "survivors" were beginning to come forward in this decade. Cf. Richardson, Best, and Bromley, "Satanism as a Social Problem," 11. An exploration of the "survivor" accounts resulting from the Satanism Scare can be found in Möller, *Satanismus als Religion der Überschreitung*, 40–57.

120. Wright, *In de ban van Satan*, 126.

121. Ellis, *Raising the Devil*, 117 (also on the influence of Pazder, who was called in as an expert); see Debbie Nathan, "Satanism and Child Molestation: Constructing the Ritual Abuse Scare," in Richardson et al., *Satanism Scare*, 75–94, there 81, for some earlier cases.

122. An overview of cases in the United States and Canada between 1983 and 1987 can be found in Victor, *Satanic Panic*, 355–361. See Nathan, "Satanism and Child Molestation," and Joel Best, "Endangered Children in Antisatanist Rhetoric," in Richardson et al., *Satanism Scare*, 95–106.

123. Wright, *In de ban van Satan*, 58.

124. On the role of the media, see Richardson, Best, and Bromley, "Satanism as a Social Problem," 12; Victor, *Satanic Panic*, 253–255. On "cult cops" and police involvement in spreading the Satanism Scare, see Robert D. Hicks, "The Police Model of Satanic Crime," in Richardson et al., *Satanism Scare*, 175–189, and Ben M. Crouch and Kelly Damphouse, "Law Enforcement and the Satanism-Crime Connection: A Survey of 'Cult Cops,'" in ibid., 191–204. Victor, *Satanic Panic*, 69, singles out "small town police and fundamentalist churches" as the two groups that were especially "ideologically receptive to the symbolism of Satanic cult rumors and are more likely to actively disseminate them."

125. Best, "Endangered Children," 97. The figure of 50,000 was reached by adopting the number of children reported missing in the United States each year and assuming that all or most of these children had fallen victim to Satanists. In reality, the majority of these cases were solved within days and most of them involved "abduction" by one of the parents in custody conflicts. Only two hundred to three hundred American children per year, it is estimated, fall victim to stereotypical kidnappings by strangers, none of which have been known to involve Satanists. On the ever wilder conspiracy thinking that accompanied the Satanism Scare, see Bromley, "Satanism," 56, 64; Mulhern, "Satanism and Psychotherapy," 159; Victor, *Satanic Panic*, 16, 294–295.

126. On rumor panics during the Satanism Scare, see Victor, *Satanic Panic*, with a chronological inventory on 330–354, as well as Jeffrey S. Victor, "The Dynamics of Rumor-Panics about Satanic Cults," in Richardson et al., *Satanism Scare*, 221–248; and Robert W. Balch and Margaret Gillam, "Devil Worship in Western Montana: A Case Study in Rumor Construction," in ibid., 249–262. On "occult" graffiti, "legend trips," and other folkloric and ostentive traditions that became elements in the Satanism Scare, cf. Bill Ellis, "Legend-Trips and Satanism: Adolescents' Ostentive Traditions as 'Cult' Activity," in Richardson et al., *Satanism Scare*, 279–295.

127. Richardson, Best, and Bromley, "Satanism as a Social Problem," 3.

128. Victor, *Satanic Panic*, 273–290; Medway, *Lure of the Sinister*, 1–3; Malcolm McGrath, *Demons of the Modern World* (Amherst, NY: Prometheus, 2002), 95, 108–109 (with qualifications).

129. Medway, *Lure of the Sinister*, 239. On the "inverted world" character of the Satanism attribution during the Satanism Scare, see Bromley, "Satanism," 58. Sometimes atavistic elements from the traditional attribution complex reappeared: for instance when one "occult survivor" reported on national television about the prevalence of ritual infanticide among American Jews (Jenkins and Maier-Katkin, "Occult Survivors," 131). This was one of the few cases in which survivors' allegations evoked public opposition; antisemitism clearly did not fit in the Satanist stereotype anymore.

130. Bromley, "Satanism," 68.

131. Ellis, *Raising the Devil*, 2–3, 5, 118–119; Victor, *Satanic Panic*, 55–56, 190–194; Victor, "Dynamics of Rumor-Panics about Satanic Cults," 227. Wuthnow, *Restructuring of American Religion*, 201, provides the following intriguing figures: "The media also began to feature much more prominently articles about sexual morality and abortion. By one estimate, the number of articles on abortion in the late 1970s was about four times as high as in the early 1960s, while the number of articles on 'sexual ethics' was more than five times as high." On anxiety about children and/or sexuality, see Best, "Endangered Children," 100. On the ambivalent nature of SRA fantasies (and earlier Satanism allegations) as both accepted outlets for "erotic fantasies of transgression" and forms of taboo affirmation, see Frankfurter, *Evil Incarnate*, 132, 140, and Möller, *Satanismus als Religion der Überschreitung*.

132. Nathan, "Satanism and Child Molestation," 82–83.

133. James T. Richardson, Jenny Reichert, and Valery Lykes, "Satanism in America: An Update," *Social Compass* 56 (December 2009) 4:552–563, there 555.

134. Victor, *Satanic Panic*, 112–113, 119–122; see also the particularly pertinent passages in Medway, *Lure of the Sinister*, 346–347, and McGrath, *Demons of the Modern World*, 98–102, 182.

135. Nathan, "Satanism and Child Molestation," 76. On local cases of violence and ostracism related to the Satanism Scare, cf. Victor, *Satanic Panic*, 176–179. In addition, huge public resources have been spent by U.S. government agencies in attempts to locate Satanist crimes. Cf. Bromley, "Satanism," 59–60.

136. An elaborate account of this story can be found in Wright's *Remembering Satan*, which I consulted in its Dutch translation, *In de ban van Satan*.

137. Medway, *Lure of the Sinister*, 343–344; http://en.wikipedia.org/wiki/Thurston_county_ritual_abuse_case, accessed 6 May 2013.

138. Ellis, *Raising the Devil*, 238–239.

139. Medway, *Lure of the Sinister*, 253–255; Lewis, *Satanism Today*, 180–181, 809.

140. Frankfurter, *Evil Incarnate*, 94.

141. Frankfurter, *Evil Incarnate*, 2–3, 97.

142. Frankfurter, *Evil Incarnate*, 97.

143. David Orr and Ilona Eveleens, "Kenyans Fear Satanism Charges Mask a Witch Hunt," *Independent*, 12 October 1996, consulted at http://www.independent.co.uk/news/world/kenyans-fear-satanism-charges-mask-a-witchhunt-1357944.html, accessed 7 May 2013; http://www.masonicinfo.com/kenya.htm, accessed 7 May 2013.

144. Diane LaVey to Charles Steenbarger, 6 March 1973, in Aquino, *Church of Satan*, 277.

145. Aquino, *Church of Satan*, 176–177, 258–259. LaVey's tendency for automystification, it must be said, may also have been motivational for his frequent use of other postal addresses.

146. Mike Warnke fabulated that he had met LaVey in 1966 but had found him slightly phoney and the public ceremony over which he presided "like going back to kindergarten" compared with the secret cult activities Warnke by that time was involved with (Ellis, *Raising the Devil*, 189). Raschke, *Painted Black*, 36, 131, suggests a darker role for the Black Pope.

147. In fact, LaVey is known to have actively cooperated with law enforcement agencies regarding rumors connected with Satanism; cf. Ellis, *Raising the Devil*, 260–261, 299n.

148. Bromley, "Satanism," 60. Several U.S. states issued legislation against blasphemy, ritual abuse, or ritual mutilation during the Satanism Scare (ibid.).

149. Raschke, *Painted Black*, 155.

150. Barton, *Secret Life of a Satanist*, 205; Barton, *Church of Satan*, 50–54, LaVey, *Satan Speaks*, 6.

151. LaVey, "Time to Start Kicking Ass," in *Devil's Notebook*, 126–129, there 126.

152. LaVey in Barton, *Church of Satan*, 79.

153. LaVey, *Devil's Notebook*, 82–83. LaVey was probably winking here to Crowley's exclamation "The Christians to the lions!" which is repeated threefold in the latter's commentary on the *Book of the Law*, 2:21; see Mathews, *Modern Satanism*, 38, quoting from Aleister Crowley, *The Law Is for All*, ed. Israel Regardie (Phoenix, AZ: Falcon, 1966), 177.

154. LaVey's (and much of modern Satanism's) inclination toward Right-wing ideology is commented upon in much of the literature on the Church of Satan or modern religious Satanism, but it is seldom deeply analyzed. An exception is Mathews, *Modern Satanism*, who concentrates most of his criticism on modern Satanism on its Right-wing tendencies and its affinity with "nineteenth-century philosophical misadventures." Mathews's criticism is often apt, but I still feel he has missed one side of the coin, as well as the considerable amount of irony in LaVey's writings. (Mathews's blind spot with regard to irony is symptomized by his serious mention of a "Satanist" Sammy Davis Jr. album entitles *Satan Swings Baby!* [p. 58] while failing to notice that the whole thing was an April Fools' Day prank by jazz critic Trevor Maclaren—cf. http://www1.allaboutjazz.com/php/article.php?id=21092, accessed 29 April 2011.) Another exception is Jesper Aagaard Petersen's interesting article "The Carnival of Dr. LaVey: Articulations of Transgression in Modern Satanism," in Faxneld and Petersen, *Devil's Party*, 167–188.

155. Barton, *Secret Life of a Satanist*, viii; see also the essay "Get a Life" in LaVey, *Satan Speaks*, 163–164. Again, the resemblance to Crowley is conspicuous—compare the latter's utterances in *Magick*, xxi: "Frater Perdurabo is the most honest of all the great religious teachers. Other have said: 'Believe me!' He says: '*Don't* believe me!' He does not ask for followers; would despise and refuse them. He wants an independent and self-reliant body of students to follow out their own methods of research." Like Crowley, LaVey nevertheless kept a tight grip on his organization as long as he lived.

156. LaVey, *Satanic Bible*, 45.

157. LaVey, "The Jewish Question? or Things My Mother Never Taught Me," in *Satan Speaks*, 69–72, there 71.

158. LaVey, *Satanic Bible*, 104.

159. LaVey, "Church of Satan, Cosmic Joy Buzzer," *Devil's Notebook*, 28–34.

160. LaVey, *Devil's Notebook*, 31.

161. Barton, *Church of Satan*, 59; Barton, *Secret Life of a Satanist*, 119–120.

162. Barton, *Church of Satan*, 121, 123.

163. Barton, *Church of Satan*, 121.

164. LaVey, *Devil's Notebook*, 93–96; the publication date is mentioned in Barton, *Church of Satan*, 135.

165. LaVey, *Devil's Notebook*, 93.

166. LaVey, *Devil's Notebook*, 93–94.

167. LaVey, *Devil's Notebook*, 93.

168. LaVey, *Devil's Notebook*, 96, 95, 146.

169. LaVey, *Devil's Notebook*, 95; LaVey, *Satan Speaks*, 30.

170. Nietzsche's inspiration with Plato is well attested; cf. Young, *Friedrich Nietzsche*, 515. LaVey also explicitly referred to Plato at least once when writing to the Church of Satan hierarchy that all Satanists were "supposed to be—at least in potential—Plato's philosopher-kings": "Phase IV Message to the Priesthood of Mendes, all Regional Agents," 27 September 1974, in Aquino, *Church of Satan*, 810–811.

171. Compare Péladan, *Introduction aux sciences occultes*, 71: "N'est-ce pas étrange, que l'on ait pu concevoir la justice sans l'accompagner de cette erreur impardonnable pour une époque qui s'attribue l'esprit scientifique: l'égalité! La nature n'est qu'une hiérarchie d'espèces, non de fonctions. Si l'on veut que les enfants, les infirmes et les vieillards puissent cueillir les fruits d'un arbre, on devra le tailler de façon à diminuer sa hauteur. Ainsi l'esprit démocratique qui a toujours rêvé l'uniformité des intelligences, arrive logiquement à l'abolition des hautes études parce qu'elles sont impossibles à la pluralité," as well as his *Vice suprême*, 391; Naglowska, *Lumière du Sexe*, 43: "la Justice appartient au plus fort, car c'est lui qui impose sa loi. *La loi est la volonté triomphante du plus fort.*"

172. Crowley, *Liber L vel Legis*, 2:58, 2:21, and 2:18. For the reference to Nietzsche, see Crowley, *Confessions*, 746; cf. also 539.

173. Mathews, *Modern Satanism*, 38, quoting from Crowley, *Law Is for All*, 177 (see note 153).

174. Naglowska, *Lumière du Sexe*, 14–15: "ceux—très rares—qui ne gouvernent pas et ne sont point gouvernés"; see also 103.

175. Aquino, *Church of Satan*, 75, quoting from David Gumaer, "Satanism: A Practical Guide to Witch Hunting," *American Opinion*, September 1970. Already in a publication from 1966, John Birch chairman Robert Welch had reappropriated classic antisemitic and anti-Masonic conspiracy theories into his anti-Communism, while also alluding to the "cult of Satanism" of the past as a sort of prototype for "our contemporary tyranny, Communism." See Ellis, *Raising the Devil*, 132.

176. Bonewits was even captured on film during a church ritual in the 1970 "documentary" *Satanis: The Devil's Mass*.

177. Cited in Ellis, *Raising the Devil*, 172.

178. See the correspondence in Aquino, *Church of Satan*, 378–380, where the National Renaissance Party is mentioned by name. In addition, see La Fontaine, "Satanism and Satanic Mythology," 113. The reasons why these Right-wing groups were interested in LaVey's church still have to be explored by scholarly historiography. Jacob C. Senholt's "Radical Politics and Political Esotericism: The Adaptation of Esoteric Discourse within the Radical Right," in *Contemporary Esotericism*, ed. Egil Asprem and Kennet Granholm (Sheffield, UK: Equinox, 2013), 244–264, which covers cross-overs between esotericism and Right-wing politics in general, offers some clues about possible areas of convergence.

179. LaVey cited in Michael Moynihan and Didrik Søderlind, *Lords of Chaos: The Bloody Rise of the Satanic Metal Underground* (Venice, CA: Feral House, 1998), 236; cf. similar utterances in Baddeley, *Lucifer Rising*, 76.

180. "Die elektrischen Vorspiele," LaVey, *Satanic Rituals*, 106–130. In one of his essays in *Satan Speaks*, 70, LaVey claimed that the rite originated with Erik Jan Hanussen, a famous Jewish clairvoyant with close connections to the Nazi elite. Compare Barton, *Church of Satan*, 34–35.

181. Aquino, *Temple of Set*, 95–107; Drury, *Stealing Fire from Heaven*, 218–220. For the history of popular lore about Nazi occultism, see Senholt, "Radical Politics and Political Esotericism," 251 (with further references).

182. LaVey, *Satanic Bible*, 82.

183. LaVey, *Satanic Bible*, 104. LaVey was evidently not aware of the low regard Hitler actually had had for Rosenberg's ideas.

184. Petersen, "Carnival of Dr. LaVey," 176–178.

185. LaVey, "A Plan," in *Satan Speaks*, 20–22.

186. LaVey, *Satanic Bible*, 104; Moynihan and Søderlind, *Lords of Chaos*, 236.

187. Aquino, *Church of Satan*, 264–276.

188. Cited in Barton, *Church of Satan*, 59–60.

189. LaVey to Aquino, 5 July 1974, cited in Aquino, *Church of Satan*, 380–381.

190. Aquino in a letter to Paul Pipkin, 25 November 1974, in Aquino, *Church of Satan*, 350. See also his letter to various grotto leaders, 1 July 1974, in ibid., 379–380.

191. Barton, *Church of Satan*, 59. Of course, LaVey does not refer to Aquino as his source here. The implication of identification is emphasized further by the sentence almost directly preceding this quote, where LaVey says: "We'll follow Huey Long's directive: 'When Fascism'—or Satanism—'comes to America it will be in the form of Americanism.'" This popular dictum is often misattributed to the populist interbellum governor Huey Long or to the American playwright Sinclair Lewis, but it seems to have been introduced to the public by Professor Halford E. Luccok of the Yale Divinity School. In the *New York Times* of 12 September 1938, he was reported to have said during a sermon: "When and if fascism comes to America it will not be labelled 'made in Germany'; it will not be marked with a swastika; it will not even be called 'fascism'; it will be called, of course, 'Americanism.'" I owe this reference to http://technoccult.net/archives/2010/03/03/who-really-said-when-fascism-comes-to-america-it-will-come-wrapped-in-the-flag-and-waving-a-cross/, accessed 29 May 2013.

192. LaVey, "Letters from the Devil," *the eXploiter*, 6 June 1971, 18, reproduced in LaVey, *Letters from the Devil*, [38].

193. Dvorak, *Satanismu*s, wrote (in 1993) that the Church of Satan was "kaum mehr aktiv"; in 1987, Melton, *Handbook of Cults*, 79, stated that the Temple of Set was "the only viable Satanic group . . . operating in America."

194. Aquino, *Church of Satan*, 433; Lyons, *Satan Wants You*, 122.

195. LaVey, "Evangelists vs. the New God," in *Devil's Notebook*, 84–85, there 85; Barton, *Church of Satan*, 58, where the Church of Satan is described as "the organisation that devised and manipulated the madness from the beginning." LaVey sometimes seemed to waver between two positions: one in which the coming of the Age of Satan was merely an inevitable process, much like the rise of the proletariat in early Marxism; and one in which he and the Church of Satan played a crucial and active role in orchestrating its advent.

196. Letter from LaVey to Aquino, 24 June 1971, in Aquino, *Church of Satan*, 378.

197. See Jacob C. Senholt, "Secret Identities in the Sinister Tradition: Political Esotericism and the Convergence of Radical Islam, Satanism, and National Socialism," in Faxneld and Petersen, *Devil's Party*, 250–274; the more elaborate 2009 conference paper by the same author, "The Sinister Tradition: Political Esotericism and the Convergence of Radical Islam, Satanism and National Socialism in the Order of the Nine Angles," which I accessed on 29 May 2013 at http://www.scribd.com/doc/38118165/The-Sinister-Tradition; and the conference paper by George Sieg mentioned in one of the notes below.

198. LaVey, *Satanic Rituals*, 173–201. The ritual was written by Aquino and based upon the horror stories of H. P. Lovecraft, but the "Nine Angles" appears to have been Aquino's own invention, representing, according to his own elucidation, the five points of the pentagram and the four-edge angles of the "phi-trapezoid," the pentagon within the pentagram (Aquino, *Church of Satan*, 693–697 [Appendix 72]). In his introductory text to the ritual, Aquino speculated about "the possibility that the Old Ones are the spectres of a future human mentality" (p. 178). Given his general program, this may well have attracted the interest of Long. The ONA itself denies this derivation and points out that its interpretation of the "Nine Angles" was different from that of Aquino. See, on this matter, Senholt, "Sinister Tradition," 20–21.

199. The Kabbalistic Sephiroth, for instance, is replaced with the neopagan "Tree of Wyrd."

200. George Sieg, "Angular Momentum: From Traditional to Progressive Satanism in the Order of the Nine Angles," [10–14], 2009 conference paper, http://www.ntnu.no/c/document_library/get_file?uuid=a827e3e1-3b8e-447a-b641-7d5285eb96f1&groupId=10244, accessed 14 May 2013.

201. See Myatt's digiscript *Recuyle of the Philosophy of Pathei-Mathos*, available via http://davidmyatt.files.wordpress.com/2012/11/myatt-recuyle-of-pathei-mathos.pdf, and his latest autobiography, *Myngath: Some Recollections of a Wyrdful and Extremist Life*, available via http://davidmyatt.files.wordpress.com/2013/04/david-myatt-myngath.pdf, both accessed 14 May 2013. Myatt accedes in this autobiography that he had set up a "secret Occult group" to serve as a "honey trap" for converting "respectable" people to the Right-wing political cause and/or for blackmailing them by their involvement in sex rites. He does not identify this group, however; cf. Myatt, *Myngath*, [91–92]. Myatt's strange ideological odyssey, moreover, is presented as a genuine spiritual quest—although this does not necessarily contradict interpreting them as a sequence of insight roles, as the latter also encompass a serious effort to broaden one's mental horizon. One of Myatt's more bizarre "insight roles" might have been his prolonged stay in a Roman Catholic monastery, at the end of which, according to his own recollections, one of his fellow monks remarked that he was eminently fit for the monastic life.

202. LaVey, *Satanic Bible*, 31.

203. LaVey, ' "Nonconformity: Satanism's Greatest Weapon,' " in *Devil's Notebook*, 63–65, there 63. I have reversed the original sequence of the two parts of this quotation.

204. LaVey, "Don't Be a Slave to (Other's) Subliminals," in *Satan Speaks*, 79–80,; LaVey, *Devil's Notebook*, 84, 86; LaVey, "The Death of Fashion," in *Satan Speaks*, 115–117, there 115; LaVey, "Clothes Make the Slave," in *Devil's Notebook*, 98–99, there 98.

205. LaVey, *Satan Speaks*, 177.

206. LaVey, "Nonconformity," *Devil's Notebook*, 63.

207. LaVey, *Devil's Notebook*, 15.

208. LaVey, *Satan Speaks*, 117, 162.

209. Baddeley, *Lucifer Rising*, 132.

210. LaVey, "Sleepers, Orphans, and Scarcity," in *Satan Speaks*, 41–42.

211. LaVey, *Devil's Notebook*, 63.

212. LaVey, *Devil's Notebook*, 64.

213. LaVey, *Devil's Notebook*, 63. Elsewhere, LaVey argued that "magical power is accrued by reading unlikely books, employing unlikely situations, and extracting unlikely ingredients, then utilizing these elements for what could be considered 'occult ends' " (ibid., 44).

214. LaVey, *Devil's Notebook*, 44.

215. LaVey, *Devil's Notebook*, 94.

216. LaVey, "Total Environments: Some Further Suggestions," in *Satan Speaks*, 152–154.

217. LaVey, *Devil's Notebook*, 63.

218. LaVey, *Devil's Notebook*, 96.

219. LaVey, *Satanic Rituals*, 12.

220. LaVey, *Devil's Notebook*, 84, 14, 86–88.

221. LaVey, *Devil's Notebook*, 88.

222. LaVey in Barton, *Church of Satan*, 82; compare ibid., 60–61. Strikingly enough, LaVey's idea concurs with the self-image of many Satanists (and neopagans), who often feel they did not convert to their religion but simply found a religious or philosophical system that fits with how they always were. Cf. James R. Lewis, "Conversion to Satanism: Constructing Diabolical Identities," in Faxneld and Petersen, *Devil's Party*, 145–166, there 147–156.

223. LaVey in Barton, *Church of Satan*, 82: "we must breed our new race of Satanists. We're interested in preserving and improving our genetic integrity."

224. Faxneld, "Secret Lineages and de Facto Satanists," 83, discounts these utterances as a pseudoscientific "garb" and rather suggests that LaVey was proposing "a form of Satanist perennialism: there is a worldview which has always existed, in all cultures and times, but has never been known under a single name." Although the element of perennialism is certainly prominent, the striking consistency of the genetic hypothesis with both LaVey's social Darwinism and his "Romanticism" suggests to me that he may have been dead serious about it.

225. See LaVey, *Satan Speaks*, 172–173, and his various authorized biographical accounts.

226. LaVey, *Devil's Notebook*, 95; compare also pp. 141–142, 146. In fact, LaVey seems to determine three classes of people: the true nonconformist, who creates his own world; an intermediate stratum of people, who join the nonconformist in this world (e.g., total environment); and the mindless herd, who are good for "target practice." Cf. *Devil's Notebook*, 63, 146.

227. LaVey, "Million d'Arlequin, Vesti la Giubba, et al.," in *Devil's Notebook*, 61–62, there 61.

228. Aleister Crowley, *Liber Oz. Liber LXXVII* (Los Angeles: O.T.O., An. Ixv [1941]). Crowley himself also spoke of this text as "The Rights of Man"; see Symonds, *King of the Shadow Realm*, 549–551. Symonds's commentary on this publication cannot be called other than utterly strange when he compares Crowley's *Liber Oz* with Sergei Nachayev's extremist *The Revolutionary's Catechism* and derides the former as "tame stuff." Pasi, *Aleister Crowley*, 271, has some pertinent analysis of the nature of the "elite" and the "slaves" in Crowley's thinking. As Crowley himself noted in *Confessions*, 539, "There will always be slaves, and the slave is to be defined as he who acquiesces in being slave." The similarities to LaVey's ideas are once again striking.

229. Barton, *Church of Satan*, 45.

230. A selection of which was republished in the slim collection *The Devil's Notebook* from 1992, while additional material would appear posthumously in *Satan Speaks*. LaVey stated his preference for reclusiveness in *Satan Speaks*, 169, among other places.

231. Wolfe, *Black Pope*, 216.

232. On frolicking with "student witches" and LaVey's bad odor, see Wolfe, *Black Pope*, 19. LaVey tells about his resolution to bathe as little as possible in the essay "Don't Bathe," in *Satan Speaks*, 134–136.

233. Wolfe, *Black Pope*, 205–210.

234. For LaVey's initial reaction to the Manson case, see, for instance, his column in *the eXploiter* from 3 January 1971, 18, reproduced in LaVey, *Letters from the Devil*, [25].

235. To be sure, her alliance with the Temple was also temporary. In 2002, Zeena LaVey left the Temple of Set to found the Sethian Liberation Movement, taking a substantial number of adherents with her. By then, she was already living in Austria with her husband or consort, Nicolas Schreck, where she authored a book on "Left Hand Path Sex Magic" and practiced as a "professional bereavement counsellor." On Zeena's recent career, see http://en.wikipedia.org/wiki/Zeena_Schreck, which I accessed on 5 June 2012. The further career of the various members of the LaVey family is described, although in a not very impartial way, by Wolfe, *Black Pope*, 232–239, 243–249. (Zeena's son Stanton, it may be added as an amusing sideline, at the time of writing tried to supplement his income by selling [replicas of] LaVey memorabilia. On sale for instance was a reproduction of the original Church of Satan membership card for $666, a price that included a thirty-minute phone call with Stanton himself, "World Famous Artist, Writer, Life Coach & Spiritual Healer." As seen on http://www.etsy.com/shop/ODIUM and http://www.etsy.com/listing/92952528/cos-card-phone-call-with-stanton-lavey, both accessed 7 June 2012.)

236. Wolfe, *Black Pope*, 204–205.

237. LaVey, "Erotic Crystallization Inertia," in *Devil's Notebook*, 72–75.

238. LaVey, "What's New," in *Satan Speaks*, 108–111, there 111.

239. LaVey, *Satan Speaks*, 110.

240. Wolfe, *Black Pope*, 198–199, 223.

241. LaVey, "Misanthropia," in *Devil's Notebook*, 139–142, there 139—I reversed the sequence of this quote. See also "The Merits of Artificiality," in *Devil's Notebook*, 130–132, and "The Construction of Artificial Human Companions," in *Devil's Notebook*, 133–138, as well as the LaVey interview in Baddeley, *Lucifer Rising*, 75–76. LaVey seems to have fostered this project at least as early as 1971, as is suggested by a letter from Diane LaVey to Michael Aquino dated 20 September 1970, cited in Aquino, *Church of Satan*, 147; see also Aquino, *Church of Satan*, 251, 400.

242. Wright, "Sympathy for the Devil," cited from Aquino, *Church of Satan*, 902–916, there 910; cf. Wolfe, *Black Pope*, 250–253.

243. Wright in Aquino, *Church of Satan*, 915; Hertenstein, *Selling Satan*, 419–431.

244. Wright, *Saints and Sinners*, 150. On LaVey's conspiracy thinking, see Asbjørn Dyrendal, "Hidden Persuaders and Invisible Wars: Anton LaVey and Conspiracy Culture," in Faxneld and Petersen, *Devil's Party*, 200–225, and "Hidden Knowledge, Hidden Powers," 207–209.

245. Here again, LaVey was probably indebted to Crowley; see the image of Crowley carrying out a "mudra" or yoga seal in Bessy, *Pictorial History of Magic*, 263 [pl. 850].

246. Moynihan and Søderlind, *Lords of Chaos*, 240.

247. The amendment was signed by Zeena LaVey and her partner, Schreck. The original death certificate can be seen on http://www.etsy.com/listing/152579638/the-official-court-certified-birth and http://www.churchofsatan.org/fake.html, both accessed 7 June 2013. For the death-bed confession rumor, see http://www.youtube.com/watch?v=Ga5P6ZTm81g, accessed 8 June 2013. I have failed to locate the original source of this rumor. LaVey had long maintained that he refused to die out of misanthropy, because "it would please so many people" (*Devil's Notebook*, 140).

248. In addition, it organizes an annual "Black X-Mass" party, with goth bands and adult entertainment. See http://www.satanicchurch.com/content/news, accessed 13 June 2013.

249. Maxwell Davies, "Self-Conscious Routinization and the Post-Charismatic Fate of the Church of Satan from 1997 to the Present," in Petersen, *Contemporary Religious Satanism*, 75–84.

250. Wolfe, *Black Pope*, 221.

251. Letter from Blanche Barton to Elizabeth Benford, attorney for Diane LaVey, 6 June 1990, cited in Aquino, *Church of Satan*, 438.

252. Don Lattin, "Satan's Den in Great Disrepair," *San Francisco Chronicle*, 25 January 1999, cited in Wolfe, *Black Pope*, 228.

253. Wolfe, *Black Pope*, 229–330; Aquino, *Church of Satan*, 447.

INTERMEZZO 4

1. Rock and metal music's adventures with the "Satanic" are recounted in Moynihan, *Lords of Chaos*. More historical data and lots of interviews in Baddeley, *Lucifer Rising*, 113–133, 160–211. On Black Metal specifically, see the excellent article by Gry Mørk, " 'With My Art I Am the Fist in the Face of God': On Old-School Black Metal," in Petersen, *Contemporary Religious Satanism*, 171–198, and the relevant sections in Moynihan, *Lords of Chaos*.

2. Moynihan, *Lords of Chaos*, 233.

3. Didrik Søderlind and Asbjørn Dyrendal, "Social Democratic Satanism? Some Examples of Satanism in Scandinavia," in Petersen, *Contemporary Religious Satanism*, 153–170, there 157.

4. Some individual cases of self-made religious Satanism with adolescents outside the metal subculture can be found in Dvorak, *Satanismus*, 319; Medway, *Lure of the Sinister*, 362–365. As might be expected, "adolescent Satanism" has often been used in a vague and confusing way in popular and scholarly publications; striking examples of such inappropriate usage are cited in Schmidt, *Satanismus*, 210–219.

5. Richardson, "Satanism in America," 559.

6. Introvigne, *Enquête sur le satanisme*, 391.

7. Victor, *Satanic Panic*, 153; Schmidt, *Satanismus*, 211–219; Andrea Menegotto, "Italian Martyrs of 'Satanism': Sister Maria Laura Mainetti and Father Giorgio Govoni," in Petersen, *Contemporary Religious Satanism*, 199–209, there 205. A more balanced attitude can be found in Petersen, "Introduction," 15; Lewis, "Conversion to Satanism," 147. The classic academic discussion of adolescent Satanism remains Kathleen S. Lowney, "Teenage Satanism as Oppositional Youth Subculture," *Journal of Contemporary Ethnography* 23 (1995) 4:453–484, which stands out for the way it takes this phenomenon seriously as a religious expression.

8. Lewis, "Conversion to Satanism," 148. Lucifer's Den is the only example I know of a Satanist organization that started as a high school group and was later resurrected as an adult religious organization; see Lewis, *Satanism Today*, 155.

9. Menegotto, "Italian Martyrs of 'Satanism.'"

10. For a particular sweet-flavored expression of adolescent Satanism, see Wenisch, *Satanismus*, 26, citing *Bild* from 28 May 1986: ". . . Sechs Schülerinnen (14 bis 17) streichelten sich bei Musik von sogenannten Satans-Rockern wie Death Kiss (Todeskuß) gegenseitig am ganzen Körper, baten Satan, einen Jungen von seiner Freundin zu befreien. Sie waren selbst in ihn verliebt."

11. Victor, *Satanic Panic*, 151.

12. Ellis, *Raising the Devil*, xix.

13. Victor, *Satanic Panic*, 155–179; Best, "Endangered Children in Antisatanist Rhetoric," 100–103. For court cases against metal bands, see Richardson, "Satanism in the Courts," 210–213.

14. As far as I know, only Peter Paul Schnierer has made a very slight suggestion of a possible family resemblance when he points out how the lyrics of Cradle of Filth have their roots in late Victorian poetry, especially that of Swinburne. See Schnierer, *Entdämonisierung und Verteufelung*, 211.

15. "Euronymous" (Øystein Aarseth) cited by Baddeley, *Lucifer Rising*, 203–204. Euronymous, who was the frontman of the band Mayhem and founder of the prominent Black Metal label Deathlike Silence Records, would be killed two month later by Count Grishnackh (Kristian Vikernes, who later was renamed Varg Vikernes) of Burzum during an inner-circle feud.

16. Wright, *Saints and Sinners*, 128.

17. Lyons, *Satan Wants You*, 170–171.

18. LaVey, *Satan Speaks*, 16–17; compare *Satan Speaks*, 63–64, 114, and Lyons, *Satan Wants You*, 170–171, for similar utterances.

19. Baddeley, *Lucifer Rising*, 133.

20. LaVey, *Satan Speaks*, 85. I think LaVey was clearly referring to rock or metal concerts here, as when he was talking about "many thousands of kids cheering real Satanic symbols and giving the sign of the horns" on p. 127. Compare Barton, *Church of Satan*, 61–62.

21. LaVey in Baddeley, *Lucifer Rising*, 239–240.

22. This is suggested by LaVey, *Satan Speaks*, 159; for the Church of Satan's Internet presence, see Jesper Aagaard Petersen, "From Book to Bit: Enacting Satanism Online," in Asprem and Granholm *Contemporary Esotericism*, 134–158, there 140.

23. Baddeley, *Lucifer Rising*, 77. Similar sentiments are voiced by LaVey in *Satan Speaks*, 159.

24. On "Cyber-Satanism," see Petersen, "From Book to Bit," 134–158; Milda Alisauskiene, "The Peculiarities of Lithuanian Satanism: Between Crime and Atheism in Cyberspace," in Petersen, *Contemporary Religious Satanism*, 121–128; Rafal Smoczynski, "Cyber-Satanism and Imagined Satanism: Dark Symptoms of Late Modernity," in ibid., 141–151. Further references are in Petersen, "From Book to Bit," 137n.

25. LaVey in Barton, *Church of Satan*, 129–130.

26. Rafal Smoczynski, "The Making of Satanic Collective Identities in Poland: From Mechanic to Organic Solidarity," in Faxneld and Petersen, *Devil's Party*, 189–203, there 194.

27. In his last "Satan Survey," James Lewis found that most Satanists found their way to their religion by way of books or the Internet. Forty-five percent of these people never speak

to another Satanist in person, while 70 percent have daily contact on the Internet with other Satanists by public or private messages. Lewis, "Conversion to Satanism," 157–161.

28. For Satanism in Italy (which has roots to at least the early 1970s): Introvigne, *Enquête sur le satanisme*, 378–392, and the same author's "Le satanisme moderne et contemporain en Italie," *Social Compass* 56 (December 2009) 4:541–551. The United Kingdom: Dave Evans, "Speculating on the Point 003 Percent? Some Remarks on the Chaotic Satanic Minorities in the UK," in Petersen, *Contemporary Religious Satanism*, 211–228. France: Alexis Mombelet, "Entre metanoïa et paranoïa: Approches sociologique et médiatique du satanisme en France," *Social Compass* 56 (December 2009) 4:530–530. Scandinavia: Søderlind, and Dyrendal, "Social Democratic Satanism?"; Titus Hjelm, Henrik Bogdan, Asbjørn Dyrendal, and Jesper Aagaard Petersen, "Nordic Satanism and Satanism Scares: The Dark Side of the Secular Welfare State," *Social Compass* 56 (December 2009) 4:515–529. Poland: Rafal Smoczynski, "Making of Satanic Collective Identities in Poland," and Smoczynski, "Cyber-Satanism and Imagined Satanism." Estonia: Ringo Ringvee, "Satanism in Estonia," in Petersen, *Contemporary Religious Satanism*, 129–140. Lithuania: Alisauskiene, "The Peculiarities of Lithuanian Satanism." The Islamic world (particularly with respect to Black Metal): Mark Levine, "Doing the Devil's Work: Heavy Metal and the Threat to Public Order in the Muslim World," *Social Compass* 56 (December 2009) 4:564–576.

29. Smoczynski, "Cyber-Satanism and Imagined Satanism," 146–150.

30. For the Rastafarian Satanists, see First Rastafarian Church of Satan, *The Rastafarian Satanic Bible* ([Los Angeles]: s.i., 2005). This very small Los Angeles group went defunct after its primary organizer moved to Ethiopia, at least according to a likewise defunct website I accessed somewhere in 2008 or 2009. For the Satanic Reds, cf. Petersen, "'We demand bedrock knowledge' Modern Satanism between Secularized Esotericism and 'Esotericized' Secularism," 96–99. See also the outdated but nevertheless extensive list of schismatic and affiliated Satanist groups in Barton, *Church of Satan*, 49.

CONCLUSION

1. This and earlier citation from *Report to the Council of the League of Nations on the Administration of the Territory of New Guinea from 1st July, 1934, to 30th June, 1935* (Commonwealth of Australia: Canberra, 1936), 19–20, citing an original report by a colonial officer who is not mentioned by name. I owe the reference to Marafi to Peter Worsley's classic book *The Trumpet Shall Sound: A Study of the "Cargo" Cults in Melanesia* (New York: Schocken, 1968), 101–103.

2. *Report on the Administration of the Territory of New Guinea 1934–1935*, 19–21. Worsley, *Trumpet Shall Sound*, 101–103, maintains that another outburst of this Papuan Satanism occurred in 1936, but the articles in the *Neuendettelsauer Missionsblatt* he gives as reference (February 1936, p. 13; May 1936, pp. 35–36) seem to describe different examples of Papuan millennialism in the same region.

Roughly similar examples of "native" adoption of the devil have been reported from Latin America. Fernando Cervantes describes several cases from marginal areas of colonial Mexico in which the Spaniards' identification of indigenous deities with Satan had a reverse effect and encouraged the Indians "to collaborate actively in the process of their own demonization" by venerating the devil or the demons as the new version of their old gods (see Cervantes, *Devil in the New World*, 92, 46–53, 56, 91–94). In one particularly confused case of syncretism, a cult to Satan was rendered by converted Indians in their local church and parallel with normal Roman Catholic services; the devil, moreover, seems to have been identified by them with both the pre-Hispanic god of thunder, and James the Apostle, a saint often associated with thunder and lightning (ibid., 51–53). Similarly, the anthropologist Michael T. Taussig reports that even in the 1960s, Bolivian tin miners placed statues of "Tio," or the devil, in their mines and held traditional rites of sacrifice for him. According to Taussig, the "Tio" ultimately derived from the pre-Incan god of the mountain: as the Christian god ruled above, the devil ruled below the ground. Consequently, Roman Catholic priests were not allowed to enter the mines because their presence would cause the tin to disappear. See Taussig, *Devil and Commodity Fetishism*, 143–228, in particular 143–144, 147–148.

3. Although reliable statistical data about adherents to modern Satanism are lacking, an ongoing series of surveys among (primarily American) Satanists by James R. Lewis shows that the average Satanist of today is a white male raised in a Christian household. However, Lewis concludes that "though a reaction against Christianity may well have been a factor for some, too many respondents indicated that their religious upbringing was superficial, nominal, or nonexistent to explain why most people become Satanists" (Lewis, "Infernal Legitimacy," 52; see also Lewis, "Conversion to Satanism," 148). Similarly, many Norwegian Black Metal Satanists only had superficial experience with Christianity before they got into Black Metal; as "Ihsahn" of Black Emperor observed, it was only after being exposed to the anti-Christian rhetoric within their subculture that they adopted a militantly anti-Christian stance (cited in Moynihan and Søderlind, *Lords of Chaos*, 196). Anton Szandor LaVey may himself be considered an early example of a Satanist who was not marked by a Christian upbringing or a personal conflict with the Christian faith.

4. *Report on the Administration of the Territory of New Guinea 1934–1935*, 20.

5. Gregorius IX, "Vox in Rama," 1:433, ll. 43–44: "Omnia Deo placita non agenda fatentur, et potius agenda que odit."

6. Among the extensive literature on conspiracy thinking, see especially Alain de Benoist, "Psychologie de la théorie du complot," *Politica Hermetica* 6 (1992): 13–28, and Dieter Groh, "Die verschwörungstheoretische Versuchung oder: Why Do Bad Things Happen to Good People?," *Anthropologische Dimensionen der Geschichte* (Frankfurt am Main: Suhrkamp, 1992), 267–304; valuable observations about the "redemptive" qualities of such theories can be found in Dyrendal, "Hidden Knowledge, Hidden Powers," 222–223. The role of childhood fantasies has been suggested by McGrath, *Demons of the Modern World*; similar theories had already been suggested by the Freudian Hanns Sachs in 1915; see Dvorak, *Satanismus*, 372 (and compare Frankfurter, *Evil Incarnate*, 209). The noted Dutch expert on primate behavior, Frans de Waal, remarks, "Obviously, the most potent force to bring out a sense of community is enmity towards outsiders. It forces unity among elements that are normally at odds. This . . . is definitely a factor for chimpanzees in the wild, which show lethal intercommunity violence." See his *Primates and Philosophers: How Morality Evolved* (Princeton, NJ: Princeton University Press, 2006), there 54–55.

7. This is suggested with regard to the Satanism Scare by Ellis, "Legend-Trips and Satanism," 292, who formulates the hypothesis that Satanists were only "proxy targets" in an internal conflict between traditionalists and modernists within American Christianity. In a broader sense, this hypothesis perfectly agrees with the evolutionary perspective offered by De Waal.

8. Rubin, *Gentile Tales*, 194.

9. Cited in Mandrou, *Possession et sorcellerie au XVIIᵉ siècle*, 300: "le diable n'ayant pas voulu d'elle."

10. Muchembled, *History of the Devil*, 149. This practical attitude is even in evidence with the first (and unconfirmed) case of Satanism we find in history: the "Satanians" whose existence is reported by Epiphanius of Salamis in the fourth century. According to Epiphanius, they turned to Satan because he was "great and the strongest, and does people a great deal of harm." See Epiphanius of Salamis, *Panarion: Book II and III*, 630 [8, 3, 1].

11. The Romantic rehabilitation of Satan should not be confused with earlier notions about the eventual *redemption* of Satan that had been espoused by Christian theologians like Origen. The Romantic Satanists praised Satan *because* of his act of rebellion; earlier ideas about Satan's redemption saw his rebellion as a transgression but speculated he would eventually be redeemed from its consequences by divine grace.

12. The difficulty to gain trustworthy data on the number of Satanists in the world will be obvious to the reader. Introvigne, *Enquête sur le satanisme*, 375, suggested a number of 10,000 adherents in 1997; Mathews, *Modern Satanism*, 160, proposes 30,000 to 100,000 Satanists globally, an estimation that is described as "quite reasonable" in Faxneld and Petersen, "Introduction," 5. At present, the only sizable Satanist presences can be found in the Anglophonic world and in Scandinavia. A 2006 census in Australia resulted in a number of 2,247 self-designated Satanists, while a 2001 National Census in England and Wales brought out 1,500. The total number of Satanists in the United Kingdom may be higher, but as Dave Evans states: "My own work leads me to believe that there might actually now be more academics researching occultism in general in the UK than that there actually are Satanists practicing their version of it." Evans, "Speculating on the Point 003 Percent," 226; see 214–215 for census data.

13. Faxneld, "Secret Lineages and de Facto Satanists," 81, also points to Dashwood and the Hell-Fire Clubs as "one of the most important sources of historical inspiration" of LaVeyan Satanism. I have not explored this line of influence in this study.

14. Frankfurter, *Evil Incarnate*, 198–203.

15. Compare Wouter J. Hanegraaff, "How Magic Survived the Disenchantment of the World," *Religion* 33 (2003): 357–380. Partridge, *Re-Enchantment of the West*, 41, criticizes Hanegraaff on this point and argues that "secularized" magic is in essence the same as premodern magic. But if we compare, say, early modern necromancy, the "Magism" of Éliphas Lévi, and LaVeyan magic, profound differences are obvious; in addition, doing the same thing in different circumstances can make it something very different after all.

16. Cf. the short discussion of "disembedding" and "de-embedding" in Asprem and Granholm, "Constructing Esotericisms," 29.

17. See LaVey's utterances in Barton, *Secret Life of a Satanist*, 207.

18. Bellah, "Religious Evolution," 85.

19. Hanegraaff, *New Age Religion and Western Culture*, 415–421, 494; Partridge, *Re-Enchantment of the West*, 72.

20. Armand Snijders, "Leve satan, God is een slappeling," *Dagblad De Pers* (18 October 2007): 12: "God is een slappeling, . . . Satan echter is een krachtige figuur. Als je hem aanbidt en een trouwe volgeling bent, kom je in zijn paradijs. Maar stel je hem teleur, dan zul je branden in de hel." The Black Metal fan is only identified as "Jerrel, a fourth grade high

school pupil." The interview seems genuine to me but appeared in a context of wild rumors about Satanism in Surinam, during which claims were being made that 16,000 adolescents were involved in Satanism in the small Latin American country. See "Meer dan 16.000 jongeren in het Satanisme," *Dagblad van Suriname*, 10 February 2007 on www.dbsuriname. com, accessed 6 February 2008.

21. Compare Godwin, *Theosophical Enlightenment*, 379.

22. Frye, *Study of English Romanticism*, 125–126. Cf. Hexham and Poewe, *New Religions as Global Culture*, 70: "New religions are what we call šhuman religions. They sanctify (š) things human (human). Šhumanists cannot free themselves of nor undo Enlightenment teaching that made the human being and the material world the starting point of all else."

23. Barton, *Church of Satan*, 5.

24. Similar objections against "theologically" informed demarcations of religion are raised by Granholm, "Secular, the Post-Secular and the Esoteric in the Public Sphere," 313.

25. And also one of marginality, as Mathews, *Modern Satanism*, 175, rightly remarks. LaVeyan Satanism's self-conception as an "elite" religion thus becomes a self-fulfilling prophecy, as Mathews aptly adds.

26. In *Liber Librae*, Crowley wrote, "Remember that unbalanced force is evil; that unbalanced severity is but cruelty and oppression; but that also unbalanced mercy is but weakness which would allow and abet Evil": closely paraphrasing, in fact, the Golden Dawn Neophyte ritual, which will have been inspired by similar statements by Lévi. See Kaczynski, "Continuing Knowledge from Generation unto Generation," 147 and 172n.

27. Introvigne, *Enquête sur le Satanisme*, 15.

28. Faxneld, "Secret Lineages and De Facto Satanists," 83.

29. Similar musings can be found in Introvigne, *Enquête sur le satanisme*, 393–394. Despite the attitude of antimodern nostalgia these words evoke, Introvigne undoubtedly has a certain point when he describes modern Satanism as "la métaphore d'une modernité brutale à laquelle on aurait arraché tous ses paravents rhétoriques."

30. For instance, in LaVey, "Church of Satan, Cosmic Joy Buzzer"; LaVey, *Devil's Notebook*, 31. Compare *Devil's Notebook*, 38, and "The Third Side: The Uncomfortable Alternative," in *Satan Speaks*, 29–32, there 30, as well as LaVey's utterances in Lyons, *Second Coming*, 185.

⌒──

Aagaard, Johannes, "Occultisme/Satanism and the Christian Faith." In *Le Défi Magique II: Satanisme, sorcellerie*, edited by Jean-Baptiste Martin and Massimo Introvigne, 259–267. Lyon: Presses Universitaires de Lyon, 1994.

Abrams, M. H., "English Romanticism: The Spirit of the Age." In *Romanticism: Points of View*, edited by Robert F. Gleckner and Gerald E. Enscoe, 314–330. Englewood Cliffs, NJ: Prentice-Hall, 1970.

Ach, Manfred, and Jörgensen, Johannes, *Joris-Karl Huysmans und die okkulte Dekadenz*. München: Arbeitsgemeinschaft für Religions- und Weltanschauungsfragen, 1980.

Ackroyd, Peter, *Blake*. London: Sinclair-Stevenson, 1995.

Agulhon, Maurice, *Marianne au combat: L'imagerie et la symbolique républicaines de 1789 à 1880*. Paris: Flammarion, 1979.

———, "Paris: A Traversal from East to West." In *Realms of Memory: The Construction of the French Past. Volume III: Symbols*, edited by Pierre Nora and Lawrence D. Kritzman, 523–553. Translated by Arthur Goldhammer. New York: Columbia University Press, 1998.

Alfred, Randall H., "The Church of Satan." In *The New Religious Consciousness*, edited by Charles Y. Glock and Robert N. Bellah, 180–202. Berkeley: University of California Press, 1976.

Algra, Keimpe, "Stoics on Souls and Demons: Reconstructing Stoic Demonology." In *Demons and the Devil in Ancient and Medieval Christianity*, edited by Nienke Vos and Willemien Otten, 71–96. Supplements to Vigiliae Christianae: Texts and Studies of Early Christian Life and Language, no. 108. Leiden: Brill, 2011.

Alinsky, Saul D., *Rules for Radicals: A Practical Primer for Realistic Radicals*. New York: Random House, 1971.

Alisauskiene, Milda, "The Peculiarities of Lithuanian Satanism: Between Crime and Atheism in Cyberspace." In *Contemporary Religious Satanism: A Critical Anthology*, edited by Jesper Aagaard Petersen, 121–128. Farnham, UK: Ashgate, 2009.

Altermatt, Urs, "L'engagement des intellectuels catholiques suisses au sein de l'Internationale noire." In *The Black International/L'International noire 1870–1878*, edited by Emiel Lamberts, 409–426. Leuven: Leuven University Press, 2002.

Ambelain, Robert, *Adam Dieu Rouge: L'ésotérisme judéo-chrétien, la gnose et les Ophites lucifériens et rose + croix*. Paris: Éditions Niclaus, 1941.

Amirav, Hagit, "The Application of Magical Formulas of Invocation in Christian Contexts." In *Demons and the Devil in Ancient and Medieval Christianity*, edited by Nienke Vos and Willemien Otten, 117–127. Supplements to Vigiliae Christianae: Texts and Studies of Early Christian Life and Language, no. 108. Leiden: Brill, 2011.

Andrey, Georges, "La Croisade antimaçonnique (XIXe–XXe sicècles)." In *La Franc-maçonnerie à Fribourg et en Suisse du XVIIIᵉ au XXᵉ siècle*, edited by Yvonne Lehnherr, 177–186. Gèneve: Slatkine, 2001.

Angenendt, Arnold, "Die Liturgie und die Organisation des Kirchlichen Lebens auf dem Lande." In *Cristianizzazione ed organizzazione ecclesiastica delle campagne nell'alto medioevo: espansione e resistenze*, 1:169–226. Spoleto: Centro Italiano di Studi sull'Alto Medioevo, 1982.

Ankarloo, Bengt, and Gustav Hennigsen (eds.), *Early Modern European Witchcraft: Center and Peripheries*. Oxford: Clarendon, 1990.

Anonymous, "Chez le Sar." *Le Jour*, 28 April 1891, 1–2.

———, "Diana Vaughan." *L'Éclaire*, 10 December 1896.

———, *Diana Vaughan: Haar persoon, haar werk en haar aanstaande komst*. Leiden: J. W. van Leeuwen, 1897.

———, *Ergänzungsband zum Bilder-Lexikon: Kulturgeschichte—Literatur und Kunst—Sexualwissenschaft*. Bilderlexikon der Erotik, vol. 4. Wien: Verlag für Kulturforschung, 1931.

———, "Gestorum Treverorum Continuatio IV." *Monumenta Germaniae Historica inde ab Anno Christi quingentesimo usque ad annum millesimum et quintegentesimum: Scriptorum*. vol. 23. Hannoverae: Impensis Bibliopolii Hahniani, 1879.

———, *Gremoire du Pape Honorius: Avec un recueil des plus rares secrets*. 1670. Reprint, Paris: Éditions Bussière, 2012.

———, *Grimoire du Pape Honorius, avec un recueil des plus rares secrets*. Rome [Lille]: Imprimerie Du Blocquel, 1760.

———, *Joris-Karl Huysmans: Du naturalisme au satanisme et à Dieu*. Paris: Bibliothèque Nationale/Bibliothèque de l'Arsenal, 1979.

———, *Le Crapouillot: Magazine non conformiste* 78 (November 1984)—*Sexe et magie*.

———, *Le labarum anti-maçonnique: Statuts de l'ordre, déclaration de principes et grandes constitutions, cérémonial des grand'gardes, extraits du rituel des chevaliers du Sacré-Cœur*. Paris: Librarie Antimaçonnique, s.a. [1895].

———, *Lettre de Satan aux Francs-Maçons, suivi d'une réponse à Satan*. Paris: Potey, 1825.

———, *Mariken van Nieumegen: Ingeleid en toegelicht door Dirk Coigneau*. 's-Gravenhage: Martinus Nijhoff, 1982.

———, *Mensonges cléricaux*. Paris: Imp. Rinuy, s.a. [1897].

———, "Miss Diana Vaughan." *Le Matin*, 23 November 1896.

——, *Réflexions sur le procès intenté à M. Waille, au sujet de l'écrit intitulé: "Lettre de Satan aux francs-maçons". Extrait du Mémorial Catholique (février, 1826).* [Paris]: Impr. De Gueffier, 1826.

——, *Report to the Council of the League of Nations on the Administration of the Territory of New Guinea from 1st July, 1934, to 30th June, 1935.* Commonwealth of Australia: Canberra, 1936.

——, *Satan. Les Études Carmélitaines* 27. Paris: Desclée De Brouwer, 1948.

——, "Satan." In: *Encyclopaedia Judaica*, 14:901–903. Jerusalem: Keter, 1972.

Aquino, Michael A., *The Church of Satan.* San Francisco: s.n., 2009 [e-book published by the author, sixth edition].

——, *The Temple of Set.* San Francisco: s.n., 2002–2010 [e-book published by the author, draft 11].

Asad, Talal, *Genealogies of Religion: Discipline and Reasons of Power in Christianity and Islam.* Baltimore, MD: John Hopkins University Press, 1993.

Ashe, Geoffrey, *The Hell-Fire Clubs: A History of Anti-Morality.* Stroud: Sutton, 2001.

Asprem, Egil, "*Kabbalah Recreata*: Reception and Adaptation of Kabbalah in Modern Occultism." *Pomegranate* 9 (2007) 2:132–253.

——, "Magic Naturalized? Negotiating Science and Occult Experience in Aleister Crowley's Scientific Illuminism." *Aries* 8 (2008): 139–165.

Asprem, Egil, and Kennet Granholm, "Introduction." In *Contemporary Esotericism*, edited by Egil Asprem and Kennet Granholm, 1–24. Sheffield, UK: Equinox, 2013.

——, "Constructing Esotericisms: Sociological, Historical and Critical Approaches to the Invention of Tradition." In *Contemporary Esotericism*, edited by Egil Asprem and Kennet Granholm, 25–48. Sheffield, UK: Equinox, 2013.

Assmann, Jan, *Moses the Egyptian: The Memory of Egypt in Western Monotheism.* Cambridge, MA: Harvard University Press, 1997.

Atkins, Susan, with Bob Slosser, *Child of Satan, Child of God.* Plainfield, NJ: Logos International, 1977.

Awn, Peter J., *Satan's Tragedy and Redemption: Iblīs in Sufi Psychology.* Studies in the History of Religions, no. 44. Leiden: Brill, 1983.

Baal, J. van, "Magic as a Religious Phenomenon." *Higher Education and Research in the Netherlands* 7 (1963): 3–4, 10–21.

Baddely, Gavin, *Lucifer Rising: Sin, Devil Worship and Rock 'n' Roll.* London: Plexus, 1999.

Bainbridge, William Sims, *Satan's Power: A Deviant Psychotherapy Cult.* Berkeley: University of California Press, 1978.

——, "Social Construction from Within: Satan's Process." In *The Satanism Scare*, edited by James T. Richardson, Joel Best, and David G. Bromley, 297–310. New York: Aldine de Gruyter, 1991.

Bakunin, Michael, *God and the State.* New York: Dover, 1970.

Balch, Robert W., and Margaret Gillam, "Devil Worship in Western Montana: A Case Study in Rumor Construction." In *The Satanism Scare*, edited by James T. Richardson, Joel Best, and David G. Bromley, 249–262. New York: Aldine de Gruyter, 1991.

Baldick, Robert, *The Life of J.-K. Huysmans.* Oxford: Clarendon, 1955.

Barbeau, Raymond, *Un prophète luciférien: Léon Bloy.* Aubier: Éditions Montaigne, 1957.

Barbey, Léon, *L'âme du Chanoine Schorderet.* Fribourg: Éditions de l'Imprimerie St-Paul, 1943.

Barbey d'Aurevilly, Jules, *Les Diaboliques*. Paris: Alphonse Lemerre, s.a.

Baron, Louis, *Réponse aux polissonneries de Léo Taxil et aux divagations d'Andrieux*. Toulouse: Orient de Toulouse, 1886.

Barr, James, "The Question of Religious Influence: The Case of Zoroastrianism, Judaism, and Christianity." *Journal of the American Academy of Religion* 53 (June 1985), 2:201–235.

Barrès, Maurice, *Un rénovateur de l'occultisme, Stanislas de Guaita (1861–1898)*. Paris: Chamuel, 1898.

Barrucand, Pierre, "Quelques aspects de l'antimaçonnisme, le cas de Paul Rosen." *Politica Hermetica* 4 (1987): 91–108.

Barruel, Augustin, *Mémoires pour servir à l'histoire du jacobinisme*. 4 vols. London: Ph. Le Boussonnier, 1797.

Barry, Jonathan, and Owen Davies (eds.), *Palgrave Advances in Witchcraft Historiography*. Houndmills: Palgrave Macmillan, 2007.

Barton, Blanche, *The Church of Satan: A History of the World's Most Notorious Religion*. New York: Hell's Kitchen, 1990.

———, *The Secret Life of a Satanist: The Authorized Biography of Anton LaVey*. London: Mondo, 1992.

Bartrina, Joaquín Maria, *Obras poéticas*. Barcelona: Bosch, 1939.

Baskin, Wade, *Dictionary of Satanism*. New York: Philosophical Library, 1971.

Basset, Serge, "Une messe noire: Chez les adorateurs du prince des ténèbres." *Le Matin*. 14 (27 May 1899) 5571:1–2.

Bastiaensen, Toon, "Exorcism: Tackling the Devil by Word of Mouth." In *Demons and the Devil in Ancient and Medieval Christianity*, edited by Nienke Vos and Willemien Otten, 129–142. Supplements to Vigiliae Christianae: Texts and Studies of Early Christian Life and Language, no. 108. Leiden: Brill, 2011.

Baudelaire, Charles, *Curiosités esthétiques, L'Art romantique et autres œuvres critiques*. Paris, Éditions Garnier Frères, 1962.

———, *Journaux intimes. Fusées—Mon cœur mis á nu—Carnet. Édition critique établie par Jacques Crépet et Georges Blin*, Paris: Librairie José Corti, 1949.

———, *Les Fleurs du Mal: Texte de la seconde edition suivi des pieces supprimées en 1857 et des additions de 1868. Édition critique établie par Jacques Crépet et Georges Blin*. Paris: Librairie José Corti, 1968.

———, *Le spleen de Paris: Petits poèmes en prose*. Paris: Librio, 2010.

Bataille, "Docteur." *Le Diable au XIXᵉ siècle: La Franc-Maçonnerie luciférienne ou les mystères du spiritisme. Révélations complètes sur le Palladisme, la théurgie, la goétie et tout le satanisme moderne. Récits d'un témoin*. 2 vols. Paris: Delhomme and Briguet, [1892–1893].

Bavent, Madeleine, *The Confessions of Madeleine Bavent*. Translated by Montague Summers. London: Fortune, 1933.

Beaufils, Christophe, *Joséphin Péladan (1858–1918): Essai sur une maladie du lyrisme*. Grenoble: Jérôme Million, 1993.

Behringer, Wolfgang, "How Waldensians Became Witches: Heretics and Their Journey to the Other World." In *Communicating with the Spirits*, edited by Gabor Klaniczay, Eva Pócs, and others, 155–192. Budapest: Central European University Press, 2005.

Bekker, Baltasar, *De Betooverde Weereld, zynde een grondig ondersoek van "t gemeen gevoelen aan-gaande de geesten, derselver Aart en vermogen, Bewind en Bedryf: als ook "t gene de Menschen door derselver kraght en gemeenschap doen*. Amsterdam: Daniel van den Dalen, 1691.

Bel, Jacqueline, "Satan in Holland. Over *Goëtia*, de salon-sataniste van Frits Lapidoth." In *Teruggedaan: Eenenvijftig bijdragen voor Harry G.M. Prick ter gelegenheid van zijn afscheid als conservator van het Nederlands Letterkundig Museum en Documentatiecentrum*, edited by Th. A. P. Bijvoet, S. A. J. van Faassen, Anton Korteweg, and others, 27–35. 's-Gravenhage: Nederlands Letterkundig Museum and Documentatiecentrum, 1988.

Bellah, Robert, "Religious Evolution." In *Reader in Comparative Religion: An Anthropological Approach*, edited by W. A. Lessa and E. Z. Vogt, 73–87. New York: Grune and Stratton, 1965.

Beller, Steven, *Antisemitism: A Very Short Introduction*. Oxford: Oxford University Press, 2007.

Belval, Maurice M., *Des ténèbres à la lumière: Etapes de la pensée mystique de J.K. Huysmans*. Paris: Maisonneuve and Larose, 1968.

Bénédictins de la Congrégation de S. Maur (ed.), *Recueil des Historiens des Gaules et de la France*, vol. 10. Paris: Chez Gabriel Martin, H. L. Guerin and L.F. Delatour, Antoine Boudet, 1760.

Bénichou, Paul, *Le sacre de l'écrivain, 1750–1830: Essai sur l'avènement d'un pouvoir laïque dans la France moderne*. Paris: Éditions Gallimard, 1996.

———, *Le temps des prophètes: Doctrines de l'âge romantique*. [Paris]: Éditions Gallimard, 1977.

———, *Les mages romantiques*. [Paris]: Éditions Gallimard, 1988.

Benko, Stephen, "The Libertine Gnostic Sect of the Phibionites According to Epiphanus." *Vigilæ Christianæ* 21 (1967): 103–119.

Benoist, Alain de, "Psychologie de la théorie du complot." *Politica Hermetica* 6 (1992): 13–28.

Berend, Nora, *At the Gate of Christendom: Jews, Muslims and "Pagans' in Medieval Hungary, c. 1000–c. 1300*. Cambridge: Cambridge University Press, 2001.

Berger, Peter, Grace Davie, and Effie Fokas, *Religious America, Secular Europe? A Theme and Variations*. Aldershot, UK: Ashgate, 2008.

Berlin, Isaiah, "The Romantic Revolution. A Crisis in the History of Modern Thought." In *The Sense of Reality: Studies in Ideas and their History*, 168–193. London: Pimlico, 1996.

———, *The Roots of Romanticism*. Princeton, NJ: Princeton University Press, 2001.

Bessy, Maurice, *A Pictorial History of Magic and the Supernatural*. Translated by Margaret Crosland and Allan Daventry. London: Spring Books, 1964.

Best, Joel, "Endangered Children in Antisatanist Rhetoric." In *The Satanism Scare*, edited by James T. Richardson, Joel Best, and David G. Bromley, 95–106. New York: Aldine de Gruyter, 1991.

Bieberstein, Johannes Rogalla von, *Die These von der Verschwörung 1776–1945: Philosophen, Freimaurer, Juden, Liberale und Sozialisten als Verschwörer gegen die Sozialordnung*. Frankfurt am Main: Peter Lang, 1978.

Billy, André, *Stanislas de Guaita*. Paris: Mercure de France, 1971.

Blake, William, *Poems and Prophecies*. London: J. M. Dent, 1972.

———, *The Marriage of Heaven and Hell: With an Introduction and Commentary by Sir Geoffrey Keynes*. Oxford: Oxford University Press, 1975.

Blavatsky, H. P., *Isis Unveiled: A Master-Key to the Mysteries of Ancient and Modern Science and Theology*. 2 vols. Pasadena, CA: Theosophical University Press, 1972.

————, *The Secret Doctrine: The Synthesis of Science, Religion, and Philosophy*. 2 vols. London: Theosophical Society Publishing, 1888.

Blécourt, Willem de, "The Witch, Her Victim, the Unwitcher and the Researcher: The Continued Existence of Traditional Witchcraft." In *Witchcraft and Magic in Europe, Volume 6: The Twentieth Century*, edited by Willem de Blécourt, R. Hutton, and J. La Fontaine, 141–218. London: Athlone, 1999.

Blok, Anton, "The Bokkerijders Bands 1726–1776: Preliminary Notes on Brigandage in the Southern Netherlands." *Papers on European and Mediterranean Societies*, no. 7. Amsterdam : Antropologisch-Sociologisch Centrum Universiteit van Amsterdam, 1976.

Bloy, Léon, "L'expiation de Jocrisse." *Gil Blas* 5 (24 January 1893), 4816:1.

————, *Sur Huysmans*. Bruxelles: Éditions Complexe, 1986.

Bobineau, Olivier, "Le satanisme ou le 'religieusement incorrect.'" *Social Compass* 56 (December 2009) 4:503–514.

Bocquet, Leon, "Édouard Dubus (1863–1895)." *Le Nord littéraire et artistique*, 19 January 1928, 10–11.

Bogdan, Hendrik, "Envisioning the Birth of a New Aeon: Dispensationalism and Millenarianism in the Thelemic Tradition." In *Aleister Crowley and Western Esotericism*, edited by Henrik Bogdan and Martin P. Starr, 89–106. New York: Oxford University Press, 2012.

Bois, G[eorges], "La fin du Palladisme." *La Vérité*, 21 April 1897.

Bois, Jules, *Les noces de Sathan*. Paris: Albert Savine, 1890.

————, "L'envoûtement et la mort du docteur Boullan." *Gil Blas* 5 (9, 11, and 13 January 1893), 4801:2, 4803:2, 4805:2.

————, *Les Petites Religions de Paris*. Paris: Ernest Flammarion, s.a.

————, *Le Satanisme et la Magie: Avec une étude de J. K. Huysmans*. Paris: Ernest Flammarion, 1895.

————, *Le monde invisible*. Paris: Ernest Flammarion, s.a.

Bosch, Firmin van den, *Impressions de littérature contemporaine*. Bruxelles: Vromant, 1905.

Boss, Valentin, *Milton and the Rise of Russian Satanism*. Toronto: University of Toronto Press, 1991.

Bossier, Herman, *Geschiedenis van een Romanfiguur: De "Chanoine Docre" uit "Là-bas" van J.-K. Huysmans*. Brussel: De Lage Landen, 1942.

————, *Geschiedenis van een romanfiguur: De "chanoine Docre" uit Là-bas van J.-K. Huysmans*. Second, revised edition. Hasselt: Heideland, 1965.

————, *Un personnage de roman: Le chanoine Docre de La-Bas de J.-K. Huysmans*. Bruxelles: Les Ecrits, 1943.

Boureau, Alain, *Satan the Heretic: The Birth of Demonology in the Medieval West*. Translated by Teresa Lavender Fagan. Chicago: University of Chicago Press, 2006.

Boutet, Frédéric, *Tableau de l'au-delà*. Paris: Gallimard, 1927.

Bouton-Toubolic, Anne-Isabelle, "Le *De diuinatione daemonum* de Saint Augustin." In *Fictions du Diable. Démonologie et littérature de saint Augustin à Léo Taxil*, edited by Françoise Lavocat, Pierre Kapitaniak, and Marianne Closson, 15–34. Genève: Librairie Droz, 2007.

Bowie, Fiona, *The Anthropology of Religion: An Introduction*. Malden, MA: Blackwell, 2006.

Boyce, Mary, *Zoroastrianism: A Shadowy but Powerful Presence in the Judaeo-Christian World*. London: Dr William's Trust, 1987.

Braekman, W., *Magische experimenten en toverpraktijken uit een middelnederlands handschrift*. Gent: Seminarie voor Volkskunde, 1966.

Brevannes, Roland, *Les Messes Noires: Reconstruction dramatique en III parties et IV tableaux. Donnée au Théâtre de la Bodinière, le 17 février 1904*. s.l.: s.i., s.a..

Breytenbach, C., and P. L. Day, "Satan." In *Dictionary of Deities and Demons in the Bible*, edited by Karel van der Toorn, Bob Becking, and Pieter W. van der Horst, 726–732. Leiden: Brill, 1999.

Bricaud, Joanny, *Huysmans, Occultiste et Magicien: Avec une Notice sur les Hosties Magiques qui servent à Huysmans pour combattre les Envoûtements*. Paris: Bibliothèque Chacornac, 1913.

———, *J.-K. Huysmans et le Satanisme: D'après des documents inédits*. Paris: Bibliothèque Chacornac, 1913.

———, *L'abbé Boullan (Docteur Johannès de Là-Bas): Sa vie, sa doctrine et ses pratiques magiques*. Paris: Chacornac Frères, 1927.

Broek, Roelof van den, "Sexuality and Sexual Symbolism in Hermetic and Gnostic Thought and Practice (Second–Fourth Centuries)." In *Hidden Intercourse: Eros and Sexuality in the History of Western Esotericism*, edited by Wouter J. Hanegraaff and Jeffrey J. Kripal, 1–21. Leiden: Brill, 2008.

Bromley, David G., "Satanism: The New Cult Scare." In *The Satanism Scare*, edited by James T. Richardson, Joel Best, and David G. Bromley, 49–72. New York: Aldine de Gruyter, 1991.

———. "The Satanism Scare in the United States." In *Le Défi Magique II: Satanisme, sorcellerie*, edited by Jean-Baptiste Martin and Massimo Introvigne, 49–64. Lyon: Presses Universitaires de Lyon, 1994.

Bronowski, J., *William Blake and the Age of Revolution*. London: Routledge and Kegan Paul, 1972.

Brooke, Stopford, "Byron's Cain." *Hibbert Journal. A Quarterly Review of Religion, Theology and Philosophy* 17 (1919): 74–94.

Bucher, Rainer, *Hitlers Theologie*. Würzburg: Echter, 2008.

Buet, Charles, *Grands Hommes en Robe de Chambre*. Paris: Société Libre d'Édition des Gens de Lettres, 1897.

Bugliosi, Vincent, and Curt Gentry, *Helter Skelter: Het ware verhaal van de Manson-moorden*. Translated by Frédérique van der Velde. Bussum: Van Holkema and Warendorf, 1978.

Burton, Richard E., *Baudelaire and the Second Republic: Writing and Revolution*. Oxford: Clarendon, 1991.

Butler, Marilyn, "Romantic Manichaeism: Shelley's 'On the Devil, and Devils' and Byron's Mythological Dramas." In *The Sun Is God: Painting, Literature and Mythology in the Nineteenth Century*, edited by J. B. Bullen, 13–37. Oxford: Clarendon, 1989.

Byron, Lord [George Gordon], *The Poetical Works of Lord Byron*. Oxford: Oxford University Press, 1961.

———, *Selected Letters and Journals*. Edited by Leslie A. Marchand. Cambridge, MA: Belknap Press of Harvard University Press, 1982.

Byron, Lord [George Gordon], and Truman Guy Steffan, *Lord Byron's Cain: Twelve Essays and a Text with Variants and Annotations*. Austin: University of Texas Press, 1968.

Cahill, E., *Freemasonry and the Anti-Christian Movement*. 2nd revised edition. Dublin: M. H. Gill, 1930.

Bibliography

Caldan, Jean de, "Le Satanisme est-il pratiqué aujourd'hui?' *Le Matin*, 21 april 1908.

Camporesi, Piero, "The Consecrated Host: A Wondrous Excess." In *Fragments for a History of the Human Body*, edited by Michel Feher, 1:220–237. New York: Urzone, 1990.

Casis, M., "M. Taxil chez Chopinette." *La Verité*, 15 April 1897, 2.

Cazotte, Jacques, *Le diable amoureux, et autres écrits fantastiques*. Paris: Flammarion, 1974.

Céard, Jean, "Démoneries du XVIe siècle et diableries du XIXe. Collin de Plancy et les démonologues de la Renaissance." In *Fictions du Diable. Démonologie et littérature de saint Augustin à Léo Taxil*, edited by Françoise Lavocat, Pierre Kapitaniak, and Marianne Closson, 297–311. Genève: Librairie Droz, 2007.

Cervantes, Fernando, *The Devil in the New World: The Impact of Diabolism in New Spain*. New Haven, CT: Yale University Press, 1994.

Cerza, Alphonse, *Anti-Masonry: Light on the Past and Present Opponents of Freemasonry*. Fulton, MO: Ovid Bell Press, 1962.

Chacornac, Paul, *Éliphas Lévi: Rénovateur de l'occultisme en France (1810–1875)*. Paris: Librairie Géneral des Sciences Occultes Chacornac Frères, 1926.

Chadwick, Owen, *The Secularization of the European Mind in the Nineteenth Century: The Gifford Lectures in the University of Edinburgh for 1973–4*. Cambridge: Cambridge University Press, 1975.

Chethimattam, John, "The Concept and the Role of the Demon in Indian Thought." In *Le Défi Magique II: Satanisme, sorcellerie*, edited by Jean-Baptiste Martin and Massimo Introvigne, 311–320. Lyon: Presses Universitaires de Lyon, 1994.

Chick, Jack T., *The Curse of Baphomet*. Ontario: Chick Publications, 1991.

———, *Spellbound?* Ontario: Chick Publications, 1978.

———, *The Unwelcome Guest*. Ontario: Chick Publications, 2006.

Cholvy, Gérard, *La religion en France de la fin du XVIIIᵉ à nos jours*. Paris: Hachette, 1991.

Churton, Tobias, "Aleister Crowley and the Yezidis." In *Aleister Crowley and Western Esotericism*, edited by Henrik Bogdan and Martin P. Starr, 181–207. New York: Oxford University Press, 2012.

Clark, T. J., *The Absolute Bourgeois: Artists and Politics in France 1848–1851*. London: Thames and Hudson, 1973.

Closson, Marianne, "Le *Diable au XIXe Siècle* de Léo Taxil, ou les 'mille et une nuits' de la démonologie." In *Fictions du Diable. Démonologie et littérature de saint Augustin à Léo Taxil*, edited by Françoise Lavocat, Pierre Kapitaniak, and Marianne Closson, 313–332. Genève: Librairie Droz, 2007.

Cohn, Norman, *Europe's Inner Demons: An Enquiry Inspired by the Great Witch-Hunt*. London: Sussex University Press, 1975.

———, *Warrant for Genocide: The Myth of the Jewish World-Conspiracy and the Protocols of the Elders of Zion*. Harmondsworth, UK: Penguin, s.a.

Collin de Plancy, J., *Le diable peint par lui-même, ou galerie de petits romans, de contes bizarres, d'anecdotes prodigieuses, sur les aventures des démons*. Paris: P. Mongie Ainé, 1819.

Constant, Alphonse, *Dictionnaire de littérature chrétienne*. Paris: Migne, 1851.

———, *Doctrines religieuses et sociales*. Paris: Aug. le Gallois, 1841.

———, *L'Assomption de la femme ou Le Livre de l'Amour*. Paris: Aug. le Gallois, 1841.

———, *La Bible de la Liberté*. Paris: Le Gallois, 1841.

———, *La Mère de Dieu, épopée religieuse et humanitaire*. Paris: Librairie de Charles Gosselin, 1844.

———, *Le dernière incarnation: Légendes évangeliques du XXIe siècle*. Paris: Libraire sociétaire, 1846.

———, *Le Testament de la Liberté*. Paris: J. Frey, 1848.

Corelli, Marie, *The Sorrows of Satan or the Strange Experience of One Geoffrey Tempest, Millionaire: A Romance*. London: Methuen, 1895.

Corfield, Penelope J., "Historians and the Return to the Diachronic." In *The New Ways of History: Developments in Historiography*, edited by Gelina Harlaftis, Nikos Karapidakis, Kostas Sbonias, and Vaios Vaiopoulos, 13–34. London: Tauris Academic Studies, 2010.

Corneille, Thomas, and Donneau de Visé, *La Devineresse: Comédie. Introduction et Notes par P. J. Yarrow*. s.l.: University of Exeter, 1971.

Crabtree, Vexen, "Reflections on Satanism." In *Contemporary Religious Satanism: A Critical Anthology*, edited by Jesper Aagaard Petersen, 231–238. Farnham, UK: Ashgate, 2009.

Craciun, Adriana, "Romantic Satanism and the Rise of Nineteenth-Century Women's Poetry." *New Literary History* 34 (2004), 4:699–721.

Crispino, Anna Marie, Fabio Giovannini, and Marco Zatterin (eds.), *Das Buch vom Teufel: Geschichte—Kult—Erscheinungsformen*. Translated by Werner Raith. Frankfurt am Main: Vito von Eichbon, 1987.

Crouch, Ben M., and Kelly Damphouse, "Law Enforcement and the Satanism-Crime Connection: A Survey of 'Cult Cops.'" In *The Satanism Scare*, edited by James T. Richardson, Joel Best, and David G. Bromley, 191–204. New York: Aldine de Gruyter, 1991.

Crowley, Aleister, *777 vel Prolegomena Symbolica ad Systemam Sceptico-Mysticæ Viæ Expliciandæ, fundamentum Hieroglyphicum Sanctissimorum Scientiæ Summæ*. London: Walter Scott, 1909.

———, *The Book of Lies, which is also falsely called Breaks: The Wanderings or Falsifications of the one thought of Frater Perdurabo (Aleister Crowley)*. Boston: Weiser, 2001.

———, *The Confessions of Aleister Crowley: An Autohagiography*. London: Jonathan Cape, 1969.

———, *Liber Oz: Liber LXXVII*. Los Angeles: O.T.O., An. IXV [1941].

———, *Magical Diaries of Aleister Crowley: Tunisia 1923*. Edited by Stephen Skinner. York Beach, ME: Samuel Weiser, 1999.

———, *Magick*. Edited by John Symonds and Kenneth Grant. London: Routledge and Kegan Paul, 1973.

D'Arch Smith, Timothy, *The Books of The Beast: Essays on Aleister Crowley, Montague Summers and Others*. [London]: Mandrake, 1991.

D'Hoore, Marc, "Goblet d'Alviella, un intellectuel en politique. Commentaires sur son œuvre et sa pensée." In *Eugène Goblet d'Alviella, historien et franc-maçon*, edited by Alain Dierkens, 19–34. Problèmes d'histoire des Religions, no. 6. Bruxelles: Éditions de l'Université de Bruxelles, 1995.

D'Olivet, Fabre, *Caïn, mystère dramatique en trois actes de Lord Byron, traduit en vers français et réfuté dans une suite de remarques philosophiques et critiques*. 1823. Reprint, Genève: Éditions Slatkine, 1981.

Dachez, Roger, "Freemasonry." In *Dictionary of Gnosis and Western Esotericism*, edited by Wouter J. Hanegraaff, 1:382–388. 2 vols. Leiden: Brill, 2005.

Daoust, Joseph, *Les débuts bénédictins de J.-K. Huysmans: Documents inédits receuillis avec le concours de dom J. Laporte et de dom J. Mazé, Moines de Saint-Wandrille*. Abbaye Saint Wandrille: Éditions de Fontenelle, 1950.

Davies, Maxwell, "Self-Conscious Routinization and the Post-Charismatic Fate of the Church of Satan from 1997 to the Present." In *Contemporary Religious Satanism: A Critical Anthology*, edited by Jesper Aagaard Petersen, 75–84. Farnham, UK: Ashgate, 2009.

Dehau, Émile, "Le culte de Lucifer." *Charente*, 13 April 1895.

Delvaux, Peter, "Hexenglaube und Verantwortung zur Walpurgisnacht in Goethe's *Faust I.*" *Neophilologus* 83 (1999), 4:601–616.

Dennis, Ian, "*Cain*: Lord Byron's Sincerity." *Studies in Romanticism (Boston University)* 41 (Winter 2002): 655–674.

Desjardins, Jean F., "Huysmans fut-il anarchiste? À propos des collaborations retrouvées." *Bulletin de la Société J.-K Huysmans* 37 (1959), 36:366–374.

Dinzelbacher, Peter, "Die Realität des Teufels im Mittelalter." In *Der Hexenhammer: Entstehung und Umfeld des Malleus Maleficarum von 1487*, edited by Peter Segl, 151–175. Köln: Böhlau, 1988.

Disreali, Benjamin, *Lord George Bentinck: A Political Biography*. London: Colburn, 1852.

Djurdjevic, Gordan, "The Great Beast as a Tantric Hero: The Role of Yoga and Tantra in Aleister Crowley's Magic." In *Aleister Crowley and Western Esotericism*, edited by Henrik Bogdan and Martin P. Starr, 107–140. New York: Oxford University Press, 2012.

Drumont, Édouard, *Le Testament d'un Antisémite*. Paris: E. Dentu, 1891.

Drury, Neville, "An Australian Original: Rosaleen Norton and Her Magical Cosmology." In *Occultism in a Global Perspective*, edited by Henrik Bogdan and Gordan Djurdjevi, 231–243. Durham, UK: Acumen, 2013.

———, *Stealing Fire from Heaven: The Rise of Modern Western Magic*. Oxford: Oxford University Press, 2011.

Dubois, Dominique, *Jules Bois (1868–1943): le reporter de l'occultisme, le poète et le féministe de la belle époque*. s.l.: Arqa, 2006.

Dubus, Edouard, "L'art de envoûter." *Le Figaro* 39 (29 January 1893) 29:1.

Dufay, Pierre, "L'Abbé Boullan et le 'Chanoine Docre.'" *Mercvre de France* 882 (15 March 1935): 509–527.

Duffy, Eamon, *Saints and Sinners: A History of the Popes*. New Haven, CT: Yale University Press, 1997.

Duggan, Colin, "Perenialism and Iconoclasm: Chaos Magick and the Legitimacy of Innovation." In *Contemporary Esotericism*, edited by Egil Asprem and Kennet Granholm, 91–112. Sheffield, UK: Equinox, 2013.

Dülmen, Richard van, "Imaginationen des Teuflischen. Nächtliche Zusammenkunfte, Hexentänze, Teufelssabbate." In *Hexenwelten: Magie und Imagination*, edited by Richard van Dülmen, 94–130. Frankfurt am Main: Fischer Taschenbuch Verlag, 1987.

Dvorak, Josef, *Satanismus: Schwarze Rituale, Teufelswahn und Exorzismus. Geschichte und Gegenwart*. München: Wilhelm Heyne Verlag, 1993.

Dyrendal, Asbjørn, "Darkness Within: Satanism as a Self-Religion." In *Contemporary Religious Satanism: A Critical Anthology*, edited by Jesper Aagaard Petersen, 59–73. Farnham, UK: Ashgate, 2009.

———, "Hidden Knowledge, Hidden Powers: Esotericism and Conspiracy Culture." In *Contemporary Esotericism*, edited by Egil Asprem and Kennet Granholm, 25–48. Sheffield, UK: Equinox, 2013.

———, "Hidden Persuaders and Invisible Wars: Anton LaVey and Conspiracy Culture." In *The Devil's Party: Satanism in Modernity*, edited by Per Faxneld and Jesper Petersen, 200–225. Oxford: Oxford University Press, 2012.

———, "Satan and the Beast: The Influence of Aleister Crowley on Modern Satanism." In *Aleister Crowley and Western Esotericism*, edited by Henrik Bogdan and Martin P. Starr, 369–394. New York: Oxford University Press, 2012.

Ebon, Martin (ed.), *The World's Weirdest Cults*. New York: Signet, 1979.

Edelman, Nicole, "Diable et médium. Histoire d'une disparition." In *Le Défi Magique II: Satanisme, sorcellerie*, edited by Jean-Baptiste Martin and Massimo Introvigne, 321–329. Lyon: Presses Universitaires de Lyon, 1994.

Egmond, Daniël van, "Western Esoteric Schools in the Late Nineteenth and Early Twentieth Centuries." In *Gnosis and Hermeticism from Antiquity to Modern Times*, edited by Roelof van den Broek and Wouter J. Hanegraaf, 311–346. Albany: State University of New York Press, 1998.

Egmond, Florike, *Underworlds: Organized Crime in the Netherlands 1650–1800*. Cambridge: Polity, 1993.

Eliade, Mircea, *The Quest: History and Meaning in Religion*. Chicago: University of Chicago Press, 1969.

Ellis, Bill, "Legend-Trips and Satanism: Adolescents' Ostentive Traditions as 'Cult' Activity." In *The Satanism Scare*, edited by James T. Richardson, Joel Best, and David G. Bromley, 279–295. New York: Aldine de Gruyter, 1991.

———, *Raising the Devil: Satanism, New Religions, and the Media*. Lexington: University Press of Kentucky, 2000.

Emmanuel, Pierre, *Baudelaire: The Paradox of Redemptive Satanism*. Translated by Robert T. Cargo. Tuscaloosa: University of Alabama Press, 1970.

Encausse, Philippe, *Sciences occultes ou 25 années d'occultisme occidental: Papus, sa vie, son œuvre*. Paris: Éditions Ocia, 1949.

Epiphanius of Salamis, *S.P.N. Epiphanii, Constantiae in Cypro episcope, opera quae repriri potuera omnia*. 3 vols. Patrologiae Cursus Completus: Patrologiae Graecae no. 41–43. Paris: J.-P. Migne, 1863.

———, *The Panarion: Book I (Sects 1-46)*. Translated by Frank Williams. Nag Hammadi Studies, no. 35. Leiden: E. J. Brill, 1987.

———, *The Panarion: Book II and III (Sects 47-80, De Fide)*. Translated by Frank Williams. Nag Hammadi Studies, no. 36. Leiden: E. J. Brill, 1994.

Erdan, Alexandre, *La France mystique: Tableau des excentricités religieuse de ces temps*. 2 vols. Amsterdam: H. C. Meijer, 1858.

Erhard, Johann Benjamin, "Apologie des Teufels." In *Über das Recht des Volks zu einer Revolution und andere Schriften*, edited by Hellmut G. Haasis, 109–134. München: Carl Hanser Verlag, 1970.

Ertl, Thomas, *Religion und Disziplin: Selbstdeutung und Weltordnung im frühen deutschen Franziskanertum*. Arbeiten zur Kirchengeschichte, no. 96. Berlin: Walter de Gruyter, 2006.

Esquiros, Alphonse, *Le Magicien*, Lausanne: L'Age d'Homme, 1978.

Essarts, Fabre des, *Sadisme, Satanisme et Gnose*. Paris: Bodin, 1906.

Evans, Dave, "Speculating on the Point 003 Percent? Some Remarks on the Chaotic Satanic Minorities in the UK." In *Contemporary Religious Satanism: A Critical Anthology*, edited by Jesper Aagaard Petersen, 211–228. Farnham, UK: Ashgate, 2009.

Fanger, Claire, "Medieval Ritual Magic: What It Is and Why We Need to Know More about It." In *Conjuring Spirits: Texts and Traditions of Medieval Ritual Magic*, edited by Claire Fanger, vii–xviii. Magic in History, no. 4. Thrupp: Sutton, 1998.

Fava, Mgr., *La Franc-Maçonnerie: Doctrine, histoire, gouvernement. Lettre à la Revue Catholique des Institutions et du Droit*. Paris: Librairie de la Société Bibliographique, 1880.

Faxneld, Per, "Blavatsky the Satanist: Luciferianism in Theosophy, and Its Feminist Implications." *Tenemos* 48 (2012) 2:203–230.

———, " 'In communication with the powers of darkness': Satanism in Turn-of-the-Century Denmark, and Its Use as a Legitimating Device in Present-day Esotericism." In *Occultism in a Global Perspective*, edited by Henrik Bogdan and Gordan Djurdjevi, 57–77. Durham, UK: Acumen, 2013.

———, "The Devil Is Red: Socialist Satanism in Nineteenth and Early Twentieth Century Europe." *Numen: International Review for the History of Religions* 60 (2013) 5.

———, *Satanic Feminism: Lucifer as the Liberator of Woman in Nineteenth-Century Culture*. Stockholm: Molin and Sorgfrei, 2014.

———, "Secret Lineages and de Facto Satanists: Anton LaVey's Use of the Esoteric Tradition." In *Contemporary Esotericism*, edited by Egil Asprem and Kennet Granholm, 72–90. Sheffield, UK: Equinox, 2013.

———, "The Strange Case of Ben Kadosh: A Luciferian Pamphlet from 1906 and Its Current Renaissance." *Aries: Journal for the Study of Western Esotericism* 11 (2011) 1:1–22.

———, "Witches, Anarchism, and Evolutionism: Stanislaw Przybyszewski's Fin-de-siècle Satanism and the Demonic Feminine." In *The Devil's Party: Satanism in Modernity*, edited by Per Faxneld and Jesper Petersen, 53–77. Oxford: Oxford University Press, 2012.

———, "Woman Liberated by the Devil in Four Gothic Novels: William Beckford's *Vathek* (1786), Matthew Lewis' *The Monk* (1796), Charlotte Dacre's *Zofloya, or The Moor* (1806), and Charles Maturin's *Melmoth the Wanderer* (1820)." In *Grotesque Femininities: Evil, Women and the Feminine*, edited by M. Barrett, 29–43. Oxford: Inter-Disciplinary Press, 2010.

Faxneld, Per, and Jesper Aagaard Petersen, "Introduction: At the Devil's Crossroads." In *The Devil's Party: Satanism in Modernity*, edited by Per Faxneld and Jesper Petersen, 3–18. Oxford: Oxford University Press, 2012.

Felix, Minicius, *Octavianus*. In *Tertullian, Apology. De Spectaculis. Minicius Felix*. Translated by Gerald H. Rendall, 303–437. 1931. Reprint, London: William Heinemann, 1960.

Ferrer Benimeli, José A., "L'antimaçonnisme en Espagne et en Amérique latine." In *Les courants antimaçonniques hier et aujourd'hui*, edited by Alain Dierkens, 77–86. Problèmes d'histoire des religions, no. 4. Bruxelles: Éditions de l'Université de Bruxelles, 1993.

Feuerbach, Ludwig, *The Essence of Christianity*. Translated by George Eliot. 1854. Reprint, Buffalo, NY: Prometheus, 1989.

Fersen, M. de, *Messes Noires: Lord Lyllian*. Question de Genre 62. Montpellier: GayKitchCam p, 2011.

Fiard, Abbé, *La France trompée par les magiciens et démonolatres du dix-huitième siècle, fait démontré par des faits*. Paris, Grégoire and Thouvenin, 1803.

———, *Lettres magiques, ou lettres sur le diable*. "En France": s.i., 1791.

First Rastafarian Church of Satan, *The Rastafarian Satanic Bible*. [Los Angeles]: s.i., 2005.

Fiume, Giovanna, "The Old Vinegar Lady, or the Judicial Modernization of the Crime of Witchcraft." In *History from Crime*, edited by Edward Muir and Guido Ruggiero, 65–87. Selections from *Quaderni Storici*, no. 3. Baltimore, MD: John Hopkins University Press, 1994.

Flowers, Stephan E., "Excerpt from Lords of the Left-Hand Path: A History of Spiritual Dissent." In *Contemporary Religious Satanism: A Critical Anthology*, edited by Jesper Aagaard Petersen, 239–245. Farnham, UK: Ashgate, 2009.

Fögen, Marie Theres, *Die Enteignung des Wahrsager: Studien zum kaiserlichen Wissensmonopol in der Spätantike*. Frankfurt am Main: Suhrkamp, 1997.

France, Anatole, *La révolte des Anges. Préface de Pierre Boulle*. Paris: Calmann-Lévy, 1980.

Frank, Frederick S., *Montague Summers: A Bibliographical Portrait*. The Great Bibliographers Series, no. 7. Metuchen, NJ: Scarecrow, 1988.

Frankfurter, David, *Evil Incarnate. Rumors of Demonic Conspiracy and Ritual Abuse in History*. Princeton, NJ: Princeton University Press, 2006.

Franz, Adolph, *Die kirchliche Benediktionen im Mittelalter*. 2 vols. Freiburg im Breisgau: Herdersche Verlagshandlung, 1909.

Fresnois, André du, *Une étape de la conversion de Huysmans: D'après des lettres inédites à Mme de C . . .* Paris: Dorbon-Ainé, s.a.

Freud, Sigmund, "Eine Teufelsneurose im siebzehnten Jahrhundert." In *Gesammelte Werke*, edited by Anne Freud, and others, 13:315–353. 18 vols. 1940. Reprint, London: Imago, 1947.

Frick, Karl R. H., *Die Satanisten: Materialen zur Geschichte der Anhänger des Satanismus und ihrer Gegner*. 3 vols. Graz: Akademische Druck- u. Verlagsanstalt, 1985.

Fry, L., *Leo Taxil et La Franc-Maçonnerie: Lettres inédites publiés par les amis de Monseugneur Jouin*. Chaton: British-American-Press, 1934.

Frye, Northrop, *A Study of English Romanticism*. New York: Random House, 1968.

Gallagher, Eugene V., "Sources, Sects, and Scripture: The Book of Satan in *The Satanic Bible*." In *The Devil's Party: Satanism in Modernity*, edited by Per Faxneld and Jesper Petersen, 103–122. Oxford: Oxford University Press, 2012.

Garçon, Maurice, "La société infernale d'Agen." *Mercvre de France* (15 July 1928): 271–304.

———, *Trois histoires Diabolique*. [Paris]: Librairie Gallimard, 1929.

———, *Vintras: Hérésiarque et prophète*. Paris: Librairie critique Émile Nourry, 1928.

Gardner, Gerald B., *Witchcraft Today*. London: Rider, 1954.

Gareis, Iris, "Feind oder Freund? Der Teufel in Spanien und in der Neuen Welt im 16.-18. Jahrhundert." *@KIH-eSkript. Interdisziplinäre Hexenforschung online* 3 (2011) 1:77–84, at http://www.historicum.net/no_cache/persistent/artikel/9107 (accessed 14 December 2011).

———, "Wie Engel und Teufel in die Neue welt kamen. Imaginationen von Gut und Böse in kolonialen Amerika." *Paideuma: Mitteilungen ur Kulturkunde* 45 (1999): 257–273.

Garinet, Jules, *Histoire de la magie en France, depuis le commencement de la monarchie jusqu'à nos jours*. Paris: Foulon, 1818.

Gauguin, Paul, *Sous deux latitudes, suivi de Natures mortes*. Paris: L'Échoppe, 2000.

Gautier, Théophile, "Le club de Hachichins." *Revue des Deux Mondes* 1 (1846): 248–259.

Gelas, Bruno, "Le satanisme et le roman Là-Bas de Huysmans." In *Le Défi Magique II: Satanisme, sorcellerie*, edited by Jean-Baptiste Martin and Massimo Introvigne, 271–277. Lyon: Presses Universitaires de Lyon, 1994.

Gerber, Hildebrand, [= Hermann Gruber], *Betrug als Ende eines Betruges. Oder: Die Kundgebung Leo Taxil's vom 19. April 1897 under der Hereinfall, bezw. die Schwindeleien, deutscher "Kulturkämpfer" anläßlich derselben.* Berlin: Germania, 1897.

Geyraud, Pierre, *Les petites églises de Paris.* Paris: Éditions Émile-Paul frères, 1937.

——, *Les religions nouvelles de Paris.* Paris: Éditions Émile-Paul frères, 1937 [=1939].

——, *Les sociétés secrètes de Paris.* Paris: Éditions Émile-Paul frères, 1938.

——, *Sectes & rites, petites églises, religions nouvelles, sociétés secrètes de Paris.* Paris: Éditions Émile-Paul frères, 1954.

Gillet, Oliver, "L'antimaçonnisme roumain depuis 1989. Ses origines et son développement actuel." In *Les courants antimaçonniques hier et aujourd'hui*, edited by Alain Dierkens, 145–161. Problèmes d'histoire des religions, no. 4. Bruxelles: Éditions de l'Université de Bruxelles, 1993.

Ginzburg, Carlo, *Ecstasies: Deciphering the Witches' Sabbath.* Translated by Raymond Rosenthal. London: Hutchinson Radius, 1990.

——, *The Night Battles: Witchcraft and Agrarian Cults in the Sixteenth and Seventeenth Centuries.* Translated by John and Anne Tedeschi. Baltimore, MD: Johns Hopkins University Press, 1983.

Godechot, Jacques, *La Grande Nation: L'expansion révolutionnaire de la France dans le monde de 1789 à 1799.* Paris, Aubier Montaigne, 1983.

Godwin, Joscelyn, *The Theosophical Enlightenment.* Albany: State University of New York Press, 1994.

Godwin, William, *Political and Philosophical Writings of William Godwin.* Edited by Mark Philp. 7 vols. London: Pickering, 1993.

Goethe, [Johann Wolfgang], *Faust: Eine Tragoedie.* München: Droemersche Verlaganstalt, 1949.

Goetz, Hans-Werner, "Was wird im frühen Mittelalter unter 'Häresie' verstanden? Zur Häresiewahrnehmung des Hrabanus Maurus." In *Die wahrnehmun anderer Religionen in früheren Mittelalter: Terminologische Probleme und methodische Ansätze*, edited by Anna Aurast and Hans-Werner Goetz, 47–88. Hamburger geistwissenschaftliche Studien zu Religion und Gesellschaft no. 1. Berlin: Lit Verlag, 2012.

Goffman, Erving, *Stigma: Notes on the Management of Spoiled Identity.* New York: Jason Aronson, 1973.

Goodman, Felicitas D., *How about Demons? Possession and Exorcism in the Modern World.* Bloomington: Indiana University Press, 1988.

Gougenot des Mousseaux, Roger, *Les Hauts Phénomènes de la Magie, précédés du Spiritisme Antique.* Paris: Plon, 1864.

——, *Le Juif, le judaïsme et la judaïsation des peuples chrétiens.* Paris: Plon, 1869.

——, *La magie au dix-neuvième siècle, ses agents, ses vérités, ses mensonges. Précédée de quelques lettres adressées à l'auteur.* Paris: Plon, 1864.

——, *La magie au dix-neuvième siècle: Ses agents, ses vérités, ses mensognes.* Paris: Henri Plon and E. Dentu, 1860.

Gourmont, Remy de, "Souvenirs sur Huysmans." *Promenades Littéraires: Troisième Série*, 5–18. Paris: Mercvre de France, 1916.

Granholm, Kennet, "Embracing Others Than Satan: The Multiple Princes of Darkness in the Left-Hand Milieu." In *Contemporary Religious Satanism: A Critical Anthology*, edited by Jesper Aagaard Petersen, 85–101. Farnham, UK: Ashgate, 2009.

———, "The Left-Hand Path and Post-Satanism: The Temple of Set and the Evolution of Satanism." In *The Devil's Party: Satanism in Modernity*, edited by Per Faxneld and Jesper Petersen, 209–228. Oxford: Oxford University Press, 2012.

———, "The Secular, the Post-Secular and the Esoteric in the Public Sphere." In *Contemporary Esotericism*, edited by Egil Asprem and Kennet Granholm, 309–329. Sheffield, UK: Equinox, 2013.

Gray, L. H., "Demons and Spirits." In *Encyclopaedia of Religion and Ethics*, edited by J. Hastings, 4:565–635. 12 vols. Edingburgh: T&T Clark, 1911.

Gregorius, Fredrik, "Luciferian Witchcraft: At the Crossroads between Paganism and Satanism." In *The Devil's Party: Satanism in Modernity*, edited by Per Faxneld and Jesper Petersen, 229–249. Oxford: Oxford University Press, 2012.

Gregorius IX (Pope), "Vox in Rama." In *Monumenta Germaniae Historica inde ab Anno Christi quingentesimo usque ad annum millesimum et quintegentesimum: Epistolae Saeculi XIII E Regestis Pontificum Romanorum selectae*, edited by G. H. Pertz and Carolus Rodenberg, 1:432–434. Berolini: apud Weidmannos, 1883.

Griffiths, Richard, *The Reactionary Revolution: The Catholic Revival in French Literature, 1870–1914*. London: Constable, 1966.

Grillet, Claudius, *Le Diable dans la littérature au XIXᵉ siècle*. Lyon: Emmanuel Vitte, 1935.

Groh, Dieter, "Die verschwörungstheoretische Versuchung oder: Why Do Bad Things Happen to Good People?' *Anthropologische Dimensionen der Geschichte*, 267–304. Frankfurt am Main: Suhrkamp, 1992.

Grundmann, Herbert, "Der Typus des Ketzers in Mittelalterlicher Anschauung." In *Kultur- und Universalgeschichte: Walter Goetz zu seinem 60. Geburtstage dargebracht von Fachgenossen, Freunden und Schülern*, 91–107. Leipzig: B.G. Teubner, 1927.

Guaita, Stanislas de, *La Muse Noire*. Paris: Alphonse Lemerre, 1883.

———, *Le Serpent de la Genèse. Première Septaine (Livre I): Le Temple de Satan*. Paris: Hector and Henri Durville, 1915.

———, *Le Serpent de la Genèse. Première Septaine (Livre II): La Clef de la Magie Noire*. Paris: Henri Durville, 1920.

———, *Lettres inédites de Stanislas de Guaita au Sâr Joséphin Péladan*. Neuchâtel: Éditions Rosicruciennes, 1952.

———, *Rosa Mystica*. Paris: Alphonse Lemerre, 1885.

Guérard, M., *Cartulaire de l'abbaye de St.-Père de Chartres*. Collection des Cartulaires de France, no. 1. Paris: Imprimerie de Crapelet, 1840.

Guillemain, Charles, "Joanny Bricaud (1881–1934). Révélateur de J.-K. Huysmans occultiste et magicien." *Bulletin de la Société J.-K Huysmans* 38 (1959) 37:375–381.

Guthke, Karl S., "Der Mythos des Bösen in der westeuropäischen Romantik." *Colloquia Germanica. Internationale Zeitschrift für germanische Sprach- und Literaturwissenschaft* (1968): 1–36.

Haag, Herbert, *Teufelsglaube*. Tübingen: Katzmann Verlag, 1974.

Habermas, Jürgen, "An Awareness of What Is Missing." In Jürgen Habermas and others, *An Awareness of What Is Missing: Faith and Reason in a Post-Secular Age*, 15–23. Translated by Ciaran Cronin. Cambridge: Polity, 2010.

Hakl, Hans Thomas, "The Magical Order of the Fraternitas Saturni." In *Occultism in a Global Perspective*, edited by Henrik Bogdan and Gordan Djurdjevi, 37–55. Durham, UK: Acumen, 2013.

———, "The Theory and Practice of Sexual Magic, Exemplified by Four Magical Groups in the Early Twentieth Century." In *Hidden Intercourse: Eros and Sexuality in the History of Western Esotericism*, edited by Wouter J. Hanegraaff and Jeffrey J. Kripal, 445–478. Leiden: Brill, 2008.

Hale, Wash Edward, *Ásura—in Early Vedic Religion*. Dehli: Motilal Banarsidass, 1986.

Hales, E. E. Y., *Mazzini and the Secret Societies: The Making of a Myth*. London: Eyre and Spottiswoode, 1956.

Hamilton, Victor P., "Satan." In *The Anchor Bible Dictionary*, edited by David Noel Freedman, 5:985–989. New York: Doubleday, 1992.

Hammond, D. Corydon, "Hypnosis in MPD: Ritual Abuse." At http://whale.to/b/greenbaum. html (accessed 28 August 2013).

Hanegraaff, Wouter J., "The Beginnings of Occultist Kabbalah: Adolphe Franck and Eliphas Lévi." In *Kabbalah and Modernity: Interpretations, Transformations, Adaptations*, edited by Boaz Huss, Marco Pasi, and Kocku von Stuckrad, 107–128. Leiden: Brill, 2010.

——— (ed.), *Dictionary of Gnosis and Western Esotericism*. 2 vols. Leiden: Brill, 2005.

———, "The Dreams of Theology and the Realities of Christianity." In *Theology and Conversation. Towards a Relational Theology*, edited by J. Haers and P. De Mey, 709–733. Leuven: Peeters/Leuven University Press, 2003.

———, "How Magic Survived the Disenchantment of the World." *Religion* 33 (2003): 357–380.

———, *New Age Religion and Western Culture: Esotericism in the Mirror of Secular Thought*. Leiden: E. J. Brill, 1996.

———, "Occult/Occultism." In *Dictionary of Gnosis and Western Esotericism*, edited by Wouter J. Hanegraaff, 2:884–889. 2 vols. Leiden: Brill, 2005.

———, "Romanticism and the Esoteric Connection." In *Gnosis and Hermeticism: From Antiquity to Modern Times*, edited by Roelof van den Broek and Wouter J. Hanegraaff, 237–268. Albany: State University of New York Press, 1998.

———, "The New Age Movement and the Esoteric Tradition." In *Gnosis and Hermeticism: From Antiquity to Modern Times*, edited by Roelof van den Broek and Wouter J. Hanegraaff, 359–382. Albany: State University of New York Press, 1998.

Hanson, Ellis, *Decadence and Catholicism*. Cambridge, MA: Harvard University Press, 1997.

Harmening, Dieter, *Superstitio: Überlieferungs- und theoriegeschichtliche Untersuchungen zur kirchlich-theologische Aberglaubensliteratur des Mittelalters*. Berlin: Erich Schmidt Verlag, 1979.

Harrison, C. G., *Das Transcedentale Weltenall: Sechs Vorträge über Geheimwissen, Theosophie und den katholische Glauben, gehalten vor der "Berean Society."* Translated by Carl Graf zu Leiningen-Billigheim. 1897. Reprint, Stuttgart: Engel and Seefels, 1990.

Hartmann, Georg, *Das Wirken Rudolfs Steiners von 1890–1907: Weimar und Berlin*.Vier Bildbände zu Rudolf Steiners Lebensgang 4. Schaffhausen: Novalis Verlag, 1975.

Harvey, David Allen, "Lucifer in the City of Light. The Palladium Hoax and 'Diabolical Causality' in Fin de siècle France." *Magic, Ritual, and Witchcraft* 1 (2006) 2:177–206.

Harvey, Graham, "Satanism in Britain Today." *Journal of Contemporary Religion* 10 (1995): 353–366.

———, "Satanism: Performing Alterity and Othering." In *Contemporary Religious Satanism: A Critical Anthology*, edited by Jesper Aagaard Petersen, 27–39. Farnham, UK: Ashgate, 2009.

Haubtmann, Pierre, *P.-J. Proudhon, genèse d'un antithéiste*. [Tours]: Mame, 1969.

Häll, Mikael, " 'God is caught in Hell, so it is better to believe in the Devil': Conceptions of Satanists and Sympathies for the Devil in Early Modern Sweden." In *The Devil's Party: Satanism in Modernity*, edited by Per Faxneld and Jesper Petersen, 23–40. Oxford: Oxford University Press, 2012.

Hemmings, F. W. J., *Baudelaire the Damned: A Biography*. New York: Charles Scribner's Sons, 1982.

Hertenstein, Mike, and Jon Trott, *Selling Satan: The Evangelical Media and the Mike Warnke Scandal*. Chicago: Cornerstone, 1993.

Hexham, Irving, and Karla Poewe, *New Religions as Global Culture: Making the Human Sacred*. Boulder, CO: Westview, 1997.

Hicks, Robert D., "The Police Model of Satanic Crime." In *The Satanism Scare*, edited by James T. Richardson, Joel Best, and David G. Bromley, 175–189. New York: Aldine de Gruyter, 1991.

Hiel, Emanuel. *Lucifer: Oratorium*. Brussel: J. Nijs, 1866.

Hill, Douglas, Pat Williams, Frank Smyth, and Tessa Clarke, *Witchcraft, Magic and the Supernatural: The Weird World of the Unknown*. London: Octopus, 1974.

Hitler, Adolf, *Mein Kampf: Zwei Bände in einem Band Ungekürzte Ausgabe*. München: Zentralverlag der NSDAP, 1943.

———, *Mein Kampf*. Translated by James Murphy. 1939. Reprint, Mumbai: Embassy Book Distributions, 2005.

Hjelm, Titus, "Introduction." *Social Compass* 56 (December 2009) 4:499–502.

Hjelm, Titus, Henrik Bogdan, Asbjørn Dyrendal, and Jesper Aagaard Petersen, "Nordic Satanism and Satanism Scares: The Dark Side of the Secular Welfare State." *Social Compass* 56 (December 2009) 4:515–529.

Hobsbawm, Eric, and Terence Ranger (eds.), *The Invention of Tradition*. Cambridge: Cambridge University Press, 1983.

Hoeven, T. H. van der, *Het imago van Satan: Een cultureel-theologisch onderzoek naar een duivels tegenbeeld*, Kampen: Kok, 1998.

Holt, Cimminnee, "Death and Dying in the Satanic Worldview." *Journal of Religion and Culture* 22 (2011) 1:33–53.

Hoog, Armand, "La révolte métaphysique et religieuse des petits romantiques." In *Les petits romantiques français*, edited by Francis Dumont, 13–28. Paris: Les Cahiers du Sud, 1949.

Howe, Ellic, *The Magicians of the Golden Dawn: A Documentary History of a Magical order, 1887–1923*. London: Routledge and Kegan Paul, 1972.

Hugo, Victor, "Eloa ou la Sœur des Anges, mystère par le comte Alfred de Vigny." In *La Muse française 1823–1824*, edited by Jules Marsan, 2:247–258. Paris: Édouard Correly, 1907.

———, *Le texte de "La Fin de Satan" dans le manuscrit B.N. n.a.fr. 24.754*, edited by René Journet and Guy Robert. Contribution aux études sur Victor Hugo, no. 2. Annales Littéraires de l'Université de Besançon, no. 232. Paris: Les Belles-Lettres, 1979.

———, *Les Contemplations* (Paris: Éditions Gallimard and Librairie Général Française, 1965.

———, "Sur George Gordon, Lord Byron." In *La Muse française 1823–1824*, edited by Jules Marsan, 2: 297–309. Paris: Édouard Correly, 1907.

Huret, Jules, *Enquête sur l'évolution littéraire*. Vanves: Éditions Thot, 1982.

Hutton, Ronald, "Crowley and Wicca." In *Aleister Crowley and Western Esotericism*, edited by Henrik Bogdan and Martin P. Starr, 285–306. New York: Oxford University Press, 2012.

———, "Modern Pagan Witchcraft." In *Witchcraft and Magic in Europe, Volume 6: The Twentieth Century*, edited by Willem de Blécourt, R. Hutton and J. La Fontaine, 1–80. London: Athlone, 1999.

———, *The Triumph of the Moon: A History of Modern Pagan Witchcraft*. Oxford: Oxford University Press, 1999.

Huxley, Aldous, *The Devils of Loudun*. London: Chatto and Windus, 1953.

Huysmans, J.-K., *À Rebours*. Paris: Bibliothèque-Charpentier, 1919.

———, *Certains*. Paris: Tresse and Stock, 1889.

———, *Croquis parisiens*. Paris: Éditions Slatkine, 1996.

———, *En Route*. Paris: Plon, 1955.

———, *Là-Bas*. Paris: Plon, s.a.

———, *Là-Bas: A Journey into the Self*. Translated by Brendan King. Sawtry: Dedalus, 2009.

———, *Lettres inédites à Jules Destrée*. Genève: Droz, 1967.

———, *Lettres inédites à Arij Prins, 1885–1907*. Genève: Droz, 1977.

———, *Marthe: Histoire d'une fille*. Paris: Le Cercle du Livre, 1955.

———, *Sainte Lydwine de Schiedam*. Paris: Plon, 1901.

Institoris, Henricus, and Jacobus Sprengerus, *Malleus Maleficarum*. Translated by Montague Summers. 1928. Reprint, New York: Benjamin Blom, 1970.

———, *Malleus Maleficarum*. Edited and translated by Christopher S. Mackay. 2 vols. Cambridge: Cambridge University Press, 2006.

Introvigne, Massimo, "The Beast and the Prophet: Aleister Crowley's Fascination with Joseph Smith." In *Aleister Crowley and Western Esotericism*, edited by Henrik Bogdan and Martin P. Starr, 255–284. New York: Oxford University Press, 2012.

———, "Diana Redux: retour sur l'affaire Léo Taxil-Diana Vaughan." *Aries: Journal for the Study of Western Esotericism* 4 (2004) 1:91–97.

———, *Enquête sur le satanisme: Satanistes et antisatanistes du XVIIe siècle à nos jours*. Translated by Philipp Baillet. Paris: Éditions Dervy, 1997.

———, "Huysmans." In *Dictionary of Gnosis and Western Esotericism*, edited by Wouter J. Hanegraaff, 1:579–580. Leiden: Brill, 2005.

———, "Le satanisme moderne et contemporain en Italie." *Social Compass* 56 (December 2009) 4:541–551.

———, "Satanism." In *Dictionary of Gnosis and Western Esotericism*, edited by Wouter J. Hanegraaff, 2:1035–1037. Leiden: Brill, 2005.

Irvine, Doreen, *From Witchcraft to Christ*. Cambridge: Concordia, 1973.

———, *Van hekserij tot Christus: Mijn ware levensverhaal*. Translated by Loek Visser. Den Haag, Gazon: s.a.

Jacques-Lefèvre, Nicole, "Michelet et les démonologues: lecture et réécriture." In *La Sorcière de Jules Michelet. L'envers de l'histoire*, edited by Paule Petitier, 90–107. Paris: Honoré Champion, 2004.

Jacquinot, Jean, "En marge de J.-K. Huysmans. Un Procès de l'Abbé Boullan." *Les Cahiers de la Tour Saint-Jacques* 8 (1963): 206–216.

Jarrige, Michel, *L'église et les Francs-Maçons dans la tourmente: Croisade de la revue "La Franc-Maçonnerie Démasquée" (1894–1899)*. Paris: Éditions Arguments, 1999.

Jaquerius, Nicolaus, *Flagellum Haereticorum Fascinariorum*. Francofurti ad Moenu: [Nic. Bassaeus], 1581.

Jenkins, Philip, and Daniel Maier-Katkin, "Occult Survivors: The Making of a Myth." In *The Satanism Scare*, edited by James T. Richardson, Joel Best, and David G. Bromley, 127–144. New York: Aldine de Gruyter, 1991.

Jenkins, Richard, "Continuity and Change: Social Science Perspectives on European Witchcraft." In *Palgrave Advances in Witchcraft Historiography*, edited by Jonathan Barry and Owen Davies, 203–224. Houndmills: Palgrave Macmillan, 2007.

Jerouschek, Günther, " 'Diabolus habitat in eis.' Wo der Teufel zu Hause ist: Geslechtigkcit in rechtstheologischen Diskurs des ausgehenden Mittelalters und der frühen Neuzeit." *Rechtshistorischer Journal* 9 (1990): 301–329.

Jésus-Marie, Bruno de, "La confession de Boullan." *Satan: Les Études Carmélitaines* 27 (Paris: Desclée De Brouwer, 1948): 420–426.

Jones, W. R., "Palladism and the Papacy: An Episode of French Anticlericalism in the Nineteenth Century." *Journal of Church and State* 12 (1970) 3:453–473.

Jong, Albert de, *Traditions of the Magi: Zoroastrianism in Greek and Latin Literature*. Religions in the Graeco-Roman World, no. 133. Leiden: Brill, 1997.

Jouvin, Henri, "Les Lettres de J.-K. Huysmans. Essais de Bibliographie." *Bulletin de la Société J.-K Huysmans* 22 (1949) 21:27–31, 24 (1951) 25:146–153, 28 (1953) 27:288–296.

Kaestli, Jean-Daniel, "L'interprétation du serpent de Genèse 3 dans quelques textes gnostiques et la question de la gnose 'Ophite.' " In *Gnosticisme et monde hellénistique: actes du colloque de Louvain-la-Neuve (11–14 mars 1980)*, edited by Julien Ries, 116–130. Publications de l'Institut Orientaliste de Louvain, no. 27. Louvain: Université Catholique de Louvain, Institut Orientaliste, 1982.

Kahaner, Larry, *Cults That Kill: Probing the Underworld of Occult Crime*. New York: Warner, 1988.

Karimi, Annette, "Satanisch seksueel misbruik: Hulpverleners vragen aandacht slachtoffers sekten." *Spits* (7 November 2011), 1.

Katz, Jacob, *Jews and Freemasons in Europe, 1723-1939*. Translated by Leonard Oschry. Cambridge, MA: Harvard University Press, 1970.

Kaczynski, Richard, "Continuing Knowledge from Generation unto Generation: The Social and Literary Background of Aleister Crowley's Magic." In *Aleister Crowley and Western Esotericism*, edited by Henrik Bogdan and Martin P. Starr, 141–179. New York: Oxford University Press, 2012.

———, *Perdurabo: The Life of Aleister Crowley*. Berkeley, CA: North Atlantic, 2010.

Keller, Barbara G., *The Middle Ages Reconsidered: Attitudes in France from the Eighteenth Century through the Romantic Movement*. New York: Peter Lang, 1994.

Kelly, Henry Ansgar, *Satan: A Biography*. Cambridge: Cambridge University Press, 2006.

Kershaw, Kris, *The One-eyed God: Odin and the (Indo-)Germanic Männerbünde*. Journal of Indo-European Studies Monograph, no. 36. Washington, DC: Institute for the Study of Man, 2000.

Kesteren, Ronald van, *Het verlangen naar de Middeleeuwen: De verbeelding van een historische passie*. Amsterdam: Uitgeverij Wereldbibliotheek, 2004.

Kieckhefer, Richard, "The Devil's Contemplatives: The Liber Iuratus, the Liber Visionum and the Christian Appropriation of Jewish Occultism." In *Conjuring Spirits: Texts and Traditions of Medieval Ritual Magic*, edited by Claire Fanger, 250–265. Magic in History, no. 4. Thrupp: Sutton, 1998.

———, *European Witch Trials: Their Foundations in Popular and Learned Culture, 1300–1500*. Berkeley: University of California Press, 1976.

———, *Forbidden Rites: A Necromancer's Manual of the Fifteenth Century*. University Park: Pennsylvania State University Press, 1998.

———, *Magic in the Middle Ages*. Cambridge: Cambridge University Press, 1990.

Kinney, Jay M., "Shedding Light on a Possible Inspiration for Taxil's Hoax Letter: Pike's *The Masonry of Adoption*." *Heredom* 11 (2003): 149–157.

Kippenberg, Anton, *Die Sage vom Herzog von Luxemburg und die historische Persönlichkeit ihres Trägers*. 1901 Reprint, Niederwalluf bei Wiesbaden: Dr. Martin Sändig oHG, 1970.

Kister, M. J., "Ādam: A Study of Some Legends in *Tafsīr* and *Hadīt* Literature." *Israel Oriental Studies* 13 (1993): 113–174.

Klaassen, Frank, "English Manuscripts of Magic, 1300–1500: A Preliminary Survey." In *Conjuring Spirits: Texts and Traditions of Medieval Ritual Magic*, edited by Claire Fanger, 3–31. Magic in History, no. 4. Thrupp: Sutton, 1998.

Klaassen, Frank, and Christopher Phillips, "The Return of Stolen Goods: Reginald Scot, Religious Controversy, and Magic in Bodleian Library, Additional B. 1." *Magic, Ritual, and Witchcraft* 1 (Winter 2006) 2:135–75.

Knight, Mark, and Emma Mason, *Nineteenth-Century Religion and Literature: An Introduction*. Oxford: Oxford University Press, 2006.

Koomen, Martin, *Het ijzige zaad van de duivel: Geschiedenis van heksen en demonen*. Amsterdam: Wetenschappelijke Uitgeverij, 1973.

Korteweg, Theodoor, "Justin Martyr and His Demon-ridden Universe." In *Demons and the Devil in Ancient and Medieval Christianity*, edited by Nienke Vos and Willemien Otten, 145–158. Supplements to Vigiliae Christianae: Texts and Studies of Early Christian Life and Language, no. 108. Leiden: Brill, 2011.

Kostka, Jean, *Lucifer démasqué*. Paris: Delhomme and Briguet. [1895].

Krampl, Ulrike, "When Witches Became False: Séducteurs and Crédules Confront the Paris Police at the Beginning of the Eighteenth Century." In *Werewolves, Witches and Wandering Spirits. Traditional Belief and Folklore in Early Modern Europe*, edited by Kathryn A. Edwards, 137–154. Kirksville, MI: Truman State University Press, 2002.

Kreyenbroek, Philip G., *Yezidism—Its Background, Observances and Textual Tradition*. Lewiston, NY: Edwin Mellen, 1995.

Kurze, Dietrich, "Zur Ketzergeschichte der Mark Brandenburg und Pommerns vornehmlich im 14. Jahrhundert." *Jahrbuch für die Geschichte Mittel- und Ostdeutschlands* 16–17 (1968): 50–94.

Kusters, Wouter, *La Sorcière: Nouvelle édition critique avec introduction, variantes et examen du manuscrit*. Nijmegen: s.i., 1989.

L., X. [=Julien Osgood Field], *Aut Diabolus Aut Nihil, and Other Tales*. London: Methuen, 1895.

La Fontaine, Jean, "Satanism and Satanic Mythology." In *Witchcraft and Magic in Europe, Volume 6: The Twentieth Century*, edited by Willem de Blécourt, R. Hutton, and J. La Fontaine, 81–140. London: Athlone, 1999.

LaChapelle, Sofia, *Investigating the Supernatural: From Spiritism and Occultism to Psychical Research and Metapsychics in France, 1853–1931*. Baltimore, MD: John Hopkins University Press, 2011.

Ladous, Régis, "Le spiritisme et les démons dans les catéchismes français du XIXe siècle." In *Le Défi Magique II: Satanisme, sorcellerie*, edited by Jean-Baptiste Martin and Massimo Introvigne, 203–228. Lyon: Presses Universitaires de Lyon, 1994.

Lambert, Pierre, "Adèle Chevalier raconte . . .", *Les Cahiers de la Tour Saint-Jacques* 8 (1963): 217–226.

———, "Annexes au dossier Van Haecke-Berthe Courrière. Lettres inédites de Gourmont et de Firmin Vanden Bosch à Joris-Karl Huysmans." *Les Cahiers de la Tour Saint-Jacques* 8 (1963): 180–189.

———, "En marge de *Là-Bas*. Une Cérémonie au 'Carmel de Jean-Baptiste,' à Lyon, d'après une relation de Boullan." *Bulletin de la Société J.-K Huysmans* 28 (1953) 27:297–306.

———, "Un culte hérétique à Paris, 11, Rue de Sèvres. Avec des textes inédits de Huysmans." *Les Cahiers de la Tour Saint-Jacques* 8 (1963): 190–205.

———, "Une lettre de J.A. Boullan à Huysmans." *Bulletin de la Société J.-K Huysmans* 25 (1952) 24:203–207.

Lamberts, Emiel, "Conclusion. The Black International and its Influence on European Catholicism (1870–1878)." In *The Black International/L'International noire 1870–1878*, edited by Emiel Lamberts, 464–480. Leuven: Leuven University Press, 2002.

———, "L'internationale noire. Une organisation secrète au service du Saint-Siège." In *The Black International/L'International noire 1870–1878*, edited by Emiel Lamberts, 15–101. Leuven: Leuven University Press, 2002.

———, "Political and Social Catholicism in Cisleithania [Austria] (1867–1889)." In *The Black International/L'International noire 1870–1878*, edited by Emiel Lamberts, 298–317. Leuven: Leuven University Press, 2002.

Lamers, Maarten Joost, *Vlucht in de Werkelijkheid: Inleiding tot het Satanisme*. Amsterdam: Satanisch Seminarium, 1983.

Lancre, Pierre de, *L'Incrédulité et mescréance du sortilège plainement convaincu*. Paris: Nicolas Buon, 1622.

———, *Tableau de l'inconstance des mauvais anges et démons, où il est amplement tracté des Sorciers, & de la Sorcellerie*. Paris: Nicolas Buon, 1613.

Lantoine, Albert, *Lettre au Souverain Pontife*. Paris: Éditions du Symbolisme, 1937.

Lap, Amina Olander, "Categorizing Modern Satanism: An Analysis of LaVey's Early Writings." In *The Devil's Party: Satanism in Modernity*, edited by Per Faxneld and Jesper Petersen, 83–102. Oxford: Oxford University Press, 2012.

Lapidoth, Frits, *Goëtia*. 2 vols. Leiden: S. C. van Doesburg, 1893.

———, *Goëtia: Die Priesterin der schwarzen Kunst*. Dresden: Heinrich Minden, [1897].

Larmore, Charles, *The Romantic Legacy*. New York: Columbia University Press, 1996.

Laurant, Jean-Pierrre, "Le dossier Léo Taxil du fonds Jean Baylot de la Bibliothèque Nationale." *Politica Hermetica* 4 (1990): 66–67.

LaVey, Anton Szandor, *The Devil's Notebook*. Los Angeles: Feral House, 1992.

——, *Letters from the Devil*. s.l.: Underworld Amusements, 2010.

——, "On Occultism in the Past." *Cloven Hoof* 3 (1971) 9: http://churchofsatan.com/occultism-of-the-past.php, accessed 15 January 2015.

——, *Satan Speaks!* Los Angeles: Feral House, 1998.

——, *The Satanic Bible*. New York: Avon, 1969.

——, *The Satanic Rituals*. New York: Avon, 1972.

——, *The Satanic Witch*. Los Angeles: Feral House, 2003.

Lavocat, Françoise, "L'Arcadie diabolique. La fiction poétique dans le débat sur la sorcellerie (XVIe–XVIIe siècles)." In *Fictions du Diable: Démonologie et littérature de saint Augustin à Léo Taxil*, edited by Françoise Lavocat, Pierre Kapitaniak, and Marianne Closson, 57–84. Genève: Librairie Droz, 2007.

Laycock, Donald, *The Complete Enochian Dictionary: A Dictionary of the Angelic Language as Revealed to Dr John Dee and Edward Kelly*. London: Askin, 1978.

Lea, Henry-Charles, *Léo Taxil, Diana Vaughan et l'Église Romaine: Histoire d'une mystification*. Paris: Société Nouvelle de Librairie et d'Édition, 1910.

Lefèvre, Frédéric, "Une heure avec M. Léon Hennique de l'Académie Goncourt." *Les Nouvelles Littéraires, artistiques et scientifiques* 9 (10 mai 1930) 395: 1–2.

Legge, F., "Devil-Worship and Freemasonry." *Contemporary Review* (October 1896) 70: 466–483.

Legué, G., *Médecins et empoisonneurs au XVIIᵉ siècle*. Paris: Bibliothèque-Charpentier, 1895.

Leland, Charles G., *Aradia, or the Gospel of the Witches*. London: David Nutt, 1899.

Lemaire, Jacques, "Les premières formes de l'antimaçonnisme en France: les ouvrages de révélation (1738–1751)." In *Les courants antimaçonniques hier et aujourd'hui*, edited by Alain Dierkens, 11–23. Problèmes d'histoire des religions, no. 4. Bruxelles: Éditions de l'Université de Bruxelles, 1993.

Lenfant, Jacques, *Histoire de la Guerre des Hussites et du Concile de Basle*. 2 vols. Amsterdam: Pierre Humbert, 1731.

Lennep Jacques van, *De 19e-eeuwse Belgische beeldhouwkunst*. Brussels: General Bank, 1990.

Lévi, Éliphas, *La Clef des grands mystères, suivant Hénoch, Abraham, Hermès Trismégiste et Solomon*. Paris: Félix Alcan, [1923].

——, *Dogme et rituel de la haute magie*. 2 vols. Paris: Félix Alcan, 1910.

——, *Histoire de la magie, avec une exposition claire et précise de ses procédés, de ses rites et de ses mystères*. Paris: Germer Ballière, 1860.

Levine, Mark, "Doing the Devil's Work: Heavy Metal and the Threat to Public Order in the Muslim World." *Social Compass* 56 (December 2009) 4:564–576.

Lewis, James R., "Conversion to Satanism: Constructing Diabolical Identities." In *The Devil's Party: Satanism in Modernity*, edited by Per Faxneld and Jesper Petersen, 145–166. Oxford: Oxford University Press, 2012.

——, "Infernal Legitimacy." In *Contemporary Religious Satanism: A Critical Anthology*, edited by Jesper Aagaard Petersen, 41–58. Farnham, UK: Ashgate, 2009.

——, "The Satanic Bible: Quasi-Scripture/Counter-Scripture." http://www.cesnur.org/2002/slc/lewis.htm, accessed 1 February 2011.

——, *Satanism Today: An Encyclopedia of Religion, Folklore, and Popular Culture*. Santa Barbara, CA: ABC-Clio, 2001.

Lewis, Matthew Gregory, *The Monk: A Romance*. London: Brentano's, 1924.

Lézinier, Michel de, *Avec Huysmans: Promenades et souvenirs*. Paris: André Delpeuch, 1928.

Liagre Böll, Herman de, *Herman Gorter 1864–1927: Met al mijn bloed heb ik voor U geleefd*. Amsterdam: Olympus, 2000.

Lidaka, Juris G., "*The Book of Angels, Rings, Characters and Images of the Planets*: Attributed to Osbern Bokinham." In *Conjuring Spirits: Texts and Traditions of Medieval Ritual Magic*, edited by Claire Fanger, 32–63. Magic in History, no. 4. Thrupp: Sutton, 1998.

Lillie, Arthur, *The Worship of Satan in Modern France*. London: Swan Sonnenschein, 1896.

Lindsey, Hal, and C. C. Carlson, *Satan Is Alive and Well on Planet Earth*. Grand Rapids, MI: Zondervan, 1972.

Lipp, Wolfgang, "Außenseiter, Häretiker, Revolutionäre. Gesichtspunkte zur systematischer Analyse." In *Reliogiöse Devianz in christlich geprägten Gesellschaften. Vom hohen Mittelalter bis zur Frühaufklärung*, edited by Dieter Fauth and Daniela Müller, 12–26. Würzburg: Religion and Kultur Verlag, 1999.

Lorain, Alphonse, "La question Diana Vaughan." *La France Libre*, 13 November 1896.

———, "L'Entreprise Diana Vaughan." *La France Libre*, December 1896.

Lord, Evelyn, *The Hell-Fire Clubs: Sex, Satanism and Secret Societies*. New Haven, CT: Yale University Press, 2010.

Loriga, Sabina, "A Secret to Kill the King: Magic and Protection in Piedmont in the Early Eighteenth Century." In *History from Crime*, edited by Edward Muir and Guido Ruggiero, 88–109. Selections from *Quaderni Storici*, no. 3. Baltimore, MD: John Hopkins University Press, 1994.

Lory, Jacques, "La 'Correspondance de Gèneve' (1870–1873). Un organe de presse singulier." In *The Black International/L'International noire 1870–1878*, edited by Emiel Lamberts, 102–131. Leuven: Leuven University Press, 2002.

Lowe, Thompson, R., *The History of the Devil: The Horned God of the West*. London: Kegan Paul, Trench, Trubner, 1929.

Lowney, Kathleen S., "The Devil's Down in Dixie: Studying Satanism in South Georgia." In *Contemporary Religious Satanism: A Critical Anthology*, edited by Jesper Aagaard Petersen, 103–117. Farnham, UK: Ashgate, 2009.

———, "Teenage Satanism as Oppositional Youth Subculture." *Journal of Contemporary Ethnography* 23 (1995) 4:453–484.

Luhrmann, T.M., *Persuasions of the Witch's Craft: Ritual Magic and Witchcraft in Present-day England*. Oxford: Basil Blackwell, 1989.

Luijk, Ruben van, "God, Satan, Poetry and Revolution: Romatic Satanism in the Nineteenth Century." *Religion and Theology* (2016) 1.

———, "Searching for Marafi: A Short History of Satanism in the Western World." *@KIH-eSkript. Interdisziplinäre Hexenforschung online* 3 (2011) 1, 23–30: http://www.historicum.net/no_cache/persistent/artikel/9102.

———, "Sex, Science and Liberty: The Resurrection of Satan in 19th Century (Counter) Culture." In *The Devil's Party: Satanism in Modernity*, edited by Per Faxneld and Jesper Petersen, 41–52. Oxford: Oxford University Press, 2012.

Lyons, Arthur, *Satan Wants You: The Cult of Devil Worship in America*. New York: Mysterious Press, 1988.

———, *The Second Coming: Satanism in America*. New York: Dodd, Mead and Company, 1970.

MacCarthy, Fiona, *Byron: Life and Legend*. London: John Murray, 2002.

MacMullen, Ramsay, *Christianity and Paganism in the Fourth and Eight Centuries*. New Haven, CT: Yale University Press, 1997.

Maeyer, Jan De, "La Belgique. Un élève modèle de l'école ultramontaine." In *The Black International/L'International noire 1870–1878*, edited by Emiel Lamberts, 360–385. Leuven: Leuven University Press, 2002.

Maigron, Louis, *Le Romantisme et les mœurs: Essai d'étude historique et sociale d'après des documents inédits* Paris: Librairie Ancienne, 1910.

Maistre, Xavier de, *Voyage autour de ma chambre*. [Paris]: Librairie Arthème Fayard, 2000.

Mali, Joseph, *Mythistory: The Making of Modern Historiography*. Chicago: University of Chicago Press, 2003.

Mandrou, Robert, *Magistrats et sorciers en France au XVIIe siècle: Une analyse de psychologie historique*. Paris: Éditions du Seuil, 1980.

——— (ed.), *Possession et sorcellerie au XVIIe siècle: Textes inédits*. Paris: Librairie Arthème Fayard, 1979.

Margiotta, Domenico, *Le Palladisme: Culte de Satan-Lucifer dans les triangles maçonniques*. Grenoble: H. Falque, 1895.

———, *Souvenirs d'un Trente-Troisième: Adriano Lemmi, chef suprême des Franc-Maçons*. Paris: Delhomme and Briguet, s.a.

Martin, Daniel, and Gary Alan Fine, "Satanic Cults, Satanic Play: Is 'Dungeons & Dragons' a Breeding Ground for the Devil?' In *The Satanism Scare*, edited by James T. Richardson, Joel Best, and David G. Bromley, 107–123. New York: Aldine de Gruyter, 1991.

Martin, Philippe, *Le théâtre divin: Une histoire de la messe du XIVème au XXème siècle*. Paris: CNSR Éditions, 2010.

Marquès-Rivière, J., *La trahison spirituelle de la Franc-Maçonnerie*. Paris: Éditions des Portiques, 1931.

Massignon, Louis, "Huysmans devant la 'confession' de Boullan." *Bulletin de la Société J.-K Huysmans* 22 (1949) 21:40–50.

———, "Le témoignage de Huysmans et l'affaire Van Haecke." *Les Cahiers de la Tour Saint-Jacques* 8 (1963): 166–179.

Masters, Anthony, *The Devil's Dominion: The Complete Story of Hell and Satanism in the Modern World*. New York: G.P. Putnam's Sons, 1978.

Mathews, Chris, *Modern Satanism: Anatomy of a Radical Subculture*. Westport, CT: Praeger, 2009.

Mathiesen, Robert, "A Thirteenth-Century Ritual to Attain the Beatific Vision from the *Sworn Book* of Honorius of Thebes." In *Conjuring Spirits: Texts and Traditions of Medieval Ritual Magic*, edited by Claire Fanger, 143–162. Magic in History, no. 4. Thrupp: Sutton, 1998.

Matuszak, Gabriela, *"Der geniale Pole"? Stanislaw Przybyszewski in Deutschland (1892–1992)*. Translated by Dietrich Scholze. Paderborn: Igel Verlag, 1996.

Maxwell-Stuart, Peter, "The Contemporary Historical Debate, 1400–1750." In *Palgrave Advances in Witchcraft Historiography*, edited by Jonathan Barry and Owen Davies, 11–32. Houndmills: Palgrave Macmillan, 2007.

McGrath, Malcolm, *Demons of the Modern World*. Amherst, NY: Prometheus, 2002.

McIntosh, Christopher, *Eliphas Lévi and the French Occult Revival*. London: Rider and Company, 1972.

McLeod, Hugh, *Secularisation in Western Europe, 1848–1914*. Houndmills: Macmillan, 2000.

Medway, Gareth J., *Lure of the Sinister: The Unnatural History of Satanism*. New York: New York University Press, 2001.

Melton, J. Gordon, "Satanism and the Church of Satan." In *Encyclopedic Handbook of Cults in America*, edited by J. Gordon Melton, 76–80. New York: Garland, 1986.

Menasce, P. de, O.P., "Note sur le dualisme mazdéen." *Satan: Les Études Carmélitaines* 27 (1948): 130–135.

Menegotto, Andrea, "Italian Martyrs of 'Satanism': Sister Maria Laura Mainetti and Father Giorgio Govoni." In *Contemporary Religious Satanism: A Critical Anthology*, edited by Jesper Aagaard Petersen, 199–209. Farnham, UK: Ashgate, 2009.

Mercer, Joyce, *Behind the Mask of Adolescent Satanis*. Minneapolis: Deaconess, 1991.

Mery, Gaston, *La vérité sur Diana Vaughan: Un complot maçonnique*. Paris: Librairie Blériot, s.a.

Meurs, Jos van, "William Blake and His Gnostic Myths." In *Gnosis and Hermeticism: From Antiquity to Modern Times*, edited by Roelof van den Broek and Wouter J. Hanegraaff, 269–309. Albany: State University of New York Press, 1998.

Meurin, Léon, *La Franc-Maçonnerie, Synagogue de Satan*. Paris: Victor Retaux and Fils, 1893.

Michelet, Jules, *La Sorcière: Nouvelle édition*. Bruxelles: A. Lacroix, Verboeckhoven, 1867.

Michelet, Victor-Émile, *L'Amour et la Magie*. Paris: Librairie Hermetique, 1909.

———, *Les compagnons de la hiérophanie: Souvenirs du mouvements hermétiste à la fin du XIXIe siècle*. Paris: Borbon-Ainé, [1938].

Milner, Max, *Le diable dans la littérature française: De Cazotte à Baudelaire 1772–1861*. 2 vols. Paris: Librairie José Corti, 1960.

———, "Signification politique de la figure de Satan dans le romantisme français." In *Romantisme et politique 1815–1851. Colloque de l'Ecole Normale Supérieure de Saint-Cloud (1966)*. Edited by Louis Girard, 157–163. Paris: Librarie Armand Colin, 1969.

Milton, John, *Paradise Lost*. London: Penguin, 2000.

Mola, Aldo A., "La Ligue antimaçonnique et son influence politique et culturelle aux confines des XIXe et XXe siècles." In *Les courants antimaçonniques hier et aujourd'hui*, edited by Alain Dierkens, 39–55. Problèmes d'histoire des religions, no. 4. Bruxelles: Éditions de l'Université de Bruxelles, 1993.

Mollenauer, Lynn Wood, *Strange Revelations: Magic, Poison and Sacrilege in Louis XIV's France*. University Park: Pennsylvania State University Press, 2006.

Möller, Helmut, and Ellic Howe, *Merlin Peregrinus: Vom Untergrund des Abendlandes*. Würzburg: Köningshausen + Neumann, 1986.

Möller, Horst, "Die Gold- und Rosenkreuzer. Struktur, Zielsetzung und Wirkung einer anti-aufklärischen Geheimgesellschaft." In *Geheime Gesellschaften*, edited by Peter Christian Ludz, 153–202. Wolfenbütteler Studien zur Aufklärung, no. V/1. Heidelberg: Verlag Lambert Schneider, 1979.

Möller, Melanie, *Satanismus als Religion der Überschreitung: Transgression und stereotype Darstellung in Erfahrungs- und Aussteigerberichten*. Marburg: diagonal-Verlag, 2007.

Mœller, Henry, "Lettres inédites de J.-K. Huysmans à l'abbé Henry Mœller." *Durendal: Revue Catholique d'Art et de Littérature* 5 (1908): 37–44.

———, "Joris-Karl Huysmans d'après sa correspondence." *Durendal: Revue Catholique d'Art et de Littérature* 5 (1908): 100–104, 169–173, 248–251, 438–446; 6 (1909): 273–282; 7 (1910): 166–177, 221–225, 493–502, 553–560, 730–741.

Mombelet, Alexis, "Entre metanoïa et paranoïa: Approches sociologique et médiatique du satanisme en France." *Social Compass* 56 (December 2009) 4:530–530.

Monsabre, T. R. P., *La Croisade au XIXe siècle: Discours prononcé à Clermont-Ferrand à l'occasion du 8e centenaire de la 1re Croisade, le 18 Mai 1895.* Paris: Bureaux de La Revue Thomiste, s.a.

Montero, Feliciano, and Robles, Cristobal, "Le mouvement catholique en Espagne dans les années 1870." In *The Black International/L'International noire 1870–1878*, edited by Emiel Lamberts, 427–446. Leuven: Leuven University Press, 2002.

Moody, Edward J., "Magical Therapy: An Anthropological Investigation of Contemporary Satanism." In *Religious Movements in Contemporary America*, edited by Irving I. Zaretsky and Mark P. Leone, 355–382. Princeton, NJ: Princeton University Press, 1974.

Moore, R. I., *The Formation of a Persecuting Society: Power and Deviance in Western Europe, 950–1250.* Oxford: Basil Blackwell, 1987.

Moore, R. Laurence, "Spiritualism." In *The Rise of Adventism. Religion and Society in Mid-Nineteenth-Century America*, edited by Edwin S. Gaustad, 79–103. New York: Harper and Row, 1974.

Moynihan, Michael, and Didrik Søderlind, *Lords of Chaos: The Bloody Rise of the Satanic Metal Underground.* Venice, CA: Feral House, 1998.

Mørk, Gry, " 'With my Art I am the Fist in the Face of god': On Old-School Black Metal." In *Contemporary Religious Satanism: A Critical Anthology*, edited by Jesper Aagaard Petersen, 171–198. Farnham, UK: Ashgate, 2009.

Muchembled, Robert, *A History of the Devil: From the Middle Ages to the Present.* Cambridge: Polity, 2003.

Mulhern, Sherrill, "Satanism and Psychotherapy: A Rumor in Search of an Inquisition." In *The Satanism Scare*, edited by James T. Richardson, Joel Best, and David G. Bromley, 145–172. New York: Aldine de Gruyter, 1991.

Müller, Daniela, "Aspekte der Ketzerverfolgung unter den römischen Kaisern bis Justinian." *Journal of Eastern Christian Studies* 60 (2008) 1–4:175–193.

———, *Frauen vor der Inquisition: Lebensform, Glaubenszeugnis und Aburteilung der deutschen und französischen Katharerinnen.* Veröffentlichungen des Instituts für Europäische Geschichte Mainz, No. 166. Mainz: Von Zabern, 1996.

———, "Gott und seine zwei Frauen: Der Teufel bei den Katharern." *@KIH-eSkript. Interdisziplinäre Hexenforschung online* 3 (2011) 1:69–76, at http://www.historicum.net/no_cache/persistent/artikel/9107 (accessed 14 December 2011).

———, "Les historiens et la question de la vérité historique: L'église cathare a-t-elle existé?' In *1209–2009. Cathares: Une histoire à pacifier? Actes du colloque international tenue à Mazamet les 15, 16 et 17 mai 2009*, edited by Anne Brenon, 139–154. Portet-sur-Garonne: Nouvelles Éditions Loubatières, 2010.

———, "Our Image of 'Others' and Our Own Identity." In *Iconoclasm and Iconoclash: Struggle for Religious Identity*, edited by Willem van Asselt, Paul van Geest, and others, 107–123. Leiden: Brill, 2007.

Murawski, Roman, "The Philosophy of Hœne-Wronski." *Organon* 35 (2006): 143–150.

Murray, Margaret Alice, *The God of the Witches*. London: Faber and Faber, 1956.

———, *The Witch Cult in Western Europe*. Oxford: Clarendon, 1962.

Naglowska, Maria de, *La Lumière du Sexe: Rituel d'initiation satanique, selon la doctrine du Troisième Terme de la Trinité*. Montperoux: Ordo Templi Orientis, Oasis Sous les Étoiles, 1993.

Nathan, Debbie, "Satanism and Child Molestation: Constructing the Ritual Abuse Scare." In *The Satanism Scare*, edited by James T. Richardson, Joel Best, and David G. Bromley, 75–94. New York: Aldine de Gruyter, 1991.

Nemours Godré, L., "La fin de Diana." *La Vérité*, 21 April 1897.

Nietzsche, Friedrich, *Also Sprach Zarathustra: Ein Buch für Alle und Keinen*. Leipzig: Alfred Kröner Verlag, 1930.

———, *Der Antichrist: Versuch einer Kritik des Christentums*. Berlin: Nordland Verlag, 1941.

———, *Jenseits von Gut und Böse/Zur Genealogie der Moral*. Leipzig: Alfred Kröner Verlag, 1923.

Oexle, Otto Gerhard, "Das Mittelalter und das Unbehagen an der Moderne: Mittelalterbesc hwörungen in der Weimarer Republik und danach." In *Geschichtswissenschaft im Zeichen des Historismus: Studien zu Problemgeschichten der Moderne*, 137–162. Kritische Studien zur Geschichtswissenchaft, no. 116. Göttingen: Vandenhoeck and Ruprecht, 1996.

Ogrinc, Will H. L., "Frère Jacques: A Shrine to Love and Sorrow. Jacques d'Adelswärd-Fersen (1880–1923)." semgai.free.fr/doc_et_pdf?Fersen-engels.pdf, 2006.

Olbrich, Karl, *Die Freimaurer im deutschen Volksglauben: Die im Volke umlaufenden Vorstellungen und Erzählungen von den Freimauern*. Breslau: M. & H. Marcus, 1930.

O'Neddy, Philotée, *Feu et Flamme*. Paris: Librairie orientale de Dondey-Dupré, 1833.

———, *Lettre inédite de Philothée O'Neddy, auteur de Feu et Flamme, sur le groupe littéraire romantique dit des Bousingos (Théophile Gautier, Gérard de Nerval, Petrus Borel, Bouchardy, Alphonse Brot, etc.)*. Paris: P. Rouquette, 1875.

Osterkamp, Ernst, *Lucifer: Stationen eines Motivs*. Berlin: Walter de Gruyter, 1979.

Owen, Alex, "The Sorcerer and His Apprentice: Aleister Crowley and the Magical Exploration of Edwardian Subjectivity." In *Aleister Crowley and Western Esotericism*, edited by Henrik Bogdan and Martin P. Starr, 15–52. New York: Oxford University Press, 2012.

Oyen, Geert van, "Demons and Exorcism in the Gospel of Mark." In *Demons and the Devil in Ancient and Medieval Christianity*, edited by Nienke Vos and Willemien Otten, 99–116. Supplements to Vigiliae Christianae: Texts and Studies of Early Christian Life and Language, no. 108. Leiden: Brill, 2011.

Pagels, Elaine, *The Origin of Satan*. London: Penguin, 1996.

———, "The Social History of Satan, the 'Intimate Enemy': A Preliminary Sketch." *Harvard Theological Review* 84 (1991) 2:105–128.

Paine, Thomas, *The Age of Reason*. 1794/1795. Reprint, New York: Prometheus, 1984.

Pals, Daniel, *Seven Theories of Religion*. New York: Oxford University Press, 1996.

Papus, *Catholicisme, satanisme et occultisme*. Paris: Chamuel, 1897.

———, "La-Bas. Par J.-K. Huysmans." *L'Initation: Revue philosophique indépendante des Hautes Études* 11 (May 1891): 97–114.

———, *La Caballe: Tradition secrète de l'Occident*. [Paris]: Bibliothèque Chacornac, 1903.

———, *Le Diable et l'Occultisme*. Paris: Chamuel, 1895.

———, *Peut-on Envoûter? Étude historique et critique sur les plus récents travaux concernant l'envoûtement*. Paris: Chamuel, 1893.

——, *Traité élémentaire de science occulte*. Paris: Albin Michel, 1926.

Parker, Fred, "Between Satan and Mephistopheles: Byron and the Devil." *Cambridge Quarterly* 35 (2006) 1:1–29.

Parker, John, *At the Heart of Darkness: Witchcraft, Black Magic and Satanism Today*. London: Sidgwick and Jackson, 1993.

Partridge, Christopher, "Occulture Is Ordinary." In *Contemporary Esotericism*, edited by Egil Asprem and Kennet Granholm, 113–133. Sheffield, UK: Equinox, 2013.

——, *The Re-Enchantment of the West. Volume I: Alternative Spiritualities, Sacralization, Popular Culture, and Occulture*. London: T&T Clark, 2004.

Pasi, Marco, *Aleister Crowley und die Versuchung der Politik*. Translated by Fredinand Leopold. Graz: Ares Verlag, 2006.

——, "Dieu du désir, dieu de la raison (Le Diable en Californie dans les années soixante)." In *Le Diable*, edited by Jean-Claude Aguerre, Jean Céard, Antoine Faivre, and others, 87–98. Paris: Éditions Dervy, 1998.

——, "Varieties of Magical Experience: Aleister Crowley's Views on Occult Practice." In *Aleister Crowley and Western Esotericism*, edited by Henrik Bogdan and Martin P. Starr, 53–87. New York: Oxford University Press, 2012.

Patschovsky, Alexander, "Der Ketzer als Teufelsdiener." In *Papsttum, Kirche und Recht im Mittelalter: Festschrift für Horst Fuhrmann zum 65. Geburtstag*, edited by Hubert Mordek, 317–334. Tübingen: Max Niemeyer Verlag, 1991.

——, "Zur Ketzerverfolgung Konrads von Marburg." *Deutsches Archiv für Erforschung des Mittelalters* 37 (1981): 641–693.

Peckham, Morse, "Toward a Theory of Romanticism." In *Romanticism: Points of View*, edited by Robert F. Gleckner and Gerald E. Enscoe, 231–257. Englewood Cliffs, NJ: Prentice-Hall, 1970.

Péladan, Joséphin, *Comment on devient artiste: esthétique*. Paris: [Chamuel], 1894.

——, *Comment on devient Fée*. 1893. Reprint, s.l.: Paréiasaure, 1996.

——, *Comment on devient Mage*. Paris: Chamuel, 1892.

——, *Introduction aux sciences occultes*. Paris: E. Sansot, [1911].

——, *L'Art idéaliste & mystique: Doctrine de l'Ordre et du Salon Annuel de Rose + Croix*. Paris: Chamuel, 1894.

——, *"Pereat!' (La décadence latine. Éthopée XV)*. 1902. Reprint, Génève: Editions Slatkine, 1979.

——, *La vice suprême (La décadence latine. Éthopée I)*. 1896. Reprint, Genève: Editions Slatkine, 1979.

Pelikan, Jaroslav, *The Emergence of the Catholic Tradition*. The Christian Tradition: A History of the Development of Doctrine, vol. 6. Chicago: University of Chicago Press, 1971.

Pessoa, Fernando, *Het uur van de Duivel*. Translated by August Willemsen. Amsterdam: Uitgeverij De Arbeiderspers, 2000.

Peters, Edward (ed.), *Monks, Bishops and Pagans: Christian Culture in Gaul and Italy, 500–700*. Philadelphia: University of Pennsylvania Press, 1975.

Petersen, Jesper Aagaard, "The Carnival of Dr. LaVey: Articulations of Transgression in Modern Satanism." In *The Devil's Party: Satanism in Modernity*, edited by Per Faxneld and Jesper Petersen, 167–188. Oxford: Oxford University Press, 2012.

——, "From Book to Bit: Enacting Satanism Online." In *Contemporary Esotericism*, edited by Egil Asprem and Kennet Granholm, 134–158. Sheffield, UK: Equinox, 2013.

————, "Introduction: Embracing Satan." In *Contemporary Religious Satanism: A Critical Anthology*, edited by Jesper Aagaard Petersen, 1–24. Farnham, UK: Ashgate, 2009.

————, "Satanists and Nuts: Schisms in Modern Satanism." In *Sacred Schisms: How Religions Divide*, edited by S. Lewis and J. R. Lewis, 218–247. New York: Cambridge University Press, 2009.

————, " 'We demand bedrock knowledge': Modern Satanism between Secularized Esotericism and "Esotericized' Secularism." In *Religion and the Authority of Science*, edited by Olav Hammer and James R. Lewis, 67–114. Leiden: Brill, 2011.

Phayer, J. Michael, *Sexual Liberation and Religion in Nineteenth Century Europe*. London: Croom Helm, 1977.

Pike, Albert, *The Book of the Words*. Whitefish, MO: Kessinger, 1992.

————, "Hymns to the Gods." *Blackwood's Edinburgh Magazine* 45 (June 1839) 284:819–830.

————, *Morals and Dogma of the Ancient and Accepted Scottish Rite of Freemasonry, Prepared for the Supreme Council of the Thirty Third Degree for the Southern Jurisdiction of the United States*. Charleston, SC: s.i., A. M. 5632 [1871].

Piper, H. W., *The Active Universe: Pantheism and the Concept of Imagination in the English Romantic Poets*. London: Athlone, 1962.

Plard, Henri, "Anticlérical, anticléricalisme: évolution des ces termes." In *Aspects de l'anticléricalisme du moyen âge à nos jours*, edited by Jacques Marx, 15–22. Bruxelles: Éditions de l'Université de Bruxelles, 1988.

Pluquet, Marc, *La Sophiale: Maria de Naglowska. Sa vie. Son œuvre*. Paris: Ordo Templi Orientalis, 1993.

Pögeler, Otto, "Hegel und die Anfänge der Nihilismus-diskussion." *Man and World* 3 (September 1970) 3:163–199.

Poliakov, Léon, *Histoire de l'antisémitisme: Du Christ aux Juifs de cour*. Paris: Calmann-Lévy, 1955.

Poorthuis, Marcel, "Mani, Augustus en de Kabbala over eten en sex: een vergelijking." In *Augustinia Neerlandica: Aspecten van Augustinus' spiritualiteit en haar doorwerking*, edited by P. van Geest and J. van Oort, 55–71. Leuven: Peeters, 2005.

Praag, Marcus van, *Pantheïstisch pleidooi*. Weesp: s.i., 1976.

Praz, Mario, *The Romantic Agony*. Translated by Angus Davidson. Oxford: Oxford University Press, 1951.

Proudhon, Pierre-Joseph, *De la justice dans la Révolution et dans l'Église. Études de philosophie pratique*. 3 vols. Paris: Garnier Frères, 1858.

————, *De la justice dans la Révolution et dans l'Église: Études de philosophie pratique*. 2 vols. [Paris]: Fayard, 1988.

————, *Système des contradictions économiques, ou philosophie de la misère*. 2 vols. Paris: Guillaumin, 1846.

Przybyszewski, Stanislaw, *Die Synagoge Satans: Entstehung und Kult des Hexensabbats, des Satanismus und der Schwarzen Messe*. Berlin: Verlag Clemens Zerling, 1979.

————, *Ferne komm ich her . : Erinnerungen an Berlin und Krakau*. Translated by Roswitha Matwin-Buschmann. Studienausgabe Werke, Aufzeichnungen und ausgewählte Briefe, 7. Paderborn: Igel Verlag, 1994.

————, *Homo Sapiens (Unter Bord. Unterwegs. Im Malstrom). Satans Kinder*. Studienausgabe Werke, Aufzeichnungen und ausgewählte Briefe, 8. Paderborn: Igel Verlag, 1993.

Puissant, Jean, "Démocratie, socialisme, anticléricalisme, et inversement." In *Aspects de l'anti-cléricalisme du moyen âge à nos jours*, edited by Jacques Marx, 135–147. Bruxelles: Éditions de l'Université de Bruxelles, 1988.

Python, Francis, "Diable, les Franc-Maçons sont de retour! 1877–1903." In *La Franc-maçonnerie à Fribourg et en Suisse du XVIIIᵉ au XXᵉ siècle*, edited by Yvonne Lehnherr, 153–175. Gèneve: Slatkine, 2001.

Rachilde, *Alfred Jarry ou le surmâle de lettres*. Paris: Bernard Grasset, 1928.

Raine, Kathleen, *Blake and Tradition*. 2 vols. Princeton, NJ: Princeton University Press, 1968.

Rand, Ayn, *Atlas Shrugged*. New York: Penguin Putnam, 1992.

Rapisardi, Mario, *Lucifero: Poema*. Rome: Eduardo Perino, 1887.

Raschke, Carl A., *Painted Black: From Drug Killing to Heavy Metal—The Alarming True Story of How Satanism Is Terrorizing Our Communities*. San Francisco: Harper and Row, 1990.

Ratner, Lorman, *Anti-Masonry: The Crusade and the Party*. Englewood Cliffs, NJ: Prentice-Hall, 1969.

Ravaisson, François (ed.), *Archives de la Bastille*. 19 vols. Paris: A. Durand and Pedone-Lauriel, 1866–1904.

Règnier, Philippe, "Le chaudron idéologique de La Sorcière: féminisme, homéopathie et saint-simonisme." In *La Sorcière de Jules Michelet: L'envers de l'histoire*, edited by Paule Petitier, 127–148. Paris: Honoré Champion, 2004.

Rheinfelder, Hans, "Giosue Carducci und sein Werk." In *Carducci. Discorsi nel Cinquantenario della morte*, 501–524. Bologna: Zanichelli, 1959.

Rhodes, Henry T. F., *The Satanic Mass: A Sociological and Crimonological Study*. London: Rider, 1955.

Richardson, James T., "Satanism in the Courts: From Murder to Heavy Metal." In *The Satanism Scare*, edited by James T. Richardson, Joel Best, and David G. Bromley, 205–217. New York: Aldine de Gruyter, 1991.

Richardson, James T., Joel Best and David G. Bromley (eds.), *The Satanism Scare*. New York: Aldine de Gruyter, 1991.

——, "Satanism as a Social Problem." In *The Satanism Scare*, edited by James T. Richardson, Joel Best, and David G. Bromley, 3–17. New York: Aldine de Gruyter, 1991.

Richardson, James T., Jenny Reichert, and Valery Lykes, "Satanism in America: An Update." *Social Compass* 56 (December 2009) 4:552–563.

Richmond, Keith, "Through the Witch's Looking Glass: The Magick of Aleister Crowley and the Witchcraft of Rosaleen Norton." In *Aleister Crowley and Western Esotericism*, edited by Henrik Bogdan and Martin P. Starr, 307–339. New York: Oxford University Press, 2012.

Ricoux, Adolphe, *L'existence des loges de femmes affirmée par Mgr Fava, évêque de Grenoble, et par Léo Taxil: Recherches à ce sujet et réponse à M. Aug. Vacquerie, rédacteur du Rappel*. Paris: Téqui, 1891.

Riley, G. J., "Demon." In *Dictionary of Deities and Demons in the Bible*, edited by Karel van der Toorn, Bob Becking, and Pieter W. van der Horst, 235–240. Leiden: Brill, 1999.

Ringvee, Ringo, "Satanism in Estonia." In *Contemporary Religious Satanism: A Critical Anthology*, edited by Jesper Aagaard Petersen, 129–140. Farnham, UK: Ashgate, 2009.

Rive, A. C. de la, *La Femme et l'Enfant dans la franc-maçonnerie universelle*. Paris: Delhomme and Briguet, 1894.

———, *Le Juif dans la Franc-Maçonnerie*. Paris: Librairie Antimaçonnique, 1895.

Roberts, J. M., *The Mythology of the Secret Societies*. London: Secker and Warburg, 1972.

Roberts, Susan, *Witches U.S.A*. New York: Dell, 1971.

Rogers, Matthew D., "Frenzies of the Beast: The Phaedran *Furores* in the Rites and Writings of Aleister Crowley." In *Aleister Crowley and Western Esotericism*, edited by Henrik Bogdan and Martin P. Starr, 209–225. New York: Oxford University Press, 2012.

Rolland, Paul-Antoine-Honoré, *Étude psychopathologique sur le Mysticisme de J.-K. Huysmans*. Nice: Imprimerie de l'Éclaireur du Nice, 1930.

Rollo, Ahmed, *The Black Art*. London: Jarrolds, 1968.

Rose, Elliot, *A Razor for a Goat: A Discussion of Certain Problems in the History of Witchcraft and Diabolism*. Toronto: University of Toronto Press, 1989.

Rosen, Paul, *L'Ennemie Sociale: Histoire documentée des faits et gestes de la Franc-Maçonnerie de 1717 à 1890 en France, en Belgique et en Italie*. Paris: Bloud and Barral, 1890.

———, *Satan et Cie: Association Universelle pour la destruction de l'ordre social. Révélations complètes et définitives de tous les secrets de la Franc-Maçonnerie*. Paris: Veuve H. Caterman, 1888.

Rosweyde, Herbert (ed.), *Vitae Patrum: De Vita et Verbis Seniorvm sive Historiæ Eremiticæ Libri X. Avctoribus fuis et Nitori pristino restituti, ac Notationibvs illustrati, Operâ et studio Heriberti Ros-Weydi Vltraiectini, e Soc. Iesu Theologi*. Antverpiæ: Ex officina Platiniana, 1628.

Rousse-Lacordaire, Jérôme, *Rome et les Franc-Maçons: Histoire d'un conflit*. Paris: Berg International Editeurs, 1996.

Rowe, Laurel, and Gray Cavender, "Caldrons Bubble, Satan's Trouble, but Witches Are Okay: Media Constructions of Satanism and Witchcraft." In *The Satanism Scare*, edited by James T. Richardson, Joel Best, and David G. Bromley, 263–275. New York: Aldine de Gruyter, 1991.

Rubellin, Michel, "Au temps où Valdès n'était pas hérétique: Hypothèse sur le rôle de Valdès à Lyon (1170–1183)." In *Inventer l'hérésie? Discours polémiques et pouvoirs avant l'Inquisition*, edited by Monique Zerner, 193–218. Nice: Z'éditions, 1998.

Rubin, Miri, *Gentile Tales: The Narrative Assault on Late-Medieval Jews*. New Haven, CT: Yale University Press, 1999.

Rudwin, Maximilian, *Supernaturalism and Satanism in Chateaubriand*. Chicago: Open Court, 1922.

Russell, Jeffrey Burton, *The Devil: Perceptions of Evil from Antiquity to Primitive Christianity*. Ithaca, NY: Cornell University Press, 1977.

———, *Lucifer: The Devil in the Middle Ages*. Ithaca, NY: Cornell University Press, 1984.

———, *Mephistofeles: The Devil in the Modern World*. Ithaca, NY: Cornell University Press, 1986.

———, *The Prince of Darkness: Radical Evil and the Power of Good in History*. Ithaca, NY: Cornell University Press, 1988.

Saget, Justin, "Notes pour servir à la Grande Histoire de la Vieille Dame." *Cahiers du Collège de Pataphysique* 5–6 (1952): 17–23.

Salemink, Theo, "Die zwei Gesichter des katholischen Antisemitismus in den Niederlanden: Das 19. Jahrhundert und die Zeit zwischen den Weltkriegen im Vergleich." In *Katholischer Antisemitismus in 19. Jarhhundert: Ursachen und Traditionen im Internationalen Vergleich*, edited by Olaf Blaschke and Aram Mattioli, 239–257. Zürich: Orell Füssli Verlag, 2000.

———, "Politischer Katholizismus in den Niederlanden." In *Die Rolle des politischen Katholizismus in Europa im 20. Jahrhundert: Band 1*, edited by Heiner Timmermann, 161–175. Münster: Lit Verlag, 2009.

Sand, George, *Consuelo. La Comtesse de Rudolfstad*. 3 vols. Paris: Éditions Garnier Frères, 1959.

Sande, Anton van de, "Antimaçonisme bij katholieken en protestanten." In *"Een stille leerschool van deugd en goede zeden": Vrijmetselarij in Nederland in de 18ᵉ en 19ᵉ eeuw*, edited by A. van de Sande and J. Roosendaal, 137–155. Hilversum: Uitgeverij Verloren, 2005.

———, "Freemasons against the Pope: The Role of Anti-masonry in the Ultramontane Propaganda in Rome, 1790–1900." In *The Power of Imagery: Essays on Rome, Italy and Imagination*, edited by Peter van Kessel, 212–230. Sant'Oreste: Apeiron Editore, 1993.

Sansweet, Stephen J., "Strange Doings. Americans Show Burst Of Interest in Witches, Other Occult Matters." *Wall Street Journal* (23 October 1969): 1, 32.

Sauvestre, Charles, *Les congrégations religieuses dévoilées*. Paris: E. Dentu, 1870.

Schaapman, Karin, *Zonder moeder*. Amsterdam: Muntinga Pockets, 2005.

Schäfer, Volker, "Tübinger Teufelspakte." In *". . helfen zu graben den Brunnen des Lebens": Historische Jubiläumsausstellung des Universitätsarchivs Tübingen*, edited by Uwe Jens Wandel, and others, 72–77. Tübingen: Universitätsbibliothek Tübingen, 1977.

Schaik-Willing, Jeanne van, *Dwaaltocht: Een stukje eigen leven*. 's Gravenhage: Nijgh and Van Ditmar, 1977.

Schiff, Gert, "Füssli, Luzifer und die Medusa." In *Johann Heinrich Füssli 1741–1825*, edited by Werner Hofmann, 9–22. München: Prestel-Verlag, 1974.

Schimmel, Annemarie, *Mystical Dimensions of Islam*. Chapel Hill: University of North Carolina Press, 1975.

Schipper, Bernd U., "From Milton to Modern Satanism: The History of the Devil and the Dynamics between Religion and Literature." *Journal of Religion in Europe* 3 (2010) 1:103–124.

Schmidt, Joachim, *Satanismus: Mythos und Wirklichkeit*. Marburg: Diagonal-Verlag, 1992.

Schnierer, Peter Paul, *Entdämonisierung und Verteufelung: Studien zur Darstellungs- und Funktionsgeschichte des Diabolischen in der englischen Literatur seit der Renaissance*. Tübingen: Max Niemeyer, 2005.

Schock, Peter A., *Romantic Satanism: Myth and the Historical Moment in Blake, Shelley, and Byron*. Houndmills: Palgrave Macmillan, 2003.

Schöne, Albrecht, *Götterzeichen, Liebeszauber, Satanskult: Neue Einblicke in alte Goethetexte*. München: C. H. Beck, 1982.

Schuré, Édouard, *Le théâtre de l'âme*. Paris: Perrin, 1900.

Scott, Gini Graham, *The Magicians: An Investigation of a Group Practicing Black Magic*. New York: ASJA, 2007.

Scrivener, Michael Henry, *Radical Shelley: The Philosophical Anarchism and Utopian Thought of Percy Bysshe Shelley*. Princeton, NJ: Princeton University Press, 1982.

Ségur, Louis Gaston Adrien de, *Les Francs-Maçons: ce qu'ils sont, ce qu'ils font, ce qu'ils veulent*. Paris, Simon Raçon, 1867.

Senholt, Jacob C., "Radical Politics and Political Esotericism: The Adaptation of Esoteric Discourse within the Radical Right." In *Contemporary Esotericism*, edited by Egil Asprem and Kennet Granholm, 244–264. Sheffield, UK: Equinox, 2013.

———, "Secret Identities in the Sinister Tradition: Political Esotericism and the Convergence of Radical Islam, Satanism, and National Socialism." In *The Devil's Party: Satanism in Modernity*, edited by Per Faxneld and Jesper Petersen, 250–274. Oxford: Oxford University Press, 2012.

———, "The Sinister Tradition: Political Esotericism and the Convergence of Radical Islam, Satanism and National Socialism in the Order of the Nine Angles." 2009 conference paper, at http://www.scribd.com/doc/38118165/The-Sinister-Tradition (accessed 29 May 2103).

Sewell, Brocard, "The Reverend Montague Summers." In *Montague Summers: A Bibliographical Portrait*, edited by Frederick S. Frank, 3–23. The Great Bibliographers Series, no. 7. Metuchen, NJ: Scarecrow, 1988.

Sharrock, Robert, "Godwin on Milton's Satan." *Notes and Queries for Readers and Writers, Collectors and Librarians* 9 (December 1962) 12:463–465.

Sedgwick, Alexander, *The Ralliement in French Politics 1890–1898*. Cambridge, MA: Harvard University Press, 1965.

Shelley, Mary Wollstonecraft, *Frankenstein; or the Modern Prometheus*. 1912. Reprint, London: J. M. Dent and Sons, 1927.

Shelley, Percy Bysshe, *The Complete Poetical Works of Percy Bysshe Shelley*. Edited by Neville Rogers. 4 vols. Oxford: Clarendon, 1972–1975.

———, *Essays and Letters by Percy Bysshe Shelley*. Edited by Ernest Rhys. London: Walter Scott, 1905.

———, *The Letters of Percy Bysshe Shelley*. Edited by Frederic L. Jones. 2 vols. Oxford: Clarendon, 1964.

———, *Shelley's "Devils' Notebook": Bodleian MS. Shelley adds. E.9. A Facsimile Edition with Full Transcription and Textual Notes*. Edited by P .M. S. Dawson and Timothy Webb. New York: Garland, 1993.

———, *Shelley's "Prometheus Unbound": The Text and the Drafts*. New Haven, CT: Yale University Press, 1968.

Siefener, Michael, "Der Teufel als Vertragspartner." *@KIH-eSkript: Interdisziplinäre Hexenforschung online* 3 (2011) 1:61–68, at https://www.historicum.net/themen/hexenforschung/akih-eskript/heft-3-2011/artikel/Der_Teufel_als_Vertragspartner/ (accessed 14 January 2012).

Sieg, George, "Angular Momentum: From Traditional to Progressive Satanism in the Order of the Nine Angles." 2009 conference paper, at http://www.ntnu.no/c/document_library/get_file?uuid=a827e3e1-3b8e-447a-b641-7d5285eb96f1&groupId=10244 (accessed 14 May 2013).

Smoczynski, Rafal, "Cyber-Satanism and Imagined Satanism: Dark Symptoms of Late Modernity." In *Contemporary Religious Satanism: A Critical Anthology*, edited by Jesper Aagaard Petersen, 141–151. Farnham, UK: Ashgate, 2009.

———, "The Making of Satanic Collective Identities in Poland: From Mechanic to Organic Solidarity." In *The Devil's Party: Satanism in Modernity*, edited by Per Faxneld and Jesper Petersen, 189–203. Oxford: Oxford University Press, 2012.

Snijders, Armand, "Leve satan, God is een slappeling." *Dagblad De Pers* (18 October 2007): 12.

Somerset, Anne, *The Affair of the Poisons: Murder, Infanticide and Satanism at the Court of Louis XIV*. London: Weidenfeld and Nicolson, 2003.

Southey, Robert, *A Vision of Judgement*. London: Longman, Hurst, Rees, Orme and Brown, 1821.

Søderlind, Didrik, and Asbjørn Dyrendal, "Social Democratic Satanism? Some Examples of Satanism in Scandinavia." In *Contemporary Religious Satanism: A Critical Anthology*, edited by Jesper Aagaard Petersen, 153–170. Farnham, UK: Ashgate, 2009.

Sperlinger, S. D., "Belial." In *Dictionary of Deities and Demons in the Bible*, edited by Karel van der Toorn, Bob Becking, and Pieter W. van der Horst, 169–171. Leiden: Brill, 1999.

Starkie, Enid, *Petrus Borel, the Lycanthrope: His Life and Times*. New York: New Directions, 1954.

Steiger, Brad, *Sex and Satanism*. New York: Ace, 1969.

Steiner, Rudolf, *Christus in verhouding tot Lucifer en Ahriman: De drievoudige gestalte*. Translated by J. Stolk-van Greuninge. Driebergen: Zevenster. 1986.

Steinmetz, Jean-Luc, *Pétrus Borel. Vocation: Poète maudit*. [Paris]: Librairie Arthème Fayard, 2002.

Stevenson, David, *The Origins of Freemasonry: Scotland's Century, 1590–1710*. Cambridge: Cambridge University Press, 1988.

Stoecklin, E., *Instructions au 18me grade*. Fribourg: Souv:. Chapitre L'Amitié de Lausanne, 1882.

Stronks, G., "The Significance of Bathasar Bekker's The Enchanted World." In *Witchcraft in the Netherlands from the Fourteenth to the Twentieth Century*, edited by M. Gijswijt-Hofstra and W. Frijhoff, 149–156. Rotterdam: Universitaire Pers, 1991.

Stuckrad, Kocku von, "Discursive Transfers and Reconfigurations: Tracing the Religious and the Esoteric in Secular Culture." In *Contemporary Esotericism*, edited by Egil Asprem and Kennet Granholm, 226–243. Sheffield, UK: Equinox, 2013.

Summers, Montague, *Antinous and Other Poems*. London: Cecil Woolf, 1995.

——, *The Galanty Show: An Autobiography*. London: Cecil Woolf, 1980.

——, *The Geography of Witchcraft*. Evanston: University Books, 1958.

——, *A Popular History of Witchcraft*. London: Kegan Paul, Trench, Trubner, 1937.

——, *Witchcraft and Black Magic*. London: Rider, [1945].

Suster, Gerald, *The Hell-Fire Friars: Sex, Politics and Religion*. London: Robson, 2000.

Swinburne, Algernon Charles, *The Poems of Algernon Charles Swinburne*. 6 vols. London: Chatto, 1904.

Symonds, John, *The King of the Shadow Realm. Aleister Crowley: His Life and Magic*. London: Duckworth, 1989.

Taussig, Michael T., *The Devil and Commodity Fetishism in South America*. Chapel Hill: University of North Carolina Press, 1984.

Taxil, Léo, *À bas la calotte!* Paris: Strauss, 1879.

——, *Confessions d'un ex-libre-penseur*. Paris: Letouzey and Ané, [1887].

——, *Le Culte du Grand Architecte*. Paris: Letouzey and Ané, [1886].

——, *Les amours secrètes de Pie IX, par un ancien camérier du Pape*. Paris: Librairie Anti-Cléricale/Librairie Populaire, [1881].

——, *Les Frères Trois-Points*. 2 vols. Paris: Letouzey and Ané, [1885].

——, *Les mystères de la Franc-Maçonnerie dévoilés*. Paris: Letouzey and Ané, [1887]

——, *Les sœurs maçonnes: La Franc-Maçonnerie des dames et ses mystères*. Paris: Letouzey and Ané, [1886].

——, *Pie IX devant l'histoire: Sa vie politique et pontificale, ses débauches, ses folies, ses crimes*. 3 vols. Paris: Librairie Anti-Cléricale, [1883].

——, *Pie IX franc-maçon?* Paris: Téqui, 1892.

——, *Y a-t-il des Femmes dans la Franc-Maçonnerie?* Paris: Delhomme and Briguet s.a.

Taxil, Léo, and Tony Gall, *Les admirateurs de la lune à l'Orient de Marseille: Histoire Amusante d'une Loge de Francs-Maçons*. Paris: Agence Centrale des Bons Livres, s.a.

Taylor, Charles, *A Secular Age*. Cambridge, MA: Belknap Press of Harvard University Press, 2007.

Tertullian, *Apology. De Spectaculis*. Translated by T. R. Glover. 1933. Reprint, London: William Heinemann, 1960.

Theißen, Gerd, "Monotheismus und Teufelsglaube: Entstehung und Psychologie des biblischen Satansmythos." In *Demons and the Devil in Ancient and Medieval Christianity*, edited by Nienke Vos and Willemien Otten, 37–69. Supplements to Vigiliae Christianae: Texts and Studies of Early Christian Life and Language, no. 108. Leiden: Brill, 2011.

Thérèse de L'Enfant-Jésus et de la Sainte-Face, Sainte, *Œuvres complètes (Textes et derniers paroles)*. Paris: Éditions du Cerf/Desclée De Brouwer, 2004.

Thiele, Rita, *Satanismus als Zeitkritik bei Joris-Karl Huysmans*. Frankfurt am Main: Verlag Peter D. Lang, 1979.

Thomas, Marcel, "Un aventurier de la mystique: L'abbé Boullan." *Les Cahiers de la Tour Saint-Jacques* 8 (1963): 116–161.

Thorey, M. J. C., *Rapports merveilleux de Mme Cantianille B . . . avec le monde surnaturel*. 2 vols. Paris: Louis Hervé, 1866.

Thorndike, Lynn, *A History of Magic and Experimental Science during the First Thirteen Centuries of Our Era*. 1932. Reprint, New York: Columbia University Press, 1964.

Todd, Janet, *Death and the Maidens: Fanny Wollstonecraft and the Shelley Circle*. London: Profile, 2007.

Tuczay, Christa, "The Nineteenth Century: Medievalism and Witchcraft." In *Palgrave Advances in Witchcraft Historiography*, edited by Jonathan Barry and Owen Davies, 52–68. Houndmills: Palgrave Macmillan, 2007.

Trachtenberg, Joshua, *The Devil and the Jews: The Medieval Conception of the Jew and Its Relation to Modern Anti-Semitism*. Philadelphia: Jewish Publication Society of America, 1961.

Trevor-Roper, H. R., *The European Witch-Craze of the Sixteenth and Seventeenth Centuries and Other Essays*. New York: Harper and Row, 1969.

Tristan, Flora, and Constant, A., *L'Émancipation de la Femme, ou le testament de la paria*. Paris: Bureau de la direction de *La Vérité*, 1846.

Truzzi, Marcello, "Towards a Sociology of the Occult. Notes on Modern Witchcraft." In *Religious Movements in Contemporary America*, edited by Irving I. Zaretsky and Mark P. Leone, 628–645. Princeton, N.J.: Princeton University Press, 1974.

Union Antimaçonnique Universelle, *Actes du Iʳᵉ Congrès antimaçonnique international, XXVI-XXX Septembre M DCCC XCVI, Trente*. 2 vols. Tournai: Desclée, Lefebvre, 1897.

Urban, Hugh B., "Magia Sexualis: Sex, Secrecy, and Liberation in Modern Western Esotericism." *Journal of the American Academy of Religion* 72 (September 2004) 3:695–731.

———, "The Occult Roots of Scientology? L. Ron Hubbard, Aleister Crowley, and the Origins of a Controversial New Religion." In *Aleister Crowley and Western Esotericism*, edited by Henrik Bogdan and Martin P. Starr, 335–367. New York: Oxford University Press, 2012.

Valente, Michaela, "Witchcraft (15th–17th centuries)." In *Dictionary of Gnosis and Western Esotericism*, edited by Wouter J. Hanegraaff, 2:1174–1177. 2 vols. Leiden: Brill, 2005.

Van Gchuchten, François, *Bokkenrijders: Late heksenprocessen in Limburg. Het proces van vier bokkenrijdersgroepen in Limburg (1773–1795)*. s.l.: s.i., 2002.

Varma, Devandra P., "Montague Summers: A Gothic Tribute." In *Montague Summers: A Bibliographical Portrait*, edited by Frederick S. Frank, 24–34. The Great Bibliographers Series, no. 7. Metuchen, NJ: Scarecrow, 1988.

Vaughan, Diana, *La restauration du paganisme: Transition décrétée par le Sanctum Regnum pour préparer l'établissement du culte public de Lucifer. Les hymnes liturgiques de Pike. Rituel du néo-paganisme*. Paris: Librairie Antimaçonnique, [1896].

———, *Le Palladium régénéré et libre. Lien des groupes lucifériens indépendants*. Paris: Bureau Central de la Propaganda Palladiste Indépendante, 1895.

——— (Jeanne-Marie-Raphaëlle), *Mémoires d'une ex-Palladiste Parfaite Initiée, Indépendante*. Paris: Librairie Antimaçonnique, 1895–1897.

——— (Jeanne-Marie-Raphaëlle), *La Neuvaine Eucharistique pour réparer*. Paris: Librairie Antimaçonnique, [1895].

———, *Le 33ᵉ:. Crispi: Un Palladiste Homme d'état démasqué. Histoire documentée du héros depuis sa naissance jusqu'à sa deuxième mort (1819–1896)*. Paris: Librairie Antimaçonnique, [1896].

Velde, H. te, *Seth, God of Confusion: A Study of His Role in Egyptian Mythology and Religion*. Probleme der Ägyptologie, no. 6. Leiden: E. J. Brill, 1977.

Viaene, Vincent, "A Brilliant Failure. Wladimir Czaki, the Legacy of the Geneva Committee and the Origins of Vatican Press Policy from Pius IX to Leo XIII." In *The Black International/ L'International noire 1870–1878*, edited by Emiel Lamberts, 230–255. Leuven: Leuven University Press, 2002.

———, "The Roman Question. Catholic Mobilisation and Papal Diplomacy during the Pontificate of Pius IX (1846–1878)." In *The Black International/L'International noire 1870– 1878*, edited by Emiel Lamberts, 135–177. Leuven: Leuven University Press, 2002.

———, " 'Wagging the dog'. An Introduction to Vatican Press Policy in an Age of Democracy and Imperialism." In *The Papacy and the New World Order. Vatican Diplomacy, Catholic Opinion and International Politics at the Time of Leo XIII, 1878–1903 = La Papauté et le nouvel ordre mondial. Diplomatie vaticane, opinion catholique et politique internationale au temps de Léo XIII*, edited by Vincent Viaene, 323–348. Bruxelles: Institut Historique Belge de Rome/Belgisch Historisch Instituut te Rome, 2005.

Viatte, Auguste, *Victor Hugo et les Illuminés de son temps*. Montréal: Les Éditions de l'Arbre, 1942.

Victor, Jeffrey S., "The Dynamics of Rumor-Panics about Satanic Cults." In *The Satanism Scare*, edited by James T. Richardson, Joel Best, and David G. Bromley, 221–248. New York: Aldine de Gruyter, 1991.

———, *Satanic Panic: The Creation of a Contemporary Legend*. Chicago: Open Court, 1993.

Vigny, A. de, *Œuvres Complètes*. Edited by F. Baldensperger. 2 vols. Paris: Librairie Gallimard, 1950.

Villeneuve, Rolland, *Le Diable dans l'Art: Essai d'iconographie comparée à propos des rapports entre l'Art et le Satanisme*. Paris: Éditions Denoël, 1957.

Vinchon, Jean, "Guillaume Apollinaire et Berthe Courrière, inspiratrice de 'Là-Bas.' " *Les Cahiers de la Tour Saint-Jacques* 8 (1963): 162–165.

Volney, C.-F., *Les Ruines*. 1822. Reprint, edited by Jean Tulard. Paris: Slatkine, 1979.

Voltaire, *Essai sur les mœurs et l'esprit des nations et sur les principaux faits de l'histoire depuis Charlemagne jusqu'à Louis XIII*. 2 vols. Paris: Éditions Garnier Frères, 1963.

Vondel, Joost van den, *Lucifer: Treurspel*. Edited by W. J. M. A. Asselbergs. Zwolle: Tjeenk Willink, 1954.

Vos, Nienke, "The Saint as Icon: Transformation of Biblical Imagery in Early Medieval Hagiography." In *Iconoclasm and Iconoclash: Struggle for Religious Identity*, edited by Willem van Asselt, Paul van Geest, and others, 201–216. Leiden: Brill, 2007.

Waal, Frans de, *Primates and Philosophers: How Morality Evolved*. Princeton, NJ: Princeton University Press, 2006.

Waardt, Hans de, "Met bloed ondertekend." *Sociologische Gids* 36 (1989): 224–244, 288–289.

Waite, Arthur Edward, *Devil-Worship in France, or the Question of Lucifer: A Record of Things Seen and Heard in the Secret Societies according to the Evidence of Initiates*. London: George Redway, 1896.

Waite, Gary K., *Eradicating the Devil's Minions: Anabaptists and Witches in Reformation Europe, 1525–1600*. Toronto: University of Toronto Press, 2007.

Walker, D. P., *Spiritual and Demonic Magic from Ficino to Campanella*. London: Warburg Institute, 1958.

Wardinski, Nathan, "The Satanic Politic." In *Contemporary Religious Satanism: A Critical Anthology*, edited by Jesper Aagaard Petersen, 255–258. Farnham, UK: Ashgate, 2009.

Warner, Sylvia Townsend, *Lolly Willowes or the Loving Huntsman*. 1926. Reprint, London: Women's Press, 1978.

Washton Long, Rose Carol, *Kandinsky: The Development of an Abstract Style*. Oxford: Clarendon, 1980.

Watson, Nicholas, "John the Monk's *Book of Visions of The Blessed and Undefiled Virgin Mary, Mother of God*: Two Versions of a Newly Discovered Ritual Magic Text." In *Conjuring Spirits: Texts and Traditions of Medieval Ritual Magic*, edited by Claire Fanger, 163–249. Magic in History, no. 4. Thrupp: Sutton, 1998.

Webb, James, *The Occult Underground*. La Salle, IL: Open Court, 1974.

Weber, Eugen, *Action Française: Royalism and Reaction in Twentieth Century France*. Stanford, CA: Stanford University Press, 1962.

———, *Fin de siècle: La France à la fin du XIXe siècle*. Translated by Philippe Delamare. Paris: Fayard, 1986.

———, *Satan franc-maçon: La mystification de Léo Taxil*. Paris: Julliard, 1964.

Weber, Max, *Wissenschaft als Beruf*. München: Duncker and Humblot, 1919.

Wellek, René, "The Concept of "Romanticism' in Literary History." *Comparative Literature* 1 (1949) 1:1–23, 2:147–172.

Wenisch, Bernhard, *Satanismus: Schwarze Messen—Dämonenglaube—Hexenkulte*. Mainz: Matthias-Grünewald-Verlag, 1988.

Wheatley, Dennis, *The Devil and All His Works*. London: Book Club Associates, 1977.

———, *The Devil Rides Out*. London: Reed International Books, 1996.

———, "Letter to Posterity." http://www.bbc.co.uk/bbcfour/documentaries/features/wheatley_letter.pdf, accessed 4 April 2011.

———, *The Satanist*. London: Arrow, 1975.

———, *To the Devil a Daughter*. Ware: Wordsworth, 2007.

Whitehead, Harriet, "Reasonably Fantastic: Some Perspectives on Scientology, Science Fiction, and Occultism." In *Religious Movements in Contemporary America*, edited by Irving I. Zaretsky and Mark P. Leone, 547–587. Princeton, NJ: Princeton University Press, 1974.

Wilder, Eleanor, *Gathering the Winds: Visionary Imagination and Radical Transformation of Self and Society*. Baltimore, MD: John Hopkins University Press, 1975.

Wilson, A. N., *God's Funeral: The Decline of Faith in Western Civilization*. London: John Murray, 1999.

Wilson, Leslie A., "Dichter-Priester. Bestandteil der Romantik." *Colloquia Germanica: Internationale Zeitschrift für germanische Sprach- und Literaturwissenschaft* (1968): 127–136.

Wippermann, Wolfgang, *Agenten des Bösen: Verschwörungstheorien von Luther bis heute*. Berlin-Brandenburg: be.bra verlag, 2007.

Wirth, Oswald, *Stanislas de Guaita: Souvenirs de son Secrétaire*. Paris: Éditions du Symbolisme, 1935.

Witte, Els, "Pierre-Théodore Verhaegen et la franc-maçonnerie." In *Pierre-Théodore Verhaegen: l'homme, sa vie, sa légende. Bicentaire d'une naissance*, edited by Jean Stengers, 47–60. Bruxelles: Université Libre de Bruxelles, 1996.

Wolf, Ole, "The Culture Cult." In *Contemporary Religious Satanism: A Critical Anthology*, edited by Jesper Aagaard Petersen, 259–265. Farnham, UK: Ashgate, 2009.

Wolfe, Burton H., *The Black Pope: The Authentic Biography of Anton Szandor LaVey*. s.l.: s.n,. 2008 [e-book published by the author].

Wood, Juliette, "The Reality of Witch Cults Reasserted: Fertility and Satanism." In *Palgrave Advances in Witchcraft Historiography*, edited by Jonathan Barry and Owen Davies, 69–89. Houndmills: Palgrave Macmillan, 2007.

Worsley, Peter, *The Trumpet Shall Sound: A Study of the "Cargo' Cults in Melanesia*. New York: Schocken, 1968.

Wright, Lawrence, *In de ban van Satan: Over ritueel seksueel misbruik en de mysteries van het geheugen*. Translated by Nicky de Swaan. Amsterdam: L. J. Veen, 1994.

———, *Saints and Sinners*. New York: Vintage, 1995.

Wurmbrand, Richard, *Was Karl Marx a Satanist?* s.l.: Diane Books, 1979.

Wuthnow, Robert, *The Restructuring of American Religion: Society and Faith Since World War II*. Princeton, NJ: Princeton University Press, 1988.

Wyllie, Timothy, *Love, Sex, Fear, Death: The Inside Story of the Process Church of the Final Judgment*. Edited by Adam Parfrey. Port Townsend, WA: Feral House, 2009.

X***, Abbé, *La Messe d'amour: Scènes de la vie religieuse*. Paris: E. Dentu, 1889.

Young, Julian, *Friedrich Nietzsche: A Philosophical Biography*. New York: Cambridge University Press, 2010.

Young, Mary de, "Breeders for Satan: Toward a Sociology of Sexual Trauma." *Journal of American Culture* 19 (1996) 2:111–118.

York, Michael, "Le neo-paganisme et les objections du wiccan au satanisme." In *Le Défi Magique II: Satanisme, sorcellerie*, edited by Jean-Baptiste Martin and Massimo Introvigne, 174–182. Lyon: Presses Universitaires de Lyon, 1994.

Zacharias, Gerhard, *Satanskult und Schwarze Messe: Die Nachtseite des Christentums. Eine Beitrag zur Phänomenologie der Religion*. München: F.A. Herbig, 1990.

Zander, Helmut, *Anthroposophie in Deutschland: Theosophische Weltanschauung und gesellschaftliche Praxis 1884–1945*. 2 vols. Göttingen: Vandenhoeck and Ruprecht, 2007.

Zayed, Fernande, *Huysmans: Peintre de son époque*. Paris: Nizet, 1973.

Zech, Kerstin, "Heidenvorstellung und Heidendarstellung: Begrifflichkeit und ihre Deutung im Kontext von Bedas *Historia Ecclesiastica*." In *Die wahrnehmun anderer Religionen in früheren Mittelalter: Terminologische Probleme und methodische Ansätze*, edited by Anna Aurast and Hans-Werner Goetz, 15–45. Hamburger geistwissenschaftliche Studien zu Religion und Gesellschaft no. 1. Berlin: Lit Verlag, 2012.

Zerner, Monique (ed.), *Inventer l'hérésie? Discours polémiques et pouvoirs avant l'Inquisition.* Nice: Z'éditions, 1998.

Zumthor, Paul, *Victor Hugo, poète de Satan.* Paris: Robert Laffont, 1946.

PERIODICALS

Annales de la Sainteté au XIXᵉ siècle. Paris: Au Bureau des Annales de la Sainteté au XIXe siècle, 1873–1875.

L'Assiette au beurre 141 (12 December 1903)—*messes noires.*

La Croix du Dauphiné 3 (1895).

La Flèche. Organe de action magique 1–5 (1930–1935).

L'Écho de Paris 8–10 (1891–1893).

L'Écho de Rome. Organe de la défense du Saint-Siège 27 (1894).

Le Nouveau Moniteur de Rome 1 (1894).

La Petite Guerre. Organe populaire de la lutte contre la Franc-Maçonnerie 1–2 *(1887–1889).*

Revue Bénédictine 13 (1896).

Revue mensuelle religieuse, politique, scientifique: Complément de la publication Le Diable au XIXᵉ Siècle 1–3 (1894–1896).

INDEX

Abrasax, 311

Affair of the Poisons, 11, 45–57, 59–63, 125, 186, 197, 290, 295, 391, 435n, 523n

Agapemonites, 9

Agrippa, Heinrich Cornelius, von Nettesheim, 44

Ahreman/Ahriman, 18, 64, 110, 146

Ahremanists, 18

Ahura Mazda, 17–18

Aiwass, 307, 309, 312

Alinsky, Saul, 120

Ambrose of Milan, 32

Anabaptists, 1–2, 39, 430n

Anger, Kenneth, 534n

Angra Mainyu, 18

Antichrist, 83–84, 95, 118, 212, 215, 226, 240, 258, 272, 325–326, 357

Aquino, Michael A., 344, 348–356, 363, 365, 369–371, 377, 548–549n, 557n

Argenson, René Voyer, Conte d', 56–61, 435n

Asmodeus, 20, 48, 197, 212–215, 226, 294, 349

Astaroth, 48, 54, 64, 197

Auerhahn, 58, 61

Augustine of Hippo, 26, 32, 42, 53, 405, 424n, 532n

Azazel, 20, 105

Baalzebul. *See* Beelzebub

Balaak, 19

Bakunin, Mikhail, 119–120, 149, 401

Baphomet, 136–137, 139–140, 144, 174, 208, 210, 212, 222, 253, 269–270, 279, 285–286, 294, 310, 346, 385

Barruel, Augustin, 232–233, 235, 237, 241–244, 257, 270–271, 316

Barry, James, 70

Barton, Blanche (Sharon Densley), 379–380, 403

Bartrina y de Aixemús, Joaquín María, 516n

Basilius, 41

Basset, Serge, 269–270

Bataille, Dr., 211–212, 215–216, 221, 223, 225, 227–228, 230, 241, 250, 258, 260, 267, 275, 279

Baudelaire, Charles, 1, 10, 151–163, 172, 175, 189, 193, 195, 197–199, 285, 290, 323, 332, 401, 440n, 471n

Bavent, Madeleine, 44, 199, 316

Bayle, Pierre, 65

Beatles, The, 1

Beelzebub, 21, 226, 294, 349

Beelzebuth, 5, 64, 161–163, 191, 197

Bekker, Balthasar, 64, 437

Belial, 20–21, 73, 197, 294

Beliar, 20
Bellah, Robert, 4–5, 109, 403
Bénichou, Paul, 90, 448n
Bertier, Ferdinand de, 233
Bessonies, Gabriel, 225, 260, 514n
Bilger, Barbe, 501n
Bismarck, Otto von, 1, 245, 247, 249
Bizouard, Joseph, 508n
Blake, William, 7, 69, 71–72, 78, 84–85, 87–97,
    99–103, 105, 110–113, 115, 133, 141, 157, 162,
    308, 333, 336, 350, 385, 392–394, 400–401,
    403, 405, 451–452n, 456n, 533n
Blavatsky, H.P.B., 144–146, 149–150, 173, 227,
    302, 306, 320, 324, 352, 395
Bloy, Léon, 486n
Bockeryders, 65
Bodin, Jean, 49, 170, 176, 475n
Bogomils, 28
Bois, Jules, 164, 187, 193, 203–207, 225, 227–228,
    268, 279, 282–283, 285, 300, 488–489n,
    523–525n, 540n
Bonewits, Isaac, 368–369, 372
Borel, Pétrus, 153, 156, 460n, 471n
Bosch, Firmin Vanden, 188–189, 192
Bossier, Herman, 189
Boullan, Joseph–Antoine, 14, 175–197, 200–207,
    221, 241, 243, 281, 388, 479–483n, 507n
Boutet, Frédéric, 269
Bouzingo(t)s, 152–156, 259, 381
Brevannes, Roland, 292, 346, 526–527n
Byron, Lord, 7, 69, 72–76, 78–81, 84, 87–88, 91,
    99–104, 107–110, 132, 136, 141, 152, 156, 158,
    162, 285, 323, 350, 353, 392–394, 405, 440n,
    452–453n, 455n, 542n

Cain, 27, 73–74, 79–81, 84, 90, 99–104, 106,
    110–111, 114–115, 131–132, 136, 158, 350, 453n
Cainites, 27
Camus, Albert, 386
Cantianille B., 191–192
Carbonari, 79, 235, 241
Carducci, Gisouè, 116, 266–267, 285, 322, 516n
Cathars, 1, 28, 31, 229, 232
Cazotte, Jacques, 161
Chrysostom, John, 29
Claraz, Lucie, 251–254
Clarin de la Rive, Abel, 225–226, 253–254, 261,
    272, 278, 280, 290
Coleridge, Samuel Taylor, 73

Constant, Alphonse-Louis. See Lévi, Éliphas
Constantine, Emperor, 31–32
Corneille, Thomas, 63
Courrière, Berthe de, 185–286, 192–193, 202,
    483–484n
Crispi, Francesco, 214, 250, 254, 258, 260–261
Crowley, Aleister, 1, 9, 270, 302, 306–314, 318,
    332–336, 339–342, 352, 367, 376, 398–399,
    401, 405, 524n, 532–535n, 538n, 542n,
    554n, 565n
Czacki, Wladimir, 256, 259

Dale, Anton van, 64
Danton, Georges Jacques, 1, 191
D'Arch Smith, Timothy, 317
Darwin, Charles, 324–327, 357, 367, 369, 371,
    401, 407
Dashwood, Sir Francis, 66–67, 108, 307,
    532n, 564n
Davis Jr., Sammy, 369, 554n
Defoe, Daniel, 65
Demogorgon, 99
Diderot, Dénis, 6
Diocletian, Emperor, 32
Disney, Walt, 1
Disraeli, Benjamin, 259
Doinel, Jules, 229, 271
Dreyfus, Albert, 265, 270, 274, 278
Drumont, Édouard, 273–276, 280, 521n
Dubus, Edouard, 186, 203
Dumont, Auguste, 117
Dvorak, Josef, 9

Eliade, Mircea, 15, 412n
Encausse, Gérard. See Papus
Epiphanius of Salamis, 26–28, 59
Erhard, Johann Benjamin, 529n
Esquiros, Alphonse, 121, 142, 467–468n
Essenes, 1, 263, 421n
Euronymous (Øystein Aarseth), 561n
Evola, Julius, 1

Faust, 16, 41, 51, 61, 74, 90, 100, 102, 110, 453n
Fava, Amand-Joseph, 210, 224–225, 237–238,
    271–272, 278
Faxneld, Per, 7, 12, 282–284, 286–288
Fersen, Jacques d'Adelswärd-, 526n
Feuerbach, Ludwig, 1, 328
Fiard, Jean-Baptiste, 242–244, 537n

France, Anatole, 116, 457n, 532n
Franco, Francisco, 521n
Frankfurter, David, 35, 396
Franklin, Benjamin, 67
Fratecelli, 28
Fraternitas Saturni, 301–303, 305–306, 395
Freemasons, 207–280, 302, 307, 340, 396
Freud, Sigmund, 175, 309, 333–334, 357, 360, 364, 436n
Frick, Karl H., 8–9, 155
Frye, Northrop, 90, 112, 330, 402
Fuseli, Henry or Heinrich, 69–70

Gambetta, Léon Michel, 217
Gardner, Gerald, 303, 312–314, 535n
Garibaldi, Giuseppe, 1, 250
Gaufridy, Louis, 45
Gautier, Théophile, 75, 153–155
Geertz, Clifford, 4, 413n
Geyraud, Pierre (Raoul Guyader), 268–270, 301, 517n
Gilmore, Peter, 380
Ginzburg, Carlo, 38–39
Gnostics, 1, 3, 26–27, 43–44, 121, 134, 136–137, 146, 229, 334, 340, 395, 422n
Godechot, Jacques, 77
Godwin, William, 71–72, 74, 77–78, 100, 103, 112, 120, 308, 392, 394
Goethe, Johann Wolfgang von, 41, 74, 100, 102, 110, 457n
Golden Dawn, Order of the, 306–308, 336, 531–532n, 543n, 565n
Goliards, 1
Görres, Joseph, 170, 176, 199, 476n, 491n
Gougenot des Mousseaux, Henri-Roger, 243, 271–272, 276
Gourmont, Remy de, 185–186, 189–190
Granholm, Kennet, 6–7
Gregorius I, Pope, 24
Gregorius VII, Pope, 33, 34
Gregorius IX, Pope, 29, 31, 33–34, 388
Gregorius XVI, Pope, 234–235
Grimston, Robert de (Robert Moor), 303–306, 535n, 539–540n
Grosche, Eugen, 301–302, 305
Guaita, Stanislas de, 171–175, 179–182, 187, 194, 200–206, 228–229, 290, 309, 313, 336, 390, 476n, 481–482n, 494n, 528n
Guibourg, Étienne, 46–49, 51, 67, 176

Hacks, Charles, 216, 218, 223–224, 227–228, 230–231, 255
Haecke, Lodewijk Van, 185–188, 192–193, 200–201, 485n
Haim, Georg Friedrich, 58, 436n
Haitzmann, Christoph, 436n
Hanegraaff, Willem, 3
Hanson, Ellis, 199
Hartman, Moses, 120
Hecate, 294, 314
Hecht, Ben, 326, 367
Helms, Jesse, 363
Hitler, Adolf, 1, 9, 280, 308, 369, 521n, 556n
Hobsbawm, H.B., 13
Hoëne-Wroński, Józef, 134, 465n
Horus, 17, 307, 309, 318
Hubbard, Ron L., 311
Hugo, Victor, 69, 75–76, 81–82, 84–85, 87–88, 90–91, 99, 105–113, 115, 117, 122–124, 127, 133, 145, 158, 162, 220, 324, 392–394, 405, 443n, 455n
Hussites, 2, 121, 227, 395
Huysmans, Joris-Karl, 7, 14, 164–205, 209–210, 218–219, 221–222, 225, 253–254, 263, 270, 281–283, 285, 290–292, 295, 308, 314, 316–317, 319, 323–324, 388–389, 396, 401, 480n, 482–486n, 489n, 491n, 493n, 522–523n

Iblis, 208
Illuminati, 1, 122, 232, 263, 270, 358, 396, 550n
Innocent IV, Pope, 34
Introvigne, Massimo, 3, 5, 10–13, 43, 45, 48–49, 53–55, 59–60, 65, 193, 254, 268, 309, 405, 415n, 565n
Irvine, Doreen, 358, 361, 551n
Isis, 10, 107, 139, 144–145, 173, 193
Isodore of Sevilla, 55

Jaquerius, Nicolaus, 37–39, 53
Jesus of Nazareth, 20–22, 24, 35, 53, 64, 76, 84–85, 106–107, 109, 119, 121, 124, 123, 127, 129–133, 137, 139, 146, 148–150, 162, 167, 174, 177, 183, 202, 206, 210, 237, 239, 253, 294, 303–308, 324, 326, 337, 356, 359, 368, 446n, 533n
Johnson, John, 70–71, 78
Jung, Carl Gustav, 175, 333
Jupiter, 23, 83, 95, 99
Justin Martyr, 21, 23, 26

Kadosh, Ben (Carl William Hansen), 12, 286–288, 395, 524–525n
Kali, 6, 227
Kiekhefer, Richard, 43
King Diamond, 384
Kolbe, Maximilian, 266
Kostka, Jean. *See* Doinel, Jules
Kuyper, Abraham, 522n

Lafargue, Paul, 120
Lamers, Maarten, 344, 346, 545–546n
Lapidoth, Frits, 491–492n
Lautier, Pierre, 214
LaVey, Anton Szandor, 7, 10, 12, 294–299, 305–306, 311–315, 322–358, 363–381, 383–385, 395–402, 405–407, 415n, 527–528n, 531n, 534–535n, 540–541n, 543–544n, 547n, 549n, 554–556n, 558–559n, 563n
LaVey, Karla, 379–380
LaVey, Zeena, 297, 377–378, 559n
Lazzareschi, Cardinal, 215, 230, 260
Leipzig or Lipsius, David, 58, 61, 436–437n
Leland, Godfrey, 125–126, 149
Lemmi, Adriano, 213–214, 230, 250–251, 254–255, 258, 267–268, 275, 517n
Leo XIII, Pope, 1, 195, 218–219, 226, 228, 234–235, 237–238, 240, 246–249, 253, 256–262, 264, 276–278, 513n
Leopardi, Giacomo, 1
Lévi, Éliphas (Alphonse-Louise Constant), 127–145, 149–150, 155, 171, 173–175, 179, 194, 221–222, 228, 243, 264, 270–272, 283, 285–286, 288–290, 292, 295, 300, 310, 312, 320, 322–324, 332, 334, 336, 339–341, 348–349, 367, 398–399, 401, 405, 463–469n, 476n, 483n, 499–500n, 515n, 531n, 540n, 564–565n
Leviathan, 5, 294
Lilith, 81, 107, 314, 354
Lindsey, Hal, 357–358, 363
Loki, 6
Lollards, 121
Long, Anton (David Myatt), 371–373, 557n
Longfellow, Henry Wadsworth, 165, 176, 190
Lord, Evelyn, 66
Lorenzelli, Monsignor, 277
Lovecraft, H.P., 337, 340, 557n
Lucifer, 5, 12, 18, 20, 22, 24, 26, 28–32, 34, 36, 38, 40, 42, 44–46, 48, 50, 52, 54, 56–58, 60, 62, 64, 66, 68, 70, 72–78, 80, 82, 84, 86–88, 90, 92, 94, 96–98, 100–104, 106–108, 110, 112, 114–118, 120, 122, 124–126, 128–138, 141–148, 150, 152, 154, 156, 158, 160, 162, 166, 168, 170, 172, 174, 176, 178, 180, 182, 184, 186, 188, 190–192, 194, 196, 198, 200, 202, 204, 206–214, 216, 218–220, 222–224, 226–232, 234, 236, 238, 240, 243–244, 246, 248, 250–252, 254, 256, 258–262, 264, 266–268, 270–272, 274, 276, 278–280, 282–288, 290, 292, 294, 296, 298, 300–306, 308–310, 312, 314–316, 318, 320, 322, 324, 326, 328, 330, 332, 334, 336, 338, 340, 342, 344, 346, 348, 350, 352–354, 356, 358–360, 362, 364, 366, 368, 370, 372, 374, 376, 378, 380, 382, 384, 395, 405, 407, 454–457n
Luciferians (medieval heretics), 29–31, 34, 44–45, 121, 388, 424n, 490n
Lueger, Karl, 274, 277, 521n
Luhrmann, T.M., 349
Luther, Martin, 29, 266, 275
Luxembourg, François-Henri de Montmorency-Bouteville, Maréchal de, 1, 46, 50–51, 433n
Lyons, Arthur, 9–10, 414n

Maboya, 54
Maclean, Mary Anne, 303–305, 531n
Maigron, Louis, 154–155
Maistre, Joseph de, 155, 233, 237, 259, 270
Maistre, Xavier de, 442n
Mandrou, Robert, 56
Manicheans, 26, 28, 32–33, 37, 44, 53, 73, 84, 122, 135–136, 146, 232, 244, 270
Mansfield, Jayne, 342
Manson, Charles, 1, 359
Manson, Marilyn, 384
Marafi, 386–387, 391–392
Marat, Jean Paul, 1, 191, 237
Marburg, Conrad of, 29, 34
Marduk, 6
Margiotta, Domenico, 213–216, 222, 224–225, 228, 230, 249–251, 254–255, 258, 260, 267, 275–276, 501n
Mariken van Nieumegen, 24, 42–43
Marlowe, Christopher, 16
Martinism, 173, 286
Marx, Karl, 1, 118, 357, 458n
Mazzini, Giuseppe, 1, 234–235, 246, 250
McLeod, Hugh, 87
Mead, George Robert Stowe, 227

Medway, Gareth J., 10
Melkina, 20
Mencken, H.L., 326, 367
Mephistopheles, 74, 100
Merimée, Prosper, 2
Meurin, Léon, 210, 225, 259, 271–273, 276,
    279, 508n
Michelet, Jules, 113, 122–126, 149, 170, 189, 194,
    288, 290, 292, 312, 324, 395, 398
Miller, Max, 78
Milton, John, 1, 70–72, 77–79, 83, 92–95, 97,
    100, 102, 110–111, 120, 152, 163, 308, 323,
    332, 349, 392, 539n
Minck, Paule, 120
Mirville, Jules Eudes de, 243
Mollenauer, Lynn Wood, 55
Moloch, 73, 197, 226
Montespan, Madame de, 1, 47–48, 50–51, 176,
    190, 434n
Montvoisin, Catherine. See Voisin, Madame La
Monroe, Marilyn, 296
Mormons, 1
Mugnier, Arthur, 189, 202, 205
Murray, John, 74
Murray, Margaret, 10, 39, 312–313, 536n

Naglowska, Maria de, 300–302, 305–306, 344,
    368, 392, 395, 530n, 534n, 539n
Napoleon Bonaparte, 99, 105, 109, 123–124,
    143–144, 234, 271, 367
Napoleon III, 143–144, 156, 237, 367, 469n
Naturalists, 169–170, 198
Neo-Palladists, 268–270, 287, 524n
Nietzsche, Friedrich, 1, 283–284, 287, 291, 309,
    324–328, 331–332, 344, 350, 367–369, 399,
    401, 405–406, 524n, 540–542n
Norton, Rosaleen, 314, 536n

Odin, 24
Olivet, Fabre d', 136
Oosterdagh, Jan Hartman, 58
Ophites, 27, 302, 306, 395
Orazi, Manuel, 292
Origen of Caesarea, 21–22, 564n
Ormuzd, 18, 208
Osiris, 17, 208

Pace, Charles, 313, 535n
Paine, Thomas, 70, 78, 83, 85, 89, 101

Palladism, 207, 209–219, 221–228, 230–231,
    244–245, 249–251, 257–260, 262–263,
    267–270, 278–279, 282–283, 287–288,
    500–501n, 517n. See also neo-Palladists
Pan, 14, 109, 116, 124, 137, 189, 282, 287, 294,
    311–314, 318, 392
Papus (Gérard Encausse), 164, 171, 173, 175, 194,
    200–201, 204–207, 221, 227–229, 286, 288
Paracelsus, Philippus Aureales, 95, 140
Parrochi, Cardinal, 219, 226, 259–261
Parsons, Jack, 311
Patschovsky, Alexander, 34
Paulicians, 25, 28, 84, 425n
Pazder, Lawrence, 360, 552n
Peckham, Morse, 101
Péladan, Joséphin, 171–175, 179, 181–182, 187,
    194, 200–205, 229, 243, 309, 313, 476n,
    476–478n, 485n, 494n, 544–545n
Pessina, Giambattista, 250
Petersen, Jesper Aagaard, 6–7, 337
Pierret, Alfred, 214, 222–223, 226, 268, 278, 288,
    496n, 511n, 517n
Pike, Albert, 210, 221–222, 250, 264–265, 267,
    279, 363, 515n, 524n
Pius IX, Pope, 1, 195, 217, 234–237, 240, 246–247,
    255–256, 267, 274, 276
Polycarp, 24
Presbyterians, 1
Praag, Marcus van, 529n
Prins, Arij, 175–176, 182–183, 189, 192, 200
Priscillian of Avila, 32
Process, The, 303–306, 336, 359, 531n, 534–535n,
    539–540n
Prometheus, 83–84, 96, 99, 110, 117, 123, 132, 141,
    174, 267, 330
Proudhon, Pierre-Joseph, 117–120, 149, 155, 159,
    222, 401, 460n
Przybyszewski, Stanislaw, 12, 281–288, 395, 522–525n

Quietists, 65

Rabelais, François, 307, 532n
Rais, Gilles de, 165, 198, 204, 292
Rampolla, Cardinal Mariano, 1, 219,
    256–257, 277
Rand, Ayn, 326, 367
Rapisardo, Mario, 267
Rasputin, Grigori, 1, 327, 365
Rastafarian Satanists, 385, 562n

Ratzinger, Cardinal Josef, 1
Raynouards, François Just Marie, 341
Reclus, Elisée, 120
Redbeard, Ragnar, 327, 374, 540–541n
Reuss, Theodor, 307
Reynie, Nicolas de la, 45, 49–51, 56
Robespierre, Maximilien Isidore de, 1, 107, 191
Roca, Canon, 179, 481n, 484n
Rolling Stones, The, 381
Rollo, Ahmed, 319
Rops, Félicien, 170, 189, 522n
Rosen, Paul, 207, 221, 230, 238, 240, 259,
    264–265, 275, 290
Rosenberg, Alfred, 327, 369, 556n
Rosicrucians, 1, 171–175, 179–183, 194, 197,
    201–206, 209, 263, 388, 482n, 495n
Rote Armee Fraktion, 9
Rousseau, Jean-Jacques, 106, 157, 328–329, 441n
Rubin, Miri, 390

Sade, Donatien Alphonse François, Marquise
    de, 67–69, 125, 158, 185, 200, 316
Samael, 20, 136
Sand, George, 121–122, 124, 126, 128, 152, 158,
    227, 395
Sanders, Alex, 314, 536n
Satanians, 27–28, 59, 422n
Satie, Erik, 172
Saturnus, 23, 301–302, 310
Schiller, Friedrich, 70
Schmidt, Joachim, 9
Schock, Peter A., 73, 78, 87, 91, 111, 393, 399
Schorderet, Joseph, 252–253, 256–257, 259, 262
Schreck, Nicolas (Barry Dubin), 378
Schuré, Edouard, 147–148, 150, 470n
Seabrook, William, 314
Ségur, Louis Gaston Adrien de, 237, 241, 537n
Semihazah, 20
Semyaza, 20–21
Seraffini, G.-G., 266
Set(h), 6, 17–18, 307, 309–310, 351–356, 400,
    402, 418n
Shelley, Mary, 71–72, 78
Shelley, Percy Bysshe, 69, 71–74, 77–79, 82–85,
    87–88, 90–91, 95–101, 104–105, 109–115,
    117, 121, 133, 141, 145, 149, 159, 308, 323, 329,
    332, 392–395, 400–401, 446n, 453–455n
Simonini, Jean-Baptiste, 270, 518n
Sloane, Herbert, 302–303, 305–306

Słowacki, Juliusz, 285, 523–523n
Socrates, 17
Somerset, Anne, 49–50, 55, 60
Soumet, Alexandre, 75–76
Southey, Robert, 73, 75, 81
Spencer, Herbert, 326
Stalin, Josef, 308
Steiner, Rudolf, 146–150, 173, 395, 532n, 535n
Stoecklin, Ernest, 251–253, 257
Summers, Montague, 315–320, 536–537n
Swedenborg, Emanuel, 91–93, 95
Swinburne, Algernon Charles, 332, 561n

Tamalyon, Ben, 29
Tardivel, J.-P., 225, 261
Taxil, Léo (Marie-Joseph-Antoine-Gabriel
    Jogand-Pagès), 208–231, 236, 238–245,
    249–263, 265, 267–268, 270, 272, 274–283,
    285, 287–290, 292, 314–315, 319, 388, 498n,
    500–504n, 512n
Taylor, Charles, 82, 112
Templars, Knight, 1, 31, 136, 208, 212, 232, 263,
    271, 337, 341, 396
Tertullian, 21, 23, 420n
Themis, 10
Theodosius, Emperor, 31–32
Theophilus, 41, 61
Theosophists, 144–146, 149, 223, 227, 302, 306,
    309, 320, 395, 535n
Theresa de Lisieux, 226
Thibault, Julie, 179, 182, 187, 202–203,
    492–493n
Thomas Aquinas, 41–42
Thompson, James, 341
Thorey, Charles, 191–192
Todd, John, 550–551n
Tolkien, J.R.R., 1
Tournet, Bernard, 60
Tristan, Flora, 128–129, 131–133, 300,
    463–464n, 532n
Twain, Mark, 350
Tylor, E.B., 3

Vaughan, Diana, 207, 212–216, 222–230, 241,
    255, 258–262, 265, 268, 275, 278, 286, 289,
    351, 501n
Verzichi, Rodolfo, 260
Vico, Giambattista, 448–450n
Vigilantes, San Francisco, 1

Vigny, Alfred de, 74–76, 103, 107, 115, 152, 392, 394, 443n
Vintras, Eugène, 178–179, 182–184, 190–195, 200–202, 221–222, 241, 243, 281, 315
Visé, Donneau de, 63
Voisin, Madame la (Catherine Montvoisin), 46–49, 51, 54–55, 60, 125, 292, 295, 391
Voltaire, 64, 70, 101, 106, 217, 237, 275, 328
Vondel, Joost van den, 77, 105, 444n

Wagner, Christophor, 61
Wagner, Richard, 172, 198, 384
Waite, Arthur, 200, 228, 308
Waite, Gary K., 63
Waldensians, 28, 31, 37
Walder, Sophie 'Sapho', 212–213, 215, 221, 223, 258, 267
Warnke, Mike, 358, 361, 550n, 554n

Weber, Eugen, 255
Wheatley, Dennis, 315, 317–321, 324, 328, 358, 538n
Wiccans, 270, 303, 312–314, 336, 344, 356, 358, 395, 401, 535n
Wiener Aktionstheater, 1, 8–9
Wirth, Oswald, 181, 201, 203–205, 482n
Wolfskehl, Karl, 529n
Wollstonecraft, Mary, 70, 78
Wordsworth, William, 73, 102

Yezidi, 7, 312, 341, 416n

Zacharias, Gerhard, 8
Zarathustra, 18, 325, 331
Zola, Émile, 168–169, 176, 274
Zoroaster, 18. *See also* Zarathustra
Zoroastrianism, 18, 20, 27, 84, 146